INDIA AND WORLD CIVILIZATION

D. P. Singhal, Professor of History at the University of Queensland, received an MA from Panjab University and a PhD in History from the University of London. A Fellow of both the Royal Historical and Royal Asiatic Societies, London, he was a lecturer in Asian History at the University of Malaya before moving to the University of Queensland.

INDIA
and
WORLD CIVILIZATION

D. P. SINGHAL

RUPA

Published by
Rupa Publications India Pvt. Ltd 2014
7/16, Ansari Road, Daryaganj
New Delhi 110002

Sales centres:
Allahabad Bengaluru Chennai
Hyderabad Jaipur Kathmandu
Kolkata Mumbai

ISBN: 978-81-291-3092-1

10 9 8 7 6 5 4 3 2 1

Typeset by Saanavi Graphics, Noida

Printed at Shree Maitrey Printech Pvt. Ltd., Noida

For Devahuti

CONTENTS

Part I

CONTENTS

Part II

Since verbal science has no final end,
Since life is short, and obstacles impend,
Let central facts be picked and firmly fixed,
As swans extract the milk with water mixed.

The PANCATANTRA

India and World Civilization

Part I

Foreword

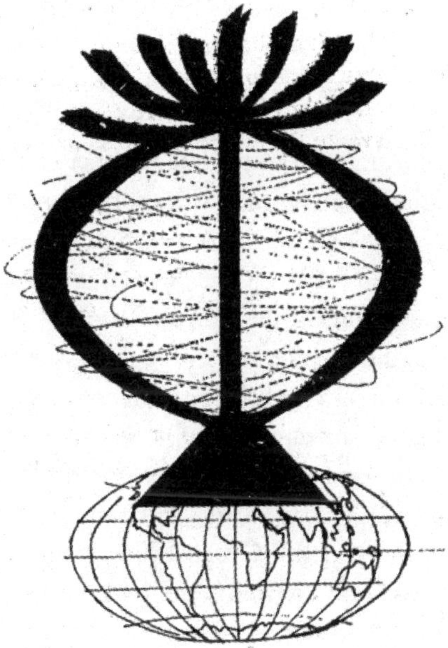

IF THE EVOLUTION of world-civilization could be reduced to a simple graphic illustration, the above symbol would perhaps be an accurate representation. The symbol's base is a solid figure, a pyramid, representing the community of those early cultures in which man sought to solve the problems of his environment. From the top of the pyramid spring divergent branches, bending first away from each other and then back again to form a new conjunction in modern times. These branches represent the diffusion of cultures and their later gradual reunification by new scientific and technological advances. Between these branches, even at their point of greatest dissociation, run slender criss-cross filaments linking them together, and representing the various ideas and skills which the civilizations of the world continued to borrow from one another throughout history. After the branches rejoin a cluster of divergent radians appear, representing the many unique developments which have resulted from the new cross-fertilisation of cultures, reaching out towards the future. The present study is an account of India's role in this cultural phenomenon.

Indian civilization is distinctive for its antiquity and continuity. Apart from its own vitality, the continuity of Indian civilization is largely due to its ability to adapt to alien ideas, harmonise contradictions and mould new thought patterns. Her constant contacts with the outside world also gave India the opportunity to contribute to other civilizations.

The earliest origins of the Indian civilization are traced to the period of the highly advanced urban Harappan cities. Since then, and even before, trade between India and the West had been an important contact which continued until the decline of the Roman Empire.

During the second millennium B.C. the Aryans came to India laying the foundation of Vedic Civilization. There are close resemblances between the language and mythology, religious traditions and social institutions of the Indians and Iranians on the one hand, and those of the Greeks, Romans, Celts, Germans and Slavs on the other. Contact between the Indians and the Greeks during the period of Persian ascendancy was close and constant, and became even closer after the military campaigns of Alexander. After Alexander's death his Empire dissolved, but for some two centuries Greek or semi-Greek principalities continued in the north-western regions of India.

By this time the Romans had become the dominant power in the West and Christianity had begun to spread. India and Rome maintained friendly relations—intermittent diplomatically but constant commercially. This brisk trade led to Indian settlements in Alexandria and to Roman and Egyptian settlements in India, and provided further opportunity for a cultural dialogue between Indian philosophy and science and the Hellenistic schools of Western Asia and Egypt. The accomplishments of this era of cultural syncretism have seldom been surpassed.

However, from the fall of the Roman Empire until the discovery of the direct sea-route between India and Europe in 1498 there was little direct contact between the two. This was a period of gradual social disintegration, political upheaval and intellectual stagnation in India. In Western Asia the Arabs were gaining power and it was they who transmitted Indian scientific thought and fables to Europe. At some stage during this period the Romanies began to move out of India towards the West carrying with them certain segments of Indian culture, especially music and dance.

The Europeans came to India in the last decade of the fifteenth century but their interests were mainly commercial. It was not until the last quarter of the eighteenth century that a real understanding of Indian learning began. The European intellectual world, Germany in particular, gradually became receptive to Indian religious thought and Sanskrit literature.

In recent times, in consequence of the frequent exchange of Indian and European scholars, and of improved technology, greater dissemination of Indian knowledge and thought took place. This includes Gandhi's ideas—especially his doctrine of non-violence and Satyagraha—which came to be known widely in the West.

Northwards, Indian cultural contacts extended through Central Asia to East Asia. Central Asia had been in the closest contact with India, and remained a thriving centre of Buddhist culture for nine or ten centuries. From Central Asia Buddhism travelled to East Asia and helped to build the philosophical and metaphysical framework of East Asian thought, and to mould the distinctive civilizations of China, Korea, Japan and Tibet.

Indians came into contact with the countries of Southeast Asia principally for commercial reasons. But wherever they settled they introduced their culture and civilization. In turn, they were influenced by the indigenous culture, laying thus the foundation of a new culture in the region. Indian cultural contact with Southeast Asia covers a period of more than thirteen hundred years, and segments of Indian culture even reached eastwards of this region, across the Pacific Ocean, the periphery of ancient America.

India was influenced by Iran, Greece and then Islam. The synthesis between Islamic and Indian cultures took several centuries to complete, and throughout India the pattern was an initial clash followed by fusion.

FOREWORD

While India was in a state of political unrest and cultural stagnation, European powers and influences appeared in the country. The introduction of Western culture, English education and scientific techniques gave a jolt to India's traditional life. The long dormant intellectual impulse suddenly became active and a new Indian spirit was born, leading to the modernisation of India.

Whilst the transmission of ideas, goods and influences was mainly from India to the outside world in ancient times, in modern times it has been the other way round. If a broad generalisation is permitted, it would appear that there is hardly a major school of thought with which Indian thought has not entered into a dialogue at one time or the other, directly or indirectly.

The story has been told in bits and pieces in hundreds of works. This study seeks to put these pieces together in a co-ordinated whole to synthesize the original research of numerous authorities, including scientists, philosophers, historians, linguists, archaeologists and anthropologists. Most of the judgments are of specialists but have been woven together in a wider historical context. Often they appear in a new guise and give rise to new overall conclusions.

Transmission of ideas proceeded in a variety of ways. During the early phase it was mainly through the large-scale migrations of nomadic peoples. Later, as life became more settled, merchants, settlers and, to some extent, soldiers were the principal transmitters. With the expansion of intellectual life and organised religions, new classes of cultural couriers, such as scholars and missionaries, were added. Mediaeval military conquests, such as the Islamic, also transmitted ideas to and fro. In modern times, with scientific and technological advances, cultural exchange became prodigious.

The problems involved in the study of such a vast and varied subject are many and complex. When an encounter between two powerful civilizations takes place, its vibrations are felt at all levels and cultural synthesis proceeds in a variety of ways, some of which are not detected for a long time, and some never. During the long, evolutionary process of assimilation, the original character of an idea may be retained wholly, partly, or not at all. It is a kind of chain reaction giving rise to new ideas. All this, strictly speaking, is part of the impact of the new culture but, for a historian, it would be impossible to determine such influences with even rough accuracy.

Moreover, such impact generates both positive and negative response. Positive response would include direct borrowing, while endeavouring to bring out one's own inherent vitality of traditions and purity of beliefs. Negative response would include rigid defence of all traditional concepts and institutions which cements conservatism and leads to rigidity in society. Defence also often leads to irrational defiance, even to counter attacks. Reluctant to accept new ideas and yet unable to reject their validity, conservative resistance sometimes gives birth to further new ideas. Arnold Toynbee calls the three responses on the part of receiving civilizations "recoil," "adaptation" and "synthesis." No amount of human ingenuity can trace the full course of cultural interaction in all its ramifications through all these stages. At best the assessment of mutual influences must remain partial and even at times subject to divergent opinions.

Cultural interaction is not a wholesale transplantation of a culture. It assumes a certain degree of cultural development on the part of the participant groups. In assessing the degree of mutual influence, allowance must be made for the independent development of intellectual traditions in the various areas. For all ideas and concepts have a common beginning, however small and remote, in the primitive societies to which we trace our common ancestry; all human groups have, in their respective ways, wondered at the surrounding universe and have sought to see reality beyond it. The common nature of inquiry can lead to similar results, reached independently. Again, certain ideas of a fundamental nature, from which further theories have developed—some form of monism or dualism, for instance have been common to all communities. Man's methods of reasoning are somewhat similar all over the world, as are human reactions. It is therefore to be expected that attitudes towards certain concepts would be common to all human groups. If, however, the cultural resemblances are too close in detail, too frequent in a given situation, or are accompanied by evidence of contact, mutual influence ought to be accepted.

The uncertainties of Indian chronology present a most difficult problem. Five thousand years or more of Indian history is generally classified into three periods: ancient, mediaeval and modern. There are differing views on both the nomenclature and dates covering each period. In fact, until some important dates were fixed with the help of Greek sources, there was an almost complete absence of dating in Indian history. Even now the dates of political events and the vast mass of literature which form the basis of cultural study are imperfectly known. Historical facts seem to dissolve in the hands of ancient Indians changing into epic poetry, sagas, mythology and legends. Time was unreal and of secondary importance. Consequently genetic analysis of philosophical ideas had little relevance to the value of ideas.

Considerable work, however, is being done in fixing Indian dates and a break-through may occur soon. Unless this happens the antiquity of a concept and consequently its nationality cannot be finalised. For instance, if an idea is known to have existed both in India and Greece at about the same time, by our present system of dating, it is not possible to know precisely whether it was of Indian or Greek origin.

There is, at present, a broad working outline of Indian history which has been compiled with the help of foreign sources. Naturally not all scholars accept its accuracy; Indian scholars generally suggest earlier dates for Indian works and events than do others. Until this dispute is resolved, the conservative dates, which are acceptable to those who assign later dates to Indian historical events, have been used in this study.

The vague usage by authorities of the terms Oriental, Western and Eastern in relation to cultural influences and concepts, without distinctly identifying the exact known or accepted area of their origin, presents no less a problem for the student of comparative culture. For instance, Iranian, Egyptian, Jewish, Chinese and Indian are often grouped under the term Oriental or Eastern and all Greek and Roman heritage as Western.

This work, I am aware, should have included many more illustrations than it does, but the consideration of cost and space imposed severe restrictions. Sometimes the difficulties of reproduction and copyright also narrowed the choice.

As no single system of transliteration of the non-English names is recognised as standard, and as my own linguistic equipment is too limited to opt for one or the other with conviction and finality, I have tried to use such versions of these names as are commonly used in modern standard writings, aiming at internal consistency and uniformity.

Because of the variety and technicality of the subject matter, the problem of detailed editing, despite the extreme care taken both by the author and the publishers, has presented numerous questions, some of which may not have been adequately resolved.

My debt of gratitude to numerous authorities, scholars, friends and colleagues is endless. Even if I tried I could not acknowledge by name my indebtedness to the authorities whose writings gave me inspiration, direction and support. Perhaps all historians face in some measure such a predicament. Without the contributions of many scholars upon whom I have drawn freely this work could never have been written. My friends and colleagues have been most generous in their help through discussion, encouragement and criticism. Again, it would be impossible to identify my debt to each of them individually. How does one trace the origins of ideas acquired consciously or unconsciously through reading, and discussions with colleagues or students?

I am particularly grateful to Professors K. A. Nilakanta Sastri and A. L. Basham who read through the whole manuscript with extreme care and patience and made numerous suggestions and criticisms without which the value of the work would have been considerably less. Whilst I have profitted a great deal by their most valuable comments, I alone am responsible for the opinions expressed.

I must also acknowledge my gratitude to Mrs. Mariel Tisdell (neé Eckermann) who helped me with research in a variety of ways and did many long and tedious translations from European languages, especially German. My thanks are due to Professor Namik Oğuztöreli, Dr. Paul Crook, Mr. John Harris, Mr. Clayton Bredt, Dr. Chris Penders, Dr. Sutjipto Wirjosuparto, Mr. Larry Sitsky, and Mr. Wei Ying Wan for reading various parts of the work and commenting upon them, to Mr. Barry Scott for helping me in compiling the bibliography, and to Mrs. Magda Sitsky, Miss Maria Chodzinski and Miss Mary Jane Emerson for typing the various drafts.

I would like to record my thanks to the University of Queensland for providing facilities for research and assistance with grants for travel and collection of material, and to the Social Science Research Council of Australia for assisting me with a grant to visit India on a study trip. Of all the University authorities, I am most appreciative of the help and encouragement generously given to me by Professor Gordon Greenwood. Finally, I would-like to thank Miss Cheryl Malmborg for her industry and help in preparing the indexes.

Despite the wealth of scholarship available to me, this work suffers from various limitations because of my own incapacity to profit more by it.

D.P.S.

Chapter I

HARAPPA TO ATHENS

MAN IS MUCH older than civilization. The written records forming the basis of history reveal only a fraction of our past, a fraction which is at best fragmentary and at worst chaotic. However, with the help of the relatively recent discipline of archaeology, the vista of history has been extended from about five thousand to almost a quarter of a million years, thus enabling the various pieces of the jig-saw puzzle of culture to fall into a somewhat more coherent pattern, even though many large sections of the puzzle remain missing. For thousands of years man lived as any other animal did. But, although one of the weakest of all animals, man alone was capable of adapting himself to his environment and of moulding it to suit his requirements. In many areas, including Europe, he merely adjusted his habits to natural conditions, in others he attacked nature. Consequently, by the seventh millennium B.C., man had begun to settle along areas watered by rainfall, rivers that did not freeze over, and inland lakes. He began cultivating the land and raising domestic animals whilst living in relative harmony with his kind.

The first signs of civilization emerged in the territories stretching westward from the Indus Valley to the Atlantic across western Asia, along the North African shore, and eastward to the Yangtze Valley.[1] In these areas well-organized village life soon developed. Improved agricultural techniques and growing stability led to a closer social organization in which each individual surrendered part of his freedom for the collective gain. As time passed large cities emerged with all the complexities of urban civilization. The earliest known civilizations were founded almost contemporaneously in India, Egypt, and Mesopotamia.

In spite of the paucity of evidence, there is enough to suggest that mankind has always pooled its knowledge and that even at the dawn of civilization there was regular contact between societies and frequent exchange of ideas and artistic techniques. Indeed, the speed of cultural evolution has been so extraordinarily rapid, when compared with the organic evolution of man, that it "seems to be due to the distinctively human capacity of learning from one's neighbour; inventions and devices, created by one society as adjustments to its special environment, can be adopted by another to its rather different requirements."[2] It is, therefore, not surprising that Indian contact with other civilizations should be as old as history itself.

Whilst other ancient civilizations have long ceased to exist, Indian civilization has continued to grow despite revolutionary changes. The ancient cultures of Egypt, Mesopotamia, and Persia have not survived and their present cultures no longer form an unbroken chain linking past with present. Modern Egyptians, for example, are almost completely dissociated from the civilization which flourished on the Nile thousands of years ago. But in India today, Hindus seek inspiration from concepts similar to those originally advanced by their ancestors. Social institutions and relationships, language and literature, are far more continuous than even those of Greece and Italy. The antiquity of Indian civilization may in itself be a doubtful virtue, but the fact that it has survived would imply an extraordinary vitality and self-perpetuating quality surpassed nowhere and only approximately matched by Chinese civilization. Apart from this innate vitality, the continuity of Indian civilization has been largely due to its ability to adapt to alien virtues, to harmonize contradictions, and assimilate new ideas. No country was more frequently invaded and occupied by foreigners, yet, in ancient times, no civilization spread abroad more extensively than that of India.[3] And thus, occupying a central position in the cultures of the world, India has contributed enormously to human civilization.

Indian contacts with the Western world date back to prehistoric times. Trade relations, preceded by the migration of peoples, inevitably developed into cultural relations. This view is not only amply supported by both philological and archaeological evidence, but by a vast body of corroborative literary evidence as well: vedic literature and the Jatakas, Jewish chronicles, and the accounts of Greek historians all suggest contact between India and the West.

It is only during the past few decades that the prehistory of Asia has come to be studied seriously. The skeletal evidence of the archaeological excavations made thus far reveals that the earliest traces of farming communities in the Indian sub-continent are to be found in the area contiguous to Sind, on the western bank of the lower reaches of the Indus River. The region is arid at present but there are indications—for example, stone-built dams erected to control floods—of greater rainfalls in the third millennium B.C. and of a jungle fauna including tigers, elephants, and rhinoceroses. Several distinct varieties of wheel-turned pottery—differing in colour and the character of painted designs—have been found in the region. Too little is known about these antecedent stages of human settlement in the Indus Valley from which emerged the earliest known civilization of India: the Harappan civilization which flourished around 2500 B.C. In this period great cities existed with well-planned houses (equipped with baths, chutes, sanitary arrangements), citadels, communal granaries, highly developed drainage systems and dockyards. There was an organized city government and a settled society. This advanced urban civilization represented an exceptional adjustment of human life to a specific environment.

Whilst the exact area and period of the Harappan or Indus civilization have yet to be firmly fixed, it is now accepted that it extended east and southward far beyond the Indus Valley and that it was certainly contemporary with the other earliest-known civilizations: Egypt and Mesopotamia where two non-Aryan races, the Sumerians and Semites, created amazing civilizations. Geographically, the Harappan civilization was probably twice the size of the old kingdom of Egypt and four times the size of Sumer and Akkad. The main settlements of Harappa, Mohenjo-daro, and Lothal are considerable distances from each other. Mohenjo-daro on the lower Indus River and Harappa on the Ravi River were separated by over three hundred and fifty miles. The smaller township trading centres and farming communities occupied a much more extensive area. Archaeological excavations of the last decade have resulted in a considerable extension of what were formerly believed to be the boundaries of the Harappan civilization to now include areas of Uttar Pradesh, north Rajasthan, and Gujarat. The Harappan civilization, therefore, occupied an area of approximately 840,000 square miles, stretching almost from Delhi to Bombay.[4]

Although these ancient civilizations were largely independent entities, the fact that direct contacts between them existed is supported by concrete evidence, mainly in the form of small objects of value. A number of seals of Indus Valley design and workmanship have been found at various sites in the Euphrates and Tigris areas. Close scrutiny of the seals found in Mesopotamia and a comparison with seals from various regions of western Asia positively indicate that they were either manufactured in the Indus cities or were close copies of Indus types.[5] The form of writing used in the Indus Valley, still to be deciphered, resembles in many respects those used in Sumer and Egypt. This script is pictographic in character and, insofar as it has survived, is almost exclusively engraved on seals in the form of texts, some of which are accompanied by pictures of animals. The paucity of the known inscriptions, the absence of long texts in Indus characters, and the variety and multiplicity of the signs employed have made decipherment impossible so far, although several scholars claim to have discovered a clue to the Indus script. Hopefully more knowledge of the cultural and commercial intercourse between these civilizations will be available once these seals are adequately deciphered. However, it is not unlikely that the seals may be found to contain nothing of great importance.

Characters similar to those on the Indus seals have also been found on tablets excavated from Easter Island. This discovery has presented a difficult problem for the prehistorian. It is not known if the two belong to a common source, if one provided the model for the other, or if the similarity is purely accidental due to inaccuracies of drawing. If the Indus models travelled about thirteen thousand miles eastward, it seems strange that the characters should have remained unaltered, because figures generally do not remain identical during prolonged transmission. And, if the seals were actually made in the Indus Valley and taken to Easter Island, what is the explanation for the differences in arrangement between the two groups of seals? The Easter Island tablets have a boustrophedon arrangement—the alternate rows are upside down—which has not been discovered in the Indus seals so far. Furthermore, the Easter Island tablets are made of local or drift wood. Still, the parallel characters are close enough to suggest contact.

Evidence of Indian contact with the ancient civilizations to her west, however, is certain. Knobbed pottery vases came to Sumer from India and so did cotton. The historical origins of cotton are somewhat uncertain, but the antiquity of the Indian cotton trade is undoubted. In the Akkadian tongue, Indian cotton was expressed by ideographs meaning "vegetable cloth." Assurbanipal (668-626 B.C.) cultivated Indian plants including the "wool-bearing trees" of India. When the Greeks first saw Indians. the latter were dressed in "wool grown on trees." Herodotus mentions Indian cotton, and the first account of cotton grown outside the western boundaries of India was given in 350 B.C. by Theophrastus, who described the "wool-bearing trees" of Tylee (Bahrein), stating that cotton was cultivated in India as well.[6] When perennial cotton plants—originally native only to India—were first grown in western Asia is a matter of conjecture, but "since there is known to have been contact between Mohenjo-daro and contemporary civilizations in Babylonia, it seems likely that the cottons of the Indus Valley were distributed along the Persian coast and as far up the Persian Gulf as perennials could be successfully grown."[7]

Commercial intercourse between the Indus and the Tigris-Euphrates civilizations is also demonstrated by the Harappan manufactures found in Mesopotamia. Semi-precious stones, such as amazonite, came from Gujarat or even the Nilgiri Hills; food stuffs and metal from Rajasthan or Baluchistan: and shank shell from southern India. All these reached Mesopotamia during 'the last half of the third millennium B.C. Indeed, a colony of Indus merchants may well have settled in a Sumerian city. On the other hand, a white marble seal, an adze, pottery rings, and horned figures are some of the items imported from Sumer into the Indus region. Furthermore, some of the numerous naturalistic figurines of baked clay found in Indus cities depict persons of distinctly Mongolian features. Archaeological researchers have also brought to light Indus remains, belonging to 2000 B.C.–1000 B.C., in Southern Turkmenia in Soviet Central Asia.

In southern Afghanistan, French excavators have discovered remains of huge granaries, akin to those of Harappa, and a great mud-brick building belonging to the third millennium B.C., with a facade of half-columns suggestive of Mesopotamia. The full implications of these remains, insofar as they throw light on international contact, have yet to be properly assessed, but their discovery has led Sir Leonard Woolley to suggest, as an explanation of the similarities between the Indus and Sumerian civilizations, that the people of Surner were newcomers from the East who had brought their arts and crafts with them, and that both peoples probably had a common origin.[8]

Indirect contact between ancient India and Egypt through Mesopotamia is generally admitted, but evidence of a direct relationship between the two is at best fragmentary and inconclusive. There are elements in the folk art, language, and rural culture of Bengal which have an affinity with their Egyptian counterparts and which have not been explained satisfactorily in terms of Aryan, Mongolian, or Dravidian influences. There are also similarities between place names in Bengal and Egypt,[9] and recently an Egyptian scholar, EI Mansouri, has pointed out that in both Egypt and India the worship of cow, sun, snake, and river was common. These and other resemblances—such as a likeness between certain pottery ornaments of Mohenjo-daro and those of Egypt, between the Indus script and the Elamite script, between the caste system of India and a similar classification in ancient Egypt—are attributed to "ties of common Dravidian and Aryan blood." Furthermore, the Indian gods, Siva, Visnu, and Brahman, are likened to the solar gods of Egypt; as are Iswara to Osiris; Nandi to Apis; and Hanuman to Cynocephalus. Both in India and Egypt the lotus flower, too, was held sacred.

Of all the Egyptian objects and motifs indicating some contact between India and Egypt during the Indus Valley period, "the cord pattern occurring in a copper tablet in the Indus Valley and on three Egyptian seals is the most striking link between the two countries."[10] Indian products were certainly known since indigo, muslin and tamarind, for example, have been found in Egyptian tombs, and ebony, ivory, sandalwood, and cotton goods reached Egypt from India in the second millennium B.C.

Whether direct or through Mesopotamia, there is "concrete evidence of a network of trade linking up the whole area from the Tigris to the Indus and the Oxus and its extension west of the Euphrates as far as the Nile."[11] International trade on such a scale presupposes efficient organization and attractive profits. Trade was mainly overland, but the discovery of Indus-like seals in Bahrein in the Persian Gulf, the dockyard at Lothal in Gujarat, and a steatite seal at Lothal with two jumping gazelles flanking a two-headed dragon suggest that maritime trade existed as well. Flourishing commercial traffic naturally involved the movement of people. Skilled artisans travelled freely and settled wherever they found a demand for their skills. Agencies and depots must have been established for the collection and storage of freight and cargo. Trade always encourages the pooling of human experience and in the ancient world it was perhaps a more potent agency in the diffusion of culture than it is today. City life, cultivation of cereals, domestication of cattle and sheep, metallurgy, a textile industry, the manufacture of bricks and pots, and the drilling of hard stones for beads were some of the common features of these early civilizations. It cannot be stated with any certainty where these inventions originated, but their dissemination must have been due to mutual borrowing.

The Oriental Institute near Baghdad excavated at Tell Agrab a green steatite vase of typical Sumerian workmanship, portraying a humped bull in front of a manger. As the vase depicts a characteristic scene of an Indus cult, it is clear that by the middle of the third millennium B.C., an Indian cult was already being practiced in Mesopotamia. As in modern times, ancient foreigners demanded the comforts of their religion in a strange country, and this led to the transmission of cults and general religious dissemination. Since Indus manufactures were imported to Sumer and Akkad, and Indus cults were certainly known and possibly celebrated there, the Indus culture must have made contributions, however slight or obscure, to the traditions inherited by Europe from Sumer and Babylonia. Archaeology thus has shown that two thousand years before the earliest references in cuneiform texts to contact with India, she was sending her manufactures to the land where the roots of Western civilization lie. "In other words," as Gordon Childe puts it, "in the third millennium B.C.

India was already in a position to contribute to the building up of the cultural tradition that constitutes our spiritual heritage as she notoriously has done since the time of Alexander."[12]

In both western Asia and the Indus Valley men wore a long beard, shaved their upper lip, and kept their hair very long. The swastika and cross were their religious and magical symbols. The demonolatry of Babylonia with its malignant serpents came to be known in India, and their Babylonian names are preserved in the *Atharva Veda*. The serpent Taimata against whom the *Atharva Veda* prescribes a charm, and who bears a non-Sanskrit name, appears to resemble closely the Assyrian dragon Tiamat. Both in India and Babylonia, physical and mental abnormalities were attributed to demons, and in both regions several powerful demons were believed to cause certain cosmic disturbances. Also fire was the messenger between gods and men in Babylonia as in India. Amongst the other striking similarities between the two cultures are the organization of society into cities; the use of picture signs for writing; and the continued but sparing use of stone, along with copper and bronze, for the manufacture of weapons, tools, and vessels.

Despite these similarities, the Egyptian, Mesopotamian, and Indus civilizations undeniably developed in their own independent ways and assumed distinct personalities. Their tools, weapons, and vessels have different forms, and the symbols of their scripts differ. The Indus civilization itself was thoroughly individual, deeply rooted in Indian soil, and was already forming the basis of modern Indian culture.[13]

The civilizations of Egypt and Mesopotamia were attacked, destroyed and were replaced from about 2000 B.C. by successive military empires which dominated western Asia. At about the same time the Indus civilization was also overrun by the Aryans. During the second millennium B.C. the continuous area of civilization extended from the alluvial valleys to cover most of western Asia and India, with an outpost as far distant as China. The political history of Mesopotamia, however, for the two thousand years before it came under Persian domination, is full of military conflict. Information concerning Indian contacts with the West during this, the later Indus, period is not precise, although documents from Babylonia and Asia Minor testify to some interchange. Recently, in the Babylonian texts of the kings of Akkad and in lexical texts, Leemans has identified two names, Magan or Makkan and Meluhha, with Makran in Baluchistan and with western India respectively.[14] The names of kings recorded in the Kassite documents (*ca.* 1760–1600 B.C.) recall Indo-Aryan deities. It was the Kassites who introduced into Babylonia the use of the horse for drawing chariots, and the late Babylonian name for a horse, *Susu,* seems to be derived from the Sanskrit *asva.*[15] The Kassites, who ruled for several centuries after 1800 B.C., and who were probably not entirely of Indo-European stock, appear to have borrowed some of their gods from the Aryans, for example *Surias* (Sanskrit *Surya,* sun god), *Maruttas* (Sanskrit *Marui,* wind god), *Bugas* (Sanskrit *Bhaga), Simalia* (Sanskrit *Himalaya), Dakas* (Sanskrit *Daksa,* a star god).

The kings of Mittani on the Upper Euphrates, of the fifteenth or sixteenth century B.C., frequently bore Aryan names, such as *Artatama, Sutarna,* and *Dusratta,* and they worshipped the vedic gods, *Mitra, Varuna* (u-ru-v-na), *Indra* (in-da-ra), and the twins *Nasatya* (na-sa-at-ti-i-ia) , an alternative name for the *Asvins,* all of whose names are found in their cuneiform inscriptions. In 1907 Hugo Winckler startled the academic world by identifying four of the numerous gods mentioned in a treaty signed between the kings of Mittani and the Hittites in 1360 B.C. with those already known in vedic literature.

A fragmentary handbook on chariot racing found in the documents at Boghaz Koi, the Hittite capital in Asia Minor, further endorses the Indo-Europeans' common cultural heritage. Many of the technical terms used for so many circuits of the course are very close to Sanskrit. For example, *aikauartanna, teravartanna, panzavartanna, shauaoartanna,* are used for one, three, five, and seven laps of the race. In Sanskrit *uartanam* means a turning. In discussing the Hittite deities, the Bull god and the Mother goddess, Garstang is most arrested by "the obvious parallelism with the symbolism and the ritual of the Indian god Siva, a result for which, however surprising, we are prepared by the inclusion of *Mitra, Varuna* , and *Indra* among the deities of Mittani."[16] The *Marianna* class of warriors among the Mittani is reminiscent of the vedic *Marya,* "the heroes." Numerals and other words of Aryan origin have also been identified in Mittanic texts. During the same period the Tell-el-Amarna tablets mention Aryan princes, such as Biridaswa of Yenoam and Suwardata of Keilah, in Syria and Palestine. The language of the

Mittanis was not Indo-European, and although the Anatolian Hittites were mainly of Indo-European stock, having emigrated from the Araxes Valley sometime in the third millennium B.C., their subjects were non-Aryan Asians and it was the native language, the Babylonian script, and the local gods which the Hittites adopted. The numerals and divine and personal names referred to are actually the oldest specimens of any Aryan speech known to scholars and, significantly, they are in this form very nearly pure Indian, being much more akin to Sanskrit than to any Iranian dialects.[17]

The Phoenicians of the Levant, important in the ancient world as traders, explorers, and craftsmen, were also in contact with India.[18] The Phoenicians were immigrants to Syria from the Persian Gulf. They set up harbour towns and guarded them jealously throughout their history. The Phoenicians were possibly the most adventurous and skilled tradesmen of the ancient world, and their trade with India was profitable and lucrative. Although their territory was neither large nor fertile, their commerce made them rich and powerful. According to Jewish chronicles, as early as 975 B.C., Hiram, the King of Tyre, acting jointly with Solomon of Judah, demanded triennially a fleet to bring ivory, apes, peacocks, almug or algum trees, and precious stones from the port of Ophir. This may have been a port on the western Indian coast—there continues to be much speculation about its location—as the objects imported were unmistakably of Indian origin. Ophir was so famous for its gold that the expression "gold of Ophir" became proverbial in Hebrew.

The sources for ivory in ancient times were Syria, the Sudan, Somaliland, and India. The Phoenicians, who first seem to have imported it from Syria, found this source exhausted by the eighth century B.C. It was then that they turned their attention to India as a fresh source of supply and organized expeditions for that purpose.[19] Logs of Indian teak have been found in the Temple of the Moon at Mugheir built during the sixth century B.C. under the Chaldean Empire, and in the palace of Nebuchadnezzar (604–562 B.C.), who raised Babylonia to a new epoch of greatness. In addition to ivory, the Indians also exported at this time various kinds of birds and beasts (including the valuable Sind horses), cotton goods, gold, silver, and jewels. The Arab traders originally brought rice to Europe from the south Indian ports. Other Indian articles reaching the West from these ports at different times included cinnamon, ginger, pepper, and beryl.

Some of the articles of commerce mentioned in the Jewish annals bear names of Indian origin. For instance, *Kophu* (ape) in Hebrew. is *kapi* in Sanskrit: *eleph* (ivory) in Hebrew, is *ibha* in Sanskrit; and the Hebrew *almug* (sandalwood) is probably from the Sanskrit *valeu*. In tracing similarities in literature, scholars, moreover, have noted the curious resemblance between the *Maha-Ummagga Jataka*[20] and the story of the judgement of Solomon.

During the reign of Solomon (973–933 B.C.) the position of Palestine, situated in easily accessible proximity to India, western Asia, and Africa, became much clearer than before. Solomon's father, David, during his campaigns, had occupied Ezion-Gaber on the Gulf of Akabah. Solomon retained this position because Ezion-Gaber, or the neighbouring port of Elath, was the point of embarkation for India and the Far East, and "he who possessed it and Palestine commanded the bridge which joined three continents."[21] After the death of Solomon, the Persian Gulf became the chief trade route between India and Asia Minor.

The recent finding in 1963 of a round stone-seal from Pandu Rajar Dhibi in Bengal and the identification of its script and pictographs with the Phaistos pictographs and "Linear A" scripts point to the possibility that the Indians of Bengal were in trading contact with the inhabitants of Crete during the second half of the second millennium B.C.[22]

There is considerable evidence to suggest that the ancient Indians were accomplished sailors and enterprising merchants. Allusions to Indian ships and seafaring activities in the vedic and Buddhist literatures are numerous and extensive. The *Baveru Jataka*[23] describes periodic voyages of Indian merchants to the kingdom of Baveru. Scholars equate this kingdom with Babylon, which had become a commercial metropolis after the overthrow of the Assyrian Empire in 606 B.C. The crowded marketplaces of Babylon were filled with merchants from distant lands—Phoenicians, Ionians, and Indians amongst them. References to ships holding seven hundred people are found in Jataka stories. These stories may exaggerate but there is no doubt that Indian seamen built ships larger than those usually employed, even at a much later date, in the Mediterranean.

Assyrian and Babylonian influence on India during the prehistoric and early historic periods must have been significant, although the nature and extent of this influence are very obscure. Bühler suggests that the Brahmi script used in Asokan inscriptions—the parent stock from which all Indian alphabets have been derived—was borrowed from Semitic sources, probably in the seventh century B.C. Other scholars, such as Rawlinson, find Bühler's arguments somewhat unsatisfactory. It has been generally held that the Brahmi script was derived from a foreign source, although there are wide disagreements as to the identity of that source. Since the discovery of the seals at Mohenjo-daro, however, scholars have begun speculating on the possibility that this alphabet may have developed from an earlier ideographic form of writing used in the Indus Valley itself. Therefore, judgement must be suspended until the writing is deciphered. Excavations in the Indus Valley have already led to a revision of the earlier view that Indian art had originated from a foreign source not much earlier than the third century B.C., and additional investigation may well lead to further reconsiderations. The influence, too, of Babylonian mythology on Indian literature, and of Chaldean astronomy on Indian scientific thought, has been suggested and disputed.[24]

The second stage of civilization in India began around 1500 B.C. with the coming of the Aryans who brought a civilization very different from that of the Indus. Still semi-nomadic, the Aryans were mainly occupied with war and cattle-raising and only secondarily with agriculture. The exact location of their origins has been a debatable point in history, sometimes vitiated by nationalistic feeling. Various theories, claiming north, central, or southeast European, or Asian origin, have been put forward. Some scholars even hold that not only did they originate in India but that the vedic civilization preceded the Indus civilization.[25] Most scholars, however, considering the evidence of philology and archaeology, maintain that the Aryans, or Indo-European peoples, originated somewhere in Central Asia or south Russia. It appears that around 2000 B.C. there existed at least a loose confederacy of tribes, stretching from south Russia to Turkistan, who shared certain elements of a common culture and who spoke closely related dialects within the Indo-European linguistic framework. Near the beginning of the second millennium B.C. these Indo-European peoples began to march out of their ancestral home in successive waves towards Europe and India. They reached India around 1500 B.C. Some historians believe they then destroyed the Indus Valley civilization, but evidence for this belief is inconclusive, and it appears to be a bold suggestion by Mortimer Wheeler.[26]

Thus began the period of the *Rig Veda,* one of the oldest and noblest books of mankind. Rabindranath Tagore has described the *Rig Veda* as "a poetic testament of a people's collective reaction to the wonder and awe of existence." In some ways a curious document, it is undoubtedly the earliest monument of Indo-European language, thought, and literature, and reveals a very high level of civilization, even though the Aryans were unfamiliar with the art of writing and possibly did not have a centralized and organized form of government. The *Rig Veda* represents the earliest developed phase of the evolution of religious consciousness and man's response to the immensity of the universe and the inexhaustible mystery of life.[27] The vedic culture, originally foreign to the country, gradually adapted itself to the Indian environment greatly changing its own religious, ethical, and economic content and at the same time permeating deeply into Indian life, thought, and society. Indeed, it is this blending which forms the basis of Indian culture.

At about the time the Hittites emerged in Anatolia the Aryans were spreading into northwest India. They probably proceeded in two directions in successive waves—westward and eastward. The Celts, the Greeks, and the Germans are the descendants of the former branch whilst the Indians and the Iranians are descendants of the latter. There are close resemblances between the language, mythology, religious traditions, and social institutions of Indians and Iranians on the one hand, and those of the Greeks, Romans, Celts, Germans, and Slavs on the other. The theory that the Indo-Europeans were one people is mainly based on linguistic evidence, which has been successfully tested against archaeological studies in western Asia and eastern Europe. Even if they began as one people ethnologically, the complexity of the anthropological evidence suggests that many native groups mixed with them in the various lands where they settled and that they adopted many of the features of the local cultures, including the language.

The Indo-European group of languages—formerly known as the Aryan or Indo-Germanic group—includes most of the languages of Europe,

North America, and India. Despite certain anomalies, the linguistic resemblances between the languages in this group can be presented in a convincingly systematized form which indicates a common source.[28] The grammatical forms and the basic words of the vocabulary, like father and mother and the numerals, are strikingly identical.[29]

The eastern branch of the Indo-European movement is often referred to as the Aryan movement, because the ancient peoples belonging to this group called themselves Aryas, a word which later acquired the meaning of "the noble ones."[30] The Aryans were further subdivided into the Iranians and the Indians. It is inevitable, therefore, that Indian contacts with Iran should be the oldest and the most prolonged. These contacts began in prehistoric times and continued into the Mughal and modern periods. Situated between the plains of the Euphrates and the Indus, Iran has occupied from the earliest times a position which made her one of the principal routes of commerce conquest, and civilization. She has, through successive periods of history, influenced the culture of both her eastern and western neighbours, and has provided a bridge between India and the West. The Persian language, like French in Europe, became the language of cultured people over wide areas of Asia. Persian was the court language of mediaeval India and even today is one of the principal Indian classical languages. Its influence on modern Indian languages is enormous, and India has produced many excellent Persian scholars, both Hindu and Muslim.

The area lying between modern Iran and India, comprising parts of West Pakistan and Afghanistan, was culturally and, at times, politically a part of India. Until the rise of Islam this area was under the influence of Hinduism and Buddhism. Afghanistan was an integral part of the Mauryan kingdom (325–185 B.C.) and later of the Mughal Empire, and many Afghan rulers, including the Turki-Afghans, ruled over Indian territories. Consequently, there are many cultural similarities between the Indian and Afghani peoples. Furthermore, both in its vocabulary and grammatical structure, Afghani is very close to Sanskrit.

Even during pre-Aryan days, contact existed between India and Iran. This is indicated by such evidence as the parallels between the pottery motifs of the two countries and finds of identical objects in both countries. But close resemblances between Indian and Iranian culture date from the days of their common Indo-Aryan origin. It seems most likely that the Indians and the Iranians lived together for some time, perhaps on the Iranian Plateau, before the Indian group moved into India. It is, however, surprising that the cultural link between pre-Aryan India and Iran should have been severed, rather than strengthened, as a result of the migrations of the Aryans into India through Iran.[31]

Although evidence of continued contact between the vedic Indians and the Iranians is not explicit, there is no doubt that the vedic religion has much in common with Zoroastrianism, and that vedic Sanskrit closely resembles the language of the *Avesta.* The Iranian god Mithra, who centuries later found his way into the Roman world and became a popular sun god of the Roman troops, and the vedic Mitra were undoubtedly originally identical. He is invoked as god of light in both religions together with the god of heaven, who is called Varuna in the Vedas and Ahura in the *Avesta.* The beginnings of Zoroastrianism, however, mark a dividing line between the vedic and Iranian Aryans. In the *Avesta* many of the vedic deities became devils,[32] whilst on the other hand, Ahura, asura, came to mean "demon" in the Vedas. By changing the relative statures of the gods, Zoroaster endeavoured to convert the old polytheism into a spiritual monotheism. Varuna was raised to a position of supremacy, having been invested with the sublime majesty of the guardian of the cosmic order (Old Persian *Asa* or Sanskrit *Rta)* and Indra was relegated to the armies of evil against whom the righteous man must fight on the side of Ahura Mazda.[33] Zoroastrianism was almost contemporary with Buddhism, and it is significant that both religions were a protest against the archaic practices of the old Aryan religions.

India was closely allied to Iran in commerce, and indeed through Iran to the areas further west. This commercial contact between India and the West was an important feature of the ancient period and continued unbroken until the decline of the Roman Empire. Merchandise, although it travelled from India to Europe, changed hands at various prominent emporia and was bartered many times in transit. Trade was brisk, and was conducted over both land and sea routes.

The existing overland trade route to the West, largely unheard of before the time of Darius, probably because of the dangers of the journey, lay through northwestern India to the Khyber Pass and thence across the

Hindu-Kush to Balkh which stood on the silk route, the main highway linking East and West. Through this route India had connections with Iran, Greece, Rome, Central Asia, and China. Several routes ran from Balkh to Central Asia and China, as well as two routes to the West. One western route crossed the Oxus River (Amu Darya) to the Caspian Sea and then to the Euxine (the Black Sea); the other, entirely by land, lay above the border of the Karmanian Desert to the north, passed through the Caspian Gates and reached Antioch (now Antakya in Turkey) by way of Hecatompylos. Another important route, probably the oldest and easiest, was through the Persian Gulf, from the mouth of the Indus River along the coast to the mouth of the Euphrates River. The ships then proceeded up the Euphrates and joined the overland route at Seleucia which connected Antioch and the Levantine ports.[34] Another sea route, somewhat circuitous, followed the Persian and Arabian coasts to Aden and then to Suez through the Red Sea. From Suez the goods were carried overland either to Egypt or to Mediterranean ports, such as Tyre and Sidon.

Although a very strong probability of constant communication by land and sea between India and western Asia is clearly indicated, real evidence of political and cultural intercourse emerges only with the rise of the Achaemenians in the sixth century B.C. after the overthrow of Babylon, the last of the great Semitic empires of western Asia, by Cyrus (559-530 B.C.) who laid the foundations of a vast Persian Empire. This event marked a major advance in the history of Iran, and in fact in the history of the world, for the Achaemenians conceived Iran as a state and made it a reality. An extensive Persian empire emerged through a series of conquests stretching from the Indus to the Aegean. It included the ancient kingdom of Egypt, Sind and Western Punjab in India and some Greek city states in Ionia. Darius (521–486 B.C.) reorganized the Empire, throughout the length and breadth of which ran good roads punctuated by imperial military posts.[35]

This great and powerful Empire lasted until it was demolished by Alexander in 331 B.C. It is not known exactly how far Persian power extended, but it is said that the Indian province was the twentieth and the richest *satrapy* added to the Persian Empire. Herodotus tells us of the wealth and density of the population of India, and that it paid 360 talents of gold dust to Persia per year as tribute, an amount which was almost one-third of the revenue of Darius' whole Empire.[36] There is no doubt that Darius, who according to Herodotus was called a merchant by his subjects, and his successors were not satisfied with the existing trade and sought its extension. They wished for oceanic trade with direct contact between India and Egypt, and a direct sea route around Arabia to Africa, through the Red Sea, and thence by some sort of a canal to the Mediterranean.

During the early period of the Mauryan administration, palace organization, court etiquette and deportment were still greatly influenced by Persian ideas and models. Even the Mauryan idea of empire was perhaps inspired by the Iranian example. The imperialism of the Maurya monarchy, especially of Asoka, was a synthesis of Indian, Achaemenian, and Hellenistic ideas.[37] The Maurya Empire was conterminous with the Seleucid Empire of Syria and Iran, because it included within its boundaries parts of modern Afghanistan and Baluchistan which belonged physically to the Iranian Plateau.

The Indian national emblem which contains four lions and a wheel borrowed from the Sarnath pillar of Asoka, is faintly reminiscent of Assyro-Persian prototypes, although clearly modified by Indian sentiment; the *dharmachakra* (the wheel of the law) is, however, also a symbol of the Buddhist faith. As examples of ancient animal sculpture, Asoka's pillars, combining realistic modelling with idealistic dignity and finished in every detail with perfect accuracy, are hardly surpassed in any country or, indeed, in later Indian art.[38]

The use of stone for columns and statues during the Mauryan period instead of ivory, wood, or clay, is also attributed to Graeco-Persian influence. Some scholars have noticed Iranian influence on Chandragupta's system of communications and in Asoka's practice of inscribing rocks and columns, although Asoka's use of such inscriptions to promulgate edicts was profoundly original. Through these edicts he spread the simple and human teaching of the Buddha and preached that true conquest was the conquest of self and the conquest of men's hearts through dharma.[39]

Indian punch-marked silver coinage was on a Persian standard, and the Kharoshthi script was derived from Aramaic, used by the Achaemenians in their official documents.[40] This Kharoshthi script remained in use in the northwestern region of India until the fourth century. The origin of Mauryan court art, however, is a subject of keen controversy, although general opinion appears to favour some Iranian inspiration. Havell, for instance, pointing out that symbolism in Indian art is thoroughly characteristic of Indo-Aryan thought, attributes the resemblances between early Indian and Iranian art to these peoples' common racial origin and imaginative heritage.[41] Certainly, differences of form and type separate the Mauryan columns from those of Achaemenian Iran.[42]

The modern term Hindu, by which the majority of the Indians are now known, is of Persian origin. Indians were known to Persians as the inhabitants of the land of Sindhu, the Indus River. The Persians softened the initial S to H, thus making it Hindu, a name which has survived and come to be applied in a much wider and more complex sense. The Ionian Greeks, who came to know of India through the Persians, transformed the word into Indus (Ιvδύs), and the land of Indus came to be known as India.[43]

Iranian political contact affected India in another important way during this period. India's relationship with the Western world from this time on became increasingly political as Persia provided a common meeting-ground for Greek and Indian merchants, warriors, scholars, and travellers. Perhaps at no other period in early history was communication by land more open, or conditions more favourable for the interchange of ideas between India and the West.

It was during this period (*ca.* 510 B.C.) that the first Greek, Scylax of Caryanda, is known to have visited India.[44] A mercenary sea captain, he was sent by Darius to explore India beyond the Indus, to trace the river down to its mouth, and then to sail back to Persia examining the coastline. After an eventful journey of over two years, he reached Arsinoe, modern Suez. He is thus not only the first Greek known to have visited India but also the first known to have made the Red Sea voyage.[45] It was probably Scylax's account of his adventures, now lost, which formed the basis of Herodotus' narrative of India. Herodotus' account, however, is full of inaccuracies and is hardly more than a medley of travellers' tales. Hecataeus of Miletus, a contemporary of Scylax and the father of Greek geography, was the first Greek to mention India, having also gathered his information most probably from Scylax's account. Hecataeus' work, too, is unfortunately lost.

Another Greek account of India, *Indika,* was partially preserved in the Library of Photius (ninth century). Ctesias (*ca.* 400 B.C.), the author, lived at the Persian court for seventeen years as a royal physician, but in spite of his excellent opportunities for acquiring knowledge about India, he packed his narrative with deliberate lies.[46] The unreliability of Ctesias' information has seldom been disputed. In a recent study, A. R. Burn reaffirms this opinion of Ctesias, describing him "as reckless of truth and concerned only to make an impression; and even when he does tell us a detail which might be true, it is always well to remember the Martichora."[47]

Indian soldiers, clad in cotton garments and equipped with bows and arrows of cane, formed part of the Persian army which fought heroically against the Greeks under Xerxes (468-465 B.C.). India also supplied Persia with chariots and horses, and an Indian contingent formed a part of Darius III's forces which fought Alexander at the historical Gaugamela battle in 331 B.C. These are the earliest known instances of Greeks and Indians facing each other in large numbers.

Although parts of India and Greece were joined in the same state, being the two ends of the Persian Empire, there is a great scarcity of historical materials which might determine with any degree of certainty the nature and volume of the cultural intercourse involved, especially before the campaigns of Alexander. This was the time of the rise of philosophical reflection in Greece and the revolt against the traditional Homeric religion. In India, as well, it was the time of the Buddha and Mahavira who had protested against the finds of the Vedas. Both India and Greece produced civilizations during this period which were to determine for generations the habits of thought and ways of life not only of their own peoples but of many races far beyond their frontiers. The fact that both India and Greece were going through a phase of spiritual unrest and intellectual agitation must have increased not only the ease but the frequency and volume of the exchange of ideas.

In fact, all over the world an unprecedented intellectual revolution was taking place which was to have a lasting influence on human thought. Prophets emerged proclaiming revelations from God, and philosophers appealed to the inherent reason in man. In the Middle East, a succession of outspoken Jewish religious and social reformers appeared, commonly known as "the prophets"—Amos, Hosea, Isaiah, and others. In China, Confucius taught rational morality and in Iran, Zarathustra (Zoroaster) endeavoured to purify the prevalent religion of polytheism, ritualism, and magic.[48] It is noteworthy that this widespread intellectual revolution in the ancient world which was probably the first of its kind in history, should have been preceded by the rise in India of the Upanishads, whose authors were also urged on in their quest for reality by their dissatisfaction with the existing forms of vedic teachings and practices.

During such a period of intense intellectual activity, free contact between India and Greece may reasonably be assumed to account for some of the parallels between Indian thought and Greek philosophy. Ardent classicists dispute the existence of Indian influence as vigorously as any other influence, because according to some, such as Sir Henry Maine, no progress at all would have been possible for the Romans, the Germans, or the English without the Greek heritage.[49] But there has been too much inclination among Western writers to idealize the Greeks and their civilization, and they have tended to discover too much of the contemporary world in the Greek past. Greek patrimony was claimed not only in the realm of thought, but in handicrafts, the techniques of mining, the essentials of engineering, the processes of finance and trade, political systems, trial by jury, civil liberties, schools and universities, gymnasia and stadia, games and sports, art and literature, and Christian theology and practice. In fact almost everything was traced to ancient Greece. In all that concerned intellectual activity and even faith, modern civilization was considered to be an overgrown colony of Hellas. The obvious Greek failings, their shortcomings and the unhealthy features of their civilization, were rationalized and romanticized.[50]

Modern research, however, has marred this comforting image and is helping to put Greek culture into its proper historical perspective showing that, like any other culture, it inherited something from preceding civilizations, profited from the progress of neighbouring cultures and, in turn, bequeathed much to later generations. The Greeks are now regarded as simple, natural, and reasonable people, responding healthily to their environment. A people of mixed descent, like the rest, the classical

Greeks were not pure Hellenes by blood; they were not even a nation. It was during the Persian wars that the tribes in the various regions around the Aegean Sea first achieved a kind of national identity against what they called the "barbaroi." Driven mainly by the fear of foreigners and the need to organize a common defence, the various tribes banded together, and, in this respect, Greek nationalism could be termed a Persian contribution. Though abundantly patriotic, the Hellenes never desired a Greek nation common to all. Their patriotism seems to have been mainly confined to the narrow limits of a particular glen or district, and this is well illustrated by their regional hatreds. Athenian Greeks disliked Ionian Greeks, and fought Sparta in disastrous wars; Boeotia hated Attica, and Attica despised Boeotia as much as it did the Scythians.

It is significant that, although the Indians and the Greeks had come from the same Indo-European stock, they met as strangers in the sixth century B.C. Persian Empire. Soon, however, the cousins became associates in a common cultural enterprise. Similarities in language, accompanied by similarities in religious beliefs, indicate that these two peoples must have either been in close contact at some early period or have had a common origin, even though neither had any recollection of those times. For example, the gods of heaven (Varuna—Ouranos; Dyaus—Zeus) and the dawn (Ushas—Aurora) were common to the Greeks and Indians. The most prominent characteristic of the gods of both races was their power of regulating the order of nature and banishing evil. The Olympian religion of the Greeks and vedic beliefs had a common background. The Greek concept of *logos* was very close to the vedic *Vac,* which corresponds to the Latin term *Vox.* In a passage of the *Rig Veda,* Vac is praised as a divine being. Vac is omnipotent, moves amongst divine beings, and carries the great gods, Mitra, Varuna, Indra, and Agni, within itself.[51] The doctrine of Vac teaches that "all gods live from Vac, also all demi-gods, animals and people. Vac is the eternal being, it is the first-born of the eternal law, mother of the Vedas and navel of immortality." Vedic Aryans attached such great importance to the spoken word that one who could not correctly pronounce Sanskrit was called *barbar* (meaning stammering). The Greek *barbaroi* had the same meaning. There is also a striking similarity between the social life described in the Homeric poems—the *Iliad* and the *Odyssey*—and that found in the Vedas.[52] Homeric gods, like the heroes who believed in them, often rode in horsedrawn chariots. Horse-chariotry was a feature of the life of the Indo-European people, and appeared in western Asia sometime after 2000 B.C. The Homeric idea of a language of the gods is also found in Sanskrit, Greek, old Norse, and Hittite literatures.[53] Some scholars, like Fiske, have even asserted that elements of the Trojan war story are to be found in the war between the bright deities and the night demons as described in the *Rig Veda.*[54] On the other hand, the Indian epics, the *Ramayana* and the *Mahabharata,* also works of great literary merit and deep cultural significance, have been said by some scholars, like Weber to have been inspired by the Homeric poems. Few, however, hold this view now, and most authorities agree with Winternitz that the Indian epics have an indigenous tradition of their own. Whilst the artistic quality and superficial resemblances between these Greek and Indian works are undoubted, the characters they describe are in every instance remote, having only a superficial basis in actuality, and the historicity of the narratives must remain open to doubt.[55]

Although the ancient Greeks did not possess any real knowledge of India, from Homer it is clear that even then they used articles of Indian merchandise which were known by names of Indian origin, such as Kassiteros (Sanskrit, *Kastira)*, elephas (Sanskrit, *ibha*), and ivory.[56]

The earliest beginnings of Greek philosophy lie in the Milesian or Ionian school of the sixth century B.C. Thales of Miletus, regarded as the father of Greek philosophy, was a merchant of whom little is known. He was, however, the first philosopher to express his ideas in logical terms.[57] He predicted the correct time of an eclipse which occurred in 585 B.C.—the first fixed date in Greek philosophy and generally regarded as its starting point. The Ionian philosophers were mainly regarded by later generations as "men of science." Extremely curious about the nature of the external world, a *cosmos* as they called it, the pre-Socratic Greek thinkers, Thales, Anaximander, and other Milesians did not exclude the possibility of a divine agency, but their conception of such an agency differed from the contemporary Greek polytheism. The Ionian philosophers paid no attention at all to the Olympian gods and ignored the Greek *theologia,* the stories or legends of the gods. Yet they had religious ideas and principles, such as the conceptions of *Moira* and

Dike—of purity and impurity—and the concept of the universe as an ordered cosmos and therefore one.[59] Whilst the idea of cosmic law and order appears in simple form in Anaximander, Xenophanes clearly sets forth the concept of a divine intelligence pervading and regulating the world, and Anaxagoras advances the idea of a world-arranging Mind. The Milesians also reflected on the question of the one and the many, and held that all things emanate from a single living substance. They believed that the world arose out of a primal unity, and that this one substance was still the permanent base of all its being, although now appearing in different forms and manifestations.[60] Before the end of the century, however, philosophical speculation in Greece underwent a change of spirit under Pythagoras (532 B.C.) and Greek thought became essentially mystical.[61]

By contrast, philosophical thought in India in the sixth century B.C. had become quite mature. It had reached a stage which could have been arrived at only after long and arduous philosophical quest. Jainism and Buddhism, the latter enormously influential in Indian and neighbouring cultures, had emerged by this time. But even before their advent, the philosophical reflections of the early Upanishads (900–600 B.C.) had set forth the fundamental concepts of Hindu thought which have continued to dominate the Indian mind.

It is perhaps necessary to point out that there has often been a wide divergence between Indian and Western interpretations of Indian thought. Coomaraswamy once even declared that a true account of Hinduism may be given in a categorical denial of most of the interpretations that have been made by Westerners or Western-trained Indians.[62] For example, whilst Western scholars have generally suggested that monotheism arose late in Indian thought, growing out of an earlier polytheism, Indian scholars have pointed out that there was more polytheism in the later vedic hymns than in those of the earlier period. Distorted analyses of Indian thought are, however, rapidly declining both in influence and frequency and an accepted and more accurate interpretation has begun to emerge. Certainly, the divergence of opinion has never proceeded completely along nationalistic lines. In fact, many Western scholars, such as Guenon, are apt to be too generous and too ready to admit that "the position of the West in relation to the East is that of a branch growing out of the trunk,"[63] or like Evans-Wentz, who declares: "Today as it did in the days of Pythagoras, of Plato, of Plotinus, of Appolonius of Tyana, and of other truth-seekers who have been the shapers of the culture and faiths of the occident, 'From the Orient cometh the Light.'"[64]

The tradition of Indian philosophic thought is as complex as it is long, but because of the Indian indifference to chronology, it is impossible to present the detailed development of this thought in its proper historical perspective. Similarly, little is known about the individual thinkers of Indian philosophy, although our knowledge of its various systems is relatively rich. Ancient Indians, it appears, concentrated almost exclusively on philosophies and disregarded philosophers. The complexities of Indian philosophy have arisen through centuries of deep reflection on the many aspects of human experience, and, in the search for some reality behind the external world, various methods have been resorted to ranging from the experimental to the purely speculative. In consequence there developed six basic systems of Hinduism, four main schools of Buddhism, two schools of Jainism, as well as the materialist thought of Carvaka.[65] In spite of this diversity, Indian philosophy in general is distinguished by a concentration upon the spiritual; a belief in the intimate relationship of philosophy and life; an introspective approach to reality which does not however neglect the study of the physical world; a tendency towards monistic idealism, which has not been oblivious to the claims of materialism; and an extensive use of intuitive reasoning for the realization of the ultimate.

Probably the oldest philosophical tradition in the world is to be traced in the ancient Vedas, although there are some prominent pre-vedic elements even in this tradition such as: the influence of forests in the life of the people; temple worship accompanied by the contemplation of the divine in a more concrete form; the elevation of animals, birds, and trees to a position of importance in the scheme of the universe; and the exaltation of the female aspect of the divine.[66]

Although the religious and philosophical spirit of India emerges distinctly in the *Rig Veda,* the Upanishads are its most brilliant exposition, for the vedic civilization was naturalistic and utilitarian, although it did not exclude cosmological and religious speculation. Man offered sacrifice to God as if bound in a contract with Him to obtain material prosperity.

One of the most significant concepts of vedic India was that of *rta,* the idea of thc true order of the world, a concept that may be considered the forerunner of *dharma* of ancient and even modern times.[67] In the Vedas a unique march of the human mind from the worship of half-personified powers of nature, such as fire, wind, and rain, to the conception of the Absolute, the One, is clearly seen. In the beginning there was no clear distinction between one deity and another as all were phenomena of nature. The same name was employed to signify more than one deity, and the same power was attributed to a number of gods. This led to the belief that they were all one in reality. Later, there arose a series of deities, Prajapati, Aditi, Prana, and Kala. But gradually the vedic thinkers, discarding all anthropomorphism, arrived at a single primordial reality, the underlying unity. They call him "many who is really One." It was this tendency towards monism which was later systematically developed in the Upanishads.

Older than Plato or Confucius, the Upanishads are the most ancient of philosophical works and contain the mature wisdom of India's intellectual and spiritual attainment.[68] They have inspired not only the orthodox systems of Indian thought but also the so-called heterodox schools such as Buddhism. In profundity of thought and beauty of style, they have rarely been surpassed not only in Indian thought but in the Western and Chinese philosophical traditions as well. The Upanishads have greatly influenced Indian culture throughout history and have also found enthusiastic admirers abroad. Schopenhauer was almost lyrical about them and Max Müller said: "The *Upanishads* are the ... sources of ... the Vedanta philosophy, a system in which human speculation seems to me to have reached its very acme." The Upanishads are saturated with the spirit of inquiry, intellectual analysis, and a passion for seeking the truth. Being works of a host of sages and scholars, speaking out of the fullness of their illumined experience over a period of centuries, they contain, naturally, many ambiguities and contradictions. The spirit of all upanishadic inquiry, however, was that the final essence or truth was the *Atman—the* spark of divinity within all beings—and that a search for this was man's highest duty. Although a logical and coherent system of metaphysics may be lacking in the Upanishads, it does not matter in comparison with their outburst of the joy and emotion of intuitive experience. The general and overriding tendency found in these texts is toward absolute monism, contained in the recognition of unity between Atman, the individual principle, and *Brahman,* the cosmic principle or essence of the universe, with the emphasis on self-realization. "The Universe is Brahman but the *Brahman* is the Atman." The Upanishads do not argue against the existence of many different gods, but argue that there is one Being of whom all the gods are manifestations, and the real, which is at the heart of the universe, is in the infinite depths of the self. Brahman is Atman and the Truth is within us. Brahman is the universal spirit approached from the objective side; Atman, the self, is the same universal spirit approached from the subjective side. Atman is imprisoned in man's body, mind, and understanding, all of which foster in him a congenital ignorance of his own infinitude and of his oneness with all beings. The true goal of human life is liberation, *moksha,* from this captivity. During the period of the Upanishads, moksha became the end and transcendent knowledge, *jnana,* the means. The gods and sacrifices were dethroned from their position of supremacy, religious formalism and ritualism were discarded, and even the knowledge of the Vedas was considered inadequate. Knowledge is exalted above works as the means of realizing truth, and the highest wisdom is to know the self (*atmanam viddhi*) which is the primal spirit, or pure awareness, distinct from bodily states and mental happenings. "I am *Brahman*" and "Thou art That" are the two key teachings of the Upanishads.[69]

The Upanishads form a principal source for the Indian schools of philosophy. In fact, whilst the Upanishads were being compiled or arranged, the Indian philosophical systems began to be formulated into recognizable traditions. It is difficult to tell how these systems were formulated, but they are generally classified into two major divisions; the *nastika* and the *astika.* The former includes those schools of thought, such as the Buddhist, Jain, and the Carvaka, which neither regard the Vedas as infallible nor attempt to impose their own validity on vedic authority. These schools deny the Atman doctrine of the Upanishads. The latter division, astika, comprises the six main orthodox schools of thought, Samkhya, Yoga, Vedanta, Mimansa, Nyaya, and Vaisesika, which accept the upanishadic teaching.

Indian philosophical thought, in contrast to the Western tradition has remained more stable and more clearly continuous. In spite of its metaphysical nature and religious overtones, Indian philosophy is essentially practical, aiming at realizing spiritually what is known intellectually. Knowledge without vision is meaningless. Hence Indians call their philosophy *darshana,* vision. One progresses from knowledge gained through study, *sravana,* through contemplative meditation and ethical discipline, *nididhyasana* and *manana,* to the final vision, *saksatkara.* Philosophy and religion in India are intertwined, because religion for the Hindu is experience or an attitude of mind, a transformation of one's being, a consciousness of the ultimate reality, not a theory about God. Whatever view of God the Hindu may adopt, he believes that the divine is in man. The supreme being, which is both absolute and God, is conceived as the object of philosophical inquiry, or jnana, and as an object of religious devotion, *upasana.* In religious experience the conception of ultimate reality and that of a personal god are reconciled, although in religious thought the reconciliation is not easy to effect. Philosophy, as religion, is seen in India as a means to an end, not as an end in itself. Hence, there is no room for dogma or intolerance in Indian tradition because the roads to truth are more than one. The infinite reality cannot be comprehended by the finite human mind.

Indian philosophy developed over a period of many centuries in various widely separated regions, yet the philosophers traversed more or less the same path and in many aspects closely anticipated the same philosophical concepts which emerged later in the West. The Indian conception of the bearing of philosophy on life is uniformly the same in almost all systems of Indian philosophy and has inspired all philosophical and religious teachings. That philosophy should not remain just an academic theory but should transform the whole life and lead men to the path of self-realization, ultimately bringing them back to the level of other men, making them share the common duties of social life in a perfected form, and binding them with ties of love together in one humanity, is the final wisdom of Indian thought.[70]

As the principal systems of Indian philosophy originated in times for which there is little chronological data available, their beginnings cannot be traced with any exactitude. There is some disagreement amongst scholars as to the period and order of emergence of the six systems, darshanas, of Indian philosophy, but it is generally agreed that the foundations of these schools had been laid before the time of the Buddha, although further developments may have taken place later. Some of these schools, such as the Samkhya, were probably well established by the time of the Buddha's birth.[71]

Thus, perhaps, India is the home of philosophy. Certainly India is a country where philosophy has always been very popular and influential. An American scholar has stated that teachers of philosophy in India were as numerous as merchants in Babylonia.[72] The sages have always been heroes of the Indians, and some of their festive celebrations were marked by relentless debates between the chief exponents of rival schools of thought. If philosophy did emerge in India earlier than in Greece and if the two countries were in close contact soon after this emergence, it is not unlikely that Indian thought had some influence on Greek philosophy, especially on those aspects which appear somewhat alien to the Greek tradition and resemble the Indian. Theoretically, it is quite feasible, however, that the Greeks had reached their conclusions independently or that they were influenced, as has often been postulated, by the older civilizations of the Nile and the Euphrates.

The similarity between the theory of Thales, that water is the material cause of all things, and the vedic idea of primeval waters as the origin of the universe, was first pointed out by Richard Garbe. The resemblances, too, between the teachings of Pythagoras (*ca.* 582–506 B.C.) and Indian philosophical beliefs are striking. Whereas the Milesians, or Ionians, in eastern Greece had sought the first principle of all things in matter and were absorbed in a scientific explanation of the universe, Pythagoras in western Greece sought it in form. The answers given by Pythagoras and his followers to questions about man represent a more developed stage in abstract thinking and constitute a distinct stream in Greek thought, which had the greatest influence on later developments of Greek philosophy and was notably influential on the thinking of Plato. Pythagoras was an exceptionally outstanding thinker, a founder both of Greek mathematical science and of philosophical cosmology. He was the first to give the name cosmos—an untranslatable word combining notions of order, fitness, and beauty—to the world and to call his own pursuit of knowledge *philosophia* (the love of wisdom) rather than *sophia* (wisdom) which he thought pretentious. He was also the first Greek to teach the doctrine of metempsychosis in the Hellenic world. Pythagoras drew inspiration from the legendary Thracian poet and bard, Orpheus, whose cult included several features absent in the Homeric religion, such as the belief in the immortality of the soul, in its transmigration from body to body, in the existence of an individual and a universal soul, and in the purification of the soul.[73] Connected with the belief in the transmigration of the soul is the most important of the Pythagorean taboos, the abstention from taking animal life. The beast or bird that one eats may be inhabited by the soul of one's ancestor. Initiation into the Pythagorean society required, in addition to the purification of the body by abstinence and self-control, a purification of the mind by scientific study. If the transmigration of souls is possible and usual, then all life is akin. In common with the early thinkers of the Upanishads, Pythagoras believed that "all souls are similar in class and the apparent distinctions between human and other kinds of beings are not ultimate."[74] As in Indian thought, the purpose of life in the Pythagorean system is to gain release from reincarnation through virtue. Pythagoras' cosmic dualism of matter and form—on one side the world of nature and the elements, on the other the spirits, both being combined in organic nature—is also vaguely reminiscent of the *dvaita* (dualistic) philosophy of the *Samkhya*, which recognizes two ultimate realities, *prakriti* (nature) and *purusha* (spirit).

Pythagoras, being a mathematician, expressed his cosmology in mathematical terms. The world in his philosophy is a mixture of light and darkness, good and evil, the formless and the form. The imposition of limit (*peras*) on the unlimited (*apeiron*) created the limited (*peperasmenon*). In the Indian scheme, prakriti is the ultimate cosmic energy—primal matter which exists externally—and is the basis of all objective existence, physical and psychical. Purusha, the conscious principle of creation, coexists eternally with prakriti. The evolution of unconscious prakriti can take place only through the presence of conscious purusha. Both are eternal, devoid of characteristics, and formless. Prakriti in its transformations becomes a perceivable object, whilst purusha, the self, remains the perceiving subject. Pythagoras' doctrine that nothing can arise which has not existed before, and that nothing existing can be annihilated is exactly parallel to the Samkhya doctrine about eternity and the indestructibility of matter. The Samkhya system is so termed because it observes a precision of reckoning in the enumeration of its principles; Samkhya being understood to signify "numeral." Hence its analogy to the Pythagorean philosophy has been presumed. It was Sir William Jones, the founder of comparative philology, who first pointed out the similarities between Indian and Pythagorean beliefs. Later, other scholars such as Colebrooke, Garbe, and Winternitz also testified to the Indian inspiration of Pythagoras.

The history of Pythagoreanism is a particularly controversial subject in Greek philosophy. Early evidence is lamentably scanty, and it is almost impossible to recover the earlier forms of Pythagorean speculation. An insight into Pythagoras' thought during its formative stages might well have led historians to the source of his inspiration. Herodotus, like Plato and others who attributed all wisdom to Egyptian sources, suggested that Pythagoras obtained the doctrine of rebirth from Egypt. This was natural as the Greeks were deeply impressed by the antiquity of Egyptian civilization.[75] However, it is now quite evident that the Egyptians did not believe in the transmigration of souls at all.[76] In discussing the sources of influences on Pythagoras, Gomperz points out, "There is a far closer agreement between Pythagorism and the Indian doctrine not merely in their general features, but even in certain details, such as vegetarianism, and it may be added that the formulae which summarize the whole creed of the 'cycle and wheel' of births are likewise the same in both. It is almost impossible for us to refer this identity to mere chance."[77] It does appear more logical to believe that Pythagoras accepted the most popular Indian theories of the time, which he could well have been aware of, than to speculate that he invented a theory alien to Greek tradition yet firmly held in neighbouring regions. Almost all the doctrines ascribed to him, religious, philosophical, and mathematical, were known in India in the sixth century B.C. The coincidences are so numerous that their cumulative force becomes considerable. The transmigration theory, the assumption of five elements, the Pythagorean theory in geometry, the prohibition on eating beans, the religiophilosophical character of the Pythagorean fraternity, and the mystical speculations of the Pythagorean school all have their close parallels in ancient India. Everyone of the Pythagorean doctrines "which we know formed the 'gospel' of Pythagoras and the Pythagorean brotherhood at Crotona, was an almost exact reproduction of the cardinal doctrines of the Indian Vidya and the Indian Yoga—so much so that Indian Vedantins today do not hesitate to claim Pythagoras as one of themselves, one of their great expounders ...."[78]

Pythagoras' doctrine of metempsychosis appears without any connection or explanatory background, and it was regarded by the Greeks as foreign in origin. Where did Pythagoras gain access to Indian doctrines? Did he travel to India? Although he was a great traveller, it seems impossible that Pythagoras should have made his way to India at so early a date, but he could quite well have met Indians in Persia.[79] Such a possibility seems more likely when it is recalled that Pythagoras was still living in his Ionian home when Ionia came under the Persians, and that it was an age of intellectual ferment. It is also not unlikely that the early immigrants who peopled Greece had come from the East and brought with them some ideas of Indian origin.[80]

Pythagoras also created an organized celibate brotherhood somewhat like the Buddhists, but for political, economic, and religious purposes, which exercised a very wide influence. In fact, the influence of the Pythagorean order grew to such an extent that it incurred the wrath of the tyrant Cylon. Pythagoras himself is said to have met his death by assassination, and after his death many of his followers were burned at the stake in mass executions. After these massacres Pythagoreanism came to an end as a political force, although it continued to survive as a religious cult.

In contrast to Pythagorean dualism, there developed at about the same time in southern Italy, an offshoot of Milesian thought of monistic character, known as the Eleatic school, which incorporated the foundations of Greek metaphysics.[81] In 545 B.C. Ionia had become a Persian province, which led Xenophanes (*ca.* 570–475 B.C.) to move to a new home in Elea. Xenophanes, Parmenides, and Zeno of Elea sought for the one reality underlying material phenomena in very much the same spirit as some of the later vedic hymns and the Upanishads. They tried to prove, unlike Heraclitus, that neither multiplicity nor movement could exist, and they concluded in favour of a stricter notion of unity and the existence of an absolute being. They taught "of a single god who worked by intellection alone, and posited an essential connection between divinity, eternity, reality, and spherical shape."[82] This Eleatic philosophy of a basic unity in all things, the whole of reality consisting of a single, motionless and unchanging substance, is similar to the upanishadic doctrine of the All-one.

Born about 515 B.C., Parmenides was the founder of the Eleatic school and furthered the Greeks on the path of abstract thought, setting the mind working without reference to external facts. He "dealt a death blow to material monism of the Ionian type."[83] His philosophy of the one absolute existence which is being and thought (*sat* and *cit*) at the same time, his recognition of not-being (*maya*) as conceptually antithetical to the idea of being and as essentially non-existent, his explanation of the plurality of the world which is only apparent, his distinction of the phenomenal and the noumenal (the *vyavaharika* and *para marthika*) are akin to the upanishadic teachings as interpreted by Samkaracharya.[84] Gomperz finds an exact parallel to the blissful primary being of Melissus, with its total lack of initiative and influence, in the lore of the vedantic philosophy in which the world is similarly represented as a mere delusive appearance with a central being whose sole attributes are essence, thought, and bliss (*sat, cit,* and *ananda*).[83]

Eleatis criticism of the Ionian philosophy gave rise to a school of pluralist thinkers who saw truth on both sides and attempted to reconcile the two lines of reasoning. This school included Empedocles (*ca.* 495–435 B.C.) who sided with the Eleatics in his denial of becoming but assumed the reality of motion, Anaxagoras, and the founders of Atomism, Leucippus and Democritus. Although the Atomic theory would appear to be the natural outcome of the mathematical knowledge of the Greeks, F. Schlegel has suggested its inspiration in the atomistic notions existing in India at the time. Both Leucippus and Democritus had travelled widely in the East and possibly met Indians in Persia.

Early Greek philosophy was principally metaphysical and only with the emergence of the sophists did it become predominantly humanistic. Born in Thrace about 485 B.C., Protagoras was the first to call himself a sophist. He taught neither science nor scholarship, but conduct. His famous saying, the Protagorean dictum, that man was the measure of all things, became a philosophical doctrine. The sophists were highly expensive travelling professors in the art of success. Little is known about them, and they were not very serious thinkers. They were generally uninterested in absolute religious or moral values, having accepted the widespread notion that morality was a relative concept and a matter of the conventions of particular societies. Socrates (*ca.* 470–399 B.C.) disagreed with this sort of moral relativism, and this eventually led to his conflict with Athenian society. Ironically, sophistic humanism found perfection in Socrates, who regarded the sophists of his day with a certain derision.

With Socrates, as with Plato later, the central preoccupation came to be man, and it was through an understanding of man's nature and behaviour that philosophical thought reverted to questions relating to God and the universe. Socrates preached that the most important thing in life was for man to know what he was and what he was for, and to care for his soul, and he believed that "virtue is knowledge." Socrates wrote nothing and claimed to know nothing, except that whilst he knew that he knew nothing, others did not. Socrates' most lasting contribution was the inspiration he gave to his pupil, Plato.

Historically, Socrates marks a decisive point in ancient Greek thought; whilst restraining the excesses of dogmatism, he did not relinquish the possibility of a knowledge suited to human faculties. Socrates did not precisely formulate a doctrine and is therefore hardly assigned a place in philosophy. He devised the process of induction and founded the study of ethics in its own right, having detached it from religion. Yet he was a deeply religious man and often talked of his inner voice. During the course of his trial, he said that this voice first came to him when he was a child and that it always forbade but never commanded him to do anything which he did not want to do. Unlike most thinkers, Socrates never claimed that he had seen the truth himself, and, in fact, he delighted in confessing his ignorance. Yet he had some convictions of truth which he called inspirations. He *knew* that reality is good and nothing but good, and that this reality could be found, if the search were earnest enough. He arduously sought to find the secret of life and that knowledge which serves the soul. He sought for the truth which reveals God, for the reality which makes goodness real, makes virtue unshakeable and *realizes* the perfection of the soul's relations to all existing things. It was his faith, which he did not attempt to prove, that reality, goodness, and God are all one. He could not think of a real cause which was not good, nor a good which was not nous (wisdom), nor a universe which was not basically both nous and good. In fact, all his questions were but variations of a single question. What are knowledge and ignorance? What is the one? What are the many? What is right? What is the ideal state? Each and all of these were different aspects of his supreme quest: "How shall we find God and be like Him?" It was in this respect that he, and later Plato, turned philosophy into religion and fused metaphysics, ethics, politics, and all other disciplines into an indissoluble unity, just as the Indian thinkers had done in relating all their thought to the one reality.[86]

The view that Socrates could have been aware of Indian philosophy receives added support from the fact that Indian scholars visited Athens during his time. Aristoxenus (*ca.* 330 B.C.), the author of the *Harmonies* and a pupil of Aristotle, is reported by Eusebius (*ca.* 264–364 A.D.) to have mentioned that certain Indian scholars visited Athens and that one of them asked Socrates his views on the scope of philosophy, "An inquiry into human phenomena," replied Socrates. "How can we inquire into human phenomena," the Indian exclaimed, "when we are ignorant of divine ones."[87]

The whole history of Greek and Indian philosophy seems to be a continual dialogue between rational thought and analysis on one side, and religious mysticism on the other, although in India religious mysticism, not in the sense of ecstatic exaltation of the soul but the realization of God within the soul, or "integrated thought" or creative insight, has a more central place. These lines of development have progressed separately and simultaneously and have crossed and recrossed frequently. Intellectualism and mysticism sometimes ran separate courses, and at other times combined to form new ideas.[88] Finally, rational thought was exhausted and philosophy was transformed into mysticism in the form of Neoplatonism. Indian influence upon mysticism is more easily admitted, for instance in the mystery cults of Orphics and of Eleusis.[89] Orphic beliefs common with Indian doctrine were those of rebirth, the immortality and godlike character of the soul, the bondage of the soul in the body, and the possibility of its release by purification. It was a simple concept of union with the divine and of an immortality consequent upon that union. The Orphic was an ascetic who believed that the source of evil lay in the body with its appetites and passions and these had to be subdued before any progress could be made.

The mystic tradition found in these movements, as well as in the doctrines of Plato and Pythagoras, is certainly un-Hellenic.[90] The Greeks generally regarded the corporeal man as the real man and the soul merely as a sort of image. But in the Orphic philosophy the soul is eternal and indestructible whilst the body is transient, unclean, and contemptible. The Greeks also generally enjoyed life on earth, but the Orphics regarded it as a sort of imprisonment. An Orphic phrase, "the wheel of birth" may be a literal translation of the Sanskrit *janmachakra.* Zeller, who upholds the independent tradition of Greek philosophy, concedes that the central idea of the Orphic cult of the liberation of the soul from the body is wholly foreign to Greek nature, and is of Indian origin, acquired by the Greeks through Persia.[91]

The Orphic movement began in the sixth century B.C. and lasted well into the Christian era, and, although it comprised only a small minority of religious devotees, it exercised a profound influence on Greek and Christian religious thought. A concept of sin and conscience, a dualistic view of the body as evil and of the soul as divine, entered into Greek thought; and the subjection of the flesh as a condition of release for the soul became one of the main purposes of religion.[92] Pythagoras probably got some of his concepts from them. The pantheism and asceticism of stoicism and the mysticism of the Neoplatonists can also be traced in part to Orphism, as can Plato's diametrically opposed body and soul. "Plato was not only the greatest original genius of Greek religious thought" writes Guthrie, "but also the one to whom the Orphic cycle of beliefs made the strongest appeal."[93]

The Eleusinian cult does not differ from the Orphic cult in theoretical background except that it places greater emphasis on the correctness of ritual. Although it offers supernatural hopes, it makes salvation dependent upon ritual purification rather than upon nobility of life. This cult also wielded extensive and enduring influence both on later Greek thought and Christianity. The great Greek poets, such as Sophocles (*ca.* 495–406 B.C.) and Euripides (*ca.* 480–408 B.C.), often referred to both cults in their writings.[94]

The mystic tradition finds its fullest expression in Plato (427–347 B.C.), a great admirer of the Pythagorean school. It is significant that Pythagoras is the only great Greek thinker whom Plato never criticizes. In fact, he speaks of him with the utmost reverence, and resembles him in spirit and aim as well as in substance.

Plato lived in a period when the great classical age was coming to an end in Greece. The fratricidal strife of the Pelopornnesian War (431–404 B.C.) had weakened the Greek city states, and Plato wrote in a period of transition. He participated in politics for a while during his early life and wrote mostly on this subject. Behind his writing, however, there lay a profound philosophy and his thought has had an extensive, deep, and lasting influence on the European intellectual tradition.[95] Indeed, the influence of Platonic philosophy on world history can hardly be overestimated. At first it was disseminated through the Academy Plato had founded and later through a variety of philosophical systems, such as the Aristotelean, Jewish-Hellenistic, Neoplatonist, and Christian.

In Plato's philosophy the central issues concern man and his social, political, and religious conduct. But for his solutions he looks beyond appearance to reality. The material world is made up of "appearances," or phenomena, which are only shadows of reality. These phenomena may be perceived by the senses but are unreliable as sources of truth. The truth or truly real is something unchanging, eternal, and divine. It is the world of forms or ideas with its ultimate principle, the good. Plato's idea of the good is very close to the supreme God of the Upanishads. The prayer of the oldest Upanishad

> From the unreal lead me to the Real
> From Darkness to the Light
> From Death to Immortality[96]

is frequently reflected in Plato's *Dialogues.* The dominating thought in Plato is that ordinary man is not truly awake but is walking about like a sleep-walker in pursuit of phantoms. The things which we see are our shadows, and the realm of truth and reality lies beyond. The well-known analogy of the cave[97] in which he illustrates the position of those who are unaware of the truth, reminds us of the Hindu doctrine of maya, the "illusion of the senses." Plato likens the human race to men assembled in a cave, bound, with their backs to a burning fire, and seeing the shadows projected on the wall before them of the people passing behind them, they mistake them for real objects. He made a clear distinction between appearance and reality, as well as between the worlds of thought and sense.

Plato considered the soul to be indissoluble and immortal and the body a fetter to which men were chained "as an oyster to his shell." The body is a tomb of the soul, the source of evil from which the soul longs to be purified.[98] After death the soul passes into other organisms, higher or lower depending on the extent to which the knowledge of good and evil has been pursued by the soul in its previous incarnation. The soul ascends to the vision of divine reality, which Plato calls "The Good" and which is the highest of the ideas or forms, or God himself. To perceive this good is the loftiest goal of knowledge, and the pursuit of wisdom is to loosen the soul from being fastened or glued to the body. For Plato asceticism is one of the most effective ways of liberating the soul from its physical encumbrance, because each emotion of pleasure and pain is a nail riveting the soul to the body. This concept is somewhat alien to the Greek spirit.

To the ordinary Greeks the body counted for a good deal. They made physical education an important part of their training by placing considerable emphasis on games. The essential unity of human soul and divine spirit, the immortality of the human soul, its escape from the restless journey of reincarnation, contempt for the body and the phenomenality of the material world, are all ideas that clash headlong with Greek popular beliefs. Until the fifth century B.C. the word "soul" (psyche) did not have any flavour of puritanism or metaphysical status for a Greek, nor was the soul regarded as the reluctant prisoner of the body; it was the life or spirit of the body and was perfectly at home there. The lasting contribution of the new religious ideas was the suggestion of the divine origin of the soul which was continually at odds with the body. It was this innovation which Rohde has called "a drop of alien blood in the veins of the Greeks."[99] Where did this drop come from? Scholars have given a variety of answers, but most suggest Eastern origins in Asia Minor or beyond in India.

The essence of mysticism, that reality cannot be perceived by sense but can only be reached by inner experience, is present in some form or other in Greek thought from Pythagoras to Plato. In an analysis of Indian and Western religious thought, Radhakrishnan observes:

> The divine origin of the soul, its pre-existence, its fall into corporeality, its judgment after death, its expiatory wanderings through the bodies of animals or men according to its character, its final redemption from the cycle of rebirth and return to God, are common to the mystery cults of Plato and Empedocles. This tradition is something which Hellenic thought, untouched by alien speculation, was perhaps not very likely to have developed, and we have it in a striking form in Indian religion.[100]

Oriental influence on Plato, especially Persian, has been acknowledged by a host of European scholars, such as Jaegar, Reitzenstein, Bidez, and Cumont.[100] If Plato's thought could be influenced by outside ideas such as the Orphic-Pythagorean doctrines, it could be so influenced again. Indeed, there is good reason to believe that he had learned something of Persian religion from a Chaldaean pupil at his Academy and from his friend, Eudoxus, the astronomer, and an admirer of Zoroastrianism. There are also a significant number of scholars, such as Colebrooke, Royle, Pococke, William Jones, and Enfield, who support the theory of Indian influence on Plato's thought.[102]

In a relatively modern and comprehensive study, E. J. Urwick has analyzed Plato's thought and pointed out striking parallels, both in fundamental concepts and in details, between Plato's teachings and those of the vedantic philosophy in India. Urwick is not so much concerned with tracing the degree of Indian influence on Plato as in claiming that platonic doctrines are not easily understood without reference to Indian teaching. He does not claim that all of Plato's writings must be interpreted from a transcendental standpoint and are beyond ordinary rational criticism. But he does maintain that behind his works as a whole there is a background of faith which does not conform to any intellectual philosophy. It is in this sense that Plato's metaphysics, ethics, politics, and science are fundamentally religious rather than rational.

Urwick concentrates his attention on the *Republic,* which he regards as the comprehensive epitome of Plato's thinking, and suggests that Plato and the Indian sages were "occupied with the self-same search, inspired by the same faith, and drawn upwards by the same vision."[108] Urwick has argued at length with great detachment and a remarkable understanding of both the Indian and the Greek traditions of thought.

Impossible as it is to represent his view with justice without writing at some length, it must be observed that he illustrates parallelism not only in Indian and Greek thought, but in the words used to express them as well. He finds that Plato's

> conceptions, arguments, and conclusions are in most cases identical with those of the Hindu Scriptures; the language in which he clothes them is often extraordinarily similar; several of his metaphors are repetitious of metaphors found in the older writings; and the psychological and ethical terms to which he gives a semi-technical use might serve excellently as translations of the corresponding technical terms in the Sanskrit.[104]

The three Indian *gunas* (qualities or elements—or the constituents of prakriti), *tamas, rajas,* and *sattva,* have exact equivalents in Plato's *epithumia, thumos,* and *logistikon,* which both constitute and explain the nature of the soul and the state. Epithumia, like tamas, represents blind desire with its character of ignorance; thumos, like rajas, is the element of power and passion; and logistikon, like sattva, is the rational quality which harmonizes the soul and illumines it. The Indian triad, however is more ethical in its connotation than Plato's terminology.

Just as Manu described the Hindu *Varna* system as having been based upon the three principles in the individual soul, so did Plato divide his state into three classes—guardians, auxiliaries, and craftsmen—representing the three psychical elements.[105] Furthermore, the old Ionian society in Attica was divided into four tribes, associated in tradition with Ion and his four sons, and thus this system is said to have been of Asian origin, presumably Aryan. Aristotle mentions this system as the first and the earliest.[106] Both in Ionia and India, certainly there once existed a social state which was adapted to the fourfold way of life. But in the former the priests were put after the agriculturists. Plato however was inclined to place the priests first, as had been done in India.

Plato's conversion of the soul is identical with the *vairaga* of the Vedas; his contrast between ordinary knowledge and true wisdom corresponds to the contrast between *vidya* in the sense of knowledge and *adhyatmavidya* or direct perception of the spiritual universe; his *nous,* the higher arc of soul divine and immortal, is the *atman* or the spiritual consciousness of the vedantic doctrine; his *dikaiosune* or righteousness is the dharma of Indian philosophy, which appears as the crown and glory of each path, but with a very different meaning in each case. His doctrine of *Anamnesis* or recollection is identical with the doctrine of the origin of all true knowledge proclaimed by Vedantins, and his correlative theory of eternal ideas, designated as his greatest contribution to Western metaphysics, has an astonishingly close counterpart in the vedanta doctrine.[107]

The doctrine of reincarnation has been a common belief in numerous religions from the Hindus to the Druids, and the Greeks could have acquired it from anyone of them.[108] But when it appears side by side with many other essential elements of Hindu teaching, as it does in the philosophies of Pythagoras and Plato, it is fair to assume that it was derived most directly from India.

It seems, however, somewhat surprising that in spite of such close parallelism there should be no specific acknowledgment of the awareness of Indian thought in Plato's writing. It is also strange that such detailed information should have been transmitted to Plato without the aid of any written works; for which, once again, there is no historical evidence, although Plato had hinted as early as the *Phaedo* at his willingness to learn from barbarians as well as Greeks. Whether he meant by the term barbarians, Indians, or only Persians, or both, cannot be deduced by such a vague reference. It is true that Plato was not habitually used to making acknowledgments, but he does acknowledge, even if vaguely, his Greek theological sources. Would he not have done the same for the Persian or the Indian sources, if he had really relied on them? Lack of reliance, however, does not indicate the absence of awareness. Indeed, awareness does not even imply acceptance. Even the rejection of an alien thought must leave behind some legacy of intellectual stimulation. If Plato were aware of Indian thought—and there is enough evidence to reason that he could have been providing his friend Eudoxus was—it would be abusing his intellectual integrity to suggest that he had not reflected upon it, and that he had rejected Indian ideas, banishing them from his mind, just because they were alien. Ancient scholars were much more intellectually receptive than they are generally credited with being. Greek and Indian thinkers were amongst the least prejudiced of them all. Their intellectual arrogance never followed the lines of national distinction. Their contempt was directed, if at all, not at the men of different nations or cultures, but at those who possessed no culture at all. An untutored Greek surely would have been held in much less regard by Plato than a barbaric scholar or a Vedantin from India. Could not the absence of definite acknowledgment of Indian thought on the part of Plato be explained, therefore, by the fact that his knowledge of it was indirect, fragmentary, and, at best, uncertain? Few scholars, even today when it is so fashionable to litter one's writing with prodigious footnotes, would specifically acknowledge their debt unless they were sure of their source and accuracy of understanding. Yet it is equally, or even more, difficult to accept the theory of a completely independent intellectual growth in the face of such striking similarities both in fundamental ideas and in details, particularly in view of the evidence of political and commercial contacts between the two peoples.

One enormous difficulty in appreciating commentaries on Plato and in resolving divergent opinions stems from the very nature of his writings and personality. Both are rich and complex, and an ingenious scholar can easily dig out extracts from Plato's *Dialogues* to suit his objective. In fact, many students have done so, and Plato has been revealed at various times "as a complete sceptic and as a complete mystic, as a pupil of Aquinas, as a Cambridge Platonist and as one of Nature's Balliol men, as an early Christian and as a very early Nazi."[109]

Whether Plato was influenced by Indian doctrines or not, his philosophy, as that of Greece in general, has its own distinctive personality. Whilst the sages of the Upanishads were principally concerned with moksha, release from the cycle of births, Plato mainly preached about the formation of an ideal state. He raised the concept of dualistic mysticism from a religious belief to scientific theory and made it a dominant principle of Western philosophy by transforming it into a philosophic system embracing the whole cosmos.[110] Again, there are many things in Plato's *Dialogues* which are alien to the Indian mind.

Just as Plato departed from his teacher, Socrates, so did his greatest pupil, Aristotle, depart from him, although Aristotle later kept a good deal more Platonism in his thinking than is often admitted. He shared Plato's concern for the goodness of personal and social life, and his ideal of certain and unchanging knowledge. But, although he did not completely reject transcendent realities, he did think that "the objects of philosophic knowledge must be found in and through the world our senses show us, and not in an altogether transcendent world of eternal realities knowable only by the disembodied reason.[111] Less attractive ideologically than Plato, although more orderly, Aristotle refused to believe that the world was anything but real. Yet he had accepted as a young pupil the whole of Plato's philosophy, including the doctrine of ideas, and the immortality and transmigration of the soul. If he later felt compelled to depart from it, he could not make a clear break. Plato's legacy never fully left him and his metaphysics fundamentally remained the same. "For all his reaction towards the standpoint of common sense and empirical fact," observes Cornford, "Aristotle could never cease to be a Platonist."[112] His idealism, however, takes a definite shape in his humanistic works, the *Ethics* and the *Politics,* and his best known contribution thus lies in the sphere of moral philosophy.

Although no one has suggested any contact or mutual influence between Aristotle and the famous Indian political thinker, Kautilya, Saletore, an Indian historian, has noted in a recent study sufficient parallels and contrasts between the systems of these two philosophers to suggest the value of a close comparative study of their ideas. Kautilya was a contemporary of Alexander, though younger in years than Aristotle. It was, in fact, only two years after the death of Aristotle in 322 B.C. that Kautilya became the prime minister of Chandragupta Maurya (320–296 B.C.).[113] Saletore suggests that in spite of divergences, there is a fundamental similarity between their views concerning the nature and functions of the state. For instance, both regard justice as the basis of the state, and self-sufficiency in matters of food, armed forces, and so on as its general function. Both share the view that the state must be concerned with virtue, and both stress the idea of happiness in relation to the state. Amongst the contrasts, Saletore points out that whilst Aristotle's state is to be happy in isolation, well administered with good laws and without conquests, Kautilya could not conceive of a happy state unless it had conquered its neighbouring states.[114]

During the period when Aristotle flourished, contact between India and Greece became much closer, almost direct. His prince-pupil, Alexander, had established Greek paramountcy in the northwestern part of India. And, if the premature death of Alexander in 323 B.C. had not been followed by that of Aristotle himself a year later, it is not unlikely that Aristotle would have visited India, meeting the scholars he so much wanted to, or else, would have received Indian scholars in Greece. Whatever may have been the political consequences of Alexander's death and the disintegration of the Macedonian Empire, the Indo-Greek cultural partnership did not receive as much impetus for expansion as it might otherwise have.

Amongst the factors that contributed to cultural intercourse between India and Greece, a major one must have been the affinity between Indian and Greek attitudes. Both were inquisitive peoples, firmly believing in reason. In India, one often finds the *guru* (teacher) asking the *sisya* (pupil) to be sceptical and always questioning; *sanka* (doubt) is the stepping-stone to spiritual knowledge. Never considered to be in conflict with the right kind of faith, honest doubt, in fact, was considered a corrective to the excesses of the latter. The divine value of an honest doubt is not to be denied. Whilst the guru is the guide in the quest and he alone can dispel the darkness of ignorance, the sisya must draw the guru out by his intellectual scepticism, exercised with the utmost respect for the guru. An Indian disciple is a blend of intellectual independence and extreme devotion for his teacher, attributing all of his accomplishments to the latter. Plato, in this respect, was a true Indian sisya, for he gave Socrates all the credit for his own wisdom. The Jnana Yoga of the *Bhagavad Gita* literally means the path of union through the knowledge and perception of God achieved by intellectual realization. The importance attached to reason in the *Gita* is very great. Krishna asks Arjuna to seek salvation in the wisdom of reason.[115]

The teachings of both the ancient Greeks and the Indians are often in a dialogue form, either between the "knowing guru" and the "doubting sisya" or between two equally matched intellectuals holding divergent views. Already in the early Upanishads, the dialectic method was used to explain empirical and transcendental truths. Knowledge about Brahman was imparted through a system of *samvada* (discussion)—distinct from *vivada* (dispute)—and the discussion progressed gradually from the empirical to the transcendental interpretation. The dialectic method of the Buddha's argument, in which he starts by putting himself in the mental position of the questioner gradually leading his opponents up to his conclusions, is the same as that of the Socratic dialogue.[116] The Greeks, like the Indians, were constantly seeking a religion and philosophy of life which would affect all their activities and produce equilibrium and a sense of harmony.

Geographically and climatically India is very different from Greece. Comprising as it does the land and islands scattered around the Aegean Sea, Greece has, unlike India, no real rivers that are navigable and suitable for ports, and no forests, although in ancient times it is said to have been more wooded than now. But in spite of these differences it is noteworthy that both nations chose mountains as the abode of their gods: the Greeks chose Olympus and the Indians the Himalayas.[117] By and large, neither the Greek Olympian gods, nor the Indian Himalayan deities are credited with having created the world. In fact, Zeus is "one of the very few gods with recognizable and undoubted Indo-Germanic names, Djeus, the well-attested sky and rain-god of the Aryan race."[118] Divinity in Greece, as in India, was cheap; in fact, in India, all beings are supposed to have the divine spark within them. There was a god for everything. Both in India and Greece, gods, such as Indra and Zeus, occasionally came down and practiced deceit, disguising themselves in order to obtain the affections of mortal women. Both races addressed their gods on equal terms. Unlike the Indian gods, however, the Greek gods were malicious, twisting human beings they did not like. And there was no higher god, as there was in India, to check their arbitrariness.

Both Indians and Greeks were fascinated by mathematics and metaphysics. Mathematics excited the Greeks most; Plato was an ardent student and over the door of his Academy was inscribed "a credit in Mathematics is required." Fond of geometry, the Greeks instinctively looked for unity and order in the universe.

Most Greeks were neither pleasure-seekers nor ascetics and accepted life as it came. In ancient India, although there were ascetics, the great majority of people led a healthy life of comfort and, in fact, revelled in physical pleasures without regarding them as evil or immoral. The common conception of ancient India as a country of forest retreats, hermitages, and saint-philosophers is grossly incorrect. Life in ancient India was divided between a highly organized and sophisticated temporal life on the one hand, and the simple and austere life of religious faith and spiritual advancement on the other. It was a materially advanced, socially enlightened, and psychologically uninhibited society in which the pleasures of the flesh received healthy attention.

Although at times saints may seem to be more than abundant in India she has had her share of sceptics and heretics. Even the beliefs of Hinduism prescribed the fourfold goal of human life: *dharma, artha, kama,* and *moksa.* These are not easily translatable terms, but they generally mean righteousness, prosperity, enjoyment, and liberation. Hindu piety which aimed at moksa (integration of the individual with the universal resulting in the cessation of transmigration) through *jnana yoga* (meditation), *karma yoga* (selfless action), and *bhakti yoga* (devotion), allowed all three avenues to run through the four *ashramas,* or stages of ideal life of equal duration. The young aspirant began as a *brahmachari* pledged to a life of abstinence and study, at the end of which he entered the life of a *grihastha* (householder), raising a family and discharging his duties to society. Pursuit of wealth and pleasure was permitted within the bounds of moral law. After the expiry of the period of active life, the grihastha with his wife retired to a forest retreat to meditate on things of the spirit in quietude and live the life of a *vanaprastha.* Free from social bondage, and enriched by knowledge as well as experience, he could reflect more profitably on the problems of life and reality. It was only after this, a kind of refresher course, that the recluse could qualify to become a *sannayasin,* renouncing all worldly possessions, pleasures, and ties of family, nation, and community. A sannayasin had no caste, no religion, and no home. He led the life of a wandering preacher, feeling at home everywhere and exclusively devoted to the service of God. This was the peak of the ideal life and had enormous prestige with Hindus. The fact of its great prestige alone suggests that it was seldom attained. In fact, more often than not the whole scheme of life was not practiced as prescribed.

Whilst the Greek civilization, brilliant for its splendid achievements, was unhappily short-lived, the ancient Indian civilization has continued to grow and, in spite of its various vicissitudes, has retained its original spirit. This spirit is best described as the tendency, whilst finding joy and harmony in the present, to reflect, as the Greeks did, on the supremacy of an inner life.[119] Although ancient Greece is supposed to be the fountainhead of European civilization, it is India, because of her organic continuity in cultural development, which is perhaps closer in spirit and outlook to ancient Greece than the nations of present-day Europe. Without questioning the immense legacy of Greece to Western civilization, it must be observed that the modern Europeans are in many ways different from the ancient Greeks.

The most typical feature of the ancient Greek mind was a sense of the wholeness of things. For example, a typical Greek was several things at once, just as Solon was political and economic reformer, man of business, and poet. The *polis* itself was not a machine for governing, but something which touched almost the whole of life. In contrast, the modern mind divides, specializes, thinks in categories. This difference is reflected in the contrast between Greek and, for example, Gothic arts; between Greek tragedy and English classical drama. In contrast to the Greek heritage, Gothic architecture delights in a multiplicity of parts and Elizabethan tragedy in the whole complexity and richness of life. One could cut a scene from Shakespeare—and he has often been abridged—but not from a Greek play. The Greek hero was an attempt to combine the virtues which the later Western world divided between the knight and the churchman. The sharp distinction which is normally drawn between the physical and the spiritual world, the body and the soul, was foreign to the Greeks at least until the time of Socrates and Plato.[120] The Greeks had a sense of beauty, particularly in connection with the human form and its surroundings, which led to perfect order and balance, even an aesthetic mysticism, in their art and literature.

Yet it was this Greek insistence on the wholeness of things, on reason as much as form, on seeking boldly to explain all nature in nature's terms, that laid the foundations of science and of Western civilization. With all their love of philosophy, the Greeks examined nature not only affectionately but critically. For centuries they combined philosophy and science in one adventurous quest, and set out to explain the world in all its aspects. Although they were hardly scientists in the modern sense, for they lacked the methodical, accurate, and detailed power of observation and of relating observed facts to theory, it was their philosophy which gave birth to science. They considered wisdom not as a "mere theoretical explanation of the world but also a definite practical attitude towards life. In this respect Greek thought shows a striking similarity with the main trend of the Indian philosophical system."[121]

Amongst the Western peoples, the Greeks were the first to attempt to devise an articulate system of concepts concerning the universe and the unknown. They invented the word "philosophy," and their observations and reflections on such problems as the origin and nature of matter, of mind, of goodness, of truth, of reality, and on a vast variety of other themes all constituted part of their philosophy. But they distinguished philosophy from mythology and also from the pursuit of knowledge for utilitarian ends. A philosopher was a disinterested seeker of knowledge wanting to know for the sake of knowing.[122]

The origins of the cultural greatness of ancient Greece lie, significantly, in Asia Minor. Ancient Greece, it may be recalled, comprised two parts, European and Asian, divided or joined by the Aegean Sea. The Asian part of Greece, Ionia, was colonized, according to early tradition, by refugees from the European side of Greece or the Greek mainland, who were escaping from the Dorians and other tribes, and the general similarity between Ionians and Greeks was fostered and increased by the frequent and growing intercourse between them. Although they sprang from the same stock, they were not the same people. The European Greeks were a mixed race as were the Iomans; the intermixing elements in European Greece came from the north, and in Ionia they came from Asia. Later, a large Ionian immigration into Europe formed an important section of European Greece. Indeed, between these two peoples there had always existed bitter rivalry. It was these Ionians, the Graeco-Asians, who not only ushered in an era of intellectual revolution in Greece, but constituted its most progressive and enterprising section. Greek thought, rationalistic as well as empiricist, owes its inception to the Ionian school of philosophy comprising Thales, Anaximander, Anaximenes, Anaxagoras, Herachtus, Pythagoras, and others. Herodotus, the father of history, and Hippocrates, the founder of scientific medicine, although both Dorians, wrote in Ionic. Homer, too, most likely came from Smyrna (Izmir) located in the northern part of the Asian west coast. Aesop, the Greek author of the *Fables*, came from Asia Minor. Even the humble origins of the classical drama, a real literary achievement on the part of Attica, are sought in Asia Minor and the Ionic element of the Athenian population. Delivering the Gifford lectures half a century ago, Sir William Ramsay observed: "The general tendency in modern estimates of Greek thought is to regard Athens as the 'Eye of Greece, Mother of Arts, and Eloquence,' whereas the true source of almost every branch of literature and science, and the earliest great names in almost every department, belong to the cities and colonies of the Old-Ionians."[123]

In tracing the origins of abstract ideas in remote antiquity, it must be admitted that one can hardly be certain or expect unanimity amongst scholars. Whilst scholars during the last century were generally receptive to the theory of Eastern influence on Greek thought, the modern tendency has been to deny or diminish it. Typical of this attitude is Nilsson who denies the origin of Greek dualism in the doctrine of Zoroaster concerning the contest between good and evil in the world but traces it in "Plato's doctrine of the antithesis between the perishable and changeful world of phenomena and the eternal and higher world of the Forms."[124] This may be an overstretched interpretation of Platonic thought but the theory of substantial Eastern influence, too, can be an exaggerated estimate. The communication of philosophy is in general exceedingly difficult; at best, only fragments of thought can be transmitted through layers of peoples, periods, or religions. No record has been found to suggest that the Greeks possessed any written Indian works or vice versa. Furthermore, even if they had had access to some, it is doubtful if they could have read them or had them translated. Whatever scholarly communication there was between the two peoples was oral.

There is no documentary evidence to prove Indian influence on Greek thought. The evidence which has survived is largely circumstantial and is far from being conclusive. In fact, it consists of deductive reasoning, not of certain proof; however, it is strongly suggestive and renders the theory of Indian influence on Greek thought well within the realm of probability. First, there is considerable evidence of close contact between India and Greece. Second, according to Greek tradition, Thales, Empedocles, and others travelled to Oriental countries to study philosophy.[125] Third, the mystical resemblances and parallels at times are too close and too frequent to be purely coincidental. Fourth, features which are attributed to an Indian origin are much in character with Indian thought and alien to Greek attitudes. Finally, these concepts and ideas were definitely known to have existed in India long before they emerged in Greece. This is quite an impressive array of evidence, even if it is not conclusive. Hence, one may be inclined to agree with E. R. Dodds, who suggests an "Oriental background against which Greek culture arose, and from which it was never completely isolated save in the minds of classical scholars."[126] In any case it can hardly be denied, as Macdonnell puts it, that "there is at least the historical possibility of the Greeks having been influenced by Indian thought through Persia."[127]

Much of the uncertainty about the influence of India upon Greece is because most of the contemporary literature on the Greek side has been lost and on the Indian side it was perhaps never preserved. The Indian lack of an historical sense is proverbial and may well be attributed to the attitude reflected generally in Indian philosophy that time is of secondary importance and that the historical context of philosophical ideas can have little relevance to their quality. The Indians possibly concentrated more on absorbing and reflecting upon foreign influences and ideas in order to fit them into their own mould and reproduce them in modified forms. They were not concerned with names or origins; only the content mattered.

Chapter II

CONTACT BY CONQUEST

UNTIL THE GREEK cities of Ionia were captured by Cyrus in 546 B.C., the Greeks lived undisturbed by neighbouring powers. At first the Greek cities offered little resistance and Persian domination was mild. The Greeks were left to develop their own culture and institutions, except for what they voluntarily adopted from the Persians, whose king was looked upon by the distant Greeks as the supreme embodiment of earthly power and glory. Later, however, the conflict became more serious. A Persian punitive expedition against Athens and Eretria was defeated in 490 B.C. Athens became the champion of Greece, and fear of Persian power compelled the Greeks to organize into a nation. They were unable to achieve political unity, but, a cultural unity, with local divergences, was developed. Thus began the great classical age of Greece. It was the period of Socrates, Plato and Aristotle, Pericles, Herodotus, Sophocles and Euripides, the Athenian democracy, and unparalleled prosperity.

During the fourth century B.C., however, internal strife and conflict set in followed by chaos. Between 354 and 338 B.C. Philip of Macedonia completed his conquest of Greece and united it under his rule. After his death two years later, he was succeeded by his son, Alexander, who rose to become one of the most famous conquerors of history. Once Greece was stabilized and reorganized, it was inevitable that they should proceed against their traditional enemy, Persia. In 333 B.C. Alexander soundly defeated the Persian army led by the king himself. Two years later he finally demolished Persian power by defeating their army (which included

Indian contingents under the command of the Bactrian and Arachosian satraps) at Gaugamela. Alexander's victory was an exceptional feat, for few empires in history have been as powerful as that of Darius, and Alexander emerged as the unchallenged ruler of a vast empire stretching from Greece well into Iran. The meteoric rise of Alexander marked a new epoch in world history and introduced an era of Graeco-Macedonian ascendancy which, though short-lived, left an indelible mark on Western civilization. Few periods of European history have seen greater political changes than the century and a half that followed the emergence of Alexander's power.[1]

Determined to conquer the eastern part of the Persian Empire and India, Alexander with a Graeco-Persian army crossed the Hindu Kush, invaded the Punjab in 326 B.C. and defeated, at heavy cost to himself, its ruler Paurava (Porus). Alexander wanted to press eastward toward the Ganges Valley and Magadha, but his troops refused to advance, for they were too tired to face the powerful monarch of Magadha. They had heard rumours of a vast nation Prasioi (Sanskrit Prachya, eastern) ruled by a king named Xandrames with a mighty army. Alexander himself was anxious to keep going till he reached the sea which he believed, as did Aristotle, encircled the earth and communicated with the Caspian and the Persian Gulf. He was also anxious to see the Ganges and the area through which it flowed, because he had been told that the Ganges was much more impressive than the Indus, the sheer magnitude of which had already filled him with surprise, despite already having seen the Nile, the Euphrates, and the Tigris: "No country he had hitherto visited was so populous and well cultivated, or abounded in so many valuable productions of nature and of art, as that part of India through which he had led his army."[2] And when he was informed of the even greater riches and beauty of the country ahead, he was naturally eager to continue on.

The enforced withdrawal from India was a shock to Alexander from which he never recovered. He suffered a further serious blow when his most trusted commander drank himself to death. In the midsummer of 323 B.C. at the age of thirty-two, he fell ill; heavy drinking aggravated his illness and resulted in his death.[3] Although extreme alcoholism was rare in Greece, Alexander was much addicted to drinking and, according to

Polycleitus of Larisa, was always accompanied to camp by flute players, both male and female, who drank with him until daybreak.

The military and political greatness of Alexander is beyond question, and even before his early death he had become a legendary figure. Had he lived longer, there is no telling what influences he might have brought to bear on world history.[4] He had become increasingly ambitious and dreamed of conquering the world. He considered himself a divine hero and employed his power ruthlessly to gain success and obedience. In a state of anger and drunkenness, he murdered his friend Clitus with his own hands, and his best general, Parmenion, was dispatched by hired assassins. In the pursuit of power he had lost personal peace.[5] If Alexander was vainglorious, and at times cruel and vengeful, it was probably the legacy of his superstitious, scheming, and hate-ridden mother, Olympias. Although only half-Greek himself, Alexander was full of the Greek spirit of inquiry, having been tutored by Aristotle. In spite of the fact that the Macedonians regarded themselves as Hellenes, the Greeks refused to treat them as a part of the Greek nation and, indeed, called them barbaroi. Aristotle himself was not, strictly speaking, a Greek, but came from Stagirus in Chalcidiee, east of Macedonia.

Alexander was frustrated in his plans to advance further east, to build great roads, and to set up sea communications, but he did succeed in establishing a Graeco-Asian empire. Although this empire did not survive his death, it left behind a bridge connecting the principal centres of ancient civilizations. Across this bridge began a traffic in ideas and culture, thus enriching the course of human history. His expedition to India, in terms of cultural intercourse between East and West, can only be compared to the discovery of a direct sea route to India by Vasco da Gama. Like da Gama, Alexander did not discover a new country, nor did he open up a forbidden land, but he did inaugurate a new process of cultural fusion, and greatly increased and enhanced the existing cultural relationships.[6]

Alexander founded about seventy new cities with the aim of creating a mixed Greek and Asian empire; of these Alexandria in Egypt was the greatest, later becoming an important centre of commerce and culture for the Hellenic and Roman worlds.[7] Aiming by marriage to bring the Asians and Greeks together in common military service and thus create a joint commonwealth, he took two Asian brides—Roxane, daughter of Oxyartes of Bactria, and Statira, daughter of Darius from Iran—and more than ten thousand of his troops including eighty of his principal associates, such as Hephaestion and Seleucus, married Asian women. Naturally, these Asian brides transmitted some of their culture to Greek families.[8]

On his Indian expedition Alexander was accompanied by a number of scholars whose purpose was to acquire knowledge about ideas and religions. His staff also surveyed the roads in the Asian areas, which led to increasing traffic both in commerce and culture. Many of Alexander's companions and officers were men of high attainments in literature and science. Some of them wrote their memoirs recording their impressions of India. Whilst some wildly exaggerated tales received currency due to inaccurate observation and imprecise writing, the Greeks learned much about Indian thought and lore. Aristotle, having retired to Athens, could not accompany Alexander but had sent in his stead his nephew Callisthenes of Othlynthus, a philosopher and historian.[9] Anaxarchus, a Democritean, and his pupil Pyrrhon (275 B.C.) who formed the Pyrrhonian school of sceptic thought before the time of the Stoics and Epicureans, are also said to have accompanied Alexander on his eastern campaign. Alexander's first halt beyond the Indus was at the great seat of Indian learning, Takshashila, a large and prosperous city from which he sent his ultimatum to Porus.

Anxious to acquaint himself with Indian thought, Alexander made contact with Indian sages and scholars. According to Arrian, he had very much wanted one of the Indian ascetics to join him, "since he so much admired their endurance." The Indian ascetics, however, rejected Alexander's overtures pointing out that his conquests meant nothing to them and that they had no need of anything he had. An old Indian sage, Dandamis, dismissed both offers of wealth and threats of death with equal contempt. After this invitation had been rejected, Alexander finally persuaded another Indian, Calanus, to accompany him.[10] So keen was Alexander to have Indian sages with him, that, having failed to persuade more than one to join him, he began capturing many of them charging that they had helped the enemies of the Macedonians.

Alexander's expedition appears to have made little impact on the contemporary Indian mind, for no mention of the event occurs in the literature of the period. It seems that India did not view the appearance of Greeks on her soil with undue worry or fascination. The Greeks were known to Indians under the Persian form of their name *Yavana* (also *Yona* and *Yonaka*) which was the Sanskrit form of the Persian *Yauna,* which in turn was a derivative of *Ionian.* The Indians did not even learn that the Greeks called themselves Hellenes, and India received nothing of the culture of their country from them.[11] Indeed, Alexander's expedition to India has been described by scholars, such as E. B. Havell, as nothing more than a mere raid, making little difference to India and leaving behind no impression on Indian civilization. For the conditions "which made Greek culture an inspiration for her Roman conquerors had no counterpart in India. The Indo-Aryans, unlike the Romans, had their classic literature, their epics and philosophy, before Athens was built… and at the closest contact of Hellenic and Indo-Aryan culture the latter had by far the greater vitality and creative power."[12] Havell points out, as does Coomaraswamy, that no Greek inscriptions have yet been discovered in India. Yet there are scholars, such as Weber, Windisch, and Niese, who have claimed that Indian civilization was a by-product of the Macedonian civilization. Whilst it is understandable that there should have been a tendency in the West to exaggerate the influence of Greece on India, it is fantastic to assert that "… we can say that Greek culture in western Asia, caused by Alexander, led to the growth there of the idea of spiritual unity, as pointed out by Christianity, and that by inspiring Chandragupta to form the Maurya Empire Alexander caused the spread of Buddhism and perhaps the union of China under the first. Han Dynasty."[13] In one statement all considerations of historical evidence, context, and chronology have been subordinated to wishful thinking.

The only permanent effect of Alexander's raid seems to have been the establishment of a number of Yavana settlements in the Uttarapatha.[14] Even the short-lived administration Alexander tried to establish was copied from the Achaemenian model not unfamiliar to India. Furthermore, negotiations between the Indians and Greeks were channelled through Persian interpreters. An indirect political result of Alexander's incursion, however, was the destruction of the petty states of the northwestern parts of India, thus paving the way for the rise of the

Maurya Empire. Although on the whole the country was left undisturbed, one cannot deny that Hellenism had been brought to the very doorstep of India and that the centuries-old indirect and sporadic contact between Indians and Greeks was thereafter made direct, extensive, and close, leading to an intensification of the processes of cultural interaction. These processes were in no small measure sustained and advanced by the subsequent emergence of the Indo-Greek kingdoms in northwest India.

The death of Alexander in 323 B.C. precipitated the Greek world into an emergency for which no provision had been made, and serious repercussions followed. Alexander, who even in his own short life span had come to be known as the Great, was in fact a restless person who preferred conquest to the consolidation of power, and, possibly, even war for its own sake. He gave, in any case, less attention to the organization and administration of the territories he conquered than "to purely military problems and matters affecting the basis of his own personal power."[13] He gathered a vast empire stretching from the Aegean Sea to the Indus, but, if he had lived longer, it is said that he would not have known what to do with it, except conquer more. Disregard of organization, coupled with Alexander's extreme concentration of power in his own hands and the ruthless execution of his expansionist designs, left behind no powerful body to effectively fill the vacuum created by his death. Disaffection, dissensions, and distrust had already exacerbated relations between his commanders in his own lifetime. In the latter years of his life, Alexander had become far more despotic and tyrannical, even more so than he had been in the early days when he had destroyed the ancient city of Thebes to warn the Greeks not to repeat their efforts to throw off the Macedonian yoke. Having styled himself a god, he had come to lean heavily on the Persian aristocracy. Old friends were considered more dangerous than adversaries, and they were promptly eliminated on the slightest suspicion. His progress "through Asia was marked by court intrigues, political trials, and the liquidation of subversive elements. His last two years saw a reign of terror among his high officers and provincial governors, and his death may have anticipated a major rebellion in Greece."[16] The absence of a legal heir, or a recognized successor, or an outstanding soldier provided the opportunity for Alexander's generals to eliminate the remaining members of his family, including his posthumously born son, and to fight it out for power amongst themselves. Personal ambition dominated their devotion to the dynasty. It was fortunate for them that at this time no foreign power was strong enough or aggressive enough to take advantage of their conflict. A prolonged struggle for domination inevitably followed (*ca.* 322 to 281 B.C.), and Alexander's loosely knit empire split into a number of component parts, each ruled by a Macedonian dynast with all the pomp of monarchy. Of these, three kingdoms were most important: Syria including the eastern part of Alexander's kingdom, Egypt, and Macedonia. The largest and the richest was Syria, where Seleucus established his dynasty with his capital in the great city of Antioch; the Ptolemies, descendants of Ptolemy Lagus, ruled Egypt with Alexandria as their capital, and controlled the sea; and Macedonia, of which Greece was still a dependency, after much bloodshed and strife passed on to the descendants of Antigonus. Seleucus tried to expand into India in 306 B.C. but had to retreat before the forces of the powerful empire of Chandragupta Maurya. The Mauryan king probably married a Greek princess, acquired large parts of the former Greek-Asian kingdom, and received at his court a Greek envoy, Magasthenes, who has left behind invaluable information on the India of his day.

The founders of these dynasties were soldiers who were principally concerned with retaining their power and who were "generally expected to marry their sisters to keep the stock pure."[17] Macedonia was the original national monarchy, and the other two were in a way usurpers. Each of them, especially at the beginning of their rise to power, had ambitions of gaining absolute supremacy over the others and restoring Alexander's empire. Consequently, these kingdoms fought themselves to exhaustion before the Romans, who had begun to emerge as a dominant international power during this period, established their sovereignty over them. Macedonia was the first to fall to Rome in 167 B.C., and it was followed by Egypt in 30 B.C. The Syrian kingdom, plagued by rebellions and succession troubles, pursued a precanous existence in varying degrees of independence between the Romans on the one side and the Parthians, the inheritors of the Achaemenian Empire' and the Mauryans on the other, until the rise of the Arab power in the seventh century. But for all practical purposes, the Syrian kingdom ceased to be important after about 160 B.C.

These powers are commonly called "Hellenistic," a term originally applied to non-Greeks who admired and copied Greek civilization, and the period of their independent existence (323 to 30 B.C.) is similarly designated.

Whatever the political consequences of these conflicts and strifes may have been, they certainly caused large-scale movements of peoples, as distinct from armies and hordes of nomads, from one area to the other. Thus, people living in distant regions came into closer contact with each other and accelerated the processes of cultural intercourse. Asia became a land of opportunity for Greeks. Greek soldiers were soon followed by Greek traders and settlers in large numbers to Egypt and the far corners of the former Persian Empire. Inevitably their Asian counterparts responded in a similar manner. Consequently, the following Hellenistic Age saw the development of thought, both scientific and philosophical, in which a variety of national traditions were freely mixed.

The Mauryan kings, especially the first three, maintained close diplomatic relations with the Hellenistic kingdoms. Syria, which was the home province of Seleucus and his successors, was in close diplomatic contact with the Mauryan Empire of India. Megasthenes lived at the court of Chandragupta, and Deimachos came on an ambassadorial mission to King Bindusara.[18] The Thirteenth Rock Edict of Asoka refers to five Greek rulers—Antiochus, Ptolemy, Antigonas, Magas, and Alexander—and there are indications that Asoka's missionary activities had reached Greek states. A. S. Altekar suggests that "Asoka's Buddhist missions were operating in western Asia, Egypt and Macedonia and the rise of the Essene sect, to which Jesus belonged, has been attributed to the influence of the Buddhist missions."[19] Asoka's Greek-Armenic inscription recently excavated at Karidahar would further strengthen the view that there was close contact between Mauryan India and the Hellenistic world, and that there must have been a well-established colony of Greek settlers or Greek-speaking people to justify inscriptions in Greek. Megasthenes tells us that there was a separate department at Pataliputra to look after foreigners, which would indicate the usual presence of a number of foreigners, such as envoys, tourists, and traders in the Mauryan Empire.

After the decline of the Mauryan Empire, Indo-Greek principalities emerged in the northwestern region of India, providing yet another bridge between India and the Hellenistic world. Alexander's Indian expedition, followed as it was by the rise of the Seleucid kingdom in western Asia, created settlements of Greeks—Indo-Greeks or Yavana—in the northwestern regions of India, although there is considerable evidence, both literary and numismatic, that even before Alexander's advent, Indo-Greek colonies had existed in this area. Whilst the Mauryans were powerful, the Indo-Greeks remained subdued. They were far removed from the centre of Mauryan power, and the influence of the Seleucids had always been at best precarious. The decline of the Mauryan power on the one hand, and the rise of the Parthians challenging the Seleucid supremacy on the other, made it possible for these Indo-Greeks to set up their own independent or semi-independent states. By about 250 B.C. they had disavowed the Seleucid Empire which at that time covered Persia and Syria, and forty years later their independence was recognized by Antiochus. In about 190 B.C. Demetrius I had established his authority in the Indus region and for the rest of the century the area remained under Indo-Greek rule. By this time, these peoples had become essentially Indian in religion and thought. Buddhism had been prevalent in India for well over two centuries, and its exponents had developed an exceptionally dynamic character, a highly sophisticated creed, and, under Asoka's inspiration, an unprecedented zeal for missionary work. The greatest of the Indo-Greek kings was Menander (Milinda) (*ca.* 180–160 B.C.), and he was converted to Buddhism by Nagasena.[20] The Mauryan domination of the Indo-Greeks for a long period possibly expedited their adaptation to Indian ways. Indeed, to describe the Indo-Greeks as Greek at all is somewhat misleading; they were even less Greek than modern Australians are English.

These Indo-Greek principalities which survived for some two centuries played a very significant role in both Hellenistic and Indian history. During this period many Greeks settled in India and gradually became integrated into Indian society. Trade between India and the Hellenistic world increased considerably, and was regarded as enormously important to Seleucia. The outburst of prosperity in that city between the years 175 and 150 B.C., and the heavy increase in the output of its mint; almost exactly coincides with the great period of Indo-Greek rule in India, from Demetrius to Menander. Enormous quantities of ivory and spices from

India were exhibited by Antiochus IV in his triumph at Daphne in 166 B.C.[21] The Indo-Greek trade was so brisk that Parthia, through which the land trade passed, also grew wealthy.[22] The Greek word *drachma* passed into Indian languages through Prakrit *dramma* to *dam.*

Although no trace of Greek architecture has ever been found in either India or in the borderlands, India is indebted to Greece for improvements in coinage, astronomy, and sculpture.[23] Greek sculpture appealed to the Indian imagination, and the Gandhara school of sculpture, which flourished in the northwestern parts of India and Central Asia, is a fine example of this assimilation. The sculpture is usually described by the name of the ancient territory where it primarily flourished, Gandhara, the capital of which was Purusapura (modern Peshawar), although other finds of this art form in Khotan and in the vicinity of Kabul render this title somewhat misleading. Gandhara sculpture is also described as Graeco-Buddhist after the statues of the Buddha cast in Graeco-Roman style, although this sculpture really developed only after the Greek domination of this part of India was in the historical past, and its principal patrons were the Sakas and the Kushans who came from Central Asia.

The precise chronology of Gandhara sculpture is uncertain and the questions posed by its different styles are an art historian's delight. The school began to emerge in the middle of the first century B.C. after the decline of Greek power and before the rise of the Kushans. It reached its peak roughly between 50 and 200 A.D., coinciding with the reign of the great Kushan kings. None of the sculptures found is later than 400. The best period of Gandhara art was contemporaneous with the Flavian and Antonine periods in western Asia and Europe, and with the reliefs at Amaravati in South India, as well as with many sculptures at Mathura. The Gandhara school, however, stands apart from the main current of the evolution of Indian art. The technique used is, no doubt, basically Hellenic, but it is modified by Iranian, Scythian, and Indian traditions and trends, for the period during which Gandhara art evolved witnessed the advent not only of the Greeks, but of other foreigners who ruled these territories. About the beginning of the first century B.C., the Indo-Greeks had been overpowered by the Parthians and Sakas, a warlike people of Scythian extraction. They ruled over the northwestern parts of India until the end of the first century A.D. The new invaders, called Yueh-chih by the Chinese and Kushans by the Indians, first settled briefly in Bactria and in the valley of the Oxus; they then penetrated into the Indus territory. Their empire, which attained its peak under Kaniska, was on the crossroads of the Hellenistic, Persian, Chinese, and Indian cultures, and in terms of cultural intercourse it was one of the most productive periods in ancient history.[24]

The themes depicted by the Gandhara school are purely Indian and almost exclusively Buddhist, and the image of the Buddha in numerous guises dominates the compositions. A major explanation of this appears to be that in the area concerned Indian cultural and religious influences had been at work for a long time, and Gandhara art, devoted to Indian culture but employing an eclectic technique, really represents a stage in the process of assimilation of the Greeks in this region.[25] Once Indianization had commenced, the Greeks placed their artistic skill at the service of a foreign religion, an act unparalleled in Hellenistic history, and helped create for it a new art form. Whether the Greeks were Buddhist or not, they worked for the Buddhist world. "Nothing can be more eloquent of the Indianization which was taking place and of the attitude of Greeks generally to Buddhism; it has been well said that the art of Gandhara was born of Buddhist piety utilising *Yavana* technique."[26] Coomaraswamy, however, does not view Gandhara art very kindly. He regards it as a phase of Roman provincial art mixed with Indian elements, which gives the impression of profound insincerity and only faintly expresses the spiritual energy of Buddhist thought.[27]

The Gandhara artist's portrayal of the Buddha in human form was in itself an innovation, probably Greek, and to render him in terms of the Graeco-Roman divine figures with their typical features, such as robed in a Roman toga with wavy hair, was wholly foreign to Indian notions. The Gandhara artist turned the Buddha into an Apollo, but the image bore all the iconographic marks and traits of the Indian tradition, all the canonical symbols traditionally belonging to him, and the reliefs depicting scenes from the Jatakas remained unchanged even in the minutest details. The Gandhara image of the Bodhisattva starving himself to death is perhaps "the most incongruous example of the mixture of India and Greece. Here a thoroughly un-Greek theme has been rendered in an equally un-Indian style."[28]

Whilst the influence of the Gandhara style did not penetrate India proper, it did continue to influence the art of Central Asia until the destruction of the Buddhist monasteries in the second half of the fifth century by the Ephthalites or White Huns, who, having overpowered Persia, advanced towards India. But, in its way, it deeply impressed Indian and Asian cultures. The iconographical, rather than the aesthetic, representation of the Buddhas, Bodhisattvas, and scenes from the Buddha legend gripped the Indian imagination and thereafter it travelled with Buddhism to Indonesia, Burma, Cambodia, Thailand, Ceylon, and other Buddhist settlements. Through Central Asia it penetrated to China, Japan, and Tibet. Consequently, countless statues of the Buddha and the Bodhisattvas are found in the Buddhist world, many of which are excellent examples of the exquisite local artistic traditions.

Vedic religion did not provide for idol-worship and there were no temples in vedic India. In vedic times, conception of a personal deity, which is the indispensable psychological basis of iconographic representation, did not exist. Although Visnu, of whom many iconographical representations are found, is a vedic deity and his personality is vividly described in a few hymns, the earliest iconographical representations of him (dated 401) are two four-armed figures standing one on either side of the door guarding the Chandragupta cave at Udayagiri.[29] The teachers of the upanishadic period were only interested in liberation from the realm of name and form, and they did not ask artists to represent sages or saviours. They were so disinterested in external appearances that their strict monism was not conducive to iconographical reproduction. Early Buddhism was strongly opposed to the Buddha being represented by statues. In Indian art the Buddha's presence was indicated by the Bo-tree, or the wheel of law, or some other symbol. For centuries Indian Buddhists felt a repugnance to depicting the Buddha in human form. Even the great royal patron of Buddhism, Asoka, who experimented with various styles of representational art and pioneered the growth of lithic art in India, felt neither the need nor the compulsion to cast a single image of the Buddha or his disciples.[30] But Greek influence in Bactria was strong and statues of Apollo—like statues of the Bodhisattvas—began to appear, and these were soon followed by images of the Buddha himself. This, in turn, gave tremendous impetus to image-worship amongst the Hindus, which has come to form such a dominant feature of popular Hinduism that images are to Hindu worshippers what diagrams are to geometricians.

Opinion, however, is divided as to whether image-worship was practiced by the Indians before Alexander's campaign or not. It should be noted that in the popular religions of the early Indians a strong anthropomorphic undercurrent was present. It remained subdued under the dominance of the vedic religion, but later it received impetus under the theistic devotional cults. There is epigraphic data revealing Vaisnava shrines in the various parts of India during the pre-Christian and early Christian periods, and it may be that very early images, of which there is definite evidence, have been lost because of their perishable materials. Finally, this innate anthropomorphism and iconolatry asserted itself with vigour and found expression in images of the divinities or saviours, especially the Buddha, during the period of Mathura art, which, although contemporary with if not anterior to the Gandhara school, had its own independent and unbroken sequence of development. And it has been argued that the Gandhara Buddhas had little or no influence, and that all the later Buddha statues were derived from the purely Indian art of Mathura.

The isolation of India has never been absolute, and Mathura, being the converging point of ancient routes from all directions, was one of the principal areas visited by travellers. Whilst Mathura art has a long and glorious tradition of continuous and autonomous evolution occupying a very important place in the history of Indian art, no one has dated the Mathura Buddhas before the Christian era, and they are usually assigned to the second century. Thus, in chronological order the Gandhara Buddha is older than the Mathura Buddha. When this order of priority is considered together with the knowledge that the Mathura artists were aware of the contemporary Gandhara tradition, the possibility of Mathura having borrowed the idea of Buddha statues from Gandhara becomes very strong. Features alien to the Indian tradition and in conformity with that of Gandhara, such as drapery hanging in curved folds from the figures of the Buddha and certain motifs such as the woman and the acanthus, appeared on some of the Mathura figures of the later period.[31] It appears that Mathura art developed its own tradition of iconographical representation, but the Gandhara influence accelerated this process and gave it a new dimension by introducing the expression of the divine image in human form. Between them, these two schools introduced the figures of the Buddha and Bodhisattvas into Buddhist art. In this enterprise the Gandhara school may well have been the dominant partner, for it is extremely unlikely that without its inspiration, direction, and competition the Mathura school could have, on its own, given rise to mass worship of images. Although this cult had existed in some parts of India before the advent of the Greeks, it remained on the whole insignificant and fragmentary until the Greeks gave it impetus.

The Greek influence on Indian coins and gems is undoubted. The datable history of Indian coinage begins in 600 B.C. with silver and copper punch-marked coins.[32] These coins were primitive in conception, irregular in shape, and crude in execution, and whilst important to historians, their aesthetic value is negligible. With the penetration of Hellenistic, Roman, and Parthian influences through the Indo-Greeks, the form and character of Indian coins changed radically. Artistically interesting, the chaste and elegant workmanship of the early coins from the second century B.C. to the first century A.D. clearly reveals the Hellenistic tradition. With the passage of time, the Hellenistic influence weakened and Indian characteristics began to assert themselves. However, the Indians learned from the Greeks the art of embossing both sides of their coins.

A large number and variety of engraved gems have been found all over northwest India, and these are undoubtedly Hellenistic in conception and workmanship. The motifs and themes employed are Greek and the gems often bear legends in Greek and early Brahmi or Kharoshthi scripts. In the first and second centuries the Greek inspiration gave way to the Roman.

Yavana bodyguards, engineers, and girls were in demand in India. Even in the extreme southern Tamil country, the Greeks were sought after. In the very early Tamil literature of the Sangam period (first three centuries), clear references are found to Yavana traders, soldiers, palace guards, night-watchmen of the streets, and lamps of Yavana workmanship. Kalidasa (fifth century) in one of his plays represents the king as being accompanied by a body of Yavana women. These girls had already appeared much earlier in the plays of Bhasa. This is confirmed by other evidence, including Greek. Amongst the articles which Indian kings would buy, as listed in the *Periplus,* occurs "good looking virgins for concubines" and it appears to have been a standing order. Poseidonius also testifies to this traffic in girls.

Greek influence on the Indian theatre has also been suggested, for the first curtain is called *Yavanika* (the Greek curtain). It is also claimed that the Indians borrowed from Greek drama their ideas of the screen, the parasite, and the clown, but there is little evidence to support the assertion that the Greek tragedies and Homer's works were known in early India, and Yavanika could not have been borrowed from the Greek stage for there the curtain was not used. Although Greek dramas were not acted against a curtain, Roman, and possibly Greek, mimes were, and Yavanika may suggest the influence of Greek mime on Indian drama. A more likely origin of this word would appear in a Prakrit modification of the Sanskrit word *Yamanika* from the root yam, meaning "to bind," "to fix," used for a curtain with ropes to fix it.[33]

By the time Greek influence had emerged in India, Hindu drama had already assumed a distinctive personality with a highly evolved form. Indeed, the art of the drama seems to have been well established in India from the earliest times. Apart from the tradition of the divine origin of Sanskrit drama, there is in the *Rig Veda* a remarkable series of dialogue-hymns with a dramatic element, such as the famous "Pururavas and Urvasi" hymn.[34] The grammarian Panini refers to acting in the fifth century B.C., and in the fourth, Kautilya describes theatrical companies. In the art of puppet plays, which certainly appears to have developed a couple of centuries before Christ and possibly even earlier, a point of culmination can be seen in the development of drama, as well as an impetus for it. At the Sitabenga and Jogimara Caves in the Ramgarh Hills in Bihar, inscriptions can be found dating from the third century B.C. which suggest the existence of a developed dramatic art, and at Sitabenga Cave, even a sort of crude stage has been excavated in the rock. The earliest available specimens of literary drama are found, however, in the fragments of some Buddhist dramas of Asvaghosa, the court poet of Kaniska, and the earliest available dramatic works are the thirteen plays ascribed to Bhasa (*ca.* 200–300).

Basic differences in approach and style between Indian and Greek drama are also revealed upon close scrutiny. It was during the fifth century B.C. that drama emerged in Greece as a highly developed art form. Furthermore, whilst the Hindu theatre was intimate and restricted to a limited audience of scarcely four hundred spectators, the Greek amphitheatre could seat twenty thousand. Greek drama was not divided into acts, but the Sanskrit *natakas* (plays) had definite divisions ranging from four to ten acts. The unities so rigidly adhered to by the Greeks were unknown to Sanskrit dramatists either in theory or practice. For example, the unities of classical drama were not strictly observed by Sanskrit dramatists, although each act was usually limited to "one course of the sun" and each play to one year, but unity of place was not regarded as a necessity, and subsidiary plots entwined the main trunk of Sanskrit plays. A Hindu play was composed expressly to mark a certain occasion, such as a coronation, triumphal procession, religious festival, or marriage, and was generally not revived after the occasion had passed. The Greek concepts of tragedy and early Attic comedy, as in Aristophanes, were totally alien to the spirit of Indian drama. The latter in general is more romantic, mythological, and metaphysical than the Greek. However, Indians must have had opportunities to watch Greek plays, as a scene from *Antigone* appears on a fragment of a locally manufactured vase found near Peshawar.

A few common Greek words, such as the words for pen, ink, book, and camel found their way into Sanskrit, and a few Sanskrit words reached the West, but on the whole there was surprisingly little exchange of language.

It is also somewhat surprising that India, who had borrowed freely from Persia and had never been averse to foreign ideas because of the all-inclusive nature of her thought, should have refrained from profiting by Greek art. A possible explanation may be found in the different concepts of art and beauty held by the Greeks and Indians. The Greeks loved beauty for its own sake and found not only joy but truth in it, whereas the ancient Indians, whilst loving beauty, sought some deeper significance in their work, some vision of the inner truth as they saw it. Whilst the Greeks had a passion for form, the Indians were obsessed by the formless. Indian art was much too firmly embedded in Indian religious thought and its metaphysical basis to find an affinity with Greek art. Another reason for India's failure to profit from Greek art may have been the inability of the Indo-Greeks to transmit Greek influence to India, for they were only remotely in contact with Hellenic culture and, in fact, became Indianized themselves during the period of Mauryan domination. Furthermore, the Greeks came to India not with the zeal of missionaries but on military campaigns and remained to carry on commerce.

Discussing in some detail this interaction between Greek and Indian civilizations during the Indo-Greek period, W. W. Tarn, a great admirer of Greek civilization and of its intrinsic vitality, observes that although two peoples living side by side for a long time on good terms must be mutually influenced, India adopted little of Greek culture. And whatever little she did adopt, did not last. In explanation he suggests that "Indian civilization was strong enough to hold its own against Greek civilization, but, except in the religious sphere, was seemingly not strong enough to influence it as Babylonia did; nevertheless we may find reason for thinking that in certain respects India was the dominant partner."[35] Indians living in Greek principalities as Greek citizens did not even take Greek names, as was common enough amongst Asian people at the time. They kept their own customs and culture. Greek rule was eventually overthrown everywhere and by the middle of the first century nothing of them was left. Tarn says that "... except for Buddha-statues, the history of India would in all essentials have been precisely what it has been had Greeks never existed"[36]

As the era of classical antiquity and Greek exclusiveness declined, an enervated Greek culture was accorded rejuvenating influences by Eastern cultures. The limited world of the city-state was transformed into large-scale government, the Greek polis was replaced by the world-state, and a new conception of world power was born. The old distinctions between the Greeks and the barbarians were replaced by world culture, and Hellenism, under the impact of Asian culture, became elastic and cosmopolitan. The repercussions of this change were almost all-embracing. Social and economic life had to be remodelled, political institutions and religious beliefs had to be recast, and experiments had to be made with new ideas. Concepts of a universal state, universal monarchy, universal law, and universal religions and philosophies began to spread. During this period there developed the conception of an emperor's divinity and absolute monarchy which played an outstanding part in European thought and political life. It enshrined Julius Caesar in a state cult as "Divus Julius"; it inspired Augustus (the assumption of this name, which has strong associations with divinity, by Octavian is in itself significant); it helped the Papacy and the Holy Roman Empire during the early mediaeval period; and it later led to the extravagant claims of the Tudor and Stuart kings in England, the Bourbons in France, and the Czars in Russia. The theory originated in an age in which religion, theology, and politics were inextricably mixed, and it came to be articulated in mediaeval times during the conflict between Pope and Emperor to assert the claims of sovereignty of the latter, and to find a positive theoretical support for the rejection of papal claims to spiritual, as well as temporal, overlordship.

It is commonly suggested that Persia provided Alexander with the inspiration for this theory of the divine right of kings, for after his remarkable military successes he pronounced himself a god. It is impossible, however, to obtain unanimity on a question which cuts deeply into national pride, but the dispute can be narrowed. The widespread cult of the divine rulers, which progressively developed into a dominant force in Europe, was entirely an internal growth evolved in a Western environment. Alexander had realized it, if at all, only briefly and almost in passing, in western Asia and the Levant. Taylor's contention that the monarchy which Alexander established was itself a combination of Greek and Macedonian traditions and the Persian conception of the king as an absolute power, the ideal representative of his people in every secular and religious office, is historically invalid.[37] Tarn, for example, strongly disputed Taylor's assertion that the Persians worshipped their kings and that their practice had influenced Alexander in his claim to divinity.[38] Consequently, Taylor partly revised his earlier opinion but maintained that the Persians had a form of ruler-worship, which must be considered in discussing the Hellenistic ruler cult, thus presumably conceding that the evidence of direct Persian influence on Alexander's deification is negligible.

The Achaemenian kings were not gods and did not claim divine rights. In Egypt there existed a cult according the king a divine status and authority. But the influence of Egypt on later Greek king-worship, and in the transformation of the Macedonian monarchy into a Ptolemaic god-kingship, seems to have been comparatively unimportant. If the Persians prostrated themselves before their king, it was a perfectly respectable form of court etiquette which in no way implied worship, and which has parallels in many other countries, such as kowtowing in China. Kings, modern or ancient, have always demanded and received from their subjects devoted respect far above that which is normally given to an elected head of state. King-worship is in reality nothing more than a form of flattery. Before, during, and after the Hellenistic age, and even in modern times, king-worship has always been at best deference, and ordinarily hypocritical and insincere—a political gimmick. Seldom have people anywhere seriously believed in the divinity of kings, although they may have acknowledged it in helpless dependence on his power, from fear of punishment, in the expectation of reward, or simply as a trivial irrelevancy, immaterial one way or the other. It is also doubtful whether even the kings, who never tired of claiming it, seriously believed in it beyond its efficacy as a political device to command blind obedience. Hence, to regard the Persian custom of prostration as indicative of king-worship is erroneous. It is also true that Macedonians and Greeks found this custom repugnant. In fact, Callisthenes, who had done more than anyone else to spread Alexander's fame through his writings, who had even extravagantly invented the story that the oracle of Apollo at Dityma had broken its long silence to endorse the oracle of Ammon that Alexander was the son of Zeus, and who had supported Alexander in his claims to divinity, refused to submit himself to this Persian custom even at the risk of Alexander's displeasure, thus courting certain execution which followed soon after on a charge of alleged conspiracy.

If in Persia and Egypt there was some evidence that men had come to believe in a single universal society under the authority of a powerful king who could receive undivided obedience from his subjects, it could hardly be taken as constituting indisputable proof of prevalent king-worship. In return the king received devotion, loyalty, and gratitude. To receive adoration is not to be a divine incarnation. In Greece too, long before Alexander, some Greek rulers had claimed divinity and had been worshipped during their lifetimes, although this may have been a political measure rather than an official cult.[40] The Hellenistic historian, Duris of Sames, tells us that the Spartan leader Lysander, the first man to gain widespread power in the Hellenic world, was also the first man to be worshipped, and that he would very likely be a man "to whom Alexander might naturally look back as a forerunner of his power in the Greek world."[41] The tyrant Heraclea (363–352 B.C.), intoxicated with power and wealth, called himself the son of Zeus and thought of himself as Zeus in person. He used his divine pretensions deliberately to strengthen his tyrannical rule.

Of course, in contrast to the Semites, who markedly distinguished between God and man, the Greeks conceived gods in human form and elevated men to the rank of gods. It was common practice in Greece to promote founders of cities to the rank of hero and to offer them "hero-worship" after their death, although in later times the term "hero" came to be used for men whom death had removed from the envy and rivalry of their companions. But there were some men—such as Dion, given heroic honours in 356 B.C. by the Syracusans—who were accorded this status in their lifetime. Homer, certainly, uses the Greek word *heros* freely for his heroes while they were still alive.[42] Hero-worship—for example the cult of Hercules and of Ammon—was quite common in Greece, and the distance between hero-worship and king-worship surely must be a short one.

It is true, however, that the worship of kings by Greek cities was somewhat different from the official cults instituted by the kings themselves. In Persia too there was no such official cult at the time. The oracle of Ammon, which had pronounced Alexander to be the son of Zeus, was well known in the Greek world for its incorruptibility, and Alexander, like all Greeks, believed in it and insisted on its validity. Lysander sought its aid unsuccessfully in his efforts to give himself divinity. Alexander's father, Philip, was deified by some of his followers, and Plato was similarly honoured by his scholars. Aristotle, Alexander's tutor, argued in a famous passage of the *Politics,* presumably with Alexander in mind, that there might exist in a state an individual so pre-eminent in political insight and virtue that he should be followed as "a god among men" and for whom there was no law, because it would be wrong to treat a person, so unequalled in virtue and political capacity, as an equal. He should not be a member of the state at all; he should be above it. So Alexander's deification, even if it had received any impetus from the Egyptian or Persian examples, had deeper roots in Greek concept and practice. Sir Ernest Barker put it clearly that "However foreign it may seem to the Greek idea of the state as a free association of citizens, the conception of the deified ruler was none the less rooted in Greek habits of thought; and the actual deification of Alexander may be traced among the Ionian Greeks in the beginning of his campaign before he touched the soil of Egypt or of Persia."[43] In addition to Egypt, Greece also began and perpetuated the deification of rulers. For a full half-century after Alexander's death no ruler claimed divinity for himself, but, during this interval, "many Greek communities voted of their own accord divine honours (temples, images, altars, priests, processions, games, sacrifices) to their rulers."[44] There was nothing oriental in this king-worship, it was a purely Greek political phenomenon. To the common man the power of a king was self-evident whilst that of a god had to be accepted on trust.

In a recent 'reassessment of Alexander, E. Badian has attempted to explain Alexander's claims to divinity in terms of his growing insanity. He suggests that the severe psychological impact on him caused by his failures in India led Alexander to discover the insecurity of power, which all his scheming could not overcome, and this in turn drove him to seek refuge in the greater exercise of power, and finally to seek and believe in his own divinity. His success in his purges and in the Susa marriages and his dealings with the mutineers only increased the resulting instability and led him to ask for absolute authority, like that of a god dispensing the fate of mortals.

He had always liked and encouraged the story that he was the son of the god Ammon (a Libyan god whom the Greeks identified with Zeus and whose oracle he had visited). The myth had been useful to inspire loyalty, particularly in Greeks, whose religion had a place for such things. But he now actually began to believe in his own divinity. About the middle of 324, he sent envoys to Greece demanding that he should be worshipped as a god. There are many anecdotes about the reluctance with which the Greeks complied .... Nor had he anything to gain by deification of this enforced sort: divine status would give him no significant political rights in a Greek city state, and men's opinion of him would not change for the better. There is no escape from the conclusion that he wanted deification purely for its own sake, for psychological and not for political reasons. As for the Greeks, they had to obey.[45]

Considering that stories were afloat even during his own lifetime which cast doubt on his paternity—that Alexander was not the son of Philip but the begotten son of a god—it would seem logical that Alexander should have been anxious to establish his divinity and establish his kinship with Zeus-Ammon. Tarn, however, who took a view of Alexander that was somewhat romantically coloured, says that Alexander never called himself son of Ammon, resented being called so, and that he similarly never called himself son of Zeus, although he allowed others to call him so. He became god of his empire for entirely political reasons.[46] Whether he was being vainglorious or Machiavellian would make little difference to the main argument that Alexander introduced the element of divinity into kingship.

An historical reason, which has not often been emphasized, for the currency of the cult of king-worship may have been that of the three kingdoms which acceded to Alexander's heritage only Macedonia had a legal right to this heritage. The Seleucids and Ptolemies were illegal intruders or usurpers. They naturally desired some basis for their power other than force, and this they found in making themselves divine rulers. The Seleucids became gods after death—although later divine status was bestowed upon living Seleucids as it was upon the Roman Emperors—but the Ptolemies, following the practice of the Pharaohs, became gods during their lifetime.

Besides the new concepts of kingship and kingdoms, the Hellenistic age saw the development of the universal philosophies of Stoicism and Epicureanism, the two most profound systems of antiquity to emerge after Aristotle's death. The popularity of mystery cults, such as the Eleusinian and the Orphic, also increased. The chief feature of this period was that as philosophy and science parted ways, philosophy and religion united. The Hellenistic age, especially the period between the foundation of the Lyceum about 325 B.C. and the end of the third century, saw the transformation of Greek science from an untidy heap of scattered observations into systematic disciplines. In some branches, such as mathematics and astronomy, it reached a level that was not attained again until the sixteenth century. Giving expression to the newly emerged world consciousness in Greece, the two chief philosophical systems of the period—the Stoic and the Epicurean—revived the old principles of Ionian monotheism.

As an inevitable consequence of Alexander's conquest, much of Greek thought was rendered obsolete and useless, especially those theories of morals and of social organization which were the most typically classical and which taught that happiness in the highest sense was possible for members of limited and self-governing societies. Now the very structure and nature of society underwent change; the sovereign city-state ceased to exist. With the expanding state, the horizons of the mind also widened. For the first time in Greek history, Greek institutions stood exposed to rational criticism and traditional ways of life were subjected to the pressures of cosmopolitan culture. Also for the first time in Greek history, "it mattered little where a man had been born or what his ancestry was: of the men who dominated Athenian intellectual life in this age, Aristotle and Theophrastus, Zeno, Cleanthes, and Chrysippus were all of them foreigners; only Epicurus was of Athenian stock, though by birth a colonial."[47]

For a time Greek philosophy kept its concern for the ordering of human life in accordance with the earlier concept, but it became increasingly interested in the individual rather than the community. The process of change was initiated by the nihilistic pronouncements of Pyrrhon (*ca.* 360–270 B.C.) who, together with Anaxarchus, had accompanied Alexander to India. He questioned the validity of existing presuppositions; for him the only certainty was that of no certainty at all. He declared that definite knowledge of any subject was impossible and that the principal aim of man was to lead a virtuous life. He wrote no works except a poem addressed to Alexander, but his philosophical system was recorded by his pupil, Timon of Philius. Although his school did not expand greatly, the Pyrrhonian scepticism may be regarded as a forerunner of the Stoic and Epicurean schools. Only a short time later the Stoic philosophy was introduced into Athens by Zeno of Citium (335-263 B.C.), who established a complete system of philosophy encompassing logic, epistemology, physics, and ethics. Stoicism, which taught a natural unity of men amongst themselves, a moral and spiritual community with all peoples and gods, and that happiness was the result of freedom from physical appetites and of obedience to the will of the gods, was the most inspiring of Hellenistic philosophies and by far the most dominant. Its teachings exerted a greater influence on the lives of men and the development of states than either the Academy or the Lyceum.[48]

Zeno came to Athens from Cyprus but he was a Phoenician. The population of his native city, where a number of Asian relics have been excavated, included settlers from Phoenicia and his mother tongue was Phoenician. In the beginning his followers were known as Zenonians but they later came to be known as Stoics because he used to discourse promenading up and down the colonnade or porch (stoa) of Peisianax. Not only was he a Phoenician but three of his immediate successors—Heraclides, Antipater, and Zeno of Tarsus—also came from Phoenicia, having been born at Tarsus, on the coast of Cilicia, which had become a kind of outpost of Stoicism. Considering that all of them came from the west Asian territory, which at the time was a principal meeting-ground between Asia and Greece, it is not unreasonable to assume that some sections of Zeno's philosophy, particularly those which sharply depart from classical Greek thought and resemble Indian doctrines, may have been influenced by the latter. Some scholars, however, in an effort to show historical and natural continuity have suggested that Stoicism was an attempt to simplify Aristotle's views on metaphysics, psychology, and ethics. It is unnecessary to stretch one's imagination in accepting the view which suggests historical continuity, because alien ideas are seldom imported wholesale and seldom supplant existing systems of thought in a well-developed society. Alien ideas certainly cannot alter the thinking processes of those philosophers who have received most of their training in native traditions and who continue to work in their native land. But to deny an Asian impetus to Zeno's philosophy altogether would be untenable. Whilst he carried over from Aristotle an interest in the physical world, it cannot be denied that Zeno introduced a new moral tone and religious earnestness into his philosophy. Thus, the whole system was transformed, and it is difficult to justify assertions that the end product is a natural continuation of Aristotelean thought.

It must be recalled that during this period, the post-classical age, the individual came to use tradition, instead of being used by it. Indeed, "it is in this age that the Greek pride in human reason attains its most confident expression."[49] Although this process began with Aristotle, it was first sharply defined by Zeno. He and the early Stoics came from Asia and "though they might inherit Greek physics and metaphysics, they were free from the prepossessions and prejudices of Greek political thought."[50] A possible channel of contact the Stoics had with Indian thought lay in the Cynic school. The Cynic philosophy of Hellenistic times sought virtue and moral freedom in liberation from desire and rejected worldly goods. It may very well have been influenced by Buddhism, since Buddhism at this time was a vigorous proselytizing religion, and Asoka had sent embassies, possibly including some missionaries, to Ptolemy of Egypt, Antiochus of Syria, and others, just before 250 B.C. "with healing herbs and yet more healing doctrines." Stoics were certainly influenced by the Cynic doctrines, and it is therefore quite likely that the *Koinos nomos* of the Stoics was influenced by the Buddhist universal "law" of karma.

The Stoics were not concerned with the idea of community in a limited, self-governing city-state but visualized a universal society, a brotherhood of man. Thus, they introduced into Western thought an ethic of universal brotherhood based on a direct altruistic relationship between man and man, overlooking the differences of race or colour. In Stoic philosophy the whole universe is conceived of as only one substance, one *Physis,* in various states, and that one substance is reason, which is, in turn, God. Reason, God, nature, Zeus, fate, world-soul, and providence are all simply different names for the same reality. Everything is a derivative of God and therefore is God. God is reason, pure and whole, and man has a fragment of divine reason in him. This fragment is the ruling principle which determines his way of life. Absolute conformity and submission to the divine reason, which permeates the universe, is virtue, and virtue is the only thing that matters. The law of the universe is also the law of our own nature, and we can only realize ourselves truly by conforming to the purpose of God, whose service is perfect freedom. This links man with God and with his fellow man. From this general philosophical principle flowed all the Stoic concepts: a world-state, the brotherhood and equality of human beings, and an all-pervading natural law based on the reason and instinct of man in harmony with the logos, the spirit of universe, a concept which strongly influenced the Roman legal system.[51] The power of this belief comes out clearly in the prayer of the Stoic Emperor of Rome, Marcus Aurelius, to the divine universe:

> Everything suits me that suits you well, O Universe: nothing in your good time is too early or too late for me: everything is fruit for me which your seasons bring, O Nature: from you all things, in you are all things, to you are all things. The poet says 'Dear city of Cecrops': will you not say 'Dear city of God'?[52]

The founders of Roman or later Stoicism were possibly Panaitios and his pupil, Posidonius of Apamea in Syria (*ca.* 135–51 B.C.).[53] The latter, after travelling a good deal, settled at Rhodes where in 78 B.C. Cicero, amongst others, studied under him and reproduced many of the ideas of his teacher in his Latin philosophical treatises. Virgil also drew from his ideas. Posidonius, a man of immense learning, was not an original thinker but a brilliant exponent of a blend of Stoicism and Platonism and of the religious doctrines of the East. He epitomized the Hellenistic culture and his writings represented with unique completeness the general mind of the Greek world at the dawn of the Christian era.[54] The main object of his philosophy was "to make men at home in the Universe" which was one great city of gods and men alike, with fiery ether above and the world of men below, in which the human soul sought to rejoin its own element by soaring upwards after death. In this system room could be found for the deification of rulers which was shown to have been common in the Hellenistic world. For if the dead moved upwards or went home to God, it was natural to think of them as being deified. Following this, even the great living might be regarded as sent by "Providence" or "the eternal and immortal Nature of the Universe," to be saviours of the community of the human race.[55]

It was during the latter period of the Roman Republic that Stoicism developed as a powerful force, and it has often been said that it gave a soul to the young emerging Roman Empire. It was certainly the greatest system of organized thought in the Roman world, and its influence on Roman jurisprudence was considerable. It influenced, amongst others, Seneca, the tutor of Nero; Epictetus; Marcus Aurelius; and Aratus of Soli, who amply compensated for his somewhat mediocre poetry by revealing the hand of Providence behind the movement of the stars.[56]

Stoic ideas, in fact, provided an almost perennial source of inspiration to later thinkers, such as Erasmus, Montaigne, and Grotius.

The rival system to Stoicism was Epicureanism, so called after its founder Epicurus (341-270 B.C.), who was a native of Samos off the coast of Asia Minor. He came to Athens and founded his school in 306 B.C. The two schools were continually engaged in controversy, but although they were essentially very different, there were many points of agreement between them. Based on an entirely naturalistic interpretation of the universe, Epicureanism taught that pleasure and the absence of pain were the principal aims of life. Pleasure came from virtue, reason, justice, and knowledge of nature. It did not specifically deny the existence of gods but it did not admit their control of human affairs. The Epicureans shared Stoic monism but they did not find a moral pattern behind society and rejected the idea of a natural law, excluding all divine interference in the course of the world. The gods, if they existed, did not interfere with human life. By keeping the gods out of worldly affairs, the Epicureans hoped to secure the peace of mind to contemplate the true nature of the gods. Their aim was to liberate mankind from superstition and the fear of death by insisting upon pleasure as the prerequisite of a wise and righteous existence. Epicurus discovered very early in life that men torture themselves with unnecessary fears of evil stemming either from their fellow men or God. Man had to rid himself of this fear, and depend on his own resources to reach inner peace by living in accordance with truth without fear or desire. Death was like sleep, an unconscious state and not to be feared: "God is nothing to be afraid of: death is nothing to worry about: good is easy to get: evil is easy to bear." The Epicureans were not sensualists or godless scientists as they have often been described. The aim of life was happiness, which could not be achieved as long as men were ridden with passions, and a sensible moderation and self-control alone could achieve serenity.[57] They had much in common with the Taoists who advocated a similar withdrawal and contemplation and "they were influenced by Indian philosophies, with their negative but benevolent attitude to life."[58] Epicureans are chiefly noted for their strong sense of reality, which found its expression in physics as materialism, and in ethics they focused interest on the present life with a special insistence on its corporeal side.

Both Stoicism and Epicureanism appear to be a response to Alexander's dream of human brotherhood in which Macedonians and Persians, Greeks and barbarians, were all alike. Both, in transcending the city-state, conceived of a universal life process. Both discerned a pattern behind life and institutions. Both regarded death as a release, the Epicureans from everything and the Stoics from the corruption of the body. Both emphasized individualism—the solitary, self-centered individual. Both aimed not at the discovery of truth but at the satisfaction of practical needs. Both stressed happiness as the aim of life and preached detachment from passions and emotions, because unfulfilled desire brought unhappiness; indeed, happiness was to be achieved in Epicureanism by holding no opinion at all. Both schools made the same arrogant claim that without philosophy there can be no goodness—a claim which neither Aristotle nor Plato ever made.[59] But Stoics went a good deal farther, striving not only for happiness, but aiming at an ideal of selfless duty. In this burdensome life the noble deed was its own reward. The Stoic philosophy was in this sense more constructive, and more greatly influenced the Romans and later Christianity, and, through its influence on men in positions of power, it contributed to the efficiency of government.[60]

Emphasis upon selfless action, the conception of the world-soul with man containing a spark of the divine fire, and the renunciation of sensual pleasures are doctrines which have an upanishadic ring, although their development from early Greek thought is also possible. The idea, however that an individual can be self-sufficient and have no business with the world, remarks John Bowie, "is profoundly alien to earlier Greek thought. It is more akin to the political abnegation of the East; it destroys the assumption, so attractive in the writings of Plato and Aristotle that the moral interest of the State and the individual naturally coincide."[61] Both Hinduism and Buddhism stress that complete detachment from the world of fear and desire is the supreme goal of wisdom. In this respect, "The *Bhagavad Gita* and the Buddhist scriptures present strange harmonies of language with the Stoic teachings .... "[62]

The fact that during this period the Eleusian and Orphic mystic cults reappeared and increased in popularity further supports the view that Indian ideas were current in the Hellenistic age and were gaining converts. The reappearance of mystery cults in its turn was influenced, as were other schools of thought, by the changed nature of the Greek world. The establishment of Greek kingdoms further east encouraged increasing numbers of Greeks to travel to Asian lands in the performance of varied civil, military, and commercial services. Many of them stayed for prolonged periods and often married into Asian families. It was, therefore, only natural that together with other ideas and experiences, Asian mystery gods and cults should have travelled back with the Greeks to the West, and provided stimulus to those cults which, although somewhat dormant at this time, had existed there for several centuries.

Chapter III

THE AGE OF SYNCRETISM

WHILST AN INTELLECTUAL transformation was taking place in the Hellenistic world, India was emerging as a dynamic and powerful state under the Mauryas. China, hitherto unrecognized, almost unknown, and politically divided, was assuming the forceful and unified national personality she was to maintain from the time of the Chin and Han Dynasties onward. The Greek kingdoms were gradually declining but long before Greek power collapsed in Asia by the middle of the first century, a new dominant power, the Roman, had begun to emerge in the West.

According to tradition Rome was founded in 753 B.C. and her early history is mostly shrouded in legend. The real Roman rise to world power appears to have begun in the middle of the third century B.C. when Rome rapidly extended her authority over an enormous variety of people outside Italy. Carthage, a powerful enemy, was defeated and destroyed by the Romans in the three Punic wars (264–241, 218–201, and 149–146 B.C.).

In about 212 B.C. the Romans began to interfere with the affairs of the Hellenistic world. In 205 B.C. they made Egypt their protectorate, finally annexing it to their empire in 30 B.C. after the defeat of Anthony and Cleopatra by the forces of Octavian. Africa was Rome's fifth province, and it was through Africa and the countries ringing the Mediterranean that Rome felt Indian influence. From about 200 B.C. until A.D. 300, Indian religion and thought played a considerable part in these Mediterranean countries. Whole Indian creeds and philosophies certainly were not transplanted into Roman soil, but enough fragments, combinations, and variations of Indian beliefs reached the Roman world to interact effectively on the prevalent local doctrines. Indian thought reached Rome mainly through Iran, Babylonia, and Egypt; however, whilst one can detect many remarkable resemblances between Indian thought and the philosophies of the Graeco-Roman age, there is no record of borrowing. But records can disappear, and their absence in itself is not evidence against mutual influence. For example, Indian influence on ancient Scutheast Asia is indisputable, even though it cannot be stated with certainty how or when Indians arrived there. The state of the Seleucids, although it continued to rule areas of Southwest Asia from Syrian Antioch, had been eliminated from the peninsula of Asia Minor. Macedonia was captured in 167 B.C. and finally annexed by Rome in 149 B.C. Greece followed two years later.

The annexation of Egypt brought the Roman frontiers of culture and commerce closer to India. This proximity became even greater when Rome gained her sixth and richest possession on the farthest coast of the Aegean Sea in 133 B.C. where the Attalid dynasty of Pergamum had broken away from the Seleucids. The last king of Pergamum had bequeathed to Rome his state, which comprised the most heavily populated part of Asia Minor, full of famous and highly developed cities and rich in agricultural resources, textiles, and other industry. This heritage brought Rome "a source of fabulous profit for its officials and financiers, and of potent influences upon its culture, religion and racial composition,"[1]

From the beginning the Roman Empire was divided into two distinct parts—the Hellenized East and the Roman West. The former was an amalgam of Eastern and Greek cultures, in which Hellenic speech and culture was sometimes a veneer and sometimes a genuine influence. Beginning as Greek states, the kingdoms in Asia Minor and Egypt gradually absorbed local concepts and customs, and Eastern thoughts and habits, Alexandria, founded by Alexander in about 332 B.C. and situated on the western edge of the Nile delta, was the capital of the Ptolemies in Egypt,[2] and as the glory of Athens wilted away, Alexandria gradually became the cultural capital of the new scientific, literary, and philosophical studies, and the commercial emporium of the East and

West. It was second only to Rome in importance. Alexander could not have foreseen that one day, because of its connection with India, Africa, and Rome, his city would become so cosmopolitan, with a fine library and museum, and attracting philosophers, artists, scientists, and others from the Mediterranean and Indian areas. The greatness of Alexandria began when the body of Alexander was enshrined there in a magnificent mausoleum, the Sema, after Ptolemy had diverted the funeral cortege to Egypt, whilst it was proceeding from Syria to Macedonia, on the pretext that Alexander had expressed the wish to be buried in the oasis of the god Ammon.

At the same time Ptolemy transferred his capital from Memphis to Alexandria. New influences began to pour in and the city grew in stature and importance. It became a busy harbour, a thriving centre of international trade with its splendid commercial facilities, and above all the repository of a cosmopolitan culture.[3] It had the biggest lighthouse of antiquity, 480 feet high, and a zoo for which rare animals were imported from all over the known world.[4] The museum, technically a temple of the Muses, the goddesses of arts and sciences, became a centre of literature and learning. Under the guidance of the first two Ptolemies it became an academy of letters and science, whose members, at times numbering about one hundred, received generous financial assistance. The library attached to the museum was liberally endowed by the Ptolemies and became the greatest library in the Hellenistic world with collections of rare and original works. At the time it was burnt when Julius Caesar, during his Egyptian campaign, set fire to the ships in the harbour, it is said to have contained about a million volumes.

A fresh beginning was made and another library was built at the Serapium a considerable distance from the harbour. This library also was destroyed, presumably by the Emperor Theodosius of Constantinople, who, being a devout Christian, did not approve of old Greek books which contained, according to him, pagan knowledge and philosophies. The contribution of Alexandria to knowledge in the realms of literature, philosophy, art, and science, is enormous, and, if its library had not twice been destroyed, our debt, no doubt, would have been incalculably greater.

Antioch, the capital of the Seleucids, was the next most important city in the Hellenistic world, and it also played a formative part in the culture of the Roman Empire for a long time. The Seleucids had founded cities throughout their dominions to help in the expansion of Hellenism. Their success appears to have been somewhat limited, however, for Greek cities in Syria, Mesopotamia, and Babylonia were like Greek islands in a sea of Asian population untouched by Hellenism. "Posidonius, himself a Syrian Greek, held no high opinion as to the purity of Hellenism among his compatriots. And this diluted Hellenism of the cities was not likely to penetrate very deeply into the thousands of villages with their Semitic population."[5]

A modern form of Greek was spoken in the Hellenistic world, including Alexandria, and Hellenistic culture was a combination of cosmopolitan and older Greek cultures. Unity of currency, new roads, improved harbours and lighthouses, and larger ships facilitated intercourse and trade. The tremendous work done by the Achaemenian rulers of Persia in opening up the lands of western Asia and linking them by means of a network of roads, including the famous "Royal Road" connecting Ephesus and Susa, and a postal system extending to Bactria and India, was continued by the Hellenistic states, and still later by the Romans after their annexation of the kingdom of Pergamum.[6]

It was from this world that the Romans acquainted themselves with the cultural and intellectual heritage of the past. Culture flourished in Egypt under the Ptolemies, and because of well-developed commerce with the outside world, Egypt became increasingly prosperous. She already had brisk trade relations with India. In fact, Indian contacts with Egypt were anterior to the emergence of Greek power in Alexandria. The tale of Egyptian explorations by land and sea from the earliest times to reach the Land of Punt (India) is a fascinating and a romantic narrative.[7] But it was at the end of the fourth century B.C., when the Ptolemies came to the throne of Egypt, that Indo-Egyptian commerce received a great impetus, especially under Ptolemy II, who also paid great attention to the African coast, where he founded colonies as far as the island of Socotra. The importance of East Africa was considerable, for here the Hellenistic armies obtained ivory, tortoise shell, slaves, and elephants.[8] The Greeks had learned from India the use of elephants in war when Chandragupta gave five hundred elephants to Seleucus.

Indian trade with Egypt, however, was by overland routes through western Asia. If there had existed an earlier sea route, it was forgotten by the time of the Ptolemies. But the anarchy reigning in Syria following Alexander's death, together with the rise of the hostile kingdom of Parthia and its defeat of the Roman legions in 53 B.C. at Carrhae, rendered the overland routes uncertain and increased the importance of the hitherto unpopular sea route.[9] During this period the Romans and the Ptolemies witnessed the development of a profitable commerce between the two great civilized regions of the time, the Mediterranean countries and India. Egypt, furthermore, unlike other parts of the Hellenistic world, could be directly reached by sea from India, and this encouraged maritime intercourse.

The perilous desert journey, however, between the Nile and the Red Sea was something of a deterrent. Attempts were made from time to time to build a canal between the waterways, but these invariably proved unsuccessful. Darius the Great tried it, and so did Ptolemy Philadelphus (285–246 B.C.), but both failed. Consequently, the latter revived the old idea of a port on the Egyptian coast of the Red Sea, connected with the Nile by a desert road furnished with convenient and comfortable resting points. The road, roughly about two hundred fifty miles long, linking Coptos on the bend of the river Nile, and the port Berenice on the Red Sea coast, was punctuated by eight watering places and the journey took eleven or twelve days under favourable conditions. In 274 B.C., Ptolemy Philadelphus built the port of Myos Hormos, one hundred eighty miles north of Berenice, thus cutting the desert journey by five days. Inevitably Myos Hormos soon became the ideal port for eastern trade and eclipsed all competitors.[10]

Almost two centuries later Strabo the geographer, who lived in the reign of Augustus, visited the port of Myos Hormos and found that it was still the greatest centre for east Indian trade, and that about one hundred twenty ships sailed from that port to India, probably in a single season. A few bold sailors even reached the mouth of the Ganges.[11]

Brisk trade led to Indian settlement in Egypt and Egyptian colonies in India. That contact between India and Egypt had become closer during this period is confirmed by Athenaeus, who says that Indian women, hunting dogs, cows, and spices carried on camels figured in the processions of Ptolemy. The saloon of Ptolemy Philopator's (221 B.C.)

yacht was lined with Indian stone. Indian figures found at Memphis may indicate the existence of an Indian settlement, and a Ptolemaic grave stone has been excavated bearing signs of the wheel and trident. The infant deity Horus is represented in Indian postures seated on a lotus. In papyrus fragments an account exists of some Greek mariners who were shipwrecked on the Malabar coast and hospitably entertained by a local king. Again, there has been discovered in the temple of Redesiya, on the desert route to the Red Sea, "a dedication by an Indian to Pan, pointing to a real and direct intercourse between the two people." Hultzsch mentions finding a solitary silver coin belonging to the period of Ptolemy Soter in a Bangalore bazaar.

From this monopoly of the sea commerce between India and Europe Ptolemaic Egypt gained the extraordinary wealth and power for which she was famous. It was fortunate for Egypt that there was no serious competition from other powers, especially Syria who could have considerably intensified her own trade with India through the Persian Gulf. Possibly the internal situation in Syria was too chaotic to encourage international trade.

A striking piece of evidence of the Egyptian-Indian trade is provided by Rostovtzeff, who points out that the financal and economic organization of Ptolemaic Egypt was very similar to that of Chandragupta Maurya and his successors as set forth in Kautilya's *Arthasastra.* For instance, the three state monopolies, oil, salt, and mines and their organization, as well as a far-reaching state socialism under the rule of "enlightened monarchs," were common to both India and Ptolemaic Egypt.[13]

The date of the *Arthasastra,* which is unique for its compression, carefully compiled detail, and political realism, is somewhat controversial—and probably will always remain so—but most scholars accept it as a work of the early Mauryan period. The volume of polemical writing surrounding the dating of this work is much too large to lend itself to brief review.[14] Of those scholars who place the date of this treatise much later, Keith, whose writings include such divergent subjects as the history of Sanskrit literature and the history of the British Empire, was the chief exponent: "That the work was a product of 300 (A.D.) written by an official attached to some court; is at least plausible if it cannot be proved."[15] Keith's view is surprisingly infirm and indeed appears to fluctuate. Elsewhere he "assigned it to the first century B.C. while the matter very probably is older by a good deal than that."[16] A number of scholars have disputed this somewhat indecisive opinion and, whilst admitting to some later interpolations in the work possibly to bring it up-to-date, have endorsed the opinion originally advanced by Shamasastry that it is a Mauryan document based upon the knowledge and experience of the pre-Mauryan administrative practice and theory of state craft. Even if parts of the *Arthasastra* reflect Mauryan or pre-Mauryan conditions, Indian influence on Egyptian administration or vice versa may be significantly indicative of a much closer exchange of ideas between India and ancient Egypt than has hitherto been believed.

During the unsettled period when the strong rule of the early Ptolemies was declining and the Romans were not yet firmly in command of Egypt, the eastern trade suffered a brief set-back. Once Rome had established its authority, however, it took positive measures to continue and in fact to vigourously encourage, the Ptolemies' policy of trading with India directly through sea or land routes which, although still in use, lay through hostile Parthia. In 25 B.C. Augustus, whose cold-blooded cruelty during the Roman civil war aroused repulsion but did help to restore order and prosperity in Rome, sent an expedition to secure command of the sea route to India, having perceived it to be in the interests of Rome to encourage the lucrative trade of Arabia and India. To secure this trade the Romans attempted to make the highways safer, improve the existing facilities, and acquire new areas for better routes. Military expeditions were also organized to cope with piracy and raiders. The road across the desert from Coptos to Myos Hormos was carefully marked into stages, depots were made for storage, water reservoirs were built, and armed guards provided protection for traders and travellers. A fleet was stationed in the Red Sea at the time and there are some accounts of merchants' ships having been armed for defence against raids. Later Hadrian (117–138) built an entirely new road to the Red Sea through level country and furnished it with halting stations.

A few decades later, in 45, the epoch-making discovery of the monsoon winds (attributed to Hippalus during the reign of Claudius) drastically altered the whole aspect of sea-borne trade between India and Rome. Strabo mentions that by a strange though eventually happy mischance an Indian sailor mistook his course and reached Egypt half dead. The Greeks in Egypt nourished him back to health and the Indian, in gratitude, piloted Hippalus back to India along the monsoon routes. Whilst knowledge of these winds was probably new to the Greeks, the Indians and the Arabians had known and made use of them for centuries.[17]

The monsoon winds blow over the Indian Ocean from the northeast in winter and from the southwest in summer. Once their currents were known it became possible to sail far more speedily and directly from Indian to Egyptian ports. Alexandria could now be reached within two months or even less, as against the thirty months taken by Scylax, the pioneer Greek sailor, to sail from India to Suez. A trader could now leave Egypt in July and reach the Indian ports by the end of September. There he could dispose of his merchandise and acquire a cargo of the luxuries so much in demand in Rome and begin his return journey by the end of November. Helped by the northeast monsoons he would sail to Aden and then, via the Red Sea, reach Alexandria about February, thus easily completing the entire trip well within a year. In fact the journey from Rome to India could be completed in less than sixteen weeks. It took about two weeks from Rome to Alexandria, about three and a half weeks from Alexandria to Berenice, a month for descending the Red Sea, and forty days from Ocelis (Cella), a port on the Red Sea coast of Arabia, to the nearest port in India.[18] Also, the ships could now sail on the high seas away from the pirate-infested coast. Furthermore, the trade monopoly of the Arab towns was broken up and, although they attempted to create difficulties, they were firmly suppressed. The West was determined to trade with India without any intermediary. The voyage could be undertaken either from the Egyptian or Nabataean side, although the former was more usual. There were three Egyptian ports: Arsince at the Gulf of Suez; halfway down the coast was Myos Hormos; and finally the distant Berenice. Traffic in goods and people now increased enormously, and whereas about twenty ships a year made the journey before the discovery of the monsoon winds, a ship now left Egypt for India almost every day.

Rome, enriched by the spoils and tributes from so many foreign lands, had acquired a taste for luxuries of every kind. The capital of the greatest empire ever established in Europe was filled with people who had inherited great wealth and whose sole occupation was the enjoyment of these riches. The returning generals found their villas dull, rustic, and old-fashioned, made all the more unbearable because they had brought back with them masses of coinage, bullion, and slaves. They had developed expensive tastes whilst in other continents, and now they had the means to indulge those tastes at home. They did so with feverish haste and great display. Oysters were brought all the way from Spain or Brittany, and wild beasts were imported from the farthest corners of Egypt to be featured in games. Common men, always keen to emulate the fashion determined by the elite, soon followed, and before long even the country surrounding Rome was involved. One may gain some conception of the vast wealth of the generals from the inheritance of the Emperor Augustus who, despite his claims to divinity and pursuit of sexual debauchery, had amassed nearly forty million pounds in twenty years. In modern values this would be many times more. Senators owned property in every province, had incomes of over a hundred thousand pounds per annum, and kept thousands of slaves. Seneca himself owned several hundred citronwood tables imported from Mauritania. The senators would spend forty thousand pounds on a single carpet for their homes. Pliny relegated to second rank those whose annual income was less than sixty thousand pounds. Even men of infamous character were rich. As for the emperors and their favourites, "they strove to astound the world by their fantastic follies. Luxury in food, in attire and in furniture surpassed every example of sumptuous idiocy which our own epoch can show."[19] Gaius (Caligula) (37–41), whose chief obsessions were cruelty and sexuality, wore cloaks adorned with emeralds and robes woven of pure silk—an extremely expensive article in Rome at the time, especially purple silk. He drank precious stones dissolved in vinegar and served his guests with gilded bread and meat. At Lucullus' triumphal feast about three million litres of wine were consumed. Roman banquets were remarkable by any standards for the enormous quantities of food and drink consumed, but they were crude, and at times repulsive, affairs, totally lacking in the elegance of the Greeks. It was, for example, considered an accomphlishment to be able to vomit at will in order to resume eating. Roman sexual life was equally uncontrolled, sadistic, and full of crude perversions. The youth of the country, clad in garments laden with gold and pearls, poured out their wealth at the feet of fashionable courtesans and would squander a fortune in a matter of hours. Greek sexual life was also extravagant, but it was remarkably immune from inelegance and perversions, if homosexuality is not included in this category. Roman pursuit of pleasure was spectacular but repulsive, lacking dignity, restraint, and an understanding of the very nature of pleasure. Even the greatest of the Mughals or the Sungs would have envied the extravagance, although not the crudity, of the Roman Emperors. Whilst the rich led a life of unparalleled laxity, kept armies of servants and slaves, and gave interminable feasts, millions of hungry men were wandering through the streets of Rome and the surrounding countryside.

Of all the goods in particular favour with the luxury-loving Romans, Indian products were the most popular. To meet the demand, new and greater efforts were made to increase trade with India and this was accomplished to a degree which would appear astonishing even today. The Romans demanded Asian luxuries on an unprecedented scale. Chinese silk, Indian pearls, jewels, fine muslin, drugs, spices, condiments, incense, ghee, ivory, dyes, cosmetics, oils, and perfumes, all fetched high prices.[20] It appears that toward the end of the first century the greatly prized Chinese silk (Sericum or Seric silk) as well as furs were being shipped from Indian ports to the western countries, because the land routes were blocked by Parthia and the sea route had gained such popularity. Cinnamon was also one of the most important exports and its price in Rome was high—about 1500 denarii per Roman pound for the best quality cinnamon and fifty denarii for the cheapest *cassia.* One of the most sought after Indian products was cotton muslin, which was so fine that the Romans called it *nebula.* Pepper, which remained one of the most highly prized luxuries of the West until modern times, was very expensive—about fifteen denarii a pound—and yet greatly in demand.[21] It was consumed in such large quantities that, as a concession to the people, no import duty was placed on it in Rome.

In return, Western merchants carried tin and lead to India, minerals which India herself did not possess, as well as wine, coral, and glass—a widely exported Roman product, especially coloured glass—brightly coloured girdles, and gold and silver coins. Special presents were carried for kings, including maidens for harems. However the principal means of exchange with India was gold. Pliny bewailed the enormous drain on Rome's resources created by the demand for eastern luxuries. There was not a year in which India did not take at least 550 million sesterces from Rome,[22] an equal amount going to Arabia and China. The gold which came from taxation and pillage in Spain and Dacia, stayed in Rome only briefly before transit to Asia. Great quantities of Roman coins found in South India where jewels and spices were sold bear Pliny out. He also tells us that Indian wares cost a hundred times more in Roman markets than in Indian markets.[23] Later, Vespasian's policy in 69–79 of cutting down extravagant expenditure may have made some difference in the import of luxury goods from India but there is no concrete evidence that it did. At the same time commerce in cotton and other industrial goods continued steadily. This is supported by the fact that Roman coins belonging to the period after the reign of Nero (54–68) are more often found in those parts of India where cotton was grown. There are considerably fewer Roman coins of the third century to be found in India, which may indicate a decline in commerce.

Trade between Europe and Asia was so brisk that, despite the hostility of Parthia towards Rome and their periodic clashes, and despite the increasing popularity of the Red Sea route, the Persian Gulf route nevertheless carried a flourishing trade and land-borne trade also grew considerably. This trade led to the rise of great cities along the routes, and of new ports on the coasts. Petra, the town of Nabataeans, and Palmyra, which commanded the caravan routes to Asia, served as terminal points for the maritime trade of the Red Sea and the Indian Ocean. Gerra, Ommana, the Charax Spasini, were all large mercantile towns to which Indian vessels regularly brought cargoes of timber, blackwood, and ebony, whilst Arabia sent the frankincense and spices of Cana. In return for these goods the region exported pearls, which, however, were not as valuable as the famous Indian ones. From Charax a route ran up to the Euphrates joining the well-known overland route near Seleucia.[24]

Both Ptolemy in his *Geography* and the unknown author of the *Periplus Maris Erythraei* testify to the number of merchants engaged in Indian trade, and thus to its volume. Ptolemy draws his information from men who had been to India, many of whom had lived there for a long time. The *Periplus*, which is a kind of practical handbook for merchants presumably written by an Egyptian Greek merchant from Berenice, contains a detailed account of its author's coasting voyage to India. The *Periplus* amongst other things mentions the import of Greek girls for Indian harems and various references are found to Indian residents in Alexandria. The Jatakas are full of references to Buddhist merchants and their adventures on voyages to distant countries, and to the overland caravans that took days and nights travelling east and west across deserts.

Trade inevitably led to some tourism and especially to Roman and Indian settlements in their respective areas of influence. There was a Yavana colony at the mouth of the Kaveri River and foreign populations were known to have existed in the Madura district. Mercenary Roman soldiers attending Indian princes are mentioned in Tamil literature. The Tamil area was one with which the Romans had considerable commercial relations, for it had cloth, dyes, and pearls to offer. Hence, it is not surprising that Tamil poems sing of Yavana ships bringing wine and other wares to their ports.[25] A late map shows a temple of Augustus at Musiris on the west coast of India (Cronganore in Kerala) which would indicate that there must have been a large enough Roman settlement to erect a temple honouring their deified Emperor. Sir Mortimer Wheeler, however, boldly declares that the "Temple of Augustus" at Musiris indicates an "official arm" long enough to reach the Malabar Coast.[26] No trace of this temple has yet been found, but the probability of its existence cannot be excluded. To regard it as evidence of a kind of imperial outpost, however, rather than a normal structure built by a colony of foreigners, is beyond understandable historical speculation.

Dion Chrysostom, the Greek rhetorician and sophist, who lived in the reign of Trajan (98–117) mentions that the population of cosmopolitan Alexandria included many Indians who had come there to trade.[27] Pausanias refers to the merchants of India and to the marvellous creatures they brought, including parrots.[28]

Of the several branches of natural science that flourished in the Hellenistic and Roman world, the revival of geography was one. Several works on Indian geography appeared describing the country with varying degrees of accuracy. Some well-known works in this area are Strabo's

Geography, regarded as the most important geographic work of antiquity; Arrian's *Indika;* the Elder Pliny's *Natural History;* and Ptolemy's *Guide to Geography*.[29] The unknown author of *Periplus Maris Erythraei* travelled through India and left an eye-witness account of the Red Sea and of the Arabian and Indian coasts.[30]

Trade between India and Rome continued to thrive steadily during the second and third centuries A.D. With the rise of the great Gupta power the heart of the Indian Empire moved inland toward central India, and a splendid cultural renaissance set in with a distinctive Indian character. This, however, interrupted the maritime trade between Rome and India. The emergence of the Sassanian Empire in 227 also checked direct communication between the two nations. But contact continued through Alexandria, to which Indians flocked in increasing numbers, until the fall of the Roman Empire in the fifth century and the consequent decline of Alexandria.

Indian trade with Rome had an extremely important influence on Indian contacts with the countries of Southeast Asia. Rome's appetite for luxuries was so great that India could not satisfy it. Indian supplies of precious stones, ivory, and spices had begun to run out. Consequently, Indian traders began searching eastward for fresh sources of supply. They imported goods from the countries of Southeast Asia and then exported them to the Roman world. This Indian commercial contact with Southeast Asia gradually bloomed into an exceptionally fruitful cultural intercourse. With the decline of the Roman Empire, the Roman demand ceased and the entrepôt trade of India collapsed.[31]

Roman emperors took an increasing interest in Indian affairs and, in marked contrast to their commonly arrogant attitude toward foreign ambassadors, accorded dignified and courteous receptions to Indian envoys. The political importance of the Indian states as allies against the Parthians and later Sassanians was a major reason for Rome to cultivate the Indian 'kings, especially those who occupied the northwestern and Indus Valley regions. Drawn more and more eastward by the problems of internal political turbulence and expanding eastern frontiers, the Roman emperors succumbed with fascination to Asian institutions and religions.

Although India had had diplomatic relations with Syria, Egypt, and other countries, she had not dispatched a mission to Rome before the time of Augustus. An Indian embassy was sent to the Roman Emperor, when he was on the island of Samos in 21–20 B.C. by the Indo-Parthian 'King Azes II.[32] It was mainly Augustus' realization of the value of Indian trade and, possibily the value of a political alliance against hostile powers in western Asia, which was responsible for an era of Indo-Roman diplomatic contact that was to last for the next three centuries.[33] With Kushan power replacing that of the Indo-Creeks in India, this diplomatic contact became much more regular. The vast Kushan Empire, which included Afghanistan, Bactria and much of Central Asia, comprised a variety of nationalities—Indo-Greeks, Parthians, Scythians, Iranians, Chinese, and others. The role of the Kushans in providing a meeting ground for the great civilizations of the time, and in disseminating Buddhism to Central Asia and beyond, has been extremely important.

It is true that contact between India and other civilizations was anterior to the rise of the Kushans but at no time was it greater. The cosmopolitan nature of the Kushan Empire is aptly illustrated by their coins, many of which carry a Persian title for the king in Greek letters and the effigy of the king in Turkish dress. The Kushan kings were in close contact with Roman authority in western Asia. The political ambition of the Romans to expand into India also brought them nearer to the Kushan frontiers. The Kushans, it is suggested, also imported a large number of Greek sculptors from Asia Minor, who settled in the Punjab and were associated with the Gandhara school of art.

Roman historians, discussing Indian missions in Rome, make specific references to the Indian embassies that visited Trajan (98–117), Hadrian (117–138), Antoninus Pius (138–161), Marcus Aurelius (161–180), Heliogabalus (218–222), Aurelian (270–275), Constantine (323–353), and Julian (361–363).[34] Two Indian embassies were probably sent to Justinian (527–565). The ancient Romans, who had dealt with a variety of foreign emissaries from both within and without their vast empire, had usually disregarded all diplomatic etiquette and theory. In contrast, India, who never acquired territorial possessions outside her own national frontiers, had a highly developed and clearly prescribed theory of the art of diplomacy. The Persians were also noted for their cultured diplomatic behaviour. The Roman rulers did not provide for a distinct foreign affairs department, and they appear to have cared even less for diplomatic negotiations. It was mainly the Greeks who acted as intermediaries between the foreign powers and the Roman emperors. Gibbon has described graphically the treatment Aurelian accorded the ambassadors of the Alemanni, who were required to prostrate themselves on the ground in front of the king, before they were commanded to rise and permitted to speak. Aurelian treated them with contempt, reproached them, and finally dismissed them.[35] "A crude haughtiness," says Saletore, "marked the dealings of the Romans with the foreign monarch which had something of the Macedonian insolence in it. Their entire diplomacy was directed towards one end—the display of their military might."[36]

Indeed despite their many brilliant achievements in political and military organization, jurisprudence, communications, and architecture, the Romans were on the whole a very unimaginative people. In marked contrast to the small city of Athens, they contributed very little which was original to human heritage during the long centuries of their domination. Culturally, they were a destitute relative of the Hellenes. Even their accomplishments were drawn, at least partially, from the experience of Greeks, Egyptians, and Persians. The Persian system of satrapies presents many parallels to the Roman provincial system, and Darius possessed many of the qualities for which Augustus is so admired. The Roman system of internal communications, including the network of roads and the postal system, is reminiscent of Iran. In fact, only in recent years has the Roman debt to Persia been fully realized.

The Romans added little to what had been devised by Greek philosophers in about 300 B.C., although some of them expressed Greek thought better than the Greeks had done. For example, Lucretius stated the doctrines of Epicurus with a much greater intensity.[37] The only Greek school of thought which found firm roots in Rome was Stoicism. Although the Romans borrowed much from the Greeks, felt a passionate admiration for Greek culture, and suffered from a sense of inferiority to the Greeks, they disliked the contemporary Greeks and denounced them as unscrupulous. At times, even Greek philosophy suffered in popularity.

In architecture, the Romans were technical innovators and although they inherited much from the Etruscans and the East, it was they who invented concrete and devised the dome.[38] Their sculpture, also an important contribution, was very significant in Byzantine art where Eastern influences were also active.

The ordinary Roman was generally ignorant of the history of mankind and of foreign peoples, and he had no knowledge of economic laws or of social possibilities. In some ways, the Romans were even primordial. In the third century B.C., whilst Asoka had renounced war and was preaching non-violence and compassion for all other beings, the Romans were indulging in human sacrifice, and "much that we learn of the religion of republican Rome carries us far back beyond the days of decent gods, to the age of Shamanism and magic."[39] Their slavery practices were infamous for their savagery. The gladiatorial combats, which the Romans introduced in 264 B.C., are illustrative of a morbid mentality and the extremes of cruelty—even by Roman standards. It was not until the first century A.D. that Seneca expressed the protest of the human conscience against such barbarism.

Gilbert Murray, whilst pointing out that of the three most important strains—Greek, Hebrew, and Roman—in the Western inheritance, the Roman influence is by far the most striking and visible, further comments that behind almost everything Roman the real moving spirit is Greek, including the Latin alphabet, Roman law and political ideas, scientific knowledge, architecture, and literature.[40] The Romans, however, were able rulers; they had courage and a sense of justice, but were otherwise ruthlessly practical men. They were a receptive people, willing to copy and imitate whatever they regarded worthwhile, and were tolerant of the ideas and institutions of others. They drew upon Greek and Asian cultures whose moral excellence they admitted. The Roman role in spreading Greek philosophy and in helping it to survive the gradual decay of Greek culture would alone render our debt to them great. In addition, Rome, gave a practical, revitalizing turn to philosophical thought.

But in spite of their superiority in armed strength and political organization, the Romans were often haunted by the fear of an Eastern empire. The influx of the Eastern peoples into Rome was so great that some historians have characterized the history of the Empire during the first three centuries as "a 'peaceful infiltration' of the Orient into the Occident."[41] An important factor which contributed to the mounting influx of Asians and Africans into Rome was the Roman lack of racial or colour prejudices. It is said that Romans were more friendly with Afro-Asians than with the Jewish people. Then too, a great many of Nero's senators and knights were of slave or foreign descent.[42]

In such an atmosphere of flowing diplomatic and commercial contacts it was natural that Indian thought should have reached the Romans. The existence of such contact is supported by the recent discovery of a third century work attributed to St. Hippolytus,[43] and entitled *Kata Pason Aireseon Elenchos* (Refutation of all Heresies) also known as *Philosophoumena*, which contains a brief exposition of the Brahmanas of Tagabena (Tungabhadra) in South India. A detailed study of the text made by Jean Filliozat has shown that Hippolytus, in championing the cause of Christian orthodoxy, was attacking the doctrine of the Upanishads. That such an attack on the Indian scriptures was made would suggest that Roman intellectuals had become greatly interested in the doctrines which came from India during the third century.[44] No wonder Plotinus, who wrote approximately a decade after the *Elenchos*, developed such a keen desire to know more of Indian thought that he joined the military expedition of Gordian in order to travel in the East. It was perhaps the rise of Christianity that put an end to the influx of Indian doctrines into Rome.

Indian commerce and culture possibly travelled even farther west than Rome to Scandinavia. This possibility is suggested by the second century inscriptions found at Junnar in western India which refer to the benefactions of two Yavanas, Irila and Cita, who have been interpreted as the amber merchants of Scandinavia. Kushan coins have been discovered in Gaul and Scandinavia, further suggesting commercial relations between India and Scandinavia. The excavations carried out in the mid-nineteen fifties on a small island called Lillion, or Helgo, in Lake Malaren, about twenty miles west of Stockholm, uncovered many foreign objects, including an exquisite bronze statue of the Buddha seated on a lotus throne with crossed legs. According to Wilhelm Holmqvist, who conducted the archaeological investigation, the Buddha is of Indian or Central Asian origin. This is an amazing discovery which may lead to even more surprising knowledge about the cultural contacts between ancient India and the West.[45]

It was at this time, when the commercial, diplomatic, and intellectual contact between India and the West was at its height, that Buddhism began to spread in the regions of Central and Western Asia.

The missionary zeal of the Buddhist *Sangha* was responsible for the expansion of Buddhism abroad. Buddhism was the world's first proselytizing religion. It is said that after attaining enlightenment the Buddha was at first reluctant to preach his doctrine, because he feared that people would be unable to understand it, but later he decided to spread his teaching for the benefit of those who could grasp something of its meaning. Consequently, he organized the Buddhist Sangha, which was to consist of men, who, having learned the doctrine themselves, would wander from place to place preaching the doctrine to laymen and disputating it with followers of other faiths. The Sangha was to be run on democratic lines in which the individual monks were subordinated to the collective authority of the monastery. An important instruction to the *bhikshus* or monks was: "Let no two of you go in the same direction," the implication of which was that a new area of activity should be selected by each individual monk. Not only were the members of the Sangha thus compelled to look for distinct spheres for themselves, but in due course they also acquired the will to do so. Whilst the Sangha initiated the process and encouraged monks to go out and preach, it did not direct, superintend, control, or co-ordinate their activities thus allowing unfettered scope for individual initiative to adjust itself to a new environment. This, perhaps, may explain the successful, enthusiastic, and many-sided missionary activities of the individual Buddhist monks.

The Sangha has a two-sided meaning in Buddhism. It is a fraternity of the entire body of monks, and at the same time a bond of association amongst monks. In the former sense the word refers to a "body of persons" and in the latter to the "confederation which makes them one body." Both concepts of the Sangha, concrete and abstract, appear in usage. In its abstract aspect Sangha is a spiritual unity, and in its concrete aspect it is an institution of Buddhism. In the beginning the abstract aspect was more important, and each individual monk was a Sangha in spiritual communion with other monks. Later as Buddhism spread the concrete aspect became uppermost from the historian's viewpoint. The unitary Sangha became plural and the wandering monks came together in monk communities. Each community came to be called a Sangha, and Sangha continued to multiply, finally assuming the form of monastic establishments, functioning as centres of learning and culture, and thus playing a remarkable and dynamic role in the history of Buddhism. Buddhist monasticism was a source of authority and intellectual advancement, and a stabilizing influence in society. Wherever Buddhism spread, monks came, settled, and built monasteries. Buddhist monk communities and monasteries, unlike their counterparts in the Christian world, were never isolated from society.[46] The monk-and-laymen intercourse remained an essential feature of Buddhist monastic life, enabling the monks to influence the life and culture of the people, and in return be influenced by them.

However, it was not until the reign of Asoka, the first great royal patron of Buddhism, that missionary efforts to preach the gospel of the Buddha abroad were set into motion. Before Asoka dispatched his emissaries abroad, however, he insisted that his own people, as is indicated by his pillar edicts, practice the observance of truth, restraint, kindness, charity, purity, respect for elders and teachers; and to control evil thoughts, such as anger, ferocity, conceit, envy, and misguided selfwill. He advocated complete religious tolerance and respect for all pious men, irrespective of their denomination, including even the materialists, and called upon all religious denominations to refrain from self-praise and denunciation of others. Deeply influenced by the Buddhist ideas of compassion and *ahimsa*, nonviolence for all living beings, he sought to bring all people closer to the gods in virtue. To help his people understand and follow his lead, he appointed religious officers in different regions and had his edicts carved on rocks and stone pillars. He himself undertook tours, contacting scholars and ascetics to enrich his knowledge, and performed numerous acts of charity and piety.[47]

It was during Asoka's time that the third Buddhist Sangili Council was held at Pataliputra in 247 B.C. to discuss religious affairs and to determine the true nature of the Buddhist faith, *dhamma*.[48] A major consequence of this Council appears to have been the decision to send religious missions to various regions of India and to other countries. Buddhist literary sources reveal that such missions were sent to the country of the Yavanas (Ionian Greeks); to Gandhara, Kashmir, and the Himalayan regions in the north; to the western part of India, Aparantaka; the southern parts, Vanavasi and Mysore and farther south to countries as far as Ceylon and the Malay Archipelago. The celebrated thirteenth rock edict of Asoka (probably belonging to 256 B.C.) refers to his religious missions to such far off kingdoms as those of Antiochus (Antiyoka) II, King of Syria; of Ptolemy (Turamaya) of Egypt; Antigonos (Antakini) of Macedonia; Alexander (Alikasundara) of Epirus, an ancient district of northern Greece; and Magas of Cyrenia, in North Africa. Asoka compares his missionary triumphs to the military conquests of other monarchs. Whether or not Asoka's endeavours to spread the dhamma, both at home and abroad, were of the dimensions suggested by the evidence of Buddhist texts there is no doubt that his efforts were mainly responsible for the popularization of the teachings of the Buddha both in and out of India. Once the process was initiated, however, the inherent quality of the creed, backed by the zeal of its monks, began to gain converts and adherents with increasing speed.

By the time Buddhism began travelling abroad, it was already centuries old and had become a well-organized, articulate doctrine, with a powerful and widespread base in India, well poised to infiltrate into other lands. During Asoka's period the bulk of the Theravada Buddhist Canonical works was in existence. The Pali Canon was settled during his reign and committed to writing later in 88–76 B.C. Being a proselytizing religion by nature, in the second century B.C. Buddhist ascetics (*Samanas*) were found in western Persia and in Bactria in the first century. B.C. Later, nascent Christianity met full-grown Buddhism in the academies and markets of Asia and Egypt.[49] Following Asoka's missions, Indian sects gamed a firm foothold in Egypt during the Ptolemaic period. Traces of an Indian settlement at Memphis have been found in the form of Indian figures and a Ptolemaic grave stone bearing the signs of the wheel and trident. References to a flourishing Buddhist convent, with a Greek chief, Mahadhammarakkhita, who went to Ceylon with other monks to attend a religious ceremony in the second century B.C., are found m the Buddhist *Mahavamsa,* as well as other works.[50] Photius refers to the presence of Brahmana in Alexandria.

Buddhism was founded in the sixth century B.C. by Siddhartha Gautama who, having renounced the life of royal luxury and worldly pleasures, set forth on a spiritual quest for a remedy for man's ills. Four experiences were the immediate causes of his "Great Renunciation": the sight of an old man, a sick man, a dead man, and a wandering *Sadhu*. The first three represented the misery of existence, and the fourth suggested a possible way out. Through a long period of spiritual ordeals and experimentation, physical suffering, ascetic practices, and meditation, he finally gained the supreme Enlightenment, becoming the Buddha. He did not claim revelation or divinity; indeed, he preached a religion of intense self-effort in which there was no need for God or the supernatural. His teaching was empirical, scientific, and therapeutic, and one which was free from tradition and clerical authority. Developing over a period of twenty-five centuries and gaining a vast following in numerous countries, Buddhism today is a highly sophisticated and complex religion, but its whole doctrine revolves around *Ariyasaccani*, the four Ariyan truths: that there is *dukkha*, suffering; that it has a *samudaya*, cause; that there can be *nirodha*, suppression of it; and there is a *magga*, path, known as the Middle Way in principle and the Noble Eightfold Path in practice, to accomplish this. Thus *nirvana* or *nibbana* can be achieved.[51]

In its early phase Buddhism in India was not very different from other ascetic movements, but during the period of Mauryan ascendancy it emerged as a distinct religion. In the following Sunga-Kanva period, despite the loss of royal patronage, Buddhism retained its hold on the Indian mind. A number of famous Buddhist establishments like the Bharhut stupa, the Karle caves, and the Sanchi stupa belonging to this period, testify to the great prosperity enjoyed by Buddhism. It had developed from a monastic religion into a popular one, and had become theistic with the Buddha and his relics as objects of worship.

It was during this early phase that Buddhism began to be adopted by some of the Greek populace settled in the northwestern regions of India; others, as shown by the Besnagar Column, became Hindus. The Greek King Milinda (Menander) was a great champion of Buddhism. In the Pali text *Milinda-panha* ("Questions of Milinda"), Menander figures as one of the characters and is described as Yonakanam raja Milinda, the king of the Yonakas.[52] Subsequently many Greeks in India adopted Buddhism and generously donated to Buddhist establishments. If Buddhism had not established itself in this region as firmly as it did, its further expansion into Western and Central Asia would have been very difficult, if not impossible.

After the period of Asoka, the reign of Kaniska (first century A.D.) marks the next prominent landmark in the annals of Buddhism. Tradition represents Kaniska as a great patron of Buddhism, and associates him with Buddhist scholars who shaped it in later times. Kaniska's reign marked a turning point, not only in the history of Buddhism, but also in Buddhist art and literature. It witnessed the rise of Mahayana Buddhism, which later developed into one of the chief schools of Buddhist doctrine, and the magnificent literary activity begun by Parsva, Asvaghosa, Vasumitra, and others. Pali was replaced by Sanskrit. The celebrated Gandhara school of art reached its peak and sculptures of the Buddha and Bodhisattvas began to appear. It was also largely through Kaniska's efforts that Buddhism was carried into Central and eastern Asia. There was ceaseless missionary activity throughout his empire which reached from central India to Central Asia. His reign may be characterized as the starting point of Asian culture.

Once Buddhism had reached Central Asia there would seem to have been every reason to aim primarily at those areas west of Asia with whom India had been in commercial and cultural contact for centuries. However, traces of Buddhist impact that far west are very few and inconclusive. Possibly this is because the West had been an almost endless scene of wars or it may be that Buddhism was too formidably opposed by various other organized religions, particularly Zoroastrianism, Islam, and Christianity.

References to the Asian countries west of India are found in Buddhist literature, for instance in the *Baveru Jataka* (No. 339) and possibly in *Sussondi Jataka* (No. 360). Indeed, it would appear that Asoka had focused his attention more on the West than on the East. After all, Indian contact with Persia had been close and dated from the Achaemenia period. Although Persian interest in Buddhism really developed after its establishment in Tokharestan under the Kushans, it is not unlikely that some fragments of Buddhism had filtered through to western Asia during Asoka's period. The *Mahavamsa* which contains the traditional account of the early Buddhist proselytizing efforts, mentions the country of the Yavanas where the Buddhist monk Maharakkhita preached the

Kalakarama Suttanta to large audiences and is said to have converted one hundred seventy thousand Greeks, ten thousand of whom entered the Sangha. Further accounts of Buddhist activity among the Yavanas are inevitably garbled but there is some historical support for the prevalence of Buddhism there. Whilst the figures quoted are evidently a gross exaggeration, the suggestion that the country of the Yavanas should be identified with some district in the Kabul valley and not further westward is contradicted by the thirteenth Rock Edict of Asoka, which refers to the distant realms of the Yavana kings. The Pali texts even represent the Greeks as taking part in missionary work. For example, the third Buddhist Council held at Pataliputra not only decided to send Buddhist missionaries to the distant Yona countries, but also called upon a Greek *bhikshu,* Yona Dhammarakkhita, to go to the Aparantaka country, the western region of India, and preach the dhamma there.[53] This would suggest that the teachings of the Buddha had begun to appeal to Greeks even before the time of Menander, and that they had begun to produce monks of such ability and accomplishment that they could preach Indian doctrines to Indians.

Writing centuries later, the famous Arab scholar Al Biruni also acknowledged the existence of Buddhism in western Asia, although his sequence of historical narrative is obviously confused and disorderly. According to him, Khurasan, Persia, Iraq, Mosul, and the country stretching up to Syria, had at one time been Buddhist. Later, Buddhism was replaced by the doctrine of Zarathustra (Zoroaster), who went from Adharbaijan and preached Magism in Balkh. King Gushtasp and his son Isfendiyad patronized this religion and spread the new faith by both force and treaties. They founded fire-temples throughout their empire, from the frontiers of China to the Greek Empire. The succeeding kings made Zoroastrianism the state religion of Persia and Iraq; as a result, the Buddhists were banished and forced to emigrate to the countries east of Balkh. Then came Islam. Whilst Al Biruni's account of Buddhism's prevalence in western Asia before Zoroastrianism is obviously inaccurate, it would be erroneous to disregard the whole statement. It is possible for a chronicler or a historian to confuse dates of events which occurred centuries ago, but it is extremely unlikely that he would confuse facts. That Buddhism was practiced in this area during the ancient period and first suppressed by Zoroastrianism, and later by Islam, must be accepted as substantially true, particularly when viewed in the light of other similar literary references. The hostility between Buddhism and Zoroastrianism is hinted at in the *Bhuridatta Jataka* (No. 543), and Zoroastrian texts mention disputes with Buddhists.[54]

Hsüan-tsang, the Chinese scholar, wrote in the seventh century that Lang-kie (ka) Lo, a country having a separate government for each of its valleys under the sovereignty of Persia, contained more than a hundred monasteries with over six thousand Buddhist monks, and that there were several hundred Hindu temples, many of which belonged to the Sáiva Pasupata sect. In the capital, Su-tu-le-ssu-fa-lo, there was a large and very handsome Mahesvara statue, highly revered by the Pasupatas. As in India, both Hinduism and Buddhism, orthodoxy and heterodoxy, were accepted beliefs.[55] Hsüan-tsang, who possibly did not visit Persia (Po-la-sse) personally, says it contained many Deva-temples and that there were two or three Sangharamas, with several hundred priests who principally studied the Hinayana teaching according to the Sarvastivadin school. The *patra* of the Buddha was in the palace of the Persian King. The fact that it was the Hinayana school which was prevalent in Persia would suggest that Buddhism had been established there very early.

Archaeological evidence also supports the presence of Buddhism in western Asia. Aurel Stein discovered a Buddhist monastery in the area around the Helmund River in the Sistan region on the Afghan-Persian border. In Turkistan at a place called Dandan-Viliq, a picture of a four-armed Bodhisattva in the guise of a Persian with black beard and whiskers and holding a *vajra* (thunderbolt) in his left hand has been found. This suggests not only the existence of Buddhism in Persia but also that it had assumed a distinctive character in its new environment, a phenomenon which generally comes after a long period of localization.

Mani, the founder of Manichaeanism, who preached his doctrine during the third century, speaks of the Buddha as a messenger of God in his work *Shaburqan* (Shapurakhan). That Manichaeanism was influenced by Buddhism is further supported by the fact that a Manichaean treatise written in the style of a Buddhist sutra, speaks of Mani as the Tathagata, an attribute of the Buddha and Bodhisattvas. There are close resemblances between certain Manichaean works and the Buddhist

Suttas and the *Patimokkha,* and, according to Cyril of Jerusalem, the Manichaean scriptures were written by one Scythianus and revised by his disciple Terebinthus who changed his name to Buddas.[56]

Although there are no remains of old Parthian translations of Buddhist texts, it is known from Chinese accounts that a number of Persian Buddhist scholars, after studying at the Buddhist centres of Tokharestan, went to China in the second and third centuries and collaborated in the translation of Buddhist texts into Chinese. The names of Parthian Buddhist monks in Chinese are distinguished by the prefix An (Ngan) from the old Chinese name of Parthia An-she (Arsak). Indeed, it was a Parthian prince, known to Chinese history as Ngan-she-kao or Lokottama, who made the first organized effort to translate the Buddhist canon into Chinese. He lived it the monastery of Pa-ma-ssee (the White Horse Monastery) during the second century and founded a school of translators known because of its excellence as "unrivalled" in the systematic interpretation of Buddhism. He himself translated more than a hundred Buddhist texts into Chinese, of which fifty-five are available. It was at this school that the first Chinese monk, Yen-Fo-t'iao or Buddhadeva, learned Sanskrit.

The reasons for the decline of Buddhism in western Asia, in marked contrast to its brilliant successes in other areas of Asia, are somewhat obscure. But some explanation may lie first in the inhospitable attitude of the powerful Sassanin Empire (226–651) with its intense Iranian nationalism towards religious and cultural proselytization, and later in the phenomenal spread of Islam, which not only cut off the West from Buddhist spiritual influences, but actually dislodged it from Central Asia.

Hinduism, although not a proselytizing religion, had also reached western Asia. A Hindu settlement was established in Armenia in the Canton of Taron in the second century B.C. under the patronage of King Valarasaces of the Arsacidae dynasty. These Hindus built fine cities and temples, but the temples were destroyed early in the fourth century by St. Gregory the Illuminator.[57]

Of the various intellectual and religious movements that developed in the Graeco-Roman world during this period, the three most important were Christianity, Gnosticism, and Neoplatonism. All three were, either directly or indirectly, influenced by Indian concepts.

The historical origins of Christianity are inexactly known and the traditional story reverentially accepted by the faithful is a subject of dispute amongst historians. The problems—textual, literary, and historical—presented by the New Testament are being consciously scrutinized in a scientific manner by scholars, many of whom are devout Christians. Albert Schweitzer, who is regarded almost as a modern Christian saint, declined to accept the historicity of the traditional view of Jesus. In a similar vein Mahatma Gandhi said in an address on Christmas Day, 1931: "I must say that I have never been interested in an historical Jesus. I should not care if it was proved by someone that the man called Jesus never lived, and that what was narrated in the Gospels was a figment of the writer's imagination. For the Sermon on the Mount would still be true for me."[38] It seems natural enough to assume that the teachings of Jesus, as in any religious belief, would be the core of the Christian faith rather than the evidence of his historical existence.[59] Yet, it has frequently been asserted by Christian theologians, such as Reinhold Niebuhr, that Christianity is the only fully historical religion and it stands or falls on the truth of certain events which took place nearly two thousand years ago. On the other hand, a body of Christian thinkers is developing which does not believe that the abandonment of Christianity's claim to historicity would injure the ends of the faith.

Irrespective of the historical character of Jesus and of an intimate connection between the activity of God and the course of human history, Christianity is basically an historical religion in the sense that it was not sudden 'or miraculous transformation but an amalgam of slow, tedious, and laborious growth to which both the accidents of history and the deliberate decisions of eminent theologians have contributed their full measure.

Although the exact time and year of his birth are uncertain, it was during the reign of Augustus Caesar that Jesus of Nazareth was born, probably in 4 B.C., in Judaea, and it was in 29 that he was crucified whilst Tiberius was the Roman emperor. Reverent disciples trace his ancestry to the royal dynasty of David and his birth is ascribed to immaculate conception, an act of God, and they, as distinct from historians, believe him to be an incarnation of God, whom the Jews were the first to recognize.

Little is known of his childhood—beyond the dramatic stories of his birth—and little of his manner of life before he began to preach his divine message at about the age of thirty. Very shortly afterward, possibly between eighteen months and three years, he was accused by his countrymen of trying to set up an independent kingdom of Judaea and found guilty.[60] Consequently, he was crucified along with two thieves by the Roman authorities. Having died as Messiah and Redeemer, Jesus Christ, it is believed by his followers, arose from the dead and founded the Christian Church which gradually spread throughout the world beginning with the work of the apostles. The believer admits that Jesus was a Jew who inherited Judaic tradition, but he disregards the continuity between Christianity and earlier doctrines, and the fact that Jesus lived in Galilee, the northern part of Palestine, which was closely connected with Syria by highways, and where there was a far greater mixture of races and ideas than in Jerusalem. Ignoring these things, he assumes the originality of the Christian faith. Jesus knew classical Hebrew and some Greek, but his mother tongue was Aramaic, which was spoken all over the Syrian world. He was a popular teacher attracting audiences from various sections of the populace.

The traditional account of Christian origins concentrates almost exclusively on the incidents connected with the rise of Christianity, giving the impression that nothing else was happening at that time in the area. Actually the situation was vastly different. It was a period of intense political activity and diverse religious practices, and it would hardly be an overstatement to suggest that in every city and village in the Roman Empire there were activities, customs, and rituals that eventually played a part in the moulding of Christianity. Everywhere there were signs of religious restlessness. The vacuum created by the decline of authority of the official religions of the city-states was filled by the cults of salvation. The stars were worshipped, and the legions of demons were regarded as having infested both earth and sky. A wide variety of beliefs and disbeliefs from all corners of the Hellenistic world and its neighbouring areas intermingled to produce a miscegenous brook of faiths and fears. The world of the first century was indeed one of transition and there were great forces at work which paved the way for Christianity. A major contributing factor to this spiritual restlessness may well have been the very nature of Roman society, which, like the Greek was based on slavery and by modern standards was callous and sensual. The unfortunate were despised and the fortunate were insecure. Despotism and tyranny were the order of the day as well as indiscriminate displays of pride without honour. Life revolved around violent sports in which men and beasts were tormented and killed, giving morbid pleasure to spectators. The uneasiness of men's hearts expressed itself in profound religious unrest.[61]

Some kind of religion has always existed in human society, although, until the rise of universalized religions, it was extremely local and personal. Early religions may appear crude or illogical to the modern mind but their adherents were next to none in the intensity of their conviction and faith in their deities. Yet they were most tolerant of each other's gods and beliefs. Religious intolerance appears to be one of the consequences of the quest for a universal religion, and a phenomenon previously almost unknown. The later introduction of organization into religious orders increased the scope and depth of religious strife and persecution. In antiquity, once the armed conflict was resolved, both the conqueror and the conquered consciously or unconsciously allowed the fusion of their gods, a process called theocrasia. A good example of such a fusion can be seen in the assimilation of Aryan and Dravidian gods in India. The process of assimilation, grouping, or rationalization of the new and old gods, however, varied with local conditions. The history of early theology is full of compromises and mutual adaptations.

When Roman rule extended to include the Hellenistic world, the existing local cults could not serve the needs of an expanding state comprised of distinct and distant nations. Greek philosophy itself was in a transitional stage, seeking new expression to fit the new world through Scepticism, Stoicism, and other schools. Along with this a tide of mysticism was developing, encouraging people to seek satisfaction through personal mystical experience. A common and new religion was needed, and the Romans, although generally disinterested in religious speculations, had to attend to it. They experimented with *Dea Roma,* the Goddess of Rome, as the supreme deity presiding over all the other local deities, but it did not succeed, possibly because of its obvious artificiality.[62] An exceedingly practical and hardy people, the Romans were singularly ill-equipped to work out a synthesis of philosophy and religion, or a common form of worship, or to produce doctrines dealing with unseen reality. They sought the satisfaction of their most personal religious emotions in exotic cults, for state religion rather inspired patriotism than stimulated spiritual life. Their hard-headed political attitude subordinated the religious urge. The glamorous potency of Jupiter, the sky god, of Juno and Minerva in their capitoline temple, and of the household gods (penates), Vesta the hearth-goddess, Janus the guardian deity of gates, and many others, as well as the careful measures taken to maintain their rites and sacred buildings with great pomp and show, and their insistence on superstition, must have held them in awe of their gods. It was left to history to answer the needs of the time.

The syncretic nature of Christianity is well known, although its historical evolution has been a complex phenomenon in which theological disputes and religious strife have frequently been interlinked with political conflicts. Founded in Judaism, which in its turn was a development of Hebrew religion, it soon came into close contact with a variety of Greek and Eastern religions and philosophies prevalent in the Hellenistic world and with Roman paganism which in itself was equally complex: "Not only did it preserve the heritage of Greek culture; it was also enlivened and enriched by the influx of religions from the Near East."[63]

Christianity has been described as a Graeco-Roman phenomenon in a Jewish mask. Enslin expresses the same opinion somewhat more forcefully, stating that the claim for Christianity as the "faith once and for all delivered to the saints" is, to an historian, utterly untenable. For Christianity was the child of Judaism, which, within a score of years, became a Gentile cult, adopted new concepts, and borrowed from all with which it came into contact.[64] It was a product of its times, combining the Graeco-Judaic heritage of exclusiveness with the newly emerging trend for universalism in a growing world of mixed peoples living in distant lands. Universalism gave Christianity its proseletyzing zeal and its exclusive claim to complete monopoly of the approaches to God.

Indeed, Jesus furthered the prophetic teachings of Judaism. He employed the old phraseology and imagery but gave them new meaning. He used the traditional material, gave it his own emphasis, and moulded it into a distinct doctrine. The core and strength of his teaching was the doctrine of the kingdom of Heaven, in which the sovereignty of God was supreme and absolute, and the nature of God was fatherly, loving, and forgiving. Jesus was not greatly concerned with speculative questions about God, or with abstract theories of his relationship to the soul and to the world. His fatherly love, his transcendent righteousness, his mercy, his goodness, were the facts of immediate experience. The certainty of God lay in the reality of consciousness and not in deductions by formal logic.[65] The love of one's fellow men and the renunciation of worldly possessions were the important ethical tenets of Jesus' teachings.

Jesus called himself the Son of God and also the Son of Man, but he made little distinction between the two; in fact, he did not even stress very much who or what he was. He emphasized his teachings. Furthermore, in the Hellenistic world the title "Son of God" did not have the same connotation as the faithful give it today. It was in fact fairly common. Greek gods had sons, and famous men were often regarded as sons of particular gods; for instance, Plato and Augustus as sons of Apollo, Alexander of Zeus-Ammon. The Gnostics, too, were more or less treated as divine. The title that occurs most often in the Gospels is "Son of Man," as used by Jesus himself. The implications of these terms have been long disputed, but it appears that Jesus was reluctant to assume the title "Son of God."[66] However, the New Testament refers to Jesus throughout as the Messiah. The title "Son of God" was frequently used for Jesus Christ when Christianity spread into the Mediterranean world. It was borrowed from the Old Testament where it was applied to David and other leaders. As the Jews were expecting the arrival of a Messiah, it was perhaps convenient to describe Jesus in Jewish terms. The title "Lord and Saviour" was also used for Messiah and was more comprehensible and agreeable to the Greeks.

Christian indebtedness to the Jewish scriptures is more than amply demonstrated by the fact that the Christians regard the Jewish Bible as the Old Testament or Covenant of God with the ancient Israelites, and their own Bible as the New Testament or Covenant made by God through Jesus Christ. It has long been said that the New Testament lies hidden in the Old Testament, and that the Old is made explicit in the New.

If the evidence of the recently discovered Dead Sea Scrolls is considered, Christianity would appear all the more to owe its existence not to divine intervention but to the processes of social and political evolution. It was by sheer accident that in early 1947 some Bedouin Arabs, whilst replenishing their freshwater supply at a spring on the northwestern shore of the Dead Sea, seven miles south of modern Jericho, found these scrolls in the caves of Qumran. Some six hundred manuscripts have emerged from these caves but only a dozen are complete. News of the first discovery was greeted with great excitement on all sides, and amongst the seven scrolls then recovered from the tall jars in the shepherd's cave were copies of the biblical book Isaiah a thousand years older than any Hebrew Old Testament then known. Whereas the translators of the Scriptures had had to rely on mediaeval copies no older than the ninth or tenth centuries, texts were now available which the palaeographers dated as belonging to a century or so before Christ.[67] Within a year the scrolls were widely known amongst scholars and the intense debate, the so-called "Battle of the Scrolls," began concerning their exact date.

These scrolls contain accounts of the puritanical and covenanting Jewish sect, the Essenes, about whom a good deal was already known from the ancient historians, particularly from Josephus of the first century. The accounts bear such close resemblances to the New Testament, particularly to St. John's Gospel, that, if they are anterior to the beginnings of Christianity, Jesus would appear, according to scholars such as Dupont-Sommer of the Sorbonne and the more popular Edmund Wilson, an astonishing reincarnation of the earlier Essene teachers, and their ideas and beliefs would have anticipated Christianity. The Essenes were conspicuous for their quietism, extreme piety, asceticism, abstinence from sensuous pleasures, adherence to the Mosaic Law, communism, and secretiveness about their sectarian teachings. They lived in a communal settlement, a sort of monastery, by the shores of the Dead Sea. They were also known for their faculty of beauty and clairvoyance. The oldest manuscript recovered so far is a small papyrus palimpsest whose pre-Exilic Hebrew script has been dated to the sixth or seventh century B.C. Other documents inscribed on parchment, papyrus, potsherds, and even slats of wood, range in date from the third century B.C. to mediaeval times. The buildings at Qumran were destroyed by Vespasian in 68 during the First Jewish Revolt.

Opinion amongst theologians and scholars is sharply divided and the volume of their interpretations is continually mounting. The Christian scholars, however, point out that similarities between the priestly Essene Teacher and Jesus Christ were slight and irrelevant compared to the differences. The former, a leader of an extremist, exclusive sect living a puritanical life, may well appear quite contrary to Christ, who freely mixed with people and claimed to be the prophet of God. Even if the Essene Teacher was crucified, the Christian apologists argue that his death was not held as an atoning martyrdom as was Jesus' crucifixion Whatever the final verdict, if agreement is finally reached at all, the new evidence has certainly caused a close re-examination of primitive Christianity, which may well revolutionize the approach of traditional Christian beliefs to Judaism.[68]

When conscious adaptation is viewed along with the indirect and imperceptible influence of other religions prevalent at the time and in the regions where Christianity first emerged, the syncretic nature of early Christianity becomes markedly visible. Syncretism, adaptation, and resemblances between religious faiths, however, must be qualified by the consideration that all religions are fundamentally the same and that their missions are not competitive but complementary.

Of the mystery cults—including those of Demeter; Dionysos Isis and Serapis, the religion of the Great Mother (Magna Mater) Cybele and Attis, Jehovah and Baal—which were prevalent in the Roman world, the Persian cult of Mithraism, named after the faithful saviour who gave his life in sacrifice for his people, was the most widespread, the most moral, and commanded the highest devotion. At one time, especially in the second and third centuries, it appeared that Mithraism would fill the widespread religious need. In Rome alone there were at one time or another more than a hundred temples dedicated to Mithra. Considering the immense popularity of the Egyptian goddess Isis throughout the Roman Empire, the emergence of Mithraism as the dominant faith clearly testifies to its power and prestige.

Mithraism was a formidable competitor of early Christianity. Renan's observation has often been quoted that if Christianity had failed, the whole of Europe would have been Mithraist. Before Mithraism, which no longer survives as a form of worship, could be suppressed and its temples in Rome demolished by Christians, Christianity adopted many of its doctrines and ceremonies. The Mithraic traditions and doctrines are collected in the *Avesta,* and a *yasht,* a special hymn of praise is dedicated to Mithra. Mithra is the Persian name of the vedic Mitra, the deity of light and truth, warning against the powers of darkness in association with Varuna. In India he was, in fact, regarded as the sun. In vedic texts, the connection between Mithra and the bull, which dater became the focal point of Mithraism is perhaps more clearly found than in the *Avesta.* But the club of Mithraism appears to have come to the Roman Empire from Iran, having been introduced to Rome by Cilioian seamen in about 68 B.C. In Zorastrianism, Mithra held a subordinate place amongst the gods with a status of a Yasita but his worship, fostered by the Persian kings and modified by Semitic influence, took deep root in western Asia under the successors of Alexander, from where it expanded further westward. Mithra was conceived as the intermediary between man and the Supreme God and the redeemer of the human race. Mithraism, in contrast to other mystery religions, contained a long and detailed account of the life of Mithra from his miraculous creation from a rock by the good power of Ahuramazda, to his ascension in the chariot of the sun into heaven. He was the invincible warrior who attended upon the Lord of Life, Ahuramazda, in eternal opposition to the evil god of Death, Angra Mainyu.

Mithraism was enormously popular in the Roman army, especially amongst the officers, for Mithra was the unconquerable hero and a symbol of bravery and skill against the toughest possible enemy. Therefore, the chief instrument of the faith's dissemination was the army, which included large numbers of Asian soldiers. Thus, Mithraism was gradually carried to the remotest corners of the empire. In the garrison areas on the Rhine, the Danube, and the British frontier, numerous shrines dedicated to Mithra have been found. Over twenty Asian regiments of auxiliaries are known to have been stationed in various parts of Europe, the ranks of which were regularly refilled from the same areas. During the third and fourth centuries there were frequent shiftings of forces between the eastern and the western parts of the Roman Empire. But despite these opportunities for spreading the cult and its own great popularity, circumstances conspired against Mithraism and "the ultimate success, permanent and undoubted, fell to the combination of Jewish and Greek worship called Christianity."[69]

There are, however, many similarities between Christianity and Mithraism. Besides sharing faith in a divine mediator and the hope of resurrection, both taught the efficacy of prayer, sacramental union with God, and his providential presence in all events of daily life. Baptism, Confirmation, and the Eucharist of the Christians are analogous to certain rites of Mithraism. It is not unlikely that Mithraic usages may have passed into the practice of the Christian Church, and the influence of Mithraic architecture on its Christian counterpart is undoubted. But the redeemer, Mithra, unlike Christ, had no historical personality.[70] Both faiths borrowed from each other, although Christianity appears to have done so more extensively.

The early Christians were also profoundly impressed by the personality and legends of Orpheus. This is attested to, for example, by his presence in the art of the Roman catacombs. The much discussed haematite seal-cylinder, or amulet, of possibly the third century, now preserved in Berlin, shows a crucified man with the name "Orpheus" inscribed around it in Greek letters. This is regarded as evidence of the syncretism of Orphic and Christian ideas. It is also suggested that the crucifixion of Orpheus was an old tradition, and that Christian representations of the crucifixion in art do not go back beyond the fifth or sixth century.[71] Both the Orphic Dionysos and Jesus Christ were the sons of God; both suffered, died, and were resurrected. In fact, in the Hellenistic world other gods, such as Osiris and Adonis, were associated with similar legends. It is suggested, therefore, that if Christianity borrowed, it did so from the general religious trend of the period rather than from Orphism alone. Some Christian eschatological dogmas are traced to Orphic beliefs. The idea of purgatory has its origin in the Orphic notion of an intermediate state of life on earth after death and the final bliss of the deified soul.[72] However, the most characteristic parts of Orphic eschatology, reincarnation and the wheel of birth, find no place in orthodox Christianity.

By this time the Jews had dispersed throughout the Mediterranean world, building their synagogues, and retaining their distinct identity.

Rome recognized Judaism as a permitted (licit) religion. The gospel had to be preached to the mixed audiences of the Hellenistic world in intelligible terms. These audiences, in turn, interpreted the teachings in a way that suited their own spiritual needs. Hellenistic Christianity thus came to vary from the original Palestinian version. "Hellenistic Christianity was no unitary phenomenon, but mainly a remarkable product of syncretism. It was full of tendencies and contradictions some of which were to be condemmed later on by orthodox Christianity as heretical, and which also explain the struggles between the various tendencies, of which the Pauline Epistles give such a vivid impression."[73] Examples of such contradictions and alterations are innumerable. The person of Jesus is sometimes defined in terms of Jewish and apocalyptic categories, sometimes as the "Lord" of the cultus, as a mystery deity, yet sometimes as the Gnostic redeemer, the pre-existent being from the heavenly world, whose earthly body is only an outworldly garb. The Christian community is sometimes described in Jewish terms as the people of God and in Gnostic terms as the "body of Christ," into which individuals are incorporated by means of the sacraments of Baptism and the Lord's Supper.[74]

These contradictions were inevitable for Christianity was in its formative stages struggling to gain converts in a highly complex and mixed community. It not only profited by the concepts and experiences of others but sometimes made concessions to them to gain their acceptance. For example, the view of Jesus as a redeemer of mankind was not a Judaic concept, nor was it held by the first Christians in Palestine. The Messiah the Jews and the Christians expected was not the Son of God, but a messenger of God. But Mithra was a redeemer of mankind and so were Tammuz, Adonis, and Osiris. It was when Christianity spread into the pagan world that the idea of Jesus as a saviour God emerged, emulating already existing concepts. It may be recalled that during the early days little was said of Jesus the teacher; it was Christ the Saviour who was the Christian Lord. Whether it had been Jesus or Mithra, it would have made little difference in the redemptionist doctrines, sacraments, and observances. It was only in 324, several centuries later, that the Church at the Council of Nicaea, called by Emperor Constantine, formally accepted by a majority vote Jesus Christ as the Saviour God.[75] It was the birthday of Mithra, 25 December (the winter solstice), that was taken by the early Christians as the birthday of Jesus. The need and urgency for early Christianity to compromise with existing traditions are further illustrated by the fact that even the Sabbath, the Jewish seventh day, Saturday, appointed a day of rest by God in the Mosaic Law and hallowed by his own resting on this day after the work of Creation, was abandoned in favour of the Mithraic first day, the Day of the Conquering Sun, Sunday. The worshippers of Mithra were called "Soldiers of Mithra" which is probably the origin of the term "Soldiers of Christ" and of the exhortations to Christians to "put on the armour of light," Mithra being the God of Light. The most frequent theme of Christ as the Good Shepherd is reminiscent of a similar identification of Mithra who was often called the Good Shepherd. And it is interesting to note that since Mithra was addressed as *Dominus,* Sunday must have been "the Lord's Day" long before Christian times. Concepts such as "the blood of the Lamb" or "Taurus the Bull" were similarly borrowed from Mithraism. The Last Supper (the Eucharist) was taken from Mithraism to combine with the sacred meal of Palestinian Christianity. The ceremony of eating an incarnate god's body and drinking his blood is of remote antiquity, with its origin in cannibalistic practices, and there could have been several sources for the Christian rite, but its connection with the Mithraic Eucharist is most apparent.[76] The Mithraic Eucharist is the commemoration of Mithra's Last Supper in a cave with Sol Helios before ascending to heaven. Some scholars believe the Resurrection of Christ derived from the Vigil of Mithra, who after his death reappeared to watch continuously over the faithful. The extent of the indebtedness of Christianity to pagan religion is so great that, "provided there was a Judaic-Christian nucleus at all, very little indeed need have been supplied by the Palestinian Christians."[77]

No country affected the development of the Christian religion more profoundly than Egypt; indeed, no city affected the development of the Christian religion more profoundly than Alexandria. In Horus, who was at once the son of Osiris and identical with Osiris, the Christians found an illuminating analogue. And, like Isis, the mother of Horus, Mary was elevated to a rank of quasi-divinity. Christianity also adopted the forms and symbols of popular cults. For instance, its priests copied the characteristic garments of the Egyptian priests. One accretion followed another and the original revolutionary teaching was buried under acquired customs.

In monasticism alone Egypt laid an indelible mark on Christianity. The formation and development of monasticism did not take place in the Greek-speaking capital Alexandria, but amongst the native Coptic-speaking Christians of Egypt. The influence on the Church of early ascetics produced by Coptic Christianity proved to be considerable. "Although monasticism spread quickly thence to Syria, it is admitted that the first Christian hermits and monasteries were Egyptian and there is some evidence for the existence there of pagan hermits. Egypt was a most religious country, but it does not appear that asceticism, celibacy or meditation formed part of its older religious life, and their appearance in Hellenistic times may be due to a wave of Asian influence starting originally from India."[78]

The most outstanding legacy of Egypt, which deeply influenced all later history of the Church, "has been the scientific Platonizing theology, which the Catechetical school of Alexandria was beginning to fashion at the close of the second century and which the comprehensive genius of Origen carried to a successful issue in the first half of the third century."[79] Pantaenus, the founder of this famous Christian college at Alexandria, who played a significant role in the spread of Christianity in Egypt, was one of the earliest Christian missionaries on record to visit India in the third century. It was he who found that there was a Christian church in India reputed to have been founded by St. Bartholomew. Clement of Alexandria, whose knowledge of India was remarkably accurate for the time, was Pantaenus' pupil and occupied the chair vacated by his teacher for the last twenty years of the second century. A pupil of Pantaenus and Clement, as well as of the Neoplatonist, Ammonius Lacoas, Origen became the head of the Catechetical school in 203. Origen was a man of enormous learning and greatly influenced Christian thought. His belief in metempsychosis, described as heretical, was possibly determined by Indian doctrine. Pointing out that mankind has two different ideals, detachment and love, Bevan comments that the Christian doctrine has also preached detachment in much the same way as did ancient Greece and India.[80]

A number of scholars, including those who accept the intrinsic superiority of Christianity, have maintained that Christianity's rise in the

Roman world was largely due to its syncretic nature. Christianity acquired greater strength in its struggle against existing faiths by voluntarily adopting their better elements. People, regardless of their colour or nationality, travelled freely in the Empire and Eastern peoples visited Rome in increasing numbers. Their religious beliefs won large numbers of converts in Roman society, thus narrowing "the gap between the old religions and Christianity, and in such a way as to make the triumph of Christianity an evolution, not a revolution."[81]

Religions spread generally through immigration, conversion, and conquest. The expansion of Islam was largely a matter of conquest, which did not figure at all in the spread of Buddhism. Christianity, however, spread in all three of these ways, although during the early centuries it was mainly carried across national frontiers by missionary zeal and the movement of people. In spite of the inadequacy of reliable information on the subject, there is considerable evidence to suggest that there was a great deal of racial intermixture in Rome. By the time of Nero, a great many of Rome's senators and knights were descendants of slaves, many of Eastern stock, and the native population had dwindled to a surprisingly small proportion of the whole; by far the largest part of the populace—perhaps ninety percent—had Oriental blood in their veins. When Paul reached Rome as a prisoner, the city itself had an Eastern population of above half a million. The immense popularity of the Eastern mystery cults in Rome, as testified to by the frequent street processions of devotees celebrating exotic rites, songs, and dances, and by widespread discussions about purification from sin, immorality, and the imminence of God in the soul, would indicate not only the increasing number of non-Roman peoples but also the growing influence of imported doctrines. Authorities, such as Cumont and Dobschutz, hold the view that a great religious conquest can be explained in moral terms alone. In other words, these Eastern cults offered something of greater moral value and stronger human appeal than the old Roman religion,[82] whilst the socially altered character of Rome and the diffusion and popularity of these new religions had prepared the Roman people for the reception of Christianity.[83]

India had been in close contact with the areas in which the accounts of the Gospels originated and the Jewish faith flourished, and it is more than likely that Indian religious ideas and legends were well known there. Indians possessed a greater missionary zeal for spreading ideas, rather than making converts, than they are generally credited with. Some Indian influences on the developing ideas of early Christianity were felt directly, whilst others were transmitted through other prevalent religions and intellectual movements. Even to understand the Jewish religion, which formed the immediate background of Christianity, non-semitic influences on Palestine and Syria must be considered.

Numerous authorities, such as Hilgenfeld and Renan, maintain that there was Buddhist influence on the Essene doctrines. And it was through this Jewish sect that Buddhist influences reached Palestine and later filtered through to Christianity. On the authority of Philo (25 B.C. A.D. 40), Josephus, and Pliny, the Essenes were a peace-loving people who despised riches and lived in villages because the cities were rife with evil. Extremely charitable, they practiced love of God, virtue, and man. They thought of pleasure as evil, objected to animal sacrifice, abstained from temple-worship, ate no meat, and drank no wine. They abjured marriage but adopted other peoples' children. They were known for their simple piety, sense of justice, powers of endurance, and brotherly love. Admission into their sect was difficult, requiring years of probation, oaths of rigorous discipline, good conduct, and secrecy. They regarded the body as corruptible, but the soul as immortal, entombed for a time in the flesh, from which, when released, it rejoices and mounts upward. They accepted the doctrine of the pre-existence of the soul. The life led by the Essenes was "just as might have been evolved by seekers after truth who were trying to put into practice in another country the religious ideals of India. There are differences: for instance these communities laboured with their hands and observed the seventh day, but their main ideas, retirement from the world and suppression of the passions, are those of Indian monks and foreign to Egyptian and Jewish thought."[84]

Although few in number—about four thousand—their influence was totally out of proportion to their numbers. John the Baptist was possibly an Essene who had spent his period of preparation in the vicinity of the Dead Sea. The evidence of the Dead Sea Scrolls clearly suggests that the community of Qumran near the Dead Sea represented a type of Judaism which was "particularly subject to external influences."[85] Moffatt remarks, "Buddhistic tendencies helped to shape some of the Essenic characteristics."[86] Jesus himself was greatly influenced by the tenets of the Essenes, even if he did not actually belong to this sect or live with them at Qumran during the time preceding his ministry. His teachings of non-resistance to evil and salvation by the forgiveness of sins, like those of John the Baptist whom Jesus regarded as his master and forerunner, have been attributed to the Essenes. It is significant that the Essenes, who, through the discovery of the Dead Sea Scrolls have come to claim a share in the development of Christian doctrine, were in 1867 described by a German scholar, Hilgenfeld, as Buddhist.[87]

The Book of Enoch, a remarkable Hebrew work which was written before the rise of Christianity in about 80 B.C., is believed to be the source of some Christian beliefs. Although full of non-Jewish speculations, the book was written for the Jews and deals with their final deliverance, the blessed lot of the righteous, and the damnation of the wicked. The older of the two forms of the book never mentions the speculations about the Son of Man, the later one does. Enoch, the saint of hoary antiquity who was transported alive to heaven, preaches of the coming world judgment. His sermons lack the charm and elegance of the parables of Jesus, but Jesus' maxims are related to and dependent on this literature in style and construction, and "the contents of many sayings of Jesus are related to those of Enoch and some may almost appear as quotations."[88] The four titles attributed to Jesus in the New Testament—the Christ, the Righteous One, the Elect One, and the Son of Man—are all to be found in the Book of Enoch. But the idea of a Son of God who was also a Son of Man, as Rudolf Otto points out, certainly did not originate in Israel but has its roots in Aryan antiquity. Although what ancient figure was once the starting point of this concept is unknown, there is no doubt that "the phrase, 'this Son of Man' points back in some way to influences of the Aryan past."[89] Radhakrishnan carries the argument a little further and concludes: "When Jesus manifests His spiritual insight by His suffering unto death He inherits the Kingdom. He is the Son of Man and the Son of God. It is the ancient Hindu tradition which Enoch illustrates and Jesus continues."[90]

In a detailed analysis of non-Jewish influences on early Christianity, Otto has traced the Indian influence on a number of the ideas set forth by Enoch. The process of spiritual ascent, unclothing and reclothing, described in the Book of Enoch, has a clear analogy in the Indo-Aryan East. Altered and abridged but unchanged in essence, the process is found in India in the *Kaushitaki-Upanishad.* Composed long before the birth of Christianity, this text details the ascent of the soul and its journey through the higher spheres: the sphere of the moon as entrance to the lower celestial region, the sphere of fire, the ever higher spheres, and finally the Brahman sphere where the soul enters the world above and meets Brahman itself.[91] The predicates which are attributed to Enoch's God are also found in the Upanishads.[92] Eschatological systems put forth in the apocalyptic Book of Enoch, on which the Christian eschatology was modelled, had a more remote origin in ancient Aryan sources. The concept of the Kingdom of God, although its interpretation is a controversial topic in Christian theology, is one of the most fundamental of the beliefs which are generally held to have been appropriated from Judaism.[93] "The ultimate source of the idea of the Kingdom," observes Otto, "lies still farther back in the prehistoric period of Aryan religion, viz. in Asura religion. The latter arose before the separation of Iranians and Indians, whose oldest sacred documents exist interspersed in the Veda of India."[94] By the time of the *Rig Veda,* however, this concept of Kingdom had become a definite term, *Kshatra Varshishta,* the most glorious Kingdom. It is described as spiritual, truthful, and purposeful. And the prayer is offered:

> O, that we
> In your far extended Kingdom
> Which protects many, may be made one.[95]

The Hindus, the Buddhists, and the Zoroastrians, like the Christians, have maintained that the Kingdom of God is not of this world, and is not to be identified with a paradise on earth. The universalism and pacifism of Jesus conflicts with the Jewish exclusiveness and militarism. His Kingdom was open to all alike, irrespective of race and nationality. His preachings of a life of self-control tantamount to asceticism and other-worldliness, forsaking parents and possessions, are not in accordance with Jewish tradition, which has little in it of an ascetic character and has accepted the uninterrupted continuance of the present world order. But self-control and asceticism were emphasized centuries ago both by the Upanishads and the Buddha. "It is not too much to say," wrote Rhys Davids, "that almost the whole of the moral teaching of the Gospels as distinct from the dogmatic teaching, will be found in Buddhist writings, several centuries older than the Gospels; that for instance, of all the moral doctrines collected together in the so-called Sermon on the Mount, all those which can be separated from the theistic dogmas there maintained are found again in the Pitakas."[96] The Christian view of future life, again, was not determined by Jewish nor by prevalent Hellenistic conceptions. The Jews were satisfied with the conception of Sheol, because the jurisdiction of Yahweh, a god of the living, did not extend to it, and they stressed the importance of life on earth. Excepting the mystery cults of Plato and Pythagoras, Greek eschatology was primitive and singularly unattractive whilst Roman belief in immortality was feeble. Christian ideas of eschatology, such as the consciousness of sin, the need of healing and redemption, or rewards and punishments, which were so different from those of the Old Testament and yet so well-developed, may well have been formulated in the atmosphere where Eastern mystical experience and intellectual speculation had reacted on Western concepts.

Jesus, no doubt, principally enlarged, and transformed the Jewish conceptions but he did so in the light of personal experiences in a cosmopolitan area where a variety of cultures, including that of India, had intermingled to produce a distinct religious environment. "In his teaching of the Kingdom of God, life eternal, ascetic emphasis, and even future life, Jesus Christ breaks away from the Jewish tradition and approximates to Hindu and Buddhist thought. Though his teaching is historically continuous with Judaism, it did not develop from it in its essentials."[97] Whilst Judaism was not a proselytizing religion, Christianity and Buddhism were.

Jesus has been described in a variety of ways, ranging from a nationalist leader to a messenger of God, and even God Himself. This diversity of opinion arises mainly because knowledge of his brief and stormy career is at best fragmentary and, more significantly, owes its existence to the early Church. The four Gospels which preserve the memory of facts were based on a living tradition and written long after the crucifixion of Christ at various dates from 65 to around 100. These Gospels agree in most essentials but differ in minor details. The New Testament comprises these four Gospels, a Church history, twenty-one epistles, and an apocalypse. Most of these were originally written in Greek—although perhaps some Gospels were based on prototypes composed in Aramaic. The Gospels are attributed to four saints, Mark, Matthew, Luke, and John in this chronological order; and the Church history, or the Acts of the Apostles, to Luke.[98] Of the thirteen epistles attributed to St. Paul six are of major significance. The Apocalypse, or the Revelation of St. John The Divine, is attributed to the apostle John but is almost certainly the work of some unidentified Ephesian mystic. It is addressed, in epistolary form, to the seven churches in Asia. Most of the canonical books of the New Testament, especially the epistles of St. Paul and St. John, do not belong to the Palestinian tradition. And the Greek influence on them is keenly debated.[99]

Scholars have been profoundly struck and at times perplexed by the remarkable similarities between the Gospel story and the life and teaching of the Buddha, as told in the *Lalitavistara,* and between the Buddhist and Christian parables and miracles. Both the Buddha and Christ were miraculously conceived and wondrously born and angels rejoiced at both births,[100] although there is no story of a virgin birth in Buddhism, the paternity of Suddhodhana never being questioned.[101] It is also not claimed that the Buddha was the Enlightened One from birth. The annunciation of the child to Mary is, however, paralleled—although remotely—by the dream of Maya at the commencement of her conception. Again, Christ was born in the royal tribe of Judah and not the priestly tribe of Levi; the Buddha was born in a royal household of the *Kshatriya* (warrior), and not the Brahman (priestly) caste.[102] An identity in the names of the mothers, Maya and Mary, through Maia, the mother of the Greek Hermes and Roman Mercury, the messenger of the gods to man, has been suggested.[103] Mary is luminous before the birth of Christ and the child is born without pain or impurity. Just as the aged Simeon sang worshipping the infant Christ, "Lord, now lettest Thou Thy servant depart in peace, for mine eyes have seen my salvation," so the old hermit Asita, who visited the infant Buddha, paid homage and lamented that he would not live to see the Great Enlightenment which he prophesied. Whether the Evangelists appropriated the Buddhist tale and grafted it into their own conceptual tradition or not, there is no doubt of the antiquity and originality of the Buddhist legend. Both Jesus and Siddhartha revealed their unusual wisdom at about the same age, twelve: Jesus through learned discourses, Siddhartha through meditation.

Nothing is known of Jesus' life during the next seventeen years and there have developed a variety of legends and literature suggesting that he travelled in India, or Egypt, or lived with the Essenes at Qumran. The Gospels, however, refute these suggestions by implication. Whether Jesus travelled abroad or not, that he chose to remain unknown after having revealed himself and his wisdom causes some surprise. As Jesus is claimed to be God, it could not have been a period of preparation. In contrast, more is known of the Buddha's life, his childhood, youth, marriage, increasing discontent with the world, renunciation, quest of Enlightenment, and finally his attainment of the Buddahood, followed by a long period of missionary activity until he died. Whilst Jesus was born as the Christ, Siddhartha became the Buddha.[104]

Christianity, like Buddhism, is based on the teachings of a divine founder, in contrast to the two semitic religions, Islam and Judaism. In the Quran the prophet Muhammad is categorically asserted to be a man like any other, and Judaism has no single founder. "Christ" is the Greek rendering of the Hebrew "Messiah," the "Anointed" who had long been awaited, whilst the Buddha is "the incarnation of *buddhi,* the Sanskrit word for divine, intuitional intellect, the intermediary between Absolute Truth and man's mind, and therefore fundamentally the same as the Word or Logos which descends from God to man, from Absolute Being to limited and reflected being."[105] If Christ was betrayed by Judas, the Buddha was harassed by Devadatta. The parallel of the beloved disciple John can be found in Ananda, yet neither of these two was chosen to step into the shoes of the Master after his death. Both the Buddha and Christ were miraculous healers, although miracles play a smaller part in Buddhism. There is a sense of expectancy in both religions; the Christians await the second coming of Christ and the Buddhists the Maitreya Buddha.[106] Both the Buddha and Christ command their disciples to collect a treasure which neither moth nor rust would corrupt, nor thieves steal. Indeed, the similarities even in detail are many and close. For instance, in *Illisa Jataka* (No. 78) the Buddha miraculously feeds five hundred "Brethren" with a single cake, just as Christ fed a multitude of four thousand with a few loaves of bread. In the *Silanisamsa-Jataka* (No. 190) an eager disciple of the Buddha, who finds no boat to take him across the river and who was deeply absorbed in thoughts of his Master, walks on the water which solidified under his feet. In the middle the waves rise and he loses his faith and begins to sink. When a renewed mental effort fortifies his faith in the Buddha, he goes safely to the other side. Max Müller remarks that mere walking on water is not an uncommon story, but walking by faith and sinking for want of it can only be accounted for by some historical contact or transference, "and in this case we must remember that the date of the Buddhist parable is chronologically anterior (some centuries) to the date of the Gospel of St. Luke."[107] Winternitz suggests that a number of Buddhist legends in the Apocryphal gospels are so clearly Indian in character that their Egyptian or Palestinian origins can hardly be sustained. Images prostrate themselves before the young Christ in a temple in Egypt just as they do before the young Buddha in the temple of Kapilavastu. The similarity between the temptations of the Buddha and Christ and their transfiguration is too close for them to be wholly independent of each other. Both the Buddha and Christ, as was Zoroaster, were tempted by the Evil One at about the same time in their careers. All the accounts of the transfiguration of the two teachers agree not only in describing the shining body but in including a reference to impending death. Even in the most Judaic of the epistles in the New Testament the phrase "the wheel of birth" occurs, which Schopenhauer ascribed to Indian influence. The ethical system of Buddhism is substantially reproduced in Christianity. "To love one's enemies, to bless them that curse, to do good to them that hate, to turn the other cheek, to leave the cloak with him who takes the coat, to give all to him who asks, which are the teachings of Jesus," observes Radhakrishnan, "are precepts not only taught but practiced in their extreme vigour by the Buddha in his many lives, according to Jatakas."[108] Both Christ and the Buddha, as did the Upanishads before them, demanded the sacrifice of natural existence as the condition of a new richer life. Possibly some of the stories and incidents are common tales of a widespread folklore. Yet, not all similarities between the two religions can be traced to natural evolution.

Many similarities between Christian and Buddhist monastic systems, vestments and rituals, the worship of saints, images, and conceptions of heaven and hell are remarkably close. All religions have sacrifice, priests, incense, and an idea of faith, but when these universal similarities are accounted for and when all allowance is made for similar causes and coincidences, it is hard to believe that a collection of practices such a clerical celibacy, confession, the veneration of relics, and the use of rosary and bell, could have originated independently in both religions.[109] Celibacy, relics, and confession have no counterparts in Jewish, Syrian, or Egyptian antiquity, whereas they are known to be old Buddhist institutions. In 1842 two French missionary travellers to Tibet, Hue and Gabet, were shocked at the close resemblances between Catholic and Lamaistic ritual.[110] Indeed, Lamaistic Buddhism, which did not follow the serene metaphysical teaching of the Buddha closely, represented demons and torments of hell as lurid as those of mediaeval Christianity. The similarities between the Tibetan religion and Christianity are so close that the former has often been designated as a corrupted form of Christianity.

In spite of these many parallels and similarities, the two religions are greatly different in temperament. Whilst Buddhism is rationalistic, non-dualistic, and even agnostic, Christianity is completely devotional and dualistic. The Buddha did not teach of God and His relation with this world, but Christ's main thesis was that God created this world which He loves deeply. The Buddha preached that nirvana was unobtainable by pleasure or rites but only through an unselfish life of renunciation. Christ taught neither asceticism nor metempsychosis. Unlike the Buddha, Christ ate flesh, allowed himself to be anointed, and drank wine—indeed is credited with miraculously producing it when wine-cellars ran out—and prescribed it for religious purposes. He praised poverty and the poor. Keyserling, however, noticed a great affinity of spirit between Mahayana Buddhism and Christianity; and although he considered Mahayanism to be far superior to Christianity philosophically, he felt that it could not be compared with Christianity in efficaciousness. In a recent study, Osborne discusses the two doctrines in some detail and suggests that in spite of their diversities, the same fundamental doctrines do exist in both religions. Apart from the many other similarities, he has endeavoured to show that "the Christian doctrine of original sin and redemption corresponds to the Four Noble Truths that form the doctrinal basis of Buddhism; that there is suffering, that there is a cause for suffering, that there is a cure for suffering, and that there is a path to this cure."[111]

Broadly speaking, both religions were missionary, zealous to bring other men into their fold, and were universal in outlook postulating that all men share a common human nature, feel a common need for salvation, and have a capacity to avail themselves of that salvation. A number of scholars from different countries, such as Rudolf Seydel, A. J. Edmonds, and Richard Garbe, have insisted on the Christian indebtedness to Buddhism. Others, apart from those who instinctively find it uncomfortable to acknowledge Christian obligation to non-Christian sources and insist on its originality and divine revelation, deny such an indebtedness and attribute all similarities to parallel development. There is no documentary proof of borrowing or of the suggestion that Jesus had travelled in the East. However, in the nineteenth century, Nicholas Notovitch published a study, *The Unknown Life of Christ,* asserting that during his long period of obscurity Jesus had stayed with Brahman and Buddhist monks, who had initiated him into Indian religions. The book was first published in French and was edited, abridged, and translated into English by Violet Crispe in 1895. This study was based on the materials Notovitch had collected during his travels in India and Tibet, particularly on the records of Saint Issa discovered by him at the convent Himis. Inevitably the book excited fierce controversy and reproach from some theologians. Max Müller disputed Notovitch's assertions and questioned the authenticity of the latter's evidence. Despite this, Notovitch reaffirmed his views when the English version was published.

Equally unknown is how Christianity arrived in India during the first century. The Syrian Christians of Malabar believe that their form of Christianity is apostolic, derived directly from the Apostle Thomas.[112] The Apostle is said to have landed at Malankora near Cronganore, then a thriving port on India's west coast, in 52 and to have founded a number of churches in southern India. He then crossed over to the east coast where he died in 68. Over the place he was buried at Mylapore, then called Calamina in Madras, there still exists the magnificent Tomb of St. Thomas which is, however, now empty, the Portuguese having removed the remains to Lisbon in 1523.[113] The evidence certainly does indicate that India and Christianity were in close contact during the period of the latter's formative stages. If Christianity could reach India during the first century and find a sanctuary so firm that it has survived all these hundreds of years, why could not Indian religions, especially Buddhism which was equally proselytizing, reach western Asia and the Graeco-Roman world and find a footing there? The road surely must have been open both ways.

Once Christianity was introduced into India, it was inevitable that it should have had some influence on Indian religious thought. In fact, it is surprising that it did not have more influence, fertilizing Indian thought in much the same way as Buddhism did in China. For, whilst retaining an identity of its own, Buddhism also gave rise to a new syncretic philosophical school, Neoconfucianism. In contrast, Christianity retained its separate identity and inspired no new schools of philosophy. However, in the last century Albrecht Weber and other scholars suggested that the cult of Krishna with it emphasis on *bhakti,* love or devotion, was a corrupt form of Christianity. Weber's theory aroused lively literary debate, and many Indologists opposed his view. Bhandarkar pointed out the positive existence of the Krishna cult in India prior to the advent of Christianity; Krishna is mentioned in Panini's *Vasudeva Sutra* and in the works of Patanjali. Supported by this evidence, Garbe exploded Weber's assertion finally by pointing out that the cult of Krishna was already of some importance in the first century B.C. The priority of the cult of Krishna, however, cannot rule out the possibility that it later adopted some legends or features from Christianity.

WHILST CHRISTIANITY WAS forming, other religious movements were afoot. Some neglected the Old Testament altogether and relied on the prevalent and peculiarly Hellenistic fusion of concepts of philosophy and science. Amongst the better known religious movements of Alexandria are Jewish Platonism, Gnosticism, and Neoplatonism. Despite their distinct personalities and varied inspirations, they all shared certain beliefs, such as an abstract concept of God as the transcendent absolute unity, the notion of an intermediary power to bridge the chasm between God and the world, the connection of matter with the principle of evil, and an emphasis on the ability of asceticism to realize absolute truths. Mysticism was particularly stressed and the dominant belief was in the immortality of the soul, imprisoned in a mortal body, which expressed itself in the Greek words, *soma sema,* the body a tomb. Belief in the Ptolemaic system of astronomy and in the auxiliary systems it created was also popular. These concepts which were widely held in the Graeco-Roman world during the first two centuries were neither Jewish nor Christian in origin. It is extremely significant that it was against this background, and indeed during the period of ascendancy of non-Jewish and non-Christian doctrines, that these syncretistic religious movements developed. These movements were so alien to Greek traditions that M. Vacherot asserts that the philosophy of the Alexandrians derived nothing from Greek philosophy except its language and its methods; the essentials were all Eastern.[114]

With Philo (*ca.* 25 B.C.-A.D. 40), Jewish philosophy reached full maturity. He interpreted Jewish scriptures freshly and systematically. Not much is known of his life, but his pious and generous character clearly emerges from his many works expounding Judaism to the Hellenistic world. Deeply impressed by Greek philosophy, he aimed to reconcile Jewish thought and customs with Greek ideas, particularly Plato's. The biblical concept of God emphasized both the transcendence and the immanence of the Supreme Being, which did not quite agree with either the Platonic notion of God as the idea of the good which was the measure of all things, or the Stoic concept of Logos as an all-pervading divine principle. Plato's God was wholly transcendent, and the Stoic one wholly immanent. In working out a reconciliation between the biblical and the Greek concepts, Philo treated the Universe as a graded hierarchy of beings from stones to plants, animals, men, demons, and gods. Philo's God is the essential being of the world, eternal, indescribable, and omnipresent. Yet, he saw matter also as distinct, eternal, and increate, although it has no life, motion, or form until infused with divine force. To create the world by giving form to matter and to establish a link with man, God employed a variety of intermediary beings, designated as angels by Jews, *diamones* by Greeks, and ideas by Plato. The world, which was a stage in the ascent of the soul to God, is God's only beloved Son produced by the union of God with , his knowledge. The distinction which Philo made between a transcendent God and wisdom or knowledge departs from the Hebrew doctrine of creation, because it admits the pre-existence of wisdom, although this distinction between God and wisdom is also made by an earlier Jewish text, *The Book of Wisdom*. In spite of his devotion to Jewish thought, Philo was very appreciative of the contemplative monks of Egypt, the Therapeutae, and also of the Essenes in whose precepts the influence of Hindu and Buddhist thought has already been noted.[115] There is a distinct mystic element in Philo's thought. The way to a vision of God lay through a detachment from the world and an embracing of the contemplative life, which must be preceded by "excising desires, pleasures, griefs, fears, follies, injustices." The body is the source of evil and man must free himself from its chains. Divine vision can be gained only when he is "lifted above and out of himself." Philo's insistence on monotheism, his contempt for idolatry, and his claim that the Jews had in the Mosaic revelation the highest religious knowledge were, no doubt, Judaic, but other elements in his mysticism which are paralleled in Hindu thought could have been influenced by Indian mysticism. For there is no doubt that genuine Indian mysticism had found a firm foothold in western Egypt, and its first fusion appears to have been with the Egyptian Judaism of Alexandria.[116]

Another important school of thought in the first century was Neo-pythagoreanism. Very little is known of but two of its members, Apollonius of Tyana (born in 4 B.C.), and Moderatus of Gades.[117] Apollonius of Tyana came to study at Taxila in India about 50. The knowledge of this visit comes from his biography written by Philostratus about 217, although the authenticity and reliability of this work has frequently been questioned. Apollonius, a Gnostic, preached and practiced strict asceticism. He renounced wine, meat, and other physical pleasures. He was opposed to blood sacrifices and insisted on prayer and contemplation. Freedom from wealth, possessions, and desires was the only worthwhile goal of life. He acquired so great a reputation as a saint and wandering prophet that he came to be worshipped as a god. Temples and shrines were erected in his honour in Asia Minor and he was held to be a rival to Jesus Christ by the opponents of Christianity.

Others accused him of sorcery and called him the prince of impostors, but, according to his disciples, he "taught the purest of religions, and in India especially, a country which long before Egypt and in different fashion had enjoyed the favour of divine wisdom, had found the evidence and inspiration to support his faith."[118]

Neopythagoreanism was the first product of an age in which abstract philosophy had begun to lose prestige, and it attempted to introduce a religious element into pagan philosophy in place of what had come to be regarded as an arid formalism. Many Neopythagoreans, like many Neoplatonists, made conscious efforts to arrest the growth of Christianity by converting philosophy to a non-Christian religion. The founders of this school sought to invest their doctrines with the halo of tradition by ascribing them to Pythagoras and Plato. They identified the good with the one and emphasized the fundamental distinction between the soul and the body. God was to be worshipped and the soul freed from the body, and, in the interest of the spiritual purity of the soul, sensuous pleasure was to be abandoned. It is said that Neopythagoreanism provided a link between the doctrines of Plato and Neoplatonism. Certainly, the similarities between Essene thought and Neopythagoreanism are close and striking. In any case there are elements in this philosophy not only of Pythagoras' and Plato's systems but also of Indian philosophy.

Jewish philosophy as interpreted by Philo may or may not have been influenced by Indian thought, but the speculations of its rivals, the Gnostics, including Valentinus and Basilides, definitely were, for Gnosticism was a deliberate attempt to fuse Christian, Platonic, and Indian ideas. Most Gnostics were strongly anti-Jewish, professedly Christian, and regarded the God of the Old Testment as an inferior being. The nature and significance of Gnosticism, however, has been a matter of controversy since its inception. A very significant product of the Hellenistic age, it is sometimes stretched to cover all varieties of Hellenistic mysticism, including the doctrines of Plotinus in spite of his criticism of the Gnostics. It is common practice nowadays to include the Mandaean and Manichaean religions, as well as part of the Hermetic literature, as "gnostic." In antiquity the followers of the gnostic systems did not usually describe themselves as "Gnostics," and the Christian preachers spoke of them as members of various sects often named after their founders. Apart from the reason that different interpretations were given to the term "gnostic," which is held to be the distinctive feature of the movement, a major reason contributing to this confusion must be the religion's very syncretistic nature for it was a movement which covered many sects and widely differing tenets prevailing in the Graeco-Roman world during and prior to the early days of Christianity when it was gradually crystallizing into the ancient Catholic Church.[119]

The gnostic movement came into prominence at the beginning of the second century and reached its height in the latter half of that century. By the middle of the third century it had begun to wane, although it continued in other forms for a century or two, and many of its ideas survived in later mysticisms. Its last, and perhaps greatest, manifestion was in the composite religion of Mani. It was revived in mediaeval Europe and is reputed to be connected with the downfall of the Templars. In modern times much of the symbolism of the Freemasons is held to be unmistakably Gnostic in origin.[120]

Gnosticism, as an intellectual activity, was chiefly concerned with attempting to work out a reconciliation between philosophy and theology, although, during its heyday, it had support from men of both philosophy and science. Its fundamental concept, gnosis, or the knowledge of God, is similar to the *Jnanakanda* of the Hindus, but many of its adherents interpreted "gnosis" not as "knowledge" or "understanding," but as "revelation." It was deeply mystical, and like other mystical religions, subscribed to the ultimate object of individual salvation, seeking a secure and comfortable habitat for the soul after death, and worshipping a redeemer or deity. Gnosticism also emphasized the special value of sacraments, rituals, acts of initiation and consecration, and symbols and formulae.

Only a few of the Gnostic texts, which were extraordinarily numerous, survived destruction by their Christian opponents. Consequently, our knowledge about the Gnostics is derived almost exclusively from the extracts and fragments found in the writings of those Christians who attacked and sought to discredit Gnostic doctrines. Broadly speaking, Gnosticism is regarded as having descended from Indian mysticism, heterodox Judaism, heterodox Christianity, or Hellenism. All these views are widely held. The controversy, however, appears to be futile because

Gnosticism, being a deliberate syncretism, contains certain elements from all these blended into its own mould. It was regarded for a long time as an "acute Hellenization of Christianity" and as a movement within Christianity, but further research has now established that it was "really a religious movement of pre-Christian origin, invading the West, from the Orient as a competitor of Christianity."[121] Kennedy has described it as "Orientalism in a Hellenic mask" and to a careful student the close similarity amongst the teachings of the Upanishads and early Buddhism and Gnostic theories is obvious.

Although Gnosticism began as a synthetic phenomenon, it soon assumed a distinctive and integrated personality of its own. It had a definite attitude toward life and a clear interpretation of human existence. The various Gnostic sects differed in detail and emphasis, but in basic beliefs they shared a similar philosophy. They all believed that the world was bad, being controlled by evil or ignorance, and could not be redeemed. But the divine spark imprisoned in men could attain salvation by divine grace. A cardinal feature of Gnostic thought is the dualism of God and world, of man and world, and of man within himself. The Gnostic God is transcendent and alien in nature to the universe, which He neither created nor governs. There are two worlds, the spiritual (good and light) and the material (evil and dark). The highest goal of the soul, or, in the language of Gnosticism, man's true inner self which originated in the world of light, is to shake off its imprisonment in the body, give up its fallen and alien life on earth, and find its way back to the world of light ascending through lower worlds and the spheres of heaven—the seats of archons (rulers). The soul is a part or spark of the Primal or Heavenly Man, who existed before the world began. Ignorance is the essence of mundane existence, hence the need for divine revelation. The soul, entombed in the body, is assisted in its efforts for freedom by the Supreme Deity, who in his pity for the captive sparks of light sends down his Son, the heavenly figure of light, to redeem them. In Christian systems this saviour figure is identified with Christ. Hence, Gnosticism was a "redemptive religion based on dualism," which gave it an affinity with Christianity. Whilst the idea of the *demiurge* (artificer), the leader of the archons, who created the world and rules it, is related to the Hindu idea of Isvara, no distinction is recognized in Gnosticism between the creator of the world and the Supreme Deity, although in Indian thought it is. The Indian emphasis on dualism may have been inspired by Persia.

Even though some of the gnostic ideas found a place in Christian thought, Christianity gradually came to look upon it as a heretical perversion and bitterly resisted its ideas. W. R. Inge has called the Gnostics representatives of "barbarised Platonism."[122] Yet, it was Gnosticism which in the initial stages gave an enormous impetus to many of the sacramental and mystical ideas in Christianity. The Christian emphasis on salvation in religion and the consolidation of its Church are the result of Gnostic influences.[123] Gnosticism had, in fact, an even wider impact on the religious and philosophical literature of the Hellenistic period. It is found in the Jewish philosopher Philo and in Neoplatonism, despite Plotinus' polemic against it.

THERE IS NO doubt that the Gnostic dualism is somewhat weak and ambiguous. There are two opposed principles at the root of all things—the kingdoms of light and darkness in perpetual conflict, but there is one God over all. Matter is a force of blind desire opposed to the force of light, but light will triumph and matter will be dissolved. The identity of the Gnostic tenets with Buddhistic views, such as the quality of the divine emanations, asceticism, penances, self-collection, and absorption into the godhead, is obvious.[124] The Gnostic aphorism "split the stick, and there is Jesus" is parallel to the Indian "Brahman sleeps in the stone."

Indeed, many of the Gnostic sects believed in pre-existence and the rebirth of human souls. The great Gnostic teacher Basilides, who taught at Alexandria about 120-130 and was a contemporary of Valentinus, produced an independent system which did not attract as many followers as did Valentinus' system, but which did make a deep impression. Basilides certainly borrowed his philosophy from the East, which he ingeniously interwove into the framework of Christianity. He conceived of 365 heavens, each superior to the other and each less concrete, less material, than the one below it. The only way to escape reincarnation was to rise to a superior sphere of peace. Through *Karma* action souls came to the world tainted with the guilt of evil deeds done in another existence. He firmly believed in the transmigration of the soul, and his pessimism and theory of personality have strong Buddhist affinities. The redemption through the ascent of the self, a kind of rebirth; belief in the unity of the human race, for all men are fundamentally endowed with divine spark; and the belief in ascetic practices to purify and strengthen the self bring to mind Indian thought. He described God as devoid of all attributes—like the Hindu concept of the *Nirguna* God.

Basilides was an Egyptian who embraced Christianity. Before his conversion he had followed the doctrines of the Eastern gnosis. Judging by the account left by his contemporary Clemens, Basilides appears to have never been a Christian—Tertullian calls him a Platonist—but rather to have joined the new notions of Buddhism, which is regarded by King as the true source of many of the primary Gnostic ideas, to the esoteric doctrines of the Egyptian priesthood. Indeed, "the introduction of Buddhism into Egypt and Palestine affords the only true solution of innumerable difficulties in the history of religion."[125]

The Gnostic doctrine of the plurality of heavens is essentially Indian; its "three qualities" resemble the "three *gunas*" of the Samkhya system. The resemblances between Gnostic doctrines and Mahayana Buddhism are well known, particularly between the *Pis tis Sophia* and the *Saddharma Pundarika.* The Pistis Sophia refers to the methods by which ecstatic experiences are obtained, and it is indicated that salvation can be achieved by a knowledge of the mysteries and by renouncing the world. It is said to have been derived from the philosophical formulations of Valentinus—probably the most famous of all the Gnostics whose activity may be dated from about 130 to 150. In his "System of Emanations" all proceed from the First Calise in pairs, male and female—a feature which pre-eminently stamps his scheme as borrowed from Indian theosophy, in which every principle is divided into a male and female energy, each exactly like the other, "the same distinguished by their sex alone."[126]

Epiphanius in his *Life of Manes* details the circumstances which introduced Buddhistic theories into Gnostic teaching. Manes or Mani (215–276), before beginning his Gnostic mission, had been the slave and later the sole heir to a wealthy widow, who had herself inherited all the belongings of a certain Terbinthus, surnamed in Assyrian, Budda. Terbinthus, in his turn, had been the servant of a wealthy merchant Scythicus, who had a knowledge of Indian religions through his frequent trade-trips to India. Later he began to preach new doctrines and there can be little doubt that these were not original but had been learned in India. His tradition was carried on by his slave and sole disciple, Terbinthus, and finally manifested itself in the mission of Manes.[127]

Bardesanes (Bardiasan, 155–233), the highly esteemed Gnostic teacher whose treatise on Indian Gymosophists is frequently quoted by later writers, such as Porphyry, evidently had learned much about India from an Indian embassy to Syria (218-222). He describes in accurate detail life in a Buddhist monastery, a visit to a cave temple in India, and the discipline and mode of life of the Brahmans and Buddhists.

Radhakrishnan takes the discussion of Indian influence on Gnosticism further. He finds the Gnostic dualism ambiguous and illustrates a number of parallels between Gnosticism and the Upanishads. According to his reading of Gnostic teaching, the perfect Gnostic is the man who is free from the world and master of himself and who having broken off from the outward symbols of religion, has realized the truth. Furthermore, he agrees with Bousset that the basic Gnostic tenets were well developed before Christianity. Gnosticism was not the child of Christianity but in fact a parent of its philosophy. It was a serious attempt to identify Christianity as a religion with Eastern speculations on the origin and end of things. This correlation of religion and philosophy is typically characteristic of Hindu thought. During the first century the Gnostics supplied Christianity with the philosophy it was seeking. "Gnosticism is by no means a mere attempt to reject the Old Testament and hellenize the Gospels. What it did was to introduce into Christianity not the pure spirit of Greek philosophy but conceptions of Eastern religions which by the first century had taken their place everywhere in the Roman Empire."[128]

The Hermetic tradition of Egypt, which flourished during the first three centuries, is somewhat Gnostic in character and a most interesting variety of Hellenistic mysticism. It is considered to be "the development of religious thought in Egypt under Persian and Indian influence which formed a basis of later Jewish and Greek developments."[129] Although it originated in Egypt, the authors of this movement were Egyptian Greeks. The Hermetic texts, intended to guide men to mystical experience, do not contain any suggestions of ceremonies, sacraments, or of a hierarchy.

Nor does God need gifts, except those of praise and adoration, for He is all things that exist. For the Hermetics God is ineffable—and He is the Supreme Reality transcending all pre-eminence and excelling all praise. He is the Creator and Father of the Cosmos, which is in His image. Man is of a divine nature, and he who knows himself passes into God. The Hermetic mystic sees unity in all things, and the purgation and illumination of the soul brings him the consciousness of a universal fellowship. The Hermetics were possibly an esoteric brotherhood, consisting of small groups with a teacher who, like a Hindu guru, guided them in their quest for truth.

Gnosticism found new life in the third century in the rise of the Manichaean religion in Sassanian Persia. Its founder, Mani, a native of Ecbatana, had travelled to India and aimed to establish a universal religion which was a fusion of Zoroastrianism, Buddhism, and the Gnostic doctrines. Many Manichaean books have been discovered in Central Asia, but in most other places the followers of Mani were persecuted and their books destroyed. A Manichaean treatise, found at Tun-huang in China, is in the form of a Buddhist sutra. It speaks of Mani as the Tathagata, a synonym for the Buddha, and refers to the Buddhas of Transformation (Hua-fo) and the Boddhisattva Ti-tsang. A confessional formula, *Khuastuanift,* found in the same area, is akin to the Buddhist *Patimokkha.* It advocated asceticism, metempsychosis, and celibacy, and emphasized the contrast between the principles of light and darkness. Until recently Mani's teaching was regarded as clearly dualistic in the metaphysical sense; it is now accepted that his outlook was substantially the same as that of the Gnostics.[130] During the fourth century Manichaeanism spread widely both in the East and the West. Because it forbade the worship of images and animal sacrifices, it incurred the wrath of the Roman emperors. It also entered into a prolonged struggle against Christianity throughout the fourth century. Augustine was a Manichaean for nine years from 373–382.

Gnosticism was one of the most powerful movements affecting Christian doctrine and thought, and, although it had passed its peak by the latter part of the third century, it continued to be influential until the decline of the Roman Empire in the fifth century. At the height of its power, it influenced two of the chief exponents of Alexandrian

Christianity, Clement and Origen. Clement was deeply influenced by Basilides and thus by Buddhist thought. A person of great learning, he worked to achieve a consistent theology. He wrote his *Stromata* nearly sixty years after the death of Basilides, and used Greek philosophy to interpret the Christian tradition liberally—not merely as a missionary expedient but in order to weave it into the texture of Christian theology. He refers to the universality of suffering; pain and fear are as inherent in human nature as rust in iron, and, quoting Basilides on rebirth, he suggests that every human act is fruitful and that if its consequence is not apparent in this life, it will be in a future one.[131] It was however, in his brilliant successor, Origen—born about 185 and the first important theologian to appear after Paul and John—that the Church had someone who could firmly blend the two streams of Greek thought and Christian tradition. A pupil of the founder of Neoplatonism, Ammonius Saccas, Origen's Supreme Being is the Neoplatonic One. He spoke of Christ as God-Man. The Father is the origin of all being and is purely spiritual, whilst the Son of Logos, begotten by the Father, is essentially God, though subordinate to Him. The doctrine of the incarnation of the Logos gave the Christian faith a medium for interpreting itself to Greek-thinking people. Origen admits pre-existence and the future rebirth of souls. For him Christ, who possessed a soul like any other, was more a teacher than a redeemer. He advocated prayer in the name of Jesus but refused to address it to Him. He distinguished between a mystery religion for the educated and a mythical one for others and justified this by the examples of "the Persians and the India."[132] Origen preached asceticism and taught that at the end of the present world dispensation many men would follow reversing the cycle of destruction and restoration. His thought sometimes reveals striking parallels with that of his great contemporary, Plotinus, perhaps due to their common master Ammonius Saccas. Origen's chief doctrines were given up by the Christian Church but the tradition of Clement and Origen was continued by the three Cappadocians, Basil of Caesarca, and the two Gregories.

Meanwhile, there emerged a somewhat alien movement, Neoplatonism, which marked the last phase of Hellenistic thought and which, following tradition, was a distinctive blend of old ideas, especially Platonic, and new ideas drawn from various schools. It developed essentially in an age of transition.[133] After a long period of preparation Neoplatonism reached its culmination in the work of Plotinus (205-*ca.* 270), one of the greatest thinkers of the ancient world.[134] The teachings of Plotinus and his school in Rome set forth doctrines which were essentially Hellenistic and syncretic. In its later forms, characterized by the Syrian school led by Iamblichus and the Athenian school of Proclus, it was transformed into a well-developed scholasticism of dynamic poly theism—a designation often given to Indian theology, which regards God in Himself as Nirguna and yet the source of all power behind the universe. Neoplatonism then underwent a further change, passing into a theurgical mystery cult. It is, however, its first phase which is of greater historical importance. In any case it continued to be the dominant philosophy of the ancient world within which the Christian culture in both its forms, Byzantine and Western, was taking shape. Many of the eminent Christian thinkers of this period, which has been designated as the most formative period of Christian theology, were greatly influenced by Neoplatonic thought.

The relationship between Neoplatonism and Christianity was somewhat precarious and fluctuating in the beginning. A period of compatability was followed by antagonism, but finally various Neoplatonic principles were absorbed by Christian thinkers.

In his own writings Plotinus tells us little about himself so that any personal information comes from the biography his disciple and editor, Porphyry, wrote as an introduction to the *Enneads.* It is curious that Plotinus, whose ideas and teaching have deeply influenced the intellectual history of the world, did little to perpetuate his thought.[135] A native of Egypt, probably of Locopolis in Upper Egypt, the modern Assiut, he spent his formative years at Alexandria. Having studied under several philosophers there, he became a disciple of the Platonic teacher Ammonius Saccas (175-242) who had abandoned Christianity. Plotinus came to study at Alexandria at the somewhat advanced age of twenty-seven and attended Saccas' lectures for ten years. Besides Plotinus, Saccas had other pupils including Erennius and Origen.[136] In 243 at the age of thirty-nine, Plotinus was greatly attracted by Eastern thought, and, in the hope of learning Indian and Persian philosophy at first hand, he accompanied the military expedition of Emperor Gordian against the

King of Persia. The expedition, however, ended in the assassination of the Emperor, and Plotinus, having escaped with some difficulty to Antioch, returned to Rome in 244, where he lived and taught for the rest of his life. It is not known if he succeeded in contacting any Indian philosophers on his somewhat abortive trip.

Plotinus believed that there is a transcendent First Principle behind everything, which he calls the One or the Good, and which is beyond the reach of human thought or language. It is a positive and dynamic reality and is the source of all defined and limited realities. From the One proceeds, by a timeless generation, the first of the derived realities, named by Plotinus *Nous,* which is the Divine Mind and also the world of forms and ideas. From Nous proceeds soul which is universal and is the intermediary between the "intelligible" world of Nous and the phenomenal world of sense. The individual souls are like parts of the Universal Soul. The highest ideal of the good and wise man, and the supreme goal of human endeavour, is contemplation of and gradual union with the Good, the Absolute.

Plotinus intellectualized religion. He saw the world indivisible as a realm of values, highest of which was the Deity of Logos. He proceeded from the idea of God and concluded with the demand for union with God—God is the ultimate source and the final goal of all being. He is without limit, form, or definition. "The One is the One and nothing else, and even to assert that it 'is' or that it is 'one' is false, since it is beyond being or essence. No 'name,' can apply to it; it eludes all definition, all knowledge, it can neither be perceived nor thought. It is not in movement, nor is it at rest. It is infinite, without limits, and since it has no parts, it is without structure and without form."[137] Everything flows from God, but what is derived is an image and reflection of the original essence. The first emanation of the Being is Nous, thought, which is at the same time the highest Being; Nous engenders soul, which is the creator of the universe in time and space. There is thus an eternal process of emanation and continuous interpenetration of being. The universe is the soul, soul is contained in Nous, Nous is contained in the One and the One contains all.

Plotinus' conception of the One has undeniable affinity with the Hindu doctrine of Spirit, "the seed of all seeds," and his conception of soul corresponds with the Hindu teaching of the Atman. His idea of God as the One, "the good, the pure thought, the pure actuality," reminds one of *Sachchidananda* of the Upanishads. The absorption of the individual soul into the world-soul as described by Plotinus shows Indian influence: "Souls which are pure and have lost their attraction to the Corporeal will cease to be dependent on the body. So detached they will pass into the world of Being and Reality." Plotinus' theory of distinction between emanation and creation is similar to that of *Advaita Vedanta* between *Vivarta,* or appearance, and *parinama,* or modification.[138]

The Neoplatonist strives to free his soul from his body through modification and to attain union with the Supreme, in the same way as the Yoga doctrine of Patanjali. Whilst Pythagoras taught rebirth (remembrance) and abstention from the flesh, he said nothing about the end—*moksha*, or liberation—which the Neoplatonist sought and which is the cardinal Hindu doctrine.

Plotinus believed in rebirth, transmigration of soul, and the law of *karma.* Until highest wisdom is attained and the individual soul is absorbed in the Universal Soul, successive births occur which are like one dream after another. A man's destiny is conditioned by his search for truth, beauty, and goodness, and failure involves reversion to a lower life-form—which is an Indian doctrine.[139] Plotinus, somewhat like the Upanishads which placed more stress on jnana than on *karma,* regarded action as a feeble result of contemplation. He taught that nothing possessing real value can perish. In India this "knowledge of God" is known as "Brahma-Vidya," which claims an insight into the divine nature superior to science, and holds that through the development of higher faculties an individual can obtain divine revelation. Nous is both individual and universal, like Atman and *Paramatman.* The true way of life for Plotinus is the way which leads the soul to itself in its unity with Nous and so to the One. The soul must be inwardly detached from the activity of the senses and the bondage of matter. Matter is evil, although Plotinus did not approve the Stoic practice of gaining freedom from matter by suicide. He sums up his doctrine of mystical purification in the command: "cut away everything." Renunciation of this world and detachment from all activity for the sake of a better world, however, did not imply condemnation of this world. This detachment from external being is reminiscent of Hindu teaching in which the soul must be freed from the subjection of the body to attain union with the Supreme through meditation. Like the Upanishads, Plotinus also said that since the One is "within, at the innermost depth" we must turn our gaze within, ignoring the external world, to seek the divine vision or the Supreme Light. The term "vision" is in itself insufficient, since it implies the duality of seen and seer, which does not exist. The light by which we see the One is the radiance of the One. The vision of the One or the attainment of direct contact with reality is the transformation of our being, reaching our goal, and is to become divine ourselves. Self-realization through wisdom, jnana, and meditation is an old teaching of the Upanishads.[140] Plotinus practiced meditation and concentration intensely. "Four times while Porphyry was staying with him, the wise heirophant 'went beyond the choir of virtues as a man leaves behind him the statues of the gods to enter the sanctuary' and reached ecstasy or communion and identification with the Infinite."[141] Although his philosophy is highly religious, he was indifferent to public worship. To find God, Plotinus had no need to enter a temple or bow before an image. Our destiny is entirely in the life within us; the soul has only to turn again towards the lost communion. Prayer is the silent yearning of the soul for affinity with the Supreme One. Plotinus refused to regard the soul as a prisoner in a satanic jail with no hope of salvation except by the supernatural intervention of a redeemer. For him the soul could force itself to rise to ecstatic union with the One. Mainly interested in contemplative and spiritual life Plotinus devoted little attention to the questions of social morality and wrote no treatise on ethics.

Plotinus himself led a simple life, disregarding the body and practicing vegetarianism. The abstention from sacrifices and animal food of Neoplatonism is, of course, in agreement with Buddhism. Actually Buddhism appears to have been so popular at Alexandria that Clement of Alexandria (150–218) declared that "the Greeks stole their philosophy from the barbarians." Indeed, he was the first Greek to mention the Buddha by name.[142]

Christian scholars, such as F. C. Burkitt and W. W. Inge, although admitting Plotinus' interest in Indian thought and even his journey to the East in quest of further knowledge, insist that there are no traces of Indian influence in his work, and that Neoplatonism is a true child of Hellenism.[143] In sharp contrast to these views there are a number of scholars, including some pro-Hellenes, who accept the theory of Eastern influence. Considering that Plotinus had studied in Alexandria where Eastern religious thought was prevalent, and that his journey to the East, at some risk to himself, would not have been undertaken unless he had not only a keen interest in the East but had actually acquired a competent knowledge of Indian thought, it seems likely that Plotinus was influenced by Indian ideas. He was, it is true, not primarily interpreting Indian philosophy, but rather clarifying and elaborating Plato's teaching with his knowledge of Greek tradition and Indian concepts. Numenius, whose influence on Plotinus was considerable, had himself sought confirmation of the fusion of the doctrines of Pythagoras and Plato in the religions of India, Persia, and Egypt.[144] Some classical authorities, such as Zeller, who maintain the independence of Greek thought would not consider Neoplatonism to be a part of the Greek philosophical tradition because it is contaminated by Eastern features. Similarly, Bacherot and Brehier are also convinced of Indian influence on Neoplatonism. Indeed, most scholars, including those who reject the theory of indebtedness to India, such as Keith, readily admit Indian influence on Neoplatonism.[145] One may conclude then that Neoplatonism was certainly influenced by Indian philosophy, although it is not always possible to distinguish what was taken from Pythagoreanism or Buddhism. It would be wrong to claim that the movement or its character was predominantly Indian, but to disclaim all Indian influence is untenable. It does draw heavily upon Plato's "Good," Aristotle's "Spirit," Stoicism, and Philo but the similarities between Neoplatonism and the Vedants and Yoga systems are likewise obvious.

Plotinus had many points of agreement with Gnosticism. For example, he agreed that the Supreme Being is beyond existence, and that the soul has a divine spark but has lost its way and must return to its original home. Yet, he criticizes the Gnostic doctrine of total depravity, holding that vice is always mixed with some good and no human being is completely bad. He also disputed the Gnostic view of the creation of the world in time. Some of his disagreement with the Gnostics may have arisen from the fact that whilst Gnostics looked upon themselves as Christians, Plotinus did not consider himself as such.

Plotinus' pupils were not of the same intellectual stature as their master. Malchus, a Phoenician better known by the Greek form of his name Porphyry (232–304), was a man of great learning but not of striking originality. Other Neoplatonists who commanded respect were Iamblichus and Proclus.

Prophyry collected, arranged, and edited the writings of Plotinus in the famous work entitled *The Enneads.* Porphyry, before he became a pupil of Plotinus, had written a treatise, *Philosophy from the Oracles*, showing his deep interest in Eastern religious thought. Differing from his teacher, Porphyry advocated image worship and strict asceticism. For him, the source of evil was not so much in the body as in the desires of the soul. Porphyry is famous for his work *Against the Christians* in which he criticized Christian doctrines, and although he was filled with the lofty philosophy of Plotinus, "the need of revelation, redemption, asceticism and immortality inspires him with a faith like that of his opponents."[146]

Porphyry's pupil Iamblichus more than anyone else was responsible for the conversion of Neoplatonism into a theurgic spiritualism, as found in the schools of Athens and Pergamum. By the beginning of the fifth century the academy founded by Plato had become Neoplatonist and it was here that Neoplatonism reigned for two centuries under the Christian Empire. It was also taught at Alexandria by Hypatia. Proclus (416–435) was not a creative thinker but a systematizer who "carried to its utmost limits the ideal of the one comprehensive philosophy that should embrace all the garnered wisdom of the ancient world."[147] In an ordered exposition of the system, Proclus methodically defended Neoplatonism and gave it a somewhat devotional orientation. His influence upon early mediaeval thought was considerable, although somewhat accidental. The school at Athens was closed by Justinian in 529, and the murder of Hypatia put an end to the Alexandrian school. But by this time Christian theology had accepted and absorbed the spirit of Neoplatonism, which became a potent factor in the growth of Christian mysticism. It was a striking end for a movement which had been opposed by Christianity, and whose works had been condemned to be burned by a decree of the Council of Ephesus in 431 and later in 448 by a law of Theodosius II.

St. Augustine, who was born in 353 in Thagaste in modern Algeria, was successively a pagan, a Manichaean, and a Neoplatonist before his conversion to Christianity. He was violent tempered and his sexual morality was loose. Later, tormented by conscience, he developed a remarkable degree of intuitional insight into the processes of his own mind. It was through his reading of Plotinus that he came to Christianity and he naturally tried to introduce the central principles of Neoplatonism into Christianity. Augustine admits his great indebtedness to the works of Plotinus and Porphyry in his *Confessions.* So deep was the influence of Neoplatonism on Augustine's spiritual evolution that he has been described as a "Christian Plotinus," and it was mainly through his writings that the tenets of Plotinus were transmitted to the Middle Ages in the West.

Augustine's mysticism was intellectual, and his vision of God was on a far higher level than that of the mystics who followed him. His views on God and matter, freedom and evil, and the relation of God with the world were adopted from Neoplatonism. It was he who conceived the idea of a universal church. Where Neoplatonism and the Christian faith came into conflict, Augustine subordinated the latter to the former. In his peculiar fusion of the two different doctrines, Neoplatonic mysticism had precedence. For the goal of all prayer was the return to the infinite One, the essential unity with the highest good.[148]

Neoplatonic ideas also came into Christian theological tradition through that most successful of pseudonymous writers, "Dionysius the Areopagite" (*ca.* 500), who expounded Christian mystical theology in Proclus' terms and whose writing had an exceptionally great influence both in Europe and Asia.[149] Dionysius the Areopagite was a Syrian and is traditionally the founder of Christian mysticism. He claimed to have enjoyed ecstatic union and preached quietism as a preparation; to speak without words and understand without knowledge: "seek therefore silently and mystically, that perfect and primitive union with the Archgood." Dionysius' system is described by Inge as "the ancient religion of the Brahmins masquerading in the clothes of Gnostics, Manichaeans, Neoplatonists and others."[150]

It was perhaps this influence of a diluted and diffused Neoplatonism on Christian theology which was the most historically important part of the Neoplatonic contribution to European thought and culture. Indeed, Neoplatonic influence can be detected in many places, not only in theology, in metaphysics, in logic, and in moral philosophy but also in the early history of European science and mediaeval and Renaissance art. From the twelfth century on it was reinforced in the West by the mediaeval Latin translations of Proclus and of the great Arabic philosophers who owed much to Neoplatonism. In the sixteenth century the Greek texts of the Neoplatonist philosophers themselves became available in the West again. Even in modern times, despite criticism, its influence has been significant, and without an understanding of Neoplatonic thought it is not possible to properly appreciate European culture.

However, Christianity, despite frequent doctrinal menaces from other contemporary syncretistic philosophies, continued to spread throughout the Roman Empire, weaving an increasing number of converts into a new commumty of ideas and religious order. The attitudes of the rulers varied between uncompromising hostility and toleration. The Roman emperors were generally intolerant to religions, including Christianity which they regarded as a Jewish sect. The Christians refused to pay homage to the Emperor's image and challenged the divinity of Caesar, thus incurring charges of treason. At the end of the third and the beginning of the fourth centuries, Christianity clashed openly with the Roman Empire. After years of persecution under the Emperor Diocletian, the associated Emperor Galerius issued an edict of toleration in 317. In 324, Constantine, who was well disposed toward Christianity and who had been an associated emperor, became the sole ruler of the Roman Empire. He embraced Christianity on his death bed in 337, having earlier abandoned all pretentions to divinity and having put Christian monograms on the army banners and shields. Thus, Christianity became the official religion of the Roman Empire.

Whilst Christianity as a united front was engaged in its struggle against the Roman Empire, it also was engaged in violent internal disputes, many of which were about the divinity of Jesus. Ignoring the teachings of charity, service, and brotherhood, the Christians became involved in torturous, agitated, and elusive argument, calling each other heretics and persecuting, excommunicating, and executing each other.

The chief disputants were the Arians, who taught that Christ was less than God; the Sabellians, who taught that he was a mode or aspect of God; and the Trinitarians, who taught that the Father, the Son, and the Holy Ghost were three distinct persons, but one God. Spite, dogmatism, and rivalry over theological refinements threatened to destroy Christianity. It was at the Council of Nicaea, convened by Constantine in 323, that the view of the Trinitarians was upheld. Christ, the Son, was declared to be consubstantial with God the Father and coeternal.[151] Although these controversies and persecutions against the spirit of Jesus produced a succession of unhappy and cruel disputes which injured Christianity as a whole in the fourth and fifth centuries, they also generated a zeal, often base and malicious, amongst Christians to propagate their faith.

Chapter IV

PAX ARABICA, THE CHANNEL-BED OF CULTURE

FOLLOWING THE DEATH of Marcus Aurelius in 180, the Roman Empire began to decay because of corruption and indiscipline, and declined in power because of internal strife and mounting outside pressure. Toward the end of the third century the Empire nearly disintegrated under attacks from Germans and Persians. But it was saved and reformed into a new empire by Diocletian (284–305), and later reorganized and further restored by Constantine (288–337). The efforts of these two Emperors, however, only succeeded in prolonging the process of dislocation. Whether the rise of Christianity with its train of bitter religious conflicts and persecutions was a contributing cause of the Roman decline or not, the two certainly coincided. During the following hundred years, Roman authority gradually weakened, Roman armies suffered defeats, and Rome was sacked. By the end of the fifth century there was nothing left of the Roman Empire in the West. Europe lapsed into the Dark Ages for centuries. Total and devoted acceptance of the authority of the new faith, as interpreted by its priests or guardians on earth, inculcated amongst the people an attitude of surrender and they handed over the right and responsibility of thinking to others. Passive submissions suppressed scientific inquiry and academic integrity, the main characteristics of the preceding age of Alexandrian syncretism. Intellectual stagnation, religious intolerance, and racial and regional exclusiveness characterized Europe for the next thousand years.

Meanwhile, Constantine had founded Constantinople (Nova Roma), present-day Istanbul, in 330 as the capital of the eastern branch of the Roman Empire. Later, when the West fell, the eastern branch, as the Byzantine Empire, maintained the Graeco-Roman tradition against and alongside the rising power of Islam until it collapsed before the Ottoman Turks in 1453.

Whilst the Roman Empire was declining, in India the Gupta Empire, noted for its exceptional cultural advancement and dissemination, had emerged early in the fourth century. Not since the days of the Mauryas had India been united under one political power. By the end of the fifth century, however, Gupta power had declined. It was revived somewhat in the seventh to the tenth centuries under Harsha the Palas and the Gurjara-Pratiharas but the forces of decline had set in and the great ancient period came to an end. In India, too, thought lacked creativity and social institutions had lost their vigour and freshness. Except for an occasional spark, intellectual curiosity had given way to religious superstitions.

During the seventh century (when Harsha Siladitya was in power In India, the West had retired into seclusion, the great Persian and Byzantine powers had exhausted each other in a series of wars and China had begun to re-emerge into greatness under the T'angs) there arose in Arabia a unique combination of the forces of a new religion and a new political power. The Islamic religion and Arab power changed the course of history decisively and created one of the world's most brilliant civilizations. The power of faith gave the Arabs, a Semitic people separated from their main stock, national consciousness and a vast empire, and it gave the world a religion and a culture. It is a unique historical episode that the Arabs, who were traders and travellers, lived in a desert country and had no high degree of civilization, should have been so suddenly transformed by Islam as to reach great heights in cultural and political advancement. In its triple role—faith, state, and culture—Islam dominated the Middle Ages and continues to be one of the most significant forces in human society. During the period of Arab hegemony Islam assimilated in its creed people of different nationalities or races more successfully than did the Greeks, the Romans, or the Anglo-Saxons, and inspired in them a strong feeling of brotherhood and a measure of harmony. There is nothing comparable until the nineteenth-century expansion of

Christianity, and that too is said to have been much less successful in inculcating a sense of brotherhood. Despite their frequent cruelty and ruthlessness, civilization is deeply indebted to the mediaeval Arabs for the development, preservation, and dissemination of both the Western and Eastern cultural heritages. They founded universities at Baghdad, Cairo, and Cordova, and for several centuries made more contributions in science and philosophy than any of their contemporaries.

Although most Muslims today are neither Arab nor speak Arabic, their culture is the product of Arab inspiration and enterprise. The Arabs at the peak of their power and creative effort, in Damascus and Baghdad, in Toledo and Cordova, either by original contributions or by what they learned and transmitted from ancient Greece, Persia, and India, played a vital role in human progress.

Information on pre-Islamic Arabia is scanty, but in the seventh century, Mecca, like Petra and Palmyra before it, had come to be known as a financial and commercial centre in the Arab world.[1] Mecca's rise as a mercantile city may be due to the conflict between the Persian Empire and Byzantium, because the wars between them resulted in the closing of the more northern trade routes between East and West. Indeed, the dismembering of the Greek Empire after the death of Alexander had led to the growing importance of Arabian routes in international trade. During the Hellenistic period the monarchs of both Syria and Egypt had attempted to monopolize these trade routes, but neither Alexander nor his successors could conquer Arabia. However, in spite of its increasing importance in trade, Mecca still remained politically and socially very much a city organized to conform to a nomadic way of life. There was practically no centrally organized and uniform system of government, and the city was ruled by a group of clans. Lawlessness and violence were common and moral life was lax, centring around dancing girls, slavery, and harems.

The religion of the pre-Islamic Arabs was inarticulate and polytheistic. Ridden with superstition, they worshipped a multiplicity of deities and sacred stones, and gave little thought to the question of a life after death. A legion of *jinn* (genii), good or evil, were subordinate to a rich pantheon of deities. The centre of stone worship was the temple of Mecca known as the *Kaaba*, which attracted pilgrims from all over Arabia. There were a number of idols in the temple, representing various gods, one of whom was called Allah (Al Ilah). Allah was probably the tribal god of the Quraish, amongst whom Muhammad was born. Muhammad preached that Allah was the only God. He transformed the existing emblems into Islamic objects. He purged the Kaaba of its images and, having first prescribed prayer towards Jerusalem, later altered the direction toward the Kaaba. Thus, the relentlessly iconoclastic Muslims revere as immeasurably holy a temple which was once a flourishing seat of idol worship. A significant feature of Arabic life around the year 600 was a number of wandering hermits and ascetics with a monotheistic tendency and a craving for solitude.

Considering that from the earliest times the Arabs had always been enterprising in international trade and commerce, and that Arabia was so close to the spheres of earlier civilizations and of later religions, Christianity and Judaism, it is indeed a puzzle that it should have remained almost unaffected by any of them. Islam, like Christianity, is based on God having revealed himself, although the means and nature of that revelation differ in the two religions. However, Islamic theology is simple. The term Islam in its Arabic form means surrender, a submission to the will of God, and, in its Hebrew origin, it means peace. Founded by Muhammad (*ca.* 570–8 June 632), who combined religious genius with political finesse, the Islamic religion is detailed in the Quran; the word "Quran" literally means a discourse. The Muslim holy book, like the Jewish-Christian Bible, is a compilation and the orthodox followers assert that every word in it was inspired by Allah.[2] It is, however, unlike the Bible, principally the word of one person. At different times over a period of about twenty-two years, Muhammad dictated his revelation in fragments of unequal length which were written down by scribes on parchment, leather, or palm leaves and stored without any consideration of order and care. By order of the Caliph Abu Bakr in 633, after the death of the Prophet, the remaining fragments were collected and arranged according to length—with the longest first and the shortest last—in complete disregard of logical or chronological order. The task was carried out by Zaid ibn Thabit, who had been Muhammad's secretary. From Zaid's manuscript several versions of the text gained currency and, as there were no vowels in the script of the time, people read and interpreted the text differently. In 651, therefore, Caliph Othman appointed a commission of three Quraish scholars to scrutinize and standardize the work. The revised version was widely circulated and since then the text, consisting of 114 chapters or suras, has been preserved with exceptional purity.[3] Muslims hold the Quran as the word of God and inimitable in style, and it has thus exercised a unique influence on the Arabic language and literature. The need to keep the holy book uncorrupted, unfold its deeper meaning, and elucidate its obscurities caused Muslims to devise a science of grammar and lexicography, and to compile and interpret the pre-Islamic literature verses, and traditions.

Muhammad's central message is uncompromising monotheism and the perdition of idolaters. He preached the existence, the unity, and the perfection of Allah—of whom Moses, Jesus, and others were the earlier prophets, and Muhammad the last. He taught kindness, honesty, and Islamic brotherhood. He respected both the Law (*Torah*) and the Gospel as true revelations, the word of God to Jews and Christians. He did not claim any divinity for himself, or perform any miracles—other than transmitting the revelation of the Quran. He sought nothing beyond the acknowledgment that he was Allan's apostle. It is not, however, enough for a Muslim to believe in the message given by Muhammad but also in Muhammad as the Seal of the Prophets: *"Lailaha illa-l-lah, Muhammadun rasulu-l-lah."* (I testify that there is no god but God, Allah and that Muhammad is the Messenger of God.) Allah is the source of creation and knowledge and the object of worship, and to believe in his messenger requires a perfect belief in the angels, the scriptures, the messengers, the day of resurrection, and the principles on which the code of laws is based.

In style the Quran follows the model of the Hebrew prophets, and is largely an adaptation of Judaic doctrines, tales, and themes. Its monotheism, prophecy, faith, repentance, the last judgement, heaven and hell, appear to be Jewish in form and origin. It departed from Judaism mainly in asserting that the Messiah had come. The separation of the divine and the human is emphasized in the Quran even more than in Judaism. Quranic teaching is less indebted to Christianity than to Judaism, although its earnest preaching of repentance in fear of the coming judgement perhaps has a Christian ring. The Quran, however, has great reverence for other Prophets, including Jesus, whom it calls "Son of Mary," Messiah, Prophet, Word, and acknowledges his miracles. But it does not call Jesus the Son of God, denies the Trinity, and deplores the divisions within Christianity. Although the teachings of Islam are rooted in the Judaeo-Christian tradition, they are shaped into a distinctive doctrine by the original thinking of Muhammad and by the assumptions and preconceptions natural to Arabs.

In 610 Muhammad began to preach publicly the divine knowledge he had received. Whilst he secured some converts, the majority of the Meccans adopted a hostile attitude. Consequently, in 622 Muhammad was forced to migrate with a small band of followers to Medina (Yathrib) over two hundred miles north. In Medina he found greater support and, through his sagacity, statesmanship, and military genius, he soon built up his prestige and power, both temporal and spiritual. From then on his cause prospered. Within ten years he became the undisputed ruler of Medina, Mecca, and the neighbouring areas. Many other tribes throughout Arabia also acknowledged his suzerainty and subscribed to the new faith.

The system of political organization which Muhammad devised, weaving the nomadic tribes into a new community which demanded surrender of personal independence and of ancestral tradition, was alien to the Arabs. Yet, with remarkable ingenuity he succeeded in subduing tribal rivalries and prejudices. Thus, the emergence of Islam as a state or political entity began with Muhammad's military conquests and pacification of the hitherto unruly Arabs, mostly Bedouins. After his death both Islamic religion and polity developed and flourished under the Caliphate.

Muhammad appointed no successor and after some conflict and rivalry Abu Bakr, a faithful friend of the Prophet, was elected the first Caliph or Khalifa of Islam; Khalifa literally means "deputy" or "representative." Despite dissensions and underlying disunion, which gave birth to permanent schisms in the body politic of Islam, the new regime was extraordinarily successful. The Arabs were now firmly welded together into a theocratic community, *Umma*, under the command of "Allah and his Prophet" and soon they were joined by countless people of non-Arab origin in Islamic brotherhood.

At the beginning of the seventh century western Asia was divided between the two rival powers of Byzantium and Persia. The former was Greek in culture, Christian in religion, and mainly Roman in administration, and was in a state of disarray because of internal quarrels. The Persian Empire was ruled by the Sassanians, was Zoroastrian in religion, Persian in culture, and weakened by external wars. The two powers were unable to successfully confront the Arab advance which suddenly burst upon them. In 642 Alexandria, protected by walls and towers and guarded by the Byzantine fleet, fell to the Arabs. The hub of intellectual and cultural life for about a thousand years and the proud possessor of some of the best monuments of antiquity, Alexandria lay in ruins before the arms of the Arab commander Amr ibn al-As.[4] According to a well-known story, the manuscripts from the famous library supplied fuel for the public baths for six months. The story also relates the oft-quoted remark allegedly made by Caliph Omar ibn al-Khattab (*ca.* 634–44) when he consented to the destruction of the library: "If these writings of the Greeks agree with the book of God, they are useless and need not be preserved; if they disagree, they are pernicious and ought to be destroyed." The story, however, is no more than a fable. It makes its first appearance in the solitary report of a stranger, Abul Faraj, who wrote five hundred years later.[5] The reported sentence of the Caliph is alien to the traditional precept of the Muslim casuists who had expressly commanded the preservation of captured religious texts of the Jews and Christians, and had declared that the works of profane scientists and philosophers could be lawfully applied to the believer.

Seldom in history has there been a parallel for transcribing a falsehood with such persistence, conviction, and indignation, in spite of contrary evidence. Gibbon, like many other scholars, denied both the fact and the consequences. In fact, the Arabs were far too fond of books and knowledge to behave in this manner. They built a number of famous libraries in their empire, and their librarians were often men of high learning. But many other Asian conquerors, such as Mahmud of Ghazni, Holagu, and Genghis Khan, destroyed libraries. European invaders from Palestine and Syria burned the magnificent library at Tripolis during the First Crusade. Many early and mediaeval Christian enthusiasts burned libraries, archives, and works of art in North Africa, pre-Columbian America, Rome, and Asia. It is likely that Emperor Theodosius of Constantinople destroyed all or part of the library of Alexandria because, as a devout Christian, he did not approve of pagan books—Greek or Asian.

During the reign of Walid (705–715), Arabs landed in Spain in 709 and soon conquered the Iberian peninsula. The Arab expansion in the West was only checked in 732 by the Franks under Charles Martel on the plains of Tours. By this time Persia, and Western and Central Asia were under their domination.[6] The vast empire, which the Arabs had conquered for Islam and its Caliphs between northern Spain and Transoxiana, was twice as large as the Roman Empire had ever been.

THE STAGGERING RAPIDITY with which the Arabs expanded westward may have been partly due to the internal conflicts within the Christian world and the Western persecution of the Eastern Christians, who consequently were alienated from their Western co-religionists. Also, it appears that Arab expansion was an unintentional extension of internecine wars; civil wars imperceptibly developed into wars of conquest. Whether or not the spectacular conquests were initially an expansion of the Islamic religion or of the Arabian nation is much debated. Whilst the role of religion as an inspiring force in the Arab conquest must be admitted, it would be wrong to underestimate the part played by Arabism. In fact, in the early phase of its expansion Islam was identified with Arabism, as is suggested by the attitude of the Arabs who held the non-Arab Muslims to be somewhat inferior. The newcomers could only enter the faith by becoming *malawi* (clients) of one or the other Arab tribes. There is no doubt that first in Arabia, then in the neighbouring areas of western Asia, and finally in successive waves of conquests the Arabs organized their own lives and those of the conquered according to the ordained way of Islam and the evolving patterns of cultural interaction between their own and local traditions.

Arab penetration of India began in 712 under Muhammad bin Kassim through the defeat of Dahar, the ruler of Sind. This action was not followed up and Arab rule in India remained confined to the small desert principality in Sind for the next five hundred years, during which time Arab relations with the neighbouring Indian states were cordial.

The Arab conquest of a variety of peoples under one hegemony gave fresh impetus to cultural exchange and a cultural dimension to Islam. But, despite their brilliant military victories, the Arabs failed to suppress factionalism and dissension within their own body politic. The rivalries over the Caliphate led to frequent armed conflicts to a change in the capital of the Islamic Empire, and to fragmentation of the Caliphate into splinter groups. It is often said that the rule of the first four Caliphs (632–660) was the only period when the Muslim state was run according to the Islamic concept. These Caliphs are therefore called *al-Khulaja al-Rashidun,* rightly guided Caliphs. Under their rule Islam was firmly established in Arabia and spread far beyond its borders. Yet, dissensions were so deep that the last three of these Caliphs were murdered. In 656 when the fourth Caliph Ali was engaged in fighting a combination of his adversaries, the seat of the Caliphate was transferred from Medina to Kufa. Five years later, following the murder of Ali, Muawiya, the ruler of Syria and an enemy of Ali, became Caliph and founded the Umayyad Caliphate with Damascus as the new capital of the Muslim world.[7] By the eleventh century the Arab Empire had begun to disintegrate. In the thirteenth century the Mongol attacks under Genghis Khan and his grandson Hulagu, dealt Arab power a shattering blow. Their successors reigned in Persia until the second wave of invaders from Central Asia under Timur (1380–1405) spread devastation throughout western Asia. The unity of Islam was, in a political sense, destroyed. The defeated Abbasids, who had succeeded the Umayyads, established their line of the Caliphate in Cairo. This lasted until 1517 when it was overthrown by the Ottoman Turks who retained the Caliphate until it was abolished by Kemal Ataturk in 1924.

The replacement of the Umayyads by the Abbasids in 750 was a landmark in Islamic history. Arab nationalism and Islam were no longer identified as one and Arab dominance of the Islamic world was supplemented by Persian ascendancy. Thus, the Arab kingdom became increasingly cosmopolitan, although the centre of Islamic power moved from the Mediterranean province of Syria to Persia, a country intersected by many trade routes and with a long, rich history.

The Abbasid Caliphate was stronger than the Umayyads, although no less despotic. The Caliph, accorded new dignity and titles plus the pomp and ceremony of an elaborate and hierarchic court, came to be regarded as the deputy of God himself rather than the deputy of the Prophet of God. Although the seat of Islamic power was now located in Persia, Arab aristocracy retained its supremacy. Yet the Abassids were not quite as "Arab" as the Umayyads were. The Caliph himself belonged to a great Arab family although the mothers of the Abbasid Caliphs for generations were Persians. Persian nobles filled the court and Persian soldiers the army. For a time Arabs and Persians forgot their national differences under their obedience to Islam but this position could not last indefinitely; political rivalries and dormant ambitions were bound to come to the surface eventually.

In 762 the capital of the new Caliphate was moved from Damascus to Baghdad, which, occupying a commanding position on the overland route between India and the West, assumed the role of Alexandria and kept the torch of learning alive when Europe was plunged into barbarism. Baghdad remained the centre of intellectual life until about the end of the tenth century when this function was transferred to Cordova in Spain. Both capitals were focal points of Arab culture. The cultural atmosphere of Baghdad was so magnificent that it became a true *Dar al-ulum,* or House of Learning, and during this period scholarship reigned supreme. The nation of warriors rapidly became both the patrons and cultivators of intellectual pursuits. Piety was no longer its own reward, and learning was accorded munificent patronage. This was Islam's age of glory which reached its peak under the most eminent of the Abbasid Caliphs, Harun Al Rashid (786–809). The famous *Arabian Nights* have made his name almost a household word. He defeated the Byzantine Emperor Nicephorus and occupied Constantinople in 782. Although the solidarity of the Islamic power was broken up into splinter Caliphates—Spain in 756, Morocco in 788, and Tunisia in 800 became virtually independent under local dynasties, and Egypt fell out in 868—one of the most momentous periods in the history of thought and culture began.

Always great travellers and world traders, the Arabs, taking advantage of their political supremacy, became the chief navigators and merchants of the early Middle Ages. It was, in fact, an Arab pilot who took Vasco da Gama across the Indian Ocean in 1498. Arab ships sailed the length of the Mediterranean and there was great activity between the ports of the Persian Gulf, such as Siraf, Basra, and Ubulla, and India and beyond. The rivers of Iraq linked the Gulf with Baghdad, and the direct Red Sea route between the Indian coast and the Egyptian ports, too, continued to be dominated by the Arabs. Thus, East-West contact during the period of Arab ascendancy became still closer. Within a few years of their occupation of the Syrian and Egyptian coastlines the Arabs built and manned great war fleets which were able to defeat the powerful and experienced Byzantine navy and to control the Mediterranean, so vital for the security and expansion of their empire.

It is said that the ascent of Arab greatness was due to their commercial enterprise. In addition to the sea routes, the overland routes connecting Arabia, western Asia, India, and China were extremely busy. The merchants of Baghdad imported Chinese silks and Indian spices, as well as tigers, panthers, elephants, panther skins, rubies, white sandalwood, ebony, and coconuts. Cotton was originally imported from India but later it was cultivated in eastern Persia and spread westward as far as Spain. From Baghdad the merchandise was dispatched to Spain and thus to Europe. Land routes also linked Baghdad with Africa and Russia. The number of Arab coins dating from the late seventh to the early eleventh centuries, found not only in the Volga basin but also in Scandinavia, especially Sweden, and some even in Britain would indicate how widespread Arab commercial influence was in the early Middle Ages.

The extensive and prosperous commercial life of the Arab world was inevitably reflected in its thought and literature. Merchants, soldiers, and scholars travelled the Islamic Empire from Spain to India in search of knowledge, glory, and profit, thus accelerating cultural intercourse. The Islamic civilization which resulted did not possess a well-defined personality, having acquired regional variations over its long period of historical development. Fluidity and diversity were the principal characteristics of classical Islamic civilization. But, although the Islamic culture is highly syncretic, it is founded in Arab culture initiative, and endeavour.

In turn, however, Arab culture itself was rooted in an amazing synthesis of the intellectual achievements of older civilizations. The Arabs had little indigenous culture, and much that was not very attractive. They mainly borrowed from Indian, Greek, and Persian sources. The preservation and the integration of these various streams of thought was the principal Arab contribution to world civilization. The syncretic nature of Arab culture is well illustrated by the fact that three of their most important gifts to the West—Aristotle, Arabic numerals, and paper—came from Greece, India, and China respectively.

Arab culture developed in western Asia where the scientific heritage of the Greeks, enriched by contributions from Persia and India, was translated and publicized in Syrian, Hebrew, Aramaic, and Pahlavi. In the neighbourhood of Baghdad the Nestorians founded a school at Jundishapur which was primarily concerned with the study of Greek philosophy and science. At the same time Indian philosophical and scientific works were also studied and translated. Al Kindi, commonly regarded as the greatest philosopher of the Arabs, wrote in the Preface of his *Metaphysics:* "It is fitting then for us not to be ashamed to acknowledge truth and to assimilate it from whatever source it comes to us, even if it is brought to us by former generations and foreign peoples. For him who seeks the truth there is nothing of higher value than truth itself; it never cheapens nor abases him who searches for it, but ennobles and honours him."

The Arabic translations of Greek and other philosophical texts began in early Abbasid times under the patronage of the Caliphs, Al Mansur and Al Rashid. But with the reign of Al Mamun (813–33) a brisk, new phase of development in Arabic literature began. The Caliph was an extraordinary man and he used his authority to enforce a liberal standard of orthodoxy. He wholeheartedly supported the pursuit of knowledge and he himself participated enthusiastically in academic discussions. The *Bayt at hikma* (the House of Wisdom, a kind of a library and museum reminiscent of the Alexandrian Library), founded at Baghdad in 830, with its impressive library and observatory, attracted scholars and encouraged intellectual pursuits, and in the *divans* of the Caliphs the most renowned scientists, poets, and scholars assembled to debate their views. The most illustrious name in this circle was that of Al Khwarizmi, who wrote on mathematics, astronomy, and geography.

Whilst Harun Al Rashid was fond of literature and philosophy, Al Mamun was interested in the sciences, especially biology. Thus, in order to enable Arab culture to assimilate the neighbouring cultures, Al Mamun encouraged exchange with India. Arab scholarship, in direct contact with Indian, Greek, and Persian systems of thought, now bloomed into its most brilliant period of development. Hitherto Muslim learning had been influenced only indirectly by the older centres of culture. The impact of the foreign systems of thought on Arab learning was so great that it has been compared to the reintroduction of Greek literature into Europe at the Renaissance.

Al Mamun's immediate successors followed his example enabling foreign influences to find fullest expression throughout the empire. Thus, the period of rich new developments in Arab learning which began with the reign of Harun Al Rashid reached its zenith during the reign of Al Mamun and his successors. However, from 850 to 950, whilst Baghdad remained the chief cultural centre, various other centres sprang up challenging Baghdad's supremacy. Cordova in Spain became quite famous, and Ghazna, Samarkand, Merv, Herat, Tus, Nishapur, Ray, Isfahan, Shiraz, Musul, Damascus, Jerusalem, Cairo, Qairawan, Fas, Marrakush, Toledo, Seville, and Granada also played significant roles in the spread of learning. It was from Toledo, for instance, that Europe first learned that scholarship had no national frontiers but belonged to the whole of mankind. At Toledo Arabs, Jews, Greeks, Christians, Spaniards, Frenchmen, Germans, and others worked together.

Scholars and translators counted amongst themselves persons of pure and mixed Arab descent, converts to Islam, and Christians, some of whom belonged to the Greek Orthodox Church although the majority were Nestorians or Jacobites. Even many of the mediaeval Arab philosophers were not of Arab descent. For example, Al Farabi was a Turk, and Al Razi (Rhazes) and Ibn Sina (Avicenna) were Persians. This led the Arab historian Ibn Khaldun to comment that it was strange that most of the learned Muslims were, with rare exceptions, *Ajam* (non-Arabs); and even those savants who claimed Arab descent spoke a foreign language, had grown up in foreign lands, and had studied under foreign masters. The peoples of Islam were bound together by religion and language but included peoples of varied nationalities. More important, they were in close contact with a variety of non-Muslims, such as Chinese, Indians, Mongols, Malays, Greeks, Copts, Syrians, Magians, Berbers, Sicilians, Spaniards, Franks, and Jews. Consequently, many important scholars who published their work under Islamic patronage were not Muslims. For example, the great chemist; Jabir ibn Hayyan, was probably a Sabian; the physicians, Hunayn ibn Ishaq, Ibn Butlan, and Ibn Jazla were Christians.

In different groups and schools the activity of translators continued in degrees of varying intensity until the eleventh century. Whilst during this period a number of original Arab works were also written, translation work was not regarded as merely mechanical or inferior. Although there were some Greek manuscripts available in the cities of western Asia at the time, these were mainly Syriac translations of the Greek originals. Many of the translators were not accomplished philosophers, but without their painstaking work the development of Western thought would have been seriously impaired, and its link with the Greek past would never have been forged. Even Arab philosophy would have hardly come into existence, as these translations laid the foundation of an Arab style and built a complex framework of Arab philosophical terminology. The translations also made it possible for the Greek and Islamic systems of thought to pass on to mediaeval Jewry, giving Jewish philosophy a much needed intellectual stimulus.

The Arabs of the day were enthusiastic, accurate, and prolific translators and they would often undertake long journeys in search of manuscripts. It is not commonly realized that, in addition to a number of Greek works, they also translated many Indian and Persian studies, with the help of Persian and Indian translators. In fact, the translation movement began when a Persian Muslim master of the Arabic language and style, Abu Muhammad ibn al-Muqaffa (*ca.* 760), rendered the *Pancatantra* into Pahlavi, and several works on medicine and logic into Arabic. Ibn al-Muqaffa served under Isa ibn Ali, uncle of the first Abbasid Caliph, Al Suffah (750–54). His Arabic version, *Kalila wa Dimna*, of the splendid Indian tales led to translations into some forty European and Asian languages.

The Arabs had studied Indian and Persian works long before becoming interested in Greek thought. By that time, at least one thousand years had intervened between the Hellenic and Arab cultures and whatever Hellenic heritage had reached the Arabs came to them through Syria and Alexandria and was already influenced by Eastern ideas. The classical period of Greek philosophy was long over, and its original flavour had been highly spiced by later schools, such as Neoplatonism. Plato and Aristotle were read through their later exponents' interpretations and these in the Syriac versions. From the fourth century Greek philosophy and its Neoplatonic commentaries, and Greek science were studied in the schools and monasteries of Syria and Mesopotamia. In fact some Greek philosophical texts, lost through Byzantine neglect or deliberate destruction are preserved only in Arabic translations. For example, the lost treatises of Galen, Greek commentaries on Aristotle, and sections of a paraphrase of Plotinus are found only in the Arabic version. The value of Arab translations of the works of Aristotle and his exponents is appreciably great. Whilst Neoplatonism gave rise to acute controversies involving the relationship between pantheism and the unrelenting monotheism of the Quran, a number of scholars were engaged in making Greek science and philosophy accessible to the Arabic-speaking world. The history of this literary activity is somewhat uncertain. The earliest known translator was Qustah ibn Luqa of Baalbak, who lived about 835 and who not only translated Aristotle and other writers but wrote profusely himself on scientific subjects. Later, Arabic learning was enriched by even more prominent and prolific writers, such as Humayan ibn Ishaq (d. 873); Al Kindi (d. 850), called the philosopher of the Arabs because he was of pure Arab descent and who is credited with no fewer than 265 treatises on a wide range of subjects from music to medicine; Al Khwarizmi, who studied not only the Greek works on mathematics and astronomy but also the Indian systems, and who by the use of Indian numerals revolutionized mathematical calculations; and Al Farabi (870-950).

Arabic literature reached across the Islamic world with exceptional rapidity, and the intellectual stimulation it provided to the regions between China and Spain laid the foundation of a new age. The Arabs not only preserved old knowledge, but, by providing a bridge between cultures, rejuvenated Western civilization.[8]

The Arabs transmitted Hellenic and Eastern knowledge to the West at a time when the latter needed it most, and they also gave the West an extremely rare gift, the spirit of scientific inquiry, observation, and experimentation. European science owes its existence to the Arabs. They elevated science from metaphysical speculation and put it on the path of experimentation and operation. Their concern with identification and verification, and thus with observation, accurate description, and measurement helped to develop an objective scientific attitude. The Arabs had, of course, acquired this disciplined approach to scientific observation from Alexandria where it had existed for some time. It must also have partially originated in the East because, although the Greeks systematized, generalized, and theorized, they did not practice sustained observation, collection of data and positive knowledge, minute methods of science, and investigation and experimentation. They were inquisitive and curious, but curiosity alone is not enough for science.

Contact between India and the Arab world goes back to the beginnings of recorded history. The long-established trade between the Persian Gulf and India resulted in several notable Arabic works, such as the *Chain of Histories* and *Marvels of India,* in addition to manuals of navigation in prose and verse. With the rise of Islam these ties were intensified, and the transfer of the capital of the Arab Empire from Damascus to Baghdad in 762 established closer links with the sea routes to India and China. Merchandise was carried from Baghdad to Basra, and thence to Siraf, the main Arabian port of embarkation situated in the Persian Gulf. From Siraf goods were transported to India, Southeast Asia, and China. The proximity of the new capital to the Persian Gulf gave a fresh impetus to trade with southern India. The Arabs exchanged goods with Gujarat, Kathiawar, Konkan, Malabar, the Coromandal coast, Bengal, the Andaman and Nicobar Islands, western Sumatra, Malaya, Indochina, and China. Close cultural and commercial contacts between the Arabs and southern India continued until the arrival of the Portuguese in India at the end of the fifteenth century.

The Arabs appear to have had a high regard for India. *Saif-i-Hindi* (the Indian sword) was their favourite weapon. There is some evidence to suggest that at the time of Prophet Muhammad, Indian tribes resembling the Jats were settled in Arabia and Iraq. When Ayasha, the favourite wife of the Prophet, fell ill she was reported to have been treated by an Indian physician from the Jat tribe. Arab interest in India is also well attested to by the record of the numerous Arab travellers to India, such as Sulaiman the merchant, Abu Zaid Sirafi, Dulaf bin Muhalhil, Buzurg bin Shahryar, Masudi, Istakhri, Ibn Haukal, Muqaddisi, Al Biruni, and Ibn Battuta, who has been called "The Traveller of the Arabs" because of his extensive journeys. Arab historians were generous in their appreciation of India. Said Al-Andalusi in his *Tabaqat al-Ulam* called India "a mine of wisdom, a source of law and politics," and Indian scientists were acknowledged to be masters of the science of numbers (*ilm al-adad)*, of geometry and astronomy, and to have surpassed all other peoples in their knowledge of medicine. Yaqubi characterized the Indians as men unsurpassed in science, especially astronomy. The period between 500 and 800 was indeed a remarkable period of scientific activity in India, especially in astronomy and mathematics. Abu Mashan described India as a noble country and said that all ancient peoples acknowledged the excellence of her peoples' wisdom, knowledge, and sense of justice. The Abbasid Caliphs, Al Mansur, Harun Al Rashid, and Al Mamun, even recruited Indian or Indian-trained ministers during their administrations. These ministers were known as Barmaks (a derivative from Pramukha); Barmakites, or Barmecides who were originally Buddhists and Heads (Pramukha) of the Nava Vihara at Balkh.[9] This temple later came to be known as the great Magian fire temple, and its high priest bore the title of Barmak. Upon the foundation of the Abbasid Caliphate, Khalid was the first Barmak to hold the important office of state under Saffah and Mansur (754-775) and his son Yahya was the tutor of Harun Al Rashid, who upon his accession to the Caliphate appointed Yahya as his grand vizier (prime minister).[10] Under the patronage and tactful administration of the Barmaks, Baghdad became a centre of Indian learning.

From this time on Arab and Muslim historians, geographers, and travellers began to visit India increasingly. Ahmad bin Yaqub bin Jafar, who came to India in the tenth century, compiled a list of Indian works translated into Arabic. Muhammad bin Ishaq ibn al-Nadim in his encyclopaedic *Kitab al-Fihrist* mentions repeatedly a wide range of works on Indian thought.

The two most eminent scholars and greatest minds of the Arab world, Al Biruni (973–1048) and Al Khwarizmi (d. *ca.* 850), whose works profoundly influenced the growth of scientific thought in Europe, were well versed in Indian thought and languages. Al Biruni had travelled widely in India and had painstakingly learned Sanskrit in order to translate Indian scientific writing into Arabic. It was only after visiting India that he wrote his monumental work on mathematics, physics, geography, and astronomy. He translated some works of Indian philosophy, such as *Kitab Patanjal* and Kapila's *Sanka.* He wrote *Kitab al-Bayan,* a work on the principles of Indian rhetoric, and even a history of India, *Tarikh al-Hind,* in which he pointed out that the Hindus were too arrogant about their science and country. His work on the comparative chronology of nations, *Al-Athar al-Baqiyak an al-Quran al-Khaliyah,* is well known and often quoted by European writers.

In physics Al Biruni used the displacement method to calculate the specific weight or gravity of eighteen different precious and semiprecious stones. He also experimented with great accuracy on some minerals. In mathematics he finalized Arab knowledge and the use of Hindu numerals, solving many intricate problems relating to angles, conics, and cubic equations. He also made outstanding contributions "to the principles of hydrostatics, which he investigated in the artesian wells of India."[11] His work on India, a product of some thirteen years of labour, in content and scientific method is outstanding in Arabic literature. He translated many Indian books into Arabic and, more curiously, several Arabic translations from the Greek into Sanskrit. He represented that "happy and fertile blend of Arabic and Indian literatures which is one of the best fruits of Muslim civilization."[12]

By the time the Arabs arrived the Indians had mastered many astronomical concepts, amongst them were the solar system; the lunar mansions; the *nakshatras;* the precession of the equinoxes and the determination of its rate; the establishment of the lunisolar year; the spherical shape of the sun, moon, earth, and the other planets; the calculation of mean distances of the planets based on the theory of equal linear motion; the rotation of the earth on its axis; the revolution of the earth around the sun; and the assumption of interplanetary attraction as an explanation of equilibrium.

Astronomy requires sophisticated mathematics, and the use of the trigonometric sine was introduced as a contribution to the mathematical representation of astral positions. It is in the *Surya Siddhanta,* a work of the fourth century, that the trigonometric sine is first mentioned. The most renowned of all the Arab astronomers, Muhammad ibn Jabir al-Battani

(877–918) whose astronomical tables superseded Greek knowledge and were widely diffused throughout mediaeval Europe, introduced into Arab science the use of ratios, sine, and tangent, which were contained in Aryabhata's geometry. When Copernicus (1473–1543) replaced the hitherto prevalent concept of the closed and hierarchical cosmos which had survived since antiquity, with that of the homogeneous and infinite universe of modern science, he extensively used the contributions to trigonometry made by Abul-Wafa (940–998) who continued the work of Al Battani. In fact, trigonometry was first studied by the Arabs as a branch of astronomy, and only later studied independently.

The Indian decimal notation and the concept of zero were similarly passed on to Europe through Arab scholarship when Al Fazari translated Brahmagupta's *Siddhanta* in 771 under the title *Sindhind*, although it was not until in the nineteenth century that Colebrooke first noticed the connection between the two. This treatise was brought to Baghdad by an Indian astronomer, who had come on a political mission from Sind to the court of the Caliph Al Mansur. Ibn al-Adami, confirmed by Al Biruni, has recorded in detail the manner in wich Indian astronomy was introduced at Baghdad. Later, Yaqub ibn Tanq incorporated in his *Tarkib al-Aflak* principles of Indian astronomy. The *Khanda-Khadyaka* of Brahmagupta, called by the Arabs Al Arkand, and Aryabhata's and Varahamihira's works on astronomy were also studied. Al Biruni translated *Surya Siddhanta* of Varahamihira.

Al Khwarizmi, who laid the foundation of Arab astronomy and higher mathematics, and to whom the world is indebted for its present knowledge of algebra, was greatly indebted to Indian scholarship. In his work on algebra entitled *Book of Calculation of Restoration and Reduction,* Al Khwarizmi used Indian as well as Greek and Babylonian sources. His arithmetic was based on the Indian decimal notation and numerals and had tremendous influence on mathematics in Europe through its translation into Latin in the twelfth century. During the latter half of the eighth century an Indian brought to Baghdad two important scientific treatises on astronomy and mathematics. Al Khwarizmi abridged the astronomical work, *Siddhanta,* into Arabic about 820 and used its tables in revising Ptolemy's and constructing his own. The trigonometric tables of Al Khwarizmi were translated into Latin by Adelard of Bath in 1126.

Through the replacement of Ptolemy's calculus of chords by the calculus of sines or trigonometry, astronomical knowledge made great advances. Other contemporary writers such as Fazl bin Hatim Naziri and Hassen bin Misba also made use of the Indian system. In the ninth century Al Kindi wrote a tract on Indian computation, *Hisabul Hindi.* It was through the Arabs that Indian astronomy, despite the complete isolation of India from Europe during the Middle Ages, exercised an indirect influence on modern Western astronomy. The Indian system with its theory of the "trepidation," or pendulum movement, of the fixed stars found wide acceptance amongst the Arab astronomers of Spain, but since it conflicted with the Ptolemaic system of the continuous precession of the equinoxes, it gave rise to a considerable body of polemical and critical writing. This reached its peak in the thirteenth century and influenced Christian circles in Europe. One positive aspect of the Crusades was that they, unintentionally although unavoidably, provided an opportunity for cultural intercourse between Europe and Asia during the mediaeval period.

Long before the Arabs began translating Indian scientific works, the Persians had begun the process of synthesizing Indian knowledge with Persian, which had reached its zenith during the reign of Anushirwan (Kushro I, 531–579). Syrian astronomers, such as Severus Sebokht, also knew of Indian achievements and in 662 he wrote of Hindu numerals—the first known mention of them outside India—and of Hindu computation which excelled the spoken word and was done with nine symbols. Hence, the possibility of Indian ideas having reached the Arabs through Persian texts cannot be ruled out.

Whilst the development of Arab science, especially astronomy and mathematics, was largely inspired by the various prevalent Alexandrian traditions and sustained by the qualities of Arab scholarship, the first major impulse came from India. But the Arabs' own tradition of astronomy—in their long desert journeys they depended on the stars for the direction—had received considerable encouragement through the establishment of several observatories under the Umayyad and Abbasid Caliphates. The Muslims looked upon astronomy as the noblest and most exalted of sciences, for the study of stars was an indispensable aid to religious observances, determining for instance the month of

Ramadhan and the hours of prayers. The observatory at Jundishapur in Iran, a centre of learning especially in medical science, was particularly suited as a focal point for Western and Indian contact. Even after the decline of the Abbasid Caliphate, interest in astronomy continued. In the thirteenth century the Mongol conqueror Hulagu Khan, who had deposed the Caliphate of Baghdad, and who was led by his superstitious belief in astrology, founded the great Margha observatory at Azerbaijan, This observatory was well known for its monumental instruments, and India was always in close contact with it. Here Arab, Persian, Greek, Chinese, and Indian learning interacted on one another.

About a century and a half later in the fifteenth century, Ulug Begh, grandson of the Turkish conqueror Tamurlane, built an observatory in Samarkand and it was here that new planetary tables and a new star catalogue were prepared, the first since Ptolemy's. It is quite possible that the renewed inspiration for erecting observatories at Jaipur, Delhi, and elsewhere in the seventeenth and eighteenth centuries, with their wonderfully accurate instruments, came from Central Asia. They almost certainly had their ancient counterparts although no material evidence is now available. In the seventeenth century, despite traditional objections, certain Indian astronomers began to introduce Arab and Western ideas. For example Kamalakara borrowed generously from the Arabs when he wrote his *Siddhantaviveka* in 1658.

When the Arabs assumed the position of political ascendancy in the world, medical science in India was already mature. It was inevitable, therefore, that the Arabs should have been attracted by Indian developments in this field. Even at the time of Alexander, says Garrison, "Hindu physicians and surgeons enjoyed a well-deserved reputation for superior knowledge and skill," and some scholars have suggested the influence on Aristotle of Indian medical ideas.[13] Barzouhyeh, who prepared a Pahlavi version of the *Pancatantra* during the reign of Anushirvan (531–579), visited India to acquire proficiency in Indian medicine and other sciences. Ibn al-Nadirn relates that when Caliph Harum Al Rashid suffered from a serious disease which baffled his physicians at Baghdad he called for an Indian physician, Manka (Manikya), who cured him. The Caliph rewarded him richly and Manka settled at Baghdad and was attached to the hospital of the Barmaks.

Having acquired a thorough knowledge of Islamic religion and languages, he translated several books from Sanskrit into Persian or Arabic. There are records of many other Indian physicians who practiced medicine amongst the Arabs; two of them were Ibn Dhan and Salih, reputed to be the descendants of Dhanapati and Bhela respectively. Ibn Dhan was appointed the director of his hospital by the Barmak Yahya, and he is credited with having translated books from Sanskrit into Arabic and Persian. Indian physicians were superintendents of the hospitals at Baghdad. Indian medical works were rendered into Pahlavi and Arabic during the Abbasid Caliphate; amongst them were Caraka, Susruta, the *Ashtangahrdaya,* the *Nidana,* the *Siddhayoga,* and other works on diseases of women and their treatment, poisons and their antidotes, on drugs, medicaments, intoxicants, nervous diseases, etc. Susruta's manual was translated by Manka and entitled *Sasru;* Ibn Dhan translated two other Sanskrit works, describing them as *Sindhstan* and *Istsangir.* Greek medical works were also translated and the Arabs were quite familiar with them as well.[14]

Ali bin Rabban's pupil, Abu Bakr Muhammad ibn Zakariya al-Razi (865–925), began the golden age of Arab medicine. He anticipated Pasteur by more than one thousand years, for when ordered by the Caliph to build a new hospital, he hung up pieces of fresh meat in various parts of Baghdad and chose the site where the meat putrefied most slowly, because, as Pasteur was to demonstrate, the atmosphere was pure and bacteria less active. Al Razi was a Persian who knew Greek, Persian, and Indian medicine. He was one of history's great doctors and one of the two greatest Muslim physicians and chemists; the other being Abu Ali Ibn Sina (Avicenna). He was a prolific writer who produced about two hundred books, half of them on medicine. His greatest work on general clinical medicine, *Al Hawi,* was translated into Latin by Gerard of Cremona and remained a standard text in European medical colleges until the seventeenth century. It draws heavily on Graeco-Arabic and Indian sources.[15]

Al Razi and Al Ashau propounded the Arabic system of atomism. That this system was founded by someone very familiar with Indian sciences would explain the Arab adoption, almost wholly, of the Indian atomic theories, as enunciated by the Nyaya-Vaisesika and the Jain and Ajivika schools of thought, in marked preference to the Greek atomic theory founded by Leucippus and Democritus.[16]

As Arab medicine developed, it spread through North Africa and reached its highest expression in the University of Cordova in Spain. In addition, other streams of thought converged on the College of Salerno near Naples, the first medical school in the Christian world. The Church played no part in its foundation, for it was reputedly started by four masters—Elinus the Jew, Pontus the Greek, Adale the Arab, and Salernus the Latin—in the tenth century, perhaps even earlier. It was certainly much older than the Universities of Paris and of Bologna, which are regarded as the two archetypes of the European university.

Arab toxicology, which marked the advance from alchemy to rational medicine, was, as reflected in the works of Ibn Wahshiya, Jabir, Maimonides, and others, greatly influenced by Indian concepts, and especially the *Book of Shanab*. *Shanab* may well have been the Arabic version of *Caraka* for the work is based on the *Carakasamhita*, particularly in its identification of poisonous substances and distinctions between "mobile" and "immobile" poisons.[17]

Arab and, indirectly, European indebtedness to Indian science is indeed great. Mediaeval Europe miserably lacked any scientific culture until Eastern knowledge reached them through Arabic translations. The Romans, being a practical people, were uninterested in speculative or pure scientific thought, and in consequence they completely disregarded the progress made in scientific fields in the schools of Alexandria and elsewhere: "Not a single Roman left his mark on mathematics, mechanics, or technology."[18] Without the Arabian contribution it is unthinkable that the West could have absorbed the scientific knowledge of India, Persia, Greece, and Alexandria as it did, thus laying the foundation of its own superb progress.

It was in Spain that the Arabs achieved their greatest conquest in Europe and it was through Spain that they made their most enduring contributions to European civilization. On the eve of Arab conquest Spain was in a weak and deplorable state. The Arab rule was tolerant, liberal, and a welcome change. The Arabs introduced scientific irrigation and a number of new crops, such as cotton, rice, sugar cane, and citrus fruits, the first three having originated in India.[19] The changes they brought about in the system of land tenure paved the way for Spanish prosperity. Industries such as textiles, wool, pottery, paper, silk, and sugar-refining were developed and important gold, silver, and other mines opened up. In architecture there developed the new Hispano-Moorish style, which produced such world-famous buildings as the Alcazar in Seville and the Alhambra in Granada.

There are Spanish historians who attempt to minimize the Arab heritage of Spain, and some even conclude that Arab domination retarded Spanish life, but there is considerable evidence pointing to the deep indebtedness of Spain to the Arabs. The Amirs of Arab Spain were enthusiastic patrons of scholarship, and Arab Spain was a citadel of cultural heritage and progress. Whilst most of Europe was in a decadent decline, both materially and spiritually, the Spanish Muslims created a splendid civilization and an organized economic life. During the reign of Abdurrahman (912–961) Spain rose to the foremost place in European civilization. The Umayyad ruler, with his capital in Cordova, was exceptionally talented, a valiant soldier, and a wise ruler with many intellectual interests.[20]

The great variety of races in Muslim Spain probably hindered the immediate integration of societies and cultures. But once momentum gathered, development was impressive. Arab science and philosophy dominated Spanish thought and life from the beginning of the ninth to the end of the thirteenth century. In practical life, including legal and military organization, Arab influence was so great that some Christian writers, such as Alvaro of Cordova, lamented the situation. The official language of Muslim Spain was classical Arabic; the Arabs were the backbone of the Spanish army, and they married freely into Spanish families. The study of Muslim law and theology introduced Arab books giving a fresh impetus to Arab learning. Scholars, students, and booksellers flocked to Cordova and it soon became the intellectual capital of the Western world. The royal library was one of the best in Spain, and there were, in addition, a number of celebrated private libraries in Cordova. The impact of Arab culture on Spain eliminated the local distrust of philosophy and astronomy and cleared the way for their study and growth, first in Spain, and later throughout Europe. Spanish scholars, attracted by this movement, travelled in the East, read the works of

Greek and other philosophers, and, upon their return, served as another channel of communication with the rest of Europe. "Muslim Spain played a decisive part in the development of art, science, philosophy, and poetry, and its influence reached even to the highest peaks of the Christian thought of the thirteenth century, to Thomas Aquinas and Dante. Then, if ever, Spain was 'the torch of Europe.'"[21]

With the destruction of Cordova at the beginning of the eleventh century by the Berbers, Toledo became the centre of Muslim learning in Spain, and it retained this position after the Christian conquest in 1085.[22] Toledo attracted scholars from all parts of Europe, including Britain. The Italian Gerard of Cremona, who is credited with having carried more of Arabic science into Europe than any other single scholar, Alfred the Englishman, Michael the Scot, Hermann the German, Herman Dalmata the Slav, all worked in Spain during the twelfth and thirteenth centuries. The greatest name in English science before Robert Grossetete and Roger Bacon, Adelard of Bath, was a student of Arab science and philosophy in the twelfth century. He learned Arabic, as did the other scientists of the day, and by the end of the thirteenth century, Arab science had been transmitted to western Europe and absorbed, and Spain's work as an intermediary was done.

A major reason why the Arabs left a vast heritage of scientific conceptual synthesis and not of speculative thought, may be because religiously and philosophically their implicit faith in Islamic thought did not allow them sufficient receptivity to other influences. But, in science and commerce they were not so inhibited and thus absorbed freely from whatever quarters they could.

Chapter V

NATURALISM AND SCIENCE IN ANCIENT INDIA

SCIENCE AND PHILOSOPHY were both highly developed disciplines in ancient India. However, because Indian philosophic thought was considerably more mature and found particular favour amongst intellectuals, the tradition persists that any early scientific contributions came solely from the West, Greece in particular. Because of this erroneous belief, which is perpetuated by a wide variety of scholars, it seems desirable to examine briefly the history of Indian scientific thought.

The history of science in general is a comparatively new field and a comprehensive account of Indian science and technology has yet to be written. Despite the fact that a vast literature in Sanskrit is no longer available, there are many documents waiting to be investigated.[1] Beginning with the earliest known Indian civilization, the Indus Valley, with its pottery wheel, cotton textiles, Indus script, and two wheeled carts, there is a good deal of material and texts to work from. By the beginning of the third millennium B.C. in India, as in China, Egypt, and Mesopotamia, scientific development was well advanced. Excavations carried on at the sites of the Indus civilization have revealed remnants of an ancient civilization unsurpassed in civil engineering accomplishments, particularly baths and drainage. Whilst much is known of the hygienic measures of the period, little is known of the scientific knowledge upon which they were based.

In ancient India, as in Greece, there was much speculative thought about astronomy, mathematics, physics, and biology. But mathematics and mysticism are inextricably mixed in early Greek thought, and Greek belief in magic, divination and oracles was perhaps more pronounced than its counterpart in India. It is therefore untrue to assert, as recent European writers particularly have done, that Greece was the home of pure science. Equally untenable is the claim of those Indian historians who overemphasize India's contribution to scientific thought. Both India and Greece, whilst having their own traditions, had direct and indirect effects on each other in science as they did in philosophy. In fact, long before the Greeks, the Indians had learned to employ the dialectic method to grasp empirical and transcendental truths, although in India, more perhaps than in ancient Greece or the modern West, reason and truth, logic and mysticism, the visible and invisible, have always been regarded as inseparable.

The practical application of science to human affairs was as poor in India as in any other ancient society. In fact, this was not achieved until the eighteenth century; until then science and technology developed separately. In the seventeenth century, called "the cradle of modern science," Francis Bacon (1561–1626) through his *Novum Organum* established a new methodology in the experimental interpretation of nature. Although he failed to appreciate that the new science must be based on mathematics, he wrote as a philosopher exposing the inadequacy of old theories. He believed that mind, liberated from prejudice and generalization, could by knowledge attain sovereignty over nature. With little aptitude for practical science he yet understood the enormous importance of a new way of investigating nature. He considered that "the purpose of science was not to make up new theories about the nature and principles of things, but to lay firmer foundations of human power and greatness. So Science was to minister to the Arts—to medicine, navigation, industry of all kinds."[2] At about the same time René Descartes (1596–1650), the founder of analytical geometry in France, also insisted on a new methodology basing his concept more on deduction than experience. He commenced by subjecting everything to the test of doubt, including doubt itself. He insisted upon proof by experiment, thus laying the foundation of modern scientific research, and advocated the practical application of scientific conclusions. The Italian astronomer and experimental philosopher, Galileo Galilei (1564–1643), was the first, however, to employ the modern scientific method in its fullness. He was an enthusiastic and versatile man, skilful with his hands, a fine writer, and a competent mathematician. He founded the science of mechanics in physics. However, his brilliant researches and remarkable work incurred the wrath of the Church and he was incarcerated by the Inquisition at the advanced age of seventy. (There is hardly a parallel in India where a difference in interpretation either in metaphysical or scientific thought was so unkindly suppressed.) In view of the work of Galileo and other Italian scientists, it is suggested that modern science, like modern art, sprang from Italy. It was then that scientific thought emerged from the realm of natural philosophy and formed the basis of modern technology. It is this scientifically based technology upon which contemporary civilization is built. Whilst science makes technology possible, technology, in turn, widens scientific horizons.

The spirit of scientific enquiry and a rigorous correlation of cause and effect in explaining natural phenomena were particularly evident in ancient India. The connection between Indian philosophy and medicine, mathematics, astronomy, and technology is, strangely enough, seldom realized much less recognized. Indian thought contained a strong element of philosophical naturalism or realism from which stemmed scientific ideas. These, however, did not always come to fruition with the same consistency and speed as in Italy or Europe during the modern period. Yet, "concrete ideas on the ultimate structure of matter, the evolution of elements and their combination to form diverse substances of the earth, the classification of the compounds, etc., clothed in speculative language peculiar to them, appear to have been put forward first by the Indians."[3] Ancient Indians "measured the land, divided the year, mapped out the heavens, traced the course of the sun and the planets through the zodiacal belt, analyzed the constitution of matter, and studied the nature of birds and beasts, plants and seeds."[4]

Whilst in Western civilizations the interest has been increasingly focused on single sciences, in the Indian world the ontological viewpoint has been generally preferred, and it would thus appear that "in India, through all periods, the special sciences are rooted in and developed on the underlying unifying cosmic concepts and presuppositions of which the single scientific result is only a special case and phenomenon, a demonstration and a facet, as it were, of the universal cosmic law. This universal vision in India has never been lost."[5]

The beginnings of Indian scientific thought are traced to the same source as those of Indian metaphysics and religion, the *Rig Veda.* The Vedas, being essentially works of poetic imagination, cannot be expected to contain much spirit of scientific inqury, yet there are remarkable flashes of intuitive conjecture and reason. In some of the hymns, especially in Book X, strong naturalistic trends are found, whilst many of them make the gods appear only slightly removed from the natural phenomena which they represent. They express a kind of simple nature worship in which man, who is regarded as "king of animals" and "first of beasts," is wonder-struck at the mighty forces of the universe. Indeed, in one of the most remarkable of the vedic hymns—the "Song of Creation"—a searching inquiry as to the origin of the world is made; it is certainly the earliest known record of philosophic doubt.

> Then was not non-existent nor existent;
> There was no realm of air, no sky
> beyond it.
> What covered in, and where? and what
> gave shelter?
> Was water there, unfathomed depth
> of water?

The hymn goes on to say that in the beginning there was neither death nor immortality, not day nor night. All that existed was void and formless. Then arose desire, the primal seed and germ of spirit. But,

> Who verily knows and
> who can declare it,
> Whence it was born and
> whence comes this creation?
>
> The gods are later than this
> world's production
> Who knows, then, whence it
> first came into being?[6]

In this hymn, which contains the essence of monism, can be seen a representation of the most advanced theory of creation. Reality is not named here; it is not identified with any of the gods. Indeed, the gods come after the world's creation. The vedic cosmos was self-sufficient and self-perpetuating, unlike the Greek cosmos which implied pre-established harmony and a stabilized order brought within the phenomena from outside. Order is immanent in the Indian cosmos, not an externally determined law.

The vedic civilization was naturalistic and utilitarian although it did not exclude cosmological, religious, and mythical speculations. The Vedas also allude to many scientific notions, some of which are also found in ancient Iranian texts. In addition to detailed information about diseases, drugs, and stars, some rather remarkable ideas relating to the order of the world were common to both the Vedic and Iranian documents. The world was conceived as governed by a cyclical law, *rita* (the world-balance or world-course), meaning both normal and true. Rita, of which Varuna was the custodian, was the law of nature and its normal course was illustrated by the revolution of the planets and the rhythm of the seasons. A balance was conceived of between the universe and the human and animal kingdoms. Unlike its Greek equivalent, in which a planned order was introduced by an all-powerful creator, vedic rita was the functional balance of an already existent single phenomenon in which each part functioned according to its own law of activity, and all of them together balanced each other in the general rhythm of the universe. In the ancient Iranian *Avesta,* this law was called *asha* and in Achaemenian texts *arta.* One of the Achaemenian inscriptions even refers to an *arta brazmaniya,* (Brahmanic order). The notion of rita "is very important, since, referring as it does not only to the natural but also to the moral order, it represents an overall determinism. It differs from strict scientific determinism in that it rejects all apparent irregularities out of hand, simply because they are irregular. It is less concerned with physical laws than with norms, less with order, as such, than with 'good' order."[7] The idea of Brahman was associated with that of *vak* ("the word") which made the sacred rites effective, and regulated the movement of the world. Cosmophysiology and astronomy were the two fundamentals of vedic science based on the observation and understanding of real phenomena, although an irrational magic element flourished side by side with them.

It was in the later vedic period, however, that scientific thought or the philosophy of naturalism became articulate. There is some evidence to suggest, despite the destruction by priests and others of materials pertaining to materialist ascendancy, that at times it even dominated the Indian scene. The authority of the vedic hymns declined and intuition gave way to inquiry, religion to philosophy. It was an age keenly alive with intellectual interest and inevitably one of many-sided, even divergent, development. Whilst there were many anomalies, contradictions, and complexities in Indian thought, in which sorcery and science, scepticism and faith and licence and asceticism co-existed, the emphasis was on intellectual fervour and inquiry and on acceptance of the independent and objective world. Formalized Indian logic was empirical. Indeed, the two trends in Indian thought, trancendentalism and naturalism, have always been neatly bound together without any obvious contradictions. The germs of free speculation and scepticism were already present in the *Rig Veda.* The Upanishads developed this spirit of inquiry, and traces of naturalistic and scientific thought in them are quite significant. Consequently, the worship of imaginary gods, the vested interests in religion and theology, and speculation about things that could not be perceived or subjected to sense experience were clearly denounced. In upanishadic cosmology, Brahman is not like the conception of God, a demiurge, seated outside the world which he created and controlled. There was no extraneous matter from which God created the universe. The direction of the world was caused by the world itself and natural phenomena were not concerned with human values; moral rules were humanistic conventions made by men living in society. Truth was seen through direct perception, *darshana. Lokayata,* or materialism, literally the philosophy or worldliness of the people, was the only Sastra for which perceptual evidence was the authority. Matter became the only reality which alone was cognizable by the senses. The ultimate principles were the four elements—earth, water, fire, and air—which were eternal. Akasa (space) was believed to be a substance from which nature derived its whole structure, and from which were evolved the other four elements: "From that Self (Brahman) sprang ether (Akasa, that through which we hear); from ether air (that through which we hear and feel); from air fire (that through which we hear, feel and see); from fire water (that through which we hear, feel, see, talk, and smell)."[8] (It is very interesting that early Indians seemed to know that sound was transmitted through the air and not through a vacuum.) Thought was a function of matter, and nature operated without any interference from the gods.

The Upanishads were the key to the mysterious relationships of the things of this world. Their main purpose was to look at the world objectively. In attempting to explain the multiplicity and diversity of phenomena by simple natural laws, they did sometimes confuse the superficial with the fundamental. They declined to submit, however, to the inevitable destiny, which indicated their desire to comprehend nature in terms of reason. In the early Upanishads, Uddalaka, possibly a fictitious character, is portrayed as representing a naturalistic point of view in marked contrast to Yajnavalkya, who represents the idealistic view. Uddalaka's hylozoistic view of the world was quite distinct from the vedic cosmological and theogonic tradition, and is anterior in Indian literature to that of the Ajivikas, or of Carvaka or Lokayata, usually called the first materialistic school. Indeed, it was a period in which man rejected the principle of authority and insisted on the validity of reason. The Indians propounded natural philosophy through various systems—the Samkhya-Yoga, the Nyaya-Vaisesika, and the theories of Carvaka and Uddalaka are clearly naturalistic.

According to the Carvakas there was no world beyond the present one, and knowledge could be acquired only through sensory perception; what could not be perceived did not exist. Their metaphysics was an unqualified materialistic monism, claiming that the world was made up of the four elements and consciousness was a material and transitory modification of these elements; their ethics were hedonistic. Virtue and vice were not absolute values; they were merely social conventions. Life was to be lived joyously. The end of man was unrestrained enjoyment. God, religion, and immortality were illusions. Their system assumed various forms of philosophical scepticism, logical fatalism, and religious indifference. Its origins are traced as far back as the *Rig Veda,* but the main work *Brhaspati Sutra* (*ca.* 600 B.C.) is not available. Fragments of information found in other texts reconstruct their materialist doctrine. They played a role in Indian thought somewhat similar to that of the atomists and sophists in Greece. In fact, the philosophies of Buddhism, Jainism, and the Ajivikas are strongly rationalistic. The Buddha has often been called atheist, because of his indifference to God. According to Buddhism, man must depend upon himself for salvation, not upon divine intervention. Buddhism is not incompatible with scientific research, and it fostered scientific speculation in India and elsewhere: "The Buddha's purpose was primarily philosophical, ethical, but his thought was distinctly of a scientific nature."[9]

Jainism also contains outstanding naturalistic elements. The world (loka) consists of matter, of atomic particles, whilst man controls his own moral life without supernatural assistance.

The Samkhya system, which has been described as the ruling philosophy of pre-Buddhist India and an orthodox system having its roots in the Upanishads, is essentially rational, anti-theistic, and intellectual. The major concern of Samkhya is to explain the workings of nature through perceptual knowledge. It contradicts the tenets of supernatural religion by substituting evolution for creation. The world is not a creation of God but the product of the interaction between the infinite number of spirits and the ever active *prakriti* or the potentiality of nature. According to Richard Garbe, it was in Samkhya doctrine that complete independence and freedom of the human mind was exhibited for the first time in history.[10] Samkhya, probably the oldest Indian philosophical system, furnished the background for the Yoga system, and the early Buddhist biography *Lalitavistara* includes both Samkhya and Yoga in the curriculum of study for the young Buddha.[11] Samkhya is generally ascribed to Kapila and Yoga to Patanjali. The general metaphysical position of these two systems with regard to soul, nature, cosmology, and ultimate goal is almost the same except that Yoga acknowledges a god (Isvara) and stresses yogic practices for the liberation of the atman, while Samkhya denies Isvara and suggests that sincere philosophic thought is sufficient to reveal truth and thus bring about liberation. Samkhya looks upon the individual as a dynamic complex of material processes arranged around an immaterial, fundamental principle of consciousness, and this distinction between *purusha* and prakriti and their conjoint functioning is the principal doctrine of this system. Prakriti is the sum-total of material processes, but without the light of consciousness, purusha, it is blind and ineffective. On the other hand, light without means of action is in the same position. Purusha, as the unchanging principle of intelligence, reflected in prakriti creates the visible universe. This heterogeneous universe (*srishti*) is a development out of homogeneous prakriti, and to prakriti it returns. There has been no creation nor will there be a destruction. The present world is but one of a series which have existed and are yet to be.[12]

Whilst the Samkhya-Yoga system confined itself to the principles of cosmic evolution, the Nyaya-Vaisesika dwelt on the method of science, elaborating the concepts of mechanics, physics, and chemistry. Nyaya-Vaisesika combined two systems embodied in the sutras attributed to Gotama and Uluka respectively. Both are realistic systems based on independent reasoning, opposing earlier phenomenalism and idealism. Nyaya stresses logic and epistemology; Vaisesika, physics and metaphysics. Both, however, have the liberation of self as their goal and agree in essential principles, such as the nature of self and the atomic theory of the universe. The Nyaya-Vaisesikas regard existence as the most obvious characteristic of things. Atoms and souls, space and time, are mere sounds and symbols having no meaning apart from experience. They dismissed Samkhya cosmology but accepted the atomic doctrine of the four elements. Thus, in spite of the strong current of idealistic thought which finally eclipsed naturalism in India, science figured prominently in Indian intellectual life.

Ancient Indian work on grammar was not only more objective, systematic, and brilliant than that done in Greece or Rome but is illustrative of their scientific methods of analysis. Although the date of Panini's grammar, the *Ashtadhyayi,* which comprises about four thousand sutras or aphoristic rules, is uncertain, it is the earliest extant scientific grammar in the world, having been written no later than the fourth century B.C. But prior grammatical analysis is clearly evidenced by the fact that Panini himself mentions over sixty predecessors in the field. For example, the sounds represented by the letters of the alphabet had been properly arranged, vowels and diphthongs separated from mutes, semivowels, and sibilants, and the sounds had been grouped into gutturals, palatals, cerebrals, dentals, and labials. Panini and other grammarians, especially Katyayana and Patanjali, carried the work much further, and by the middle of the second century B.C. Sanskrit had attained a stereotyped form which remained unaltered for centuries. Whilst Greek grammar tended to be logical, philosophical and syntactical, Indian grammar was the result of an empirical investigation of language done with the objectivity of an anatomist dissecting a body. It was the discovery of Sanskrit by the West and the study of Indian methods of analysis that revolutionized Western studies of language and laid the foundation of comparative philology.

Science is essentially a series of experiments requiring various external aids. Lacking the finer and more precise instruments for experimentation, the ancient Indians used a careful analysis of observation. B. N. Seal, analyzing this method of scientific research, pointed out that the processes of perception, observation, experiment, fallacies of observation, inference, and hypothesis were very accurately defined and strictly followed.[13]

Hindu research in exact science, before the beginnings of modern science in Europe, covers the period from the *Rig Veda* to the middle of the fourteenth century represented by Madhavacharya's *The Sixteen Systems of Philosophy* (1331) and Gunratna's work on logic, the *Rasaratna-Samuchchaya* (1350). This period may be divided into four somewhat overlapping phases. The first phase is that of the vedic literature lasting until about 800 B.C. The second, represented by the *Vedanga Jyotisa*, the *Srauta*, *Grhya* and *Dharmasutras*, Manu and Yajnavalkya, Garga and the Jain works, came to an end about the third century A.D. The third, the period of the Siddhantas, which gave rise to the important works of Aryabhata (born 476), of Varahmihira (*ca.* 475–550), and of Brahmagupta (born 598), lasted until the rise of Islam. The fourth covered the mediaeval period of Indian history.

There is a divergence of opinion as to the scientific importance of the vedic texts. According to J. Filliozat and other recent scholars, these texts were the first attempts to systematize and codify scientific thought in astronomy and physiology.[14] In contrast, early Indologists, such as Macdonell and his pupil Keith, looked upon them as somewhat vague cosmological fancies and found extremely little sign of astronomical study in the vedic period. Nevertheless, it is certain that the vedic Indians knew something of astronomy and that it had a high utilitarian value for them, as it did for all peoples of antiquity who possessed some elementary knowledge about the celestial bodies and meteorological phenomena. The priest-astronomer, for example, could give information of utmost value to a people who were largely agricultural. The vedic priests had to make careful calculations of time for their rituals and sacrifices, and also the headman of the tribe, as in other ancient societies, had to determine the time of sowing and harvest. Moreover, astronomical periods played an important role in vedic thought, for they were considered to be successive parts of the ever returning cosmic cycle. The temporal aspect of that cycle was only one facet of the creative cosmic power, of the "word" of Prajapati, the world spirit whose wisdom was expressed in the Vedas. The year was the Prajapati's unit of time and the *Satapatha Brahmana* states that the Veda contains as many metrical divisions (10,800), as there are "moments" in the year of the world spirit.[15]

The *Rig Veda* lists a number of stars and mentions twelve divisions of the sun's yearly path (rashis) and also 360 divisions of the circle. Thus, the year of 360 days is divided into twelve months. The sun's annual course was described as a wheel with twelve spokes, which correspond to the twelve signs of the zodiac. In the *Vedanga Jyotisa,* a brief treatise of which there were two recensions, one with forty-three verses and the other thirty-six concerned exclusively with chronological calculations, the vedic Indians determined the equinoctial and solstitial points and associated them with Agni and Indra, and Mitra and Varuna. Composed at the close of the vedic period, the *Vedanga Jyotisa* contains the most important of the short texts on the principles of the calendar. Its main purpose was to fix the dates of ceremonies so that they could coincide with the given moments in the cosmic cycle thus ensuring its regularity. The principles listed are, however, too condensed to give direct information about the prevalent astronomical concepts. The calendar was arranged on the basis of a five year cycle of 1830 days, with a 366-day year divided into three equal seasons. The cycle equalled approximately sixty-seven sidereal months and contained sixty-two syndocal months. To keep each year to the traditional twelve months, two months—the thirty-first and the sixty-second—were omitted in each cycle. Thus, lunar and solar reckoning coincided at the beginning and middle of a cycle. Asoka is known to have used these figures in calculating the precise duration of his intended Buddhist pilgrimage.

In the *Yajur Veda* are listed twenty-seven or, if *abhijit* is added, twenty-eight constellations called nakshatras, unquestionably the most important astronomical item in the vedic texts. For a long time the nakshatras were regarded as lunar mansions or divisions in the path of the moon. It was also thought that lunar reckoning was used to calculate months, and a period of five years with sixty-two lunar months, called *yuga,* was established to make it correspond with the solar year. In reality, the nakshatras were used to follow the motions of the sun, as well as those of the moon and the planets. The calendars of the vedic and later periods were never either purely lunar or purely solar but lunisolar, for Indian astrologers have always looked upon astronomical phenomena as indivisible.[16]

As this list of nakshatras is virtually identical with the Chinese *sieu* or *hsui,* J. B. Biot, in the middle of the last century, and de Saussure, at the beginning of this, mistakenly suggested that India borrowed it from China. But since Biot formulated his opinion, it is now accepted as certain that the first complete list of sieu is later than the Indian nakshatras.[17] It would now seem that China probably borrowed from India. With Buddhism a good deal of Indian scientific knowledge travelled to China. Hindu astronomical instruments were introduced into China and there were Hindu astronomers on the astronomical board of the Chinese government. However, at present there is no proof of contact between India and China at the time of the *Yajur Veda,* and it is possible that China developed her system independently. It has been somewhat hesitatingly asserted by J. Needham, well-known for his generous view of Chinese science, that both systems, Indian and Chinese lunar mansions, were probably originally Babylonian.[18] This is clearly untenable because, although astronomy was studied in Mesopotamia, there is no trace of such a system having existed there. If it had existed, it would have survived as an alternative to the zodiac, a much less precise system for calculating the position of the sun by the heliacal rising and setting of the stars. The nakshatra system, associated with the vedic religion of sacrifices, not only continued to grow in India uninfluenced by the Greek zodiac when Alexandrian astrology was introduced, but it spread to other countries. The Sassanid Persians, the Arabs, and the Copts in Egypt all marked the moon's course of approximately twenty-eight days by that number of asterisms, regarded as "lunar houses." Even before the Arabs, this idea is found in a Hermetic Greek text. Since no equivalent of the nakshatras has been discovered in ancient Iran, or any other western country, it must be assumed that the Arabs had taken it from Indian astronomy.[19]

The Indian theory of the great cycles of the universe and the ages of the world is of older origin than either Greek or Babylonian speculations about the "great year," the period within which all the stars make a round number of complete revolutions. But there is remarkably close numerical concordance in these theories.[20] The Indian concept of the great year (*mahayuga*) developed from the idea of a lunisolar period of five years, combined with the four ages of the world (yugas) which were thought to be of unequal perfection and duration, succeeding one another and lasting in the ratio of 4: 3: 2: 1. The last, the *kaliyuga,* was one-tenth of the mahayuga or 432,000 years. This figure was calculated not only from rough estimates of planetary and stellar cycles, but also from the 10,800 stanzas of the *Rig Veda,* consisting of 432,000 syllables. The classical astronomers calculated the great period as one of 4,320,000 years, the basic element of which was a number of sidereal solar years, 1,080,000, a multiple of 10,800. According to Berossus, the Babylonian great year was a period of 432,000 years, comprising 120 "saroi" of 3,600 years apiece.[21]

Although the Vedas have survived the onslaughts of time and climate, it is common knowledge that many other works dealing with Indian culture, including science and astronomy, have been lost. After the vedic literature, the next existing scientific works belong to the early Christian era—a gap of more than a thousand years. During this period there appears to have been a great upsurge in astronomical studies. By the early Christian era, India had had a long period of contact with Greece, Persia, and western Asia. Consequently, it was at this time that the *Siddhanta* astronomy, filled with notions of Greek astrology, first made its appearance. The five astronomical systems, the Siddhantas—*Surya*, *Paitamaha, Romaka, Paulisa,* and *Vasistha*—are summarized by Varahamihira, the sixth century astronomer, in his *Panchasiddhantas.*

The *Romaka* and the *Paulisa* may well have been influenced by Rome and Paul of Alexandria, although some scholars maintain the theory of their independent growth. The *Paulisa,* however, seems to have been a purely astronomical, not astrological, work, and, if it was influenced by some unknown Greek work, the influence cannot be defined accurately. The *Romaka* is the more likely text of the two to have come under Greek influence, but it is quite likely that the *Romaka* was composed by a Greek who had settled in India and who was familiar with Indian as well as Alexandrian astronomy. None of these systems, however, stood the test of time, each being dislodged by a new one. Of the Siddhantas only the *Surya Siddhanta* is extant. It has been described as "a pocket-book for accomplished scholars rather than a textbook for students." Although the Indian astronomers had noticed very early, because of their fairly accurate determinations of the sun's position through their nakshatra system, that the equinoctial and solstitial points do not remain stationary, it was centuries later before reference was made to this fact in the *Surya Siddhanta,* which speaks of a libratory motion rather than a rotatory precession. It has therefore been suggested that this concept was a Greek contribution to Indian astronomy. There are, however, many divergences between the numerical elements of Ptolemy and of the *Surya Siddhanta.* Hence, if there were some Greek influence on this work, it must have been before the Ptolemaic period.

The Indian astronomer, Aryabhata, lived during the period in which the *Surya Siddhanta* was composed. He was born in 476 and reputedly completed his famous work, *Aryabhatiya,* at the age of twenty-three. A concise and brilliant work of astronomy and mathematics, containing the customary four sections and 121 couplets written in terse style, the *Aryabhatiya* must have followed a long tradition of scientific thought to have attained the maturity it did. The *Aryabhatiya,* whilst mainly in agreement with the *Surya Siddhanta,* introduced certain concepts of its own. Aryabhata's new epicyclic theory, the sphericity of the earth, its rotation on its axis and revolution around the sun, the true explanation of eclipses and methods of forecasting them with accuracy, and the correct length of the year were his outstanding contributions. The Arabs preserved the theory of the sphericity of earth, and Pierre d'Ailly employed it in 1410 in his map, which was used by Columbus. Aryabhata was one of the most original and brilliant Indian scientific thinkers, yet his work did not exert much influence on Indian thought inside or outside the country. His theory of the earth's rotation remained isolated and no later works alluded to it. It was the *Surya Siddhanta* that exercised the greatest influence on those countries neighbouring India.

Varahamihira who wrote the *Panchasiddhantas* summarizing the astronomy of the five Siddhantas, flourished in the middle of the sixth century. In his work the *Brhatsamhita* (the Great Compendium), which describes the motions and conjunctions of celestial bodies and their ominous significance, he shows a mastery of wide fields of knowledge and is thoroughly skilled in language and metre. In his two books on purely horoscopic astrology, *Brhakjataka* and *Laghujataka,* the earliest works of Indian astrology, he used many Greek astrological terms, beginning with the *hora.* It was Varahamihira who asserted that although the Yavanas were Mlecchas and their astronomy inferior to Indian, they must be honoured like rishis or seers for having originated the science of astrology. He does not pay the Greeks any similar compliment for their accomplishments in astronomy or mathematics. Speaking of the Siddhantas, he observes that the *Paulisa* and the *Romaka,* which were inspired by European treatises, were accurate, but the Hindu standard work, the *Surya Siddhanta,* was more accurate. Indeed, the credit for developing astrology as an extension of astronomy must go to the Greeks. Even though it is a popular pastime of the Indian priesthood, no astrological considerations are found in any vedic, Buddhist, or Jain texts before the Christian era. During the period immediately prior to the Christian era, however, it appears, some Indians were named after stars, for instance Brihaspatimitra, friend of Brihaspati (Jupiter). But it was much later, under the influence of the Greeks, that horoscopic astrology gained immense popularity in India.

The classical period of ancient Indian astronomy is considered to have ended with Brahmagupta, who was born in 598 and worked in Ujjain. He wrote his Brahma *Siddhanta* in 628, and the *Khandakhadyaka,* a practical treatise on astronomical calculations, in 664. He rejected Aryabhata's doctrine of the earth's rotation saying: "If the earth move a minute in a *prana,* then whence and by what route does it proceed? If it revolve, why do not lofty objects fall?" Al Biruni, whilst criticizing him for his unjust attack on Aryabhata, calls him the most accomplished of Indian astronomers. He was, like his predecessor, an excellent mathematician.

By this time, Indian contributions to astronomy included the solar system in which the earth and the planets move around the sun; the lunar mansions or the nakshatras; the precession of the equinoxes and the determination of its rate; the establishment of the lunisolar year; the names of the week days; the calculation of the mean rates of motion of the planets (bhaganas) based on continued observations; the construction of an astronomical calendar on a scientific basis; the spherical shape of the sun, moon, earth, and the other planets; the calculation of the mean distances of the planets based on the theory of equal linear motion; the rotation of the earth about its axis; the assumption of interplanetary attraction in order to explain equilibrium; and the measurement of the position of the sun, the latitude of the place of observation and time, etc. with the help of the shadow of the gnomon.[22]

Several other eminent astronomers are known to have flourished, such as Lalla and Bhoja. But it was not until 1150 that the *Siddhantaasiromani* of Bhaskaracarya (Bhaskara) appeared, and after Bhaskara no appreciable progress in Indian astronomy is recorded, although some popular works were written. Changadeva founded a school in 1205 to carry on the work of his grandfather, Bhaskara, but it was short lived. It appears that Indian scholars devoted most of their energies to expounding the ancient traditions, and, in marked contrast to their ancient counterparts, were uninfluenced by Persian influences.

According to Burgess, there was "very little astronomical borrowing between the Hindus and the Greeks ... since in no case do the numerical data and results in the system of the two peoples exactly correspond."[23] Moreover, the Hindus possessed an important body of astronomical knowledge no less significant than that of the Hellenistic astronomers long before they came into contact with Greece itself or with Alexandrian science. But it would be unnatural not to expect intellectual stimulation on both sides and exchange of ideas during a period of close contact between India and the Western world. Whilst the tradition of astronomy in India was ancient and independent, it certainly received impetus from Alexandrian science. There are, furthermore, some technical terms in both Greek and Indian astronomy which were borrowed from each other. For instance, *aux* of European astronomy is from the Sanskrit *ucca,* borrowed through the Arabs; Greek *pepton* has become *lipta* in Sanskrit; *dekanos, drkana; trignos, trikona.*

It is practically impossible to separate mathematics from astronomy during the period of Arab ascendancy, for almost every mathematician was also an astronomer or an astrologer or both. In India, mathematics was also pursued in close connection with astronomy; hence, the astronomical works of Aryabhata, Brahmagupta, and Bhaskara also carry important sections on arithmetic and algebra.

Recent research has led to a greater acceptance of the theory of Indian contribution to mathematics, a science far more advanced in India than in any other nation of antiquity. Both ancient Indians and Greeks were extremely fond of mathematics and both made important discoveries, but their outlooks were somewhat different.[24] The Greeks devoted their attention to geometry, subordinating arithmetic, algebra, and astronomy and looked upon magnitude not as number but as length, whilst the Indians based their mathematics on numbers. They had a clear conception of abstract number, as distinct from the numerical quantity of objects or spatial extension, which enabled them to develop algebra and to make more complicated calculations than could the Greeks.

Whilst rigorous logic and systematic treatment are the outstanding features of Greek geometry, boldness of conception, abstraction, symbolism, and ingenuity are the main features of Indian mathematics.[25] In India, as in Greece, science and philosophy interacted on each other. For example, the Greeks being fond of geometry saw a symmetry in the universe, and in India, the conception of *sunya,* void or nothingness in Hindu and Buddhist philosophies, suggested to Indian mathematicians the power and utility of symbols. The philosophy of the void or *sunyavada* urged that the world was neither real nor unreal, nor both nor neither. Bringing this metaphysical notion into the realm of science and giving this conception a form, a shape, and a symbol must be regarded as one of the greatest events in the history of human thought and progress, indeed the basis of all scientific calculations. The concept of sunya or zero is not just a mathematical and scientific discovery, but is deeply rooted in all branches of Indian thought, especially metaphysics and cosmology. Zero is the transition point between opposites, it symbolizes the real balance between divergent tendencies. It transcends all empirical data, and yet it is the basis of all empirical data. It is simultaneously the All and the None. It was originally conceived of as a symbol of Brahman or Nirvana, expressing the sum of all distinct forms. In the third century B.C. the eminent mathematician Bhaskara wrote a treatise dealing in great detail with the concept of Nirvana. The term sunya occurs in vedic literature and is used in Sanskrit literature in the sense of blank (*abhava*), insignificant or negligible (*tuccha*), incomplete (*a-sam purana)*, and less (*una*). Most of the ancient Indian mathematicians defined zero as the sum of two equal and opposite quantities.[26]

For a long time it was believed in Europe that the symbol of zero and the decimal system of notation were of Arab origin, but it is now universally acknowledged that these passed from India through the Arabs to Europe.[27] The numerals first appeared in Arabia in 830 and were written in Arabic from right to left and, according to their position, counting from the right, they represented units, tens, hundreds, thousands, etc. Whenever the number to be expressed lacked units, tens, or hundreds, a point was placed in the appropriate place of the "word," which was the forerunner of the modern zero.

The mathematical implications of zero and infinity were never more than vaguely realized by the Greeks. Until the appearance of the Indian system, the nations of antiquity did their fundamental arithmetical operations by using symbols for writing numbers. They did not use the zero symbol and their task was thus extremely tedious and limited. In the Indian notation, unlike that of any other ancient people, any number no matter how large could be easily expressed. Instead of assigning a distinct symbol to each number, Indian mathematicians introduced a place-value notation, which made it simple to produce numbers of indefinite length. The introduction of the Indian system led to remarkable scientific progress first in mathematics and then in the broad sphere of the exact sciences. Most of the great discoveries and inventions of the West would have been impossible without a developed system of mathematics and this, in turn, would have been impossible if European science had remained saddled with the unwieldy system of Roman numerals. "The unknown man who devised the new system was from the world's point of view, after the Buddha, the most important son of India. His achievement, though easily taken for granted, was the work of an analytical mind of the first order, and he deserves much more honour than he has so far received."[28] Praise for the unknown scholar must be unreserved, but would it have been possible for anyone, however ingenious, to achieve such heights of analytical scholarship without a sound tradition and a well-developed school of mathematical learning? Even if there is only scattered and fragmentary evidence, it must be clear that to not only give rise to such theories but to sustain and transmit them to other cultures required a highly intelligent school of mathematical thought. Little is known of the development of Hindu mathematics, but the few manuscripts that are available bear ample testimony to the sophistication it had achieved by whatever route.

Some scholars definitely date the origins of zero (sunya), and possibly of place-value notation, to as early as *ca.* 200 B.C. because reference to sunya is found in the *Pingala-Chandah-Sutra* composed at about that time. There is general agreement that this system of zero and place-value notation was in use in India in the fifth century A.D., and that the Syrians and the Indochinese had come to know of it by the end of the sixth century. The old system of numeration was still widely used in Europe even as late as the fourteenth century; however, no work on arithmetic using the old system has been found in India. The *Bakshali Manuscript,* alleged to belong to the fourth century A.D., uses the new system, giving general solutions of numerous mathematical problems on which other texts are silent.[29] The precise date, however, of this manuscript is uncertain, and, unless the date of the Bakshali Manuscript is definitely settled, any argument concerning the antiquity of zero must remain tentative. However, Aryabhata, who wrote *Aryabhatiya* in 499, and who had extracted square and cube roots by the method in use today, must have either used a decimal notation with nine figures plus a zero, or an abacus, where empty spaces represented the zero symbol.[30]

J. Filliozat, however, believes that the zero was either borrowed by the Indians through Babylonian officials, or more likely, "was reinvented during the earliest centuries of the Christian era by the Indian scholars." However, he does not question that it was from India that the zero spread during the Middle Ages to Asia and through the Arabs to

Europe.[31] It appears that the principle of local value was used in the sexagesimal system found on Babylonian tablets dating from about 1600 B.C. Babylonian records from the centuries immediately preceding the Christian era contain a symbol for zero, which, however, was not used in computation. But India was the first country to use the complete decimal system of place-notation. What suggested the form for the zero is, of course, a matter of conjecture; the actual form of the zero symbol varied from region to region.

It was probably in the twelfth century that Europeans learned this Indian system through the Arabs. Leonardo of Pisa, also called Fibonacci, an Italian merchant, who published his *Liber Abbaci* in 1202 laying the foundation of modern mathematics in Europe, was educated in Barbary where he became acquainted with the so-called Arabic numerals. Of all the methods of calculation, he found this to be the best.

In algebra, too, the Indians made outstanding and lasting contributions. It is now commonly accepted that the Arabs were not the discoverers, but merely the transmitters of algebra. Indians were the first to recognize the existence of absolutely negative quantities. They differentiated between positive and negative quantities by attaching to the one the idea of "possession," and to the other the idea of "debts." The conception of opposite directions on a line, as an interpretation of plus and minus quantities, was familiar to them. Being a science dealing with unknowns, algebra could make definite progress only when a proper symbolism was devised. The Indians, accustomed to abstract thinking, evolved the appropriate symbolism by using the letters of the alphabet to denote unknowns together with arithmetical signs and suitable rules for calculations. Once this symbolism was devised, advance was rapid. In the fifth century, for example, Aryabhata could express large numbers by means of syllables, for Indian phoneticians had devised a phonetic alphabet including fifteen vowels, twenty-five stopped consonants, and eight other letters. Indians evolved a sound system of extracting square and cube roots, wrote numerical co-efficients and algebraic equations, evolved the rules of transportation of terms, classified equations according to degrees, and solved quadratic and indeterminate equations. Indian contributions in the field of the theory of indeterminate equations has been hailed as one of their greatest contributions to algebra.[32]

The Greeks, hampered by their emphasis on geometry and the lack of proper symbolism, tackled indeterminate equations but with much less success. In the seventh century, Brahmagupta (598–660) was the first to discover the complete solution of the quadratic equation. His work was furthered by Mahavira in the ninth century. In the twelfth century, Bhaskara framed rules for finding permutations and combinations, and invented the fraction form. The Arabs and later the Europeans made great advances in algebra, but up to the end of the eighteenth century this progress was along Indian lines. Although modified, the present day algebraic symbolism remains Indian in all essentials. According to Hankel, algebra was really invented by the Indians, if algebra is defined as the application of arithmetical operations to both rational and irrational numbers of magnitudes. "Both the form and the spirit of arithmetic and algebra of modern times are essentially Indian."[33]

Diophantus of Alexandria (third century), the first Greek algebraist and the father of algebra in Europe, may have gotten his inspiration from India. Whilst there is no definite proof of this, it is significant that his work *Arithmetica* appeared quite suddenly, ran counter to all previous mathematical trends, and was a far cry from pure Greek geometry.[34] Without him, it has been said that there would have been no Greek science of algebra. He introduced the idea of an algebraic equation expressed in algebraic symbols and his treatment is purely analytical and completely divorced from geometrical methods. In addition to introducing various algebraic symbols, he also discovered new properties of numbers and solved many kinds of determinate and indeterminate equations. His system is very similar to that of Indian algebra. Struik points out that the first general solution of indeterminate equations of the first degree, $ax + by = c$ (a, b, c integers), is found in Brahmagupta. It is therefore incorrect to call linear indeterminate equations Diophantine equations. Furthermore, while Diophantus still accepted fractional solutions, the Hindus insisted on integer solutions. They also advanced beyond Diophantus in admitting negative roots of equations.[35] That communication of thought from India to Alexandria did take place is evident from the fact that certain philosophical and theological doctrines—for example, those of the Manichaeans, Neoplatonists, and Gnostics—show unmistakable resemblances to

Indian teaching, and it is difficult not to suspect Indian inspiration behind Diophantus' work.[36]

Whilst Indians made their mark primarily in algebra and arithmetic, the beginnings of their mathematics strangely enough are found in geometry, the field in which they were least proficient. The knowledge of geometry began in the vedic age, and the earliest examples are found in the Sulvasutras (the rules of the chord which form part of the vedic Kalpasutras). This was largely a practical and empirical geometry, dealing with the exigencies of religious life and rituals.

Vedic altars and sacrificial places were constructed according to strict geometrical principles. The *Vedi* (altar) had to be stacked in a geometrical form with sides in fixed proportions, and brick altars had to combine fixed dimensions with a fixed number of bricks. Again, the surface areas were so designed that altars could be increased in size without change of shape, which required considerable geometrical ingenuity. Geometrical rules found in the *Sulvasutras*, therefore, relate to the construction of squares and rectangles, the relation of the diagonal to the sides, equivalent rectangles and squares, equivalent circles and squares, conversion of oblongs into squares and vice versa, and the construction of squares equal to the sum or difference of two squares.[37] In such relations a prior knowledge of the Pythagorean theorem, that the square of the hypotenuse of a right-angled triangle is equal to the sum of squares of the other two sides, is disclosed. In these treatises are also found a few interesting approximations in terms of unit fractions. The fractions used are all unit fractions and the expression yields a result correct to five decimal places. The vedic Indians knew the mensuration of the triangle, the parallelogram, the rectangle, and the rectangular parallelepiped. The constant ratio between the circumference and the diameter of a circle was known to the Indians later. They also studied the mensuration of the circle, the cone, the sphere, and the pyramids.

It is curious, however, that these geometrical constructions which were remarkable for their age do not occur in later Hindu works, which appear to have disregarded completely the mathematical results of the Sulvasutras. If the continuity of tradition had been maintained and developed as in Egypt and Mesopotamia, the story of Indian geometry might be different. Jainism, however, did encourage mathematical studies, and in its sacred books the value $\pi = \sqrt{10}$ is found.

Indian attainments in geometry fall short of those of the Greeks; Indians were mainly interested in mensuration and practically ignored giving definitions, postulates, axioms, or steps of logical reasoning. The possibility, however, of the Greek mathematician Hero of Alexandria who flourished at about the beginning of the first century B.C., having been influenced by the *Sulvasutras* cannot be ruled out. It is also possible that the Indian mathematician, Brahmagupta, was familiar with Hero's work. Whilst distinguishing between approximate and exact areas, he gives Hero's formula for the area of a triangle as a function of the sides, $\sqrt{p(p-a)(p-b)(p-c)}$. Brahmagupta and later Mahavira, however, made a remarkable extension of Hero's formula by giving $\sqrt{(p-a)(p-b)(p-c)(p-d)}$ as the area of a quadrilateral whose sides were a, b, c, d, and whose semiperimeter was p. In spite of the Greek superiority in geometry, it was Aryabhata who gave the usual modern approximate value of π. The Greeks put it as $\pi = 22/7$ whereas the Indian mathematician expressed it in the form of a fraction

$$\pi = \frac{62,832}{20,000} = 3.1416.$$

Later mathematicians improved this value, already far more accurate than that of the Greeks, to nine places of decimals. The correct value of π was not known in Europe before Peurbach (1423–61).

Considerable work was done in trigonometry, and Indians were familiar with some formulae not even known to the Greeks. In Varahamihira's *Panchasiddhantas* are found notations for unit radius $\pi = \sqrt{10}$, $\sin 30 = \frac{1}{2}$, $\sin 60 = \sqrt{1-\frac{1}{4}}$, $\sin^2 Y = (\sin 2Y)\, 2/4 + [1 \sin (90^0 - 2Y)]\, 2/4$, and a table of twenty-four sines. The Greeks calculated in terms of chords and used the ratio of the chord of the circle to its diameter. Ptolemy's chords were reckoned on a diameter of 120. By using the half-chord and a radius of 120, the Indians obtained a table of sines directly. Every Indian treatise on astronomy contained a table of sines, and functions of the trigonometric sine were clearly known and applied. The following formula given in the *Surya Siddhanta* (*ca.* 400)

$$\sin (n + 1)\,\theta - \sin n\,\theta =$$

$$\sin n\,\theta - \sin (n - 1)\,\theta - \sin n\,\theta - \frac{\sin n\,\theta}{225}$$

used for calculating the tables of sines was not known either to the Greeks or the Arabs.[38] The Sanskrit term *jya* or *jiva,* a derivative from *ardhajya* or *ardhajiva,* half-chord or bow-string, became first *jiba* and then *jaib* in Arabic and finally sinus in mediaeval Latin.

Nothing like a true system of natural philosophy existed amongst the ancient peoples of Greece and India, although in their writings many brilliant conceptions are seen. Hindu physicists, however, made some comprehensive and co-ordinated efforts to advance hypotheses about nature, matter, and energy, although they were closely linked with religion and philosophy. The greatest weakness of Indian science, as that of Greece, was its vision of physics as philosophy and not as mechanics. Yet, it was an attitude which was not entirely unfruitful. Natural philosophy as propounded by the Indians conformed mainly to three systems: (a) the Nyaya-Vaisesika, dealing principally with the method of science and elaborating the concepts of mechanics, physics, and chemistry; (b) the Samkhya-Yoga, which confined itself to the principles of cosmic evolution; and (c) Vedanta and other systems, which contributed little directly to the development of the physical sciences. As early as the time of the Buddha, possibly even before him, the universe was classified by the elements, and most schools of thought believed that the elements, other than ether, were atomic. The Nyaya-Vaisesika school of physicists especially propounded the atomic theory and "believed the single atom to he a mere point in space completely without magnitude." They also analyzed the general properties of matter, such as elasticity, cohesion, impenetrability, viscosity, fluidity, porosity, etc. They asserted that atoms cannot exist in an uncombined state, and they could not believe matter to be infinitely divisible. The Jains regarded the atoms not only as infinitesimal, but also as eternal and ultimate. Umasvati analyzed in 50 the mutual attraction or repulsion of atoms in the formation of molecules.

The Samkhya system, in attempting to explain the process of cosmic evolution on a scientific basis in relation to energy as the principle, may have foreshadowed Darwin in some ways, although its ideas, embodied as they are in metaphysical language, are not easy to correlate with the modern scientific terminology of evolution. Almost every school conceived motion, both atomic and molecular, as underlying the physical phenomena of sound, light, and heat. Motion was defined somewhat as it is today, as the change of position of a particle. Not only molar and molecular motions were postulated but also the subtle motions inside the atoms themselves. Both matter and energy were known to be indestructible; and although constant, they were subject to changes in collocation, with this transformation going on continually. Brahmagupta foreshadowed Newton by declaring that "all things fall to the earth by a law of nature, for it is the nature of the earth to attract and keep things." But the law of gravitation itself was not anticipated.

Great progress was made in India in mineralogy and metallurgy. The mining and extensive use of gold, silver, and copper was undertaken in the Indus Valley in the third century B.C. In the vedic period extensive use was made of copper, bronze, and brass for household utensils, weapons, and images for worship. Patanjali, writing in the second century B.C. in his *Lohasastra,* gives elaborate directions for many metallurgic and chemical processes, especially the preparation of metallic salts, alloys, and amalgams, and the extraction, purification, and assaying of metals. The discovery of aqua regia (a mixture of nitric and hydrochloric acid to dissolve gold and platinum) is ascribed to him. Numerous specimens of weapons made of iron have been excavated, probably belonging to the fourth century B.C. Iron clamps and the iron stag found at the Bodhgaya temple point to the knowledge of the process of manufacturing iron as early as the third century B.C. The famous iron pillar in Delhi belonging to the fourth-fifth century A.D. is a metallurgical wonder. This huge wrought iron pillar 24 feet in height 16.4 inches in diameter at the bottom, and 6½ tons in weight has stood exposed to tropical sun and rain for fifteen hundred years, but does not show the least sign of rusting or corrosion.

The *Periplus* mentions that in the first century A.D. Indian iron and steel were being exported to Africa and Ethiopia. Indian metallurgists were well known for their ability to extract metal from ore and their cast products were highly valued by the Romans, Egyptians, and Arabs. Their skill in tempering steel, the secret of manufacturing the so-called "Damascus blades," was well known.[39] Although no definite judgement can be reached until rigorous metallurgical analysis has been made of the "damascened" swords found throughout Eurasia, Edouard Salin, an authority on the metallurgy of early mediaeval longswords, suggests that "the marvellously skilful twisting and fagoting of thin rods of steel and iron of different qualities that produced the laminated Merovingian blades was inspired by Indian Wootz steel, which achieved similar results by crystallization."[40] Persians considered Indian swords to be the best, and the phrase, *Jawabi hind*, literally meaning "Indian answer" meant "a cut with the sword made of Indian steel." That the art of' metallurgy was highly developed in ancient India is further reaffirmed by the fact that the Gypsies, who originated in India, are highly skilled craftsmen, and it has been suggested that the art of the forge may have been transmitted to Europe through Gypsies. Steel was manufactured in ancient India, and it was being exported to China at least by the fifth century A.D. That the Arabs also imported steel from India is testified to by Al Kindi, who wrote in the ninth century.[41]

Corresponding progress was made in the allied branches of science, for example botany, plant pathology, and zoology. Indian achievements in chemistry had some influence on the Arabs and the Chinese, although in India, as elsewhere, chemistry did not begin as a branch of science in its own right. In the beginning, perhaps, it was pure alchemy, concerning itself with the transmutation of baser metals into gold. But it soon became allied with medicine, metallurgy and the industrial arts. The earliest evidence of chemical knowledge in India is in painted pottery traced to the Indus Valley period. Chemical knowledge later became an adherent of the Tantric cult. Herbs and plants with active healing properties were deified. The juice of the *soma* plant, for instance, was supposed to confer immortality; even in the *Rig Veda* it is described as *amrita* (Greek ambrosia), giving immortality to gods and health to sick men. In *Somarasa* the dawn of Hindu alchemy is traced. But it was during the Tantric period that the practice of alchemy reached its highest development in India.[42] Nagarjuna, the reputed author of the renowned Tantric treatise *Rasaratnakara*, stands pre-eminent among the Indian alchemists.[43] He is also said to have written a treatise on metallurgy.

During the post-verlic period, when the medical system of India was rationalized, Indian chemists devoted their attention to making medicines and drugs. By the sixth century they had succeeded in producing many important aikalis (*kshara*), both for internal and external use, acids, and metallic salts by processes of calcination, distillation, sublimation, steaming, and fixing, described in *Rasaratna-Samuccaya*, a valuable medico-chemical work. Medicines were classified into two types: one promoting longevity, health, and strength, and the other curing disease.

Even in technology Indian contributions to world civilization were significant. The spinning wheel is an Indian invention, and, apart from its economic significance in reducing the cost of textiles, is one of the first examples of the belt-transmission of power. The stirrup, certainly the big-toe stirrup, is of second century B.C. Indian origin. The ancient blow-gun (*nalika*), which shot small arrows or iron pellets, may well have been a forerunner of the air-gun which is supposed to have been invented by the Europeans in the sixteenth century.

More important, however, is the fact that India supplied the concept of perpetual motion to European thinking about mechanical power. The origin of this concept has been traced to Bhaskara, and it was taken to Europe by the Arabs where it not only helped European engineers to generalize their concept of mechanical power, but also provoked a process of thinking by analogy that profoundly influenced Western scientific views.[44] The Indian idea of perpetual motion is in accordance with the Hindu belief in the cyclical and self-renewing nature of all things.

The ancient Indians were very interested in preserving life and caring for the body. Consequently medical science, including surgery, developed in India as early as the Indus Valley period and was widely studied and practiced. Indian medicine was called *Ayur Veda* and is practiced even today; in fact, in recent years it has been growing in popularity and is being harmonized with modern medical knowledge and techniques.[45] Whilst some scientists disregard Ayurvedic medicine as a relic of an antiquated past, others defend it with an overemphasized patriotic fervour as a fully mature system of medicine. Both are partisan views with only partial validity at best. At its height, however, Indian medicine was exceptionally advanced and gave evidence of a rational, scientific spirit unparalleled by other civilizations. Indeed, of all the natural sciences of ancient India, medicine was the most important. It was closely connected with the Samkhya and Vaisesika physics and was probably the basis of the logical speculations subsequently codified in the *Nyayasutras*.[46]

The beginnings of medical science in India have been traced to the proficiency of the Indus Valley people in town-planning, sanitation, and hygiene. Representing the oldest surviving examples of town-planning, the Indus cities had baths, lavatories, drains, fresh water tanks, and interior courtyards. The main drains were cleared by lifting large, specially made brick manhole covers, and the whole conception indicates a remarkable concern for public health. In the vedic hymns, especially in the *Atharva Veda,* we find the healing art along with the belief in demons of disease and magical rituals and remedial incantations to entice evil spirits away from the patients.[47] In these texts, however, references to anatomy, embryology, and hygiene are found as well as references to a great many diseases and plants with medicinal properties. Vedic medicine, in common with that of other ancient peoples, was primarily magico-religious. In Europe, as in various other areas, even as late as the fifteenth and sixteenth centuries, disease was looked upon as a punishment from God, and the cure was sought through priests rather than professional medicine.

Vedic Indians classified diseases by their major symptoms, such as pain, emaciation, and fever, without seriously examining the possible relationships between associated symptoms. They seldom investigated the pathogenic causes of the diseases. Remedies were generally based on plants, incantations, and practices of mimetic magic. Whilst there is no marked difference between diseases and demons in vedic medicine, and no sense of diagnosis in the accepted sense of the term, there are frequent indications of empirico-rational elements. Thus, magical attributes and practical knowledge were intermixed. The vedic Indians closely studied the human body and its structure as is evidenced by the richness of anatomical terminology in vedic Sanskrit.

During the period of the rise of Buddhism in India, great progress was made in medicine. Jivaka, a contemporary of the Buddha, is credited with numerous and wonderful cures, especially for children. Indian kings founded hospitals and appointed physicians for both men and animals. The canonical works of the Buddhists contain a number of medical statements, and Patanjali's reference to *vaidyaka* speaks for the development of medical science in the centuries preceding the Christian era. The famous Buddhist university at Nalanda during the seventh century comfortably accommodated ten thousand students in philosophy and medicine. The principal doctrines of the Vedas later formed the general basis of Indian classical medicine. *Ayur Veda* is the principle source for texts commonly used during the first centuries of the Christian era, but only a few works of this period have survived.[48]

The four principal ancient authorities are Charaka (first-second centuries A.D.), Susruta (sixth century B.C. to fourth century A.D.), Vagbhata (*ca.* 600 A.D.), and Atreya (sixth century B.C.). These dates are controversial and these are conservative estimates. None of the texts (principally the Samhitas) produced during this period represents an initial effort at systematic description of medical science; indeed all clearly point to an existing tradition and confine their attention to collecting the known facts and disseminating the knowledge gained. They are edited manuals rather than works of individual scholars. George Sarton accepts A. F. Rudolf Hoernle's dating of Susruta and Atreya, as the sixth century B.C.[49] Filliozat, having analyzed the evidence in some detail, suggests that *Susruta Samhita* is a work of the last centuries before the Christian era, and that *Charaka Samhita* could be slightly anterior to the Christian era.[50] The medical works of Vagbhata, of which the *Ashtangahrdaya Samhita* is best known, also probably appeared in the late classical period.

Atreya, a physician, taught at the Kasi (Benares) University, and his younger contemporary Susruta, a surgeon, at Taksasila (Taxila) University. Charaka was a physician living at the court of Kanishka and was looked upon as the spokesman for and editor of Agnivesa, a disciple of Atreya. Filliozat is of the opinion, therefore, that the famous system of medicine known after Charaka really belongs to Atreya, a contemporary of the Buddha. Susruta transmitted the doctrine attributed to Divodasa, King of Banaras and incarnation of Dhanvantari, the mythical holder of amrita, the liquid of immortality. Like *Charaka Samhita, Susruta Samhita* is based on ancient traditions and sources. These Samhitas are didactic texts in prose and verse of varied metres, and "are the products of a fully evolved system which resembles those of Hippocrates and Galen in some respects, and in others had developed beyond them."[51] The creative period of ancient Indian medicine closed with the Samhitas of Caraka and Susruta, and they have remained the standard works of Indian medicine and surgery respectively. Later medical writers either imitated or elaborated on them. The most important texts which augmented the Samhitas were the *Yogasataka* and the *Amrtahridaya.* The former is a medical compendium and was very popular and used widely at the time, having been translated into other Asian languages. It is consulted in Ceylon even to this day. Indian tradition assigns this work to the Buddhist patriarch Nagarjuna, but this is doubtful. The *Amrtahridaya* is a lengthy medical treatise in four sections and it has survived only in its Tibetan translation. Indian medicine, it would appear; progressed rapidly during the vedic and Buddhist periods, and, after a period of systematization, rationalization, and cautious advance, came almost to a standstill in the Middle Ages.

Although based on experience and observation, the doctrines of *Ayur Veda* are not empirical. A peculiar reflection of the general theory of the Samkhya in its medical conceptions can be seen as well as an enumeration of the elements (*pancabhutas*) which constitute the material content of the universe. The human body, the seat of consciousness (*cetana*), is also composed of these elements. Of these five, space and earth—which correspond to organic cavities and firm tissue—are inert, and the remaining three are active substances. Wind, fire, and water act in the body in the form of breath (*vayu*) located below the navel; bile (*pitta*) located between the navel and the heart; and mucus or phlegm (*kapha* or *sleshman*) located above the heart. These three elements are counted both as constituents (*dhatus*) and as morbid elements (*dosas*), and the doctrine is known, therefore, as either *trid* or *tridosha.* It is the basis of Ayurvedic diagnosis and therapeutics. Health consists of a normal quantitative relationship between these primary constituents, and if there is an imbalance, disease, or *dhatu-vaisamya,* results.[52]

Nosology was highly developed and diseases were classified in three ways: according to the main organic element responsible for them, according to their anatomical situation, and according to the nature of the major symptoms. Susruta paid a good deal of attention to observing the symptoms of diseases.

Anatomy was also studied in this period in India. The vedic hymns refer not only to the heart, lungs, stomach, intestines, and kidneys but also to imaginary constituents of the human body, for example, *ojas* (energy) and *rasa* (vital fluid). In the evolution of Indian anatomy, facts and data concerning the human body were accumulated and rationalized into various schools of anatomical thought, chief of which were the schools of Caraka and Susruta. In their Samhitas they deal with embryology and histology in addition to anatomy proper. The total number of muscles in the body is 513, and the ancient Hindus described 500 muscles—400 in the extremities, 66 in the trunk, and 34 in the area above the collarbone—and they were familiar with ligaments, sutures, lymphatics, nerve plexuses, fascia, adipose tissues, vascular tissue, and the mucous membrane of the digestive canal. Hindu anatomy included some fanciful numerations of the parts of the body, such as 360 bones, 800 ligaments, 300 veins, 500 muscles, and 7 layers of skin. It must, however, be pointed out that the Hindus calculated these figures by including as separate bones the teeth, nails, cartilages, and prominent parts of bones now known as "processes" or "protuberances." Whilst there were major gaps and errors in their knowledge of anatomy, it was surprisingly accurate for the age.

The formation and development of the embryo was a subject of considerable speculation and controversy in the various schools of medicine. The question of prenatal influence, which is being given increasingly serious consideration by Western physicians, was intensively studied by Hindu doctors. They prescribed detailed rules for the care of expectant mothers, who were to be given a pleasant environment, kept away from excitement, and given appetizing food in moderate quantities.

As early as the vedic period, Indians possessed considerable knowledge of physiology. The vedic term *rasa* has been likened to the "humours" of ancient Greek medicine. Physiological processes were regarded as having counterparts in nature at large, such as bile acting in the human body much as fire acts on water. The prime mover of life was the breath (*prana*) which was only a manifestation of the wind, the moving force of the universe. Vedic physiology was a highly developed pneumatic doctrine, based on the belief that multiple breaths circulate inside the organism through a system of internal canals. These breaths were given distinct names, and this vedic concept became fundamental in Indian classical medicine. However, the pathological doctrine of the tridosha, which included the notion of breath, did not appear as such in the vedic Samhitas. Breath not only governed respiration but all the other physiological processes as well. "Ancient India was familiar with a pneumatistic theory by which all human activities both bodily and mental, and all natural activities as well, were attributed to the play of puffs of air originating in the wind, the universal driving power."[53] Although this doctrine was not codified and expounded until later, all its essential elements were present in vedic texts, even to the assigning of technical names. These and other Indian texts belonging to the period between 1000 and 500 B.C. refer to the concept that bile is of an igneous nature and to the theory concerning the part played by the pituitary gland which represents the aqueous element. The basic doctrine, upon which subsequent Indian medical science was based, held that the breath, the bile, and the pituitary gland became the three associated factors. Some scholars suggest that Indian physiology was more comprehensive, and it is a mistake to believe that it consisted only of the tridhatu or vital fluids of the body. It is to this mistaken belief that the neglect of the study of Indian medicine is mainly attributed.[54] The theory, however, was far more profound, and also more ancient than that of the Greeks. Filliozat points out that the breath of life circulating in other parts of the body was a common notion in ancient times but nowhere else were its technical details so precisely listed and systematized.[55]

There are striking parallels between the ancient Greek and Indian systems of medicine, and because of this many Western writers have suggested that the Greeks influenced Indian medicine. The possibility of mutual influence cannot be ruled out, but it should be remembered that whilst Hindu writers acknowledged their debt to Greek astronomy, they made no reference to foreign influences in medicine. Nor do Hindu medical classics, as pointed out by William Jones, contain a single technical term which points to a foreign origin. On the contrary, Hippocratic doctrines such as the emphasis on prognosis, on direction to physicians, and on diet and regimen in preference to medicines, the doctrine of the four humours and conception of the influence of seasons on their fluctuations and on dietetics, the quotidian, tertian, and quarton fever, and several others, bear too close a similarity to anterior Indian practices to be coincidental.[56] Hippocrates (*ca.* 460 B.C.), who dissociated medicine from superstition, systematized the empirical knowledge then available, and founded inductive and positive medicine, was certainly familiar with Indian drugs such as pepper, ginger, and cardamom. Whilst Hippocrates was laying the foundations of Greek medicine, Indian medicine was already a well-developed system, with an extensive pharmacopoeia and intricate surgical operations. Hippocrates' treatise *On Breaths* refers to diseases as processes in nature in almost the same way as did the school of Atreya and the vedic texts on winds and organic breaths. Whilst the general agreement between these doctrines of Hippocrates and those of Indian pneumatism is unmistaken, and whilst there are recognizable similarities in details of pathogenic representations, differences do occur. For instance, whilst *On Breaths* explains epidemics through spots introduced in the body by inhaled air, the Indian texts contain nothing similar. If there was any borrowing from India, "it has been in the shape of general ideas and it has been of an entire part of the Greek medical text rather than that of the author of the manual *On Breaths* acting alone."[57] In explaining the similarity between the Greek and Hindu traditions, Sarton admits the possibility of mutual influence but does not exclude independent thought on facts of common experience.[58]

Similar analogies are also noted between Indian pathology and Plato's theory, as developed in the *Timaeus,* which is practically identical with the Indian doctrine of the tridosha, and cites the same three elements—air, fire, and water, or breath, bile and mucus. Whilst Plato's exposition is extremely rudimentary, his classification of diseases into three groups—those caused by the disequilibrium of the elements, and those due to phlegm and bile—is much in accord with the classical Indian doctrine. Whilst elements of the doctrine of the *Timaeus* may be found scattered in various texts, no Greek medical text has been found which grouped them in the same manner as Plato did. In contrast, "only in Indian doctrine is found in the form of a received doctrine a pathogeny similar to that of Plato."[59] Plato's theory of phlegm is quite similar to that of the sleshman of Indian medical men. Plato's conception of bile, its "hot and liquid" nature, agrees fully with the old vedic idea of the igneous nature of bile. Even such notions as haemorrhagic diseases caused by an eruption of the bile into the blood are common to Plato and the *Ayur Veda.* The intermittent fevers enumerated by Plato were also known to the authors of the *Atharva Veda*, although their causes were explained differently.

Despite these differences, the case for Indian influence on Plato's doctrine is somewhat strengthened when it is recalled that Plato's belief in metempsychosis and his theory of ideas are also closely parallel to Indian philosophical doctrines. As the Indian doctrines preceded Plato, Greek influence on India must be ruled out. Moreover, although Plato does not mention his sources, his doctrine is closer to the Indian than any contemporary Greek school.

That the Greeks were aware of and esteemed Indian medicine is supported by contemporary Greek writings. Arrian, in describing Alexander's Indian expedition, points out that Greek physicians had no cure for snakebite but the Indians had. Consequently, Alexander gathered a body of skilful Indian physicians to attend him and his men. Another Greek, Nearchos, also bears testimony to the skill of Hindu physicians in toxicology. It is certain that at the time of Alexander Hindu physicians and surgeons were considered superior to those of the Greeks, even by the Greeks themselves.[60] Citing Megasthenes, Strabo says that "there is a class of physicians among the Indians who rely most on diet and regimen and next on internal application, having a great distrust of the effects of more powerful modes of treatment."[61]

Indian medical knowledge, although considerable, was in many respects imperfect. Indians realized the importance of the spinal cord and knew of the nervous system but did not understand them fully. Even though they understood the functions of the heart, their ideas about its structure were rudimentary. Like Aristotle, Indian doctors held the mistaken conception that the heart was the seat of intelligence and the organ of consciousness, although some scholars dispute this on the grounds of the distinction between *mana* and *hrdaya,* two words translated as heart but having different connotations in Sanskrit. The Indians, however, knew that the heart receives impure blood, sends it to the liver, where it is purified and then returned to the heart. The sensory and motor nerves were believed to ascend to and descend from the heart. Later however this misconception was corrected. Like Galen, the Greek scientist of the second century, the Tantrists and Yogists in India came to know the real importance of the brain and the spinal cord; in fact the Tantric mystical text *Shiva samhita* describes the nervous system more accurately than medical treatises. Indian scientists made valuable observation on the senses and sense-perception but their knowledge of brain functions was limited. They knew the digestive system and its fluids well and described its processes clearly.

Diagnoses were made from symptoms and calculations of the vital elements involved. Diagnostic methods were highly advanced, and Susruta divided 1120 diseases into "natural" and "super-natural," taught palpation and auscultation of the heart, lungs, and womb, and advocated the inspection and use of the special senses.[62] He also gives a very recognizable description of malarial fever, which is attributed to mosquitoes. A favourite method of diagnosis was urinalysis. Feeling the pulse was studied with scrupulous care and thoroughness, and Hindu physicians achieved exceptional competence in the use of palpation long before Prayagoras of Cos, who is credited in the West as the first physician to teach the value of the pulse in diagnosis.

Whilst notions of hygiene were mainly based on physiological theories, treatment was based on observation. Proper diet and regimen were carefully detailed and the use of drugs was subordinated to diets: baths, enemata, emetics, inhalations, gargles, urethral and vaginal injections, and blood-letting by leeches or cups. Some scholars such as Garrison have interpreted a passage in Dhanvantari's *Sacteya* as indicative of Hindu knowledge of vaccination as early as 550; this was not known in Europe until the eighteenth century.[63] Essential diabetes mellitus was recognized as madhumeha (or "honey-urine") and its usual symptoms of thirst, foul breath, and languor were known.

Indian surgery (*salya*), was well advanced for the times. It is frequently mentioned in the *Mahabharata* that surgeons regularly accompanied the army. By the second century, surgery had become a well-developed art and was regarded as the most important branch of medicine. The methods of dissection, however, were too imperfect to give any accurate knowledge of the internal organs and of the vascular system of the body. Knowledge of the human body remained primitive in ancient India, as in other contemporary civilizations, where anatomy and physiology lagged behind clinical practice. Priestly influence confused this and "the concepts of anatomy were weird and wonderful."[64] The Indian surgeons endeavoured to make up for their lack of precise knowledge of anatomy by the concept of *marma* (a marma is a junction or meeting place of five organic structures—ligaments, blood vessels, muscles, bones, and joints). There were 107 marmas in all divided into five groups on the basis of the seriousness of injury.

This concept made possible efficient study of regional anatomy. As early as the third century B.C. there were hospitals in India and the numerous rock inscriptions of Asoka testify to the popularization of medical treatment of men and animals. Surgery flourished in these hospitals several centuries prior to the Christian era. Indian surgeons had attained considerable expertise in extracting the dead foetus, recovering foreign bodies from body tissues, and treating different kinds of inflammation. Their cataract operations attracted wide attention and their mode of couching cataracts has survived to the present day. The art of cutting and setting bones had reached a high degree of skill, as had plastic surgery. They treated fractures and dislocations with a special splint made of withes of bamboo, which was subsequently adopted in the British army as the "patent rattan cane splint."[65] Indian surgeons were expert at the repair of noses, ears, and lips; and it was from them that the army surgeons of the East India Company learned the art of rhinoplasty (which means turning down a flap of the skin of the forehead to repair unsightly nose defects).

Susruta describes a surgical technique of dissecting organs, after they have begun to disintegrate in water, which makes him a forerunner of Lacanchie, who introduced hydrotomy in the nineteenth century. Susruta, marred somewhat by excessive scholasticism and classifications, describes many surgical operations—hernia, cataract, lithotomy, caesarian section—and about 121 surgical instruments—scalpels, lancets, saws, scissors, needles, hooks, probes, detectors, forceps, and syringes—all of which belong to modern surgical practice. These instruments were properly handled and carefully prepared according to elaborate rules. The sterilization of the wound by fumigation is one of the earliest known examples of antiseptic surgery. Three surgical methods were prescribed: instruments, caustic, and cautery (*agni karman*), but as a rule the Indians believed in helping nature to effect a cure, rather than in resorting to more violent methods.

In certain cases they employed anesthetics, even at a very early date.[66] Insensibility to pain was produced by the use of medical liquors, drugs like belladonna, and Indian hemp (*cannabis indica*). The one operative process the Hindus did not know was ligaturing—the method of tying the end of a blood vessel. Whilst skilfully amputating limbs, they checked haemorrhage by cauterization, boiling oil, or pressure. More than a thousand years prior to Oliver Wendell Holmes' "wandering friar" they "cut for stone." The Indians even introduced a special method of tying intestinal wounds. Since normal sutures caused the intestines to become constricted, they joined the lips of the wound and had them bitten by large ants. Later the body of the ant was cut off leaving behind the mandibles as clamps which were acceptable to the human system. The abdominal wall was closed by ordinary sutures. The Arabs later adopted this system and passed it on to the West. It survives to this day, especially on the Somali coast.[67]

The Indians were particularly adept in teaching surgery. Having realized the value of rapid, dexterous incision in operations without anesthesia, they required the students to begin by practicing on plants. The hollow stalks of water-lilies, or the veins of large leaves, or the blood vessels of dead animals, were punctured and lanced. Soft fruits or leather baas filled with water were incised or tapped as training for operation: on hydrocele or any other disorder of a hollow cavity. Fresh hides of animals or dead bodies were used in the demonstration of scarification and bleeding. Flexible models of the human body were used for practice in bandaging. The use of the probe was practiced on hollow bamboos. In training students in this way the Indians were the pioneers of many recent teaching techniques in experimental surgery.[68]

The ancient Indians undoubtedly excelled all other nations of their time in operative surgery. Their concern for physical health and their achievements in medicine must confuse the image of India as a land of pure metaphysics and otherworldliness. Yet, it may well have been this very Hindu attitude towards life, their very theory of nature, which led to their success in medicine. They did not look upon the universe as a mere fortuitous concourse of atoms, or as a puzzling labyrinth of purposeless activities and inactivities, but as a cosmos capable of consistent explanation, an ordered sequence of cause and effect, a mighty whole of which human beings were just one part. For the Hindus, philosophy, science, and religion were inseparable, being different aspects of real knowledge. This belief led them to study medicine, not as an isolated art but as a branch of their pursuit of reality. In classical Greece too a similar belief in the systems of nature—philosophy regarding the human being as part of the whole of nature—had governed the art of medicine. A number of the alleged treatises of Hippocrates reflect this attitude. The philosophy of nature influenced medicine and began to transform it. It was only later that an adverse reaction set in and medicine became more of an empiric art.[69]

Not only human beings and animals, but plants are also part of the cosmic immanent life-force, and all are interrelated. This concept significantly conditioned the Indian attitude and had a bearing on their accomplishments in pharmacology. The nourishment received from the plant's vitality transformed itself naturally into the strength of the animal and human body. Western intellectuals have often been surprised by the discoveries in plant pathology and crystallogeny of the Indian scientists trained in their own traditional way.[70] A modern Indian scientist, Sir J. C. Bose (1850–1937), was able to demonstrate the pulsating life-force in plants and their biological changes in his laboratories at Calcutta and Darjeeling, with the help of accurate modern Western instruments. He demonstrated the effects of air, sleep, food, drugs, etc., on plants and established a complete parallel between the responses of plant and animal tissues.[71]

The Indian pharmacopoeia, consisting mainly of vegetable substances and herbs, was particularly rich and remarkable for its range and value. Susruta listed 760 medicinal plants, many of which came into the *materia medica* of the West and are still there. Special emphasis was given to aphrodisiacs and poisons along with antidotes for snake and animal bites. Garlic was praised in a hymn in the Bower manuscript found in 1890, and is now accepted as possessing the ability to check gastric ulcers. The soporific effects of *hyoscyamus* and cannabis indica were known, and so was the purgative effect of honey in the newborn infant. Mercury was used as an internal remedy from a very early date. Even more significant was the drug *rauwolfia serpentine,* extracted from the leaves of a plant in the Himalayan foothills, which was in use from antiquity as a tranquilizer.

Present day medicine, having extracted its active principle *reserpine,* now uses it in cases of hypertension and as a treatment for mental cases. Amongst other Indian drugs adopted for use in modern pharmacopoeia are *ishabgol* and *triphala.* Turmeric *(haridra)* is used in Indian curry as an antiseptic ingredient. Triphala, like other Indian drugs, was perhaps known to later Greek authors such as Actuarius and Myrepsus through the Arabs. What Actuarius calls *trypala* or *tryphera parva* was Indian *triphala,* both in name and the constituents of the compound, and was recommended for use as in India.[72]

Apart from using plants for dietetic purposes, Indian physicians also used them as electuaries, infusions, powders, ointments, and enemas, as well as errhines; which were not commonly prescribed by Western physicians. Indian physicians were not content with merely growing, gathering, and compounding the various medicinal herbs, but they even studied the effect of the seasons upon plants.

The Indians gave careful and thorough attention to hygiene and diet. They studied climatic influences on various diseases and examined hydropathy. Hindu medical texts recommend rinsing the mouth with warm or cold water before and after meals, as well as at other times. The use of oil as unguent for massage, for dropping into the ears, and for rubbing into the soles was suggested for general physical fitness, as was regular exercise. The anointing of the whole body before taking a bath was suggested for its invigorating effect. Rules pertaining to diet were elaborate in relation to various ailments and governed even the daily intake of food for a healthy person. Generally, half the stomach was to be filled with food, a quarter with water, and the rest left empty.[73] Cleansing the teeth was particularly advocated, and massage was a favourite remedy for both physical and mental ailments. Regular sleep and early rising, and the drinking of a certain quantity of water daily at sunrise were believed to be an aid to good health and long life. Indians even today follow many of these recommendations.

The ancient Indian medical system is being scientifically studied and restored in India today, and many of its early drugs and medicines are finding their way into modern medicine. The physician (vaidya) was a respected member of society and was expected to maintain the very high standard cf professional and ethical conduct prescribed in medical texts.

Hypnotism as therapy, according to Garrison, appears to have originated with the Indians who often took their sick to temples to be cured by hypnotic suggestion. The Englishmen responsible for this technique in England—Braid, Esdaile, and Elliotson—certainly got their ideas from their contact with India. In India hypnotism had been practiced as a cure in certain diseases, because Indian physicians devoted their attention to the psychic as well as the physical side of life. In the *Mahabharata* there is mention of the two classes of diseases, physical and mental, which were interlinked and interdependent.[74]

Since animals were regarded as a part of the same cosmos as humans, it is not surprising that animal life was keenly protected and veterinary medicine was a distinct branch of science with its own hospitals and scholars. Numerous texts, especially of the postclassical period, *Visnudharmottara Mahapurana* for example, mention veterinary medicine. Megasthenes refers to the kind of treatment which was later to be incorporated in Palakapyamuni's *Hastya yur Veda* and similar treatises. Salihotra was the most eminent authority on horse breeding and hippiatry, and Jadudatta gives a detailed account of the medical treatment of cows in his *Asva-Vaidyaka.*

Indian ability to make surgical instruments, astronomical instruments, and other scientific apparatus, as well as their meteorological accomplishments would imply a certain competence in mechanical devices and technological proficiency. Although not conclusive, there are ample references in Indian literature to mechanical devices beginning with the *Rig Veda,* the epics, and the Puranas, to the *Meghaduta,* the *Rajatarangini,* and the various *Yantras.* How far applied science was developed in India cannot be stated with any certainty, but the *Samarangana-sutradhara* ascribed to Bhoja includes a brief narrative of Indian technology and technonomy which makes it appear to be both ancient and accomplished.

Whilst science developed in the West during the Renaissance, changing the whole character of society and attaining unbelievable successes, India entered a mediaeval period and science declined. The reasons for this decline are complex and still largely speculative, because investigation is seriously handicapped by the pathetic lack of information. Various explanations are given, none of which is wholly convincing. Even in China where the scientific tradition was continuous and productive, it declined during the mediaeval period. What is more surprising is that in China, with all her emphasis on things material and concrete, and her progress in the application of science to human affairs, medical progress remained almost stationary until the present day, although the Chinese knowledge of anatomy and anthropometric measurements was exceptional. A possible explanation for the decline in Indian science may be that it proceeded in the wrong direction by pursuing alchemy and occultism. But the major reason must lie in the general stagnation of thought and learning during this period in India and the disappearance of the tradition of university and secular education. Despite its loss of creative activity, however, Indian science continued to have some influence over other regions such as Central Asia and the Indonesian Archipelago.

Chapter VI

MYTHS, FABLES, MUSIC AND GAMES

IT HAS BEEN claimed that India is the original home of literary fiction and intellectual games. Whatever be the merits of this assertion, there is no doubt that stories of Indian origin have long been told in distant lands of Asia and Europe in a variety of forms, giving delight to countless people, often without reference to or awareness of their sources. Centuries before Kalidasa's *Sakuntala* captured the fascination of Western intellectuals at the end "of the eighteenth century, Indian myths and tales were widely known, and the influence of Visnusarman, the mythical author of the *Pancatantra,* the most famous collection of Indian fables, was widely felt.

Once again it was mainly the Arabs, and the Iranians before them, who transmitted Indian fables and folklore to Europe, either through Turkey or Spain. From Constantinople Indian stories were transmitted to Venice and Naples through trade contacts and thence they found their way into the works of Boccaccio, Chaucer, Cervantes, Shakespeare, Le Sage, La Fontaine, Voltaire, and other famous Western writers. With each story-teller the story assumed a new look, eventually reaching a stage at which it often bore only a feeble resemblance to the original. It was not until Western scholars discovered Sanskrit language and literature in the latter part of the eighteenth century that the Indian contribution to the world's fiction came to be appreciated, although its full extent is yet to be systematically assessed. This discovery of Sanskrit led to the beginnings of comparative philology, the study of comparative religions and philosophies, knowledge of Indo-European antiquities, and to the recognition of parallels between Indian and Western literatures, especially in fables and fairy tales.

The story of how Indian fables reached the remote corners of Europe, Asia, and even Africa is a fascinating study; for it is not merely a case of single or isolated stories reaching other countries by way of merchants and travellers from India, but of entire Indian books becoming the common heritage of mankind through the medium of translations.

There are, of course, various kinds of folklore and folktales, and scholars have devoted much effort to give them exact descriptions. At present we are chiefly concerned with fables and myths. Although these are somewhat interrelated and difficult to separate into their respective traditions, it is generally accepted that the story which is embedded in rituals, morals, and cults and which endeavours to explain some natural phenomena or religious problem is a myth, whilst the story which is intended to amuse, to instruct, and to point out a moral is a fable. Myths generally deal with the deeds of gods or heroes and man's primitive beliefs and intellectual attempts to explain nature. Myth is now commonly associated with the incredible or the wholly imaginary. But this was not the original sense in which the ancient Greeks, who coined the term, used it. Many ancient myths even describe the creation and organization of the universe, the evolution of mankind, and the emergence of civilization.

Despite the resemblances between the mythologies of the ancient peoples, myths differ widely in plots, motifs, and treatment, reflecting the characteristics of the respective environments in which they were produced, and scholars hold divergent views about their scope and importance. About a century ago mythology was regarded as a study of ancient peoples, mainly those of Greece and Rome. Modern scholars, despite their recognition of a close association between myth and religion, take a wider and more accurate view of the subject. Some scholars, however, look upon myths as hardly more than superstitious fairy tales of little intellectual importance and historical significance. Yet, others see in myths a remarkable expression of human insight and spirit. Whatever be its actual nature, scope, and significance, the value of mythology in understanding the mental processes of early man, his beliefs and feelings as expressed in writing and visual art, can hardly be denied. Goethe maintained that the early peoples had their ideas in intuitions of fancy, whereas modern men articulate them into notions.

Originally a fable was just a tale, a simple expression of man's desire to amuse himself, but over a period of time it was provided with a "moral," and became a vehicle for teaching a lesson in morality or wisdom in an entertaining style. It has, therefore, acquired a twin objective, to amuse and to instruct. With the surprising exception of the pre-Buddhist Chinese, all peoples in all societies have incorporated in their literature entertaining yet instructive stories.[1] Most fables are beast fables because they describe imaginary adventures of animals who act and feel like human beings. An explanation for this characteristic may well be the close proximity primitive man had with wild and domestic animals, and his dependence on them.

This distinction between myth and fable, although somewhat valid by virtue of common concurrence, is not quite applicable to Indian tradition. For whilst the ancient civilizations of Greece, Iran, Egypt, and other countries have disappeared and their mythologies have been displaced by well-defined and well-organized religious beliefs, such as Christianity and Zoroastrianism, thus allowing their folklore to develop distinctly, the Indian civilization and religion has been a continuous organic growth which did not displace mythology. Again, the amorphous nature of India's religious beliefs, and the fact that her religion and philosophy are inseparable from her literature, make it difficult to distinguish Indian myth from fable. For example, stories found in vedic literature, such as that of Pururavas and Urvasi, can be both myths and fables.[2] The Jataka tales, dealing with the birth stories of the Buddha, and the stories in the *Mahabharata,* although rooted in religious culture, are considered to be fables.

Sanskrit achieved excellence in most forms of literature. Sanskrit works on religion and philosophy are unsurpassed, and Sanskrit poetry, as contained in lyrical and dramatic works, compares favourably with the most beautiful European works Although the qualities of Sanskrit literature are not well known in the West outside a limited circle of specialists, it is outstanding in its imagination and perception, especially in gnomic poetry. The Sanskrit aphorism and didactic style of verse, best illustrated in Indian fables and folklore, are most valuable contributions of Indian literature.[3]

Ancient Indian fiction is especially notable for its diversity of theme, setting, situation, and characterization. Whilst some stories are filled with a spirit of piety and religious devotion, others advocate a secular and even naturalistic attitude towards life. There are realistic images of noble sages, profound thinkers, detached men of wisdom, distraught poets, restless wanderers, voluble astrologers, credulous peasants, greedy priests, flattering courtiers, arrogant scholars, cunning traders, and a wide variety of people, many of whom are recognizable today in Indian society. Whilst some stories are pure flights of fancy, others provide a necessary corrective to the excesses of imagination through their realism; and whilst some are profound and substantial, others are simply interesting and amusing.

India has often been characterized as the most religious country in the world in somewhat the same way as China is described as pre-eminent in porcelain, Japan in drawing, and the West in technology. Porcelain is made throughout the world, but it is in China that the art bas reached perfection. So in India has "man gone to the farthest limit of his religious faculty."[4] Consequently, mythology is one of India's richest traditions. It is also one of the oldest, and, because of the common origins of the Indo-European peoples, it is connected with the mythologies of Greece, Iran, and Italy. Such similarities of religions and mythical ideas, however, are only limited: partly because the Greeks, having left the Indo-European peoples, entered regions where more complex societies already flourished, and partly because it appears that the themes of Indo-European mythology were relatively simple.[5] Reflections of the ancestral links in mythologies can be seen in the tales of Hercules, Thor, and Indra. Whilst Hercules was a son of Zeus by Alcmene, and was later deified, Indra is described in the vedic hymns as a national god of the Aryans and the patron of the military nobility with the thunderbolt as his principal weapon. He is, however, a wholly anthropormorphic deity, and his passion for *soma* borders on intemperance. Like a simple mortal, however, he is formidable and bellicose to his enemies, but good and generous to his followers, helping them in war. His struggles against the Dasyus may be somewhat reminiscent of Hercules' heroic exploits and there is some resemblance between Indra and Zeus. Both were principal gods, and both had salaciously succumbed to the charms of pious mortal women and impersonated their husbands to seduce them.

Kern has suggested a comparison between the ape king, who in a Jataka tale makes himself a bridge over the Ganges for his following, and a similar episode involving the Irish King Bran, and further suggests that the function of the Roman pontifex may be pertinent.[6] In fact, similar features of the Irish and Greek mythologies can be explained only by their common Aryan mythological heritage. Whilst little is known of the mythology of the continental Celts, and Irish mythology is fragmentary in form and distorted by its transmission through the centuries, mythical conceptions and visions in Ireland are more archaic, even if recorded much later, than those of Greece and India. The Celts were known in the ancient world for their positive beliefs concerning the survival of the soul, and their conception of a "happy otherworld" was similar to that of the early Greeks. Of all the Indo-European peoples, the Greeks and the Irish alone have fully preserved the early version of this conception. Similarly, the myth of Oedipus, essentially Greek in its mature construction, reflects an Indo-Aryan influence.

The myth of the "world-egg," which was designed to describe the origins of the universe, and which relates that heaven was formed from the upper shell of the egg laid by Nyx and earth from the lower, cannot be purely Greek in origin as alleged. It is also found amongst the Persians, the Indians, and other peoples in varying versions. In fact the vedic *Brahmanda* is much older. The Greeks, no doubt, placed their own construction on an original Indo-European tale, whilst the vedic hymns preserved the myths in their primitive forms. Max Müller observes: "Nowhere is the wide distance which separates the ancient poems of India from the most ancient literature of Greece more clearly felt than when we compare the growing myths of the *Vedas* with the full grown and decayed myths on which the poetry of Homer is founded. The Veda is the real Theogony of the Aryan races, while that of Hesoid is a distorted caricature of the original image."[7] However, in the early Vedas the story material is limited, and, despite the fact that the vedic hymns are voluminous in comparison with Homeric hymns, the latter on the whole narrate a story more consistently. The fact that certain chief gods were common to all of them would lend weight to the view that the earliest hymns of the Aryans may have constituted the nucleus for many Greek, Celtic, and Persian myths. The Sanskrit *deva* (god) is the Latin *deus,* Greek *theos,* Lithuanian *dewas,* Irish *dia.* The greatest of the heavenly beings, who was heaven himself, was *Diu.* He is addressed as *Dyaus Pita* in vedic hymns, he is *Zeus Pater* in Greek. *Jupiter* in Latin, *Tius* in German. The Greeks appear to have regarded him as the supreme god, the giver of all things, and in some contexts, as just God. Vedic *ushas* (dawn) is Greek *eos; haritas,* another name of *surya* (sun) is Greek *charites.* The "Sons of Zeus," the two Dioscuri, are compared to the twin Asvins of Indian mythology. Some Greek gods, such as Earth (*Gaea*), Dawn (*Eos*), Sun (*Helios*), and Moon (*Selene*), are also common nouns, which may suggest that some vague divinity was attached to them from Indo-European times. Therefore, one often notices similarities amongst the names of the peoples, and sometimes the exploits of gods or heroes, in the legends of the Indo-European peoples. Many of the outstanding tales and motifs in several European mythologies bear so strong a likeness to each other that they can only have originated from a common prototype, and these similar features are in common with the myths of India. Beyond the proof of common origin, the Greeks and the Indians developed their own independent and complex tradition in mythology.

The spread of Indo-European myths and legends, dating from a common ethnic past, and the similarities amongst the mythologies of Indo-European peoples are a distinct branch of study, which has little to do with the migration of fables in strictly historical times from India to Arabia, to Greece, and to the West, either orally or, more importantly, by translations or adaptations. The two migrations—that of the Indo-Europeans and their myths and the migration of the fables of their descendants—were separated by about two thousand years. It is, therefore, not surprising that when the history of fables and their journeys is examined, the emerging picture is somewhat more definite as there is relatively more material available from which to draw conclusions.

It is possible to follow the passage of certain fables from one country to another; however, it must be pointed out that the art of story-telling is far older than history. As a popular tale is copied and recopied from one collection to another over a period of centuries and across continents, it seldom remains intact, often undergoing even changes of plot and characterization. Hence, to trace the history of a story, which, for example, may have been transmitted from India to Persia and western Asia, thence to Italy, France, and finally to Britain, must remain an exceedingly complex investigation. Yet, sometimes resemblances between various tales are so close, and their interrelation so inextricable, that the hypothesis of common origin becomes inevitable.

Scholars have now been engaged in the study of folklore for more than a century, and there is much material setting out divergent views on the questions of the origin, dissemination, meaning, and nature of folktales. Serious consideration of these questions appeared for the first time in the second edition of the Grimms' *Kinder und Hausmärchen* (folk tales for children and the home, more usually known as *Grimm's Fairy Tales*) in 1819. The Grimm brothers, Jacob and Wilhelm, had given little thought to the problem of the origin of folktales when they issued their first edition, but between the first and second editions similar tales from other countries had been published, especially from Serbia, raising the need to explain the similarities and identical plots. Also, the discovery of Sanskrit had opened up new vistas in comparative literature. More than a quarter of a century later, in 1856, Wilhelm Grimm suggested that the resemblances found not only amongst the stories of nations widely separated by time and distance, but also amongst those which are neighbours, consisted partly in the basic plot and the delineation of characters, and partly in the weaving together or disentangling of incidents. There are, however, certain situations which are so commonplace and natural that they occur anywhere, in the same way as some thoughts seem to emerge simultaneously. Hence, it is possible that the same or very similar stories arose in different countries quite independently of each other. To Grimm the fairy tale was an inheritance from the remains of Indo-European mythical poetry. He was, however, talking of the folktale in a broad sense, but he did distinguish between two types of tales: one, which showed close resemblances to others in the Indo-European language family, was doubtless inherited from a common Indo-European antiquity; the other, which contained dissected or broken-down myths, could be understood only by a proper interpretation of its parent-myths. Perhaps an example of this is the

Anglo-Saxon epic *Beowulf,* comprising more than six thousand verses or half-verses, which was composed before 750. Certain of its features which resemble those of Asian mythology can be more easily explained by the common Indo-European past than by suggesting the migration of ideas so far westward at that time, although the possibility cannot be altogether ruled out.

With the awareness of the importance of Sanskrit at the beginning of the nineteenth century, many eminent European scholars and linguists, especially German, took an exceptionally keen interest in the problem of reconstructing the parent speech from which most of the languages of India and Europe descended. Although many details remained unsolved, the overall framework with its various subdivisions had become clear by the middle of the nineteenth century. The general approach to the subject was well illustrated in the works that followed, such as those of Max Müller, Angelo de Gubernatis, John Fiske, and Sir George Cox, who all stressed that the parallels in folklore and myths from Ireland to India were principally an inheritance from a common Indo-European past, and traced their origins to the *Rig Veda.* For instance, the trick of dragging stolen cattle backwards into their place of hiding without leaving behind their footprints to escape detection appears again and again in the mythology of different Indo-European peoples.[8]

Whilst some scholars were exploring the *Rig Veda* and its influence on the folktale, others were also finding India the origin of folktale tradition from another point of view. As early as 1838, Loiseleur Deslongchamps suggested that European folktales could probably be traced to India, but it was Theodor Benfey who took up this suggestion and carried it to its logical conclusion. Although he had already advanced this view in some of his previous studies, it was expressed with clarity and authority in the Introduction to his edition of the *Pancatantra* in 1859. Whilst Benfey believed that most of the animal fables originated in the West and were, more or less, transformations of the so-called *Aesop's Fables,* he believed folktales had originally come from India. He found fairy tales which had been included in Indian works such as the *Pancatantra,* the *Sukasaptati,* and the *Vetalapancavimsati,* in later Indian languages referred to as *Baital Pachisi.*[9] He pointed out, however, that some animal fables give the impression of having an Indian origin, for many considerations indicated that the Indians, well before their acquaintance with the animal fables of Aesop, had invented a good many stories of a similar kind. The difference between Indian fables and Aesop's is that whilst Aesop's animals act in conformity with their own nature and characteristics, the Indian fables treat the animals as if they were men masked in animal form. When the essentially didactic nature of the animal fable, which is exclusively an Indian characteristic, and the Hindu belief in the transmigration of souls are taken into consideration, the theory of Indian origin of fables is further reinforced.

Benfey's arguments were very convincing. To each story from the *Pancatantra* he appended exhaustive notes elaborating and illustrating his opinion with scrupulous and profound scholarship. Jacob Grimm agreed with him and the students of folklore in the nineteenth century generally accepted the position, although there was some criticism. For example, it was claimed that too much reliance was placed on literary sources and that insufficient attention was paid to the actual movement of fairy tales from one nation to another.

Another important scholar in the field was Reinhold Köhler (1830–1892), who published annotations of the main collections of European tales, and thus helped to clarify the mutual relationship of the various tales and motifs. He was, however, mainly an editor and commentator and was little concerned with theories of historical origins. A strong supporter of Benfey's basic ideas was Emmanuel Cosquin (1841-1921), who published an extremely valuable series of monographs. His *Contes populaires de Lorraine* (1887) is regarded as the French equivalent of *Grimm's Fairy Tales.* He studied numerous motifs and tales, always emphasizing their relationships with Indian parallels which he was convinced represented the originals. His studies paved the way for more definitive work by other scholars. Cosquin, however, was also impressed by the antiquity of Egyptian folklore, and he felt that even though all tales may not have originated in India, India had certainly served as the great reservoir for tales of varied nationalities which, in turn, flowed out all over the world.

The Finnish school, distinct in its method of investigation whereby a fairy tale was analyzed according to its events and motifs, worked through all available sources item by item and tried to find the original parts of each fairy tale. They emphasized the fact that folktales may be composed by any people, and that the possibility cannot be ruled out that a variety of tales may have spread from various centres. But whilst it was theoretically possible for folktales to originate in any country, they attributed most of them to India. It was suggested that there were "streams of fairy tales" and "waves" in which everybody participated because every listener became a narrator afterwards.

In the 1870's, however, a reaction against the theory of folklore diffusion set in. Reinforced by the Darwinian concept of organic evolution, the British school of anthropology gave rise to the anthropological theory. E. B. Tylor claimed in his book *Primitive Culture* (1871) that a number of customs, ideas, and religious convictions could be traced in like form in all primitive and civilized people, so that similar intellectual prerequisites producing similar forms of fairy tales must be assumed.

Andrew Lang insisted that folklore was close to the surface of civilized life, being the remains of ideas as old as the stone elf-shots and older than the cult of bronze. He detected in proverbs, riddles, nursery tales, and superstitions, the relics of a stage of thought which was dying out.[10] In support of his view that folklore beliefs were not peculiar to any one race he cited the story *The Mystery of the Pezazi*, which was current in a very similar form in Ceylon and Mexico. The curious coincidence of the "midnight axe" described in both versions was held by him as the expression of a common state of superstitious fancy, not an indication of common origin. If Lang had known there was considerable evidence of cultural diffusion between southern Asia and ancient America, he would not have found this parallelism so striking.

Andrew Lang's anthropological theory asserted that the fairy tale had been common to all primitive peoples, and thus had the tradition of parallel development. He used the discovery of Egyptian folktales along with the stories mentioned in Herodotus and Homer in his sometimes satirical opposition to the theory of Indian primacy in folklore. He also pointed out many primitive ideas in modern folktales and suggested that these tales had survived from a very ancient time. Lang's position of parallel development of culture everywhere is untenable for it would manifest itself in analogous tales. Without undermining the considerable value of Lang's reasoning and conclusions, his interest in the contributions of primitive man may have been somewhat over pronounced because of the remarkable work with the concept of organic evolution done by British anthropologists during the second half of the nineteenth century.

Besides Lang, other scholars had come to take an interest in the beliefs and practices of primitive peoples and begun to collect and compare data, pointing out various parallels in development. They attempted to show that all mythological stories said the same things in different ways. The most famous example is Sir James George Frazer's *Golden Bough* originally published in twelve volumes. A remarkable collection of logically arranged data on primitive beliefs and practices, Frazer's work attempted to show that story motifs, practices, and beliefs were almost identical amongst the American Indians, the natives of Australia, and those of South Africa. The assumption was that all peoples had gone through the same stages of culture in a direct line of evolution and that in each stage they reacted to the world and expressed themselves in the same way. In higher stages there may be survivals of the earlier stages. This theory of the direct and parallel evolution of cultures and of survivals in culture, as illustrated by Lang and Frazer, and later by J. A. MacCulloch in *The Childhood of Fiction,* is undoubtedly of great interest, but it neglects to consider that culture is a matter of historical development for each people who are subjected to a wide variety of internal and external influences. Except in the vaguest and most general sense, therefore, parallelism between different peoples, especially if they are far removed, must remain an uncertain and untenable inference. At best, it could be only a rare coincidence. This theory also underestimates the role which the diffusion of the elements of tribal life has played, and pays little attention to the great community of interest amongst peoples within particular "cultural areas." Noting similarities in the tales of distant lands without adequate consideration of the possibility of their being connected in human tradition, could hardly sustain the theory of independent and parallel growth. The value of the work done by Frazer and other scholars, however, is considerable because it notes a vast number of interesting similarities in narrative patterns and poses important questions.

There were three principal theories about the origins of folktales: the mythological school, mainly German, subscribed to the view of common Indo-European ancestry and inheritance; the anthropological school, mainly British, advocated the parallel development of culture all over the world; the Indianist school traced every tale to India. All of these theories were partially correct and incorrect. In spite of divergent theories, however, the doctrine of integration prevailed, and the migration of folktales has been like the rings formed when a stone is thrown into a pool, spreading equally in all directions. The mythological school, like the anthropological school, was not primarily interested in how tradition was diffused from one place to another, or from people.

Modern anthropological research has led to revisions in the generalizations about primitive man, and the realization that many of the resemblances in the cultures of primitive peoples are not real identities either from the psychological or historical viewpoint. In fact, systematic examination of the geographical and historical factors clearly reveals a particular culture being continually influenced by its neighbours. The problem of the dissemination of cultural traits, including the folktale, is admittedly a complex one. Examination of the folktale involves the reconstruction of the original story form by unwrapping the layers imposed by time and locality and then tracing its passage through history. Moreover, the fact that the Benfey school and the Finnish school maintain their "Indian theory"; the fact that the question as to the relationship between the fairy tale collection of *Alf Laila Wa Laila* (literally, *The Thousand Nights and One Night*, or the *Arabian Nights*) and older European collections has not yet been answered; the fact that the anthropological theory becomes problematic in light of Peuckert's theory that the origin of all fairy tales dealing with magic must be connected with the observation and use of herbs and plants; and finally, the fact that De Vries' theory of archetyes has not been effectively dealt with must suggest, amongst other things, the complex nature of the problem.

The earliest Indian fables are found in the vedic literature, the *Mahabharata*, the Jatakas, and the famous collections known as the *Pancatantra* and the *Hitopadesa*. These collections fall broadly into two categories: those compiled for the purpose of religious preaching, such as the Jatakas and the other storybooks of the Buddhists and Jains written in Prakrit; and those intended to inculcate political doctrines and worldly wisdom, and to entertain, written Sanskrit, such as the *Pancatantra*. The oldest beast fables known in India occur in the *Chandogya Upanishad*,[11] in which animals are introduced as actors and speakers. There are other stories dealing with the metamorphosis theme representing the gods in the forms of animals associating with men. Indeed, there are even earlier illustrations of this form of story: for instance, the story of Manu and the fish, that of Indra's metamorphosis into a bird, and the Rig Vedic simile of the sun as a vulture or falcon hovering in the air.[12] The theory of the transmigration of souls, applied equally to both man and animal, must have favoured the development of this form of tale. Indeed, the Buddha himself—during the period of his previous incarnations—appears in the guise of various animals in the old Jatakas.

The great variety of anecdotes with animal heroes throughout world literature is quite impressive. For the tellers of folktales everywhere and in every age, the human and animal worlds are never too distinct. The idea of a hunter disguising himself in the skin of an animal is quite common. This ambiguity extends even to mythologies, and as a consequence many deities appear one day in human guise and the next in the image of a beast. Folk tradition is generally very careful in its choice of animals, selecting only those that can make their actions appear as nearly human as is possible, and, of course, keep their character constant. Thus, the jackal is crafty, the hare is swift and wily, the cat is a hypocrite, and the lion is strong but gullible.

Whilst Indian fables and tales date from remote antiquity, they were, perhaps, not used for a definite purpose and not reduced to a literary form until a much later period. The ancestor of the popular tale may have been such vedic *akhyanas* as are preserved, for instance, in the Rig Vedic dialogue-hymn of Pururavas and Urvasi, or in such early legends as that of Sunahsepa. But it is going too far to seek the origin of the beast fable in the Rig Vedic hymn[13] in which the chanting Brahmans are compared to croaking frogs who are portrayed as more magical than didactic, or in the upanishadic parable of the dogs searching out a leader to howl for food for them, which may have been a satire or an allegory. It may also be somewhat questionable to clearly identify in the *Mahabharata* fables a distinct literary form although the motifs of the clever jackal, the naughty cat, and the greedy vulture are employed for moral instruction. All these, as well as the Jataka technique of illustrating the virtues of Buddhism by means of beast stories, may have been the basis for the well-developed beast fable in the *Pancatantra.* In its mature form, it departed from the simple parable or beast tale by bringing out the latent didactic motive clearly and deliberately and setting it artistically in a framework of connected stories in which the thoughts and deeds of men were attributed to animals.

It is not possible to neatly separate the Indian fable from the tale. The *Pancatantra,* although mainly composed of beast fables, also includes folktales and stories of human adventure, whereas the tale, as represented by the *Brihatkatha,* sometimes contains elements of the fable and a didactic motive.[14] However, the beast fable diverged considerably as all independent literary creation from the popular tale, which was not didactic and in which the stories of human life and popular ideas in myth and magic found expression.

The Jatakas are a collection of over five hundred stories, arranged in twenty-two *nipatas* (sections). They reflect an aspect of the literary, as well as popular, taste of the land. Each story gives an account of an incident in the previous existences of the Buddha as a Bodhisattva. These stories are held by the believer to be true, but they are really an assorted collection of popular folklore and historical tradition in the form of fables, fairy tales, riddles, puzzles, legends, humorous superstitions, and accounts of the social life of ancient India. At some period in antiquity, certainly well before 300 B.C., it had become customary to identify the principal hero of each of these popular stones with the Buddha himself in a previous birth, and this identification was not entirely imaginary. Indeed, it is solely due to the growth of this idea that there is preserved "the most complete, the most authentic, and the most ancient collection of folklore in the world—a collection entirely unadulterated, as modern folklore stories so often are, by the inevitable process of passing through a Western mind."[15] In each story, the Buddha narrates, although not in first person, an experience of a past life to explain a present incident showing its moral implications. Because these tales bear upon the previous lives of the Buddha, scholars fix their origin in a period after his death. Yet, they have not explained how the tales can be attributed to men of later times if the Buddha were the actual narrator of each story. In fact, this mode of telling tales was an old one; it was not difficult to replace a sage or a wise man with a Bodhisattva. Any story, however secular or frivolous, could easily be transformed into a Buddhist tale by having its principal character identified with the Bodhisattva. There were several diverse types of Jatakas and in the early forms there was no place for Bodhisattvas. They were largely folk literature in which beast fables and fragments of historical tradition, as well as tales of wisdom, had been collected for instructive or didactic purposes.

The Jataka tales, however, have a definite religious significance. The only secular surviving collection of beast fables in Sanskrit is the *Pancatantra,* which exists in various versions and has, perhaps, a more interesting history than any work in world literature. Over two hundred different versions of the work are known to exist in more than fifty languages, and about three-quarters of these languages are not Indian.[16] Its range has stretched from Java to Iceland. As early as the eleventh century the *Pancatantra* had reached Europe, and by the end of the sixteenth it had been translated into almost all the major languages of Europe. Few books in history have been translated into so many languages and it is doubtful if any secular book has had a wider readership.

All the versions emanate from a single original text which has not been preserved. Its earliest recensions have been classified into four main groups, each representing a diversity of tradition. The first is the lost Pahlavi version from which the old Syriac and Arabic versions were derived, and it was through this source that the *Pancatantra,* in a somewhat modified form, was introduced into the fable literature of Europe. The second is a lost northwestern recension from which the text was incorporated into the two Kashmirian Sanskrit versions of Gunadhya's *Brihatkatha,* made respectively by Ksemendra and Somadeva (eleventh century). The third is the common lost source of the Kashmirian version, entitled *Tantrakhyayika,* and of the two Jain versions, the Simplicitor Text, well known from the Bühler and Kielhorn edition, and the Ornatior Text of Purnabhadra (1190), called *Pancakhyana.* The fourth is also the source of the southern *Pancatantra,* the Nepalese version, and the Bengali *Hitopadesa.* Of these, the *Tantrakhyayika* best represents the original. The nature and extent of the transformation to which the work was subjected in course of time make the problem of reconstruction extremely complicated, but the close examination of the various existing versions made by Hertel and Edgerton succeeded to a great extent in recreating the original *Pancatantra.*

From the very beginning the *Pancatantra* had a deliberate literary form, being the instruction in the art of statecraft given by a learned scholar, Visnusarman, to three unintelligent but impressionable young princes. Its theme is not morality but practical wisdom in the affairs of life. It passed as a text book of *artha* (worldy wisdom) or *niti* (polity), which is one of three objects of human desires for the Hindus—the other two being dharma and kama. It repeatedly quotes verbatim from the celebrated Indian text on polity, the *Arthasastra:* "Like that work, it is designed especially to advise rulers in the arts of government. It is then, a 'Mirror for Magistrates' or 'Fiirstenspiegel.'"[17] It teaches the art of being an accomplished, successful, and happy social being; it does not concern itself with the possibility of living as a saint or an ascetic. Whilst insisting on the misery of poverty—"twas better to be dead than poor"—the *Pancatantra* does not glorify the acquisition of wealth. Money is a means to an end, to be able to live—"a Man to thrive must keep alive." Once security and freedom from worry are obtained, real joy comes from resolute and wise action, from contact with friends, and especially from the worthy exercise of the intelligence. Niti is the integrated development of the powers of man, in which security, prosperity, resolution, friendship, and learning are harmoniously blended to produce the utmost joy of life. The *Pancatantra* is therefore closely related to the *Nitisastra* and *Arthasastra,* although not directly opposed to the *Dharmasastra.* This is important, because even if the beast fable stresses the practical art of diplomacy in human affairs, rather than the strict code of uprightness, it does not teach the politics of profit at the expense of morality. Its five parts—*mitrabheda, mitraprapti, samdhivigraha, labdhanasa,* and *apariksitakaritana*—from which it derives its title, deal respectively with how friends and allies are lost; how they are won; the principles of war and peace; how gains are lost; and the dangers of hasty action. Each part is a narrative complete in itself, and together they constitute a perfect whole.[18] The stories are recounted in a simple and graceful prose narrative without attempting to create elaborate stylistic effects or sentimental digressions. Its technique of inserting a number of stories within the framework of a single narrative is distinctive, although this feature of combining a number of fables is also used in the popular tale. In bringing together unconnected stories, considerable ingenuity has been employed to achieve unity and completeness of effect. The numerous general gnomic stanzas which punctuate the narrative are dictated by the didactive motive of the fable.

Originally intended as a work for imparting political wisdom to princes, the *Pancatantra* is now principally a storybook in which the story-teller and the political teacher are unified in one personality. At times the charm of story-telling is subordinated to the professed practical objective, and the tedious exposition of polity prevails over simple and vivid narrative. Such instances, however, are not numerous. Discrepancies doubtless appear in the different versions, but most of the stories are well and amusingly told, showing the author as a master of narrative, as well as a perfect man of the world, who never departs from an attitude of objective observation and whose considerable fund of wit and humour is often disguised behind his pedagogic seriousness. Because of its beauty and its wisdom the *Pancatantra* is one of the best storybooks ever composed.

In the absence of the original text it is impossible to determine the age of the *Pancatantra* with accuracy. The original version could have been composed any time between 100 B.C. and 500 A.D. However, it is certain that by the middle of the sixth century A.D. it had acquired wide fame even outside India. Its popularity within India is well illustrated by the various abridged versions of it available from Nepal to South India.

The Pahlavi translation was made by Barzuyeh (or Burzoe), the physician of the Sassanian King Khusru Anushirvan (537–79), by royal command.[19] This translation was obviously made from a Sanskrit version. Soon after, in 570, it was rendered from Pahlavi into Old Syriac by Bud, and his version, although imperfectly preserved, is still extant. It was thus virtually contemporary with the lost Pahlavi version. The Bud translation has been edited and translated twice into German by modern scholars. Almost two centuries later, about 760, the Pahlavi version was translated into Arabic by Abadallah ibn al-Muqaffa under the title *Kalila wa Dimna.* The title appears to have been taken from the names of the two jackals, Karataka and Damanaka, who play prominent parts in the original Sanskrit version of the *Pancatantra.* The diffusion of translations from then on was much wider still, and the Arabic version became the source of numerous versions in several continents.

Comparatively few Indian fables reached the West before the tenth century. Apart from those contained in the translations of the *Pancatantra,* there were stories handed down by oral tradition. In the tenth century, India became better known to the Islamic world, and from then on literary sources became more important than the oral tradition. Indian scientific and literary works were now translated into Persian and Arabic, were diffused all over the Islamic world in Asia, Africa, and Europe, and, because of the frequent conflicts between the Muslims and the Christians, also throughout the Christian West, particularly the Byzantine Empire, Italy, and Spain.

Hindu and Buddhist classical works had spread earlier to those countries and regions in the vicinity of India, primarily because of Buddhist missionary expansion. With this literature, from about the first century on, tales and fables penetrated without interruption into China and further east. They also reached Tibet and from there travelled with Buddhism to the Mongols, who adapted them to their own language with many changes and modifications. In addition to the *Vetalapancavimsati* and the *Vikramacaritra,* it is certain that the Mongols were also familiar with a third collection of stories, the *Sukasaptati.* Considering that the Mongols were in power in Europe for almost two hundred years, it seems more than plausible that many of these stories reached Europe through them. In the introduction to his translation of the *Vetalapancavimsati,* Heinrich Uhle points out that there is a Mongolian version of many of the Vetala stories in the language of the Kalmucks—a Mongolian race living on the Caspian Sea—called *Siddhi-Kur.* This Mongolian version became known in 1804 through Benjamin Bergmann's book *Nomadic Wanderings in the Region of the Kalmucks* but was not identified until 1857 by Benfey as being borrowed from India.[20] A Mongolian translation of the Arabic version of the *Pancatantra, Kalila wa Dimna,* is ascribed to Malik Said Iftikhar uddin Mohammad bin Abu Nasr, who died in 1280.

Another Syriac translation was made from this Arabic version in the tenth or eleventh century, and in about 1080, a Jew, Simeon Seth, translated it into Greek entitling it *Stephanites kai Ichnelades,* and stating in the Preface that the book originally had come from India. This, in turn, led to an Italian version by Giulio Nuti in 1583, two Latin versions, one German, and various translations in the Slavonic languages. At the beginning of the twelfth century, a Hebrew version was made by Rabbi Joel; this was translated into Latin by an Italian, John of Capua, between 1263 and 1278, was called *Liber Kalilee et Dimnae, Directorium vitae humanae,* and attained great popularity in the later Middle Ages. In 1480 two printed versions of this book appeared, and it has been reprinted in modern times. In 1483 a German translation appeared by Antonius von Pforr called *Das Buch der Beispiele der alten Weisen,* which is the best and most famous mediaeval version of the *Pancatantra.* It was repeatedly printed and, besides influencing German literature, was rendered into Danish, Icelandic, and Dutch.[21] The fact that four dated editions appeared at Ulm within four years of its first publication in German, followed by thirteen more during the course of the next hundred years, shows the importance of the *Pancatantra* at the time. A Spanish version appeared in 1493 and from it two Italian renderings by Firenzuola and Doni were made in 1548 and in 1552 respectively. In 1556 a French translation was made from Firenzuola's version. From Doni's version Sir Thomas North, the translator of Plutarch, made an English rendering under the title *The Morall Philosophie of Doni* in 1570, almost exactly one thousand years after the Syriac translation. No less than six renderings had intervened between the original Sanskrit and the English version. North's translation was reprinted in 1601, the year after the East India Company had been given a royal charter to trade with India and further east.

After the Islamic conquest of Spain, numerous works were translated from Arabic into Latin or Spanish, including a Spanish translation of *Kalila wa Dimna* in 1289, entitled *Calila c Dymna.* This, or another translation from Arabic, was rendered into Latin verse by Raimond de Beziers in 1313, but it was not published. In the thirteenth century, another translation from Arabic straight into Latin verse was made by Baldo under the title *Aesopus alter.* These renderings of the Indian fables were extremely popular, and indeed were read more widely in Europe, according to Max Müller, than the Bible or any other book.[22] Not only were complete translations read but individual stories were incorporated into sermons, homilies, and works on morality. Inevitably they were modified, improved, and localized to the extent that the original forms were forgotten. The speed and ease with which such tales spread testifies to the pleasure and joy with which they were heard and repeated. Because of their appeal, the tales from India seem to have been quickly assimilated, and their specifically Indian features could not be preserved in the rapid transit from one people to another.

Another Indian work, the *Sukasaptati* (seventy stories of a parrot), similar to the *Pancatantra,* also travelled westward through translation. During the fourteenth century it was translated into Persian under the title *Tutinameh,* and later rendered into Turkish. From the Persian account many tales passed to Europe through western Asia, and one of these was made famous by Gottfried V. Strassburg's *Tristan and Isolde.*

In 1026 a work on Indian history, originally translated from the "Indian language" into Arabic by Abu Salih bin Su'ayb bin Jami was rendered into Persian. This version, by Abu-l-Hasan Ali, was quoted or summarized in a later Persian work of unknown date known as the *Mujmil al-Tawarikh.* It was actually a version of the *Mahabharata* story translated from a late Prakrit version.[23]

Another mediator of Indian tales was the famous *Arabian Nights.* Muslim fundamentalists consider this collection noxious, because they believe that pleasant stories stimulate sinful desires as much as wine, music, or sculpture. This work, however, has been instrumental in fashioning Western man's image of romantic love. Many of its approximately two hundred stories (264 in the Arabic version) are from Indian storybooks, and all the main elements of its framework are derived from Indian ideas. The prologue is very similar to that of the *Pancatantra* as is the idea that the stories are recounted to save someone's life. The *Samugga Jataka* (No. 436) tells the story of the *asura* (demon) who unsuccessfully put his beautiful wife in a box to guard her from going astray. The tale in all its essentials recurs in the *Arabian Nights.* Numerous animal fables contained in the *Arabian Nights* are traceable to Indian sources: for example, "The Barber's Fifth Brother" (6ee), "The Merchant's Wife and the Parrot" (134b), "The King's Son and the Afrit's Mistress" (134w), "The Fakir and His Pot of Butter" (161b), "The Hedgehog and the Pigeons" (17). The world-famous story of Sindbad is a tale of Indian origin. The Arab historian Al Masudi expressly said that the *Kitab el Sindbad* was derived from India. This work is identical with the Persian *Sindibad-namah*, the Syriac *Sindban*, an Arabic version contained in the *Arabian Nights*, the Hebrew *Sandabar*, the Greek *Syntipas*, and a number of other books in European languages. The Greek *Syntipas* contains numerous passages that can be understood properly only by recognizing that they are merely variations of a Sanskrit original, and everything supports the conclusion that here is yet another case of an Arabic work rendered from a Pahlavi translation of a Sanskrit text.

Most probably Jewish writings were also responsible for the dissemination of Indian tales in Europe, especially in the Slavonic countries. The influence of the *Haggadah*, a Jewish collection of tales and parables, on mediaeval and modern European fiction has been very great. From literature these stories were passed on to the people, and after being modified went again into literature, to the people, and so on, assuming in this process of alternation between literature and folklore the character of national truth and individual unity which gives many of them their great poetic quality. The very fact that a work can sustain the interest of a wide variety of peoples living in distant lands for more than a thousand years indicates its great intrinsic merit.

It was, however, in 1859 that the first direct translation of the Sanskrit *Pancatantra* was made in a European language by the German scholar Benfey. In 1952 the *Pancatantra* was newly translated into German by Alsdorf. Although available in English in several editions for centuries, it was not directly translated from the Sanskrit into English until 1924 by Stanley Rice who entitled his work *Ancient Fables and Stories*. A year later, Arthur W. Ryder also translated the *Pancatantra*.

The most important of all the later adaptations of the *Pancatantra* is the *Hitopadesa* (Salutary Advice) which, owing to its excellent literary merit, is one of the most popular and best known Sanskrit works in Europe. Containing twenty-five of the *Pancatantra's* stories, it is in fact a new work. Its authorship is uncertain as well as the date of its compilation. Probably composed in Bengal somewhere between 1000 and 1300, it contains seventeen stories which are not found in any of the recensions of the *Pancatantra*.[24] Besides Indian languages it has been repeatedly translated into European languages. It was in 1861 that Sir

Edwin Arnold, the celebrated poet of *The Light of Asia,* translated the *Hitopadesa* from Sanskrit to English.

Apart from these literary channels, individual Indian tales must have reached Europe through Arab merchants, travellers, and Gypsies. Somewhat similar to the story-tellers in rural communities of India, Gypsy story-tellers all over the world take their recitals very seriously, and firmly adhere to a certain form, consisting of definite openings, links, and tags as common and stereotyped as in India. However story-telling in most societies tends to conform to a set pattern.

One of the most remarkable examples of the migration of Indian tales is the acceptance of the Buddha as a Christian saint. During the eighth century, a Christian, St. John of Damascus, was living at the court of Caliph Al Mansur, during whose reign the Arabic version of the *Pancatantra* was prepared. John wrote a story of *Barlaam and Josaphat* in Greek as an exposition of Christian doctrines and theology, enlivening it by fables and parables. The Christian clergy did not like it because it was a religious novel. Nevertheless, it became immensely popular and was translated into numerous languages. As early as 1204 it was even translated into Icelandic. The major theme is accompanied by a body of fables and parables mostly of Indian origin. Although the Barlaam story is not a direct translation of any Indian original it is in fact, the story of the Great Renunciation of the Buddha. Recent researches suggest that the Greek version of St. John had originated from *Balavariani,* a Georgian version of the Buddha story. *Balavariani,* in its turn, was a derivation from an Arabic version.[25] In the sixteenth century Josaphat was made a saint both in the Greek Orthodox and Roman Catholic Churches. That the founder of an "atheistic" Asian religion should have been transformed into a Christian saint is, indeed, an amazing episode in religious history. In spite of striking similarities between the careers of the Buddha and Josaphat, it was only in the last century that the Buddhist origin of this Christian cult was realized.

Throughout mediaeval Christendom, *Barlaam and Josaphat* was accepted as an exposition of the ideals of Christian monasticism and asceticism. The churches celebrated the festival days associated with the Indian hermit Barlaam and his royal pupil Prince Josaphat with appropriate solemnity, and "their relics were invested with exceptional healing power." In the literary world too, the influence of the Barlaam story was deep and lasting. It inspired outstanding writers such as Guv de Cambrai, Rudolf Von Ems, Lope de Vega, Leo Tolstoy, and Shakespeare, who borrowed from it the story of the Caskets.[26]

The introduction of delightful Indian tales into mediaeval Europe at a time when asceticism was strong there is of considerable significance. The worldliness and sensuality of the Indian fables must have helped to bring European literature back to its natural course. Hence, almost immediately after their arrival in Europe, Indian fables appeared in Giovanni Boccaccio's (1313-1375) *Decamcron* and Don Juan Manuel's *Conde Lucanor,* unrivalled examples of mediaeval prose. The *Decameron* is an extraordinary work of literary art, containing witty and amusing tales of adventure and the love of people of every class and character. Its influence on European literature has been incalculable, especially on Italian fiction. Whether Boccaccio was aware of it or not, many of his tales, which he either heard in Naples or collected from other works such as the *Gesta Romanorum,* were of Indian origin.

Other popular European storybooks such as the fourteenth century *Gesta Romanorum,* whose authorship is uncertain; Chaucer's (*ca.* 1340–1400) *Canterbury Tales*; La Fontaine's *Fables;* St. Rapola's *Märchen;* and Grimm's *Tales* include fables of Indian origin. For instance, "The Passion of St. Eustace and his Companions" included in the *Gesta Romanorum* (Tale CX) has its origin in the Jataka tale *Mahasutasoma* (No. 537). The Indian fables became known in Europe as the *Fables of Bidpai* (Pilpay), because in the translation one of the wicked kings is reclaimed to virtue by a Brahman sage, Bidpai. La Fontaine in the second edition of *Fables,* published in 1678, expressly confessed his indebtedness to Indian tradition. In the Preface he says: "It is not necessary that I should say whence I have taken the subjects of these new fables. I shall only say, from a sense of gratitude that I owe the largest portion of them to Pilpay the Indian sage."[27]. The story of the ebony horse in Chaucer's "Squires' Tale" came from India via Persia, Egypt, and Spain to France (*Le Cheval de Fust)* and thence to Chaucer's ears. The theme of the three caskets and of the pound of flesh in the *Merchant of Venice* are of Buddhist origin, and stories derived from the *Pancatantra*—the "Gullible Husband" and the "Butler and the Blinded Brahman"—were adapted by Boccaccio. Many of the inmensely popular tales found in Hans Christian Andersen's fairy tales, such as the "Magic Mirror," the "Seven-leagued Boots," "Jack and the Beanstalk ," and the "Purse of Fortunatus," have been traced to Indian sources. Chaucer's "Pardoner's Tale" is an adaptation of a story in the *Vedabbha Jataka* (No. 48) or of the ploughshares eaten by mice in the *Kula Vanija Jataka* (No. 218). The story "The Three Fastidious Brahmans" found its way to Siberia and Lapland through Central Asia, and from there to Jutland, where Hans Christian Andersen wrote his "Princess on the Pea." The *Jungle Books* of Kipling are a revival of the beast fables. "The Transposed Heads" from the *Brihat Kathasaritsagara* inspired Thomas Mann to write a delighful story *Die Vertauschten Kopfe.*

One of the most popular fairy tales in Europe is the romantic story of "Beauty and the Beast." It is found in its numerous variations in practically every country of the world. For centuries children have sympathized with its amiable heroine. It first appeared in Europe in 1740 in Madame de Villeneuve's *Contes Marines.* Ralston has examined in detail its numerous variants, compared their similarities, and has demonstrated it to be of Indian origin.[28] According to Max Müller, the "Story of the Master Thief," the complex legend of *Rhampsinitos* as reproduced in *Gesta Romanorum,* appears to be an adaptation of a story in *Hitopadesa.* The Sanskrit tale is that of a Brahman who, upon being told by three thieves in succession that the goat he was carrying was in fact a dog, throws away his load for the thieves to pick. The essence of the story is that a man will believe almost anything if three people, seemingly unconnected with each other, repeat the same thing. The story of the "Judgement of Solomon" may be one of the earliest examples of Indian fable migration and is based on a story in the *Maha Ummagga Jataka* (No. 546). In the Indian story, the real mother lets the child go at once when he cries upon being pulled apart by the two claimant mothers. The story of the "Dog and the Sparrow" in Grimm's collection is remarkably close in details to the story of "The Nautch-Girl and the Parrot," in the *Baital Pachisi.* In both, a bird vows to bring about the ruin of a human being; in both, the bird helps avenge unjust injury; and in both, the guilty come to grief in consequence of their own voluntary acts. Such a series of events is not likely to have been imagined independently by different tale-tellers in almost identical forms, and one is inclined to accept the chronological influence of the stories. Numerous Jatakas, such as *Virocana Jataka* (No. 143), *Jambu Khadaka Jataka* (No. 294), *Dipi Jataka* (No. 426), have parallels in such well-known fables as "The Ass in the Lion's Skin," "The Fox and the Crow," and "The Wolf and the Lamb." The Russian popular story "The Friend," like other stories about evil spirits, has been traced to Indian sources. Marusia's demon lover is akin to the Arabian ghoul or the Rakshasa of Indian mythology, as described in the Arabic story of Sidi Noman and the Indian story of Asokadatta and Vijayadatta in the fifth book of the *Kathasaritsagara.* Another Russian story, the "Fox-Waier," which is a variant of "Jack and the Beanstalk" in which a fox is described as wailing, is said to be of Indian origin. For de Gubernatis points out that such "howling" is more in keeping with the nature of the Eastern jackal than with that of its Western counter-part, the fox.[29] The Russian story of Norka corresponds to an Indian one. Again, the story *Schastie and Neschastie* (Luck and Bad-luck) is a variant of the story of Vira-Vara found in the *Hitopadesa* and of a similar one in the *Pancatantra.*

How stories undergo change during the course of migration is illustrated by Max Müller with *La Laitiere et le Pot au Lait* from La Fontaine's *Fables.*[30] Few stories have travelled through so many translations. A milkmaid, Perrette, carrying a pail of milk on her head to market, indulges in daydreams. From the proceeds of the sale of the milk she will buy eggs, and then from the profits made on the eggs will buy chickens, and so on. At the prospect of her approaching wealth she suddenly gives a jump of joy, thereby dropping her pail of milk. Her milk is spilt and her riches are gone. In the original from the *Pancatantra,*[31] Svabhava Kripana (a born miser), a Brahman, having filled his bowl with rice hangs it near his bed and dreams of the profits he will make in time of famine from his hoarded rice, buying goats and cows, marrying a rich girl, and living in luxury. Imitating the ways of the rich, he dreams himself attempting to assert authority over his family, and he kicks the bowl over. The moral of this Indian story, that "he who makes foolish plans for the future will be white all over," became transformed through La Fontaine's adaptation of it, into what is a popular proverb in English—"don't count your chickens before they are hatched."

Again, the well-known Welsh story of Llewellyn's dog Gelert, as told in William R. Spencer's ballad, "Bedd Gellert," is the Welsh transformation of the *Pancatantra* story[32] of the Brahman who, having left a mongoose to guard his child in a cradle during his absence, returns and finds the mongoose with its mouth covered with blood. Assuming that the mongoose had bitten the child, he kills it at once. Later he discovers a dead cobra near the child and is filled with great remorse. In the Welsh version, the mongoose and the snake are altered to a dog and a wolf. The idea of killing hastily a faithful animal under such circumstances has occurred independently to different peoples in distant lands, but in this case, scholars have been able to trace back the successive stages of transformation of the story from the *Pancatantra* version to the Welsh version.[33]

The story of the fox who succeeds in stealing the young magpies originated in the *Pancatantra,* and was later incorporated in the Reynard cycle and in the work of Hans Sachs. Along with this artistic tale, and undoubtedly influenced by it, there developed a folktale, well known in northern and eastern Europe, in which the fox threatens to push down the tree in which the magpie has its young. The crow gives good advice to the magpies and saves them. The fox avenges himself by playing dead and catching the crow. The action in the latter part of the tale is the opposite of that in the literary fable.

Another tale which appeared first in the Jatakas and then spread widely is the story of the tar baby, the essential point of which is that the trickster, generally a rabbit, is caught by a tar baby, some kind of sticky image. Often the rabbit's enemies dwell upon how he could be punished. Very ingeniously, the rabbit pretends to agree to various kinds of punishment suggested, begging not to be thrown into the brier patch. His enemies, misled into thinking that it would do him most injury, throw him into the briers and the rabbit escapes. This tale of the tar baby was studied very thoroughly by A. M. Espinosa in more than one hundred and fifty versions. Later he supplemented the original number by an additional one hundred and fifteen. It seems this story reached the Negroes and Indians of America through several routes. It came from India to Africa, where it is very popular and where it underwent some characteristic modifications before being carried, presumably by slaves, to America. Another route lay through Europe to Spain and then to

American colonies. Yet, it could have travelled across the Pacific many centuries earlier.

Before any overall assessment of the Indian inspiration of European beast fables is made, it should be pointed out that the literary fable collections from India are only one of four principal sources upon which Western tradition appears to have drawn. The other three are Aesop's fables, the mediaeval literary animal tales brought together in the cycle of Reynard the Fox, and the purely oral tradition, a very important part of which was developed in Russia and the countries of east Europe. The interrelation of all these influences is extremely complicated, and the writing of the history of a particular animal tale extraordinarily difficult.

India's influence on the mediaeval fables is not seriously questioned and fable migration during the Middle Ages can be traced through the translations of Indian tales. But when parallels and identities are noted in the ancient tales, and where there is no concrete evidence of borrowing other than through human contact, analysis of the historicity of oral tradition has to rely to some extent on conjecture, which no matter how valid is frequently disputed.[34]

Parallels and similarities between Greek and Indian fables are quite obvious, and a number of scholars have carefully analyzed both their historical roots and internal structure. Since the beginning of scholarly interest in fable migration in the middle of the nineteenth century, arguments have been sharply divided on the question of the historical relationship between the so-called Greek *Aesop's Fables* and Indian fables. Although the debate is somewhat subdued at present, opinion is no less divided. As far as the antiquity of the fable itself is concerned, the case for India is unassailable. The dispute is over the priority of the beast fable.

The argument favouring the Greek origin of the beast fable is based almost entirely on chronology, and the main confusion arises because Indian chronology is not firmly fixed. Disputes concerning the dates of major Indian works, although considerably narrowed, remain unresolved. Max Müller held the opinion that in almost every case of parallelism, the borrowing was done by the Greeks. Amongst the many scholars who shared this view were Otto Keller and Johannes Hertel. Against them, Theodor Benfey, who regarded India as the home of all folktales, held the view that India had borrowed animal fables from the Greeks, although he also stressed the existence of an independent Indian tradition in this respect. Another Sanskrit scholar, A. Weber, first subscribed to the theory of Indian origin but later reversed his opinion. A. Wagener (*Essai Sur La rapports qui existent entre les apologues de Inde et apologues de la Grece*) shared Weber's former view that in almost every case the Greeks were the borrowers. Weber's latter view was vigorously opposed by Keller in his work *The History of the Greek Fable* (1862). He fully believed in the Indian origin of the fables and that they were transmitted to Greece through an ancient Assyrian connective link.

The Greek fables belonging to different dates were collected in *Aesop's Fables* in the third century by Valerius Babrius, a Hellenized Roman who, in his Preface, refers to two sources for his material: Aesop for the Hellenic fable and Kybises for the Lybian fable. This is the oldest non-Indian collection of fables available, although Demetrius reputedly made a collection in Athens in 300 B.C. Three-quarters of the fables are about animals, and the rest deal with planets, natural elements, such as the sea, rivers, and the sun, and a few with gods and men. The work was soon translated from its original Greek and Latin versions into a variety of European languages. It is said that a French collection appeared in the tenth century, followed by many others and culminating in the seventeenth century in La Fontaine's *Fables*. Evidently, not all of the stories are of Greek origin—although some certainly must be. The collection comprises the *Life of Aesop;* four books derived from the *Romulus,* a collection of the mediaeval prose renderings of Phaedrus, a Greek freedman of Augustus in the first century; a selection of the *Fables* of Avian; and some fables from other sources. The bulk of the stories are the renderings of Phaedrus, who refers not only to Aesop but also to Anacharsis the Scythian, a possible source of Indian influence.[35]

Jacobs has suggested that Babrius' collection, which ran to about one hundred fables, was derived directly or indirectly from a Sinhalese embassy which came to Rome in 52. It is suggested that the *Life of Aesop* itself was modelled on the Persian or Babylonian "Story of Ahiqar," which Benfey has "identified with a well-known Indian type."[36] Indeed, the historicity of Aesop is doubtful, although Herodotus mentions him as a maker of stories who lived in the sixth century B.C. and who was the slave of a Samian citizen called Iadmon. Considering Herodotus' undeveloped sense of history, his uncritical reliance on oral tradition, and his gift of imagination, his testimony must be accepted with caution. Later writers also refer to Aesop but there are inconsistencies in their accounts.

However, Aesop's historical existence is immaterial; his name was certainly common in fifth century B.C. Greece as the author of fables, whilst the earliest Indian fables on record date back to the upanishadic period—the *Chandogya Upanishad*—and the tradition may have been much older.

Those who assert the priority of the Greek fable maintain that the Indian fable cannot be older than the fourth or fifth century B.C. This date is based on the assumption that Indian folktales and the *Pancatantra* are of Buddhist origin, and that the Buddhist Jatakas, another source of Indian fables, were composed after the Buddha. There are several flaws in this argument and its assumptions. The Buddha, accepting the conservative estimate, was born about a century before Herodotus who was supposedly born between 490 and 480 B.C. Hence, it is not unlikely that the tradition of Buddhist birth stories had become quite powerful in India before the time Aesop began his compositions. Jataka legends occur even in the canonical *Pitakas* and it is now generally accepted that the *Sutta* and *Vinaya Pitakas* containing Jataka tales are at least older than the Council of Vaisali (*ca.* 380 B.C.). This conclusion is confirmed by the bas-reliefs depicting scenes from the Jatakas in the Stupas of Sanchi, Amaravati, and especially of Bharhut, where the titles of several Jatakas are clearly inscribed. If there were a collection in existence in the fourth century B.C., the oral tradition upon which it was inevitably based must have been considerably older.

Most of the tales in the Jatakas open with "once upon a time when Brahmadatta was reigning in Banaras"; the previous incarnation of the Buddha was in the reign of Brahmadatta's son Kashyapa. "It is therefore possible, that a separate collection of beast-fables existed, connected with this Kashyapa, which was incorporated in the *Jatakas* assuming him to be a pre-incarnation of the Buddha."[37]

More important, however, are the flaws in the assumption that the tradition of folklore in India is of Buddhist origin. Fables, as mentioned above, had been found in vedic literature which by even the most conservative chronological standards predates Aesop by at least five centuries. The most dominant form in Aesop, that of the beast fable, is recorded in the Upanishads, definitely pre-Buddhist and pre-Homeric.

The fact that the Jataka tales are Buddhist does not by itself prove that the folklore tradition behind them is also Buddhist. Moreover, there is definite evidence that the Jatakas are related to pre-Buddhist Indian works. R. P. Mehta wrote an account of pre-Buddhist India in 1939 mainly from the Jatakas. He has also shown the pre-Buddhist ancestry of the Jatakas, which, without the idea of the Bodhisattva, originally consisted of a verse or verses and a prose narration embodying a folktale, and were generally intended to impart a moral.[38] That the Jatakas have a non-Buddhist Indian ancestry has been suggested by other scholars too, such as Franke, who points to the parallels between the *Mahabharata* and the Jatakas and suggests that the common tales in these two works are not the outcome of direct borrowing but are connected through some other common source.[39] If the Buddhist tales themselves are of pre-Buddhist origin, then the argument that the stories collected in the *Pancatantra* were originally Buddhist tales and as such belong to a later period is invalid. Yet, it may be observed that although Buddhism certainly influenced many tales in the *Pancatantra,* and that this fact led Benfey to conclude that the Indian fables were of Buddhist origin, it is now certain that the work originated from Hindu sources and later was revised by Buddhist and Jain editors. Hertel proved quite effectively that in its earlier form the *Pancatantra* was purely a Hindu work. Macdonnel endorsed Hertel's opinion that there could be no doubt that, in the style of the *Tantrakhyayika,* it was one of the earliest products of the artificial literature of India. "The general atmosphere is that of Brahmanism, while no relation to Buddhism can be found in the book. The view once rather widely held that the *Pancatantra* was of Buddhist origin must therefore be rejected."[40] Hertel's work did not quite solve the problem of the comparative antiquity of the Indian and the Greek fable, although he maintained that the *Pancatantra* was written down in the second century B.C. but that the actual stories were probably much older. Furthermore, he insisted that the Indian fables were original, because the use of fables to give instruction in politics was essentially Indian.

Indeed, apart from the historical evidence, the literary evidence also leans to the Indian side. The fables have had too luxuriant a growth in Indian literature to admit the theory of borrowed origins without more substantial evidence. No other literature can vie with Sanskrit in the richness of fables and stories when we consider the Jatakas, Buddhaghosa's *Dhammapada Commentary*, the *Pancatantra*, and the *Hitopadesa.* In Greek literature before Aesop only eight complete fables are known, with a dozen others merely referred to, including "The Ass's Heart," "The Countryman and the Snake," "The Dog and the Shadow"—all of which can be traced to India. When one remembers also that many of the stories in the *Arabian Nights* are of Hindu origin, it is not easy to accept the view that the Indian tales could have a Greek source. The Indian mentality was particularly favourable to the growth of fables, animal stories, and fairy tales, because of the Indian belief in transmigration, which effaces the difference between the human and the animal worlds. Indians are extremely kind to animals for they believe in their independent existence, and without such sympathetic treatment it seems unlikely that the beast fable could have been written.

In supporting the theory of Indian origin, Keller pointed out that the relation existing between the fox and the lion has no real basis in the nature of the two animals, whereas the jackal does relate to the lion as portrayed in Indian fable. Weber, who later advanced the theory of a Semitic origin for the Greek fable, contended that the jackal existed in the land of the Semites, and that the Greeks changed the jackal to a fox, and when the Indians took over the story they changed the fox back to a jackal.[41] This is a plausible explanation, but in the context of all the evidence its efficacy is much reduced. That the migration of fables was originally from East to West, and not vice versa, is clearly illustrated by the fact that the animals and birds who play the leading parts—the lion, the jackal, the elephant, the peacock, the tiger, the monkey, and the crocodile—abound in Indian jungles and rivers, but not in Greece. It is not possible to read Indian literature without being constantly impressed by the sense of the forest.

Evidence in the Talmudic-midrashic literature and the parallels between Indian, Jewish, and Greek fables and parables also lend weight to the theory of the early westward migration of the fable from India to

Greece. The parable of the blind and the lame, for instance, which is so popular in Jewish literature, and which is most likely of Indian origin, was known to the Greeks of the fourth century B.C. It is possible that the Palestinian writers got it directly from India, but it is more likely that it came from the Greeks or Hellenistic Jews in the second century A.D. Again, the legend about David's harpstrings has a parallel not only in Indian folklore in the *Pancatantra,* but also in the Greek legend of Aeslus' harp. The description of the world as a wheel frequently found in rabbinic writings could have been borrowed from India through the Greeks; although in rabbinic literature it is used as a metaphor, whilst in India it is associated with the dominant philosophical concept—transmigration. In *Midrash Rabba,* a commentary on the Pentateuch (*Five Rolls*), Indian fables are found and appear to have been taken directly from India, because they have Indian features but not Greek. For example, the Jewish story of the bird who has built a nest on the sea shore only to find it threatened by the waves and who tries to bail out the water with its beak, but is rebuked by another bird, has no parallel in Aesop, but is similar to the *Kaka Jataka* (No. 146). It is also possible that the *Pancatantra* fable in which the mouse, transformed into a girl by Yajnavalkya, declines in succession to marry the sun, the clouds, the wind, and the mountain could have formed the basis of the famous Abraham legend in which Abraham observes that one element subdues another: fire is extinguished by water, and clouds are dispersed by wind.

The *Pancatantra* is distinguished from the Greek *Fables* of Babrius by its purpose. In the guise of witty fables, the *Pancatantra* teaches the lessons embodied in such famous works of polity as Kautilya's *Arthasastra.* The technique of moralizing the various stories in pointed memorial passages, not general maxims but special labels to distinguish the points of individual fables, is novel and interesting, and the essential nature of the stanzas is gnomic or recapitulatory rather than dramatic or interlocutory. A great deal of floating gnomic literature in Sanskrit must have existed prior to this, paving the way for these passages of didactic wisdom. The fact that the *Pancatantra* is a *Nitisastra,* the book of niti and that the Greeks had no equivalent term, plus the fact that the purpose of political instruction was essentially Indian and not Greek, would further endorse the originality of the *Pancatantra.* Wherever the introduction of the fable is traced, it is almost invariably associated with political applications. Rabbi Joshua ben Hananiah applied the fable of "The Wolf and the Crane" to prevent a revolution of the Jews against Romans. Krylor and his followers in Russia made use of the fable to reflect upon the bureaucracy; and when Aesop was first translated into Chinese, the officials soon suppressed the edition because they considered the fables to be directed against them.[42]

Whilst the relation between the mass of *Aesop's Fables* and the *Pancatantra* stories cannot be demonstrated, in some cases there is plausible evidence of borrowing. Edgerton has recently analyzed two tales which seem certainly to have been borrowed from India: "Ass in Panther's Skin" and "Ass Without Heart and Ears" of *Pancatantra* Book III and Book IV respectively.[43] However, even if the priority of the Indian fable is conceded, it does not explain the existence of a vast number of Greek fables which have no parallel in Indian literature. No one could seriously suggest that all Greek fables have been borrowed from India. Clearly, both countries had an independent tradition of fables and it is likely that the fable as a type did not arise exclusively in either India or Greece, but that some migration of fables occurred when communication between the two countries arose.

SANGITA, THE INDIAN tradition of music, is as old as Indian contacts with the Western world, and it has graduated through various strata of evolution: primitive, prehistoric, vedic, classical, mediaeval, and modern. It has travelled from temples and courts to modern festivals and concert halls, imbibing the spirit of Indian culture, and retaining a clearly recognizable continuity of tradition. Whilst the words of songs have vaned and altered from time to time, many of the musical themes are essentially ancient.

Sangita, which originally meant drama, music and dance, was closely associated with religion and philosophy. At first it was inextricably interwoven with the ritualistic and devotional side of religious life. The recital and chant of mantras has been an essential element of vedic ritual throughout the centuries. According to Indian philosophy, the ultimate goal of human existence is moksha, liberation of the atman from the life-cycle, or spiritual enlightment; and *nadopasana* (literally, the worship of sound) is taught as an important means for reaching this goal. The highest musical experience is ananda, the "divine bliss." This devotional approach to music is a significant feature of Indian culture.

The origin of Indian music is enshrined in beautiful tales and legends. It is a common Hindu practice to attribute the beginning of a branch of learning to a divine origin through the agency of a rishi. Siva, also called Nataraja, is supposed to be the creator of Sangita, and his mystic dance symbolizes the rhythmic motion of the universe.[44] He transmitted his knowledge of cosmic dance to the rishi Bharata, through one of his *ganas,* Tandu. The dance was called *tandava* and Bharata thus became the first teacher of music to men, and even to *apsaras,* the heavenly dancers. Similarly, the rishi Narada, who is depicted as endlessly moving about the universe playing on his *vina* (lute) and singing, is believed to be another primeval teacher of music.

The Indian musical tradition can be traced to pre-vedic times in the Indus Valley civilization. From the excavations at Mohenjo-daro and Harappa, musical instruments such as crude flutes, vinas with seven strings, drums, and a bronze statue of a dancing girl, have been found. During the vedic period a wide variety of musical instruments—wind, string, and percussion—were in use. The goddess of music, Sarasvati, who is also the goddess of learning, is portrayed as seated on a white lotus playing the vina.

The ancient Hindus were familiar with the theory of sound (*Gandharva Veda*), and its metaphysics and physics. The hymns of the *Rig Veda* contain the earliest examples of words set to music, and by the time of the *Sama Veda* a complicated system of chanting had been developed. By the time of the *Yajur Veda,* a variety of professional musicians had appeared, such as lute players, drummers, flute players, and conch blowers. Buddhist texts also testify to the prevalence of Sangita, both religious and secular, in early India. Music in India, however, reached its zenith during the Gupta period, the classical age of Indian art and literature.

Indian music is based upon a system of *ragas* and is improvised or composed at the moment of performance. The notes which are to convey certain definite emotions or ideas are selected with extreme care from the twenty-five intervals of the *sruti* scale and then grouped to form a raga, a mode or a melodic structure of a tune. It is upon this basic structure that a musician or singer improvises according to his feeling at the time. Structural melody is the most fundamental characteristic of Indian music.

Every classical Indian tune must be in a particular raga or *ragini;* the latter term, the feminine of raga, implies an abridged or modified raga. The word raga is derived from a Sanskrit root, *ranj* or *raj,* literally meaning to colour but figuratively meaning to tinge with emotion. The essential feature of a raga is its power to evoke emotion. The term has no equivalent in Western music, although the Arabic *maqam iqa* corresponds to it. Oversimplified, the concept of raga is to connect musical ideas in such a way as to form a continuous whole based on emotional impact. There are, however, mixed ragas combined in a continuous whole of contrasting moods. Technically, a raga is defined as "essentially a scale with a tonic and two axial notes," although it has additional characteristics.

The word raga appears in Bharata's *Natyasastra,* and a similar concept did exist at the time, but it was Matanga (fifth-seventh century) who first defined raga in a technical sense as "that kind of sound composition, consisting of melodic movements, which has the effect of colouring the hearts of men." This definition remains valid today. Before the evolution of the raga concept in Bharata's time, *jati* tunes with their fixed, narrow musical outlines constituted the mainstay of Indian music. These were only simple melodic patterns without any scope for further elaboration. It was out of these jati tunes that a more comprehensive and imaginative form was evolved by separating their musical contents and freeing them from words and metres.

Indeed, a raga is basically a feeling, the expression of which has come to be associated with certain notes and twists of melody. A musician may compose in the same raga an indefinite number of times, and the music can be considerably different each time. Although a raga is inexhaustible, it can be recognized in the first few notes, because the feelings produced by the musician's execution of these notes are intensely strong. The effect of Indian music is cumulative rather than dramatic. As the musician develops his discourse in his raga, it eventually colours all the thoughts and feelings of the listeners. Clearly, the longer a musician can dwell on and extend the theme with artistic intensity the greater the impact on the audience.

Unlike Western music, which from the mid-eighteenth century constantly changes and contrasts its moods, Indian music, as well as Arabic and Iranian, always centres in developing and exalting one particular emotion. The musician, if he is sufficiently skilled, can "lead his audience through the magic of sound to a depth and intensity of feeling undreamt of in other musical systems."[45] Indian music is essentially impersonal, reflecting "an emotion and an experience which are deeper and wider and older than the emotion or wisdom of any single individual. Its sorrow is without tears, its joy without exultation and it is passionate without any loss of serenity. It is in the deepest sense of the word all-human."[46] It is an art nearest to life; in fact, W. B. Yeats called Indian music "not an art, but life itself," although its theory is elaborate and technique difficult.

The possible number of ragas is very large, but the majority of musical systems recognize seventy-two (thirty-six *janaka* or fundamental, thirty six *janya* or secondary). New ragas, however, are being invented constantly, as they have always been, and a few of them will live to join the classical series. Many of the established ragas change slowly, since they embody the modes of feeling meaningful at a particular time. It is for this reason that it is impossible to say in advance what an Indian musician will play, because the selection of raga is contingent upon his feelings at the precise moment of performance.

Indian music recognizes seven main and two secondary notes or *svaras.* Representing definite intervals, they form the basic or *suddha* scale. They can be raised or lowered to form other scales, known in their altered form as *vikrita,* The chanting of the *Sama Veda* employed three to four musical intervals, the earliest example of the Indian tetrachord, which eventually developed into a full musical scale. From vaguely defined musical intervals to a definite tetrachord and then to a full octave of seven suddha and five vikrita was a long, continuous, and scientific process. For instance, Bharata's *Natyasastra,* the earliest surviving work on Indian aesthetics variously dated between the second century B.C. and the fourth century A.D., in its detailed exposition of Indian musical theory, refers to only two vikrita notes, *antara* and *kakali.* But in the *Sangita Ratnakara,* an encyclopaedia of Indian music attributed to Sarngadeva (1210–1247), the number of vikritas is not less than nineteen; *shadja* and *panchama* also have acquired vikritas.[47] It was during the mediaeval period that Ramamatya in the south, and Lochana-kavi in the north in his *Ragatarangini* referred to shadja and panchama as constant notes. Indian music thus came to acquire a full fledged gamut of *mandra, madhya,* and *tar saptak.*

The scale as it exists today has great possibilities for musical formations, and it has a very extensive range included in the microtonal variations. The microtones, the twenty-two srutis, are useful for determining the correct intonation of the notes, their bases, and therefore their scales (gramas). The Indian scale allows the musician to embellish his notes, which he always endeavours to do, because grace plays the part in Indian music that harmony does in European music.

Whilst Indian music represents the most highly evolved and the most complete form of modal music, the musical system adopted by more than one-third of mankind is Western music based on a highly developed system of harmony, implying a combination of simultaneously produced tones. Western music is music without microtones and Indian music is music without harmony. The strongly developed harmonic system of Western music is diametrically opposed in conception and pattern to the melodic Indian system. Harmony is so indispensable a part of Western music today that Europeans find it difficult to conceive of a music based on melody alone. Indians, on the other hand, have been for centuries so steeped in purely melodic traditions that whilst listening to Western music they cannot help looking for a melodic thread underlying the harmonic structures.

The fundamental and most important difference between the European and Indian systems of rhythm is respectively one of multiplication and addition of the numbers two and three. The highly developed *tala,* or rhythmic system with its avoidance of strict metre and its development by the use of an accumulating combination of beat subdivisions, has no parallel in Western music. On the other hand, the Indian system has no exact counterpart to the tone of the tempered system, except for the keynote, of Western music. Consequently, just and tempered intonations are variously conceived which eliminate the possibility of combining the melodic interval theory of the sruti system with the Western modulating, harmonic, arbitrarily tempered theory of intervals. With its tempered basis, larger intervals, and metred rhythms, Western music is more easily comprehended than Indian music, which seems to require a certain musical aptitude and ability to understand its use of microtones, the diversification of the unmetred tala, and the subtle and minutely graded inflection.[48]

Considering the divergence between these two systems, it would be difficult to imagine that one is indebted to the other, even in a small measure, or that there could have been any points of contact between the two. But Western music, as it appears today, is a relatively modern development.

In early times melody was the sole component of Western music as is revealed by the Gregorian chants, which may well be the archetype of Western classical music. One or more male voices used to sing these single threads of notes without accompaniment. Pope Gregory, in the seventh century, revised them into their present form. During the long period between Pythagoras and Bach, who successfully incorporated the Pythagorean comma in *The Well-tempered Clavichord,* Western music, like Indian music, was not modulating and largely free in improvization and ornamentation. Because of Western music's assimilative character and genius for compromise, however, notes in the harmonic series gradually began to dominate it. This made it, on the one hand, increasingly sophisticated and complex, and, on the other, reduced progressively its freedom of elaboration and improvization, subordinating it firmly to the direction of the conductor. And, whilst it has been much poorer modally, melodically, and rhythmically than Indian classical music, it is perhaps that very restriction and constriction that provided the essential compression necessary before polyphonic counterpoint, and finally harmony, offered new and promising avenues for development and expansion.[49]

The real indebtedness of European music is to Greece and Arabia. When, after the fall of Rome, music began to be fashionable again, it was the understanding of the Greek theory and of Byzantine practice, imperfect as it was, which led to the systematization of music in Europe. Later, some Arab influence percolated through the Romance countries. But Arabia, Persia, and the countries of the Greek and Roman world were in contact with India, and it is not unlikely that some Indian influence in this sphere had reached Europe well before the advent of the Gypsies.

The ancient Western world was aware of the existence of a highly developed system of Indian music. According to Curt Sachs, it was the South Indian drum *tambattam* that was known in Babylonia under the name of *timbutu,* and the South Indian *kinnori* shared its name with King David's *kinnor*. Strabo referred to it, pointing out that the Greeks believed that their music, from the triple point of view of melody, rhythm, and instruments, came to them originally from Thrace and Asia.[50] Arrian, the biographer of Alexander, also mentions that the Indians were great lovers of music and dance from earliest times. The Greek writers, who made the whole of Asia, including India, the sacred territory of Dionysos, claimed that the greater part of music was derived from Asia. Thus, one of them, speaking of the lyre, would say that he caused the strings of the Asian cithara to vibrate. Aristotle describes a type of lyre in which strings were fastened to the top and bottom, which is reminiscent of the Indian type of single-stringed *ektantri vina.*

The vina is really neither a lute nor a harp, although it is commonly translated into English as lute. Generally known in its construction as bow-harp, the vina must have originally been developed from the hunting bow, a type of a musical bow, *pinaka,* on which a tightly drawn string was twanged by the finger or struck with a short stick. To increase the resonance a boat-shaped sound box was attached, consisting of a small half-gourd of coconut with a skin table or cover, through which a bamboo stick was passed longitudinally, bearing a string of twisted hair resting on a little wooden bridge placed on the skin table. This was the *ekatari,* or one-stringed lute of India, which soon produced its close relative, the *dvitari* or two-stringed lute. Later, additional strings were inevitably added. Whilst it is possible to trace the passage of the slender form of the fingerboard instrument, *pandoura,* from Egypt to Greece, it was not until they came into contact with the Persians that the Greeks became acquainted with the bow, a fact which may reinforce the view of the Indian origin of the Greek lute.

Although many varieties of the vina have been evolved, it existed in its original form, now extinct, in the vedic and pre-vedic times. This is known from the excavations at Mohenjo-daro and Harappa. There is sufficient evidence that some of these musical instruments were constructed according to the heptatonic, *sampurna,* scale with seven notes. However, in the other contemporary civilizations of Egypt and Mesopotamia, similar instruments have also been found. The vina is often shown in the hands of the musicians on the early Buddhist sculptures at Bhaja, Bharhut, and Sanchi and is still in use in Burma and Assam. In Africa it is used by many Nilotic tribes. A bow-harp, known as an angle-harp, closely resembling the Indian vina can be seen in the mural-paintings at Pompeii.

The two earliest Greek scales, the Mixolydic and the Doric have an affinity to early Indian scales. Some recent British writers, for example the editors *The New Oxford History of Music,* have attempted to exclude Indian influence by making the somewhat strange suggestion that the term "India" meant countries much nearer. Whilst the evidence pointing to the direct influence of India on Greek music is slight, there is enough of it to suggest serious Greek interest in Indian art. In addition, there are parallels between the two systems, which may or may not be connected. It is certainly true that the seven note scale with three octaves was known in India long before the Greeks were familiar with it. Pythagoras' scheme of cycle of the fifth and cycle of the fourth in his system of music is exactly the same as the *sadjapancama* and *sadja-madhyama bhavas* of Bharata. Since Bharata lived several centuries after Pythagoras, it has been suggested that he borrowed the scheme from Pythagoras. At the same time it has been pointed out that Indian music, dating as it does from the early vedic period, is much anterior to Greek music, and that it is not unlikely that Pythagoras may have been indebted to Indian ideas. In almost all other fields of scholarship in which he was interested, a close identity between his and the older Indian theories has already been noted.

Whilst no title of any Sanskrit work on music translated at Baghdad is available, there is no doubt that Indian music influenced Arab music. The well-known Arab writer Jahiz, recording the popularity of Indian music at the Abbasid Court, mentions an Indian instrument known as *kankalah,* which was played with a string stretched on a pumpkin. This instrument would appear to be the *kingar,* which is made with two gourds. Knowledge of Indian music in the Arab world is evidenced by an Arab author from Spain, who refers to a book on Indian tunes and melodies. Many technical terms for Arab music were borrowed from Persia and India. Indian music, too, was influenced in return, incorporating certain

Persio-Arab airs, such as *Yeman* and *Hiji* from Hijaz. At the beginning of their rise to power, the Arabs themselves had hardly any musical system worth noting and mainly practiced the existing systems in the light of Greek theory. Since Indian contact with western Asia had been close and constant, it would appear likely that the Arabic maqam iqa is the Persian version of the Indian melodic rhythmic system, traga tala, which had existed for more than a thousand years before maqam iqa was known.

Yehudi Menuhin is convinced that

> we would find all, or most, strands beginning in India; for only in India have all possible modes been investigated, tabulated, and each assigned a particular place and purpose. Of these many hundreds, some found their way to Greece; others were adopted by nomadic tribes such as the Gypsies; others became the mainstay of Arabic music. However, none of these styles has developed counterpoint and harmony, except the Western-most offshoot (and this is truly our title to greatness and originality), with its incredible emotional impact corresponding so perfectly with the infinite and unpredictable nuances, from the fleeting shadow to the limits of exaltation or despair, or subjective experience. Again, its ability to paint the phenomena of existence, from terror to jubilation, from the waves of the sea to the steel and concrete canyons of a modern metropolis, has never been equalled.[51]

It was during the fifteenth and sixteenth centuries, after the discovery of the direct sea route, that India came to be directly known in Europe. It also happened to be the period of the Renaissance, the advent of the Gypsies in Europe, and of the first flood of progress in Western music. Indian music came to be better known in the West during the eighteenth and nineteenth centuries but a wide appreciation of Indian music in western Europe has yet to articulate and mature.

Western interest in Indian music during the past century has proceeded along two distinct lines: first, a purely academic interest by scholars in the nature of Indian music especially in France, Germany, and Britain; and second, adoption by Western composers of Indian themes. This interest in Indian music was, in fact, a part of a wider interest in Indian culture which had fascinated some European intellectuals after their discovery of Sanskrit's rich heritage.[52]

In 1863 Albrecht Weber published in Berlin a critical study of some of the earliest texts on Indian scales. Later in 1888, Hermann Oldenberg published a book about the hymns of the *Rig Veda,* which included a lengthy chapter dealing with vedic metres. About the same time, Martin Haug's work on the *Sama Veda* appeared giving the particulars of accents and notations. At the turn of the century Ludwig Reimann, in a book about various instruments located in European museums, gave a detailed description of several Indian instruments. Richard Simon published with notations a critical edition of the compositions of Somanatha. He attempted an interpretation of the system of grace notes adopted in the *Ragavibodha.* The French scholars have included J. Grosset and Victor Charles Mahillon and more recently, Alain Danielou.[53] Amongst the English writers, the best known are C. R. Day, who in 1891 published a book on *The Music and the Musical Instrument of Southern India;* Anne Wilson, who wrote a short book on Indian music; Alexander Ellis; Charles Myers; and E. Clements who published his *Study of Indian Music* in 1913. A year later, A. H. Fox-Strangway's famous and profound book *Music of Hindustan* was published, and in 1921 Herbert A. Popley brought out his work *The Music of India.*

With the advance of learning and national consciousness in India, it was inevitable that Indian scholars should write in English on Indian music, aiming their interpretations at Western or Westernized readers. By far the most effective and brilliant exponent of Indian art, including music, was Ananda K. Coomaraswamy, whose writings are as remarkable for their depth of investigation and reflection as for their masterly exposition.

Excluding works which have mainly employed Asian themes in a purely Western idiom to provide for novelty or colour, such as *Lakme* by the French composer Delibes or *Madame Butterfly* by Puccini, there have been a number of Western composers, such as Gustav Holst, Albert Roussel, Oliver Messiaen, Paul Dukas, Vincent d'Indy, and Florent Schmitt, whose interest in Indian music has been serious and artistic. Richard Wagner (1813–1883) was indebted to Indian music, especially for his theory of the "leading motive," *leitmotiv.*[54] He had been influenced by Indian thought, especially Buddhism, and probably was familiar with Asian music through Latin translations and conversations with the German philosopher Schopenhauer on the subject.

Maurice Delage and Albert Roussel consciously embodied the result of Indian inspiration in their work with great skill and success. Albert Roussel (1869–1937) was a French composer who visited India as a young man and spent some time at Bombay, Ellora, Jaipur, and Varanasi. The influence of this visit can be seen in two of his major works, *Evocations* and *Padmavati.* The first is a work in three movements and is inspired by his recollections of the Ellora Caves, Jaipur (or Udaipur?); and Varanasi and the River Ganga. The second work is an opera-ballet in two acts which deals with the story of the legendary Queen of Chittor. The general treatment of the work is in the romantic heroic model of Western opera, but there are many instances, such as rhythms in 5/4 and 7/4, which testify to Roussel's deep interest in the melodic and rhythmic devices of Indian music. One of the songs, sung by Nakamati, is supposed to be based on an Indian melody. Various other melodic passages—modal in character—and their harmonic treatment have also been affected by Indian rhythmic devices. Maurice Delage, known for his study of and admiration for Indian music, incorporated his Indian inspiration in *Quatre Poems Hindous* and *Raga Mallika.* Gustav Holst, who studied Sanskrit seriously, dealt with Indian themes in his fine settings of the *Hymns from the Rig Veda,* the settings of several songs from Kalidasa, and two operas *Sita* and *Savitri,* based on a well-known Indian legend.

Indian music has apparently come to fill a need in Western art, and provide inspiration to Western composers who are looking beyond the Western heritage for fresh stimulus. Not unnaturally they find the highly developed, sophisticated, and complex Indian melodies very attractive. Amongst such composers are Oliver Messiaen, Henry Cowell, Colin McPhee, Alan Hovhannes, and Peggy Glanville-Hicks. Henry Cowell, amongst other works, has written a *Madras Symphony* dedicated to the Music Academy of Madras. Peggy Glanville-Hicks' opera, *The Transposed Heads,* based on a story by Thomas Mann which, in turn, was based on an Indian tale, stimulated an exciting controversy on the validity of its form when it was produced in New York. The composer had reversed the traditional basis of composition, and instead of using melody and harmony as structural assets, with minimal rhythm, she used melody and rhythm as the basic structural elements underscoring the harmony, thus to some extent following the Indian system.

A modern Indian scholar of Western music, Kaikhosru Sorabji, points out that although there has been little understanding of Indian classical music, the rhythm of which is far too subtle and complex "to be transcribed so as to be within the technical and musical capacities of suburban drawing rooms," the attraction and awe of Asian culture, religion, and philosophy is so great for Westerners that Asian themes are accepted with alacrity by many of them. It is, therefore, not so much in the adoption of these themes and in superficial extremes that the influence of Indian music is felt, but rather "in rhythmic intricacy, in richness and efflorescence of elaborate detail, in abundant, intricate arabesque, in melodic lines which, without imitating, suggest by their contours relationship with melodies of Oriental types."[55] There are a number of European musicians who accept Eastern inspiration without making a point of acknowledging it. For example, Claude Debussy did not consciously acknowledge his extra-European inspiration but it is quite clear that without it certain very typical aspects of his art would have remained either undeveloped or underdeveloped, and he could not have produced such masterpieces as *L'Enjant Prodigue, L'Aprés-Midi, La Mer, L' Île Joyeuse,* and *Les Parjums de la Nuit:* "In all these there is a suppleness of rhythm, a richness and delicacy of colouring, and a flexibility of melodic line that shows very plainly their Asiatic affinities and sympathies."[56] Strauss' music-drama *Salome* also clearly shows marks of Asian inspiration.

In recent years, Indian music, like other forms of Indian art, has had a great revival both in India and abroad. Yehudi Menuhin has been mainly responsible for introducing Indian music to contemporary Western audiences. He went to India in 1952 on a concert tour and was immediately captivated by the music. From this time on he has taken every opportunity to write and speak of Indian music. In 1958 after Indian musicians had begun to visit Britain, Lord Harewood travelled widely in India listening to the music. In 1963 he sponsored a large-scale Indian participation at the Edinburgh Festival, and Indian music has now become one of the chief features of this annual festival.

For several years a number of leading Indian musicians have visited Western, as well as Asian, countries. Their performances have gained increasing popularity. Commenting upon the growing popularity of

Indian music in the West during the Edinburgh Festival of 1963, the music correspondent of *The Times* said: "The impact of Indian music is immediate, although like any subtle art it needs a lot of understanding fully to appreciate it. I was once asked to arrange for a famous Indian musician to play at a British university, but the professor of music warned me that the performance should not be long, since the audience was not used to Indian music. After the concert, which was shorter than it need have been, the professor came up with beaming face and said 'But why didn't you tell me it would be so enjoyable?'"[57]

The advent of Indian music in the West has inspired promising young composers to weave the two musics—Indian and Western—into a new syncretic composition. For example, Mr. Peter Feuchtwanger, whose works have recently been gaining increasing recognition in the United States and Europe, has been commissioned by Yehudi Menuhin to compose a work for violin, sitar, tabla, and tambura. Menuhin himself has made a best selling record, "East meets West," in which he plays raga with Ravi Shankar. And strangely enough the emergence of pop music in Europe has led to an increase in the popularity of Indian music in the West. The Beatles, Rolling Stones, Yardbirds, and other groups have created a mounting enthusiasm for Indian music amongst young people by using the sitar in their recordings.

Inspired by Western interest in their music, Asian countries have also begun to organize international musical gatherings. In 1961 there was a major conference in Tokyo which brought together artists from both East and West. Nicholas Nabokov inspired the Tokyo conference and one of the major outcomes of it was the establishment of the International Institute for Comparative Music Studies at Berlin. Two years later, in 1963, the conference was repeated in Israel, although on a somewhat less ambitious scale. Later, Delhi became the venue of an International Festival and the first Commonwealth Arts Festival in 1965. This expanding mutual interest amongst musicians and musicologists of Europe and Asia will no doubt have wide repercussions on both sides.

Although Western interest in Indian music has been serious and continuous, recordings of Indian music are rarely found in Western homes and markets. In contrast, Indians play Western music more frequently and widely, but have made hardly any sustained study of it.

Whilst European research on Indian music is meagre, there is hardly any Indian scholarship on Western music; the works of Sorabji are a rare exception. Yehudi Menuhin believes that Western music has reached a point where there is very little room left for the personal expression of the performer, and it is at this moment particularly ripe for Indian influence, which might be most helpful in

> the flexibility of the tone-row, melodic freedom and invention, including ornamentation; the peculiar technique of uniting melody and pulse of Indian music; the ability to improvise with requisite training and the release of creative energies in the performers; the quality of serenity, a type of unique, exalted and personal expression of union with the infinite; and study of the incredibly complex rhythmic organisation of Indian music. The rhythmic patterns in Indian music are as determined and precise as the patterns of ornamentation, again leaving no margin for the minute ebb and flow of the individual pulse. This is a prime example of unbounded intellectual complexity holding the emotional surge in check.[58]

For a long time the invention of chess was ascribed to various peoples ranging from the Egyptians to the Welsh, and ever since the Arabs transmitted it to Europe more than a thousand years ago, it has been held in great esteem there. It commands an authority which no other board game has ever attained, and has been described as "a philosophy, a contest of mental athletics to which the very young bring an instinctive genius, and the old the distillation of their experience." The complexities of tactics and the almost unending possibilities of manoeuvre have made chess the pastime of the intellectual élite. It began as a war game to be fought between the contesting maharajas, and it was regarded in mediaeval Europe as one of seven knightly accomplishments—a release and pleasant diversion from the monotony and tedium of aristocratic life. Today, its enthusiasts belong to a common fraternity in which all class distinctions are subordinated to the supremacy of the skilled.

At first the Church frowned upon chess, but later St. Thomas Aquinas discovered in it a useful allegory of life, death, and the social structure. The black squares on the chessboard symbolized vice, the white ones virtue, and the game ended in all the pieces being swept off the board into the democracy of death. This imposed spiritual analogy possibly added to the mysterious power of the game, but, as time went on, this alien and mystical character which inhibited chess during the Middle Ages gradually vanished, and once again it assumed the role of a pleasant pastime.

It was after the discovery of Sanskrit by European scholars that the Indian ancestry of chess was realized and acknowledged, although Thomas Hyde, the first writer to deal with non-European games, suggested the Indian theory in 1694 in his *De Ludis Orientalibus*. Towards the end of the eighteenth century, Sir William Jones wrote that chess had been known to Indians in antiquity as *caturanga,* meaning the four wings of the army, which are described in the *Amarakosa* as elephants, horses, chariots, and infantry. One of the early Sanskrit texts, the *Bhavishya Purana,* contains a tale of a prince who lost all his possessions in a game of chess played with dice. Chess must indeed go deep into early Indian history, because it was associated with astronomical symbolism throughout its growth. According to H. J. R. Murray, who published his monumental study *A History of Chess* in 1913, chess descended from an earlier Indian game called *astapada,* played on a board containing 8 × 8 cells.[59] Whilst it is certain that games have travelled from one country to another, gaps in information and changes in names and rules often blur the course of diffusion.

Chaturanga was taken to Persia in the sixth century during the reign of Anushirvan (531–579) where it came to be known as *chatrang,* which according to the Arabic phonetic system became *shatranj.* The earliest reference to chess in Persia is found in the *Karnamak-i-Artakh Shatr-i-Papakan,* written about 600. In the tenth century, the poet Firdusi related a traditional story in his epic poem *Shahnama* of how chess came to Persia through an envoy of the King of Hind. Subsequently, it became known to the Arabs and also to the Byzantine court through the marriage of Khusru Parviz, the grandson of Anushirvan, to the daughter of the Byzantine Emperor Maurice. There are numerous Arabic references to chess. For example, Al Masudi, writing about 950, mentions that chess had existed possibly as long as a thousand years before his generation.

The earlier theory of the Persian origin of chess has now been discarded, because the evidence supporting the Indian theory is overwhelming. The Arabic word shatranj is not only an exact derivation of the Sanskrit chaturanga but is regarded as a foreign word by the Persians and Arabs. Furthermore, *al-fil,* the Arabic name for the bishop, means the elephant, otherwise *alephhind,* the Indian ox. From Persia the Arabs took it to Spain, and from there it spread to the court of Charlemagne about 760. It is also possible the game may have reached France from the Byzantine court for the monarchs of the two courts exchanged diplomatic missions and courtesies, and amongst the presents from the aged Empress Irene to Charlemagne was a chess set in which the two prime ministers (vazirs) had been replaced by two powerful queens. Another theory holds that chess was introduced to Europe during the period of the Crusades, but there is evidence to suggest that chess was known in Italy before the First Crusade.

From India, chaturanga travelled to China and then to Japan. The earliest reference to chess in China is found in Niu Seng-Ju's *Yu Kuai Lu* (Book of Marvels) written at the end of the eighth century. The countries of Southeast Asia learned chess both directly from India and, as in the case of Siam, indirectly through China. Modern Japanese chess is very different from its immediate parent in China, and both differ from European chess, although all share a common ancestry.

Indeed, the earliest recognizable diffusion of games from India is to China, and this is possibly a result of the spread of Buddhism from India to China. During the first millennium A.D., Indian racing games began to reach China. Karl Himly, an authority on the history of Chinese games, on the strength of a passage from the *Hun tsun su,* a work of the Sung period (960–1279), suggests that the Chinese game *k'shu-pu* was invented in western India and spread to China in the time of the Wei Dynasty (220–265). Again, according to *Wei-shu,* k'shu-pu was brought to China in ancient times from Hu country, which at the time meant a country somewhere in the vicinity of India. K'shu-pu is, in fact, the Chinese adaptation of the Indian *chatush pada* (in modern Indian language, *chaupur*). The game apparently had four other successive names in China, *wu-sho* (spear-seizing), *thshan-han* (long row), *po-lo-sai-hi,* and *shwan-liu* (double sixes). The last of these names however, may belong to *nard,* a different game related to the Greek *table,* and which, according to a Persian tradition, was introduced into northern India towards the end of the sixth century by a Persian minister of Anushirvan. Nard is mentioned in the mediaeval Iranian romance, *Chatrang-namak* (probably written between 650 and 850), which also speaks of the introduction of chess into Iran.

However, the ninth century Arab writer, Al Yaqubi, and other early sources refer to nard as an Indian invention to illustrate man's dependence on chance and destiny. The board stands for the year; it has twenty-four points representing the hours of a day. It is divided into two halves of twelve points each, signifying the months in a year. The thirty men (*kilab*) stand for the days in a month. The two dice are day and night, and the sum of opposite faces of the dice is seven for the days of the week.[60] As this symbolism was also known to Byzantine Greeks, it is not conclusive evidence of the Indian origin of nard. But as far as China is concerned, shwan-liu was introduced from India in the seventh century, whilst wei-ki, the oldest and best of the native Chinese games, originated around 1000.[61] Cubical dice (*chhu-phu* or *yu-phy*), although found in ancient Egypt as well as in India, are generally thought to have reached China from India, possibly quite early. The prominence of the number six in the *Book of Changes* is said to have been derived from the six sides of a cubical die.

The Japanese game *sunoroku* (or *sugoroku,* backgammon), which was played at the royal court of the Nara rulers, and which is still a popular game in Japan, may well have originated in India, for it is derived from the Chinese game k'shu-pu, which as stated earlier is known in its original Indian form as *chatush-poda.*

What is perhaps more significant is that the dice used in Japan today —cubes, each six-faced, numbered one to six—have exactly the same form as the dice found amongst the relics of the Indus Valley civilization.[62] The significance of this point becomes greater when it is noted that dice are marked similarly throughout the world from ancient times. But the Indus dice, cubical or tabular and made of pottery, were marked, except in one example from Harappa, not so that the sum of two opposite sides is seven as they are today but rather, with one opposite two, three opposite four and five opposite six.

Indian games appear to have reached as far west as ancient Mexico. Writing in 1881, Edward Tylor, the first important exponent of parallelism in cultural development, pointed out that the ancient and popular Mexican game of *patolli* was very similar to the Indian *pachisi*, and concluded that it must have come from Asia. Pachisi is a very popular game in India with almost all classes of people. Mogul emperors, especially the great Akbar, were very fond of the game and played it with all the regal trimmings on courts made of inlaid marble, the remains of which can still be seen at Agra and elsewhere. Patolli also was popular with the Mexican aristocracy as well as the peasantry. Mexican gamesters would walk about with their patolliztli mat and markers, and the Emperor Montezuma reputedly watched his nobles playing at court. Addicted to gambling, the Mexicans were also passionately fond of another dice game, *tlachtli*.

About seventeen years after Tylor, Stewart Culin showed that even the cosmic meaning of the Mexican game, its relation to the four quarters of the world and to the colours ascribed to them, was essentially the same as in pachisi, particularly in its Burmese variation. Kroeber, who did not find much evidence of contact between India and ancient America, conceded that the mathematical probability of the two games being invented separately, agreeing by chance in so many specific features, was very low. Also, the close correspondence between the rules of the two games does indicate a firm connection.

Pachisi, in fact, is played all over the world, and, as expected, it has acquired certain local characteristics and is called by different names in different countries. However, its Indian ancestry is easily proved. In Burma it is known as *posit*, in Somaliland *bakkis*, in Persia *pachis*, in Arabia *barjis*, and in Spain *parchis*. In Britain it is popularly known as Ludo, a modified version of the Indian pachisi, having been patented and introduced in 1896.[63]

Chapter VII

ROMANIES: LORDS OF THE OPEN COUNTRY

ROMANIES, OR GYPSIES as they are popularly known, had their origin in India. They are the descendants of tribes who left the banks of the Indus, traversed a number of intervening countries over a period of centuries, and arrived in Europe more than five hundred years ago. For a long time they were mistakenly believed to have come from Egypt and the word "gypsy"—a misnomer—is a derivative of Egyptian. Today there are six million or more Gypsies scattered throughout Europe and North and South America.[1] They are found throughout Asia and Africa and there are even isolated bands in Australia and New Zealand. Their love of nature and liberty is unrivalled in history. These gay, colourful, unique, and somewhat mysterious people wander about the world in small groups never demonstrating a definite pattern of movement. Romanticized for their music, dancing, and folklore, they are a people with identity but no nationality, political rights or freedoms, written history, art or science, or any international organization, agency, or movement to plead for them.[2]

Despite their significant contributions to European cultural life over a period of centuries, Europe on the whole has not accepted them with kindness. They have been frequently persecuted throughout the period of their known history. The Nazis alone killed about half a million Gypsies in concentration camps for the sole crime of possessing an irrepressible urge for freedom and an attitude of defiance against any kind of regimentation.[3] The very presence of such a group in their midst made the Nazis uneasy. Other European countries also have a sordid record of Gypsy-persecution. Whatever their faults, the Gypsies did not come into Europe as bandits or as tramps. They have always been skilled in metal work and music and dancing. At worst, Gypsies have been guilty of trivial crimes, such as theft without violence, generally involving items of food and clothing—much less serious crimes than are common occurrences amongst most advanced and modernized communities.

Soon after their arrival in Europe they were characterized as a people who spoke a strange language and practiced sorcery. The peasants were alarmed and the state officials in towns disturbed by their presence. In 1427 the Bishop of Paris excommunicated them and they were driven out of the city. They were blamed elsewhere, as they are even today, for thefts, exactions, and black magic, but above all for being foreigners. The Parliament of Paris ordered their expulsion in 1539. In 1560 the Estates General of Orleans called upon "all those imposters known by the name of Bohemians or Egyptians to leave the Kingdom under penalty of the galleys."[4] The decree was applied with extreme severity, and penalties, ranging from cutting off ears to hanging and "breaking on the wheel," were carried out indiscriminately and expeditiously. There are many other early accounts which refer to similar repressive laws and punishments. No matter how hard it is for us to imagine the dark depths of superstition and fear that prevailed in Europe at the time, the ruthless persecution of Gypsies must invite severe comment.

The period when the Gypsies first appeared in Germany was fraught with extraordinary events: the coming of the Black Death, the quarrels of the three Popes, the burning alive of John Huss, and the Battle of Agincourt. These tragedies, epidemics, and scourges of nature were attributed to Gypsies. The Reichstag held at Speyer in 1489, regarding them as "traitors to Christian countries," ordered their banishment from the Rhineland and the Palatinate. The Prince Elector of Mainz even congratulated himself for having put to death all the male Gypsies in his region, and for flogging and branding their women and children.[5] In the sixteenth century in Bavaria alone, hundreds of peaceable Gypsies, including children, were put to death by torture and fire on charges of witchcraft and communion with spirits. In 1724 in Beyreuth, fifteen

Gypsy women, aged from fifteen to ninety-eight, were hanged in a single day. Two years later, Charles VI ordered the death of all male Gypsies in Austria. In the early eighteenth century, Gypsies were arrested on sight, flogged and branded, and if found again put to death without mercy.

In Spain their persecution was equally harsh. They were banished by royal edict under threat of terrible penalties as early as 1499. Later in Toledo in 1523, and in Madrid in 1528 and 1534, edicts revived this order and threatened the *Gitanos* with the galleys. But many hid in caves and avoided the merciless persecution of Ferdinand, Charles V, and Philip II. The Spanish kings made many laws for what they regarded as thc protection of their subjects from pernicious people. "Perhaps there is no country in which more laws have been framed," wrote George Borrow, "having in view the extinction and suppression of the Gypsy name, race, and manner of life, than Spain."[6] It was during their successive banishments from Spain that many Gypsies temporarily overcame their fear of the sea, sailed for South America, and penetrated into Brazil, Peru, and Chile. Later a somewhat more liberal policy was introduced—they were to be called neo-Castilian—and Gypsies in Spain multiplied with surprising rapidity. They were, however, not permitted to use their own language, Romani, or to wander about the country. This prohibition is still in force and, discriminatory as it appears, it did force many of them to settle down. Since 1873 they have been allowed to do more or less what they please in Spain.

Poland, Sweden, Norway, and Denmark also tried to expel Gypsies from their territories. In Romania they were enslaved and forced to work under inhuman conditions without any wage except a small meal of maize porridge. In addition they were flogged naked, for little or no reason, and iron hooks were fixed in their necks as a punishment and to prevent them from sleeping. There were slave markets where Gypsies were sold by public auction in groups or whole families. It was only in 1852 that slavery ended and their situation improved somewhat.

In Hungary and in Transylvania also, Gypsies were forced into slavery. Under the pretext that the Gypsies had committed heinous crimes, charges never supported by evidence, the authorities imposed unspeakable penalties on them. In 1782 the Hungarians hanged, beheaded, or broke on the wheel forty-one Gypsy men and women. Others were driven by soldiers into dangerous swamps to die by drowning.[7] Yet, in Hungary Gypsies enjoyed, in the midst of slavery, more freedom than anywhere else.

Gypsies were also severely persecuted in Britain and it was infinitely more difficult for them to escape detection there because England has little wilderness to offer as means of escape or protection. They arrived there some time in the middle of the fifteenth century and quickly dispersed throughout the British Isles. (How, with their fear of water, they crossed the North Sea or the English Channel is somewhat of a puzzle.) For a while the Gypsies remained unmolested, but during the reign of Henry VIII severe measures were taken against them. In 1537 Lord Thomas Cromwell, the keeper of the Privy Seal, advocated the wholesale banishment or execution of Gypsies, and a dreadful campaign of persecution was begun. Merely being a Gypsy was esteemed a crime worthy of death, and "the gibbets of England groaned and creaked beneath the weight of Gypsy carcasses, and the miserable survivors were literally obliged to creep into the earth in order to preserve their lives."[8] During the reign of Elizabeth I (1558–1603), who accused the Gypsies, amongst other misdeeds, of hiding priests and emissaries of Rome, even more extreme measures were introduced. In 1563 they were ordered to leave the country within three months under penalty of death. As late as 1882, by an Act of Parliament, all persons purporting to be Gypsies, telling fortunes, wandering abroad, or lodging under tents or carts were to be treated as rogues and vagabonds. Legal discrimination against the Gypsies continued in Britain in varying degrees until the beginning of this century. In 1908 the laws were relaxed and they were given relative freedom and accommodation to settle down to their traditional life and culture. However, a strong prejudice still exists in parts of Britain, and "No Gypsies Served" is a sign openly displayed in the windows of many English village inns today.

In Scotland, after a brief period in the sixteenth century during which they were in favour with the kings, Gypsies were condemned in 1573 as murderers, thieves, and sorcerers, and their execution was sought. The Privy Council of Scotland promulgated a decree giving Gypsies the choice between sedentary work and expulsion. In 1597 an Act of Parliament was passed, which was reaffirmed in 1600, authorizing the government to punish Gypsies along with vagabonds and beggars with penal servitude for life. In 1627 all Gypsies were ordered to be forcibly recruited into the army, and in 1665 they were to be banished to the West Indies, Jamaica, and Barbados. In 1715 nine Scottish Gypsies were transported to Virginia, and they appear to be the first British Gypsies in America, the forerunners of the many thousands now living there. France deported Gypsies to America; Portugal and Spain sent them to Africa and South America. Britain also banished Gypsies to Australia. In fact, deportation appears to have been a common practice, and at one time or another almost every European country deported Gypsies to distant lands.

In Russia, however, Gypsies did not encounter any serious hostility, although life for them must have been harsh in the wintry vastness. They are mentioned as being in Russia since 1500, and there are no records of oppression or persecution under either the Tsarist or Soviet regime. On the contrary, there seems to have been a bond of friendliness between Russians and the Gypsies. Local governments in Russia are known to have made sincere efforts to integrate them into a settled life, although they were not completely successful. Gypsies continued to wander about the country unmolested for some time, although since 1956 they have been prohibited by law from leading a nomadic life. In Russia, Gypsy music and dance have always enjoyed popular, as well as aristocratic, appreciation, and today in Moscow there is a Gypsy theatre, "Romen," and the study of their culture is encouraged.

During the nineteenth century, although generally less persecuted in Europe than before, Gypsies were automatically regarded as criminals. They were accused of kidnapping children, suspected of sorcery, and invariably treated with scant justice. Even today they are looked upon with extreme suspicion, apprehension, and contempt. A stereotyped image of the Gypsies dominates the thinking about them. No people in history have been made to suffer what they have. Suffering is so much a part of their life that a Gypsy proverb designates it as "a badge of honour."[9]

Existing knowledge about Gypsies is hopelessly inadequate and this ignorance has resulted in either unreasonable fear, prejudice, and antagonism, or in the myth of the noble savage. Articles, newspaper reports, or television programs seldom attempt a true representation of their life and history. They are, perhaps, victims of their determined refusal to lead a settled life, believing that those who are prejudiced against them have no understanding or appreciation of their adherence to true liberty. No wonder the Spanish novelist, Miguel de Cervantes, who was familiar with Gypsy life and culture, acclaimed the Gypsies in his *La Gitanilla* as "the Lords of the Universe, of fields, fruits, crops, forests, mountains, of rivers and springs, of the stars and all the elements."

In spite of persecution, hostility, and apathy, the Gypsies could not be exterminated or even subdued for any length of time. They have survived all over the world; have remained the happiest, gayest, and the most light-hearted of people; have achieved a gigantic migration without losing their identity; and represent an exceptional example of a well-defined cultural group. It is almost incredible that the group of over a hundred which first appeared in Germany in 1417 should have not only survived but grown into the millions spread throughout the world today.

If settled peoples hold them in contempt, the Gypsies reciprocate the attitude in equal measure, but they most dislike those amongst themselves who desert the realm of open space. Their stock of abusive epithets, mainly reserved for the semi-settled Gypsies, is quite rich, and they have derogatorily designated non-Gypsies as *gadjo* or *gaujo* (peasant, yokel, bumpkin, or clodhopper). English Gypsies call half-breeds *posh-rat,* and less than half-blood Gypsies and vagrants *didakyai.* Muslim Gypsies of the Balkans call Christian Gypsies *das* (Sanskrit *dasa,* infidel, non-Aryan). Whilst they themselves infiltrate everywhere, they allow little penetration from the outside. They consider themselves superior to all other peoples, unequalled in purity, health, and Wisdom, and zealously guard the purity of their Romany blood. A Gypsy marrying a non-Gypsy is excluded from the Romany community for all time, and children of mixed marriages cannot even call themselves Roms.

A Gypsy on the road knows the taste of real liberty and he regards modern man as little more than a mere cog in a gigantic machine bed to money, convention, and a timetable. Throughout the centuries Gypsies have fought, lied, cheated, and suffered numerous humiliations and penalties to retain their own individuality, language, and cultural identity.

Attempts have been made in the past, and are still being made, to turn Gypsies into useful citizens, to show them the advantages of education and fixed employment, to integrate them in settled societies and to rehabilitate them. Maria Theresa, the Empress of Austria, initiated a movement to integrate Gypsies into European society in 1761. She called them New Hungarians, but her efforts were largely unsuccessful. Later nineteenth-century efforts were somewhat more successful: Archduke Joseph of Prussia set up Gypsy settlements, and Catherine II of Russia gave them crown lands. In Britain Gypsy societies were founded for their reform and education. In central Europe today they receive special encouragement, scholarships for education, and consideration in employment. In a ceremonious procession in Delhi, Nehru led these "followers of Rana Pratap," a liberty loving king of Rajasthan who suffered a homeless existence in preference to submission and a life of comfort and riches, to free allotments of land on the outskirts of the city. But their love for open spaces has been far too deep to be easily uprooted. Or perhaps it is their pride in being different from the rest of mankind and their unwillingness to make concessions that have enabled them to survive both repressive measures and encouragements to incorporate themselves in a community. Their persistent refusal to align themselves with non-Gypsies baffles European sociology just as it humbles non-Gypsy pride. Even today the majority of Gypsies are relentless nomads, although there are some, especially in Britain and eastern and central Europe, who live a partially settled life in villages or suburbs. But they too hasten to take to the road during fine weather.[10]

The genealogy of the Gypsies is highly complex, but they are divided into three principal tribal groups—the *Kalderash*, the *Gitanos*, and the *Manush* (also called the *Sinti*). Outside these major groups there are other Gypsies, as distinct from non-Gypsy nomads, as for example those in Britain who appear to resemble all three in part but none wholly. Charles Duff places the British Gypsies into a fourth category of their own. All these groups are authentic Romanies, and are generally of dark appearance with black hair, white teeth, brown eyes, and supple gait, except the Kalderash, many of whom have fair skin and some even blue eyes and fair hair. The Kalderash, who came westward from eastern Europe and now live mainly in northern and northwestern Europe, and the Manush, who wander about generally in Germany, France, and Italy, consider themselves the oldest and the best; the former even look upon themselves as the only "true" Romanies. The Gitanos, called *Gitanes* in France, are mainly concentrated in Spain and France, with an offshoot called *Ciganos* in Portugal. This differentiation is of Gypsy origin, and each group seeks to project an inflated image of themselves. They speak diverse dialects and rarely intermarry. In spite of the dispersion of their groups and lack of uniformity in many of their customs, all Gypsies regard themselves as one people and are very proud of their race:

> I wouldn't be a noble
> My birth is no disgrace
> I'd rather be a Gypsy,
> The same as all my race.[11]

The basic language of all Gypsies is Romani, although each group inevitably grafted on the foreign idiom, vocabularies, and pronunciation through centuries of living in various countries.[12] Although Gypsies have never had a written language and have retained the tradition of their language by word of mouth over generations, they have kept it relatively pure. The social customs and manners, taboos and superstitions, laws and religious beliefs, and their *patrin* (or *patteran*), although varying from group to group, are fundamentally the same.

Few scholars today doubt that the original home of the Gypsies was India. Whilst the case for their Indian origin is overwhelming, it is not definitely known when they first began to leave India and under what circumstances and on what scale they did, or were compelled to do so. Nor has it been settled exactly where in India they originated, just as it is uncertain that Gypsies were originally a nomadic people. Jan Kochanowski, a Gypsy scholar, has recently suggested that they were not nomads in the beginning.[13] Should this be accepted as historically valid it will substantially affect prevalent ideas of Gypsy history and sociology. Indian history is very indifferent on the subject, and the paucity of relevant material is disconcerting.[14] The Indian aspects of Gypsy history must be extremely fascinating and instructive, but they remain obscure and complex.

Considering that there are many Greek words in the Gypsy language, and that all Gypsies still count in Greek, Verovici is of the opinion that the first exodus of the Gypsies from India happened at the time of Alexander's invasion. On the other hand, Grellmann believed that the Gypsies had been driven out of India by Timur and his savage hordes at the end of the fourteeth century. This view appears to rely partly on a reference to Gypsies made by Arab Shah in a chapter of his biography of Timur, which is a classic in Arabic literature. But this reference describes not only some curious details of Gypsy life in Samarkand, but also their extermination by Timur because the Gypsies were constantly rising in rebellion against him. Since Timur had annihilated the Gypsy population of Samarkand before he invaded Indian territory, the theory that his invasion caused the wandering of the Gypsies must be abandoned. Moreover, this theory is contradicted by the evidence of the existence of Gypsies in Europe before this date.

According to Jan Kochanowski, Gypsies were the original survivors of the army of the famous Chauhan Rajput ruler of Delhi, Prithvi Raj, after its disastrous defeat by the forces of Muhammad Ghori in 1192. They carried out guerilla campaigns against the Ghorid rulers for some time from their mountain resorts and jungle hideouts, but were not victorious and lost most of their men. The remaining few split into three groups, one of which left India through Afghanistan to Europe, founding the modern group of Gypsies, whilst the other two remained in India and mingled with the peasants and artisans.

Another theory holds that the Gypsies came to Europe from India through Persia. The Persian poet, Firdusi, mentions in his *Shah Namad* that about the year 420 the Sassanian King of Persia, Bahram Gur, requested Shankhala, the Maharaja of India, to send him people capable of entertaining his poor subjects whose lives were miserable without music and amusements. Soon Bahram Gur had collected twelve thousand Indian musicians men and women alike, to amuse his people. The Indians were assigned land and given facilities to cultivate it. But the musicians neglected agriculture, consumed the corn seed, and incurred the wrath of the Persian King, who seized their musical instruments and commanded them to roam the country earning their living by singing.

The accuracy of Firdusi's narrative may be coloured with some literary imagination, but his account is supported by the Arab historian, Hamza of Isfahan, who wrote in 940, about half a century earlier than Firdusi. Both writers called these musicians by terms which later came to mean Gypsies. Firdusi uses the ordinary Persian word *Luri,* and Hamza the word *Zott,* which is merely the common Arabic pronunciation of the Indian word *Jat,* and which is also one of the modern Syrian words for Gypsies. It is possible that Firdusi borrowed the episode from Hamza. His account, nevertheless, testifies to the presence of Indian musicians in western Asia from early times. The Arab conquest of Sind in the eighth century may have provided further impetus to Indian artists and entertainers to travel westward.

Charles Leland, who identifies the Gypsies with the Jats of northern India, suggests that they were taken away in large numbers as slaves by Mahmud of Ghazni during his Indian invasions. Mahmud, having later acquired fairer slaves from Persia, released many of his Indian captives, who then wandered westward. This theory, however, does not explain why the prisoners chose to wander westward upon their release rather than return home. An explanation, if the story is true, may perhaps be sought in the caste structure of Hindu society. The released slaves, who by the rigid code of caste may have performed prohibited deeds, would have had little hope of rehabilitating themselves in Hindu society. Disinclined to return, and detached from their natural habitat, they may have opted for the life of freedom without losing their identity.

In Arab chronicles there are frequently references to wandering tribes called Zotts. Evidence is also found of a tribe of roaming cattle breeders, who lived long ago at the mouth of the Indus, and who raised their tents wherever their black water buffaloes could graze. The Arabs tried several times to conquer them, but were driven back each time.

Under Walid (705-715), during whose reign the Arabs landed in Spain, the Zotts agreed to terms of peace but Walid later realized that their loyalty could not be relied upon. In 710 he took a great many of them prisoner and led them to the borders of the Tigris in Kurdistan. Six years later, under Yazid II, still more prisoners were transported to Antioch with their cattle and tents. About a century later, in 820, the Zotts had become so powerful that they defied the Arab power and for fourteen years waged a continuous war against the Arab armies, inflicting heavy losses and capturing a great quantity of booty. It was only after long and costly warfare that the Zotts were subdued by the Arabs under Al Motasim in 834. The Arab commander took about twenty-seven thousand prisoners—men, women, and children—with him to Baghdad and then deported them, first to Khanikin, northeast of Baghdad, and then to Ainzarba and to other places on the northern frontier of Syria.

In 856 the Byzantians, called the "Rums," captured Ainzarba from the Arabs and took the Zotts prisoner. The year 856 is the approximate date of the first appearance of Gypsies in Byzantine territory. That the Byzantians were called Rums and that the Gypsies later called themselves Roms may be significant, or pure coincidence. But the whole episode is too well authenticated and well knit to be lightly dismissed. This evidence indicates that the migration of the Gypsies from India occurred during or before the eighth century, and that in the ninth century Gypsies were living in Lower Mesopotamia. This is supported by Byzantine records, which speak of a people closely resembling Gypsies, called *Athinganoi* (or *Azingahoi*), who are characterized as magicians, and who were living in Constantinople about 810. About two hundred years later a Georgian monk noted the arrival at Mount Athos of a group of people, *Atisincani*, who were forthwith styled as "sorcerers and thieves."

John Sampson seems to have come to the conclusion that the Gypsies were in Persia before 900.[15] He believed that in Persia they divided into two bands: the one, called *Ben* Gypsies, travelled southward into Syria and became the ancestors of the present Gypsies of Syria, Palestine, Egypt, Persia, and Transcaucasia; and the other, the *Phen* Gypsies, first settled in Armenia and then migrated westward through Byzantine Greece.

Other philologists, such as Miklosich, believe, however, that Gypsies could not have left India before 1000 because the evolution of the modern Indian languages, with which Romani is associated, did not take place until that date. Whilst serious consideration must be given to such opinions, it cannot be overlooked, as Sampson argued, that the huge gap between the break up of the Prakrits and our first knowledge of the modern languages does not allow any positive statement to be made in this respect. In fact, Miklosich himself did not altogether reject the possibility of an earlier Gypsy exodus from India. At a time when modern Indian dialects were taking definite shape, the Gypsies may have taken with them the germ of corruption and developed an analytic form of language similar to that of the other Indian idioms. A contemporary scholar, Brian Vesey-Fitzgerald, whilst claiming no expertise in philology and not denying the Indian origin of Gypsies, does not quite accept the accuracy of the dates advanced by the experts. For philologists "are at work on something, an indefinite something at that, which happened at least eight hundred years ago, before the earliest of them set to work. Can they be definite to a century or two or three?"[16] The bulk of opinion, however, accepts the view that their dispersion began somewhere about the tenth century.

Whilst the date and manner of the Gypsy exodus from India remain somewhat uncertain, there is relatively better evidence available regarding the times of their recorded appearances in the various countries of the West. These records, however, cannot exclude the possibility that the Gypsies may have been in Europe long before official mention was made of them.

For some time the generally accepted date for the first appearance of the Gypsies in Europe was 1417 when a small band of men and women were discovered in Germany at Luneburg, bearing letters of safe conduct from various princes, such as Emperor Sigismund, and the King of Hungary. In that year Gypsies were also noticed in other parts of Europe, in Moldavia, Hungary, and Switzerland. But there is a good deal of evidence that they had been in Europe for quite a while before this date.[17] Their leaders bore Christian names, such as Andrew, Michael, and Thomas, which suggests a long stay amongst Christian peoples and nations. Gypsies may have reached Spain or Bohemia, part of present-day Czechoslovakia, before the fourteenth century, or the lower Balkans as early as the eleventh century.[18] They were certainly on the Greek island of Corfu early in the fourteenth century, which would mean that the Italians had come into contact with them quite early, for the island belonged to Venice from 1401 to 1797.[19] Indeed it is known from a Venetian Viceroy, Otkaviano Buono, that there were Gypsies in Peloponnesus even before the end of the fourteenth century, for some time about 1395 he confirmed the privileges granted to the *Acingani* of Nauplion by his predecessors. At about the same time there is evidence of the presence of Gypsies in Moldavia and Wallachia. In 1387 Mircen I, Prince of Wallachia, renewed a grant that had been made by his uncle Vladislav to the monastery of St. Anthony at Voditza of forty *salaschi* (tents or families) of Atsegane.

Bataillard, who held the opinion that the Gypsies had reached Europe in prehistoric times and that it was they who had brought the knowledge of metallurgy to Europe, sought to prove that the alien people known as *Bemische,* living in the bishopric of Wurzburg before 1400, were Gypsies. Also, in 1348 Gypsies were present in Serbia. The records and town accounts of the fifteenth century contain notices of payments made to Gypsies in Central Europe.[20] There were Gypsy settlements at Hildesheim in 1407, at Basle in 1414, and at Meissen in 1416. From that time on there is no scarcity of records.

By 1438 thousands of Gypsies had begun to pour into Europe overrunning Germany, Italy, and France. They were highly disciplined and well led, and they travelled with astonishing speed. They reached France in 1419, arriving in Paris in 1427, in Britain about 1430, in Spain by 1447, and in Russia in 1500.[21] And within a few years of their arrival, measures were being taken in every country for their suppression and banishment.

Inevitably these people, who suddenly descended at about the same time, were called by different names in different countries, although they were most commonly known as Gypsies, Bohemians, and at one time Saracens. They were called Assyrians or Ethiopians in England, Ismaelites in Hungary and Romania, *Tatem* (Tartars) in Germany, *Taltera* in Sweden—remarkably close to the name of a tribe of smiths in northern India called *Tathera—Pagans* in Bavaria and the Low Countries, Wanderers in Arab countries, Philistines in Poland, *Luri* in Iraq, *Karaki* and *Zangi* in Persia, *Caraque* and *Romanichel* in France, *Cinghames* or *Tchinganes* in Turkey and Syria, and *Katsiveloi, Tsiganos, Atsincanoi,* or *Athinganoi* in Greece.[22] Most of these epithets were employed to point them out as foreigners and heretics.

There are some obvious and close resemblances between the Jewish *diaspora* and the Gypsy dispersion. No other human migration in history can be compared with these two. Both peoples were reputedly compelled under a curse to wander about indefinitely. Both have been persecuted throughout history and both have, in spite of it, stoutly managed to preserve their distinctive identity. In a way the Gypsy diaspora has been far more widespread even than that of the Jews. Inspired by such superficial similarities, a relationship between the two has been suggested, but this theory has never left the sphere of hypothesis or found any valid support. Apart from a variety of differences of language and culture, the Jews have never shunned sedentary civilization and have integrated themselves into the national cultures of the lands of their adoption.

For several centuries after their first appearance in Europe, no systematic study was made of the Romanies, and the history and culture of these people remained heavily overlaid by a variety of myths, legends, and fantastic hypotheses. It seems incredible that a people should have lived so long in Europe, suffering general contempt and state persecution, and yet not have attracted academic curiosity and attention. But then Europe itself was in a state of transition and intellectual rejuvenation, and was not well equipped, until the rise of comparative philology, to seriously examine the Gypsy problem.

Some scholars of the Bible regarded Gypsies as the cursed descendants of Cain, whereas others claimed Egyptian origin for them. But in either of these views there is little evidence of a non-legendary nature. A major reason for attributing Egyptian origin to the Gypsies may well have been the inexplicable mediaeval European custom of dubbing all travelling showmen and mountebanks as "Egyptians." With the passage of time, it is not unlikely that the real usage of the term Egyptian was forgotten, making it possible for its literal meaning to give rise to an erroneous belief. A few of the Gypsy legends speak of their Egyptian origins, but it is doubtful if these legends were invented by the Gypsies themselves. A people who had lost all definite recollection of their past during their wanderings might easily incorporate the commonly held belief of their origin in some of their stories. In any case, such legends are few and not very definite. If early generations of Gypsies knew their exact origins, they did not transmit the knowledge to their descendants. When they first appeared in Germany, however, they claimed to have come from Lower Egypt, doing penance, by a seven years' wandering for the sin of their forefathers, who had refused hospitality to the Virgin and Child.

Other legends pointing to their origin in the regions of Mesopotamia and ancient Asia also do not withstand serious scrutiny.[23] In contrast, however, Gypsy legends identifying India as the country of their origin are far more numerous and carefuly preserved. In Gypsy lore India is commonly referred to as the *Baro Than* (the Great Land). One of their legends, told with slight regional variations, claims their antiquity in India as far back as the invasion of Alexander. They had to leave India under the curse of a sorcerer, who condemned them to wander over the face of the earth forever, never to sleep twice in the same place, never to drink water twice from the same well, and never to cross the same river twice in one year. There are also some old Persian legends which tell of a people called *Mutes* coming from India before the time of Alexander.

Of all the evidence linking the Gypsies with India, the linguistic one is the most important. Andrew Borde, an eccentric physician who lived during the reign of Henry VIII, was the first person to make a vocabulary of the Gypsy language in 1542 under the mistaken belief that it was the current language of Egypt. In 1597 Bonaventura Valcanius, in his curious book *De Literis et Lingua Getarum,* also gave specimens of Romani as Nubian. But it was in the eighteenth century that the increasing contact with India led scholars to notice linguistic similarities between the Romani and Indian languages; to investigate deeper into the origins, manners, and customs of Gypsies; and finally to fix India as their original home. It was a fortunate accident of history that a Calvinist cleric at Almas in Hungary, Stefan Valyi, met three Indian students from Malabar whilst he was studying at the University of Leiden and noticed the close resemblances between their language and that of the Romanies of his country. He drew up a vocabulary of one thousand Indian words, put it before some Gypsies at Raab, and found that they understood most of it. The publication of his unexpected, although very important, discovery in 1763 gave rise to further investigation which shattered the theory of the Romanies' Egyptian origin, although it did not remove the possibility that they might have come to Europe by way of Egypt. J. C. Rüdiger published his discoveries regarding the Indian origin of Romanies in a book entitled *Neuester Zuwachs der Sprachkunde* in 1782. He was followed a year later by H. M. G. Grellmann, whose much more copious work firmly established the Indian origin of Gypsies.

It was translated into English at the beginning of this century and has passed through three editions.

According to John Sampson, however, it was an English scholar, Jacob Bryant—and not Rüdiger—who was the earliest to discover the Indian origin of the Romanies.[24] It was not until 1844–45, however, when the German philologist, August Friedrich Pott, who strangely enough had never come into contact with Gypsies, published his famous work. *Die Zijeuner in Europa und Asien,* that the foundations for really scientific, especially linguistic, research into the Gypsy question were laid. In consequence, the theory of the Indian origin of the Gypsies came to be systematically investigated and increasingly accepted. The study of the Gypsy language was greatly helped by the development of comparative philology, which came into vogue after the discovery of Sanskrit in the early nineteenth century. Later, Alexandros Georgios Paspates (usually called Paspati), Max Müller, Weislocki, von Sowa, Kopernicki, Franz Miklosich, A. C. Woolner, and a host of other scholars who were primarily philologists, agreed in assigning the birthplace of the Romani language to India.

A major study was made by Paspati and published in 1870. He was a Greek doctor of medicine but had devoted much of his life to the study of the Gypsies, the *Tshinghanes* , of the Ottoman Empire. He believed that the true history of Gypsies, especially in the absence of written history and definite oral traditions, was to be found in their language. The language of the Gypsies in Turkey was a kind of halfway house in the path of evolution of the Romani language from India to the West. Hence, Paspati's able study proved to be of great value to the students of Romani. Between 1872 and 1881, the Austrian philologist, Franz Miklosich, published his monumental studies on Gypsies, specializing in Romani dialects.

Meanwhile, George Borrow, in his novels *Lavengro* and *The Romany Rye,* published about 1845, and in *The Gypsies in Spain,* had told the public for the first time much about this subject, and his influence was great both in England and on the European mainland in awakening an interest in Gypsy history and culture.

John Sampson (1862–1931) was an eminent comparative philologist and a sound classical scholar who devised an excellent phonetic alphabet for writing spoken Welsh Romani. He devoted a lifetime of study to the Gypsy language, and it took him thirty-two years of painstaking effort before he could publish his work on Welsh Romani in 1926, *The Dialect of the Gypsies of Wales.* This was a major landmark in the study of the subject, because the Gypsies of Wales preserved the purity of their traditions most loyally, so much so that "they are almost the only ones in the world to use Romani language in a state of purity, including grammar and syntax." Thus, philologists after careful research spread over a century established a definite identity between the various dialects of the Romani.[25] They also established a certain relationship amongst Romani, Sanskrit, and the modern Indian languages. The resemblances are so close and so numerous that even a non-specialist can detect them. More than half of the fundamental vocabulary of Romani is related to languages spoken today in northern India. Romani grammar and vocabulary cannot be explained except by Sanskrit.

However, there is no general agreement on the exact locality of the origin of Romani in India. Miklosich, in his *Beitrage Zur Kenntniss der Zigeunermundarten* in 1878, argued that Romani had some kinship with the Dard and Kafir dialects. His view was followed by Pischel and later by J. Block in the brilliant introduction to his *Formation de la Langue Marathe.* Sampson, however, opposed this connection of Romani with the Dard group. A. C. Woolner connected Romani with languages spoken farther into India and drew some striking parallels with Western Indian Pahari. In Grellmann's opinion, the original home of these people was the same as that of the Jats. Pott, Bataillard, Trumpp, and Burton also concluded that the relation between Romani and the dialect of the modern Jats was so close that there could be no doubt that the roots of Romani lay in the north of India. De Goeje, relying on Arab chronicles, believed that the Jats, Zotts, and Doms were related to Gypsies. John Beames, an Indian civil servant who was a reputed scholar of Sanskrit, considered the language more closely related to Sindi. The localities suggested ranged from the Hindu Kush Mountains area to the Indus region. A present-day authority on the Indo-European languages, Sir Ralph Turner, however, has argued that Romani originally belonged to a central Indian group of dialects and subsequently migrated to the northwestern group.[26] The problem remains unresolved mainly because knowledge of the Indian dialects of the period when the Gypsies left India is unavailable. But the fact that Romani appears to be related to several dialects may suggest that the Gypsies were already a nomadic people at the time of their departure from India.

Although the Gypsies have no system of writing, they do possess a comprehensive list of conventional signs which they use to communicate with each other. This secret code is called *patrin* and consists of items chosen from nature, such as cocks' feathers, pieces of trimmed wood, etc. These are made into signs which can be carved or drawn on trees, gates, and wood. Patrin in Romani means a leaf, and is related to Sanskrit *patra* which is variously used for designating letter and leaf. By arranging these signs in a certain way, one tribe can easily communicate with other tribes along its route of travel.

Romani is related to Sanskrit in the same way as the Romance languages are to Latin.

The following list of cardinal numbers illustrates the point:

Romani	*Hindi*	*English*
yek	ek	one
dui	do	two
trin	tin	three
star or chtar	car	four
pansh	panc	five
sho	che	six
eft (haft in Persian)	sat	seven
okht-octo	ath	eight
nu	nan	nine
dash	das	ten

The following are afew examples of Romani words with their Hindi and English equivalents:

Romani	*Hindi*	*English*
yakh	ankh	eye
yag	ag	fire
kalo	kala	black

ker	kar	to do, make
kan	kan	ear
devata	devata	deity
nak	nak	nose
bal	bal	hair
rat	rakt	blood
tud	dudh	milk
marva	marna	to die
amaro	hamara	ours
gra	ghora	horse
dant	dant	teeth
lon	lun	salt
kameva	kam	love
than	sthan	land
mas	mans	meat
tu	turn, tu	you
chib	jibh	tongue
manush	manush	man
puro	burha	old
salo	sala	brother-in-law
phen	bahin, Ghen	sister
phral	bhrata, bhai	brother
dzamutro	jamatar	son-in-law
sasro	sasur	father-in-law
sasuy	sas	mother-in-law
kak	kaka	uncle

The sentence is generally constructed In the same way in Romani and Hindi. For example:

Romani: Ja, kik kon chalavelo a vurdo.
Hindi: Ja, dekh kaun chalaaya dvar ko.
English: Go and see who has come to the door.

Romani: Main hun kalo.
Hindi: Main hun kala.
English: I am dark.

Romani: Mero sera dukkers.
Hindi: Mero sir dukhe.
English: My head aches.

Conjugations of verbs and declensions of nouns, etc., follow the Hindi pattern. The feminine ending *i* is found in both. Romani has two genders: *o* represents the masculine and *i* the feminine. For instance *boro rye,* a great man, and *bori rani,* a great lady. In Romani the feminine of *kalo* is *kali,* as in Hindi the feminine of *kala* is *kali;* in both the adjective means "black."

As in Hindi, the Gypsies use the same word (*kaliko*) for tomorrow and yesterday, which again is very close to Hindi *kal* (or *kalko).* Similarly, Gypsy *shoshoi* signifies both hare and rabbit as does Sanskrit *sasa.* The Gypsy habit of coining new words by compounding two or more words is also reminiscent of the Sanskrit *Sandhi Samasa* system. However, the Romani vocabulary is very limited, and it has few verbs.

It is inevitable that the Romani vocabulary should include a number of words from the languages of those countries through which the Gypsies wandered. There are, consequently, many words in Romani of Iranian, Greek, and Armenian origin. Furthermore, the Gypsies from the time of their arrival in Europe readily assimilated many words from Russian, German, Polish, Hungarian, and other languages. In fact, the careful scrutiny of these borrowings has been the chief means of establishing their routes of dispersion. For example, as the language of the Gypsies of Finland contains Swedish words, but not Russian, scholars have concluded that the Gypsies entered Finland from the west. The presence of over two thousand Arabic words in the Romani dialect of the Spanish Gitanos confirms their passage to Spain through Arabia and North Africa. The presence of as many as two hundred Greek words in all the European Romani dialects suggests that Gypsies spent a good deal of time in Greece before spreading over Europe.

As most legends suggest, metal working, including bronze, gold, and precious stones, has always been the principal vocation of Gypsies. It is well known that the art of metallurgy was widespread and very proficiently practiced in ancient India. Some of the tools used by Gypsies, the technique employing forge and simple goatskin bellows, and the designs they engrave are used even today by certain tribes in India. Again, the mythical association of the practice of metallurgy with the occupations of those possessed by the devil is reminiscent of Indian mythology. Gypsies are regarded in Europe today as amongst the most highly accomplished and skilled enamellers, goldsmiths, silversmiths, and blacksmiths. They are also good mechanics and motor vehicle dealers.

Fortune-telling is invariably associated with Gypsies, although only their women tell fortunes and they practice the art only on non-Gypsies. It appears that despite pronouncements of disbelief and even derision, people still flock to wandering Gypsies to listen eagerly to their forecasts. Brian Vesey-Fitzgerald testifies that he had his fortune told by Gypsies on more than one occasion with remarkable accuracy.

It is significant that the professions practiced by the Gypsies are exactly the ones which were prescribed for the outcaste in caste-ridden Indian society. If the list of curses and occupational prohibitions contained in the *Manusmriti* (the Laws of Manu) is consulted, it will be seen that Gypsies have followed precisely those occupations condemned by Manu. Trading in horses or cows; driving wagons; professional dancing, singing, or playing instruments; training elephants, bulls, horses, or camels; and gambling and professional fortune-telling were amongst the occupations forbidden to upper caste people. Those who engaged in these or similar vocations were driven into the ranks of the depressed castes or outcastes, and required to dwell in the mountains and woods. The Gypsies, however, did not adopt all the professions prohibited by Manu; they chose the ones which suited their nomadic way of life. The combination of the Gypsy occupations of smith and musician is reminiscent of some Indian tribes which occupy an unenviable lower power position in the caste hierarchy; for example, the *Ghasis,* the *Luris,* and the *Asuras.*

The code of Manu is, however, extremely complex and intricate. It classifies mixed castes and other outcastes into a wide variety of categories, and accordingly prescribes professions and other laws for each one of them. If a detailed analysis is made of the professions prohibited by Manu, as well as by other ancient Indian law-makers, and if these professions are correlated with those practiced by various Gypsy groups, some further light may be thrown on the origins of Gypsies. It is possible that they may emerge as the offspring of intercaste marriages or of outcastes rather than the descendants of the depressed classes. The name, *Zingary,* which the Gypsies bore when they first appeared in Germany and which is still in use, is in fact a derivative of the Sanskrit word (*Varna) sankara*, meaning children of mixed castes or of adulterous union.

Since the Gypsy heritage of laws and customs was transmitted orally, its origin is naturally somewhat blurred. Yet many of them can be identified with ancient Indian practices. If they are a people who were expelled from India as outcastes, or who emigrated under priestly persecution, it is not surprising that all Gypsies have a peculiar dislike of priests. Yet, wise and learned men, called *rashey,* reminiscent of the Indian rishi, occupy, as in India, a highly esteemed place in Gypsy society. Amongst the authentic signs on the sceptre of a Gypsy tribal chief is the *trishul* (trident), the insignia of Siva. Gypsy chiefs are still called *Thakur.* They regard excommunication from the tribe, as did the Hindus from the caste, as the most severe punishment that can be inflicted.[27] An expelled Gypsy can be rehabilitated, as could a Hindu outcaste, by going through a process of repentance and restitution prescribed by the tribe elders. In both groups membership is strictly hereditary, and the collective authority of the group is supreme, exercised either by a chief or a council of elders. The elders of the tribe are addressed respectfully as *kako,* meaning uncle, a Hindi word of the same meaning. The feminine version of the tribal chief is called *phuri dai,* which in Hindi is *burhi dai,* the old lady. The Gypsy council of elders is clearly a replica of the Indian *panchayat,* and the Gypsy chief corresponds to the head of the panchayat. The Gypsy family system is a joint one, as is the Hindu, embracing parents, children, aunts, uncles, and all kinds of cousins. Likewise, property belongs to the family and not to the individual.[28]

Even in the primarily Gypsy traditions, taboos, beliefs, superstitions, social customs and manners, many Indian· counterparts can be seen. The Gypsy's love for and importance attached to the horse, and the injunction against killing horses or eating horsemeat, except amongst the *Gitanos* of Spain, have parallels in several Indian tribes. Surprisingly, Gypsies are poor horsemen, despite their abilities in horse training and trading. Again, in common with many Indians, Gypsies regard dogs and cats as unclean (*mochardi*).[29] Gypsy women are also regarded as mochardi during menstruation. A pregnant Gypsy woman is treated with careful consideration and as suggested in the Hindu *Kama Sutra,* her women friends place beautiful picture icons of gods and goddesses within her sight in the belief that the child will be cast in a similar image of physical perfection. A woman in childbirth is regarded as unclean until the child is christened and this ritual is somewhat similar to one prevalent amongst the primitive castes in India. Gypsy marriages are generally arranged by the parents, and early marriage is common. Both the bridegroom and the bride are customarily bashful, and, despite the European atmosphere, Gypsy courtship is extremely brief and restrained. Hindus, however, have no courtship at all. The Gypsy marriage ceremony is accompanied by elaborate ritual and feasting. Although divorce exists, Gypsy marriage is a sacred bond as is the Hindu. Sterility is the greatest misfortune possible for a Gypsy woman, and some of their ceremonial cures, such as the marriage between the trees planted by the childless couple, are common in India. The planting of a grove of trees is generally held by Hindus as a religious work. The Gypsies in Germany honour the fir tree, the birch, and the hawthorn, and in Wales venerate the fascinating vegetable growth known to them as the *broado koro.* The Gypsy method of foretelling the sex of a child by casting grains of maize into a basin and observing the way they settle was a custom practiced in vedic India. By no means fond of bathing, Gypsies have ideas of ritual purity somewhat like those of the Hindus.

Gypsies have displayed an adaptability towards the religious beliefs of the countries in their paths. Hence, there are Christians and Muslims of various denominations amongst them. Many practice their faith with deep devotion. They call the Bible the Sastra, the Sanskrit name for scriptures. Underneath, however, all of them enthusiastically retain the peculiar heritage of their ancient beliefs, and it is in these traditional beliefs that Indian parallels are seen.

Strict monotheists, Gypsies use a word of Indian origin *O'Devel* (or *O' Del* or *O'Delore*), which is translated as *the* God. Somewhat like the early Rig Vedic Aryans who composed the "Song of Creation," they do not conceive of God as the creator of the universe. The universe or the earth, *phu* (Sanskrit *bhu*), has always existed independently. The Gypsy worship of Sara is significantly reminiscent of a Hindu form of worship. The Gypsies call Sara the Kali, which is the name of the Hindu goddess of power, and, during the period of worship, take turns in a night-long vigil over the statue of Sara in the church with bare feet but covered head, a Hindu custom.[30] Gypsies seldom need cathedrals and altars for worship. Images placed in a corner of their caravans are regarded as adequate. In this they again reflect the Hindu way of worship. Whilst the Hindus often go to temples, they do not have an overwhelming need for them and most Hindu homes have a small corner reserved for prayers.

Although generally unconcerned about the unknown world or the next life, Gypsies believe in Karma and some kind of continuation of life after death. They accept the fluctuations of fortune with resignation and unconcern. This perhaps explains why they have retained their innate cheerfulness, despite repeated persecutions and injustices.[31] Terms such as *tatva* (the first principle, the reality) and *mukti* (liberation) are familiar to them, although their actual significance has become somewhat blurred over the centuries.

Evidence of similarities between many of the Gypsy tribes of Europe and existing communities in India is both vast and varied. The Gypsy name for themselves, Rom, is linked with the Dom tribe in India. Dom became Lom in Armenia, and then Rom. These names are in exact phonetic correspondence with the Sanskrit *domba* and the modern Indian dom, which means "a man of low caste who gains his living by singing and dancing." Charles Leland first suggested in *English Gypsies and their Language* that the true origin of the Roms (or Romani) was to be found amongst the Doms, a very low caste of India, which sprang from the *Domar*, a mountain tribe of shepherd-robbers. Later, researches by Grierson amongst the Bihari Doms went far to confirm this conjecture. He discovered that there existed in India a wandering tribe known as *Trablus*, who called themselves Roms, and who were in all respects identical with the Syrian and European Gypsies. The Doms of modern India are vagrant tribes, found mainly in Bihar and in the west and northwest areas, and they have many features in common with the Gypsies. They wander about with tattered reed tents which they pitch in the vicinity of villages. Some of them make baskets, mats, and similar articles; and in Darkistan, where they form a considerable part of the population but still constitute the lower caste, they are musicians, smiths, and leather workers. They are today *Doma* and Doms and the name may well have no more racial significance than, for instance, "smith" or "tinker." One of the explanations of the origin of the tribal name Dom is that it imitates the sound of a drum or tomtom. Dom may merely mean a professional musician, or it may simply be applied to any and every outcaste tribe.[32] Present-day Doms are described as sleeping, dreaming, sitting, talking, gambling, smoking, drinking, fighting, and, above all, singing. They improvise songs, play various instruments, and dance immodestly. This description might fit various primitive races but not to the same degree as it fits the Gypsies.

Close parallels between the Romanies of Europe and various other Gypsy-like tribes of India have been noted. *Lovari* in eastern Europe corresponds with *Lahar* in India, *Sinti* with *Sindhis*—although the Sindhi are not a tribe but a linguistic group—Zotts with Jats. Again, there are several Indian tribes which approximate Gypsics closely in both appearance and way of life, such as the Asuras; Luris; Ghasis; *Kamis,* the smiths and metal workers of Nepal: *Kasars* or *Kasera,* the copper smelters and metal workers of northern India; *Koravas* of South India; *Banjaras* of Bombay; *Chharas; Thatharas;* and others. Of these the Luris and the Doms have been the most extensively studied.

Parallels between Gypsy and Indian folklore also invite attention. The publication of *Gypsy Folk-Tales* by Francis Hindes Groome in 1899 brought to light a wealth of hitherto unexplored stories. In asserting the significance of identical tales, allowance must be made for the fact that many stories, in spite of their numerous variations, are common to all Indo-Europeans, that many Indian tales had travelled to Europe through other routes, and that the Romanies have freely borrowed tales from the lands they visited. Therefore, it is not always possible to definitely identify a Gypsy tale as having a purely Indian origin. Yet, there are a few examples, typical of the Indian and the Gypsy traditions, and foreign to other intervening cultures, which suggest a possible direct link. For example, the Gypsy tales "God and the Woodcutter" and "Jack and the Cabbage" have Indian analogues in "The Weaver and the Prophecy" and "The Weaver and the Watermelon."[33] A Gypsy legend as to how God made the different races of man has a striking parallel in an Indian myth. According to the Nagas, a hill tribe in northeastern India, God made a model of man and slipped him into the oven. Being new at the job, he took the model out too soon, and the pale and pasty creature became the white man. The next time, afraid of repeating the mistake, he left it too long and the outcome was the Negro. The third time, he timed it accurately and the result was the perfect brown man, the Indian. In the Gypsy version the perfect man, naturally, was the ancestor of the Gypsies.[34] Both the importance the Gypsies attach to the art of story-telling, and their insistence on following a set pattern, are somewhat reminiscent of traditional story-telling in India.

If the mediaeval wandering jugglers, story-tellers, and entertainers, in whose songs specimens of the oldest secular folk music are found, are considered to be early Gypsies, the Gypsy influence on Western folklore would appear to be considerable. The Gypsy musicians and showmen who have been travelling about in western Europe for several centuries easily resemble a similar class which existed there in mediaeval times. This class consisted of itinerant showmen, mountebanks, jugglers, story-tellers, singers, dancers, and the like. They appeared suddenly in large numbers in France, Germany, Italy, Spain, and England. In Germany they were considered vagrants and tramps. In France, especially in Provence and Normandy, they were known as *jongleurs* and *menestriers*, men who were clowns, acrobats, or musicians, and who recited fables and stories to the accompaniment of music. In England they were called minstrels, and they sang, danced, joked, tossed balls and knives. Gypsy showmen today are clowns, story-tellers, and they recite poems and fables to the accompaniment of music. In fact, the Kurds call Gypsies *A'shuk,* from the Turkish *Ashek*, meaning a story-teller. In Italy these travelling showmen gave performances similar to the Gypsies of today who frequently visit the fairs and country districts of southern Italy. They play, dance, sing, perform acrobatic and riding feats, toss balls and knives, walk on stilts, and do other jugglers' tricks; and they have trained bears, monkeys and other animal acts. They are expert at training all kinds of animals for public entertainment and many Gypsies are found today in the circus world.

Some scholars have described these itinerant entertainers as the descendants of old gladiators and comedians who, after the fall of Rome, were compelled to seek their living amongst the barbarians by trading "what had been introduced into Rome from Asia." There is no doubt that there were such showmen and musicians in the Roman Empire but they originated in Asia, for Rome had imported large numbers of Asian showmen both before and after the beginning of the Christian era.

When the players moved about in companies, women and children formed part of the troupe, the former taking part in the performances as dancers and singers, skilfully using the Asian tambourine and Egyptian clapper in their wanton dances. Although this was about fifteen hundred years ago, there is no other class of showmen today, except the Gypsies, who roam about Europe with their families performing for their livelihood. Some mediaeval wanderers were employed by the nobility as couriers, bearing secret messages or professions of love. Similarly, Gypsies have traditionally been employed as spies, messengers, and "go-betweens," in both Asia and Europe, and Gypsy women in Egypt, as elsewhere, are noted for arranging meetings for lovers. There were two main types of minstrels in England: those in the service of a court and those who wandered about freely. Both types persisted even in the Elizabethan period, when Gypsies reputedly appeared in England, at which point the minstrels faded away.

Whilst these wandering showmen were very popular—in fact, indispensible at court festivals, feasts, tournaments, and other gatherings—and their art was regarded as traditional, they were treated with contempt and denied civil rights. They were tolerated, but not given the real protection of law. Upon sustaining physical injury they could not even claim redress or charge their assailant. Like the Gypsies, these people retained their romantic spirit throughout the Middle Ages whilst remaining homeless outcasts. Even the Church excluded them from partaking in communion and the sacraments. The Church saw in their secular music, in their instinctive and genuine love of life and its pleasures, and in their indomitable determination to hold on to their way of life, a serious danger to the spiritual well-being of its followers. If these minstrels were the early Gypsies of Europe, the hostility of the Church towards them could explain some of the later persecution of the Gypsies in European countries, as well as the Gypsy desire at first to appear as Christians.

Whilst the Gypsies borrowed cultural traits from their adopted countries, they also inevitably transmitted many of their own characteristics, some of which are now completely unrecognizable. It is interesting to note that the Gypsies, afraid of water, nevertheless invented bait for fishing lines. Adept with their hands and nimble on their feet, it is not surprising that the Gypsies have produced most of the bull fighters in Spain, and, in the bare-knuckle days of boxing, they were a power in the British professional ring. Jem Driscoll, a remarkable boxer commonly known as a Welshman, was really a Gypsy.[35] Gypsy women, such as Zora Kostich, have been famous for their breathtaking horse riding tricks in the circus.

If the various Romani dialects borrowed abundantly from the vocabularies of the countries they passed through, they have also contributed in some degree to the enrichment of European languages. The secret slang of evil-doers has drawn most profitably from Gypsy sources. The early history of English slang and cant, the language of the underworld, is obscure, but the impact of the Gypsy language during the early sixteenth century stimulated the English to improve their own rude and scanty jargon. Although the Gypsy contribution to canting was not extensive, it was much larger than many writers on the subject have supposed. A number of the most characteristic English slang words, such as row, shindy, tool (in driving), mash (i.e., to fascinate), pal, chivvy, and especially the term "slang" itself are Romani.[36] "Slang" was derived from the Hindi *swang* (artificial or a show). In the middle of the nineteenth century slang was used to mean a travelling show.

Slang easily advances to the rank of accepted popular language, and there are many English words which owe their origin to Romani. For example: the English words, pal, cosh, bloke, jockey, are derived from Romani.[37] The English dick, meaning to see, is found in all Gypsy dialects. Its Hindi equivalent is *dekh.* Shakespeare's character Caliban is the Gypsy name for "darkness," "blackness," *kaliben.*

The Spanish Gitanos have evolved a distinct dialect of their own called *calo*, which has left many traces in everyday Spanish. For example: *gacho,* meaning lovers, and its feminine *gachi,* meaning mistress; *gili* (fool); *sandunga* (elegance); *chunga* (fun, joke); *mangante* (beggar, vagabond); *terne* (bully); and *manteca* (butter).

The list of Gypsy contributions to French, made chiefly during the last century, is a long one. If some words of Romani origin, which were part of the slang vocabulary in Balzac's time, have now become extinct, there are others which have survived, although their "bohemian" origin is seldom suspected. For example, the word *bath* (popular term for excellent, fine as in C'est *bath!)* is pure Romani. *Bakht* means luck, usually good luck. A toast is proposed saying, "Bakht to ke!" (Good luck be on you!)

This is the *baraka* of the Arabs which, in its original Indian form, *bhakti,* carried with it a more subtle meaning of devout abandon or devotion to the Divinity. There are some twenty to thirty French words currently used which can be traced to Romani with certainty, such as *berge* (ear) from *bers ; surin* (knife) from *tchuri; rupin* (rich) from *rup* (money, as in the Indian rupee); *ouste* (an exclamation, as in Allons, ouste! Come, let's go! or Let's get a move on!) from *ustel* (Get up!); and *costaud* (strong, strapping, hefty) from *kusto* (strong).[38] The term bohemian, popularized by Murger in *La Vie de Bohème,* comes from the French word for Gypsy, employed to portray the gay, Gypsy-like, lives of youthful groups of poets, painters, and musicians.

Deriving from Indian castes to whom formal education was denied, Romanies are not a learned people. Their significant contribution has been in those spheres where they have gained a certain proficiency, such as metal working, music, and dancing. Whilst it is common knowledge that the art of metallurgy was widespread in ancient India, it is not definitely known when and how it first appeared in Europe. According to Gabriel de Mortillet, an eminent prehistorian, European metallurgy owes its origins to the immigration of nomad peoples, presumably Gypsies. "Jules Bloch even pinpoints the fact that the link between India and Greece was made by the cauldron makers, the Gaordari of Astarabad, south of Caspian, and the Gypsies of the Khorassan (northeast of Iran), who were chain makers and, at the same time, makers of combs and sieves."[39] Some scholars ascribe the rise of European metallurgy to the Phoenicians, but Paul Bataillard (1814–1894), the French writer, maintains that the credit for introducing bronze into Europe belongs to the Gypsies. It is also possible that the adventurous Phoenician seafarers learned much of their handicraft from the travelling Sygynes, who camped in their towns and villages, and are described by Homer as a wandering tribe beloved by Vulcan, the god of furnaces, because of their great skill in metal work.

Franz de Ville carries Bataillard's theory even further and states that it appears certain that the Gypsies made bronze in Europe.[40] He cites in support of this theory the evidence of the weapons and jewellery recently excavated along the Baltic, ornamented with the *swastika*, an original Indian symbol.[41] Well before the advent of Nazism some

Norweigan Gypsies had the swastika tatooed on their right shoulder. Musical instruments called lures, which are of foreign origin and have been skilfully smelted, have been found at the same location.

Music plays an extremely important part in Gypsy life. Irrespective of his profession, every Gypsy—except possibly some English Gypsies—knows how to play the violin. Many Central European Gypsy songs express the utmost veneration for the violin. Their regard for musical instruments is so great they never sell them. Their intense love for music has been known throughout the world for centuries. It should be recalled that the ten thousand Luris who went over to Iran at the invitation of Bahram Gur were accomplished musicians and expert lute players. There are also early documents referring to the musical abilities of the Gypsies in Europe. In Scotland, they danced for King James in Holyrood Palace, and in France they danced at the court of Louis XIII, in spite of a decree forbidding their entry to the kingdom. In the second interlude of *Le Malade Imaginaire,* Moliere speaks of Egyptians, presumably Gypsies, dressed like Moors, who mingle songs with dances. Even today Gypsy musicians are found everywhere. Hungarian music is greatly indebted to the Gypsies. This is equally true of Romania, Bessarabia, Bulgaria, Turkey, and the whole Balkan Peninsula. In Serbia, Herzegovina, Bosnia, and Croatia, Gypsy musicians and music are as popular as they are in Hungary. The intense love of the Russians for their Gypsy singers and choruses is well known. The Russian Gypsy songs, such as "Ochi Chorniya" ("Dark Eyes"), are known and sung universally. In Spain many of the large Gitano population are musicians, singers, and dancers, and some have risen to positions of eminence in the musical field. In Persia, where there are well over one hundred thousand Gypsies, practically all of the public musicians, singers, and dancers are Gypsies. They are known as *Karachi, Luli, Luri,* and *Mutrib.* In Syria, Mesopotamia, and Egypt, where Gypsies are called *Nuri, Rawazi,* and *Alimah,* the story is much the same.

The Gypsies mentioned by Firdusi and the Arab historian, Hamza, were expert lute players, and it has been suggested that it was possibly they who introduced the lute to Europe. The name of the instrument is borrowed from the Arabic *al-ud*, literally meaning wood. But there is some doubt that the Gypsies were responsible our introducing this instrument to Europe, although it is certain that the lute is of Indian origin. At the time of the Arab conquest of Persia, Persian music was a highly developed art. The Arabs took Indo-Persian music with them to other areas which they occupied, such as Syria, Egypt, North Africa, and Spain. They also took with them a musical instrument, called *rebab*, which was the forerunner of the modern violin.

The guitar, a unique instrument of the lute class capable of playing both harmony and melody simultaneously, and which is indispensable to Gitano musicians, is a variation of the Indian sitar (or cithara), which has mobile frets, and the *tambura,* which does not. There are different theories about the introduction of the guitar (or *guitarra)* into Spain. One theory suggests it was brought by the Arabs, whereas another suggests that it was derived from the Roman cithara of Graeco-Asian origin, which was brought to Spain by the Roman conquerors before the advent of the Arabs. Spanish texts of the Middle Ages mention two types of guitar, the *Latina* and the *Morisca* (Moorish). The earlier guitar was essentially the same stringed instrument that it is today, having an incurved body shaped like the number eight, with flat top and bottom and a finger board with frets, and was played directly by the fingers. It originally had four strings, a fifth was added later on, and was very similar to the Spanish guitar of today. Later, a sixth string was added and tuned in "e" like the first, but two octaves lower.

The Spanish guitar, whilst ideal in some ways, does not perfectly suit the needs of the Gitanos. The Gypsy style of playing has its own distinctive character, the main element of which is rhythm, and the fundamental mood, whether gay or sad, is that of passion. Each type of Gypsy song has its own special accompaniment. In the *taranta,* for instance, the guitar plays an important role. The guitar gives a long prelude and postlude, but remains silent during the singing, or, at the most, plays a few scattered notes. Guitar and voice give the impression of being independent of each other. This is essential, especially in the deeper and more Gypsy-like varieties, in which glides and microtones play an important part. The fixed keys of the instrument are constructed on the guitar system which does not allow it to follow the voice, and the guitar has to play the role of bridging the pauses between verses.

The typical Gypsy instrument is partly made of cypress in order to give it a metallic tone. Often a clamp is put across the neck at varying intervals to shorten the length of the strings and make the tone still more brilliant. Gypsies, who cannot afford this clamp, often use a knife tied in place by a handkerchief instead.[42] The ideal instrument for accompanying this type of *cante gitano* would be either the Indian sitar or the *tambura,* which is the name used by the nomads and some eastern Gypsies for any kind of guitar.[43] An instrument of the same name is in use amongst some of the Balkan Gypsies, with the frets so arranged that one may play microtones. It is probable that the Gypsies brought it with them from India.

In the Balkans, mainly in Bulgaria, the Gypsies have borrowed the *cobza,* a sort of lute with pizzicato strings, and the *naiou* (pipes of Pan). In Romania they use the *tsimbal,* a rudimentary and portable piano. This instrument, which Liszt calls the zymbala (cimbalum), and which is an ancestor of the Western keyboard instruments, appears to be of Indian origin (*svara-mandala*), and it seems very likely that it was the Gypsies who brought it into southern Europe in the fifteenth century.[44] Also, according to Elizabeth Robbins Pennell, the Gypsies introduced the bagpipe into Europe.

Other instruments greatly appreciated by the Gypsies are the drums and tambourine. Considering that Asia furnished the West with a number of wind, string, and percussion instruments, such as the flute, trumpet, horn, bagpipe, cymbal, drum, psaltery, harp, and lute, which were popular with itinerant musicians, it would not be surprising if some of these originated in India. Amongst the percussion instruments, numerous kinds of drums dominate the musical scene in India. Of these, the *mridangam* is the most common, and probably the most ancient; the *tabla* (an Arabic term), equally popular in northern and central India, is almost similar to a *mridanga* but is divided in the middle with each of the two parts sealed at the bottom. Although the tambourine is not exclusively Gypsy or Asian, since it is found everywhere in Mediterranean countries, the use the Gypsies make of it suggests that it is of Indian origin. The tambourine is still reserved either for women to accompany the dances, or for bear leaders to give rhythm to the movements of the animal. In India, whilst drums are used in numerous forms and ways, its *dholak* version is principally played by women, and *damaru* is used for the animal dance.

In some countries of Europe where the number of Gypsies was small, Britain and France for example, Gypsy music was not much appreciated; in others, such as Hungary and Spain, it made a great impact. Franz Liszt, who knew Gypsies and who had made a close study of their music, regarded all Hungarian music as simply Gypsy music.[45] A modern music critic, Sinclair, agrees with this opinion and even suggests that this "statement can be applied to Rumania and Bessarabia with almost as much truth as to Hungary. It is the same in Bulgaria, European Turkey, and the whole Balkan peninsula."[46] Other scholars advocate the originality of Hungarian music. At the beginning of this century, two musicians, Béla Bartok and Zoltan Kodaly, emphasized the independence of Hungarian music by exhuming melodies and rhythms different from those of Gypsy music and authentically Hungarian. The protagonists of the priority of Gypsy music, however, cite ancient documents, which clearly record the presence of Gypsy musicians of high reputation in Hungary and do not mention any other musicians at all. Reference is found in an official register that Gypsy musicians were in the service of Queen Beatrice of Aragon at the end of the fifteenth century. They often played in the palaces, in most great celebrations and processions, and nearly every nobleman owned a Gypsy orchestra. From the seventeenth century, at the courts of the noblemen and at village dances alike, Gypsies accompanied the singing of *kuruc* (songs) with their cymbalums, pipes, and violins. Because of their extremely popular rhythmic chants, the Gypsy singers Michel Varna and his granddaughter Panna Cinka gained fame throughout Europe. They even played the violin for the armies marching into battle. At the end of the eighteenth century they made a specialty of playing the *Verbunkos,* the famous dance of the recruiting sergeants which marked the renaissance of Hungarian music.[47]

The Hungarian csardas is similar to Gypsy dances, and has a peculiar step (knocking the heels together) found in some Eastern dances. According to Liszt, no one can play or dance the csardas like the Gypsies themselves. Gypsy music in Hungary has been developed to an almost unequalled state of perfection in composition and execution. Their music, soft, sweet, weird, and wailing, can suddenly transform into the fierce, wild, fiery strains of a battle song or csardas. Some of the most famous violin performers in the world have been Gypsies, amongst them the nineteenth-century virtuoso, Eduard Remenyi.[48]

Although a certain amount of specialization exists amongst the Gypsy entertainers, the majority are skilled dancers as well as singers. It is likely that the first Gypsy dancers from India were professionals, but it is equally possible that the origin of Gypsy dances is ritualistic, and that "in some way they represent an everyday or commonplace rendering of the sacred dances of Vedic India."[49] The Romanian "Dance of the Kalus" (sticks), also known in Hungary as the Stick Dance (Rovl'enca Khelen), is reminiscent of the *chatia* dance, which with regional variations, is widespread in India. The English Morris (Moorish) dance is said to have been inspired by Gypsies, although the Romanies of Britain have never rivalled the musical skill of their fellow Romanies of Hungary, Spain, or Russia.

In Spain conditions for the growth of Gypsy music were particularly suitable. For centuries Spain was under Arab domination, and during this time the country, especially the southern part, absorbed many Asian characteristics. The presence of the Jews, another Semitic race, also aided this absorption. During the Islamic period music became a highly cultivated art, especially in Seville. Gypsies arrived in Spain nearly half a century before the expulsion of the Muslims and the Jews, and it was only natural that their Asian music and dancing were appreciated. The ease with which the Gypsies took to flamenco music would suggest that Hispano-Arabic music was similar to their own. It must be remembered that the Gypsies reached Spain by the same route as the Arabs had before them. Consequently, whilst they borrowed from flamenco as easily as they contributed to it, Gypsy music in Spain has retained much of its original flavour. It is said that in matter of pure rhythm Spanish Gypsies have few equals. In accompanying a song or dance by only handclapping, they attain an astonishing variety of complex rhythms. Many Spanish dances, such as the bolero, the fandango, the seguidilla, and the malaguena, seem to be of Asian origin. The saraband, the name of one Spanish dance, is a Persian word derived from the beautiful saraband Persian carpet. Spanish folk music is commonly regarded as one of the richest in the world, mainly because a variety of foreign influences have mingled with it, including that of the Gypsies.

Most of the Gypsies settled in Andalusia and the Andalusian influence predominates in Spanish music.

Although Gypsy music scores are not written down—except by non-Gypsies—their musical themes have gained widespread fame throughout Europe. Many lesser-known as well as eminent composers such as Haydn, Beethoven, Schubert, and Brahms occasionally used Gypsy themes.[50] Gypsy music fascinated Wilhelm Friedemann Bach, the eldest son of Johann Sebastian Bach. Once a teacher of mathematics and organist at Halle, Wilhelm left everything to follow a tribe of Gypsy musicians. Scholarly opinion is somewhat divided over the question of Gypsy influence on either Spanish flamenco or east European music. Scholars have hesitated to make definite statements, partly because it is extremely difficult to isolate the importations or alien elements in music. Yet, there are themes in both Hungarian and Spanish music which are clearly of alien origin. At the same time, Hungarian and Spanish Gypsy music have common peculiar characteristics. And, as Spain and Hungary are at opposite ends of western Europe, the mutual similarity must be due to a common third source, which, in this case, would appear to be more likely Gypsy than any other. It is also significant that the musical accomplishments of Spain became noteworthy after the advent of Gypsies in the country in 1447. Unless one insists on a series of unexplained coincidences, the theory of Gypsy inspiration in music must command serious attention.

In Indian and Spanish Gypsy music there is, unlike in Western music, a luxuriance of cross rhythms, a freedom, a richness, a fluidity, and a multiplicity of rhythms, whereas harmony is much neglected.[51] Similarly, the characteristic rhythms, elaborate ornamentation, and quarter tones, unknown to Western music, are common to both Hungarian Gypsy and Indian music. Hungarian Gypsies employ various scales or modes not used in Western music, for example c, d, e, f#, g, a, b. They employ in the minor scale the augmented fourth, the minor sixth, and the major seventh. Often they also use the minor seventh and the dominant with an augmented fifth. Asian music, Arabian for example, contains the same peculiarities. Indian and Gypsy melodies have many similarities which are easier to perceive than to explain. Both in Indian and Gypsy music melodic themes are more fluid and complex than they are in

European music. Gypsy melodies, like the Indian, are elusive, delicate, and subtle. The *Indiana* of the Spanish Gypsies corresponds to the Indian *Bhairavi.* The use of microtones, such as quarter and third tones, is alien to Western, but common to Gypsy and Indian music. For this reason it is almost impossible to transcribe Spanish Gypsy folk songs, as it is Indian songs, by the European system of notation and to play them on European instruments with fixed keys. Grace notes and the use of the flowing glide, producing what the Indians call "curves of sound," are essential to Spanish Gypsy music as well as to Indian. The melody seems to flow like water in a river, rising and falling in rapids, halting in still pools, and dashing over falls.[52] Even in the orchestral music of the Gypsies, harmony and counterpoint play a subordinate role to rhythm and melody. Liszt states that in the Hungarian Gypsy orchestra the violin is really a solo instrument; the rest of the instruments merely intensify its shadows and illuminate its joys. Both Indian and Gypsy music are relatively indifferent to the quality of the tone. In contrast, Western music pays much attention to it. Although the Gypsies charmed people throughout Europe with their music, it received its warmest reception and accommodation in those countries which already had some tradition of Eastern music.

Musical improvisation is a favourite art amongst the Gypsies of Spain. In India, whilst waiting for the marriage feast to begin, the Doms will often take turns at improvising. In fact, improvisation in music and poetry is quite common in India, and is sometimes even expected by the audience as a light touch in a serious performance.

On the whole, the dances of the Gypsies in Spain appear to be nearer those of India than those of Spain. As in India, great emphasis is laid on the graceful curving movements of the fingers, the hands, and the arms which glide through the air like winged snakes, whilst the feet, in a violently contrasting tempo, drum a devil's tattoo. In the dances of Andalusia, the movements of arms and hands, and the play of the body muscles, are especially prominent. The combination of song and dance, the cries of "Ole! Ole!" echoed from all directions to animate the performer, the rapid gyrations, the undulations of the body suggesting dunes of sand or wind-blown fields of ripe wheat, all characteristic of the entertainments given by families of Indian Gypsies, have their definite counterparts in the zambras and danzas given by the Gitanos of Granada.[53]

A classic performance of Gypsy women is the snake dance, which is often confused with the "belly dance" of Arab women. But, as Martin Block has pointed out, this dance is not at all erotic, because Gypsy women, unlike their Arabian counterparts, never dance undraped. Like the Indian woman dancer, the Spanish dancer dresses unrevealingly, thus making herself more mysterious and inviting. References are found in European literature which confirm that the relationship between the Gypsy and Indian dances was at least vaguely recognized. For instance, the Badminton volume on dancing quotes Walter Thornbury (*Life in Spain*): "Seville is the headquarters of the gipsy girl who is going to show us how the Egyptian ghawassees and the Hindoo nautch girls dance. She will dance the Romalis, which is the dance Tiberius may have seen, and which no one but a gipsy dances in Spain. She will dance it to the old Oriental music and handclapping and to an old religious Eastern time, low and melancholy, diatonic, not chromatic, and full of sudden pauses, which are strange and startling."[54]

Chapter VIII

BUDDHIST PROSELYTISM IN CENTRAL ASIA

ONE OF THE remarkable characteristics of early Asian history—in fact of the ancient world until the Christian suppression of non-Christian religions in the Roman Empire—was the receptivity to cultural ideas regardless of their nationality, and a lack of religious bigotry. Prejudice against a foreign belief was uncommon; it certainly was never strong enough to cause total rejection of a different faith. The civilized peoples of those days seem to have implicitly accepted the proposition that there were numerous approaches to truth, and, without any false sense of pride or violated nationalism, they readily accepted knowledge, alien or otherwise, if they thought it worthwhile. This free flow of ideas, unimpeded by preconceptions and national barriers, made the ancient world in some ways far more international in its cultural outlook and social behaviour than our present-day society.

Trade and commerce dominated India's relations with the countries to the West of her, and cultural intercourse remained a subordinate partner throughout the long period of contact. Ideas inevitably moved with goods, soldiers, and travellers; but few journeys were undertaken just to seek knowledge and learning. In marked contrast, Indian contacts with the countries on her north, east, and southeast were mainly cultural, with trade playing a significant but secondary role. Commerce may have initiated contact but it was soon outpaced by culture. Again, the marks of Indian culture in these areas are far more clearly seen, and more readily conceded, than those in the West. It has, therefore, often been said that India's finest contributions to human civilization lie in Central Asia, East Asia, and Southeast Asia. Whatever the sum total of Indian influences on Western civilization, there is no doubt that ancient India was the radiating centre of a civilization which left a deep mark on the greater part of Asia.

Buddhism was the principal vehicle of Indian ideas and culture in Asia and is still the religion of millions of Asians. In many countries it became the national religion; in others it produced great intellectual stimulation, controversy, and, eventually, rejuvenation. It brought the uniquely rich and creative cultures of India, Indochina, Indonesia, China, and Japan into contact with each other and, over a period of more than a thousand years, gave rise to a great spiritual and cultural community throughout Asia.

The most remarkable feature of the Buddhist missionary activity, however, was that it was never fanatical, bigoted, or obtrusive, and Buddhist missionaries never served the interests of a militant political power. In the true spirit of its faith, Buddhism prevailed peacefully through force of conviction. Like Hinduism, it did not lay claim to exclusiveness and remained exceptionally tolerant of other beliefs. Its intrinsic quality of being able to accommodate alien doctrines and adopt local cultural traditions, without surrendering its fundamental concepts, was principally responsible for its remarkable success in distant lands of divergent cultures. Buddhism acted as a catalyst in different societies, helping them to bring out their dormant strengths and to release their creative energies. Its capacity to absorb, to impart, and to fertilize remains unmatched in the history of cultural expansion.

Much of the history of the ancient states of Central Asia has been reconstructed from Chinese sources, which naturally deal with the life and events of these neighbouring states from the Chinese viewpoint and as an adjunct to Chinese history. But the Chinese accounts are valuable in providing corrective or corroborative evidence to Buddhist narratives. Without archaeological work, however, the reconstruction of Buddhist Central Asia would have remained less comprehensible and reliable.

It was only after the northern boundary of Afghanistan had been demarcated and an agreement signed between Britain and Russia in 1887 that Central Asia was visited by European soldiers, adventurers, and civil and military officials. In the beginning there were only stray archaeological finds but they drew the attention of a wide circle of scholars. In 1890 two Turks found a birch bark manuscript in the vicinity of Qum-Tura, which they sold to a British army officer, Colonel Bower, at Kucha. The text is commonly known as the Bower Manuscript and is a Sanskrit treatise on medicine belonging to the fourth century. A few years later, in 1893, a French traveller, M. Dutreuil de Rhins, acquired two birch bark manuscripts in the vicinity of Khotan. Expert examination found they contained a Buddhist text in an Indian language and script of the second century—a new version of the *Dhammapada* in Prakrit written in Kharoshthi script. These discoveries kindled a widespread interest in the area. In 1898 a Russian archaeological mission led by Klements visited the northern parts of eastern Turkistan. This had been inspired by the remarkable finds of the Russian Consul-General, Petrovsky, at Kashgar, but not much further archaeological exploration of the region was undertaken. In 1896 Hedin's march through the areas of sand-buried ruins in the desert northeast of Khotan, although not producing any historical evidence, succeeded in demonstrating the accessibility and suitability of these sites for excavation. Soon, urged by the recommendations of Hoernle, the Indian government deputed Aurel Stein, a trained archaeologist, to carry out exploration in the region of Khotan in 1900–1901. Encouraged by the remarkable results of his first expedition Stein then explored regions beyond Khotan in the southern part of eastern Turkistan up to the borders of China. On his third expedition, he covered a wider area including Khotan, Niya, Loulan, Tun-huang, Borkul, Guchen, and Jimasa Kucha.[1]

His greatest discoveries were made in 1907, when he found more than twenty thousand manuscripts and 554 separate paintings. The collection included five hundred complete Buddhist canonical works and three thousand works in Sanskrit or Brahmi. He filled twenty-four heavy cases with manuscripts and five with paintings, embroideries, and other remains of Buddhist art. Amongst his many fascinating discoveries was that of the "Old Wall." The Great Wall of China in its present form is of Ming date and was designed to protect China from Mongol attack;

but Stein found an extension of the original wall nearly two hundred miles east of the Jade Gate where the silk road passes through the frontier rampart. The wall, traced for one hundred miles, was first built for protection against the ancient Huns in the second century B.C. by the Han rulers.

Meanwhile, other European scholars also carried out explorations in this region. Three German expeditions were conducted between 1902–1903 and 1913–1914 under the direction of Albert Grunwedel and Albert Von Lecoq. These archaeologists worked mostly in the northern part of eastern Turkistan. A French scholar of Chinese, Paul Pelliot, led an expedition in 1906 which worked for two years, mainly at Tunhuang, studying manuscript collections and the remains of art in the caves of the Thousand Buddhas. In fact, Stein had bought a large collection of manuscripts for a small sum of money in 1907 from a discharged soldier, Wang Yuan-Lu, who had discovered the hidden library in the cave in 1900. A year later Pelliot made a similar but smaller find, although his knowledge of Chinese enabled him to be more discriminating than Stein. The Chinese understandably regard Stein and Pelliot as robbers because they acted in accordance with the nineteenth-century European attitude of the right to carry off "finds" made in non-European lands. Despite this, there was enough of the collection left behind that in 1910 the Chinese government was able to bring to Peking some ten thousand manuscripts. Many fell into private hands and a year later the Japanese managed to smuggle out six hundred manuscripts.[2] Most of the treasures are now housed in various countries—Britain, China, Japan, India, Russia, and Germany. During the last war, however, a large number of those kept in Berlin were destroyed.

This remarkable burst of archaeological work done during the first seventeen years of this century has not been followed up for political and financial reasons. There remains a good deal more to be done and signs have appeared in recent years suggesting a renewal of interest in the exploration of this area, especially by Soviet and Chinese archaeologists. In 1946–1947 the Russian Tolstov mission systematically explored the enormous castle at Toprak-Kala in Chorasmia and later published their valuable findings.

The limited work which has been done clearly reveals that the ancient civilizations of the Central Asian states were of a somewhat cosmopolitan character, in which Indian, Chinese, Persian, and Hellenistic influences intermingled with local heritages. Although Zoroastrianism, Manichaeanism, and Nestorian Christianity were prevalent amongst some of the people, Buddhism was most popular, and Central Asian cultural life was dominated for about a thousand years by Indian religion, literature, arts, and sciences. The different religious groups lived in harmony. For instance, at a ruined city called Turfan (Idiqut-i-Shanri, Chotsche) the remains of Manichaean, Nestorian, and Buddhist art and architecture are so closely associated that one must conclude that full religious tolerance prevailed there. However, evidence has also been found of a massacre of Buddhists by the Chinese about the ninth century. Von Lecoq discovered a chamber packed with the skeletons of monks still wearing fragments of their robes and bearing marks of ruthless slaughter.

By far the largest part of the vast material discovered is of Buddhist origin, although other documents, including many Manichaean books have also been found. Numerous Sanskrit writings have been found dealing with religious or semi-religious subjects—as medicine, astronomy, and grammar were then considered to be. Documents from as early as the second century have been discovered, some of them in Prakrit written in the Kharoshthi script of Asoka's time. Some were written on wood, some on birch bark or palm leaf, and others on leather. During the first three centuries the Kharoshthi script was in use from Khotan to Kroraina in the Lobnor region. Kharoshthi documents, numbering into hundreds, have been found, mainly on the sites at Niya, Endere, and Kroraina. In the fourth century in Khotan, Kucha, and Karashahr, Kharoshthi was replaced by a form of Brahmi adopted from the script of fourth-century Gupta India. The Chinese records date from even earlier periods; some are written on bamboo, others on silk, and other later ones on paper. Recent excavations in Chinese Turkistan have brought to light a large number of flourishing cities with rich sanctuaries. Recently, Soviet scholars discovered Sanskrit birch bark dating back to the sixth century in a castle called Zangtepe in Uzbekistan. These are in the Central Asian Brahmi script, and have thrown additional light on the cultural contact between India and Central Asia.

The religious structures excavated in Central Asia comprise stupas, caves, and *viharas.* The architecture appears to owe almost nothing to China but to include Indian and Persian features. Whilst numerous representations of Hindu deities have been found, Hinduism does not seem to have existed, except in Afghanistan. Buddhist missionaries transmitted to Central Asia not only religion, art, and literature but also scientific knowledge, as is evidenced by the discovery of the Sanskrit medical texts. It is not unlikely, therefore, that Indian ideas in other branches of science, such as mathematics and astronomy, may also have reached Central Asia and beyond.

AFGHANISTAN, ESPECIALLY ITS northern regions around Balkh called Tokharestan, was the crossroads of Central Asia. It was here that the nomadic peoples first learned the ways of settled life, and thus Tokharestan played the significant role of a cultural intermediary.[3] Of all the neighbouring cultures, it was with India that this region was most closely connected. In fact, there is some sense in the suggestion that the territory between the Indus and the Oxus Rivers was a domain of Indian culture during the ancient period. Until the rise of Islam, Afghanistan was Hindu-Buddhist. The Parthians called the province corresponding to modern Kandahar and Sistan "White India," because Indian culture prevailed there. The Sassanians of the third century regarded even Bactriana, or the region of Balkh, as virtually an Indian country and the Oxus as a river of the Buddhists and the Brahmans. The ancient Greek writers coupled Bactriana with India and stated that thousands of Brahmans and Buddhist monks resided there.

Buddhism was the predominant religion in the various states of Tokharestan from the second century B.C. to the beginning of the eighth century. Hsüan-tsang (Yuan-chuang)[4] (602–664), who visited the region on his way to India, testifies that Balkh was a great centre of original Buddhist studies, and gives a vivid description of the Buddhist establishments there. Except for Hsüan-tsang's account, there is no systematic account of Buddhism in the early period in Tokharestan and adjoining territories. From his record it appears that Buddhism was most prosperous in the cities, and that there were Buddhist monasteries in every state. According to a legend recounted by Hsüan-tsang, the first two lay disciples of the Buddha, Trapusa and Bhallika, laid the foundations of Buddhism in that country. Regardless of the authenticity of this evidence, there is no doubt that Buddhism was carried to Balkh during the period of Asoka's reign. Later, the Yueh-chih, who conquered the area, adopted Buddhism. The Kushans, who ruled over Tokharestan, became great patrons of Buddhism, and Tokharestan became a thriving centre for Buddhist studies. It produced famous scholars, such as Ghasaka, who played an important part in the compilation of the *Vibhasa*, a monumental Buddhist commentary, at the Buddhist Council held in Kashmir under the patronage of Kaniska. It was from Tokharestan that the Chinese ambassador Tsing Kiang received Buddhist texts as presents to take back to the Chinese court in 2 B.C., thus beginning the inflow of Buddhist culture to China. Later, Buddhist monks went to China from Tokharestan to preach their faith and culture.

Archaeological data pertaining to the Buddhist period of Tokharestan are only gradually coming to light. Various sites have been noted, and some excavations have been carried out by French scholars in Afghanistan, and, since the war, by Russian archaeologists on their side of the Soviet-Afghan border. But much more needs to be done. However, the explorations that have been carried out have led to the discovery of very important finds. Situated about one hundred and fifty miles northwest of Kabul, at the intersection of two major routes—one leading from China to Persia across the Pamirs, and the other from north Bactria to the Indus Valley—and commanding a major pass, Bamiyan (Fanyen-na) was the first important way-station on the route from the Kabul region to Balkh (Balhika or Fo-ho). It was a major seat of Buddhist culture, as is revealed by the ruins of a very large monastery which provided travellers with necessary facilities. It continued to be a flourishing centre of Indian culture, attracting pilgrims and monks, until the eighth century. A number of grottos in the hills around Bamiyan were converted into Buddhist temples, and colossal figures of the Buddha were carved on hillsides. Writing at the end of the seventeenth century, Abul Fazl estimated the number of these caves to be about twelve thousand. Some of the caves housed monks, others enshrined the images of the Buddha and Bodhisattvas. Manuscripts of Buddhist texts in Indian scripts found at the site testify further to the Buddhist past of the region.

These remains reveal clearly that Buddhist art in Balkh, at least on the south side of the Oxus, was flourishing. Beyond Bamiyan on the ancient site of Balkh, ruins of stupas and other antiquities have been excavated. As late as the time of Hsüan-tsang the Buddhist monasteries of Balkh were thriving. However, the city suffered much from foreign invasions, and was destroyed by the Arabs towards the end of the seventh century, soon after the departure of Hsüan-tsang.

Greek culture had been superimposed on the Persian cultural background of this region, until the penetration of Buddhism about the first century. Although the country came under the rule of a number of different peoples—the Greeks, the Sakas, the Yueh-chih, and the Huns—it remained Buddhist until the end of the seventh century, when the Muslim conquerors destroyed the great monastery, converted the chief priests to Islam, and took them to the court of the Caliph. On the authority of Al Biruni, these priests—Barmaks—inaugurated the study of Indian astronomy and mathematics at Baghdad.

Elsewhere in Tokharestan, where foreign invasions were not as destructive, remains of Buddhist art have even been discovered above ground. For example, in Haibak, which is situated on the Khula River, a stupa of the type of the Kailasa temple of Ellora was found. A group of interesting ruins have also been discovered at Kundus and its neighbourhood. These include remains of Graeco-Buddhist art, and other evidence which reveals direct Indian influence from the fourth to the fifth centuries. At Termez, which suffered considerably at the hands of invaders, such as the Arabs and Mongols, old coins including those of Kaniska and Huviska, the majority of which belong to the Indo-Greek period have been excavated, as well as remains of Graeco-Buddhist art. Other ruins yielded the Kata-stupa which is of the type found in Gandhara and statues of Bodhisattvas similar to those found in Kucha and Taxila. Recently, first in 1958 and later in 1963, Asokan inscriptions have been found in the vicinity of Kandahar. These inscriptions were written in Aramaic and Greek for the benefit of the Iranian and Greek subjects of the Maurya Emperor.

BUDDHISM SPREAD NOT only westward from Tokharestan to Parthia, but eastward to China and northward to Sogdiana (or Sodgh), the ancient name of Samarkand. Sogdians were known to the ancient Greeks and Iranians, and were in close contact with India, where they were known as Sulika, a name derived from the Iranian Sughdik (or Suwdik). The people and their language have long since disappeared, but remnants of the language have been discovered in a few Sogdian translations of Buddhist texts excavated from parts of eastern Turkistan. Sogdians were well-known traders and visited various regions of Central Asia from Samarkand to the Great Wall, carrying with them Buddhist theory. The Sogdian monks' Chinese name was prefixed by Kang, derived from Kang-kiu, the ancient name for Sogdiana in Chinese. A prominent Sogdian monk, Seng-hui, introduced Buddhism to southern China via India and Tonkin in the third century, and founded a Buddhist school and a monastery at Nanking.

The eastward march of Buddhism into Chinese Turkistan is a story not only of rare courage and conviction but also of enormous significance in world history, for it provided the first major bridge between the two great civilizations of India and China. Some idea of the success of Buddhist missionary activity in this area can be gauged by the fact that the civilization of Chinese or eastern Turkistan was so close to that of India and Iran about the tenth century that Sir Aurel Stein referred to it by the ancient Greek name "Ser-India."

Lying beyond Tibet hundreds of torturous miles away from India, and bounded on the south by the wild and untrodden Kun-iun mountain ranges, on the west by the Pamirs, on the north by the T'ien-shan mountains, and on the east by the treacherous Gobi Desert, Chinese Turkistan is practically a vast wasteland of gravel and shifting dunes. Political and cultural activities, therefore, were confined to towns which were situated in most cases along the northern and southern edges of the Tarim Basin, where the rivers and streams in the T'ien-shan and Kun-lun ranges made irrigation possible and agriculture practicable. These oasis cities were capitals of states of varying and fluctuating sizes, as well as important commercial centres on the silk road for more than a thousand years.

Along the edge of T'ien-shan, in the northern part of Chinese Turkistan, there were four important states culturally similar: the modern Aksu, (Sanskrit, Bharuka); modern Kucha (Sanskrit, Kuchi); modern

Karashahr (Sanskrit, Agnidesa; Chinese, Yenki); and modern Turfan (Chinese, Kao Chang, Chotsche). Of the southern states along the foot of the Kun-lun Range the most important, from the viewpoint of cultural influences, were Kashgar (Sanskrit, Sailadesa) ; Yarkand (Sanskrit, Chokkuka); and Khotan (Sanskrit, Kustana; Chinese, Yutien). The two Pamir states, Kie-Pan-to (Sarikol) and Wu-Sha (Yangi-Hissar), in the east of Shughnan are included in the Kashgar group. At the eastern extremity of these routes, the famous city of Tun-huang was located.

The chief sources of information about this region are the Chinese and Tibetan annals, the narratives of Chinese pilgrims, and modern archaeological excavations undertaken by Aurel Stein, Albert Grunwedel, Paul Pelliot, and others mainly between 1900 and 1914, and by Soviet and Chinese archaeologists recently. The authenticity of the traditional accounts, preserved in the Chinese and Tibetan literatures, as well as in Buddhist texts, may be open to further verification. However, there is reliable archaeological evidence to suggest that there were small Indian settlements in existence in the southern part of this region before the Christian era, and that the wandering peoples of Central Asia, such as the Sakas and the Kushans, together with Indian merchants, were amongst the first to carry Indian culture and Buddhism to eastern Turkistan. An Indian dialect similar to that of northwestern India was the official language in some of these states. It is not unlikely that in certain areas Indians had settled in large numbers and set up their own principalities. These kingdoms of Central Asia were centres of extraordinary religious, literary, and artistic activity. Indian settlements were periodically reinforced by people from India, and many of these people would themselves set out on missions, for example, to China. Many of these Indians were from South India. From recent excavations at Toprak-Kala, Tolstov has suggested that the kings of this region employed Dravidian Indians as palace guards.[5] In the southern kingdoms of Kashgar, Yarkand, and Khotan, there was a strong Indian element in the population, and Khotan appears to have been the most important Indianized kingdom in Central Asia.

At the junction of one route running southeast to Khotan and another northeast to the Kucha region, Kashgar, from ancient times, played a significant role in the transmission of culture to the northern and southern states of the Tarim Basin. In Kashgar a script of Indian origin based on Brahmi, was current, and possibly the language was a dialect of eastern Iran. Fa-hsien, who visited Kashgar during his Indian journey at the end of the fourth century, found Buddhism prospering there with more than two thousand monks and their disciples, all followers of the *Theravada* school. Two centuries later, Hsüan-tsang found that the people were sincere Buddhists. There were hundreds of monasteries, and Sanskrit was seriously cultivated. It was common for Indian scholars to visit Kashgar; the Buddhist teacher, Kumarajiva, stayed there for about a year on his return journey from Kashmir. Numerous relics of Buddhist stupas have been found in this locality.

The adjoining area of Khotan was also a flourishing centre of Buddhism. There is more information about Khotan revealed in Chinese, Tibetan, and archaeological sources, than there is about Kashgar.[6] A Buddhist legend describes the conversion of Khotan as early as the time of the Buddha. Another legend refers to the political supremacy of Kunala, Asoka's son, in Khotan. Also, according to ancient Khotanese traditions, a son of Asoka named Kustana founded the kingdom about 240 B.C., 234 years after the *Nirvana,* and it was Vijayasambhava, the grandson of Kustana, who introduced Buddhism into Khotan. A Buddhist scholar named Arya Vairocana, who was regarded as an incarnation of the Maitraya Buddha, and who had miraculously brought Buddhist relics from Kashmir, is said to have come from India and become the King's preceptor. The tradition further claims the rule of an Indian dynasty in Khotan for fifty-six generations—all the kings' names of this line begin with Vijaya—during which period Buddhism remained the dominant religion of the state. According to the Tibetan annals, the first monastery, which Chinese records describe as "the stupa of up-turned bowl," was built about 211 B.C. A Chinese scholar-monk, Song-yun, mentions a monastery called Tsan-mo which is known as Tsarma in Tibetan sources. The Chinese annals more or less confirm Tibetan accounts of ancient Khotan, which are substantially reinforced by the archaeological finds of Aurel Stein, who identified the old site of Tsarrna with Chalma-kazan in the vicinity of Yotkan. The remarkable sculptures and paintings which the ancient shrines and dwelling places have yielded, despite centuries of burial beneath the dunes indicate that the painters of Central Asian regions followed Indian models during the seventh and eighth centuries.

When Buddhism first began to expand into Central Asia a synthesis between the Indian and Graeco-Roman art forms was taking place in Gandhara (northwestern India). The emergent form utilized Greek architectural motifs, such as the Corinthian pillar, and Greek drapery, but also contained characteristics of Indian art, which was flourishing in the interior of the country. The life of the Buddha and stories from his former incarnations were generally portrayed and for the first time the image of the Buddha was carved on the model of Apollo. This gave rise to the whole iconography of later Buddhism, which has inspired the art of various countries, and has become an integral part of Buddhist worship. Until then neither the Buddha nor the Boddhisattvas were represented in pictorial form. In contrast, the worship of "images," a pan-Hellenic phenomenon, was very popular throughout the Hellenistic civilization.

Later, as art developed in India, some of its influences, particularly Gupta art, were passed on to Central Asia through the routes travelled by monks and merchants. Figures became slenderer, poses more graceful, draperies more transparent. Buddha images were portrayed cooling their feet on the beautiful lotus, an Indian symbol of purity. The art of Ajanta appears to have been reborn in Central Asia. In fact, these paintings from Central Asia have helped to bridge a gap between Ajanta and Akbar in the story of Indian painting.

Central Asian art bore Persian, Chinese, Graeco-Buddhist, and Indian influences. The Khotanese were very fond of music and drama, and this fondness found an expression in the annual procession of images called *Buddha Yatra,* like the Indian *Ratha Yatra.* Close Indian contact is also indicated by a find of coins, a Kharoshthi inscription, and a text of the *Dhammapada* near Khotan. The Sino-Kharoshthi coins are the most important of these finds and were probably issued after 74 when Khotan had passed under effective Chinese suzerainty.

Numerous fresco or distemper paintings on wood and plaster have been found at Dandan-Uiliq, the Chinese garrison headquarters which was deserted soon after 791. A number of old Buddhist sites excavated in the desert of Dandan-Uiliq have yielded many stucco images and relics, manuscripts and records in Brahmi as well as in Chinese script.

Khotan's famous monastery, Gomati Vihara, was widely known as a seat of learning from very early times and attracted scholars from India and China. In 259 a well-known Chinese monk Chu She-ling, who compiled one of the first catalogues of Buddhist texts in Chinese, came to Khotan to study Buddhism, taking back with him ninety bundles of original Buddhist texts. In Central Asia numerous Sanskrit texts have been found that are not extant in India, amongst them the *Udanavarga*.

Buddhism flourished in Khotan until about the eighth century and at its peak boasted nearly four thousand monasteries. According to Fa-hsien, Mahayana Buddhism was the more prevalent type and its priests numbered in the thousands. He mentions a monastery which took eighty years to build and was two hundred and fifty feet tall, overlaid with gold and silver carvings.

At the height of her power, the kingdom of Khotan extended from Chokkuka (Yarkand, Sokiu) in the west to Niya (Ni-jang) in the east. Khotan became the centre for the dissemination of Buddhism to other states, such as Niya, Calmadana (Cherchen), Kroraina (Loulan), and even China. It was from Khotan that Buddhism travelled to China reaching Korea and Japan by the sixth century. The Chinese, during the later Han and Tang periods, maintained effective control over the kingdom of Khotan. This fact is recorded in the Chinese annals and illustrated by finds of Chinese documents on wood or paper, Chinese coins, and other articles. Whilst China maintained political supremacy over Khotan and exercised an influence on Khotanese culture in the realms of art and religion, it borrowed a good deal more than it gave. A Khotanese embassy was sent to China for the first time during the reign of Emperor Wu (140–87 B.C.). Chinese ascendancy in Khotan ended about 791 and contact between the two became infrequent. It is possible that historians may well have overestimated Khotan's importance in this process of cultural diffusion simply because the materials available on the subject are plentiful in comparison with other principalities.

East of Khotan was Niya, also an important centre of Buddhism. The discovery of some seals and effigies of Kubera and Trimukha at Niya, and the painted Ganesha at Endere, suggest some Hindu influence. But the discovery of the remains of Buddhist stupas, viharas, and texts written in Sanskrit and Prakrit indicate that Buddhism was the predominant religion in all these localities. A variety of other documents written in Indian languages and scripts on leather, paper, silk, and wooden tablets have also been found. East of Niya is the modern site called Endere, the ancient Tu-ho-lo, which has also yielded Kharoshthi tablets and manuscripts of the type found in Niya, as well as the ruins of a Buddhist stupa.

Archaeological work has revealed a chain of sites in the east and northeast which also testify to the preponderance of the Buddhist culture in this region for several centuries. In the Chinese records of the Han period, this country is referred to as Shan-Shan, the new name for Loulan which in turn was the Chinese transcription of the original Kroraina (or Krorayma) found in the Kharoshthi documents. Evidence indicates that Kroraina was a thriving centre of Buddhism and Indian culture; according to Fa-hsien there were four thousand monks there. The Kharoshthi documents excavated from the various sites of Kroraina are written in Prakrit and contain names of Indian origin: for example, Caraka, Kumudvati, Vasudeva, and Budhamitra.

The story of Buddhist expansion along the northern route is somewhat the same. Kucha was the most powerful state in this region and played a predominant role in the spread of Buddhism to other northern states and to China. The exact date of the arrival of Buddhism in China is unknown, although it was probably in the first century. The Chinese annals of the third century state that there were nearly one thousand stupas and temples in Kucha. Buddhist monks from Kucha went to China and took an active part in translating Buddhist texts into Chinese. Po-yen, who was probably a member of the Kuchean royal family, became a Buddhist monk, and rendered six Buddhist texts into Chinese. Buddhist activity reached a peak during the fourth century with Kucha an almost entirely Buddhist city. Kumarajiva, the Buddhist monk-scholar who introduced Mahayana Buddhism to the states of the Tarim Basin and also to China, was born in Kucha of an Indian father, who was the Rajaguru of the state, and of a Kuchean princess. Kumarajiva was taken to China as a prisoner when Kucha was destroyed by a Chinese expeditionary force in 382. He lived there until his death in 413 and his work gave rise to an exceptionally brilliant and productive phase in the history of Chinese Buddhism.

Archaeological finds show that Buddhism was a flourishing religion in the north until about the eighth century. In the early period, Buddhist culture in Turfan drew upon the Buddhist church in Kucha and Karashahr but after about the fifth century it increasingly assimilated Chinese influences. Buddhism continued, however, as the religion of the people for many centuries. Hsüan-tsang, who received a warm reception in Turfan and was given generous help so that he might continue his pilgrimage to India, speaks of the prosperous condition of Buddhism there. His account is supported by Chinese inscriptions which contain many references to the influences of Buddhism on the life and culture of the inhabitants.

In 507, Kiu, a Chinese dynasty, was established in Turfan, and more than a century later, in 640, it was brought under the direct control of China. At about this time the conflict for power with the Uigur Turks, one of the Hun tribes, began. During the sixth century a Turkish kingdom stretched from the Altai Mountains eastward to the Pacific Ocean and westward to the Black Sea. In the seventh century, Balkh, Bamiyan, the Hindu Kush, Badakshan, and Belehan were under Turkish control. But soon central authority began to weaken, the conflict with the rising power of the Arabs began, and the Turkish Empire split into two parts. The western part gradually became Islamic between the eighth and tenth centuries, and the eastern part was consolidated under the Uigur Turks. The Uigur Empire was the most important power in Central Asia between 755 and 840. After a prolonged war amongst the Tibetans, the Chinese, and the Uigurs, the latter triumphed and set up their rule in Turfan in 870 with Qarakhodjo as their capital. Uigur rule lasted in Turfan until the eleventh century, and during this period the region played a significant role in the history of Central Asia.

The ascendancy of the Uigurs, who were enthusiastic Buddhists, acted as a new impetus for the further advance of Buddhism. The Turks had embraced Buddhism quite early in Tokharestan and it had a powerful influence over their lives until their conversion to Islam. By the time they appeared in Turfan they had already absorbed a good deal of Buddhist culture. During their struggle against the Arabs, they built a huge Buddhist monastery near the Sogdh River. The name of the City, Bokhara, is derived from the Turkish and Mongol word *bukhar* for vihara. It is said that a Chinese princess, who was given in marriage to a Turkish ruler, brought with her an icon of the Buddha. A vihara was built for the image and the town of Bokhara later developed around this monastery. Most of the Buddhist sites in the region of Turfan belong to the Uigur period, and include cave temples with frescos representing Buddhas or Bodhisattvas, and numerous other Buddhist shrines. Buddhist texts in Tokharian are found together with Uigur translations.

Buddhism did not retain its original Indian character in Central Asia. During the course of its migration from India to Tokharestan, Khotan, and Turfan, Buddhism inevitably absorbed local characteristics. In the western part of Central Asia around Kashgar and in the northern part stretching eastward beyond Kucha, Theravada Buddhism was prevalent but at places along the southern route, especially in Khotan and in the northeastern part around Turfan, Mahayana Buddhism was practiced.

Despite the enormous pressure of Islam in the eighth century, Buddhism held on until the eleventh century in the lines of oases lying north and south of the desert. Islamic attacks must have caused extensive destruction of religious art and sacred manuscripts since these Buddhist monasteries and sanctuaries were deserted in the eleventh century; whatever escaped the iconoclastic zeal of the Muslim conquerors has been well preserved in the dry climate of the region for the past nine hundred years.

India's immediate neighbours, Nepal and Tibet, owe much of their cultural inheritance to contact with India. Modern Nepal, an expanded version of the ancient country, is 525 miles long and about one hundred miles wide, and lies between India and Tibet. Originally the word Nepal implied the Valley, which, surrounded by the peaks of the Himalayas, is about fifteen to twenty miles long and ten miles wide, with its three capitals, Kathmandu, Patan, and Bhatgaon lying within a radius of seven miles of one another. Contact between the two countries is so close and ancient that it is impossible to trace the origins of Nepalese culture separately from Indian culture. It was in one of the republics of ancient India, at Lumbini in the city of Kapilavastu, within the boundaries of modern Nepal, that Gautama, the founder of Buddhism, was born. Consequently, Nepal holds a unique position in the Buddhist world, even though today it is the only country professing to be a sovereign Hindu state.

According to tradition, however, it was Asoka who introduced

Buddhism as an organized doctrine into Nepal. He visited Lumbini and erected an inscribed pillar to commemorate the sacred birthplace of the Buddha. This event is an important landmark in the history of Buddhism. It is said that Charumati, a daughter of Asoka, married a Nepalese prince and built several stupas and monasteries, some of which have survived to the present day. Later, the imperial Guptas imposed their sovereignty on Nepal, and the reigning dynasties of Nepal and India began to intermarry. Nepal has often changed her religion according to whichever faith prevailed in the neighbouring parts of India—having embraced Hinayana, Mahayana, Vajrayana, and Hinduism in their respective ages of supremacy. The Rajputs and the Brahmans—and probably Buddhist monks from Nalanda and elsewhere—escaped to Nepal when Islam triumphed in India. In the eighteenth century Nepal was conquered by the Gurkhas, who trace their descent from the Rajputs, and who in the sixteenth century conquered the little state of Gurkha. Their language, Khas, is a Rajasthani dialect of Sanskrit origin, and under their influence Hinduism became the state religion of Nepal.

Nepal has never known religious conflicts and persecutions, and even today Hinduism and Buddhism live together in complete harmony. In the early centuries A.D. the disciplinary rules applicable to the monks of the *Mulasarvastivada* school of Buddhism in Nepal were somewhat modified to suit the rigid climatic conditions of that region. Nepal attained prominence both as a political and religious state during the reign of King Amsurvarman in the seventh century, who was as remarkable an administrator as he was a conqueror. Although he was perhaps a Sivaite Hindu, he contributed generously towards the growth of the Buddhist faith and institutions.

Later, Buddhist monks escaping from the encroachments of Islam in Bihar and Bengal took refuge in Nepal, carrying with them numerous valuable manuscripts, some of which were later transmitted to Tibet where they are still preserved. Thus some of the many Buddhist works which were lost in India are available in Chinese and Tibetan translations, and it is in Nepal that the nine Sanskrit works forming the Nepalese Buddhist canon are preserved. They are considered the original works of the Sanskrit canon which became the official scriptures of Mahayana Buddhism; the *Prajnaparamita* is amongst these nine. Nepal has been a link between the regions lying on the two sides of the mid-Himalayan ranges, and, until recently, the normal road of communication between India and Tibet lay through Nepal via Kyirong.

With the decline of Buddhism in India, Nepalese Buddhism became increasingly self-contained, gradually abandoning some of its original features, such as monastic life and opposition to caste. Until recently four main sects of Buddhist philosophy have been prominent in Nepal: Svabhavika, which emphasizes that all things in the world have their own ultimate characteristics; Aisvarika, which believes in a self-existent god, who is perfect and infinite; Karmika, which believes in a conscious moral effort through which the world-phenomenon is developed; and Yatrika, which believes in the existence of conscious intellectual agency and free will. These represent an almost complete fusion of the various philosophical theories that emerged in India and Tibet under the stimulus of either Hinduism or Buddhism.

The small valley of Nepal reputedly contains more than two thousand temples. The most famous of these is the Temple of Pashupatinath. Most of the stupas of Asoka have disappeared and those that have survived, such as at Sanchi, Taxila, and Sarnath, have been so enlarged that the original structures are no longer clear. Only in Nepal have Mauryan stupas retained their original shape. Hindu religious architecture in Nepal is characterized by the stone temple with a massive tower above a comparatively small shrine. Because of the Buddhist periods in her history, Nepal has also developed temples of the pagoda type made of wood with copper roofs. Nepalese sculpture and painting is in a style derived from the Pala art of Bihar and Bengal. In the realm of art, Nepal was, in fact, practically an exclusive province of Pala, India, between the ninth and twelfth centuries. Tibet, whose art is close to that of Nepal, adopted the Pala tradition through Nepal and Kashmir. Many of the laws of Nepal and its social organizations naturally reflect Hindu models, and the Nepalese language is very close to Sanskrit. But the Hindu civilization in Nepal has evolved a distinct character of its own, effected through a blending of its own traditions with those of Tibet.

Wherever Buddhism spread it was able to ignite a new historical consciousness. This was the case in some measure even in India where

Indian recorded history began in inscriptions and other forms from the time of Asoka. But it is in Tibet that the best example of this is seen. The history of Tibet was first recorded in the seventh century during the reign of Songtsan-Gampo, who first conceived the idea of reducing spoken Tibetan to a system of alphabetic writing to facilitate the arrival of Buddhism from India. However, Tibet's great altitude, the deeply religious character of its society, and its political organization have isolated it from other lands. When the Tibetans, who are ethnologically similar to the peoples of the Himalayan regions, settled in the area is not known; from time immemorial they have lived in an isolation imposed by the peculiarities of their environment. Except for Buddhism in the seventh century, Tibet scarcely allowed any other foreign cultural influence within her national frontiers. In fact, Tibet was the last country to embrace Buddhism, which by the seventh century was thriving in many other lands.

Traders, soldiers, and pilgrims had long been crossing her borders, and cultural contacts between Tibet and the Buddhist world surrounding her must have been established centuries before the actual arrival of Buddhism. According to a Tibetan legend, in the fifth century some Buddhist missionaries from India approached the Tibetan King Thothori with presents of Buddhist books, but none at the royal court could make out what they meant, since an alphabetic script was then unknown in Tibet.

Although Buddhism was finally welcomed and encouraged by the powerful ruling Tibetan dynasty, it did not take root as easily as might have been expected. Before it was accepted by the people, it encountered prolonged opposition from the traditional ritualistic and sacrificial faith. This faith endorsed a nature worship, and believed that human ills were caused by the activities of evil spirits who were controlled by magic and spells. Buddhism had to wage an incessant and arduous struggle for over three centuries against these indigenous beliefs and old superstitions, and adapt its own doctrines to placate them. Many setbacks occurred until the arrival of Atisa in the eleventh century, when Buddhism finally became the national religion of Tibet.

Matrimonial alliances were instrumental in starting the growth of Buddhism in Tibet. In the seventh century, Tibet had emerged as a strong kingdom extending to the borders of India, Nepal, and China. In the south, Nepal's King was Amsuvarman; in the east, China was ruled by the powerful Emperor Tang Tai-tsung. According to the Tibetan chronicles, the talented Tibetan King, Songtsan-Gampo (or Srong-btsan Bam-po) married the daughter of Amsuvarman, Princess Bhrikuti, who was a devout Buddhist and who brought an image of the Buddha to Tibet with her. Songtsan, in deference to the new queen's beliefs which he himself already favoured, built a great temple known as Jokhang to house her image of the Buddha. Songtsan's power was so great that he compelled the Emperor of China to give him Princess Wen Ch'eng in marriage. She too was Buddhist and brought to Tibet the famous Buddha image now enshrined in Jokhang. This statue originally came from Magadha in India. It forms, together with two other statues preserved at the monastery of Kum-bum and at Santal temple at Peking, one of a triad celebrated in the Buddhist world. Whilst the arrival of these two queens did much to help the king introduce Buddhism into Tibet, he had, in fact, already selected a brilliant Tibetan in his court, Thonmi Sambhota, along with sixteen others, to travel to the famous centres of learning in southern India to study Indian writing, phonetics, and grammar.

Upon his return from several years of study in India, Thonmi Sambhota not only composed eight independent treatises on Tibetan writing and grammar, but also prepared the first Tibetan translations of Sanskrit texts of Buddhism.[7] Thus, he was both the pioneer of Buddhist learning in Tibet and the father of Tibetan literature. A grammar and a new script on the lines of the Khotanese alphabet, derived from Sanskrit prevalent in the Gupta period, were evolved for the Tibetan language.

Once the practice of visiting India had begun, many Tibetan students went to India to study Buddhism, and Sanskrit texts began to pour into Tibet. Indian and Chinese scholars visited Tibet and helped in translation and interpretation. It was during this period that the celebrated sandalwood image of Avalokitesvara, the compassionate Buddha, now worshipped in the palace of the Dalai Lama, was supposedly brought to Tibet by Indian scholars.

Songtsan, a contemporary of Muhammad and Harsha, introduced a number of social and cultural reforms, made Buddhism the state religion, and actively encouraged the study of Buddhism during the thirty years of his reign. He promulgated laws to harmonize with the Ten Virtues of Buddhism. He built the temples of Ramoche and Jokhang in Lhasa, and laid the beginnings of the magnificent palace of the Dalai Lama, the Potala, which exists to this day. He is regarded by the Tibetans as a national hero and a spiritual guide. For his respect for learning, and love of Tibet and its people, he is worshipped as one of the incarnations of Avalokitesvara.[8]

By the middle of the eighth century, Tibet had become so powerful under Trisong-Detsan that it was able to dictate terms to the kingdoms of Central Asia, control the nomads in the Tarim Basin, and even defeat Chinese armies and force the payment of tribute. Trisong-Detsan's victory over China is commemorated in a pillar inscription in front of the Potala. He enthusiastically supported Buddhism, and invited Santarakshita, a famous Indian scholar from Nalanda University, to Tibet to preach Buddhism and initiate regular conversions. But Santarakshita faced bitter opposition from the Bonists and his sermons elicited little response. Storms and epidemics raging at the time provided "heaven-sent" opportunities for the Bonists, who were supported by dissident elements in the palace. These natural calamities were interpreted as the wrath of the gods at the perverse teachings of Santarakshita and finally the King was compelled to advise Santarakshita to retire to Nepal until public passions had subsided. In the end, however, the King triumphed over the Bonist rebellion. Santarakshita saw that in Tibet, immersed as it was in primitive sorcery and love of ritual, only a man versed in the esoteric practices and beliefs of Tantrism could command attention, and on his advice in 747 the King invited the great Tantric teacher, Padmasambhava (known in Tibet as Guru Rinpoche), to Tibet.

Born in Udayana, the border region between Kashmir and Afghanistan famous for its sorcery and magic, Padmasambhava had studied at Nalanda and was reputed to possess great supernatural powers. Before starting for Tibet, Padmasambhava prepared himself thoroughly for his task. He carefully studied the Bon doctrines and practices, and realized that only a person who could claim power over evil spirits and demonstrate this supremacy could possibly succeed. He took Mahayana Buddhism tinged with Tantric ideas to Tibet and, by incorporating many gods as Tantric guardian deities, he laid the foundation of Tibetan Buddhism or Lamaism. He replaced the Bon cult of animal worship with symbolic worship and its practice of black magic with inner purification.

It is, however, not easy to ascertain the truth about Padmasambhava because his life is so enshrouded in myth and legend. Nor is it easy now to define the details of the primitive Lamaism he devised and taught. But it is evident that his teaching was Tantric and a magical type of Mahayana Buddhism, to which he added a portion of the ritual and demonolatry of Bon. The Tantric Buddhism of Padmasambhava has been subjected to a good deal of criticism by some commentators, mainly because they have misunderstood the nature of Tantrism and the large part which sex played in it. The standards which these critics apply to Padmasambhava and his doctrine are unenlightened. Tantrism, whether Hindu or Buddhist, aims to interpret human nature pragmatically, and, unlike most faiths, it preaches understanding and sublimation of the reproductive force in direct opposition to the common but scientifically unsound teaching concerning the forcible suppression of it. Science recognizes today what Tantric thinkers accepted centuries ago, that "there is direct relationship between the highest mental and psychic powers in mankind and the secretions of the sex glands and, that physical youthfulness and efficiency are dependent upon conservation of the reproductive essences. All religions, likewise, even the most primitive, have recognized that there is inseparableness between the sex-energy and spiritual growth."[9]

Having been engaged in an unending war against evil spirits and demons, the Tibetans had acquired a tradition of discipline and organization, which made it easy for Padmasambhava to develop organized Buddhist life in Tibet. The first great monastery, in fact the greatest ever built in Tibet, the Samye monastery, which today contains many shrines and a large library of Sanskrit and Tibetan books, was built in 749 at Bsam-yas on the model of the Udayantapuri in Bihar. Santarakshita laid the foundation and was appointed its abbot. He held office for thirteen years until his death. He and Padmasambhava collaborated in teaching the Tripitaka, the Tantric doctrines, and the philosophical system of Yogacara. Having established Tibetan Buddhism or Lamaism, Padmasambhava disappeared from Tibet. However, the deep respect held for him even today indicates the impression he made on his contemporaries.

An important feature of this period was the reorganization and systematization of the translations of Santarakshita, and the preparation of the first catalogue of all translated Buddhist works. Meanwhile, Buddhist texts and scholars had also begun to arrive from China, some of them opposed to Lamaism. To meet their challenge the King invited Santarakshita's able disciple and commentator, Kamalasila, from Nalanda to deal with them. A debate was held between a Chinese scholar, the Mahayanist Hwashang, and Kamalasila in the presence of the King, and Kamalasila was the winner. The Chinese scholar, having lost the argument, left the country, but feelings amongst his defeated partisans were so embittered that the Indian scholar was murdered. His body was embalmed and is still preserved in a monastery in the north of Lhasa. Kamalasila was the author of *Tarka*, a work expounding the various philosophic systems of India, and of many other treatises which are still extant in the great Lamaist canon, *Tan-gyur* (or *Tanjur). Mahavyutpatti*, the excellent Sanskrit-Tibetan dictionary, also dates from this period.

Buddhism made steady progress and was actively patronized by Trisong-Detsan's successors, especially by Rapachen (or Ralpachen) (817–836). His reign is considered a glorious period of Tibetan Buddhism, and it was under his patronage that the first history of Tibet was written. He made his young son take monastic vows, gave various privileges and administrative authority to the priesthood, built libraries, monasteries, and temples, encouraged Buddhist painting and sculpture, and even allowed his long locks of hair to be used as a mat by the Buddhist abbots associated with him. In the first year of his reign, he convened a Great Council of Indian and Tibetan scholars to discuss ways of spreading Buddhism. It was a period of great literary activity in which numerous Indian scholars, such as Jinamitra, Silendrabodhi, Surendrabodhi, Prajnavarmam, Danasila, and Bodhimitra, co-operated with the Tibetan scholars, Dpal-brt segs, Ye-ses-sde, Chos-kyirgyalmthsan, and others, in translating many Sanskrit works, which constitute more than half of the two large Tibetan collections, *Kanjur* and *Tanjur*.

Perhaps the very fact of Rapachen's devotion to Buddhism and the intensity of Buddhist activity caused the opposition to react violently, and in a palace revolution Rapachen was murdered by the supporters of his elder brother Glandarma, who, upon accession, became a professed enemy of Buddhism. A violent persecution followed. Buddhist images were burned, monasteries closed, religious ceremonies banned, and monks forced to return to the life of laymen under the penalty of exile. By an interesting coincidence, Buddhism was also being persecuted in China at this time. Such excesses created widespread resentment and counteraction. Within three years of the beginning of King Glandarma's reign, in 841, a monk quietly rode up and killed him with a well-aimed arrow. Whilst Glandarma's ruthless suppression of Buddhism brought the end of early Lamaism, it marked a decisive period in the annals of Tibetan politics, for it led to the decline and fall of monarchial rule in Tibet. The banished priesthood returned to Tibet and became more powerful than ever.

Buddhism finally became the national religion of Tibet by the beginning of the eleventh century, and the flow of Buddhist monks and scholars between India and Tibet gained new impetus. Once the followers of Bon were fully reconciled, there developed a distinctive Tibetan branch of Buddhism which produced many great spiritual teachers, scholars, and preachers, well-versed in both Sanskrit and Tibetan literature. To assist in the growth of Buddhism, Tibetan scholars persuaded Atisa (980–1054)—also known as Dipankara Srijnana—of the Vikramasila monastery in Bihar, to come to Tibet in 1038. Atisa, who was nearly sixty years old at that time, lived and preached in all parts of the country for about fifteen years before he died in the Nyethang monastery, where his *Samadhi* still stands. Atisa based his teachings on the Yogacara tradition, took a synthetic view of the tenets of Hinayana and Mahayana Buddhism, enforced celibacy of monks, and discouraged magic practices. He was possibly the last great Indian scholar to carry spiritual impetus from India to Tibet, where he ranks next only to the Buddha and Padmasambhava.

Other Indian influences also found their way to Tibet. For instance, the Tibetan medical system owes its origin to the Ayurvedic system of India. Tibetan Tantric forms are almost indistinguishable from Hindu Tantras, and certain Tantric images like Halahal-avalokitesvara and Nilkant-avalokitesvara are derivatives of Siva. Tibetan art is largely a continuation of the Buddhist art of eastern India during the Pala period. The representations of the Bodhisattvas, for example, are directly reminiscent of the traditions of Pala art, and reached Tibet through the Nepalese. Nepalese craftsmen were particularly accomplished and, even as far as Peking, they were considered amongst the best in this field until the collapse of Lamaism in China. Indian influence, possibly that of Ajanta, is particularly well marked in a Tibetan painting representing Avalokitesvara and Kitigarbha, now preserved in the Musée Guimet at Paris. Tibetan art was very popular with the Emperors of China, so much so that some of its religious features were adopted during the Ming and Ching periods.

After the death of Atisa, Buddhist reform was somewhat interrupted by prolonged political unrest in Tibet. Whilst reform suffered, Buddhism itself gained fresh strength, because Buddhist monasteries provided sanctuary to soldiers as well as to refugees. In 1206 Genghis Khan, the grandfather of Kublai Khan, brought Tibet under Mongol control. In the second half of the century, the Tibetan Lamas, despite intense competition from their Christian rivals, succeeded in converting Emperor Kublai Khan to Buddhism, giving Buddhism in Tibet unique prestige and power. The most powerful of the Lamaist hierarchs was the Saskya Grand Lama, and it was his representatives who succeeded in converting the Great Khan. In return, the Lama of Saskya, with the assistance of a staff of scholars, translated the Tibetan Buddhist canon into Mongolian, and was recognized as head of the Lamaist Church and tributory ruler of Tibet in 1270. This creation of a Lamaist Papacy by conferring "divine" honours upon the acquisition of temporal power, was, however, not analogous to Indian practice. Asoka himself never claimed any divine honours other than what was implied in his cherished title, "Beloved of the Gods." Tibet remained under Saskya supremacy until the middle of the fourteenth century when the power of the Saskya abbot was broken by the Ming Emperor of China.

Meanwhile, Tibetan Buddhism had begun to split into various schools of thought. The earlier heterogenous type of Buddhism came to be called Rninmapa, or the Old Tantric or Translation School. Its followers worshipped Padmasambhava as their founder and guru, and believed in the fulfilment of both the divine and the demonical. Today they are generally recognized by their red caps. The Kagyupa school was founded by Marpa, who had studied with Atisa at Nalanda under the Indian Tantrist, Naropa, and whose teachings have some affinities with the Dhyana School of Buddhism. The Saskya School (Great Earth School, so known because of the colour of the soil where its first monastery was built in 1071 on the site of the present Saskya) was closely related to the old Rninmapa School. It sought a synthesis between the old and the new Tantrism on the basis of Nagarjuna's Madhyamika philosophy. The monks of this School did not practice celibacy, but were greatly devoted to learning, were excellent preachers, and the School produced many eminent scholars, including By-ston (1290–1364) who was a renowned commentator on fundamental Buddhist treatises, an authoritative historian, and a collector of Buddhist works.

Atisa's reformed teachings, based upon the Yogacara traditions, led to the establishment of the Bkahgdamspa School by his Tibetan disciple, Hbrom-ston. This School took a synthetic view of the teachings of both the Hinayana (Theravada) and Mahayana, enforced celibacy upon monks and opposed magic practices. This reformed School of Atisa, reorganized and purged of much of its rituals by the great Tsongkhapa, dominates Tibetan Buddhism today. The altered title was Gelugpa (popularly known as the Yellow Hats), and the first Grand Lama was Geden-dub, the nephew of Tsongkhapa. It soon eclipsed all other rival schools, and in five generations it gained the priest-kingship of Tibet, which it retains to this day. The fifth Grand Lama, Nag-wan-Lozang (1615–1680), gave Gelugpa great temporal power, and in 1650 the Mongolian chief, Gusri Khan, conferred upon him the sovereignty of Tibet and gave him the title of Dalai, meaning ocean. Whilst his successors are now commonly known as Dalai Lamas, the Tibetans call them Gyal-wa Rin-po-che the great gem of majesty.

The recognition of the complete and divine sovereignty of the Dalai Lama over the whole of Tibet is a turning point in Tibetan history. Sanskrit texts, not only on religion but also on other subjects such as grammar and medicine, continued to be translated into Tibetan under the rule of this able and widely travelled Dalai Lama. Religious and cultural relations with India increasingly declined, however, mainly because of British domination and the liquidation of the old order in India.

Relations between India and Tibet, both of a political and cultural nature, have been re-established in the recent years since Indian independence, although the political aspect has become by far the dominant. The Dalai Lama and a number of his followers are presently living in India as refugees from Chinese interference in Tibet. The close physical contact, although caused by political circumstances, must have cultural consequences which will only be realized later.

Chapter IX

THE DRAGON UNDER THE BODHI TREE

UNTIL RECENTLY, INDIA and China had coexisted peacefully for over two thousand years. This amicable relationship may have been nurtured by the close historical and religious ties of Buddhism, introduced to China by Indian monks at a very early stage of their respective histories, although there are fragmentary records of contacts anterior to the introduction of Buddhism. There are numerous references to China in Sanskrit texts, but their chronology is questionable and sketchy. The *Mahabharata* refers to China several times, including a reference to presents brought by the Chinese at the *Rajasuya Yajna* of the Pandavas; also, the *Arthasastra* and the *Manusmriti* mention China. According to René Grousset, the name China comes from "an ancient Sanskrit name for the regions to the east, and not, as often supposed, from the name of the state of Ch'in," the first dynasty established by Shih Huang Ti in 221 B.C. When necessary, the Chinese would distinguish the centre of the world where they lived from peripheral regions, and one of the ancient expressions has become the modern name for China: Chung-kuo, literally "central country."[1] The Sanskrit name *Cina* for China could have been derived from the small state of that name in Chan-si (Shan-si) in the northwest of China, which flourished in the fourth century B.C., or the name may have come down to India through Central Asia. Scholars have pointed out that the Chinese word for lion, *shih,* used long before the Chin dynasty, was derived from the Sanskrit word, *simha,* and that the Greek word for China, *Tzinista,* used by some later writers, appears to be a derivative of the Sanskrit *Chinasthana.*

The formative period of Chinese Quietism, the fourth century B.C., was not one when outside influences on thought were general, but it developed and expanded during a period when such influences were growing in importance, and scholars now agree that Chinese literature of the third century is full of geographic and mythological elements derived from India. "I see no reason to doubt," comments Arthur Waley, "that the 'holy mountain-men' (*sheng-hsien)* described by Lieh Tzu are Indian *rishi*; and when we read in *Chuang Tzu* of certain Taoists who practiced movements very similar to the *asanas* of Hindu *yoga,* it is at least a possibility that some knowledge of the *yoga* technique which these *rishi* used had also drifted into China."[2] The Chinese Quietists practiced a form of self-hypnosis which has an indisputably close resemblance to Indian Yoga. The Chinese Taoist philosopher, Liu-An (Huai-nan-tzu) who died in 122 B.C., makes use "of a cosmology in his book which is clearly of Buddhist inspiration."[3]

The first mention of India to be found in Chinese records is in connection with the mission to Ta-hsia (Bactriana) of a talented and courageous Chinese envoy, Chang Chien (kien), about 138 B.C.[4] Fourteen years later, having escaped after ten years as a captive of the Huns, he returned home and in his report to the Chinese Emperor he referred to the country of *Shen-tu* (India) to the southeast of the Yueh-chih (Jou-Chih) country.[5] Chang Chien had seen bamboo poles and cloth in Ta-hsia, which had reached there from Szechwan, a province in the southwest of China, through India and Afghanistan. Whilst his diplomatic mission did not succeed, his observations and reports impressed the Han Emperor with the need to encourage trade and contact with India and other countries to the west.

There are other traditional stories suggestive of earlier links, but Chang Chien's reference to Indian trade with the southwestern districts of China along the overland route corresponding to the modern Yunnan road indicates the existence of some sort of commercial relations well before the second century B.C. The find of a Chinese coin at Mysore, dated 138 B.C., suggests that maritime relations between India and China existed in the second century B.C. Passages in a Chinese text of the first century A.D. vaguely refer to Chinese trade relations with countries in the China Sea and Indian Ocean, such as Huanz-che (Kanchi or a place in the Ganges delta), as well as to the exchange of occasional diplomatic missions.

There can be little dispute that trade was the main motivation for these early contacts. This is supported by finds of beads and pottery, in addition to specific references in historical texts. By the early centuries of the Christian era, Sino-Indian trade appears to have assumed considerable proportions. Chinese silk, *Chinamsuka,* and later porcelain were highly prized in India, and Indian textiles were sold in southwest China. The similarity between the Chinese and Indian words for vermilion and bamboo, *ch'in-tung* and *ki-chok* , and *sindura* and *kichaka,* also indicates commercial links. At least by the fifth century, India was exporting to China wootz steel (wootz from the Indian Kanarese word *ukku*), which was produced by fusing magnetic iron ore by carbonaceous matter.

With goods came ideas. It has often been contended that merchants were not likely to have been interested in philosophy or capable of the exchange of ideas. This is an erroneous belief which disregards historical evidence and, as Arthur Waley points out, is "derived from a false analogy between East and West. It is quite true that Marco Polo 'songeait surtout à son négoce'. But the same can hardly be said of Indian or Chinese merchants. Buddhist legend, for example, teems with merchants reputedly capable of discussing metaphysical questions; and in China Lu Puwei, compiler of the philosophical encyclopaedia *Lu Shih Ch'un Chiu*, was himself a merchant. Legend even makes a merchant of Kuan Chung; which at any rate shows that philosophy and trade were not currently supposed to be incompatible."[6]

The trade routes between China and India, by both land and sea, were long and perilous, often requiring considerably more than two years to negotiate. The overland routes were much older and more often used but the sea routes gained popularity with progress in shipbuilding and seamanship. Formidable and frightening as the physiography of the land routes was, the traffic through the passes and along the circuitous routes around the mountains was fairly vigorous.

There were three overland routes between India and China. The principal route lay through the northwestern regions of India which converge upon Afghanistan, western Tibet, Russian Turkistan, and Chinese Turkistan. Piercing through the Afghan country, and proceeding along the valley of the Kabul River, with stages at Peshawar (Purusapura) and Jalalabad (Nagarahara), it reached the Valley of Bamiyan which commands a major pass from the Kabul region to Balkh in the Hindukush mountains. Beyond this region, on the famous Silk Highway between Central and Western Asia, lay Bactriana, modern Balkh, which the ancient Indians called Balhika and the Chinese Fo-ho. On the westward journey from Balkh, the silk route proceeded to Antiochia Margiana (modern Meri), then to the great Parthian cities at Hecatompylos (modern Shahrud), and Ecbatana (modern Hamadan), crossing the Euphrates at Heirapoli (modern Menbij), and finally reaching Antioch. Eastward from Balkh two roads led to Central Asia and China. One proceeded northward through Sogdiana, then crossed the Syr or Jaxartes, and went eastward through Tashkent and the passes of the Tienshan, finally reaching Ush-Turfan. The other, which was shorter and more frequently used by Buddhist monks, passed through the country of the Tokharians and the Pamirs to Kashgar, and thence led to the Tarim Basin, the modern Chinese province of Sinkiang. There was a more direct but far more difficult route from Kashmir along the Gilgit and the Yasin valleys to Tashkurghan where it joined the other route to Kashgar. It was in this region that Indian, Chinese, and Western merchants met, making it the centre of commerce for the ancient world.

From Kashgar two routes led to the borders of China, one along the southern fringe of the Tarim Basin via Khotan, and the other along its northern fringe to Turfan. Rivers and streams in the Tien-shan ranges in the north and the Kun-lun ranges in the south made irrigation and agriculture possible in the foothills. International trade along these two routes further strenghtened the economic prosperity of this area. Along the southern route, a number of flourishing states and settlements, such as Yarkand, Khotan, and Niya, practiced Buddhism and played an extremely important role for almost a thousand years in the trade and cultural relations between China and India. There were equally important states along the northern route as well, whose people and languages differed from those of the south, but who were all united in Buddhism. Turfan, situated further east on the northern route, was well within the periphery of Chinese politics, and thus made outstanding contributions to Buddhism in China.

The two routes from Kashgar met on the Chinese frontier at Yumenkuan, the Jade Gate, near Tun-huang, one of the principal centres of Buddhist learning. From the testimony of ancient travellers, it would appear that Central Asia was much more habitable during the first thousand years of the Christian era than it is now.

Long before the northwestern routes were opened about the second century B.C., and long before the development of these Indianized states, there were two other routes from India to China. One of these began at Pataliputra (modern Patna), passed through Assam and Upper Burma near Bhamo, and proceeded over the mountains and across the river valleys to Yunnanfu (Kunming), the main city of the southern province of China. The other route lay through Nepal and Tibet. We have no contemporary description of this route but there is definite evidence of its use. These routes were difficult and dangerous because they lay through inaccessible, turbulent, and barren lands offering scanty food and security. The route across Tibet was developed much later in the middle of the seventh century, when Tibet had accepted Buddhism and established political relations with China. During the second half of the seventh century, a large number of Chinese monks came to India by this route.

In addition to land routes, there was an important sea link between India and China through Southeast Asia. During the course of the first few centuries of the Christian era, a number of Indianized states had been founded all over Southeast Asia. Both cultures met in this region, and the Indianized states served as an intermediary stage for the further transmission of Indian culture and Buddhism to China.

Ancient Greek geographers knew Southeast Asia and China (*Thinae*) were accessible by sea. Ptolemy mentions an important but unidentified Chinese port on the Tonkinese coast. Ports on the western coast of India were Bharukaccha (Broach); Surparka (Sopara); Kalyana; on the Bay of Bengal at the mouth of the Kaveri, Kaveripattam (Puhar); and at the mouth of the Ganges, Tamralipti (Tamluk). At least two of these ports on the Bay of Bengal—Kaveripattam and Tamralipti—were known to the Greek sailors as Khaberos and Tamalitis. At first Indian ships sailed to Tonkin (Kiao-Che) which was the principal port of China, Tonkin being a Chinese protectorate. Later all foreign ships were required to sail to Canton in China proper. Canton became a prosperous port and from the seventh century onward was the most important landing place for Buddhist missionaries arriving from India or Southeast Asia.

Reading the accounts of Chinese travellers, it is impossible not to be impressed by their intrepid spirit. The perils of the desert, the danger of the "moving sands," and the loneliness of the journey were so complete that there were not even any birds or animals to be seen. Travellers often lost their way, and the sands were littered with the bones of those who had perished. The rigours of the journey were relieved only by the hospitality offered by the few Buddhist principalities and towns. The route continued through the different crests and gorges of the sand-eroded Karakorum and Kohibaba into northern Afghanistan or into Ladhakh on the Tibetan border. South of Kapisa, then a small state to the north of the modern city of Kabul, India commenced with the kingdom of Gandhara, lying alongside the stretch of the Kabul River between the Kunar and the Indus.

The sea was only slightly less dangerous. Navigation at the time was crude and without any scientific aids except the mariner's compass. The timber ships—tall floundering vessels of three tiers—were apt to spring leaks, and there was constant danger from typhoons between China and the Indonesian islands. Fa-hsien vividly describes how he escaped a watery grave. It took him fourteen days to reach Ceylon from Tamralipti and another ninety from Ceylon to Java. On his journey from Java to Canton, his ship lost its course in a storm, and it took eighty-two days of anxious drifting to reach Shantung. Merchants and monks travelled together. Although the traders faced the same hard climatic and physical conditions as did the pilgrims, they were better organized. The pilgrims, too, were probably weaker physically because of fasts and other self-imposed restrictions. They often depended on the goodwill of the kings through whose kingdoms they passed for protection, and frequently these kings, who had only recently embraced Buddhism, would coerce the monks to stay behind. But their single-minded devotion to their pilgrimages and their irrepressible urge to acquire learning sustained the pilgrims, although tests of physical endurance did not end with the journey. Living in strange and distant lands was no less trying. Whilst some scholars and pilgrims adapted easily to the ways of the new land, where they either stayed for several years or settled permanently, others longed to return to their homes.

Generally the Chinese monks set out for the famous centres of learning in India, like the University of Nalanda, but many Chinese scholars elected to stop at places on the periphery of India, such as the seats of learning in northwest India and Kashmir. Of those who came by sea, some chose to stop at the famous Buddhist centres in Sumatra or Ceylon. Whilst some monks learned the sacred language, philosophy, and rules of monastic life, others studied a special branch or particular school of Buddhism. Some, upon their return to China, founded their own new schools.

THE SIXTH AND fifth centuries B.C., during which Chinese philosophy was systematized, is by far the most brilliant period of Chinese thought. The number of philosophies was so large that this period is commonly known as the time of the Hundred Schools. It was one of those unique moments in the history of a nation, in which political suffering and economic chaos are dwarfed by the brilliance of its philosophic and spiritual achievement. Of the six main schools of philosophy, Confucianism and Taoism were the most important.[7]

It is misleading to use the general term Confucianism. *Ju Chia,* to define Chinese classics dealing with a wide variety of subjects, such as cosmology, ethics, morals, and theories of state and government. But it was from the time of Kung-tzu, or Confucius (551–479 B.C.), that the era of systematic philosophies began in China. Confucius was, strictly speaking, not the founder of a system but the editor, interpreter, and transmitter of ancient Chinese lore. He expounded in his *Lun-yu* (*Analects*), the old Chinese classics, such as *I-Ching, Shih-Ching, Shu-Ching, Li-Chi,* and *Chun-Chiu.*[8] In fact, the Duke of Chou, who lived many centuries before Confucius, is honoured in China as the founder of the "Confucian" tradition.

With a magnetic personality and persuasive power of speech, Confucius attracted a number of disciples—reputedly seventy-two, although in the *Analects* only some twenty persons figure—many of whom were members of the nobility. He was China's first and greatest teacher. He spent his long life as a travelling advisor to the feudal princes and as the head of a flourishing private school of ethics. China was at the time, so Confucius thought, drifting away from its ancient heritage, and he felt compelled to arrest this evil by collecting, preserving, and disseminating the records of ancient learning. The religion prevalent in Chinese society dwelt little on life after death and little use was made of it to deter wickedness and stimulate virtue. Confucius did have some religious convictions but he apparently did not use them as a basis for his philosophy. He was curious about the invisible realm or reality and believed that man had a moral force or character from which his effectiveness was derived, but he did not dwell upon the origin of this all-important essence. He condemned human sacrifice, which had been very prevalent earlier in China and which had continued to a lesser extent until his time.

Confucius, despite his deep influence on intellectual history, was not himself, strictly speaking, an intellectual. He was mainly a moral teacher, aiming at improving the conduct and values of the people. The central theme of his doctrine was the perfect development of personality, and the proper standardization and adjustment of human relations for the attainment of the supreme good. Until Confucius' time, the term *Chun-tzu*, son of a ruler or gentleman, meant a man of superior birth. But Confucius changed this meaning completely, asserting that any man who was noble, just, kind, and unselfish could be a gentleman. The criterion was not birth but conduct.

He considered man to be essentially a social being, emphasizing the virtues of *jen* (human-heartedness) and *yi* (righteousness). Jen, which has been described as his "golden rule," implies "Do not do to others what you do not wish for yourself." It is imperative for the individual to act rightly and morally, but not just because it is personally advantageous to do so.

Confucius made no claim to possessing the ultimate truth; he only claimed to be advancing towards it through the empirical method of observation and analysis. Perhaps more than any other thinker of comparable stature, he made a clear distinction between metaphysics and ethics, basing his ethics upon the nature of man and society. Confucius purposely refrained from teaching metaphysics, but his disciples, especially Meng-tzu or Mencius (371–289 B.C.) and Hsun-tzu (298–238 B.C.), included metaphysical speculations in Confucianist thought. Whilst

Mencius emphasized the idealistic aspect of Confucianism, saying that human nature was good, Hsun-tzu stressed its realism, holding that human nature was originally and intrinsically bad.

Teaching, however, was not Confucius' ultimate goal; he planned to reform society through government. Society to him was an ordinance of heaven and was made up of five relationships, between ruler and subject, husband and wife, father and son, elder and younger brothers, and friends. And since the government was to work righteously for the welfare and happiness of society, and was in return entitled to the sincere obedience of the people, the country should be ruled by the most capable man available. Few could be better equipped for this task, he believed, than himself. He patiently waited for the right opportunity to capture political power and prove himself to be the model ruler. In this he was sadly disappointed, although many of his disciples held government posts and he did become for a short period *Shih-Shih,* Leader of the Knights, which was not, politically speaking, a position of importance. His doctrine that any man, regardless of birth, could become a gentleman was a revolutionary concept in feudal Chinese society, and it is therefore scarcely surprising that Confucius was not very successful in his lifetime. Frustrated in his bid for political power, he died a broken-hearted and rather pathetic old man who thought himself a failure. Indeed, his ideas did not gain supremacy during the first century or so after his death until they were lifted out of obscurity by Mencius, who emphasized the idealistic trend in Confucianism, postulating that human nature was intrinsically good. Since then, Confucianist ideas, in one form or another, have continued to influence men. Even some of the Chinese Communists trace the beginnings of their revolutionary tradition to him.

Taoism (or *Tao Chia,* or *Tao Chiao)* belongs to a much later period than Confucianism. It begins with Yang-chu, probably a contemporary of Mencius and Chuang-tzu, but it is based on the *Tao Te Ching* which is reputed to be the work of Lao-tzu (b. 604 B.C.) whose actual existence, however, is doubted today. Some of the teachings of the *Tao Te Ching* can be traced to ancient Chinese classics, and some bear close resemblance to Indian thought. The text was edited during the Han period, having been given state recognition as a classic in the middle of the second century B.C. It is a small book of about five thousand characters with two large divisions entitled *Tao* and *Te*. The former deals mainly with metaphysics and the latter with ethics and politics. Although the beginnings of Taoist thought can be traced back to a time before Confucius, it is commonly regarded as an intellectual reaction against Confucianist thought.

Taoism is both a religion (*Tao Chiao*) and a philosophy (*Tao Chia*), and the teachings of the two are in a way mutually contradictory. As a philosophy Taoism teaches the doctrine of following nature, whilst as a religion it teaches men to work against nature. Taoism as a philosophy is theoretical, and as a religion it is quite practical in outlook and aims; its philosophy is anterior to its religion. Taoist thought is mainly a form of escapism, preaching abandonment of human society which is considered evil, and retirement to a life of seclusion in natural retreats. It is, however, as a philosophy that Taoism is seen as a competitor of Confucianism. Whilst Confucianism was originally a social philosophy emphasizing the responsibilities of man, Taoism was originally an anti-social philosophy emphasizing what was natural and spontaneous in man. It opposed the educational activities of the Confucianists, and advocated that the people should be kept in innocence. Opposed to a highly centralized system of government and all forms of legal restraint, it condemned militarism and exalted non-resistance. Whilst Confucianists advocated a carefully ordered system of government for the benefit of the people, Taoists claimed that the best government was one which left the people alone.

Whilst Confucianism was prepared to accept the world without speculating on the origins of the universe or the nature of being, Taoism penetrated behind the visible to explore the ultimate reality. Taoism stands for conformity with nature and its laws. Only by the proper development of his nature through the use of his *te* (power or virtue), and by recognizing the relative nature of things and identifying himself with the whole, can man achieve his chief purpose, happiness. Gradual recognition that all distinctions, including that between life and death, are merely relative conventions and not absolute can lead to this state of happiness. Nature is regulated by exact principles, but it never explains them. The perfect man penetrates the mystery of the order of heaven and earth, and comprehends the principles of nature. He does nothing and originates nothing; he merely contemplates the universe. The perfect man only needs to be one with the Great One. The end of knowledge is its own banishment, it is no-knowledge. Hence the doctrine of *wu-wei,* do-nothing or inaction. By doing nothing there is nothing which is not done.

Both tao and te are important concepts of Taoist metaphysics. The term tao originally meant the way in which the heavens caused the phenomena on earth. The tao was located about the celestial pole, which was the seat of power because all revolved about it. Later, tao was thought of as the universal cosmic energy behind the visible order of nature. The tao, omnipotent and eternal, produced *yin* and *yang,* the negative and positive, female and male principles of nature, which gave birth to heaven and earth, which in their turn produced all beings. It is conceived as unnameable, the ultimate and absolute principle that lies beyond good and evil, not moral but supra-moral. It is the oneness in which both being and non-being are dialectically embraced.

Chuang-tzu (*ca.* 369–286 B.C.) was the earliest and most brilliant Taoist. Original both in thought and literary expression, he sought to defend and develop the *Ching* philosophy, and he reacted strongly against all traditional thought, particularly Confucianism.

Until Buddhism entered China, the rivalry between the Confucianist and Taoist philosophies dominated Chinese thought. Confucianism, however, gained ground during the Han period, but not without incorporating some Taoist doctrines. Consequently, a culture based on the canonical writings, as edited and interpreted by Confucius and his school, had emerged. The Former Han dynasty, in contrast to the active policy of its predecessors, encouraged scholarship and adopted Confucianism as the state religion. Confucianist scholars were given high positions, and a rationale for political, bureaucratic, and social relationships was sought in the Confucianist classics. The intelligentsia and the ruling classes accepted the complete supremacy of these classics, and the government drew upon them, as they were impregnated with legalistic notions for a standard code of morals and ritual rules regulating conduct of the rulers and the ruled. During the Later Han period, rigid Confucianist "ceremonialism" dominated the whole society. The Confucianist classics had become highly formalized, verbose, and specialized. *Li,* or procedural rules, actually divided society into ranks of social positions. Even nations had come to be placed in hierarchial positions; China was "the Middle Kingdom" and other nations were "Barbarians." Within nations there were lords, aristocrats, officials, common people, and slaves.

In the Later Han period the literati, mentally exhausted and physically weakened by the successive incursions of the hordes from the north, were disinclined to follow the Confucianist principle of restraint. Fond of explaining the matters of state and society by relating them to the phenomena of nature, the Confucianists had pushed analogies so far that they could not be sustained against the attacks of the iconoclasts and sceptics, such as Wang Chung (27–97), the chief exponent of the Old Text School that purged Confucianism of its yin-yang elements. Through his criticism of the yin-yang theory, especially its belief that an interaction exists between heaven and man, and by pointing out that man's position in the universe was no better than that of a flea under a robe, Wang Chung prepared the way for a revival of Taoism a century later. The increasing belief in the supernatural also undermined Confucianist authority. Doctrinal and internal conflicts concerning the interpretation of classical texts also had enervating effects. Powerless to obtain relief from the oppression of the great families which maintained their authority by driving the peasantry to slavery, extreme poverty, and deep discontent, the Confucianists became receptive to superstition and miracles. Whilst dynastic quarrels pulled the Empire apart from the top, the peasants were alienated at the bottom. Furthermore, a system of thought so completely interwoven with the Han political order as was Confucianism was bound to be weakened and discredited once the Han Empire declined.

It was at this time that Buddhism arrived in China. Disillusioned in Confucianist thought, both the literati and the masses alike turned to Taoism and Buddhism, seeking an escape into spiritualism. The golden images of the Buddha, the burning of incense, and the changing of sutras by the yellow-robed Buddhist monks captivated the Chinese mind. Consequently, Buddhism was welcomed by all classes as a religion holding the promise of relief from misfortune.

The Later Han period is conspicuous for its political decadence, economic stress, and opulence in the urban areas, which combined to add to the general poverty of the common people. Whilst the lax life led many of the rich to renounce worldly pleasures by turning to Buddhism, the peasants hoped for equality in the new faith. Chinese traditional thought had little left of its earlier vitality and intellectual curiosity to resist the influx of Buddhist ideas.

Buddhism was more developed religiously than Confucianism and more sophisticated philosophically than Taoism. Buddhism made no class distinctions and thus appealed to both the educated and uneducated the rich and poor. Mou-tzu (170–225) wrote a treatise in which he compared the doctrines of Buddhism with the teachings of Confucius and Lao-tzu, and tried to establish Buddhist superiority. Such writings created a favourable climate for Buddhist teachings.

In spite of the recognition given to Buddhism by the Han Emperor Ming, there were many Chinese literati who opposed it because their own political, intellectual, and social interests clearly would have suffered from its predominance. Hence, the Later Han official classes were hostile to the introduction of Buddhism, and, since Confucianism continued to be a powerful factor in Chinese society, Buddhism has always been subject to the pressures of Confucianist beliefs and politics and its fortunes have varied accordingly.

THE EXACT DATE of the introduction of Buddhism into China is controversial. Chinese historians, as a rule, excluded religion from their chronicles unless it was directly related to politics or the court. They were even less interested in foreign religions, because they were orthodox Confucianist scholars. The Chinese peasants were generally unfamiliar with Chinese ideographs and literature, and the contemporary Chinese writings that have survived come from a small group of government intellectuals who, trained in the tradition of Confucianism, suffered from a marked attitude of superiority and exclusiveness towards foreign countries. Chinese history was written "by bureaucrats for bureaucrats." References in these records to early Buddhism, therefore, are too few and often too casual, if not altogether adverse, to give a clear picture. These annals give scarcely any account of the people and life in the provinces. In reconstructing the history of Buddhism on the basis of such material, extreme care must be taken. On the other hand, the Buddhist accounts were naturally written less as history than as a means of enhancing the prestige and popularity of the faith, often recording easy conversions and exaggerated triumphs of Buddhism at the Chinese Court.

Buddhism is generally said to have entered China during the reign of Ming-ti (58–75), but it is certain that it had been heard of in China before this time. According to a Chinese tradition, which cannot be fully substantiated, Buddhist missionaries reached Chin China from Mauryan India. *Li Tai San Pao Chi* (The Record Concerning the Three Treasures Under Successive Dynasties), written at the end of the sixth century, states that eighteen Buddhist monks headed by the Shrmana Shih-li-fang, carrying a number of Buddhist scriptures, reached the Chin Court early in the third century B.C., but the historicity of this reference is doubtful.[9] Only a few recent scholars accept this tradition as valid, but it is significant that one of them should be Liang Chi-chao (1873–1929), because he is otherwise quite critical in dealing with early Buddhism.[10] According to a legend, the source of which, the *Lieh-tzu*, is a forgery of the third century or later, Confucius knew 'of the existence of the Buddha. Amongst other evidence cited to connect Asoka with the introduction of Buddhism into China, mention is made of his eighty thousand stupas some of which were said to have been discovered in China, and of relic bones of the Buddha said to have been excavated from one of them. Significantly, the first reference to Buddhist missionaries is in the period of Asoka, the founder of proselytism.

Whilst Asoka was engaged in humanizing politics by incorporating the spirit of the Buddha's compassion into his administration, and by promulgating the doctrine that "victory through the *Dharma* is the highest victory," China was beginning to emerge from an age of chaos and civil wars as a unified state. This was the period of the Chin dynasty from which China is generally believed to have gotten its name. Its first ruler, Shih Huang-ti (246–210 B.C.), sometimes called the Chinese Caesar, suppressed the turbulent Yueh-chih (Jou-Chih) in the south and the Huns in the north, and built the famous Great Wall. He founded a centralized state which was to last under different dynasties with varying authority and changing frontiers for more than two thousand years. Shih Huang-ti, however, in marked contrast to his contemporary, Asoka, violently suppressed certain philosophical and political ideas. This policy culminated in the outrageous "Fen-shu-keng-ju" incident in which scholars were buried alive and books were burned. The report that Shih Huang-ti imprisoned a group of Buddhist monks may lend some strength to the view that Buddhism had begun to trickle into China in the time of the Mauryas. After the death of Asoka in India, the great Han dynasty (206 B.C.–A.D. 220) arose in China, extending the Chinese frontiers, establishing internal peace and prosperity, and laying the foundations for the greatness and continuity of the Chinese state and culture. During the second century B.C., the Han dynasty adopted an aggressive policy towards its western neighbours, and opened up the Central Asian traffic routes over the Sinkiang Desert. These routes, which first carried Chinese political domination, later brought Indian culture.

In the spring of 121 B.C. the Han Emperor Wu dispatched a Chinese cavalry general, Ho Chu-ping, on a military expedition against the Hsiu-tu king in the northern territories. It is reported that Ho Chu-ping found a golden statue of a human form which the defeated king worshipped and to which, except for burning incense and ceremonial bowing, no sacrifices were offered. It has been suggested that this statue was a Buddhist image, and, if true, it is the earliest record of Chinese contact with Buddhism. The general opinion, however, is that it was instead a symbol of some local deity.

In 120 B.C. whilst a huge artificial lake named Kun-ming was being dug in Shansi, a mysterious black substance was excavated. Emperor Wu is said to have been informed that it was the residual ashes left behind after the conflagration of the world at the end of a *kalpa* or aeon. The digging of the lake is historically correct, and such an explanation could only have been given after the introduction of Buddhism. Consequently, this is regarded as evidence of the existence of Buddhist monks at the capital, Chang-an, in the last half of the second century B.C.

Wei-shou (506–572), the author of the history of the Topa Wei, *Wei-shu,* mentions that Chang-Chien, who had been sent to Central Asia in 138 B.C. to remonstrate with the Yueh-chih, reported on Indian Buddhism and that this was the first Chinese exposure to Buddhism.

According to *Wei-Lueh,* the history of the Wei dynasty written about 280, the envoy of the Yueh-chih king orally transmitted a Buddhist scripture to an official of the Han Court in the year 2 B.C. This account is credible because it includes accurate biographical details of the Buddha, and mentions some technical terms of the Buddhist order. By the first century of the Christian era, some small Buddhist communities were in existence in the capital itself. An official Chinese history, *The Record of the Later Han,* mentions that Liu Yang, the Prince of Chu and the half-brother of Emperor Ming, was a practicing Buddhist with the Emperor's approval. He worshipped the Buddha along with Huang-ti and Lao-tzu, and gave alms to Buddhists from a foreign land in Hsu-chou, which lay to the east of Loyang, the new capital of the Later Han. There were already Buddhists amongst the gentry, and missionaries were freely received in their homes. If Buddhism was being adopted by the nobility and if foreign missionaries were active in the district of Loyang and Hsu-chou, it is likely that Buddhism had already been known in the western provinces of Shensi and Kansu for some time. For those who came from Central Asia, it was customary to pause at Tun-huang in Kansu province after crossing the desert before entering China and proceeding to Loyang by way of Lian-chou and Chang-an. These major cities and provinces along the trade route already bustled with foreign caravans and the Buddhist missionaries who came with them.

At first Buddhism flourished in China chiefly amongst the foreigners, including merchants, refugees, hostages, and adventurers, who had brought it from their own countries. The official histories of China, however, do not concern themselves with the social and cultural life of these foreign groups on Chinese soil: "The Confucian World-conception recognized only one kind of relation between the inhabitants of the barbarian wastelands and the Middle kingdom: they are the people from afar, who attracted by the radiance of the emperor's virtue, came to offer their 'tribute of local products' as a token of their submission."[11]

According to a famous story, which is based on Chinese historical sources such as the *Mou-tzu,* the validity of which has been questioned in recent years, Buddhism was first "officially" introduced into China during the reign of Ming-ti of the Later Han dynasty. He is said to have had a vision of a golden man with sunlight passing from the back of his neck who flew about in space and came to earth. Upon being advised by a court scholar that the man in the vision was probably the Indian Buddha, he sent envoys to the country of the Yueh-chih to procure Buddhist sacred texts. The envoys returned, accompanied by the Indian monk Kasyapa

Matanga. They also brought an image of the Buddha and a number of Buddhist scriptures.[12]

Variations in the details of this story found in different sources, and the remarkably accurate description of the Buddha of the dream, have cast doubt on its authenticity. Since Buddhism had already been introduced into China before the time of Ming-ti's dream, there would appear to be little justification for fabricating the story unless it was considered expedient to do so, and the chief purpose of this story was perhaps to make the entry of Buddhism into China appear official and "by appointment." It claims that Chinese Buddhism had its beginning when the Emperor himself ordered the importation of Buddhist teaching and provided it with images, temples, scriptures, and monks. Nevertheless, it is certain that during Ming-ti's reign many foreign monks, whose names have not been preserved, were in Loyang and Chang-an. From this time onward, China began to receive a succession of Indian monks and texts.

Around the middle of the first century, Buddhism, regardless of its reception at the Chinese court, had found acceptance in the region north of the River Huai, in eastern Honan, southern Shantung, and northern Kiangsu. The most important city of this region was Peng Cheng (Hsu-chou), a flourishing centre of trade on an eastern extension of the Silk Highway. Some scholars have suggested that the "Church of Loyang" was a later offshoot of the "Church of Peng-Cheng." Tonkin, now in Vietnam but part of southern China at that time, was also a principal seat of Buddhism. This centre, however, was set up by monks who had arrived by sea, and who were possibly in contact with the Buddhist centre of Peng-Cheng in the north.

From the middle of the second century the growth of Buddhism in China began to accelerate. Emperor Huan (147–167), like Ch'u-wangying (Liu Yang, The Prince of Chu), enshrined the Buddha in his palace together with the Huang-ti (Yellow Emperor) and Lao-tzu. In 166, Siang-Chieh of Shantung Province came to the capital and presented the emperor with a letter admonishing him for his excesses and reminded him of the teachings of the Buddha, which implies that Buddhism had already gained a widespread following in China.

The steady translation of the Buddhist scriptures into Chinese began in the middle of the second century. If any Buddhist scriptures had been translated into Chinese before this, there is no record of them. A Parthian monk, An Shih-kao, arrived at Loyang in 148, marking the beginning of a period of intense literary activity. He is the first of those personalities of Chinese Buddhism whose historicity is not questioned. He was followed by Chih-lou-chia-chian (or Lokakshema) from the Yueh-chih country. An Shih-kao chiefly translated Hinayana into Chinese, and Chih-lou-chia-chian translated Mahayana scnptures. Soon Chinese intellectuals became interested in Buddhism, and began to make their own annotations and commentaries. From the middle of the second century to the beginning of the third, a number of Buddhist teachers, translators, and scholars were active at Loyang. According to Tao-an's catalogue, some ten *acharyas* translated about fifty-one Buddhist scriptures during this period.

Information about the organization of the monasteries and monks at Loyang is scanty, but it is known that the missionaries were cosmopolitan. Their group is known to have included at least two Parthians, one of whom was Shih-kao, three Yueh-chih, two Sogdians, and three Indians. Hardly anything is known about the relations of the Buddhist community at Loyang with its immediate surroundings and with the Chinese court, but it is clear that it was not an isolated enclave of foreign culture. Many of its Chinese lay devotees belonged to the cultured classes. It has been generally thought that there were no Chinese monks until the fourth century because the Han Emperors permitted only foreigners to embrace Buddhism; there is, however, evidence to the contrary. At the end of the second century a Chinese monk Futiao, a convert of Shih-kao, not only helped the foreign monks in their translations but did some of his own. He also wrote an original work *Sha-mi-shih-hui Chang-chü,* the Preface of which is still extant.

The gradual disintegration of the Han Empire began around the middle of the second century, and the authority of the central government was undermined by a variety of disruptive forces, including the provincial warlords. The Han hold over the western regions slackened, and a civil war began which brought about the downfall of the dynasty in 220. The Later Han dynasty was succeeded by three states, the Three Kingdoms: Wei in the north with its capital at Loyang, Wu in the central and lower part of the Yangtze Valley with its capital at Nanking, and Shu in Szechwan with its capital at Chengtu. Their rule lasted for about half a century, but it was a period of almost constant war whose prominent heroes have since filled the pages of Chinese literature. The fortunes of war varied with no single power dominating. Political unity was restored briefly in 281 by the Western Chin dynasty with its capital at Loyang, but it too collapsed in 316 under the mounting pressures of internal uprisings and Hun invasions.

The Eastern Chin dynasty began in 317 with its capital at Nanking. It lasted until about 420 when its rule was terminated by an ambitious general, Liu Yu, who set up the Liu Sung ruling house, bringing under its control the territory along the Yangtze Valley and south of it. There was a succession of short-lived Chinese dynasties in southern China: the Liu Sung (420–479), Chi (479–502), Liang (502–557), and Chen (557–589). The capital of the Southern Dynasties remained Nanking.

In northern China, the Northern Wei dynasty was founded by the Toba people in 386 with Loyang as their capital. Wei or Toba kings were of the Turkic race. Having unified northern China in 440, the Toba Wei remained in power until 534. Their kingdom was then divided into two states, the Eastern Wei (534–550) and the Western Wei (535–557), with capitals at Yeh and Chang-an respectively. These in turn were replaced by the Northern Chi (550–577), with Yeh as capital, and by Northern Chou (557–581), with Chang-an as capital; both were of non-Chinese origin.

With the unification of northern China under the Northern Wei dynasty in 440, there began the era commonly referred to as the Northern and Southern Dynasties. This lasted more than a hundred and fifty years until China was finally unified in 589 by the Hui house. This was a period of political and social unrest with frequent dynastic and regional wars, but it was also a period of transition in which Buddhism helped to bring about major changes in Chinese life and learning.[13]

Under the patronage of the foreign dynasties, Buddhism became firmly established in northern China where there was already a large non-Chinese population. Some of the rulers who invaded northern and western China were already devout Buddhists, and, by the end of the third century, Buddhist establishments in the two northern capitals of

Chang-an and Loyang numbered 180 and their clergy 3,700. By 381 nine-tenths of the people of northwest China were Buddhists. Emperor Wu (265–290) of the Chin dynasty showed great interest in Buddhism and built many monasteries throughout his empire. Emperor Min (313–316), during his brief reign, also built two monasteries at Chang-an. Yuan-ti (317–322) and his successors, during their rule of about a century, founded 17,608 Buddhist institutions throughout the kingdom and 263 volumes of Buddhist texts were translated. The Northern Wei dynasty favoured Buddhism, and during their reign Chinese Buddhist art made spectacular progress. An exception in this dynasty was Emperor Tai-Wu who decreed the suppression of Buddhism in 446. But other Wei kings made Loyang and Chang-an the greatest centres of Buddhist activity in China. Thousands of temples were built and the number of monks and nuns allegedly rose to two million. Many important monk-scholars, both Indian and Chinese, such as Kumarajiva, Bodhiruci, Tao-an, Hui-yuan, and Fa-hsien, worked and lived in China during this period.

In southern China also, Buddhism was accorded royal patronage by the Eastern Chin dynasty. Some of the rulers of the succeeding houses were also practicing Buddhists. For example, the founder of the Liang dynasty, Emperor Wu (502–549), a Confucianist, was converted to Buddhism, and frequently gave public lectures on Buddhist scriptures. He collected the first Chinese Buddhist canon, wrote on Buddhism, and even entered a monastery three times to lead the life of an ascetic. Yang-ti, the Sui Emperor, also declared himself in favour of Buddhism.

The Eastern Chin dynasty hoped to reassert Chinese supremacy and culture over the entire country. Although they adhered to traditional Chinese culture, there was some doubt in their minds about its total efficacy. Consequently, they turned towards Buddhism as a rallying force to strengthen them for the recovery of the north. Buddhist monks and scholars responded to this attitude in full measure, and they intensified their missionary and religious activities, incorporating in their discussion and writing Confucianist and Taoist learning. Soon an alliance between the monks and the elite emerged, rendering the monastic community powerful enough to assert its independence from the weakened secular authority of the Chin rulers, and "to maintain what amounted to an empire within an empire."[14]

By the time the Han dynasty had declined, different trends had already begun to develop in Buddhism in China. One, with its emphasis on control of the mind, concentration, and the suppression of the passions, was inspired mainly by the translations of An Shih-kao and was Hinayana in nature. The Prajna School, based largely on the translations of Chih-ch'an, favoured Mahayanism and was more inclined to probe into the ultimate reality behind external appearances. This aspect of Buddhism began to develop in the middle of the third century and ultimately became the dominant tenet of Buddhism in the South. At about the same time, during the fourth century, Neotaoism was gaining wide acceptance amongst literary circles in southern China, and this factor made a rapprochement with Buddhist thought somewhat easier. The Prajna School preached the philosophy of *Sunyata,* or emptiness, somewhat resembling the Neotaoist doctrine of non-being. A Taoist, once united with the tao or non-being, could become eternal and manifest himself in any form at any place, just as the Buddha was eternal and formless. The recognition of this affinity paved the way for closer interaction between these two schools, and for a gradual growth of Buddhism in China. Another fact encouraging closer relations between the Buddhists and Neotaoists was that some of the Buddhist monks originated from the same social class as the Neotaoists. The head of the powerful Wang family of the early Eastern Chin dynasty, Wang Tao (276–339), who was also the Prime Minister of the Empire, was a devoted patron of Buddhism. Other members of his family were equally enthusiastic and some of them had even joined the order of monks. Foreign monks also actively participated in this rapprochement. In southern China, at the end of the fourth century, under the patronage of the Eastern Chin ruler, the number of Buddhist establishments in the Kingdom alone was 1,786 temples and there were 24,000 monks and nuns. In Chien Wing, the capital, the names of thirty-seven temples have survived. Thus, during the third and fourth centuries, Buddhism became firmly rooted in the middle Yangtze Valley, as well as in the older centres of the north. Between the years 265 and 317, sixteen translators are known to have rendered 491 works into Chinese.

Rarely in history does a movement receive support from two mutually opposed forces for separate political reasons. At this time Buddhism in China was supported by both the traditionalists and the foreigners; either party would probably have taken a hostile attitude in different circumstances. Buddhism developed along different lines in northern and southern China, reflecting the needs of local polity. For instance, in the north it was associated with state control, and in the south it asserted its independence of the state and worked in association with the Chinese élite.

Although Buddhism was at times helped by certain political situations, it would be wrong to overemphasize this point. It was not always supported by the ruling and official classes and at times faced intense resistance and hostility. Without the inherent vitality of its doctrine, its sense of purpose, the capacity to endure suffering, the devoted service of its monks, and the brilliant intellectual activities of its scholars, Buddhism could not have evoked such a response from people as culturally advanced as the Chinese. Buddhists not only had to make Chinese society more receptive to their teachings, but they also had to translate Buddhist doctrine into Chinese.

The task was spread over several centuries. Sanskrit and Pali are completely different from Chinese in form and style. Sanskrit has a highly elaborate grammatical system, whilst Chinese has no systematized grammar; Sanskrit is highly inflected, alphabetic, and polysyllabic, whilst Chinese is uninflected, ideographic, and mainly monosyllabic. And whilst Indian literature is reflective, imaginative, and discursive, Chinese literature is terse, concrete, and practical. Even in temperament the two peoples differed: "The Chinese had shown little disposition to analyse the personality into its components, while India had a highly developed science of psychological analysis. In concepts of time and space there were also striking differences. The Chinese tended to think of both as finite and to reckon time in life-spans, generations, or political eras; the Indians, on the other hand, conceived of time and space as infinite and tended to think of Cosmic eons rather than of units of terrestrial life."[15]

The political and social values of the two peoples were equally alien. Whilst love of the family dominated Chinese society, Buddhism taught a universal ethic and a doctrine of personal salvation outside the family. The Buddhist ideal was ascetic and celibate, and it clashed with the Chinese popular view that to have a son was not only a duty but also essential for those sacrifices without which the departed spirit could not have peace. Whereas the Chinese aimed at establishing a good society, Indian thought went far beyond this goal and reflected upon the ultimate reality which was inseparably bound with what was visible. Despite the decline of Confucianism, the task of the initial Buddhist missionaries was a formidable one.

A factor which must have helped the early Buddhist missionaries was the absence of a complex and highly developed Chinese religious system. The ancient Chinese had to struggle against the forces of nature in northern China to build their civilization. This made them intensely practical and disciplined, but allowed them little time for reflection. Thus, the Chinese religion was a set of simple beliefs of a plain-thinking people, comprising the worship of ancestors and the forces of nature, a belief in a supreme god or heaven, a belief in divination, and a vague concept of the retribution of good and evil. By the time Buddhism appeared in China, however, Chinese religion had matured somewhat, but it did not approach the richness of Buddhism. The concepts of karma, the transmigration of the soul, the world as illusion, worldly pleasures as impediments to spiritual advancement, celibacy and asceticism, charity, compassion, and love of all beings, are only "a few drops in that vast flux of Indian religious and cultural invasion."[16]

Most of the Indian monks who migrated to China did so during the five centuries following the third century. During that time a stream of Chinese monks arrived in India to study Buddhism in its homeland, and to collect authentic Buddhist texts. Many of them left records of their experiences and observations. Most of these records have perished, some are known only by their titles, whilst brief extracts or stray passages from others appear in China's vast literature. Only three records are preserved in full: Fa-hsien's *Fo-Kuo-chi,* Hsüan-tsang's *Hsi-yu-chi,* and I-tsing's *Nan-hai-ki-kuei-nai-fa-chuan.* Whilst nearly all the Chinese monks eventually returned home, most of the Indian monks who went to China remained there.

Much less is known of the Indian monks who went to China than of the Chinese pilgrims who went to India. The Chinese had a deeper interest in objective observation and in recording history. Consequently, none of the numerous Indian monks who went to China has left a record of his experiences and impressions. Three Indian monks, Kumarajiva, Paramartha, and Bodhidharma, are held in particularly high esteem by Chinese Buddhists. Bodhidharma has even been deified by Chinese Buddhists, and the school of Dhyana Buddhism, which he founded and which is known as Ch'an in China and Zen in Japan, is still alive in East Asia, especially in Japan where its main centre is Kyoto. There were many others who enjoyed local or regional fame and are mentioned in Chinese dynastic histories. A host of others were absorbed in translating Sanskrit texts, working singly or jointly with Chinese scholars.[17]

The first recorded Indian missionaries to China are Dharmaratna (Chu-Fa-Lan) and Kasyapa Matanga (Chu Mo-t'eng) who reputedly arrived at Loyang at the invitation of the Han ruler Ming-ti in 67, and for whom he built the White Horse Monastery.[18] These two monks initiated the work of translating Buddhist texts.[19] The great emphasis placed on these translations by the missionaries may have been, apart from the need to interpret the Buddhist doctrine to the Chinese people, motivated by the traditional Chinese reverence for the written word. Kasyapa Matanga wrote a treatise entitled *Sutra of Forty-two Sections,* known by Chinese Buddhists as "the first ray of the Law," which has since gone into numerous editions and versions. Four other works, now vanished, are also attributed to him. The *Sutra* is not a translation but an original work written to introduce the essentials of Buddhism to the Chinese.

Despite unending wars and political unrest in China, Buddhist missionaries continued to arrive with new texts. They poured into China through different routes, but mainly from Central Asia. Towards the middle of the second century, Ngan Shih-kao (An-Shih-kao or Lokottama) , the famous Parthian prince of Pakor who had renounced his throne, arrived and embraced Buddhism. He settled in the White Horse Monastery at the Chinese capital, and spent the rest of his life from 148 to 168 propagating Buddhism and encouraging the work of translation. He himself translated more than thirty texts into Chinese and had a great influence on his Chinese followers, who considered his school of translators unrivalled.

One of the important Central Asian monks was Dharmaraksha, better known by his Chinese name, Chu Fa-hu. Born in Tun-huang, he was a Yueh-chih and went to China in the third century after travelling and studying widely in India. He was an accomplished linguist and an authority on Buddhism. Most of his life was spent at the White Horse Monastery where he worked for the expansion of Buddhism and translated Sanskrit texts into Chinese. He died about 317 at the age of eighty-seven. He reportedly knew thirty-six languages, and he translated at least two hundred and eleven works into Chinese in the years between 284 and 317, including the *Lalita Vistara;* ninety of these translations have survived.

At the invitation of a Hun king of the northwestern region of China, Dharmakshema (Fa-feng) , an outstanding Indian monk, came from Central Asia to the Hun court at Liang-chou in 414. The King, Meng-hsun, became a Buddhist and Dharmakshema, after prolonged study of the Chinese language, translated about twenty-five works, twelve of which have survived. They include *Maha Sannipata Sutra,* an important canonical work of Mahayana Buddhism, and Asvaghosa's *Buddha Charita.* Rivalry over Dharmakshema arose between the Hun king and the Chinese Toba Wei rulers, and the scholar met a tragic death at the hands of his patron in 434 because he was anxious to return to India. He served as royal adviser to Meng-hsun, and reputedly possessed remarkable occult powers.

Whilst Dharmakshema was working at Liang-chou, the followers of Kumarajiva, who had initiated a new epoch in the transmission of Buddhism to China, were engaged in their prodigious translation work at Chang-an, then the capital of a small state of Later Chin. Kumarajiva (343–413) was the son of an Indian scholar, Kumarayana, who had renounced his hereditary title to a ministerial position in Kashmir. From early childhood, Kumarajiva was educated in India in Buddhist doctrines and literature under the celebrated Bandhudatta, who was later converted to Mahayanism by his former pupil. Kumarajiva became widely known for his scholarship and attracted disciples from Khotan, Kashgar, Yarkand, and other parts of eastern Turkistan. Indeed, his reputation as a superb Buddhist teacher was the cause of his imprisonment. The Emperor of northern China, Fu Kien (or Fu-Chien), sent for him, but the Kucha ruler was reluctant to release him. A war ensued and Kumarajiva was taken to China in 383 as a prisoner. This was a period of political upheavals and Fu Kien, whilst attempting to conquer the Eastern Chin, was himself defeated and killed in 383. General Lu Kuang, a non-Buddhist, subsequently captured Kumarajiva and badly mistreated him during his long period of captivity, refusing to release him in spite of repeated pleas from the Yao family to send him east to the capital at Chang-an. It was not until after the accession of the Chin Emperor Yao Hsing (or Yo Chang, reign 393–415) that Kumarajiva was freed and invited to Chang-an in 401. Chinese chronicles record that the Chin Emperor was a devoted follower of Buddhism, that he held Kumarajiva in great respect, and appointed him the Rajguru or Kuoshih.

Welcomed as a national preceptor, he was accommodated at the monastery known as the "Great Monastery" of Chang-an. During the last twelve years of his life, when he was free to preach, his prestige rose immensely and he won an unsurpassed reputation as an interpreter of Buddhism. Through his efforts, a large number of Buddhist monasteries were established in northern China, and an overwhelming majority of the people were converted to the new faith. Having mastered the Chinese language during his captivity, he plunged directly into literary work. He corrected many earlier imperfect translations, made new ones, and founded an immense bureau of translators with over eight hundred scholars on the staff. More than one hundred and six Buddhist texts, mostly Mahayana, were translated, fifty-six of which are still extant. Amongst the translations were the works of Nagarjuna, the great second-century exponent of the Madhyamika school and one of the greatest names in Mahayana literature. No books are as popular with Chinese Buddhists as Kumarajiva's translations of *Vimalakirtinirdesa* and *Saddharma Pundarika,* the most important scripture of Mahayana Buddhism.

Kumarajiva was much more than a brilliant translator, for he was an original thinker of great genius as well. He gave Chinese Buddhism a philosophic basis and created a sound Buddhist literary tradition in China. He wrote several original works in Chinese, including the *Life of Asvaghosa* based on a vanished Sanskrit source. He is traditionally regarded as the first exponent of Madhyamika doctrine, and his work introduced a new era in Buddhist China. From then on Mahayanism became the dominant school of East Asian Buddhist thought. Through his propagation of Nagarjuna's doctrine of Sunyata, Kumarajiva was able to overthrow the general practice of interpreting Buddhism in the light of Lao-tzu and Chuang-tzu. Because of the imprint he left on the intellectual history of Asia, he may be regarded as one of the greatest Indians of all time. But he was more than an Indian, for he symbolized, as Bagchi points out, "the spirit of cultural collaboration between Central Asia and India and the joint effort made by the Buddhist scholars of these countries for the dissemination of Indian culture in China."[20]

According to contemporary Chinese records, he was honest, loyal, humane, tolerant, hard-working, and self-sacrificing, although according to some legends he was once tempted into marriage by the beauty of a woman. He repented of his lapse, and it is reported that thereafter he would always begin his sermons with the apologetic exordium: "Follow my work, but not my life which is far from ideal; But the lotus grows out of mud. Love the lotus; do not love the mud."

The main burden of transmitting Buddhist knowledge to China fell on Kashmir, because of its physical proximity and because of its well-developed tradition of Buddhist studies. Amongst Kashmir's more famous scholars are Sanghabhuti, who reached China in 381; Buddhabhadra, the translator of *Avatamsaka Sutra;* Gautama Sanghadeva; Punyatrata (404), and his pupil Dharmayasas; Buddhayasas, who was Kumarajiva's teacher in Kashmir; and Vimalaksa, an associate of Kumarajiva.

Many Indian monks went to China by sea. Two Kashmiri teachers, Dharmayasas and Buddhabhadra, used this circuitous route at the beginning of the fifth century. Buddhajiva, a collaborator of Fa-hsien, reached Nanking in 423. In 431 he was followed by Gunavarman (Kiu-na pa-mo). The Emperor invited Gunavarman to his court at the request of the Chinese monks of Nanking, and did the monk the unique honour of receiving him personally. Gunavarman died within a year, but so great was his scholarship and industry that he translated eleven texts, five of which are still extant. Gunavarman was a royal prince from Kashmir and had travelled throughout India as a *bhikshu*, as well as working for over thirty years in Ceylon and Java. In Ceylon he had helped develop the Buddhist Sangha and in Java, where Hinduism prevailed at the time, he founded the first Buddhist monastery on the island. Another of his important contributions to Buddhism in China was the help he rendered towards the conferment of higher ordination on the Buddhist nuns or bhiksunis.

In 435 Gunabhadra (Kiu-no-po-to-lo) reached Canton by sea. For the next thirty-three years, until his death in 468, he continued to work in Nanking. He was a great authority on Mahayana and specialized in the *Avatamsaka Sutra.* Welcomed and encouraged by the Emperor Tai-tsu of the Sung dynasty, he translated seventy-six works of which twenty-eight have survived. The political disorders which broke out in China during 453–454 did not result in the loss of royal favour for Gunabhadra even though he was working at the monastery of Sin-See at the invitation of the rebel chief Yi-Siuan, who was defeated and beheaded.

During the sixth century, amongst the Indian monks who went to China by sea, Paramartha (*ca.* 498–569) is the most famous. He was widely recognized in India as a distinguished and accomplished scholar, and took with him to China a large collection of Buddhist texts. Arriving in Canton in 546 at the request of the Chinese Emperor Wu-ti of the Liang dynasty, who had dispatched a goodwill mission to India asking the King of Magadha to send a Buddhist scholar, Paramartha was given a Chinese escort to assure his safety during his journey to the capital at Nanking. Paramartha worked incessantly for the next twenty-three years, first at Fuchuang, and later at Nanking and other Buddhist centres. He did much original writing besides translating seventy Buddhist works, of which only thirty-two are extant. His contribution to Chinese Buddhism rivals that of Kumarajiva. War, chaos, and famine had caused Buddhism to decline in China, but Paramartha, through his immense literary activity and religious enthusiasm, gave it a new and vigorous life during the latter days of the Liang dynasty (502–557) and the early part of the Chen dynasty (557–589). He, Bodhiruci, and Hsüan-tsang are the three most important Vijnanavadin translators of Sanskrit texts into Chinese. Paramartha established a Buddhist philosophical system, the *She-lun-tsung,* the basic text of which was his translated work *Mahayanasamparigrahasastra.* This school had eminent disciples and prevailed for about eighty years before it was finally absorbed by the Dharmalakshana school founded by Hsüan-tsang.

Of all Indian monks, the most celebrated in China is Bodhidharma (or Dharmabodhi). Son of an Indian king, he is an almost legendary figure and several miracles are attributed to him.[21] He was regarded as the twenty-eighth Patriarch in India. The arrival of Bodhidharma in Canton in about 526 at the invitation of the Liang Emperor Wu was very significant in the history of Buddhism, because he introduced into China the Ch'an (a phonetic variation of the Sanskrit Dhyana) school, and thus became the first Patriarch (Tsu or Tsung) of this school in China. He did not undertake missionary tours and he wrote no books. He disapproved of reading the canonical texts of the Tripitaka, although he used to recommend the *Lankavatara Sutra.* He taught the value of meditation to find the Buddha in one's own heart, and he himself meditated in silence for nine years in the Shao-Lin monastery on the Sung Mountain. Because of his influence, Buddhist monasteries became much less intellectual and more meditative. It is not surprising that a practical people like the Chinese should have preferred those aspects of Buddhism which seemed to them more natural and practical, such as the Dhyana exercises.

By the end of the sixth century the long period of political unrest in China had come to a close, and the beginning of the seventh century saw the emergence of the T'ang dynasty (619–907). Despite the opposition of the Confucianist literati, Buddhism continued to gain ground in China where it had already assumed a distinctive Chinese personality. Before the T'ang period there was some persecution but it was ineffective and intermittent and failed to arrest the progress of Buddhism. In 405 nine out of every ten families in northern China embraced the Buddhist faith. By the end of the fifth century, it is asserted that the whole of China, north and south alike, was Buddhist. According to an official census made between 512 and 545 in the kingdom of Wei in northern China, there were thirteen thousand Buddhist shrines and monasteries and three thousand foreign monks living in the capital alone, whilst an even greater number of indigenous monks were scattered throughout the country. In the sixth century both northern and southern China had staunch imperial patrons of Buddhism: for example, Queen Hu of the Wei dynasty in the north and Emperor Wei of the Liang dynasty in the south. Thousands of Indian merchants, monks, and travellers had settled in the principal cities of China, and in the sixth century there were probably more than three thousand Indian Buddhist monks and ten thousand Indian families in the Loyang province alone.

Soon after the T'angs came to power in China, northern India was ruled by one of the most famous patrons of Buddhism, Harsha, and the Buddhist University, Nalanda Mahavihara, was the most important centre of learning in India. It had been founded in the fifth century by the Gupta ruler Kumaragupta I (*ca.* 415–455).[22] The intellectual demands of Nalanda were severe, and discipline was strict. Only the most distinguished and talented could teach at Nalanda. The routine of daily life was rigorous, divided mainly between study and religious rites. The prestige of the University was high in Indian society and in the Buddhist world. Throughout the T'ang period, the most glorious of Chinese history, Nalanda attracted numerous Chinese pilgrims and visitors. In fact, the story of the Nalanda Mahavihara has been reconstructed mainly from accounts left by Chinese pilgrims, particularly Hsüan-tsang and I-tsing.

An accomplished scholar at Nalanda, Prabhakaramitra (Kuang che), whose pupils later became famous professors at Nalanda, was the first Indian scholar to go to China during the T'ang period. He arrived in 627 at the age of sixty-three. The Emperor Tai Tsung was deeply impressed and gave him a very courteous reception. Prabhakaramitra rendered some Buddhist texts into Chinese which have survived, but he lost the King's favour because of the Confucianist literati's machinations and died disappointed in 633.

Of the monks who followed Prabhakaramitra to China, the best-known was Bodhiruci (Fa-hi) from South India.[23] Reaching China by sea in 693, he translated one of the most extensive works of Mahayana, the *Ratnakuta Sutra.* Hsüan-tsang, who brought the manuscript back with him from India, died before he could make much progress with its translation. Bodhiruci, after seven years of strenuous labour, completed the work in 713, and his Chinese biographer recounts that the Emperor himself took down the final notes in his own hand at a ceremonial gathering when the translation was completed. This was the last of Bodhiruci's fifty-three translations. He died in 727, it is said, at the age of one hundred and fifty-six.

Vajrabodhi and his disciple Amoghavajra were amongst the last Indian teachers to go to China. Born a royal prince and educated at Nalanda, Vajrabodhi reached Canton in 720 in his fifty-eighth year to present to the Chinese Emperor a copy of *Mahaprajnaparamitasutra* on behalf of the King of Ceylon. Before he died at Loyang in 732, he had translated a number of mystical Buddhist works into Chinese and had numerous disciples. Famed for his mastery of Tripitaka and Tantric Buddhism, he introduced the Mantra sect of Tantric esotericism, based on *Mulamantras,* into China. The doctrines and practices of the Mantra cults were confined to circle of initiates, and Vajrabodhi initiated only two monks into the Tantric rituals during his stay in China. Amoghavajra carried on his work more successfully, and translated about seventy-seven texts, mainly dealing with *tantras* and *dharanis,* before he died in 774. He was the spiritual adviser of three emperors of the T'ang dynasty—Hsüan-tsang, Shu-tsung, and T'ai-tsung.

China, in the latter part of the T'ang period, was somewhat politically disturbed, as was India, and contact between the two countries had virtually come to an end. Yet, a few Indian missionaries went to China and, whilst they did some valuable work, they lacked the zeal and ability of their predecessors. The most important missionary of this later period was Dharmadeva (Fa-tien), who came to China in 973 during the Sung period, and translated about 178 Sanskrit texts. He headed a board of translators which was responsible for rendering 201 volumes of the Sanskrit texts into Chinese between 982 and 1011, despite his death in 1001.

Recalling the story of these monks and the enormous difficulties involved in translation, admiration for their patience, perseverance, and faith is increased. To learn Chinese with modern aids and techniques is a formidable enough task, but in those days to learn it and also communicate doctrinal beliefs intelligibly to a people whose own tradition of reflective thought was relatively less developed and accommodating, was a monumental achievement.

Although a large number of Indian monks and scholars had already visited and worked in China, it was not until the end of the fourth century that a notable Chinese scholar, Fa-hsien, visited India.[24] Until Buddhism had been established in China and Chinese monks had acquired intellectual proficiency, the long and arduous pilgrimages to India were infrequent. There are stories of some Chinese princes captured by Kaniska who had lived in northern Punjab, and stories of Chinese scholars who may have visited India in the third century. A

Chinese monk, Chu-She-Ling, set out in 260 for India but elected to stay in Khotan where he found the Indian knowledge he was seeking. On the authority of I-tsing, the Chinese scholar who visited India in the seventh century, it is said that twenty Chinese monks went to India by the Yunnan-Burma route, and a monastery called China-Sangharama was especially built for them near Bodhgaya by King Sri Gupta. However, evidence of Chinese visitors to India from the fourth century on is more definite, and the flow of pilgrims during this period was far greater than the few surviving names would suggest.

By the fourth century China had developed her own powerful tradition of Buddhist philosophy. The two most illustrious names in Chinese Buddhism during this period were Tao-an of Hsiang-Yang and Hui-Yuan of Lu-Shan. Tao-an (312–385) carried on his missionary activities north of the Yangtze River and was undeterred by the hardships prevalent at the time, thus exemplifying the true spirit of the Buddha. He converted a great many Chinese intellectuals to the Buddhist doctrine, sending them afterwards to different parts of the country to preach Buddhism. Through his disciples and his writings he created a new spirit in Buddhist China. He was the first Chinese scholar to reexamine and correct earlier translations of Buddhist texts and to compile commentaries on them. The foreign monks rarely knew Chinese well, whilst their Chinese collaborators were ignorant of Sanskrit and Pali. More important, he became acutely aware of the invalidity of interpreting the Buddhist scriptures in the light of the Chinese classics, a practice which had become common during the preceding century, mainly because the Chinese intellectuals did not have access to the originals or even to scholars who were masters of the original texts. Tao-an's organization of intensive translation activity at Chang-an later provided the much-needed trained Chinese talent to help Kumarajiva. Realizing the need for closer contact between Indian and Chinese scholars, he invited a number of Indians from Central Asia to China, and, more important, encouraged the Chinese to visit India. It was he who had initiated steps to invite Kumarajiva to China.

After the fall of Hsiang-Yang, Tao-an's disciple, Hui-Yuan (344–416), founded the monastery of Lu-Shan and initiated a new school of Buddhist thought, the White Lotus Society, which introduced the cult of Amitabha. The Society has left an indelible mark on Chinese Buddhism, because it was the origin of *Ching-tu* (the Pure Realm movement), still a major philosophical doctrine of eastern Asia. Hui-Yuan was closely associated with the metaphysical speculations carried on in Chien-Kang and Kuai-chi on the philosophies of Lao-chuang and Prajna, and also with the propogation of dhyana exercises. Under his direction, Neotaoist metaphysical speculations were mixed with Prajna thought, and the purity of his monastic discipline attracted Confucianist literati. He was the epitome of the "gentry Buddhism" of South China. He laid the foundation of the independent status of the Buddhist community there. His disciple, Tao-Sheng (*ca.* 360–434), provided a bridge between the Buddhist centres at Lu-Shan and Chang-an, and made a significant contribution to Chinese Buddhist thought, especially the Nirvana School.

Whilst the tradition of Buddhist thought was thus maturing in its new environment, the appeal made by Tao-an for Chinese scholars to undertake religious study-tours to India had begun to draw responses. In 399, fourteen years after Tao-an's death, Fa-hsien, accompanied by four other Chinese monks, set out on his pilgrimage from Chang-an to India by the Central Asian land route. Emperor Yao Hsing, the royal patron of Kumarajiva, was still ruling in northern China. At the frontier Fa-hsien and his companions met another party of five Chinese monks who were also going to India. They joined forces, taking the southern route through Khotan and Kashgar. Negotiating difficult terrain, Fa-hsien and his companions entered India through Kashmir. He stayed at Pataliputra for three years, studying Sanskrit and collecting manuscripts. There was as yet no Chinese translation of the entire *Vinaya*, the Buddhist rules of monastic discipline, and Fa-hsien strongly felt the need for one. Whilst he was still in India, however, Kumarajiva arrived in Chang-an in 401 and was instrumental in translating the *Vinaya* of the Sarvastivadin School. For another two years Fa-hsien stayed at the monastery of Tamralipti copying Buddhist sutras and images. He returned to China in 414 and collaborated with Buddhabhadra, an Indian monk, in translating some of the works he had taken back with him. Fa-hsien left behind a record of his travels, *Fo Kuo Chi,* which gives an individual account of India during the period of the Gupta Empire.

Little is known of the companions of Fa-hsien, except for Pao-yun, who learned Sanskrit in India and, after his return home, translated a number of Buddhist texts. A succession of Chinese pilgrims followed Fa-hsien. Of those who travelled to India in the fifth century, five names are known, but information about them is fragmentary.[25]

Whilst Fa-hsien was in India, a group of fifteen Chinese monks led by Che-mong started for India in 404 through Khotan and the Pamirs The difficult mountain routes compelled nine of them to return to China, and one died of fatigue, but the remaining five completed their journey. They visited places of Buddhist learning, collected texts, and set out on their return journey by the same route. Three of the five died on the way back and Che-mong reached China in 424 with only one companion. The account of his travels, which he composed in 439, is lost.

Another party of twenty-five monks led by Fa-yong commenced its journey to India in 420 following the northern Central Asian route via Turfan and Kashgar and passing over the Pamirs to Kashmir. Not much of their travels in India is known, except that Fa-yong, having visited important Buddhist centres throughout northern India, returned home by sea.

In 518 an empress of the Wei dynasty sent an official mission to India under Song-yun to offer presents to Buddhist sanctuaries and bring back texts. Song-yun's mission toured the northwestern regions of India and returned in 522.

The Wei rulers, who were such great patrons of Buddhism, lost their authority in 535. Until the rise of the Sui dynasty in 589, royal interest in Buddhism was somewhat diminished. Although the Sui dynasty (589–618) was short-lived, it revived the efforts for direct contact with India. Emperor Yang (605–616) dispatched a mission led by Wei-tsie and Tu Hing-man; this mission travelled by the overland route and toured extensively in Central Asia and northern India.

After the rise of the T'ang dynasty, Chinese monks began to visit India in unprecedented numbers. During the seventh century, Sino-Indian cultural relations were particularly strong. Although the imperial clan claimed descent from Lao-tzu and thus favoured Taoism, they exercised a policy of religious toleration. Nestorian Christianity, Islam, and Manichaeaism were introduced during the T'ang period and found

Chinese converts. Buddhism gained unprecedented influence under the patronage of some of the T'ang rulers, and had far more support than Taoism. In the eighth century in the imperial capital Chang-an alone, there were ninety-one Buddhist monasteries compared to sixteen Taoist monasteries. Over the whole country, Buddhist temples numbered more than three times those of the Taoists. Buddhism was supported by all factions of society, no doubt aided by the peaceful conditions and the patronage of the rulers. But the rise of Harsha in northern India, the enormous reputation of Nalanda University as a seat of Buddhist learning, and the fame of Indian mathematics, art, medicine, and astronomy must also have been largely responsible for the sudden influx of Chinese scholars to India.

The first monk to visit India during the T'ang period, and by far the most eminent, was Hsüan-tsang (*ca.* 596–664). A Chinese nobleman and the son of an orthodox Confucianist scholar, he embraced Buddhism at an early age and acquired a national reputation as a learned and eloquent monk, well-versed in the Confucianist classics. He left China for India in 629, two years after the accession of the T'ang Emperor, Tai-tsung (627–649), who was even more disposed towards Buddhism than his father, Kao-tzu.

Hsüan-tsang travelled by the northern route through Central Asia, and, after a perilous journey through the desert, reached Kapisa in 630. For the next fifteen years he travelled extensively throughout northern and southern India. Charming, courtly, and learned as he was, he was honoured by the great rulers of the time, Harsha of Kanauj and Bhaskaravarman of Kamarupa. Hsüan-tsang stayed at Nalanda for five years studying Buddhist philosophy with the greatest scholar of the age, Silabhadra. It was customary for a monastery to honour a learned visiting monk with the presentation of a precious holy book, and Hsüan-tsang collected 657 volumes, many of which were rare texts and prize possessions. So heavy were his manuscripts and sacred relics that they were carried by twenty horses. He was remarkably methodical and industrious in making notes of his observations, and enjoyed a reputation both as a writer and as a translator. Yet it is surprising that he does not mention the great Buddhist stupa at Sanchi, which he must have visited, since it is of exceptional importance to the Buddhists. Nor does he allude to Ajanta, which was at the height of its glory when he was there. In 645 he returned to China by the southern Central Asian route. He left a detailed account of his travels, *Si-yu-ki* (or *Ta-Tang Hsi-yu-chi*), which is an invaluable source of information on Central Asian and ancient Indian history. Indian culture owes a great debt of gratitude to Hsüan-tsang, for he came to India at a time when Buddhism was in a state of decline, and by taking away many texts of Buddhist philosophy, he made it possible for them to be preserved in their Chinese versions. The Sanskrit originals of many of these texts have been completely lost in India.

When Hsüan-tsang left India, Emperor Harsha, who had received him with honour and reverence, gave him an almost royal send-off, as well as generous gifts of money to defray his expenses. His Indian farewell was more than matched by the elaborate royal reception prepared for him in China. From the border to the capital he was conducted with state dignity, and, on his arrival at Chang-an, he was given a great ovation by the people, and the emperor declared a holiday in his honour. It is rare in history that such a reception is bestowed on a scholar, much less on a teacher of an alien creed.

For the next nineteen years until his death Hsüan-tsang worked incessantly, translating the Sanskrit texts he had brought from India. Altogether, he translated seventy-five works. It was principally due to the efforts of Hsüan-tsang, supported by I-tsing, that the essence of all the five courses of Buddhism—*Hetuvidya, Abhidharma, Vinaya, Madhyamaka*, and *Yogacara*—taught at Nalanda University during its most flourishing period, was introduced into China. Whilst these courses later underwent certain changes, their fundamental teachings conformed to the doctrines introduced by these two Chinese scholars.

The Emperor T'ai-tsung sent his second embassy to the court of Harsha in 643 whilst Hsüan-tsang was still in India. The ambassador Li Yi-Piao was assisted by a Chinese officer, Wang Hsüan-tse. The latter led the third imperial mission to India in 647.[26] He helped Hsüan-chao, a visiting Buddhist monk and scholar, to return to China. In 664 Hsüan-chao returned to India to collect medicines and contact physicians. From 643 to 758 the T'angs maintained occasional diplomatic relations with several Indian kingdoms, including Udayana in the Swat Valley, Magadha, Kashmir, Gandhara, and with Ceylon.

Biographies survive of sixty Chinese monks who visited India during the latter half of the seventh century. The best-known of these monks is I-tsing (also spelled Yi-Ching or Yi-tsing) whose scholarship at the time was excelled only by that of Hsüan-tsang in China. He was, however, not as interested as Hsüan-tsang was in Buddhist philosophy, but, like Fa-hsien, laid greater emphasis on the observance of monastic rules. In 671, soon after Hsüan-tsang's death, I-tsing set out for India on board a Persian vessel which arrived at Tamralipti in 673. He was the first important Chinese pilgrim to travel by sea to India, and he appears to have done so because of the unrest caused in Central Asia by Arab and Tibetan invasions. From this time on, more and more pilgrims and visitors followed the maritime route. Before I-tsing reached India, he stayed for about two years in Sumatra, which was at that time part of the Srivijaya Empire. He left a record of Buddhism there in *Nan-hai-chi-kuei-fa Chuan (A Record of the Buddhist Kingdoms in the Southern Archipelago)*.

In India, I-tsing spent ten years at Nalanda, visited places of Buddhist interest, and collected about four hundred manuscripts which he took back to China in 695. He was mainly interested in visiting Buddhist stupas, shrines, and monasteries, as well as centres of learning. He made a special study of Indian medicine and often made comparative references to the Chinese system. On his return he devoted himself to interpreting and propagating Buddhist doctrine. His most monumental work of translation was one of the Buddhist codes of monastic discipline, entitled *Mulasarvastivinaya.* He also completed a short Sanskrit-Chinese dictionary, and wrote brief biographical notes on fifty-one Chinese pilgrims who visited India between the reigns of T'ai-tsung and Empress Wu.

The last Chinese to come to India during the T'ang period was Wu-kong. He was a layman, and was dispatched in 751 to escort an Indian ambassador back to his kingdom, Kapisa. During his Indian visit Wu-kong was converted to Buddhism. He spent many years studying Buddhist texts and travelling about the country before returning to China in 790.

During the later years of the T'ang Empire, Chinese monks ceased travelling to India, presumably because of the political unrest in China, the loss of Chinese authority in Central Asia, and the decline of Buddhism in India. The breakdown of Chinese authority in Central Asia is of significant importance in the history of Sino-Indian relations and of Buddhism. China's retreat from this area at a time when Islamic power emerged left a vacuum which was to be filled by Muslim domination, thus separating the areas of Indian and Chinese culture. But by this time the Chinese need to draw upon Indian learning had considerably diminished. For, by the end of the T'ang dynasty, the Chinese Buddhist canon was practically complete, and almost all the important Sanskrit sutras had been translated into Chinese.

After the downfall of the T'ang dynasty, there was a short period of political anarchy in China, during which five military leaders made themselves kings in Kaifeng and Loyang, and about thirty thousand Buddhist monasteries were destroyed. In 960 the Empire was reunited by Chao Kuang-yin, who founded the Sung dynasty (960–1270). Between 960 and 1039 it appears that a number of Chinese pilgrims went to India, but their travels have only a limited interest. Contact between India and China practically ceased after the eleventh century.

Whilst the last emperors of the Sung dynasty were still ruling, Gengis Khan was emerging as a world power. He and his descendants, the Mongol or Yuan dynasty, were to govern China from 1206 to 1368, and to play a significant role in the development of Buddhism. However, before the Yuans, three other alien ruling houses had established themselves contemporaneously with the Sungs, and these are worth notice in the history of Buddhism in China. One, the Liao (907–1125), was established by the Mongol tribe called the Khitans, and, during its rule, Buddhism spread in Mongolia and Manchuria. The Khitans subjugated northern China and set up a large number of Buddhist temples throughout their kingdom. During their rule, between 1031 and 1064, the Liao edition of the Chinese Tripitaka was printed. The Liao rulers were also responsible for engraving the sutras on stone.[27]

Whilst the Liao dynasty was still ruling Manchuria, a chieftain of the Ju-chen (Jurchen) tribe, Akuta, successfully broke away from the Liao rule and set up the Chin dynasty (1115–1234). He sacked the Liao capital in 1122, and in 1126 he even captured Kaifeng, the capital of the now declining Sungs, forcing them to move southward and extending the frontiers of his empire as far south as the Huai River. Peking became the Chin capital, until they were forced to evacuate it in 1215 under pressure from the Mongols, who brought the Chin dynasty to an end in 1234. Buddhism was already flourishing in the areas the Chin dynasty had taken over, and the new rulers continued to support the Indian religion. The Chin dynasty sponsored the printing of an edition of the Chinese Tripitaka during the period 1148–1173.[28]

The third northern dynasty was the Hsi-Hsia which ruled Kansu, including the famous Buddhist centre at Hun-huang, from 1038 to 1227. Although they claimed descent from the Toba, their language seems to have been related to Tibetan rather than to Turkish. Buddhism was their official religion and, under the auspices of the Imperial House, the last of the extensive Buddhist translating or publishing projects was undertaken, involving the production of a mass of Buddhist texts in their language. Hsi-Hsia manuscripts and printed books have survived in large numbers, and were still being printed in Hsi-Hsia well into the Mongol period.

The Mongols, the first foreign conquerors to dominate the whole of China, came into closer contact with Buddhism after their conquest of northern China. Kublai Khan was the greatest ruler of this dynasty, and it was during his rule that Marco Polo visited China. Kublai Khan had been converted to Buddhism and was especially well disposed towards the Lamaistic Buddhism of Tibet. Probably the Great Khan sought to use the support of Buddhist and Taoist churches for political ends: to subdue the stubborn Sung legitimism of the Confucianists. Although tolerant of other faiths, he was an enthusiastic Buddhist. Whenever he was called upon to act as arbitrator in the ecclesiastical debates between Buddhists and Taoists, an important feature of the times, his verdict always favoured Buddhism. He had relics of the Buddha brought from Ceylon, and appointed a young but learned Tibetan Lama, Phags-pa or Matidhvajasribhadra (1240–1280), as imperial preceptor; this office was held in the greatest respect by the Mongol royal family, and Lamaistic Buddhism was made the national religion of the Mongols.

Kublai's successors patronized Tibetan Buddhism with even greater fervour. How highly Lamaism was held in the imperial estimation is illustrated by the edict of 1309 which stated that anyone guilty of striking a Lama could have his hand cut off, and that anyone insulting a Lama would lose his tongue. The Confucianist literati criticized the Mongols for granting excessive privileges to their rivals, and accused the Lamas of committing acts of cruelty and debauchery. Whilst this is the usual Confucianist literati criticism of Buddhist monasticism, some of their accusations were valid. Buddhist temples were favoured by the Imperial Court with huge grants of land. According to the registry of the *Hsuan-Cheng Yuan*, there were 42,318 temples and 213,418 monks and nuns in China.

The Mongol rule was terminated in 1368 by Chu Yuan-chang, who founded the Ming dynasty which ruled China for about three centuries. Chu Yuan-chang came from a poor farm labourer's family and was a former Buddhist monk at the Huang-ch'ieh monastery in An-hui.[29] The first Ming emperor often organized Buddhist assemblies and discussions. The last great emperor of the Ming dynasty was Yung-le (1403–1424), who was himself a Buddhist, although he raised the Neoconfucianist texts to the status of the ancient Confucianist canon. By this time, however, Buddhism had lost contact with India and had become an independent and integral part of Chinese life.

The Manchu or Ching emperors, although not Chinese themselves, were great supporters of Chinese culture. They continued to patronize Buddhism, especially Lamaism. They were also interested in Ch'an Buddhism.[30] During the reign of Kang-hsi (1662–1721) there were 79,622 temples and 118,907 monks and nuns in the country. Whilst the number of monks was rather small, when compared with the estimate of 740,000 monks during the T'ang and Sung periods, the number of temples was the highest in history.[31]

The outstanding feature of Ming Buddhism was the achievement of harmony between the different schools, largely brought about by Chu-hung, a sixteenth-century monk. He also inaugurated a movement for the development of Buddhism amongst the laity. Intellectuals and wealthy Buddhists organized groups of laymen in the cities and founded societies for welfare and missionary work. This movement gained considerable strength, and even university scholars began to study Buddhist philosophy and history. This lay movement reached its peak during the closing years of the Manchu dynasty, and the unique role played by laymen has continued in modern Chinese Buddhism. The growing popularity of this movement probably aroused the anti-Buddhist feelings of the Confucianist literati, and, consequently, Buddhism, which had always faced considerable indifference and apathy from the officials and intellectuals of the Ming and Manchu dynasties, now faced active hostility. An expression of this antagonism is seen in the 1898 publication of a work by Chang Chih-tung entitled *Chuan Hsueh-pien*, in which he advocated the reorganization of Chinese education by appropriating Buddhist property for schools. His theories commanded considerable support from the Chinese intelligentsia. More than three hundred Buddhist temples were destroyed during the first quarter of the present century.

However, Buddhism has always remained important in China, especially amongst the common people. The new pressures of the late nineteenth and early twentieth centuries even forced something of a revival of Buddhism, and it subsequently played some part as an intellectual force in the revolution that overthrew the Manchu dynasty.[32] The Chinese could more effectively combat the Western cultural invasion by centring their defence around their Buddhist traditions, which, they contended, were democratic, humanistic, liberal, and in fact contained all that the West could claim and more. The Buddhist reformer, Liang Chi-chao, for instance, said that the doctrine of karma was superior to the theories of Darwin and Spencer. Another stimulus, of somewhat doubtful value, came during the period of the Sino-Japanese War and World War II when some Buddhist temples were rebuilt in the Japanese-occupied areas, and links between China and Japan were strengthened for political reasons.

The revival of Buddhism in China was aided by the foundation of the Mahabodhi Society in 1891 with its headquarters in Ceylon. The Society was begun by Dharmapala with the declared objective of reviving the Dhamma. Its activities since then have included holding international Buddhist conferences, publishing Buddhist literature in Asian as well as European languages, and sending missions abroad.

Aroused by the anti-Buddhist measures of the various administrations, and by the criticisms of the Chinese Renaissance leaders in the twenties and thirties as well as by the criticisms of Marxist thinkers, learned

Buddhist monks, such as Ti-hsien, Yin-kuang, Tao-chieh, and Tai-shu, intensified their work to revive and reform their faith. Buddhist centres attempted to restore and update the true teachings of the Buddha. The most active reformer was Tai-hsu (1889–1947), who led a movement to reform the clerical system, temple property, and teachings. He established contact with Buddhism abroad, sent monks to study in India, Tibet, and Japan, and founded *Shih-chieh fo hsueh Yuan* (the Universal Buddhist College), with the declared objective of modernizing Buddhism. Consequently, numerous works of Buddhist literature began to appear in ever-increasing numbers. Between 1920 and 1935, as many as fifty-eight Buddhist periodicals were published in China.

The growing popularity of Buddhism in Western countries, the emergence of the Buddhist countries of Asia as free nations, and the rehabilitation of Buddhism in independent India have all led to the intensification of Buddhist activity everywhere.

Whilst it is not easy to assess accurately the position of Buddhism under the Peoples Republic of China since 1949, there is no doubt that it has been confronted with extraordinary difficulties. It not only has incurred resistance from the conservative and nationalistic Confucianists, but has also encountered opposition from a highly autocratic and centralized régime which is based on an openly materialistic, atheistic, and anti-religious ideology. The Communist government has instituted anti-Buddhist measures, confiscating temple lands, taking over schools and publishing houses, and reducing the Sangha in size. Until 1950 the Buddhist monasteries of China derived most of their income from land holdings received as gifts from their patrons. The Land Revenue Act of June 1950 led to the confiscation of agricultural land belonging to Buddhist temples and monasteries. This economic loss to the monasteries compelled a large number of monks to leave them. In the cities the monks were made to set up light industries on the premises of the monasteries or vacate them for the use of local factories. Buddhist monks and nuns were compelled to study the works of Mao Tse-tung and were subjected to "thought reform." However, realizing the significance of Buddhism and its value in Chinese life and society, the government has adopted a policy of controlling rather than suppressing it. They formed the *Chung kuo fo chiao hsieh hui* (the Chinese Buddhist Association) in 1953, bringing all Buddhist monks and laymen into one organization under central control. In 1958 the Association claimed to represent about half a million monks and one hundred million followers. During the course of this revolutionary process Buddhists have no doubt been used by the government as instruments of propaganda, mainly directed at the large Buddhist populations in other countries. Peking's refusal to allow the Chinese Buddhists to participate in the Seventh Congress of World Fellowship of Buddhists, held at Sarnath in 1964, disturbed Buddhists all over the world and deepened their anxiety about the fate of Buddhism in present-day China; they suspect that this religion of peace is being turned into a tool of political propaganda and international conflict. They fear that the Peking regime has been particularly severe on Buddhism, because of the great hold this religion has always exercised, and perhaps still exercises, over the minds of the Chinese people.

THE HISTORY OF Buddhism in China is like that of any powerful foreign culture, which, on encountering an equally powerful local culture, has to undergo the varying processes of confrontation and assimilation. During the initial period of impact, the local people remain indifferent to or even unaware of the gradually mounting influence of the foreign culture. It is only when the alien culture begins to assume sizeable proportions that it is generally regarded as threatening, and reaction sets in. But the struggle is not then between a purely foreign and a purely local culture, because the so-called foreign culture by that time has come to acquire some native character, and its opponents have become conscious of the shortcomings of their own heritage. Finally, there begins a period of compromise on both sides, conscious and unconscious, during which the foreign culture is either naturalized or nationalized, serving as a distinct group within a changed pattern of the society, or it is assimilated in the traditional culture giving rise to an entirely new culture. This formative period of imperceptible growth is vital, because if the roots of the incoming thought are not firmly planted, it cannot survive the inevitable reaction against it. And no foreign culture, however advanced or backed by political power, can find strong roots unless it meets a definite need in the local culture.

Buddhism has often been denounced in China, not so much for its philosophical content as for its foreign character. The fact that Buddhism dominated Chinese thought for centuries and continues even now in its naturalized form as a principal factor in Chinese life, plus the fact that it reached this position through voluntary acceptance in a society which regarded itself as superior to all others, are not so much a unique testimony to the brilliance of its teachings but indicative of the vast gap in Chinese cultural life which it must have filled.

At the time Buddhism was introduced into China, the cultural atmosphere of the country was quite conducive to its development. Neither Confucianism nor Taoism possessed a highly developed spiritual character. Confucianism, with all its emphasis on the adaptation of human personality to the social order, or on welding together the cult of heaven, the family system, and the state, neither sought nor provided answers to metaphysical or religious questions. It gave the ordinary man neither strength to see him through the ordeals of life nor solace in the hour of death. If Confucianism—begun primarily as a political theory prescribing a moral code for the ruling class—served as a religion in later forms, it was because its social basis was supported by a spiritual faith acquired under the influence of Taoism and Buddhism.

Taoism, on the other hand, indulged in religious speculations in search of an undefined something which would offer hope of eternity. Like Confucianism, it sought to bring man's life on earth into harmony with the life and law of the universe (Tao), but unlike Confucianism it set out to attain this ideal not by laying down rules for human conduct but by an intuitive emotional method.

Buddhism seemed to meet the intellectual needs of both the traditional creeds, and it fitted neatly into the emotional gaps left by them. The glowing spirituality of Buddhism and its elaborate forms of worship greatly attracted the Chinese, who also found in it fulfilment of the natural human hope for life beyond death. The Buddhist emphasis on salvation through moral effort and the law of karma made a deep impression on the moral nature of the Chinese. For the middle and lower classes, Buddhism declared that the humbler folk, who suffered so unjustly at the hands of the Confucianist nobility, would be reborn into higher rank, whilst the cruel officials and noblemen would descend the ladder to suffer for their misdeeds. Buddhism, as it was being elaborated in northern India in the first centuries A.D., substituted the hope of a blissful rebirth, at the feet of the various Buddhas and Bodhisattvas, for Nirvana, the final delivery from the cycle of rebirth. The paradises of Avalokitesvara and Amitabha thus became most popular in China: "The beatific vision thus took the place of the former desire for extinction; the wisdom—a little arid perhaps—of primitive Buddhism gave way either to a powerful esotericism, in the last analysis fairly close to Chinese neo-Taoism, or to a religion of the heart, full of tenderness and forgiveness, likely to appeal to the loftiest souls as well as to console the afflictions of the masses. In both cases Buddhism, with its religiosity, with its charity, with its faith, brought to China spirituality that it still lacked."[33]

Yet, Buddhism was in several respects alien to the Chinese temperament. Its doctrines were too subtle and metaphysical for the essentially practical and material Chinese mind. The Buddhist negation of life, renunciation of family relationships, and practice of celibacy were contrary to Chinese, especially Confucianist, ideas and traditions. Monkhood meant that men avoided their primary task of parenthood, thus failing to continue the family line, and it made them live on charity.

The period of the great expansion of Buddhism, after the collapse of the Later Han dynasty, was one in which China was divided into three states and suffered from foreign invasions; wars and political upheavals were common, life and property were constantly in danger, and it is possible that the intellectuals and the masses alike turned to Buddhism seeking religious salvation. Only a literate could get satisfaction from Confucianism and only an exceptional man could become immortal in Taoism, but Buddhism offered salvation to everyone. Monks were few, but anyone could be a lay Buddhist and there were always Bodhisattvas anxious to help him. The self-denial, hard work, and reforming zeal of the missionaries must have elicited the admiration of the simple people, whereas the Buddhist writings, mainly translations of the scriptures, attracted the intelligentsia.

Changes in the thinking habits of the intellectuals made China more receptive to Buddhism. The young scholars were up in arms against the hair-splitting and formalized interpretations of Confucianism, and a new mood had emerged throughout the country opposing the fetters of

Confucianist propriety, seeking man's liberation into a life beyond the sphere of all restraints: a life in which man could act, think, and speak freely according to the dictates of human emotions. Such a mood could have easily led to admiration for the Buddhist renunciation of worldly pleasures in quest of freedom and the true path.

Magnificent monasteries, towering pagodas, and temples, and beautiful statues, with which the country abounded, drew admiration even from the opponents of Buddhism. A letter from a Confucianist scholar to the prime minister of the Western Chin dynasty describes the monastery built by Tao-an in the fourth century: "Teachers and disciples total seven hundred, and of fasting and study there is no wearying. There is no dazzling of the eyes and ears of common men by resort to magical tricks, nor is there any trampling on the difference among the lesser monk by resort to threats or authority. Furthermore, teachers and pupils courteously respect one another. It is a magnificent sight, and one such as I have never seen before."

The tolerance of the Chinese Buddhists and their willingness to make adjustments to indigenous doctrines must have made them more acceptable. The Chinese deity of Heaven, for example, has a place of honour in certain Buddhist ceremonies; a Bodhisattva was introduced as an incarnation of Confucius; Buddhist temples were built in conformity with the Chinese system of magical ideas, known as *feng shui;* Buddhists occasionally adopted Tao, the key term of philosophic Taoism, for Buddhist dharma; and translations of phrases or passages which might offend traditional Chinese susceptibilities, conditioned by concepts of Confucianist morality, were deleted or edited. For instance, Indian words indicating love and respect for a Bodhisattva—"kiss" and "embrace"—were dropped; and phrases such as "the husband supports his wife" were replaced by the "husband controls his wife" and "the wife comforts her husband" became "the wife reveres her husband." Buddhism gave women a higher place in society than did Chinese traditional concepts.

Buddhist monks also borrowed the Taoist vocabulary because of the purely linguistic difficulty of translating Buddhist concepts into Chinese. The Sanskrit language had nothing in common with Chinese. Every Chinese character carries a traditional connotation which is liable to lead to strange distortions when employed to interpret foreign concepts.

Consequently, the Buddhist adopted Tao (absolute, cosmic force) for *bodhi* (illumination), for *arhat* (Buddhist saint) the Taoist expression, *chen-jen* (true man) was used, and so on. It is, however, also possible that in the initial stages Buddhism found Taoism a convenient medium for the spread of its own ideas. Buddhist nirvana and arhat were, for instance, more easily acceptable to the Chinese as Taoist *wu-wei* and chen-jen. Buddhists made use of some Confucianist expressions also; for example, for *sila* (morality or pious conduct) they used the Confucianist *hsiao-hsun* (filial submission and obedience). In the sixteenth century when the Catholic missionaries faced the same problem they solved it in a similar way, by borrowing equivalent terms from Confucianist philosophy.

Since tenants on the Buddhist temple lands were better treated than those on lands owned by Confucianist aristocrats, poorer people readily became Buddhist tenants, later accepting the faith. Merchants made use of the Buddhist monasteries as banks, stock exchanges, and warehouses, and the monasteries grew in importance as repositories of capital. The temples bought more and more land, thus gaining an increasing influence in the country's economic life. Habitual association with Buddhist monks, even if it were for material reasons, encouraged the people to be well disposed towards Buddhist doctrine, because the monks worked so selflessly and the inevitable human response to this example was one of sympathy.[34]

As time passed, not only did the emperors and the common people become Buddhists, but even distinguished men of learning increasingly turned towards Buddhism. In the eleventh century the famous reformer-statesman, Wang An-shih, whose tablet was placed in the Confucianist temple next to that of Mencius, deplored the fact that scholars sought new ideas and inspiration in Buddhism. Yet his son wrote books on Buddhism. Even the chief exponent of Confucianist orthodoxy, Chu Hsi, complained in the twelfth century that the educated man now found himself compelled to draw upon Taoism and Buddhism for religious and ethical concepts.

But the rise of Buddhism in China was not without religious struggles, controversies, and persecutions. Confucianism and Taoism have always been jealous of Buddhism and have often persecuted it, Confucianism persistently appealing to Chinese nationalism and cultural pride. There were four major anti-Buddhist persecutions in 466, 574, 845, and 955. None of these, however, was nation-wide or lasted more than a few years. Upon the death of the persecuting king, almost invariably the policy of suppression was reversed by his successor and Buddhism resumed its former influence. Chinese persecution of Buddhism tended to be directed mainly against monastic establishments rather than against monks and devotees. That such persecution was political is clearly suggested by the fact that all edicts for the persecution of Buddhism emphasized that it was a national disaster and a humiliation for the celestial kingdom to be influenced by an alien creed.

As long as Buddhism remained alien it was tolerated and was even popular, but as soon as it sought naturalization it aroused opposition. Confucianists and Taoists, often in conflict with each other, combined to resist the ideas from India, which had come to be looked upon by the Chinese people as "the Land of the Buddha" and even as "the Western Heaven" from which nothing but the great truth could come.[35] In the fifth century, Ku Huan wrote *I-hsia-lun,* a treatise against Buddhism, denouncing it as inferior to the Chinese system. He was not the first scholar to criticize Buddhism, but he was the first to do so at length. He sought to prove that Indian nature and customs were evil, and thus that Buddhism was unsuited to Chinese culture. Whilst Ku Huan's criticisms were essentially motivated by nationalistic prejudice, there were other Chinese scholars, such as Fan Chen and Hsun-chi, who were motivated by intellectual and political considerations.

Buddhism was widely popular under both the Southern and Northern dynasties, although Confucianist and Taoist scholars demanded its outright suppression. Persecution in the south, however, was not nearly as bad as in the north. It is indeed surprising that the first major persecution should have taken place under a dynasty which is chiefly remembered for its patronage of Buddhism. In 446 Toba Emperor Tai-Wu or Shih-tsu (424–451) of the Northern Wei dynasty, after a series of anti-Buddhist measures, finally decreed that the Buddhist religion was to be completely wiped out. Not one monk, one scriptural text, or one image was to remain in existence.[36] Consequently, there was a wholesale destruction of Buddhist temples, stupas, and texts and numerous monks were executed. It is thought that the Taoist Kou Chien-chih and his friend the Confucianist minister, Tsui Hao, were instrumental in instigating this persecution.

The persecution lasted for seven years until reversed by the new Emperor, Wen-Chang, in 454. The new decree, in fact, commenced by praising the Buddha, and then endeavoured to explain the persecution as an attempt to eliminate certain evil elements from the monastic order. Buddhism emerged from this persecution with increased vigour and determination to expand. The Buddhists renewed their work by constructing the world-famous caves of Yun-kang. This undertaking of large-scale rock sculpture is a monument as much to the artistic techniques and religious zeal of the Buddhists as to the prestige and graceful restitution of the ruling dynasty under whose patronage these caves were constructed. Within sixty years of the Buddhist revival there were about fourteen thousand temples in the Northern Wei territory alone, and during the next twenty years the number reached thirty thousand with more than two million monks and nuns. At this time, Buddhism was more widespread in northern China than it was in the south. In the southern kingdoms, for example, under the Liang dynasty (502–556) there were, according to a T'ang source, about 2,864 temples and 82,000 monks and nuns.

More than a century later, in 574, before Buddhism reached its peak during the Sui and T'ang dynasties, Emperor Wu (reign 561–577) of one of the short-lived dynasties, the Northern Chou, anxious to make Confucianism the state religion, ordered the abolition of all Taoist and Buddhist organizations. There had long been a fierce controversy between Buddhists and Taoists about the priority of Lao-tzu (now considered a mythical figure) over the Buddha. The Taoist claimed that Lao-tzu had gone to India where he had become the Buddha. Both sides fabricated evidence to support their contentions. In 520 a historic debate over this question was held in the presence of Emperor Hsiao-ming, at the conclusion of which the Taoists were severely defeated and their claim was pronounced unfounded by a committee of one hundred and seventy scholars headed by Wei-shou. This brought Hsiao-ming's wrath down upon the Taoists, whose chief spokesman in the debate, Chiang Pin, escaped execution only by the intercession of the Buddhist monk, Bodhiruci. Later, in the reign of Emperor Wu, this debate started again with such acrimony that even the Imperial presence could not assuage it. Probably disgusted by this unending and bitter debate, Wu decided in 573 to rank Confucianism first, Taoism second, and Buddhism third as religions of the Empire. It is said that his decision was influenced by the machinations of Wei Yuan-sung, who had been a Buddhist monk and who had dabbled in the occult sciences, and Chiang Pin, who had lost the Taoist argument in the debate of 520. The Buddhists resented this decision, thus infuriating the Emperor who retaliated by proscribing Buddhism. In his decree he ordered the destruction of Buddhist temples, images, and scriptures; monks and nuns were to return to the laity; and the treasures of the monasteries were to be confiscated for distribution amongst the officials and royal princes. It is noteworthy that the Buddhists had so successfully exposed the flagrant forgeries perpetrated by the Taoists that Emperor Wu had to also include Taoism in his decree of suppression. These persecutions, however, were short-lived. Wu died in 578, and three years later the Northern Chou dynasty was overthrown by Emperor Wen of the Sui dynasty. He immediately reinstated both Buddhism and Taoism. The recovery of Buddhism was extraordinarily rapid, and it soon enjoyed a new peak of popularity.

The T'ang rulers generally preferred Taoism, but did not interfere with Buddhism, except on two occasions. The first T'ang Emperor, Li-yuan (or Kao-tzu), was quite antagonistic, but, conscious as he was of the size and influence of the Buddhist community in China, he did not risk open hostility. Therefore, instead of trying to suppress Buddhism outright, he placed various restrictions on its activities. He regarded Confucianism as essential to China, and under the influence of the Imperial historian, Fu-i, who was a staunch Confucianist, he issued an edict ordering magistrates to inquire into the lives of the Buddhist monks and nuns. But before the decree could be fully implemented, he was murdered, and there emerged a succession of T'ang rulers who were well disposed towards Buddhism.

Two centuries later the Taoist emperor, Wu-tsung, during his brief reign of five years attempted to suppress Buddhism. He decreed in 845 that, except for the four temples in each of the capital cities and one in each of the provinces, all Buddhist temples and monasteries were to be demolished and monks and nuns unfrocked. More than sixty-five thousand temples were desecrated, millions of acres of monastic land confiscated, and more than a quarter of a million monks and nuns forced to return to lay life. They were even denied Chinese nationality. These figures may be somewhat exaggerated, but they at least indicate both the scale of the suppression and the hold Buddhism had acquired in China. This persecution was certainly the most widespread of its kind in China, for previous persecutions had been mainly confined to northern China. It is said that Han Yu (768–824) was the intellectual father of the persecution of 845. He coined such slogans as: "Restore their people to humanity! Burn their books! And convert their buildings to human residences!"[37] Whether this persecution was a sudden development or another episode in the long ideological struggle between Taoism and Buddhism is a matter of controversy amongst historians. Economic considerations, such as the desire of the Emperor for the enormous wealth deposited in the thousands of Buddhist stupas, cannot be overlooked.

This persecution was also short-lived. In 846 Emperor Wu-tsung died, probably affected by the longevity potions he had been taking, and his successor, Hsüan-tsang, immediately cancelled the persecution. The number of temples and monks increased at once. Some scholars, however, hold the view that after the persecution of 845, Buddhism did not completely recover, and that the Sangha declined as an intellectual and spiritual force.

After the downfall of the T'ang dynasty in 907, China was divided into a dozen kingdoms and Buddhism again came under the state ax with some thirty thousand monasteries being destroyed. The Sung dynasty (960–1127) reversed this policy. At state expense a project was instituted for the translation and publication of the Buddhist scriptures. State assistance came at a most opportune moment, because by this time contact with India had ceased. The Sung period, however, soon witnessed the revival of Confucianist bureaucracy. Because of the constant infiltration into Sung China from the north by the Khitans and Juchens, nationalist feelings were unusually high. Taking advantage of the situation, the Confucianists intensified their efforts to have the alien creed expelled. Meanwhile, there arose a new syncretic school of thought, Neoconfucianism, which had absorbed some Buddhist philosophy and metaphysics, and which was adopted by the Sungs as their official doctrine.

The Mongols (1279–1368), who dislodged the Sungs, protected Buddhism because they were themselves Tibetan Buddhists. But under the Ming dynasty opposition to Buddhism increased and continued into the Manchu dynasty, except for a respite during the reign of the first two Manchu emperors who were devout Buddhists. Buddhism was subjected to suppression by the state and the bureaucracy. Emperors persecuted Buddhism, philosophers accused it of superstitions, statesmen were disturbed that some of the most able people in the country were lying idle in the monasteries, and Confucianist and Taoist literati denounced it as an alien import. But in the end the emperors made peace with Buddhism, the monks were allowed to collect alms and raise temples, and the bureaucracy was compelled to keep Confucianism as its own aristocratic creed.

The introduction of Buddhism is one of the most important events in Chinese history, and since its inception it has been a major factor in Chinese civilization, exercising a great influence on religion, philosophy, art and literature. The Chinese have freely acknowledged their debt to India often referring to her as the "Teacher of China," and Chinese Buddhists have pictured India as a Western Paradise, *Sukhavati.* The advent of Buddhism meant for many Chinese a new way of life, and for all Chinese, whether they accepted it or not, a means of reassessing their traditional beliefs. A new conception of the universe developed, and the entire Chinese approach to life was slowly but surely altered. The change was so gradual and so universal that few people realized it was happening. For over a thousand years the Chinese mind was dominated mainly by Buddhism. The decline of Buddhism in China during the last few centuries cannot obscure the fact that whilst Buddhism enjoyed prestige and popularity, it influenced Chinese culture in many ways and left lasting impressions on Chinese life.[38] Being a strong and self-confident civilization, however, China fitted Buddhist ideas into her own texture of life, and the ascetism of Buddhism, for example, could not suppress the Chinese love of life and gaiety.[39]

There has been, however, no scarcity of historians who have been unable to appreciate adequately the extent and depth of Buddhist influence on Chinese culture. Whilst Western writers, with notable exceptions, have found it difficult to comprehend the variety and complexity of Buddhist doctrines, texts, and traditions, and have been somewhat disabled by their own predispositions, Confucianist historians have looked upon Buddhism as an alien intrusion, regarding the Buddhist ascendancy in Chinese life as indicative of a weakness in the culture of a great people, a weakness which they would like to confine to obscurity. Even some rationalist historians are not altogether free from this somewhat irrational, although natural, feeling, as is shown by Hu Shih's comment that "with the new aids of modern science and technology, and of the new social and historical sciences, we are confident that we may yet achieve a rapid liberation from the two thousand years' cultural domination by India."[40]

India never imposed her ideas or culture on any nation by military force, not even on the small countries in her neighbourhood, and, in the case of China, it would have been virtually impossible to do so since China has usually been the more powerful of the two. So the expansion of Indian culture into China is a monument to human understanding and cultural co-operation—the outcome of a voluntary quest for learning. Whilst China almost completely suppressed other foreign religions, such as Zoroastrianism, Nestorian Christianity, and, to some extent, Manichaeanism, she could not uproot Buddhism. At times Buddhism was persecuted, but for two thousand years it continued to Indianize Chinese life even after it had ceased to be a vital force in its homeland and long after it had lost its place as the dominant religion of China. In fact, Indianization became more powerful and effective after it was thought that Buddhism had been killed in China.[41]

By far the most significant contribution of Buddhism to China was that it made knowledge available to the lower strata of society and introduced a democratic element into learning. Popular education was unheard of, but Buddhism broke open the gates of learning for all alike; the powerful and the rich could no longer monopolize knowledge. Indeed, the Buddhist neophytes were usually taken from humbler classes. Hu Shih, who considered that Indian influence had harmed the natural development of Chinese culture, and who led the modern Chinese intellectual renaissance, commented: "Never before had China seen a religion so rich in imagery, so beautiful and captivating in ritualism and so bold in cosmological and metaphysical speculations. Like a poor beggar suddenly halting before a magnificent storehouse of precious stones of dazzling brilliancy and splendour, China was overwhelmed, baffled and overjoyed. She begged and borrowed freely from this munificent giver. The first borrowings were chiefly from the religious life of India, in which China's indebtedness to India can never be fully told."[42] Through its compassionate Buddhas and Bodhisattvas, its promise of salvation to all alike, its emphasis on piety, meditation, and restraint of passions, its attractive rituals and festivals, its universality and its tolerance, "the religious life of the Chinese has been enriched, deepened, broadened" and made more meaningful in terms of human sympathy, love, and compassion for all living creatures."[43]

Certain theistic beliefs—the doctrine of rebirth, the idea of causality, the belief in reward and retribution, the conception of reality which permeates every living thing in nature, and the notion of universal impermanence—had an abiding influence on Chinese life, literature, and thought. The old simple idea of retribution of good and evil was replaced by the law of karma (yeh in Chinese) which controls all past, present, and future existences. The doctrine of karma brought spiritual consolation to innumerable people. That Chinese philosophy blossomed afresh after the impact of Buddhism indicates both a response to and a borrowing from Indian ideas. Buddhism not only offered paradise to the good, but also threatened the wicked with a multiplicity of hells. The Chinese, who have always regarded ancestor-worship as important, found this Buddhist doctrine impressive and convincing. Compassionate concern for all living beings naturally expressed itself in practical ways, including the establishment of charitable institutions, such as hospitals, orphanages, resthouses, and old peoples' homes. Emotional attachment to religion encouraged pilgrimages to distant Buddhist establishments, thus making the Chinese better acquainted with other parts of their country and its environs.

Broadly, Indian influence on Chinese thought proceeded along two lines: ideas which were assimilated as part of the indigenous tradition, and those ideas so radically different that they were distinctly identified as Indian. Fung Yu-Lan expressed this by pointing out that there is a distinction between "Chinese Buddhism" and "Buddhism in China."[44] For example, the school of subjective idealism of Hsüan-tsang, known in Chinese as the *Hsiang tsung* (or Wei-shih), is obviously Indian, whilst the Ch'an school developed in China through interaction with Taoism. Of the two, the latter line of Indian influence was more successful, and, as Buddhism adapted more and more to China, it was able to make a greater contribution to Chinese culture.

The famous disciple of Kumarajiva, Seng-chao (374–414), first compared Indian and Chinese thought. He wrote several essays, collected as the *Chao Lun*, and found that the systems of Nagarjuna and of Lao-tzu were not dissimilar. At an early stage in its development, two schools of Mahayana Buddhism emerged—Madhyamika and Yogacara—and Nagarjuna was the founder of the Madhyamika school. This school held the doctrine of the middle view between existence and non-existence, affirmation and negation, eternity and transience, self and 'non-self. Although the Buddha in his first sermon at Banaras preached the middle path, his doctrine differed from that of Madhyamika. Buddha's teaching had an ethical meaning, preaching neither a life of material pleasure nor of self-mortification. Nagarjuna's concept was metaphysical, advocating neither the theory of reality nor that of unreality. Nagarjuna taught that nothing is existent per se; it exists only in relation to other things; everything is sunyata (void) and its individuality is imaginary, *samvriti.* The sunyata is the absolute, corresponding to the *Nirguna Brahman* of the Upanishads; and there is no difference between *samsara,* the world of vision, and nirvana or sunyata. True knowledge is that which discloses the supreme identity beyond all opposites. Seng-chao interpreted the philosophy of Nagarjuna in Taoist terms and approximated the two doctrines. For instance, in his essay, *On the Immutability of Things,* he observed that Buddhist thought presented the contrast between the immutable reality (*bhuta-tathata*) and the temporal (*utpada-nirodha*), between permanence and change, and between nirvana and rebirth. These were very similar to the Taoist contrast between non-being and being, immutability and mutability, and *wu wei* (non-existence) and *yu-wei* (existence). Philosophical controversy in China at the time was centred mostly on *ti* (noumenon, or substance) and *yung* (phenomenon or function). Seng-chao held that ti and yung are not opposed but are the same. He sought to synthesize, which was his middle path. His synthesis of the absolute and the relative was no doubt based on the system of Nagarjuna, but it was expressed in Taoist phraseology. Because of its Chinese exterior, it was accepted as Chinese, and, in this, Seng-chao paved the way for Buddhist assimilation into Chinese philosophy.

Hui-Yuan, a disciple of Tao-an and a contemporary of Seng-chao, laid the foundation for the White Lotus Society of Lushan School, later known as the Pure Land School. In 402 Hui-Yuan assembled a group of one hundred and twenty-three of his chosen followers before a statue of Amitabha where they made a collective vow to be reborn in the Western Paradise. Thus the cult of Amitabha, the compassionate Buddha who became a Buddha only on the condition that he could distribute his accumulated good to others as he chose, was initiated. Those who live righteously and who piously repeat daily the words *namo Amitabha-ya,* or who meditate properly on him, can reach his paradise, the Pure Land (Sukhavati) in the West. This concept of the splendid Pure Land of Amitabha, one of the most magnificent in Buddhist imagery, had great success throughout Eastern Asia and inspired many works of art in both China and Japan. It was a non-intellectual and extremely simple form of Buddhism, involving an attitude of complete and enthusiastic bhakti (devotion) to Amitabha—a new type of Buddhist theism.

Hui-Yuan emphasized meditation and actively promoted dhyana exercises in South China. He was so enthusiastic that he sent emissaries to Central Asia to obtain relevant texts and instruction. Well-versed in Confucianist and Taoist classics, he frequently relied on Taoist terms to express Buddhist principles. He believed that Buddhist and non-Buddhist learning could be fused into one doctrine. In his writings he mixed the metaphysical speculations of Neotaoism with the Prajna thought of Buddhism, thus making the monastic ideal all the more attractive to the literati and gentry of South China.

A disciple of Hui-Yuan, Tao-sheng (also a fellow student of Seng-chao's under Kumarajiva) was a monk of wide learning and great brillance who served as a bridge between the Buddhist centres at Lu-Shan and Chang-an. He preached such revolutionary theories that he was once publicly banished from Nanking by the conservative monks. Two of these theories are important: "good action requires return," and "sudden enlightenment" as opposed to all forms of "gradual attainment." These doctrines were not really new but were actually Buddhist with a Chinese emphasis, demonstrating the Chinese assimilation of Buddhism. For example, Tao-sheng's doctrine of the true self was the logical culmination of Buddhist thinking on the subject. He taught that every sentient being possesses the Buddha-nature of universal mind, but is ignorant of it. It is this *avidya* (ignorance) which chains him to the wheel of birth and rebirth. Therefore, it is necessary for him to realize and learn to "see" the Buddha-nature within him, thus gaining freedom from illusion and returning to the ultimate. This realization of the Buddha within through sudden enlightenment also meant being one with the Buddha-nature of wu or universal mind, and this was the state of nirvana. Many Buddhists did not approve of Tao-sheng's doctrine since it implied that there is in reality no pure land or other world; the world of Buddha is around us; anyone could attain Buddhahood by sudden enlightenment. The idea of the Universal Mind is an Indian contribution to Chinese philosophy. The tao of the Taoists is the "mystery of mysteries," yet it is not Mind.[45] After Tao-sheng, Chinese philosophy had not only mind but also Mind, and his emphasis on meditation as a means of attaining enlightenment prepared the way for the development of the Ch'an (Dhyana) school of thought, which influenced not just Buddhism but all Chinese thought.

Tao-an and Hui-Yuan also emphasized the importance of Dhyana. Yet it was not until a century after Tao-sheng's death in 434 that the Dhyana school of thought was introduced to China by the Indian monk Bodhidharma. Bodhidharma had evolved a system through which Buddhahood could be attained only by the conscious identification of both the absolute and the relative. According to the traditions of the Dhyana school, this was an esoteric teaching of the Buddha transmitted from disciple to disciple, independently of written texts, until it reached the twenty-eighth Indian Patriarch, Bodhidharma, who taught that the Buddha was not to be found in images and books but in the hearts of men. The heart of every man is in communion with all time and all space. This heart is the Buddha and the Buddha is the heart. There is no Buddha outside the heart. Enlightenment and nirvana are also in the heart. Outside the reality of the heart, everything is imaginary. To search for something outside the heart is an attempt to seize emptiness. It is therefore essential to look within and to contemplate the Buddha-nature of the self. Bodhidharma's teaching was derived from the *Vijnana Vada,* but if Brahman is substituted for the Buddha, it appears remarkably similar to the Vedanta philosophy.

The Ch'an school presented a challenge to Buddhist scholasticism and monasticism. Throughout China there were thousands of monasteries with innumerable monks and nuns and a vast literature of Buddhist texts. And then the Ch'an philosophy arrived, ignoring all scriptures, disregarding asceticism and all forms of worship, even the concept of good and evil, preaching deliverance by knowing one's own self. Dhyana Buddhism was the very antithesis of the easy and popular way of gaining salvation through devotion and worship of Amitabha. It opposed the worship of images and the authority of the priesthood and emphasized instead the application of one's own strength, the sense of inner freedom, detachment from worldly things, and ceaseless meditation and self-discipline. Bodhidharma is said to have told the devout Buddhist, Emperor Wu of the Liang dynasty, that all his good works did not accumulate any merit. To Bodhidharma the scriptures were nothing more than the finger that points to the moon of enlightenment, no longer useful once the moon is seen. Because of the difference between the existing Buddhist scholasticism and Bodhidharma's Dhyana, it has been suggested that the Dhyana movement was not really Buddhism at all, but a Chinese revolt against Buddhist verbalism and scholasticism, as well as a movement to make Buddhism more Chinese in character by detaching it from intellectualism. If this be true, then the Chinese alternative to Indian Buddhism emerged from Buddhism itself. But there is little substance in this assertion, because, whilst the Dhyana school rejects many features of Mahayana Buddhism, much of what is left is still remarkably close to early Indian Buddhism. "Chari Buddhism differs from the orthodox and popular Mahayana of the theistic Sutras just as the teaching of Christ and of the Christian mystics differs from the systematic Christianity of the Churches."[46] Indeed, the Ch'an doctrine of introspection in order to discover the essence of perfection in the depths of the heart and to bring about its mystical cleansing can doubtless be traced back to the practices of the Indian Yogis, both Hindu and

Buddhist. However, it would be wrong to deny the influence of Taoism in the development of the Ch'an movement in China. The emphasis of Ch'an writers, teachers, and artists on spontaneity and naturalness is reminiscent of many passages in Taoist philosophic texts protesting the artificial restraints of society against the natural development of man. The Dhyana emphasis on the Buddha-nature of the self may have a parallel in the Taoist immanence of the Tao. Both Dhyana and Taoism stress the idea of the wordless doctrine, and Dhyana contemplation differs little from Taoist ecstasy. It is probable, however, that these common features illustrate Buddhist influence on Taoism.

Whatever the Taoist content in Ch'an, it certainly was not as speculative as some other schools of Buddhism were. Ch'an bore an affinity with Taoism in its philosophical ramifications, but did not antagonize Confucianist thought. Inevitably, it had great appeal for the Chinese and became widely popular in China. This sect "completed the transformation into Chinese thought of the fundamental ideas brought from India, thus achieving a Buddhist equivalent of the highest Taoism."[47]

The concept of Dhyana is sometimes hailed as an internal Chinese Buddhist movement independent of Indian influence. It is argued that Bodhidharma was a legendary figure invented later to give the doctrine weight and authority, and that Dhyana was, psychologically if not doctrinally, the descendant of the early Chinese Quietism. Whilst this theory is somewhat far-fetched, some scholars maintain that the Quietism of China during the fourth and third centuries B.C. was to some extent moulded by Indian influence. This does seem possible but there is no definite proof of it. Whilst it is not altogether true that the formative period of Chinese Quietism, the fourth century B.C., was a time when outside influences on thought were general, Quietism did develop and expand when such influences were demonstrably beginning to be of importance. Scholars are now agreed that the literature of the third century B.C. is full of geographical and mythological elements derived from India.[48] Moreover, the Chinese Quietists practiced a form of self-hypnosis remarkably close to Indian Yoga.

The only flourishing Buddhist school in China today is the Tien-Tai school, founded by Chih-i (or Chi-kai) (538–597). This school was eclectic, saw no antagonism between the Hinayana and Mahayana, and accepted all sutras as true words of the Buddha. Following Nagarjuna's doctrine that all component things are impermanent, that all dharmas are without self, and that only nirvana is quiescence, it established a threefold system of perfect comprehension, *chi-kwan: kung,* empty or void; *chia,* hypothetical or temporariness; and *chung,* medial or mean. These three modes of comprehending beings can be likened to the three eyes of Siva. The "empty" mode destroys the illusion of sensory perception and constructs supreme knowledge, prajna; the "hypothetical" mode dispenses with the defilement of the world and establishes salvation from all evils; and the "medial" mode demolishes hallucination born of ignorance, avidya, and establishes the enlightened mind. Through these three truths the Tien-Tai school emphasizes the idea of totality and mutual identification; the whole and its parts are identical. The entire cosmos and all the Buddhas may be present in a grain of sand or the point of a hair. The Tien-Tai identification of phenomena with the absolute is further illustrated by their doctrine of the Absolute Mind, which embraces the universe in its entirety.

The Tien-Tai tenets are a brilliant product of Buddhist thought in China, because they harmonize and synthesize all doctrines, even the most contradictory, affirm the existence of the Buddha-nature in all sentient beings and assure universal salvation. Tien-Tai Buddhism is the most comprehensive system of Mahayana and is held as an authoritative model for East Asia, particularly for Japan. Its main text, *Saddharma-Pundarika-Sutra* (*Fa-hua-Ching* in Chinese and *Hokke-kyo* in Japanese), has provided more themes for Buddhist art in China than any other source.

Whilst Chinese scholars, such as Seng-chao, Hui-Yuan, Tao-sheng, and Chih-i, adapted Indian thought to Chinese patterns, there were others, like Hsüan-tsang and his chief disciple Kuei-chi, who founded schools which seem wholly Indian in character, some of which still survive. Hsüan-tsang founded a school called Fa hsiang-tsung (Dharma lakshana, known in Japan as Hosso) which taught that the world of phenomena is a projection of Vijnana, consciousness. Phenomena are illusory and only consciousness is real; the purpose of life is to free oneself from fear of and attachment to the external world, which is a fabrication of one's own consciousness. This system, explaining all phenomena psychologically and rationally, evoked a new interest amongst Chinese intellectuals, but could not wield great proselytizing power, because its deep and complex metaphysical speculations had little appeal to the average Chinese. Moreover, the Chinese language was just not flexible enough to translate and expound the subtle distinctions of terms and phrases of this school, which in its vast literature developed a most abstruse system of introspective psychology, analyzing consciousness into more than five hundred states of mind and their corresponding faculties and objects.[49] Although no Chinese sect exclusively follows this philosophy, it is still studied and has had considerable influence on East Asian thought.

Amongst other Buddhist schools of China are the Kiu-she, based on the *Abhidharma-kosa;* the Liu (Vinaya) school, founded by Tao-Shiuan; and Chen-Yen (the School of the True Word), based on Tantric Buddhism introduced by Vajrabodhi in the eighth century. Tantrism or Vajrayana, named after its chief symbol, *vajra* (thunderbolt), is a combination of mystical speculation and secret magic rites expressed in a complex symbolism. These speculations involve the relationship between empirical reality and true essence, illustrated by a hierarchy of sacred figures and culminating in the *adi* (absolute) Buddha. The meditations, rites, and symbols aid the practical realization of the identity existing between the devotee and the Buddhanature within him.

Whilst some Buddhist influence can still be seen in practically every aspect of Chinese cultural life, much is hardly recognizable. The transformation of Buddhist deities in China is a good illustration of this point. It is not often realized that the pot-bellied, exuberant Buddha, so popular as a tourist souvenir and as a model of art practically everywhere, is a Chinese version of the Indian Maitreya Buddha, who is yet to come and who is at present in the Tusita Heaven. The Indian Bodhisattva, Avalokitesvara, a sort of Buddhist Providence, on his arrival in China assumed by a curious metamorphosis a feminine guise, becoming the Goddess of Mercy, Kuan-yin, often represented as a beautiful woman with tiny feet sometimes bound in the traditional Chinese way. This goddess is extremely popular in China. Practically every household contains her image in wood, ivory, or porcelain, and she has temples in all parts of the country. The same Chinese tendency to adapt, assimilate, and integrate Indian elements is evident in other aspects of cultural life such as music, painting, sculpture, and architecture.

The most outstanding product of the cultural dialogue between Buddhism and Chinese thought was Neoconfucianism, unquestionably one of the greatest philosophies of China. The impact of Buddhism gave rise to a renaissance of Confucianism under the Sung and Ming dynasties. Many Chinese scholars of traditional learning recognized the superiority of Buddhist teachings, especially in metaphysics and methodology. Hence, they were inspired to rejuvenate Confucianism, grafting onto it what they regarded as the merits of Buddhism. But the Chinese, deeply imbued with a sense of this-worldiness and social responsibility, could not be completely reconciled with the other-wordliness of Buddhism. Therefore, the interaction between metaphysical Buddhist thought and Confucianist ethics led to the emergence of a new philosophical movement, commonly known as Neoconfucianism, during the Sung period (960–1279). Just as Buddhist interaction with Taoism gave rise to Ch'an, so with Confucianism it produced Neoconfucianism or *Li*. Thus, Buddhism finally succeeded in stirring the Chinese intellect to respond in a positive way to new stimuli. This Confucianist response to Buddhism was characteristically Chinese: having failed to silence a critic, denounce him but act on his criticism. Whilst Confucianism underwent drastic changes under the Buddhist impact, Buddhism itself, except in minor concepts, absorbed little of Confucianism.[50]

Neoconfucianism was a deliberate attempt to show that Confucianism could offer everything that Buddhism offered. Neoconfucianists found fault with Buddhist doctrines but endeavoured to crystallize their own philosophical thinking. In doing so, they had to borrow a good deal without specifically acknowledging their debt. Often they overstretched their interpretations to prove the continuity and purity of their interpretation of Confucianism, since the new movement was partly a nationalist reaction against Buddhism. But in fact, Neoconfucianism contains less Confucianism and more Buddhism, and to call it Neoconfucianism, therefore, is strictly speaking a misnomer. A contemporary Chinese scholar, Chou Hsiang-kuang, calls it Sung Rationalism or *Li Hsueh* of the Sung dynasty.[51]

Neoconfucianism explicitly undertook to match the Buddhist

cosmology, explain the world metaphysically, and show how man could attain happiness within the ordinary pursuits of life. It was impossible to produce a system of cosmology and metaphysics from the *Analects* of Confucius, who was much too practical. Many Neoconfucianists appealed to Mencius, who, although a Confucianist, had diverged considerably from the master's practicality and adopted an almost mystical attitude similar to that of a Taoist. Whatever could not be explained was attributed to the esoteric teaching of Confucius, which was imparted not to the masses but to the select few. Four books came to be regarded as the main scriptures of Neoconfucianism during the Sung period: the *Analects,* the *Book of Mencius,* the *Great Learning,* and the *Doctrine of the Mean.* The last was held to contain the esoteric teaching of Confucius. It is significant that whilst some Confucianist scholars continued to deprecate Buddhism as a foreign religion, Confucianist temples from the eighth to the sixteenth centuries contained images of Confucius, his disciples and other notables, like the images in Buddhist temples.

That Neoconfucianists felt the need to discover scientific thought to match the notions of positive sciences as applied to philosophy shows that Indian concepts, such as the dualism of Samkhya and the atomism of Vaisesika, were too popular and well known to be liked by the revivalists. Compelled thus to offer a cosmology that could compete with that of the Buddhists, "the Neo-Confucians took over bodily some of the ideas of their rivals. Thus we find them echoing the Buddhist idea that the Universe is ceaselessly destroyed and recreated. This is interpreted in Chinese terms, however, as a function of the operation of the *Yin* (regression) and *Yang* (progression), the five forces, mystic numerology, and the diagrams which are the basis of the *Book of Changes.*"[52] The Confucianists claimed that this work was written by Confucius, but in fact it is an ancient fortune-teller's manual. However, for many Neoconfucianists it virtually became a bible for their cosmology. It is so alien to the whole of early Confucianism that it is impossible not to believe that its metaphysical speculations were derived from Taoism and Buddhism over a period of time.

But each rival school of the many varieties of Neoconfucianism claimed Confucianist purity for itself and accused the others of having been influenced by Taoism and Buddhism. Later, many Chinese scholars, such as Ku Yen-Wu (or Ku Ting-Lin, 1613–1682), also attacked Neoconfucianism for its debt to Buddhism.

The Neoconfucianist movement was initiated by Chou Tun-i (1017–1073), who introduced into Confucianism the doctrine of the Supreme Ultimate, or first principle, which he called by the ancient name, *tai-chi* (meaning literally "supreme-limit") and which was conceived of as the primordial unity like the ancient Tao. However, in common with the Neotaoists of his time, Chou Tun-i envisaged this primordial essence as purely cosmogonic and not metaphysical. In modern terms, it resembled the infinitely rarefied and diffused matter of nebulae, a dust which consolidates itself into things by the laws of nature, and which produces the universe through the process of evolution. He criticized the Buddhist doctrine of sunyata, which maintained that the phenomenal world was illusionary.

Similar ideas were developed by other scholars, such as Shao Yung (1011–1077); the two brothers, Cheng Hao (1032–1085) and Cheng Yi (1033–1107); Chang Tsai, their uncle; and Chu Hsi (1130–1200).[53] Of these exponents of Neoconfucianism, Chang Tsai was probably the one most responsible for the introduction of acceptable elements from Buddhism. Chu Hsi, hailed by Needham as "the supreme synthetic mind in all Chinese history," was born in Fukien and is alleged to have once been a Buddhist monk. About 1154 he renounced Buddhism and returned to official Confucianism. His philosophical writings so completely dominated those of his predecessors, and wielded such an extensive influence, that his system is generally distinguished as Chuism. Like Confucius he was "a transmitter rather than an originator" of thought. His main object was to further the new approach to the Confucianist classics as taught by the Cheng brothers.[54] Perhaps his central concept is that the whole universe is composed of two co-eternal principles which are *li* and *chi*—the norm or reason, and matter or energy. These two are inseparable, yet possess distinctive characters. They existed before heaven and earth, and li set chi in motion which produced the world. In regard to the relation between the norm and the world, the noumenon and the phenomenon, Chu Hsi and the Neoconfucianist philosophers seem to accept the Buddhist concept of nirvana and samsara. But the li principle is not the same as the concept of a universal consciousness, an affable spirituality, the soul of souls and of worlds of Indian pantheism. Li action is necessary inevitable and unconscious, which excludes any idea of spirituality. All things and all human relationships consist of li and chi, which, as one, are infinite, eternal, immutable, unalterable, homogenous, unconscious, and unintelligent. Li is pure, vast, without form, and unable to create. Chi is alone responsible for existent things and for change. In this Chu Hsi was, no doubt, influenced by the Indian idea that only the permanent and unchanging is good in the highest sense.

Man's nature is his li, which is part of the Supreme Ultimate. It is only human desire that obscures his true nature, and if he could but realize this fact he would be enlightened. This is remarkably similar to the doctrine of the Dhyana school of Buddhism, and much of this philosophy is so alien to early Chinese thought that "it would be easy to conclude the Neo-Confucians have been converted to Buddhism in everything but name."[55] Chu Hsi, in common with Shao Yung (1011–1077), believed that at the end of an epoch lasting 129,600 years the existing world system would come to an end and be replaced by another. This concept was alien to the Chinese and must have been derived from the well-known Indian ideas of aeons and recurring world systems.

Chu Hsi's greatest rival was Lu Hsiang-Shan (or Lu Chiu-Yuan, 1139–1193), the founder of the rival school of Sung Rationalism. He stressed meditation and intuition, and wielded much influence over Chinese thinkers of the day, especially in eastern China. Whilst his emphasis resembles that of Dhyana Buddhism, it also has roots in ancient Chinese thought, especially that of Mencius. Chu Hsi's system, with its vagaries and universality, is marked by an element of caution and consideration, whilst Lu Hsiang-Shan's is characterized by sharpness and penetration. Lu Hsiang-Shan did not share Chu-Hsi's dualistic philosophy, but propounded a monistic doctrine stating that everything that exists is li. Nothing is finite; man, heaven, earth, and all things exist in the infinite. Man is personally concerned in every affair of the universe, and the universe is concerned in all man's personal affairs. Early Chinese thought was closer to Lu Hsiang-Shan's than to Chu Hsi's. Lu said, "the Universe is my mind, and my mind is the Universe," in somewhat the same way as Mencius said, "all things are complete within me." But the type of monism which Lu Hsiang-Shan preached is also akin to Dhyana

Buddhism, and for this reason Chu Hsi's disciples criticized Lu. Whilst Chu Hsi taught that man's nature is pure and unchanging, and that mind is composed of li and chi, Lu regarded nature, mind, and feeling as the same thing seen from different aspects, and believed that the process of moral cultivation consisted of looking for one's own "lost mind," one's true nature which was originally good, but had been led astray through desire. Lu advocated practical methods for regaining the lost mind. For man there is nothing prior to knowing himself. For attaining knowledge of one's own self or lost mind, he suggested meditation, much in the same manner as the Dhyana Buddhists did. Practiced assiduously, meditation would lead to the sudden realization of the oneness of one's own mind with the totality of all things. This concept of lost mind resembles the upanishadic teaching, "thou art that," and the theory of sudden enlightenment of Dhyana Buddhism.

The Chu Hsi school was closer to the whole rationale of Confucianism, whilst the Lu School was more akin to Indian Buddhism. The Neoconfucianists of the Chu Hsi School began by examining the external world, and this determined their conception of li as heaven or nature. Because the exponents of the Lu School endeavoured to permeate Confucianism with Buddhist thought they began by looking inward upon themselves, but defined their theory of li as the mind in an attempt to modify Buddhism with Confucianist teaching. Irrespective of the validity of this distinction, there is no doubt that the Neoconfucianist doctrine of mind and the advocacy of concentration of mind were influenced by Buddhism. The controversy raging within Buddhist society concerning sudden and gradual enlightenment is reflected "in the discussions of the Neo-Confucianists, with Chu Hsi representing the gradual rational approach and Lu Hsiang-Shan the intuitive instantaneous approach."[56] Even in the motto of the Sung political reformer, Fan Chung-Yen, "to be first in worrying about the world's troubles and last in the enjoyment of its pleasures," one can detect overtones of the Bodhisattva ideal of seeking the salvation of others before passing to one's own reward as a Buddha.[57]

The most outstanding Neoconfucianist philosopher of the Ming dynasty, and a statesman of high calibre and integrity, Wang Yang-ming (or Wang Shou-Jen, 1472–1529) echoed the doctrine of Lu Hsiang-

Shan. Mind covers the whole range of existence and nothing exists independent of and apart from it. An individual may understand the fundamental principles of life and of things by understanding his own mind and by developing his own nature. Each individual has the solution of the problems of the universe within himself.

In his early days Wang Yang-ming was an ardent follower of Chu Hsi, but upon further investigation and reflection he moved to Lu Hsiang-Shan's concept of Universal Mind. In the exposition of this doctrine, Wang's writings are more comprehensive than those of Lu. Although his doctrine is hardly different in essence from that of his predecessor, he organized it more systematically and expressed it more precisely and convincingly. He was tolerant of both Buddhism and Taoism. His system was denounced by his opponents as being Buddhism in disguise and was criticized as heretical, and the Ming Emperor forbade its dissemination after the death of the philosopher. But his influence on later Chinese thought was extensive. Whilst Wang Yang-ming did not consciously attempt to reconcile Buddhist and Confucianist ideas, his stress on individual intuition, innate knowledge of the good, and the inseparability of knowledge and practice led to a "rejection of all formal and traditional standards of Confucian morality, a positive contempt for book learning as an intellectual discipline, and a conscious desire to arrive at a syncretism of Buddhism and Taoism with Confucianism."[58]

Buddhism had become such an integral part of Chinese thinking that it was impossible for the exponents of Sung Rationalism to discount it. They used Confucianist terms to interpret Buddhist concepts, or interpreted Confucianist concepts in the light of Buddhist knowledge. Without understanding the Buddhist ideas of Sung China, the Neoconfucianist system cannot be properly comprehended. Yet, several doctrines central to Buddhism, such as reincarnation and the concept of heavens and hells, have no place in Neoconfucianism. The Neoconfucianist emphasis on the problems of society is in marked contrast to the Buddhist indifference to the fate of society. Buddhist asceticism and pessimism are very different from Neoconfucianist optimism. Unlike Buddhism, Neoconfucianism neither counsels withdrawal from life nor regards it as evil.

Taoism also leaned heavily on Buddhism, and, in fact, was far more affected by Buddhist ideas. The Taoists had no notion of their system as a religion until they appropriated the idea from the Buddhists. Having done so, they decided to imitate the Buddhist example. They borrowed their views on cosmology from Buddhism, as well as their pantheon, their literature, and their doctrines: "Instead of Taoism swallowing up Buddhism, as was feared at the end of the Han Dynasty, the Taoists were themselves overwhelmed by the Buddhists."[59] Taoism borrowed the concept of heavens and hells from Indian Buddhism, and the indefinable Tao is very close to the indeterminate "thusness" of Buddhism. Taoist and Buddhist ethics teach returning good for evil, in marked contrast to the Confucianist doctrine of reciprocity. Chuang-Tzu's emphasis on self-identification with the universe as a means of entering a state of pure experience and higher happiness, having discarded intellectual knowledge, reveals Indian influence. He was presumably acquainted with Yoga techniques, and several of his passages describing a state of self-induced trance are reminiscent of dhyana.

Whatever the extent and nature of Buddhist influence on Taoism, there is no doubt that Taoism and Buddhism were commonly associated in the Chinese mind. Buddhists were often very tolerant of Taoists and sometimes even included Taoist deities in their temples. Taoism also copied Buddhism in establishing temples and an order of monks. The Taoist Trinity created by deifying Lao-tzu and associating him with Panku and Yu Huang Shangti is on the pattern of the Three Jewels of Buddhism. In an interesting work called *Mou-tzu,* after its author, Buddhism is in fart regarded as simply an older and more elaborate version of Taoism.[60]

Buddhist elements are found in Chinese festivals, local beliefs and practices. Certain features of the clan organizations, notably the idea and function of charitable estates for the benefit of the entire clan, are of Buddhist origin.[61] Buddhist symbolism is seen in the ideologies and rituals of the secret societies, which have been so important in Chinese life and history. The concept of karma is to be found in all types of Chinese literature from poetry to popular tales.

BUDDHISM ALSO MADE contributions from areas of Indian culture other than the philosophic—such as art, astronomy, mathematics, medicine, and fables. The great literary activity of the Buddhist scholars naturally had a permanent influence on Chinese literature, one of the oldest and richest in the world.[62] Whilst the antiquity of Chinese literature is apparent, its literary forms were slow in evolving. In fact, they did not begin to articulate and crystallize until after the impact of the Buddhist translations, literary themes, and techniques. There was no epic poetry or short story form until the T'ang period; no recorded dramas until the Mongol period; and no development of the novel until the Ming period.[63] In a recent study a Chinese scholar, Lai Ming, says that a significant feature in the development of Chinese literature has been "the immense influence of Buddhist literature on the development of every sphere of Chinese literature since the Eastern Chin period (317 A.D.). We cannot say that without this influence Chinese literature would have remained static and only poetry and prose been its principal literary forms, but we can safely say that it certainly would have been different from what it is today."[64]

The earliest works of Chinese literature are the Confucianist classics.[65] The ancient Chinese, such as the Ch'an masters, wrote their *Recorded Sayings* without much attention to literary organization and clarity of presentation. With the advent of the Buddhist classics, Chinese writing became more systematized, lucid, and logical. Indian *hetuvidya*, methodology, and Buddhist translations in both prose and verse led to a new era in literature.

Buddhist influence on Chinese literature, as on other aspects of cultural life, was not a deliberately initiated and directed process but a natural growth dictated by the needs of religious propaganda. The sutras were written in combined prose and rhymed verse, a literary form unknown in China at the time. It was possible to communicate the meaning, but the tonal harmony and the beauty of the verses could not be translated. The Chinese language when pronounced in the Sanskrit polyphonic manner was likely to sound hurried and abrupt, and to chant the Sanskrit verses in monophthongal Chinese prolonged the verses so much the rhymes were lost. Hence, to make the Chinese sutras pleasant to listen to, the Chinese language had to be modified to accommodate Sanskrit sounds, and greater attention paid to *fan-chieh*, the Chinese method of phonetic spelling, by joining the initial or consonant sound of a word to the end or vowel sound of another word. Consequently, in 489,

Yung Ming, Prince of Ching Ling, convened a conference of Buddhist monks at his capital to differentiate between, and define the tones of, the Chinese language for reading Buddhist sutras and for chanting the verses. Their deliberations improved and more accurately defined the sound of monophthongal Chinese, and a new theory, called the Theory of Four Tones, was established: *ping* or "soft" tone; and three "hard" tones, *shang* or acute tone, *chu* or grave tone, and *ju* or abrupt tone.

The emergence of the Theory of Four Tones led to the rise of a new prosody. Instead of using a single rhyme for a poem, poets started to write poems which changed rhymes every two, four, or eight lines and greater attention was given to the balance of tonal values: "The 'new style' poetry of the Tang Dynasty, *tse* of the Sung Dynasty and *chu* of the Yuan Dynasty, all followed basically the same theory which had grown out of the necessity to adapt the Chinese language to translating Buddhist sutras and propagating Buddhism."[66] A new form of prose, *pien-ti-wen,* also developed because of the new emphasis on tonal value. The new prose style introduced pleasing tones and flowery phrases, which, in turn, brought about a greater consciousness of the subtle distinctions between works of philosophy and history and those literature.

The introduction into China of highly imaginative literature, such as the Mahayana sutras and the Indian epics, infused into Chinese literature the quality of imagination which had been hitherto lacking. Taoist literature, such as the book *Chuang-tzu,* did perhaps show some quality of imaginative power, but on the whole Chinese literature, especially Confucianist, was narrow, formal, restricted, and unimaginative. It recorded daily routine and historical events but seldom told interesting tales. *The Biography of Emperor Mu,* which comprises the barest possible outlines of stories, can be cited as an example of Chinese writing of the pre-Buddhist period. By contrasting this work with Wu Cheng-en's *Hsi Yu Chi,* the great romantic novel written after Buddhist influence had permeated Chinese literature, the enormous contribution of Indian imaginative literature to creative writing in China is apparent.

The literary masterpiece of the Buddhist poet, Asvaghosa: *Buddha-carita-kavya,* translated into Chinese by Dharmaraksa, influenced not only Chinese Buddhism but Chinese literature as well. The long Chinese poems, *A Heroine of the Molan* and the *Peacock Flying towards the South-*

east, reflect the style of Buddhist literature. The novels and dramas of the Yuan and Ming dynasties were influenced by Buddhism either directly or indirectly. China has no epic poetry; but what is the most surprising feature of the history of Chinese literature is the conspicuous absence of fiction until almost the end of the eighth century. The Chinese sense of realism was so intense that there was hardly any mythology in ancient China, and they have produced few fairy tales of their own. Most of their finest fairy tales were originally brought to China by Indian monks in the first millennium. The Buddhists used them to make their sermons more agreeable and lucid. The tales eventually spread throughout the country, assuming a Chinese appearance conformable to their new environment. For example the stories of Chinese plays such as *A Play of Thunder-Peak, A Dream of a Butterfly,* and *A Record of Southern Trees* were of Buddhist origin.

Many ghost stories were written during the Three Kingdoms and Chin periods (220–419), a time when China was passing through a succession of wars and natural disasters, and even the ultrarealistic Chinese were receptive to some kind of emotional escape. Buddhist influence on the rise of story-telling can be seen in the collections of tales published of the period of the Northern-Southern dynasties for example, *Yuan Hun Chi* (Accounts of Avenging Spirits) by Yen Chihtui, and *Ming Hsiang Chi* (Records of Mysterious Manifestations) by Wang Yen. But the fables which became so popular in western Asia, Europe, and elsewhere did not find acceptance in China. The Chinese did not much care for animals who assumed human characteristics.

The stories found in the Buddhist sutras were changed into Chinese scenes and characters and passed off, possibly unconsciously, as Chinese stories. For example, the story, "A Scholar of Yang Hsien," included in the *Sequel to Tales of Chi-Hsieh,* is a replica of a Buddhist story found in the *Samyuktavadana Sutra,* which was rendered into Chinese in the Three Kingdoms period by Kang Seng-hui. Buddhist ideas influenced many short story writers: for example, Lee Kung-tso's *The Governor of Nan-ko* and Shen Chi-chi's *Records of a Pillow,* both of which dwell upon the transience of life and the futility of worldly possessions and fame. An outstanding example of this is the well-known Chinese novel *Hsi Yu Chi* (Records of a Trip to the West, known in its English adaptation by Arthur Waley as *Monkey*) by Wu Chengen (1505–1580), which is a modified version of an earlier story *The Story of Hsüan-tsang's Search for Buddhist Sutras,* which in its turn was based on the life of Hsüan-tsang. It has seventeen chapters in three volumes, and is the first Chinese novel to be divided into chapters, each of which has a couplet for the title. More important, however, is the fact that it was the first and remains one of the very few novels of romantic fantasy. The story has a Buddhist theme, is based on the actual journey of Hsüan-tsang, and was written by someone who, if not a Buddhist monk, was familiar with Buddhist literature. On his journey, Hsüan-tsang takes a monkey who looks like a scholar, has magical powers, writes poems, and has a striking similarity to Hanuman, the monkey god of the Indian epic *Ramayana.* This can hardly have been a coincidence. This monkey so fascinated the Chinese that this story continued to be popular throughout the Sung, Mongol, and Ming dynasties. The popular novel, *Plum of the Golden Bottle,* written in the Sung period and narrating the story of a young man learning the teachings of the Buddha, and *Feng-Shen-Chuan* (Annals of the Investiture of Deities) of the Ming period, are other examples of Buddhist influence on the Chinese novel. Still other stories are pure adaptations of Indian legends. Amongst these are *The Story of Hsiao Tung-hsien* which was based on an Indian legend mentioned by Hsüan-tsang in his *Hsi Yu Chi.*

A Chinese style of essay-writing called *san wen* or *pien wen,* consisting of short prose which combines straight narration, rhymed verses, descriptive prose, and allegories, is of Buddhist origin. To propagate their faith Buddhist monks used to explain the often obscure meaning of Buddhist sutras by telling anecdotes in order to arouse and hold the interest of the people. This method of expounding the sutras in story-telling form proved very effective and popular, and gradually gave rise to the pien wen stye of writing.[67]

Whilst there were numerous references to pien wen in standard works, literature written in this style was first discovered in 1907 amongst the manuscripts, scrolls, and drawings found by Sir Aurel Stein in the cave temples of Tun-huang. These included some forty stories. Some of these, for example, *Shuntse Chih Hsiao Pien Wen* (The Most Filial Shuntse), *Lieh Kuo Chih Pien Wen* (The Story of Lieh Kuo), *Ming Fei Pien* (or

Ming Fei), *Chiu Hu Pien Wen* (or *Chiu Hu*), have nothing to do with Buddhism in subject matter but are historical or legendary stories retold in the pien wen literary form.

Pien wen occupies an important place in the evolution of Chinese literature, because it is the forerunner of hua pen, the texts of the story-tellers of the Sung dynasty. It is through hua pen that Buddhist literature contributed most to the development of Chinese novels, for Chinese novels are a literary form evolved and adapted almost indiscriminately from hua pen.

Pien wen also indirectly influenced Chinese drama although the influence is less obvious, because not enough manuscripts have survived to allow a full examination. Since pien wen is the first known Chinese literary form to contain both prose and rhymed verse, it must have contributed to the emergence of *chu kung tiao,* an art form of the Sung and Chin dynasties. Chu kung tiao consists of sets of lyrics composed according to musical scores in various keys, linking descriptive passages and dialogues. It was from this that Northern drama or *tsa chu* evolved.

Chinese drama assimilated Indian features in three stages. First, the story, characters, and technique were all borrowed from India; later, Indian technique gave way to Chinese; and finally, the story was modified and the characters became Chinese also. There are many dimensions to Chinese drama, and it is not easy to place them accurately in history. However, the twelfth century provides the first-known record of the performance of a play, a Buddhist miracle-play called *Mu-lien Rescues his Mother* based on an episode in the Indian epic *Mahabharata.* The subject matter of the Buddhist adaptation of the story, in which Maudgalyayana (Mu-lien in Chinese) rescues his mother from hell, occurs in a Tun-huang pien wen. Significantly, the play was first performed at the Northern Sung capital by professionals before a religious festival.

Phrases and words coined by Buddhist scholars enriched the Chinese vocabulary by more than thirty-five thousand words. As the assimilation was spread over a long period of time, the Chinese accepted these words as a matter of course without even suspecting their foreign origin. Even today words of Buddhist origin are widely used in China from the folklore of peasants to the formal language of the intelligentsia. For example, *poli* for glass in the names of many precious and semi-precious stones is of

Sanskrit origin. *Cha-na,* an instant, from *kshana; t'a,* pagoda, from *stupa; mo-li,* jasmine, from *mallika*, and terms for many trees and plants are amongst the many thousands of Chinese words of Indian origin.

These words were coined principally in two ways. One method combined single Chinese words to evolve a new meaning, similar to the method followed by Sanskrit. An example of such a word is *Chin Ju. Chin* means real, *ju* means likely, and together they mean *bhutatathata,* implying the absolute, ultimate source and character of all phenomena. The word is fundamental to Mahayana Buddhism. The other method adopted a Sanskrit word with its original sound: for example *ni pan,* which is the rendering of *nirvana; cha-na* of *ksana; she-men* of *sramana.* The legacy of transliterative devices, first developed to render the untranslatable words and concepts of Indian origin, still survives in China. These devices are now used to translate Western ideas and concepts. Indian grammar also undoubtedly stimulated Chinese philological study.

Chinese script consists of numerous symbols, which in their earliest stage were chiefly pictographic and ideographic. This was awkward to work with so Buddhist scholars set out to devise an alphabetical system. The first system was called *Hsi Yu Hu Shu* (Foreign Writing of the Western Countries), or *Po La Men Shu* (Brahmanical Writing). Later, during the latter half of the T'ang dynasty, the Indian Buddhists helped Chinese scholars form a system of thirty *tzu-mu,* phonetic symbols divided on the model of Sanskrit into gutturals, glottals, linguals, dentals, and labials. Shen-kung, a Buddhist monk, is the reputed author of the system, and the dictionary, *Yu Pien* (Discrimination of Language), was one of the first extensive works in which it was used. Chinese phonetic spelling, the *fan ch'ieh* system of employing two characters to indicate the pronunciation of the third character, was no doubt, the result of Chinese knowledge of the Sanskrit alphabet. Previous to the fan ch'ieh system the Chinese had endeavoured to indicate the pronunciation of a character by the use of homonyms, but the fan ch'ieh system combines the initial sound of the first character with the final sound of the second to indicate the pronunciation.

INDIAN ART ALSO reached China, mainly through Central Asia, although some works of Buddhist art came by sea. Monks and their retinues, and traders brought Buddha statues, models of temples, and other objects of art to China. Chinese pilgrims also enthusiastically collected works of art on their travels. Fa-hsien made drawings of images whilst at Tamralipiti; Hsüan-tsang returned with several golden and sandalwood figures of the Buddha; and Hui-lun with a model of the Nalanda Mahavihara. Wang Huan-ts'e, who went to India several times, collected many drawings of Buddhist images, including a copy of the Buddha image at Bodhgaya; this was deposited at the Imperial palace and served as a model of the image in Ko-ngai-see temple. The most famous icon of East Asian Buddhism known as the "Udayana" image was reported to have been brought by the first Indian missionaries in 67, although there are various legends associated with this image and many scholars believe it was brought by Kumarajiva. However, this influx of Indian art was incidental and intermittent, and was destined to be absorbed by Chinese art, which had a strong tradition of its own. This combination resulted in a Buddhist art of exceptional beauty.

There were three main centres of Buddhist art in China–Tun-huang, Yun-kang in the north of Shansi, and Lung-men near Loyang. Tun-huang is located on the northwestern frontier of China near an oasis known as Yumen or the Jade Gate, where the northern and southern routes from Central Asia converged. For travellers to China it marked the last stage of an arduous journey, and it became a thriving centre for Buddhist activities. During the fourth century, Tun-huang provided refuge to numerous monks escaping from the upheavals prevalent in the rest of northern China. These monks contributed to Tun-huang's importance as a centre of Buddhist learning. For accommodation they dug cave monasteries in the hillsides. The earliest dated cave temple was built by a monk, Lo-tsun, in 366, although Tun-huang had been a flourishing colony of monks long before this date. In the most famous of these caves there is a wall painting which was executed in 344. Several monks, such as Dharmaraksa, had travelled from there to China. The site is called Ch'ien-fo-tung, "Caves of the Thousand Buddhas," because there were supposedly more than a thousand caves in 698. So far, about five hundred caves have been discovered. These caves were painted throughout with murals, and were frequently furnished with numerous Buddha statues and sculptured scenes from the Jatakas.

The murals have been well preserved in the dry climate. Besides wall paintings and paintings on silk and paper, a large number of ancient manuscripts and art relics remained hidden in perfectly good condition in a walled-up rock temple library for about nine hundred years. Many of the scrolls and drawings belong to the T'ang period, and many of the manuscripts are in Sanskrit. These paintings are an invaluable record of the history of Chinese art, not only because they cover a period of a thousand years to the end of the thirteenth century, but also because only a few other T'ang paintings have survived. Whilst the numerous cave sanctuaries of Central Asia have preserved an incalculably rich art treasure, the implications and interpretations of which embrace most of the known ancient world, the history of Chinese art would have remained far more obscure without the yield of Tun-huang.

Tun-huang art mainly follows Chinese and the Serindian (Central Asian Indian) traditions. There is some evidence of Turkish and Iranian influences in the later paintings. The grottos were begun in the Northern and Western Wei periods, but their art attained its peak form later. Mural painting in cave temples, or in sanctuaries dug in cliff walls is most likely due to Indian influence, although tombs have painted walls at least as far back as the Han dynasty. These cave paintings portray the entire system of Indian mudras (expressive gestures of the hand) and motifs of Indo-Buddhist Art: for example the Bodhi tree, the nimbus, and the *yaksas* guarding the temple. Later on, as might be expected, Chinese traditions became increasingly predominant, and the Tun-huang paintings represent an increasing synthesis of Indian and Chinese ideas. On some silk paintings are found pictures of Vaisravana, the *lokapala* or guardian king of the North in Indian mythology, featured as a formidable T'ang warrior with dazzling armour and adornments in golds, reds, blues, and greens. He is supposed to be the protector of the Buddha, of his sanctuary, and of his doctrine. The Tun-huang banners exhibit Buddhist doctrines in the process of evolution. The cult of Maitreya is depicted alongside the heavens of Avalokitesvara, the Buddhist Providence. They also show the transformation of the Indian Avalokitesvara into the Chinese Kuan-yin, the Goddess of Mercy. Thus, Tun-huang is "not only the junction where one passes from the art of the Tarim Basin, still permeated with Indian influence, to a purely Chinese art; it also remains a unique testimony, after the conquest of China by Buddhism, to the counter-annexation of Buddhism by China."[66]

In China proper the earliest traceable influence of Indian art is found in the Yun-kang caves. So far, twenty-eight major caves, revealing art of different periods, have been discovered. These caves were constructed from about 453 onwards to commemorate the reversal of the policy of Buddhist persecution initiated in 446 by the Toba Wei Emperor, T'ai Wu. The work continued throughout the Wei period and for several centuries thereafter. The leading role in the resumption of work on these caves in 453 was played by the Buddhist monk, Tan Yao, who came from Central Asia, and whose doctrine was based on the *Lotus of the True Law* and on the teachings of the Indian arhat Vimalakirti. Later, the Wei Emperor, Wen-hsien himself directed the work on the caves at Yun-kang between 460 and 465, including the enormous Buddha seated in Indian fashion in cave Number 20.

The conversion of the Toba Wei rulers to Buddhism had an enormous influence on the development of Chinese art. The Wei sculpture includes some of the finest religious art of all time. Similar to the way Romanesque and Gothic artists adapted the traditions of Graeco-Roman plastic art to purely spiritual ends, the sculptors of the Wei period drew upon the Gandhara technique of drapery and the Apollo-like features of its statues to more effectively express the pure spirituality of Buddhism.[69] However, in recent years the art of Yun-kang has come to be regarded as somewhat of an improvement on Gandhara art in purity of line and elegance.

Although colossal images of the Buddha, like those at Bamiyan in Afghanistan, and smaller statues in cliff niches of the Buddha and the Bodhisattvas were predominant, some caves (Nos. 7, 8, and 10) also contain many images of Hindu deities, such as Siva on Nandi and Vishnu on Garuda. Two Japanese scholars, Mizuno and Nagahira, in their fifteen-volume work on the art of these caves, find not so much of the mature Gupta style, as seen in the seated Sarnath image, as of the Mathura style of the earlier Gupta period. If these images had come from India and were considered holy, as is suggested by Omura who, in his *History of Chinese Sculpture,* drew upon Chinese literary references, it would significantly underline the depth of Chinese acceptance of Indian thought.

The art in the caves at Lung-men is a continuation of that at Yun-kang, and carries mysticism and stylization even further. In 494 the Wei kings moved their capital from Peng-Cheng to Loyang, which led to the construction of Buddhist rock shrines near the new capital in 508. Beginning in the reign of Emperor Hsuan-wu, the chiselling of the caves continued through the rest of the dynasty. Emperors, officials, monks, and laymen cooperated in cutting the hard rocks and filling niches with images of the Buddha. The number of Buddha statues according to one count, totals 142,289.

The most important of the Lung-men caves are the Ku-yang-tung and Pin-yang-tung. The Buddha and Maitreya were the chief deities portrayed in the Ku-yang-tung. The Pin-yang-tung cave was patronized by the ruling house and is the more imposing. Here, figures of the emperors and empresses can be seen paying their respects to the Buddha. The sculpture in the Pin-yang-tung is based on two widely known Jatakas, the *Sudassanajataka* and *Mahasattvajataka.*

The sculptures produced during the Pei-Ch'i period (550–577) are of considerable importance. Carved in white sandstone in the caves on the cliffs of T'ieh-lung-shan, they bear marks of Gupta art, as do the limestone sculptures of Hsiang-tang-shan on the border of Hopei and Honan, which were still being produced during the T'ang period. In the cave temples of T'ieh-lung-shan, statues of Bodhisattvas have been discovered, which are apparently contemporary with the T'ang dynasty, and which are direct imitations of Indian Gupta art. They have a softness of modelling, a rounded charm, and a blending of forms which are strikingly un-Chinese but do represent the Indian sense of beauty with its inherent tropical sensuousness.[70] Oswald Siren has pointed out that certain Buddha figures at T'ieh-lung-shan were obviously inspired by models from Mathura and Sarnath. One of the Bodhisattvas seated on a lotus is cast in a graceful and recognizably Indian posture and costume. Other Bodhisattvas, for example in cave Number 17, are seated in *lalitasana,* a posture which brings out the beauty and suppleness of the body, with the upper part of the body bare except for a necklace and a thin scarf; these appear to have been directly inspired by Indian examples. Considering how foreign the nude is to Chinese art, it is interesting that Indian aesthetics for a brief period wholly reshaped

Chinese taste.[71] In the cave temples of Hsiang-tang-shan the influences of the Gupta style are also seen in the representation of jewellery, lotus leaves and vine stems, and in the rounded style and graded modelling of the seated Buddhas.

From the T'ang period onwards Indian art was increasingly absorbed by Chinese art traditions. Indeed, the faces of all the Buddhist deities became Chinese in appearance. In the Tun-huang caves, one can see how the distinct Indian figures of the Wei period went through physiognomical changes to become Chinese by the Sung period.

The oldest Chinese aesthetic traditions go back to the fourth or fifth century when Buddhism was in ascendancy, and they are strongly reminiscent of the Indian principles of aesthetics. The six principles of painting of Sie-Ho (479–501) are parallel to *shadanga,* the six principles of painting described in ancient Indian literature—*rupa, pramana, bhava, lavanya, sadrsya,* and *varnikabhanga.*[72]

Ku Kai-Chih, one of the earliest and most famous Chinese masters, employed Buddhist themes in the fourth century. By the time of the T'ang period Indian influence appears to have found a dominant place in Chinese painting. For example, the T'ang ideal of feminine beauty—a more pointed face and rounded figure (compared to the slender elegance of previous periods), with hair collected around and above the head and an air of cheerful health—was the result of this influence. The most splendid paintings of the T'ang period were of Buddhist inspiration, such as those by Wei-Chih I-Seng, Yen Li-pen, and Wu Tao-tzu.

A remarkable school of painting directly connected with Indian thought, although not with an Indian artistic tradition, was inspired by Dhyana Buddhism. This school gained popularity during the twelfth and thirteenth centuries and had a closer approach to nature than other schools. Landscape painting had become an independent art during the T'ang period, but the landscape works of the Sung artists inspired by Ch'an Buddhism are the best. Before this, the most famous landscape painter was Li Lung-mien (*ca.* 1040–1106) who relied upon Buddhist themes for his works. A romantic attraction for nature became the dominant inspiration of the landscape painter, and was strengthened by Ch'an Buddhism with its reliance on intuition and contempt for appearances. The elements of nature were transformed into abstract ideas. The Sung painter saw the mountains as if floating in the distance, having no real existence. Ma Yuan's (1190–1224) picture of a solitary fisherman, lost in the middle of a lake in the winter with no bank visible, is a most poignant painting. Another outstanding artist of this school was Liang Kai, whose masterpiece is a picture of the Buddha, leaning on his stick near a stream in a strange landscape of steep mountains. The greatest of them all was Muchi, who worked in a Ch'an monastery near Hangchow, but whose work is now mainly preserved in Japan. His painting, "The Ch'an Master in Meditation," in which a serpent is curled around an ascetic or a holy man who is completely unconcerned, is a familiar scene in Indian art, but in China it is particularly characteristic of the Ch'an School.

Ch'an influence is similarly seen in the painting of flowers. The Ch'an artist saw in flowers a reflection of the Buddha essence and he sought to capture its spiritual significance by identifying himself with the object through intense mental concentration. Favourite themes were plum blossoms, vines, orchids, and narcissi—messengers of spring. A vast literature has grown up around these motifs. Another favourite theme was the bamboo, which, by its uprightness and the inner emptiness of its hollow stem, symbolized the Buddhist ideal. Hence, to paint bamboo with devotion was an ascetic exercise leading to a state of spirituality.

By the thirteenth century Indian influence in painting waned, although images of the Buddha continued to be made in the traditional manner. With the decline of Buddhism in China, Buddhist art also declined.

In architecture, India's contribution is not as notable as it is in painting or sculpture, although some influence can be seen in the temples. The pagoda type of temple is of Indian origin, but it appears that the traditional Indian style of stupa did not catch on in China. The architecture of all Chinese temples, Buddhist, Taoist, or Confucianist, is much the same. Even the mosques are, in general, identical with the temples, except that they use extracts from the Quran as exterior decorations. It is the interior decoration that distinguishes one from the other. There is virtually no difference in the architectural design of temples and palaces. Certain official rules prescribing the dimensions of all Chinese habitations were taken from the architectural texts of India.[73]

Chinese musical theory is based on the foundation tone, the pitch of a man's voice when he speaks without passion, *huang-chung*, which was conceived as an abstract eternal principle; it was the basis of the Chinese system of measures, of the calendar and of their astronomical calculations, and a definite pitch in music. Everything, a ruling dynasty, political order, or music, must have the correct pitch. From the foundation tone, other higher notes were derived, and a five note scale was developed in which the vibration frequencies were on the powers of numerals 2 and 3; 3 being regarded as the number of heaven and 2 that of the earth, the sounds in the ratio 3: 2 expressed the harmony of heaven and earth. Ancient classical music was almost exclusively confined to temple worship, religious rites, and court ceremonies. There was no well-organized class of professional music teachers, no accomplished amateur musicians practicing music purely for aesthetic satisfaction, and ballads and folk-singing were not very common. The Chinese did not regard music as an art to be cultivated outside temples and theatres. Buddhist monks who reached China brought the practice of chanting sacred texts during religious rites. Hence, Indian melody was introduced into Chinese music which had hitherto been rather static and restrained.[74]

Dancing and singing no doubt originated in ancient times but a combination of the two does not seem to have existed in China before the period of the Wei and Chin dynasties. The earliest known opera, *Po-tow* (The Wedge), is reported to have been introduced from India. By the end of the period of the Northern and Southern dynasties, several musical instruments had been introduced into China through Central Asia. Many foreign instruments also came during the T'ang period, and the stringed instrument *ya-cheng*, played by rubbing the strings with a slip of bamboo, came through Tibet. The Chinese *hu-ch'in*, a foreign importation, is exactly like the two-stringed sitara of India. A popular stringed musical instrument of the time, the *K'ung-hou* came from India during the Han period. The Chinese guitar, called the *p'i p'a*, which was another popular instrument during the Han and T'ang dynasties, possibly came from India.

Indian music was at one time so popular in China that Emperor Kao-tsu (581-595) tried unsuccessfully to proscribe it by an Imperial decree. His successor Yang-ti was also very fond of Indian music. In Chinese annals, references are found to visiting Indian musicians, who reached China from India, Kucha, Kashgar, Bokhara, and Cambodia. Even Needham, the well-known advocate of Chinese cultural and scientific priority, admits "Indian music came through Kucha to China just before the Sui period and had a great vogue there in the hands of exponents such as Ts'ao Miao-ta of Brahminical origin."[75]

By the end of the sixth century Indian music had been given state recognition. During the T'ang period, Indian music was quite popular, especially the famous Rainbow Garment Dance melody. There were Indian, Central Asian, and Southeast Asian orchestras, and each year the Emperor invited musical parties from abroad to the T'ang court. A contemporary Chinese poet, Po Chu-yi, wrote a poem in praise of Indian music. "It is little wonder," an official publication of the Chinese Repubhc says, "that when a Chinese audience today hears Indian music they feel that while possessing a piquant Indian flavour it has a remarkable affinity with Chinese music."[76] However, Chinese music has always retained its own character and values.

One reason for the early success of Buddhism was the Chinese fascination for Buddhist science and knowledge of elixirs and practices that were thought to promote longevity or produce levitation. However, the history of the migration of Buddhism to China has not yet been seriously examined with a view to tracing the exchange of scientific ideas; the study of the history of Indian science itself has hardly begun. Broadly speaking there are two reasons for this: the interest in Buddhist religion and philosophy, which constitute the more fascinating and spectacular side of the story, has been, understandably, too concentrated to allow specific investigation of secondary concepts relating to science; and, second, such a study would require exceptional scholarship, including competence in several languages, such as Chinese, Sanskrit, Pali, Persian, plus a keen sense and understanding of history and philosophy, and a thorough knowledge of science. Joseph Needham, in his multi-volume history of Chinese science, alludes to Indian ideas, but only very briefly and he has used a limited range of sources. He prefers to rely on Chinese materials and some well-known but hopelessly out-of-date Indian commentaries, such as V. A. Smith for Indian history and G. R. Kaye for Indian mathematics. Perhaps the limitations of an arbitrary selection of Indian references, more than his generous disposition towards China and his reliance on Chinese sources which were disinclined to admit to any substantial "barbarian" influence on Chinese achievement, have tilted his scientific objectivity towards China.[77]

A major Buddhist influence on Chinese science was in scientific thought itself. Buddhist concepts, such as the infinity of space and time, and the plurality of worlds and of time-cycles or kalpas (*chieh*), had a stimulating effect on Chinese inquiry, broadening the Chinese outlook and better equipping it to investigate scientific problems. For example, the Indian doctrine of *pralayas*, or recurrent world catastrophes in which sea and land were turned upside down before another world was recreated to go through the four cycles—differentiation (*ch'eng*), stagnation (*chu*), destruction (*huai*), and emptiness (*kung*)—which was later adopted by Neoconfucianists, was responsible for the Chinese recognition of the true nature of fossils long before they were understood in Europe. Again, the Indian doctrine of karma (*tso-yeh*), or metempsychosis, influenced Chinese scientific thought on the process of biological change involving both phylogeny and ontogeny. Buddhist iconography contained a biological element. Buddhism also introduced a highly developed theory of logic, both formal and dialectical, and of epistemology.

Tantric Buddhism, which reached China in the eighth century or before, and in which the worship of personal gods was mixed with strong magical elements, may have contributed to the scientific development in the sense that it asserted the validity of the principle that magic and science were originally united in a single undifferentiated complex of manual operations.[78] The greatest Chinese astronomer and mathematician of his time, I-hsing (682–727), was a Tantric Buddhist monk.

Whilst the work of Indian mathematicians was carried westward by the Arabs and transmitted to Europe, it was taken eastward by Indian Buddhist monks and professional mathematicians. There is some evidence that works on Indian astronomy were in circulation in China well before the T'ang period. In the annals of the Sui dynasty, numerous Chinese translations of Indian mathematical and astronomical works are mentioned, such as *Po-lo-men Suan fa* (The Hindu Arithmetical Rules) and *Po-lo-men Suan King*. These works have vanished, and it is impossible to assess the degree of their influence on Chinese sciences. However, there is definite evidence of Indian influence on Chinese astronomy and calendar studies during the T'ang dynasty. During this period, Indian astronomers were working at the Imperial Bureau of Astronomy which was charged with preparing accurate calendars. Yang Ching-fang, a pupil of Amoghavajra (*Pu-k'ung*), wrote in 764 that those who wished to know the positions of the five planets and predict what Hsiu (heavenly mansion) a planet would be traversing, should adopt Indian calendrical methods. Five years earlier, Amoghavajra had translated an Indian astrological work, the *Hsiu Vao Ching* (Hsiu and Planet Sutra), into Chinese.

At the time there were three astronomical schools at Chang-an: Gautama (Chhuthan), Kasyapa (Chiayeh), and Kumara (Chumolo). In 684 one of the members of the Gautama school, Lo, presented a calendar, *Kuang-tse-li,* which had been in use for three years, to the Empress Wu. Later, in 718, another member of the school, Hsi-ta (Siddhartha), presented to the Emperor a calendar, *Chiu-che-li,* which was almost a direct translation of an Indian calendar, *Navagraha Siddhanta* of Varahamihira, and which is still preserved in the T'ang period collection. It was in use for four years. In 729 Siddhartha compiled a treatise based on this calendar which is the greatest known collection of ancient Chinese astronomical writings. This was the first time that a zero symbol appeared in a Chinese text, but, even more important, this work also contained a table of sines, which were typically Indian. I-hsing (682–727) was associated with the Kumara school and was much influenced by Indian astronomy. In 720 he was employed by the Emperor to revise the calendar. Whilst I-hsing's works on mathematics have been lost and the exact nature of his work is not known, Indian influence can be seen in the nine planets he introduced into his calendar, *Ta-yen-li.* The nine planets included the sun, moon, five known planets, and two new planets, *Rahu* and *Ketu,* by which the Indian astronomers represented the ascending and descending nodes of the moon. I-hsing organized an astronomical expedition to the southern seas to chart stars that could not be seen in China, and he also conducted a valuable project for measuring latitudes. He made measurements in ecliptic co-ordinates, constructed armillary spheres with ecliptically mounted sighting-tubes, and invented the first escapement for a mechanical clock.[79]

Evidence of Indian influence on Chinese medicine is even more definite. A number of Indian medical treatises are found in Chinese Buddhist collections: for example, the *Ravanakumaratantra* and *Kasyapasamhita.* From its very inception, Buddhism stressed the importance of health and the prevention and cure of mental and physical ailments. Indeed, the Buddha is credited with some miracle cures, and he described his teaching as a therapy for the ills of the world. The main emphasis of Buddhism has always been on the relief of pain and suffering. An important Bodhisattva in the pantheon was Bhaishajyaguru, the master of medicine. There were always many Buddhist monks noted for their medical skills. Indian medical texts were widely known in Central Asia, where parts of the original texts on *Ayur Veda* have been found as well as numerous translations.

A basic doctrine of Indian Ayurvedic medicine is that of the tridhatus (tridoshas), or organic functions and disturbance. The elementary substances of the universe also make up the human body, and the proper equilibrium of these elements ensures good health. Malady or disease occurs when this equilibrium is disturbed, and the function of medicine is to restore the right balance. The Chinese adopted this theory, as is seen in the writings of one of the leading T'ang physicians, Sun Ssumiao, who, despite his adherence to Taoism, was nicknamed the "new Vimalakirti" because of his interest in Buddhist medicine. In his *Ch'ien Chin Yao fang* (Book of Prescriptions Worth a Thousand Gold Pieces), he explicitly subscribed to the Indian theory, and strongly recommended the study of Buddhist medical literature to those who aspired to become great physicians. His advice on medical ethics, requiring practitioners to subdue desire and ambition, to develop love and compassion and to treat all, rich and poor, Chinese or barbarians, intelligent or stupid, with affectionate care and strict impartiality, is Buddhist inspired. In contrast, the famous monk of the period, I-tsing, although he was a Buddhist and respected Indian physicians, regarded the Chinese art of healing as unsurpassed.

The T'ang emperors patronized Indian *thaumaturges* (Tantric Yogis) who were believed to possess secret methods of rejuvenation. Wang Hsüan-chao, who returned to India after the death of Harsha, had been charged by the Chinese Emperor in 664 to bring back Indian medicines and physicians. Wang Hsüan-chao succeeded in finding a physician, presumably So-po-mei or Lu-chiai-to, and he may have persuaded other physicians to go to China, although there is no evidence for it. Nor is there any evidence of Chinese physicians ever visiting India; although the possibility cannot be ruled out.

Considering that Indian medicine, especially operative surgery, was highly developed for the time, and that the Chinese genius for practical knowledge somehow did not work in medicine, it is not surprising that the Chinese, like the Arabs, were captivated by Indian medical skills and drugs.[80] In fact, until recently Chinese medicine had progressed very little.[81] Whilst the Chinese used dry cupping and massage effectively, they did not practice venesection but substituted acupuncture, which was introduced into China, as it was into Europe, from Egypt. Castration was performed by Chinese methods but other surgical techniques, such as laparotomy, trepanation, and removal of cataracts, as well as inoculation for smallpox, were influenced by Indian practices.[82]

THE FAMOUS SHAO-LIN style of boxing is also attributed to Indian influence. Bodhidharma, who believed in a sound mind in a sound body, taught the monks in the Shao-lin temple this style of boxing for self-defence and for rejuvenating the body after exacting meditation and mental concentration.

During the first millennium, Indian racing games reached China. The well-known expert on the history of Chinese games, Karl Himly, on the authority of a passage from the *Hun Tsun Su*, a work of the Sung period (960–1279), suggests that the Chinese game *t'shu-p'u* was invented in western India and spread to China in the time of the Wei dynasty (220–265). T'shu-p'u is, in fact, the Chinese adaptation of the Indian *chatus-pada* (modern *chaupur)*. Chess was introduced from India *ca.* 700 through the ancient trade route from Kashmir. The oldest and best of the native Chinese games, *wei-ch'i*, did not appear until 1000.[83] Cubical dice (*ch'u-p'i* or *yu-p'i*), although found in ancient Egypt as well as in India, are generally believed to have reached China from India, possibly quite early. Arthur Waley is of the opinion that the prominence of the number six in the *Book of Changes* was derived from the six sides of cubical dice.[84]

DURING THIS PERIOD of Sino-Indian contact, one would expect to find some Chinese influence on India, but there is little evidence of such influence. Since the overwhelming majority of the scholars and monks who travelled between the two countries were Indians going to China, China quite naturally assimilated more Indian culture than vice-versa. Most of the Indian monks who went to China settled there permanently, and consequently, India did not have the opportunity of exposure to the knowledge these monks had acquired in China. The Indian monks felt their primary loyalty to Buddhism and went where they thought they were most needed. Historical accounts tell us that these monks lived and worked until their death in the temple cells of China, on a simple vegetarian diet, carefully translating and interpreting Buddhist texts. They were above worldly temptation, and the very nature of their faith precluded attachment to either nation or family.

By contrast, the Chinese monks and pilgrims who came to India returned home, thus disseminating Indian ideas in their country. They returned, not necessarily because of nationalism, but because of their sense of duty to transmit their newly gained knowledge to those people in China who were not able to undertake similar journeys. Moreover, many of the Chinese travellers to India were simply pilgrims, who could not be expected to have fully subordinated national attachments to their faith.

Furthermore, whilst Chinese monks came to acquire knowledge and take it back, the Indian monks went to China on specific religious missions to impart knowledge. There is hardly any evidence that the Chinese monks brought with them any work which was translated into an Indian language. It seems that during this period of Sino-Indian contact, the psychological atmosphere was one in which India was naturally accepted as the giver and China as the taker. Whilst the best in Indian thought was carefully studied and carried back to China, Chinese ideas filtered through to India whether they represented the best of their culture or not. This mixed quality of assorted ideas operating in a limited area could not approach the impact of the best of a vital culture working in a much larger area.

Yet Chinese culture had some influence on India. The gabled roofs of houses on the western coast of India show a Chinese influence, as do the temples and houses in the Himalayan regions. Some Chinese influence is noted on Gupta coins, and the story framework of Kalidasa's *Meghaduta* suggests Chinese inspiration.[85] Chinese influence can also be seen in Mughal miniature paintings, but this influence reached India indirectly through Iran. The use of a certain kind of silk (china-msuka) in India, different kinds of fruits including pears (cinaraja-putra), peaches (cinani), and lichis, vermilion (sindura), the technique of fishing in the backwaters, and the porcelain industry all owe something to Chinese influence. Indians also learned the art of papermaking from China.[86]

The Kamakhya cult in Assam, the Chinachara, a recognized form of Tantrism in which the sage Vasistha was made to travel to China to be initiated into this cult, is reputed to have been influenced by Taoist mystic discipline. Although early visitors from India to China were struck by the similarities between Indian and Taoist philosophies, it was not until much later in the seventh century that India took a noticeable interest in Taoism. By that time, however, Taoism had interacted with Indian thought in China for more than six centuries and had acquired certain Buddhist features. The main evidence for this Indian interest in Taoism is the request of a king of Kamarupa, Kumara Bhaskara Varman (seventh century), to the Chinese envoys, Li Yi-piao and Wang Hsüan-ts'e to send him a portrait of Lao-tzu and a Sanskrit translation of *Tao Te Ching*, the book of the Taoist philosophy. Whether this text was ever sent is unknown; certainly the Chinese text had been rendered into Sanskrit by 647.[87] Bagchi is of the opinion that the translation reached India and was known in Buddhist mystic circles where it influenced the Buddhist School known as *Sahajayana*, which later influenced a Vaisnavite sect of eastern India, called *Sahajiya*.

After the decline of Buddhism in China and India, contact between these two countries ceased. Except for occasional sparks of brilliance, both India and China allowed their best accomplishments to stagnate, deteriorate and even be forgotten. In China, technology, and in India, philosophy, ceased to progress; both neglected to adapt their traditions to contemporary situations. Politically, however, China continued to be unified and more or less stable. Only since the end of Western domination have these two countries established direct contact and resumed the process of cultural intercourse.

During the period of Western domination of Asia, when Mahatma Gandhi was engaged in his unique fight against oppression of all kinds through love and non-violence, multitudes of peoples both in India and abroad heard in his voice an echo of the Buddha and the Christ. Gandhi's emphasis on non-violence and abstinence was well appreciated by Chinese Buddhists who had known these concepts for centuries, and also by Confucianists, because similar standards of moral values and the same appreciation of human character prevailed in both China and India. Certain social values were also common to both countries, and the most important of these was the solidarity of the family.

India, on her part, despite certain fundamental differences of approach and values, found much to admire in the Chinese revolution and in China's practical techniques of national reconstruction. The patriotic fervour and single-minded devotion of the Chinese people, their intense self-discipline, industry, and sense of national unity, their self-sacrificing spirit to work in increased austerity to build future prosperity and their almost contemptuous disregard of uninvited Western criticism have made a deep impression on many Indian visitors to China. It appeared in the 1950's that an era of unparalleled cultural collaboration between these two civilizations might be opened up, but the divergence of political ideologies and systems, accentuated by border disputes, diplomatic tension, national vanity, and armed conflicts, have rudely interrupted this interaction. Despite all this, a mutual respect for and the desire to learn from each other's culture seems to have survived.

India and World Civilization

Part II

Chapter I

THE EASTERN HORIZON OF BUDDHISM

ONCE BUDDHISM HAD a firm foothold in Central Asia and China, it was inevitable that it should spread into neighbouring areas, such as Korea, Japan, and Mongolia. These countries had some direct contact with India, although part of the Buddhist influence in Mongolia was the result of contacts with Tibet. Whilst the exact origins of Buddhist penetration into Korea are obscure, there is no doubt that Korea, like China, felt the effect of two great waves of influence: one from the north, originating in Central Asia and travelling to Korea and Japan by way of the Wei Empire; and the other from the south, originating in India and Southeast Asia and travelling through southern China, towards northern China, Korea, and possibly also to Japan.

It was in the latter half of the fourth century that Buddhism reached Korea. At the time Korea was divided into three kingdoms—Koguryu in the north, Pekche in the southwest, and Silla in the south-east. These states were continually engaged in warfare, and their boundaries fluctuated. Although all of these states welcomed Buddhism and the fortunes of Korean Buddhism, like Korean politics, were linked with developments in China, the history of Buddhism in these three regions is not identical.

Buddhism was brought to Koguryu in 372, reputedly by royal invitation, by a Chinese monk, Shun Tao (or Sundo), who came from a small kingdom—China at the time was divided into sixteen states—on the upper borders of Korea. He was followed by another Chinese monk, A Tao, and in 375 the King built two temples, one for each monk. Buddhism came to Pekche in 384 from the south through an Indian or Tibetan monk named Marananda. It is said that the Pekche King came to the outskirts of the capital to receive him. Marananda was soon followed by other monks from China. Temples began to appear and Buddhism became the state religion. Because of its isolated position, Silla was the last kingdom to receive Buddhism, more than thirty years after it had been introduced into Koguryu. According to tradition, a Buddhist priest, Mukocha, having cured the King's daughter of illness by offering prayers to the Buddha, persuaded the King of Silla to send for monks from China.

It is quite possible that Buddhism reached Pekche by sea even before it was introduced into Koguryu, because Pekche had maritime links with South China. Establishing this fact is difficult for very few Buddhist works of art from this period have survived in Pekche as is also the case in Koguryu. In both kingdoms, art works were destroyed during their dynastic wars with Silla. The absence of definite information is particularly regrettable, since it was Pekche which established contact with Japan and, in the middle of the sixth century, acted as a launching pad for Buddhist doctrine and art into Japan.

In 668 Korea was united under the Silla dynasty which ruled until 935. Many Korean monks went to China to study Buddhist doctrines and some even went to India. According to I-tsing, five Korean monks visited India during the seventh century. Prajnavarman, a Korean monk, travelled by sea to Fukien in China and then, after learning Sanskrit and studying Buddhism for ten years at the Monastery of Great Faith, proceeded to India in company with a Chinese monk. Of those who went to China to study, Yuan-tso (613–683) of the Fa Sian sect and Yuan-hiao (617–670) and Yi-siang (625–702) of the Huayen sect are best known. An outstanding monk of the period was Wonhyo, who laid the firm foundations of Korean Buddhism, and whose works are highly esteemed, even in China and Japan. However, he did not go to China, which was under the Tang dynasty at the time, although it was the fashion for scholars to do so. The Huayen doctrine, proclaiming the Buddha-nature of all beings without distinction, was first introduced into Korea in the latter part of the seventh century. As a result of the work of Yui-shih, a Korean monk who had been actively associated with the learned circles of Tang China, the "consciousness-only" doctrines of Yogacara Buddhism spread in Korea. Korea borrowed profusely from the Chinese civilization, and this tendency helped the development of Buddhism at the time even though Confucianism, its formidable rival, was also introduced in the early eighth century. '

Kyongu, the capital of Silla, was a flourishing centre of Buddhist culture and trade, attracting merchants from India, Tibet, and Iran. With the expansion of Buddhism, monasteries, temples, and stupas appeared. Today a number of ruins survive in the vicinity of Kyongu, and some of the early Sillan art is distinctly Indian in style.

The next dynasty, the Koryo which replaced the Sillas in 935, was devoted to Buddhism.[1] Consequently, Buddhist art and learning were extensively practiced, and the eleventh century became the period of greatest prosperity for Buddhism in Korea. It was, however, a time of recurrent pressures and invasions from people beyond the borders. Despite success against these intruders, a feeling of insecurity remained in Korea which may have increased the need to seek solace in religious escape and consolation. At the end of the century, the crown prince became a monk, went to China to study, and upon his return propagated the teaching of T'ien-t'ai Buddhism. On his initiative, numerous Buddhist texts were imported from neighbouring areas and published in Korea. During the Koryo period, Buddhism became the entire basis of Korea's religious life, affecting the ideology, customs, and morals of the people as well as the political and economic life of the state. Festivals were celebrated by the Court with great splendour, and magnificent monasteries were founded. Many Buddhist monks even occupied high positions in the administration. Buddhist participation in politics, however, caused increased opposition which had begun to emerge during the latter part of the Koryo ascendancy.

Buddhism, hitherto the religion of the Korean aristocracy related to the Silla dynasty, became the faith of the common people through the efforts of such eminent monks as Pu-chao, who introduced Korea to Son (Dhyana or Ch'an) Buddhism, and who is famous for his editing of the catalogue of the Chinese Tripitaka, known in Korean as the *Taejang*, published in 1010. Son Buddhism spread widely in Korea and during the twelfth century it became extremely popular as taught by Chinsul. Son Buddhism eventually assumed predominance in Korea, although during the period of Mongol ascendancy in China, Lamaism was introduced into Korea.

After the decline of the Koryo dynasty in 1392, Buddhism was generally suppressed by the state with only occasional periods of respite. Reflecting Chinese Neoconfucianism, the Korean rulers of the Yi Chosun dynasty (1392–1910) encouraged the revival of Confucianist teachings. Confucianism was accorded such enthusiastic royal patronage that the Confucianists became extremely intolerant of other faiths. The feudal lords who had suffered loss of power and prestige because of the Buddhist emphasis on the equality of man, sided with Confucianism. Despite the state policy of suppression, which became severe under King Taijong (1401–1418), Buddhism continued to flourish as the religion of the masses. A monk, Hanho, published a famous book denouncing the severe persecution. The next king, Sejong, who in fact styled himself as the Buddha's protector, managed to end the persecution. A wise and perceptive ruler, he realized the great literary value of the Buddhist scriptures, which he helped translate. He is also regarded as the inventor of the Korean alphabet, the *Hangul.*

In the fifteenth century, when Korea fell under Chinese domination, the fate of Buddhism in Korea became all the more contingent upon the fluctuations of its counterpart in China. However, with the rise of Japan as a major power, Korea came increasingly under Japanese domination, and in 1910 was annexed by Japan. Taking advantage of the changed political situation, Japanese Buddhists intensified their activities to encourage Buddhism in Korea and recast it on the model of their own. Whilst Korean Buddhism retained its own distinctive personality, it certainly benefited by the efforts of Japanese monks. According to the figures compiled in 1926, Korea had 1,363 temples and 7,188 Buddhist clerics.

Buddhism in Korea is still held in high esteem, and, despite the influence of Confucianist ethics on Korean thought and life, Korea is one of the countries where Buddhists are still actively engaged in public welfare activities, especially education. Modern Korean Buddhism is Zen tinged with a belief in Amitabha Buddha and Maitreya Bodhisattva.

Although Korea did not contribute a school of her own to Buddhism, and made no notable developments in its doctrine, she acted as a cultural intermediary between China and Japan, and thus transmitted Buddhism to Japan.

Before the arrival of Buddhism in Korea, the existing local belief was rooted in a form of Shamanism, a combination of cults of the sun, earth, and natural forces, in addition to ancestor worship. In the days of the Three Kingdoms, Koreans believed that the ultimate objective of man was to understand, obey, and worship a heavenly emperor, who was the judge of all human affairs. To this society, Confucianism introduced its ethic and Buddhism its divinities. Buddhism came not only as a well-developed philosophy but also as a mature religion. Soon it permeated all segments of society and began to influence and enrich Korean culture, arts, music, and all branches of scientific learning. It gave Koreans what they lacked most: a sense of security and hope. When Buddhism first entered the peninsula, it absorbed the local deities into the Buddhist pantheon in the same manner as it had in China and Japan, hailed them as previous incarnations of the Buddha and gave them new names. For instance, the spirit of the Ever-White Mountains, the Virgin in Ever-White Robes, was called Manjusri, whose abode was in the unmelting snows.

Korean Buddhism has frequently been a powerful factor in national affairs, and at times it practically controlled the state. A major reason for this was, apart from its popularity amongst the common men and a certain military nature in its organization, its appeal to the intellectuals and men of learning. Often Buddhists actively participated in patriotic wars against aggression. An important example of this was the resistance movement organized by Sosan, a monk , against invasion by the Japanese war-lord, Hideyoshi. In war and peace Buddhists co-operated with the state by mobilizing labour from their monastic order for works of public welfare. For instance, the Manhan mountain fortress was built by the Buddhist monks under the direction of the monk, Pyogam. As Buddhism came to be associated more and more with secular affairs, the construction of temples and pagodas and the publication of scriptures came to be considered symbols of state protection against enemy powers. Buddhist structures were also built for defence and security, although their primary objective had always been religious advancement.

During the period of the Silla Empire, when Korea was united under one dynasty, Korean culture made great advances in all spheres. This period witnessed, amongst other things, the construction of the magnificent cave temples at Sokkulam, southeast of Kyongu. These caves form a link in the long chain of cave temples extending from India to Korea through Central Asia and from China to Japan. Sokkulam is constructed according to a remarkably symmetrical plan and is decorated with brilliant reliefs and statues. It was probably built in the middle of the eighth century, although some scholars give it an earlier date. The foundations of Korean temple architecture, however, were laid during the period of the Three Kingdoms.

The sites and general environment of Buddhist temples and monasteries in Korea closely resemble those of China and Japan. Usually situated on hills or high mountains, they are walled around by tall and imposing trees inspiring awe and devotion. An impressive gateway is erected at some distance in front of the temple. On the frieze of the portal, the name of the temple is inscribed, occasionally in Sanskrit letters. The most impressive of the thirty-four Buddhist retreats in the Diamond Mountains is Yu Chomsa , which features fifty-three diminutive sitting and standing figures of the Buddha placed on the roots of an upturned tree. According to an ancient Buddhist legend, this structure commemorates the foundation of the monastery by fifty-three Indian monks who came to Korea many centuries earlier, and triumphed over the hostile dragons by placing an image of the Buddha upon each root of the tree.

Another art developed by the Koreans was the casting of bronze bells, impressive and artistic features of every Buddhist temple and important in Buddhist ritual. In Korea, however, they are particularly fine in form, and are embellished with relief decorations of figures and ornaments. The Buddhist art of Silla was taken to China and Japan by many emigrants. For instance, temples in the Shantung province of China were built on the Korean model.

In China, or in those neighbouring countries where Chinese culture penetrated, learning was the prerogative of a few noblemen and officials, who guarded it jealously from the masses. But Buddhism broke these barriers, and whilst the Confucianist classics formed the basis of courtly and aristocratic education in Korea, Buddhism appealed to the intellectuals and to the common people, and formed the basis of popular education. Indeed, by purposely recruiting converts from the humbler classes, Buddhism made a significant contribution in tile diffusion of culture. Wherever Buddhists went, religious literature was published in the local languages. Even the statues, pictures, and scrolls carried vernacular explanations.

China gave her language and ideographs to Korea. India contributed Sanskrit and phonetic letters from which syllabaries or alphabets were constructed, not only for vernacular writing and printing, but also as aids to the popularization of Confucianist teachings. The Korean syllabary, called *nido,* was, like the *kana* of the Japanese, a collection of syllables and not a true alphabet. The nido gave a phonetic value to some of the more common Chinese characters, although the idea of having a vernacular system of writing was probably suggested by Sanskrit letters, some of which represented Korean sounds accurately. The Korean alphabet, *unmun* (common language), was invented by a Buddhist monk named Syel-chong (or Sye-chong), one of the ablest scholars in Korean history.[2]

The fourth King of the Yi dynasty, Sejong, encouraged the translation of Buddhist scriptures, and is credited with having made a few translations himself. The real efforts at translation, however, were made by the seventh ruler, Sejo, a devout Buddhist and a great ruler of the dynasty. He created an office for Buddhist affairs and had many Buddhist scriptures translated.

FROM KOREA, BUDDHISM spread to Japan. Although a small country, Japan has played an extremely important role in history. Despite the limitations of their physiographic environment, the virile and dynamic people of Japan were able not only to maintain their independence at a time when almost all of Asia had succumbed to Western domination, but also to make remarkable progress in modernizing their industry and technology without losing the distinctive character of their traditional culture. A major reason for this unique blending of tradition and modernity is her readiness to receive and adapt alien contributions. Japan has demonstrated that the willingness to borrow and assimilate foreign traits is not a mark of cultural inferiority but evidence of vitality. Japanese culture is a compound of Shinto, Confucianism, and Buddhism. Prince Shotoku Taishi, who laid the foundations of Japanese civilization, likened these three systems to the three parts of the tree of Japanese culture: Shinto being the root embedded in the soil of national traditions and disposition, Confucianism the stem and branches of legal and educational institutions and of ethical codes, and Buddhism the blossoming flowers of religious sentiment and the fruit of spiritual life. The Japanese people may follow Buddhism, Shinto, or Confucianism, or any combination of these. Indeed, at the beginning of the nineteenth century there was a movement called Shingaku (heart learning) advocating such a combination. Whilst proud of their traditional culture, the Japanese have often consciously endeavoured to acquire knowledge from other lands. As early as the seventh century, Japanese leaders would carefully select able and promising young scholars and attach them to their embassies abroad, especially in China, charging them to bring back foreign knowledge. Few parallels can be cited from history to match this Japanese practice of importing knowledge. Even though the Japanese Emperor did not at times agree with the Chinese Emperor on the question of rank, the Japanese desire to acquire all that was useful from China was not diminished.[3] Because the Japanese eagerly sought foreign knowledge and have guarded and enriched it with extreme care, Japan is often justifiably described as a storehouse of East Asian culture. Indeed, this characteristic has made it possible for historians to gain valuable insight into the processes of the evolution of Asian culture itself. The history of Asian music, of the theatre, and of ritual dancing would have been imperfect without the aid of Japanese material. Some cultural forms, extinct in their homelands, still survive in Japan: for example the music-drama of seventh-century India.

Shinto, the indigenous religion of Japan, reflects the life and temperament of the people and is closely connected with national traditions and social institutions.[4] At first, it was an inarticulate religion and preached no fixed doctrines; it was an unorganized worship of the deities and spirits of nature and of the dead, although some authorities deny that Shinto originally included the veneration of ancestors. Whilst the spirit of ancestor worship and the desire to preserve one's house and family possible existed, there was no clear conception of loyalty or filial piety, now an integral and important part of the moral life of the people. Earlier religion was indistinguished from administration and this practice enabled the imperial family to become the head household of the nation and for the Emperor to assume divinity.

Chinese thought and religious practice played some part in pre-Buddhist Japan, but these had degenerated into methods of divination. It was only after Japan had been exposed to Confucianist ethics with a metaphysical background, as modified by Buddhist thought, that Chinese ideas made an impact on the Japanese mind. Confucianism gained popularity with the royal court, and was later to exercise a real influence on Japanese legal and educational institutions, and to contribute a systematic method of teaching morality. Taoist thought also had some influence on Japan but it was never very significant. Real advances in Japanese thought and civilization were made only after the advent of Buddhism.

With Buddhism came its rich heritage of learning in arts and sciences, letters and philosophy, which inspired higher ideals and encouraged indigenous art and literature. Buddhism provided a wealth of material for metaphysical speculation, satisfying Japanese yearnings for the unseen. Indeed, it gave them a clear and deep insight into a profound mysticism hitherto unknown to them. It resulted in the development of elaborate methods of spiritual training and the organization of ecclesiastical institutions, and led to the teaching of a system of cosmology and eschatology. The Mahayana form of Buddhism which was introduced into Japan had acquired various ideas and practices on its journey from India across Central Asia, China, and Korea, but Japan was able to impress upon it a distinctive Japanese character.

Whilst there is general agreement that Buddhism first came to Japan from Korea, the records differ as to the exact date of its advent. Buddhist figures have been found on bronze mirrors dating from about 300, but it is not certain whether their real significance was known to the Japanese at the time. The first known prominent Buddhist is Shiba Tachito, who went to Japan as a refugee in 522. Later his family produced more eminent Buddhists, including the first Japanese Buddhist nun and the greatest artist of the seventh century, Tori, who cast the main image of the Horyuji Temple at Nara.

The history of Buddhism in Japan is generally divided into three broad periods: the period of importation lasting from the sixth to the eighth century (known as the Asuka and Nara period); the period of nationalization from the ninth to the fourteenth century (the Heian and Kamakura periods); and the period of continuation from the fifteenth to the twentieth century (the Muromachi, Momoyama, and Edo periods, and the modern age).

Officially; Buddhism came to Japan for diplomatic reasons with a delegation from the Kingdom of Kudara (Pekche). The delegation was accompanied by Buddhist priests, and they presented to the Japanese Court of Yamato a gold-plated image of the Buddha with some other ceremonial articles, sutras, banners, and a letter praising the doctrine.[5] The Emperor is reported to have been extremely delighted at what he thought was "an exquisite teaching" and a radiant and beautiful figure. The generally accepted date of this event is 552, one hundred and fifty years after the introduction of Confucianism in Japan. Certain militarist factions inside the Court and some conservative sections outside it opposed Buddhism, but the Court supported the administrators and diplomats who favoured a progressive policy. The scales were soon tipped in favour of Buddhism with the growing influx of Buddhist missionaries, artisans, and other immigrants. The introduction of medicine, arts, and sciences, and especially of writing and astronomy, which invariably accompanied the Buddhist missions, helped to further break the conservative opposition.

Emperor Yomei, who came to the throne in 585 for a brief period, was the first Mikado to embrace Buddhism. He commissioned an image of Bhaishajyaguru, the Buddha of Healing, which was completed after his death and later installed in the world-renowned Horyuji Temple where it can still be seen. It was during his reign that for the first time a Japanese, Tasuna, renounced the world to become a Buddhist monk.

Emperor Yomei's son, Prince Shotoku Taishi, ensured the permanence of Buddhism through a variety of ordinances and legal measures. He became regent in 593 during the reign of his aunt, Emperor Suiko (573–628), and was extremely popular with his people.[6] He and other Japanese dignitaries adopted Buddhism because they believed it was the world trend of the time in philosophical thought. In February

594, he issued his first Imperial ordinance as Regent of the Empire, proclaiming Buddhism as the state religion and urging the development of the *Triratna,* the three basic tenets of Buddhism: the Buddha, the Dharma, and the Sangha. They were to be the principal objects of faith and undivided devotion, and were to constitute the fundamental basis of an upright life.

During Prince Shotoku's regency (593–621), the state built the first Buddhist pagodas, seminaries, hospitals, dispensaries, and homes for the aged and destitute. The temple of Kokoji was built in 596 and the temple of Horyuji in 607.[7] At the latter, Prince Shotoku himself gave lectures on the Mahayana sutras, especially on the *Saddharma bundarika* (The Lotus of the True Law), the *Vimalakirtinirdesa* and the *Srimala devi-simhanada-sutra.* Later the Horyuji Temple became an important centre for the study of Buddhist idealism of the *Vijnaptimatrata,* or Yogacara School.

Officials competed with one another to express their gratitude towards Shotoku for erecting Buddhist temples. These temples and their art were effective means of attracting the people's admiration and reverence for the Buddhist religion. The mural paintings, panel decorations, ceilings, and pillars provided the settings for Buddhist worship and ceremonies, which were performed with musical accompaniment around the statue of the Buddha installed on a dais in the central part of the temple. Thus, all the fine arts were a part of Buddhist worship, which not only captivated the devotees, but also automatically and almost imperceptibly released and refined the aesthetic energies of its followers. The Japanese were fascinated by these temples, and by 624 there were forty-six temples, eight hundred and sixteen priests, and five hundred and sixty-nine nuns in Japan. Japanese temples have always been built to honour emperors and ancestors and, although the temples of all sects have mainly functioned as centres of learning, worship, and the expansion of Buddhism, they have also performed functions connected with funerals and the custody of family graves. Thus, the Japanese worked out a harmony between the family system, the emperor, and Buddhism.

Shotoku sent envoys to China for Buddhist texts, and he himself wrote commentaries and expositions which have survived intact. He did not interpret the Mahayana philosophy literally but according to his understanding of its true meaning. The value of his work for Buddhism in Japan is perhaps as great as Asoka's work in India. He set up direct diplomatic relations with China, introduced reforms in administration, and laid down fundamental principles of state organization in his *Kempo* (known as the Constitution in Seventeen Articles). He thus provided the basis of national unity, guided and inspired the country with the spiritual ideals of Buddhism, and educated the people in arts and sciences.

With the establishment of a new and impressive capital at Nara (literally meaning the "abode of peace") in 710, Buddhism received further impetus, and a new phase in its history was begun. Emperor Shomu (701–756) played the central part in this progress; he spent the last seven years of his life in monastic robes, having renounced the throne after a rule of twenty-five years. Indeed, many Japanese emperors retired from the burdens and pleasures of secular power to the ascetic and peaceful life of the Buddhist monk. Known as the Era of Heavenly Peace, Shomu's reign marks a climactic period in the development of religion and art, as well as in government administration. He built temples and monasteries throughout the country as centres of religious observance and discipline as well as of social work, especially medical care. He erected the impressive temple, Todaiji, at Nara which houses the imposing image of Roshana (or Vairocana Buddha) cast in a mood of calm reflection and superb dignity. The dedication ceremony of this statue took place in 752, with many Indian monks and visitors in attendance, and it is regarded as the most brilliant event in the history of Japanese Buddhism. Emperor Shomu also constructed the Daibutsu, the great bronze Buddha statue rising forty-nine feet from the ground, which has come to be looked upon as a symbol of a united nation.

In 794, a grandiose new capital was built at Heian, modern Kyoto, a few miles north of Nara. The capital of Japan remained in Kyoto until 1868 when it was moved to Tokyo. With the change of capitals, a new phase in Buddhist activity began and new Buddhist structures were built at Kyoto. It was during the Heian period (794–1191) that the Kana alphabet was invented and widely used. *The Tale of Genji,* perhaps the finest literary masterpiece of Japan, in which the pessimistic views of Buddhism are interwoven with the sensuality of life, was also written during this period in the eleventh century.

As Buddhism began to permeate Japanese society, its adherents began to show preference for one or the other of its several imported varieties, but later Buddhism in Japan began to develop its own distinctive local schools of thought. During the ninth century two new sects were founded: the Tendai by Saicho, and the Shingon by Kukai. Their principal object was to present Buddhist doctrines in Japanese terms, and to discipline the monks. Both sects stressed not only spiritual salvation, but also its fulfilment in this world. It was through the efforts of the monks of these two sects that Buddhism became firmly and popularly nationalized.

Despite its growing success, however, Buddhism still remained too scholarly to be easily comprehended by common men, who were prone to ignore its intellectual content and to respond only to its devotional aspects. Consequently, a new Buddhist movement arose in the tenth century preaching faith in the Amitabha Buddha as the best means of salvation. The believers of this school needed only to recite the name of Amidabutsu (the Japanese form of the Amitabha Buddha), praying to be reborn in Jodo, the Pure Land, and thus obtain *satori* or enlightenment. Various other sects, such as Yuzu-nenbutsu, Jodo-shu, and Ji-shu, similarly emphasizing devotion for the Amitabha Buddha, arose during the Kamakura period (1192–1333). Because these sects made efforts to purify as well as simplify the doctrine and its practice, they were able to command a large following amongst the peasants.

During the Kamakura period, when the devotional sects were gaining popularity and feudalism was growing in strength, two new schools of Buddhist thought emerged in the country. One was the Zen (Ch'an or Dhyana) introduced by Eisai and Dogen, and the other was the Nichiren founded by Nichiren. Whilst these schools shared some of the characteristics of the contemporary sects of the Pure Land, they were based on different principles. Pure Land Buddhism believed in salvation through faith in others, whereas the doctrine of salvation through one's own enlightenment was the basis of the Zen and the Nichiren sects. Zen Buddhism found its adherents mainly amongst the warriors, or *samurai,* and gave rise to *bushido,* the characteristic Japanese ideal of chivalry, which is the most notable cultural development of this period. The samurai attached special value to loyalty, self-denial, temperance, and the power of mind and will. Whilst the growth of these sects was the outcome of the process of adjustment between traditional Japanese thinking and the vast and varied body of past Buddhist experience, the emergence of sectarian differences, in turn, increased religious activity and the acceptance of Buddhism by the masses.

After the Kamakura period no new major sect was founded in Japan. But as a result of the cultural processes having been firmly set into motion, there developed during the fifteenth and sixteenth centuries, literary activities, as represented by the *kyogen* or no plays and the tea cult, which, combined with Zen Buddhism, symbolize the culture of this era.

Later, during the Edo or Tokugawa period (1603–1867), Buddhism was used to combat the influence of Christianity. The Tokugawa shoguns required everyone to belong to a temple, called *danka,* which meant that all Japanese families during this period were at least nominally Buddhist. The Buddhist clergy was also compelled to co-operate with the feudal society of the Shogunate.

After the Meiji (meaning enlightened) Restoration in 1868, Buddhism stood in danger of being deprived of public support because of the hostility of nationalistic Shinto, although the new constitution guaranteed freedom of religion. However, loss of state patronage and the challenge of modernization compelled Buddhist scholars to investigate the doctrines of Buddhism scientifically and to find new meaning in the old doctrines. The Meiji government, whilst granting religious freedom to all, reasserted the independence of Shinto from Buddhism and set it up as a state religion. For a thousand years Shinto had more or less been absorbed by Buddhism, and Buddhist priests had moulded Shintoism according to their will. Even the fact that Shinto itself had profited enormously by this long tutelage under Buddhism did not discourage the new rulers from making it independent and supreme. Moreover, as Buddhism was favoured by the defeated Tokugawa shogunate, it was looked upon as a dangerous political adversary. Consequently, Buddhism suffered from 1867 to 1872 under a policy of ruthless oppression; Buddhist temples were reorganized and their economic foundations shaken; large parts of the temple properties were confiscated; and Buddhist statues, scriptures, paintings, carvings, and ceremonial instruments were destroyed in misplaced patriotic zeal. Buddhist monks and nuns were compelled to take up secular work. Debarred from participating in Shinto ceremonies, they were subjected to beatings and threats. Members of the royal family were no longer allowed to continue in Buddhist orders, and Buddhist ceremonies in the Imperial Palace were discontinued. But Buddhism survived this period of hostility and humiliation through the zealous efforts of monks such as Ekido, Nisshu, Tetsujo, Dokuon, Sesso, Unsho, and Mokurai, who realized the need for further reforms in their order to adapt it to the changing times. The state, for its part, realized the futility of repression against a faith which had become an integral part of Japanese culture and life. Even if there were to be no counterrevolution to the anti-Buddhist policy, which seemed unlikely, Shinto-Buddhist bonds could at best be severed in official areas and in the public institutions of the two religions, but never in the homes. The beliefs of the common people were too inextricably a blending of Shinto and Buddhism to allow the continuation of any open policy of Buddhist suppression. In any case, exclusivist policies are alien to the Japanese temperament, and even the official recognition of Shinto as a state religion was abolished after World War II.

The technological progress of Western civilization which deeply impressed the Japanese mind proved another challenge to Buddhism. But it also stirred the Japanese Buddhists to emphasize their own original rationalism and spirit of inquiry, thus bringing their faith in line with the demands of changing times. Simultaneously, the missionary activities of Christian missions, which invariably came with Europeans, gave a strong impetus to Buddhist revival. In fact, the forces of opposition, persecution, rationalism, and evangelism served to fill the Buddhists with a new zeal to modernize and sharpen their doctrine.

Meanwhile, Europe had begun to study Buddhism with scientific scrutiny, some scholars with sympathy and admiration but none with devotion. This movement gave a further helping hand to Japanese Buddhism, although by far the most energy and ability to reform came from within. Eminent Japanese scholars, such as Masaharu Anesaki Junjiro Takakusu, Bunyo Nanjio, and Bunzaburo Matsumoto, studied in Europe and returned to direct modern Buddhist studies in Japan. Their efforts, despite some opposition from orthodoxy, bore remarkable success, culminating in a movement amongst the clergy, laity, scholars, intelligentsia, artists, and others to advance the new scientific Buddhism.

Few Indian Buddhist monks came to Japan; Buddhism was spread there largely through the efforts of Japanese and Chinese monks. During the reign of Emperor Kotoku (645–654), a scholarly Indian monk, Hodo (Dharmamarga or Dharmapatha), is said to have come to Japan from Rajagrha, India. However, evidence supporting this visit is inconclusive. Japanese chronicles mention Bodhisena as the most prominent amongst a number of early Indian monks who came to Japan. Whilst the details of his life in India are not known, he is much revered in Japan. Having received mystic inspiration from the Bodhisattva Manjusri, he set out from India for China and arrived there in 730. Young in years but mature in wisdom, he was welcomed by both the clergy and laity. Impressed by his integrity and reputation, some Japanese monks and envoys who were on a mission in China at the time persuaded Bodhisena to come to Japan. Accompanied by monks and musicians, including a Vietnamese monk, Fu-che, and a Chinese monk, Tao Hsuan, Bodhisena arrived in Japan on 18 May 736 after a stormy sea journey. By this time Japanese Buddhism was more than two hundred years old and visiting monks were, as would be expected, accorded an honourable reception. Bodhisena settled in Japan and taught Sanskrit and preached Buddhism until he died in 760 at the age of fifty-seven. When the statue of Vairocana Buddha (Daigutsu), the biggest in the world, was cast and installed at Nara, it was Bodhisena who presided over the religious ceremony of dedication. A stupa known as Baramon Sojo (Brahaman Archbishop) was built in his memory.

There are many distinctive features in Japanese Buddhism. For instance, it abolished all discrimination between priestly life and secular life, the prayers of saints and common people are of the same merit, and people are instantaneously saved by Amidabutsu merely by reciting prayers. An important aspect of Japanese Buddhism has been that the worship of Avalokitesvara as Kwannon is not an exclusive characteristic of one sect.

However, today there are thirteen representative Buddhist sects in Japan: the Kegon (the Avatamsaka school), the Ritsu (the Vinaya school), the Hosso (the Dharmalaksana school), the Tendai, the Shingon (Tantric Buddhism), the Jodo, the Jodo-shin, the Yuzunenbutsu, the Ji-shu the Rinzai, the Soto, the Obaku, and the Nichiren. There were three others—the Sanron (the Three Sastra school of Madhyamika), the Kusha (the Abhidharma-kosa school), and the Jojitsu (the Satyassiddhisastra school)—but they are more or less extinct and have little independent influence. Most of these sects originated in China. The Kegon, the Ritsu, and the Hosso have retained their Chinese character, whilst the others are Japanese creations. The three Chinese sects were influential in the Nara period but they lost much of this influence afterwards as they were opposed to the new Buddhism. The Hosso sect is a type of Buddhist idealism, derived from the Yogacara School, and regards everything as the manifestation of the fundamental mind-principle. The Kegon sect centres around the worship of the Vairocana Buddha.

The thirteen sects are generally grouped into five major sects—the Tendai, Shingon, Zen, Pure Land or Jodo, and the Nichiren. The Tendai sect, founded in 804 by Saicho (767–822), better known as Dengyo-Daishi, greatly influenced the cultural and spiritual life of the Japanese. Saicho sought to harmonize all beliefs with the teachings of the *Hokke-kyo* (Lotus sutra); he taught that all men can become Buddhas and urged them to attempt to do so. An offshoot of the Chinese T'ien-t'ai, the Tendai sect absorbed the ideas and principles of other doctrines, such as the Tantric, the Dhyana, and the Vinaya Schools. It differs from the Chinese T'ien-t'ai in its practical approach, although both base their teachings essentially on the Mahayana text, the *Saddharmapundarika,* laying stress on the Ekayana theory.

A younger contemporary of Saicho, Kukai (774–835) also known as Kobo Daishi, founded the Shingon sect, which is the third largest religious organization in Japan with approximately twelve thousand temples. An ascetic, a traveller, an accomplished calligrapher and sculptor, Kukai was a versatile and remarkable scholar. In the records and legends of Japanese Buddhism there is no more celebrated name than his.[8] Shingon literally means "true word," the *mantra* or sacred formula, and its doctrine, based mainly upon the *Mahavairocana-sutra,* is essentially magical or mystical. According to this sect, enlightenment can be attained through the recitation of a mantra or *dharani.* It is now the only sect in Japan which retains Tantric ideas, and it has successfully avoided the shortcomings of Indian and Tibetan Tantrism. Like

Tendai, Shingon also endeavoured to effect a unification of Buddhism with Shinto.

Pure Land Buddhism embraces the Jodo-shu, Shin-shu, Yuzunenbutsu, and Ji-shu sects. The last two of these are much less important than the others. All these sects believe that salvation can be attained only through undivided faith in the saving power of the Amitabha Buddha, Amidabutsu. The followers of this system recite Nenbutsu, the name of Amitabha, praying to be reborn in his paradise called Jodo (Sukhavati). The emphasis, however, is on faith, not on recitation.

Founded in 1175 during the Heian era by Genku, better known as Honen (1133–1212), the Jodo sect was mainly inspired by the teachings of Shan-tao (613–681) of the Amitabha School in China. Honen selected the *Sukhavativyuha Sutras* and the *Amitayurdhyana Sutra* as his canonical texts. In the thirteenth century Shinran introduced several important reforms in the Jodo sect and its monastic order, seeking to remove the division between the clergy and the laity. According to him, all living beings will be saved because of the vow taken by Amitabha. Hence, the recitation of the name of the Buddha is but the expression of gratitude. The Jodo sect as reformed by Shinran is known as Shin-shu. Being a simple creed, it suited the common man admirably and rapidly became popular. Today it has the largest following in Japan.

As a specific form of Buddhism, Dhyana or Zen was first founded in China by Bodhidharma in the early sixth century, but ultimately it is a variation of the Mahayana School of Buddhism of northern India. Zen Buddhism has three branches in Japan: the Rinzai, the Soto, and the Obaku. Sote-Zen has the largest following, being second only to Shin-shu. Rinzai-Zen was founded by the Japanese monk, Eisai (or Yesai 1141–1215); Soto-Zen by his disciple, Dogen (1200–1253); and Obaku-Zen by a Chinese monk, Igen (or Yin-yuan) in about 1653. Eisai and Dogen had spent several years studying in China. Dogen is known not only for his strict religious discipline but also as one of the most prominent philosophers of Japan. He led a life of stern discipline and devoted himself to discovering persons who could competently spread the teaching of Zen Buddhism. His sermons were collected and published by his disciples after his death. The most important of these,

Sho-bo-gcn-zo (the Essence of the True Doctrine) is considered to he one of the best philosophical works in Japan. He preached: "All human beings have already been enlightened. They are Buddhas by nature. The practice of meditation is nothing but the Buddha's act itself."

All sects of Buddhism emphasize tranquillity of mind but Zen Buddhism stresses it most strongly. Zen teaches that tranquillity of mind is the same as the Buddha's ideal. Zen doctrine emphasizes that meditation or contemplation alone can lead one to enlightenment. The essence of Zen Buddhism is: "Look into the mind and you will find Buddhahood." This philosophy found great favour amongst the warriors who valued tranquillity of mind. Patronized and encouraged by the Shozuns, Zen Buddhism rapidly spread throughout the country, and made far-reaching contributions to Japanese culture.

The Nichiren sect was founded in 1253 by Nichiren (1222–1282), the son of a fisherman who became a patriot and saint of Japan. He lived at a time when Japan was in danger of invasion by the Mongol Emperor of China. Nichiren declared: "I will become the loyal pillar of Japan, the eyes of Japan, the ship of Japan." After wandering about the country and long years of study of various doctrinal beliefs, he concluded that the *Saddharma Pundarika* was the final revelation of the truth and that the deliverance of the country from suffering could best be achieved by following its teaching. Perhaps to counteract the influence of Nenbutsu of the Jodo sect, he introduced the use of the mantra formula, *namu myoho renge kyo* (homage to the Sutra of the Lotus of the True Law), the recitation of which could give men the power to fuse themselves with eternal life. Because of his rudeness and violent expressions, Nichiren was frequently in trouble with the authorities, and his story is a long catalogue of persecution, although he always miraculously escaped.

These Buddhist sects were not free from rivalry and conflict, and disputes between monasteries were at times settled by force of arms. There was much antagonism between the followers of Nichiren and those of Shinran in the last half of the fifteenth century, mainly because Buddhism in Japan was too closely associated with the political and social affairs of the country. Consequently, during periods of political upheaval, religious leaders combined religious ambition with the contest for power. Buddhism in Japan has often been a major political force and, as in the Fujiwara period (858–1068), even threatened the sovereignty of the state. Buddhist militancy, as reflected both in sectarian disagreements and interference in power-politics, was also conditioned by the prevalent feudal divisions, which became more pronounced in times of political agitation.

However, it would be wrong to characterize Japanese Buddhism as militant or aggressive, because if this were true, its missionary activities would have invited military reaction and its highly developed philosophy and intellectual equipment would have crushed many primitive beliefs mythologies, and superstitious traditions. It never declared a holy war *jihad* (crusade), although for patriotic reasons, Japanese Buddhism has sanctioned national wars as crusades for peace and goodwill on earth. Because of its spirit of accommodation, Buddhism did not encounter sustained hostility from traditional beliefs, except for brief occasional spells.

Although both Buddhism and Shinto have survived and have interacted on each other, there has been, in marked contrast to China, no persecution of "foreign" Buddhism by the "nationalistic" Shinto. Shinto is a Chinese word (Shen-tao) and means "way of the spirits"; in Japanese it is called *Kami no Michi.* Buddhism adopted a characteristic policy of tolerance and assimilation towards Shinto. It accepted the Shinto cult of ancestor worship, and the Shinto deities or *Kamis*—Kami has a wide meaning, which may signify a natural object, or a god, or the original spirit itself—as the temporal manifestations of Buddhist divinities. To the early Japanese, Kamis were superior to men but, although powerful (chi-haya-baru), they were not omniscient. This made it relatively easy for the Buddhists to designate Kamis as the earthly incarnations of the Buddha. The Buddhist pantheon was generally thought to represent the "Indestructibles" (*Honji*), whilst the Shinto deities were interpreted as their partial appearances *(suijaku).* Thus, every Kami was regarded as a manifestation of a certain deity. The chief Shinto deity, the Sun goddess, was identified with the Buddha Vairocana. Buddhists made a practice of reading the Sutras before the altar of the Shinto deities. They worshipped publicly at the Meiji and other Shinto shrines, and incorporated Shinto deities and doctrines into their body of beliefs, including the doctrine, given up since World War II, that the Emperor was the direct descendant of the sun goddess and divinely authorized to rule.

Shinto was mainly a primitive form of nature worship based on a simple feeling of awe at the forces of nature, and anything awe-inspiring was called Kami. It had no moral code, and its prayers and sacrifices did not aim at seeking spiritual blessings. Shinto, like Confucianism, had nothing to say about the state of the dead. Shinto had no educational function; its priests did not preach or teach. The theorists of this simple faith, which in fact has no philosophy, leaned heavily on the well-developed philosophy of Buddhism in attempting to interpret Shinto ideas. Hence, Buddhism so influenced Shinto that it is claimed that without Buddhist umbrage for more than a thousand years Shinto could hardly have survived as an organized religion; "Buddhism imparted a depth and meaning to the old Shinto mythology and made it philosophically respectable and acceptable to educated men. In others words Buddhism equipped Shinto—a primitive religion—with a worthy doctrinal and ethical content."[9]

Whilst it is true that there has been no sustained and violent hostility between Buddhism and Shinto, it would be wrong to deny the existence of disharmony between the two. Several Neoshinto movements arose in the mediaeval period to emphasize the differences between Shinto and Buddhist thought, and to assert the supremacy of the former. For example, *Yui-itsu Shinto,* prominent at the end of the fifteenth century, was the only school that sought to reverse earlier Buddhist interpretations of Kamis and declared that the Buddhist deities were not the primordial powers, but the temporal manifestations of the Kamis. In the eighteenth century a similar movement, Return to Antiquity Shinto (*Fukko* Shinto), emphasized the divine origins of kingship and exhorted the people to return to pure Shinto. For a brief period after the Meiji Revolution in 1868 it appeared that Buddhism might suffer under the instigation of Shintoist revivalists, but the Constitution guaranteed freedom of religion to all and the fear proved unfounded. Much of the limited and intermittent religious hostility was the result of Buddhist involvement in state politics. It could be said with reasonable justification that it was the politics of the Buddhist order, not the doctrine of Buddhism, that spurred occasional resentment. For example, the resistance exhibited towards Buddhism at the time of its official entry in the sixth century was the undoubted outcome of political rivalry between two warring factions—the militarists and the administrators—at the royal court; the militarists sought to exploit the foreign origin of Buddhism in their favour. This conflict lasted about forty years, and it became menacing enough at one stage to threaten the stability of the state and the life of the sovereign.

Shinto opposition to Buddhism has generally taken the line of an expression of patriotic resentment towards an alien creed. Shintoists tend to glorify the pre-Buddhist culture and belittle Buddhist contributions, but this feud, although real, must not be magnified. After all, the overwhelming majority of the Japanese people are Buddhist; Japan is the leading Buddhist nation today; and Buddhism is inseparably woven into the national fabric of Japan.

As in China, there was considerable Confucianist opposition toward Buddhism in Japan. But Confucianism was also a foreign doctrine, and appears to have kept its antagonism subdued until the seventeenth century, even though Confucianist hostility in China had been active for centuries. These two systems did not come into conflict in Japan until the seventeenth century when Confucianists began to attack Buddhism from motives which were not purely religious. Their censure was not directed against Buddhist thought; rather, they denounced Buddhist political influence upon the nation and the administration. Antagonism between the two came to the surface again during the early Meiji era when some Confucianist scholars aligned themselves with a powerful group of Shintoists to vent their doctrine of *Haibutsuorn* "Down with Buddhism." But this movement was short-lived.

Approximately two-thirds of Japan's inhabitants profess Buddhism. The various Buddhist sects combined maintain about eighty thousand temples and one hundred and fifty thousand clerics, and there are several colleges and institutes primarily devoted to Buddhist studies. There is no doubt that Buddhism is an integral part of Japanese life and a powerful force in the country. Throughout the country, countless images of the Buddha and the Bodhisattvas, sutras, paintings, and other sacred objects have been preserved, both for the tourist and the devotee. Buddhist festivals not only perform an attractive religious function in keeping the spirit of the religion alive, but lend colour to the cultural life of the country. For example, on 15 July every year Buddhists celebrate *Ulambana,* a principal event in Japanese Buddhist life. It is a service to pacify the souls of the dead, who are believed to return to their old homes on that day. There are also the *higan* periods in spring and autumn each period comprising seven days spread around the two equinoctial days, called *chunichi.* On higan, Buddhist services recall the memories of the dead. At midnight on the last day of the year bells begin to sound in Buddhist temples. Through the ringing of the bells the worldly passions of the previous year are supposed to be completely eradicated.

Whilst Buddhism provided a bridge between Indian and Chinese civilizations, it also linked Chinese and Japanese culture. Those Indian ideas which found their way to Japan were transmitted through China or Central Asia, although there was some direct contact between India and Japan by sea. According to a scholar of ethnology, there is evidence of the presence of an Indian community in the Shima district in Mie Prefecture.[10] These Indians were called *Tenjiku Renin,* meaning the "masterless Indian samurai."

Although China and Japan had always been in contact, it was not until Buddhism was firmly entrenched in Chinese life that China was able to influence Japanese culture. Before the arrival of Buddhism, Japan led a fairly isolated, primitive life; writing was unknown, and religious beliefs centred around the worship of natural forces and ancestors. But once Buddhism had become an integral part of Japanese life and thought, Japan appears to have begun to seek and adopt new ideas with amazing aptitude.

The best way of assessing the influence of Buddhist thought and practice on Japanese cultural life, suggests Suzuki, is to wipe out all the Buddhist temples together with their treasures, libraries, gardens, anecdotes, tales, and romances, and see what is left in the history of Japan: "First of all, there would be no painting, sculpture, architecture, or even music and drama. Following this, all the minor branches of art would also disappear—landscape gardening, tea ceremony, flower arrangement, and fencing (which may be classed as art since it is the art of spiritual training and defence of oneself against the enemy, morally as well as physically). The industrial arts would also vanish, the first impetus to which was given by Buddhism."[11]

The advent of Buddhism made Japan India-conscious, eager to know the country and the original texts of its new faith. The Japanese became familiar with Indian culture and studied the Sanskrit language and literature. Even today, outside of India, "there is no country in the world where so many students are learning a rudimentary knowledge of Sanskrit and Pali languages. There are many universities where they are taught these languages. A great many books concerning these languages have appeared in recent times."[12] In some Japanese temples, very ancient manuscripts in Sanskrit are preserved intact. It is significant that many of those manuscripts found in Japan are much older than those preserved in India.

Kukai started the study of Sanskrit letters, known as *Shittan*, a Japanese equivalent of the Sanskrit word *Siddham*, with which ancient Indian inscriptions and works often begin. Before this, during the Nara period, the Vinaya; the *Abhidharmakosa* by Vasubandhu; the *Satyasiddhi* by Harivarman; the works of Nagarjuna and Aryadeva; the *Vijnaptimatrata*, Buddhist idealism; and the *Gandavyuha sutra* had been studied. These are called "the Six Schools of the Ancient Capital."[13] In addition, Buddhist logic had been introduced into Japan in 661 by Dusho. In the seventh century Dusho went to China with Tzu-en (Jion) and, under Hsüan-tsang, studied the system of Buddhist idealism, which was then the newest system of Buddhist logic. Later, in the beginning of the eighth century, further impetus was given the study of logic through the efforts of Genbo. In Japan, Dusho's tradition is called "the teaching at the Southern Temple" and Genbo's "the teaching at the Northern temple," because they taught at Gango-ji Temple and Konfuku-ji Temple respectively. Since then this system of logic has been studied in the Hosso sect as a discipline subordinate to the study of Buddhist idealism and the *Abhidharmakosa*. The study of logic became very popular and it appears that prior to Western influence, more than two hundred works were composed on Buddhist logic in Japan.[14]

After Kukai, the other prominent name in the history of Japanese Sanskrit studies is Jogon (1639–1702), who edited some Sanskrit *dharanis* (magic verses or syllables) and composed a remarkable Sanskrit work entitled *Shittan-Sanmitsu-Sho*. Jiun (1718–1804) compiled a thesaurus of many extant Sanskrit manuscripts of the kind which consisted of one thousand volumes.

Although common people in Japan do not know Sanskrit they are to some extent familiar with the Devanagari alphabet. It is not uncommon to find wooden tablets written in Devanagari characters in Japanese cemeteries. Japanese temples contain images of the Buddha Bodhisattvas, and other divinities with nagari characters inscribed beneath them. These letters are called seeds, (*bija,* a Sanskrit term), with each identifying a single divine being. In mediaeval times some Japanese warriors went into battle wearing helmets with Sanskrit characters for *mangala* (blessing).

Japanese characters are undoubtedly constructed on the lines of Chinese characters. Whereas Chinese characters are ideographic, Japanese characters are phonetic like the Devanagari letters and are arranged in a sentence in the same order as in Sanskrit—subject, object, and verb. Word order is not in itself indicative of family affinity in languages, but there is further evidence suggesting constructional similarities. The Japanese used certain shortened Chinese characters to develop a syllabic alphabet of their own. The older method of using Chinese characters with a similar pronunciation to render certain Japanese words phonetically did not work satisfactorily, because it was neither simple nor well regulated. A Chinese character represents a whole syllable and thus the Japanese did not think of spelling the sounds of their language by separate signs for vowels and consonants until they came into contact with the Indian alphabet, which, regarding the consonants as the most important letters, indicated the vowels by additional signs placed around the consonants. In the Japanese syllabary the vowels are arranged in exactly the same order as in the Indian alphabet: a,i,u,e,o. The groups of consonants then follow accompanied by vowels: for example, ka, ki, ku, ke, ko. A Japanese song, *irohauta,* attributed to Kukai, the supposed inventor of Japanese letters, is made up of all the forty-seven letters, and is nothing but a free translation of a Buddhist poem written in ancient India.[15]

The arrangement of the Japanese syllabary into fifty phonetic sounds is regarded by Japanese scholars as no more than an adaptation of the Sanskrit alphabet. The system is undoubtedly the work of a Buddhist, perhaps Bodhisena. If the Chinese language and script had not penetrated deeply into Japan before the Indian alphabet, there is little doubt that the

Japanese would have found it far more convenient to adopt the Indian script rather than Chinese characters.[16]

Unlike Chinese, but like Korean, Japanese has a well-developed verbal system. In their phonetic systems Chinese and Japanese have nothing in common. In Chinese, inflection is unknown and tenses and modes of action are indicated if necessary by isolated words. The idea of a sentence is implicit in Chinese by the syntactic relations of the meaning of characters, and, strictly speaking, it is not possible to differentiate between nouns and verbs.

The development of a simple writing method and the perfection of the Kana syllabary, together with the introduction of Buddhist texts, inevitably influenced Japanese literature and learning. Indeed, a remarkable process of literary activity commenced which was to bloom in the Classical Age of Japanese literature during the Heian period. The first philosophical works ever written by a Japanese, although in Chinese, were Prince Shotoku's commentaries on the three Buddhist scriptures—the *Hokke-kyo*, the *Yuima-kyo*, and the *Shoman-kyo*. The first legendary tale, *Taketori Monogatari* (Tale of a Bamboo Cutter), the story of a divine maiden written in the ninth century, drew inspiration from various Buddhist works, such as the Jatakas, and embodies the Buddhist idea of moral causation. The fullest development of the monogatari tale is found in Japan's first novel, the *Genji Monogatari* (the Tale of Genji), written in the early eleventh century and a masterpiece of Japanese classical literature. In the novel, the sensuality of worldly life is interwoven with the pessimistic doctrines of Buddhism. This work, probably the earliest novel of its kind in world-literature, was written by Murasaki Shikibu, a lady-in-waiting at the royal court.

Buddhist influence with its stress on asceticism and didacticism can be seen in the twelfth century collection of about two hundred stories, entitled *Uji Shui Monogatari* (Gleanings at Uji), which includes a number of Buddhist morality tales. The thirteenth-century work, *Jikkinsho* (Section of Ten Teachings), contains ten stories illustrating Buddhist moral principles.

Indian legends also found their way into Japanese literature. An example of this is the legend of *Rishyasringa* in which a rishi who had never seen a woman was seduced by Santa, the daughter of King

Lomapada. This is a very famous story in the *Mahabharata.* In the Japanese version the saint is named Ikkaku Sennin, that is Ekasrnga (Unicorn). The Kabuki drama, *Narukami,* was derived from this legend. Many such Indian stories were incorporated into Buddhist literature and conveyed to Japan.

Painting was allied to literature, and received added impetus because of the Buddhist keenness to disseminate knowledge through this medium. One of the most celebrated Buddhist empresses of Japan, Komyo, had a million miniature pagodas made for distribution. Each pagoda contained a print of a short Buddhist *dharani,* or text.[17]

Buddhists also were remarkably successful in preserving the existing knowledge of rival faiths. Buddhist institutions in Japan acted as custodians of Japanese learning, whether Shinto, Confucianist, secular, or religious. Without the protection of the Buddhist order, much of the documentary material of Shinto would not have survived. The increasing power of war-lords in various regions of the country, and the rise of a warring feudal society in the mediaeval period, naturally put a greater premium on martial skill than on intellectual learning. Therefore the Buddhist monasteries rather than the official academies became the repositories and guardians of knowledge and the chief sources of education.

Numerous Buddhist deities were introduced into Japan and many of these are still very popular. Some Hindu gods, who had been incorporated into the Buddhist pantheon, were amongst them. For example, Indra, originally the god of thunder but now also the king of gods, is popular in Japan as Taishakuten (literally the great King Sakra);[18] Ganesa is worshipped as Sho-ten (literally, holy god) in many Buddhist temples, and is believed to confer happiness upon his devotees. A sea-serpent worshipped by sailors is called Ryujin, a Chinese equivalent of the Indian *naga.* Hariti and Dakini are also worshipped, the former as Kishimojin, and the latter by her original name. Bishamon is a Japanese equivalent of the Indian Vaisravana (Kubera), the god of wealth.

Even Shinto adopted Indian gods, despite its desperate efforts after the Meiji Revolution to systematically disengage itself from Buddhism and assert its own independent identity. Indeed, Shinto, before it felt the influence of the Buddhist iconography, did not cast deities into human form but represented them with symbols such as a mirror, a jewel, a sword. The Indian sea god, Varuna, is worshipped in Tokyo as Sui-ten (water god); the Indian goddess of learning, Sarasvati, has become Benten (literally, goddess of speech), with many shrines dedicated to her along sea coasts and beside lakes and ponds. Siva is well known to the Japanese as Daikoku (literally, god of darkness), which is a Chinese and Japanese equivalent of the Indian Mahakala, another name of Siva. Daikoku is a popular god in Japan. At the Kotohira shrine on the island of Shikoku, sailors worship a god called Kompira, which is a corruption of the Sanskrit word for crocodile, *kumbhira.* The divine architect mentioned in the *Rig Veda,* Visvakarma, who designed and constructed the world, was regarded in ancient Japan as the god of carpenters, Bishukatsuma. The Indian Yama, the god of death, is the most dreaded god of Japan, under the name Emma, the king of hell. The idea of rewards and punishments after death was introduced by Buddhism; early Shinto texts do not refer to this subject.[19]

The climbers wearing traditional white dress, who scale the sacred Mount Ontake as a religious observance, sometimes have inscribed on their robe Sanskrit *Siddham* characters of an ancient type. Sometimes they put on white Japanese scarfs *(tenugui)* which carry the Sanskrit character *OM,* the sacred syllable of the Hindus.

The Japanese customs of cremation and ancestor worship were influenced by India. Until the Meiji Revolution all funerals were performed by Buddhist priests, and even now many Japanese who are not Buddhist prefer Buddhist burial rites and ceremonies. To enjoy good incense with a calm mind has become a cultivated art amongst educated Japanese. The varieties of incense popular in Japan and China were partly supplied by India. Specimens of ancient incense from India have been preserved as national treasures in the Imperial Shoso-in repository.

The profundity of Japanese mythology and philosophy has its roots in traditions that have been dominated by Buddhist thought since the days of Shotoku Taishi. Both the individual and national dispositions of the Japanese people have been conditioned by the teachings of Buddhism. Even the common ideas and ideals that inspire and guide the Japanese in their daily life are a reflection of Buddhist ideas. The notion that everyone can attain Buddhahood is common to all Buddhism, but it is particularly popular in Japan. The Japanese faculties of precise observation, concentrated reflection and efficient transmission, humility and perseverance, and the stress on the fulfilment of duties and national obligations are attributed to Buddhism which is no doubt "the greatest promoter of the culture of the intellect."

An example of Buddhist influence on modern Japanese thought can be seen in the philosophy of Nishida Kitaro (1870-1945), who is regarded as the most stimulating thinker Japan has eyer produced. In the latter part of the nineteenth century a movement to blend Buddhist philosophy with Western thought emerged in Japan. This philosophical blending is perhaps best represented in Nishida's doctrine in which he sought "to give to oriental culture its logical foundation" or to see "a form in the formless, hear a voice in the voiceless."[20] In the formulation of his theory he drew upon the Buddhist concept of *sunyata*.

Buddhist influence can also be seen in the Japanese theory of government. Initially, Buddhism was officially recognized in Japan for diplomatic reasons, and the first Japanese constitution, promulgated in 604 by Prince Shotoku Taishi, was inspired by Buddhist ideals. Buddhist monasticism played a significant role in practical politics in the tenth and eleventh centuries. Nichiren, in the thirteenth century, sought to identify religion with the state, and nationalism with Buddhism. Buddhist monasticism in the sixteenth century has been described as the greatest power in Japan at the time. The gallant samurai and *daimyo* classes were influenced deeply by the various schools of Zen Buddhism. Although Zen doctrines had been taught in Japan before the Nara period, it was not until the Kamakura period that the various Zen schools profoundly influenced the government and the military classes. In 1916 the Buddhist Church publicly encouraged and welded the spirit of nationalism, and protected the Imperial family and state. When Japanese militarism was at its peak in 1937, the Buddhist Movement of the Imperial Way became very powerful. Indeed, the Chinese Buddhist Society severely criticized the Japanese Buddhists for co-operating so enthusiastically with Japanese imperialist policies. The demands of religion and the pressures of patriotism are not always easy to reconcile. Japanese Buddhism departed from the principles of the Buddhist Sangha, and adopted the distinct role of lending its support to a totalitarian state ideology.

Japanese education and social service originated in Buddhism. Education began in the Horyuji and other Buddhist temples, and a scheme of general education was designed for the first time by Kukai when he built his school in 829 known as Sogei Shuchi-In. The monks not only taught religion and philosophy but also practical arts and sciences. They even taught the people how to read and write, and initiated the compilation of Japanese histories. Above all, they fostered the love of nature and humanity, and broadened the religious outlook of the people, instilling a compassionate idealism both in their thought and conduct. They founded hospitals, dispensaries, health-resorts, taught the art of healing, built alms houses, conducted free funerals for the poor, and brought widespread relief from famine and pestilence.

Buddhist social welfare programs continue to be exceptionally impressive. Having recovered its balance from the Shinto-Confucianist attack of the nineteenth century, Buddhism applied itself to alleviating some of the damaging consequences of a capitalistic economy on society. Today Buddhism maintains an imposing array of social welfare activities, such as public dispensaries, hospitals, infirmaries, maternity homes, asylums, nurseries, kindergartens, schools, homes for the disabled and the aged, libraries, information bureaus, social education institutions, settlement houses, continuation schools, reform schools, employment offices, and legal offices for the protection of the poor and needy.

Through the journeys of indefatigable Buddhist monks the whole country was opened up, mountains were conquered, harbours were made, roads were built, rivers were bridged, wells were dug, and swamps were drained. These monks promoted agriculture and forestry, planted trees, constructed irrigation canals, and opened up new and extensive tracts of land to a more enlightened industry and agriculture than primitive Japan had ever known. For example, the cultivation of cotton in Japan is traced to an Indian who had drifted to the shore of Aichi Prefecture in 799. To commemorate the event, the Japanese named the village wherc the shipwrecked Indian had landed Tenjiku; Tenjiku was the Japanese name for India, and means Heaven. The Japanese also erected a shrine in his honour and installed in it his statue cast in Indian costume.

Japanese art, remarkable for its distinctive beauty, dexterity, and dignity, bears some imprints of Indian styles. "The debt of art to

Buddhism is even greater in Japan than in China, for on the whole the gift of Buddhism to China was ideas rather than technique, whereas in ancient Japan there was no art worth mentioning. Painting, sculpture, and architecture, as well as engraving, printing, and even writing, were all introduced in connection with Buddhism."[21] Pre-Buddhist Japanese art is important to history and to the understanding of Japanese society of the time, but it is a very remote, almost unrecognizable and poor parent of the rich Japanese art one is most familiar with. Buddhism provided the spiritual inspiration that caused the Japanese to either refine their own traditional art styles, or import Chinese or other styles.

Earlier Japanese paintings, found mostly on the walls of chambers of burial mounds, consisted mainly of totemic symbols and geometric patterns in colour. Of the early Buddhist paintings, the most famous is the one found on the panels of a portable wooden shrine, the *Tamamushinozushi* shrine. It was done during the period of the Emperor Suiko (592–628) and is preserved today in the Horyuji Temple. The oil painting shows landscapes and Buddhist figures with slender limbs and faces, which are regarded as the typical features of the Chinese art of the period of Six Dynasties. Much of early Japanese art was produced with the help of Chinese and Korean artisans, but they too were mainly Buddhists who had been inspired by Indian tradition. Architectural development also began to bloom as Buddhist temples were built on a grand scale with elaborate detail. The Horyuji Temple, the oldest wooden building in the world (with the possible exception of the treasury at Nara, the *Shoso-in*), dates from the beginning of the seventh century.

In the eighth century when Buddhism had almost become the national religion, Japanese painting embarked on a fresh and brilliant course of development under the influence of the Indian chiaroscuro style transmitted through T'ang China. A unique illustration of this is found in the fresco painting, closely resembling the Ajanta art, in the Golden Hall of the Horyuji Temple. In contrast to the romantic and transcendental figures of the preceding period, the figures in this painting are rotund and human.[22] During the Nara period, encouraged by royal patronage and enthusiasm for their faith, Buddhists made magnificent contributions in art, architecture, sculpture, painting, and music. The accomplishments of this period were so brilliant that even today Nara is the most impressive site in Japan from an artistic standpoint. Typical of the excellence of the Nara art is the nine foot seated bronze Buddha, attended by the sun and moon.

Japan by this time had matured artistically and had developed indigenous traditions. Furthermore, her contact with China was broken around the end of the ninth century. Japanese art began to assume its own character with the paintings of Kanaoka Kose, who flourished in the ninth century and who is traditionally regarded as Japan's greatest painter. He painted secular scenes as well as Buddhist subjects. Genshin, better known as Eshin Sozu (942–1017), is particularly associated with the beatific vision of the Amitabha Buddha. He was a profound thinker and held the view that the Buddha-nature was inherent in everyone and that by contemplation of the innermost depths of the soul a manifestation of the Buddha's wisdom and power could be realized. This philosophy gradually led him to concentrate on Amida Buddha, and he painted the Pure Land in graceful lines and harmonious colours. Indeed, the surviving pictures of the early period are all Buddhist, although the artists also painted secular themes.

Kamakura painting, which is the most truly national, was deeply inspired by Buddhism. Nobuzane, one of the outstanding masters of the period, is famous for a series of portraits of poets, but his masterpiece is the portrait of the Buddhist saint, Kukai, depicted as a child kneeling upon the lotus. The great bronze Buddha Daibutsu, although an emulation of Nara style, is in fact characteristic of the art of the period, reflecting the mood of Amidism as influenced by the widening of Buddhist consciousness. Temple architecture of the Kamakura period witnessed a variety of styles, some incorporating Nara features and some influenced by the emergence of Zen Buddhism, which became the premier spiritual force in Japanese life during the Muromachi period (1336–1753). Zen Buddhist influence on art can be seen on the ink paintings of the period, including the extensive work done by the Zen monk Sesshu (1420–1506), and the paintings of Arhats or Buddhist saints by Mincho (or Cho Densu) (1341–1427). The Zen emphasis on contemplation reduced the importance of icons in religious worship. Consequently, sculpture declined in importance.

After this period the influence of Buddhism, which had been thoroughly localized in any case, began to decline; or more accurately, it began to lose its Buddhist identity as it assumed a Japanese character. However, a good deal of it can yet be recognized in the works of the Zen monk-painters, such as Hakuin and Sengai, and the poet-painters of the Tokugawa period (1420–1868).

In modern times, when art began to depart from religion and head towards secularism, it was inevitable that Buddhist inspiration should lose much of its force. Still, modern Japanese art bears marks of the Buddhist ideals of simplicity, restraint, and dignity. Buddhist ideals and traditions are reflected perhaps to a greater degree in sculpture and architecture, because of the utilitarian value of those arts in religious life and ritual. The art of the woodcut, which has been brought to a remarkable perfection in Japan, is a by-product of Buddhism, since woodcut engraving was first used for printing Buddhist sutras and pictures. In fact, the earliest specimen of extant printed texts are Buddhist charms enclosed in miniature wooden pagodas distributed amongst the temples of Japan in the eighth century.

Japancse music and dance was in a state of primitive development until the arrival of Buddhism, in whose religious observances music played an important role. Young Japanese musicians went to China and Korea to study. The earliest known music-dance of Japan is Gigaku, a kind of primitive mask-play which was brought to Japan in 612 from Korea by Mimashi. Although Mimashi learned his art in China, the Gigaku was of Indian origin, as is indicated by the masks representing Indian features. More than two hundred of these masks are still preserved in the temples of Nara. The masked dancers were led by *Chido*, a figure, whose function was to clear the way. Even today religious processions in Japan are headed by a person wearing a long-nosed mask, who is called *Tengu.* Amongst the dancers were characters representing a lion and an eagle, which also suggests links with India, because there were no lions in Japan (or in China) and the term for the eagle character, *Karura,* is a derivative of the Sanskrit *Garuda.*

Whilst most parts of Gigaku have been lost, some fragments of it later merged with the elegant and grateful *Gagaku.* Gagaku is the name for a piece of music, but it brought with it the dance called *Bugaku.* Both were introduced to Japan by Bodhisena. This court dance and music was performed for the first time in 752 in celebration of the opening of the Todaiji Temple at Nara. At this ceremony the Emperor Shomu unveiled the Vairocana Buddha statue, and hundreds of foreign musicians, a number of whom were Indians, performed. Many of the instruments used on that occasion are still in the Shoso-in Treasure House at Nara. Buddhism was a strong inspirational force, and there is little doubt that the orchestras of Japan were first organized to meet Buddhist needs. Although this music-drama is more than twelve hundred years old, it is still preserved in Japan in its original form, not only in records, musical instruments, and masks, which are kept in the Horyuji Temple, but in the dance form itself.

From the beginning, the Japanese aristocracy patronized this dance and music. Consequently, the Gagaku and Bugaku became the music of the court itself, both for ceremonial use and for entertainment. During the eighth century, a Gagaku institute was founded, and was directed on a national scale by professional musicians and officials. Many local variations of the Gagaku resulted, but a clear distinction was made between the local and foreign varieties. Those derived from India and China were called *Saho-no-mai.* In the eighteenth century, it was decided to designate only music of foreign origin as Gagaku, but at present the term embraces both foreign and indigenous dances. The Bugaku is still played in some Buddhist temples and shrines, but the formal stage for this art is found only in the Royal Palace. However, during its long journey from the Nara period Bugaku has influenced the music of Japan in a variety of ways, including the national anthem, as well as the *Kurodabushi,* a popular drinking song. These court dances and music are now extinct in India, their original home.

Japanese dance music is composed of eight, possibly more, pieces: *Bosatsu, Garyobin, Konju, Bairo, Bato, Riowo* (or *Ryo-o), Ama Ninomai,* and *Banshuraku.* Some of these names can be easily traced to Indian origins; for example, *Bosatsu* is the Japanese adaptation of Bodhisattva, *Bairo* of Bhairava, *Garyobin* of Kalavinka, a sonorous, sweet voiced bird. The *Riowo* dance, according to the famous scholar Takakusu, is a part of an ancient Indian opera, *Nagananda* (The Joy of the Snake) written by Emperor Harsha. I-tsing, during his pilgrimage to India, saw a performance of this music-drama and, presumably, it was he who brought it back to China, from where it was later transmitted to Japan.

The *no* plays of Japan were developed during the thirteenth to the fifteenth century from what was called *Dengaku-no-noh,* meaning field-music performance. The no owes its present form to two men: Kanami (1333–1384), who was a priest of the Kasuga Shrine near Nara, and his son Zeami (1363–1443), who was an outstanding actor, author, and composer. The intricate term *yugen,* meaning "what lies beneath the surface," which occurs throughout Zeami's writings, is derived from Zen literature. During the sixteenth century, comic interludes called *kyogen* were incorporated in the traditional no performances. Kyogen was the name of secular entertainments given to relieve the strain of long religious ceremonies and the term implies a prayer to the Buddha that the chatter of the mountebank may be transformed into a hymn of praise.

Certain analogies between Indian drama and the Japanese no play have been pointed out. Just as Indian drama was originally a combination of song and dance performed for inspiration at sacred festivals, so was the Japanese no. Again, the development of Indian drama was from narrative recitation to dialogue, first sung then spoken, just as in Japan the recitative of the "tonsured lutist" was followed by the sung and spoken dialogue of the no. Furthermore, in Indian drama the narrative connection was often preserved by interpreters whose function closely resembled that of the chorus in Japanese no. Both dramas were performed in the open courts of palaces or temples, and artificial scenery was necessarily absent. Neither drama considered it strange that a character should make journeys on stage. Both dramas excluded performance of the vulgar acts of life: actors did not die, eat, sleep, or make love on the stage. Indian dramatists invariably used classical phraseology which was generally incomprehensible to the majority of their audiences, just as no plays were written in the classical language of the period, although the kyogen used the common vernacular of the day.

By the seventeenth century the no play had become essentially an aristocratic art. However, Okuni, a woman dancer from the Buddhist shrine at Izumo, in the beginning of that century became the leader of a movement to expound and popularize Buddhist religious dances to the accompaniment of flute and drum. Through Okuni's originality of interpretation the dance took the form of a simple operetta, which appealed to the people. The new popular form was called *Kabuki.* The Kabuki borrowed extensively from the no plays, and eventually the no play became less exclusive and Kabuki less traditional.

Flowers, symbolizing joy, purity, and good luck, play an important role in Buddhist worship. Incense, light, and flowers are regarded as the best offerings to Buddhist deities, who are said to live surrounded by beautiful flowers; Buddhist images are always placed on a pedestal of lotus flower. The Goddess of Mercy, Kwannon-Bosatzu, always carries flowers in her hand. Various Buddhist ideas are expressed by the different colours of flowers; for example, white flowers denote safety and health, red respect, and yellow wealth. Inspired with religious fervour, the Japanese perfected their art of flower arrangement. This art was, indeed, one of the remarkable outcomes of the period of warriors. Its name, *ikebana* (living flower), explains the fundamental principle underlying the art: the flowers must be so arranged as to convey the idea of life, they should look as if they were growing, and not as though they had been cut. Preserving the living aspect of flowers is derived from the Buddhist injunction against the destruction of life.

The tea ceremony of Japan also has its origin in Buddhism. The ceremonial came from China, but its elaborate conventions and its complexity as practiced in Japan would be utterly alien to China. It became immensely popular during the mediaeval period of militarism. The principles of tea-making were prescribed by the celebrated Buddhist monk, Dagen. The etiquette observed during the tea ceremony ought to become part of daily routine because all outward formalities are merely expressions of the inner spirit. Tea must be offered with reverence, purity, and calmness of mind: an expression of Zen Buddhism. The history of tea in Japan goes back to the time of the Buddhist Emperor Shomu in the eighth century. It is said that tea was offered to the image of the Buddha, and after the service to the monks. Possibly, the use of tea was encouraged to keep the monks from drinking wine, as well as to keep them awake during long ceremonies.

The popular Japanese game of *sunoroku* or *sugoroku* (backgammon), played at the royal court of the Nara rulers and still popular in Japan, is of Indian origin. In Japan the game is played as nard. Nard is generally regarded as an Iranian game, but the ninth century Arab scholar, Al Yaqubi, considered nard an Indian invention used to illustrate man's dependence on chance and destiny. The board stands for the year, and it has twenty-four points for the hours of the day. It is divided into two halves, each of twelve points for the months in a year. The thirty men stand for the days in a month. The two dice are day and night, and the sum of opposite faces of the dice is seven for the days of the week. However, this symbolism was also known to Byzantine Greeks, and this fact disputes the theory of Indian origin. Whatever the paternity of nard, sugoroku came to Japan from India by way of Central Asia and China. *Shwan-liu,* the Chinese name for sugoroku was introduced into China from India in the seventh century, possibly earlier. According to *Wei-Shu,* sugoroku was brought to China in ancient times from Hu country, which at the time meant a country somewhere in the vicinity of India. Again, as Karl Himly has pointed out, the *Hun Tsun Sii,* written during the Sung period (960–1279), states that t'shu-pu, another Chinese name for sugoroku, was invented in western India, that it was known in its original form as *chatushpada,* and that it reached China during the Wei period (220–265).[23]

Because the whole framework of Japanese culture has been provided by Buddhism, it is only natural that the Japanese should take a deep interest in Indian studies. In modern times there are few countries where Indian studies are so widespread as in Japan. In 1881 a regular course in Indian philosophy was formally instituted at the University of Tokyo. In 1904 an independent chair of Indian philosophy was established in Tokyo. Also situated in Tokyo is the Centre for East Asian Cultural Studies under the directorship of the eminent scholar Naoshiro Tsuji. At other national universities, such as Kyushu, Hokkaido, Nagoya, and Osaka, Buddhism and Indian studies are systematically pursued. Consequently, there have emerged from Japan numerous Buddhist works and scholars of world repute.

In the changed political and cultural climate of Indo-Japanese relations after World War II, renewed interest in Indian studies developed in Japan, particularly in the exploration of the socio-political, as well as intellectual, background of early Buddhism. Consequently, Indian society and history are also studied at various universities in Japan. Hajime

Nakamura has played a significant role in this renewal of interest in Indian studies.

Japan's industrial and political achievements in this century have inspired the Indians, and Japan is playing an important role in the repatriation of Buddhism in India, as well as in Indian economic advancement. Buddhist studies in India have begun at university level, and much of what Indians now study comprises contributions made to Buddhist thought and literature by the Japanese and other Asians. Courses of Japanese language and literature have been established at Indian universities: for example at the Vishvabharati. The exchange of leading statesmen and scholars in recent years has also helped to reactivate cultural contact. The first president of the Republic of India, Rajendra Prasad, paid his first official visit to a foreign country when he visited Japan in 1958. In the same year, a Japan-India Society was founded in India to further the cultural ties between the two countries. Independent India declined to demand reparations from Japan after World War II, and indeed it offered to return all Japanese property which had been seized by the former British Government of India.

Chapter II

RED INDIANS OR ASIOMERICANS[1] — INDIAN FOAM ON PACIFIC WAVES

HISTORY IS FULL of misnomers; one such term is the New World, as applied to the Americas. The landing of Columbus in 1492 undoubtedly created a new life on the continents, but it neither created nor discovered a new world. Many centuries earlier, Asian migrants had come to the western shores in substantial numbers and in successive waves across the Bering Sea, as well as across the Pacific; later, the Europeans landed on the Atlantic coastline. The Norsemen or the Vikings founded a colony in Vinland in the early eleventh century on the eastern coast of America, probably as far south as present-day New England. And, according to the archaeological researches of Paul Norlund, who excavated bodies in Greenland that were clothed in mid-fifteenth century European garments, the contact between Europe and the American region continued until the so-called discovery of America.[2]

The first Maya Empire had been founded in Guatemala at about the beginning of the Christian era. Before the fall of Rome the Mayas were charting accurately the synodical revolutions of Venus, and whilst Europe was still lingering in the Dark Ages the Maya civilization had reached a peak of greatness.

The most significant development of the ancient American or Asiomerican culture took place in the south of the United States, in Mexico, in Central America, and in Peru. The early history of Asiomericans is shrouded in mystery and controversy due to the absence of definitive documentary evidence, which was destroyed by the European conquerors in their misguided religious zeal. However, it appears that after the discovery or introduction of maize into Mexico, Asiomericans no longer had to wander about in search of food. Men in America, as in other parts of the world, settled down to cultivate food, and culture, a byproduct of agricultural life, inevitably followed.

Of the Asiomerican civilizations, the best known are the Maya, the Toltec, the Aztec, and the Inca. The Mayas were possibly the earliest people to found a civilization there; they moved from the Mexican plateau into Guatemala. They were later pushed out, presumably by the Toltecs who, in turn, were dislodged by the Aztecs.

The Mayan civilization was certainly in existence in the early seventh century B.C., and there is strong evidence that it had existed prior to that time. According to their calendar, which is extant, the time record of the Mayas began on 6 August 613 B.C. It is an exact date, based upon intricate astronomical calculations, and prolonged observations. To work out this kind of elaborate calendar must have taken well over two thousand years of studying stars, and the Asiomericans must have been remarkably shrewd observers. The Mayan calendar was adopted by other Asiomerican civilizations: amongst them, the Aztecs.

Indeed, one of the most characteristic features of the Asiomerican culture has been the use of this calendar with certain variations in different ages and areas, dividing the year into eighteen months of twenty days with an additional month of only five days to complete the full 365 days of the solar year. The Mayas divided a month into twenty days, possibly because they counted by twenties instead of tens. Each month and day had a name, the days also being numbered progressively from one to thirteen, then starting again from one. The 365 days divided by thirteen left a remainder of one, but each of the thirteen numbers could begin the new year. Hence, it was not until fifty-two years had elapsed that a year could begin with the same day-name and numbers. Thirteen twenty-day months made another wholly arbitrary period of 260 days, which the Aztecs called *tonalamatl.* This system, with no basis in nature or astronomy, was a pure invention, a reckoning device. It ran simultaneously with the other astronomical 365-day calendar as two wheels of time. The two wheels came together again after fifty-two years.

The Aztecs adopted this fifty-two year cycle, and called it a "bundle of years" and two such cycles "an age."

Lacking accurate clocks, Asiomericans must have needed long periods of astronomical observations to calculate the mean duration of the day. They became aware of the increasing discrepancy between their calendar and the celestial phenomena, and succeeded in working out the error with remarkable accuracy. The Mayas calculated the length of a year to 365.2420 days; the present corrected Gregorian or New Style Calendar reckons it to 365.2425. Whilst Asiomericans did not interpolate any leap days, they computed the necessary correction at twenty-five days in 104 years or two calendar rounds. They brought the revolutions of the moon into accord with their day count with an error of only one day in three hundred years. In addition to this general division of the year, the Mayas were using a long count, connecting their dates with a zero point of their own, and "position numbers" for each day of a month. This zero date represented some unknown or mythical event or perhaps the day of creation, somewhat similar to the birth of Christ or the supposed date of the creation in 3761 B.C. of the Jewish calendar. Because the Mayas, unlike the Aztecs, did not content themselves with a fifty-two-year period but calculated time by *katuns* of twenty (a *katun* was equal to twenty *tuns* and a tun was equal to 360 days) and cycles of four hundred years, and because the dates of Maya inscriptions are mostly from their eighth, ninth, and tenth cycles, which roughly correspond to the first six centuries of the Christian era, their fixed zero date or tile starting point of their first cycle would be the cycle before 3000 B.C. The experts generally place it on or about 12 August 3113 B.C. There is, however, no absolute evidence at present to substantiate that their calculations of time had begun that early.

The calendar did not exhaust the astronomical and mathematical accomplishments of the Mayas. Although they did not know that the earth and Venus revolve about the sun, they had worked out that eight solar years correspond almost exactly with five years or the revolutions of 584 days each of Venus, and that sixty-five years of Venus coincide with 104 solar years. Indeed, in astronomy the Asiomericans, particularly the Mayas, reached the peak of their scientific achievement. They made remarkable accomplishments for a people without astronomical instruments, and without any real contact with other civilizations.

The Mayas of Yucatan were the first people besides the Indians to use a zero sign and represent number values by the position of basic symbols. The similarity between the Indian zero and the Mayan zero is indeed striking. So far as the logical principle is concerned, the two are identical but the expressions of the principle are dissimilar. Again, whilst the Indian system of notation was decimal, as was the European, the Mayan was vigesimal. Consequently, their 100 stood for 400, 1000 for 8000, 1234 for 8864, and so on. Whilst the place of zero in the respective systems of the Indians and the Mayas is different, the underlying principle and method are the same, and the common origin of the Mayan and Indian zeros appears to be undoubted. But dispute continues amongst scholars in the absence of any conclusive evidence, apart from that of cultural parallels. As chronological evidence stands today, the Mayan zero would appear to be anterior by several centuries to its Hindu counterpart.

The Mayas had a practical knowledge of physics and geometry, were exceptional draughtsmen, and used a form of hieroglyphics. They were also accomplished builders and artists. Their architecture, sculpture, and painting, especially of their peak period from 450 to 600, are skilfully and artistically conceived and executed.

It is significant that the zenith of Maya civilization was reached at a time when India had also attained an unparalleled cultural peak during the Gupta period, and Indian cultural intercourse with Southeast Asia, as well as with Central and East Asia, was exceptionally close. In fact, the Gupta period had begun more than a century before the Mayan classical age in 320 and Buddhism and Hinduism had been well known in neighbouring regions for several centuries. If there was contact between Mayan America and Indianized Southeast Asia, the simultaneous cultural advance would not appear surprising. In marked contrast, this was the darkest period in Europe's history between the sack of Rome and the rise of Charlemagne; China was in a prolonged state of political unrest following the collapse of the Han dynasty.

At the end of the twelfth century the Mayas of Yucatan were overthrown by Quetzalcoatl who came from the Mexican plateau. Thus began the period of the Toltecs or Master Builders' ascendancy in Asiomerican history. The Teotihuacan Toltecs were accomplished architects, carpenters, and mechanics. Their era saw the blossoming of a unified Central American civilization: the Toltecs were so prosperous that their foodstuffs were not even priced. Quetzalcoatl was king, hero, priest, astronomer, and the embodiment of all wisdom and compassion for his people. He is identified with gods, and a vast legend has developed around him. He adopted the Mayan calendar, reducing it to a system of signs and ideographs to make it comprehensible to the diverse peoples of Central America.

The succeeding era in Asiomerican history was a chaotic one, generally referred to as the period of Aztec supremacy, which lasted with varying degrees of authority until the Spanish conquest. Before their decline the Aztecs made some striking cultural advances. They developed a lake civilization based on the island in Lake Texcoco, where they built their remarkable city, Mexico-Tenochtitlan, which was linked to the shores by causeways, and surrounded by the colourful *Chinampas,* floating gardens which were really artificial islands made by scooping up mud from the marshy borders of the lake and holding it in place by a breastwork of reeds. The roots of the trees planted on them cemented the earth together. Thus the Aztecs converted the barren marshy land into a grid of waterways and productive areas. This city was described by Bernal Diaz, the companion of the Spanish commander Cortes, as a dreamland which inspired the Spanish invaders to lyrical adulation and murderous plunder. Diaz wrote that the Mexicans were like the Romans, and that there was nothing in Spain to match the royal palace of Montezuma.[3]

The Asiomericans had an advanced system of medicine and herbal remedies, including digitalis. They had extensive knowledge of the human body, its muscles, skeleton, and nervous system, and the Mayas were particularly skilled in treating eye diseases. The Aztecs had well-organized hospitals, which even their Spanish conquerors admired, and their sanitation system was so far in advance of anything the Spaniards had left behind in Europe that they were unable to operate it.

At the time of the Spanish conquest none of the nations of Europe was much superior to the Mexicans in botanical knowledge, and their botanical gardens were more elaborate than any in Europe. They had, in addition, developed an aesthetic appreciation of plants, and the Valley of Mexico was full of cultivated flowers. Their cultivation of crops was also highly skilled and sophisticated.

By the time of the Spanish conquest in 1519, however, the Aztec Empire had degenerated to the extent that the Spanish triumph and its accompanying ruthless slaughter and destruction appeared less savage than they really were. Past-master of intrigue, betrayal, and wholesale massacre in Cholula, the most important sanctuary in pre-Columbian America, Cortes slaughtered, in less than two hours, six thousand people who had gathered in a temple patio. Destruction of Aztec cities was so complete that almost everything lay in ruins. The elite of the Asiomericans were put to death almost to the last man. After his entry into the conquered capital Tenochtitlan, Cortes wrote that "you could not put down your foot without stepping on an Indian corpse." In addition, his soldiery, as that of Pizarro a few years later in the Inca Empire, driven by their lust for gold, melted down irreplacable works of art by the ton to get the precious metal. The Aztec civilization thus came to a violent end, but the Aztecs live even now, for without their Asiomerican ancestry and heritage, there would be no Mexican people or civilization today.

If the history of pre-Columbian America is obscure, it is because after the Spanish conquest, the first Bishop of Mexico, Juan de Zumarraga, burned all the records of the Library of Texcoco in Tlatelolco market square as "the work of the devil," and religious fanatics destroyed temples and statues. Zumarraga, gloating over his success, wrote to his superiors in 1531 that he alone had had five hundred temples razed to the ground and twenty thousand idols destroyed. Diego de Landa, the second Bishop of Yucatan, following the pattern, reduced the Maya Library in Yucatan to ashes in 1562. These libraries contained records of ancient history, medicine, astronomy, science, religion, and philosophy. What Emperor Theodosius of Constantinople did to the library at Alexandria to save Christianity from the Greek and Oriental pagan knowledge deposited there, these priests did in Central America with similar motives but larger success. The burning of manuscripts continued for decades. Soldiers were encouraged to ransack palaces, public buildings, and private houses to find manuscripts. Pablo Jose de Arriaga, the head of the Jesuit College in Peru, in almost unparalleled fanaticism, caused the systematic and wholesale destruction of all state archives, customs records, royal and imperial archives, codes of laws, temple archives, and historical records. Less than a score of manuscripts escaped annihilation.

The Spaniards destroyed whatever they could, but they could not, for instance, burn the great Pyramid of the Sun and the remains of Teotihuacan, which speak of the splendid bygone civilization. The memory as well as the material evidence of Asiomerican past greatness was lost in the excitement of the discovery and conquest of the new and rich lands offering prospects for migration. No matter how much historians stretch their imagination, it will never be possible to reconstruct a picture of these advanced civilizations which would do them justice, and yet be held historically acceptable. Thus, today the sources of ancient Mexican history comprise about ten codices or books of pictures written principally in ideographs but also in the partially phonetic representation of Nahuatl, the language of the Aztecs and Toltecs; some folios written by Asiomericans in the Nahuatl language using the Latin alphabet manage to salvage something of their folklore, literature, and archaeological findings.

Beyond Mexico to the south flourished the civilization of the Incas in Peru, which remained stable and prosperous for at least three centuries prior to its subjugation by Spain. The ancient Andean or Peruvian civilization also has an obscure history, although there is enough evidence to support its existence and general nature. The first known Inca chief was Sinchi Roca, who possibly began his rule in 1105. The Incas suffered an even worse fate at the hands of the Spaniards than did their neighbours in Central America. The Spanish assault on the Incas, the Spanish avarice for gold, and the barbarities perpetrated in the wake of victory, including the inhuman tortures publicly inflicted on the Inca King, Atahuallpa, are illustrations of savagery seldom surpassed in history. So complete was the destruction of historical materials pertaining to the Peruvian culture that there are no extant records except those left by the Spaniards; these are, of course, terribly inadequate and partisan. Perhaps the Incas did not have a written language in the generally accepted sense of the term.

Despite the Spanish conquerors, the Inca culture survives today. Inca government, based on a unique village system, was remarkable even by modern standards. The village was not only a community of people but a communion of these people with the soil; there was complete identification between men and land. They were skilled farmers, and it is said that the Incas lived as if they were to die the next day but farmed as if they were to live forever. The soil belonged to the community of the people, but the metals underneath were state property. In criminal law, which was rather severe, the Incas made a distinction between stealing for want or necessity and stealing from malice or avarice. Of the two, the latter was a capital offence, but the former entailed punishment of the offender's village official for allowing his administration to create a situation in which theft became necessary.

The Inca communication and road systems were elaborate. Two main roads ran the length of the kingdom, one along the coast and the other in the highlands, whilst transverse roads connected all the important towns. The coast or Royal Road ran through the Andes south through Ecuador, Peru, Bolivia, Argentina, and Chile. It covered about three and a quarter thousand miles, which makes it longer than the longest Roman road which ran from Hadrian's Wall, separating England from Scotland to Jerusalem. Baron Von Humboldt claimed that as an engineering feat, the Inca road system surpassed that of the Romans.[4]

Little is known of the pre-Inca Meche and Chimu cultures, except what can be gleaned from archaeological remains. But these speak eloquently of their skills, ingenuity, and accomplishments. The dry desert climate along the coast has preserved surprisingly well the remains of its early inhabitants, including bones, textiles, pottery, and temples. The Moches perhaps developed a means of communication by signs incised on lima beans, and their pottery is particularly interesting. The canals and aqueducts, bringing water from the mountains to irrigate the parched coastal valleys, speak highly of their engineering skill; the aqueduct at Ascope is nearly a mile long and fifty feet high. Their carefully controlled hydraulic system in the fields was, perhaps, even more remarkable. If the water flowed too fast, it could erode the banks; if it flowed too slowly, it could silt up the conduits. By control of the imported water, terracing, and natural fertilizer, the desert was made productive enough to support a population far larger than any living there since.

Why did the Aztecs and the Incas submit to such inhuman and merciless punishment from the Spaniards, and how was it that a handful of mercenaries and adventurers were allowed to wipe out the highly advanced civilization of an entire continent? The Spaniards had four hundred men, fifteen horses, and seven light guns, whilst Montezuma had at his command thousands of brave, experienced warriors with bows and arrows, as well as the macquaitl sword which was so sharp that it could lop off a human head with a single stroke. The Aztecs and the Incas did not offer any resistance at first, allowing the Spaniards to roam the streets, enter the most sacred places, destroy the idols they so fervently worshipped, and even capture King Montezuma in the midst of his own people. It was not fear that kept them submissive, for the Asiomericans did eventually resist. The only explanation that appears somewhat convincing is that the Asiomericans believed that at some period of their prehistory, white men with beards had landed on their shores and had given them all their knowledge. They were the white gods, who had left with a promise to return one day. Hence, the Spaniards were mistaken by Asiomericans for their legendary white gods, who were to be made welcome, and if they inflicted suffering it was to be accepted as a divine judgement. And, by a tragic coincidence, the Spanish conquerors invaded Mexico at about the time, in 1519, as the Aztec priests and tradition had predicted the return of the white gods.[5] The Aztecs even offered the Spanish conquistadores the vestments of Quetzalcoatl and other gods and considered performing human sacrifice to them in case they were fatigued after such a long journey. Throughout the Inca Empire, the Spaniards were greeted as *Viracocha,* the Inca name of the great White God they had been waiting for. It is only when the Asiomericans were completely horrified and disillusioned by the brutalities and merciless killings, that they recognized their mistake. The realization that the Spaniards were not gods but *popolocas* (barbarians), however, came too late.

The European conquerors of South and Central America not only destroyed practically all the records and literature of Asiomerica, but created an utterly distorted image of the American past by taking some of its ugly features out of context and magnifying them out of proportion. For instance, the human sacrifice practiced by the Aztecs was repeatedly stressed without explaining its extenuating features, and without pointing out that human sacrifice had not been unknown to other peoples, such as in Egypt and Rome. Taking their technique a step farther they contrasted this picture with that of their own deeds in Asiomerica in which European misdemeanour, caprice, and criminality were soft-pedalled and civilized and humane behaviour emphasized. No wonder the Asiomerican past did not attract much attention and even today remains popularly unknown and historically uncertain. Most people believe that Asiomericans were uncivilized hordes with an occasional freak of knowledge, who had contributed nothing of permanent value to civilization by 1492. Despite a good deal of information to the contrary, there is resistance to accepting a change in this image. Misconceptions multiply fast but die slowly.

In the second half of the eighteenth century explorers and historians began to take an interest in America's ancient history. Alexander Von Humboldt was the first man to recognize the Inca and Aztec civilizations in their own right, and the first to give a serious account of their religious traditions. He also saw the manifestations of artistic achievement in Aztec monuments.

As interest grew, many explorers and writers gave their lifetimes and even their fortunes to reconstructing America's past. Lord Edward Kingborough, who attempted unsuccessfully to prove that Asiomericans were one of the ten lost tribes of Israel, painstakingly collected enormously valuable data and published nine volumes of his *Antiquities of Mexico* between 1831 and 1848, but ended in a debtors' prison. Yet, without his work the ancient American history would be much poorer.

Good luck played a part in John Lloyd Stephens' discovery of the first major complex of pyramids, temples, and terraces covering twelve acres—the Copan ruins in Honduras—in November 1839. He bought the site from the local owner for fifty dollars, and although Stephens was not a professional archaeologist but an American lawyer and antiquarian, his find opened the way to Asiomerican archaeology. Edward Herbert Thompson discovered the Chichen Itza in 1855, with its brilliant temples, pyramids, and sculpture. Soon, others pursued similar work with as much devotion as skill and competence.[6] Amongst the pioneer scholars, the works of William Prescott, who wrote during the second quarter of the nineteenth century, are commonly accepted as standard writings.[7] They are still of incalculable value and in some respects remain unsurpassed, certainly in the English language.

However, such was the nature of the discoveries and research that it was inevitable that this subject should have lent itself to divergent interpretations and conflicting opinions. In this battle, not only historians, anthropologists, archaeologists, and, of necessity, scientists, especially botanists, actively participate, but also institutions and Church organizations, such as the Rosicrucians, the Theosophists, and the Church of Jesus Christ of Latter-day Saints (the Mormons), maintain strong positions. It is indeed ironic that the world should have so little information about the origins and early civilization of a people who first cultivated the food its inhabitants eat in various regions; after all, civilization began as a result of cultivation. Potatoes, maize, beans, yams, squash, mangoes, peanuts, cashews, pineapples, cacao, avocados, tomatoes, peppers, papaya, strawberries, and blackberries, are all Asiomerican contributions to civilization.

Much of the discussion revolves around the origin of man in America, and consequently early civilizations of ancient America. It is generally conceded that man is not indigenous to America, for no anthropoid apes, the ancestors of man, either extant or fossil, have been found in America. The absence of such remains, however, is not definite proof of their non-existence, yet, until such evidence turns up, the theory of indigenous Americans would remain untenable. Even the theory of Continental Drift, propounded by Wegener in 1912, which has recently been considerably reinforced by studies in rock-magnetism, and which claimed that the world was once a solid land mass that broke up into continents and islands, may explain certain facts of geology, geography, and prehuman biology, such as South American monkeys, but cannot account for man's presence on the American continent. For the continents would have drifted away from each other before any form of man existed in terms other than those of his simian ancestors. Even if man had existed originally in America, this cannot exclude the possibility of early human migration, of which there is undoubted evidence. But the great debate that has already lasted for centuries continues and seldom has so much bitterness, so much militancy, not principally overlaid by nationalistic passion, been noted in academic disputes as in this one.

Some of the theories which have been advanced to account for the presence of the Asiomericans on the continents are hardly more than extravagant assumptions. Of those that have enjoyed popularity at one time or another, the following are regarded as major hypotheses. Some religious zealots have suggested that Asiomericans are the descendants of the Lost Tribes of Israel who had wandered to America. This theory was something of a fad with the earliest explorers. On the other hand, the eighteenth and early nineteenth-century classicists liked to find Carthaginian-Phoenician traits in Asiomerican culture. Later, the Egyptian origin theory became the favourite, and even now enjoys occasional currency.

Of the numerous Egyptian enthusiasts, the most devoted was Augustus Le Plongeon, whose intellectual arrogance and egotism initiated a militancy, acrimony, and bickering in this academic debate which has filled proceedings of numerous congresses of Americanists and pages of historical writings. But he died a disappointed and discarded scholar. After him, the greatest champion of Egyptian origins was Elliot Smith, who wrote *Elephants and Ethnologists,* and who was ably supported by William Perry. They amassed a staggering body of evidence in their support, but before they could gain general acceptance of their theory, they were confronted by one of the most meticulous of scholars, Ronald B. Dixon, who minutely scrutinized their evidence. His verdict was categorically against this theory which was seriously discredited, despite the bitter counterattack against Dixon. Yet, this Egyptian theory, in complete disregard of professional and scholarly opinion, stubbornly persists, presumably because Egyptian archaeology is so well known to European scholars, and because they are so used to tracing their own early culture to Egypt. It is one of those academic irrationalities which has gradually built up immunity to its own antidotes.

Similarly, two other schools, the Lost Tribes of Israel and the Lost Continent of Atlantis, have substantial supporters who refuse to respond to the weight of evidence to the contrary. Both these beliefs use Egyptian parallels with ancient America but claim that Egypt acted only as an intermediary. The Lost Tribes of Israel theory is held by, amongst others, the Mormons, and members of other religious organizations. The theory of the Lost Continent of Atlantis is almost as old as the Columbian discovery of America itself. It was championed by Gonzalo Fernandez de Oviedo y Valdes in 1535, and later held by many eminent European scholars. As late as 1924 and 1925 it was effectively advocated by H. Lewis Spence in his works, *Atlantis in America* and *The Problem of Atlantis*. This theory of Lost Atlantis continues to be a favourite and is revived now and then by new editions of the Spence and Ignatius Donnelly best sellers. There is a Pacific counterpart of Atlantis, popularly called Mu, or the lost continent of Lemuria. Its best known exponent was James Churchward, who published his last book on the subject in 1931. The idea of the lost continent of Atlantis providing a partial land bridge from Europe or Africa to America, or that of a transatlantic sea-migration which would conveniently explain the vague affinity between the Aztec and Mayan calendar systems and those of the Nile Valley, or that of a Pacific Ocean lost continent, Mu, linking Asia with America, are all far too speculative to merit serious attention.

A post-war theory of Thor Heyerdahl, widely known as *Kon-Tiki*, bravely supported by a daring voyage on a balsa raft, advances the view that Asiomericans sailed westwards across the Pacific and populated Polynesia. Heyerdahl does not deny, however, the Indonesian or Melanesian origin of the present Polynesian race and culture, but suggests that Indonesian culture reached Polynesia through a circuitous northern route via Japan, America, and thence to Polynesia. Before Heyerdahl, a Spanish missionary, J. de Zuniga, in 1803, and a British missionary, William Ellis, in the 1830's had similarly suggested that the eastern group of Polynesian islands was peopled from America.

An Atlantic Kon-tiki was proposed by De Bourbourg, who argued that the Egyptian civilization was derived from the Atlantean colonists from America. Recently a view has been put forward that the Mayan script came from Crete and the entire civilization revolves round the emergence of a White God in ancient America, who may have come from the Western world.

Some scholars, such as A. Hyatt Verrill, believe that men came to America in a variety of ways, some from Europe via Greenland, others across the Atlantic, some from Lost Atlantis or southern Europe, some via the Bering Straits, and many more across the Pacific. He suspected that professional archaeologists suppressed information contrary to their theories.

An eminent amateur anthropologist, Harold S. Gladwin, who also distrusted the common sense of the professionals, wrote in his book *Men Out of Asia*, of a series of waves of migrants going out from the various parts of Asia to settle in ancient America. He also suggested that after the death of Alexander in 323 B.C., some survivors of the wrecked fleet under Nearchus sailed eastwards, picked up artisans from India and Southeast Asia, crossed the Pacific and reached America, where they and their descendants founded the ancient civilizations. Whilst the feasibility of such a voyage cannot be conclusively refuted, it is not generally accepted.

Without diverting attention from subtle distinctions, it may be said that all these divergent opinions fall into two broad groups—the transatlanticites, who believe in western migration across the Atlantic, and the transpacificites who support Asian settlers having gone across the Pacific either through a northern route, a middle route or both. Of these, the former view has been considerably challenged by later researches, but lingers on.

Divergent views prevail amongst the enthusiasts of the Asian origins of Asiomericans. Baron Von Humboldt, whilst visiting Mexico, found similarities between Asian and Mexican astrology.[8] He founded the systematic study of ancient American cultures and was convinced of the Asian origin of the American-Indian high civilization. He said, "if languages supply but feeble evidence of ancient communication between the two worlds, their communication is fully proved by the cosmogonies, the monuments, the hieroglyphical characters and the institutions of the people of America and Asia."[9] In 1761 a French scholar, De Guignes, published his opinion that some Buddhits were sent from China to Mexico, which was identified as Fu-Sang in early Chinese annals, in the fifth century. He appears to have based his hypothesis on the tradition of a Chinese legend which spoke of a Buddhist priest, Hwui Shan, who was said to have come from ancient America. Later, H. J. Von Klaproth endeavoured to disprove this theory on the grounds that the monk in question had come from southeastern Japan, and not from America. Many scholars since, however, especially from France and some from Germany, have rallied round the theory of Buddhist influence. M. de Paravey renewed the theory of Buddhist influence in 1844. A year later, a German orientalist, Friedrich de Neuman supported the view. Rivero and Tschudi urged that Quetzalcoatl in Mexico and Mango-Capac in Peru were Indian missionaries. Channing Arnold and F. J. T. Frost even traced the chronological passage of Buddhism from India to Central America. They argued that as Buddhism had spread all over eastern Asia by the eighth century, it was rightly poised to launch itself farther eastward across the sea.

Considering that at this time Buddhism was flourishing in Southeast Asia, as well as in China and Japan, and was backed actively by powerful Asian kingdoms, such as that of the Khmers, it would not appear surprising that some Buddhist monks had voyaged across the Pacific. Meanwhile, John Ranking, in his *Historical Researches on the Conquest of Peru, Mexico etc.*, suggested in 1827 that the Inca Empire was founded by the crews of a few ships of Kublai Khan wrecked and driven across the Pacific. In 1834, John Dunmore Lang, a minister of the Scots Church at Sydney, declared that Polynesians had crossed the Pacific Ocean from Easter Island to America under a violent gale of westerly wind, landing somewhere near Copiapo in Chile. It was the descendants of these Polynesians, he claimed, who progressively populated and civilized the whole continent of America from Cape Horn to Labrador.[10] In 1836, J. Mackintosh favoured the view that· Koreans were the first to visit ancient America. In 1866, the French architect, Viollet-le-Duc, also noted striking resemblances between ancient Mexican structures and those of South India.

All these scholars were also greatly impressed by the similarity between the Hindu Trinity—Brahma-Visnu-Siva—and the Mexican Trinity—Ho-Huizilopochtli-Tlaloc—as well as the likeness between Indian temples and American pyramids. Later, two English scholars, Channing Arnold and Frederick J. Tabor Frost, in their *The American Egypt,* made a detailed examination of the transpacific contacts, reinforcing the view of Buddhist influences on Central America. In 1947, Harold S. Gladwin suggested successive waves of Asian migrants belonging to specific archaeological cultures and linguistic groups, including Alexander's sailors. The most recent and by far the most systematic, well-reasoned, and effective case has been advanced by the eminent archaeologists, R. Heine-Geldern and Gordon Ekholm, who favour Indian and Southeast

Asian cultural influences on ancient America through migrations across the Pacific.

It is likely that man first came to America from Asia towards the end of the last glacial period, probably between twenty thousand and ten thousand years ago, across the Bering Straits. He may have gone by sea or, more likely, crossed on ice. The water distance is only about sixty miles, interrupted by the Diomede Island almost in the middle of the gap, and ice may have paved the whole way at the time. The Aleutian Islands have also been suggested as a route of migration, but the chain of islands is long, and the gap at the western end of about a hundred miles would have required skilful negotiation. Whether there was a land bridge so far south of the Bering Straits is questionable because of the ocean depths of ten to twenty thousand feet. Long before, in geological antiquity, there was a land bridge from Siberia to Alaska which horses, camels, cattle, elephants, deer, and other species had crossed. This, however, does not explain human migration, for man's entry belongs to a much later period when the two continents had probably separated.

There are just as many conflicting opinions about the Bering Straits theory as any other. Arguments in favour of the theory are: many Asiomericans share physical characteristics with North Asians; even today there is some migration between northeastern Asia and the extreme tip of northwestern Alaska; and, distinctively Asian dialects are spoken by many Alaskan and northwestern American tribes. Examples of arguments against this theory are: the physical characteristics of it race are likely to be altered by environment, or admixture of blood with other races if encountered during the course of migration; not all Indians of North, Central, and South America possess Mongoloid or North Asian features; the Asian dialects disappear completely as soon as one goes far from the northwestern coast tribes.

Widely distributed over the vast continent, Asiomericans show considerable ethnic diyersity. Generally speaking, Asiomericans are yellowish or reddish brown in skin-colour, and usually have coarse black hair, broad faces with prominent cheek-bones, and often a well-developed chin. They are described broadly as Mongoloids, but they are a composite race. Whilst they have some characteristic Mongoloid features, they lack others. For example, the pigmentation of their skin, usually darker than that of the Asians and sometimes more reddish than yellow, their hair-form, and their facial size are Mongoloid, but the Mongoloid eye-fold appears only occasionally. Their eyes do not slant. Their browridges are often well-developed, whilst the Mongoloid forehead is typically smooth. The nose of any American Indian is very rarely as flat as that of a typical Mongoloid; it may be hooked, straight, or sometimes concave. The hawk-nose of so many of the Asiomericans is, in fact, recognized as inherently Aryan, associated with the races of the Iranian plateau. Asiomerican types have also been identified with the Dravidians of the Indus Valley. There is concrete evidence to support the belief that many of the early American peoples were of Indo-European stock. For instance, the Toltecs, apart from various references to bearded white gods, were, as Edward Tylor has pointed out, large of stature and fair in complexion. In contrast, the Aztecs of later times were small and dark.

Again, the Sirionos of Bolivia, an isolated, primitive tribe with slightly wavy, fine hair and great bushy beards, who bear no resemblances at all to any other known Asiomerican tribe, resemble Polynesians. Also amongst nearly all the tribes of western South America are found words—not one or two but scores—which are strikingly like and, in many cases identical with, words of the same meanings in Oceanian dialects. In some of their arts, habits, and religious beliefs there is a great similarity between the Polynesians and the Asiomericans of western South America. The evidence of blood grouping would indicate kinship between the Asiomericans of North America and Polynesians. They share a relatively high incidence of M, and they also share some of the highest known frequencies of the rhesus gene cDE. This similarity may imply transpacific contact.

In the 1930's, Baron Erland Nordenskiold noted numerous cultural traits—forty-nine to be exact—common to both South America and the Pacific islands. This could have been due either to accidental or deliberate migrations from Polynesia to America, or simply to parallel and independent growth. It is significant, however, that four-fifths of these common traits were found in Colombia and Panama, the precise areas where Polynesian sailors would land if they were drifting with the Equatorial Counter-current.

This evidence would seem to support the view that during the course of the uncounted thousands of years, successive waves of immigrants spread over the two continents of America. The migrants had clearly been filtering across Asia and had added to their respective characteristics—Eurafrican or Dravidian or Iranian—traits which they shared with the Mongols. Gladwin, pointing out that the Americas are populated by many different kinds of men, recounts no less than five successive migratory waves of Pygmies, Australoid Negroid, Mongoloid and Melanesian-Polynesian peoples to America.

At the time of the discovery of America, there were perhaps thirty million Asiomericans distributed over the two Americas, comprising more than six hundred distinct societies. Hence, it would require far more time than is usually allowed for a few nomadic people to multiply, develop an ethnic admixture, spread from the Arctic Circle to Cape Horn, and to give rise to the diversity of tribes, dialects, customs, and beliefs found amongst the original inhabitants of America.

As THE INQUIRY into the cultural past of ancient America has to rely heavily on anthropological data, its students have come to reflect the controversies that divide anthropologists. Broadly speaking, cultural historians of Asiomerica are divided into two camps, "diffusionists" and "evolutionists." The former believe in an early diffusion of Asian and Pacific culture through America, whilst the latter assert the independent and local development of the American-Indian culture. Inevitably both sides have their relentless and uncompromising champions many of whom, by reversing the process of historical scrutiny, mould evidence to fit their conclusions, rather than draw conclusions from actual material. There are some extremely plausible arguments on both sides but it appears that more and more material is coming to light reinforcing the diffusionist theory.

According to the evolutionist, man, being a creative animal, can invent in one place as easily as he can in another. And under similar circumstances and needs, and at similar cultural levels, widely distributed men can produce similar inventions. Hence, identity in achievements is no evidence of cultural borrowing. The diffusionists accept the fundamental basis of this assertion, but go a good deal further in interpretation. They argue that whilst coincidences are possible, identical complex inventions in details of common cultural trends cannot be purely coincidental. In any case, for every instance of parallelism, many more of diffusion—almost in the ratio of one to a hundred—can be traced in history.

In the second half of the nineteenth century ideas based on Adolf Bastian's concept of the *Elementargedanke,* psychic unity of mankind, captured the imagination of anthropologists. Whilst Bastian recognized the importance of geographical conditions on the development of culture, he did not ascribe any creative power to them; they could only modify a culture, not create one. Hence, he explained the sameness of thought in widely separated lands as due to the similarity of the psychic structure of man the world over. However, the evolutionists appear to have disregarded Bastian's stress on the similarity in elementary ideas and on his admission that at a higher stage contact with other cultures might constitute a superior external stimulus. As they interpreted this theory, the psychic unity, together with the similarity of circumstances in which culture tends to develop, was bound to lead to parallel and independent developments which produced similar or even identical results. Even the most highly complex beliefs and myths were regarded as natural products of the human mind. The underlying thought of these conceptions was that the manifestation of ethnic life represents a time series, which progresses from simple beginnings to complex modern civilization.

The publication of *The Origin of Species* in 1859 and the popularity of Charles Darwin's concept of evolution also had repercussions on the writing of cultural history. Cultural historians borrowed the concept of evolution from ethnologists, who in turn had borrowed it from biology and applied it, somewhat indiscriminately, to cultural phenomena. In their zeal to make use of new-found knowledge, nineteenth century anthoropologists failed to reflect sufficiently on the capacity of man, as of all living beings, as Darwin himself had pointed out, to respond to changing environmental conditions and to improve his position. Only now has anthropological inquiry begun to note the concepts of function and adaptation. Broadly speaking, evolutionist historians applied the theory of evolution to culture in the same way as it is applied to biological organisms; one form grows out of another. Elaborate arts, complex institutions, and abstruse knowledge were held to be the results of gradual development from an earlier and simpler form.

The earliest pioneers of cultural evolutionism, Herbert Spencer, Edward Tylor, and Morgan, however, were somewhat anterior to Darwin, although their ideas gathered force after Darwin had published his thesis. In 1852, Spencer had published a paper, *Development Hypothesis,* a brilliant defence of the theory of organic evolution which laid the beginnings of cultural evolutionism. Edward Tylor pioneered cultural evolutionism in Britain and introduced the term culture into anthropological literature as a specific technical term. He was, however, always willing to concede transmission of cultural traits if he were satisfied with the evidence. Franz Boas (1858–1942), whilst accepting the validity of the concept of evolution in biology, was opposed to its application to cultural history. He could not accept the contention that cultural similarities were the outcome of identical processes, because it was based on the assumption that the human mind behaves identically everywhere. He had wide support amongst fellow anthropologists.

England was the main home of evolutionist theories and, despite its far-flung empire, it remained partial to its island mentality and isolationist theories long after the weight of opinion had moved away from evolutionism elsewhere. Whilst on the Continent evolutionist concepts had been considerably discredited by the last quarter of the last century, it was not until 1911 that W. H. Rivers, a leading British exponent of evolutionism, announced his conversion to diffusionism. Since then evolutionist concepts, which were found very convenient by writers seeking to fan nationalist-purism, have lost much of their impact, although the discussion has by no means ended either amongst ethnologists or historians. With some exceptions, mainly in Britain, most historians today seem to agree with V. Gordon Childe in making a clear distinction between cultural evolution and biological evolution and oppose notions of total parallelism in cultural growth.[11]

The opposition to the isolationist theory gained credence in 1949, when two eminent scholars, Robert Heine-Geldern and Gordon F. Ekholm, presented overwhelming evidence of innumerable Asian-Pacific-American similarities before the Congress of Americanists at New York.

The theory of identically independent cultural development in distant lands can be, as it has often been, taken too far. Like any other people, Asiomericans, no doubt, have made original contributions to civilization, such as rubber and numerous foods, including the development of tapioca from a poisonous root called manioc, but it is a very different matter to independently duplicate those inventions previously made in other parts of the world. It seems almost unbelievable that the evolutionists are prepared to concede to Asiomericans what is not conceded to the inhabitants of the British Isles nor to Europeans in general. No serious and non-partisan scholar today credits prehistoric Europe with having independently invented the wheel, bronze-casting, writing, pottery, weaving, and similarly important innovations. Europe borrowed them from Asia. Thus, whilst Europe invented with the assistance of Asian experience and heritage, ancient America is not supposed to have borrowed from or been influenced by anyone else. What is still more baffling is the premise that a series of complex techniques, such as casting by the lost wax method, the extraction of tin from cassiterite, the alloying of copper and tin, the colouring of gold by chemical processes, weaving, tie-dying, and batik could have been invented twice, independently of each other, in two different areas of the world.

Whilst the diffusionist theory has been gaining popular support, there is no conclusive evidence to dissuade the isolationist or evolutionist. Whatever evidence there is, is fragmentary, insufficient, and mainly in the form of parallels between the cultures of Asia and ancient America. But these parallels are so many and so close in detail, that the theory of contact and exchange is quite logical. Many of these similarities, identified as emanating from a single source, belong to much later periods, cutting well into historical times, and suggest that periodic migrations from Asia to America continued to take place until the first century, and possibly later. Many of the Asian parallels with America are of Indian origin. As direct migration from India has not been suggested, it is claimed that diffusion of Indian ideas and cultural traits took place through the media of China and especially Southeast Asia.

The first Asians to travel to America during prehistoric times were perhaps East Asians. The archaeological work done since 1961 on the Pacific Coast at Valdivia in Ecuador, by scholars such as Emilio Estrada,

Betty J. Meggers, and Clifford Evans, has added considerably to the documentation of similarities between South America and eastern Asia, and suggests that the Japanese crossed the Pacific in prehistoric times. Pottery made by shellfish-gathering people of Ecuador and that of Japan (Honshu island)—both belonging to the same period of prehistory, between 3000 and 2000 B.C.—are very similar. Whilst Valdivian pottery is different from other early Asiomerican artifacts and archaeological finds, it is very close to the pottery from the Jomon period of Japan which would suggest Japanese landings in Ecuador. Other items, belonging to a much later period, the last two centuries B.C., include pottery, house models with certain alien architectural features, neck rests, seated figurines, symmetrically graduated Pan pipes, net weights, ear ornaments, coolie yokes, and sea-going rafts with centreboards.

The first Asians to travel to America during historical times were possibly the Chinese, as is suggested by some of the sculptures of the Chavin culture, the oldest of the higher civilizations of Peru. This most ancient site of all the American civilizations discovered so far, was not found until 1941. It was discovered by Julio C. Tello, the Asiomerican archaeologist, and derived its name from Chavin de Huantar in the north Peruvian highlands. Chavin sculptures show motifs which closely correspond to those found only in China of the ninth and eighth century B.C. (848 B.C. ± 167 years), which corresponds exactly with the date of the Chavin culture as determined by the Carbon-14 method.

There was no prior local tradition, no bridge or direct transition from an earlier beginning to explain satisfactorily the evolution of this era of Chavin culture. It appeared suddenly, embracing the whole of Peru and producing works of art that were inspired by profound religious feeling. Maize (radio carbon dating 714 B.C. ± 200 years) and decorated ceramics for ceremonial use also appeared in Peru during this period. Traces of metal (gold only) and weaving appeared for the first time in South America during this period. The art of the goldsmith required metallurgical techniques, such as hammering, embossing, annealing, welding, soldering, strap joining, incising, champleve, and cut-out designs. From where did these techniques suddenly emerge? Whilst scholars such as Heine-Geldern suspect a Chinese link, Vale and Clifford Evans suggest Central America, and Julio C. Tello favours its local evolution. Archaeological investigations on this site have to be carried further before puzzling questions can be, if at all, resolved.

The art of the following period, the Salinar culture at El Salinar in Chicarna Valley, again contains motifs that correspond with those of seventh and sixth centuries B.C. China. Chinese influences probably came from the ancient eastern states of Wu, in the lower part of the Yangtze Valley, and Yueh, in modern Chekiang. After some interruption, presumably caused by the unsettled conditions in China, it appears that Asians resumed migratory voyages from the coasts of Vietnam and traces of Dong-son culture are far more numerous in South America than those of Chinese influence. These migrations, possibly, came to an end with the conquest of Tonkin and north Annam by China during the first century.

It appears that the vacuum created by the disappearance of Vietnamese and Chinese transpacific voyages to South America was filled by the Indianized peoples of Southeast Asia. This view has gained strength from the recent researches of Heine-Geldern and Ekholm. They have unearthed astonishing parallels in architecture and art, religious symbols, cosmological theories, government institutions and royal courts, insignia of kings and dignitaries, and even games. The contacts between Cambodia and the Maya and Olmec areas seem to have been particularly close from the seventh to the tenth century and it is likely that they more or less continued until the fall of the Kambuja Empire before the Thai incursions.

Indeed, the parallels between the arts and culture of India and those of ancient America are too numerous and close to be attributed to independent growth. A variety of art forms are common to Mexico, India, Java, and Indo-China, the most striking of which are the *Teocallis,* the pyramids, with receding stages, faced with cut stone, and with stairways leading to a stone sanctuary on top. Many share surprisingly common features such as serpent columns and banisters, vaulted galleries and corbeled arches, attached columns, stone cut-out lattices, and Atlantean figures; these are typical of the Puuc style of Yucatan. Heine-Geldern and Ekholm point out that temple pyramids in Cambodia did not become important until the ninth and tenth centuries, a time coinciding with the beginning of the Puuc period. The use of half columns flanking the doors and of groups of small columns set in panels is characteristic of both the Cambodian and Mayan civilizations. Atlantean figures, which appeared in India in the second century B.C., are found at Tula in Central Mexico and Chichen Itza in the tropical forest of Yucatan.

The oldest Mayan city to be excavated was Uaxactun, where the first Mayan observatory was found, and also the oldest Mayan fresco. Quite near Uaxactun was the city Tikal, where archaeologists have found colossal mounds of rubble and immense buildings, including five of the steepest pyramids that have ever been seen; the tallest rose to a height of two hundred and thirty feet with the temple standing at the very top. Similar towering, narrow pyramids are found in the ancient Cambodian city, Angkor Thom.

Mayan art reached its highest point in the cities of Yaxchilan, Palenque, and Piedras Negras. Numerous pyramids and sculptures have been excavated there. One of the best pieces of Mayan sculpture in the pyramid temple of Piedras Negras, Guatemala, appears to be a Buddhist scene. The subject matter of the scene is not clear but the theme is somewhat alien to Mexican art tradition. It bears remarkable likeness to a Jataka bas-relief of the Borobudur stupa in Central Java, and the technique of placing the figures at several levels in the composition is also very similar to the one used in Borobudur.

The buildings of Chichen Itza show certain influences from Southeast Asia; for example, the lotus motif occurs in the Mercado (covered market) at Chichen Itza. As a vaulted gallery, closed by a wall on one side and with pillars along the other, the Mercado is strikingly reminiscent of the galleries so typical of the Cambodian architecture that eventually blossomed into the galleries of Angkor Vat, dated about the middle of the twelfth century—the precise time that the Mercado and similar buildings at Chichen Itza were built. What is more significant is that the gradual development of these galleries follows very much the same pattern in both Cambodia and the northern Mayan region.

The lotus motif, interspersed with seated human figures, which has a deep symbolic meaning in Hindu and Buddhist mythologies and as such is an integral part of early Indian art, especially of Amaravati, is found at Chichen Itza as a border in the reliefs of the lower room of the Temple of Tigers. The lotus plant in Indian art, as reproduced on architraves and in border designs, shows not only the flowers and leaves, but the whole plant, including the rhizome, a kind of root-like stalk which grows horizontally under water or deeply buried in the mud. Whilst the flowers and leaves generally resemble their natural forms, the rhizome is represented by a decorative undulating creeper. This occurs in the art at Chichen Itza. If these two representations are not connected in some way, it must be an extraordinary coincidence that in India as well as in ancient America the generally invisible rhizome should have been not only made the basic element of a whole motif but also stylized in a similarly unrealistic manner.

Again, as in the early Indian art, the lotus motif at Chichen Itza is used as a border around an imaginary landscape and as a frame for other motifs such as the human figures. Even the figures' postures and movements are similar to those in India. Whilst the figures naturally differ in racial type and in costume, the motif is essentially the same. The similarity between the art of Amaravati and that of Chichen Itza is particularly noticeable in reclining figures holding on to the rhizome of the lotus.

In Indian art the lotus rhizome frequently protrudes from the mouths of *makaras,* sea monsters with fish-like bodies and elephant-like trunks. At Chichen Itza, stylized figures of fish are found at both ends of the lotus plant, in the same position as the makaras in India. "Such a combination of highly specific details cannot be accidental. It suggests the existence of some kind of relationship between Maya art and not only Buddhist art in general, but the school of Amaravati of the second century A.D. in particular."[12]

If the gap of almost a thousand years between the Amaravati period and Chichen Itza appears long, it is because evidence of the connecting links has not survived. In any case, it is not uncommon for decorative or symbolic motifs to survive even longer. Furthermore, the lotus occurs in Mayan art in the middle of the Classic period, several hundred years earlier than the date of the Chichen Itza reliefs. It is also a reasonable assumption that wooden sculptures and buildings, which have not survived, existed in Central America and carried on the tradition of this motif. There is evidence of wood carving amongst the Aztecs and there is little reason to believe it was not equally important in earlier times.

Eventually the lotus motif in both India and Southeast Asia assumed new forms: totally unrealistic, purely decorative designs of foliage-like scrolls. It then merged with another motif, *kirttimukha,* combining features of the lion, the death's head (*kala*) and the serpent or dragon, which appears in the Gupta art of India. The new form, found for the first time in the Pallava art of the seventh century, became a favourite in Southeast Asia, particularly Cambodia and Bali. In Cambodia, the creepers with ornamental foliage which had replaced the lotus are frequently seen on door lintels of the period between the ninth and the eleventh centuries, surging from both sides of the mouth of a demonic face without lower jaw, a mythical sea monster with a fish's body and an elephant's trunk. Lotus rhizomes extending from both sides of the mouth of a demonic face without lower jaw occur also at Chichen Itza. This similar use of the lotus motif not only indicates cultural intercourse between South Asia and America, but also suggests that it lasted well after the seventh century.

The makara motif, a makara head with upturned snout and with a human face in its mouth, from India, Java, Bali, and Sumatra, is comparable to the Mexican Xiuhcoatl, the so-called fire-serpent found at Palenque. Whilst this fire-serpent of Mayan art and its Aztec counterpart differ from the numerous more realistic representations of reptiles of the same areas, they correspond in many details, such as fish-like bodies, elephant-like trunks and forms of the teeth, to the makara. In Indian and Mayan art variants with paws occur, which resemble a crocodile rather than a fish, and in both regions a human figure often emerges from the mouth of the monster.

The makara and kirttimukha are the most frequent motifs on ancient and mediaeval temples in and outside India, and seem to have gained widespread popularity abroad in both the East and the West. Ananda K. Coomaraswamy pointed out in a study of Indian iconography in 1931 that the makara occurred frequently in mediaeval European art. Long before him, in 1875, E. Viollet-le-Duc suggested that the kirttimukha occurred at Poitiers, a twelfth-century Romanesque cathedral, but few scholars took notice of this assertion. Recently, a director of the Seattle Art Museum has pointed out further examples: "There can be little doubt that Coomaraswamy was correct, while Viollet-le-Duc's observation that the kirttimukha occurred at Poitiers was an understatement.

While makara and kirttimukha forms appear on the majority of French and Spanish Churches built in the 12th century, earlier Romanesque Churches were not decorated with such designs."[13] This makara motif seems to have been incorporated into the Chinese dragon concept. Islamic structures, such as the old Talisman gate at Baghdad, have also preserved variations of the kirttimukha. This motif was probably taken to England from France by the Plantagenets, and a motif known as the "Green Man" which appears on the Romanesque churches of some twenty-three English counties is thus ultimately of Indian origin.

The reputed "Cross" of Palenque, a stylized tree with a demonic face in its branches, appears to be a copy of the *Kalpa-Vrksa,* depicted In Indian sculpture as growing on the cosmic Mount Sumeru. The Javanese version of this tree, as seen in the *Wayang kulit,* with a demon's face between the beams of a cross, resembles the Mexican Cross. The motif also appears in a highly conventionalized form amongst the reliefs of the Angkor Vat in Cambodia. Porches with figures of monsters, lotus walls, and a "cross-shaped-holy-arch" have been discovered in the temples of Palenque, as in the temples of Cambodia, where the holy-arch was particularly common from the eighth to the tenth centuries.

Ancient American sites have revealed a galaxy of teocallis, despite the fact that many were demolished by European invaders. These pyramids are of various sizes and belong to different periods. Many of them escaped the onslaught of the intruders because they had been swallowed up by the jungles, thus remaining disguised until discovered by archaeologists. The ruins of Teotihuacan remained more or less unnoticed until the beginning of this century, even though they were not hidden by the jungle. Teotihuacan, meaning "the place where gods were made," was supposedly the most glorious and ancient city of Mexico. The two world-famous teocallis of the Sun (Tonatiuh) and the Moon (Meztli) have been excavated on this site. These pyramids are surrounded by numerous smaller pyramids. A number of scholars have suggested that the inspiration for these teocallis came from Egypt, but American pyramids are very unlike those of Egypt; it may even be a misnomer to describe them as pyramids. The teocallis of ancient America are really step-pyramids, in which several rectangular terraces, each of diminishing size, are built on top of one another, with an outside stairway leading up

Makara from Amaravati (a) and makara from Chichen Itza (b); the lotus-motif from Amaravati (c) and the lotus-motif from Chichen Itza (d). *After R. Heine-Geldern and G. F. Ekholm.*

God on the lion throne from India (e), and Mayan jaguar throne (f). *After R. Heine-Geldern and G. F. Ekholm.*

The Tree of Heaven in shadow play figure from Jave (a), and the so-called "Cross" from Palenque, Mexico (b).
After R. Heine-Geldern and G. F. Ekholm.

to the platform. The Sun Pyramid at Teotihuacan has four such terraces; the temple at Tulahas has five. At the top is a temple for which the rest of the pyramid merely serves a base, or a plinth. The Egyptian pyramids had neither platforms nor temples at the top and there was no stairway outside. Certainly, until later times their side walls were plain. The interior chamber, in which the bones of the Pharaoh were entombed, was reached by a low passage through the stone, which was sealed with earth after the entombment of the king. But the American pyramid is similar to the temple-pyramids of Cambodia, and is reminiscent of a prevalent concept in the Hindu-Buddhist world. It expresses the idea of erecting an artificial mountain, like the Indian Mount Sumeru, the Mountain ascending to Heaven.

There are however certain difficulties about the chronology of the pyramids of Southeast Asia and Mexico. The earliest American pyramids are older than the earliest similar pyramids known in Southeast Asia. For instance, the temple-pyramids of Cambodia date from the eighth century, and the Sun Pyramids of Teotihuacan, despite the difficulty of obtaining reliable radio carbon dates and taking into account the additions and alterations made from time to time, possibly had its earliest foundations laid in the second century B.C. Whilst there may be certain difficulties in satisfactorily setting out the similarities between the temple-pyramids of Cambodia and those of Mexican-Mayan areas, there are none in respect to other parallels. Nor are there any chronological discrepancies in the case of the Southeast Asian parallels in the Mercado at Chichen Itza.

Ancient Indian chronology is still subject to dispute, and any theories about Indian influences travelling across the Pacific to America must remain somewhat tentative. However, it seems that this cultural intercourse between Southeast Asia and America took place intermittently during the first six centuries of the Christian era. Whilst evidence from the Southeast Asian side would suggest the most likely period to be from the third to the fifth centuries, American evidence suggests that contact must have taken place not later than the middle of the classic period of Central America, since some Hindu-Buddhist traits appear in the Maya area at that time. This does not, however, preclude an earlier date. The lotus designs of Chichen Itza would bear testimony to cultural exchange during the first half of the first millennium. Atlantean figures and the motif of gods standing on crouching human figures may belong to the same time.

The makara motif may have been introduced more than once over a prolonged period. Indeed, a more detailed comparison of the various forms in which it appears in different regions may yield valuable chronological clues. At any rate, the combined motifs of the makara and the lotus would seem to indicate contacts in the period from the ninth to the twelfth century. And the similarities between the buildings of the Puuc style and Cambodian temples, particularly those of Isvarapura, would reinforce the evidence of contact around the tenth century. Finally, the Mercado at Chichen Itza reflects characteristics of Cambodian galleries of the eleventh and twelfth centuries.

There are indications that Java and possibly Sumatra and Champa may have participated in transpacific contacts with America but Asiomerican parallels with Cambodia are much closer. The ports from which the traffic was carried on must have been located on the coast of what now is Vietnam, a region Cambodia lost to her neighbours in the eighteenth century. Long before that, however, after a period of unprecedented political power and cultural achievements around 1200, the collapse of the Cambodian Empire must have caused the cessation of transpacific voyages.[14]

There is little material available to enable historians to visualize even the broad lines of ancient American thought. Their astronomical calculations give some indication of their concept of the universe, but they reveal little of their gods and their religious system. However, similarities between the gods and temples of Central America and those of India are far too striking not to compel consideration, even if adequate allowance is made for the fact that some kind of polytheism had existed in all primitive societies, and gods were conceived of in all shapes and sizes by primitive men. Ancient America was as rich in gods and temples as was India. The Asiomerican term for god, "teo", is close to the Sanskrit "deva." E. G. Squire noted similarities in both major and minor features of Buddhist temples of South India and Southeast Asia and those of ancient America. Both in ancient India and Mexico they were round and different colours were used on each of the four quarters. In 1866, Viollet-le-Duc pointed out some striking similarities between ancient Mexican structures and those of southern India.

The similarity extends also to their gods. The parallels between the Hindu Brahma-Visnu-Siva Trinity and the Mexican Ho-Huitzilopochtli-Tlaloc Trinity, and the resemblances between the attributes of certain Hindu deities and those of the Mayan pantheon are impressive. Discussing the diffusion of Indian religions to Mexico, a recent scholar, Paul Kirchhoff, has even suggested that it is not simply a question of miscellaneous influences wandering from one country to the other, but that China, India, Java, and Mexico actually share a common system.[15] Kirchhoff has sought "to demonstrate that a calendaric classification of 28 Hindu gods and their animals into twelve groups, subdivided into four blocks within each of which we find a sequence of gods and animals representing Creation, Destruction, and Renovation, and which can be shown to have existed both in India and Java, must have been carried from the Old World to the New, since in Mexico we find calendaric lists of gods and animals (or their substitutes) that follow each other without interruption in the same order and with attributes and functions or meanings strikingly similar to those of the 12 Indian and Javanese groups of gods, showing the same four subdivisions."[16]

There is some similarity between the iconography of American gods and Hindu and Buddhist art motifs. The disc of the sun as a quoit, the mussel shell with a plant, and the figures of Visnu, who despite his Mexican features, is so recognized from the mace (*Gada*) and *Cakra* that he holds in his two hands, appear on both sides of the Pacific. Moreover, the Mayas used the umbrella as a mark of dignity and a symbol of rank, and the umbrella comes from Southeast Asia, where it was known in the third millennium B.C. The friezes of Chacmultun in Yucatan exhibit two types of umbrellas like those still used in India and Southeast Asia. The Mayan goddess, Ix Tub Tun, who spits out precious stones, possesses attributes of an Indian *nagini* of Kubera, the Indian god of treasure.[17]

E. B. Tylor showed in a lecture in 1894 the four Mexican pictures, known as The Vatican Codex, that corresponded so closely to the pictures of Buddhist hells or purgatories painted on Japanese temple scrolls, as to "preclude any explanation except direct transmission from one religion to another."[18] He also found the counterparts of the tortoise myth of India in ancient America.

The Toltecs achieved greatness mainly because of the inspiration they derived from their white-bearded legendary god-man, Quetzalcoatl, who was exceptional in moral virtues, loved the sciences, was the source of all agricultural prosperity, and the inventor of all arts. His two institutions, priesthood and princedom, were the foundations of all Aztec social and religious life, creating a new religious concept of a higher spirituality. The historical reality of Quetzalcoatl is somewhat obscure.[19] The myth of Quetzalcoatl has been described as having its basis in a belief in a rain-and-wind god who brought fructifying showers to the dry earth of Mexico. Later, a number of stories and legends grew about him and he was credited with powers of wisdom and the attributes of a hero. Yet his humility, his burning need for self-purification, and emphasis on achieving mystic union with divinity through a life of contemplation, chastity, and penitence, could not have sprung from a society which, like that of the Aztecs, was given to armed conquests and bloodshed. Quetzalcoatl is said to have lived a rigorous life of abstinence in his palace, oriented towards the four points of the Universe, practicing several types of penance. Above all he devoted himself to meditation, *mo-teotia,* to conceive the supreme God and all that exists. It has, therefore, been suggested that behind Quetzalcoatl was Buddhist inspiration. Considering that the tradition of the Toltec beliefs is posterior to the Buddhist expansion in Southeast and East Asia, and to the fresh waves of migrants from Asia, particularly from Indo-China, It is quite likely that some Hindu-Buddhist thought had crept into Toltec beliefs.[20]

In fact, it was about the beginning of the Christian era, referred to as the classical period, that evidence appears of new ways of thinking in ancient America as well as fresh migrations from Asia. It would be extremely unlikely if these two were not connected. The new migrants are described as a people with a high degree of culture, possessing books of pictures, music and song, and worshipping a Supreme God who was Master of the Everywhere (Tloque-Nahuaque) and "was held to be the dual god (Ometiol), Master and Mistress of our flesh, who in a mysterious cosmic coupling and conception, has given origin to all that exists."[21] The Supreme God caused the birth of his four god-sons, who made up the primordial forces which were to generate the history of the world. It is from these myths and beliefs that several of their principal rites were derived. "The belief in a supreme dual principle mother and father of the gods and of man, as well as a concept of the world with the four corners of the universe, their characteristic colours, the four elements, the heavenly tiers and the nether world of the dead, are undoubtedly analogous to some concepts in the civilizations of India, China, and Tibet. Are these simply parallelisms, or did there exist in ancient times some kind of cultural dissemination ?"[22] According to Leon-Portilla, a definitive answer cannot be formulated as yet. But he reminds those who are inclined towards the idea of cultural dissemination of the inexplicable absence of such cultural elements as the practical use of the wheel, the concept of weight and the development of balance scales, amongst other things, in the pre-Columbian world. Besides, it cannot be ignored that the innate capacities of all human beings make them apply relatively similar solutions to similar problems.[23]

Mackenzie and some other scholars, however, are of the definite opinion that the ancient Mexicans and Peruvians were familar with Indian mythology and cite in support close parallels in details. For instance, the history of the Mayan elephant symbol cannot be traced in the local tradition, whereas it was a prominent religious symbol in India. It is not a motif imported from Egypt, for there are divergences between the African elephant and the American representation of it. The African elephant has larger ears, a less-elevated head and a bulging forehead without the indentation at the root of the trunk, which is characteristic of the Indian elephant. It is the profile of the Indian elephant, its tusk and lower lip, the form of its ear, as well as its turbaned rider with his *ankus,* which is found in Meso-American models. Whilst the African elephant was of little religious significance, it had been tamed in India and associated with religious practice since the early days. The elephant was associated with the Nagas, snake deities, who were rain-gods "wholly dependent on the presence of water and much afraid of fire, just like the dragons in many Chinese and Japanese legends."[24] The Nagas were regarded as the guardians of treasures, especially of pearls, and there is a good deal of additional evidence that the cults of Nagas and elephants in India had overlapped frequently. The religious significance of the elephant is typically Indian and there appears to be little doubt that the Mayan representation is similarly religious.[25] Mayan elephants are represented with the conventional ornamentation of the elephant-like figures on the bas-reliefs in Cambodia. Even Bancroft, who did not subscribe to the theory of contact between Indian and American mythologies, thought the elephant motif deserved attention.

A kind of caste system prevailed amongst the Incas of Peru. Peruvians worshipped an omnipotent and invisible Supreme Being, Viracocha, creator and preserver of the world. Imprints of the *Ramayana* and the' *Mahabharata* have been noticed on the poetry of Peru. The American story of Yappan resembles the story of Indra of the *Mahabharata* so closely that Mackenzie comments that with this piece of evidence alone a good circumstantial case can be made for the diffusion of Hindu thought, myths, and practices to ancient America.

The Mexican doctrine of the World's Ages—the universe was destroyed four consecutive times—is reminiscent of the Indian *Yugas*. Even the reputed colours of these mythical four ages, white, yellow, red, and black, are identical with and in the same order as one of the two versions of the Indian Yugas. In both myths the duration of the First Age is exactly the same, 4,800 divine years. The Mexican Trinity is associated with this doctrine as is the Hindu Trinity with the Yugas in India.[26]

Only four chemical elements were known to the peoples of ancient Greece and India. They were earth, water, fire, and air. The Hindus, in the *Bhagavad Gita*, describe the four ages of the world as corresponding to the four points of the compass, and they were the ages of earth, water, fire, and air. The Mayas divided each of their four ages into five periods, with each period ruled by a god. These are the twenty gods of the Mayan myths and they provide names for the twenty days of the Mayan months. In this way the Mayan calendar is somewhat akin to the Hindu Yugas. The Mayas distinguished between thirteen heavens, each ruled by a god; the lowest was earth. Below earth were nine underworlds with nine head gods; the lowest of these underworlds was ruled by the god of Death, Ahpuk.

Scholars who insist that pre-Columbian American religion and civilization were of independent origin are obliged to explain why the myths, beliefs, and practices of ancient America assumed such complex features at the very beginning, whilst in Asia they resulted from the fusions and movements of numerous peoples after a period of time much greater than that covered by American civilizations from beginning to end. The isolationists must also explain why the American race should have been the last to emerge from an uncivilized state and why, once they emerged, their progress should have been so phenomenally rapid.

Considering the missionary zeal and religious enterprise of Indian monks and priests, it would seem unlikely that they would have missed an opportunity to spread their respective religions. The traces of Hindu-Buddhist influence in Mexico and amongst the Maya correspond in kind precisely to those cultural elements which were introduced by Buddhist monks and Hindu priests in Southeast Asia. If Indian religions were not found in Central America at the time of the Spanish conquest, this cannot by itself be held as evidence that they had not existed at an earlier date. The history, especially of Southeast Asia, shows how easily religions may disappear or be submerged in local cults. Amongst the Cham of Annam, Hinduism and Buddhism had been firmly established for almost a millennium and a half, from the second to the fifteenth century. Yet, Buddhism disappeared completely after the fall of the Cham kingdom in 1471 and Hinduism declined so rapidly that its influence at present is hardly recognizable. Amongst the non-Muslim Badui and Tenggerese of Java, traces of Hinduism and Buddhism are exceedingly slight, although these must have been the predominant religions as late as the sixteenth century. The Batak of Sumatra were under Buddhist and Hindu influences from probably the third to the fourteenth century, but in the nineteenth century they were pagans. "We have little doubt that a sober but unbiased comparative analysis of the Mexican and Mayan religions will reveal many traces of the former influences of either Hinduism or Buddhism or of both. To mention but one instance, the conceptions of hell and of the punishments inflicted there resemble those of Buddhist and Hindu belief to such an extent, both in a general way and in specific details, that the assumption of historic relationship is almost inevitable."[27] It is, however, interesting that whilst in Mexico and amongst the Mayas, traits of apparent Hindu-Buddhist origin abound in the fields of art, religious architecture, government, cosmology, mythology, and iconography, there is hardly any Indian influence in the technical fields. Whatever little there is appears to have been the by-product of artistic and religious beliefs.

Parallels between the Pan-pipes of the Solomon Islands and those of

South America are indeed startling. The Pan-pipe is a primitive wind instrument mythologically associated with the goat-footed Greek god Pan. But here are pipes which are pre-Columbian, and have tone and pitch identical with their Polynesian counterparts. The odd pipes differ, each from the next, by the interval of a fourth. The even pipes have notes half-way in pitch between the odd ones, and thus form another "circle of fourths." What is more significant is that the absolute pitch of the instruments examined from both areas is the same. Consequently, the vibration rates in successive pipes are 557 and 560.5; 651 and 651; 759 and 749; 880 and 879: too close to be within the bounds of accidental convergence.

Elliot Smith, who had lived in Egypt for years working as a professor of anatomy, and who was a British diffusionist, points out that Asiomericans and East Asians practiced the same method of mumification. Some scholars have noted other parallels between the symbols, postures, dress, and etiquette of Indian and Southeast Asian royalty and those of Mexico and Peru. It is pointed out that the four queens of the last Ayar ruler performed *sati* after the latter had been killed by the Spaniards. The Mexican Lion-throne and Lotus-throne remind one of Indian *Simhasana* and *Padmasana.* The parasol, a mark of royalty amongst the Mayas, the Aztecs, and the Incas, may be an adaptation of the royal *Chatra* in use in India and Indianized Asia from the earliest times. Both types of parasols shown in the frescoes of Chak Multun in Yucatan correspond to types still in use in Southeast Asia. The use of the throne, of the litter, and of fans mounted like standards on long poles as insignia of rank and royalty, closely resemble similar paraphernalia of royalty and aristocracy in Southeast Asia. Not only Aztec court ceremony, but even their form of government, was similar to that of Southeast Asia; for instance, the institution of four chief officials in Mexico corresponds to the four ministers of state and governors of the four quarters of the empires of Southeast Asia. What is of particular significance is that in both cases this institution is based on Indian cosmological principles.

William MacLeod pointed out that the Mexican *Volador* ritual is similar to an Indian rite of hook-swinging, the *Charak Puja* of Bengal and South India. In Mexico the participants normally hang by their feet, and in India by their shoulders. However, an old description and illustration of hook-swinging in India in which the participants hang by their feet has been unearthed by Heine-Geldern and Ekholm. A relief at the Bayon at Angkor Thom in Cambodia represents a rite similar to the Volador of Mexico.

Similar routines of everyday life of Indians and Asiomericans have also been noted. For instance, betel-chewing with lime and coca-chewing and tobacco, as well as the gourd-container for the lime are common to both peoples. The Peruvian substitute for tobacco, which was used for medicinal purposes, was a shrub, called cuca (coca). The leaves are first dried in the sun and then mixed with a little lime to constitute "a preparation for chewing, much like the betel-leaf of the East."[28] Vegetarianism has been popular both in India and Mexico, and Indian food is similar to Mexican. The Indian *roti* or *chapati* and the Mexican *tortilla,* similar in size and shape, are made in the same way. Both peoples have an unusual respect for corn, and share the custom of offering bits of food, before eating, to God in expression of their gratitude for the meal provided.

Mirrors of pyrite; shell money; birchbark shelters canoes and containers with identical curvilinear design from Siberia and North America; string crosses for prayers from Tibet, India, Assam, Mexico, and Peru; the custom of fishing with poison; shell fishhooks; the use of agricultural terraces in Southeast Asia, Peru and Bolivia; and the cultivation of cotton, were common from early days in both Asia and Amenca.

Some linguistic kinship between India and ancient America has also been suggested. Miles Poindexter, a former ambassador of the United States to Mexico, proposed that primitive Aryan words and people came to America by the island chains of Polynesia. The Mexican name for boat is a South Indian Tamil word, *Catamaran,* and Poindexter gives a long list of words of the Quichua languages and their analogous forms in Sanskrit.[29] Similarities between the hymns of the Inca rulers of Peru and Vedic hymns have been pointed out.[30] Kroeber has also found striking similarities between the structure of Indo-European and the Penutian language of some of the tribes along the northwestern coast of California.

Tylor, writing in 1881, pointed out that the ancient Mexican game, *patolli,* a favourite of the Aztecs, was very similar to *pachisi,* played in India. The two games were connected in a series of independent features, such as divining by lot, a sportive wager, realization of the law of chance, transfer of the result to a counting board, and rules of moving and capturing.

ETHNOBOTANY, A RELATIVELY recent discipline not hitherto fully utilized, provides conclusive evidence of both cultural contacts between Southeast Asia and ancient America, and of transpacific crossings. The publication of *The Evolution of Gossypium.* in 1947 by Hutchinson, Silow, and Stephens brought home to many historians the value of the study of ethnobotany in tracing the processes of cultural diffusion and the migrations of people through plants.

A study of cultural intercourse would reveal that the transfer of knowledge is a slow and uncertain process. Intermittent contacts lasting even over centuries may not result in any influence. Settlement, on the other hand, may result in the rapid introduction of numerous culture traits. As far as plants are concerned, their transplantation is a very complicated procedure. It requires the adoption of a whole complex of knowledge about the plant's ecological requirements, and often also about its human uses. Hence, the presence of even one transferred plant would mean that a quite effective and probably relatively durable contact had been made between two peoples. The presence of a number of plants would indicate a major cultural contact.

Cotton, which plays such an important part in world economy and is grown at present in Asia, Africa, the Americas, and to some extent in Europe, is one of the tantalizing mysteries of history and science. In Egypt, the first definite proof of its use dates from the fourth century B.C. But long before this, about 3000 B.C., cotton was cultivated in the Indus Valley. During the excavations at Mohenjo-daro a small fragment of cotton fabric and a small piece of cotton string in the neck of a silver vessel were recovered. These fragments were made from raw material indistinguishable from the indigenous coarse *bengalese* cottons found in the region today. The quality of both the fabric and the string leaves no doubt that a mature textile craft had existed in the Indus Valley civilization. It is from this cotton that the perennial forms of East Asia, Africa, and the West have developed.

Although it is certain that cotton was first used in the Indus Valley, no evidence of its wild ancestors has been found in India. There are various interpretations of the cytogenetic evidence but it is suggested that the progenitors of the early cottons of India may have been introduced from southern Arabia or northeastern Africa. This is puzzling enough, but when South American cotton is studied scholars and scientists are thoroughly baffled. Evidence of the Asian ancestry of American cottons is irrefutable, but substantial proof of the migration of Gossypium is inconclusive.

On the north Peruvian coast known as the Huaca Prieta woven fabrics of unexpectedly elaborate pattern, dated about 2400 B.C. and made from a highly cultivated species of cotton, have been discovered. Archaeological evidence concerning cotton is incomplete because both cotton plant material and cotton fabrics have survived only in the driest areas. It is, therefore, principally the botanical evidence, together with whatever archaeological finds there are, which is relied upon in fixing the origins of the cotton plant of America.

American cottons are tetraploid in chromosome constitution and their chromosome complement is made up of one set homologous with the complement of the diploid Asian cottons and one set homologous with the complement of the diploid species of America.[31] After a series of painstaking experiments, experts have agreed that one parent of the American cotton undoubtedly came from Asia: in other words, from the Indus Valley area.

The vast diversity of cultivated cottons falls into four species, distinguished from each other by their respective number of chromosomes. The species, Gossypium herbaceum and Gossypium arboreum, are diploid (with thirteen chromosomes each) and the other two, Gossypium hirsutum and Gossypium barbadense, are a more sophisticated species, the tetraploid, with twenty-six chromosomes each. The first two are of Asian origin, with Gossypium arboreum coming from the Indus Valley region, the other from Africa and Arabia. The two tetraploids are of Amerilcan origin and are hybrid, with half Asian ancestry. The linted diploid species which were the Asian ancestral species of the Peruvian tetraploid cotton was Gossypium arboreum, which is typically an Indus diploid widely distributed over Southeast Asia.

But how did the two come together? Did the Indus ancestor travel through Africa across the Atlantic to Peru? This view has been rejected—not so much because of the inability to explain the feasibility of its transatlantic journey, which is in itself a difficult problem—because of the difficulty in understanding how the two parents came in contact, once the

Asian species had reached South America. Not only is the closest known American wild ancestor of the Peruvian cotton confined to the Peruvian coast, but the whole group of the American wild species of Gossypium are found on the Pacific side of the continent. Since the American diploids are all static or relic species with limited distribution, it would appear that the two met because the Asian diploids are aggressive and spread rapidly. And as the centres of variability of these major allopolyploids are within the area at present occupied by the American diploid on the Pacific side, it would also support the theory that the Indus diploid entered Peru from the Pacific. If this is true the Asian diploid must have been the Gossypium arboreum or a species ancestral to it, for no other linted diploid species could have been carried across the Pacific to western South America. "There is no evidence that Gossypium herbaceum ever reached the Pacific and the present eastern limit of the distribution of Gossypium aboreum coincides apparently with the limit of the area in which it has recently been used."[32]

S. C. Harland, whose researches led to the modern studies of the origins and evolutionary history of cultivated cottons, suggested that they met on a land bridge across the Pacific Ocean. But objections to this theory are insuperable. Neither birds nor winds could carry cotton seeds for a distance of at least three thousand miles and, in fact, the Pacific Ocean from New Guinea to Peru is about ten thousand miles wide. In any case, birds do not eat Gossypium seeds, and sea-water would have destroyed their germinal power. Recently, Skovsted, carrying Harland's researches further, has demonstrated that the American cottons are amphidiploids of the constitution 2 (AD), which makes it essential that an A genom diploid cotton must have reached Central America through man's efforts, where it hybridized with an ancestral D.

Again, from the longitude of Guam to that of the Revillo Gigedo islands there is no record of the occurrence of a diploid cotton north of Australia. This fact, together with the scientific evidence suggesting that the growth of A-genom bearing linted allopolyploids has taken place only since the origin of human civilization, would lead to one conclusion; cotton seeds must have been carried by man who took them with other seeds of his crop plant and with the tools of his civilization.[33]

Also, the contact between the Asian and the American species could not have come about by migration around the Pacific, either by a northern route, by way of China and Alaska, or by a southern route, by way of the Antarctic. For, as Hutchinson points out, "Gossypium is a genus of Xerophystic perennial shrubs adapted to the arid tropics. No member of the genus would grow in an ecological situation where temperate woodlands existed and until the modern development of short-term annual cottons under domestication, no member of the genus would survive in a climate with winter frosts ."[34]

Scientific evidence is supported by archaeological remains. In the pre-Inca Peruvian graves not only have woven fabrics been found but also instruments for weaving and spinning. This would amply support the theory that cotton was introduced by civilized men, for the development of fibres into threads and thence into weaving is an important advance in the skills of man, and a landmark in the history of civilization. It is also significant that the spindles in Peru used the same device as did the fine spinner of the Dacca muslins in India. Their two-barred type of cotton loom has been used in Asia, Europe, America, and everywhere else. But, as Crawford points out, the fact that this two-barred type of loom originated in India and spread to Europe, and that it is found with its technical subtleties of fabric construction in the cotton areas of South America, would be difficult to explain except in terms of direct or indirect cultural contact between India and ancient America.

Contact between Asia and America probably was two-way. If Asians went with the intention of permanently settling in America, this cannot exclude the possibility that some may have returned, possibly accompanied by some descendants of the early settlers. It is not unlikely that early American cultures were founded by the impact of Asian immigration, but they then developed mainly under their own stimulus. Later the Americanized Asian cultures might have diffused back across the Pacific giving a new impetus to their original homelands. Cotton is such an example. It was the Indus cultivated cotton that crossed over to America, and, having been hybridized with American cotton returned to Asia in a new and more advanced form.

Another plant which appears to have been imported to America from Southeast Asia is the coconut, *cocos nucifera,* which is regarded as characteristic plant of the Pacific. It is a pan-Pacific species which probably originated along the shores of the Indian Ocean. Because of the uniformity of its nomenclature throughout the area stretching from Madagascar to Tahiti, it is concluded that its distribution must have taken place through the agency of man. However, as "coco" is a Portuguese word, it is likely that it was the Portuguese who carried it to South America. Ridley's suggestion, made in 1930, that the original home of the coconut must have been Costa Rica and Panama was probably based on the Spanish traveller Oviedo's accounts of the early sixteenth century. It is refuted by the references made by Marco Polo to coconut in Sumatra, the Nicobar and Andaman islands, and South India in the last quarter of the thirteenth century. Indian sources from about the first century refer to coconuts. Again, coconut palms are represented in the carvings of both Angkor Vat in Cambodia, and the Borobudur in Indonesia. The coconut plant was already widespread in Polynesia on the eve of the first European contact. The suggestion that the coconut could have drifted from America to Polynesia during the pre-Columbian period is invalidated by the absence of any evidence that coconuts have floated to and established themselves on remote islands. The embryo within the fruit can survive only for a limited period, and the waves could at best carry it to near-by islands, although there is no evidence that this occurred. It must have been planted throughout Polynesia by man before the arrival of Europeans in the Pacific.

Maize, *Zea Mays,* is widely grown in Asia and Africa. At one time it was believed to have originated in Asia, but evidence of extensive cultivation in pre-Columbian America made an American origin seem most likely. Early this century, Laufer and Merril concluded that the Spaniards took maize to Asia, by way of the Philippines, from America during the early modern period. Since then further research has renewed claims that maize was in use in Asia he before Columbus discovered America. There is no doubt that maize was of enormous importance in pre-Columbian America. It was, as it is now, the basic staple of life in Mexico. Consequently, there are various versions, including mythical and speculative, about its origin. The Aztecs believed that their herogod, Quetzalcoatl, who created the human race with his own blood, assumed the shape of an ant to steal away a single grain of maize from the mountains where the ants had hidden it. This grain he gave to man to cultivate. Whilst evidence supporting the claims of maize originating in Asia is at present inconclusive, it is more misleading and unwarranted to assert for instance as Van Hagen has recently done, that maize was cultivated at Huaca Prieta in Peru as early as 3000 B.C. In fact, the Huaca Prieta site is noted for its lack of maize pods, although the evidence of the most ancient maize has been found in other regions of Peru. The earliest remains of an extremely primitive form of cultivated corn came from a once-inhabited rock shelter at the Bat Cave in New Mexico. Excavated by Herbert Dick between 1948 and 1950, these remains have been dated by radio-carbon analysis as belonging to the mid-third millennium B.C., but there is no evidence for maize agriculture in the Valley of Mexico until more than a thousand years later.

The maize plant has never been found in a wild state and its immediate progenitor, despite several speculative theories, is unknown. One theory is that maize developed from a wild ancestor that was at once a popcorn and a podcorn; another is that it descended from teosinte or tripsacum. Two scientists, C. R. Stonor and Edgar Anderson, working independently, concluded that certain distinctive varieties of maize widely cultivated by the Nagas in Assam in India, had been in cultivation there from the pre-Columbian period. Whilst, on the whole, these varieties were similar to those of maize grown in early Peru and Chile; the popcorns, green corns used as a fresh vegetable, and brewing corns did not fit into the picture at all. The Asian popcorns are not at all like the popcorns of Central America. After a period of collaboration and further experimentation these two scientists found the conclusion inescapable, that "there are at least two races of maize in Asia and that one of these must have crossed the Pacific in pre-Columbian times. The direction (or directions) in which it travelled, however, is still uncertain."[35] It seems somewhat surprising that the post-Columbian maize should reach such remote areas as the Naga hills and the interior of New Guinea, and be cultivated by the hill tribes of Upper Burma and Siam, the Lolo of Central Asia, and the Aborigines of Hainan, without reaching the surrounding highly civilized Asian countries. Yet it is a significant crop of Asian countries. Why should India, China, and other Asian countries have taken maize from the hill tribes, and not from the Europeans before it passed through their territories on its way to these hinterlands? It may be possible that maize, like cotton, crossed the Pacific from Asia to America in prehistoric times, and was later repatriated.

Whatever its exact origin, the maize plant certainly went through a long process of skilful cultivation in the hands of Asiomericans. Thin pancake-like bread made of maize flour, called *tlaxcatti* by the Aztecs and *tortillas* by the Mexicans today, accompanied by beans and peppers, and washed down with drinks made from maguey or cacao were the standard diet of the Aztecs and other Asiomericans.

Evidence of the origin of the sweet potato, *Ipomoea batatas,* mainly cultivated in Southeast Asia and Central America, is inconclusive despite numerous studies. Various hypotheses on its original home have been proposed by scientists supporting Southern Asia, Central and South America, or Africa. Of these, the theory of its American origin is generally accepted, for it is datable in Peru at least to the beginning of the Christian era. However, recent cytological research has thrown considerable doubt on this theory. In spite of its wide distribution, it is a single species, as is suggested by the continuous ranges in individual morphological characters, and the consistent chromosome numbers. Although the sweet potato came to be widely distributed throughout Europe and Asia during the post-Columbian period, it existed in Polynesia well before that. It is known that the sweet potato was in Hawaii by about the middle of the thirteenth century, and no more than a century later it was in New Zealand. The American prehistorian, Ronald B. Dixon, was convinced that the sweet potato had reached Polynesia before Columbus reached America. Whether the original species travelled from Southern Asia or the Pacific areas to America or vice versa, the fact of its common origin and diffusion would lend further support to the theory of transpacific contact. What makes this plant more important for the historian is that if the transpacific voyages were long and arduous, the sweet potato tubers would have either been eaten or spoiled. But this did not happen. The migration of the sweet potato alone shows that voyages were made relatively easily across the Pacific.[36] At any rate, the sweet potato was certainly transplanted via the Pacific irrespective of the direction of the journey. This is further substantiated by the fact that the name for the sweet potato, *kumara* or *kumala,* is found in the entire Pacific area, and that cognates were prevalent amongst the Aztecs and the peoples of Panama and the Caribbean.

Another typical feature of American culture, the *quipu,* the device of the ancient Peruvians for recording events, sending messages, etc., consisting of cords or threads of various colours knotted in various ways, has a replica in Hawaii. Something like quipu was used in early China and is referred to in the Tao-toh-chiang.

Whilst the importance of cultural similarities must not be overemphasized, it would be equally untenable to regard them as incidental results of sporadic or accidental transpacific crossings from Southeast Asia. To justify the volume of the cultural parallels, there must have been repeated and consciously undertaken voyages between the two continents. But the evidence of ethnobotany must clinch the argument in favour of the transpacific voyages during historic times. Indeed, acceptance of the theory of Asian migration to Central America across the Pacific would resolve a problem in tracing the origins and interrelationships of world cottons. Scientists have provided definite proof of cultural diffusion; historians must now provide the evidence of migrations.

The only plausible argument against cultural diffusion from southern Asia to the Pacific is the distance involved. It is asserted that it would have been unlikely for a large number of people to have crossed the vast expanses of the Pacific without well-equipped boats and skilful voyagers. The argument, however, falls upon closer scrutiny. It would not be at all difficult for a large canoe or catamaran to cross from Polynesia to South America even at the present time, and the ancient Asians were skilled and enterprising seafaring men. Also, in prehistoric times the Pacific was divided into relatively small areas of navigability studded with small islands. Within these areas, off-shore voyages of two hundred miles or so were practical.

However, the migrations with which the present argument is most concerned are the ones which took place later in historic times, when cultural traits were sufficiently developed to be transmitted. Asian ability to cross the seas during that period is undoubted. The art of shipping and navigation in India and China at the time was sufficiently advanced for oceanic crossings. Indian ships operating between Indian and Southeast Asian ports were large and well equipped to sail across the Bay of Bengal.

When the Chinese Buddhist scholar, Fa-hsien, returned from India, his ship carried a crew of more than two hundred persons and did not sail along the coasts but directly across the ocean. Such ships were larger than those Columbus used to negotiate the Atlantic a thousand years later. According to a work of mediaeval times, *Yukti Kalpataru,* which gives a fund of information about shipbuilding, India built large vessels from 200 B.C. to the close of the sixteenth century. A Chinese chronicler mentions ships of Southern Asia that could carry as many as one thousand persons, and were manned mainly by Malayan crews. They used western winds and currents in the North Pacific to reach California, sailed south along the coast, and then returned to Asia with the help of the trade winds, taking a more southerly route, without, however, touching the Polynesian islands.[37]

In ancient times the Indians excelled in shipbuilding and even the English, who were attentive to everything which related to naval architecture, found early Indian models worth copying. The Indian vessels united elegance and utility, and were models of fine workmanship. Sir John Malcolm wrote: Indian vessels "are so admirably adapted to the purpose for which they are required that, nothwithstanding their superior science, Europeans were unable, during an intercourse with India for two centuries, to suggest or at least to bring into successful practice one improvement."[38] It is also known that in the third century a transport of horses, which would have required large ships, reached Malaya and Indochina. '

Emilio Estrada, Clifford Evans, and Betty J. Meggers, who have pointed out many striking similarities between Ecuadorian archaeological remains of the early Bahia and early Jama-Coaque cultures (the last two centuries B.C.) with relics of approximately the same period of Japan, India, and Southeast Asia, also support the feasibility of transpacific voyages. The Equatorial Counter-current, running eastward just north of the equator, leads directly towards the northern coast of Ecuador, and farther to the north the Japanese current flows eastwards to join the Mexican current moving down along the Pacific coast to Ecuador. Asian vessels were already carrying a flourishing trade and traffic from East Asia to the western world via Southeast Asia. By the third century, their ships were capable of carrying six hundred men and one thousand metric tons of cargo. The nineteenth-century geographer and Confederate naval Commander, Matthew Fontaine Maury, believed that Chinese mariners would have had no serious difficulty in discovering America. "One could go from China via Japan, the Kuriles, the Kamchatka coast, and the Aleutians to Alaska without losing sight of land for more than a few hours."[39]

The New Zealand prehistorian, S. Percy Smith, tries to show in his *Hawaiki—the Original Home of the Maori* that the ancient Polynesian wanderers left India as far back as the fourth century B.C. and were daring mariners who made, more often than not, adventurous voyages with the definite object of new settlements.[40] A people who reached as far east as Easter Island could not have missed the great continent ahead of them.[41]

In contrast to the Pacific, the Atlantic is comparatively small and its winds and currents bead directly toward Central America. Hence, one may ask why the Asian, rather than the Mediterranean, migration to Central America be found more feasible? The answer lies in the art and technique of shipping. The Pacific people first developed advanced watercraft. Their oceangoing canoes were equipped with masts, sails, paddles, bailers and stone anchors; some boats even had three masts. For a long time the Mediterranean-Atlantic propulsion technique was rowing, which did not give way exclusively to sail propulsion until the end of the Middle Ages. Indopacific people had made this shift much earlier due to their two pieces of sophisticated sailing equipment—the fore-and-aft-rigged sail made of plaited pandanus mats sewn together in a triangular form with wooden yards and booms to strengthen the long sides of the triangle, and the centreboard, both of which employ the same aerodynamic principle of lift as does the airplane wing. Consequently, they could paddle forward much more freely and efficiently. Whilst the Vikings were sweeping across the northern seas in their long ships, the Polynesians in their long canoes, mounted with reinforced triangular sail, were negotiating thousands of miles of sea, often at seven knots an hour if favoured by a powerful wind.

What was the motive that urged Asians to undertake long journeys to America? It was probably gold, which initially attracted Indian adventurers and merchants to Southeast Asia. The remains of Dong-

Son culture are mainly found in gold-producing areas. It is also possible that the daring ancient mariners were looking merely for new areas for food and settlement. But it seems more likely they were prospecting for precious metals, stones, and pearls to cope with the demand in the centres of ancient civilization. This view is substantially reinforced by W. J. Perry who was the first scholar to point out the distribution of the pearling beds of the world, and why, wherever pearls are found, similar complex religious myths, beliefs, and practices are also found. It is therefore significant that the mythology of the pre-Columbian American civilizations "was deeply impregnated by the religious beliefs and practices and habits of life that obtained amongst the treasureseekers of the Old World."[42] Equally significant is the fact that the Mayas preferred to settle in that part of Central America which was unhealthy but rich in precious stones and gold. Somewhat like the Indians, the Asiomericans accumulated stones and gold and made symbolic ornaments from them. Mexican temples and idols, as in India, were lavishly decorated with gold and precious stones.

Whatever the motive, transpacific traffic would seem to have gone on regularly for about two thousand years, from about the eighth century B.C. to the twelfth century. The number of Asian migrants was perhaps not very substantial and they were absorbed in the local populations of early Asian settlers, but their cultural influence was profound. The foreign civilization implanted upon more primitive indigenous cultures by small groups of immigrants was soon absorbed by the local population and, in consequence, new civilizations were born which, despite their original character, nevertheless also reveal the features of both foreign and indigenous sources.

In view of so many parallels in fundamental conceptions and detail, in mythology, ritual, iconography, architecture, religious beliefs, crowns, thrones, plants, together with the evidence of migration, it appears incredible that isolationists should continue to insist on the independent evolution of Asiomerican civilization. Each correspondence in itself, with the exception of a few very unusual ones, may not amount to much, but in aggregate the evidence of cultural diffusion is formidable. Heine-Geldern and Ekholm declare unequivocally:

The large number of highly specific correspondences in so many fields precludes any possibility of mere accidental coincidence. Nor would it help us to take refuge in any kind of explanation based on some alleged psychological laws. There is no psychological law which could have caused the peoples on both sides of the Pacific to stylize the lotus plant in the same manner and to make it surge from the mouth of a jawless demon's head, to invent the parasol and use it as a sign of rank and to invent the same complicated game. There is no explanation other than the assumption of cultural relationship. We must bow to the evidence of facts, even though this may mean a completely new start in our appraisal of the origin and development of the American Indian higher civilization.[43]

Chapter III

SUVARNABHUMI: ASIANIZATION OF INDIAN CULTURE

ONLY SINCE WORLD War II has the term Southeast Asia been used to describe the area to the east of India and to the south of China, which includes the Indochinese Peninsula, the Malay Archipelago and the Philippines, roughly forming a circle from Burma through Indonesia to Vietnam. Before the term Southeast Asia became common usage, the region was often described as Further or Greater India, and it was common to describe the Indonesian region or Malay Archipelago as the East Indies.[1] The reason may be found in the fact that prior to Western dominance, Southeast Asia was closely allied to India culturally and commercially.

This region was broadly referred to by ancient Indians as *Suvarnabhumi* (the Land of Gold) or *Suvarnadvipa* (the Island of Gold), although scholars dispute its exact definition. Sometimes the term is interpreted to mean only Indonesia or Sumatra. It has been suggested that the term was mainly applied to Burma, but this interpretation is not convincing. Arab writers such as Al Biruni testify that Indians called the whole Southeast region *Suwarndib (Suvarnadvipa).* Hellenistic geographers knew the area as the Golden Chersonese. The Chinese called it *Kin-Lin; kin* means gold. Although the exact region meant by the term is not clear, it is not unlikely that the name was applied to the whole Indochinese Peninsula and the Malay Archipelago.

Southeast Asia is a complex of races and languages. In its mountains and jungles live a wide variety of peoples with varying degrees of advancement and divergent historical experiences. During the last two thousand years, this region has come under the influence of practically all the major civilizations of the world: Indian, Chinese, Islamic, and Western. Of these, Indian culture appears to have blended best with the indigenous culture.

It is not known precisely when contact began between India and Southeast Asia, for Indian writers seldom recorded historical or topographical details with any degree of accuracy. The modern historian has to reconstruct the picture from fragmentary references in literary sources, archaeological remains, and non-Indian writings. The archaeological sources remain insufficiently tapped. Nor are the excavations always conducted by experts, for easy accessibility to the sites and the chance of generous rewards often attract pseudo-scientists.

Contemporary indigenous historical narratives are conspicuously inadequate, and the information in Greek literature is casual and defective. The references made by the Arab travellers of the ninth century onwards and by Marco Polo, although of great importance, are impressionistic and insufficient. Chinese sources reveal considerable information about the areas geographically and historically close to her, but distant countries such as Malaya and Indonesia are inadequately treated.

Modern historical research on Southeast Asia is in its formative stages and the attention accorded its ancient past has been much less than that given to later periods. Western scholars were mainly stimulated by their colonial involvement in the area and generally concentrated attention on their own activities. An idea of the extent of knowledge about Southeast Asia may be gained from an European scholar who wrote in 1861, that, except for Burma, "the Indian countries situated beyond the Ganges hardly deserve the attention of History."[2] Burma was presumably excepted because the British by that time had fought two successful wars against her and had annexed Lower Burma to their Indian Empire, and a few British administrators, such as John Crawford, Henry Yule, and Arthur Phayre, had written accounts of their missions and the country. Stamford Raffles in 1817 produced *A History of Java* from materials collected by a staff of collaborators but it does not seem to have stimulated much interest amongst British writers who remained, almost until the end of World War II, excessively preoccupied with the British in India. Neither the realization of the close and ancient Indian cultural contact with Southeast Asia nor the fact that Burma, Malaya, and their other territorial possessions in eastern Asia were tied to Indian administration, evoked British interest in the study of early Southeast Asia. Even today, with the exception of a few notable orientalists and scholars of cultural history such as Richard Winstedt, G. H. Luce, H. G. Quaritch Wales, Reginald Le May, and Roland Braddet, British historians have made little serious inquiry into the cultural past of these Asian countries. A people with no long cultural history of their own perhaps could not be expected to be attracted by the ancient cultural past of the people they dominated. What is surprising, however, is that British intellectual interest in Asian culture remained much less and much more inhibited than even that of France and Holland whose own cultural pasts were only, if at all, slightly better, but whose political and economic interests in Asia were less than those of the British.

Equally strange is the attitude of Indian historians towards the cultural past of Southeast Asia. With their appetite for knowledge Indian scholars could be expected to make an impressive study of Asian culture. But on the whole they have remained generally indifferent, not even attempting to integrate their own ancient history with that of their neighbours. Presumably this is because they have generally followed a prescribed course of study and inherited a set system of academic training, which is only gradually adapting itself to new consciousness and need. Indeed, in their newly found zeal of independence and Asianism, they tend to lean too much on the nationalist side, although there are notable exceptions, such as K. A. Nilakanta Sastri, R. C. Majumdar, B. R. Chatterjee, B. Ch. Chhabra, H. B. Sarkar, and Manmohan Ghosh. Indian interest, however, has been growing in this field and various publications have emerged in recent years.

Although the interest of the French and Dutch scholars in early Southeast Asian history was also limited, it was, in fact, their work which paved the way for its advancement. Studies concerning the ancient past of Indochina were stimulated by the discovery of the temples at Angkor in 1862 and of the account of the exploratory voyage of Doudart de Lagree and

Francis Garnier. Later, works by E. Aymonier, Victor Goloubew, George Coedès, H. Parmentier, M. G. Maspero, Renè Grousset, G. de Coral-Remusat, Philippe Stern, S. Lèvi, B. P. Groslier, and others, appeared.

The Dutch set up a society to study the culture of the Indonesian people in 1778 in Java and this inspired numerous studies in early Indonesian history and culture. Hendrik Kern, Brandes, Cohen Stuart, and Holle published important studies on Indonesian epigraphy. Later, N. J. Krom, W. F. Stutterheim, R. Goris, P. V. Van Stein Callenfels, F. D. K. Bosch, C. C. Berg, J. C. Van Leur, H. J. de Graaf, J. G. de Casparis, and many other Dutch writers made notable contributions on Indonesia's early history. Amongst the better known Indonesian scholars in this field are R. Ng. Poerbatjaraka, Sanusi Pane, Mohammad Yamin, Prijono, and Hussein Djajadiningrat.

But the eastward expansion of Hindu civilization has not yet been fully traced. Whilst historians have begun to understand its results, its origin, and its progress in the various individual countries, there still lies a long road ahead before a substantial assessment of the entire regional phenomenon can be made. There is, of course, less expectation of reaching agreement on detailed interpretations. There is a tendency amongst some Indian scholars to overemphasize Indian influence on Southeast Asian civilization, and some of them insist on analyzing the process in terms of cultural domination or colonization. On the other hand, some non-Indian scholars, especially modern writers of secondary works, tend to play down India's importance in the evolution of Southeast Asian civilization. For a balanced and dispassionate interpretation the degree of Indian influence should not be overemphasized nor the local genius overestimated. Dispute amongst historians, however, is not always along nationalistic lines; often there are genuine differences of well-considered opinion. For example, whilst F. D. K. Bosch, Parmentier and E. B. Havell suggest limited local contribution, others, such as Coedès, Quaritch Wales, and Stutterheim see more surviving influences of the local cultures.

Sociologists who have entered the field in recent years tend to disregard the evidence of literary sources, philology, archaeology, and epigraphy, and overrate somewhat uncertain and overstretched ethnological formulations, and the surviving features of pre-Indian civilization. Briefly discussing the limitations of this approach, and emphasizing the need for the greater study of inscriptions in local languages, Georges Coedès says, "I am convinced that such research will reveal numerous facts which will indicate a much deeper Indianization of the mass of the population than the sociologists will at present admit."[3]

The advent of Indians in Southeast Asia has hardly a parallel in history. It cannot be equated with the arrival of Europeans in America, because the Indians did not go to Southeast Asia as strangers. There appears to have always been some form of contact. But at a certain point which is at present indefinite, and due to circumstances which are not yet determined, an influx of merchants and immigrants into Southeast Asia resulted in the foundation of indigenous kingdoms, which practiced the arts, customs, and religions of India, and used Sanskrit as the sacred language. If the Indianization of Southeast Asia appears to be a new phenomenon around the beginning of the Christian era, it is because Indians arrived at this time in noticeable numbers, accompanied possibly for the first time by educated persons who were able to spread India's religions and culture with the Sanskrit language. In fact, the most ancient Sanskrit inscriptions of Southeast Asia are not very posterior to the first Sanskrit inscriptions of India proper. However, the earliest archaeological finds in these areas are not necessarily evidence of the earliest Indian influence. The priests who consecrated the first Hindu or Buddhist temples, and the scholars who composed the first Sanskrit inscriptions, must have been preceded by navigators, merchants, or immigrants, who founded the first Indian establishments. These establishments, Oc-eo in Indochina and Kuala Selinsing in Perak, for instance, were not always completely new creations, but were founded on neolithic sites, which Indian navigators may have frequented from time immemorial.

In view of the ethnic affinities between the prehistoric Austro-Asiatic races of India and those of Suvarnabhumi, contact between the two regions may well go back to the remotest antiquity. Opinion on this question, however, is by no means united. Mainly basing their evidence on linguistic affinities between Malaya and certain tribes of India, which they believe belong to the Austro-Asiatic family, Schmidt and Kuh, for example, favour the view that the Malay race emigrated to the Malay Archipelago in prehistoric times. Some scholars dispute this theory and deny even the existence of the Austro-Asiatic family. There are other theories, one of which suggests that first the Malays went to India and then the process was reversed.

Whatever be the ethnic and cultural relationship between India and Southeast Asia during the prehistoric period, the transplantation of Indian culture into Southeast Asia began in historic times with trade contacts. The Buddhist Jatakas tell many stories of enterprising merchants and princes, sailing to Suvarnabhumi for trade. For instance, in the *Mahajanaka Jataka,* Mahajanaka, the son of a banished King of Videha, undertook trade in order to make money to finance his campaign against the usurper of his father's throne. Having collected goods, including pearls, jewels, and diamonds, he embarked on a ship with some merchants bound for Suvarnabhumi. There were seven caravans on board with their beasts (or three hundred and fifty men, depending upon the interpretation of the original text), and in seven days the ship travelled seven hundred leagues. The story is told for religious instruction; mention of trade and sea journeying is incidental. Hence, the geographical and chronological data are very inadequate.

Reference to Suvarnabhumi is also found in the accounts of the third Buddhist Sangiti (council) held at Pataliputra in 247 B.C. during the reign of Asoka. The tradition as contained in the *Mahavamsa* refers to two missionaries, Sona and Uttara, who were said to have been sent to Suvarnabhumi, possibly to Burma, with the message of Buddhism. Nothing, however, has been found in the countries of Southeast Asia to corroborate the tradition, and no reference to this incident has been found in the inscriptions of Asoka.

Accounts of sea voyages, some of which ended in disaster, are also recounted in other ancient texts, such as the various recensions of the lost Paisachi text *Brihatkatha* of Gunadhya, *Kathakosa,* and the Jain *Jnatadharmakatha.* The *Kathakosa* tells the story of Nagadatta who went to Suvarnadvipa with five hundred ships to conduct a profitable trade. Whilst this story, like similar stories of romance, adventure, and instruction, must have a touch of the imagination of the tale-teller, and the size of the merchant fleet may be somewhat magnified, it suggests that the trade between the two regions was considerable. The *Jnatadharmakatha* mentions that a party of merchants, having braved a storm, reached an island called Kaliyadvipa and found mines of gold, silver, diamonds, and other jewels. There are numerous references in the *Arthasastra* to those lands and places in eastern and Southeast Asia, which were worthy of note from, the economic, commercial, or political viewpoint. For instance, it refers to a kind of sandalwood, called *tailaparnika,* which was produced in Suvarnabhumi. The *Ramayana* reveals some knowledge of the eastern regions beyond seas; for instance Sugriva dispatched his men to Yayadvipa, the island of Java or Sumatra, in search of Sita. It speaks of Burma as the land of silver mines.

Tamil literature contains references to tall roomy ships laden with goods returning from eastern ports. Puranic cosmology and geographical divisions into *varshas* and *dvipas* point to Indian knowledge of this area, although the knowledge of the Puranic compilers was somewhat vague and inexact.

The *Milindapanha* and the *Mahaniddesa,* both Buddhist texts, ascribed to the first centuries of the Christian era at the latest, refer to trading voyages to eastern ports. The *Niddesa* enumerates a series, of Sanskrit or Sanskritized toponyms whose identification with localities in Southeast Asia has been proposed by Sylvain Lévi. At the present neither archaeological and epigraphic evidence nor the non-Indian literary sources allow historians to go further back than the *Niddesa* with any degree of certainty. However, if the *Niddesa* contains older tradition, the date of Indian voyages could be put back to a few centuries before the Christian era.

India's contact by sea with China would also imply Indian contact with Southeast Asia. On the authority of the *Annals of the Former Han Dynasty,* which gives the itinerary of a sea journey starting from the coast of Tonkin (Te-nan) and ending on the Indian coast, belonging to the period of Emperor Wu (140–80 B.C.), and which also contains a reverse itinerary relating to the reign of Wang Mang (A.D. 1–6), Bagchi suggests that regular sailing from the Gangetic Valley to Tonkin was taking place in the second and first centuries B.C.[4] S. Lévi, who was the first scholar to analyze the evidence of such itineraries and who held the view that the detailed knowledge of the sea route as contained in these accounts could not have been acquired before the second century, did not make use of the Chinese evidence, upon which Bagchi based his opinion.

Beyer, the first to conduct systematic archaeological investigations in the Philippines, finds formidable evidence to strengthen the view that there was pre-Christian contact between India and Southeast Asia. He concluded that all the artifacts found during the excavations at the Novaliches site in the late 1920's, including pottery, iron implements and weapons, beads and bangles, were brought to the Philippines from India over a long period of trade between the two countries. Both the iron and glass objects found are similar to, and in some cases identical with, the prehistoric glass and iron finds in South India. In 1948, having re-examined the theory and its criticism, Beyer substantially reaffirmed his earlier view. If Indian contacts reached as far as the Philippines in the centuries before Christ, it would be reasonable to conclude that the countries en route were also in touch, perhaps more intimately with India. If this evidence is accepted, there must have been Indian settlements in coastal Southeast Asia well before the commencement of the Christian era.

Evidence, however, of Indian migration in the first century is definite. This evidence is archaeological rather than historical, and suggests that Indians sailed as far as the Sunda Islands. Indian works of art have been found all along the route from India and, more significantly, all the cultures that emerged in the area about the same time carry unmistakable marks of Indian influence. Just why that should have happened remains obscure, for nothing in written sources explains it.[5]

Information about trade routes between India and Southeast Asia is found in Chinese and Greek sources. The Greek and Roman writers did not know of the world east of the Ganges, including China (*Sinai* or *Thinai*), until the first century but they do corroborate the Chinese evidence of the trade routes. About the middle of the first century, Pomponius Mela mentions Chryse and Argyre, the islands of gold and silver beyond the Ganges. Substantial evidence for the existence of a sea route to China via Southeast Asia comes from the anonymous author of the *Periplus of the Erythraean Sea*, who had undertaken a journey to India.[6] But the first extant description of Southeast Asia as a whole is found in Ptolemy's *Geography*, written in the middle of the second century.

Land routes between India and Southeast Asia lay through eastern Bengal, Assam, and Manipur. Proceeding to Upper Burma through the passes in the Manipur hills, travellers reached Lower Burma through

Arakan. Part of this route was common with the Indian route to Szechwan and Yunnan in southwestern China, and although difficult, it was often used.

The two extreme points in India for sailing to Southeast Asia were Bharukachha (Broach) on the western coast and Tamralipti (modern Tamluk in the Midnapore district of Bengal) on the eastern coast. Between them there were many good ports on both coasts. From Tamralipti, ships sailed regularly along the coasts of Bengal and Burma to Malaya, Indonesia, and Indochina. Some ships sailing from India for the ports in Malaya and beyond first made the journey along the coast as far as Palura in the Ganjam district, and then travelled across the high seas, to the Malay Peninsula. Further voyages to the islands of the East Indies and to the coast of the Indochinese Peninsula were routed through the Malacca Strait. However, archaeological evidence suggests that many voyagers disembarked and negotiated the short land journey across the Isthmus of Kra to the east coast of southern Thailand. From there the sea journey recommenced across the Gulf of Siam to Indochina. There were probably also direct sailings from South India through the channel between the Andaman and Nicobar Islands to Takua Pa in Siam or Kedah in Malaya. Voyages also commenced from the Andhra coast, and proceeded either along the coast or directly to Tavoy in Lower Burma. From there, the travellers headed for the Menam Delta negotiating the mountains through the Three Pagoda Pass. A route not generally used was to skirt Singapore and reach either what is now Bangkok, through the Gulf of Siam, or Funan and Champa across the China Sea. At all these points of embarkation and disembarkation, and all along the inland routes, the harvest of archaeological finds has been rich and has enabled historians to piece together a coherent account of journeys between India and Suvarnabhumi.

The popularity of these routes varied from time to time. The earliest settlers, it appears, embarked at Amaravati or at Guduru and landed at Martaban in Burma. Some of them moved up to the Pegu region and settled there, whilst others pushed southward through the Three Pagoda Pass as far as the fertile rice plains of Thailand. Later, during the reign of the Guptas, the port of Tamralipti was more frequently used, possibly because of its proximity to the Gupta capital at Pataliputra. It was from here that Fa-hsien started his sea journey back to China. In Pallava times, Kanchipuram—though not a port, being about forty miles inland—was more popular for journeys to Burma, Malaya, Java, or Sumatra.

The journey from India to Burma by land was so exacting that travellers generally preferred to take an alternate route. The Indochinese Peninsula was covered with mountain ranges, wild and thick jungles, treacherous rivers, and other perils. Inland communications were few and difficult. The major means of inland communication were the rivers—the Red River, the Mekong, and the Menam; the overland routes were, and still are, few. The only regular land route between Burma and Siam was through the Three Pagoda Pass, although at times some Burmese armies and migrants did cross over to Siam in the north. There was no regular road link between Laos, Tonkin, and Annam, and there is still none. The hostility of nature is such that more than four-fifths of Indochina is almost barren and uninhabitable.

That Indian traders and settlers repeatedly undertook journeys to Southeast Asia, despite the hazards and perils involved, speaks well for their physical prowess, courage, and determination, even if allowance for the pull of profit is made. But they were more than enterprising and courageous. This is illustrated by the fact that they were able to radically transform whole civilizations by spontaneous individual effort, without state aid, planned organizational backing, or political domination. It was the Indian merchants who opened up the region for Indian religions and settlements, and who sustained Indian cultural intercourse with Southeast Asia. In marked contrast with what happened in Central Asia and China, where once the process had been initiated the principal burden of cultural diffusion fell on scholars, pilgrims, and monks, the cultural role of Indian settlers and traders continued undiminished in Southeast Asia. There were numerous coastal merchant settlements both in India and Southeast Asia, constantly in touch with each other. To deny them the qualities of mind and body which they no doubt possessed, would be extraordinarily prejudicial. Suggestions have been made in the past, and recently repeated, that the Indian traders were poor and untutored and could not effectively transmit ideas.[7] In view of the ample archaeological evidence and of the opinions of specialist scholars in the field, such as Coedès, Winstedt, and Groslier, it is surprising that this suggestion, without any substantial arguments to back it, should ever have been put forward.

Indians were not the only people trading in Southeast Asia at the time, but it was the Indians who proved most skilful in winning the confidence and friendship of the local peoples and in transmitting their cultural influences. In ancient Indian society, the trading community was wealthy and, after the ruling houses, the chief patron of priests and learning. Even today the distinction between the trader and the labourer is clear enough to a discerning observer. In the ancient period those who came to Southeast Asia and set up establishments there, whether temporary or permanent, were wealthy merchants or their agents in charge of foreign depots: men of skill, enterprise, and culture. Reflecting upon the extraordinary difficulties involved in these journeys and remembering that often they were feats of ingenuity, stamina, and perseverance, one cannot but regard the early Indian traders as remarkably well-equipped to spread ideas. They were good traders and good sailors and loved to acquire wealth through risk and honest bargain. Not only were the Indian traders vehicles of culture in this part of the world, but everywhere trade has been a major factor in the dissemination of culture. The Indian commercial relations with the Western counties is one example of it. The Arabs, as traders, have been the most outstanding transmitters of culture. Arthur Waley, writing on a similar subject, categorically declares that merchants were undoubtedly the main carriers of information about the outside world, and disputes the assertion which is derived from false analogy between the East and West that merchants are not likely to have been interested in philosophy. Indian or Chinese merchants, in contrast to European traders, were "reputedly capable of discussing metaphysical questions" and there is ample testimony in Buddhist legend of such merchants.[8]

No doubt cultural contact was stimulated by the inherent spirit of human adventure and the desire to give and take; the main reason for Indian expansion and the eventual radiation of Indian culture was profit, not missionary endeavour. Indian trade was already brisk by the beginning of the Christian era, and later it became far more extensive. The discovery of monsoons made sea journeys between India and the Western world safe and punctual, and the Roman demand for the luxury goods of the East had reached fantastic proportions—far beyond what India alone could supply. Consequently, the Indians went in increasing numbers to Southeast Asia looking for those things that could be sold to the Romans at such good prices that Pliny the Elder was to bewail this loss of blood inflicted on the Roman economy. Spices, sandalwood, camphor, and benzoin, were amongst the products of the countries beyond the Ganges: Takkola, "cardamom market"; Karpuradvipa, "the camphor island"; Narikeladvipa, "the coconut palm island," and many more Sanskrit toponyms reveal the type of interest which attracted Indians toward these regions. The growing demands of maritime trade stimulated the development and expansion of Indian shipping. The consequent economic revolution was so vigorous that it has been compared to the epoch-making change brought about by the discovery of the direct sea route to India from Europe fourteen centuries later, which altered the entire commercial map of the world.

The attraction of lucrative trade was no doubt further strengthened by the reputation of Southeast Asia for rich gold resources. Perhaps by modern standards Southeast Asia would not seem to have been so rich as to justify this reputation, but gold was far more scarce in ancient days, and the prospects of finding gold were accompanied by a certain expectation of profitable trade. In the beginning of the Christian era, India lost Siberia as her most important source of gold, because political upheavals and large-scale movements of the peoples of Central Asia in the last two centuries B.C. cut off the trade route.

That Indonesians adopted various Indian numbers would further endorse the view that Indian trade with Southeast Asia, particularly with the East Indies, was unusually active. Numerals, terms for family relations, and terms for parts of the body, generally remain unchanged in a language affected by foreign influences.

Since profit, not religious zeal, was the driving force behind Indian cultural expansion, it is somewhat superfluous to argue whether Hinduism or Buddhism came first to Southeast Asia. At any rate no definite answer can be given, for in thought and culture both religions are inextricably interlinked and the differences are at best sectarian. Hinduism probably arrived first but certainly existed simultaneously. Whilst Hinduism must have been due to the presence of Hindus from India and those local peoples who had imperceptibly absorbed elements of Hindu culture, Buddhism, an organized missionary religion, must have been introduced by monks. That Hinduism was not a proselytizing religion, and yet had a powerful hold for centuries in Southeast Asia, would suggest the existence of large communities of Hindus or gradually converted peoples.

Although the Buddha is recorded to have instructed his disciples "let not any two of you go in the same direction," early Buddhism was not a proselytizing religion; in fact, it did not begin as a religion at all. However, it soon developed into one with an unprecedented zeal for proselytization. During the reign of Asoka, zealous missionaries carried Buddhism to foreign lands as well as the distant regions of the vast Mauryan Empire. Innumerable stupas sprang up all over the country, the finest of which, the stupa of Sanchi, still stands.[9] As communication improved between northern and southern India, Buddhism migrated to South India. After the fall of the Mauryan Empire, the Satavahanas founded the first historical empire in the west and the south. It was then that the ancient trunk route of northern India, which was the main artery of traffic linking Ujjayini, the western capital of the Imperial government, with the capital of the Mauryan Empire, Pataliputra in the east, was extended to the capital of the Satavahanas at Pratisthana. From Pratisthana the route proceeded southward, bifurcating in both eastern and western directions. Thus, centres of political power, missionary religion, and maritime commerce were linked by road transport in an unprecedentedly intimate contact, bringing Buddhism to the Indian coastal areas of brisk international trade. From there it was but a short step for a dynamic religion, as Buddhism no doubt was, to the countries of Southeast Asia.

The Hindu Satavahanas, at first, only tolerated Buddhism. Later it was actively patronized, and consequently flourished throughout the Satavahana period. It was, however, during the first two centuries A.D., after the Satavahanas had recovered from a short political set-back (*ca.* 35–90), that Buddhism had its greatest success in South India. This was also the period when Indian trade, mainly from South India, with the West had reached its height, and was expanding in the East. The Satavahanas, and the Kshaharatas, their rivals in the west, competed in building Buddhist monasteries, patronizing the monks, and granting lands and gifts of money to Buddhist temples. In the eastern sector of the Empire, particularly along the southeastern coast of India, Buddhist stupas and other structures were built mainly through private effort, which would suggest that Buddhism was even more popular in these areas. The remains of Amaravati and Nagarjunakonda lend considerable support to this view. Both cities were situated on the river Krishna; the distance between the two by land was about sixty miles, and by river a little more than one hundred. Amaravati was contemporaneous with the Satavahanas, whereas Nagarjunakonda was developed after their fall, and is associated with the Buddhist teacher, Nagarjuna. It was from this area and during this time that Indians sailed mostly to Southeast Asian ports, which makes it likely that they were either Buddhist or at least familiar with Buddhist teachings.

Whilst Hinduism may have been more popular with the settlers, courts, and aristocracy, Buddhism with its simplicity and doctrine of human equality may have gained more attention from the common people as it did in China. Both in their respective ways, however, helped cultural intercourse until the whole of Southeast Asia professed Buddhism, Hinduism, a mixture of both, or an admixture of these and their own indigenous beliefs. Practically all sects and schools of Hinduism and Buddhism, from vedic worship to Tantric beliefs, entered these countries. Siva, generally speaking, was a more popular Hindu god than Vishnu. Many Cambodian and Indonesian kings had their images installed in the likeness of the deity they worshipped, superimposing on their own personality the attributes of their favorite god. In some countries, such as Indonesia, Hinduism was so intermingled with Buddhism that Siva and the Buddha were described as brothers. Indeed, in Balinese temples where the religion is Balinese Hinduism, Saiva and Buddhist priests sit side by side, although dressed differently, as they bless the laity. Theravada Buddhism found a far greater following in Southeast Asia than the Mahayana School. In countries such as Indonesia and Malaya, which became Muslim in the fourteenth and fifteenth centuries, the earlier beliefs still survive. Most have been given an Islamic veneer, but in some cases they are still in their original form. In comparatively inaccessible mountainous regions of interior Indonesia, indigenous beliefs are combined with Hindu and Buddhist practices, and in many cities, such as Jogjakarta and Surabaya, Muslims, theoretically not supposed to worship icons, can be seen kneeling in prayer before beautifully sculptured Hindu-Buddhist images of the ninth century and later.

It seems that the Indian immigrants made no conscious attempt to convert local peoples to their faith or culture; they certainly did not impose it by force. Proselytism was precluded by the very nature of the Hindu faith, which perhaps would explain the general unconcern of Indians with the Indianization of Southeast Asia, as well as the absence of references in Indian literature relating to the processes of change. However, there were Buddhist missionaries who worked for the spread of their faith, and some centres and monasteries earned a widespread reputation for their learning.

Whether they were monks or merchants, the culture of these Indians deeply affected the countries they visited or settled. Groslier gives a graphic description of Indian traders who came to Spice Island with the southwestern monsoon looking for goods for export to the Mediterranean world. They had to temporarily settle in the deserted land waiting for the favourable wind to return, and gradually the demands of increasing trade compelled them to establish permanent depots in these lands.

Intermarriage must have played an important role in this cultural synthesis. Soon complete fusion of population and culture was achieved. This fact should dispel any arguments of Indian caste rigidity at the time. The argument, first advanced by Coedès long ago and almost mechanically repeated by certain other scholars, that since the caste system, which was an integral part of the Hindu social organization, did not exist in Southeast Asia, Indian cultural influence must have been partial, ignores the fact that the Indian culture which radiated abroad was a blending of Hinduism and Buddhism, and that the caste system was not so rigid at that time. Also, many settlers and sailors were Buddhists and opposed to the caste system.

Whilst there was a continuous influx of merchants, priests, monks, and settlers into Southeast Asia, and whereas Indian scholars and traders constantly went to other lands to preach or to make profit, unlike the Portuguese and other Europeans, there is no account of any Indian adventurer or merchant seeking employment at the local courts purely for reasons of amassing wealth. However, once Indians had become a part of Southeast Asian life, they were often employed by the local rulers. Later, Indianized kingdoms emerged either as a result of an Indian imposing himself on the local population or else through a local chief adopting the foreign civilization. With time it was inevitable that there should emerge able men of enterprise and ambition who sought power and authority. Those who succeeded in setting themselves up as rulers brought to their court and household, at least in the beginning, the required staff of priests, scribes, goldsmiths, weavers, bards, sculptors, scholars, bodyguards, and so on, as well as Indian texts on law and jurisprudence, the arts, and the like. All aspects of the culture of the rulers penetrated the society of their adoption. In time, local people were employed in various positions and local influences were assimilated by the Indian rulers and settlers.

Despite the large-scale influx of Indians of various economic classes and intellectual levels over a long period, there is no evidence of any local resistance to their arrival. The friendly reception accorded Indian settlers is in marked contrast to the strong distrust and opposition encountered by European settlers and traders practically everywhere, not only from highly civilized and sophisticated communities but also from primitive and aboriginal peoples. There is no evidence that the Indians regarded these new lands as outlets for their excessive population or an exclusive market for their growing trade, or that they insisted on the superiority of their culture. Wherever Indians settled they gave what they had and took what they could. Thus was evolved, by mutual consent, a new culture whose dominant note was Indian.

Southeast Asian traders or Buddhist pilgrims who visited India brought back Indian traditions. Consequently, an Indian political system, centring around the king, with a Hindu-Buddhist cosmological basis of kingship; Indian epic and sacred texts; Indian mathematics and astronomy; and Indian skills in husbandry and handicrafts became increasingly entrenched in the new lands. Sanskrit became the official language, and along with Pali, was used for religious texts. The various schools of Hinduism and Buddhism found a following in these countries, and even Indian Islam entered Southeast Asia. The impact of Indian civilization was such that it did not remain confined to settlements or coastal areas, as one would expect in an age of slow transport, but penetrated to the centre and distant corners of mainland and inland Southeast Asia.

According to Quaritch Wales, Indianization, although a continuing process, proceeded in successive peaks, which he calls the Four Main Waves of Indian Cultural Expansion.[10] These waves, which correspond to the peak periods of Hindu-Buddhist civilization, are the Amaravati in the second and third centuries, the Gupta from the fourth to the sixth centuries, the Pallava from about 550 to 750, and the Pala from about 750 to 900. He adds a fifth wave, supplementary to the fourth, the late Pala influence in the twelfth and thirteenth centuries, after the disruption of Nalanda University. Perhaps a sixth wave of Islam could also be added, for it was principally Indian Islam that travelled to Southeast Asia. This is a simplified classification of a complex process which does not lend itself to neat categorization, but it does reflect the fact that the Indian cultural encounter with Southeast Asia assumed different forms in different periods, and that it was closely connected with the changing patterns of Indian society. The Indian impact was a kind of chain reaction, in which each successive wave of Indian immigrants worked out a cultural synthesis with the local people, including localized Indians, with varying degrees of concentration and assimilation.

Besides commercial profit and cultural propaganda, there were other reasons that prompted this vigorous, sustained, and extraordinary maritime expansion by a people who today are not particularly noted for their adventurous spirit or material pursuits. One conclusion is obvious: the ancient Indians were very different from their modern descendants in their spirit of commercial enterprise as well as missionary zeal. They were not reluctant to go out seeking people with whom they could exchange goods and ideas. However, various other explanations have been suggested. For example, a remote cause is to be found in the third century B.C. in the conquest of Kalinga by Asoka, and in the resultant exodus of population. Others believe that the pressure felt by the mass of the Indian population because of the Kushana invasions in the first century led to Indian emigration; this would be chronologically more plausible. It is also suggested that a wholesale migration of coastal people might have been caused by Samudragupta's conquest of South India; this would explain the simultaneous rise of the Hindu states in

Southeast Asia. However, none of these explanations would appear to be correct, because the available data clearly indicate that Indian expansion in the first centuries was of a commercial nature, and not a haphazard movement of groups of people seeking asylum from unrest. No evidence has been advanced to show a systematic displacement of large Indian populations. If invasions or internal chaos were normally to cause an exodus of Indians to foreign lands, then there would have been many more migratory waves, especially during the period beginning with the disastrous incursions of Mahmud of Ghazni.

That the introduction of Indian culture was a gradual process presupposes that the indigenous cultures were sufficiently well developed to exchange knowledge. The local cultures adopted only those Indian features of which they approved. It is possible that the local element was subordinated to Indian influence but it was never eclipsed, and the local people never completely lost their freedom of initiative. A people who could feel the stimulus of an alien culture and respond to it in accordance with their need cannot but have attained a certain degree of civilization. The facility with which the Indians were able to expand their culture in Southeast Asia may lend some weight to the view that in their beliefs and attitudes the indigenous peoples could see a reflection of their own traditions.

What sort of civilization existed in Southeast Asia before the advent of Indian cultural diffusion? Because of the earliest racial and cultural movements it seems that by the last phase of the Neolithic Age, the entire region was inhabited by ethnically intermixed peoples. The most characteristic feature known of this period is the different forms of adzes with quadrangular sections. These adzes are found in North India, Burma, Malaya, China, and Japan. Probably this quadrangular adze-culture came to the Malay Peninsula and Indonesia through China and central Indochina (Laos and Siam) sometime between 2000 and 1500 B.C. It brought to Indonesia what are called the Austronesian languages (which later developed into Indonesian languages), and introduced the outrigger canoe, rice cultivation, domesticated cattle or buffaloes, head-hunting, and the custom of erecting megalithic monuments.[11] This culture was the most widespread and important of the Stone Age cultures of the region, because of its artistic development, especially in pottery and weaving.

Whilst Heine-Geldern considers that originally Indonesians migrated from Yunnan and southwestern China, Hendrik Kern, who wrote in 1889 and relied on linguistic evidence, suggested it to be Indochina and the neighbouring areas, in which sugar cane, bananas, cocoanut, bamboo, and possibly rattan were grown. Rice was the staple food of this seafaring people. The Neolithic wave of migration, however, does not seem to have gone beyond the Moluccas and did not reach New Guinea.

The next stage in the development of these countries, known as the Dong-son culture, which has been defined as the culture of the Indonesian peoples of the coastal belt of Annam, took place between the fifth and second centuries B.C. It was characterized by extensive use of bronze and considerable knowledge of iron. The bronze work was quite advanced and bronze kettledrums are a special feature of this period. Of superb workmanship, they were widely used for ritual purposes. They have very thin walls and the bronze is an alloy of copper and lead as in the mints of China in the Han times. Later, in the Indian period, the usual copper-tin alloy came back into use. In addition to the drums, swords, daggers and helmets, household utensils and small statuettes, all of bronze, and ornaments of shell and semi-precious stones have been found. The first find of drums was made near Thanh-hoa in Annam. However, they have subsequently been discovered all over the island area.

The Dong-son people were skilled agriculturists, fishermen, shipbuilders, and sailors. Their navigation was more developed than that of their predecessors and they had some knowledge of astronomy. They were well-travelled merchants and, significantly, some of their names for weights and measures, such as *kati* and *tahil,* are still used in Malaya and Indonesia.

It has been suggested recently that the Dong-son culture can be traced back to the Yueh people who inhabited the coastal regions of China about 2000 B.C., and whose typical traits, according to Eberhard, were: "A developed navigation; the practice of holding boat races, with its outgrowth, the dragon boat festival; the use of bronze drums decorated in a way showing connection with that rite; and the concept of the dragon as the river god. Elements of this culture were the worship of serpents, of sacred mountains—the latter developed into important temple festivals—and of certain trees."[12] However, as Eberhard himself points out, the subject of the affiliations of these early cultures of the Pacific lands can be tackled only in a tentative manner.[13]

There are various other theories, all disputed and unresolved, concerning the relationship between Austro-Asiatic or Austric culture—the culture which spread across the Indo-Chinese peninsula to the extremities of northeastern India—and pre-Aryan India. If some are valid, Indian contact with Southeast Asia began many cenuturies before the Christian era and continued vigorously until about 1500. Even if the possibility of cultural contacts during the prehistoric times, of which there is only fragmentary and indefinite archaeological evidence and legendary accounts, is discounted, direct Indian contact with the countries of Southeast Asia lasted for about fifteen hundred years. Whilst Hinduism stagnated and Buddhism almost disappeared in India during the mediaeval period, they both flourished in Southeast Asia. Burma, Thailand, Ceylon, Laos, Cambodia, and Vietnam are even today predominantly Buddhist nations, and Malaya and Indonesia—with the exception of Bali which still professes Balinese Hinduism—remained Hindu-Buddhist until the rise of Islam in the fifteenth century. However, Islam did not dislodge Indian culture; it became another tributary in the river of Malay culture. South India by far exerted the greatest influence on Southeast Asia, although Gujarat, Bengal, and Malwa made significant contributions.

The line of demarcation between Chinese and Indian cultural influence in Southeast Asia may be drawn from eastern central Tibet southward through the Indochinese Peninsula, then in a southeasterly direction into Indonesia; but there was much interpenetration. Formosa, Tonkin, and the Philippines remained on the Chinese side, whilst Laos, Cambodia, Siam, Burma, Malaysia, and Indonesia came within the Indian sphere. Chinese influence, however, does not seem to have been very great. Formosa is really a part of the Chinese nation, and in the Philippines, both India and China made contributions, as well as other regions, including the West. Even Tonkin, which is physically, ethnologically, and often politically allied to China, retained Buddhism and a good deal of Indian culture.

The nature and depth of Indian and Chinese influences differed considerably, as did the processes of their advance. Whilst the Chinese migrants had little inclination to mix with local populations, even though there was an ethnic affinity between them, the Indian settlers intermarried freely with indigenous people. Even within the Indian sphere of influence, the Chinese, who established themselves at selected trading points, remained colonies of foreigners with little inclination to mix with the local population. Chinese cultural expansion was the secondary outcome of political domination, for China seldom exported culture for its own sake but gave it as if to soften the blow of conquest. Except for some political interference in Ceylon and for the naval expedition sent by Rajendra Cola against the Sri Vijaya Empire in 1025, no Indian state ever made any serious effort to dictate political terms, much less culture, to the peoples of Southeast Asia. Chinese culture remained confined to the people of Chinese descent in these regions, and nowhere, with the possible exception of Tonkin, is there any trace of the total assimilation of Chinese culture.

Indian and Chinese cultures have met in other areas, but in Indochina the meeting was on a large scale, and their interaction with the existing culture has been a unique phenomenon in history. Although India was farther away from Indochina, it does not appear that this was much of a handicap. Tonkin, over which China ruled for long periods, was the only area in the whole Southeast Asian region where the local people absorbed more Chinese than Indian culture. Even then it accepted Buddhism and, in turn, transmitted it to southern China. Describing the contrast between the methods and effects of these two influences, Groslier observes: "China quite simply conquered and annexed Tonkin, making a clean slate of the past to impose her civilization and finally turn the country into one of her provinces; a province scarcely recognizable as distinct from others in her vast empire. Whereas India only touched on the southern coasts of Indo-China, and vanished again from the scene, when her seafaring activity practically came to an end in about the fifth century A.D. But in that short space of time the peoples thus drawn out of their isolation, on their own initiative took over her culture, and very soon in turn created new civilizations of profound originality. China dominated, whilst India scattered seed, and between them they were to shape the double aspect of Indo-China."[14]

Indeed, as Coedes has pointed out, Southeast Asia was able to make progress mainly during those periods of history when it was left alone by a China weakened by her own internal political upheavals. China never liked the establishment of powerful empires in her neighbourhood, and the states of Southeast Asia found a favourable climate for political and cultural progress at a time when China was politically unstable. The ascendancy of Funan during the fourth and fifth centuries coincides with the chaotic period of the Three Kingdoms in China; the consolidation of Champa's power in the seventh century, the peak of pre-Angkor Cambodia, the blossoming of Angkor Cambodia in the tenth century and the growth of the Khmer, Cham, and Burmese kingdoms at the end of the eleventh century coincide with periods of weakness in Chinese history. In contrast, the strength of cultural movements in India is reflected in similar movements in the countries of Southeast Asia.[15]

Even the remarkable Hellenization of the Mediterranean world does not compare with the Indianization of Southeast Asia. India was far from Southeast Asia and had never dominated any of the local kingdoms; nor did any purely Indian dynasty, unlike the Greeks in Egypt or Syria, ever rule the area. Hellenic civilization directly expanded in those areas that were in the Greek neighbourhood and had been dominated by Hellenic dynasts. There were far fewer Indians in Southeast Asia than Greeks in the Hellenistic world, and those Indians had to contend with an equally powerful Chinese civilization in an area mainly frequented by Chinese, and in which most of the local peoples were racially closer to China than to India. On the other hand, Greek civilization did not confront such a contrast of cultural and ethnic types. In fact, the Greeks were not successful in influencing Persians, West Asians, or Indians. On the contrary, they were considerably influenced by them. Even in effect, Indian culture in Southeast Asia left behind more than was left by Hellenism in the Mediterranean world. There is nothing in the Hellenistic world to compare with the Angkor Wat or Borobudur. Whilst Hellenism merged into Hellenisticism and absorbed many traits of other civilizations, Indian culture has continued to grow quite distinctly. Again, India contributed not only philosophy and thought, but also a religion that still survives in most areas of Southeast Asia. Greek religion is a thing of the past.

Whatever be the precise nature of the process of Indian cultural alliance and influence, its extent was deep and extensive, and its effects were felt in all aspects of culture from religious thought to the technical skills in agriculture and handicrafts. First the Indian alphabetic system, which is still used in Burma, Siam, Cambodia, and Laos, was introduced, followed by the introduction of Sanskrit and Sanskrit literature, "playing just the same part as Latin in Mediaeval Europe. India also taught her political system centred on the king, and her main religious beliefs. Her sacred texts, and her great epics, were so well learnt throughout this India beyond the seas that they became naturalised in each of these lands. Finally, India unfolded the secrets of her mathematics and astronomy, making possible calendar calculations of much greater accuracy than in the past, and all her technical skill in husbandry and handicrafts."[16]

Ceylon

Sri Lanka, Sinhala, or Ceylon, which is India's closest neighbour to the south, was possibly the first country in southern Asia to feel the impact of Indian immigration. Ceylon's cultural relations with India, often reinforced by close political ties, have been almost continuous to the present day. Strictly speaking, Ceylon is not counted as part of Southeast Asia but it did act both as an intermediary and a base for the eastward migration of Indian culture and religions. In the history of Buddhism and Hinduism, as well as in the contemporary Indian world, Lanka occupies an eminent position. The Hindu epic, *Ramayana,* narrates the story in which Rama's conflict with Ravana, the king of Lanka, is the central theme. Although the history of ancient Ceylon, when it was known as Lanka in India, is largely a complex of myths, legends, and plausible conjectures, and the beginnings of the earliest migrations are indefinite, it is undoubted that the early settlers of Ceylon came from India.[17]

The Vaddas were possibly the earliest peoples of Ceylon but it is the following Aryan migration which has been authenticated. The language of the Aryans gave rise to Sinhalese, now the national language of modern Ceylon. The Aryan migrants, members of the *Sinhalaa, Sinhalas,* or the Lion Tribe, named their new home Sinhaladvipa, from which have derived its later variations: the Portuguese *Ceilao* or *Zeylan,* and the English Ceylon.

The coming of Aryans is represented in the *Mahavamsa* by the story of Prince Vijayasimha who came from northern India in the sixth century B.C. In spite of the legends that surround him, his historical existence is generally acknowledged. It was, however, at the time of the introduction of Buddhism during the reign of Asoka that close contact between India and Ceylon began. This contact became so constant that it is not always possible to separate the history of South India from that of Ceylon. Indeed, the period before the arrival of the Portuguese in 1505 is sometimes referred to as the Indian period of Ceylonese history.

By the time Buddhism arrived, the Aryans, who were not altogether cut off from their kinsmen in India, had opened up the country, established settlements in the dry zone, introduced the use of iron, organized a system of government, and spread Hindu doctrines. The existence of Hinduism is undoubted, but the extent of its popularity is not precisely known; other faiths, such as Jain and Ajivika, were also practiced. Certain elements of Hinduism, such as the caste system, are known to have existed in pre-Buddhist Ceylon. It is also possible that the fame of Buddhism had reached Ceylon before the third century B.C. when Asoka sent in the mission headed by his son (or brother), Mahinda (or Mahendra), the first foreign missionary and the real founder of Buddhism in Ceylon. According to the *Mahavamsa,* the King of Ceylon, Devanampiya Tissa (247–207 B.C.), received Asoka's mission with great respect and, deeply impressed by the new faith, he and his people soon embraced Buddhism. Mahinda delivered a number of sermons during his initial stay of twenty-six days at Anuradhapura, the capital, and when he left there were already sixty-two monks. Whatever be the accuracy of the story of his spectacular success, there is no doubt that the visit of this young man, who worked for the next forty-eight years of his life in Ceylon, marks the beginning of Sinhalese culture as we know it, and the phenomenal rise of Buddhism throughout the country.

Because no monk was allowed to ordain nuns, Asoka later sent Sanghamitra, Mahendra's sister, to Ceylon to ordain Queen Anula and other women who expressed the desire to enter the Sangha. It is said that she brought with her a sprig of the Bodhi Tree, under which Gautama Buddha had attained enlightenment. The branch was planted at the capital in an impressive ceremony, and the sacred tree which resulted still exists.[18] The idea for this transplantation of a branch of the Bodhi Tree is attributed to Asoka. The Tree served as an inspiration to the people who had recently embraced the Buddhist religion, became symbolic of Buddhist supremacy in Ceylon, and strengthened the cultural links with India. Later, other sacred relics were imported to Ceylon from India. A returning Ceylonese mission from Pataliputra brought the alms bowl of the Buddha, which was housed in the Thuparama Dagoba, and one of the Buddha's teeth was enshrined in a specially built temple, Dhammachakka. These events in the early history of Ceylonese Buddhism left a deep impression on the Sinhalese people and still evoke pious enthusiasm amongst millions of its votaries.

There are various legends about the tooth, but it is known to have been in Ceylon when Fa-hsien visited the country in the fifth century. The tooth has a chequered history, for powerful monarchs, both within Ceylon and outside, longed to possess it. Some hostile powers sought to destroy it; the Portuguese claimed to have captured and burned it in the marketplace of Goa during their suzerainty over Ceylon from 1517 to 1600. It has, however, survived all such attempts and is now preserved in the Temple of the Sacred Tooth at Kandy where a colourful festival is held each year.

The reign of Vattagamani (*ca.* 29–17 B.C.) is an important landmark in the history of Buddhism in Ceylon, for it was then that the sacred scriptures, which had been committed to memory, were written down through the efforts of hundreds of reciters and scribes. The sacred Pali canon, the Tripitaka, which survives today and the original of which has long since vanished from India, was the result of this mass effort. Buddhism became so powerful in Ceylon that kings went out of their way to identify themselves more closely with it and to extend it special patronage. Monks began to pour into Ceylon from India and monasteries were erected all over the country with generous endowments made for their maintenance. Hundred of thousands of men and women embraced the new faith and thousands entered the Sangha.

Ceylon's particularly enthusiastic response to Buddhism was presumably because Buddhism was seeking support amongst a people who were already ethnologically and culturally closely associated with India. By the time it came to Ceylon, Buddhism had assumed a popular form. It did not stress its abstruse doctrines but sought to emphasize the personality of the Buddha as an inspiring teacher and as a saviour of supernatural power. It was this image which was most appealing and comprehensible to the common man. Buddhist literature was rich and comprehensive enough to satisfy both monks and laymen. It was therefore easy for Buddhist preachers to communicate with the masses in Ceylon.

The adoption of Buddhism as the national religion was followed by major changes in the social and religious life of the people, as well as in the royal household and court. The court was additionally influenced by India because the Ceylonese royalty established matrimonial links with South Indian royal houses, and continued to maintain them. During certain later periods, parts of Ceylon and South India were joined under one ruling dynasty, and trade contacts between India and Ceylon were further strengthened. Pali—also much Sanskrit—became the literary language of Ceylon, and Ceylonese literature has close affinities with its Indian counterpart. The art of writing possibly came to Ceylon with the Aryans before the introduction of Buddhism; the earliest known specimens of writing, however, are associated with Buddhism.[19] Whether the Ceylonese alphabet was introduced during the period of Asoka or before, it is undoubtediy Indian in origin.

The rise of Buddhism also witnessed a blossoming of Ceylonese art and architecture. King Devanampiya Tissa was the first to promote the building of sacred monuments, the earliest of which is the Thuparama Dagoba at Anuradhapura, built during the days of Asoka. A successor of his, Dutthagamani (101–77 B.C.), built the Lohapasada, the brazen palace, and began the Ruvanvelisaya Dagoba, which was completed after his death. King Mahasena (334–362), who is famous for his large irrigation tanks, also built the largest *dagoba* (or stupa), commonly called the Jetavanarama, at Anuradhapura. The 251 feet high Jetavanarama Dagoba stands on a platform which covers nearly eight acres of a fourteen acre walled enclosure. The Abhayagiri Dagoba, almost equally massive, is reputed to have been built in the first century B.C.

The main architectural remains are found at Anuradhapura and Polonnaruva, the two most famous capitals of ancient and mediaeval Ceylon. The former was the royal capital for more than a thousand years, until it was superseded about the eighth century by the latter which remained the capital until the thirteenth century. Ceylonese antiquities, therefore, belong to two widely separated periods. Anuradhapura architecture goes back to the third century B.C. although most of it dates from the early centuries A.D., whereas the important structures of Polonnaruva belong to the second half of the twelfth century. The most conspicuous structures at Anuradhapura are the Buddhist dagobas, far exceeding in dimensions anything extant in India. But the magnificent stupas and the ornamental and decorative architecture, the sculptures of dwarfs and of Naga deities, the moonstones, and the stone railings of Anuradhapura recall those of Sanchi and Amaravati. The latter phase of this period is characterized by influences typical of Andhra art, as seen in the Buddhist sculptures of Amaravati.

During the Polonnaruva period, Ceylonese architecture was mainly influenced by the South India Pallava art of the seventh century. Examples in Ceylon of the sacred shrines of the Pallava period are the Koneswara temple at Trincomallee, and the ancient temple of Tiruketiswaram. The Tivaka Vihara at Polonnaruva, built by Parakrama Bahu (1153–1186), has a high pyramidal roof in Dravidian style; indeed, the buildings at Polonnaruva in general have a distinctly Dravidian character.

In Buddhist shrines, Hindu deities occupy honoured places; Vishnu is particularly popular in Sinhalese Buddhist temples, for he is not considered a rival of the Buddha but the protector of Ceylon, and is worshipped as subordinate to the Buddha. Hindu temples were also built: for example, the Siva temple at Polonnaruva dating probably from the eleventh or twelfth century resembles the South Indian Chola buildings. Ceylonese sacred monuments and monasteries, however, are distinguished from those in India by certain features common with Buddhist structures in Indochina.

Painting and sculpture in Ceylon, although modified by indigenous influence, generally followed Indian models. But often the mark of Ceylon is so deep on certain works of art that its Indian origins are not very evident. The Ceylonese "moonstone," a semi-circular slab placed at the foot of a staircase and carved elaborately in low relief, although developed from the plain Amaravati type moonstone, is especially characteristic of Ceylonese art. Its design is invariably based on the open lotus flower.

Indian influence on Buddhist iconography is unmistakable. Large statues of the Buddha, seated, standing, or reclining, are abundant in the country, and some of them go back to the beginning of the Christian era. The earlier type of Buddha image known in Ceylon is that of the Andhra School, and the folded drapery style of the early Buddha images closely resembles that of Amaravati.[20] The stone Buddha statue, from the Toluvila ruins at Anuradhapura, with a local devotee seated beside it, is comparable to the best Gupta sculpture, and Pallava influence can be seen in the sculpture of Polonnaruva. Some Ceylonese sculpture may have even been cast in India. The human panel-figures generally resemble those at Sanchi, although they are more advanced in style.

Early Sinhalese pictorial art is said to have been inspired by Amaravati, and the frescoes at Sigiriya bear striking similarities to those of Ajanta. Situated on an isolated hill, Sigiriya was constructed as an impregnable refuge by King Kasyapa I, who reigned during the last quarter of the fifth century, and the paintings, comprising twenty-one female portraits, are placed in two irregular rock chambers, usually called pockets. Some recent observers have noticed the reflection of the Amaravati style and technique in the art of Sigiriya. Whatever be the foreign influence, the Sigiriya frescoes are remarkable productions of their age. There is nothing to suggest who the artists were, where they came from, or how they learned their art.

Apart from the ancient Pali Chronicle, *Mahavamsa,* the main sources of the history of dance and music in Ceylon are art and literature. Details of sculptured dancing figures, and wood and ivory carvings undoubtedly reveal the relationship of the Ceylonese dancers' art with that of Indian, particularly Bharata Natyam, which spread to Ceylon from South India. The *Mahavamsa* mentions musical instruments such as *mridanga, kahala, maddala,* and *vina,* which are still in common use in India. Most of the musical instruments listed in the *Thupavamsa* and *Dalada Sirita,* belonging roughly to a period between the thirteenth and fourteenth centuries, are of Indian origin. Some of the drums are identical with those of South India. A number of technical terms current in Indian music are referred to in the Sinhalese poem, *Kavislumina.*[21] In Sinhalese folksongs, for example harvest songs, is seen the reflection of the folksongs of Malabar which accompany the transplantation of paddy seedlings in the fields.

In turn, Ceylon has contributed a good deal to India and the world by carefully preserving the original Buddhist doctrine and practice. It was from Ceylon that the world learned the must authentic account of the rise of Buddhism. The Pali canon has had great influence upon Burma, Cambodia, Thailand, and Laos: the countries where Theravada Buddhism flourishes today.

Burma

Burma is the largest country in the Southeast Asian mainland with an area of a quarter of a million square miles. Although there was a land route between India and Burma from very ancient times, trade and contact between the two countries developed by sea rather than by land because Burma lay across the highly inaccessible Assam and Manipur hills, and the Arakan hill ranges. In contrast, the sea route to lower Burma was relatively easy. It was an important stage in the route from India to China, although today Burma lies off the main road of world commerce, which goes by sea through the Strait of Malacca.

It was mainly through Buddhism that Indian thought and culture made an impression on Burmese life and civilization. The Ceylonese chronicles speak of two of Asoka's missionaries, Sona and Uttara, who were dispatched by the Third Buddhist Council to Burma to revive Buddhism. This would suggest that Buddhism had been in existence in Burma for some time. Whilst the accuracy of this account has been questioned, its possibility cannot be denied outright, and there is hardly any other legend so widespread in the Buddhist tradition of Burma and held with such deep conviction. There is a Burmese tradition that Buddhism came to the country through the good offices of two Mon merchants, Tapussa and Bhallika, who were graced by the Buddha with some hair from his head and who enshrined the hair on the top of the Singuttara Hill, at the place where the famous pagoda, Shwe Dagon, now stands. Amongst other traditional accounts emphasizing the antiquity of Buddhism in Burma, a prominent story is connected with the commentator of the Pali canon in the fifth century, Buddhaghosa, who is said to have been born in Burma, went west to Ceylon, and finally returned home with a complete set of the Pali Tripitaka. Whilst the historicity of the episode is obscure, the Burmese chronicles strongly insist on its reality.

Outside the Buddhist tradition, the earliest reference to Buddhism in Burma is found in the Chinese chronicles of the third century, which mention a Buddhist kingdom of over one hundred thousand families and several thousand monks in Lin-Yang in central Burma. Chinese interest in Burma was awakened because, during the Han dynasty, parts of the land had fallen under Chinese overlordship, and occasional military expeditions were sent from China. After the collapse of the Han rule, China relaxed her hold on Burma.

Despite Chinese domination of large parts of Burma for centuries, the foundations of Burmese civilizations as we now know it were not laid until the arrival of Indian cultural influences, and there is no evidence of Chinese influence on Burmese civilization whatsoever. Except for its Buddhist content, Chinese culture remained alien to Burma. The Burmese claim that the beginnings of their culture and civilization came with the Sakyan migration from India. According to the Burmese legend, Taganng, their first capital, was founded in Upper Burma by Sakyan princes from Kapilavastu. The Chinese texts also observe that the Indians' arrival laid the beginnings of Burmese civilization, and that whilst Buddhism was strong in central Burma, Hinduism had made some progress in southern Burma.

Indians settled along the coast in Burma and inward on the river. The *Periplus* refers to Sino-Indian trade through the wild Sesatai people who possibly lived in the north of Burma, between China and Assam. Some of the Sanskrit place names mentioned by Ptolemy in the second century have been identified with places in Burma. Although his descriptions, especially of the interior, suffer from mistakes, he gives place names in abundance, sometimes as if he is enumerating numbers like a mathematician. The ports of Takkola and Vesunga appear to be Ptolemy's Takola and Besynga. Ptolemy speaks of the Irrawaddy Delta as it was at the beginning of the second century. He refers to Kirrhadia, beyond the mouth of the Ganges, in which the finest cinnamon was to be found, and above which lived the Tiladai people (variously spelled). These people are identified as the Kiratas or the Cilatas mentioned in an inscription discovered at Nagarjunakonda. They inhabited the regions now known as Arakan and Lower Burma and were converted to Buddhism about 250 by monks from Tambapanna.

Although Indian culture must have travelled to Burma well before, possibly in, the pre-Christian era, the evidence of Indo-Burmese cultural contact from about the fifth century onwards is definite. Its greatest impact came in the beginning before the Burmese national genius had attained maturity. "The basis of her script, her literature, her art, her thought, her religion, Burma owes to India, and a fair number of her economic products."[22]

The people of Burma are broadly divided into three racial groups, the Mons, the Burmese, and the Shans. Today the Burmese are by far the largest group, but the Mons, who are related to the Khmers and who once occupied wide tracts in Lower Burma and the Malay Peninsula, are the earliest known people in Burmese history. Originally they held most of Thailand and, in Burma, the eastern plains from Kyauksu to the sea, and thence to the Isthmus of Kra. Pegu remained their main centre of power and activity until 1757. The Burmese belong to the same racial stock as the Tibetans, Nepalese, and other peoples of the Himalayan region. The exact date of their immigration to Burma is not known but by the ninth century they had become the dominant power in Upper Burma. When they arrived, the Buddhist kingdom of Pyu with its capital at Sri Ksetra, was flourishing, and after the overthrow of the Pyu in 832, they settled at Kyauksu, where they adopted the language, religion and culture of the Mon. Later, they founded the kingdom of Arakan but their main centre was Pagan (Arimaddana).

The Shans, related to the Thais, came after the Burmese and acquired principalities in Upper Burma. They share the Buddhist culture of the Burmese. The Mons were often persecuted by the Burmese during the mediaeval and early modern periods, and were forced to flee to Thailand in large numbers. Today they are relatively small in numbers, mainly concentrated near Moulmein, and have more or less assimilated with the Burmese.

The Mons were, however, an accomplished people; it was they who gave Burma its writing and its religion. They were possibly the first to come into contact with Indian culture in the first century through the seafaring Telinganas of the Andhra-Pallava country of South India. The earliest Mon inscription found on a pillar at Lopburi in Thailand is in the Pallava script of the fifth century.

So far only the Pyu capital site, about five miles from Prome, has been worked with any thoroughness. Archaeological finds, ranging from about the beginning of the sixth to the end of the tenth century, comprise numerous Buddhist monuments, stone and bronze statues, terracotta tablets with inscriptions, and reliquaries. The earliest relics are fragments of the Pali scriptures discovered at Moza and Maungun, on the Pyu site. Dated approximately 500, these are written in a script resembling the Kadamba script of South India of the same period. They were first discovered in 1897 and then supplemented by further finds at Hmawza, including a manuscript of twenty gold leaves and stone statues of the Buddha, bearing imprints of Gupta style. Some of these statues carry inscriptions in Pyu and Sanskrit. These remains indicate that by this time Buddhism was widespread and well established in Burma, that Pali was known and understood—certainly in the capital city—and that Buddhism was fed and nourished from the Andhra-Pallava region of South India from centres such as Amaravati, Nagarjunakonda, Kanchipuram, and Kaveripattinam. It is significant that all these places were intimately associated with the Buddhaghosa tradition.

Epigraphic documents point to the prevalence of the Theravada School of Buddhism, stressing the doctrinal and metaphysical aspects more than anything else. Although Buddhism in Burma at this time was predominantly Theravada and was greatly influenced by the emergence of the Theravada Buddhist centre at Kanchipuram under the commentator Dhammapala, evidence is also found that Mahayanism, which probably came from eastern India, also existed there.

Kings of the Pyu dynasty and others bore the Indian titles of Varman and Vikrama: for instance, Surya Vikrama (died in 688), Hari Vikrama (654–695), and Jayacandra Varman. Their capital, Sri Ksetra, was built according to Indian cosmological beliefs, like an image of Indra's city Sudarsana—also called Amaravati—on the summit of Mount Meru, with thirty-two main gates and a golden palace in its centre. The division of the Pyu kingdom into thirty-two provinces with the king presiding over them would even suggest that the entire layout of the empire was organized as a replica of the heavenly realm of Indra. The Pyu country was mentioned by the Chinese scholars, Hsüan-tsang and I-tsing, in the seventh century as a Buddhist kingdom. The Chinese chronicles of the T'ang period provide further evidence of the flourishing state of Buddhism in the Pyu kingdom.

In addition to various Buddhist objects, images of Vishnu, Siva, Ganesa, Brahma, and other Hindu gods have been found at Hmawza, Mergui, and over a wide area of Burma. In Prome, ruined stupas and other objects going back to the sixth century have been discovered. One of the stupas is a majestic structure rising from five superimposed terraces. The stone figure sculptures attached to these temples and the terracotta votive tablets recovered from the debris of their relic chambers reveal influences not only of the contemporary Pallava art of South India, but also of the Gupta style of the north.

The principal southern Indianized neighbours of the Pyu were the two Mon kingdoms of Pegu (Hamsavati) and Thaton (Suddhammavati), where Hinduism and Buddhism flourished side by side. Sometime before the eleventh century Thaton became a very important centre of Buddhism. There is also some evidence of a Hindu dynasty, Sri Dharmarajanujavamsa, ruling Arakan from 600 to 1000.[23]

Earlier, to the north of Prome, a debased form of Tantric Buddhism seems to have prevailed: the Ari cult amongst the Mrammas, a Tibeto-Dravidian tribe who were a somewhat uncouth people and had set up a kingdom with its capital at Pagan. In 1044, Anawarhta (Aniruddha) ascended the throne of Pagan, and thus began a new and distinguished era in Burmese history. Our knowledge of the Burmese and their culture from the eleventh century onwards is more reliable and unbroken.[24] Anawarhta openly endeavoured to destroy the Ari cult, and himself embraced Theravada Buddhism from a Mon monk, Shin Arhan (Dharmadarsi). A patron of art and culture, he built numerous temples and monasteries with the zeal of a new convert. He began work on the Shwe Dagon (or Shwe Zigon) Pagoda which was completed during the reign of his son, Kyanzittha (1084–1113), and he imported complete copies of the Tripitaka from Ceylon. In 1057 he even declared war on the Thaton Mon king, Manuha, who had refused to give him canonical texts. Manuha was defeated, and Anawarhta returned with thirty-two white elephants laden with sacred texts, Buddhist relics, and monks.

The results of the sack of Thaton were of great importance for religion and art in Burma. From now onwards Theravada Buddhism became the principal religion of the state, with Pali as the language of the scriptures. Burmese law came to be based on the *Manusmriti* as interpreted and modified by Buddhist teachers. The Burmese adopted the Mon alphabet, and the great influx of craftsmen from Thaton to Pagan ushered in an era of religious and educational reform which lasted for over two centuries.

There were many features of Hinduism in the prevalent form of Buddhism at Thaton, including the place of prominence given to Hindu deities in temples. This led G. E. Harvey to call it a form of Buddhism which was largely Hindu in spirit. The artists from Thaton influenced the building of temples in the Pagan kingdom. In the Bidgat Tail Library built in the twelfth century to house scriptures from Thaton, ten Hindu avataras are reproduced with the Buddha as the ninth, and the building is dedicated to Vishnu.

During the twenty-eight years of his reign, Kyanzittha carried on the work of his father. He built numerous temples and stupas, including the great Ananda Temple, and restored the famous Mahabodhi Temple at Bodhgaya in Bihar, where the Buddha had attained enlightenment. Since Buddhism was declining in India at the time, this restoration was most opportune. By the end of the eleventh century, the Pala dynasty of eastern India, under whose rule of three hundred and fifty years both Buddhist and Hindu art had flourished, and the Nalanda University had risen to great fame, was drawing to an end,

The Ananda Temple at Pagan with its glittering gilt spire is one of the most beautiful sights in Burma. On the outside there are fifteen hundred plaques illustrating the Jataka tales, each with an inscription in Pali or Mon, and inside the aisles there are eighty niches with sculptures of the early life of the Buddha. These were made by Indian artists or by artists following Indian styles and models, and with Indian inspiration, Kyanzittha, whose mother was Indian, patronized Hinduism as well and had many Brahmans amongst his advisers. Kyanzittha's reign is regarded as the most creative age in the history of Burma. After Kyanzhitta's death, his son, Alaungsithu, came to the throne. He, too, was a great temple builder—and built the temple of Thatbyinnyu at Pagan, which, according to Harvey, dominates all others in majesty of line, and which was built after the model of contemporary temples in North India.

In the last quarter of the twelfth century, a significant episode occurred in the history of Buddhism in Burma when it was split by the establishment of a Ceylonese order of monks by Capata. From then on, Ceylonese Buddhism was the chief influence on the religion of Burma. Ceylon at that time had witnessed a revival of Theravada Buddhism under Parakrama Bahu I, and for the next four centuries was looked upon with the utmost veneration by other Theravada Buddhist countries such as Thailand, Burma, and Cambodia. During these centuries Indian trade with Burma had been as brisk as ever. An inscription at Pagan alludes to a Vishnu temple built by Nanadesi merchants and to a gift made to the temple in the thirteenth century by some Malabari merchants.

Whilst Buddhism was declining in India, many Buddhist monks crossed over to Burma, taking Pala art and Tantric Buddhism with them. But this Burmese link with India was weakened when the Turki–Afghan rulers took over northern India. Burma herself was not in a very stable condition. In 1287 Pagan fell to Mongol invaders, and Burma lapsed into a state of political disintegration, prolonged anarchy, and confusion. Buddhism suffered in the general decline. The Sangha split up into sects, and although pagodas were built, none of them could rival even the lesser temples of Pagan. This condition lasted until the second half of the fifteenth century when Dhaddacedi ascended the throne; a more stable kingdom was set up, and religious reforms were introduced, restoring the Sangha to its former prestige and power. From now onwards, Buddhism was firmly entrenched in Burmese society and although there were schisms on trivial matters, its ascendancy has never been questioned.

The rulers of the later dynasties, such as the Toungoo (1531–1752) and the Alaungpaya (1753–1886), were devout Buddhists, and Buddhism and its culture continued to grow in Burma, making notable contributions to world Buddhism. During the reign of Mindon, a remarkable statesman who ruled his country most wisely at a critical period when British pressure on Upper Burma was continually mounting, Buddhism made further progress in Burma. Under Mindon's patronage, religious studies were pursued with increasing vigour and zeal, and some of the best works of Burmese Buddhism were produced. Emulating the tradition of Asoka, Mindon summoned the Fifth Buddhist Council to make a redaction of the Tripitaka. The Council met at Mandalay from 1868 to 1871 under the direction of the King himself, and the text adopted was incised on 729 stone slabs, which are still carefully preserved. This text formed the basis of the revision of the Tripitaka carried out under the auspices of the Sixth Buddhist Council held in Rangoon during 1954–1956.

Buddhism not only dominated the cultural life of the people but played a significant role, at times decisive, in the political history of Burma. It helped to unify the peoples of Burma by bringing the Mons, the Burmese, and the Shans together into one national religion, culture, and consciousness. It encouraged the growth of art, education, literature, and social and cultural life. Although Burmese culture absorbed other influences, Buddhism represents the crystallization of Burmese national tradition. It inaugurated a society in Burma based on equality of social standards; few societies enjoy such democratic social life as does Burma.

Thailand

The story of Siam, or Thailand as it is now called, is unique in that although the country has a long history, the Thais, who dominate it today, have a common history of only about seven centuries. The Thais came to Siam in the thirteenth century, having been driven out of their former home in southwestern China by the military campaigns of Kublai Khan. They had founded in Yunnan around the seventh century a powerful kingdom, Nanchao, which played an important role in the history of Southeast Asia until their expulsion.[25]

Nanchao was in close proximity to the Indianized Pyu kingdom, and lay on a route between India and China at a time when intercourse between these two countries was active. Hence, it had been exposed to Indian culture for centuries.[26] Buddhism was popular in Nanchao. Two bells with Buddhist inscriptions in Chinese and Sanskrit that have been dated about the eleventh century have been found there. Brahman advisers to the government are referred to in their folklore. There were Indian settlements in Nanchao. The most important Thai kingdom in

Yunnan was Gandhara; one portion of it was also called Videharajya.[27] Their capital was known as Mithila, and the king, entitled "Maharaja," was reputedly descended from Asoka. The people of Nanchao used an alphabet of Indian origin, and, according to a local legend, Avalokitesvara came from India and converted the people to Buddhism. Names of places and symbols in Yunnan were associated with Buddhism: for example, the sacred hill Gridhra-kuta, the Bodhi Tree, and the Pippala Cave. According to a tenth-century Chinese traveller, there was even a local tradition asserting that the Buddha attained enlightenment in Yunnan. Writing in the thirteenth century, Rashiduddin not only calls the country Gandhara, but asserts that its people came from India and China.[28] The Pali chronicles and the Chinese annals also endorse the view that the Thais, although ethnologically related to the Chinese, had acquired more Indian culture than Chinese before they were forced out of their homeland. In northern Siam, where they settled first and which was close to southern China, there is no trace of Chinese influence either in customs, dress, literature, art, or religion.

Even before the Mongol incursions, some of the Thais had begun to move out of their state and slowly penetrate the adjoining areas to the south and west, such as the Pyu kingdom, the Shan states, and the Sip-Song Panna, a no-man's land to the northeast of Siam. According to the standard Siamese history of North Siam, the *Pongsawadan Yonaka,* the first Thai settlement of any importance was made in 860 when a Thai prince named Brahma crossed the Mekong and founded a principality at Chai Praka in the district of Cheingrai, in far northern Siam.[29] In 1215 the Thais founded the principality of Mogaung to the north of Bhamo, and eight years later, that of Mone (or Muong Nai). It was, however, after the conquest of their kingdom by the Mongols in 1253, that their mass migration from Nanchao commenced.

By the time these Indianized Thai people reached Siam, the country had been in close cultural contact with India for more than a thousand years. Whilst there is archaeological evidence indicating Indian influence on early Siamese culture, specific references to Siam in the ancient literature of India are rare. Frequent references to Suvarnabhumi, however, do suggest that the ancient Indians were familiar with the Menam Valley. The Siamese scholar, Prince Damrong, whose researches were based on Siamese annals and inscriptions as well as on Chinese chronicles, has even suggested that Suvarnabhumi was actually in southern Siam, near the mouth of the Menam Chao Phya. Coedès is also of the opinion that this region with its many toponyms like Supan, Kanburi, U Thong, all meaning gold or the land of gold, perhaps had a better claim than Burma to represent Suvarnabhumi.

Thailand comprises four geographically distinct areas—the northern region embracing the circle of Bayab, the central region formed by the valley of the Menam River, the northeastern plateau region, and the southern peninsular region. The earliest inhabitants of Siam were the Lavas—some of whom still survive in the northern hill ranges—and the Mon-khmer, who stretched from present-day Cambodia through the Menam Valley and the Malay country as far as Pegu. All these regions were deeply influenced by Indian culture. The north felt the impact for the first time when it was conquered by the Mons of central Siam in the eighth century and it seems likely that central Siam may have come into direct contact with Amaravati even before the Mons arrived from Lower Burma, as is suggested by the archaeological finds at Pong Tuk and Phra Pathom (or Nagarama Pathama). The Buddhist symbol, the *dharmacakra,* has been found amongst the relics at Phra Pathom which suggests that Buddhism possibly had reached Siam even before the Christian era, because the dharmacakra belongs to a very early period of Indian art, when the Buddha was not represented in human form but only by symbols. The specimen found at Phra Pathom may not be so old, but it is not later than the first or second century.

The northeastern area had come under the influence of the Hindu kingdom of Funan at a very early period. Later, when northeastern Siam fell to the Khmers, its Indian character was further strengthened. The southern part of Siam, however, was most directly and continuously in contact with India. Large numbers of Indian merchants, settlers, and teachers came to southern Siam in successive waves either directly from India or through Burma. Southern Siam is full of remains of Indian culture, most prominent of which is the city of Nakhon Srithammarat.

The traffic along the trade routes between India and Siam varied from time to time. It seems that the earliest Indian immigrants to Siam came by sea from the Amaravati region. Having landed at Martaban, they proceeded towards the south through the Three Pagoda Pass into southern central Siam. Later, during the Gupta period, when the capital was at Pataliputra, the routes from the ports in Bengal, such as Tamralipti, were busier. Southeast Asian travellers proceeded either to Martaban or to the Burmese ports of Akyab and Arakan, and thence overland to Siam via Thaton. During the period of Pallava ascendancy in South India, the route from Kanchi either straight to Mergui and Tenasserim, or to Takuapa in the Siamese part of the Malay Peninsula was commonly used. In addition, there was the sea route around the island of Singapore up to the Gulf of Siam where Bangkok stands today; although long, this route was often used.

Numerous excavations have yielded extensive evidence of Indianization and some remarkable pieces of art. Because Siam increasingly assimilated Indian art and culture into a local pattern, relics of pure Indian descent are more ancient than those reflecting local influence.

The most ancient objects of culture excavated in Siam in 1927 at Pong Tuk and Phra Pathom are all relics of Indian culture. Pong Tuk, situated less than thirty miles west of Bangkok on the Mekong River very close to Kanburi, was on the route to the Three Pagoda Pass leading to Martaban, and was thus in direct contact with Amaravati. Indian settlements flourished on this site for several centuries. Excavations have revealed a variety of objects, including the remains of a temple sanctuary and other buildings, a small statue of the standing Buddha and, curiously, a Graeco-Roman lamp of Pompeian style. The discovery of this lamp in Siam has been regarded as indicative of collaboration between Indian and Greek navigators east of India. Coedès considers the lamp to be of Mediterranean origin, not a copy made in Asia, and places it in the second century.[30] This date is also confirmed by the small bronze statue of the Buddha in the Amaravati style of the second century. In addition, other objects, such as votive tablets of the Bodhgaya style and bronze Buddha images, show Gupta influence and could not be later than the sixth century. Since no Khmer or Thai images or objects have been found on this site, and all the relics are Buddhist, it is suggested that a centre of Buddhist worship existed at Pong Tuk from early in the Christian era up to the sixth or seventh century. Buddhism may well have come even earlier if the representation of the Buddha by the dharmacakra found at Phra Pathom is taken into consideration. The very early inhabitants of western Siam must have principally remained Buddhist for a long time, for there are no early Hindu relics found in the area. However, Indian cultural influence continued to grow throughout; first through its contact with Amaravati in South India, and later with neighbouring Dvaravati in the Menam Valley, an Indianized kingdom of Siam of which Pong Tuk may well have been a part. Hsüan-tsang mentions that Tu-ho-lo-po-ti (Dvaravati) was a flourishing kingdom between Sri Ksetra (Pyu) in Burma and Isanapura (Khmer-lang) in Cambodia.

Situated in central Siam, Dvaravati was founded by the Mons or Talaings from Lower Burma in the second or third century. It became prominent after the decline of Funan. By the seventh century Dvaravati had become important enough to dispatch embassies to China and extend her frontiers from the borders of Cambodia to the Bay of Bengal. This kingdom flourished until the rulers of Kambuja extended their supremacy over the Lower Menam Valley in the tenth century. The bronze Buddhas of Amaravati style, Gupta images from the Ganges Valley, ruins of stupas and monasteries, and tablets bearing Buddhist beliefs written in Pallava script have been found there. The art of Dvaravati shows clear Gupta affiliations. The Hindu and Buddhist images of Vishnu, Siva, and the Buddha appear to reflect the art of Sarnath, Mathura, and Ajanta. Even after the Thais had broken the Mon power and set up their ascendancy, Dvaravati retained something of its Hindu character. Under the Thais the city came to be known as Ayuthia, which remained the Thai capital until it was captured and destroyed by the Burmese in 1757.

The archaeological and sculptural remains belonging to the succeeding period are somewhat scanty; they nevertheless point out that during the eighth and ninth centuries the people of central Siam practiced Theravada Buddhism, and that their art was influenced by Gupta art. As they were politically a part of Kambuja (Cambodia) during this period, it seems they were further influenced by Hinduism, of which many traces are found.

One of the oldest sites in central Siam, eighty miles north of Bangkok, is Lopburi (Lavo), a minor city at present but for centuries a centre of Mon-Indian culture which later became the capital of the central

Siamese province of the Kambuja Kingdom in 1002. Here are ancient monuments, including the temple of Maha-tat, and standing images of the Buddha, one of which bears a Sanskrit inscription.

One of the most remarkable sites in the centre of Siam, is Srideb (Crip-tep) , where statues of Hindu deities bearing Sanskrit inscriptions of the fifth or sixth century have been discovered. The art of Srideb is of excellent quality and provides a link between Indian art and the art of Indochina. Quaritch Wales considered Srideb the oldest known Hindu temple in Indochina. Le May, however, has some misgivings, not because of its architectural conception, which is definitely Hindu, but because of its laterite base.

In peninsular Siam, as well as in Malaya, evidence of the existence of hitherto unsuspected Hindu states and settlements has recently come to light, and some Buddhist and Hindu images have been excavated. Present knowledge is based on archaeological finds and Chinese notices, which do not easily lend themselves to interpretation. Of the several states in this region mentioned by Chinese annals, one was Tambralingo with its capital at Ligor, modern Nakhon Srithammarat. A Sanskrit inscription of not later than the sixth century has been found here. As the Pali *Niddesa* refers to this kingdom, it must have been flourishing in the second century. Although it was a strong Buddhist centre many Hindu relics have been unearthed here. Three sanctuaries—the Bot Prahm with numerous Sivalingas, the San Pra Isuon containing bronze statues of Siva, Parvati, and Ganesh, and the Na Pra Narai with its renowned statues of Vishnu—are amongst the excavations made at this site. The political history of this state is obscure, but the ambitions of one of its princes initiated an era of Indian culture which has been designated the Cambodian period of Siam.

According to the *Liang Shu,* there possibly existed in the region in the first or second century a Hindu state, Lang-ya-hsiu, which sent several embassies to China. This may have been the Lankasuka of the Malay and Javanese chronicles, located on the east coast of the Malay Peninsula, south of Ligor.[31]

The Isthmus of Kra, in addition to Nakhon Srithammarat, has produced a rich harvest of archaeological finds. The Vat Phra That at Chaiya of the Sri Vijaya period is constructed according to the classical

Indian architectural principles of *silpa-sastra.* An exquisite black bust of Lokesvara, inspired by Pala art, has been found in this vicinity.

Towards the end of the tenth century, Lopburi was seized from the reigning Mon king by a prince from Nakhon Srithammarat, thus bringing the whole of central and southern Siam under one authority. In 1002, his son, Suryavarman I, captured the throne of Kambuja at Angkor during a civil war. Although he came from southern Siam, his dynasty claimed kinship with the Khmers, and Suryavarman claimed the Khmer kingdom as his right. Thus central and southern Siam were united with Kambuja under the Khmer Kingdom of which northeastern Siam was already a part.

The Khmers or Cambodians had begun to penetrate the northeastern part of Siam from the seventh century, but it was not until Khmer ascendancy had been established that Siam felt the full impact of Khmer culture. Both regions belonged to the same Indianized culture. The Khmers patronized both Buddhism and Hinduism, leaning a little more to one or the other at different times. Whilst their temples at Panom Rung and Muang Tam are clearly Hindu in character, one of the scenes portrayed on a large square stele is of a Buddhist character which resembles reliefs from Bharhut and Sanchi.

Whilst the Khmers were ruling northeastern and central Siam, the Thais began to penetrate the land. They settled first in the north as a dependent state of the court at Angkor. Their migrations, unimportant at first, became formidable by the middle of the thirteenth century. One of their attacks led to the foundation of the Shan states in Upper Burma, and in 1229 the kingdom of Sukhotai was founded. The rise of Thai power is associated with Rama Kamheng (or Gamhen), who succeeded to the throne about 1276. During his reign the Thai kingdom was extended to include both Pegu and Nakhon Srithammarat, and political relations with China were opened up. A patron of Buddhism, Rama Kamheng was well versed in both the Tripitaka and Hindu ritual and astrology. He built a school for Hindu and Buddhist priests, and dispatched a mission to Ceylon to fetch Buddhist relics and texts. Buddhism prospered in Sukhotai, and it received impetus from Ceylon when the Thai king persuaded the Ceylonese monk, Mahasami Sangharaj, to come to Siam. Rama Kamheng was an admirer of Parakrama Bahu, the king of Ceylon, and sought to emulate him. Under Kamheng's influence, Buddhism and Pali literature were firmly established in Sukhotai and even the neighbouring Hindu kingdoms came more and more into the Buddhist orbit. Hinduism then declined, leaving its mark only on ceremonies and customs. The Sukhotai School of Buddhism is often characterized as the blending of the Chiengsen School, which may have come from China, and the Theravada School of Ceylon. In Sukhotai's many temples and remarkable bronze standing Buddha images can be seen the beginnings of Thai art, which is a fusion of the art of the Khmers and the legacy which the Thais brought with them from the north.

By the middle of the fourteenth century, Sukhotai declined and the centre of power moved to Ayuthia. A Thai prince crowned himself king in 1350 under the title of Ramadhipati, and he is traditionally regarded as the first king of Thailand. Religious contact with Ceylon continued and during the Ayuthia period, particularly the fifteenth century, Buddhist activity greatly increased under the influence of Sinhalese Buddhism. Politically, it was a period of wars with Burma on one side and Cambodia on the other. The Khmer kingdom was destroyed by the Thais in the fifteenth century, reducing it to Siamese vassalage; the Siamese captured Angkor three times, and finally annexed it in 1460. The Siamese victory over Angkor in 1431 led to an influx of Cambodian scholars and priests. The Siamese king, taking advantage of Cambodian scholars and statesmen, reorganized the state administration and remodelled the court ceremonials on Cambodian lines, a reform that survives even today.

The Thais were ethnologically Chinese and the chronicles of the Sui dynasty give details of the court life at Nanchao, which resembled that of the Chinese. Many words are common to both Thai and Chinese; for instance, most of the Siamese numerals are of Chinese origin. The only obvious Chinese influence on Siam today lies in architecture, particularly the tiers of roofs of Siamese temples. Very little else of Thai culture can be traced to China. In fact, it appears that even when they arrived in Siam, the Thais had not absorbed much Chinese culture. For in northern Siam, where they settled first and which was close to southern China, there is no trace of Chinese influence in customs, art, literature, or thought. Chinese culture, without the medium of Buddhism, has not generally attracted non-Chinese peoples, even in China's immediate neighbourhood. The

Thais do not appear to have been very culturally advanced at the time they came to Siam. When they found themselves face to face with the highly advanced kingdom of Cambodia, they were simply awe-stricken and fascinated.

It is scarcely surprising that the Thais took to the prevalent form of Mon-Khmer culture enthusiastically and in time made notable contributions of their own to it. Today Thailand is replete with temples. The present-day capital, Bangkok, alone has many famous temples, some of which are amongst the most impressive monuments in the whole of Asia; for example the Wat Phra Keo, the temple of the Emerald Buddha, next door to the royal palace. The main object of worship in this temple is a single-stone jasper image of the Buddha which is dated to a very ancient period, and around which numerous legends have grown. The image was first discovered in 1436 at Chiengrai in northern Siam. Wall paintings, bas-reliefs, and other pieces of sculptural art enhance the artistic beauty of the temple.

Although Thailand is predominantly Buddhist, there are traces of Hindu influence, visible mostly in the court ceremonials. The kings of Sukhotai recruited their court Brahmans from Cambodia and adopted much of the Cambodian Hindu court ritual. Later, during the Ayuthia period when Hinduism in Cambodia had fallen into decline, Brahmans were obtained from southern Siam. Until recently, the court Brahmans cast horoscopes, consulted omens, and performed worship of both Hindu and Buddhist deities. Ceremonies of coronation, tonsure, cremation, and lesser rites connected with agriculture were developed by the Brahmans. The Siamese call their coronation by its ancient Sanskrit designation, the *rajabhiseka.* The entire complex of coronation ceremonies, such as *homa* (sacrifices to Fire), purificatory rites, ablutions, anointment, and the actual coronation, are closely modelled on Hindu rituals, and are presided over by the *Brah Maha Raja Guru.* The Buddha, as well as the chief Hindu deities, are represented in these ceremonies. The tonsure ceremony in Siam is a rite of initiation of youths, corresponding to the Hindu *Cudakarma Mangala,* which is a very important Hindu *Samskara.* Cremation, an old vedic rite, is the only means of disposal of the remains of deceased royalty in Siam, and the chief method of disposing of all their dead. The people of Thailand take these ancient ceremonies very seriously, which partly explains why state ceremonies are still conducted by Brahmans.

There are some eight families of court Brahmans in Thailand who claim that their ancestors came originally from the sacred Indian city of Varanasi. As no Brahman women appear to have come with them, they intermarried with local people. Today they speak only Siamese, and have a very limited and corrupt knowledge of Sanskrit. Amongst their texts, which are mostly mantras, they have a Tamil hymn written in an Indian character.

Some of the domestic ceremonies performed in Siam are of Hindu origin. The royal title is Rama, a Hindu *avatara,* and the royal temple at Bangkok contains illustrations from the *Ramayana.* Hindu festivals, such as Dashahara, commemorating the victory of Rama over the demon king Ravana, are still observed in Thailand. In Chi Mai *Sankranti* (called *Songhurant*) is still observed as the New Year's Day. The Thais, like the Hindus, still believe in Vishnu or Narayana (Phra Narain), and Mahadeva or Siva, and dislike the asuras (*asuns*) as the enemies of the devas.

The Siamese lent their own ideas to Buddhist sculpture. This led to the development of the typical Siamese image of Buddha, in the form of a slender figure with flame-crowned oval face wearing a strange all-pervasive smile, and to the distinctive pagoda style which is a unique combination of Indian inspiration and Chinese architecture.

It is not always possible to separate the Indian influence in Thai language and literature from the Siamese genius. The Siamese alphabet, consisting of forty-four consonants and thirty-two vowels, is derived directly from the Kambuja alphabet which, in turn, owes its origin to the alphabet of the inscriptions of southern India during the sixth and eighth centuries. Numerous Thai words are taken directly from Sanskrit: for instance, *akas, rath, maha, racha* (raja), *cakra, sathani* (sthan). The pronunciation of the language is, of course, very different.

Siamese fiction and mythological literature have drawn freely upon Indian stories. Their religious literature is almost wholly Buddhist. Famous Indian works, such as the *Ramayana,* the *Mahabharata,* and the *Sakuntala* have formed the basis of some of the outstanding Siamese literature. The *Ramayana,* known in Siam as the *Ramakien* (or *Ramakirti*), is regarded as a Siamese classic. Knowledge of this work is as essential for a cultured Siamese as Homer used to be for an European. The characters of Rama and Sita are known everywhere by all classes of people. The epic and Puranic literature of India constituted the principal source of inspiration not only for Siam but for the whole of Southeast Asia. It provided the themes for classical theatre, shadow theatre, and marionette shows.

Indian influence is clearly seen on Siamese dance, drama, and music. Many of the themes of Siam's various dance-dramas (*lakhon-ram*) are drawn from Indian mythology: for example, the story of Savitri and Satyavan. Many Thai musical instruments closely resemble those of India. Unlike India, dancing is an integral part of the social life of Thailand, and the ancient plays and tales from Indian epics, which are almost dissociated from the artistic world of India, are continually staged in Thailand. The Siamese dance is generally performed in a very slow and steady motion, as it was done in ancient days in the presence of royalty.

The Siamese legal system is directly descended from the *Manusmriti*. The Hindu *Dharmasastras* provided the framework for Siamese justice. The earliest available legal corpus dates from 1805, but many of the earlier collections of manuscripts were destroyed when Ayuthia, the capital of Siam at the time, was sacked by the Burmese. The first volume of this work is justifiably entitled the *Phra Dharmasastra*.

Indochina

Indochina is divided into several interlinked regions with distinctive characteristics, and her states throughout the course of history have been subjected to periodic boundary changes and foreign interference and domination. These factors have rendered her culture complex, rich, and varied, giving her the quality of diversity in uniformity.

In the north is the delta of Tonkin (northern Vietnam) which had direct sea contact with India and played a significant role in transmitting Buddhism to China. South of Tonkin, divided by an almost impenetrable chain of mountains, is Annam (southern Vietnam), where the Dong-son culture developed, followed by one of the earliest and most brilliant Southeast Asian civilizations, Champa. West of Tonkin lies Laos, south of which is Cambodia. Both these countries have been important areas of contact between Indian and Chinese culture.

Because of the almost insurmountable geographical barriers, Indochina has been isolated from the mass of the Asian continent. The only overland route to India lay through Burma over the difficult mountains of Assam. The journey over the Bhamo Pass to China was also tedious. Travelling up the rivers meant reaching the inhospitable wilderness of Yunnan and Szechwan. However, the sea routes with both India and China were open and carried most of the traffic.[32]

Our knowledge of the history of Indochina, before the arrival first of the Chinese and then of the Indians around the beginning of the Christian era, is very fragmentary. The Dong-son culture flourished mainly along the coastal belt of Annam, developing remarkably between the fifth and second centuries B.C. This was the period when China was vigorously expanding her frontiers, and had come to dominate Tonkin. Consequently, China influenced the art and culture of Dong-son, especially on the eve of the Christian era. It was, however, not until Indian culture entered the scene, that Indochinese civilization got a real start and gathered momentum.

Indian and Chinese cultures have met in other areas but not on such a large scale as in Indochina, where they interacted with a vigorous local culture. Whilst China ruled over Tonkin for long periods, India only touched on the southern coasts of Indochina and vanished from the scene in about the fifth century when her seafaring activity practically came to an end. But in that short space of time the peoples of Indochina were so inspired by Indian culture that they voluntarily accepted it and in turn created new civilizations of profound originality: "China dominated, while India scattered the seed, and between them they were to shape the double aspect of Indo-China."[33]

The oldest and most important of the Indianized states was Funan occupying the lower valley of the Mekong, roughly corresponding to modern Cambodia and South Vietnarn.[34] Funan was possibly the result of a confederation of tribes. Finot suggests that Funan is a Chinese variation of the old Khmer word *bnam* (meaning mountain), *phnom* in modern Khmer. The Chinese texts on Funan were first collected and properly interpreted by Pelliot, and Coedès, as in many other sections of Indochinese archaeology, initiated the serious interpretation of the archaeological evidence. Precise information concerning the people of Funan and their civilization is still lacking. The discovery of Indian objects together with objects of advanced Dong-son style suggests very early Indian contact. However, it is generally agreed that civilization began with the arrival of Indian traders. Funan was rich in all that Indian merchants were looking for and, in addition, was an ideal halfway house on the sea journey to China.

A Chinese writer, Kang Tai, who visited Funan in the middle of the third century—the period of the oldest of four Sanskrit inscriptions found in that country—reports that an Indian Brahman, Huen-Chen of Ho-fu, led by a dream, landed in Funan, married a local princess, Lien-Ye, and founded the kingdom in the first century. A variation of this story is found in the Cambodian annals. This literary tradition is confirmed by a seventh-century inscription from Champa[35] wherein the Indian is identified as Kaundinya of the Somavamsa. Under Kaundinya's successors, Funan's domination spread over most of the neighbouring lands by the third century, and diplomatic contacts were established with India and China; one of Funan's missions visited India in the third century. It is said that the direct descendants of Kaundinya were overthrown about 200 by the commander of the troops, Fan-cheman, who founded the political greatness of Funan.

Until the fifth century the history of Funan is fragmentary, but enough is known to suggest its increasing Indianization. About 357, for instance, it is known that an Indian was ruling Funan. Local Sanskrit inscriptions, supported by the *History of the Liang Dynasty* which provides precise dates and facts, tell of the arrival of another Indian Brahman, Kaundinya-Jayavarman, who ruled over Funan between 478 and 514.[36] With the assistance of an Indian monk, Nagasena, who carried statues of the Buddha and other gifts to the Chinese emperor, he cultivated good relations with China, seeking Chinese help to defeat the neighbouring Chenla. Although the kings of Funan professed Saiva Hinduism, Nagasena reported to the Chinese emperor that both Hinduism and Buddhism were flourishing in Funan. The Funanese monks were well versed in Sanskrit and some of them went to China and translated Buddhist texts into Chinese.

Rudravarman, the son of Jayavarman, ascended the throne in 514 and ruled for the next twenty-five years. During his reign he sent at least six embassies to China. He was an ardent devotee of Vishnu, and the last great king of Funan. He was responsible for the first great work of sculpture preserved in Indochina. After a prolonged struggle, Funan was conquered by the neighbouring Indianized state of Chenla.

The country was wealthy, and its trade, stretching from Rome to China, was brisk. Even the Chinese were full of praise for Funan's material prosperity. According to them the country was overflowing with gold, silver, pearls, and spices. Considering that the Indians had already developed techniques of irrigation and land reclamation it is possible that they were responsible for the agricultural prosperity of the land.

Not much of the art of Funan has survived. The Funanese archaeological site, Oc-eo, has produced various important objects, including a gold medallion, dated 152, bearing the effigy of Antoninus Pius. The Roman medallion was found with various Hindu objects, notably intaglios and seals with Sanskrit inscriptions of the same and following periods. The medallion is striking evidence of the close Indo-Roman trade relations, which were one cause of Indian exploration of Southeast Asia.

Influence of Gupta or post-Gupta architecture is found in many Funanese buildings, and numerous statues of the Buddha and Hindu gods, such as Vishnu and Siva, gold ornaments, tin amulets with symbols of Vishnu and Siva, and merchant's seals with inscriptions in Sanskrit, have been excavated from sites in Funan. Some of these pieces were directly imported from India and others were copied locally from Indian models. A Buddha head discovered at Ba-the, clearly of Gandhara inspiration, is perhaps the oldest Indian object. The images of Harihara and Ardhanarisvara, found in southern Funan and now preserved in the museum at Phnom Penh, are brilliant examples of sculptural art, both in conception and execution.

Funan inscriptions are in pure, flawless Sanskrit. Their content shows that Indian religion, philosophy, and mythology were widely understood, and that the secular knowledge of India, such as phonetics (*sabda*), logic (*nyaya*), and political theory (*arthasastra*), were studied in Funan.

Champa, on the coast of Annam, was another Indianized state, about which more information is available. It constantly clashed with the nearby Chinese colonies established in Tonkin during the Han period, and hence Chinese historians frequently refer to Champa. The kingdom (called Lin-yi) is first mentioned in 190–193. The name Champa is clearly Indian whether it was named after the capital of the Anga country in the lower Ganges Valley, or as Sastri suggests, after the Cola capital of the same name.[37] The Chams were probably of the same Indonesian stock as the founders of the Dong-son culture further to the north.

Situated on the main sea routes from India and Java to China, and at the foot of spice-bearing mountains, Champa soon attracted the attention of Indian traders, and played a significant role in spreading Indian culture in eastern Asia. Sri Mara was the first Hindu king of Champa, and established his dynasty about 200 over an extensive area, including Tonkin and part of northern Annam. Champa maintained close relations with Funan, a fact which must have been largely responsible for the penetration of Indian influence there. Since the early history of Champa is reconstructed from Chinese sources we have the Chinese derivation of the names of Champa kings. They all begin with *Fan,* such as Fan-hiong and Fan-wen, which is possibly a corruption of the common Indian royal suffix, *Varman.* Fan-wen, who had expanded the frontiers of his empire by a vigorous, aggressive policy, died in 349. His grandson, Fan-hu-ta, was probably the kin referred to in the Sanskrit inscriptions as Bhadravarman. He was a noted commander and scholar. He dedicated a temple to Siva at Mison which was called Bhadresvarasvami and became the centre of royal worship in later centuries. It is said that Bhadravarman abdicated his throne to spend his last days on the banks of the Ganges.

Champa passed through various dynasties, and war with China continued intermittently, particularly during the third and fourth centuries. This was a period of political unrest in China, which probably gave Champa the opportunity to expand into Chinese territory. However, once China was unified under the Sui dynasty towards the end of the sixth century, Champa was attacked and its power broken by the Chinese emperor. The Chinese took back with them the golden tablets of eighteen kings of Champa and 1350 Buddhist works. Champa continued as a tributary state of China, but it never recovered its old power.

Recent excavations in Tra-Kieu, the most ancient capital of Champa, have revealed ample evidence of Indian influence in the form of Sivaite and Vaisnavite shrines and bas-reliefs. The earliest inscription found in the region and possibly the whole of Southeast Asia, is the Vo-canh inscription written in a South Indian script and dating from the second or third century. The most ancient bronze statue found in Champa is that of the Buddha of Dongduong (Quang-nam) which is one of the most beautiful specimens of Amaravati art; even a principality in that area was called Amaravati. Inscriptions of Bhadravarman, both in Sanskrit and Cham, have been found; they belong to about 350 and are the earliest inscriptions found in Champa proper. This bronze Buddha image of the Amaravati School indicates that Buddhism had obtained a footing in the country by the third century, and in 605 the Chinese captured more than thirteen hundred Buddhist monks. I-tsing also alludes to the prevalence of Buddhism in Champa. Mahayana Buddhism was possibly most generally practiced, as it was occasionally patronized by the Kings.

During this period, remarkable sculptures and original brick temples were created which are notable for their decoration and ornamentation. The doorways and pillars are adorned with an incredibly intricate stone foliation of leaves, buds and flowers, inset with medallions of anchorites and celestial dancers. Three groups of temples, Mi-song, Ponagar, and Dongduong, are very famous. In the day of their splendour the Chams were Sivaites, and Siva, his Sakti, and his two sons, Ganesa and Skanda, were prominent amongst the gods worshipped. Champa statues followed Gupta models, not only in subject matter but also in technique, which was simple, dignified, and majestic. Sanskrit inscriptions, one of which carries a date of the Saka era, have also been found.

The beginnings of Chenla, the Indianized kingdom that demolished Funan and later blossomed into the Khmer Empire, are obscure. Chenla is the name of the Kingdom as found in the Chinese texts, but the derivation of the name is not known. Chenla was certainly in existence by the end of the sixth century, and was beginning to emerge in the northeastern parts of Cambodia along the middle reaches of the Mekong whilst Funan was flourishing. It is possible that until the end of the fifth century Chenla was confined to the tableland watered by the Semun, whilst the Bassac region was dominated by the Chams. It was a vassal state of Funan and had its capital at Sreshthapura, near Vat Phu.

Chenla is claimed to have been the original home of the Kambuja people. The Kambuja royalty, however, traced its descent from rishi Kambu Svayambhuva, the king of Aryadesa (India) and the *apsara*

Mera, which is another version of the recurrent motif of foundation myths of royal families in South India. The two earliest known kings are Srutavarman and his son Sreshthavarman, who secured Chenla's freedom from Funan. About the middle of the sixth century, when the last king of Funan, Rudravarman, died, the king of Chenla, Bhavavarman—possibly a grandson of Rudravarman of Funan—undertook to conquer Funan with the help of his brother Chitrasena. Their partial conquest of Funan made Bhavavarman the undisputed master of the Mekong Valley; his successors completed the conquest of Funan. It seems that the Khmer people of Chenla, unlike the people of Funan, did not cultivate the deltas, but preferred to depend on rain in the high lands. Hence, they were possibly attracted by the rich plains of southern Funan.

A good deal is known of Bhavavarman from inscriptions, one of which written in Sanskrit verse, announces the consecration by the King, of a Sivalinga named Tryambaka. Another describes him as King of Kings, strong as Mount Meru. When he died in 598 the unification of the two kingdoms was well advanced, and he has been described, therefore, as the founder of the glory of Kambujadesa. After his death, his brother Chitrasena ascended the throne as Mahendravarman. He built numerous Siva temples throughout his domains. All the known inscriptions of Mahendravarman resemble Pallava inscriptions of the early seventh century.[38] In marked contrast to Funan and other Southeast Asian states which frequently sent embassies to China, Chenla dispatched its first embassy to China in 616–617, during Chitrasena's reign.

After Chitrasena's death, his son Isanavarman ruled over the whole of Cambodia, Cochin China, and the valley of the Mun River to the north of the Dangrek Mountains. On the site of the modern Sambor Prei Kuk (Kampong Thom) on the Mekong River, he founded a new capital city, called after his name, Isanapura. It was in this city, which served as the capital of the Kambuja kingdom until the ninth century, that the art of Chenla, known as the Sambor style, and the early phase of Khmer art developed. One of his inscriptions commemorates the consecration of a statue of Harihara and of an *asrama* for the *Bhagavata* or *Pancaratra* priests. These inscriptions attest to the power of the king and the prosperity of his reign, but say little of his conquests.

The Kambuja or the Khmer kingdom gradually emerged from the

fusion of Chenla and Funan, and became the most powerful state in Indochina. It survived for almost seven centuries and attained an unparalleled height of political prestige and cultural advancement until destroyed by the Thais in the fifteenth century. At about the same time this empire emerged, the Pyu kingdom of Sri Ksetra in Burma, the Mon kingdom of Dvaravati in Siam, and the Empire of Sri Vijaya in Indonesia were flourishing. The seventh century was a formative one in Southeast Asia.

Until the end of this century, the Khmer kings concentrated on consolidating their hold over the lower Mekong region and around Tonle Sap, Both Hinduism and Buddhism were practiced, with the former predominating; Saivism appears to have been the court religion. The worship of Harihara, in which Siva and Vishnu are united in a single body, was the main feature of this period. Most inscriptions are in Sanskrit and the literary culture was based upon the *Ramayana,* the *Mahabharata,* and the *Puranas.*

The eighth century is a complete blank in Khmer history; possibly it was a period of unrest and confusion all over Southeast Asia. But at the beginning of the ninth century the whole country came under the authority of Jayavarman II, whose long rule of fifty-two years (802–854) marks the beginning of the Angkor period and of classical Khmer art. At this time, inscriptions indicate the Khmer Empire was confined to the eastern and southern portions of Cambodia and Cochin China.

Until the rise of Jayavarman II the capital of the Kambuja was in the south at Isanapura where the earliest types of Khmer temples are found, all dedicated to the Hindu religion. Indian models, especially of the post-Gupta style, were generally imitated, but the wood originals in India have perished. Indian influence in early Khmer or Sambor art is so marked that some scholars have suggested the artists came from India. The statues are extremely beautiful, but only a few have survived. The most exquisite of these are the statues of Harihara, Uma, and Lakshmi in the Phnom Penh museum. This Sambor phase was one of the most beautiful in Khmer art, and a worthy forerunner of the brilliant later period.

There is some mystery about the exact origins of Jayavarman II. He is said to have been a descendant of an ancient dynasty of Cambodia who had lived at the court of the Sailendras in central Java, and returned to his country steeped in Javanese culture. According to one inscription he came from Java to reign in Indrapura but another records that he simply appeared like a fresh lotus. B. R. Chatterji holds the view that Jayavarman II did not come from Java in Indonesia but from a place named Java in Laos,[39] but Groslier accepts the theory that he did come from Java. Indeed the impact of the Indianized culture of Indonesia ignited the renaissance of Cambodia.[40]

Jayavarman introduced into Cambodia with the help of a Brahman guru, Hiranyadama, the cult of the Deva Raja (the king-God) which was somewhat similar to that of the Sailendra King of the Mountain cult. This cult claimed universal supremacy for the king, and inspired the period of temple-building in Cambodia. According to scholars, such as Coedès, the Sailendras had resuscitated the title of King of the Mountain which had previously been an attribute of the kings of Funan. If so, then Jayavarman was only repatriating something which the Sailendras had borrowed from his predecessors. Significantly, the proclamation styling him as the Deva Raja specified that Cambodia was no longer dependent on Java, and this may imply, as Groslier suggests, that the Sailendras had occupied parts of Cambodia during the eighth century. Jayavarman based his power on religion. He organized the state, founding several capitals—Hariharalaya, modern Roluos, Amarendrapura, probably a city built around Akyum, and finally Mahendraparvata on the Phnom Kulen—which provide impressive evidence of his progress. There are many remains from Jayavarman's reign at Sambor Prei Kuk, at Banteay Prei Nokor, at Roluos, and on the Phnom Kulen, the last being the most important. Excavations on the summit of Phnom Kulen have revealed a number of temples that were completely hidden by thick forests and were mainly discovered by Phillippe Stern and Henri Mouhot. In style, they provide a link between pre-Angkor and classical Angkor art.

The Khmers were accomplished builders: Jayavarman's successors built temples enthusiastically. The cult of the King of the Mountain inspired each king to erect a magnificent shrine to perpetuate his memory. Thus arose the complex of Angkor Thom. Yasovarman I (889–901) was one of the outstanding rulers of the dynasty, and the founder of the first city of Angkor. This covered a much larger area than Angkor Thom, which was founded later by Jayavarman VII at the end of the twelfth century. These two cities partly overlap, but the former lies outside the southern wall of Angkor Thom. Yasovarman issued a large number of Sanskrit inscriptions written in Kavya style and built the Saiva temple of Phnom Bakheng. Six of his successors ruled during the tenth century when building activity dominated political events. The last king of this dynasty was Jayavarman V (968–1001), in whose reign Mahayana Buddhism prevailed and numerous Buddhist texts were imported from abroad. He was followed by Suryavarman (1002–1050) from Siam, who initiated a new dynasty of great kings. Primarily a Buddhist, he is said to have erected temples of Siva and Vishnu. Cambodia reached its peak during the reign of Suryavarman II (1113–1152), the builder of the matchless Angkor Wat, an epic in stone. With the death of Jayavarman VII (1181–1220) the kingdom began to decline, falling finally before the advancing Thais.

After the fall of the Khmers in the fifteenth century, the temples gradually fell into disuse. Their ruins were discovered only in 1860, and are perhaps the most awe-inspiring to be found anywhere. Scattered throughout the mountains and jungles of Cambodia in an area of about ten thousand acres, more than six hundred Khmer monument ruins can still be counted. Of these, twenty are of major importance. They range from temples and palaces to reservoirs and bridges, and cover the reigns of more than twenty kings. The great monuments are near the capital Angkor Thom, which alone covers an area of two thousand acres; Angkor is a derivative of the Sanskrit *nagara,* meaning city, and *thom* a Khmer word meaning great.

The ruins of Angkor Thom are the remains of the latest city built by Jayavarman VII. He planned the whole city to give it a cosmic meaning. According to Hindu belief the world consists of a circular, central continent (Jambudvipa, the ancient name of India) surrounded by seven annular continents. Beyond the oceans an enormous mountain range encloses the world. In the centre of Jambudvipa is Mount Meru, surrounded by the moon, sun and other stars. On the summit of Meru is the city of the gods, encircled by the abodes of eight *Lokapalas,* the guardian gods of the world. Buddhist conception is fundamentally the same, with differences in detail. Both hold Mount Meru as the centre of a circular universe with concentric zones around it. Thus, a miniature image of this cosmological arrangement carries a symbolic meaning for both Hindus and Buddhists.

In Angkor Thom the central mountain is the Bayon, the temple of the Bodhisattva Lokesvara, the Lord of the Universe, and the city is surrounded by a wall and moat forming a square almost two miles on each side. The balustrades of the causeways leading over the moat to the city gates are formed by rows of giant statues, on one side of gods, devas, and on the other of demons, asuras, holding an enormous serpent. Thus, the whole city is a representation of the Puranic story of the churning of the primeval milk ocean (kshirasagara) by the gods and the demons, using the primeval snake, Vasuki, as a rope and Mount Meru as a churning stick.

Outside Angkor Thom is the Angkor Wat, covering an area of five hundred acres. This is the largest and the most impressive temple in the world. According to Henri Mouhot, who discovered it for the modern world: "This architectural work perhaps has not, and perhaps never has had, its equal on the face of the globe."[41] Since his day, countless people, both admirers and sceptics, have stood spellbound before this majestic temple of Vishnu. The genius who conceived this temple, like all other Khmer artists, is unknown to us.

A raised causeway of flagstones, lined by a naga-balustrade, leads from the main road over a moat to the main gate of the temple. This gate house, which is a spacious building forming the front part of the wall that goes around the enclosure, is in itself a remarkable creation. A paved road 400 yards long leads to the temple. At the base, the temple is 223 by 242 yards, and its main tower is about 80 yards high. Structurally it is a three-stepped pyramid. Each storey is punctuated by towers at the corners and pavilions in the centre. The main tower is on the third storey. The temple rises steeply in the form of three concentric rectangular galleries, each double the height of the preceding one, and connected by stairs and intervening open terraces. The innermost gallery is dominated by five tall domes, the central one of which dominates the plain below. The entire building is constructed in sandstone, and if any wood was used, it has long since perished.

The building has been chiselled with endless bas-reliefs and beautiful designs and patterns. Flowers, birds, and dancing maidens decorate the walls. Hundreds of Khmer artists must have spent their entire lives on the work, yet it is impossible to detect a single flaw in these acres of carved panels. The sculptors of Angkor who executed many scenes from the *Ramayana*, the *Mahabharata*, and the *Harivamsa*, must have had an intimate knowledge of Indian epic literature. Vishnu predominates but other gods also adorn the temple with their various incarnations and emanations. Kings are also introduced and the Khmer language can be seen engraved in some places. Evildoers are shown being condemned and the virtuous rewarded by Yama with Chitragupta as the keeper of the records. The outer gallery, running around the whole building, itself contains a half-mile of bas-reliefs on the back wall, and there are about 1750 life-size *apsaras*, practically every one in a different, magnificent head-dress.

Although the Khmers are so admirably remembered for their superb achievements in art, they patronized all branches of Indian learning. All the princes received training in Indian philosophy and literature. A number of persons of apparent Indian origin were present in the Kambuja kingdom and Brahmans were held in high esteem. For instance, Hiranyadama came from a *janapada* in India to teach Tantric texts to the royal priest, Sivakaivalya. According to a Chinese tradition, there were a thousand Brahmans in Tuan Siuan, an area in Funan, alone. The presence of so many Hindus presumably influenced the social structure of Kambujadesa on caste lines, creating divisions and relationships. Kambuja records mention four *varnas*, and the emergence of a new class, *Brahmaksatra*, resulting from intermarriage between Brahmans and Ksatriyas. Other classes were created during the period of Jayavarman V, such as Khmuk and Karmantara. The Brahmans seem to have enjoyed a position of privilege, and their social life, as well as marriage customs and funerary rites, was much influenced by Indian practices. Although Hinduism remained the dominant religion, Buddhism also flourished. In the ninth century, King Yasovarman erected a Saugatasrama for Buddhist monks. Suryavarman I, who came from Siam, possibly adopted Buddhism; his inscription contains an invocation to the Buddha as well as to Siva, and he was posthumously named Nirvanapada.

Jayavarman VII was an ardent Buddhist and the public utility works undertaken by him were remarkably extensive. His Ta Prohm inscription containing 145 Sanskrit verses expresses his feeling of charity and compassion towards the whole universe. The magnitude of his resources and the depth of his religious sentiments can be gauged by the scale of his donations and charities. About sixty-seven thousand people were employed in the temples and the revenues from approximately three and a half thousand villages were given to defray their expenses. More than fourteen hundred professors and scholars were engaged in study in these temples, and their daily necessities were supplied. According to the evidence of his inscriptions, there were about eight hundred temples and more than a hundred hospitals in the kingdom, that were given over thirty million pounds of rice every year. Whilst these figures must be exaggerated, they do give an idea of his devotion to Buddhism. Despite this devotion, he was "the most arrogant and the most lustful for glory of all the Khmer kings, attributes in which they all excelled themselves."[42] He built so many temples that it is said he shifted greater quantities of stone than all his predecessors put together, and put statues of himself in the chief temples of his kingdoms.

When Buddhism became the paramount religion of Cambodia is uncertain. It had long been flourishing and occasionally enjoyed royal patronage, but it was never the state religion and never held a dominant position. It seems likely that Siam, which was first influenced by Cambodia, later aided Cambodia's conversion to Buddhism. The change was almost complete; today Hinduism is practically extinct in Cambodia except in a vestigial form in certain ceremonies and festivities. For instance court Brahmans, called *Bakus,* perform domestic rituals in the royal household. These Brahmans, although a survival of Hinduism, are Buddhists as are other Cambodians; their performance of the royal ceremonies appears to be rather a matter of profession than of faith. Hindu deities have been absorbed by Buddhism and relegated to subordinate positions, and even the Hindu gods in the great temples, such as Angkor Wat, have long been replaced by the images of the Buddha. Numerous Buddhist images have been found in the temple and it appears that by 1550 it had become a Buddhist pilgrimage place.

Unlike some other countries, Cambodia does not minimize Indian influence on the local culture. On the contrary, the people of the country generously acknowledge it. For instance, inaugurating the Maha Vithei

Jawaharlal Nehru Boulevard on 10 May 1965, Prince Norodom Sihanouk recalled the close cultural ties that have existed for two thousand years between India and Cambodia. He said: "When we refer to 2000 year old ties which unite us with India, it is not at all a hyperbole. In fact, it was about 2000 years ago that the first navigators, Indian merchants and Brahmans brought to our ancestors their gods, their techniques, their organisation. Briefly India was for us what Greece was for the Latin Occident."

Malaya

Malaya has historically been a meeting ground of diverse races and cultures. Certainly, the Malay Peninsula, which includes modern Malaya and southern Thailand, has played a central role in Indian sea trade with the countries of East Asia, as well as in the transmission of Indian culture throughout Southeast Asia. Takkola, modern Takua Pa in southern Thailand, was the first landfall of traders and settlers coming from India. From here the travellers went on in different directions. Some crossed over the mountain range to the fertile plain on the eastern coast and then proceeded either by land or sea to Siam, Cambodia, and other regions of Indochina, and further east. Others went to Burma or travelled by land southward toward Malaya or by sea through the Strait of Malacca to destinations in the Archipelago or East Asia. But all who wished to travel further east had to negotiate Malaya either overland or by a circuitous coastal voyage. It is therefore not surprising that this region was much Indianized, and ruins of shrines, images, Sanskrit inscriptions, and other remains of Indian culture have been found throughout the Peninsula.

Land communications within Malaya were adequate, including rivers and elephant tracks through thick jungles. Kedah was connected with Ligor in the northeast, and with the east coast region encircled by the Patani Sai, Belum, and Pergau Rivers. The goldfields of Pahang could be reached both by land and by sailing down the Kelantan and its tributaries. The northern part of Malaya, including part of what is today southern Thailand, was more advanced than the southern part of the country, as most of the important places and harbours, such as Tambralinga, Kataha, and Takkola, were located in the north close to the trade routes.

Southern Malaya also remained in a state of neglect because of the power and prosperity of Sumatra.

Malaya's fortunes have often been subjected to external pressures. Malaya has been rich enough to attract attention but not powerful enough to repel unwanted guests. Prior to Western domination, her northern neighbours, first Funan and later the Thai kingdom, held sway over her; from the south the Sri Vijaya and Majapahit Empires dominated Malaya for long periods. All these political contacts affected her cultural life.

Of the written records tracing the antiquity of the Indo-Malay contact, one has to rely again on Chinese chronicles, which refer to Indianized principalities in the Peninsula, although many of the place names are not positively identifiable. Ancient Indian literature contains very few references to Malaya.

In the first or second century, the kingdom of Langkasuka (Lang-Kia-su, Lang-Ya-hsiu or Tun Sun), mentioned several times in Chinese chronicles, was founded on the east coast in the neighbourhood of Patani. There is some controversy as to whether Langkasuka was on the west or the east coast of Malaya, but latest opinion appears to favour the latter view.[43] More than four hundred years later, in 515, King Bhagadatta (Po-chi-ieh-ta-to) of Langkasuka sent an envoy, Aditya, to China. During the sixth century at least three other embassies were sent to China. References are also found to other states, such as Pan Pan, which was conterminous with Langkasuka and was frequented by the Brahmans from India. It was from this state that the second Kaundinya went to Funan. Southeast of Pan Pan was Kolo (Kolo-fu-sha-lo), placed by Coedès in the area of Kedah or Kra; this was prominent enough in the sixth and seventh centuries to attract envoys from China. Chinese records speak of embassies coming from Malaya to China in the sixth century and of Indian kings reigning there and using the Sanskrit language.

Indian literature also mentions kingdoms, Kalasapura and Kamalanka (Karmaranga), which were probably in the Malay Peninsula, Kala (Kedah), and Pahang. In the *Puranas,* mention is often made of Katahadvipa (Kataha), which was included amongst the nine divisions of the world across the seas, and to which regular voyages were undertaken from Tamralipti. Various other references to Katahadvipa are found in Sanskrit dramas and stories. The Tamil epic, *Silappadikaram,* of the second century contains a description of tall, roomy ships entering a city in South India laden with a variety of goods and spices from a Malayan port called Tondi.

Both Indian and Chinese literature contain references to Kedah, situated on the west coast, and the most important Indianized principality in Malaya proper. From the third to the fifteenth century, Kedah was an important port. A well-known Tamil poem, *Pattinappalai*, of the second or third century, mentions regular trade between Kalagam, possibly Kedah, and Puhar (Kavirippattinam). Later, the Chola inscriptions of the eleventh century refer to Kedah in various forms, such as Kidaram, Kadaram, and Kataha.

Although the Chinese had become aware of Langkasuka earlier, Kedah was neither noticed nor recorded until the T'ang period, presumably because it was not in contact with China. I-tsing was the first Chinese scholar to refer to Kedah (Chieh-cha), which he visited in 671. Later, the Arab writers also mention it as Kalah placing it on the way from India to China, and some mention it as a dependency of Zabaj, Sri Vijaya.

The remains excavated in the Malay Peninsula generally confirm the deductions made from literary sources, although much work still needs to be done. Excavations so far have not yielded any substantial evidence from the time of the kingdoms of Langkasuka. The Sanskrit inscriptions that have been discovered do not date back further than the fourth century, although the literary references fix the date of the Indianized states in the Malay Peninsula much earlier. Lately, however, some evidence has been building up to strengthen the conclusions reached from literary sources. It was probably an Indian ship that brought an Attic vase of the fifth century B.C. to Perlis. The Roman beads found at Kota Tinggi in Johore were probably brought by Indian traders at the beginning of the Christian era.[44] The remains of a Siva temple excavated by Quaritch Wales on a low spur of Kedah Peak have been interpreted as an important link in the transition from the sepulchral shrines of South India to the *Chandis* or tomb shrines of Java. Thus it seems that Indian culture was centuries old in Kedah in the seventh century, and flourishing enough to become the centre of cultural diffusion to Java. Malacca also must have been an early Indian centre. A *makara* fragment built into the wall of a

Portuguese church must have come from an ancient temple destroyed by the Christian conquerors.[45]

Kedah, however, is by far the most important of Malayan sites. Following the explorations of James Low and later of Evans, made in 1925, Quaritch Wales carried out extensive investigations in Kedah on about thirty sites. Further archaeological work has been done recently on these sites by members of the Malayan universities. Of the thirty sites excavated by Quaritch Wales, eight appear to be Buddhist, as many as twelve are possibly Saiva and Hindu, and three are the remains of secular buildings.

The Pallavas founded settlements in Kedah, on the Bujang River, whose temple ruins have yielded an image of Ganesa and other objects of Saiva faith. Kedah was an important centre of Indian culture in the fifth or sixth century; Indians, both Hindu and Buddhist, came continuously for several centuries to settle, and gradually Kedah became a repository of Indian art styles and cultural traits which in due course were further diffused. They came mainly from South India, but many Indians arrived from other parts of the country. A stone inscription found at Guak Kepah in Kedah mentions a *mahanavika,* literally a great sailor, Buddhagupta. He is described as an inhabitant of Raktamrittika which is identified with Rangamati, twelve miles south of Murshidabad in Bengal.

Some of the inscriptions testify to the presence of both Hinayana and Mahayana Buddhists in Kedah in the fourth century. A bronze statue of Buddha in the style of Amaravati found in Kedah and two Buddhist images of Gupta style from the Kinta Valley in Perak, belong to the fifth century. An inscribed clay tablet found near Kedah, which is assigned to the sixth century, contains three Sanskrit verses embodying some Mahayana philosophical doctrines. Two of these three verses have been found in Chinese translations of Madhyamika texts and all three are found in a Chinese translation of the *Sagaramatipariprccha.* In the eighth century the Palas of eastern India reinforced Mahayanism in Malaya.

Bruas in Perak is supposed to contain the relics of the ancient Gangga Nagara mentioned in the Blagden recension of the Malay annals. Higher up the west coast, Kuala Selinsing in Perak has been identified by Evans as the site of an ancient Indian settlement on the strength of a Sanskrit inscription "Sri Vishnuvarmmasya," found on a cornelian seal.[46] Spelled incorrectly, the inscription is written in boxheaded characters of a South Indian variety of about the sixth century or earlier; hence, it is generally regarded as a Pallava seal. This site has yielded many other significant finds pointing to the existence of a continuous settlement there for several centuries. These include a remarkable number and variety of beads, some of which, such as the complicated stone beads, appear to be imitations of those of India or cultures farther west.

Some important Buddhist relics have also been excavated from Perak, which has been a rich mining area from ancient times. A fine bronze Buddha statue from Pangkalan, and another bronze image of the Buddha mined from a depth of sixty feet in a tin mine at Tanjong Rambutan, reflect the Gupta style of the fifth century.

In the southwest corner of Kedah, in Province Wellesley, a group of seven Sanskrit inscriptions probably belonging to the fourth century, were discovered by James Low at Cherok Tokun in the central part and four more in the north. From Bidor comes a fine bronze image of Avalokitesvara with Tantric emblems in Pala style of the eighth and ninth centuries. Two more bronze statues of the same Bodhisattva, one of which is a standing four-armed image, have been found in open cast tin mines at Sungei Siput. A bronze statue representing a Brahman ascetic found recently at a site in Tinkus Valley, Sungei Siput in Perak, resembles the effigies of the vedic sage, Agastya, of whom numerous specimens have been discovered in South India, Ceylon, and Java. Whilst the Agastya cult was common in Indonesia, this is the first evidence of its presence in Malaya. Of the six hundred or so beads found at Kota Tinggi in Johore about eighty are of early Indian origin, more than a hundred are Roman (probably brought by Indian merchants), one Hittite, and two Phoenician.

The present political border between Malaya and Thailand is not a meaningful division in respect to their cultural past. The monuments in southern Siam, at places such as Chaiya, Takua Pa, Nakhon Srithammarata (Ligor), and Yala (near Patani), are impressive examples of the local Indianized art, resembling Pallava or Gupta architecture. Of all the Indianized states in the Peninsula the most important was Ligor, now Nakhon Srithammarata, in southern Thailand. It was essentially a Buddhist settlement. Some of the fifty temples that encircled the stupa belong to a very early period, yet there are also Brahmans of Indian descent at Patalung, who trace the arrival of their ancestors by an overland route from India across the Malay Peninsula. In addition, numerous relics of Hindu origin have been excavated from this area.

The history of the Malay region from the eighth century onward is a little better known, for it came under the domination of the Indonesian Empire of Sri Vijaya and the Sailendras, and the ruins of this period, which lasted almost until the end of the thirteenth century, are found throughout the Peninsula. In the fourteenth century, when the Indianized Majapahit Empire displaced Sri Vijaya, Kedah, Patani, and Kelantan were greatly influenced by Majapahit culture; for example, linguistic traces in Kedah and the shadow play in Kelantan still contain Javanese Hindu characteristics.

Although Malaya was in close contact with India for over a thousand years and Hindu and Buddhist influences were strong, the remains unearthed are surprisingly few, and Malaya proper has not yielded a single temple or stupa approximating the splendour of even a minor structure of Thailand or Indonesia. Perhaps the adverse climate and corrosive soil took their toll on early structures which may have been of wood. Moreover, the empires of which Malaya formed a part had their seats of government outside the Peninsula, particularly in Indonesia. Another possible explanation of this, as Winstedt points out, is Muslim iconoclasm: "*The Kedah Annals* record how on conversion to Islam the Malays destroyed all the idols they were accustomed to worship, together with the idols handed down from their ancestors."[47] Islam is indeed uncompromisingly iconoclastic and has a long history of image and temple destruction in other countries, including Indonesia—and India itself—where most of the many statues surviving from the pre-Muslim past are headless.

Indian contacts with Malaya during this period can be better studied as a part of the whole phenomenon of developing cultures in the Archipelago. Soon after, Islam and Europeans came to Malaya effecting deep changes in her life and culture, yet the cultural background of Islamic Malaya is distinctly Indianized. Malays still perform many ceremonies which bear the marks of Hinduism; some Sanskrit words are still used in rituals. The Malay ceremony, *Melenggang perut,* performed in the seventh month of pregnancy to achieve the birth of a son, is reminiscent of a Hindu practice. Various other rituals connected with childbirth are the relics of an Hindu past. Elaborate ceremonies pertaining to the student life, laws and customs regulating family life, inheritance and social behaviour, wedding ceremonies, and temperamental similarities all suggest the harmonious blending of the two cultures.

Concepts of state and kingship in Malaya, royal titles such as *Seri Paduka,* ceremonies connected with coronation, and royal prerogatives are clearly of Indian inspiration. Malaya's literature and folklore are deeply influenced by the Hindu epics, the *Ramayana* and the *Mahabharata.* Her language has many Sanskrit loan words, and until the introduction of Arabic and, later, Roman script, Indian scripts were used in Malaya and the Archipelago.

Indonesia

Sea trade between India and East Asia had begun to flourish in the first century, and Indian settlements had been established in Southeast Asia; Palembang in Sumatra was a port of call en route from India to China.

The oldest report on Indonesia is found in the Han annals of the Emperor Wang Mang who ruled China in the first quarter of the first century. Specimens of Chinese ceramics of the Han period found in Sumatra endorse the existence of regular contact between China and Indonesia at that time. A Chinese source mentions an embassy sent to China in 132 by King Pien (Tiao-pien) of Ye-tiao: the name is a Chinese transcription of King Devavarman of Yavadvipa (Java Island).

The fact that there was an Indianized kingdom in Java powerful enough to dispatch an envoy to China in the early second century would suggest the prior existence of Indian influence. Believing that Java was already Indianized by 132 and assuming that this Indianization had only been effected slowly in the course of many years, G. Ferrand believes that the beginnings of Hinduism in Indochina and in Indonesia must be anterior to the Christian era. Fa-hsien, who visited Java about 414 for five months, described the country as a stronghold of Hinduism. From Java, Fa-hsien sailed for Canton in a merchant vessel which had two hundred Hindu traders on board. Less than twenty-five years later, the Buddhist monk, Gunavarman, stopped in Java on his way to China and laid the foundation of Buddhism there. References to Indianized Java of later periods are numerous and specific in the Chinese chronicles.

Ptolemy's reference in the second century to *Iabadiou* certainly represents the Prakrit form of the Sanskrit Yavadvipa. He also mentions several places in the Archipelago and the Peninsula under their Sanskritic names. The evidence indicates that Indian civilization had found a firm foothold in Java by his time.[48]

The chief sources of early Javanese history are elaborate local narrative verses and poems. People in Java believed that Rishi Agastya came from India and settled there. Usually called Bhatara Guru, Agastya is an extremely popular legendary figure in Indonesia, and he was widely worshipped and venerated; numerous reproductions of his image in art and sculpture are found in the country. According to Javanese chronicles, twenty thousand Indian families came to Java from Kalinga in the second century. A century later their prince, Kano, emerged. Various other Javanese traditions and legends associate the original settlers and their leader, Aji Saka, with the heroes of the *Mahabharata.* The Javanese era commences from Aji Saka in the year 78, the epoch of the Saka era in India. Another tradition in Java mentions the foundation of a Hindu state in 56.[49]

The archaeological remains excavated so far are somewhat posterior to the literary references relating to Indian culture in Indonesia. Amongst the earliest finds are the images of the Buddha, in the Amaravati style, discovered at Sampaga in the Celebes; in the south of the Jember province in eastern Java; and on Mount Seguntang at Palembang in Sumatra. Sanskrit inscriptions of a King Mulavarman from Kutei in Borneo, dating from the fourth or the beginning of the fifth century, have also been found. These inscriptions are not dated, but their script closely resembles that of the early Pallava inscriptions of South India and the early inscriptions of Champa and Kambuja. The next series of inscriptions comes from West Java and refers to a King Purnavarman; these scripts suggest that they were engraved in the middle of the fifth century. Because of its closer proximity to India, Sumatra was probably the first island visited by Indians in this area, but it has yet to be properly investigated by archaeologists.

However, in the various parts of Indochina and Malaya numerous stone inscriptions belonging to the third century, at the latest, have been found. These inscriptions, covering a period of centuries, bear recognizable family likeness, and are usually composed in Sanskrit and written in a South Indian script. The earliest of these inscriptions is the rock inscription from Vo-Canh in Champa, written in Sanskrit, dating from the third or even possibly the second century. It is therefore plausible to assume that before Indian culture spread as far as Champa, it may have found a foothold in lands nearer to India, such as the Malay Peninsula, Sumatra, and Java.

The earliest chief Indianized kingdom in Indonesia was Sri Vijaya with its capital at Palembang, in Sumatra. The Chinese called it Shih-li-fo-shih (San-fo-tsi, Kan-te-li or, briefly, Fuche). It is generally believed that this kingdom was founded in the seventh century, but Majumdar believes, as does Ferrand, that it was founded in or before the fourth century, reaching greatness at the end of the seventh.[50] In any case, it is in the last quarter of the seventh century that the first clear allusions to this kingdom are found in epigraphy and literature. Quaritch Wales, whilst admitting the existence of Sri Vijaya in the seventh century, suggests that it was supplanted by a powerful kingdom called Javaka, under a Mahayanist dynasty of the Sailendras newly arrived from India. Whether Sri Vijaya and Javaka were one or two states, the cultural pattern of Indianization remained the same.

Sri Vijaya ruled over an extensive area stretching from Java to the Malay Peninsula and southern Siam from at least the seventh to the twelfth, possibly the thirteenth, century. A group of inscriptions found at Palembang, some of them dated 683–686, refer to the conquest of Jambi (Malayu) and the island of Bangka. An inscription dated 775 from Nakhon Srithammarat refers to the might of the king of Sri Vijaya and to several Buddhist temples built there under the king's command. Thus, it seems that by the eighth century Sri Vijaya dominated the whole of Sumatra, West Java, and the greater part of the Malay Peninsula. Control of the northern part of Malaya and the two straits added to the increasing prosperity of Sri Vijaya. Indian traders who chose the sea route had to go through one of the two straits, and those who took the overland route to Indochina and China had to cut across the northern part of the Malay

Peninsula. According to Coedes, Sri Vijaya succeeded to the commercial hegemony of Funan and control of the southern area.

Material progress accelerated the growth of learning and art. I-tsing stayed in Palembang for six months in 671 learning Sanskrit grammar, and again fourteen years later, on his return from India, spent four years, copying and translating several Sanskrit texts into Chinese. He was so impressed by the Buddhist studies in Palembang that he advised Chinese monks to go through a course of preliminary learning there before proceeding to India. He himself came back to Palembang for the third time with four of his colleagues from Canton and wrote his two *Memoirs* there. At the time, Buddhist monks in Sri Vijaya numbered more than a thousand. From the seventh to the eleventh century Buddhism remained most powerful in Indonesia, attracting famous scholars from India, such as Dharmapala, a scholar from Nalanda University, who visited Indonesia in the seventh century. Atisa Dipankara (eleventh century), the monk who became the head of Vikramasila University and inaugurated the second period of Buddhism in Tibet, went there in his early life to study Buddhism.

Whilst Sri Vijaya was at the peak of its power, another kingdom was emerging in central Java, the Sailendras, with whom Sri Vijaya had friendly relations at first. Before the rise of the Sailendra kingdom in the eighth century, there were several Indianized states in Java. Two of these, called by the Chinese Cho-po and Ho-lo-tan, sent embassies to China in the fifth century. Amongst the earliest archaeological remains of West Java are four Sanskrit stone inscriptions of a king Purnavarman of Taruma who reigned in the fifth century. As these inscriptions refer to his grandfather as a *rajarshi,* and another ancestor as a *rajadhiraja,* it would seem that an Indianized society flourished in Java during the fourth and fifth centuries.

Chinese historical works mention various kingdoms in Java and other islands, although not all of these are easy to identify. The most important kingdom in Java during the T'ang period was Ho-ling, a Chinese variation of the Indonesian Kaling or Kalinga, which was also the name of a region on India's east coast. About this time a number of Indians from Kalinga are said to have emigrated, and it is possible that they settled in a part of Java; they certainly were numerous enough to name the state after their home area.

Attempts have been made to connect the Indian Kalinga with the origins of the Sailendras in Java. It is argued that the two ruling dynasties of Kalinga, the Gangas and the Sailodbhavas, were defeated by the Calukya dynasty of the south in the seventh century. The defeated rulers thereupon set out for the renowned islands of the east and founded the Sailendra Kingdom. Nilakanta Sastri, however, finds this theory open to objection and suggests that the Sailendras may be an offshoot of the South Indian Pandyas. Various other theories of their precise origins have been advanced but none is clearly established. It seems that in Java there were numerous centres of power, usually referred to as *kratons,* which meant king and his court. The more powerful kratons struggled for political supremacy, and out of this conflict emerged the Sailendra dynasty in central Java, in the eighth century, which was to attain not only great political power but also a degree of cultural advancement seldom surpassed in history.

The accounts of Arab writers, such as Ibn Khurdadhbih, Abu Zayd Hasan, Al Masudi and Al Biruni, testify to the political, commercial, and cultural accomplishments of the Sailendras. The Sailendra Empire is referred to by the Arab writers as *Zabag (Zabaj),* from the empire of Maharaja; some scholars believe that the term refers to the Maharaja of the Sri Vijaya Empire. The most detailed account of Zabag is by Abu Zayd Hasan, who wrote about 916, basing his account on one originally written by Sulayman in 851. Sulayman recounts various islands forming part of the kingdom and speaks of the great fertility of its soil and of its dense population. The king is described as so rich that every day he threw a solid brick of gold into water saying "there is my treasure." His daily revenue amounted to two hundred *mans* of gold, fifty of which came from cock-fights. The Maharaja was the overlord of a number of islands and, according to Al Masudi, his Empire was so large that even the fastest vessels could not complete a round trip of it in two years.

The data to reconstruct the history of this Empire are inadequate, and the details of its relationship with Sri Vijaya are not clear. We do not know whether the Sailendras were a branch of Sri Vijaya, whether they had taken the latter under their protection, or whether they shared a peaceful coexistence. It is, however, generally accepted that a Sailendra prince, either having been driven out of his home or by virtue of kinship, became the ruler of Sri Vijaya at Palembang in the ninth century and his dynasty lasted there until the thirteenth century.

The Sailendras brought the greatest part of the Malay Archipelago under one central authority. Their Empire extended as far as Champa and Kambuja; the Sailendra fleet raided the distant coast more than once in the eighth century. This was a troubled period in the history of Southeast Asia, especially Indochina, and our knowledge of it is more obscure than that of others. Why these naval raids were carried out is not clear. Why did the Sailendras temporarily bring Cambodia under their domination? It is known that Jayavarman had declared the independence of Kambuja from Java in 802, and although it is not certain, there are reasons to believe that the successive Sailendra expeditions and incursions caused the collapse of the royal dynasty of Champa.

The Sailendras were evidently a great naval power, and their relations with the fellow-Buddhist Pala Kingdom of Bengal were quite close; as early as 782, Kumaraghosha of the Pala Empire was the royal preceptor, guru, of the Sailendra kings. A copper plate inscription, found at Nalanda and dated about 860, records the erection there of a monastery by King Balaputradeva of Suvarnadvipa. Visitors and scholars from Indonesia to Nalanda became so numerous that a separate monastery had to be built to lodge them. A Chola inscription from South India records that two Sailendra kings, Chudamanivarman and his son, Sri Maravijayottungavarman, constructed a Buddhist monastery at Nagapattana (modern Negapatam). In both cases the respective Indian kings granted lands and villages to these monasteries.

The Sailendras maintained good relations with the Chola rulers of South India. The Cholas were also a great naval power, and by the beginning of the eleventh century under Rajaraja the Great (985–1014) and his still more powerful son, Rajendra Chola (1014–1044), they became the paramount power in southern India. The friendly relations between these two powers deteriorated in the eleventh century, and two Chola inscriptions of 1024 and 1030 speak of Rajendra's military expeditions and conquests of several countries in Southeast Asia including Sri Vijaya and the Sailendra Kingdom. Another Chola king, Virarajendra (1063–1070), is also said to have led a successful military incursion to Sailendra. The conflict between the Cholas and the Sailendras, which persisted throughout the eleventh century, considerably crippled the power of both.

The Sailendra period is one of the most important eras in the history of Southeast Asia. Buddhist art, inspired by the Mahayanism and Tantrism of the Palas, reached a new peak. Indonesian civilization during the Sailendra period became a model for other Southeast Asian countries. The Sailendras introduced a new kind of script, Devanagari, from northern India, built world famous monuments, such as Lara Jonggrang and Borobudur, and gave Malaysia a new name, Kalinga. Whilst Mahayana Buddhism had its votaries at the court and amongst the governing classes, Sivaism was prevalent amongst the common people; whilst Borobudur represents the peak of Buddhist art in Indonesia, the temple of Lara Jonggrang at Prambanan is Saiva.

In the tenth century the scene of power and civilization moved to eastern Java. Just before the Sailendras emerged in central Java as a supreme power, a powerful dynasty was ruling there with its capital at Mataram, and, under its ruler Sanjaya, had led successful expeditions to Sumatra and Cambodia. Sanjaya is said to have been a great conqueror and he was deified as Divine Sanjaya. An inscription found at Changal in the district of Kedu mentions that Sanjaya had erected there a monument for a Sivalinga in 732. After his death, central Java was conquered by the Sailendras and his successors were pushed eastward. In the ninth century, however, it appears that Mataram had shaken off the political supremacy of the Sailendras in eastern Java, which became a prominent region where Indian culture found a strong repository for the next five hundred years.

Mpu Sindok, who ascended the throne in 929, was the first known king of the house of Mataram to settle in eastern Java, under the regal title of *Sri Isana Vikrama Dharmottungadeva.* By this time, the culture and civilization in central Java had visibly declined. Sindok is an eminent name in Javanese history, and the later kings eagerly sought to trace their descent from him, but the exact accomplishments which gave him this prestige are lost to history.

Princess Mahendradatta, the great granddaughter of Sindok, married a prince of Bali, Udayana. Their son, Airlingga, who ruled over the Mataram Kingdom from 1010 to 1049 was one of the greatest kings of

Java. He brought the whole of Java under his authority and established commercial and political relations with other countries. According to an inscription, he built a dam to stop the Brantas River from flooding. He was regarded as an incarnation of Vishnu, and at Balahan, where he was cremated, there is a fine statue of Vishnu on his mount, Garuda. He was a patron of literature, and Kanva's poem, *Arjunavivaha,* the first book of its kind, was written under his patronage.

Before he died, he divided his kingdom between two of his sons. The two resulting states, Kadiri and Djanggala, survived in eastern Java until the beginning of the thirteenth century, when a new dynasty, Singhasari, emerged. Kadiri was the center of intellectual activity during this period.

Singhasari was founded by Ken Angrok, who styled himself as an incarnation of Bhatara Guru; he has been the subject of many popular legends. But the dynasty attained its highest power and prestige under the rule of Kritanagara (1268–1292), who is portrayed in literature in striking contrasts. A Javanese chronicle, *Pararaton,* describes him adversely, whilst a well-known historical poem, *Nagara-Kritagama,* hails him as an expert in Buddhist scriptures and polity. He was certainly a devout Buddhist and practiced Yoga and Samadhi. Marco Polo, who visited Java during this period, described Singhasari as a prosperous kingdom ruled by a great king. Kritanagara initiated an aggressive imperial policy. He subdued Sumatra, Bali, parts of Borneo, and the Malay Peninsula. Emboldened by his successes, he even picked a quarrel with Kublai Khan, but before the Chinese punitive expedition could reach Java he was dethroned by an internal rebellion led by the governor of Kadiri.[51]

From the chaos and unrest that followed the rebellion in Singhasari, in which the Chinese expedition played an active part, there emerged the kingdom of Majapahit in central Java under Vijaya, a son-in-law of Kritanagara. Vijaya, having subdued other contenders for the throne, proclaimed himself the king of the whole of Java in 1294, assuming the regal name of Kritarajasa Jayavardhana. The most eminent name of this dynasty, however, is not that of a king, but of a commander, Gajah Mada, who became the prime minister and the effective ruler from 1331 to 1364. He extended the authority of Majapahit over Sumatra where he completely demolished the weakened Sri Vijaya kingdom as well as dominating Bali and other islands. He is believed to have initiated the "Javanization" of Bali.

The Empire attained the peak of its power under Rajasanagara (1350–1389), commonly known by his personal name, Hayam Wuruk. He ruled over all the principal islands in the Archipelago and the large part of the Malay Peninsula. He established cultural and trade relations with neighbouring countries, such as Kambuja, Champa, China, Siam, and India, which sent a large number of Brahmans and Sramanas to his capital. After his death the kingdom disintegrated and supremacy over the various islands, including Sumatra and some states of Malaya, gradually passed to Ming China, which became the suzerain of the Archipelago.

The Majapahit Kingdom, however, continued until 1520. About the middle of the fifteenth century Islam had begun to penetrate Java; the new religion gradually became powerful enough to bring about the downfall of the last great Indianized kingdoms in Java, as of others in Indonesia. Only a small Hindu state of Balambangan retained its independence, and continued to.do so for two and a half centuries. Today only Bali still professes a kind of Hinduism, called Hindu-Balinese.

Soon the arrival of European merchants, soldiers, and missionaries changed the pattern of Indonesian society. In fact, Western culture came to Indonesia at about the same time as Islamic culture, but whilst the former scarcely affected the indigenous culture of Indonesia at first, the latter quickly began to take root in Indonesian soil. The explanation of this contrast may be that whilst Western culture was completely alien and had come to Indonesia in association with political domination, Islamic culture was familiar and completely unattended by foreign military force.

Indian Muslim traders and teachers, chiefly from South India, embarking at Gujarat and Malabar, carried Islam to the Malay Archipelago. They were mainly interested in profit, and were not religious zealots. They were not willing to sacrifice life or property for the holy cause, nor were they the instruments of an Islamic Church. Even teachers who arrived later from Egypt, Mecca, and Arabia came in search of gain through rich patrons. Their language was Indian—Hindustani, Gujarati, Malayalam, Tamil, or some other—and the books they brought were Indian versions of Arabic or Persian originals. From these Indian versions, translations into Malay were made.

Islam made easy conversions, mainly because of the simplicity of its beliefs, in marked contrast to the complex doctrines and traditions of Hinduism and Buddhism, in which very sophisticated and varied philosophies had admitted a variety of ugly traditions and superstitions over a period of centuries; Sufism also found a ready reception in Indianized Indonesia. Whilst Islam made religious converts, it could not impose a new culture, for Indonesian culture was far too developed and distinctive itself at the time. Change of religion was bound to affect the existing religious cultural character, but even in this sphere Islam accepted many features of Indonesian culture. For instance, Islamic fasts in Indonesia are still called *puwasi upavasa,* a term of Sanskrit origin; a Muslim teacher is called guru; and Muslim sultans bear titles such as *Maharaja, Srinara,* and *Mandulika.*

Today, Indonesia is the largest Muslim country in the world, yet Indonesian culture is perhaps the only one which Islam has not penetrated beyond the surface. In Malaya, too, the culture has few Islamic features but the Malays at least have Muslim names, whilst most Indonesians have retained their original names. Islam is not a culture in the true sense of the term, but it has certain recognizable features, acquired from the Arab and Persian cultures, which it has always sought to impose on its adherents. The French traveller, Jules Leclercq, having seen *hajis* (Muslims returned from Mecca) joining in the worship of ancient Hindu images, remarked that the advent of the Muslim faith has not alienated the Javanese from their old beliefs.[52]

Indonesian language, art, social customs, legal and political systems, literature, folklore, and philosophy, were affected by Indian cultural currents. "To gain a correct idea of the extent of the influence of Hindu culture in the islands that came under it," says Sastri, "one must contrast Sumatra, Java and Bali with the islands farther east which were not touched by this influence. It will then become clear that all the elements of higher culture, the form of organized state-life, trade and industry, art and literature were practically gifts of the Hindus to these islands, and that the archipelago falls easily into two divisions—one which accepted the new culture and advanced with it into civilization, and the other which lagged behind."[53]

The Kawi language, Indonesian in essence, is full of Sanskrit loan words. The oldest extant script in the Malay Archipelago is the so-called Pallava script—the language being Sanskrit—named after the Pallava dynasty. By the eighth century Java had evolved its Kawi or Old Javanese script from the Pallava, which was given the Sanskrit appellation of Akshara Buddha, meaning Buddhist letters. Another Indian script used in the Archipelago was an early form of Devanagari, possibly introduced in the eighth century as a result of the close intercourse between the Palas and the Sailendras. Madurese, Sundanese, and Balinese scripts also derive from the Pallava. Batak writing in central Sumatra has undergone much simplification perhaps owing to the writing materials used—bark or sapwood—but it is also derived from the same source. Peoples in the south of Sumatra, the Rajang and the Lampong, use writing closely resembling the Kawi. The ancient alphabets of the Bugis and Macassars of the Celebes were derived from an Old Malay or Sumatran script of the Pallava family. The alphabets used by the Tagalogs and others in the Philippines, when the Spanish first met them in the sixteenth century, were likewise closely allied to the Sumatran script, although the number of characters had dwindled considerably. Thus at one time Indian scripts were in use in the whole of the Malay Archipelago. With the introduction of Islam they were partially superseded by the Arabic script, and with the coming of the Europeans by Roman characters.

Numerals generally remain unchanged in a language affected by foreign influences, but Indonesians adopted various Indian numerals. Before the arrival of the Indians, Indonesians had their terms for 1–10, 100, and 1000. Numbers higher than that, however, were represented by words meaning "innumerable," "obscure," or by borrowed terms. The Sanskrit *laksha,* which means 100,000, is used throughout the Archipelago to denote 10,000, so when the problem of appropriate terminology for 100,000 arose, the Archipelago adopted the Sanskrit word *koti* representing 10,000,000.

Whilst the Sanskrit laksha and koti are given a lower value than the original, Sanskrit *ayuta,* 10,000 assumes the higher value of 1,000,000 *(yuta)* in Malay and Javanese, and 100,000 *(samyuta)* in Tagalog. It is possible, however, that yuta is derived from the Sanskrit *niyuta,* meaning a very high number. In Balinese, *ha-laksa* stands for 10,000, *ha-koti* for 100,000, *ha-yuta* for 1,000,000, and *ha-bara* (in Sanskrit *bhara* means weight, a large quantity) for 10,000,000. The lower Indian numerals that have been adopted in the Archipelago are mostly used in compounds: thus *pancanana* (five-faced), or *dasaguna* (tenfold).

The formation of ordinals from the cardinals is interesting. In India, *prathama* (foremost or first) was excluded from the list of ordinals because the functions of the first are different from those of other ordinal numbers. The Malay differentiates between its first and the following ordinals by using *pertama* (prathama) with *yang* preceding it for first, but for all others it merely uses the prefix *ke* before the original cardinals; thus *ke-dua* is second, *ke-tiga* is third, and so on.

Tagalog expresses fractions by the use of the term *bahagi* (part) from the Sanskrit *bhaga* (share). In Malay bahagi means to share or to apportion. As for the numeral co-efficient *biji*, which also means seed in Malay and some other languages of the Archipelago, the origin may be sought in the Sanskrit *bija* (seed). The Javanese *siji* (one) is short for *sa-wiji* meaning one or a certain. *Wiji* alone stands for piece in counting, or for seed, and in a literary sense for offspring. Likewise in Malay it means not only seed or pip but also testicle. The Javanese wiji may share the same origin with the informal. Dayak *ije* (one), which may represent a word etymologically cognate with the Sanskrit bija. As for the connection between bija and biji, it is common to find the Sanskrit "a" being changed into "i" in the languages of the Malay Archipelago.

Language is merely a vehicle of ideas. Whilst its introduction was dictated by utilitarian reasons like the need to communicate, it soon assumed the additional role of transmitting ideas and cultural traits. Some Sanskrit inscriptions suggest that Indian philosophical and literary texts were carried to Java from very early times, although there is no record of it. The most ancient texts composed in Indonesia appear to belong to the fifth century; they deal mainly with grants of land, etc. Later, under the patronage of the great empires, Indonesian literature flourished, and Indian epics, such as the *Mahabharata* and the *Ramayana*, were translated and adapted in the Javanese language.

Several recensions of the *Ramayana* exist in both verse and prose in Indonesia. Episodes from it are used as themes in the popular Indonesian *wayang-kulit* (shadow play). The Indonesians have made alterations in Valmiki's version, combining it with material from other Indian versions of the *Ramayana* and with their own imaginative embellishments. Some scholars, such as Stutterheim, believe that some of the traditions preserved in the Indonesian version may even be anterior to Valmiki's *Ramayana*. The Rama tradition, however, principally in its Indian form, is still a living force in Indonesia. The Indonesian concept of chivalry is closely modelled on this epic and on Rama's ideals. In the education of Indonesian girls frequent references are made to the lofty examples of Sita. The main river of central Java, Sarayu, is named after the Indian river on the bank of which was situated Rama's capital, Ayodhya.

The other Indian epic, the *Mahabharata*, is even more popular. First translated into Old Javanese in the tenth or eleventh century, it has been repeatedly translated and adapted. The *Mahabharata* is like an encyclopaedia of Hinduism containing a wide variety of tales of heroic deeds and exploits. It appears to have captured the imagination of Indonesian peoples, who consider themselves to be the descendants of the heroes of the *Mahabharata*, and believe that all the drama took place on their soil. They endeavour to model their own lives and deeds in accordance with the ideals and examples of its heroes. The major hero of the epic, Arjuna, is the national hero of Indonesia. The name of the leader of the Indonesian Revolution, Sukarno, is taken from Su-Karna, a hero of the *Mahabharata*.

The style of early Javanese literature closely follows Sanskrit. Courtly poetry began in Indonesia with adaptations of Indian epics and other works. The Old Javanese work, *Amaramala*, is modelled on the Sanskrit *Amarakosa* and other Indian lexicons. Such adaptations as a category are known as *Parva*. Parvas were followed by *Kakawins*, which were the adaptations of Indian poetical works. These are called *Nitisastra-Kawin* in Java, and in Bali just *Nitisastra*. The first important literary work of Indonesia, *Arjuna Vivaha*, was written during the reign of Airlangga (Erlanga, or Rake Halu Sri Lokesvara Charmavamsa Erlanganantavikramottungodeva, the only Balinese prince to rule over both Bali and Java), and deals with an episode from the *Mahabharata*. The theme and style of this work made the Indian epic extremely popular in Indonesia and are reflected in other literary works and folk tales. During the Kadiri period two poetical works of outstanding quality *Krishnayana*, describing Krishna's fight with Jarasandha, and *Sumanasantaka*, based on Kalidasa's *Raghuvamsa*, were written. Another masterpiece, the *Bharatayuddha*, portrays the conflict between the Pandavas and the Kauravas. It was written in the second half of the twelfth century by Mpu Sedah and possibly completed by Mpu Panuluh. Many other Javanese works, such as *Harivamsa*, *Bhamokavya*, *Smaradahana*, and *Nagora Kritagama*, drew freely from Indian literature. The *Hitopadesa* and the *Pancatantra*, which so deeply influenced the fables and fairy tales of the Western world, were well known in Indonesia and other parts of East Asia. Their stories form the basis of Indonesian fables and folklore known as *Tantri*.

The Indian tradition of puppet shows, *Kathaputali*, is not only well preserved, but nowhere in the world are these shows as much an integral part of the social life of the people as they are in Indonesia. All over Java and Bali, and now also elsewhere in Indonesia and Malaya, wayang shows are frequently performed before large audiences. It is an exquisite art developed over centuries. The beautifully cut leather puppets are operated by the *dalang* (performer) with incredible ingenuity and skill. The performance is accompanied by the Javanese *gamelan* (orchestra), and the puppets represent the heroes and heroines of the Indian epics, with the size, appearance, colour, and ornaments of each character fixed by convention. The influence of the wayang on the life of the people is enormous, and even the dominance of Islam has not lessened its popularity. For the Javanese, says Wagner, "the wayang-kulit is not just a show; but represents an abstract world in which ideas take human shape and imagination becomes reality." [54] Stamford Raffles, at the beginning of the nineteenth century, found eager multitudes of people listening for whole nights with rapturous delight and profound attention to wayang-kulit. The nationalists adopted wayang for patriotic shows during their struggle for power, and without it they might not have succeeded in gaining mass support for their movement.

The origin of wayang is a subject of dispute, but there is no doubt that the culture introduced from India greatly influenced it. Indian myths, tales, and sagas were increasingly adopted; Indian gods, heroes, and demons also soon found their way into wayang. As might be expected,

Indian tales and heroes over a period of centuries were hopelessly interwoven. Indian characters and situations drawn from a variety of long forgotten tales may be woven into a new context with a local character. Indian traditions also mingled with indigenous myths and tales. Indian influence, however, is noticed not only in the subject matter of the *lakons* (stage version of stories) but also in the technique of the whole art.

Indian imprints on Javanese music, village organization, rural economy, and customary laws of property can also be seen. Hindu influence in Indonesian music was perhaps felt somewhat later than it was in Indochinese music. The reliefs on the Hindu and Buddhist shrines of the Sailendra period illustrate the musical instruments of that time. These, especially the ones depicted at Borobudur in the eighth century, contain most of the local and Indian instruments that make up the modern orchestra, which is composed almost entirely of percussion instruments. There is no doubt that the instruments found in the household of the ruling and upper classes in Indonesia mainly bore Hindu characteristics; later, in the tenth century, small ensembles such as drum, conch horn, and crooked trumpet came into use.

Of the two principal scale systems of Indonesian music, *pelog* and *slendro (salendro),* the former is indigenous but the latter is of Indian origin and was named after the Sailendras. The deity *Batara Endra* is said to have invented this system at the command of Siva, but it seems that it was really given currency by Buddhists in Sumatra. It is a five note scale with three different modes, which divides the octave into more nearly equal parts than the pelog, namely into intervals of about six-fifths of a tone. It is said that Indonesia treats slendro as masculine, exalted, and severe, and pelog as feminine, friendly, and sad. The most important influence in developing Indonesian music was the Sanskrit dance-drama which promoted the development of the wayang-kulit, providing scope for dancing and narrative song.

In Indonesia singing and poetry go together, and many ancient Indian metres are found in Javanese songs. The art of dancing matured in the kratons of central Java, and bears recognizable marks of Indian style. The symbolic gesture of the hand, *mudra,* and the meditative seated posture, with legs crossed under the body, for example, are obviously Indian. It is, however, in Bali that Indonesian dancing has found its highest expression, associated with religious worship and the traditional Hindu-Balinese ceremonials. Whilst Javanese music absorbed certain new traits under the impact of Islam, Bali retained its older traditions. In fact, it was the Balinese who fled from the advance of Islam, settled in Bali, and created the first musical notation of Southeast Asia, based on the vowels in the names of the five notes of the scale—*ding, dong, deng, dung, dang*. Islamic influence on Javanese music was not significant, and its chief legacy is a two stringed spike-fiddle called *rehab* which reached Indonesia through Muslim India.

Both Hinduism, mostly Saivism in contrast to Vaisnavism in Cambodia, and Buddhism flourished in Indonesia and both have left an indelible mark on the life and culture of her people. At about the beginning of the eighth century, the Puranic form of Hinduism, involving the worship of the Hindu Trinity, Brahma, Vishnu, and Siva, was popular in Java; in Indonesia Siva occupied the supreme position. Buddhism had very little hold on the people of Java at the beginning of the fifth century, but soon after, due to the missionary zeal of an Indian monk, Gunavarman, it gained considerable support. By the time I-tsing visited Sumatra, the kingdom of Sri Vijaya had become an important centre of Buddhist learning in southern Asia.

The influence of religion and philosophy was naturally to be felt in art and architecture. The religious structures in Java are commonly called *chandis,* a term which originally meant a commemorative building. With rare exceptions, all the relics of Indo-Javanese art are temples, sanctuaries, and sacred statues. These are found throughout the islands but chiefly in Java, where most of the Indonesian population appears to have been concentrated. In Sumatra also, many remains have been found. Bronze statues and a large stone image of the Buddha in the Amaravati style have been discovered in the district of Palembang. Considering that attention was not paid to some of these monuments until the twentieth century, it is not unlikely that most of them may have been lost forever. But there are enough left to reveal the high standard of Indonesian art. Whilst it was Indian in conception, it became increasingly local in character, evolving a well-integrated and distinctive regional style. For instance, the plan of the temple was Indian but the motifs were modified and the Indonesians excelled in the creation of decorative elements.

The numerous temples situated on the Dieng Plateau probably belong to the eighth century, and are the oldest in Java. At least some of them were erected during the dynasty that preceded the Sailendras. They are not large monuments but are fairly compact with sparse ornamentation. Images of Siva, Ganesa, Durga, Vishnu, and other Hindu deities indicate South Indian influence. Pallava or Calukya art was the main source of inspiration of these buildings, but Pala art also might have influenced the Javanese art of this period.

Chandi Kalasan is perhaps the oldest shrine to which an approximate date (778) may be given. The inscription commemorating this shrine is also the first Javanese record of the Sailendra kings. Erected by the first of the kings, it is dedicated to the Buddhist goddess Tara and appears to have been designed as a sepulchre for the king's consort. It is situated south of the Volcano Merapi in central Java. Above the entrance is found the kalamakara motif, which was originally a Pallava innovation.

The most important Indonesian monument is the stupa of Borobudur, which immediately followed Kalasan. The building is so enormous that it must have taken a decade or so to complete and is in marked contrast to the much smaller Hindu temples of the Dieng Plateau. In the Kedu Plain of central Java, Borobudur is a structure of overpowering majesty and splendour and commands an extensive view of the green rice fields and the distant towering volcanoes. It is rich and bold in conception, with grand decorations executed in an extraordinarily refined technique. Coomaraswamy describes it as a ripe fruit matured in breathless air—the fullness of its forms is an expression of static wealth that denotes the outward radiation of power rather than the volume.

Its exact origins are shrouded in mystery. Although there is nothing in India to compare with it, Havell regards it a descendant of Sanchi and Bharhut. Zimmer is more specific: "The Sailendra style is completely free of Polynesian elements. It is intrinsically Indian, even though, in the new, very gifted environment, it was guided by a new inspiration. The impulses of the Gupta style, and such subsequent mainland developments as are represented in the Pallava and Pala, have become infused in it with a new life. Specifically, its basic conceptions and formulae, as well as the refined, well-controlled execution, point to the Pallava area more directly than to the North."[55]

Unlike any other monument of the period, Borobudur is a whole mountain top carved into nine stone terraces, each of rising height and diminishing size, crowned by a simple stupa surmounted by an octagonal pinnacle. The result is a truncated, terraced pyramid supporting a relatively small central stupa, surrounded by seventy-two much smaller perforated stupas arranged in three concentric circles. The terraces have balustrades and there are galleries running around the four lower terraces. The outer side of the balustrades contains niches with 432 images of meditating Buddhas. Buddhas also appear on the other terraces. The most significant feature is the series of 1500 sculptured panels in the four ascending galleries of the lower terraces. The carvings, with extraordinary naturalness, depict the lives of the Buddha in his various incarnations, his travels throughout India, and other stories warning the wicked and inspiring the virtuous. The sculpture resembles certain Indian styles although typically Javanese scenes are depicted.

The unique beauty of Borobudur is inspired by the spirit of Buddhist devotion. Every detail is executed with care and refined realism. This freshness and originality was achieved not only by revolutionary changes in forms and techniques, but also by a novel application of the classical Buddhist vocabulary already perfected in its original Indian environment. All Buddhist monuments are associated with religious symbolism.

Borobudur represents the Mahayana Buddhist cosmic system and is one of the finest examples of iconological symbolism.

Not far from Borobudur there is an extensive group of Hindu temples, commonly referred to as the Prambanan group, which commands the veneration of the population. There are six buildings in two lines of three; the largest and the most beautiful, Lara Djonggrang, built by King Daksha of Mataram about 860, is dedicated to Siva, and the two smaller ones to Vishnu and Brahma. The largest temple derives its name from a statue of Durga Mahisasuramardini, which it contains. Opposite are the chandis of the mounts of the three gods of the Trimurti. Forty-two bas-reliefs representing the story of Rama are carved on the inner wall of the gallery. These reliefs are, if anything, superior to those of Borobudur, and certainly more dramatically conceived. The gate arches and entrances abound in ornamentation, with the head of Mahakala, an incarnation of Siva, in the centre. Both the architecture and sculpture are inspired by Indian models.

The largest and most important group of monuments in eastern Java are the temples of Panataran. Although work on this site appears to have begun during the Singhasari period, the most important was done in the time of Majapahit.

Indonesian art is a syncretism of Hindu-Buddhist techniques and of indigenous traditions. The art of the Sailendra period is probably the most Indian, but later, Indonesian features became increasingly prominent. As Indonesian culture grew and gathered momentum, the Indian element weakened for want of immigrant reinforcements. By the time of Majapahit the synthesis between the Indian and Indonesian arts was complete, and from then onward the art of Indonesia was truly Javanese.

Although information about Borneo is at present scanty, seven inscriptions found at Maera Kaman in Kutei (East Borneo), inscribed on stone pillars in the Sanskrit script of the fourth century, point to a direct relationship between India and Borneo. These inscriptions speak of King Mulavarman and his ancestors and of a sanctuary called Vaprakesvara, probably dedicated to Siva or Agastya. A beautiful bronze Buddha image of Gupta style has also been found in Kutei at Kota Bangum, and several statues of Hindu-Buddhist deities have been excavated at Mount Kombeng and in the estuary of the River Rata. Indeed, the earliest Hindu inscriptions in the whole of the Malay Archipelago have been found in Borneo. Although the Kutei inscriptions are simple, they reveal a fairly good knowledge of Sanskrit. There are other sites which have yet to be properly excavated. Two other objects, a gold Vishnu statuette and a gold tortoise, were found at Kutei and were worn by the Sultan of Maera Kaman in his necklace on state occasions. Images of Siva have been found in various parts of the island, and other remains include a Ganesa image from Sarawak and a Pallava inscription from near Sangbetrang on the east coast. The name Borneo is said to have been derived from *Porunei,* and is identified with *Purnadvipa* mentioned in Kautilya's *Arthasastra,* According to the *History of the Sung,* Sri Maharaja, the King of Borneo *(Po-ni),* sent a diplomatic embassy to China in 1082.

One of the most delightful spots in the world is the small island of Bali. In the whole of Indonesia, indeed in all Southeast Asia, it is only here that Hinduism has survived. The Hindu faith, however, has absorbed many local customs and traditions.

Little is known of the first Indian contact with Bali, and some scholars describe Balinese culture as an extension of Indo-Javanese civilization carried there by those who had escaped from the Islamization of Java. Others, such as Majumdar, hold the view that Bali had been in direct contact with India, for her inscriptions are in Old Balinese, which contains many Sanskrit loan words but is different from Old Javanese. The discovery of little clay tablets or circular seals bearing the confession of the Buddhist faith or Tantric Buddhist *mantras,* probably of the eighth century or before, suggests Indian influence for some time prior to that date. In addition to Sanskrit inscriptions and Buddhist formulae, images of Hindu gods and characters from the Hindu epics have been found. All these data indicate that Bali received Indian culture directly, but evidence of trade between India and Bali has not been discovered.

Bali has been justly called the island of thousands of temples. Despite the loss of about 2500 temples in an earthquake, it still contains more than 4500 large and important temples. The number of the temples and shrines may well be over 20,000. The most important is Pura Besakih, at the foot of the mountain Gunung Agung, and associated with the Hindu Trinity. This temple is said to have been founded by Wira Dalem Kesari (Warmadeva Keshari), probably in the beginning of the tenth century. It may have originally been a Buddhist sanctuary as well as the state temple of the Warmadeva dynasty. Even today the tradition is observed that only a Buddhist *pedanda* accompanying the ruler as his court priest may enter Pura Besakih. At important ceremonies, Buddhist and Hindu priests jointly conduct the rites and bless the devotees. Balinese literature and language, religion, worship and cremation services, and caste and social organization clearly reflect Indian influence.

Indonesia thus gives a remarkable example of a harmonious blending of local and foreign cultures. Few countries in the world have received so much from outside and yet have retained their own distinct personality. In the beginning Indian elements dominated, but they were all gradually acculturized. As an example, the Indonesian week comprised five days, called *pantjawarna of pasaran.* Indians, upon their arrival in 78, introduced the Saka calendar based on calculations made of the course 'of the sun, with a seven day week and a 365 day year. Its usage became common and at first all inscriptions were dated according to this system. But with the passage of time events were also recorded according to the Indonesian week of five days. Still later, the two systems were fused in a new one.[56]

The Philippines

Indian cultural waves went well beyond Bali and Borneo, reaching the Philippines and even Formosa. Both of these were for a time parts of the Sri Vijaya Empire, which has been described by a modern Filipino historian as "basically Malay in might, Hinduistic in culture, and Buddhistic in religion."[57] This contact of Indian culture with the Philippines also continued under the Sailendras. In the fourteenth century, the Hinduized Majapahit Empire emerged as a powerful state in Southeast Asia, extending its overlordship as far as Formosa and New Guinea. Whilst the control of Sri Vijaya and Majapahit over the Philippines was rather loose, their cultural impact was deep.

The influence of India over the Philippines was not as direct as that of China and later of Spain and the United States but, with the exception of modern European cultures, Indian influences have been the most profound. The manner in which Indian influence was brought and the date when it began are subjects of speculation; dates have been suggested ranging from the first millennium B.C. to the early fourth century.

The Philippines were near the sea route between India and East Asia, so they may have been visited by Indian sailors and traders. A series of remarkable excavations were carried out by Beyer in the late 1920's at Novaliches in the Philippines. His work was the first systematic archaeological investigation in the country, and his finds and conclusions were thoroughly examined by R. B. Dixon. Beyer concluded that all the artifacts found, including a large quantity of pottery, iron implements and weapons such as knives and axes, glass beads and bangles and beads of semi-precious stones such as carnelian, agate and amethyst, were brought to the Philippines from India over a long period of trade, well before the beginnings of the Christian era. Both iron and glass objects are similar to, and in some cases identical with, those of prehistoric South India. "There is no tribe in the Philippines," wrote the American anthropologist, Alfred L. Kroeber, "no matter how primitive and remote, in whose culture today elements of Indian origin cannot be traced."[58] Whatever its antiquity, it would be hard to deny the existence of trade between the two countries from the first centuries A.D. onwards. Pre-Spanish Philippine society with its nobility, code of laws, and political procedure, was largely of Indian cast. Some years ago when a new legislative building was put up in Manila, the capital, four figures were carved on its facade illustrating the sources of the Philippine culture, one of which is Manu, the ancient Indian lawgiver.[59]

A fleeting glimpse of Buddhism is noticeable in Philippine *Bathala* worship. The term *Bathala,* the supreme god of the ancient Tagalogs, originated from the Sanskrit *Bhattara.* The Hindu element in the ancient Philippine religious beliefs, and in the names of old Philippine gods, and of legendary heroes is quite apparent. Several religious objects which have been unearthed in the island of Mactan and in eastern Mindanao show the undoubted influence of India, but only two images of Hindu deities have so far been discovered. One image of solid gold shows "clear evidence in its tall pointed head-dress and other ornaments of the influence of Hindu-Javanese art of the tenth century."[60]

Spaniards of the sixteenth century found several related alphabets (one for each of the principal languages), all of which seemed to have derived from India some eight hundred years before. Malayan languages, including those of the Philippines, are unusually simple in their phonetic system, which caused them to discard much of the elaborate Sanskrit alphabet, but the salient characteristics of Indian writing were retained.

Whilst the most advanced Philippine peoples, such as the Tagalog and Bisaya, have long given up their old alphabets, remote descendants of ancient Indian scripts still linger on amongst the less advanced tribes in the interior of the country. Tavera and Paterno, two Filipino scholars, and Saleeby, an American, and others have concluded that about twenty-five per cent of the Philippine vocabularies is traceable to Indian influence. For instance: *bahagi* (part, portion) in Tagalog is *bhag* in Hindi; *bansa* (nation) is *bans* (family); *katha* (fiction, story) is *katha; diwata* (god or goddess) is *devata; dukha* (poor, destitute) is *duhkha; guro* (teacher) is *guru; mukh* (face) is *mukka; yaya* (nurse) is *aya:* and so on.

Philippine literature, mythology, and folklore are traceable to India. The Maranaw epic, *Darangan,* the longest in early Philippine literature, is basically Indian in plot and characterization. The tale of the *Ifugao Balituk* is reminiscent of the story of Arjunna getting water from a rock with his arrow for Bhishma who was dying of his wounds. A Philippine legend about the creation of different races from baked clay pots is quite popular in India with its local variations.

Indian influence through Sumatra brought the calendar, much of Buddhist folklore, and the syllabic alphabets; through Java came the more advanced arts of metal work, jewellery, and weaving. Modes of dress such as the *sarong* and *putong* (turban), personal ornamentation, especially by the people of Sulu and southern Mindanao, and old names for money, such as *salapi, siping, gatang, tanso, pilak,* and *bakal,* are said to be of Indian origin. The lotus design on the Philippine weapons was of Indian inspiration.

In 1762 during the Seven Years War in Europe, which was extended to the Philippines, eight hundred Indian soldiers formed a part of the British expeditionary force against Manila. A year and a half later, when the invading forces evacuated Manila, many of the Indian soldiers refused to go home, even at the risk of violating military regulations. They settled in the district of Morong in the community now known as Cainta, south of the town of Anitpolo, and married local girls. Their descendants today form an integral and useful part of the Philippine society. They have a reputation of being peaceful, law-abiding, and industrious citizens.

Except for this brief interlude, and some trade between India and Manila, nothing much was heard of India during the 333 years of the Spanish regime (1565–1898), largely because of the Spanish policy of sequestration, and also because of the similar though less severe restrictions of the British colonial government on Indians. During the American regime (1898–1946), freer intercourse with other countries was allowed, in consequence of which many British Indian subjects came to the Philippines as traders, businessmen, and a few as labourers. The contact between the two countries since independence in recent years has increased noticeably.[61]

Thus the history of Indian cultural penetration of Southeast Asia covers a period of more than fourteen hundred years up to the end of the fifteenth century. Hinduism was flourishing in Southeast Asia when it was in a state of decline in its homeland. Unbacked by political power or military conquest, the cultural development of Southeast Asia is indeed a remarkable tribute to the interaction of human ideas.

Chapter IV

IMPACT OF ISLAM ON INDIAN SOCIETY

THE ADVENT OF Islam was the most important event in the history of India since the coming of the Aryans, and it was the first major impact of an alien culture on Hindu society. So far, India had assimilated all immigrant peoples and cultures; on the other hand, Islam had usually assimilated the culture of the land to which it went. But in India, Islam neither lost its identity nor conquered the country culturally; both appropriated something of each other. The Muslims of the Indian subcontinent, who constitute the largest Muslim population found in any one country, are culturally distinct from their co-religionists in Arabia, Indonesia, or elsewhere. Although Islam assumed an Indian character, its adherents retained their distinctive religious and social organization. The political repercussions of this dichotomy have been far-reaching, resulting in the partition of India into two independent states.

The India to which Islam came was in a state of decline. Northern India especially had lost its old vigour, the reasons for which have often been debated but never conclusively, explained. But for occasional sparks of brilliance in philosophy and science, cultural activity had given way to political adventurism. An era of intellectual stagnation and social degeneration had set in. Pride in past accomplishment superseded respect for change; progress meant not evolution but preservation of the ancestral heritage. Instead of investing their cultural legacy, Indians began to hoard it.

The spirit of enterprise was dislodged first by arrogance, later by timidity. Whilst Al Biruni, who accompanied Mahmud of Ghazni, considered Hindus to be excellent philosophers, accomplished mathematicians, and remarkable astrologers, he saw clear marks of stagnation and decay and accused them of cultural arrogance rooted in past glory. According to him, the Hindus called foreigners *mleccha* (impure) and believed that there was no country but theirs, no religion but theirs, no science but theirs.[1] Having repelled the powerful Huns, who shook the roots of the Roman Empire and ravaged Europe, the complacent Hindus became consumingly conceited. The flourishing commercial and cultural intercourse which had thrived in the area from Rome to Japan, almost all of the known world, began to contract rapidly. Deprived of this stimulus, culture became static, Hinduism sectarian and ritualistic, and Buddhism gradually almost nonexistent, except in eastern India where it flourished until the thirteenth century. Common people were divided into innumerable castes and lived in narrow circles; caste discipline became corrupt and oppressive. The Brahmans tightened their monopoly of learning and took advantage of the common man's ignorance and credulity.

To the west of India the Roman world had collapsed and Europe had sunk into the Dark Ages. The Eastern Roman Empire at Constantinople, although it survived for some time, was in a state of decline. In contrast, China had emerged reunited under a powerful dynasty after a prolonged period of political unrest. In Southeast Asia and ancient America, new periods of progress began.[2]

The death of Harsha in 647 proved an irreparable loss. It marked the end of an era in Indian history. There were to be no more Asokas, Chandraguptas, or Harshas. For the next several centuries most of India, especially in the northern and central regions, was divided amongst independent kingdoms which, led by ambitious kings or pretenders, waged interminable wars against one another, often for petty ends. Although some of the rulers succeeded in establishing powerful kingdoms, they did not survive for long.

Most of the ruling dynasties of the North belonged to clans later known as Rajput. These suddenly emerged into prominence towards the end of the sixth century, and slowly gained political ascendancy in northern India which they held for the next five hundred years. They continued to play a major role throughout the mediaeval and modern periods, during which they did not dominate but were sought as allies by the paramount power in the country. After Indian independence in 1947, the numerous Rajput states, like all others, lost their identity and were merged into the Indian Union.

The origin of the Rajputs is the subject of historical controversy. The term Rajput is a derivative of the Sanskrit word, Rajaputra. According to legend, they are the descendants of either the sun, *suryavamsi,* moon, *chandravamsi,* or fire, *agnikula.* Some historians have suggested they were the descendants of the Scythians or Sakas who came to India, settled there, and eventually became unrecognizably mixed with the local warrior classes.[3] Others trace their origins to the Kshatriyas of the vedic period.

The Rajputs are renowned for their valour, chivalry, sense of honour, pride, patriotism, and lofty ideals of individual character. Indian legends and songs are full of praise for them. They were zealous patrons of Hinduism and it was, in a way, their courage and devotion which sustained Indian culture and traditions for nearly five centuries during the years of political unrest. However, their history is a wearisome chronicle of states continually rising, warring, and falling. They had no unity; they could not rise above parochialism and clan rivalries. Loyal to their personal ideals and prides, they perfected individual culture to the utter exclusion of national unity and social welfare.[4] It is, indeed, a tragedy of Indian history that such brave people, so earnestly devoted to their faith and heritage should have been inadvertently responsible for the failure to check cultural and social decline because of their constant dynastic feuds and internecine wars.

The history of South India during this period was less turbulent although there were frequent wars. However, social organization and economic activity were relatively undisturbed, and cultural continuity was maintained in South India.

Art and literature, however, flourished under Rajput patronage; this period witnessed the perfection of temple architecture and the construction of some of the greatest buildings in India. But each Rajput dynasty was keen to retain its distinctive character in art as in politics and this led to the growth of several styles of architecture of which there are five main ones. Most important of the surviving buildings of the period are the remarkable temples of Khajuraho, built between 954 and 1002.[5] They are famous for their architecture and sculpture; some of their bas-reliefs are conspicuous for their eroticism. The Muktesvara Temple at Bhuvanesvara, the most beautiful of all Orissa temples, belongs to the Rajput period, having been built at the end of the ninth century. Some treasures at the famous Ellora and Elephanta Caves also belong to this period.

Despite the growing political unrest and internal decay India remained practically free from foreign aggression from the early sixth century until the raids of Mahmud of Ghazni in the first quarter of the eleventh century, except for the brief incursion of Muhammad bin Qasim in Sind in 711–713. It is somewhat surprising that the Arabs, who had emerged as great expansionist powers and brought the lands between Spain and China under Islamic domination during this period, should have left India alone. Possibly, the prevalent reputation of Indian glory and strength deterred aggression, but once Mabmud of Ghazni exposed the myth of Indian might, numerous attacks on India were made in quick succession by foreign armies. Another reason for the Arab indifference to the expansion of Islam into India may well have been the approval of Indian faiths by the Prophet himself, who is reported to have once said: "I get cool breezes from the side of Hind." In *Sahih Muslim*, Abu Horaira says that the Prophet mentioned certain rivers as belonging to heaven and one of them was a river of India. Two Indians, Sarmanak and Ratan, who collected the Prophet's sayings, *Al Rataniyab*, are reported to have visited Arabia during his time. Many Islamic traditions support the high standing of Indian culture with the Arabs: "Ibni Ali Hatim relates on Ali's authority that the Valley of Hind where Adam descended from Heaven, and the Valley of Mecca, which had the tradition of Abraham, were the best valleys in the world."[6] Certain words occurring in the Quran, such as *tooba*, *sundas*, and *ablai*, are of Sanskrit origin. A common legend suggests that after the Deluge some of Noah's sons settled in India. A son of Adam, Shees (Seth in the biblical form), was born in India and is now said to be buried in Ayodhya. The fourth Caliph is reported to have said: "The land where books were first written and from where wisdom and knowledge sprang is India."[7]

These and other traditions may be true, wholly, in part, or not at all, but they certainly indicate the affection and respect of early Muslims for India. Considering that the Arabs were convinced of their own superiority and had imposed their culture on the conquered, their high regard for India is a rare tribute. Even the highly developed civilizations of Iran and Egypt could not withstand the Arabs.

Muslim penetration into India was not a case of wholesale colonization, but of successive military attacks, migration of small groups of West and Central Asian Muslims to India, and large-scale conversion of local Indians over a long period of time. The first wave of Muslim conquerors originated with the Arabs, who gave Islam a foothold in India but did not press on with expansion. In 636-637, the Arab Governor of Bahrein and Uman, Usman Sakifi, dispatched an expedition to the coast of India, but India was still too strong to be successfully conquered. In any case, Caliph Umar was opposed to attacking India, even when he was told that "Indian rivers are pearls, her mountains rubies, her trees perfumes," for he regarded India as a country of complete freedom of thought and belief where Muslims and others were free to practice their faith.[8] Indeed, he rebuked Usman Sakifi for dispatching a military expedition, and threatened him with severe, punishment if the experiment were repeated. About three-quarters of a century later in 711–713 during the Umayyad Caliphate of Walid, Muhammad bin Qasim conquered Sind and Multan. This intervention however was occasioned not by any calculated designs of aggression; it was in the nature of a punitive expedition against the pirates of Kutch who rashly interfered with the trade and vessels of the Hajjaj, the Viceroy of the eastern provinces of the Umayyad Empire.

Politically, Islam remained confined to Sind and Multan for the next four hundred years, but a new era of intellectual collaboration between the Arab world and India began which was to have lasting effects. Although their conquest of Sind was politically insignificant, the Arabs acquired knowledge of vedantic philosophy, astronomy, mathematics, medicine, chemistry, and the art of administration. Elsewhere, the Arabs had tried to impose a composite culture on the local peoples which was based on their own language and script, and some elements of the indigenous civilizations. In contrast, the Arab rulers of Sind adopted local practices to a much greater extent than even the later and not so accomplished, Turki-

Afghan rulers of northern India. The Arab rulers dressed like Hindu rajas, and even followed a policy of religious accommodation. Despite their uncompromising iconoclasm, they did not apply to the Hindus the stringent provisions of Islamic law regarding idol-worshippers. On the contrary, they treated the Hindus as "people of the book."

Whilst the Arabs treated Indian culture with utmost consideration and hoped to profit from it, the Indians generally remained unresponsive to Arab culture, thus gaining very little in return. There are, however, a few examples on record which are suggestive of some Hindu interest in Islamic thought. In 886, a Hindu king commissioned an Arab linguist from Mansura, one of the two Muslim states in Sind, to prepare a version of the Quran in the local language. In the eighth century, Sind produced a scholar, Abu Maashar Sindi, an authority on the life of the Prophet and held in high esteem throughout the Caliphate; several other notable scholars from Sind made their mark in the Islamic world. Jurists from Sind were particularly noted for their mastery of the Hadith. Abul Ata and Abu Zila, two Sindi poets who wrote in both Arabic and Sindi, attained great fame.

The Arabs were as skilful traders as they were conquerors, and their merchants, under the stimulus of political supremacy, intensified their commercial activity, including maritime trade with India. With the traders came the new faith, but it was only a trickle compared with what was to come later, and it was confined to a few coastal areas. South India, with which the Arabs had trade relations long before the advent of Islam, at this time was involved in political upheaval as well as in religious rethinking. The Cheras were losing power, and new ideas were emerging in Hinduism. Indicative of the Arab influence in Malabar is the conversion to Islam in the ninth century of the last of the Cherman Perumal kings who, a few years after his change of faith, went to Arabia where he died. The memory of the event was kept alive in Malabar until recently. The Maharaja of Travancore, until the end of princedom in India, used to declare at the time of his coronation that he would keep the sword of power until the uncle, who had gone to Mecca, returned. Whilst the historicity of this conversion is mainly based on legends and its details are subject to doubt, that Islam had gained a firm foothold in Malabar at the time is not questioned. The Muslims in the area were designated as *Mappillas,* a title of honour, and various privileges were granted to them.[9] Under the patronage of the Zamorin who actively encouraged conversion, the influx of Arab merchants increased, the volume of Indo-Arab trade greatly expanded, and many Arabs settled permanently in India.

The real history of Islam in India begins with the Turki-Afghan invasions, although the invaders were mainly adventurers looking for plunder. Mahmud of Ghazni, ruler of a small Turki kingdom in Afghanistan, attacked India no less than seventeen times in the first quarter of the eleventh century, and carried back immense wealth, treasures which included the pillars of the Temple of Somnath and enormous quantities of jewels and gold. He was also responsible for the destruction of countless Hindu idols and temples. His invasions ended the rule of the Arabs in Sind in 1005. After Mahmud's death, his successors were unable to hold his kingdom together, and it was left to Muhammad Ghori, ruler of a small mountainous state in Afghanistan, to found the first Muslim state in India. In 1192 Muhammad Ghori gave a crushing blow to the Rajput power in northern India and appointed one of his Turkish slaves, Qutbuddin Aibak, as the Governor of his Indian territory. After Ghori's assassination in 1206 near Damiyak, probably by an Ismailite fanatic, Qutbuddin Aibak assumed sovereign power and founded the Slave Dynasty, which turned into an oligarchy of Turks, jealously guarding its doors against men of other races, whether Muslims or not.

It was only when the Turki-Afghan rulers had established their political authority in northern India, that Islam began to make its impact on Indian society. It is, perhaps, a pity that Islam did not spread in India during its early period of Arab supremacy when it was young and vigorous. When Islam came to India, it had passed the peak of its power and glory. Worse still, it arrived through the medium of military adventurers and free booters whose own cultural attainments were almost nonexistent. The Turki-Afghans had raided and looted India for more than two hundred years before they began to organize an administration. In fact, the Turks almost devastated the Empire of Islam through misgovernment and interminable warfare. Whilst the Ottoman Turks at Constantinople were compelled to respect the dignity and traditions of Islamic culture, their kinsmen in India felt no such compulsion. The Ghaznavis, the Ghoris, the Khiljis, and the Tughluqs were much too concerned with the conquest of the country to devote much attention to religious or cultural matters. These conquerors were, in general, rough and crude people, ill-grounded in and uninspired by the Islamic faith. It was a great misfortune for both India and Islam that Islam fell into the hands of ruthless Turki-Afghan generals, whose sole aim was to establish themselves as sovereign powers and use the rich resources of India as funds for their almost ceaseless military campaigns.

When the Turki-Afghan conquests are compared with the early Arab invasions of India, the difference between the barbarity of the former and the culture of the latter stands out clearly. At first the Arab invasion was marked with cruelty, and Muhammad bin Qasim did commit rash deeds in his religious zeal or political nervousness in a foreign, reputedly mighty, country. Moreover, Muhammad bin Qasim was very young. Yet, as soon as the war ended, he compensated those whose property was wrongfully damaged, gave offices of responsibility to local representatives, permitted them to worship their own gods, practice their own customs, build their own temples, and gave protection to the people under his authority.[10] He even kept Hindu ministers and police officials in his service. Indeed, when he informed his Caliph that he had demolished temples, converted Hindus to Islam, and successfully waged war against them, he was reprimanded instead of receiving the commendation he had expected. His actions were held by the Caliph to be against the Islamic law, and he was ordered to compensate for the damage he had done.

Contests for political supremacy had been a feature of Islamic history from the very inception of the Caliphate. Whilst the first four Caliphs may have had religious motives for their political actions, the wars and conquests of later Muslim kings were never purely religious. India resisted the early Islamic invasions, as she would have any intruder, regardless of nationality or religion. Thus, the early armed conflicts between the aggressors and the nationals were not religious but simply political wars. Once Muslims states were founded in India, wars between Muslim kings were as common and natural as wars between Muslim and Hindu rulers. Most of the wars which the Muslim Emperors of Delhi had to fight were against Muslim sovereigns. All the Muslim invaders who came after Muhammad Ghori had to contend with a Muslim state. The invasions of Timur and Nadir Shah were not against Hindu kings but against Muslims. The cruelties of Timur were directed against Muslims and non-Muslims alike. It was Timur who built a human wall by piling up two thousand *shaikhs* of Islam one upon the other and plastering them alive. Babur had to defeat a Muslim king, Ibrahim Lodi, and he was opposed" by the combined forces of Rajputs and Muslims. Humayun was dislodged by Shershah, and Akbar had to defeat other Muslim rulers to consolidate the Empire, and was actively aided by Rajputs. Aurangzeb spent the last years of his life in a long struggle to subdue the Muslim states of Deccan with the help of well-known Hindu generals. Even Mahmud of Ghazni made profuse use of Hindu generals and soldiers in his campaigns.

A Muslim king was first a king and then a Muslim. Alauddin Khilji abolished the supremacy of the Ulama and asserted the King's independent authority and responsibility for good government. Even the devout Aurangzeb did not undertake the holy pilgrimage to Mecca, Haj, for he was afraid of losing his throne in his absence. Neither the Sultanate of Delhi nor the Mughal Empire was an Islamic state in the real sense of the term. Although some rulers acknowledged but did not obey the authority of the Caliph, imposed *jizya* and many laws of the *Sharia* on Hindus, and patronized Muslim saints and nobles, all of them subordinated the demands of religion to the exigencies of politics. Few went to Haj, a major requirement of Islam. They extracted far more revenue from the cultivators than was allowed under the Islamic law, indulged in the lax and luxurious life forbidden by Islam, and, by claiming to be the "Shadow of God" on earth and assigning divine rights to themselves usurped the sovereignty, which, according to Islam, belonged to none but God and which was exercised under rigidly prescribed conditions by the Caliph. Even the Caliphs did not govern according to the instructions of Islam. No Muslim rule, other than that of the first four Caliphs, was truly Islamic in character, and in a sense the Islamic state and Islamic culture lasted for only about half a century under the Prophet and the four righteous Caliphs.

The period of effective Muslim rule in India is generally divided into two parts—the Sultanate of Delhi (1206–1526) and the Mughal period

(1526–1707).[11] Whilst the latter is a glorious period of Indian history, the former was very turbulent. The Delhi Sultanate did little to synthesize Hindu and Muslim cultures. With a few notable exceptions, the rulers were incompetent, cruel, and degenerate. Dynasties were short-lived, court intrigues and palace revolutions were rampant, and learning and the welfare of the people were completely neglected.

The five dynasties that ruled at Delhi before the rise of the Mughals were the Slave (1206–1290), the Khilji (1290–1320), the Tughluq (1320–1412), the Sayyid (1414–1451), and the Lodi (1451–1526). The Slaves jealously guarded their doors against non-Turks, but the distinctions between Turks and non-Turks vanished during the Khilji period. The Lodis were the first Afghan tribe to rule at Delhi but Babur wrested control from them in 1526. The early Turkish rulers of India had been Afghanized over the period of their stay in Afghanistan. Most of the later rulers were actually born in India, and many were of part Indian parentage; the proportion of these steadily increased with the passage of time.

Most of the Sultans were busied putting down rebellions of their own subordinates. No less than thirty-five Sultans belonging to the five dynasties sat on the throne of Delhi during a period of little more than three centuries, an average of about nine years for each Sultan. Of these thirty-five, nineteen were assassinated by Muslim rebels. As if this had not done enough damage to the prestige and power of Islam, Timur came in 1398 and left behind a trail of violence. He demolished a Muslim state, converted Delhi into shambles, and laid much of northern India to waste.[12]

Yet the Sultanate of Delhi was the richest and most powerful Muslim state of the time, and attracted innumerable scholars, soldiers, and statesmen, who had been forced to leave Iraq and Iran after the fall of the Abbasid Caliphate. Whilst the frequent fluctuations in the political fortunes of the Sultans of Delhi did not allow them to either harness the accumulating talent for cultural progress or to impose their supremacy, usurping the Caliphate, over other Muslim states, the very fact that Muslim scholars poured into India stimulated Indian contacts with the outside world.

Whilst North India renewed its close contact with Western Asia and the Islamic world, South India continued some relations with Southeast Asia, and received visitors from the European world. Islam travelled to Southeast Asia from South India during this period. Marco Polo visited South India on his homeward journey from the Mongol Court of China towards the close of the thirteenth century. He commended Indian kings for good administration, and Indian merchants for their wealth, and declared that India was "the noblest and richest country in the world."

Of the visitors who came to India during this period the more prominent were: the Moroccan Ibn Batuta, who stayed in India for about twenty years in the middle of the fourteenth century; the Italian Nicolo de Conti in the early fifteenth century; the Persian Abdur Razzaq, who was an envoy to the Zamorin of Calicut in 1442–1443; and the Russian Athanasius Nikitin, who travelled through the Bahmani Kingdom in South India from 1470 to 1474, and was awed by the luxury of the nobles and the poverty of the peasants. In 1498, Vasco da Gama landed at Calicut, thus discovering the direct sea route between India and Europe which led to a regular influx of European visitors.

It was, in fact, after the commencement of European activities in the coastal areas of India that the Mughal dynasty was founded in 1526. During its rule, Indo-Islamic art and culture made rapid and memorable strides. All of the great Mughal Emperors were men of literary accomplishment and refinement and generously patronized art and learning. Akbar, although himself illiterate, far outstripped all the others in intellectual capacity, humanity, and cultural patronage. Babur wrote his memoirs, as did Jahangir, who was also interested in science and medicine. Shahjahan was well-read and knew Arabic, Turki, and Persian fairly well. His eldest son, Dara Shikoh, was a renowned scholar. Aurangzeb was proficient in several languages and a devoted student of the Quran. The last Mughal Emperor, Bahadur Shah II, who died tragically in exile in Burma after the revolt of 1857, was a sensitive and accomplished poet.

Islam expansion has been mainly attributed to coercion rather than persuasion. Whilst it is true that considerable official pressure, varying according to the zeal of the individual, and at times persecution and force were applied, much of the Hindu conversion to Islam was voluntary. Some Hindus, especially in Bengal, embraced Islam because of Hindu caste oppression, and others because they had had a genuine change of belief under the influence of Muslim missionaries. Others became Muslims in order to gain concrete benefits by embracing the religion of the rulers.

The development of Islam in India was a process of evolution rather than of imposition. Indifferent to culture, the Turki-Afghan rulers, in fact, sought neither to impose Islamic culture on India nor to enrich it by drawing upon the rich Indian heritage. But racial exclusiveness could not be maintained indefinitely. All the soldiers and officials could not be imported from Western or Central Asia. Even if there were enough men in these areas who were competent and prepared to undertake government positions in India, their recruitment would have been impossible on economic grounds alone. In addition, there were political and sectarian rivalries demanding the exclusion of alien Muslims. Muslim rule had to be Indianized to ensure success in India. This became inevitable as the Hindus who embraced Islam soon far outnumbered the few who had come from outside.[13] The Muslims in India were like the Buddhists in China, or the Christians in Europe. The Chinese Buddhists could not be called foreigners because they embraced a faith of alien origin, or the European Christians called Asians because Christianity was born in Asia. That the Muslims of India felt themselves to be Indians is well illustrated by Abul Fazl in his *Ain-i-Akbari.* He was so carried away by the beauties of Hindustan that he apologized for a digression which proceeded from "the love of my native country."

The Hindus gradually overcame their natural hostility against what had come from outside in the company of the sword. Slowly throughout India, the initial clash was followed by fusion and synthesis. In language and literature, scientific and philosophic thought, and art and architecture, a new character began to emerge which reached its peak during the Mughal period, especially under Akbar. He initiated measures to blend the two communities in a variety of ways. His *Din-i-Ilahi* (The Divine Faith), in which he sought to create a universal religion, was a noble effort. Dara Shikoh translated the Upanishads into Persian, and if he, instead of his younger brother and executioner, Aurangzeb, had come to the throne, the history of India might have been different. Both Akbar and Dara, in attempting to unite the two cultural groups, were following the main teaching of Islam, which is unity, human equality, and universal toleration. Islam rejuvenated Indian life, but it did not give rise to substantially new and enduring doctrines in Hindu culture. A possible explanation may be that Indian thought was highly intricate, whilst Islamic thought was simple and straightforward with a powerful appeal for the common man but a less strong one for the intellectual.

Islam was uncompromisingly monotheistic. The Quran lays great stress on the unity of God and on the belief that nothing can share a single attribute with God. This doctrine led to the mass destruction of Hindu temples and images, countless works of arts and learning, and created extreme bitterness in Hindu minds: but it also compelled Hindus to reflect on their own beliefs, many of which had become unrecognizable through tradition, superstition, and dogma. Consequently, Hindus began to modify their existing practice, mainly by returning to the original purity of their own scriptures. For instance, the vedantic philosophy of monism, the principal teaching of the Upanishads, was revived under the vigorous guidance of Sankaracharya (Sankara). Opinion is divided as to whether the new emphasis on the upanishadic thought was the consequence of the Islamic impact or a natural stage in the development of Hindu thought.

Whilst Islam preached the unity of God alone, accepting the universe as his creation, Sankara's vedantic philosophy stressed the unity of both the creator and the creation: the latter being *maya*, an illusion. "Brahman—the absolute existence, knowledge, and bliss—is real. The universe is not real. Brahman and Atman are one." Sankara is the unrivalled propounder of *Advaita Vedanta*, the non-dualistic aspect of the vedic teachings. His clarity, wisdom, and spirituality are deeply impressed upon the Vedanta—which is not only the primary Indian philosophy but is also widely popular abroad. However, the historical possibility that Sankara revived the upanishadic teaching because of Islamic thought cannot be altogether ruled out, for he was born about 686 in a village in Malabar, where Arab traders had introduced Islamic ideas.[14]

Islam opposed the caste system, and taught human equality and a personal pride in religion. The Sufi missionaries met with considerable success amongst the lower caste Hindus for whom conversion to Islam, as later conversion to Christianity, meant escape from a life of indignity and suffering. Islam's attack on caste and idolatory led to religious ferment which culminated in the Bhakti cult, single-minded, direct devotion to God and liberalism in religion.[15] There emerged a succession of remarkable teachers, such as Ramanuja, Madhava, Ramananda, Kabir, Vallabhacharya, Guru Nanak, Chaitanya, Dadu, and Mirabai, who advocated reconciliation of the two religious beliefs. Between them they covered a period of more than five hundred years, from the eleventh to the seventeenth centuries. Ramanuja and Madhava were amongst the early saint-reformers, and of the later ones, the most important were Kabir and Guru Nanak.

Ramanuja, of the eleventh century, ranks second only to Sankara amongst the great interpreters of vedantic thought. He argued that God and souls of men were not the same, although not separate from each other, and that the highest ideal was to love and worship God and to surrender completely to Him. Ramanuja's philosophy is known as *Visistadvaita* (qualified non-dualism), for he admitted the plurality of of both matter and souls.

Whilst Ramanuja was strict in culinary rules, his eminent follower, Ramananda, who probably lived during the end of the fourteenth and the first half of the fifteenth century, was not. Ramananda admitted disciples of all castes to his group, and they learned and dined together. His disciples included Dhanna the cultivator, Pipa the raj, Ravidas the leather worker, Sainu the barber, and Kabir the Muslim weaver. Chaitanya (1485–1533) of Bengal, in whose teaching is found the culmination and fulfilment of the religion of love, and who ushered in a new era in the spiritual life of Bengal, also had both Hindu and Muslim disciples. The cult of Krishna was particularly popular with Muslims.

Kabir (*ca.* 1440–1518), whose teaching is a synthesis of the finest Hindu and Muslim sentiment, condemned rituals and caste, opposed asceticism, and preached the religion of love.[16] He combined the zeal of a reformer with the humility of a devotee. He regarded the spiritual basis of Hinduism and Islam as one, and was revolted by the superstructures of dogma. Kabir was the embodiment of the process of Hindu-Muslim union in mediaeval India. He advocated a universal religion, to which no Hindu or Muslim could take objection. He denounced the Hindu worship of idols, ceremonial rituals and caste on the one hand, and on the other, the Muslim trust in one Prophet and his book, pilgrimage, and fasts. He repeatedly pointed out that Hindus and Muslims were one: they worshipped the same God and were children of the same ancestors.

> Make thy mind thy Kaaba,
>   Thy body its enclosing temple,
> Conscience its prime teacher.
> Then, O priest, call men to pray to that mosque
> Which hath five gates.
> The Hindus and Mussulmans have the same Lord.

Kabir had a large following amongst both Hindus and Muslims. Amongst his friends were several reformers who are remembered with respect even to this day, such as Taqui of the Sufi Suhrawardi sect, whose daughter Kamal married a Brahman, and Ravidas, who was a low caste, *chamar*, Hindu. Kabir is regarded as one of the great men of Indian history. He is an outstanding Hindi poet whose poetry is steeped in the love of God. Today there are more than half a million followers of Kabir, *Kabirpanthis*, in India. Other offshoots of his teaching are the Satnamis, Radhaswamis, and Dadupanthis.

Guru Nanak (1469–1539), a contemporary of Kabir and the Mughal ruler Babur, founded the Sikh faith.[17] Principally a social and religious thinker, Nanak lived in a period of Indian history filled with political upheavals, atrocities, and lawlessness. He condemned formalism and ritualism in religion and tried to blend the mystical ideas of the Hindu and Muslim faiths in Sikhism.[18] His first puplic proclamation was that there was no Hindu or Muslim, for all were the children of the same God. The ultimate goal of human beings was to enjoy divine beatitude. In many respects, he represents the high water mark of this Hindu-Muslim cultural synthesis and renaissance philosophy. He opposed all forms of idolatry and denounced caste and communalism. He preached devotion to one God, transcending religious divisions. His teachings were so liberal that they constitute a daily prayer not only for Sikhs, but also for many Hindus.[19]

All the reformers condemned caste, denounced polytheism and idolatry, advocated a puritanical way of life, preached communal harmony, goodwill and unity, exposed the futility of ceremonies, tended to emancipate the minds of men from the domination of priests and *mullas,* safeguarded fundamental religious beliefs, and encouraged local literature. They were nonsectarian, noncommunal, and nondogmatic. They realized the oneness of the God invoked by various religions under different names and believed in the *bhakti* as the principal means of salvation. Their chief contribution to Indian religious thought was a profoundly psychological analysis and comprehensive interpretation of bhakti.

Whether the Bhakti movement was inspired by Islam or was a logical extension of the developing Hindu thought during the mediaeval period is debatable. Certainly the excessive, if not exclusive, stress on devotion and love of God as preached by the leaders of the Bhakti movement was in contrast to the ancient Indian philosophical speculations which emphasized intellectual scepticism as the essence of religion. However, before the advent of Islam, Hindu mediaeval thought had departed from the questioning attitude, demanding logical explanations of conclusions, and had come to seek its validity in revealed truth. The earliest mention of bhakti is found in the *Svetasvatara Upanishad.* Later the *Bhagavad Gita,* composed before the Christian era began, emphasized the triple path of *bhakti, jnana,* and *karma* to obtain *moksha,* and by the middle ages bhakti had become a central doctrine of Hinduism.

The sacred language of Islam was Arabic, the mother tongue of the early invaders; later conquerors spoke Turkish and Persian, influenced and modified by Arabic. Whilst Arabic remained the language of religion, Persian became the language of the court during the Muslim rule. Persian was, therefore, studied by both Hindus and Muslims if they sought administrative positions, but it did not become the language of the masses, not even of the Muslim masses.[20] The overwhelming majority of the Muslims in India were Indian converts, and the change of religion was easier than the change of tongue. Of necessity, Arabic and Persian had to intermingle with local languages. The result was Urdu, which is spoken in northern India and is a national language of Pakistan today. A combination of Persian and Hindi, Urdu is a fine example of Indo-Islamic synthesis. The evolution of a common language was indicative of growing intimacy between the two religious groups and an assurance of future understanding.

Originally a spoken language, Urdu came to be written in Arabic script. Its basic structure and grammar are Indian, as is most of its vocabulary. The emergence of a simplified and popular language helped the development of local languages too. A flood of literature appeared in the different languages of India. The Bhakti saints wrote and preached in the local languages, which gradually gained importance and respectability, and the snobbery attached to Sanskrit, which had discouraged the development of literatures in regional languages, was overthrown.

More important, however, was the growth of a common outlook which discounted religious ritualism and led to an extensive exchange of ideas at the common man's level and, consequently, to the development of common cultural patterns. As Urdu and Hindi were the expressions of the new common culture, Hindu and Muslim scholars wrote in both languages. Whilst Amir Khusrau, Rahim Khanikhana, and Malik Muhammad Jayasi wrote classical poetry in Hindi, many Hindus contributed to Urdu literature. Muslims contributed to the development of regional literatures also; for instance, Alaol (Alaul-Husan), the son of the Nawab of Jalapur, heralded a new age in Bengali literature. He translated not only Jayasi's famous Hindi epic, *Padmavat,* into Bengali, but also the Persian romance, *Saifu'l-Muluk wa Badi'ul-Jamal.*

Hindu and Muslim rulers in practically every region encouraged Indo-Islamic culture and literature. Muslim kings endowed Hindu temples and granted crown lands to learned Brahmans. During the reign of Qutbuddin Ahmad Shah (1451–1458), the first lyrical poem, *Vasanta Vilasa,* was composed in Gujarati. The Bengali translation of the *Mahabharata* was undertaken under the order of Nasir Shah of Gaur who ruled from 1285 to 1325, and to whom Vidyapati dedicated one of his poems. Similarly, Hussain Shah commanded Maladhar Vasu to render the *Bhagavad Gita* into Bengali. In South India, the Qutbshahi and Adilshahi rulers, some of whom were poets in their own right, patronized the local languages even more than the Muslim kings of northern India.

The creative energy released by Indo-Islamic cultural intercourse achieved even better results in art. In many ways, Islamic art, which had assumed a synthetic character from a selective fusion of Arab, Syrian, Byzantine, Persian, and Central Asian traditions, was the antithesis of Hindu art. The divergence in natural background, religious beliefs, and political history of the two peoples was reflected in their respective art forms. Yet upon contact, instead of clashing they blended together, giving rise to a new form of art in India.

Because of religious taboos, Muslims were not initially interested in music and painting, but they soon acquired a deep affection for them. Before the rise of Islam, Mecca was not only noted for its shrines, but also for its dancing and singing girls. There is some evidence that even in the Quran a beautiful voice is indirectly praised. The Persians had always been fond of music. The oldest parts of the *Avesta,* named *gathas,* were recited in a musical voice. The Sassanian kings were famous for their patronage of music. With this background, Islam could not resist music for long. The serious study of this art began during the last phase of the Umayyad Caliphate and was well developed by the time the Abbasids ascended to their rule. The growth of Islamic music was a valuable contribution to world culture, as well as to that of India. Islamic music first came to Sind with the Arabs, and was soon blended with the prevalent Indian system.

The divine service in the mosque was performed without vocal or instrumental music, but when Muslim rulers saw that Hindu life was full of music, they adopted it into their social life, although they continued their *namaz* (prayer) without music. Muslim Sufi saints, who were as fond of music as the Hindu Bhaktas, even introduced it into their congregational meetings, where songs of divine love, *qawwalis,* were sung; qawwalis are extremely popular in India even today.

Some Muslim rulers became skilful musicians. A Muslim ruler of Jaunpur is credited with developing the imaginative *raga khayal* from the massive and solid *raga dhrupad*. Alauddin Khilji had a number of accomplished musicians amongst his courtiers. Singers and dancers—Hindu, Turkish, Persian, and others—resided permanently at Muslim *darbars,* often under the headship of a Persian officer. Devotional songs, such as *bhairavi, sarasrag, kalungra,* and *bhairon,* were sung at religious gatherings, and in the darbar, *malkos* and *darbari* were presented. Thus, by a fusion of Indo-Iranian music, North Indian music was formed.[20a] The Muslim poet, Amir Khusrau, was also a famous singer who introduced new styles. From the fourteenth and fifteenth centuries onwards Persian modes were introduced into the music of northern India, thereby making it a little different from that of South India where the Iranian influence was not felt. The modern ragas and raginis developed under Muslim patronage. Many Indian instruments also owe their origin to Muslim artists; for instance, the *tabla, dilruba, sarod,* and *naqqara,* were introduced by the Arabs or Iranians. Amongst the tunes believed to be Iranian in origin are *zangola, zlif, zala,* and *khamaj.*

A synthesis of Hindu and Muslim musical elements had taken place even during the period of the Delhi Sultanate, and by the time of the Mughals, a musical art form existed which became highly developed under the enthusiasm and patronage of the Mughals. Music, as other aspects of Indo-Islamic culture, reached its zenith at the time of Akbar. During his reign about two hundred tunes were modified under Iranian influence. Darbari, or chamber music, was introduced in his time. The celebrated pupil of Swami Haridas, Tansen, lived at Akbar's court, and was one of his *navaratna* (nine jewels). Tansen's disciples gave rise to various schools of music. It is said that when the Mughals returned to the north after their conquest of Deccan, they took with them the most famous South Indian musicians along with other artists and sculptors.

Music in Muslim India was far more popular than it is sometimes made out to be. A major reason for this may well be that the vast majority of Muslims in India were of Hindu descent and disinclined to give up, like their tongue, their music. Even today some of the best known Indian musicians are Muslims, such as Ali Akbar Khan, Vilayat Khan, and Bismillah Khan.

The mediaeval period, in fact, appears to have been an age of accomplished musicians, both Hindu and Muslim. The great poet-singers, Tulsidas, Surdas, and Mirabai, belong to this period. Akbar's contemporary, Sultan Ibrahim Adil Shah of Bijapur, was also a composer, a teacher of both Hindu and Muslim musicians, and the author of a book, *Nau-Ras,* on music. In Kashmir, King Zainul Abidin patronized art and music and had a large number of Central Asian musicians at his court. Shahjahan, the prince of builders, who did not care much for painting, was a great lover of music. During Aurangzeb's reign, music, as well as other art forms, lost court favour but by that time North Indian music—often called Hindustani—had already assumed its new personality.

Today, Hindustani and Karnatak schools of music are prevalent in the north and south respectively. There may be minor differences of nomenclature and articulation but basically there is only one Indian music. The raga is the basis, and its development the goal of musical expression. Both systems have the same number of notes—seven *suddha* and five *vikrita*—in the octave. The classification of ragas under parental modes is also common to both.

Because of Islam's intense aversion to images, sculpture was not a well-developed art in the Islamic countries. Pre-Islamic Arabia had idols, and a few animal figures in stone, bronze or other metals are found in the palace of Alhambra in Spain and amongst the ruins of Egypt and Spain. Pre-Islamic Iran, under the Achaemenians and Sassanians, was rich in sculpture. Sculpture was also highly developed in India and remained almost unaffected by Islam.

At first Islam did not encourage painting, but later the Caliphs declared that the religious injunction against the representation of living creatures applied only to religious structures, not to residential buildings. Hence, the Umayyads and the Abbasids in Asia and the Caliphs of Spain had their palace walls decorated with floral designs and even human figures. The Mughal rulers loved and patronized painting. Babur brought with him some of the finest specimens from the ancestral collection of Timurid paintings. The Timurid school of painting, one of the two greatest Persian schools—the other being the Safavi—was begun by Timur's grandsons. The first patron of the school was Iskandar Sultan, son of Ulugh Beg, who ruled over Fars until 1414. Soon afterwards another Timurid ruler, Baysunghur (d. 1433), attracted artists to his library at Herat; it was there that Kamaluddin Bihzad flourished in the middle of the fifteenth century. Bihzad was the greatest artist of Persia—with the possible exception of Mani—and his interpretation of the Timurid style of painting greatly influenced Indian art. Both Babur and Humayun greatly admired Bihzad, and when Humayun returned to India after his exile in Persia, he took with him two of Bihzad's distinguished pupils, Mir Saiyid Ali and Khwaja Adbus Samad Shirazi.

In the course of time, three new schools of painting—the Rajput, the Jammu, and the Kangra—emerged in northern India, appearing first in the early sixteenth century in Rajasthan. Later, the Rajput style spread far beyond Rajasthan to the Himalaya states, Kashmir, and also to Mathura and Banaras. The new style was primitive but highly expressive and colourful. The eyes of the figures were almost hypnotic, with all expression conveyed through postures and poses of the body. However, Mughal art superseded this style by the middle of the seventeenth century.

Akbar was a great admirer of the realistic and forceful simplicity of the Hindu style and of the delicacy, linear grace, and decoration of the Persian. He deliberately initiated a blending of the two styles under experts of both schools. Akbar rewarded good paintings generously, and both Hindu and Muslim artists were designated as officers of the state. His patronage, coupled with the use of paper as a medium, greatly advanced the development of the graphic arts. The importance of painting is stressed in the *Ain-i-Akbari*. Talented Iranian and Indian artists executed the miniatures of the illuminated manuscripts of *Hamzanama, Tutinama, Baburnama, Razmnama,* a Persian version of the *Mahabharata* which cost the Emperor about eighty thousand pounds, the *Akbarnama,* illustrated by Farrukh Beg, *Nala-Damayanti* of Faizi, the *Ramayana,* the *Harivamsa,* and others.[21] The *Akbarnama* paintings are noted for their unity of design, even though Mughal miniatures were usually painted by several artists. The miniatures of the Indian epics are not only fine art specimens, but also a valuable source of information about contemporary Hindu manners and customs.

At first the style was chiefly Persian in inspiration but later it was more influenced by Indian styles, and by the time of Jahangir's reign a new Mughal style of painting had been born. Jahangir, a talented painter himself, patronized painting almost exclusively; all the great painters of the school belonged to his court. He had a keen aesthetic sense and loved the beauties of nature. He was so attracted to Kashmir that he visited it thirteen times during the twenty-two years of his reign. He favoured naturalism in art, and the painting of landscapes, animals, and portraits reached its zenith during his reign. Mansur is the most renowned of the bird and animal painters of the period. From Jahangir's reign onward, the Rajput and the Mughal schools can be distinguished. Shahjahan carried on the tradition, but his chief patronage was given to architecture. His son, Dara Shikoh, patronized the arts, although he was more interested in philosophy. He left behind a valuable album of paintings, but before he could stamp his personality on Indian culture and society, he was executed by his younger brother, Aurangzeb.

Islam's richest contribution was in architecture and the whole of northern India is studded with beautiful buildings of the period. The Fatehpur Sikri complex, the Red Fort of Delhi, and the Taj Mahal are a few of the many outstanding buildings in which the blending of Indian and Islamic elements can be seen.

Muslim architecture, a fusion of Arab, Syrian, Persian, Turkish, Central Asian, and other traditions, is generally massive, with extensive buildings and mosques, mausoleums, domes, minarets, lofty portals, open courtyards, geometrical patterns, and calligraphic inscriptions. Its basic forms are the pillared hall, the dome resting on pillars, and the brick vault and cupola. The monotheistic puritanism of Islam delighted in the simplicity of the unbroken dome, the plain symbolism of the pointed arch, and the slenderness of the minaret. The inhospitable natural surroundings of Arabia had influenced the art of Islam, as they did its outlook on life, making it austere, vigorous, and purposeful. It is particularly conspicuous in mosques and sacred places by the absence of representations of living beings, whether in painting or sculpture. In contrast, Hindu architecture is renowned for its majesty, richness, and variety. Temples were carved with reliefs of all forms of the supernatural, and animal and plant life. Hindu art is decorative and at times voluptuous, whereas Muslim art is simple and puritanical.

By the time the Muslims came to India with a view to setting up an empire, they already had centuries of cultural tradition behind them which was influenced by the numerous peoples with whom they had come in contact in Europe, Asia, and Africa. Although Islamic architecture started in Arabia, it attained maturity through a period of sustained development in West and Central Asia, North Africa, and Spain, before reaching its zenith in India. Islamic architecture originated in the construction and design of the mosque and many of its finest buildings are mosques. Next in importance come tombs, followed by palaces, forts, and public buildings. In their early days in India, the Muslims were dazzled by the extraordinary richness and sumptuousness of Indian architecture. In the fourteenth century, they began to react against it, but this was a short-lived phase; soon syncretic tendencies reached their peak during the Mughal period.

The oldest extant Indian mosques are in the neighbourhood of Delhi where the Mughals built profusely. The most significant early Islamic building in India is the Qutb Minar at Delhi, which was completed about 1231 during the reign of Iltutmish. One of the most stupendous architectural achievements conceived by Muslims, the tower, comprising five stories and standing 238 feet high, forms part of the Qutb Mosque scheme. The Qutb Mosque was built by Qutbuddin Aibek in 1195 on the spacious substructure of a Hindu temple, and consisted entirely of spoils extracted from temples in the area. Such a second-hand building had little architectural beauty or order. However, four years later it was decided to project an expansive arched screen across the side of the structure facing Mecca; this screen is possibly the first surviving example of a structure in definite original Islamic style on Indian soil.

At about the time the Qutb Minar was being built in the eastern extremity of the Islamic world, Yusuf I of Spain, at the western extremity of Islam, was raising a tower even higher than the Qutb, the Giralda, at Seville. However, neither the Giralda nor any other tower in the Islamic world surpasses the Qutb in beauty. Another extremely fine example of the early Indo-Islamic style is to be seen in the adjacent Alai Darwaza, built in 1310. This and the ruined tomb of Alauddin Khilji, erected soon after, represent the early Sultanate style at the time of its greatest perfection.

Many palaces, mosques, mausoleums, baths, and educational institutions sprang up, especially during the reigns of Alauddin Khilji and Firuz Tughluq. After Alauddin's death there was a change in style, which had been foreshadowed for some time, and Tughluq architecture became marked by the absence of extravagant features. The Tughluq style, however, is vigorous and straightforward and readily adapted old structural features to its requirements. Its departure from Islamic traditions became clear; red sandstone and marble gave place to rubble and plaster.

The Lodi style was an elaboration of the Tughluq, enriched by new ornamental motifs from Iran and Turkistan. The most important feature of the tomb of Sikandar Lodi is the double dome, which subsequently played an important role in the evolution of Mughal style. This architectural invention, designed to preserve the symmetry and relative proportions of the body of the building, probably originated in Syria and came to India through Iraq and Iran.

The assimilation of forms and techniques in art naturally went on throughout the country. In Bengal, the prevalent brick construction was adopted by the Muslim conquerors who imitated Hindu motifs in their structural embellishments. The main features of Islamic architecture in eastern India are heavy stone pillars, pointed arches, and brick vaults. In Kashmir, the beautiful wooden architecture was readily appropriated, and Kashmiri tombs are quite different from similar structures elsewhere in India. In western India, Gujarati styles were similarly adapted. The rich ornamentation and delicate style of the Muslim architecture of Gujarat accord with the highly developed and rich Hindu architecture. In other regions of India, similarly, Islamic architecture absorbed prevalent local characteristics, emerging with a distinctive personality.

Unlike other Muslim rulers of India, the Bahmani rulers of the Deccan largely ignored the indigenous art with the result that the Deccan style was mainly influenced by the Imperial buildings at Delhi and the monuments of Iran. The Bahmani Kings, who were Shia Muslims, were patrons of the arts and sciences. They attracted eminent scholars and expert technicians from other countries, and it was probably because of this that their military architecture was much influenced by Europe and their civil architecture by Iran.

The Muslims acquired much from the Sassanian and Byzantine schools, and in all the countries they conquered they adapted the indigenous architecture to their own requirements. In India, mosques and temples required some ornamental decoration, and colonnades adorned the open courts of both but the contrasting styles were striking. The prayer chamber of the mosque was spacious, whereas the shrine of the temple was small; the mosque was light and open and the temple rather dark and closed in; Muslim construction was based on arches, vaults and domes, whereas Hindu construction was based on columns, architraves and pyramidal towers or slender spires. The Muslims readily adopted the Hindu trabeate, the system of using beams or long square stones as lintels and entablature instead of using the arch. They also made use of the bracket type of Hindu corbel—the stone or timber projection for support. In return, they gave to Indian architecture a sense of breadth and spaciousness and introduced new forms and colours. Like the Romans, they used concrete and mortar imaginatively. They spanned big spaces with arches, roofed large areas with magnificent domes, and introduced, amongst other architectural features, the minar. They introduced decorative arabesque or geometric devices, inscriptions in graceful lettering, gilding and painting in variegated colours, encaustic tile-mosaic and tesselate designs in coloured stones and marble.

With the establishment of the Mughal Empire in 1526, a new era of architecture dawned in India. By that time, even those Muslims whose families had come from outside had been largely Indianized, and the Indo-Islamic cultural synthesis had attained maturity. The Mughals gave it a new and vigorous impetus. In 1530, Babur, the founder of the Mughal Empire, was succeeded by his son, Humayun, who, after ten years of unsettled reign, was exiled for the next fifteen years. Because of the almost unending warfare throughout their brief reigns in India, Babur and Humayun were unable to contribute much of lasting value to Mughal architecture.

During Humayun's exile, his conqueror, Shershah Suri, famous for his revenue administration and public welfare works, ruled from Delhi, and architecture made considerable progress during the relatively brief rule of the Suri dynasty. At first Suri architecture was soberly elegant but toward the end it became highly decorative. It is the precursor of the Mughal styles, and an important stage in the development of Indian architecture. Shershah's finest building is the mosque constructed at Delhi in 1541. The mausoleum of Shershah, in Sahasram in Bihar, built in a splendid Indo-Iranian style at about the same time, is an architectural masterpiece. It is indeed a suitable tribute to the genius of a ruler and to the skill and vision of its architect. Constructed of fine sandstone, the mausoleum is 250 feet wide and stands four square in the centre of a large artificial lake so extensive that each of its concrete sides measures 1400 feet in length. Whilst the style of Babur and Humayun was foreign, that of the Suris, although Muslim in external appearance, was influenced in details by Hindu architecture especially in the construction of doorways.

The first outstanding monument of the early Mughal style is the mausoleum of Humayun (Humayun ka Makbara), built by his widow during Akbar's reign. She is said to have employed an Iranian architect Mirak Mirza Ghiyas, who introduced certain Iranian features such as a typically Iranian dome, an arched alcove as is found in the royal tombs of Iran, the interior arrangement of corridors, and the complex of rooms. Indigenous characteristics are to be found in the elegant kiosks with cupolas, and the excellent stone masonry. The style of this monument has been described as an Indian interpretation of an Iranian architectural conception. Both in spirit and in structure, Humayun's tomb is a captivating example of the synthesis of two great traditions of art.

All of the early Mughal buildings display the sober elegance of the Iranian style. At the beginning of the Mughal period, a fresh wave of Iranians came to India: this influx of noblemen and men of learning and culture more or less continued throughout the period. Iran thus played the same part in the development of Indo-Islamic art during the sixteenth century as Renaissance Italy did to the art of France. But early in Akbar's reign, Iranian influences were blended with Indian styles. This fusion is reflected in the mosque and palace buildings at Fatehpur Sikri, the capital city built by Akbar in 1570–1574 on a site near Agra. These buildings form a brilliant complex, with broad terraces and stately courtyard surrounded by numerous palaces and pavilions. The most imposing building is the Jama Masjid; its finest feature is the 176 feet tall southern gateway, the Buland Darwaza, which is made of marble and sandstone, and is architecturally the most perfect gateway in India, and the largest of its kind in the world. Indeed, the buildings at Fatehpur Sikri constitute one of the most spectacular structural achievements in the whole of India. The style of Fatehpur Sikri is mature in every respect, fully absorbing Iranian elegance into the exactness of Indian workmanship. A monument to Akbar's vision and originality, it is, after the Taj Mahal, the most notable architectural achievement of the Mughals. This capital was built purely as a retreat from military strife. But Sikri's tenure as the capital was ironically short, lasting hardly more than a generation.

Akbar left scores of buildings at Agra, Allahabad, and elsewhere. The Agra fort, built in 1565–1573, is one of his outstanding structural achievements. It is important not only in providing an example of the military architecture of the early Mughals, but in testifying that the aesthetic taste and artistic feeling of its builders influenced even utilitarian structures. Unlike most Muslim rulers of India, Akbar encouraged indigenous construction systems and borrowed from other countries only when necessary. Most of his buildings are red sandstone, with white marble here and there for emphasis, and both arcuate and trabeate styles were used.

In the secular buildings of the time, of which the most important and complete is the palace of Akbar's Hindu queen, Jodh Bai, the carved decoration was unrestrained. Figures of elephants, lions, and peacocks, and other embellishments suggest that Hindu craftsmen predominated, under the supervision of accommodating Mughal overseers. Some of the civil buildings are more Hindu than others, and copy features of Hindu and Jain temples. Although this synthesis was a natural outcome of Indo-Islamic cultural exchange, Akbar's sympathies with Indian culture as a whole partly accounts for these unorthodox intrusions into Islamic art. In mosques and religious buildings, however, traditional Muslim construction was adhered to more closely.

By the time of Jahangir and Shahjahan, both of whom were sons of Hindu queens, the situation had changed. Islam had long been Indianized and so had Mughal rule. Muslim art had already assumed a predominantly Indian personality, in which Iranian influence can be detected only by experts. Although Jahangir inherited Akbar's artistic taste and built some magnificent structures, his reign was relatively unproductive in architecture. However, other arts developed, and a new school of miniature painting was established. Of the buildings erected by Jahangir, the tomb of Akbar, at Sikandra near Agra, is the most impressive. Built in 1613–1614, it was a departure from the conventional domed structure, and is a low, truncated, three-storied pyramid shape. Reflecting something of the nature-loving monarch whose remains it enshrines, a sense of space is given by the wide-terraced flower garden which surrounds it. The carvings and paintings, in both gold and colours, are exquisite. Its four minarets are in perfect harmony; nothing like these had been built in northern India since the Qutb Minar centuries earlier. Whilst it does not compare with the mausoleum of Humayun at Delhi, it was a conception of such magnitude that it was not completed until eight years after Jahangir's accession, even though the Emperor took a personal interest in its construction.

Another interesting building of Jahangir's reign is the tomb of his father-in-law, Itmadud-daulah, at Agra, built by Empress Nurjahan. This small, elegant, and exquisitely finished mausoleum marks a transition between the styles of Akbar and Shahjahan, illustrating a fresh interpretation of the art of building. As an example of architecture in miniature, this building, with its garden and gateways, is one of the best of its kind. Built of white marble and decorated in stone of five colours, it is elaborately ornamental and embellished throughout with subtlety and delicacy. This mausoleum marks the beginning of the most sumptuous phase of Mughal building characterized by the profusion of gold, precious stones, and white marble, which replaced sandstone. The best known buildings of Shahjahan's period are the Jama Masjid; the Red Fort at Delhi, with its Diwan-i-Am, Diwan-i-Khas, and Moti Masjid; and the Taj Mahal. The Taj is the triumph of Indo-Islamic synthesis in art. Shahjahan built the mausoleum which stands on the Jamuna River at Agra, to enshrine the remains of his qeen, Mumtaz Mahal. Commencing work in 1631, twenty thousand Hindus and Muslims laboured for twenty-two years to finish it. Whilst the broad conception of this unique memorial is attributed to Shahjahan himself, there is some uncertainty about the identity of the architect who translated his ideals into stone. Some Western scholars have suggested that he was a Venetian jeweller and silversmith, Geronimo Veroneo. There is no evidence to support this suggestion except that the Italian was employed by the Mughal Court at the time and was invited, along with many others, to submit designs to a council of architects and craftsmen convened by the Emperor. But the design finally accepted was prepared by local master builders. That the Taj Mahal is wholly indigenous is obvious by the indisputably Indo-Islamic style of architecture. Contemporary manuscripts give full details of its construction, including the names of the architects and builders, amongst whom are found Hindus, Muslims, and West Asians, but no Italians.

Shahjahan's reign was followed by the long, austere, and autocratic rule of the intensely orthodox Muslim emperor, Aurangzeb, the last of the Great Mughals. Aurangzeb was not a patron of art, but was an accomplished calligrapher, and had made copies of the Quran to earn his living. After his death, the unity of India was broken and the country was plunged into political chaos and intrigue.

Just as the buildings constructed by Muslims blended Islamic designs with Indian details, the Hindu temples came under Indo-Islamic influence. The Govind Deo temple built in 1590 is the most notable of these and is a tribute to the versatility of Indian masons. It shows a sense of refinement and an appreciation of plain surfaces not often seen in temple designs. The secular architecture of Hindus, for example in Malwa and Rajasthan, was also influenced by Akbar and his successors. Royal residences and other state buildings, for instance at Bikaner, and palace fortresses, such as those at Jodhpur and Orchha, show the influence of the Mughal style.

Other arts and crafts which the Muslims transmitted from Iran to India, are enamelling, faience, the parcel gilt work of Kashmir, damascening, and papier mâché. Innovations were introduced in the manufacture of cotton and silk textiles, woollen shawls and carpets, and Nurjahan is credited with the discovery of the attar of roses.

Islamic political influence was considerable. In fact, the whole military organization was revolutionized and a new military oligarchy became the principal political institution of Muslim India. New weapons and techniques of warfare were also introduced.

The Muslims introduced into India the *Yunani* system of medicine. The large number of physicians, *hakims,* at the royal court held high *mansabs* and rendered inexpensive medical aid to the sick. The Yunani system is presumably so called because the Arabs had borrowed liberally from Greek medicine.

Islam made a greater impact on Indian urban life than on rural life. Influenced by the royal court, the urban population attained a high degree of sophistication in language and literature, arts and crafts, manners, dress, diet, luxuries and refinements. The centres of power, Delhi, Agra, and Lucknow, set fashions that were widely followed in all provincial courts, including even unfriendly states such as Rajasthan and the Deccan. This Mughal impress persisted in the parlours, the *zenana,* the wardrobe and the dining room, and continues to do so today amongst the upper classes of Indian society. Islamic court fashions, under Akbar and afterwards, exercised considerable influence on men's wear amongst the

Hindu upper and middle classes, but not so much on women's clothing except in jewelry.[22]

Whilst the court played a significant part in determining styles, dress is principally governed by climatic conditions. Consequently, in large countries, the national dress has regional style. For instance, *pajamas* are worn in the Punjab by both Hindus and Muslims, as is the *dhoti* in the south; the variations in dress more often reflect class rather than communal distinctions. Women's ornaments are common to both communities. Whilst the *shalwar* is worn by the women of the Punjab, the *sari* is the most common dress of all Indian women. In India today certain regional dresses, like dishes of food, have gained national popularity. For instance, young girls in all parts of India prefer the shalwar to the sari because of its suitability for active work and sport, and the Afghan-type *karakuli* cap is a common sight in Delhi during winter.

Even those Muslims who came to India from other countries largely adopted costumes suitable to their new country. For instance, the Arab *amama, jubba, rida, tahmad,* and *tasma,* as well as the Central Asian *kulah, nima,* and *moza,* were replaced by the Indian *pugree, chira, kurta, angarkha, patka, dupatta,* and *pajama.* The assimilation in dress was primarily an upper class problem, and the large numbers of Hindu converts felt no need to change their fashions.

In the rural Indian villages, where practically the entire Muslim population was descended from Hindu converts, the traditional Hindu outlook and social forms were retained. Even the caste prejudices, the objection to widow remarriage, and the love of ritual and image worship continued. Both Hindus and Muslims observed similar ceremonies of birth, death, and marriage, and had much the same fairs and festivals. The dress, the manner of cooking, the family system, and the style of houses continued to be the same for both, and the common language remained the regional tongue.

In social life, however, some effects of Islam on Indian society were not too healthy, for example, the development of *purdah,* the seclusion of women. Many Hindu nobles were required to offer their daughters in marriage to Muslim sultans and noblemen, a demand which the former found contrary to their religious beliefs. The caste-ridden Hindu could not contract marriages for their children outside their own caste or even subcaste, let alone their religious group. Consequently, they responded to this pressure by adopting the Muslim practice of purdah, which, in time, led to child-marriage and the general deterioration of the woman's position in Indian society. Customs such as *jauhar* and *sati* became more frequent. However, in the areas where Muslim influence was weak, such as South India, the custom of purdah was not prevalent.

For all its emphasis on human equality, Islam, like Buddhism before it, failed to demolish caste. From the Hindu point of view the Muslims became another caste, and despite cultural similarity, they remained a distinct social group. Because of the rigid Hindu caste system, intermarriage and inter-dining between orthodox Hindus and Muslims were not possible. Also, no orthodox Muslim would allow his son or daughter to marry an unconverted Hindu. There was, however, no hostility based on group prejudice or religious consciousness. Cultural dissimilarities were regional, and power conflicts political.

A COMMON INDIAN culture could not be evolved unless Islam in turn was influenced by Hindu culture and became Indian in character. Because of the Indian influence on their social life and customs, Indian Muslims today are a group distinct from Muslims elsewhere. Hindu caste affected Islam. Commonly, Muslims are regarded as belonging to two social groups—the *sharifzats* (high castes) and the *ajlafzats* (low castes). In fact, however, there are many more social castes and distinctions which divide Indian Muslims.[23] Whilst inter-caste marriages amongst Muslims were not prohibited, they generally did not take place. Social distinctions were preserved not by religious belief but by snobbery. The Muslim *bhangi* was as downtrodden as his Hindu counterpart, although the Islamic ideal of human equality was a major incentive for many caste-ridden and oppressed Hindus to embrace Islam. But in practice their social inequality remained. The foreign Muslims regarded themselves as somewhat superior to the local converts and, as a natural extension of this snobbery, the mixed Muslims, like the early Eurasians, tried to identify themselves with the ruling foreign class. Having been refused the superior status of the foreigner, they developed a class of their own. The terms *sayyid* and *shaikh*, implying Arab origin, carry highest prestige; the Mughal ranks next in importance. Outcastes and the converts from the lower Hindu castes were designated as *Nau* (New)-*Muslims,* somewhat in the same way as new migrants are called New Australians in Australia today.

Islam condemns priesthood, but it developed amongst Indian Muslims. They also showed a marked fondness for ritual and elaborate ceremony. Islam is monotheistic and iconoclastic, but Indian Muslims often venerate saints and their tombs. Numerous sacred shrines, such as Shaikh Chishti at Ajmer and Bhairava Nath at Mathura, are frequented by both Muslims and Hindus. A Muslim sect, *Panchpiriyas* (worshippers of five pirs), venerate saints to such a degree that an Indian census of 1911 described them as Hindus whose religion has a strong Mohammedan flavour. The Prophet rejected miracles, but Indian Muslims sanctify their heroes. Many Muslims even developed idolatrous practices. For example, the Chauriharas of Uttar Pradesh worship Kalka Sahja Mai and observe *sraddha ;* the Meos of the Punjab worship many gods such as Siausi, Magti, and Lachi : the Mirasis take offerings to Durga-Bhavani; the Turk-Nawas of eastern Bengal worship Lakshmi. Many Bengali Muslims worship Sitala, Kali, Dharmaraj, Baidyanatu, and other Hindu deities. The Avans of the Punjab use Brahmans as family priests, and the cow is revered by the Shins of the Indus Valley, who do not eat beef, as well as by the Momins of Kutch.[24] The Momins worship the Hindu Trinity—Brahma, Vishnu and Mahesh—and their salutation is "Ram Ram." Muslim ascetics are often tonsured and smear their bodies with ash; they also often act as guardians of shrines. The fire in some Muslim areas such as the Jhang district in West Punjab and Gorakhpur in Uttar Pradesh is looked upon as sacred. Many Muslims participate fully in Hindu festivities, such as Holi and Diwali.

Hindu women in Muslim harems formed a powerful influence in working out the Indo-Islamic synthesis. Hindu women who married Muslim men introduced their social customs and rites into the new homes. Muslims tended more toward monogamy under Hindu influence, the remarriage of widows became rarer. Many features of Muslim court life were borrowed from Hindus. The Hindu superstition of the evil eye, and Hindu habits of bathing and ceremonial purity were adopted by Muslims. Many Rajput converts retained their family names. The Malkana Rajputs, now Muslim, still perform Hindu rites and ceremonies. They prefer to be called Miyan Thakurs and admit to being a mixture of

Hindu and Muslim. The Avans, although they are nearly all Muslims, retain their Hindu names and keep their genealogies in the Brahmanic fashion. Hindu titles, such as Chaudhari, Thakur, and Raja, are also found amongst Muslims. Some Muslim groups use the Hindu marriage ceremony, or perform the Hindu rites first and the Muslim ceremony afterwards. The Hindu joint family system and, in many cases, the Hindu property law were followed by Muslims.

Islamic thought was also affected by Hindu doctrines and philosophy. There were, no doubt, a number of people amongst both communities who bitterly resisted extraneous influences or innovations, but there were many more who regarded the spirit of religion as more important than its letter. Amongst them were mystics who interpreted religion for the common man. It was because of the endeavours of such people that the closeness of the two apparently irreconcilable doctrines came to be noticed: both stressed inner discipline, purification of mind, and unification with the divine.

The most mystical Muslim philosophy is *Tasawwuf*, known as Sufism, which is essentially the doctrine of the love of God, and which has exercised an incalculable influence on the intellectual and emotional life of Muslims, as well as on Islamic culture. Although Muslim orthodoxy often persecuted the Sufis, it was their interpretation which won the most converts to Islam in India, Africa, Indonesia, and elsewhere. It has been suggested that it is only because of Sufism that Islam became an international religion.

Sufism is not regarded by its followers as something which originated at a specific place or at a certain point in time: Jalaluddin Rumi said in his *Diwan* that the Sufis drank the wine of wisdom and knowledge before there were vines on this earth. Another Sufi scholar asserts that Sufism is too sublime to have had an origin. One theory derives Sufism from the esoteric doctrine of Muhammad himself, another from Neoplatonism, whilst yet another maintains it originated independently in the inherent mystical urge in all religious men. It has also been suggested that Sufism represents the reaction of the Aryan mind to a Semitic religion imposed by force.

The term *Sufi* comes from *suf* meaning wool; a Sufi is one who wears a woollen garment. The movement represented a reaction against the worldiness, luxury, and external piety of the period which followed the Muslim conquests. The early Sufis were simple, unsophisticated and pious people, who lived a life of self-discipline and poverty (*fakr*), devoting themselves to meditation and prayer in the quest of truth and righteousness. Their meditation was originally the continuous chanting of the name of Allah. Ascetics at first, they soon easily became mystics.

It was a woman, Rabia al-Adawiyya (717–801), who introduced a new dimension, the doctrines of divine love, into early Sufism by her concentration on serving God without being motivated either by the fear of divine punishment or expectation of reward: "O God if I worship Thee in fear of Hell, burn me in Hell; and if I worship Thee in hope of Paradise, exclude me from Paradise; but if I worship Thee for Thine own sake, withhold not Thine Everlasting Beauty." She thus marks the transition from the ascetic quietism of early Sufism to the advanced form it assumed with the introduction of the doctrine of *marifat,* gnosis, by the Egyptian Dhul-Nun al-Misri (d. 861), and that of *fana,* passing away into universal being, by the Persian Abu Yazid of Bistam (d. 875). Yazid was bold in his language and scandalized the orthodoxy. He was the first of the "intoxicated" Sufis who had drunk the "wine of knowledge" and who found God within his own soul through the mystic path. He was the first Sufi to give a detailed description of his *miraj,* mystical experience. From his time onward, the doctrine of fana became a central theme in Sufi theory. It was, however, Al Junaid of Baghdad (d. 910), the most original and penetrating intellectual of his time, who was responsible for developing this doctrine as an integral part of a well co-ordinated theosophy. Mansur al-Hajjaj (858–922) carried the philosophy still further. He did not merely see in the supreme mystical experience a reunion with God, but taught that man was God Incarnate, the doctrine of *anal-haqq* (I am the Truth).

By the end of the twelfth century Sufism so dominated the Muslim mind that every school of Islamic thought had become influenced by it. Imam al-Ghazali (1058–1111), who has been described as a "Renewer of Islam," was mainly responsible for this. His philosophy was the product of varied experience. After prolonged study, he attempted to reconcile orthodox Islamic teachings with mysticism and applied rational methods in interpreting its dogmas and doctrines. He became a wandering Sufi in

1095, asserted the futility of scholasticism, and declared that philosophy cannot unfold the mysteries of God and creation. He emphasized the value of direct experience as the vital element in religion, and taught that man's duty was to seek God and to love Him, whilst the role of the intellect was to realize its own limitations in this task. Ghazali took Abu Yazid, Al Hajjaj and Abu Said ibn Abil Khayr, who had reached the "reality of realities," as his models, and used their phrases, such as "anal-haqq," to express his belief in monism and "the annihilation of the soul and the sole vision of God." The greatest Muslim mystic thinker, Muhi al-Din ibn al-Arabi (d. 1240) was influenced by Al Ghazali. He built an imposing philosophical system and through his prolific writings Muslim mysticism attained its zenith. He was a complete monist: not only is there no other god but God, there is nothing but God and the world is His external manifestation. The evolutionary cycle of Sufism was completed in the fourteenth century with the rise of the school of Wahdat-al-Wujud, existentialist monism.

The early Sufis adhered to what was prescribed by Islam, but their ideal of life was renunciation, self-abnegation, and poverty. Later, Sufism gained greater spiritual intensity and breadth of outlook. Whilst retaining its mystical content, the Sufi vision embraces both heaven and earth and seeks to penetrate the innermost secrets of creation in order to comprehend the Divine mysteries that lie beyond ordinary human perception. The Sufis came to believe in the attainment of the vision of God and union with the Divine by adhering to the mystic path, *tariqa* or *suluk*. For them, spiritual life is a journey (*safar*) along this path; the journey has many stages and each state (*maqam*) has its corresponding achievement of certain virtues (*hal*). For Sufis, God or reality is the universal will, the true knowledge, the eternal light, and the supreme beauty, reflected in the mirror of the universe. As the nature of beauty is self-manifestation and desire to be loved, Sufis consider love to be the essence of all religions and the cause of creation and its continuation. The world is unreal, merely an illusion. Sufism thus teaches the doctrine of Wahdat-al-Wujud, unity of being, that being is one, that all apparent differences are modes, aspects, and manifestation of reality, and that the phenomenal world is the outward expression of the real, anal-haqq, "Know Thyself" is the core of Sufi philosophy, as it is in the Vedanta. It is through the path of self-knowledge that truth or reality is discovered in both Sufism and Hinduism, whether it is called *Jnana* in Sanskrit, or *Man arafa Nafsah Rabbahu* in Arabic.

Mysticism of the Sufi type has no place in orthodox Islamic teaching, for the strictly monotheistic religions, with the exception of Christianity, are not conducive to mysticism. Neither the Torah nor the Quran lend themselves to a mystical interpretation, as both assert most emphatically the complete otherness of God. Yet, the fact that mystic thought did develop in Islam is an illustration both of the powerful mystical strain in all religion, and of Indian influence on it. It is, therefore, not surprising that numerous scholars, both Muslim and non-Muslim, have been struck by the remarkable parallels between Sufi doctrines and those of Indian Vedanta and Buddhism.

One of the earliest examples of India's possible influence on Islam appears to have been the rise of opposition to legal Islam, known as *Zuhd* or asceticism. But in the further advanced philosophic concepts of Sufism, more definite Indian influence is suggested. R. A. Nicholson, strongly supported by Max Horton, insists that the Sufi idea of *fana* is of Indian origin, and strikingly close to the nirvana of Buddhism. Although recently A. J. Arberry has disputed this assertion as not proven, the weight of argument and opinion would seem to favour Nicholson and Horton rather than Arberry. The founder of this doctrine, Abu Yazid of Bistam, an uneducated man who disliked books, was a pupil of Abu Ali al-Sindi, who came from Sind in India (and not from a village called Sind in Khorasan, as Arberry asserts) and who was a convert to Islam from a foreign religion, evidently Hinduism. He instructed Abu Yazid, as Yazid himself admits, in the doctrines of divine unity (*tawhid*) and the ultimate truth (*haqa-iq*)[23] Even Abu Yazid's phraseology is reminiscent of Hindu philosophical expression. For instance, his usage of "That" for God is a typically Hindu way of referring to Brahman as the absolute, *Tat*. The phrase *Takunu anta dhaka* is indeed a literal translation of the upanishadic phrase, *tat tvam asi,* meaning "Thou art That" which is exclusive to the Vedanta. Considering that the vedantic teacher, Sankaracharya, had just revived and systematized the vedantic philosophy and made it a widespread and vigorous movement in India, it seems likely that Abu Yazid knew of it through his Indian teacher. Abu

Yazid's extreme monism and his description of the world as illusion or deceit is remarkably close to Sankara's dismissal of the phenomenal world as maya, and his interpretation of vedantic monism.[26] A contemporary scholar, Zaehner, in fact, regards Sufism as "Vedanta in Muslim dress." It is indeed a remarkable illustration of cultural migration that through Sufism Indian monism should have found its way into Islamic philosophy which has been uncompromisingly opposed to any monistic or pantheistic doctrines.

Goldziher, who counsels that Sufism can be looked upon as an organized sect within Islam, points out that even the Sufi doctrine of Tawhid, or unity of God, is fundamentally different from the usual Islamic monotheistic concept, and is dependent upon Indian philosophy. "A Sufi goes so far to say it is *shirk* (giving associates to God) to assert that 'I know God': for in this sentence duality between perceiving subject and object to knowledge is involved; and this is also the current Indian view."[27]

The doctrine of anal-haqq is too reminiscent of the vedantic *aham Brahmasmi* to be attributed to parallel growth, especially since it is completely alien to Islamic thought. Its founder, Mansur al-Hajjaj, incurred the wrath of Islamic orthodoxy by his monist doctrine. He was condemned for blasphemy and was crucified in 922 for heresy. His theories were later incorporated into the system of Ibn-al-Arabi and Abdul Karim Jili. Jili's familiarity with Hinduism is testified to by his reference to ten major sects, including the Brahima (Brahman). Another exponent of Sufism, Jalaluddin Rumi (d. 1273), was also persecuted at first for opinions which were later accepted by the orthodoxy. Through his most important work *Mathnavi* containing reflections on Sufi thought, he introduced the practice of *sama,* a devotional dance akin to the Hindu *kirtan,* to Sufism. He taught that the heart is the mirror of divinity and that the "self is a copy made in the image of God," man's own true self belongs to the eternal self, which is God, to which it must return through fana, the annihilation of the self. All these doctrines closely resemble those of Hinduism.

Many of the mystical practices of the Sufis have Indian parallels. The *pasp-anfas* may have been derived from yogic breathing exercises; the Sufi *dhikr* is similar to the Hindu *japa,* and the *tasbih* (rosary) almost a replica of the Hindu *mala.* Both Indian thought and Sufism stress the approach to God not only through love but also submission to the *pir* or *guru,* who guides the way over the torturous path of self-knowledge to enlightenment.

It is probable that Sufism, although independent in origin, was assisted in its growth by contact with Indian thought. India and Iran, where Sufism developed, had long been exchanging scholars, merchants, artists, and envoys. Sufism first emerged as an eclectic philosophy in that part of Iran which is now Soviet Central Asia and Afghanistan, where Buddhist monks had been preaching for centuries, and which, until the rise of Islam, was a flourishing centre of Hinduism and Buddhism. The conversion of Ibrahim bin Adham (d. 777), prince of Balkh, to austerity became a favourite legend amongst the later Sufis. Admonished for his frivolity by an invisible voice during a hunting expedition, he is said to have pledged himself to an austere life. This story has often been compared with the story of the Buddha, and Al Junaid has called Adham the "Key to Sufism."

It is also clear that Sufism was more congenial to Iranians and Central Asians than to the Arabs. Buddhist monasteries flourished in eastern Iran and Transoxiana with a powerful centre at Balkh long before the Muslim conquest of India in the eleventh century. Wandering Indian monks were found as far as Baghdad during the Abbasid Caliphate, and are graphically described by Jabiz (*ca.* 866). A good deal of Buddhist literature had passed into Islam, often through a Manichaean medium.[28] By the eighth century, some Buddhist texts had been translated into Arabic along with many other Indian works. The Arabic version of the *Balauhar wa Budasaf* (Barlaam and Josaphat) had become a part of Arabic literature. The Buddhist story of the blind men describing an elephant according to their sense of touch recurs in the writings of Tawhidi, Al Ghazali, Sana-i, and Jalaluddin Rumi. The moral of the story is that, as each blind man felt only a part of the elephant and accepted it as the whole animal, so various religions know only partial truth, but in their spiritual blindness, claim it to be the entire truth. This denunciation of religious bigotry was an essential aspect of both Buddhist and Hindu teaching, and suited the Sufis admirably.

During the Arab period, many major Indian works were translated into Persian and Arabic. Al Kindi wrote a book on Indian religions; Sulaiman and Al Masudi collected and recorded information about India; during their travels, Al Nadim, Al Ashari, Al Biruni, and others discussed Indian religions and philosophic systems at length in their writings. Indian life and thought influenced the Islamic world in three areas: popular literature, science, and religious thought.

Indian mystic ideas were possibly transmitted to Jewish mysticism, known as *Kabbala,* through Sufism. Kabbala developed in Egypt and Western Asia and was introduced into Europe about 900. Important modifications in the doctrine were made centuries later by Isaac Luria (1534–1572) who lived in Palestine. Many features of Kabbala, such as the marvellous powers assigned to letters, the use of charms and amulets, the emanations or phases of the deity, and the theory of the correspondence between macrocosm and microcosm, are amazingly like Indian Tantrism. Hindu influence is definitely discerned in the theories of metempsychosis and pantheism, so often found to have some connection with India when they exist in an extreme form. Although alien to the spirit of orthodox Judaism, the pre-existence and repeated embodiment of the soul is taught in the Zohar, and even more systematically by Luria whose school composed works called Gilgulim, or lists of transmigrations. The ultimate Godhead is called *En soph* or the infinite and is unknowable, not to be described by positive epithets and therefore, in a sense nonexistent, since nothing which is predicated of existing beings can be truly predicated of *En soph.* These are crumbs from the table of Plotinus and the Upanishads.[20]

Many Sufis were attracted to India and settled there; eventually India became a centre of Sufism. Mansur al-Hallaj (858–922) was one of the earliest Sufis to visit India. Tradition also mentions a few other Sufis who settled in South India. However, Ali bin Uthman al-Julabi al-Hujwiri (d. 1072) was the first Sufi known to have made India his home, and in the middle of the eleventh century he wrote the first treatise in Persian on mysticism, called *Kashf-al Mahjub,* which has remained a standard text. He is revered by people of various faiths as a great teacher under the honorific title of Data Ganj Bakhsh.

Salar Masud Ghazi and Shaikh Ismail came to India in the eleventh century and made many converts to Sufism before Islam became a political force. Muinuddin Chishti came to India from Central Asia about 1192 and founded the Chishti order of Sufis, the largest Sufi order in India and Pakistan even today. His tomb at Ajmer is a popular pilgrimage place for both Muslims and Hindus. Later, Sufis came in large numbers with Muslim conquerors and began to preach Islam. They established monasteries, presided over by a pir, murshed or shaikh, who guided the disciples along the path of self-realization, *tariqa.* Their zeal, tolerance, and sympathy with Hindu thought brought success, but soon many of them gave up missionary work and devoted their attention to the study of Indian religions and thought.

Sufism in India aided the rapprochement between Hindu and Muslim beliefs and culture, for example in the Bhakti movement. Sufi thought to a limited extent inspired such eminent Indian thinkers as Kabir, Guru Nanak, Ram Mohan Roy, and Rabindranath Tagore. Sufis were influenced by Indian thought, particularly in the seventeenth century when they were repelled by Aurangzeb's intense adherence to the letter of Islam. Drawn towards the Vedanta, many Muslim mystics declared that nothing was real except God, and everything was illusion. They even adopted the doctrines of karma and the transmigration of the soul. They refrained from denouncing image-worship and preached *ahimsa,* nonviolence. Unlike the Sufis elsewhere, many Indian Sufis did not regard Muhammad as the perfect man, but as the equal of other prophets. He became a hero like Krishna in the *Mahabharata,* The Quran no longer remained the only holy book, but one of numerous holy scriptures, including those of other religions. The Sufis condemned religious bigotry and fanaticism, and preached the essential unity of all religions. In India the Sufis approximated the Hindu practices of meditation and asceticism.

As might be expected of any great religious movement with a long history and a succession of saint-philosophers, Sufism developed a number of sects. In India there were three chief ones—Dogmatics (*Kalam*), Philosophy (*Hikmat*), and Mysticism (*tasawwuf*). All these schools professed fundamentally similar philosophies but each was conditioned by a distinct intellectual tradition. The most original thinker of the Indian Dogmatics was Shah Wali Ullah of Delhi (d. 1762), who is compared with Al Ghazali. He endeavoured to reconcile theology and philosophy and entered a powerful plea for moral reconstruction and social reform. The Dogmatics did not believe in conversion and considered all religious rituals and dogmas superfluous.

Dara Shikoh stands out amonsgst those who sought to harmonize Hindu and Muslim mystic philosophies, abandoned dogma, preached simple faith founded on the love of God, and stressed the fundamental unity of faiths. The eldest son of Shahjahan, he wrote a number of treatises on Muslim mysticism and expounded the identity of Hindu and Muslim mystic thought. In his *Majma al-Bahrain*, he sought to reconcile the Sufi theory with the Vedanta. He emphasized the yearning of the soul for unity with God (tawhid) and the conception of God as absolute. His assertion of the fundamental unity of being, and his teaching that the Upanishads and the Quran both sought the same truth provoked the wrath of Muslim orthodoxy. Dara translated several of the Upanishads into Persian under the title *Sirr-ul-Akbar*, and it was in this form that they first became known to European scholars. There was perhaps no other prince in the history of Muslim India who could match his scholarship and who was so passionately devoted to the spiritual life.

Chapter V

EUROPEAN DISCOVERY OF INDIA

INDIA WAS KNOWN to Europe in ancient times; indeed, parts of both Greece and India were under Iranian domination at the same time. Greek and Indian soldiers had fought together and against each other; diplomatic, commercial, and cultural relations existed for centuries between India and the Hellenic and the Hellenistic worlds; and countless adventurers, scholars, merchants, and missonaries had travelled to and fro. However, this close contact ceased after the emergence of Islamic power in the seventh century, and during the Middle Ages there was little or no direct intercourse between India and the West. European knowledge of India was remote during the Crusades, and was, at best, fragmentary during the mediaeval period. Something of India was known through travel accounts, such as those of Marco Polo, but here reality often gave way to romantic imagination. However, Indian influence can definitely be traced in some works of literature. For instance, in the *Alexander Song,* composed by Priest Lambrecht in the twelfth century, the flower girls, in their charming existence as half flowers—half humans, show a surprising similarity to the daughters of Mara who were supposed to seduce the Buddha. From the Alexander novel, the story, *Girl with the Poison,* entered the poetry of Frauenlob, Hugo von Trimberg, and others. This story belongs to Indian tradition in connection with the Maurya king, Chandragupta, and is found in Visakhadatta's play, *Mudraraksasa.* Again, the hero, Parzival, in Wolfram von Eschenbach's poetry becomes the embodiment of compassion and mercy as the positive result of the commandment not to kill. Remarkable, too, is the description of the "schastel marvel" and the "lit marveile" which is reminiscent of the Buddhist stupas. Moreover, the development of the legend of Priest John who spread Christianity in India, and for whom the Portuguese went looking in vain, may well have a basis in some kind of cultural contact.

During the fifteenth century the Renaissance spirit drew Europe out of mediaevalism, and the new religious and commercial zeal inspired European explorers to find a direct sea link with India. It was the quest for India that led Columbus to stumble onto America in 1493. After persistent exploratory expeditions, the Portuguese, in their bid to reduce the power of the Muslims of North Africa and Western Asia, as well as in search of "Christians and spices," circumnavigated Africa, crossed the Arabian Sea with the assistance of an Indian sailor, and reached Calicut on the southwest coast of India, on 27 May 1498. This success eventually led to the almost complete elimination of Turkish supremacy on the Indian Ocean; the Arab trade monopoly between Asia and Europe was also destroyed by the incoming European powers. "It is to the discovery of the passage to India by the Cape of Good Hope, and to the vigour and success with which the Portuguese prosecuted their conquests and established their dominion there, that Europe has been indebted for its preservation from the most illiberal and humiliating servitude that ever oppressed polished nations."[1] This contact also slowly altered the whole character of Indian society. India became for the first time a political and economic appendage of another country, her weaknesses were exposed, and the processes of modernization were stirred into motion with increasing rapidity. The maritime activity of India, which had declined after the fall of the Roman Empire, was revived.

Although profitable trade was always one motive for their activities, the Portuguese, as the first European power to come to Asia, looked upon themselves as crusaders against Islam. Every injury inflicted on the Moors or Muslims was a gain for Christianity. Even the capture of the spice trade was described as a device to reduce the financial strength of the Muslims. It was both a religious duty and a patriotic pride to combat Islam everywhere. The centuries-old struggle for the Iberian Peninsula had made the Portuguese intensely hostile to Muslims. Alfonso de

Albuquerque, the Portuguese Commander, reporting the capture of Goa, an important centre of international trade and commerce, gloated over the fact that he had put every Moor he could find to the sword, filled mosques with the bodies, and set them on fire. He calculated six thousand persons had been killed, some roasted alive.

These acts of terror and brutality, initially directed principally against Muslims, gradually became typical of Portuguese colonialism. They frequently attacked vessels carrying pilgrims to Mecca and set them on fire, sometimes with the passengers on board. The Portuguese were no less severe on Hinduism: "The fathers of the Church forbade the Hindus under terrible penalties the use of their own sacred books, and prevented them from all exercise of their religion. They destroyed their temples and mosques, and so harassed and interfered with the people that they abandoned the city in large numbers, refusing to remain any longer in a place where they had no liberty, and were liable to imprisonment, torture and death if they worshipped after their own fashion the gods of their fathers."[2] The Portuguese tried to build their empire in Asia on their bitter hatred of Islam and Hinduism. Their reign was devoid of scruples, honour, and morality, and was a major reason for the decline of Portuguese power.

As the Papal Bulls of Alexander III protected Portugal from other Catholic powers, especially Spain, the Portuguese were able to carry on their trade without rival or restriction for about a century. They established a highly organized and flourishing commercial empire, stretching from the coast of Malabar to the Philippines, which was incomparable to any empire in European history. The Portuguese supplied all of Europe with Asian goods, of which spices were the most considerable and precious commodity. Almost all the writers of the Middle Ages confirm the widespread demand for Indian spices in Europe. Most European dishes were highly seasoned with Indian spices; they were regarded as essential at every entertainment and were principal ingredients in almost all medical prescriptions. Despite the reduction in the cost of transport due to the discovery of the direct sea route, and the consequent cheaper price, the Portuguese conducted such a lucrative trade that the jealousy of other European nations eventually could no longer be contained. Consequently, by the beginning of the seventeenth century, when Mughal India was at the height of its glory, Dutch and British, and later French, trading companies emerged to capture the Asian trade.

The anti-Muslim aspect of European expansion in Asia was soon replaced by the rivalry between the Catholic and Protestant powers of Europe. Holland, inspired by the Reformation which began in Germany in 1517, revolted against Spanish tyranny and assumed independence in 1579. Soon England joined in, and the Protestant nations defied the Papal Bulls allocating the two halves of the world to Spain and Portugal. Their struggle for commercial supremacy in the East was one aspect of their religious defiance. During the reign of Elizabeth I, English world interests had broadened, and their triumph over the Spanish Armada gave the English confidence to expand their mercantile activity. Consequently, the East India Company was founded in 1600 to break the lucrative Portuguese monopoly of East Indian trade. The Portuguese were soon dislodged, and the European desire for profit and power made religious rivalry insignificant; indeed, by the middle of the eighteenth century religious rivalry had assumed the pronounced character of a political and economic struggle.

For over two hundred years, however, the Western powers remained confined to coastal commerce, and acquired only small territorial possessions in Asia because at this time the Mughals in India, the Mings and Manchus in China, and the Safavis in Persia ruled prosperous and powerful states. These Asian states were strong land powers with limited interest in maritime activities. This was especially true of the Mughals, who had come to India by land from the northwest and did not appreciate the danger to their security from the sea, or the importance of maritime power. When they did realize their mistake it was too late; they had become too weak even on land to reverse the process. The early Europeans came to India as traders, not as invaders, which possibly concealed the emerging trend in their activities for some time, but it seems incredible that the Mughals, who were so jealous of the integrity of their Empire, should have failed to detect it. The era of the great Mughals ended after the death of Aurangzeb in 1707 and throughout the eighteenth century local powers continued to decline. In due course, this led to the European domination of India and the industrial and technological advance of the West.

The Mughal period was in many respects a glorious period of Indian history, and the Mughals devoted much attention to art and culture, but they completely neglected practical and secular learning, especially the sciences. Throughout their long rule, no institution was established comparable to the modern university, although early India had world-famous centres of learning, such as Taxila, Nalanda, and Kanchi. There were flourishing universities in mediaeval Europe, as in other parts of the Islamic world, some of which had been in existence for some centuries. The University of Paris, which became the model not only for the universities of France but also for Oxford and Cambridge, had an organized pattern and legal status by the early thirteenth century. By the seventeenth century, a number of universities had come into existence in Europe. These universities nurtured intellectualism and laid the foundations of Western scientific culture through disciplined thinking, systematic investigation, and free discussion of knowledge. What is significant is that the European university had borrowed freely from the ancient Asian and Islamic models, which really were a part of the Mughal inheritance. Although their court was frequented by European visitors, the Mughals took no interest in European knowledge and technological accomplishments. Akbar received many European missionaries, and Ibadat Khana discussed religion and theology with them and protected them against the fanatic mullas. Christian missionaries at Akbar's Court came fully equipped, having learned Persian and read the Quran, and repeatedly had the edge in discussion over the Muslim mullas who argued with intense faith but with no knowledge of their opponents' holy book. Neither the nobles nor the mullas was stirred into learning Latin and investigating the Bible. Nor did Akbar show any curiosity in European science and philosophy, although both Hindus and Muslims had made notable scientific contributions in the past. Akbar was presented with printed books and a printing press, yet even the Indian classics were first printed by Europeans. It is, therefore, not surprising that during the period of European struggle for power, India was in a state of unparalleled decline, which not only made it possible for the Europeans to pursue their rivalries at will but also to do so with unique success.

The Mughals' power was gone, and a long trail of political upheavals followed. Intellectual inertia, already in evidence, became the prominent feature of Indian society, and the country lapsed into chaos, anarchy, and confusion. Eighteenth century India, in contrast to renaissant Europe, was so weak that it had little control over its affairs. It could not even tip the balance in favour of one of the European contenders struggling for power over Indian territory. It was the British who eventually triumphed in this contest, although it was the French who first conceived of European hegemony over Indian rulers.

In this struggle for power, technology, rather than diplomacy, played a decisive role. In purely military terms, the West won command of the East because of two things—ships and, more important, gunpowder.[3] To these could be added military organization and strategy. Superior armoury soon bred a military mentality and an aggressive policy. Immunity from retaliatory action led, at times, to unbridled tyranny. The West developed the bronze gun out of the bell-founding industry. Spain and Portugal, the first considerable ocean-goers of the times, borrowed northern European technology and met the cost of production from their overseas trade. England entered the arena later, successfully substituted cast iron for bronze, and, with the newer and cheaper technique, asserted her supremacy over others. By 1600 England was not only self-sufficient in artillery but also exported guns profitably. About the same time, France, and a little later Germany, entered the gun-making industry and eventually surpassed the English lead. Asians did not achieve any comparable results but fell farther and farther behind, and it was not until the middle of this century that they began to catch up with Europe in the race for arms.

Whilst the British were struggling for political supremacy in India, European scholars began an investigation into Indian literature and heritage. Some of these scholars were inspired by the spirit of inquiry, others by utilitarian ends, but they all began to explore India's past by working backwards from its current phase to its earliest one. They also began, understandably, by learning the languages spoken in the areas where they carried on their commercial and political activities. They soon became familiar with Persian, the court language of Mughal India, through which modern Europe first became acquainted with Indian literature and religion. It was only later that efforts were made to gain knowledge of the ancient classical language of India, Sanskrit, and finally of the vedic literature and the early civilization.

Discounting the mythical Sighelmus alleged to have been sent by Alfred on a pilgrimage to the shrine of St. Thomas at Mailapur, the first Englishman to visit India was a Jesuit priest, Thomas Stevens. He arrived in Goa in 1579 and was one of the first Europeans in modern times to study Indian languages seriously. He published a Konkani grammar, and in 1615 a remarkable poem entitled *Kristana Purana,* which was the story of the Bible intended for Indian converts to Christianity. He was a great admirer of the Marathi language, which he described as "a jewel among pebbles."

At about the same time, a Dutchman, Jan Huyghen Van Linschoten, published his *Itineratio* in 1595–1596 in which he referred to the imprisonments and tortures inflicted upon Indians by the Portuguese Inquisition. A Florentine merchant, Filippo Sassetti, who studied at the University of Pisa for six years (1568–1574) and lived at Goa for five years (1583–1588), collected a wide variety of data on India. Most of the letters in which his information was recorded deal with meteorological observations, but others deal with Indian folklore, science, and medicine. His interest in pharmaceutical texts awakened his interest in Sanskrit. He was, perhaps, the first person to declare that some relationship existed between Sanskrit and the principal languages of Europe.

Until the last quarter of the eighteenth century, several other isolated missionaries and travellers acquired certain, chiefly impressionistic knowledge of Indian literature, language, and contemporary life but few made any serious attempt to understand Indian civilization. They accepted Indian culture at its face value without investigating its origins or studying it in its proper historical perspective.

Those Europeans who came to India at the time were a motley crowd of merchants and medicos, envoys and ecclesiastics, soldiers and sailors, adventurers and fortune seekers. They arrived from different countries by different routes with different motives; some eccentrics, such as Tom Coryat even walked all the way from Aleppo to Ajmer. Seeking pecuniary gain or excitement, these early Europeans were generally untutored and ill-equipped to either transmit or absorb ideas. The English were no exception. Trade, and only trade, was their object and they endeavoured to attain it, as merchants still do, not necessarily by sharing the beliefs of their customers or even by understanding their culture, but by making themselves agreeable to them. Consequently, they adopted Indian habits in food, often married Indian women, and respected Indian customs, beliefs, and authority. As traders they were concerned only with making money, regardless of scruples, morality, and learning. India was an "El Dorado" for enterprising young men in search of a fortune.

The travellers who carried information about India back to Europe were inadequately informed about the geography and society of the country as a whole, and their stay, in most cases, was too brief for accurate knowledge. Moreover, like most foreign visitors, they did not bring unprejudiced minds to the alien land, and whilst they fully understood and rationalized their own shortcomings and inconsistencies, they were much too willing to believe and record, if not magnify, anything which even vaguely had the ring of the extraordinary, unfamiliar, or exciting. And the complexities of Indian society and beliefs were far too paradoxical to lend themselves to easy comprehension. Furthermore, the impressions and the narratives of European travellers had unfortunately become stereotyped, and each visitor referred to practically the same things, as if he had come to India with preconceived ideas and was merely looking for reinforcement. Whilst some useful information reached Europe through these travellers, references to the exotic and romantic East became frequent and indiscriminate in European literature. At best, seventeenth-century India to the European was the India of the great Mughals, depicted with extravagant imagination. For instance Dryden's popular drama, *Aurengzebe* published in 1675, portrayed the Mughal Court quite fantastically. Unrealiable as these narratives were, they succeeded in projecting a picture of India in Europe which has never fully worn off.

It is significant that although the early European travellers were imbued with an anti-Islamic bias, they usually accepted the fanatic Muslim point of view about the Hindus, presumably because they shared the Judaic tradition with Muslims, knew a good deal about Islam which was no longer so strange by that time, and also because they were taken by the splendour of the Mughal Court. They looked upon the Hindus as degraded and superstitious. This attitude was reinforced by missionaries like Abbé Dubois, who focused their attention almost exclusively on the darker side of Hinduism, and sought to replace it with their own faith.

Alexander Pope's (1688–1744) couplet is typical of the British response to Indian ideas as they understood them:

> Lo the poor Indian whose
> untutored mind.
> Sees God in clouds or hears
> him in the wind.

The French response to India was somewhat different from that of the British, possibly because many of the French travellers who came to India were known for their literary taste and gave interesting accounts of their travels. J. B. Tavernier, Thévenot, Francois Bernier, and Abbé Carré concentrated on the Mughal Court and Empire in their travel accounts. Tavernier, a jewel merchant, travelled to India as many as five times between 1641 and 1668. A competent businessman, he had no education or refinement, however, and wrote more to amuse than to inform. He probably saw more of India than any other traveller in the seventeenth century, although he said little that is worth remembering; his anecdotes are childish and often offensive. Bernier is better known, for he was an educated man, and was responsible for bringing Indian ideas to some of the prominent French scholars of the day. He spent twelve years as a physician at the Mughal Court, and upon his return met the eminent French fabulist, La Fontaine, at Mme. de la Sablier's Salon, and shared his knowledge of India with him and Pascal, the philosopher and mathematician. Jean Racine (1630–1699) gave a flattering portrayal of Puru, Alexander's Indian adversary, in his *Alexandre.* A friend and disciple of Rousseau, Bernardin de Saint Pierre (1737–1814), who had lived in Mauritius for two years, wrote *Le Café de Surat* and other pieces with an Indian setting.

In 1778 a work was published dealing with Sanskrit literature, vedic legends, and doctrines, called *L'Ezour Vedam,* which created a sensation in the West by attracting the attention of Voltaire. But it was later shown to be a work faked by a European missionary, Roberto de Nobili, for the purpose of converting Hindus in the seventeenth century.[4] Earlier, Voltaire had published a tragi-comic story relating the adventures of a Hindu and his wife, as well as his *Historical Fragments on India.* Whilst

Voltaire's information on India came from unreliable sources, he believed that the West received its knowledge of astronomy, astrology, and metempsychosis from India, and he looked to India for truth with the eyes of a disillusioned European.

Several other well-known French writers of the Enlightenment were somewhat familiar with India. Diderot wrote several articles on Indian religion and philosophy in the *Encylopédie* of 1751. In 1770 Abbé Rayal, with the assistance of Diderot, d'Holback, and Naigon, produced the *Philosophical and Political History of the Europeans in the two Indias*.

Not long after the publication of Voltaire's works, Abbé Dubois fled France as a political refugee from the Revolution to live in India for thirty-one years. Typical of the class of people who regard themselves as charged with civilizing the heathens, and convinced of the superiority of his own civilization, he published his widely read *Hindu Manners, Customs and Ceremonies,* which, despite his laboriously collected data, is essentially a scathing criticism of Hindu belief and practices. Even if allowance is made for the Roman Catholic standards he applied to the Indian religions, many of his observations are grossly inaccurate and appear to be deliberate distortions. What is incredible, however, is that his work, despite the decisive exposition of its errors, has enjoyed almost continuous popularity in Europe, and was long accepted as a standard interpretation of Indian religions.

Jacquemont, who visited India during the reign of Ranjit Singh, wrote *Hindu Heroes and Heroines.* Lemierre's *Veuve du Malabar,* published in 1770, was epoch-making. M. de Jouy wrote the *Tipoo Sahib* and the opera, *Les Bayadères,* in 1810, which Napoleon himself attended.

Meanwhile a few missionaries had been taking a close interest in Sanskrit. In the beginning, having come first to South India, they learned Tamil or some other South Indian language. It was only after some time that they felt the need to learn Sanskrit. A German priest, Heinrich Roth (1610–1688) was the first European to produce a Sanskrit grammar, which was written in Latin and remained in manuscript form. In 1651, a Dutch preacher named Abraham Roger, who had lived at Pulicat near Madras as well as in Indonesia, published in Amsterdam *Open Door to Hidden Heathendom.* This book included about two hundred proverbs of the Sanskrit poet, Bhartrihari, from a Portuguese translation, and not only described the customs and religion of the Hindus but also mentioned the Vedas for the first time. Translated into German in 1663, it was drawn upon by Herder (1744–1813) for his *Stimmen der Volker in Liedern* (Voices of the Peoples in Songs). After the stories of the *Pancatantra,* this work was the first Indian literature to become known in Germany. A German Jesuit, Johann Ernst Hanxleden, who worked in Malabar from 1699 to 1732, compiled a Sanskrit grammar in Latin and one in Malayalam. His Sanskrit grammar also remained unpublished but was used by the Austrian missionary, Fra Paolino de St. Bartholomeo (whose real name was Johannes Philippus Wessdin), "undeniably the most important of the missionaries who worked at the earliest opening-up of Indian literature."[3] He lived on the Malabar coast from 1776 to 1789 and was well acquainted with Indian literature, languages, and religions. He wrote two Sanskrit grammars in Rome in 1790 and several learned treatises. Another missionary, Coeurdoux, suggested in 1767 that there was a kinship between Sanskrit and European languages. He reached this conclusion with the help of Maridas Pillai of Pondicherry. It appears that he was quite familiar with Sanskrit literature. He correctly describes its system of grammar and refers to the *Amarakosa* and other Sanskrit dictionaries as well as to the Indian system of poetics, called *alamkara.* He also describes the six systems of Indian philosophy, in addition to Buddhism and Jainism.

The English were most closely bound in political and cultural relations with India, and although they initiated a systematic investigation of Sanskrit literature, most of the work on the subject was done on the continent, particularly in France and Germany. Perhaps the Anglo-Indian political association, enforced and unequal as it was and often clouded by mutual distrust and fear, was not conducive to a deeper British appreciation of the Indian heritage. Morevoer, the remarkable practical qualities of the British in commerce, military organization, and administration, and their faculty for recognizing and making use of opportunities, inevitably, although not inordinately, subordinated their cultural and intellectual sensitivities. Hence it was administrative needs which initially induced the British to study Sanskrit.

Despite the loss of countless texts, today there are-scores of thousands of Sanskrit manuscripts in various libraries. When Alexander came, there existed in India an ancient literature far richer than that in Greece at the time. The first scholar to publish a real dissertation on Sanskrit learning was Alexander Dow, in a preface to his history of India, which appeared in Europe in three volumes in 1768. Whilst his history leaned heavily on Ferishta, his Preface carried a significant account of Hindu religion and customs. He pointed out the existence of innumerable ancient Sanskrit texts, observing that the authentic history of the Hindus went back farther than that of any other nation.

The turning point in the European discovery of India's past came during Warren Hastings' Governor-Generalship. By this time the British had gained control of Bengal and their commercial interests in India depended on their ability to eliminate rampant corruption in their own ranks and to rationalize the administration of their Indian possessions. The merchants of the East India Company were generally greedy and corrupt, filling their own pockets by cheating the Company and the Indians. Their contributions to India were political anarchy, economic exploitation, cruel taxation, extravagant wars, unjust intervention, and forged treaties. London was appalled at this tarnishing of the British name.

Born in 1732, Warren Hastings was the son of a clergyman from an old and once wealthy family. He went to India at the age of seventeen as a writer in the Company's service and, through his varied experiences in trade and administration, he acquired an exceptional knowledge of the Indian mind and temperament. Well-disposed towards Indian literature and culture, he stressed the need for the study of Sanskrit, albeit mainly for utilitarian reasons. Hastings also realized that British supremacy in India could rest only on a proper understanding of Indian religion and culture. Although he was impeached for acts of corruption and tyranny, he gave the beginnings of a sound administration to British India. For the codification of the laws of the land and for the efficient operation of the administration, it was essential to gain an accurate knowledge of the ancient Sanskrit legal texts. Hastings had the Indian law books compiled by the local learned pundits under the title of *Vivadarnavasetu* (meaning bridge over the ocean of dispute) but there was no one who could translate the resultant text into English. Hence, a Persian translation was made and an English translation of this was published in London in 1776. This was entitled *A Code of Gentoo Laws by* N. B. Halhead, a schoolmate of

Sir William Jones.[6] This second-hand translation introduced the study of Sanskrit philology.

The first Englishman who, urged by Warren Hastings, acquired a knowledge of Sanskrit was Charles Wilkins (1749–1836). He was a founding member of the Asiatic Society of Bengal and had acquired considerable knowledge of Sanskrit at Varanasi (Banaras). He subsequently became the first librarian of the famous India Office Library at London, then known as the East India Company Library. He is described by his contemporaries as the first European who really understood Sanskrit, and he gave Europe its earliest acquaintance with actual Sanskrit writing. H. T. Colebrooke, a founder of Sanskrit scholarship in Europe, said that Wilkins had more information and knowledge respecting the Hindus than any other foreigner since the days of Pythagoras. In 1785 Wilkins published an English translation of the *Bhagavad Gita*—the first Sanskrit work rendered directly into a European language. Later, Wilkins published the *Hitopadesa* (1787) and the Sakuntala episode from the *Mahabharata* (1795). These Sanskrit works were translated principally to familarize European intellectuals with Indian ideas; their literary merit was a subordinate consideration, if at all. Thirteen years later, in 1808, Wilkins' Sanskrit grammar appeared, using Devanagari type (which he himself had carved and cast) for the first time in Europe. Wilkins also initiated the study of Indian inscriptions and translated some of them into English.

It was, however, the celebrated Orientalist, Sir William Jones (1746–1794), who pioneered Sanskrit studies. He came to India as a puisne judge of the Supreme Court at Calcutta in September 1783, having already gained competence in Asian learning, especially Persian and Arabic, and having formed a deep appreciation of Indian culture. He had ardently sought the Indian appointment, and had waited in uneasy uncertainty for five years, first, in order to make enough money to be able to retire early and conduct his researches without financial worries, and second, to "give the finishing stroke to his Oriental knowledge." He lived in India for about ten years, until his premature death, and was extremely happy there. He said that, although he was never unhappy in England, for it was not in his nature to be unhappy, he was never really content until he was settled in India.

His admiration for Indian thought and culture was almost limitless. "It gave me inexpressible pleasure to find myself in the midst of so noble an amphitheatre, almost encircled by the vast regions of Asia, which has even been esteemed the nurse of sciences, the scene of glorious actions, fertile in the productions of human genius, abounding in natural wonders, and infinitely in the forms of religion and government in the laws, manners, customs, and languages, as well in the features and complexions, of men."[7] Even at a time when Hinduism was at a low ebb and it was quite fashionable to run it down, he held it in great esteem. Whilst Jones believed in Christ and Christianity, he was attracted to the Hindu concepts of the non-duality of God, as interpreted by Sankara, and the transmigration of the human soul. The latter theory he found more rational than the Christian doctrine of punishment and eternity of pain. Writing to his erstwhile pupil and close friend, Earl Spencer, in 1787, after three years in India, he said: "I am no Hindu; but I hold the doctrine of the Hindus concerning a future state to be incomparably more rational, more pious, and more likely to deter men from vice, than the horrid opinions, inculcated on punishments without end."[8]

Although he had nourished political ambitions, which fortunately for Oriental learning did not materialize, and although he was a professional barrister, Jones was essentially a scholar. He was a brilliant Orientalist and linguist, for whom his eminent contemporaries, such as Burke, Gibbon, Sheridan, Garrick, and Johnson, had great respect. Literary London admired him so much that he was elected a member of the Club, Samuel Johnson's immortal coterie, a month before even Boswell was given that honour. He was made a Fellow of the Royal Society in April 1772 when he was learning Sanskrit during his initial years in India. His interest in botany was much more than mere pleasure; it was stimulated by his deep religious feelings, for in every flower, every leaf, and every berry he could see the attributes of God more eloquently illustrated than in the wisdom of man.

He learned Sanskrit with the assistance and encouragement of Charles Wilkins before the latter left India in 1786. In January 1784, a few months after his arrival in Calcutta, Jones founded the famous Asiatic Society of Bengal, of which he remained President until his death. The object of the Society was to inquire into the history, culture, literature, and science of Asia; it has done enormous work to advance the knowledge of Asian civilization both in India and abroad. It was in the journal of this Society, *Asiatick Researches,* that the initial attempts were made to unearth India's past. Within three years Jones became so proficient in Sanskrit that he could converse familiarly with Indian pundits. In 1789, five years after his arrival in India, he published in Calcutta his translation of the celebrated Sanskrit drama, *Abhijnana Sakuntala,* by Kalidasa.[9] This work became so popular that it went into five English editions in less than twenty years. In 1791 a German translation of the English version was made by George Förster, the world traveller and revolutionary. This inspired men like Herder and Goethe. Many other translations of the *Sakuntala* were made in the first half of the nineteenth century from Jones' English version, and later from the Sanskrit original.

In 1792 Jones brought out an English translation of Jayadeva's *Gita Govinda,* and published in Calcutta, Kalidasa's *Ritusamhara* in the original; this was the first Sanskrit text ever printed. Of greater importance, however, was his translation of the well-known legal text of ancient India, the *Manusmriti,* which was published posthumously in 1794 under the title *Institutes of Hindu Law or the Ordinances of Manu.* Three years later, in 1797, a German translation of the book appeared. Not only did Jones produce excellent translations but he also wrote original hymns to Indian deities, which are lasting monuments of Anglo-Indian literature. By the time of his death, his reputation as a Sanskrit scholar had eclipsed all his many other accomplishments.

Jones was the first British scholar to definitely assert the genealogical connection of Sanskrit with Greek and Latin, and possibly with Persian, German, and Celtic. In his third annual discourse of the Asiatic Society on 2 February 1786, he declared that the Sanskrit language was of a wonderful structure, more perfect than the Greek, more copious than the Latin, and more exquisitely refined than either, yet bearing to both of them a stronger affinity, both in the roots of verbs and in the forms of grammar, than could possibly have been produced by accident. All three languages must have come from some common source.[10]

The greatest influence of Jones' work was, of course, on the study of Oriental learning itself. The interest in Indian literature awakened by Jones and Wilkins, led to scholars searching for Sanskrit manuscripts "with the avidity of explorers seeking Australian goldfields."[11] Of those scholars, the most outstanding was Henry Thomas Colebrooke (1765–1837), who put the study of Sanskrit on a scientific footing. "Had he lived in Germany," says Max Müller, "we should long ago have seen his statue in his native place, his name written in the letters of gold on the walls of acadamies; we should have heard of Colebrooke jubilees and Colebrooke scholarships. In England if any notice is taken of the discovery of Sanskrit—a discovery in many respects equally important, in some even more important, than the revival of Greek scholarship in the fifteenth century—we may possibly hear the popular name of Sir William Jones and his classical translation of Sakuntala; but of the infinitely more important achievements of Colebrooke, not one word."[12]

Colebrooke entered the service of the East India Company in 1782 and left India in 1815 at the age of fifty. During this period he had a distinguished career as an administrator and lawyer, but his claim to eminence is mainly based upon his being "the founder and the father of true Sanskrit scholarship in Europe."

He pursued his study of Sanskrit most energetically with the assistance of some excellent Indian instructors. A man of extraordinary industry and clear intellect, Colebrooke published many texts, translations, and essays dealing with practically all aspects of Sanskrit literature. His writings included works on Indian law, philosophy, religion, grammar, astronomy, and arithmetic. In 1797–1798, he published his first four-volume translation, *A Digest of Hindu Law on Contracts and Successions,* which immediately established his reputation as the best Sanskrit scholar of his day. His famous *Essay on the Vedas,* published in 1805, the same year as his *Sanskrit Grammar,* gave the first definite and reliable information on the sacred Hindu texts. In 1808 he published a critical edition of the *Amarakosa,* a Sanskrit lexicon. By this time Colebrooke had become President of the Court of Appeal, a high and lucrative position, but demanding; nevertheless, he continued his Sanskrit studies.

Unlike Jones, Colebrooke's interests lay chiefly in scientific literature. His love of mathematics and astronomy stirred his intellectual curiosity to investigate Indian work in these disciplines. Although some scholars such as Burrow and Strachey had preceded him, it was entirely through his work that scientists were able to form a clear idea of the Indian achievement in mathematics, especially indeterminate analysis. But it is chiefly for his philological researches and services to Indian jurisprudence that Colebrooke is remembered.

Apart from his writings, he collected a wide variety of Sanskrit manuscripts and presented them to the East India Company in 1818. This collection is one of the most valuable treasures of the India Office Library in London. In 1822 he founded the Royal Asiatic Society in London which has since done much to promote Oriental learning in Europe. He published many of his most valuable papers in this Society's *Transactions.*

An eminent English contemporary of Colebrooke, Horace Hayman Wilson came to India in the Medical Service of the East India Company and became deeply interested in Sanskrit studies. He pursued his interest with vigour and industry, and published his elegant translation of Kalidasa's *Meghaduta* in 1813; this made both an immediate and a lasting impact on European readers, and it has since been translated into many languages. In 1819, Wilson published his Sanskrit dictionary and he translated the *Visnu Parana* into English. In 1832, he became the first occupant of the Boden Chair of Sanskrit at Oxford and this provided him a fuller opportunity to advance the study of Indology. By this time, however, Indian studies in England had lost their earlier vigour. The British, now masters of India and the supreme maritime power of the day, were less inclined to learn from aliens; they listened to Macaulay instead.

Two professors of Sanskrit, Wilson at Oxford and Lee at Cambridge, bemoaned the fact that not much attention was paid at their respective universities to Sanskrit, a language "capable of giving a soul to the objects of sense, and a body to the abstractions of metaphysics." The best philological works published in England were generally translations from the German.[13]

France began to take a closer interest in Indian learning and commenced a systematic investigation by the beginning of the eighteenth century. In 1718, Bignan, the librarian of the French king, asked travellers to purchase or make a copy of every book of note, as well as grammars and dictionaries available in India or in regions where Indian culture prevailed. In response, many French officials, residents, missionaries, and visitors began to acquire Indian texts. The missionary, Calmette, obtained copies of the *Rig Veda,* the *Yajur Veda,* and the *Sama Veda,* although he failed to get a copy of the fourth Veda, the *Atharva Veda.* The *Rig Veda* was first sent to Paris in 1731, together with its *Aitareya Brahmana.* Other Sanskrit books, such as Gangesa's *Tattvacintamani,* which was very popular at the time in the southern and eastern regions of India, together with some Tamil books, a Tamil grammar, and a Tamil dictionary, were also sent to France about the same time by the Italian Jesuit, Beschi. A number of books were obtained from Bengal. Pere Pons, stationed in Chandernagore, succeeded in collecting main works in the different branches of classical Sanskrit literature. His catalogue containing one hundred and sixty-eight entries was astonishingly accurate for its time. Pons, who himself knew Sanskrit, had been assisted in the selection of his manuscripts by competent Indian scholars. His collection included a Sanskrit grammar which he had written in Latin, following the *Samkshiptasara,* and a Latin translation of the *Amarakosa.* Because of the labours of these men the first printed catalogue of Sanskrit literature was published in Paris in 1739. The following year, Pons published in a letter, which has been repeatedly reproduced since, the first sound report on Sanskrit literature.

Whilst the difficulties of reading these manuscripts held up progress. French scholars learned something of Indian thought and history through Arabic, Persian, Chinese, Greek, and Latin works. The collection of Indian materials continued, however, and Joseph Deguignes accumulated as much material as was possible from non-Indian sources. Strictly speaking, Deguignes was not an Indologist; he was essentially a Sinologist who wrote a vast history of the Huns, but he gathered remarkably accurate knowledge about India. He was perhaps the first modern European to show, through his study of Chinese sources, the wide influence of Buddhism on Central Asian and Chinese peoples, and to give a tentative translation of a part of an ancient Chinese Buddhist text, the *Sutra in Forty-two Articles.* Still greater was his accomplishment in fixing the basis of Indian chronology. In this he had received invaluable help from an Indian scholar of Tamil Maridas Pillai of Pondicherry, who knew Latin and French well. Both these contributions are extremely significant, and are worthy of much greater recognition than has hitherto been accorded to Deguignes. Possibly because of their background of English education, Indians have exhibited equal indifference to the contribution of Maridas Pillai. "All French scholars who visited Pondicherry during that period were indebted to him for most of the valuable information. He apparently played a part in the discovery of original links between Sanskrit on the one hand, and Latin and Greek on the other. The astronomer Le Gentil, one of the first who gave substantial account of Indian astronomy, wrote that he himself had been a grateful pupil of Maridas Pillai and of other Tamil scholars of Pondicherry in that matter."[14] Some of his translations and analyses of Indian texts were profitably used by French scholars. For instance his translation of the *Bagavatam* was sent to Deguignes before its publication, and it was in this manuscript that the latter found the dynastic lists of the Suryavamsa and the Somavamsa kings who had reigned since Parikshit, including Chandragupta which Deguignes immediately recognized as the Sandrokottos of the Greeks. This synchronism was published in the *Mémoires de l'Academie des Inscriptions et Belles Lettres;* this same synchronism was rediscovered by Sir William Jones, who is generally given the credit for identifying it. Whilst Jones may not have been the real discoverer of Indian chronology, he indeed popularized it.

At about this time, Anquétil du Perron (1731–1805) visited India and later prepared the first European translation in Latin of the Upanishads from the literal Persian version made for the Mughal prince, Dara Shikoh, in 1636. As a young man of twenty-three, du Perron, whilst working in the Bibliothéque de Roi at Paris in 1754, saw a fragment of a mysterious manuscript which the Bodleian Library at Oxford had acquired in 1718 and which was reputed to be a book by Zoroaster. Du Perron was so moved by it that he at once decided to visit India and learn the language so that he could read it. He arrived at Pondicherry in 1754. This was the period when the English and the French were engaged in a bitter conflict for supremacy in India and du Perron was caught in it. He finally managed to learn Persian at Surat, and returned home via England in 1762. Whilst studying at Surat, he discovered the *Avesta,* and published his *Zend-Avesta* in three volumes in 1771. He also published an account of his travels, *Voyage aux Grandes Indes,* in 1781.

Du Perron acquired the Persian manuscript of the Upanishads in

1775 from M. Gentil, the French Resident at Fyzabad in North Bengal, and he translated them into French word for word, in the Persian word-order. Realizing his error, he set out to make a Latin translation of fifty Upanishads. He finished the work in 1796, but it was not printed until 1801–1802 in Paris. It is remarkable that this translation of the Upanishads, which had so profound an influence on European thought, was an incidental product of a venture undertaken for an altogether different purpose.

With Wilkins' version of the *Bhagavad Gita,* and du Perron's translation of the Upanishads, entitled *Oupenekhat,* the fundamental texts of Indian philosophy were available to Western thinkers. Du Perron did not know Sanskrit but, despite the imperfections of his translations, it made an important contribution to European knowledge. It caught the attention of the German philosopher, Schelling, and later of Schopenhauer, who in 1813 praised it as "a production of the highest human wisdom" and adopted an upanishadic motto, "whosoever knows God, himself becomes God."

For many decades, attention in France had been centered on China, about which much was heard from the sympathetic reports of Jesuit missionaries, mariners, and merchants; on Siam with whom France had come into diplomatic contact; and on Western and Central Asia, with which Europe had been closely linked historically and culturally. To Europe, China appeared culturally unique and politically powerful. Thus China came to influence European life in many respects, ranging from religious thought to opera. Hebrew had been taught regularly at the Collége Royal, later called College de France, since its inception in the sixteenth century. Syriac, Arabic, Persian, and Turkish were also actively cultivated. Consequently, when France awakened to Indian literature, there was already an existing tradition of learning into which Indology could easily fit. French possessions in India, and later domination over Indochina, provided further incentive for French interest.

A determined French scholar of Persian studies, Leonard de Chézy had become a passionate admirer of William Jones' translation of the *Sakuntala.* He was seized by the desire to read the masterpiece in its original. With the help of Pons' grammar of the *Amarakosa,* and later of Wilkins' translation of the *Hitopadesa,* he began learning Sanskrit. By sheer perseverance and remarkable ingenuity he was finally able to realize his dream—to read and even publish, the text of the *Sakuntala.*

Leonard de Chézy, like many contemporary French thinkers, realized that Europe should be acquainted with the achievements of Asian nations. Consequently, there developed in France an influential body of opinion advocating the study of India as well as China. As a result in 1814, a Chair of Sanskrit and a Chair of Chinese were created for Chézy and Abel-Rémusat respectively. These Chairs, a radical innovation in academic life, were set up between the disasters of 1814 and Waterloo, when the whole nation was undergoing political unrest and military conflicts. Only a nation like France, whose intellectual and cultural attitudes dominated most of Europe during the seventeenth and eighteenth centuries, could turn its attention to scholarship at such a time.

Although Abel-Rémusat was a Sinologist, he made important contributions to Indology by collecting Chinese data on India and translating the account of Fa-hsien's travels. Both de Chézy and Abel-Rémusat died of cholera in 1832, but their traditions did not die with them. Abel-Rémusat's successor was Stanislas Julien, who furthered research on Indian antiquity through Chinese documents. De Chézy was followed by several outstanding pupils. Amongst these were two Germans: Franz Bopp, the founder of the comparative philology of Indo-European languages, and August Schlegel. His French pupils included Loiseleur Deslongchamps, who published the *Manusmriti* and the *Amarakosa,* and Langlois, who was responsible for the first translations made directly from the manuscripts of the *Rig Veda* and the *Harivamsa.* But the most important of all was Eugene Burnouf, who in turn had many eminent students, including Max Müller.

Eugène Burnouf's father, Jean-Louis Burnouf, had been a student of de Chézy, and was an able classical scholar who was amongst the first to realize that much progress could be made in the morphology of European classical languages by a comparison with Sanskrit. Eugène Burnouf learned Sanskrit not so much to study philology as to investigate the depths of Indian culture, as well as comprehend hitherto unknown languages and the civilizations associated with them. With the help of Sanskrit he was able to decipher Pali and discover the rules of Avestan and its relationship with Sanskrit. His *An Essay on Pali,* published in 1826 jointly with Christian Lassen, who was later to become a leading German Indologist, led to the recognition of a relationship between Pali and Sanskrit. Burnouf not only researched classical Sanskrit literature, but also the fundamental vedic literature, which had remained unused in the Royal Library for about a century. He translated the *Bhagavata Purana* into French in 1840, and devoted himself to the study of Indian Buddhism. Making use of the work done by Deguignes and Abel-Rémusat on Chinese sources, he realized the importance of Buddhism in the expansion of Indian culture abroad. He made a comparative study of Buddhist texts in Pali and Sanskrit. He wrote his famous *Introduction à l' Histoire du Bouddhisme Indien* in 1844, and published *Lotus de la Bonne Loi,* an annotated translation of the *Saddharama-Pundarika,* the most important Mahayana text. His work thus led to a great advance in the study of Indian literature and culture in Europe. He succeeded de Chézy as Professor of Sanskrit from 1832 until his untimely death in 1853. According to him, the publications of the Asiatic Society of Bengal were widely sold and read in France, and people frequently bought copies of Indian classics that were available in various languages. He also refers to the exchange of learned publications between France and India.

Meanwhile, in 1822, the Société Asiatique, the first of its kind in Europe, had been founded in Paris. Many other French scholars had now come to take a deep interest in Indian thought. One of Burnouf's colleagues, the philosopher and translator of Aristotle, Barthélémy de Saint-Hilaire, who was later swept up to the Ministry of Foreign Affairs by the peculiar current of politics, published valuable studies on the Nyaya and Samkhya systems of Indian philosophy. Burnouf encouraged his pupil Ariel to study Tamil and its literature. Ariel collected many Tamil manuscripts and translated part of the *Tirukkural* and the poems of Auvaiyar. Burnouf helped Max Müller to publish the *Rig Veda,* and Rudolph Roth and Adolph Régnier to interpret it. The Piedmontese, Gaspere Gorresio, disciple of Barthélémy de Saint-Hilaire, published in Paris a monumental edition of the *Ramayana,* in five volumes, with financial assistance from the King of Sardinia. He also published two Italian translations of the work.

Fauche translated the *Ravanavadha Mahakavya* of Bhartrihari, the *Gitagovinda* of Jayadeva, all the works of Kalidasa, the *Dasakumaracarita* of Dandin, the *Sisupalavadha* of Magha, the *Mricchakatika* of Sudraka, the entire *Ramayana,* and the first nine parvas of the *Mahabharata* into French. Having read Fauche's translation of the *Ramayana* in 1863, the French historian Michelet said: "That year will always remain a dear and cherished memory; it was the first time I had the opportunity to read the great sacred poem of India, the divine *Ramayana.* If anyone has lost the freshness of emotion, let him drink a long draught of life, and youth from that deep chalice."

With the creation of the École des Hautes Études in 1868, a new centre for the study of Indology was opened up. Amongst many other Sanskritists who flourished in France were scholars such as Paul Régnaud, whose chief work was on Sanskrit rhetoric and on *Bharatiya Natyasastra,* Hauvette-Besnault, Auguste Barth, Abel Bergaigne, and Emile Senart. Barth devoted himself for more than forty years to the study of Indian religions in their historical perspective and to the criticism of works published in every field of Indology. Bergaigne wrote an epoch-making work, *The Vedic Religion according to the Hymns of the Rig-Veda.* This was followed by other works, of which the *Researches on the Samhita of the Rig-Veda* is most noteworthy. He brought about a revolution in the realm of religious history by his tireless work on the *Rig Veda.* The vedic hymns, which had been interpreted as songs of worship dedicated to the forces of nature, came to reveal through his interpretation an artificial pedantic religion surcharged with liturgy and rituals. Bergaigne founded the teaching of Sanskrit at the Sorbonne. Although at first purely a vedic and Sanskrit scholar, Bergaigne later turned to the study of Indian civilization and to the history of Indochina. Many inscriptions in impeccable Sanskrit, frequently elaborated in kavya style, were found in Cambodia and on the eastern coast of the Indochinese Peninsula. Bergaigne and Barth deciphered and translated many of these. With the help of such data, a part of the history of Champa was disclosed.

French scholars preferred to study Indian civilization in its broader perspective, including its phase of foreign expansion, through non-Indian sources. Foucaux, Professor of Sanskrit at the Collège de France, and Leon Féér worked on Buddhist subjects from Sanskrit and Tibetan works. The former published the *Lalitavistara* in Tibetan and French, and the latter translated many texts from Sanskrit, Pali, Tibetan, Mongolian, and Chinese.

With the increasing interest in the archaeological remains of Indochina, Indian art also attracted French attention. At the beginning of the nineteenth century, Langles compiled his comprehensive *The Monuments of Hindustan.* Later, Emile Guimet founded, first in Lyons and later in Paris, a special museum of history of religions, Musée Guimet, which became a world-renowned museum of Indian and East Asian art and archaeology.

Since every major Asian country had been in the closest possible contact with India in the past, an understanding of Indian culture was essential to appreciate other neighbouring civilizations. So in addition to their interest in Indian civilization or in Sanskrit, the French need to evaluate Indochinese society and culture led them back to India, and to Central Asia. In Khotan, Dutreuil de Rhins bought a manuscript written on birch bark in Kharoshthi script. It was a Buddhist work, containing a middle Indian version of the *Dharmapada.* It was studied and published by Emile Senart. He published a new edition of Asoka's inscriptions, and of those found at Nasik and Karle. He edited the Pali grammar of Kaccayana and the *Mahavastu,* and wrote the *Essay on the Legend of Buddha,* in which he tried to show how the Buddhists introduced into the life story of the Buddha many elements taken from the saga of Vishnu-Mahapurusha.

The discovery of Dutreuil de Rhin's manuscript was the first in a series of finds. Since the end of the nineteenth century, a number of competent French scholars of Asian history and culture have undertaken historical explorations. Amongst the first of these were four friends of slightly different ages, Sylvain Lévi, Alfred Foucher, Edouard Chavannes, and Louis Finot. Edouard Chavannes was a Sinologist, but he contributed much to Indology through his studies on Chinese pilgrims, Chinese inscriptions of *Bodhgaya,* and the Chinese renderings of Buddhist stories and legends. However, his work cannot be separated from that of Sylvain Lévi.

In 1894 Sylvain Lévi, a former pupil of Bergaigne, succeeded Foucaux to the Chair of Sanskrit at the College de France, at the age of thirty-one. Earlier he had done field work in India, mainly in Nepal, looking for inscriptions and manuscripts, He was devoted to the study of Hindu-Buddhist literature and texts. He first published *The Indian Theatre* and then *Doctrine of the Sacrifice of the Brahmanas.* It was his findings in Nepal and his collaboration with Chavannes which finally led Levi to Buddhist studies. Having learned both Tibetan and Chinese, he was able to correct the Sanskrit texts he rediscovered, such as *Mahayanasutralankara* by Asanga, *Trinisika* and *Vimsatika* by Vasubandhu, and *Mahakarmavibhanga,* by checking them against their Tibetan and Chinese versions. With the help of the linguist, Antoine Meillet, Lévi also deciphered the Kuchean language. He found fragments of a Kuchean poem very similar to the *Karmavibhanga,* the sculptural illustrations of which he also later noticed in the famous Buddhist temple, Borobudur, in Java. Another French scholar, Paul Pelliot, in 1908 discovered many fragments of Indian texts in Central Asia.[15]

Albert Foucher came to India long before he succeeded Victor Henry at the Sorbonne. He was a devoted humanist who was greatly attracted to Sanskrit literature, its grammar, system of philosophy, and archaeology. It was he who connected the art of Buddhist India, widely known as the Gandhara School, with that of the Graeco-Roman world. He edited Maridas Pillai's French translation of the *Bhagavata Purana,* and in association with Finot, was responsible for the foundation of a research institute, the École Francaise d'Extreme-Orient, in Indochina, to study and preserve Indochinese culture. This institute helped to join Indology with Sinology. He also founded the French Archaeological Institute at Kabul, and the Franco-Japanese Mansion at Tokyo.

Many French Indologists, including Jean Przyluski and Jules Bloch, have worked in these institutions. Przyluski was attracted to Buddhist studies, linguistics, and ethnology, and wrote many books with the intention of tracing the remains of Munda, or popular, elements of non-Aryan origin in Indian documents. Jules Bloch, having first studied in Paris under Sylvain Lévi, Meillet, the famous linguist, and Vinson, the specialist in Tamil studies, came to India as a member of the École Francaise d'Extreme-Orient to learn modern Indian linguistics, where he worked with the Indian scholar, R. G. Bhandarkar. In addition to working on the grammatical structure of Dravidian languages and

Asoka's edicts, he wrote a study of the Gypsies, *Les Tsiganes,* His work, *Formation de la langue Marathe,* contributed greatly to the study of modern dialects as well as to the rigorous science of linguistics.

The Belgian scholar, Louis de la Vallée Poussin (1869–1938), who studied with Emile Senart and Sylvain Lévi, contributed three volumes to the famous *Histoire du Monde* series between 1924 and 1935. His volumes form a complete political history of pre-Muslim India and are outstanding works of scholarship.

The French, even after withdrawing from their Indian territorial possessions, retained their interest in Indian studies. With the concurrence of India they have founded a centre at Pondicherry to continue research on Indian life and culture. Louis Renou, who died in 1966, was not only the leading French Indologist of his generation, but the most distinguished in the West. His output was phenomenal, but he was chiefly a scholar of the Vedas. Amongst his many books and articles were a Veda bibliography, a Veda index, a study of Indo-Iranian mythology, a Sanskrit-French dictionary, and a study of Panini, the grammarian. Jean Filliozat, who has made outstanding contributions to Indian studies, especially to the history of Indian science, worked for many years at the Pondicherry institute. Filliozat, a qualified medical practitioner and an accomplished linguist, has the rare competence to study ancient Indian medicine. His work, *The Classical Doctrine of Indian Medicine,* must remain a standard text.

Germany, unlike Britain or even France, was not at all politically connected with India, but undertook Sanskrit studies most enthusiastically. German Indologists produced work exceptional both in quality and quantity, and they soon became the leaders in the study of Sanskrit language and literature, as well as Indian thought and culture. Although the English scholars were the first to study Sanskrit, they did not maintain their lead for long, presumably because they were mainly motivated by considerations other than scholarship. Whilst a Chair of Sanskrit, which was first held by August Schlegel, was instituted at the University of Bonn in 1818, it was not until 1832 that the first Chair of Sanskrit was created in England, at Oxford, to recognize the work done by H. H. Wilson. Later, Chairs of Sanskrit were established at London, Cambridge, and Edinburgh Universities, and by the first quarter of the nineteenth century practically every intellectual capital of Europe had initiated a full fledged study of Sanskrit.

A contemporary of Jones and Colebrooke, Alexander Hamilton (1765–1824), who had learned Sanskrit in India, inadvertently introduced the language to Germany. Returning from India to England in 1802, he was detained in France when hostilities were suddenly renewed between England and France. By a remarkable coincidence, the German poet and philosopher, Friedrich von Schlegel (1772–1829), was also in Paris. By that time German interest in Indian literature had already been awakened by the work of the English scholars. Consequently, when Schlegel met Hamilton in 1803 he quickly took advantage of the opportunity and began learning Sanskrit.

In 1808 Schlegel published *Über die Sprache und Weisheit der Inder* (On the Language and Wisdom of the Indians), and thus became the founder of Indian philology in Germany. This work contained the first direct translation from Sanskrit into German. It gave an account of Indian mythology, and of the theories of incarnation and the transmigration of soul, all illustrated by translations from Sanskrit texts. Friedrich von Schlegel declared that a real history of world literature could be written only when Asian literature was included in it. However, his brother, August Wilhelm von Schlegel (1767–1845), whose translation of Shakespeare's plays is a German classic, became an even more active Sanskrit scholar. He had learned Sanskrit under Leonard de Chézy in France, and led the extensive development of Indology in Germany. He edited and translated a number of Sanskrit texts and wrote works on philology. He edited the original text of the *Bhagavad Gita,* together with a Latin translation, and paid tribute to its unknown authors: "I shall always adore the imprints of their feet." Schlegel insisted that the critical methods evolved in classical philology, of which he was an expert, should be applied to Sanskrit texts. He established a Sanskrit press at Bonn, at a time when the printing of Sanskrit was only beginning in India. With painstaking care he drew the Devanagari types, supervised their casting, and invented important technical improvements for their printing. He composed his first text, a critical edition of the *Bhagavad Gita,* with his own hands. With the help of a subscription from Goethe, he then started it critical edition of the *Ramayana,* but only the first volume was published.

Franz Bopp (1791–1867), who had also studied Sanskrit in Paris was, unlike the Schlegel brothers, more interested in language than in literature. Professor of Sanskrit at the University of Berlin, he published *On the Conjugational System of the Sanskrit language in Comparison with that of the Greek, Latin, Persian, and Germanic languages* in 1816, thus laying the foundations for the new science of comparative philology. In addition, Bopp selected a number of episodes from the *Mahabharata,* especially that of Nala and Damayanti, translated them into German and Latin, and published them in 1819. His *Glossarium Sanscritum,* an important complement to this translation, appeared in 1830.

During the initial phase of Sanskrit studies, until about 1830, European attention was mainly focused on the classical period of Sanskrit. The vedic literature remained almost unknown except for Colebrooke's essay. Little was known of the extensive Buddhist literature. The Upanishads were better known through Anquétil du Perron's Latin translation from the Persian. The Indian linguistic genius, Ram Mohan Roy, edited the Sanskrit text of several Upanishads and published their English translation in 1816–1817.

Later, Paul Deussen (1845–1919) reinforced the study of the Upanishads with his translations and philosophical writings; he also made a selection of texts from the *Mahabharata* with philosophical commentary. Many Indologists reproduced consecutive depictions of the *Mahabharata.*[16] The pioneer in this field, however, was Hermann Jacobi, whose book, *Mahabharata-Inhaltsangabe, Index, Concordanz,* was published in 1903.

The real philological investigation of the Vedas began in 1838 with the publication of the first eight parts of the *Rig Veda* in London by a German scholar, Friedrich Rosen. Vedic literature contains many forms which became extinct in the later Sanskrit, but which existed in similar forms in Greek and other Indo-European languages. For instance, classical Sanskrit has no subjunctive mood unlike most of the older Indo-European languages, but it is common enough in vedic Sanskrit. Moreover, vedic Sanskrit has a tonic accent unlike the later Sanskrit, but similar to the Greek system. After his premature death, Rosen's work was continued by Eugene Burnouf.

One of Burnouf's students, Rudolph Roth (1821–1895), published his work on the history and literature of the Vedas in 1846. In association with another German scholar, Otto Bohtlingk (1815–1909), Roth produced the enormous Sanskrit-German dictionary, the *St. Petersburg Sanskrit Dictionary*, commonly known as the St. Petersburg Lexicon because it was published by the Russian Imperial Academy of Sciences between 1852 and 1875. Comprising almost ten thousand pages, this is the most outstanding of all the achievements of German Indology.

The most celebrated German Indologist, Friedrich Max Müller (1823–1900) continued vedic research by bringing out his splendid edition of the *Rig Veda* in six volumes between 1849 and 1874, and, from 1875 onwards, by editing the authoritative and annotated translation series, *Sacred Books of the East*, in fifty-one volumes, thirty-one of which are Indian texts. This work laid the beginnings of the study of comparative religion. It caused a tremendous sensation even in India, where a cultural renaissance and renewed national consciousness were taking place. Max Müller's translations of the Upanishads and the *Rig Veda* and other works, which have since been published in a variety of forms and editions, made Indian knowledge better known and appreciated everywhere. He guided considerable research in Indology, comparative religion, and mythology. The essays on mythology are amongst his most delightful writings.

Max Müller lived during the formative period of modern India. Armed resistance to the British rule in India had collapsed, having gained its momentum in 1857, but political opposition to British domination had become more organized and intensive. Whilst the Indian rebellion, especially the military revolt of 1857, enraged many British thinkers, such as Tennyson and Ruskin, to the point of writing unkindly of India, Max Müller remained a great friend and admirer, and his name is often Sanskritized as "Moksa-mula," meaning the root of salvation. Müller was the first European scholar to announce that India had a spiritual message for Europe, and he praised Indian thought and philosophy in almost lyrical terms: "If I were to look over the whole world to find out the country most richly endowed with all the wealth, power, and beauty that nature can bestow—in some parts a very paradise on earth—I should point to India. If I were asked under what sky the human mind has most fully developed some of the choicest gifts, has most deeply pondered on the greatest problems of life, and has found solutions of some of them which well deserve the attention even of those who have studied Plato and Kant—I should point to India…"

Max Müller first came under the influence of German Orientalists, and later studied in Paris under Burnout. He went to Oxford in 1848 to supervise the printing of his *Rig Veda,* and spent the rest of his long working life in England. An eminent classical scholar and a master of languages, including English, he was blocked from succeeding to the Chair of Sanskrit at Oxford in 1860 because he was of foreign birth and his liberal views on theological questions were unacceptable to the clergy in England. The Chair was given to Sir Monier-Williams, an important Sanskrit scholar who did a great deal to make Indian culture known in English-speaking countries. In 1868, however, Max Müller was appointed to a new Chair of Comparative Philosophy. Müller's influence on Indian studies has been extensive, deep, and lasting. For instance, when he pointed out that Alexander is not mentioned in the entire body of Sanskrit literature, historians felt compelled to revise their exaggerated assessment of his campaigns in India.[17]

By the middle of the nineteenth century, Indian texts began to appear in rapid succession, and knowledge about India was keenly sought. One of the most important works of this period was *Indische Alterthumskunde* by Christian Lassen (1800–1876), a pupil of August Wilhelm von Schlegel. The work was published in four large volumes between 1843 and 1862. Lassen, a Norwegian who regarded himself as a German, worked for many years as Professor of Sanskrit at the University of Bonn. His work, although somewhat obsolete today, is of outstanding merit.

The discovery of the vedic hymns also led to the emergence of a new science of comparative mythology. Theodor Benfey published in 1859 his edition of the Indian fable collection, the *Pancatantra,* which created a literary revolution. Benfey showed through meticulous research how the fables of India reached Europe, travelling step by step, through Pahlavi, Persian, Arabic, Hebrew, Latin, and the modern languages of Europe, till they supplied even La Fontaine with some of his most charming themes. Benfey's various Sanskrit grammars, founded as they were on the classical grammar of Panini, and his *History of Sanskrit Philology* are still important.

In 1852, A. Weber published his *History of Indian Literature* in German, the first connected historical account of Indian literature. The work was translated into English and has been printed several times. Weber brought out a second edition in 1876 which he updated by adding notes to the texts. He also opened up a new branch of Indian study through his work in 1883–1885 on the sacred writings of the Jains.

Towards the end of the nineteenth century, the literature on Indian studies had grown too vast and unwieldy for an individual scholar to master. Consequently, the need for an encyclopaedia surveying the work done in all branches of the subject was felt. *Grundriss der indoarischen Philologic und Altertumskunde* (Compendium of Indo-Aryan Philology and Antiquities) began to appear in 1897 under the general editorship of the versatile Sanskrit scholar, Georg Bühler (1837–1898), who had studied under Benfey, and published many works of his own. This was an attempt by thirty leading scholars from throughout the world to give an encyclopaedic view of the work done in the various branches of Indology. The publication was continued under the editorship of other scholars and was one of the important developments in the field of Indian studies. Later, in 1900, A. A. Macdonell, a successor of Wilson at Oxford, published *A History of Sanskrit Literature* and in 1907 M. Winternitz, Professor of Indology at Prague, brought out *A History of Indian Literature* in German.

Today almost every library in Germany has a special collection of books on India and every university has a departmental library of Indology. Six universities—Bonn, Tübingen, Munich, Göttingen, Marburg, and Hamburg—have Chairs of Sanskrit, and practically every university provides for the teaching of Sanskrit within its department of comparative linguistics. Three German universities have their own magazines on Indology.

Holland's interest in India was direct, because of her commercial and political involvements in the East Indies, but Indology did not begin in that country until the nineteenth century. During the seventeenth and eighteenth centuries, a number of Dutchmen learned modern Indian languages, but only one, Herbert de Jager of the University of Leyden, is known to have been familiar with Sanskrit. The first professor to teach Sanskrit was Hamaker at the University of Leyden, who encouraged the study of comparative linguistics. But the real foundation of Sanskrit studies was laid by his eminent pupil, Hendrik Kern, whose work evoked much interest. A Chair of Sanskrit was consequently established at the University of Leyden in 1865, and was filled by Kern. Before Kern began his professional career, he had taught in England and India. By his publications and through his pupils, several of whom became eminent Indologists, Indian studies made considerable progress in Holland. Later, Holland produced such scholars as Speyer, Vogel, Gonda, Th. P. Gabestios, Bosch, and Faddegon. Today Chairs of Sanskrit exist at Leyden, Utrecht, Amsterdam, and Groningen.

In Italy, also, there developed a keen interest in and systematic study of Indology. Italian missionaries, merchants, and mariners continuously visited India. Those who left valuable accounts of their travels included Marco Polo; Florentine Filippo Sassetti, who made the first suggestion in his letters of a possible link between Italian and Sanskrit in the sixteenth century; Nicolo Manucci; Florentine Francesco Carletti; Pietro della Valle; Giovanni Francesco Gemelli Careri, who wrote *Giro del Mondo,* one volume of which is devoted to India; and Roberto De Nobili. Indian studies in Italy did not begin, on a scientific basis, until the middle of the nineteenth century. Italian interest in Indian thought was initially inspired by German romanticism. The father of Italian Indology was the Piedmontese, Gaspare Gorresio. As soon as Italy achieved political harmony and the kingdom of Italy was formed in 1870, the first Chairs of Oriental Studies were set up. Since then Italy has produced famous Indologists from Graziadio Ascoli to Giuseppe Tucci of the present day.

Even in those small nations of Europe which were not directly concerned with India, the knowledge of ancient India spread. In Czechoslovakia, which has a long tradition of learning, Indology was to occupy a place of prominence. Czech scholars were first attracted to Indian studies through the work of a Jesuit missionary, Karel Prikryl (1718–1795), who arrived in Goa in 1748 as director of the Archbishop's seminary. During his fourteen years in India, he studied Marathi, and is reputed to have written several books. Only one of these, *Principia Linguae Brahmanicae* (The Principles of the Brahmanic Tongue), has survived; this was probably the first grammar of Konkani dialect to have been written. Inspired by Prikryl's works, Josef Dobrovski, a philologist and historian, learned Sanskrit during the last part of the eighteenth century and pointed out the similarities between many Indian and Slav words and forms. In 1812 Joseph Jungmann wrote on Indian prosody and metre, and nine years later his brother, Antonin Jungmann, published the first Sanskrit grammar in Czech.

Of the numerous comparative philologists, Joseph Zubaty made notable contributions to Sanskrit philology and to the history of vedic literature and classical Indian epic and dramatic literature. He published his *Qualitative Changes in the Final Syllable in Vedic* in 1888, and, two years later, a study of Indian metrics entitled *The Construction of Tristubh and Jagati Verses in the Mahabharata.*

Alfred Ludwig (1837–1912), Zubaty's teacher, and Moriz Winternitz (1836–1937) were the first scholars who advanced Indian studies from comparative philology to Indology proper. Ludwig's philological studies were important but he is better known for his German translation of the *Rig Veda* in six volumes, published in Prague in 1876–1888, and for his studies of classical Indian literature. Ludwig was the first Czech scholar to study Dravidian languages.[18]

Winternitz succeeded Ludwig to the Chair of Indology at the University of Prague and held it for several decades. He wrote the three-volume *History of Indian Literature* in German, the first two volumes of which were translated into English and published in India in 1927–1933. In addition, he wrote many shorter studies on Indian literature, some of which were published in book form in Calcutta in 1925 under the title, *Some Problems of Indian Literature.*

After World War I, a new Chair of Indology was founded at the Charles University of Prague, the oldest university in Central Europe. Its first occupant, Wincerc Lesny (1882–1953) had travelled extensively in India, and was a scholar of Indian, as well as of Iranian, languages. He published a number of books on India, including a monograph on Rabindranath Tagore, and translated many of Tagore's works directly from Bengali. His work, *Buddhismus,* analyzing the Buddhism of the Pali canon and its development in India and abroad, is yet to be translated from Czech into other languages. Lesny also founded the periodical, *The New East and the Indian Society,* before World War II.

In Hungary, Indian studies did not reach such an advanced level as in some major countries of Europe, but Indian thought made a significant impact on Hungarian intellectual life, and Hungary has made some contributions to Indology. One of these is the work of Sir Aurel Stein (1862–1943), a British citizen of Hungarian origin whose archaeological surveys and work in Central Asia are classical contributions to the study of Indian culture abroad. Born in Budapest, he studied in Austria and Germany, and taught Sanskrit at the University of the Punjab, before he led Indian archaeological expeditions to the hitherto unexcavated ruins in Serindia. He bequeathed his valuable library to the Hungarian Academy of Sciences.

The first Hungarian Orientalist was Alexander Csoma de Körös (1784–1842) who visited India in 1830 at the invitation of the Asiatic Society of Bengal, and who died at Darjeeling in 1842 during his second visit. His work and that of Tivadar Duka (1825–1908) were the beginnings of Indian studies in Hungary. Some of the scholars whose contributions to Hungarian Indology are particularly notable are Karoly Fiolk (1857–1915), who translated several Sanskrit classical texts; Sandor Kegl (1862–1920) and Josef Schmidt (1868–1933) who made Indian philosophy accessible to Hungarians; Charles Louis Fabri, whose writings on Indian art and aesthetics are well known to Indian scholars; Ervin Baktay (1890–1963); and Ferenc Hopp, who founded the Museum of East Asiatic Art in Budapest, which is named after him.

Some Rumanian scholars and poets were also fascinated by Indian culture. G. Coshbuc (1866–1918), called "the singer of the Rumanian peasantry," translated the *Sakuntala* from a German version in 1897, and compiled a Sanskrit anthology. B. P. Hashdeu studied the problems of Sanskrit literature or linguistics. His disciple, Lazar Saineanu, went to Paris where he studied Sanskrit at the Sorbonne with Abel Bergaigne. Constantin Georgian (1850–1904), who had worked with A. Weber at Berlin, was the first Rumanian Orientalist to make persistent efforts to introduce the study of Sanskrit into his country. However, the authorities did not approve of the teaching of Sanskrit; original translations from Sanskrit and works of Indology did not appear in Rumania until the 1930's.[19] Amongst many other Rumanian scholars who made Sanskrit and Indian culture their intellectual pursuit and formed a literary circle (Junimea), the names of Vasile Pogor, Vasile Burla, and Teohari Antonescu, can be mentioned as more prominent. Antonescu's important work on the philosophy of the Upanishads was the first study in Rumania to deal with such a problem in its entirety.

Information about early Russian awareness of India and Indian culture is at present insufficient. In the South Russian Steppes, some Buddhist images of the pre-Mongol period have been found. Indian fables and stories have long been known in Russia, although it is doubtful if their origins were known. A Russian traveller, Athanasius Nikitin, went to India in the fifteenth century but his diary, a valuable source of information, was unfinished. At the end of the seventeenth century a Russian merchant, Semen Malinkov, was received by Aurangzeb. A small colony of Indian traders and artisans was established in Astrakhan about 1615 and some Indian religious men settled in the region and enjoyed freedom of worship.

The first translation of a Sanskrit text was published in Russia in 1787 by N. I. Novikov. This was not a direct translation from Sanskrit but a Russian version of Wilkins' translation of the *Bhagavad Gila.* Later, a Russian musician, Gerasim Lebedev (1749–1817) who lived in India from 1785 to 1797 and played a significant role in the renaissance of the Bengali Theatre, published his *Grammar of Pure and Mixed East Indian Dialects with Dialogues* in 1801, and *An Impartial Survey of the Systems of Brahmanical East India* in 1805. He also cast the first Devanagari type by the command of Tsar Alexander I.

An Asian Academy was established at St. Petersburg in 1810, and Robert Lenz (1808–1836), who learned Sanskrit under Franz Bopp at Berlin, was appointed the first Professor of Sanskrit and Comparative Philology, but he died at the age of twenty-eight. His work, however, was continued by Pave Yakovlevich Petrov, who taught a number of Russian philologists and Indologists, including F. Korsch, F. F. Fortunator and V. F. Miller and translated into Russian the Sitaharana episode of the *Ramayana* with a glossary and a grammatical analysis.

Once the process had begun, Sanskrit studies expanded rapidly in the receptive atmosphere of Russian intellectual life, and Russia produced famous Indologists, such as V. P. Vasilyev (1818–1900) and V. P. Minayev (1840–1890). A pupil of Minayev, Sergei Fedorovich

Oldenburg (1863–1934), founded in 1897 the *Bibliotheca Buddhica*, a series devoted to the publication of Buddhist texts and monographs on Buddhist subjects. The Russian school of Indology had already produced the monumental St. Petersburg Lexicon, between 1852 and 1875. Possibly Oldenburg's greatest achievement was his archaeological explorations of Eastern Turkistan, and his participation in the organization of Russian scientific exploration of Central Asia; Russian explorers were the first to point out the rich archaeological sites on the edges of the Taklamakan Desert. Fedor Ippolitovich Stcherbatsky (1886–1941), who studied under Minayev and Oldenburg in St. Petersburg, Büehler in Vienna, and Jacobi in Bonn, published important works on Buddhist thought and edited numerous Tibetan and Sanskrit texts for the *Bibliotheca Buddhica.* Since the end of the last century, Russian interest and work in Indian studies have become even more comprehensive.

The first direct contact between India and the United States was commercial, and began in the end of the eighteenth century. By the middle of the nineteenth century, American trade with India had greatly increased. Diplomatic and missionary activity followed. American knowledge of India was at first vague, fragmentary, and indirect, acquired through the writings of European scholars. Later, however, the impact of Swami Vivekananda, Rabindranath Tagore, and other visiting Indians was clearly felt.

Since Yale University was founded in 1718 with the help of a cargo of gifts raised in India by Elihu Yale, who was a governor of Madras, it was only appropriate that it was there that Indian studies in the United States were begun in 1841. Edward Elbridge Salisbury (1814–1901), a pupil of Franz Bopp, was appointed the first Professor of Sanskrit. Later, his pupil, William Dwight Whitney (1827–1894), who had also studied with Weber and Roth, fined the Chair with distinction and made the first important American contributions to Sanskrit studies, including editions of the *Vishnu Purana* and the *Atharva Veda.*

Johns Hopkins University was next to set up a Chair in Sanskrit in 1878, within two years of its own foundation. A pupil of Whitney, Charles Rockwell Lanman, the author of the widely known *Sanskrit Reader* and the editor of the *Harvard Oriental Series,* was appointed to the position, but he moved to Harvard University two years later to set up what was to become an outstanding Department of Sanskrit. Later, several other universities, such as Columbia, California, and Pennsylvania, instituted Chairs of Sanskrit, and America produced many well-known scholars, such as Washburn Hopkins, Maurice Bloomfield, Franklin Edgerton, Arthur Ryder, A. U. William Jackson, and W. Norman Brown. Whilst American scholarship has made notable contributions of its own, Indian thought made its impact on the American mind mainly through European Indology.

Until World War II, American academic interest was primarily confined to the linguistic and literary study of ancient texts. Now, with the independence of India and the role of America in world affairs, the study of India in American universities and colleges has increased and become phenomenally diversified. Research in Indian history, sociology, politics, economics, and many other fields is rapidly expanding, and the recently established American Institute of Indian Studies has given a new impetus to American Indology. Thousands of Indian students are studying at American universities—over one thousand Indian scholars are now teaching there—and countless American scholars, journalists, artists, and tourists have visited India.

Without further straining the patience of the reader, it is not possible to mention here the considerable Indological work done in the other countries of Europe, and the many outstanding contributions made by scholars not already noted; the works of Sten Konow and Georg Morgenstierne from Norway; Jarl Carpentier and Helmer Smith from Sweden; Myles Dillon from Eire; W. S. Majewski, J. Lelewal, D. L. Boskowsk, and S. Schayer from Poland; Hermann Brunnhofer, Ernst Leumann, and Jacob Wockernagel from Switzerland; and Fausboll from Denmark are particularly valuable.[20]

Whilst a good deal of work was thus being done in Europe and America, the study of ancient Indian culture was progressing in India as well, through the efforts of both European and Indian scholars. Amongst the Indians themselves there developed during the nineteenth century a class of scholars who were educated in Western learning and were inspired by the growing spirit of cultural renaissance in India. Of these the works of R. G. Bhandarkar and Rajendralal Mitra are best known.

Their tradition gave rise to successive generations of Indian scholars who now do the vast majority of the work in Indian studies.

The initial work of the Asiatic Society of Bengal on written records was soon to lead attention to archaeological remains. Inscriptions in long-forgotten alphabets, coins, etc were closely scrutinized. Working back from current scripts the older languages were deciphered. One of the most remarkable achievements in this field was James Prinsep's (1799–1840) reading of the Brahmi script in 1837. An erudite scholar skilled in epigraphic techniques, he was able to interpret the edicts of Asoka, giving India knowledge of her noblest ruler, and placing Indian archaeology on a secure chronological basis. His death at the age of forty-one was a grievous blow to Indian studies.[21] A colleague of his, Alexander Cunningham, was an engineer with the British Indian Army and greatly interested in Indian archaeology. He continued Prinsep's work, and in 1862 became the first archaeological surveyor of India. Later, his work was carried forward by a number of archaeologists, prominent amongst whom were James Burgess, John Marshall, and R. D. Banerji, who discovered the cities of the Indus civilization in 1922.

Chapter VI

WESTERN RESPONSE TO MODERN INDIA

WHILST EUROPE'S DEBT to Greek literature is generally acknowledged, and often overemphasized, it is not always easy for modern generations to imagine the effect Indian ideas have had on European intellectual and cultural progress. The stimulus of Indian literature was such that scholars, exemplified by Macdonell, said: "Since the Renaissance there has been no event of such world-wide significance in the history of culture as the discovery of Sanskrit literature in the latter part of the eighteenth century."[1] Indeed, the impact of Indian thought on the intellectual life of renaissant Europe was so powerful that many European writers have not taken kindly to it. Driven by some strange fear of losing their cultural identity, they endeavoured to minimize or ignore the influence of Indian philosophy, and stretch logic to explain intellectual evolution purely in terms of what they call Western traditions.

India, however, was only one of the several factors which influenced European thought and life. The entire political, social, and intellectual life of Europe at this time was far more active and complex than during any previous age, and perhaps any subsequent one. France led the Age of Enlightenment. Germany was rapidly advancing, asserting its intellectual prowess in literature and philosophy; America and Russia had begun to make important contributions; and science had scored fresh advances. These were far-reaching changes, in which the discovery of Indian literature and philosophy played a limited but significant role.

Inevitably, European response to Indian ideas differed from country to country: indeed, from thinker to thinker. Some received Indian thought more readily and understood it better than others. Others reacted against it almost instinctively. Whatever the response, favourable or unfavourable, deep or fragmentary, it was entirely conditioned by the intellectual climate of Europe and its variations. There was no organized movement to advocate the adoption of Indian ideas. If there were those anxious to underline the virtues of Indian literature, they were the Europeans themselves, acting individually. Seldom were Indian doctrines adopted wholesale—to expect otherwise would be to deny the existence of a powerful indigenous tradition and the intellectual independence of the receiver. Some found in Indian thought reinforcement of their own ideas; others an escape or diversion from their own tradition.

Indian thought and literature had its finest European reception in Germany. In fact, Indology became largely a province of German scholarship, stimulated entirely by academic considerations, as Germany, unlike Britain and France, had no political ties with India or her neighbours. Although Abraham Roger's work, *The Open Door to Hidden Heathendom,* a German translation of two hundred maxims of Bhartrihari, appeared in 1663, it made little impact. Not until the end of the eighteenth century did the Germans come to know some of the famous works of Indian literature.

Europe took *Sakuntala* to heart, and in Germany the popularity of this work ensured that later translations would be welcomed. The first German to recognize the beauty of *Sakuntala* was the poet and critic, Johann Gottfried Herder (1744–1803). Although not familiar with India or its languages, he had already given a somewhat idealized picture of the Indian people in his chief work, *Ideen Zur Philosophie der Menschheit (Ideas on a Philosophy of the History of Mankind),* in 1787. According to him, mankind's origin was to be traced to India, where the "human mind got the first shapes of wisdom and virtue with a simplicity, strength and sublimity which has—frankly spoken—nothing, nothing at all equivalent in our philosophical, cold European world." He regarded the Hindus, because of their ethical teachings, as the most gentle and peaceful people on earth. His concept of India was taken up by the Romantic movement, and long dominated the fantasy of German poets. The connection which the teachings of reincarnation established between all forms of life opened a new field to Herder and his contemporaries. Herder's *Thoughts of Some Brahmins* (1792), which contains a selection of gnomic stanzas in free translations, gathered from Bhartrihari, the *Hitopadesa* and the *Bhagavad Gita,* expressed these ideals. When George Förster sent him his German translation of the English version of the *Sakuntala* in 1791, Herder responded: "I cannot easily find a product of the human mind more pleasant than this ... a real blossom of the Orient, and the first, most beautiful of its kind! ... Something like that, of course, appears once every two thousand years." He published a detailed study and analysis of *Sakuntala,* claiming that this work disproved the popular belief that drama was the exclusive invention of the ancient Greeks.

Herder's letters, published under the title, *The Oriental Drama,* claim that Kalidasa's masterpiece contains a perfection unique in world literature both in poetic substance and the characterization of the heroine. Herder hurriedly passed on his discovery of the Indian drama to his friend, Johann Wolfgang von Goethe (1749–1832), whose own enthusiasm for this play was no less exuberant. He wrote in 1792:

> Wouldst thou the young year's blossoms and the fruits
> of its decline
> And all by which the soul is charmed, enraptured,
> feasted, fed,
> Wouldst thou the earth, and heaven itself in one sole name
> combine)
> I name thee, O Sakuntala! and all at once is said.[7]

Goethe expressed this admiration for *Sakuntala* more than once. Nearly forty years later, in 1830 when de Chézy sent him his edition of the original with his French translation, he wrote to the Frenchman expressing his deep gratitude: "The first time I came across this inexhaustible work it aroused such enthusiasm in me and so held me that I could not stop studying it. I even felt impelled to make the impossible attempt to bring it in some form to the German stage. These efforts were fruitless but they made me so thoroughly acquainted with this most valuable work, it represented such an epoch in my life, I so absorbed it, that for thirty years I did not look at either the English or the German version ... It is only now that I understand the enormous impression that work made on me at an earlier age."[3] Goethe goes on to point out the beauties of the work, saying that in it the poet appears in his highest function, as the representative of the most natural state, of the most refined form of life, of the purest moral striving, of the worthiest majesty and the most solemn contemplation of God; at the same time he is lord and master of his creation to so great an extent that he may venture vulgar and ludicrous contrasts which yet must be regarded as necessary links of the whole organization. No wonder he modelled the prologue of his *Faust* (1797) on the prologue to *Sakuntala.* The jester in the prologue of *Faust* is reminiscent of the *vidusaka* in the Indian drama, a parallel first noticed by Heinrich Heme.

Goethe's friend, Schiller, who otherwise took little interest in Indian literature, was also moved to enthusiastic praise of *Sakuntala*, which he found in some respects unparalleled in the classical literature of Greece and Rome. He published part of the *Sakuntala* in *Thalia,* and in a letter to Wilhelm Humboldt he wrote that "in the whole of Greek antiquity there is no poetical representation of beautiful love which approaches Sakuntala even afar."

Goethe also admired other Indian poems, such as Jayadeva's *Gita Govinda* and Kalidasa's *Meghaduta* which he read in Wilson's English translation in 1817 and welcomed as "a great treasure." Goethe's second Indian ballad, "Der Paria" (1824), was his best. The plot for "Der Paria" comes from the work of the French traveller, Sonnerat (*Voyage aux Indes,* 1783), who had returned to Europe in 1782 after seven years in India. Goethe's first Indian ballad, "Der Gotund die Bajadere," published in 1797, was also based on Sonnerat.

Whilst Herder and Goethe shared enthusiasm for the *Sakuntala,* their attitudes toward India were very different. Herder was gradually becoming old and moralizing. The *Sakuntala* had captivated him, but it was the rich treasure of Indian gnomic and didactic poetry that appealed to him most. Herder admired India, as did Novalis and Heine, for its simplicity, and denounced the Europeans for their greed, corruption, and economic exploitation of India.

Goethe, on the other hand, reacted to Indian literature as a poet and an artist. Although he was delighted by the harmonious beauty and lyrical intensity of the epics and *kavya,* he did not care for the *Hitopadesa* and philosophy, and he took no interest in Indian mythology and sculpture. He was particularly interested in poetry that expressed human feelings and sentiments in a simple and natural way. Indian sculpture, with its variety and abundance of form, offended his classical ideal of unified beauty. His admiration for India was strong and deep, but it could not compare with his appreciation for Greece. He was fascinated by India, but he understood Greece. Consequently Goethe did not actively participate in the expansion of Indian studies and did not learn Sanskrit, although in the Goethe Archives there are some papers on which the poet tried the Devanagari script. Extreme attraction unaccompanied by proper intellectual understanding was bound to unnerve a thinking, sensitive scholar, such as Goethe. He expressed this feeling to his friend Humboldt in 1826: "I have by no means an aversion to things Indian, but I am afraid of them, for they draw my imagination into the formless and the diffuse against which I have to guard myself more than ever before."[4] However, he consistently acknowledged the tremendous stimulus of Indian thought on Western civilization, and followed the work of German Indologists such as the Schlegel brothers and Bopp with interest and approval.

Inspired by Herder's idealist concepts there developed a belief that the highest form of romantic poetry could be found only in India. The very reason which made Goethe hesitant gave the Romantics a predilection for India. Consequently, they did not content themselves with glorifying it in poetry alone; they laid the foundation for a real science of India.

Until the end of the eighteenth century, French was the language of the German élite and, together with Latin, the language of learning. During the French Revolution and Napoleonic Wars, Germany suffered heavily. After the war, educated Germans became more aware of their own language and heritage, and took an increasing pride in it. At this psychological moment Indian literature appeared in Germany; a certain undoubted cultural and historical affinity between India and Germany probably assumed greater imaginary proportions than it would have at any other time.

Shakespeare on the one hand, and Indian literature on the other, formed the main inspiration of the German Romantic movement. Both were introduced into Germany at about the same time and by the same persons, Friedrich and August Wilhelm von Schlegel. The Romantics found in India that dynamic and synthetic approach to life which they felt was lacking in the formalism and artificiality of the early European Romantic movement, and sought to substitute aesthetic standards for utilitarian ones.

The religions of India also fascinated the Romantics of Germany; throughout the nineteenth century Western religious criticism was inspired by the discovery of Indian polytheism. "If one considers," comments Schlegel, "the superior conception which is at the basis of the truly universal Indian culture and which, itself divine, knows how to embrace in its universality everything that is divine without distinction, then, what we in Europe call religion or what we used to call such, no longer seems to deserve that name. And one would like to advise everyone who wants to see religion, he should, just as one goes to Italy to study art, go to India for that purpose where he may be certain to find at least fragments for which he will surely look in vain in Europe."[5]

Amongst those men of letters who took an enthusiastic interest in Indian literature was the versatile Prussian minister of education, Wilhelm von Humboldt (1767–1835), a brilliant linguist and the founder of the science of general linguistics. He began to learn Sanskrit in 1821 and was greatly moved by Schlegel's edition of the *Bhagavad Gita,* on which he published an extensive study and which he described as "the deepest and loftiest thing the world has to show."[6] He declared that he was grateful to God for granting him a life so long that he could read the *Gita.*[7]

Ludwig van Beethoven (1770–1827) was also attracted by Indian thought, as is clearly attested by numerous passages and notes referring to Indian ideas and texts found in the Beethoven papers. He was first introduced to Indian literature by the Austrian Orientalist, Hammer-Purgstal, who founded a periodical for the dissemination of Eastern knowledge in Europe as early as January 1809. Beethoven had a dear interest in Indian knowledge long before Indological studies began in Germany. The fragments of Indian religious texts that have been discovered in the Beethoven manuscripts are partly translations and partly adaptations of the Upanishads and the *Bhagavad Gita.* It is not certain if Beethoven himself or his Orientalist friends selected these passages for him.

The German poet, Friedrich Rückert (1788–1866), Professor of Oriental Languages at the University of Erlangen from 1827 to 1841, produced, under the inspiration of August Wilhelm van Schlegel, numerous skilful translations from Sanskrit. His published translations from Indian classical poetry made Indian lyrics and poems widely popular in Germany amongst his translations are *Nalopakhyana*, the *Amarusataka*, the *Raghuvamsa*, and the *Gita Govinda*, which lost nothing of its beauty, colour, and atmosphere in Rückert's German version. The Indian poem is such a complex work from the viewpoint of rhyme, alliteration, and allusion that Rückert's version represents a brilliant accomplishment. Of all the German poets, it was he who best understood the character of Indian poetry.[8]

Novalis (1772–1801), one of Germany's greatest Romantic poets, wrote in his essay, *Christendom in Europe*, that poetry, pure and colourful like a beautiful India, stood opposed to the cold and deadening mountains of philistine reason. For him Sanskrit was the most mysterious linguistic symbol of any human expression; Sanskrit took him back to the "original people" who had been forgotten. However, in spite of his emotional enthusiasm for India, Novalis did not really understand Indian thought. Unlike those Indians who believe the objective world is an illusion, Novalis sought to perfect this world. Similarly, when E. T. A. Hoffmann (1776–1822) attempted to create Indian characters in some of his stories they were magicians who although traditionally associated with India, were not really representative.

Schelling also accorded India an important position in his *Philosophy of Mythology*. He was a great admirer of ancient Indian literature, especially the Upanishads, which he regarded, like Schopenhauer, to be the genuine wisdom of Indians and of mankind.

Heinrich Heine (1797–1856), a late Romantic lyric poet, whose influence was enormous not only in Germany but in most countries of the Western world, describes the India of his imagination: "... in the glass I saw the dear motherland, the blue and sacred Ganges, the eternally shining Himalayas, the gigantic forests of Banyan trees on whose wide shadowy paths quietly walk wise elephants and white pilgrims..."[9] His poem, "Auf Flügeln des Gesanges,"

Am Ganges duftet's and leuchtet's
Und Riesenbäume blühn,
Und schöne, stille Menschen
Vor Lotosblumen knien.

created a picture of India widely familiar in Germany.[10] Heine's acquaintance with Indian thought, acquired in Bonn under Schlegel and Bopp, remained important to him throughout his life. His approach to Indian works was intimate and sensitive, but it did not lead to uncritical enthusiasm for them. He did not care for the story of the rivalry between Vasistha and Visvamitra, in which he saw a parallel with the investiture contest in mediaeval Europe. However, he had a particular feeling for Indian scenery, as is revealed by his verses in his famous *Buck der Lieder* (*Book of Songs*). He remarked that if the Portuguese, the Dutch, and the English had carried away ships laden with Indian treasures, Germany would do likewise, but hers would be treasures of spiritual knowledge.

Although Gutzkow titled his novel *Mahaguru* (1832), he shows no evidence of real knowledge of Indian thought. F. Hebbel's attention was drawn to India by Ad. Holtzmann's *Indian Sagas.* In 1863, he wrote the story of King Sibi who by sacrificing his own life saved a dove from a hawk, and his poem, "The Brahmans," gives a moving expression of the Indian concept of the equality of all living beings.

Immanuel Kant (1712–1804) was apparently the first important German philosopher to have some acquaintance with Indian philosophy. Kant's differentiation between the physical world as seen in space and time and the unknowable thing in itself beyond these concepts, is very similar to the doctrine of Maya. There are certain parallels between Kantian thought and Buddhist philosophy. Like the Buddha, Kant declared a number of questions unsolvable, such as "Has the world a beginning or not?" "Is it finite or eternal?" Stcherbatsky has shown that Kant's doctrine of the categorical imperative has its counterpart in Hindu philosophy, and has pointed out similarities between Kantian thought and later Buddhist thinkers like Chandrakirti. Moreover according to Hermann Jacobi, Kant's *Aesthetics* had been preceded by Indian writers on poetics.

These are important parallels and strongly indicative of Kant's familiarity with Indian philosophy. But, considering that Sanskrit studies were only beginning to emerge in Europe, and Europe knew very little of Indian philosophy at the time, it seems unlikely that Kant had any direct knowledge of Indian thought. However, the possibility of his acquaintance, as distinct from knowledge, with Indian ideas through earlier Western writings and contemporary travel accounts cannot be ruled out. In his lectures at the Konigberg University in East Prussia from 1756 to 1796, he talked about the physiography of India and the customs and manners of the people, and it seems likely that an intellectual of his genius would have gathered other information about India and reflected upon it with utmost care and competence. His observations about Buddhism in Asia and about Hindus appear to endorse the view that he had extensive and accurate knowledge of Indian thought. He said the Hindus were gentle and tolerant of other religions and nations. He was very much impressed by the Hindu doctrine of transmigration, which corresponded in some respects to his own teaching about the destiny of the soul after death. Similarly, Kant's successor, Johann Gottlieb Fichte (1762–1814), includes in his *Anweisung Zu einem selingen Leben (Hints for a Blessed Life)* numerous passages which approximate the *Advaita* doctrine.

Whilst Kant and Fichte were not familiar with original Sanskrit texts, Arthur Schopenhauer (1788–1860) knew them, at least in some measure, and openly acknowledged his debt to Indian systems in *Die Welt als Wille und Vorstcllung (The World as Will and Idea):* "I acknowledge that I owe the best part of my development, beside the impression of the outward world, to thc works of Kant and to the holy scriptures of the Hindus and Plato." He believed that if "...the reader has also received and assimilated the sacred primitive Indian wisdom, then is he best of all prepared to hear what I have to say to him."[11] Schopenhauer, who was unusually free from nationalism, and who has been called the philosopher of disillusion and profound pessimism, was introduced to Indian thought in 1813 by one of Goethe's friends, the Orientalist Friedrich Mayer. From then on, Schopenhauer never lost interest. In 1818, he published his most important work, *Die Welt als Wille und Vorstellung*, in which he put forward the doctrines of pessimism and the subjectivity of will to knowledge. Although his university career had come to an abrupt end at this time, he continued to work on his doctoral thesis privately. He read whatever he could lay his hands on at the Weimar Library concerning Indian thought. Of these, Anquetil du Perron's translation of the Upanishads was his chief source of information. Schopenhauer, although working with an imperfect translation, was extremely enthusiastic about the Upanishads' philosophy and declared them to be "the production of the highest human wisdom." For him no study was so elevating as that of the Upanishads: "It has been the solace of my life, it will be the solace of my death." A few years later when he became acquainted with Buddhism, he regarded it as more profound than Christianity. He did not think that Christianity could ever displace Buddhism in the East: "It is just as if we fired a bullet against a cliff." On the contrary, he thought that Indian philosophy would profoundly alter European knowledge and thought: "The influence of Sanskrit literature will penetrate no less deeply than did the revival of Greek letters in the fifteenth century."[12] Schopenhauer, mainly influenced by the discovery of upanishadic thought, has been called the first apostle of Buddhism in Germany. He was so impressed by Buddhism that he claimed fundamental identity of his philosophy with the teachings of Buddhism, kept a bronze of the Buddha in his study, and occasionally referred to himself and his followers as "we Buddhists." But there are important differences between his philosophy and Indian thought, whether Buddhist or vedantic.

Schopenhauer regarded the Hindus as deeper thinkers than Europeans because their interpretation of the world was internal and intuitive, not external and intellectual. For intuition unites everything; the intellect divides everything. The Hindus saw that the "I" is a delusion, that the individual is merely phenomenal, and that the only reality is the Infinite One "That art Thou."

Another German philosopher, Karl Christian Friedrich Krause (1781–1832) was even more strongly influenced by Indian philosophy. He praised the Vedanta particularly in his *Vorlesungen über die Grundwahrheiten der Wissenschaften* (1829), although he wrote on Buddhism, Jainism, and the Carvakas.

Paul Deussen (1845–1919), a rare combination of a scholar of European philosophy as well as of Indology, was also greatly attracted by the Vedanta philosophy. Works on the Vedanta philosophy and his translation of the *Vedanta Sutras* were published in 1883 and in 1887 respectively. By translating the original texts of the Upanishads into German and commenting upon them he increased the understanding of Indian philosophy amongst European thinkers. He called the Vedanta system one of the greatest achievements of humanity in the search for eternal truth.

Not all German philosophers were fascinated by Indian thought. Once Europe had recovered from the ravages of the Napoleonic Wars and Indian culture lost its novelty, European intellectuals began to analyze Indian civilization, even if they had no familiarity with original texts. A typical example was Georg Wilhelm Friedrich Hegel (1770–1831), a contemporary of Schopenhauer, who, in reaction to the undiluted romanticism towards India, gave a full chapter to India in his *Philosophy of World History* (1822–1823), and drew some depressing conclusions. With his stress on reason, he criticized the Romantics for idolizing India. He considered the prevailing degenerate condition of Indian society as its natural condition, and maintained it was a society condemned by its own inability to rejuvenate itself. Hegel not only applied erroneous standards but relied on undependable sources—the writings of British administrators and Abbé Dubois' book. How ill-informed Hegel was of things Eastern can best be seen in the brief attempt he makes in his book to define Buddhism. "There is a great dispute going on," he says, "which of the two religions (Buddhism and Hinduism) is older and simpler; for both there are reasons, but one cannot discern it clearly. The Buddhistic religion is simpler, but this may be due either to the fact that it is older, or that it is the result of a Reformation. Probably, however, Buddhism is the older of the two."[13]

Yet it is interesting to notice a likeness between Hegel's famous "dialectical movement," that every idea and every situation in the world leads irresistibly to its opposite and then unites with it to form a new whole, and the Buddhist concept of the "golden mean." Hegel expressly refers to Indian predecessors of his logic of contradictions. Also, his view that man reaches his full stature only through suffering is quite close to the Buddha's declaration that life is dukkha.

Whilst Hegel reacted against Romanticism and against Schopenhauer's enthusiasm for Indian thought, Friedrich Nietzsche (1844–1900) protested as much against Schopenhauer's philosophy as against Deussen's interpretation of the Vedanta. Nietzsche, however, was deeply influenced by Schopenhauer in his youth, and regarded himself as his successor, although superior to him in some ways. He found in *The World as Will and Idea* "a mirror in which I espied the world, life, and my own nature depicted with frightful grandeur." Although he later denounced pessimism as decadent, he remained an unhappy man and under the permanent influence of Schopenhauer's thought. Nietzsche was very appreciative of the Upanishads and, indeed, contemptuous of those Europeans who, devoid of intellectual discernment, wanted to convert and "civilize" the Brahmans. When Paul Deussen told him his plan of translating ancient Hindu texts and expounding their wisdom, he expressed great enthusiasm saying that Indian philosophy was the one parallel to their own European philosophy. In *Thus Spake Zarathustra* (1883–1891), the most revealing and personal of all his writings, Nietzsche propounded his central doctrine, the gospel of the superman, which is his chief legacy to the world. Passionately individualistic he was a believer in the hero. He found in the *Manusmriti* one of the sources of his own philosophy of superman. He so highly esteemed the Hindu text that he declared all other ethical codes to be imitations and even caricatures of this. He saw the supremacy of the Indian Brahmans as the implicit obedience of the herd to the religious and moral command of the "ruling" caste. Nietzsche was not a nationalist and showed no excessive admiration for Germany; he certainly was not anti-Semitic. He wanted an international ruling race, a vast aristocracy of artist-tyrants. Seldom in Western thought is the difference between man as he now is and man as he might become more emphatically pronounced than by Nietzsche.

During the first half of the nineteenth century, interest was directed towards India as a whole, but in the second half of the century, German scholars were drawn towards Buddhist thought and literature, through the publication of Burnouf's *Introduction à l'histoire du Bouddhisme indien* (1844) and Koppen's *Buddhismus* (1857–1859). Even Nietzsche, who had moved away from Schopenhauer and Wagner, included in his book, *Revaluation of All Values,* a hymn of praise to Buddhism which he found a "hundred times more realistic than Christ's Nativity."

Richard Wagner (1813–1883) was so profoundly influenced by Buddhism as propagated by Schopenhauer and his followers that he confessed he had involuntarily become a Buddhist. He was fascinated by the doctrine of salvation and the ethics of compassion, before which every other dogma appeared to be small and narrow. In his play, *The Victors*, Wagner uses a story from Burnouf's book about a *chandala* (untouchable) female, Prakriti, who was accepted into the monastic order by the Buddha to enable her to find fulfilment in her love for Ananda who had also become a monk, and to make amends for her past sins. Prakriti and Ananda were later transformed into Kundry and Parsifal in his last opera, *Parsifal.* The flowergirls (which Wagner took from Lambrecht's *Alexander Song*) and Kingsor's lance, which hangs above Parsifal's head, have their origins in the story about the Buddha's temptation through Mara. In *Götterdämmerung (Twilight of the Gods),* Wahnheim (the abode of illusion) and Wunschheim (the abode of desire), for which the man, delivered from the necessity of having to be born again, strives, are typically Indian concepts. Countless borrowings from India are found in Wagner's work.

In 1881 Hermann Oldenberg (1854–1920) published his brilliant study, *Buddha-His Life, Teachings and Community,* which added greatly to Buddhism's popularity in Germany. Oldenberg also edited and translated the *Dipavamsa* and the *Vinaya Pitaka.* The abundance of new material and the inherent atheism of original Buddhism inspired some German poets of the following decades.

J. V. Widmann created an historically inaccurate picture of the Buddha in his epic, *Buddha,* as the Master who urged pantheism and atheism so that "a new golden age" could be achieved. Karl Bleibtreu's dramas, *Karma* (1901) and *Saviour* (1903), attempted to ease the entrance of Buddhism into Europe, but again it was interpreted inaccurately. The most complete treatment of the Buddha was achieved by Karl Gjellerup in *Pilgrim Kamanita* (1903). He tried to convey some of the nature of Buddhism, and showed much knowledge of Indian customs and Hinduism.

Whilst a general feeling of weariness towards all matters of the world encouraged the influx of Eastern, especially Buddhist, ideas at the beginning of the twentieth century, this impact was considerably increased in the years following because of the intellectual restiveness generated by World War I. Buddhism in Germany was encouraged by the poetry of P. Dahlke and Hans Much. A particularly powerful poetic treatment of the Buddha legend was achieved by Albrecht Schaffer in *The Gem in the Lotus* (1923) which was partly inspired by Sir Edwin Arnold's *The Light of Asia.* Werfel's play, *The Mirror Man,* appeared in 1920. The hero of this play leaves an Indian monastery and through the "mirror man" (the manifestation of illusion) he gradually overcomes maya (illusion) and realizes that dissociation from one's own existence is the highest possible aim.

Most poets at that time no longer believed in the superiority of Christianity. In Josef Winckler's comedy, *Labyrinth of God or the Comedy of Chaos* (1922), the Buddha has only a smile for the twelve Apostles who want to convince him that his time has ended. The hero of Stefan Zweig's *The Eyes of the Eternal Brother* (1921), the Indian *Virata,* attempts to lead a life without guilt. He moves down socially from one step to the other and finally realizes that one should strive to subject one's will but not attempt to live without guilt. The hero in Alfred Döblin's epic, *Manas* (1927), is haunted by the question of where the enemies he has slain in battle will continue to suffer. He therefore goes to the land of the dead in the Himalayas, where he witnesses such terrible things that he suffers a breakdown and dies. His wife who has followed him brings him back to life. The hero then overcomes gods and demons; he no longer rejects the world but worships the forces of nature. Döblin's descriptions of visions belonging to Siva's world show his familiarity with Indian religious literature.

Hermann Keyserling (1880–1946), who found a strong affinity between Christianity and Buddhism, was much impressed by the metaphysical profundity of India. He used Indian thought to measure European standards of conduct and morality. The influence of Keyserling on the European intelligentsia after World War I, especially in Germany, was deep but short-lived. Germany, shattered from the disastrous war, had returned its attention towards India for solace and new inspiration, as is indicated by the publication of innumerable novels and poems with a predominantly Asian background.

Hermann Hesse, awarded the Knobel Prize for literature in 1946, found in Indian thought an answer to his yearning for deliverance from "ego," and from the tyrannical dictates of temporality. Indian thought offered the most radical possibility of undoing the curse of individuation, of annihilating the "idiotic one-after-the-other" by the postulation of the eternal simultaneity of nirvana. The positive attitude of the *Bhagavad Gita* also appealed to Hesse. Yoga and maya are the background to the events portrayed in the *Glasperlenspiel (The Game of Glass Beads).* Hesse himself claimed that Yoga had an invaluable effect upon him as a means of improving his powers of concentration. The threefold sequence of sensual love, wisdom, and self-denial experienced by the poet Bhartrihari is interpreted by Hesse as the result of humble and wise humanity. In *Journey to the Orient,* Hesse, whose mother was born in Malabar, says of India that it was "not' only a country and something geographical, but the home and the youth of the soul, the everywhere and nowhere, the oneness of all times." It is significant that Hesse, although a Christian, repeatedly substituted the upanishadic *tat tvamasi,* literally "love your neighbour for he is yourself," for Christ's command, "love thy neighbour as thyself." In *Siddhartha* (1922) he tried to reconcile Christian and Indian piety.

Other prominent German writers, such as Paul Dahlke (1865–1928), H. Much, Josef Winckler, Albrecht Schaffer, Franz Werfel, Stefan Zweig, Hermann Kasack , Gustav Meyrink, and Thomas Mann, drew upon Indian materials. Thomas Mann (1875–1955) gave a new interpretation to an Indian story from the *Vatalapancavimsati* in *The Transposed Heads,* which Goethe had previously used in his poem, "Der Paria."

French interest in Indology is also reflected in their literature, especially during the Romantic period. In common with many of his contemporaries, Francois René de Chateaubriand (1768–1848), who deeply influenced the Romantic movement in France, was an enthusiastic admirer of *Sakuntala.* He had lived in England as a refugee from Napoleonic France between 1793 and 1800, when Sir William Jones' translations of Sanskrit works were published.

Victor Hugo (1802–1885) imitated an Upanishad in his poem, "Suprématie" (1870). He gathered his information from G. Pautheir's *Les Livres Sacrés de l'Orient.* Alphonse de Lamartine (1790–1869), who did for French poetry what Chateaubriand did for French prose, wrote about Sanskrit epics, drama, and poetry in his *Cours jamilier de Littérature* in 1861.

Jean-Jacques Ampère (1800–1864), a friend of Hugo, is reputed to have said that during the Renaissance Greek works were given the attention they deserved, but in his day Indian works would be studied and another Renaissance would be witnessed. Louis Revel went a long step farther when he remarked that if Greek culture had influenced Western civilization, the ancient Greeks themselves were "the sons of Hindu thought." Joseph Mery (1798–1865), who wrote satirical poems on the French Restoration, could recite the works of Kalidasa and Bhavabhuti from memory.

In 1825 Philaré le Charles (1798–1873), who did much to familiarize his readers with the literature of foreign countries, wrote *The Bride of Banaras* and *Indian Nights.* Paul Verlaine (1844–1896) wrote the poem, "Savitri," which is a short piece but is indicative that the French writers had an accurate knowledge of Indian literature. Verlaine became keenly interested in Hindu mythology during his high school days. His enthusiasm was such that he said, "Par Indra! que c'est beau, et comme ca vous dégotte la Bible, l'Evangile et toute la dégueulade des Pères de l'Eglise." (By Indra! how beautiful this is and how much better than the Bible, the Gospel and all the words of the Fathers of the Church.)

Louis Jacolliot (1837–1890), who worked in French India as a government official and was at one time President of the Court in Chandranagar , translated numerous vedic hymns, the *Manusmriti,* and the Tamil work, *Kural.* His masterpiece, *La Bible dans l'Inde,* stirred a storm of controversy. He praised the Vedas in his *Sons of God,* and said: "The Hindu revelation, which proclaims the slow and gradual formation of worlds, is of all revelations the only one whose ideas are in complete harmony with modern science." Anatole France (1844–1924) saw in the Buddha "the best adviser and sweetest comforter of suffering mankind."

English response to Indian culture in the eighteenth century was conditioned by the ostentatious "nabobs," who amassed great wealth through unscrupulousness and deceit. The nabobs "raised the price of Parliamentary seats and made themselves otherwise objectionable to the old-established aristocratic society into which they intruded with their outlandish ways."[14] The image of the epic greatness of India was thus tinctured by the money-making vulgarity of these Englishmen. Consequently, the first reaction of the English was against their own people who were spoiling the good name of Britain in the East. During this period a large number of books were published dealing satirically with the English administration in India: for example, Mackenzie's *The Lounger* (1787), Samuel Foote's *The Nabob* (1772), *Harley House* (1789), and a number of passages in Cowper's poems.

Later, English administration became firm and settled and lost some of its earlier unpopularity, and Indian philosophy and literature came to be known in England. Even before Sir Charles Wilkins translated the *Gita,* or Halhead published *Sanskrit Grammar* (1778), Alexander Dow had published an essay on Hinduism entitled *A Dissertation Concerning the Customs, Manners, Language, Religion and Philosophy of the Hindus* (1768). The first European scholar to produce a real dissertation on Sanskrit learning, he pointed out the vast quantities of Sanskrit literature in existence, plus the fact that the history of the Hindus was older than that of any other people.

Jones had come to India, unlike most of his contemporaries, not to amass a fortune or to seek adventure, but to study Sanskrit and Indian culture in order to transmit Indian learning to the West. Already a master of Greek, Latin, Persian, Arabic, and Hebrew, he had high regard for Western knowledge which had culminated in British achievements. Whilst British culture continued to advance, he believed, because of the free institutions of the West, the Eastern tradition of despotism caused cultural stagnation in Asia. Yet he had great esteem for Indian civilization. He was not a romantic admirer of India but, in fact, a conservative commentator. In assessing Indian heritage he employed his own criteria and Western standard. His initial conclusion was that Europe excelled in the realm of reason; India, in that of reflection. But, as he delved deeper into Indian literature, he modified his earlier opinion to admit the impressive Indian accomplishments in the natural sciences. In 1794, the last year of his life, he declared that "...without detracting from the 'never fading laurels of Newton,' the whole of Newton's theology, and part of his philosophy were to be found in the Vedas and other Indian works." His opinion of Indian philosophy was immeasurably high. "One correct version of any celebrated Hindu book would be of greater value than all the dissertations or essays that could be composed on the same subject."[15]

Jones' evaluation of Indian thought attracted the attention of contemporary British scholars and writers of diverse interests, such as Gibbon, Byron, and George Borrow, who acknowledge their debt to Jones' *Works* and the *Life*. His *Hymn to Narayana*, in which he described the process of creation, inspired Shelley's "Hymn to Intellectual Beauty." Southey and Moore often cite from Jones' writings, and E. Koeppel has recently illustrated that Shelley and Tennyson borrowed from Jones in their *Queen Mab* and *Locksley Hall*.[16]

William Robertson, Principal of the College of Edinburgh and a well-known historian, published his book, *An Historical Disquisition Concerning Ancient India* (1791), describing the knowledge ancient Greeks and Romans had of India, her progress, and trade activities prior to the discovery of the direct sea route between India and Europe. Robertson based his assessment of Indian works on the existing literature, supplemented by his frequent conversations with high British officials in India, whose names he, for reasons of confidence, did not specify. He found both merits and defects in Indian thought and literature.

By the beginning of the nineteenth century, whilst Britain had gained India and Canada, she had lost America. Her industrial revolution was well under way and Britain was emerging as a new type of nation-state combining an industrial capitalist society with an imperialist democratic government. The newly gained prosperity and security from foreign aggression, and the pride of possessing a vast colonial empire, produced a sense of power—a national feeling of implicit faith in her own historical processes and political institutions—which was later to manifest itself, not infrequently, in racial arrogance. These changes inevitably affected Britain's material and intellectual life. It was during this formative period that words of capital importance in the English language and way of life at present, and which illustrate the changing patterns in culture and ways of thinking, such as industry, democracy, class, art, and culture, came to be used with new meanings.

Between the appearance of William Blake's *Song of Innocence* (1789), in which he first revealed his mystical inclination, and the death of Sir Walter Scott in 1832, the English literary tradition changed its course; the

Romantic period, in essence, aimed at liberating human personality from the fetters of social conventions. Whilst English Romanticism largely provided its own momentum, it was deeply influenced by Germany in the beginning of the nineteenth century, and India played a significant part, either directly or through the medium of Germany or Neoplatonism.

William Blake's (1757–1827) belief that human life is a manifestation of eternal being has an upanishadic ring. His idea, quite different from the prevalent one in England, that soul was the true reality and its corporal form a passing shadow, an encumbrance, and his belief that the human was divine, are reminiscent of Indian monism. He declared Jesus Christ "was the only God—and so am I and so are you." He even regarded the beasts as "beings, the Living ones."

Blake's deep concern and preoccupation with fundamental questions of life, his emphasis on complete harmony between art, moral problems, and beliefs, his conviction that the human and the divine are One, and his painstaking study of Neoplatonism, Gnosticism, and the *Bhagavad Gita,* are clearly manifested in his writing. His Four Zoas appear to have a source in the Four Guardians (Lokapalas) of the four quarters of the Hindu mythology. According to Damon, Blake's zoas were derived from the three *Goons, sativa, rajas* and *tamas* described in the *Bhagavad Gita.* Blake's profound emphasis on mysticism, especially in *Songs of Experience* (1794) and his principal prose work, *The Marriage of Heaven and Hell* (1790), was radically out of character with the literary tradition in England at the time, and he was long regarded as an eccentric. In *The Marriage of Heaven and Hell* he vigorously and satirically denied the reality of matter and eternal punishment. In *Songs of Experience,* too, he protested against restrictive codes and exalted the spirit of love. His main poems were written between 1788 and 1820, the period of European discovery of Indian literature, thus Indian inspiration of Blake is plausible. Whilst some attempts to explain Blake's thought as an independent growth away from Indian ideas could have been conditioned by prejudice against alien influences others are the result of the critics' inadequate knowledge of philosophical thought in general, and of Indian philosophy in particular. Consequently, even some competent recent studies, such as Désirée Hirst's *Hidden Riches,* do not given proper consideration to the Indian inspiration of Blake or of English Romanticism.[17]

Thomas De Quincey (1785–1859), whose qualities as a writer are fascinating despite criticisms of his indulgences as a man, knew something of Indian ideas. In his famous autobiographical narrative, *Confessions of an English Opium Eater* (1822), he describes how in his opium dreams he was hounded by Brahma, Visnu, and Siva.

Thomas Carlyle (1795–1881) found a basis for his doctrine of superiority in the caste system. Carlyle, who was a radical early in life and in the course of years became more and more hostile to democracy and advocated British imperialism, divided humanity into supermen and helots. His way of combatting anarchy by finding heroes who commanded obedience is somewhat reminiscent of Indian brahmanical supremacy.[18]

William Wordsworth (1770–1850), who expressed the deepest aspirations of English Romanticism, endeavoured throughout his writing to communicate his new vision of nature, which was so alien to English tradition that it was not until 1830 that his poetry was given wide public recognition. In intimacy with nature and its beauties, he also found a corrective to his personal despondency. Apart from this, however, Wordsworth seriously attempted to work out a bridge between mental and material worlds. It is impossible for a person familiar with Indian thought not to see the reflections of Vedanta in Wordsworth when he reads:

> And I have felt
> A presence that disturbs me with the joy
> Of elevated thoughts; a sense sublime,
> Of something far more deeply interfused,
> Whose dwelling is the light of setting suns,
> And the round ocean and the living air,
> And the blue sky and in the mind of man:
> A motion and a spirit, that impels
> All thinking things, all objects of all thought,
> And rolls through all things.
>
> ("Tintern Abbey," 1798)

Although Hindu thought is recognizable in Wordsworth's poetry, it is often characterized as "unconscious" or coincidental for he is considered to have been deeply impressed in his romantic ideas by his enthusiasm for France and the French Revolution. This view, however, does not sufficiently account for the fact that, after his return from France at the age of twenty-eight, Wordsworth—together with Coleridge—gave up his dreams of political regeneration for the vision of bringing the greatest possible degree of happiness to the world through proper cultivation of sensibility and imagination in *Lyrical Ballads* (1798). By the time *Lyrical Ballads* appeared, the works of Sir William Jones had spread some knowledge of Indian thought in England.

Wordsworth's friend, collaborator, and "his spirit's brother," Samuel Taylor Coleridge (1772–1834), was also guided by the same vision. Indeed, he went a step farther in dabbling with the supernatural, as is reflected in "The Rime of the Ancient Mariner" (1798). Although Coleridge did not use Indian material, he was greatly attracted by the words and pictures of old tales, some of which must have come from India. His Eastern inspiration is to some extent attested to by the elusive yet arresting images in "Kubla Khan" (1797). This influence is also displayed in his Circassian love song, "Lewti.'

Coleridge emphasized the Neoplatonic tradition and introduced into England the new idealism of Germany, which was influenced by Indian thought. More than any other English Romantic, he was responsible for bringing about the literary revolution which regarded imagination as the most important creative faculty. His cardinal doctrine, reminiscent of the Vedanta, was the wholeness of, and continuity in, self-consciousness as the basis of mental experience which was all absorbed into a single dynamic force, the divine spark in each person, the "I" of every rational being, the free will which was the eventual source of religious faith as well as of genuine perception. Coleridge was well aware of Indian literature, as is illustrated by his letter to John Thirlwell in which he said he often wished to sleep or die, or "like the Indian *Vishnu,* to float about along an infinite ocean cradled in the flower of the Lotus and wake once in a million years for a few minutes."[19]

John Keats (1795–1821), although he knew little about India, was somewhat drawn to her as the passage about the Indian maid in *Endymion* (1818) reveals. Keats was fascinated by the romantic aspect of Greek mythology but *Endymion* was severely criticized at the time for its un-Greek quality. Keats wrote all the poems which brought him such fame within twelve months of *Endymion's* publication.

Percy Bysshe Shelley (1792–1822), who wrote *The Revolt of Islam* and was attracted by an idealized version of the Vale of Kashmir, propounds most magnificently the vedantic doctrine of maya in his elegy dedicated to Keats, *Adonais* (1821), perhaps his finest single poem.

> The one remains, the many change and pass.
> Heaven's light for ever shines. Earth's shadows fly.
> Life, like a dome of many-coloured glass.
> Stains the white radiance of Eternity,
> Until Death tramples it to fragments.

Simultaneously a song of lamentation and a song of triumph, the poem makes no distinction between mortality and immortality. Shelley's passionate conviction that Adonais is not dead, but has "awakened from the dream of Life" and is "made one with Nature," is highly significant.[20] Hindu thought maintains that the end of the journey is to become one with the absolute. Shelley's suggestion that birth interrupts a state of bliss which death restores

> That Light whose smile kindles the Universe,
> That Beauty in which all things work and move,
> That Benediction which the eclipsing curse of
> birth can quench not.... *(Adonais)*

is very close to the Indian concept. Engaged in the pursuit of an unattainable ideal of beauty, Shelley was inspired by his love for the universe, which included not only the human race or even all living beings, but all elements of nature. His identification with nature—he becomes one with the lark in "To a Skylark," with the cloud in "The Cloud," and with the wind in "Ode to the West Wind"—and penetrating perception of its hidden meaning approximate Indian thought.

In 1810, Robert Southey (1774–1843) published his long narrative poem, *The Curse of Kehama,* drawing upon romantic material from India. Although Southey had studied Indian society and literature and claimed his poem as an authentic picture of India, his knowledge was imperfect, and he graphically endeavoured to show that Hinduism was a false and monstrous religion. Based on a theme from Hindu mythology, this poem conveyed little of India, but added distortion and confusion to the British view of Indian life. Ultimately, Southey himself found the poem unsatisfactory, as did his contemporaries, such as Sir Walter Scott. Southey, neither as famous nor as brilliant as his friends Wordsworth and Coleridge, was united with them in the ardour of youthful ideas, and during the years of maturity, in reaction against those same ideas. The foreign influence in his poetry is so prominent that he is remembered primarily for his outlandish settings.

Thomas Moore (1779–1852) was also attracted by Indian material. He showed an insight into Indian society and customs in his poem *Lalla Rookh* (1817), which brought the then huge sum of three thousand guineas for the author. The first edition sold out immediately and during the course of the century it went into innumerable editions. In view of the fact that novels were far too expensive to buy in relation to the average income of the time, the rapid reprints of *Lalla Rookh* reveal more than ordinary attraction for Indian situations. *Lalla Rookh* consisted of four narrative poems woven into the romantic tale of a Mughal princess' love for a Kashmiri poet. Mainly concerned with delighting his readers, Moore presented India as a land of dazzling beauty, full of magnificent palaces, splendid temples, and perfumed gardens. His descriptions of the country, however, merely underlined the prevalent conventionally distorted picture of political India. He relied on rather undependable sources, and occasionally let his imagination get the better of him, as a result of which certain absurd, even nonsensical, descriptions crept into his work.

Many writers used India as a locale for European adventure. For instance, India figured prominently in *The Surgeon's Daughter* by Sir Walter Scott (1771–1832). However, he knew nothing of India, and hinted as much in the introduction to the novel. The story begins in Scotland and ends in the territory of Haider Ali and Tipu Sultan, the famous rulers of eighteenth-century Mysore, which had recently been conquered by the British after a series of prolonged and exacting campaigns. Scott's characters and situations were, of course, fictitious; his knowledge of Indian history inaccurate; and he had a Scotsman's love for fairy tales, fables, and folklore.

Most fiction writers of this period had no personal knowledge of India, and used Indian situations primarily to advance the popularity of their works. But the case of Lord Thomas Babington Macaulay is somewhat different and, therefore, puzzling. He was a well-known man of letters when he came to India in 1834 where he lived for four years. However, he read little of Indian literature and made no serious evaluation of India and her heritage, even though scores of European scholars had revealed the richness of Indian learning, which was available in any number of European languages. If he had done so, the history of the Anglo-Indian relationship might have been different. He wrote one small volume of essays on India, but it was written with such fervour and effect that it was the standard authority on India for many years in England. The revolt of 1857 gave these essays additional popularity as they were easy on the English ear. Despite the abundance of evidence contradicting Macaulay, later English writers continued to echo his ideas again and again, thereby keeping a falsehood alive. Macaulay's India was a distant land across boundless seas and deserts where dusky natives lived under strange stars, worshipped strange gods, and wrote strange characters from right to left.

It is not surprising that India figured in English Romanticism. What does astonish historians is that the Romantic writers found India of only passing and minor interest. Perhaps the complexities of a political relationship hampered a better understanding of Indian culture. Britons came to India to govern, acquire wealth, live without interrupting their own habits and customs, and return home in comfort and economic security. Belief in their political ascendancy and material prosperity as evidence of cultural superiority possibly rendered them unreceptive to any but the negative aspects of Indian society. There were, no doubt, some British administrators who made notable contributions to Indology, but most of the traders, as well as the adventurers serving at Indian courts, were hardly men of culture; they were merely interested in "shaking the pagoda tree." Whilst British power was reaffirmed with a certain degree of finality after the revolt of 1857, the uprising left scars on both sides. The British, proud and arrogant with success, still were mindful of how close they had come to total loss and disaster, which made them cautious, suspicious, even afraid. The Indians, on the other hand, smarting under defeat, turned to more organized preparations for their national reconstruction. Each side remembered the savagery and brutalities of the other, without recalling their own part in it. It was in this atmosphere of mutual distrust and fear, later worsened by political crises and conflicts, that cultural intercourse between India and Britain took place. For instance, John Ruskin (1819–1900), whose opinion was coloured by the events of 1857, dismissed Indians and their philosophy as "childish, or restricted in intellect and similarly childish or restricted in their philosophies or faiths."[21]

Ruskin wrote and spoke with equal authority and arrogance on subjects he knew well and those he knew nothing about. However, he was a great teacher—he was Slade Professor of Art at Oxford—and a master of prose. But he was a complex person, at once charming and sinister, righteous and satanic. He inherited a strain of madness and suffered intermittently from insanity. Tennyson expressed sentiments similar to Ruskin's in his *Defence of Lucknow*. But these are extreme examples of English response to India in which reason was subordinated to prejudice.

During the second half of the nineteenth century, Buddhism became better known in Britain, as in Europe. Indeed, since the end of the nineteenth century, many European thinkers and writers have proposed the adoption of Buddhism by the West. Whatever their success, there is no doubt that in recent times Buddhism, because of its rational and realistic character, has gained popularity in the West. Of the three Eastern civilizations, Indian, Chinese, and Islamic, the Indians have influenced the modern West most, especially through Buddhism. In fact, the West—especially Christians—regarded Buddhism as so powerful that it was dangerous.

Sir Edwin Arnold's famous poem, *The Light of Asia*, published in 1879, which is based on *Lalitavistara*, singing the praise of the Buddha has become extremely popular. In America it has gone through one hundred editions, and in England between fifty to one hundred. It has been translated into several European languages. Later, scholars like T. W. Rhys Davids (1843–1922), who greatly aided the interpretation of early Buddhism by editing Pali sources, Mrs. Caroline Rhys, Davids Paul Carus, Edward Conze, Christmas Humphreys, and others contributed to the popularity of Buddhism in the West.

In 1881 T. W. Rhys Davids founded the Pali Text Society which atracted the attention of a number of European scholars to a new and important branch of Indian thought and literature. In addition to two dozen volumes of translations, the Society published one hundred and seventeen volumes of Pali texts and a Pali-English dictionary. The Buddhist Society in London and elsewhere has also played an important role in exposing the West to Buddhist teaching. Looking at the notices of meetings and lectures in any recent issue of the London *New Statesman* for example, one must get the impression that during the past decade or so interest in Indian thought, especially Buddhism, has been steadily growing in Europe.

Actually, early in the nineteenth century, attempts were made to prove the Buddhistic origins of primitive Christianity. N. A. Notovick's book, *Inconnue Vie de Jesus Christ* (*Unknown Life of Jesus Christ*), published in 1834, sought to prove that Jesus had been initiated into his career by a sixteen-year stay with Brahmans and Buddhist monks. Many scholars from different countries later combined in trying to discover cases of Christian dependence on Buddhism, such as Rudolf Seydel (1882), A. S. Edmunds (1909), and Richard Garbe (1914). In 1882 Notovick's book came under heavy criticism. In the English translation of the work he endeavoured to answer the criticism, maintaining that the doctrine contained in the Tibetan verses was the same as that of the Gospels, differing only in outward appearance.[22]

India even partly conditioned English character, for the conquest of India made England a powerful political and military empire. A sense of racial superiority and national exclusiveness, and of a predetermined mission, inverted nationalism which often manifests itself in understatements and in deceptively disguised self-praise for which the British are well known, strict individualism neatly integrated in collective discipline, and ability for endurance under sustained pressure, are natural consequences of the British association with India.

From the early days of the East India Company, Indian words have been continuously adopted into English. Typical words are durbar, bazaar, pukka, khaki, bungalow, divan, pundit, pajamas, baksheesh, begum, chop, chit, cot, fakir, purdah, raj, nabob, darshan, verandah, vakil, zenana, palanquin, mulligatawney, chutney, swaraj, and shikar.

"The Oxford English Dictionary," observes Subba Rao "which rejects over half the words noticed by *Hobson-Jobson* and does not contain words which have become familiar only in very recent times, accords recognition to about a thousand words, apart from numerous compounds and derivatives."[23] It is, however, true that this number, large as it is, is small considering the length and intensity of Indo-British contact, and also in comparison to the English words adopted by Indian languages. The assimilation of language over this period was conditioned by the nature and need of the relationship. For instance, in the early phase when contact was predominantly commercial, the words borrowed were mainly from that vocabulary. Later, when Indian thought, literature, and philosophy began to attract the attention of the English scholars, English men of letters began to use terminology from these fields in their writing. Milton, Dryden, Orme, Burke, Scott, Thackeray, and T. S. Eliot are some of the eminent writers who made effective use of Indian words.

In a unique although incidental way, India helped to develop not only British economy and social life, but also political thought. The increasing influx of Indian wealth into England created a new class, whose widening horizon for the deployment and experimentation of political ideas required a setting of India's size. In the East India Company Adam Smith saw an embodiment of the hated "mercantile system." Many English political movements tested their strength and fought their early contests upon Indian questions. A few Englishmen had succeeded in carving out an empire and enforcing an organized, although intensely authoritarian, government. India provided the much needed efficiency in administration and the purpose in government for the dominant English Liberalism of the day, in addition to an operation base for free trade and the missionary activities of Evangelicalism. It was this Indian experience which influenced Utilitarian thought, and caused John Stuart Mill to criticize Liberty, Equality, and Fraternity. He called his book "little more than the turning of an Indian lantern on European problems." One obvious example of Indian influence is the development of British imperialism, another lies in the reform of the civil service. Maine was deeply influenced by India in his study of early societies. He wrote after the publication of *Popular Government:* "If there was an ideal Toryism I should probably be a Tory; but I should wish to win now. The truth is, India and the India Office make one judge public men by standards which have little to do with public opinion."

Echoes of Indian thought could be heard even in lands only remotely concerned with India. For instance, in the works of Mihai Eminescu (1850–1889), the greatest poet of Rumania, Sanskrit and Buddhist influences are found. Eminescu learned of Indian philosophy through Schopenhauer. He also had some knowledge of the Sanskrit language, although it is doubtful that he could read original Sanskrit texts. However, he translated Franz Bopp's *Glossarium Sanskriticum* and a part of his Dictionary. Parts of his poetry appear to be Rumanian versions of well-known Sanskrit texts. For example, in *Letter number one,* his vision of the origin of the world, when the existent and the non-existent were not, is reminiscent of the "Hymn of Creation" from the *Rig Veda.* The idea of nirvana is frequently found in his poems. The Hindu approach to reality and beauty is reflected in many of his verses. Indian literary legends and themes are also found in poems such as "God and Man" and "Looking for Sheherezade." Not only the title of his poem, "Tattwamasi," indicates his familiarity with upanishadic thought, but the content deals with the identity of Atman and Brahman. Hindu monism is reflected in his

> So it is that bird and man,
>   Sun and moon
> Are born and die in Brahma
>   the Sacred—
> Where all things become one.[25]

Eminescu's poetry also contains many erotic themes such as *Kamadeva,* after the Hindu god of love, the spark of creation. That Eminescu chose an Indian symbol to express one of his intimate sentiments is held as "yet another proof of the deep and wide contact he had with the ancient literature of India."[26]

Russian intellectuals, too, reacting against the increasing mechanization of life, turned towards the East for inspiration. Although this movement was not as powerful as the Romantic movement in Western Europe, especially in Germany, Russia, aided by her rapidly expanding territorial frontiers in Asia, acquired a new Asian awareness in her national disposition. In fact, even before the big Russian advance eastwards, Chadaiev said in 1840 that "We are the darling children of the East. Everywhere we are in contact with the East, it is from there that we have drawn our belief, our laws, our virtue ...."[27] He goes on to claim that as the East is declining, Russia is the natural successor to Eastern wisdom. Maxim Gorki (1868–1936) in a letter to Romain Rolland said that Russia was more Oriental than China. Dostoievsky declared that it would be beneficial for Russia to turn her soul towards the East. In fact, there has always been a sort of gulf between Western Europe and Russia, the former frequently referring to the latter as the East.

Leo Tolstoy (1828–1910) responded to the East with great sensitivity. At Kazan he studied Oriental languages and literature, and came into close contact with Asian people during his frequent visits to Caucasus. He acquired an early reverent interest in Indian culture which he always retained. In 1870 he published a collection of folktales which included some Indian stories. His *Confession,* in which he describes his spiritual struggles, refers more than once to the Buddha with admiration, relates some of the episodes of the Buddha's Renunciation, and seeks to demonstrate the futility of human life on earth in terms of an ancient Indian parable. Ancient Indian literature, Max Müller's series, *Sacred Books of the East,* and later, the writings of Vivekananda made a deep impression on him. He opposed the imposition of what he considered a degenerating Western structure on India, but disagreed with Hinduism on a number of points including Hindu cosmology. Indeed, he looked upon Hinduism through the eyes of a social reformer, yet Indian thought helped him to acquire new standards by which he could revaluate Christianity. Tolstoy corresponded with a number of his Indian friends, including Mahatma Gandhi and C. R. Das. In *Letter to a Hindu,* addressed to Gandhi in 1909, Tolstoy quoted from the Upanishads, the *Bhagavad Gita*, the Tamil *Kural*, and modern Hindu religious writings, including Vivekananda. He urged Indians to adopt what he called "the Law of Love," and not give up their ancient religious culture for the materialism of the West. Tolstoy was amongst the first European intellectuals who reflected on the problems facing India. It is well known that his ideas on resistance to aggression influenced Mahatma Gandhi.

Indian thought made a better impression not only in nineteenth century Germany, than in England but even in distant America. An illustration of this influence is the American transcendentalist movement inspired by Ralph Waldo Emerson (1803–1882). Emerson's central theme is that all that exists is the manifestion of a simple universal spirit. The development of Emerson's thought is revealed in his *Journals* which cover twenty years. India is first mentioned in 1842. It seems that in the beginning Buddhism aroused conflicting feelings in him. Whilst he admitted the greatness of Buddhist teaching, he was uncertain of its practicability. He was drawn by the concept of the transmigration of soul: "Then I discovered the Secret of the World, that all things subsist, and do not die, but only retire a little from sight and afterwards return again."[28]

The discovery of Hinduism and Buddhism impressed on Emerson that all religions are fundamentally the same. Eighty years later, Romain Rolland came to a similar conclusion which he described as the "predisposition to Vedantism." Repelled by the increasing materialism of the West, Emerson turned to India for solace: "The Indian teaching, through its cloud of legends, has yet a simple and grand religion, like a queenly countenance seen through a rich veil. It teaches to speak truth, love others as yourself, and to despise trifles."[29] As he grew older he became increasingly devoted to Hinduism and Buddhism. Nowhere does Emerson's transcendentalism find more complete expression than in his remarkable poem, "Brahma," which Sencourt suggests is a translation from Kalidasa through a Latin version known to Dr. Morrison of the Indian Institute.[30] The poem may not have been a direct translation from Kalidasa, but it was derived from him. In his essay on Plato, Emerson explicitly acknowledges his debt to India: "In all nations there are minds which incline to dwell in the conception of the fundamental Unity. The raptures of prayer and ecstasy of devotion lost all being in one Being. This tendency finds its highest expression in the religious writings of the East, and chiefly in the Indian Scriptures, in the *Vedas*, the *Bhagavat Gita*, and the *Vishnu Purana*. Those writings contain little else than this idea, and they rise to pure and sublime strains in celebrating it."

Another American who turned his attention towards India was Henry David Thoreau (1817–1862), a younger contemporary and friend of Emerson. He is chiefly remembered for *Walden*, which much inspired the pioneers of the British labour movement, and for his essay, "On Civil

Disobedience," in which he protested the government's interference with individual liberty. In some respect, Mahatma Gandhi's philosophy of life and programme of action were similar to Thoreau's. Both were keen naturalists; both believed in the dignity of human labour and attempted to run self-sufficient farms; both were vegetarians, teetotallers, and non-smokers; both derived their inspiration from the *Bhagavad Gita;* and both were rebels against human injustice.

There is some controversy about Mahatma Gandhi's debt to Thoreau. Thoreau partisans suggest that his "On Civil Disobedience," published in 1849, was Gandhi's source book in his political campaign for civil resistance because the Mahatma used the phrase "civil disobedience" to describe his resistance to the tyranny of the State. Beyond this use of identical phrases, there is little to substantiate this assertion. In his autobiography, *My Experiments with Truth,* Gandhi lists and analyzes the books that most influenced him during the formative period of his public life when he was experimenting with the political weapon which he called *satyagraha.* In his generous acknowledgement of debts, he does not refer to the work of Thoreau. Some weight has been lent to this misconception by an open letter that Gandhi wrote to the people of America, on the eve of the launching of his Quit India movement in 1942, in which he showed his great esteem for Thoreau, whom he called, in his characteristic humility, his "teacher." This letter, however, also clearly states that Gandhi had found in Thoreau a teacher who, through his essay on civil disobedience, furnished him with scientific *confirmation* of what he was doing, and Gandhi was punctilious in his use of language.[31]

Thoreau was deeply impressed by Hindu thought and his *Journal* contains many comments on his extensive reading of Hindu texts. He wrote in 1850 that the inspiration of the Vedas had fallen on him like the light of a higher and purer luminary, and risen on him like the full moon after the stars had come out. *Walden* contains explicit references to Indian scriptures, such as "How much more admirable the *Bhagavad Gita* than all the ruins of the East." He even followed a traditional Hindu way of life. "It was fit that I should live on rice mainly, who loved so well the philosophy of India." Thoreau invokes the language of silence, which is so common in India, in his silent communion with the old fisherman at the pond. Even more significant, perhaps, are the many references to the river and the definite equation of Walden Pond with the sacred Ganges. "To dismiss all of these references as simply part of Thoreau's temperamental affinity for India is to underestimate the extraordinary influence of the Orient on his own thinking and to misunderstand the purpose of *Walden.*"[32]

Walt Whitman (1819–1892), who championed American intellectual independence, was amongst those who came under the influence of the Transcendentalists. There are no explicit quotations from Indian literature in Whitman's writings, but he knew of Indian texts. His poems show a strong sense of the brotherhood of man, and it was possibly from the Transcendentalists that he learned an all-inclusive mystical self-identification with all men and all things. In *Song of Myself* he says that "all religions are true"; a doctrine which has always found favour with Hindu thought. In the nineteenth century, this doctrine was powerfully reaffirmed by Swami Ramakrishna. In some of his later poems Whitman shows a definite interest in Hindu mysticism. Most significant of these is *Passage to India* in which he voices the characteristic Hindu doctrine that his own soul is one with the soul of the universe.

The Christian Science movement in America was possibly influenced by India. The founder of this movement, Mary Baker Eddy, in common with the Vedantins, believed that matter and suffering were unreal, and that a full realization of this fact was essential for relief from ills and pains. In *Science and Health* she asserts: "Christian Science explains all cause and effect as mental, not physical. It lifts the veil of mystery from Soul and body. It shows the scientific relation of man to God, disentangles the interlaced ambiguities of being, and sets free the imprisoned thought. In divine Science, the "Universe, including man, is spiritual, harmonious, and eternal. Science shows that what is termed *matter* is but the subjective state of what is termed by the author *mortal mind.*" The Christian Science doctrine has naturally been given a Christian framework, but the echoes of Vedanta in its literature are often striking.

Late in the nineteenth century, Vivekananda made two trips to the United States, and was received with enthusiastic popular acclaim. There were, however, some critics who were ill-informed of his motives and of the concepts he represented, and who dreaded the influx of alien ideas.

Both the devotion and dispute which his lectures evoked stimulated further American interest in Indian religion and thought. As a result, Vedanta Centres and Ramakrishna Missions were established in various parts of the country, and they flourish today as active nuclei of Indian thought. Even before Vivekananda fired the imagination of the American people, Sanskrit philosophy had made an impact on American scholarship by the teaching of Sanskrit at leading American universities.

Later, Tagore visited the United States three times and travelled throughout the country lecturing on Indian art and philosophy and giving readings from his poetry and plays. His writings had already, and have always, received widespread appreciation.

Because of the advance in the mass communication media, the Indian national movement attracted the attention of European peoples who were themselves going through a period of democratic advance, fighting against traditional and aristocratic oppression. Some European intellectuals took a purely academic interest in India during this period, but others were inclined towards a synthesis between East and West. Amongst the latter, Romain Rolland, the French pacifist and author, is outstanding. He was deeply concerned with and championed the cause of Indian thought and culture. He saw a close affinity between the Aryans of the East and those of the West. He met Indian intellectuals, especially from the Ramakrishna Mission in Europe. He wrote the *Life of Ramakrishna* in which he said, "I am bringing to Europe, as yet unaware of it, the fruit of a new autumn, a new message of the soul, the symphony of India, bearing the name of Ramakrishna. The man whose image I evoke was the consummation of a thousand years of the spiritual life of three hundred million people."[33] He also wrote the world-famous biography of Mahatma Gandhi, which inspired many European thinkers. Having read this biography, Mira ben (Madeleine Slade), the daughter of an English admiral, renounced a life of luxury to live in the ashram of Gandhi. In Gandhi, Rolland saw the embodiment of all that was simple, modest, and pure. Surprisingly, Rolland had never visited India. In close contact on the one hand with Tagore and Gandhi, and on the other with European intellectuals, Romain Rolland was a unique mediator between India and the West. Although a devout Christian himself, he often felt that his Christianity had more in common with the religions of India than with the church in which he was brought up.

Of modern Indian thinkers, M. K. Gandhi (1869–1948) had the most influence on the outside world. Gandhi has often been described as the greatest man since Jesus; he certainly was India's greatest since the Buddha. He represented Indian idealism at its best. All his life he worked on almost all fronts of the Indian revolution, but he combatted evil with good and in the true spirit of love. Satya (truth) was his God; ahimsa (non-violence), his creed. He believed violence to be the antithesis of the spirit of truth. Inflicting physical injury or uttering an unkind word, even thinking ill of others, were serious violations of ahimsa. Indeed, to be truly non-violent meant that one must love his opponent and pray for him even when attacked. No wonder many Christians see in Gandhian doctrines a reflection of Christian thought.

Indeed Gandhi was a great admirer of Christianity, and often admitted the influence of the Sermon on the Mount which he believed contained Jesus' message of non-violence. Frequently he would read passages from the Bible in his daily prayer meetings. "When I survey the wondrous Cross" and "Lead kindly light amid the encircling gloom" were his favourite hymns. Romain Rolland described Gandhi as the "St. Paul of our own days." Gandhi was so devoted to Jesus that in the earlier phase of his career many of his Christian friends thought his conversion was imminent. But he was a Hindu to the core. Defining his attitude to a prominent Indian Christian, Kali Charan Banerjee, he said: "Today my position is that, though I admire much in Christianity, I am unable to identify myself with orthodox Christianity. I must tell you in all humility that Hinduism, as I know it, entirely satisfies my soul, fills my whole being, and I find a solace in the *Bhagavad Gita* and *Upanishads* that I miss even in the Sermon on the Mount."[34]

Kropotkin's essays awakened Gandhi's ideas of pacific anarchism. His completely non-violent society was to be stateless, for it was not possible to impose non-violence on a person or society. Tolstoy's *The Kingdom of God is Within You* and Ruskin's *Unto This Last* contributed to Gandhi's philosophy.

Gandhi, although he belonged to humanity and wielded unparalleled influence over millions of people all over the world, was, in all respects, essentially an Indian. As a London *Times* editorial said on the day after his death: "No country but India and no religion but Hinduism could have given birth to a Gandhi."

Whilst the full reprecussions of Gandhi's influence are still to be seen, there is no doubt they will be unending and inexhaustible. His philosophy has already assumed a self-perpetuating quality. His doctrines of non-violence and satyagraha have not only given Indians a new means of fighting for their rights but have become a source of inspiration to all seekers of justice everywhere. Indeed, non-Indian movements, notably those led by Martin Luther King, Jr. in the American South and Kenneth Kaunda in Northern Rhodesia, might even be regarded as more truly Gandhian in essence than similar movements within India today.

Since the days of the Montgomery bus boycott of 1955–1956, followed by the upsurge of the sit-ins and freedom rides of 1960–1961, the movement for civil rights in the United States has been strongly based on the Gandhian concept of non-violence. The movement, as expected, has assumed a distinctively local character and personality, and has gained notable successes in advancing the Negro revolution in America. Martin Luther King often acknowledged his debt to Gandhian thought and literature.

In Nazi Germany, the real resistance that developed within the country itself was inspired by Gandhian theories of passiveness and non-violent revolution. Its leader, Dietrich Bonhoeffer, was so impressed by the possibility of applying these ideas to Christianity, and employing Gandhian resistance against Hitler's tyranny that he arranged to make a "pilgrimage to India" to visit Gandhi, but political events prevented him from undertaking the journey.

Today, wherever there is a popular people's movement against injustice, it proceeds along lines inspired by Gandhian satyagraha. Indeed what Marx is to socialism Gandhi is to modern active pacifism. His doctrine of class co-operation and trusteeship inspires hope in those who loathe the prospect of achieving progress only through class conflict. Persuasion, not coercion, is the keynote of polity today. In fact, serious, and in some ways diverse, British writers, such as Sir Stephen King-Hall and Kingsley Martin, suggest that any resistance to nuclear war must be non-violent, organized on Gandhian lines. An Indian Gandhi scholar writes,

"Countries distant from India, wherever the field is ready or rather where there are workers in the field, have been influenced by the Gandhian approach to the spiritual and practical fusion. Serious studies in Group Dynamics, group and individual action-therapy are being pursued in great institutions abroad; the Gandhian quantum which stimulates higher loyalties and cohesion rather than spreads negative crowd-infection has stimulated new sociological and applicational research."[35]

Romain Rolland spoke for many of Gandhi's Western admirers when he wrote: "Gandhi is not only for India a hero of national history whose legendary memory will be enshrined in the millennial epoch. He has not only been the spirit of active life which has breathed into the peoples of India the proud consciousness of their unity, of their power, and the will to their independence. He has renewed, for all the people of the West, the message of their Christ, forgotten or betrayed. He has inscribed his name among the sages and saints of humanity; and the radiance of his figure has penetrated into all the regions of the earth."[36] The American missionary, John Haynes Holmes, declared: "If I believe in rebirth, I should—I mention it with due respect-see in Mahatma Gandhi the Christ returned to our world."

Aurobindo Ghose (1872–1950), the modern Indian philosopher, transformed the Hindu spiritual heritage into a dynamic spiritual evolution. He is the only modern Indian thinker known both as a Yogi and as a philosopher. He sought to reconcile the theories of ancient Vedanta with those of modern scientific materialism and vitalism, thus attempting to harmonize spiritual and material demands. He was opposed to scientific materialism that sought to reduce man to the position of an insect.

He believed in the omnipresence of the One and the inevitable culmination of man's evolution into an integral and dynamic union with Him in life. Reality, although manifold in self-expression, is one and indivisible. There is nothing else but Him, and to infuse His unity, harmony, and perfection into worldly life and nature is the mission of every individual human soul. This was the core of Aurobindo's philosophy and the central aim of his Yoga. His Spiritual Realism thus departs from the traditional Indian doctrine of maya. Aurobindo was educated in Europe, and his philosophy was greatly influenced by the theory of evolution and the Western positive attitude to the material world, but he discovered both of these elements in the Saiva and the Sakta forms of the Advaita.[37] Romain Rolland regarded Aurobindo as the highest synthesis of the genius of Europe and the genius of Asia. He was an Indian rishi who had gained a clear insight into the modern scientific mind. Instead of finding a conflict between East and West he saw the old heritage of the East and the new knowledge of the West as one organized whole. His philosophy, like that of Gandhi, was couched in a language drawn from India's past, but was addressed to problems posed in the modern West.

Whilst Aurobindo's philosophy was rooted in the vedantic consciousness, his Muslim contemporary, Sir Muhammed Iqbal (1876–1938), was deeply committed to Islam. Poet and philosopher, he wrote one of the most popular national songs of India, "Sare Jahan se Acchha Hindustan Hamara." He was well versed in European thought and culture but is better known as a poet than as a philosopher, although he inspired the creation of Pakistan. In Germany, where he completed his doctoral thesis on Persian metaphysics, he became acutely conscious of both the good and the evil of Western scientific materialism, and of the consequent agonizing inner conflicts amongst European intellectuals and nations. He admired the vitality and dynamism of European life but criticized its mechanistic and utilitarian aspects. In his poems and teaching he combined his Islamic beliefs with Western rationalism and was heavily influenced by Nietzsche.

Although a mystic, he preached the glorification and divination of desire rather than its negation. Somewhat like the *Bhagavad Gita,* he urged man not so much to seek God as to seek his own true self. The essence of his philosophy was the quest for perfect man which could only be achieved through persistent and continuous personal effort. During the last years of his life, Iqbal was increasingly attracted by the progress of Soviet Russia.

Rabindranath Tagore (1861–1941) was a poet, philosopher, educator, and above all, a humanist. Fundamentally inspired by the Upanishads, he did not believe the new India belonged to one race or religion but to humanity. His visits to Western capitals were invariably attended by huge crowds, and he became an object of world-wide adoration. For a poet, especially of a subject-nation, this reception was unique. Despite this, the award of the Nobel Prize in 1913 to Tagore, against the claims of such famous Europeans as Thomas Hardy, Anatole France, Tolstoy, and Zola, drew protests from certain sections of the European and American press because Tagore was not "white." Perhaps in honouring Tagore, the West was endeavouring to show its appreciation of the Indian heritage which he so nobly symbolized.

Tagore wrote in both Bengali and English, and from 1913 onwards his poetry was translated into practically every European language. No other Indian has received greater honour in the West during his lifetime. Such appreciation cannot be altogether devoid of understanding. The West, involved in the conflicts of political and military alignments, on the brink of World War I was frustrated at the futility of material advancement. At this time Tagore brought to them a message which appealed "to their intelligence, their goodwill, their longing for emancipation from the chains of dead matter, speaking to white, black and yellow in the same language with the simplicity of a child and a prophet."[38]

After the war, Europe's response to the culture of Asia took conflicting forms. Whilst some thinkers defended the West, others hailed the East. In this process of European rethinking, India and Tagore played an important role. Numerous Western readers eagerly read Tagore's works, hoping to find mystical solace from the frustrations of life. Many European intellectuals were so firmly convinced that only Eastern ideals could save them that innumerable pseudo-oriental societies were founded all over Europe. Many of these societies had inaccurate knowledge of the East and practiced popularized forms of pseudo-Buddhistic and yogic cults.

Amongst the many European intellectuals and artists Tagore met, William Butler Yeats (1865–1939) was one of his more intimate friends. He dedicated *The Gardener* to Yeats. Yeats' belief that poetry was the product of a mystical experience, a state of trance where worldly conflicts melt away and the subconscious is transformed into artistic creation, had Indian origins. Yeats had discovered India, in fact, long before his intimate contact with Tagore. He had published his essay *The Celtic Element* in 1897, followed three years later by an essay on Shelley in which he compared the ministering spirits of intellectual beauty with the Devas of the East. Impressed in his adolescence by Sinnett's *Esoteric Buddhism,* he was alienated from science; Theosophy, Buddhism, Odic Force, and poetry constituted his world for a long time. In his *Autobiography* he recalls that it was under the impact of psychical research and mystical philosophy that he broke away from his father's influence, and he spent much time in mystical gatherings during his school days. Describing his first meeting with a Hindu philosopher at Dublin, Yeats said: "It was my first meeting with a philosophy that confirmed my vague speculations and seemed at once logical and boundless. Consciousness, he taught, does not merely spread out its surface but has, in vision and in contemplation, another motion, and can change in height and in depth."[39] His appreciation of India, however, in common with many European intellectuals, was more romantic than academic. After his contact with Tagore and his discovery of the English version of the *Gitanjali,* he turned more towards the East for inspiration. When Sir William Rothenstein, the celebrated English art critic and painter who was chiefly responsible for introducing Tagore to English intellectuals, gave Yeats the manuscript of the *Gitanjali* to read before it was published, Yeats was so deeply moved by it that he carried it with him everywhere. He records in his preface to the first edition of *Gitanjali:* "The lyrics ... display in their thought a world I have dreamed of all my life long. The work of a supreme culture, they yet appear as much the growth of the common soil as the grass and the rushes."[40] He continues: "A whole people, a whole civilization, immeasurably strange to us, seem to have been taken up into this imagination; and yet we are not moved because of its strangeness, but because we have met our own image, as though we had walked in Rossetti's willow wood, or heard, perhaps for the first time in literature, our voice as in a dream."[41] Yeats wrote some poems which had an Indian setting, such as "Jealousy." "Kanva on Himself" is based on a Hindu prayer: "I have lived many lives .... Everything that has been shall be again."

The quality Yeats valued most in Tagore's poetry was his union of sensuous images and deep spiritual appreciation of life. Yeats also aspired to what he called the "unity of being," to bring together the natural and the spiritual world in his poetry. In his conception, nature and God were not separated by thought, and the constricting sense of guilt was banished by gaiety and joyfulness in which the creative mind of the artist had been freed. According to Yeats, European writing, despite its familiar metaphor and general structure, was no longer acceptable because spirit and matter were irrevocably separated and as a result nature had become evil. Yeats could not forsake nature which was so full of art, beauty, and music. In Tagore he found a saint who sang of the joy in life without disturbing its deep sense of sanctity. Unlike Tagore, however, Yeats was keenly interested in the Yoga system and the Tantra. The authoritative texts of these two systems had reached Europe at about the same time and they made a further impact on Yeats.

Towards the end of his life Yeats moved away from Tagore a little, but he continued to draw inspiration from India, which contained for him the vision of the final harmony in human life. Like another Irish poet, George William Russell (popularly known as A. E.) who had also come under the influence of the Upanishads and Theosophy, Yeats discovered an identical spirit underlying both Gaelic and Indian civilizations.

In his "Meru" (1935)—Meru is the central mountain of the world in Indian mythology—Yeats contrasts the peaceful life of the mystic, despite the hardships of nature, with the transitory cycle of creation and destruction exemplified in the world of man. Yeats was influenced not only by Indian mysticism, but also by the secular aspects of Indian classical literature and art.

Traces of the influence of Indian secular thought are also noticed in the works of other writers, such as Edward Carpenter, Havelock Ellis, and D. H. Lawrence, who found support in the *Kama Sutra* for their revolt against the rigid sexual ethics of an earlier period. This text, widely read despite restrictions on it of various kinds, has had a far more subtle effect on Western people than is often realized.

The mysticism of T. S. Eliot, Aldous Huxley, and W. H. Auden clearly stems from Hindu roots. Aldous Huxley, an exacting critic, a brilliant novelist, and a satirist of his age, was deeply concerned with Indian religions and philosophy. He was, however, a highly sophisticated European with scientific training. He tested both aesthetic enjoyment and mystic experience by what he saw in conduct and behaviour, both in himself and in the world around him. He found many faults with the Indian attitude towards life. Yet he was convinced, after prolonged reflection, that society could not be changed unless the individual sensibility, cleansed of all passions, proceeded towards selfrealization through selflessness. In *Beyond the Mexique Bay* (1934) and *Ends and Means* (1937) he suggests that the flux of time is an illusion caused by man's preoccupation with his personal affairs, and it is through contemplation that man can merge into the timelessness of reality. For the first time in *Ends and Means,* a pacifist manifesto, Huxley almost reverentially mentions Gandhi, in whose achievement means and ends are inseparable. In *Ape and Essence* (1948) he regarded Gandhi's assassination as a cosmic tragedy. *The Perennial Philosophy* (1946) is yet another illustration of his knowledge of Indian thought, especially the Vedanta.

T. S. Eliot shows considerable knowledge of and sympathy with Hinduism and Buddhism in his writings. *The Waste Land,* for instance, contains references to a sermon of the Buddha and to a famous passage of the *Brihadaranyaka Upanishad,* and concludes, like an *Upanishad,* with the Sanskrit words *Shantih shantih shantih* (Peace! Peace!! Peace!!!!). *Four Quartets* reaffirms his familiarity with and interest in the Hindu and Buddhist texts. In "The Dry Salvages," which treats time and eternity, he makes an explicit reference to the *Bhagavad Gita* and to its cardinal doctrine of *niskama karma*—that all man's actions should be motivated by rightness and goodness, not by expectation of gain or merit.

Indian influences can easily be seen in Somerset Maugham's *The Razor's Edge,* and in the writings of Edith Sitwell, Christopher Isherwood, and Gerald Heard. C. G. Jung interpreted Hinduism and Buddhism in terms of his psychological system, and pointed out the great significance of Indian thought for the modern West: "We do not yet realise that while we are turning upside down the material world of the East with our technical proficiency, the East with its psychic proficiency is throwing our spiritual world into confusion. We have never yet hit upon the thought that while we are overpowering the Orient from without, it may be fastening its hold upon us from within."

Many other Western scientists have been profoundly attracted by Indian thought, causing them to revise their own intellectual presuppositions and inheritance. The relationship between the body and the mind is as much a concern of the Western psychologist as it was of the ancient Indian philosopher. Kenneth Walker, a famous British surgeon, has devoted a good deal of time and writing to the study of Indian thought and literature in search of an answer:

From the point of view of science we see man as an elaborate piece of mechanism, his actions determined by man's endocrine glands, his central nervous system, his hereditary endowments, and his environment. From philosophy we learn that his capacity for knowledge is strictly limited, so that by means of the sense organs alone he can never know reality. This is confirmed by Eastern philosophy, but a new idea is added. Man, as he is, can see no more and do no more, but by right effort and right method, he can gain new powers, understand more, and achieve more. Finally we have the confirmation of this idea by religion. Whatever may be the differences in their creed, whatever may be the variations in their philosophy, all religions, without exception, contain this idea of the possibility of change, so that a man may become other than he is. From the point of view of all religions man is a being in whom are lying latent higher powers.[42]

Amongst contemporary interpreters of Indian culture and philosophic thought, S. Radhakrishnan (1888–) is the best known. His many works, almost thirty, written in superb English with arresting originality, his long period of teaching Indian philosophy at Oxford University, and his eloquent, lucid lectures, have made him the representative Indian philosopher for most foreigners. His scholarly status, no doubt, has been aided by his pre-eminence in Indian political life; he served a term as India's Rastrapati, President.[43] In fact, well before Radhakrishnan's work became widely known, he had made such an impact on the West that more than thirty years ago C. E. M. Joad published a book entitled *Counter-attack from the East. The Philosophy of Radhakrishnan.*

Generally, Radhakrishnan is regarded as the philosopher of a dynamic idealism characterized by a deep spiritual note, a catholic outlook, an appreciation of the eternal values of all cultures and religions, and an abiding, confident optimism as to the future of human civilization. His idealism contains certain influences of Western thinkers such as Plato and Hegel, but it is essentially upanishadic in its comprehensiveness. He accepts the monistic and the theistic view of the Upanishads, and does not subordinate the one to the other. The essence of his idealism is the primacy of the spirit and its manifestation in matter, life, mind, and self. It is not the substance of Hegel, for it is not immobile but dynamic and real. It is felt everywhere, although seen nowhere. The spirit is the absolute, and is not only imminent but also transcendent. He is a follower of Samkara, but does not regard the world as an illusion (maya), as most other Advaitins do. Although the creation of the world is inexplicable, the world is not devoid of value and importance. He would prefer to treat the world as a combination of being and non-being.

Of the other interpreters of Indian culture who have made substantial impact on Western thinking, Ananda Coomaraswamy (1877–1947) is unique. Burn in Ceylon of a highly successful Ceylonese barrister and a British mother, and originally trained as a geologist, he became a scholar and philosopher wholly wedded to the Indian tradition. His masterly analysis of Indian culture exhibits a rare combination of scientific investigation and artistic formulation. His researches include work on archaeology, philology, iconography, metaphysics, and religion. For the last thirty years of his life he worked at the Boston Museum of Fine Arts. His writing reveals a devoted, painstaking, and erudite scholarship, encyclopaedic intellect, and sensitive insight. His works have acquired such a high degree of authority that it is virtually impossible to pick up any significant modern work on Indian art which has not drawn upon Coomaraswamy.

He wanted India to remain Indian and continue to demonstrate that a pattern of life rooted in religion and philosophy can also be elegant, graceful, and fully satisfying. In India philosophy has been the key to the understanding of concrete life, not a mere intellectual exercise in abstract thought.

In Jagdish Chandra Bose (1858–1937) can be seen a remarkable Indian response to Western impact. Bose, a pioneer of modern Indian science, combined ancient Indian introspective methods with modern experimental methods to demonstrate "the universal livingness of matter" or "the omnipresence of Life in Matter." He demonstrated by laboratory tests, using special scientific instruments of extreme delicacy and precision, that plants possessed life. Modern science thus endorsed the ancient upanishadic truth that the entire universe is born of a life-force and is quivering with a touch of animation. His work represents the triumph of spirituality over extreme materialism.

In 1897, two disciples of Sri Ramakrishna, Swami Vivekananda (1863–1902) and Swami Brahmananda (1863–1922), founded the Ramakrishna Mission with its headquarters at Belur near Calcutta. Whilst Brahmananda remained in India as head of the organization, Vivekananda pioneered the establishment of Ramakrishna Missions in America and other Western countries. However, when Vivekananda first visited the United States in 1893 to attend the World-Parliament of Religions at Chicago, he did not come as a missionary of the Ramakrishna cult but as an exponent of Vedanta philosophy. Hence Vedanta philosophy got further circulation before the Ramakrishna movement gained currency. In any case, the distinction between the two is small.

Vivekananda boldly proclaimed that Vedanta was destined to be the religion of mankind. He received a spontaneous ovation at the Chicago meeting when he gave his remarkable presentation of the Hindu religion. He won popular recognition abroad for India's ancient civilization, for the Vedanta philosophy, and for India's newborn claim to nationhood. Such was the impact of his personality that wherever he went, whether in Europe, China, or Egypt, he created a minor sensation; in America he was called the "cyclonic Hindu."

The influence of Vivekananda and the Ramakrishna Missions, through their *maths* in almost every Western capital, is considerable. Although essentially Hindu, they advocate the oneness of all religions and the doctrine of "one goal of the many paths." This extreme religious tolerance has a natural appeal to many in the West. There are some, however, who dread a deeper challenge in this "live and let live" approach.

How DEEPLY INDIAN ideas have impressed the Western mind through Theosophy can be gauged by the great popularity of the works of J. Krishnamurti (1895–), who was acclaimed in his youth as "Messiah." The central theme of Krishnamurti's teaching is that it is through self-knowledge that man comes to eternal reality.

The term Theosophy is a translation of the Sanskrit term, Brahmavidya. First used in the third century by the Greek philosopher, Iamblichus, it meant the inner knowledge concerning the things of God. In its modern sense, Theosophy was a movement founded by Madame H. P. Blavatsky in 1875 in New York. The Theosophical Society is a nonsectarian body whose creed is that there is no religion higher than truth. It seeks to form a nucleus of the universal brotherhood of humanity, without distinction of race, creed, sex, caste, or colour; to encourage the study of comparative religion, philosophy, and science; and to investigate unexplained laws of nature and the powers latent in man.

Theosophy, signifying a knowledge of Brahman or the Absolute, closely follows the concepts propounded by the Upanishads and Indian philosophies. For example, the doctrine of the one transcendent, eternal, all pervading, all sustaining, self-existent life, and of the reincarnation and liberation of soul bear deep affinity to Hindu ideas. Theosophists regard India as the guardian of secret wisdom and esoteric science, and the chief exponent of the transcendent unity of all religions.

In addition to the influence of the Theosophical Society in the West, Theosophy has also had a notable impact in the countries to the east of India. In Indonesia, for instance, early nationalism came under Theosophist influence through *Taman Siswa,* literally garden of pupils, and Sukarno at one time subscribed to Theosophy. Madame Blavatsky founded a branch of the Theosophical Society in Java in 1883; by 1910 it had a membership of over two thousand, about half of which were Europeans, and the rest Indonesians and Chinese. The Theosophical movement in Indonesia also ran its own schools, called the Arjuna Schools.

Yoga, which seeks to join the unenlightened nature of man to the enlightened and divine part of himself through knowledge and discipline of mind and body, is becoming increasingly popular in the West. The Western world is best acquainted with Hatha-yoga (the yoga of body control), as is indicated by a flood of publications on the subject and the rapidly growing number of Yoga schools. Paul Brunton's *The Hidden Teaching Beyond Yoga,* published in 1941, has gone through eleven printings. The first official recognition by a British local authority was given recently when the Birmingham City Council introduced courses in Yoga, for which there had been a growing demand for some years. Reporting on the Birmingham Yoga Schools, the *Times* (London) on 23 February 1965 observed: "The attractions are often relaxation and gentle exercise, and the air of Oriental mystery which surrounds the classes. The long list of pleasures from which a full time yogi should abstain seem not to be observed by night school students. Many of them say, they would not want to 'go in any deeper,' but in subtle ways the classes have changed some of their beliefs."

The father of the Yoga philosophy, Patanjali, defined it as "restraining the mind-stuff from taking various forms." Based on psychological conception by the proper training of mind, Yoga aims to reach the higher levels of consciousness. It is a method of finding things out for oneself rather than a preconceived metaphysical theory of reality or of universe. Yoga aims at removing suffering, sin, and all imperfections caused by *avidya* (ignorance), egoism, attachment, aversion, and clinging to life, which belie the true nature of self. By eliminating these obstacles through knowledge or illumination, and by controlling the flow of ideas in one's mind, one can become a true man. It is only natural that such a widely known system should be wrongly interpreted and even denounced at times for its quaint practices. Apparently its influence perturbed a widely read naturalized British writer so deeply that he venomously attacked Indian thought, about which he knew, by his own confession, but little, and reiterated the prejudices of those who are convinced that Western philosophies are the unfailing standards of all truth.[44]

The growing influence of Indian thought in recent years has indeed frightened some Western religious writers, such as Hendrik Kraemer (*World Cultures and World Religions*), who have designated it as the "Eastern invasion of the West." Perhaps excessive anxiety to defend the Western Christian tradition may have led Kraemer to over-rate Indian influence. But there are many European scholars who have denounced Indian thought in unmistakable terms. Whether response or resistance, admiration or denunciation, all are equally indicative of impact and stimulus.

In a limited way the migration of Indian labour to other countries provided yet another link between India and the outside world, Indian settlers began to move to other countries in 1830, mainly to work on British plantations. This made the abolition of slavery commercially possible a few years later, when the notorious indenture system was introduced in the British Empire. Indian migration; enforced or voluntary, has possibly been second only to that of the Europeans.

Whilst it does not come anywhere near the combined migration of all the European countries, it exceeds—in absolute numbers, not in the proportion of population—the recorded overseas migration of any single country. According to one estimate, twenty-eight million Indians migrated to various countries between 1834 and 1932. Today there are said to be more than four million Indians in forty countries all over the globe, in some of which they form a majority, such as British Guiana, Fiji, and Mauritius. In some they constitute strong minorities; in Britain, a recent estimate would show them to be over forty thousand. Their economic and political importance is considerable, and there must also be a significant cultural impact.

An important social survey, carried out in Britain about ten years ago, produced some surprising results. A representative sample of five thousand persons, of both sexes and all ages and classes, was chosen for questioning. Nearly a quarter of the population of England did not consider that they belonged to any religion or denomination. About half the population—forty-seven per cent—expressed a positive belief in a future life; a third—thirty per cent—stated that they were uncertain. What is most significant, however, is that a quarter of all those who professed belief in an after-life—an eighth of the population—did not believe that this after-life would be eternal; eleven per cent of the believers actually declared their faith in transmigration. This was "perhaps the most surprising single piece of information to be derived from this research."[45] Belief in reincarnation is a typically Indian doctrine and is contrary to the creeds of Europe and western Asia.

Politically and intellectually it was inevitable that there should have been some reaction in Europe against an invasion of Indian learning. Reaction against alien ideas appears to be a common human irrationality. Certainly, the nature of political relationships and nationalistic pride understandably played a significant role. European nations generally were more receptive to Indian ideas during the early period of their relationship which was based on relative equality. But as European political, technological and economic supremacy over Asia came to be recognized, an attitude of superiority crept into the European—and particularly the British—outlook. The influence of political relationships on cultural intercourse is further illustrated by the fact that, once the British became overlords of India, Indian learning drew more sympathetic and imaginative understanding from other European countries than it did from the British.

The discovery of Indian thought by European scholars in the eighteenth and nineteenth centuries led to an outburst of admiration and enthusiasm, mainly because they felt that Indian thought filled a need in their European culture. Neither Christianity nor the classical cultures of Greece and Rome were considered satisfactory any more and the European intelligentsia sought to apply the new knowledge, brought in increasingly by Indologists, to their own spiritual preoccupations. Upon closer examination of Indian thought, whilst some of the deeper ideas were revealed, illusions were exposed. Even some admirers became critical and sceptical. Both reactions were based on insufficient knowledge. Goethe himself moved from one opinion to the other, although he continually acknowledged the tremendous stimulus of Indian thought. This conflicting approach is in fact characteristic of the modern European attitude towards India. Although in recent years some European writers have made a thorough and understanding study of Indian thought, India still conjures up conflicting images in Western minds, and evokes a variety of responses ranging from Kipling's caricatures to Max Müller's "the very paradise on earth."

It is significant that, with notable exceptions, India appears to have been most attractive to those Europeans who did not visit the country personally. In other words, Indian thought made a better impact on the European mind than did contemporary Indians.

Although it was uneven, intermittent, and in many ways limited, the stimulus provided to the West by Indian thought was timely and invaluable. Of all the European nations Germany's response to India was most enthusiastic and open-hearted. Perhaps the similarity between the German and the Indian mind, in the sense that both are given to contemplation, abstract speculation, and pantheism, and both have a tendency towards formlessness, inwardness, and transcendentalism, contributed toward German understanding of Indian literature. Leopold von Schroeder says: "The Indians are the nation of romanticists of antiquity: The Germans are the romanticists of modern times." He even concludes that all the romantic minds of the West turn towards India because of the deep-rooted similarity between romanticism in Europe, and, what he considers to be, romanticism in India. Sentimentality and feeling for nature are common to both German and Indian poetry, whereas they are foreign, for instance, to Hebrew or Greek poetry. The similarity between the two peoples is further illustrated, in a different area, by the Indian tendency to work out scientific systems; India was the nation of scholars of antiquity, in the same way as the Germans are the nation of scholars of the modern times.

Even if suggestions of parallels between the Germans and Indians are discounted as being over emphasized, if not altogether misleading, it cannot be denied that German response to Indian literature and philosophy was prompt and profuse, which must have been considerably conditioned by some intrinsic appeal of Indian thought for the German mind.

The French were not amongst the first Europeans to come into contact with India. But, as soon as French travellers, who are known for their literary taste, visited India and reported on their travels, French literary circles responded enthusiastically. French interest in Indian studies, which was much anterior to that of the English, was distinctive for its imaginative understanding of Indian literature and thought. There have been many eminent French Indologists, and both the volume and quality of French contributions to Indian studies are remarkable. In fact it is a matter of some surprise that Indologists working in the English speaking world have not made full use of these French contributions.

The British response to Indian learning was most mixed. Whilst India remained a trying political problem, she was a symbol of British power and achievement, as well as a major source of her economic wealth. India as a national political problem required collective reaction, but intellectual response was a personal matter. Individual thinkers studied India closely and whilst some were fascinated, others were repelled. In both cases, Indian ideas stimulated British imagination and exercised influence in a variety of ways, which at times were conflicting. Often for political expedience—for instance the need to justify domination of India to the British public—British administrators were compelled to interpret Indian culture as degenerate and decadent. Even the Utilitarians, who advocated liberty and democracy, supported the continued rule of the Company so that Indian society could be rejuvenated.

Another barrier between Indian and British cultural co-operation was the Englishmen working in India. The early administrators were indifferent to anything except trade and profits; the later ones, after 1830, suffered from a sense of cultural inferiority, which, compounded with political superiority, manifested itself in self-righteousness, prejudices, and arrogance. They often came to India for only a few years, invariably lived an exclusive life, and returned home to condemn Indian culture and traditions with gusto. Their callous indifference to Indian art is well reflected by the fact that the liberal William Bentinck, who initiated social reforms in India, seriously considered the possibility of dismantling the Taj Mahal and selling the marble to meet the shortage of money in the Company's treasury. He was prevented because "the test auction of materials from the Agra palace proved unsatisfactory." Fed on Macaulay, Mutiny, and Kipling, the English, no wonder, did not appreciate India.

In spite of these handicaps, Indian literature captured the imagination of a few British scholars and writers. This unknown land of romantic dynasties, luxury and exotic beauty, and mystic religions and developed philosophies became a source of inspiration for romantic literature. Indian peoples, scenery, costumes, courts, religious ceremonies, folk songs, tiger hunts, hermits, and buildings presented a kind of fairy tale picture, which increasingly captured popular interest.

It is a pity that Europeans did not press on with their advantage and make better use of Indian knowledge. If Indian philosophy, literature, and art had received a fuller and less inhibited appreciation in Europe, some new form of all inclusive civilization or European renaissance, more comprehensive than a mere technological and industrial revolution, might have emerged. However, a British-Indian civil servant and historian, Garratt, considered that the British rulers of India were not a good channel for cultural intercourse, for they had "failed to achieve a 'union of Hindu and European learning' or to give any scope to the technical skill and knowledge inherent among the people."[46]

Chapter VII

INDIAN RESPONSE TO MODERN EUROPE

WHILST EUROPE SOUGHT ancient Indian learning, India focused her attention on modern European knowledge. In this cultural encounter, initiative remained for the most part with Europe, for she was a young developing society with an inquisitive mind and the material resources to obtain easy access to what she fancied. In contrast, Indians even if they knew what they needed, could not get at it at will. As a result, Europe absorbed Indian wisdom within a much shorter period than Indians took to gain Western knowledge. Indeed, some Western scientific theory and technological know-how has only been acquired since Indian independence.

Once the initial period of romanticism and disillusionment had been overcome, and the Indo-British political relationship was firmly established, a new phase of cultural interaction between India and the West began. With the increasing Western domination of Asia and the advance in science and technology, the process of cultural exchange gained speed and momentum. The traffic of people and ideas between India and Europe grew correspondingly, and numerous Indian intellectuals, students, officials, soldiers, tourists, princes, and merchants began to visit Britain and Europe. The cultural encounter between India and modern Europe hardly has a parallel in history.

Western tradition is a highly generalized, extremely vague, and ill-defined concept that is often stretched to include or exclude anything at will to suit the purpose in hand. It is not a unitary system of thought, nor has it an unbroken historical continuity. There are deep controversies as to its exact nature and value, and it is a complex of diverse, even contradictory, ideologies and traditions. For instance, it is equally proud of the imprints of early Greek and Christian traditions which were relentlessly opposed to each other.

Even a casual investigation reveals the inherent contradictions of Western tradition. Western tradition is often characterized as one of material progress and scientific advancement, yet Christian mystical thought is superbly well developed, and until recently science was positively denounced in the Christian West. In most respects scientific inquiry was much more highly developed in the Hellenistic period than it was in mediaeval Europe. In fact, exactly why Hellenistic science declined needs an explanation. Again, it is repeatedly pointed out that Western tradition stems from the enlargement of individual liberties, and that individual liberty is the essence of Western civilization. Some Western scholars go much farther and assert that the West has regarded "a denial of freedom as a denial of the value of the individual and therefore as a sin against the soul of man." Yet it is not possible to completely ignore the Western institutions of slavery, feudalism, colonialism and imperialism, and racism. Western liberalism, of which the West can be justly proud, was born in the seventeenth century as a reaction against the violence and hatred that had prevailed during the almost unbelievably atrocious religious wars. But even since then, liberalism has not remained unchallenged in the West. Indeed, totalitarianism and suppression of freedom of thought and person appear to be the unbroken trend of a Western tradition that can claim most of the great despots of world history, including Alexander, Julius Caesar, Nero, Napoleon, Hitler, and Mussolini. This fact is even more startling when these dictators and conquerors are contrasted with the prophets of non-violence and peace, such as Jesus Christ, Gautama Buddha, Asoka, and Mahatma Gandhi, who were all born in Asia. Even the concept of the divine right of kings found far more serious advocates amongst Western monarchs—the Greek Alexander, the Roman Caesars, Russians Czars, French Bourbons, and British Stuarts. It is true that the Western world has continuously fought for liberty, but this only serves to illustrate the existence of anti-freedom forces and a totalitarian current in Western tradition.

Again, it cannot be claimed, as is often done, that the rise of Christianity did much to improve the position of the individual, for religious persecution has been a common feature of Western Christianity. The once persecuted Christians, having gained power, themselves became persecutors; Caesar was more, not less, divine when he became the sword of Christianity. The terrible struggles between Church and State were not fought for individual, or even religious, freedom; the Church sought to compel the secular power to serve its own purposes. Any individual who did not subscribe to the Church's belief was at once denounced as a heretic. Crusades and religious wars of extermination were often as bloody as Hitler's slaughter of the Jews and Gypsies. The Church even persecuted the mediaeval minstrels and Gypsies because they loved freedom. Once the so-called heretics came to power they were no less tyrannical and no more tolerant than their erstwhile persecutors. It was Calvin, an apostle of Protestantism, who managed to bring secular and religious life under a single authority, and thus to direct thought and action alike by "the rule of the saints." His was the first monolithic party of the Western civilization, from which all totalitarian states have learned. "Toleration, when it came did not spring from deep-rooted conviction; it originated in the boredom and weariness of the mass of ordinary men with the conflict of totalitarian rulers who had struggled to tear Europe apart."[1]

Christianity, which is in practice a unique combination of beliefs and clergy, whilst owing its religion to Jesus and his early Asian disciples, is, in strict ecclesiastical hierarchy, an essentially Western movement.' Whatever may have been the value of the Church in religious practice, it has inhibited freedom of thought and individual liberty by relentlessly enforcing its presuppositions as eternal truths. It is the Church which sets moral standards for the individual and prescribes his belief. The organization of the Church is unparalleled in history. No federation of states has been as comprehensive and universal in taking hold of the minds of people, and no monarch or dictator has been given the complete and willing obedience of such a wide and vast body of peoples as has the Church. The Islamic Caliphate and Buddhist monasticism were, in this respect, no way comparable to the Christian Church. The former was too often divided, and was always too temporal to command any control of minds, and eventually was abolished. The Buddhist Sangha was, at best, a collection of autonomous monasteries.

Communism, with all its scientific reason, humanism, and economic equality, is essentially a totalitarian doctrine, negating individual liberty, and is a typical, almost exclusive, Western concept. Communism stresses the primacy of reason, but, like a missionary religion, it has a sense of its own infallibility and an obligation to world-wide expansion. Its greatest exponents have mainly been Western or Western-trained.

Even British thought, which was more directly and closely linked with India than that of other European countries, had its own inner conflicts and contradictions in respect to India, ranging from Edmund Burke's liberalism and John Stuart Mill's utilitarianism to John Bright's radicalism. Burke desired India to stay Indian; in fact, he was rather anxious to reform the disreputable English trustees in India. He strongly condemned the facile and much used aspersion of "Oriental Despotism" and warned his countrymen against passing judgement upon a people, for ages civilized and cultivated, who formed their laws and institutions prior to "our insect origins of yesterday." The Utilitarians and Evangelicals, on the contrary, saw little good in Indian society and desired to Westernize it completely by denying individual liberty to the Indian. The Utilitarians, whilst not denying the abstract right to liberty, could see no alternative to a benevolent British despotism in India, conducted from London. India exposed Utilitarianism's paradox between its principle of liberty and that of authority. The Evangelicals' viewpoint was religious; they believed that only through Christianity could temporal welfare and spiritual salvation be achieved. Hence, they looked upon the British conquest of India as a divine act of punishment for Indian paganism, and an opportunity for Indians to redeem themselves from their depraved system of superstition. Thus they sought the rapid conversion of the peoples of India to Christian ways, as interpreted by Western clergy. If Utilitarianism provided a justification and a practical basis for British imperial rule in India Evangelicalism gave it a sense of urgency and intense zeal.

Each diverse current of thought or tradition had its corresponding influence on India, and the Indian response, consequently, was as varied as Western tradition itself.

The Portuguese were the first European power to expand into India. Their activities were essentially an extension of the Christian crusade against Islam, and a search for trade. Although they were the last of the colonial powers to leave Indian territory (in 1961), their imprint on Indian culture is negligible.

Whilst the seventeenth century marked the zenith of India's mediaeval glory, the eighteenth century was a spectacle of corruption, misery, and chaos. The glory of the Mughals had vanished, life had become insecure, the nobility was deceitful and oppressive and intellectual curiosity had given way to superstitious beliefs. The country was in a state of military and political helplessness. In this atmosphere, literature, art, and culture could barely survive. The malaise of India was aggravated in full measure by the East India Company with its indiscriminate exploitation, corruption, and bribery.

In contrast, Europe was robust and vigorous. This was the Age of Enlightenment, and Europeans had gone through a process of rebirth during which religion was detached from state, alchemy from science, theology from philosophy, and divinity from art. A Western scholar recently asserted that "Western science and philosophy as they have developed in the last three or four centuries, are the most sustained, comprehensive, and rigorous attempt ever made by man to understand himself and his environment, physical and social..."[2] Even if the achievement of the modern West is not as unprecedented as is claimed, there can be little doubt that the cultural vitality, the variety, and the spirit of scientific inquiry displayed by Europeans in the seventeenth and eighteenth centuries mark the rise of a civilization more dynamic than anything seen in the West since Alexandria's heyday. Thus, the impact of Western culture on India was that of a dynamic society on a static one. It is a cruel irony of history that whilst two major revolutions—the French and the American—upholding the human rights to liberty and equality were taking place in the West, India was in the throes of losing her own freedom to Western mercantile imperialism.

The West provided India with the necessary impetus for a real stock taking and reform. The introduction of Western culture, education, and scientific techniques gave traditional Indian life a jolt, shocking Indians into a new awareness and vitality in thought and action. Long dormant intellectual impulses emerged and a new Indian spirit was born. During the period of Western supremacy in India, the conflict of two civilizations certainly produced unrest, but it also sustained and stimulated intellectual life.

Western influences became effective in India mainly through the British, who were the pioneers of a new technological and industrial civilization. They represented a new historic force which was later to change the world, and thus were the forerunners of change and revolution. Although Indian and Western civilizations were at approximately the same level at the time, they were tending in different directions: the former was declining, the latter progressing. India lost to Europe because it lacked political organization, including a central government, and a progressive outlook.

The British domination of India has been described as a "political and economic misfortune," and in some respects it was indeed enervating and devitalizing. Dadabhai Naoroji, whilst pointing out the many blessings of law and order it had conferred on India, called the despotic system of government in British India "un-British," for it was as destructive to British ideals and honour as it was to India. In 1937, a distinguished British civil servant, G. T. Garratt, declared that the period of Indo-British civilization of the previous one hundred and fifty years had been most disappointing, and "in some ways the most sterile in Indian history."[3] This must come as a shock not only to those who have been brought up to believe in British virtue but also to those who do not take an uncritical view of British colonialism. Garratt was no Indian nationalist charged with exaggerated patriotism. He had scrupulously analyzed the problem and advanced some impressive arguments in support of his assertion, although he no doubt overstated his indignation at "what could be done but was not done." Whilst it may be irrelevant to dwell here upon the merits and demerits of British colonial policies, there can be no doubt that British impact led to such a transformation of Indian society that Indians, in retrospect, may even be thankful for what the British did, regardless of what they did not do.

Western influences were very different from any India had received before. This time the newcomers not only had a different religion but also a different outlook on life, and an economic system which was the result of new scientific and technological advances. They had firm political values, well-developed cultural traditions, and superior technical skills. Above all, their organization in all respects—military, religious, economic, and political—was remarkable and iron-cast. Whilst India has always held her own in the realm of thought, broadly speaking, organization and co-ordination have never been her strong points. Indeed, in India, as in no other civilization, except with doubtful and partial exceptions in ancient Greece and modern France, extreme intellectual individualism has been a dominant, zealously guarded characteristic. Complete freedom of individual thought, academic disputes, and philosophical debates led to an enriched Indian cultural heritage. But individualism caused frequent clashes, frustration, and indifference in political and military spheres. No serious attempt was ever made by Indian states to direct and superintend the dissemination of Indian culture. It is indeed surprising that whilst intellectually so independent and individualistic, Indians followed for centuries a caste system almost unparalleled in its rigidity. That they were unable to suppress its ugly features, and paid for it heavily in terms of social suffering and cultural decline, would further emphasize the Indian lack of collective discipline and organization.

It is not a rarity that intellectual perseverance and thoroughness of analysis add to the infirmity, rather than to the clarity, of conclusions. Having searched into all aspects of a problem, Indians do riot necessarily feel the need to opt for one view or the other. They are quite content to accept the reality of contradictions in a given situation, a quality which baffles most people but is easily acceptable to the Indian mind. Indians accept reality as it is, which may or may not be unitary, and their decisions and beliefs are generally tentative, for the finite mind cannot always comprehend totality. Contradiction, not compromise, has been the keynote of Indian intellectual and political strengths and weaknesses, and even conditions her present-day revolution. Compulsion to make a firm choice in cases of conflicting views often results in merely selecting a preference for the one against the other. There is no fervour of conviction in it. Whenever there is fervour in Indian convictions it is generally emotional and indecisive; belief based on pure emotion is passion, not conviction.

Consequently, upon being confronted with British power, India could neither penetrate the steel ring of British organization nor could she absorb their culture into her own pattern. Intellectually indifferent, spiritually subdued, and physically weak at the time, Indians found an adjustment with the newcomers not only practical but essential.

INDIAN RESPONSE TO Western impact was first noticed in religion. Indians were not unfamiliar with Christianity, nor were they ill-disposed towards it. Christianity dated to the first century A.D. in India, long before Britain had even acquired the necessary degree of cultural sophistication to be able to appreciate Christian doctrines. Whilst Indians were attracted by the practical ethics of Christianity and the social welfare activities of Christian missionaries, they were repelled by their excessive zeal, their religious arrogance, and their harsh criticism of Indian religious practices and social customs. Indians could not understand the narrowness and intolerance of the Christians, in marked contrast to India's inclusive and tolerant religion. They were prepared to admit Christ as one of the prophets of God, but not as the only son of God. Despite their indignation at the new heralds of Christianity, Indians became acutely conscious of their own inadequacies and intellectual inertia.

Even though Christian missionary activity in India became widespread during British rule, the East India Company was disinclined to mix trade and religion. From the beginning it set its face against all missionary activities, and after 1757 it decided to exclude missionary propaganda in the territories under its control. However, the Company's attempts to restrict missionary work within its territory were frustrated in 1808 by Spencer Perceval, who has been called "the Evangelical Prime Minister" because of his zeal for Church reform. He was assassinated in 1812, but by then his efforts, in combination with those of Wilberforce and the Evangelicals, had already broken the Company's resistance to missionaries. The Charter of 1813 required the East India Company to allow missionaries to travel on its ships, and to admit a British bishop at Calcutta. By this Act, however, the Company's trade monopoly was abolished and its commercial opposition to missionaries weakened.

In any case, the Company had never successfully controlled missionary activity in India. Several Christian missions had been at work in various parts of India for a long time. Catholic missions had been active since the arrival of the Portuguese, and in 1780 the Serampore Mission was established in Bengal. By 1792, the spirit of evangelism had permeated Protestant churches deeply enough to move the English Baptists into organizing the first Protestant mission. Three years later the London Missionary Society was formed, and a powerful evangelical movement began in Britain, the vibrations of which, under the direction of William Carey, were felt in British India. Whilst the Company itself, as a mercantile corporation, could not lend its support to Christian missionary activity, many individuals in the administration felt deeply convinced of the need for evangelical work in India, and gave their active cooperation to the missionaries.

Although the Christian missionaries intensified their activities under the stimulus of the Act of 1813, they met with only limited success through conversions. The impact of Christian thought itself however was considerable, culminating in a revival, reinterpretation, and reorientation of Indian thought. Just as the impact of Islam had given encouragement to the Bhakti movement in mediaeval times the advent of Western civilization caused the growth of numerous reform movements in modern times.

Bengal, where British power was concentrated at the time, and which had felt the worst of the East India Company's early misrule, took the lead in both cultural and political advances. The earliest stirrings of the Indian cultural renaissance appeared under the leadership of Raja Ram Mohan Roy (1772–1833) who made the first organized efforts to adapt Hinduism to the new situation. He made a clear distinction between good and bad traditions, and reasserted the wisdom of welcoming a good concept, regardless of its nationality.

He was a scholar of Sanskrit, Hebrew, Greek, Persian, English, and Arabic. A devout Hindu inspired by the vedantic philosophy, he was also deeply influenced by Sufism and was an admirer of Christianity and Western thought, especially the writings of Montesquieu, Blackstone, and Bentham. Towards the end of his life, he was also attracted by the revolutionary movements of America and Europe.

He was perhaps the first earnest modern scholar of comparative religion. Making a clear distinction between Western virtues and Western failings, he defended Hinduism against the attacks of missionaries as stoutly as he challenged the orthodoxy to abandon its ritualistic conventions. He kept in close touch with Oriental research and interpreted the ancient Indian texts in the light of Western doctrines and ideas. Consequently he became an uncompromising and vehement opponent of idolatry and of all rituals connected with it. At the age of thirty-one, he published a book in Persian, denouncing idolatry and advocating belief in one god and a universal religion. He conceived the idea of a universal church, somewhat in the tradition of Akbar's Din-i-ilahi, combining the best spiritual traditions of Hinduism, Christianity, and Islam and accepting equally the teachings of all religions. He looked beyond dogma, ritual, and philosophical dialectics to seek the fundamentals of each faith, and found them identical.

Although willing to join in Christian worship, Ram Mohan Roy was an ardent Hindu who found Hinduism's defence against Christianity in Vedanta, which supported his ideas on the unity of God, the futility of idolatry and pilgrimages, and the doctrine of Karma and incarnations. In an exposition on Christianity, *The Precepts of Jesus, the Guide to Peace and Happiness,* he extolled the ethical teachings of Christ but rejected the miraculous legends about his life which he said were due to a misinterpretation on the part of his followers. Moreover, he did not believe that man could atone for his sins simply by repentance. This was, in fact, a reply to missionaries rather than a call to Indians. He regarded a bigoted Christian to be as conceited as a bigoted Hindu, and ignored both. He accepted the humanism of European thought. Whilst his denunciation of Hindu orthodoxy antagonized Hindu traditionalists, his discriminating approach to Christian doctrines displeased Christian diehards. Despite strong opposition from a superstitious and indifferent people, aggressive missionaries, and a mercenary government, he persisted in his endeavours. As a result he set India on a course of cultural reformation, which gradually gathered momentum and support, and eventually made it possible for modern India to emerge.

In his attempt to bring about harmony between faiths, Roy founded the Brahmo Samaj in 1828. Brahmo Samaj was not an entirely new religion, for it was based on the vedanta philosophy, but its outlook was European, and it derived its inspiration from the intellectual movements of the eighteenth century. Doctrinally somewhat similar to Unitarianism and attempting to synthesize the cultures of East and West, it encouraged rationalism and social reform.

Ram Mohan Roy, however, was much more than a religious reformer. He was a patriot who represented Indian nationalism on the defensive; its leaders at this stage were cautious, and apprehensive. He commenced the task of national reconstruction on several fronts with vigour and industry. In 1823, twelve years before Macaulay wrote his famous minute on education, Ram Mohan Roy had petitioned the British Government to introduce English rather than continue traditional Indian education. A few years earlier he had founded a Hindu college at Calcutta, where Western learning was taught. Macaulay, who is credited with having forced the issue in favour of English education, not only followed the arguments advanced by Ram Mohan Roy, but even borrowed some of his language.

Roy relentlessly battled the ugly but hallowed custom of sati to save women from cruel deaths. This custom, for some unknown reason, increased in Bengal during British expansion. Ram Mohan filed petitions for its abolition before the British, and ten years later when William Bentinck did abolish sati, Roy was profoundly moved. When a group of reactionary Indians petitioned the Privy Council in London to reverse the abolition, he appeared before the Council personally and successfully defended Bentinck's measure. Many sincere leaders before him had exposed the evils in Indian life and religion, but none had grasped with as much clarity the passivity which had come to paralyze the Indian mind, and none had worked with such devotion, perseverance and conviction to revitalize Indian thinking.

Ram Mohan Roy was received enthusiastically in Europe and exercised a considerable influence upon liberal Protestants, especially Unitarians. He went to England ostensibly as the ambassador of the Mughal king to recover Mughal authority from the British Company. He did not succeed in his political mission, but he helped to bring India a good deal closer to the West. During his stay, he met leading British statesmen, philosophers, and historians, such as Jeremy Bentham and James Mill. So highly did Bentham hold Ram Mohan Roy in his esteem that when the Indian scholar arrived in London in April 1831, Bentham was the first man to call on Roy at the Adelphi Hotel. Bentham was eighty-three years of age at the time and fastidious—he refused to see Mme. de Staāl in 1813 because he thought she had nothing of interest to say. In welcoming Roy at the British Unitarian Association's reception, Sir John Bowring placed Ram Mohan in the same class as "a Plato or a Socrates, a Milton or a Newton." Bentham even actively agitated to secure Roy's election to the British Parliament.

The new spirit of humanism and rationalism stimulated Indian thought and literature enormously. No longer was Indian writing appended to theology, mythology, and scholasticism. No gods and goddesses descended from heaven and played a part in human life. Man now occupied the foremost place, steering his course of life without divine help. This concept of the world was somewhat similar to that which had existed in the ancient past, of which only a dim recollection had survived. Soon new ideas began to fill old patterns and Indian writers and thinkers were inspired not only by the renewed spirit of humanism but also by the French revolutionary spirit of liberty and equality.

After the death of Ram Mohan Roy in Bristol in 1833, the Brahmo Samaj remained the focus of the Hindu renaissance. Debendranath Tagore (1817–1905), who had been in intimate contact with Roy, continued the monotheistic tradition. In 1839, he founded the Tattvabodhi Sabha, which played a significant role in the cultural revival of India, especially in Bengal. Unlike Ram Mohan, however, his ideas reflect little Christian influence. In spite of his impressive missionary activity, Debendranath, who became an ascetic, seems to have embraced Brahmoism primarily out of an intense spiritual craving, not out of any inclination for social reform.

After him came the dynamic, although somewhat erratic, Keshab Chandra Sen (1838–1884), under whose direction the eclecticism of the Brahmo Samaj gathered momentum. His enthusiasm was infectious and he wielded tremendous influence upon his contemporaries. Widely read in Western philosophy, he was especially attracted by Carlyle and Emerson. His own backgorund was vaisnava, and Ramakrishna's idea of the harmony of all religions captured his imagination. He wanted the Samaj to maintain not merely that there were truths in all religions but that all religions of the world were true. Not a Christian, he was nevertheless a great admirer of Christ. Indeed, his teachings were so close to Christianity that at one time his conversion to the Christian faith was thought imminent. But he was deeply saturated in Hindu thought and often, especially in his later life, would stress the validity of many vedantic ideas. He believed that many Hindu rituals and usages could be reinterpreted and restored with new symbolic meaning to suit the Brahmo Samaj. Consequently, he retained many Hindu practices in Brahmo worship but turned to Christianity for ethical guidance. Despite his mental prowess and unquestionable integrity, clarity or consistency of thought was not his strong point. In his *New Dispensation*, published in 1881, he set out to create a third dispensation—the Old Testament being the first and the New Testament being the second—and declared himself the centre of it, as Christ was of his dispensation. But immediately he felt he was a sinner; a slave of Christ, *Jesudasa*. He called himself "a child of Asia" and loudly claimed Christianity to be an Asian religion. He asserted that Jesus was akin to his Asian nature and ways of thinking, and that Christianity was more comprehensible to the Asian mind than to the European. He made a clear distinction between the spirit of Christianity and the fashions of Western civilization. He was a relentless opponent of hypocrisy, insisted on social purity and upright individual conduct, and preached his views throughout India with unsparing energy. In some ways he was ahead of his times. He was the first Brahmo Samaj leader to advocate the welfare and rights of men, to attempt a new interpretation of history, and to evolve a modern prose style in Bengali. He took radical positions on social and religious issues which may not have endeared him to some of his contemporaries but undoubtedly left an impact on them. After his death, the Brahmo Samaj ceased to be a living force, but by that time it had served its extremely vital purpose of national awakening.

The Brahmo Samaj was an attempt to achieve a synthesis of East and West by some educated and restive men of Bengal. It did not become a mass movement, but impressive leaders gave impetus to a chain of religious reforms and social consciousness which gradually bound the whole country together. Not all of these movements were kindly disposed towards Western culture, but they all created a new spirit and the face of the country began to change. Later religious movements were mainly concerned with asserting the pure and original form of Hinduism and returning to it.

Under the stimulus of renascent Hinduism in Bengal, the Prarthana Samaj society was founded in Maharastra in 1867. Bengal and Maharastra had divergent historical experiences during the Mughal period, but they had much in common in the nineteenth century. Both had for some time been the scene of European activities and both had developed the urge to reform traditional society in a reaction against foreign domination. Eminent persons joined the Prarthana Samaj, such as M. G. Ranade (1842–1901) and Sir R. G. Bhandarkar; the former being its most outstanding leader. Somewhat milder in policy than the Brahmo Samaj, the Prarthana Samaj believed in the fatherhood of God and the brotherhood of man, but their theism rested largely on ancient Hindu thought. The Vedas, however, were not their source of inspiration, and transmigration was left an open question. The Prarthana Samaj opposed idolatry, child-marriage, prohibition of widow remarriage, and caste, but membership was not forfeited if these practices were continued. The Prarthana Samaj did for Maharastra what Brahmo Samaj did for Bengal.

Through the efforts of these cultural movements, the spread of English education, the study of Indian culture, and the increasing orderliness of political organization, there had awakened in India a deep sense of nationality and cultural pride. The emergent India demanded a more militant defence of its own inheritance, and the growth of national, as opposed to regional, movements. Soon the initiative passed to Swami Dayananda Sarasvati (1824–1883), who based his teachings entirely on the Vedas, "the primeval scripture of humanity," which he regarded as the revealed word of God. He thought the amorphous nature of Hinduism exposed it to much weakness, which could be repaired by possessing, like Islam and Christianity, a revealed work of unquestionable authority.

Born in 1824 in Kathiawar in western India, Swami Dayananda spent many years in the quest of truth. He began his public life in 1868. After an extensive lecture tour severely criticizing certain weaknesses of Hinduism, as well as those of Christianity and Islam, he founded the Arya Samaj in 1875; it has since been an active movement in Hindu life, especially in the Punjab.

Untutored in English but a profound Sanskrit scholar, Dayananda, in his most important work, the *Satyartha Prakash,* made a brilliant attempt to discover in the Vedas the bases of the Christian and Muslim religions. His chief convictions were that there was only one God to be worshipped, without the aid of idols. The many divine names which occur in the Vedas were all epithets of the one true God. Many other Hindu texts were of value but they were not to be followed where they contradict the Vedas. Swami Dayananda relentlessly opposed priests, who he believed had caused discord and disunion, in marked contrast to prophets of other faiths who had attempted to unite humanity. He emphasized the fundamental purity of Hinduism, as be conceived it, which was to him the original vedic religion.

Fearless and overpowering, Dayananda aimed at giving self-confidence back to Hindus, although he ruthlessly denounced the deplorable practices prevalent in contemporary Hinduism. He asked Hindus to adopt modern ideas that impressed him, and he introduced militancy into Hinduism. His strong urge to assert Hindu nationalism found expression in the Shuddhi movement to take Hindus who had been converted to Islam or Christianity back into the fold. This was a novel experiment which was resented by Muslims and Christians. However, belonging to proseletyzing religions themselves, they really bad no logical argument against this practice, even if it were a new one for the Hindu.

As there is no sanction in the Vedas for caste and other taboos that had gripped Hindu society the Arya Sarnaj vigorously advocated drastic social reform. For example, it spent large sums of money on sacred thread for millions of untouchables, thus making them equal to other members of the Hindu society. However successful the Arya Samaj may have been as a militant organization, its appeal was mainly confined to the Punjab, chiefly for two reasons. By exclusively emphasizing the Vedas, it ignored the rich tradition of Hindu culture which had followed them for over two thousand years. The concept of Arya and Aryavarta, inherent in vedic supremacy, excluded South India, which has been in many ways the real repository of Hindu culture in later times.

Swami Dayananda and his followers disclaimed any indebtedness to Western ideas, but this would appear rather an assertion of national pride than a statement of fact. A distinctive feature of the Arya Samaj has been its remarkable contribution to the spread of English education, through its numerous Dayananda Anglo Vedic schools and colleges throughout the country. It is significant that a movement which superficially seemed inward-looking and which raised the cry of "back to the Vedas" should have done more than any other single Indian public organization to spread Western knowledge in India.

Dayananda's contemporary, Sri Ramakrishna Paramahamsa (1834–1886), in preaching selfless devotion to God and seeking self-realization, approached Muslim and Christian mystics. He emphasized that different religions are but different paths to reach the one God, and that if one religion is true, then by the same logic, all other religions are also true.

Ramakrishna, who lived at the temple of Dakshineshwar near Calcutta, was a poor priest without any formal education. It has been claimed that what Socrates was to the Greek consciousness Ramakrishna was to the modern Indian renaissance. Max Müller said that in comparison to the illiterate Ramakrishna the brightest intellects of Europe were mere gropers in the dark. In a recent study, Christopher Isherwood has called Ramakrishna the incarnation of Siva.

Ramakrishna never claimed to be the founder of a new religion. He simply preached the old religion of India, founded on the Vedas and the Upanishads, and systematized in later commentaries. He was not an original thinker in the true sense of the word, but he could recognize many things, including the divine presence, which others could not. He never wrote a philosophical treatise, but his pithy sayings and simple, commonplace illustrations are marvels of lucid exposition. Not urbane, and often even devoid of grace, he was utterly genuine, sincere, and forthright.

His dynamic disciple, Swami Vivekananda, preached the teaching of his guru to India and to the world in somewhat the same manner as Saint Paul preached the gospel of Jesus. Whilst Ramakrishna was a mystic, depending upon intuition and vision, Vivekananda was an intellectual, relying mainly upon reason. In India he pioneered rationalism in religion and philosophy, as Ram Mohan Roy had done in the field of social thought. He preached the "oneness of all religions," asking Hindus to become better Hindus, Muslims to become better Muslims, and Christians to become better Christians. He impressively interpreted Indian thought to Western peoples and provided a bridge between the East and West, both of whom needed reform; the former lacked food and education, the latter, spirituality. Through his forceful and logical speeches, he established the inherent virtues of the Hindu religion. The period of apologies was over; his was the voice of the self-confident Hindu who expounded his faith with the fullest conviction and righteous pride. Rooted in the past and full of pride in India's heritage, Vivekananda was modern in his approach to the problems of life, providing a bridge between the past of India and her present. He foreshadowed Mahatma Gandhi in his burning enthusiasm for the uplifting of the masses. He regarded India, in spite of her degradation, as the home of spiritualism and enlightenment, but he attacked Indian inertia, disunity, and lack of national pride. He was impressed with American efficiency and equality, and British tenacity, law-abidingness, and sense of loyalty. In 1897 he founded the Ramakrishna Mission at Belur, near Calcutta, and the new institution adopted a comprehensive programme of social service. It started schools, colleges, hospitals, orphanages, and libraries, and has remained a leader in rendering humanitarian services in India.

Although Vivekananda died at the age of thirty-nine, he left a permanent mark on Indian life and thought. The great national leaders, such as Gandhi, Tagore, and Nehru, often acknowledged their debt to him. Towns, streets, bridges, and institutions are named after him in all corners of India, and it has been said that to understand India an understanding of Vivekananda is essential.

The Theosophical Society moved its headquarters from New York to India in 1879. At first the Society aimed mainly at the investigation and propagation of the belief in life beyond death, but later the scope of its inquiry was broadened considerably. Today it is a blending of the wisdom of the East and the West. Theosophists, whilst seeking liberation, are pledged to lead a life of sacrifice. They are encouraged to act according to their oft-quoted maxim, "Light on the Path," and to "try to lift a little of the heavy Karma of the world." The members of the Society are required to lead highly ethical and moral lives and oppose the increasingly materialistic outlook on life. Religious fanaticism is not allowed and the followers of any religion can become members, adhering to what is best in their own religion.

At a time when Hinduism, Christianity, and Islam were competing with each other, this stress on the unity of religions served a very useful purpose. Although not a mass movement, the Society significantly affected the outlook of the emerging nation. For a while, at least, it accommodated the urge of educated Hindus to find a common denomination for their various sects.

Annie Besant (1847–1933), who came to India in 1893, was the Society's most forceful leader. She was at one time a British socialist leader and an atheist. She said that she remembered India from her past incarnation and looked upon it as her "motherland." She adopted the Indian way of life, and translated various important Hindu texts into English. A persuasive speaker, she advanced the popularity of Hinduism and Indian culture through her widely attended public lectures. She took an active part in the Indian national movement and became the first woman President of the Indian National Congress. However, she disagreed vigorously with her contemporary Indian nationalism leaders, Lokamanya Tilak and Mahatma Gandhi.

Indian Islam also felt the impact of the West, but its response was somewhat different from that of Hinduism. Whilst many educated Hindus were eager to reconcile Western ideas to their own inheritance, Muslims remained markedly disinclined for some time to accept the validity of any knowledge not blessed by the Quran. The Muslims refused to give up Persian and Arabic to learn English. Typical of early Muslim response was Mirza Abu Talib Khan (1752–1807), who was one of the first Indians to visit Europe where he was lionized by English aristocracy. In *The Travels of Mirza Talib Khan,* he described the peculiarities of European customs and the evils of Western materialism, and advised his fellow Muslims to continue to ignore Western learning out of "zeal for their religion." In 1835, when Bentinck decreed the introduction of Western education, a number of Muslim notables of Calcutta presented a petition to the British Government asking them to rescind the decree. They felt it was a slight on their own learning and feared that It was aimed at the Christianization of India. The centuries' old rivalry between Islam and Christianity also contributed to Indian Islam's hostility.

In 1837, Persian was dicarded as the official language, Muslim laws and Muslim courts were abolished, and high positions in government and the army were closed to Muslims in the same way as they were to other Indians. The loss of political ascendancy and the secularization of government produced discontent, resentment, and resistance to the West. Many Muslims even felt, like the Arabian Wahhabis, that British India was no longer a suitable place for the Muslim community, and some of the more zealous ones, under the leadership of Sayyid Ahmad of Rae Bareli, preached the need to emigrate to other Muslim countries. The inevitable consequence of this self-imposed isolation and resistance to modernization was that by the middle of the century Muslims were left well behind the Hindus in progress.

In 1857, the Mughal Empire was irrevocably ended, and with it Muslim hopes of political supremacy in India. Not only were the Mughals dislodged but the Muslim political superstructure built upon Indian society over a period of centuries was shattered.

In 1867, the Muslim intellectuals and nationalist leaders who had taken a prominent part in the Indian revolt of 1857, set up the *Darul-Ulum* at Deoband, professing loyalty to Islamic law and religious orthodoxy. The Deoband School derived its doctrines from Shah Walli Allah Dihlawi (1703–1762), who envisaged Islam as an unfinished social movement begun by Muhammad, and who aimed at purifying the faith. The school made a vigorous and determined effort to resuscitate classical Islam. It accepted the old order but tried to revive and purify it. The Deoband School became the most important and respected theological academy of Muslim India, indeed of the entire Islamic world next to Al Azhar of Cairo. It produced some brilliant Muslim leaders and developed a strong tradition of vitality and quality.

The first concrete efforts to adapt modern thought to Islamic culture were made in the second quarter of the nineteenth century at Delhi, where a group of able men set out to revive Urdu by publishing Western works in that language. Later, in 1863, under the leadership of Nawab Abdul Latif some liberal Muslims founded the Muhammadan Literary Society at Calcutta whose main objective was to emphasize the increasing importance of Western learning and culture. In trying to assimilate Western knowledge, leaders of this movement leaned too heavily on the British for support, and primarily attracted loyalist Muslims. Even theologically the movement distinguished itself by being thoroughly pro-British. It opposed the popular Wahhabi *jihad* agitation against the British "infidels" and by this denunciation, the

Society gained the gratitude of both the British Government and the well-to-do Muslims.[4]

Continuing somewhat in the same tradition, Sir Syed Ahmad Khan (1817–1898) attempted to persuade Muslims to change their religious outlook and reconcile themselves to the changing environment. Sir Syed, convinced of the futility of fighting the British, "remained faithful to the British and helped them by saving the lives of those in danger" during the revolt of 1857.[5] He sought to improve the position of Indian Muslims through co-operation with the British authorities.

Anxious to draw the Muslims out of their shell of orthodoxy and to reconcile modern scientific thought with Islam, he actively pursued a policy of social and educational reform. He pointed out the basic similarities between Islam and Christianity, attacked the purdah system which segregated women from men, advocated the emancipation of women, opposed allegiance to the Turkish Caliphate, and, above all, advised his fellow Muslims to accept English education. He founded the Anglo-Oriental College at Aligarh in 1877; the College gained university status and played a vital role in the movement for Pakistan. He published a multi-volume commentary on the Quran in which he tried to prove that the teachings of Islam were in complete harmony with modern scientific theories, and sought to assimilate the best of Western thought into the Islamic faith. He was consequently severely criticized by the orthodox section of the community and his interpretation of Islam has generally been ignored. But his religious writings and advocacy of social reforms have made a lasting impression on Indian Islam.

Maulana Abul Kalam Azad (1888–1958) was also influential in helping modernize Indian Muslims. Unlike Sir Syed, Azad was an uncompromising adversary of the British imperial rule, and an important leader of the Indian National Congress. He was an even greater Islamic scholar than Sir Syed and a versatile litterateur, combining religious knowledge with scientific research. Azad's commentary on the Quran is universally acknowledged as an outstanding contribution to Islamic studies. Although educated entirely in the orthodox tradition, he imbibed the spirit of the modern West. He interpreted Islam as a universal religion which could embrace the diversity of all creeds. A brilliant theologian, his work is distinguished by a spirit of free inquiry. His interpretation evoked criticism from the orthodox, and admiration from liberal thinkers. A progressive revolutionary dedicated to true freedom, he is included amongst the *Ulama* (learned men) because of his religious learning, in which he was unsurpassed.[6]

There was bitter rivalry between Deoband and Aligarh. The achievement of Pakistan may be regarded as Aligarh's success, but the cultural response goes on, and it is yet to be seen which of the two schools will finally triumph in reconciling Islam to modernity. It seems likely that the uninhibited cultural response of the Muslims of India and Pakistan may well proceed along the lines of Deoband, resuscitating the purity of classical Islam with the assistance of modern concepts and needs. Looking at what has happened in these two countries since the partition, it would appear that Islam in Pakistan is primarily a political consideration, whilst in India it is more concerned with cultural and religious advancement.[7]

Whilst the Deoband and Aligarh movements represented the two divergent Muslim responses to Western impact, Muslim response generally was significantly different from that of the Hindus. The Hindu reform movements were ruthlessly self-critical, often questioning the very validity of some of their sacred texts and eager to absorb or adapt Western knowledge, and all—orthodox and unorthodox—were nationalistic in varying degrees of intensity. In contrast, the Muslims on the whole were not so anxious to accept new ideas. Whilst the orthodox movement, attempting to resuscitate classical Islam, was intensely opposed to British rule in India, the unorthodox movement, seeking to carve a new image of Islam, advocated loyalty to British power. The orthodox saw the security of Islam in a free and united India. The unorthodox, fearful of Hindu supremacy, eventually sought the partition of the country. In other words, the cultural and religious response of the Indian Muslim community to the West was largely conditioned by economic and political factors, as a result, the orthodox dreaded European Christian domination, the unorthodox dreaded Indian Hindu domination.

The British established an orderly and centralised government in India, although it was unwieldy and extremely bureaucratic. The British administration in India, by its very nature, first demolished the traditional personal rule and later brought about the development of the rule of law. In contrast to the older Indian system, the fundamental feature of the British administration was its impersonal character, which had its merits as well as its demerits. The multiplicity of governmental functions gave rise to a highly graded paternalistic bureaucracy which eclipsed the self-governing village Panchayats and at times discouraged individual initiative. But a somewhat democratic control served as a continual reminder of the superior value of parliamentary democracy.

Although independent India has borrowed profusely from other Western political systems, such as the United States and Ireland, and is inevitably developing its own body of parliamentary experience, her political values and institutions are based principally on British experience. Broadly speaking, Indian political organization is Western in its aims, assumptions, and techniques. The concepts of human rights and of human equality, implied in the ideal of democracy, are a Western legacy. These concepts are so inseparably grafted onto the Indian body-politic and appear so natural that many scholars have tried to trace their origins to early India. Democracy is working most satisfactorily in India today but not in most other countries of Asia and Africa, many of which were also ruled by the British. These facts lend considerable weight to the view that democracy was net altogether alien to Indian temperament and tradition.[8] Again, if Indians were borrowing from the British, irrespective of their own values and national considerations, they would have sought to set up a typically British, monarchical democracy, but instead they worked frantically to abolish the princedoms left behind by the British. Whilst it is possible to trace prototypes of some modern political ideas in ancient Indian tradition, such as democracy and individual liberty, it is difficult to find approximate parallels of such Western political institutions as parliamentary democracy or the cabinet system. Whatever Indian precedents there may be, there is no doubt that in contemporary India these concepts and institutions are of Western inspiration.

The Indian civil service, now called the Indian Administrative Service, was carefully built up during the British rule into a powerful and efficient, although impersonal and bureaucratic, force. Once the much criticized patronage system of recruitment was replaced by competitive examination in 1855, the service acquired a unique reputation for skill, experience, and devotion to duty. The core of the service consisted of the District Officers, modern variants of Asoka's *Rajukas,* whose duties were, similarly, to collect revenue and keep peace. Many members of the I.C.S. became deeply interested in historical research, and much of Indian historiography was pioneered by these administrators.[9]

More important, however, was the British impact on law, which has been described as the finest and the most abiding British contribution to India. Before the British period, both Hindus and Muslims merely applied, at best, the sacred law and, at worst, the will of the ruler; often there were different laws for different regions and castes. A Brahman could sometimes go free, or escape with relatively light punishment, where a sudra incurred heavy penalties for the same offence; often the former could not be punished on the evidence of the latter. In many cases Muslim law was based on religious partisanship and privileged birth. The Mughal Emperor regarded himself as the earthly Shadow of God and the source of all law and justice. The British made the law applicable to all alike, and detached it from religion.

Neither in Hindu nor Muslim India was there a law-making body. The former relied on ancient codes, as interpreted by the learned Brahmans, to regulate life and society. For the Muslim, Prophet Muhammad had revealed once and for all the divine law which was above modification. Islamic law, derived from the Quran and the *Hadith,* was all comprehensive, compulsorily regulating the public and private life of society and the individual. Thus, law was an appendix to religion until British impact liberated it and made it an instrument of social advancement. It was this changed character in Indian legal attitudes that made it possible for free India to enact laws abolishing untouchability, unequal status of women, and other social evils.

It must, however, be pointed out that law did not become fully independent of faith. During the British period it remained largely restricted by firm religious conventions and susceptibilities, especially in the social sphere. Even in India today the social life of Muslims is regulated by law based on Islamic beliefs; for instance, their marriage customs and property and inheritance rules are yet to be secularized.

With this new legal system and the monolithic administration, came a complicated structure of high and low courts, giving rise to litigation, often unnecessary and always prolonged. A poor man found justice remote and beyond his reach, for it became expensive and too technical

What was previously "known" locally now had to be "proven" in distant courts, through a tedious procedure and an often unfamiliar law. The lawyer, with his skill to convince the judge of the validity of evidence but not necessarily of the actuality of crime, assumed paramount importance. There developed a long hierarchy of judicial officials whose ranks had first to be penetrated before the case could be heard. The familiar and ancient system of the Panchayati Raj was suppressed. Whilst some of these undesirable features were inherent in the system, many were the result of misguided and ill-controlled practice.

Pre-British Indians were not litigious. Numerous authorities of the contemporary scene have amply testified to the general truthfulness and honesty of Indians, and to the integrity of Indian merchants. Typical was the comment made in 1852 by Sir Erskine Perry, who had been the Chief Justice of Bombay, that "the sanctity of mercantile books was such that in the Native Courts of justice, the production of the books was quite conclusive as to the veracity of any transaction in dispute."[10] Similarly, Colonel Sleeman reported that he had witnessed innumerable cases in which a man's property, liberty, and life had depended on his telling a lie, and he had refused to do so.

Whilst the British impact discouraged economic progress it proved beneficial in social life, despite hesitant and uncertain policy. The prohibition of sati, the abolition of child-marriage, and the undermining of caste or sex distinctions were commendable measures which, if taken to their logical end, could have purged India of its social evils long before the enactments of independent India.

The economic consequences of British rule, looking at both the credit and debit sides, leave much to be desired. Indian economy, on the eve of British expansion, was not backward for the time, and India had a flourishing export trade in silk, cotton, brocade, salt, and sugar, but economic exploitation by the new rulers led to its rapid impoverishment. Indian rural economy was transformed to suit the new modes of industrial Britain. This transformation led to drastic changes in the Indian way of life, the most fundamental of which was the disintegration of the old village community structure, partly as a result of the spread of commercial agriculture. Pre-British Indian agriculture was, by the standards of the period, robust, rich, and well provided for by widespread irrigation systems which had a history stretching back to pre-Mauryan days. The entire country was carved by an extraordinary labyrinth of canals, tanks, and dams, constructed by the state at prodigious expense. Bernier marvelled at the extent and size of the engineering works he saw in India, and in 1800, Francis Buchanan, who travelled extensively in India between 1800 and 1810 collecting agricultural data for the British Government, saw several large reservoirs which were still functioning.[11]

Indian manufacturing skills and economics were well advanced; spinning and weaving were national industries. Indian industry suffered severely because of the partisan and protective policy favouring British manufactured goods. Indian textiles, ivory works, brassware, gold and silver, filigree and luxury goods, which were once famous abroad, gradually fell into disuse, reducing millions of the artisan class to unemployment, poverty, and many to death. Vast numbers of these displaced artisans were forced to go back to their villages to live on the already fully occupied land. The crisis in industry led to a crisis in agriculture. Land holdings became smaller, the number of landless labourers increased, and villages became overcrowded. Poverty thus multiplied, famines became common, and rural India became progressively more ruralized.

Famines were not unknown in Indian history but the frequency and intensity with which they occurred during the British period were unprecedented and disconcerting. It has been estimated that in earlier times a major famine occurred, on an average, once in fifty years, and that between the eleventh and the seventeenth centuries, there were fourteen famines, almost all of which were confined to small local areas. But, from 1765, when the British took over Bengal, to 1858, when they quelled India's first major revolt, twelve famines and four "severe scarcities" occurred. This frequency increased in the latter part of the nineteenth century. Although there is no accurate record, a conservative estimate suggests that in the nineteenth century alone more than twenty-one million people died of starvation. In 1943, four years before British withdrawal from India, more than three million people perished in the Bengal Famine. It is significant that those parts of India which had been longest under British rule were the poorest at the time of Indian Independence.

Although India remained predominantly agricultural, the inflow of British capital, the development of a modern banking and communications systems, the establishment of textile, jute, sugar, and cement factories, and the European demand for tea and coffee led to the beginnings of industrialization. However, it remained extremely limited until the withdrawal of British power. Towards the latter part of British rule, the changed nature of the British economy and the demands of war rendered Indian industrial development a little more necessary, and after the British industrial revolution had reached the height of safety, it not only allowed but even required Indian small-scale industrialization in certain specified spheres.

The growth of modern commerce and industry brought urbanization. Old towns, located in religious, political, or trading centres, were now replaced by large metropolitan cities, such as Bombay, Madras, and Calcutta, and by purely industrial towns, like Ahmadabad. The densely populated cities were an inevitable source of slums, but they also became dynamic political, cultural, and economic centres of a type unknown in India before. The cities and traditions of civic life later played an important role in developing the national consciousness and progressive aspirations of India, as they had done elsewhere. Rome introduced the city into most of continental Europe, and with the city came citizenship and the civic tradition, the greatest contribution of Mediterranean culture.[12] When Rome declined, the Romanized cities upheld the Roman tradition. Later, the rise of the mediaeval city in Europe led to far-reaching changes in the intellectual life of Western society. In India, urbanization attracted landless labour from the village, which weakened the joint family system and the traditional social structure.

The growing complex of new occupations could not be accomodated within the caste system. Industrialization, secular education, and improved means of transportation and communications all operated against the institution of caste. Untouchability and caste discrimination can only survive in a small village community where everyone's caste is known. Wherever crowds of people were thrown together, caste was not visible, nor was it possible to follow all the rules of caste in modern urban surroundings. The need to survive in new conditions, the increasing knowledge of the irreligious character of caste, and crusades by national leaders, especially Mahatma Gandhi, shook the foundations of the caste structure. Consequently, when India became independent, there were, except for the inevitable orthodox, no mental reservations against the abolition of caste.

During the British period, India developed considerable interest, if not competence, in science and its application to human affairs, even though Indian technological development was still in its infancy. Scientific thought was a major part of the Indian inheritance but modern technology was a Western innovation. The British mainly encouraged humanistic and literary education in India, and neglected technical studies and sciences. Whilst there were many liberal arts colleges in India, there were only a few engineering or medical colleges. But the enthusiasm with which the Indians have taken to science and the rapid progress made in recent years is instructive, especially to those who think of them as unworldly recluses, levitating in forests and holy places.

Modern education, in which aesthetic values seldom find a place, is not conducive to artistic development, in India or elsewhere. Indian artists, however, managed to retain their traditional values and forms, partly because the modernists neglected them, and partly because of pride in their rich heritage. Consequently, the old canons are still systematically applied in every form of popular art in India, and modern Indian art, on the whole, retains the spirit of its exceedingly rich past. But it has been influenced by artistic developments in Western countries. Reflecting the new technical civilization and expressing the spirit of its time, modern Indian art has become no less experimental than that of Europe or America.

The Portuguese were the first to introduce late Renaissance and Baroque art into their Indian possessions. It had limited effect. It was with the British, and their need to build bungalows, factories, forts, cathedrals, and cities, that Indian art came under a major European influence; Bombay government offices, the Lahore railway station, the palaces of Gwalior and Baroda, and the Victoria Memorial in Calcutta are but a few examples of various European architectural styles.

Later in the nineteenth century, a reaction against imitating Europe set in, and Indian art took a new turn under Englishmen such as E. B. Havell, and Indians, such as A. N. Tagore. For a while, an art revival persisted which attempted to recreate a national style of painting. But, as in other spheres of cultural life, a process of synthesis commenced. New schools began to arise, and there is no doubt that a fully developed Indian art will be an integration of past and present, a synthesis of East and West. Modern Indian artists are expressing themselves in all the modern idioms of Europe and America, accompanied by the modes of art practiced in India. Whilst Indian painters follow the styles and techniques of modern Europe, especially of France, they depict scenes and people in recognizably Indian manner.

British-built structures guided Indian architects. The importation of European styles was soon followed by a period of blending the rich Indian tradition with European design. An example of this was the capital of British India, New Delhi, built by Sir Edwin Lutyens and his associate, Sir Edward Baker, in the 1930's. Their first designs were a type of neo-Roman style but, under severe criticism from innumerable people in England, including such outstanding names in literature and art as George Bernard Shaw and Sir William Rothenstein, the plans were revised to incorporate Indian motifs. But the product did not turn out to be a synthesis of styles but an assortment of patterns, hybrid and uninspired, partly because New Delhi was built at a time when the old style had lost all virility, and the new style was yet to be developed. However, further changes have taken place since and a composite style may well be on its way, blending elements of Hindu, Mughal, and Victorian Gothic architecture.

Dance and music remained almost uninfluenced by European styles. Certain modifications, however, are noticed in popular music, especially in Indian cinemas, and in modern musical compositions which have adopted Western techniques. Some Indian composers, such as Sarabji, have written music in Western styles, sometimes using Indian motifs. Ali Akbar Khan occasionally incorporated a certain amount of harmony and Western melodies into his improvizations.

Direct British impact on Indian social and cultural life may not have been as decisive as it was on Indian economic and political organization. But the revival of the tradition of learning and the introduction of English secular education illuminated the path of Indian modernization, just as the Indian appetite for knowledge had sustained India's greatness in the past.

Education in ancient India, though somewhat limited in scope, was not commercial; teachers were generally not paid, nor did students race through examinations to pick up lucrative jobs. It was a voluntary partnership in pursuit of truth. Standards were too demanding and academic freedom so firm that even the strongest ruler could not tamper with universities. On the whole, the system of learning was exceedingly effective. Emphasis was on philosophy but science was also studied, and in all subjects an attitude of criticism and a spirit of inquiry and reason were encouraged. However, this tradition of learning declined during the long period of changing political patterns in India.

The mediaeval rulers remained indifferent to scientific and secular education, and whilst the Western countries were making rapid scientific progress, India allowed her intellectual heritage to go unused. The spirit of inquiry was replaced by a sacrosanct attitude towards authority, and an uncritical acceptance of opinions discouraged rational analysis.

The rise of Muslim power in India did not help matters much. Islam, which had stirred Indian intellectual and cultural life into a burst of activity, did not subscribe to the absolute supremacy of the human intellect; it was decisively restricted by the holy scriptures as interpreted by the Ulama. Islam had begun as an assertion of intellectual freedom, but the initial urgency for this freedom was soon lost. Once Islam's earlier democracy was replaced by authoritarianism, Muslim education also became subject to state authority, even in the most creative centres of Islamic civilization. It is no small wonder that Muslim education in India also became increasingly dogmatic, inward-looking, and stereotyped. There was, no doubt, a wide network of schools, but the system of education, consisting chiefly of the study of theology and scripture, was not conducive to the sustained growth of higher learning. Neither science nor technology was taught, although during the reign of Feroz Shah Tughlaq an unsuccessful attempt was made to introduce a simple form of technical education.

Indian education was in an especially neglected state on the eve of British supremacy in India. Whilst the Hindu system of learning was jealously guarded in Brahman caste interests, Muslim education, although open to all, was dominated by theologians and confined to the faithful study of the Quran. Both systems neglected literary and scientific education, critical analyses, and women's education.

The East India Company was reluctant to take responsibility for expensive programs, such as religion, public welfare, and education; although there were notable individual exceptions, for example, William Carey and Sir William Jones. Until compelled to act otherwise, the British Company's rule was like that of a mediaeval police state, anxious to extract revenue and keen to maintain internal and external security with no sense of obligation and responsibility for public welfare, health, and education. Under the Act of 1813 the Company was required to promote public education, and to make a ridiculously inadequate annual grant of one lakh of rupees for educational purposes.

Many Indians were already somewhat familiar with Western education through the activities of Christian missionaries. Danish missionaries had taken the lead in starting English education in India from the middle of the eighteenth century. Ram Mohan Roy even founded an English school, the Hindu College—now known as the Presidency College—at Calcutta in 1817. Starting with a hundred students, the College soon became the leading educational institution of Bengal. In other parts of the country, English schools and colleges had been established through private efforts.

Although Ram Mohan Roy wanted Western knowledge, he wanted to use education to promote the moral and rational development of the individual. He was as much distressed at the secularism of the Hindu College as at the orthodoxy of the pundits. Whilst Roy believed that the new learning "was indispensable for the progress of the nation," he never lost his admiration for the Hindu *Sastras* which he sought to study in the light of modern thought.

After years of agitation, in 1835 Macaulay's minute was written and Governor General Bentinck took a definite decision in favour of English. However, it was not until 1853, forty years after the Act of 1813, that East India Company officials seriously investigated Indian education, as a result of which the modern system of education in India emerged. The universities of Bombay, Calcutta, and Madras, modelled on the lines of London University, were founded in 1857. For a long time these universities continued to be staffed by Europeans and taught a Western curriculum. The British were not very generous with expenditures on education; at the turn of the century, after more than a century of rule, they provided little more than a million pounds a year for the education of about 240 million Indians—a penny a head.

Widespread progress of Western education, however, was made possible by the open-door policy introduced by the British, and by the vast sums donated by Indian philanthropists. Learning, hitherto mainly confined to Brahmans, rulers, or aristocrats, was now available to all those who cared for it, although the expense involved made it still the privilege of the well-to-do few. However, the multiplication of presses meant greater production and wider circulation of books and, in turn, education. (The art of printing had been introduced by Portuguese missionaries in the sixteenth century but it made progress only after the establishment of the British rule.)[13]

Western education was like an explosive force as it shattered dogma and superstition. The Indians were compelled to reflect upon the bases of their beliefs and institutions and to measure them against European standards. If this new thinking helped the modernization of India, it also gave rise to a class of Indian thinkers who shared Macaulay's contempt of Oriental learning and, like Macaulay, without bothering to study it.

Indians took to Western learning so wholeheartedly and uncritically that many of these newly educated men became comic imitators, without any enduring contact with either West or East. They were overawed by Western knowledge and in their eagerness to profit by it, missed its very essence—intellectual scepticism and scientific investigation. Without a critical understanding of Western learning, they made no effort to learn their own. Even competent Indian scholars acquired at best a high level of scholarly knowledge, but made no creative contribution to learning. With great expertise they either elaborated Western concepts or sought endorsement of their ideas in Western literature. Whilst Western learning opened up new vistas of knowledge for the Indians, in some ways it blunted the edge of their intellectual scepticism. Consequently, English-trained Indian scholars were generally inferior to European authorities. Their intellectual subservience had been so intense that even at present, despite political independence, Indians have yet to assert their intellectual freedom.

Some effects of English education were quite ugly, for it gave rise to a cultural minority with its own distinct features and interests. Although the English-educated Indians were a very small minority in the country (less than one per cent), they were numerous enough to constitute a class of their own. Patronized by the British Government, this class soon dominated the top levels of Indian life. It became a kind of middle class interposed between the masters and the masses, often acting as an insulator protecting the former against the latter. Whilst peasants, workers, and petty tradesmen did not speak English, those above them, from clerk to councillor, did. Spurred by the class-preservation instinct, the Westernized Indian was led to rather indiscriminately adopt Western forms in speech, dress, and manners; and to isolate himself from the "illiterate" and "uncouth" masses of his own people. At best, he was a laboriously cultivated English gentleman. At worst, he was clumsy if not ludicrous, and often crude, pretending to enjoy European food, music, and painting, at times even speaking his own native language with an English accent.

The snob value of English degrees was so great that those who had any kind of degree would take care to display it meticulously, and those who could not pass their examinations would be anxious to let it be known that they had reached the take-off point, even if they could not take off. As a result, there grew up not only a class of B.A.'s, out also a class of "B.A. failed" or "Intermediate passed."

The English-educated had a hierarchy of their own; the Brahmans of this class were those who returned from England, preferably with a degree—any degree—but without it if necessary. Those Indians who desired a Western education other than English flocked to Germany and other Western centres of learning. History does not offer a parallel to this phenomenon where efforts for learning produced such a pathetic class of self-complaisant and servile scholars. The nearest example, perhaps, may be that of the English themselves during the Norman period, when it was fashionable to be French in speech, appearance, and behaviour, and English was the language of the vulgarian.

Reaction against this kind of English education inevitably set in. A number of "national" institutions which imparted both Indian and Western learning, such as the Kashi Vidyalaya, the Jamia Milia, and the Gurukula, were established. In contrast, the Anglicized schools and colleges strongly emphasized English education—not even European learning—and students learned a good deal of England, its birds, countryside, and flowers, and of English literature and history. The national institutions did not, as expected, gain widespread support in the absence of government patronage. They were not assisted financially or otherwise by the state, nor were their degrees recognized. On the contrary, the British Government looked upon them with distrust as centres of "subversive" propaganda. Indeed, these institutions did seek to inculcate a sense of nationhood and Indian-ness and therefore attracted students with nationalistic inclinations. As their degrees did not originally entitle them to government or other positions, they did not draw a response from the practical-minded. Despite their limitations and small numbers, they have produced quite a number of competent and successful national leaders, such as Acharya Narendra Deva, a much respected Indian patriot-scholar, Lal Bahadur Sastri, who succeeded Jawaharlal Nehru as India's Prime Minister, and Zakir Hussain, who was the first Muslim president of India.

The influence of English literature on the literature of Indian languages was intensive. Poetry had been composed in India since the days of the *Rig Veda,* but prose began to be written for the first time after a break of more than a thousand years. Begun as polemics for and against religious and social reform, prose forms rapidly reached maturity. Novels, short stories, essays, and modern drama developed in Indian writing—the short story particularly in the twentieth century.

Shakespeare became an integral part of Indian studies, exercising an almost hypnotic influence on Indian literature and drama. Shakespeare was not known to Indians until the beginning of the nineteenth century, although he was writing his great tragedies around the time the East India Company was founded in 1600. Once, however, English education was begun and a knowledge of Western literature and thought became a status symbol and an essential prerequisite for professional and pecuniary gain, Shakespeare became familiar reading in Indian literary and dramatic circles. For most English-educated Indians, Shakespeare's characters, the situations in his plays, and significant quotations, became almost as intimate a part of their lives as those of their own best writers.

Most of Shakespeare's better plays have been translated into Indian languages. First to appear, in 1853, was a Bengali translation by Harachandra Ghosh called *Bhanumati Chittavilasa,* an adaptation of the Portia-Bassanio theme from *The Merchant of Venice.* Since then all of Shakespeare's comedies have been translated, with the exception of the "dark comedy," (in fact unclassifiable as a kind of drama) *Troilus and Cressida.* The Marathi version of the minor comedy, *The Taming of the Shrew,* rendered by V. B. Kelkar in 1891 has been "acclaimed to be such a perfect stage version that even if Shakespeare were a Hindu, he could not have improved on it." P. Sambanda Mudaliar's Tamil adaptations of Shakespeare are well known. The four best known tragedies have been translated with alterations to suit the Indian taste, which prefers a happy ending. For instance, Hamlet and Ophelia are reconciled at the end; Desdemona is not really dead; a daughter is provided for Macbeth in answer to the famous question, "How many children had Lady Macbeth?" to make it possible for her to be married to Malcolm at the end.

However, it is doubtful if Shakespeare will continue to attract Indian universities as before, and the modern scholar's image of Shakespeare—emphasizing the technical, social, source-hunting, and temporal aspects of his work—does not appeal much to Indians, who prefer to look at him from literary and human viewpoints, as did the romantic poet-critics during the last century.

THE CONTINUAL GROWTH of secular and scientific knowledge affected the whole Indian attitude towards life. Indians were overpowered by the ideas of Western liberty, parliamentary government, and nationalism. Later, Marxism and socialism also permeated Indian thinking. Early Indian nationalists even drew their inspiration from European patriots. In the 1870's, Italian nationalist leaders, such as Mazzini and Garibaldi were popular idols of Indian patriots. The Irish movement for self-rule was closely watched and admired by many Indian leaders, for whom the Irish patriots were models of devotion and sacrifice. De Valera was as much an Indian as an Irish hero, and Subhas Bose was often called the Indian De Valera.

Two major political ideologies have dominated Indian life for about a century—nationalism and Marxism. Indian nationalism has long assumed its own individual personality, and there is every likelihood that Indian communism may well become distinctly Indian before gaining any widespread adherence in India. Indian communists already look more to Gandhi and Nehru than to Marx and Lenin. Nationalism was, no doubt, primarily a reaction against British imperialism, which gave it the consciousness of a common political community, the urge to organize, and the power to attract widespread attention. It was further strengthened by territorial unification, a uniform educational system, the establishment of a communication network, and a highly centralized administration. But its ideological rationalization and form came from the influx of Western liberal ideas and a growing pride in its own cultural past.

How much Indian nationalism owes to the direct impact of European liberalism would be extremely difficult to ascertain. The force of liberal ideas certainly made British imperialism more humane and receptive to Indian demands, although the growing power of commercial interests in an era of industrial revolution invariably counselled authoritarianism. Democracy at home was to "co-exist with despotism abroad." The conflicting principles of liberty and empire were to be blended into a new and unique doctrine of "domination for the dominated."

Many of the prophets and leaders of Indian nationalism were, no doubt, greatly influenced by European liberal thought, but their main inspiration was India's cultural renaissance, which was almost contemporary with Western liberalism. Ram Mohan Roy implored the British to introduce colleges of Western, not Oriental, learning to India. He saw no contradictions between the freedom of liberalism and the intrinsic values of Hinduism. Roy was not a product of the West, and did not visit there until the end of his life. Even Jawaharlal Nehru, who adopted British habits and thought-processes "more than even the British themselves," regarded Indian cultural heritage as the driving force behind unity and progress. Bal Gangadhar Tilak, the "Father of Indian Unrest" and the first man to suggest to Indians the goal of "swaraj (freedom) is my birth-right," did not visit England until almost the end of his career. He was deeply inspired in his political philosophy by the *Bhagavad Gita*. However, it would not be correct to assume that Western ideas did not influence their thinking.

The common people, who formed the great bulk of the Indian national movement, knew little of Western liberal ideas. The only impact they felt directly was Western imperialism. To them, Western concepts of rights and freedom were vague, hypothetical, and even hypocritical. They could see the value of these concepts only when they were presented in Indian terms. Thus, Aurobindo Ghose, a completely Westernized and English-educated intellectual, who renounced politics to retire to Pondicherry in the pursuit of Divine consciousness, spoke of nationalism as an *Avatar* (an incarnation of God), which must emancipate humanity from demonic oppression. Nationalism being God, was immortal, and therefore no government could destroy it. Aurobindo Ghose, despite his too brief incursion into politics from 1905 to 1910, was able to introduce into the Indian nationalist movement an esoteric philosophy which proved to be of immense political value both at home and abroad. The divinity of "Mother India," long cherished as an abstract and ethical conception by many generations of Indian nationalists became a political weapon of unquestionable efficacy in his hands. He preached that the sanctification of patriotism was the dedicated worship of India personified as the Great Mother. Much later Mahatma Gandhi spoke along the same lines to "the teeming millions of India" who followed him. His concept of political freedom was translated into "Ramarajya," the kingdom of Rama, which was based on principles of universal morality, and in which justice, righteousness, and the will of the people were supreme.

It was this alliance between the imported concepts of liberty and unity, and the developing ideals of renascent Hinduism which gave Indian nationalism not only a distinctive character but also a worthwhile meaning and force. The concept of nationality, that is, the existence of a community within a defined territory, and patriotism were both known to Indians throughout their history. Ancient literature testifies to a well-defined image of Mother India and to a clear consciousness of national solidarity called Bharatavarsha, or just Bharat, a name now reinstated in the republican constitution of India. Deep sentiments of love and service for India were voiced in the vedic and epic literature. The *Manusmriti* contains passages of extreme patriotic fervour such as "Mother and Mother-country are greater than Heaven." The protective natural frontiers of India helped to weld all Indian peoples into an Indian oneness. The resuscitation of this image gave a definite meaning to Indian nationalism, and Indians responded with intense feeling.

Indian leaders visualized political and social development as going hand in hand, and considered social rejuvenation essential for political and economic progress. Consequently, Indian nationalism in its early phases was closely linked with cultural renaissance. Later, it became more virile and political in character. It was not only the pride of the old, but the vigour of the new which agitated for change (*inqilab*). Liberation from alien rule was not sufficient; the nationalist movement was to be the comprehensive crusade against all kinds of oppressions—including social and economic. In the final phase, the cry for change almost subordinated the demand for political independence (*swaraj* or *azadi*).

The fact that Mahatma Gandhi, who was typically representative of the Indian synthesis of contradictions which baffles logic, was able to gain leadership of the national movement with little resistance and held it almost unchallenged until his death, would further illustrate the syncretic nature of Indian nationalism. Mahatma Gandhi, however, made a distinction between Western and modern civilizations. Although both were equally good, he believed the latter had taken a wrong turn in the West. He, therefore, asked India to keep clear of that kind of modernized West. His position was somewhat similar to that of Tolstoy—a moral man in an immoral world, which had been brought about by a materialist, militarist, and imperialist way of life. He called upon his countrymen to select those elements from Western culture, as from any other, which were essential for their own progress. The spirit of the century was to be reconciled with that of the country.

In an era of intense nationalism, cultural pride, and racial prejudice, Rabindranath Tagore sought to broaden India's outlook to one of world-wide humanism. Truly a world-citizen, he consistently warned his countrymen against the evils of nationalism, and, like Gandhi, spoke of India's self-purification and constructive work. For him, the ideal of humanity transcended the love of country. Political freedom was not necessarily real freedom but might merely be a means of becoming more powerful. Real freedom was of the mind and the spirit, and this could not come to India from outside. Tagore was not against anyone nation in particular but the idea of nationalism in general. He was, however, very proud of Indian culture, and called upon the West to understand its good qualities. Tagore's influence over the Indian mind has been incalculable; more than any of his contemporaries, he helped to harmonize the ideals of East and West, and to broaden the bases of Indian nationalism. He was one of the world's great internationalists, believing in and working for international co-operation, taking India's culture to other countries and bringing theirs to India.

Jawaharlal Nehru's greatest gift to renaissant India was to underline the intrinsic merits of Western culture. Although influenced by his Indian heritage, Nehru was completely Western in his outlook. Scientific rationalism, humanism, and socialism had a profound influence on him, enabling him to fill a gap in Indian political life, a gap that could otherwise have proven very costly. Western individualism was essential in order to give the Indian a feeling of self-reliance. Contemptuously discarding traditional self-effacement, he preached and practiced self-assertion, even at the risk of appearing arrogant; competent arrogance was preferable to empty humility in a society ridden with multiple social and economic inequalities.

Nehru was the living symbol of what was best in the West. Most Indian intellectuals saw in Nehru the ideal expression of their Westernization, and a bridge between tradition and modernity. Even at a time when Nehru lay in a British prison, he recorded in his *Autobiography*, "in spite of my hostility to British imperialism and all imperialisms, I have loved much that was England..." Yet, he spoke the Gandhian language of India: "Do away with evil, put your faith in goodness—in your goodness and the goodness of your opponent."

Influenced by the ethical norms of Western humanism, the precepts of the Upanishads, and the rationalism of the Buddha, Nehru had been attracted by Marxist theory, during the late 1920's. He was generally regarded as the patron of democratic socialism in India, although he was never a member of any socialist party. It was mainly through his efforts that Marxism, a completely Western product, was admitted to Indian political life, and it has since considerably influenced modern Indian thought, politics, literature, economic life, and social outlook. It was mainly Gandhi's moral influence and Nehru's admiration for Gandhian satyagraha that restrained Nehru from becoming a Marxist socialist.

During his visit to Europe in 1926–1927, he came into contact with numerous Marxist intellectuals and leaders, especially at the Congress of the League of Oppressed Peoples at Brussels. Later, he went to Russia and was greatly impressed by the achievements of Socialist Russia. Since then he always advocated a socialistic society for India, based on democracy and individual liberty.

From the declaration of Indian independence until his death in 1964, Nehru dominated Indian life and politics blending modern values into Indian tradition with a skill that hardly has a parallel in history. Throughout his life, despite frequent criticisms of his policy of non-alignment, he remained a key man in world politics. A leader of an anti-imperialist revolution, he embodied the hopes of peace of men all over the globe. Others looked upon him as the architect of a unique democracy, struggling between divergent forces to acquire economic prosperity and social justice. The Indian revolution, although rooted in Gandhian ethics, could be described as "Nehruesque," for it is to Nehru that it owes its present form, reflecting his typical combination of Indian idealism and Western materialism.

Nehru was not a philosopher in the sense that Gandhi was, but without him much of Gandhism would have remained in disuse, somewhat in the same way as Marxism would have without Lenin. He commanded both the respect of the intelligentsia and the love of the common man. He was not only an exponent of the cherished ideals of his people but an expression of human conscience. Few statesmen could claim his empiricism without opportunism, and doctrinism without dogmatism. He could win the personal affection of his political adversaries without compromising either relationship. He believed that the "creative mind," with its social sensitiveness, could alone solve the crisis of the human spirit. It is this humanism which made him a representative of the West in the East and of the East in the West.

A major consequence of the West's impact on Indian tradition has been in psychological attitudes. Being a self-contained, rich, agricultural community, India was conservative, hospitable, tolerant, and somewhat fatalistic. But all this changed, first under prolonged foreign domination, and later under the pressure of the newly developing competitive society. India's natural contentment has given way to a spirit of rebellion and self-reliance which, under the excessive zeal of new converts, often inclines Indians to self-deprecation and lack of collective discipline. Highly individualistic, Indians have always resisted any regimentation of thought. Extrovert, nonconformist, and informal, they express themselves uninhibitedly, and indulge too often in reflection and introspection. Whilst these qualities gave India a distinctive character, and advanced her learning and democracy, they have often enough in the past, as in the present, reached a point where they hinder organization, team work, and discipline, the essential virtues of material transformation. It is curious, for the Indian does not lack in self-discipline, or even in self-denial. In fact, self-discipline to the Indian is not denial of one's liberty but an aid to individual spiritual perfection. However, any collective political discipline is regarded as an abridgement of individual liberty. Despite exemplary devotion and the spirit of self-sacrifice, conspiracies, mutinies, and underground revolutionary movements failed in India because of poor co-ordination and the inevitable leakage of information. Mass movements, such as Mahatma Gandhi's satyagraha, succeeded because they were open, and required essentially individual effort. Whilst crowds of people participated in satyagraha, in effect, each individual was a self-contained movement, and as an individual he could successfully protest against what he thought was unjust. Gandhi often did, alone.

Indians have yet to strike a balance between these two opposites and learn to blend individual liberty with social discipline in order to speed national advance. The value of compromise and discipline in a collective effort cannot be overestimated. No chapter of history is more instructive in this respect than that of Western activities in Asia. Western domination was, in fact, the triumph of organization and team work over personal valour and an unco-ordinated approach to politics. It is this Indian inability to integrate individual qualities into a collective pattern which, more than any other, finds its expression in a variety of meaningless disagreements, consuming national effort and morale. It seems sometimes that every Indian is a walking Lok Sabha as well as a moral preceptor. What India needs, and has often stood in need of, is not so much sound advice as sustained endeavour.

Reflection and criticism are, no doubt, indispensable for both the political and spiritual health of a nation, but they can be overdone.

Democracy after all consists of both criticism and effort. In India, they sometimes part company. Excessive self-criticism soon leads to loss of self-confidence, and thoughtless and irresponsible expression creates an atmosphere of general frustration. Together they drain national energy. Today, India's most severe criticism comes from thinking Indians, especially from perfectionists and those whose expectations far exceed their competence. As perfection is unattainable, and undeserved expectations remain unfulfilled, frustration is inevitable, with the result that the very class of people who should be in the vanguard of an Indian revolution are its great liability. One often finds on the one side the educated Indians, extremely critical of everything and exuding gloom, and on the other the common people solemnly engaged in the tasks of national reconstruction. Irrespective of what awaits them—although it is prosperity they expect to find—and unmindful of the urgency of their job, the common men in India evidently find honest work for honest ends inspiring and satisfactory in itself.

The frustration of educated Indians is in no small measure conditioned by Western criticisms of Indian achievements, which are not always valid. Indians cannot shut themselves away from criticism, valid or invalid, for they respect their own right to criticize. Often Western critical analysis is more effective than it should be because it is couched in English, a language in which the Indians are at a disadvantage. Indians, however, are often reluctant to confess to this inadequacy for they still confuse knowledge of English with knowledge itself and unconsciously tend to measure the degree of a person's learnedness by his command of English.

But even well meaning critics of India, who would like to see India progress, quite often inadvertently measure India in Western terms and confuse a difference of values and emphasis with unsoundness of policy and practice. In any case, in their anxiety to achieve rapid results they have imposed a sense of urgency on the Indian experiment. Delay might explode India, they fear, and may even disrupt world order. Indisputably, the sooner Indian poverty is banished the better. But it would be imprudent to lose balance for speed. It is better to reach the goal late on one's own feet than to arrive soon on a stretcher.

India is not racing against either time, economic poverty, political rivalry, or alien criticism. She is fighting herself. If, during this period of development, she cannot keep up national morale, avoiding the frustrations inherent in partial successes or failures, and stand firmly optimistic against the unsolicited flood of gloomy prophecies, no amount of her past glory or professions of noble faith can lead her to the desired goal.

If the British brought out the best in Indian society, they also emphasized its hitherto dormant weakness. One such influence was on the social and political relationship between Hindus and Muslims, which finally destroyed the political unity of India. Before the advent of the British in India, Hindus and Muslims had lived side by side for about a thousand years in distinct social compartments, accommodating each other's religious beliefs. In political spheres, there were, as anywhere else, divisions within each community as dictated by the politics of power. Political relationship was not hinged to religious beliefs. Socially, Muslims were yet another caste in India. Just as the caste system separating Hindus from Hindus came under condemnation, so did the exclusion of Muslims from Hindu society. But Hindu-Muslim social assimilation was a very different problem because of their diverse faiths and traditions. Later, the development of modern politics, involving a relentless struggle between Indian nationalism and British imperialism, gave rise to Muslim nationalism. Whilst the ruling power remained alien, both Hindus and Muslims were equally deprived of authority, but once the prospects of democratic self-government began to emerge, the numerical superiority of Hindus caused a natural concern to Muslims.

Whether the British deliberately introduced the policy of "divide and rule" or not, they did little to maintain the separation of religion and politics, and still less to tone down the consciousness of communalism. They certainly did make positive efforts to accommodate the problems and to allay the fears of minorities. But their attitudes and statements, made either in genuine ignorance of the effect of their policy or in conscious effort to profit by it, overemphasized the problem, and even inflamed fears. Practically every Secretary of State and Viceroy kept notes for a stereotyped statement, which was repeated with necessary but minor variations on every public occasion, stressing the manifold divisions in Indian society. Referring to India's many languages, races, and creeds, it sought to mobilize all the interests opposed to Indian nationalism and unity. It paraded minority statistics, not always quite accurate, and invariably dwelt on the opposed religions and depressed classes. Sometimes this was done in a tone of fatalistic regret, sometimes with an air of polemical triumph, but always the stress was on the divisions of India. This was surely the wrong way to try to bridge such divisions. The reverse would have been more appropriate. The British might have emphasized the fundamental unity of the two religions and their common historical past.

It must, however, be pointed out that Western thought is, unlike Indian, permeated with the consciousness of religious differences and antagonisms, even amongst denominations of the same Christian faith. Religion was the keynote of British politics and education until the end of the nineteenth century. The British could have recalled that it was only in 1829, after a period of prolonged opposition, that the Catholic Emancipation Act was passed in Britain, even if they chose to ignore the terribly bitter Catholic-Protestant conflicts and other religious struggles. It was in 1836 that the Marriage Act of 1753, under which no one could be legally married except by a Church of England parson, and which was an intolerable insult to Catholics, was remedied. Religious bigotry was intense in education. Catholics could not enter the Universities of Oxford and Cambridge until 1871, after the working class of the towns had been enfranchized by the Reform Act of 1867, and long after the rise of liberalism and concepts of individual freedom.

The treatment of the Jews was no better; indeed, the Jews did not get full and equal citizenship rights until 1866. Charles Bradlaugh was not allowed to take his seat in Parliament because he was an atheist, and it took six years of painstaking struggle before he could enter the House and voice the views of his constituents. Indeed, religion in England was more than a matter of personal preference, and the Anglican Church was more than an ecclesiastical choice. Protestant ascendancy was an integral part of the British Constitution; the Coronation oath pledged the monarch to defend Protestantism by law and power, and the Act of Settlement ensured a Protestant succession.

Yet the British might have communicated to Muslims and Hindus the Western discovery made long ago, that creed was an irrelevance in modern politics, and emphasized the significance of economic and social issues. "If every day and in every way, each according to his temperament and opportunities, using the press and the wireless, schoolbooks and white papers, the officials and spokesmen of this mighty government had sought to minimise religious differences and promote an outlook of secular commonsense, and done this steadily for fifty years, is it certain that this feud would rage as it does today? They chose to make the other speech."[14]

The influx of Western culture was a gradual, persistent, and unpremeditated process, brought in by a motley crowd of Europeans ranging from unscrupulous adventurers to devoted intellectuals, missionaries, and administrators. As a class, these heralds of change, however, made no conscious effort to hasten the process. This part of Indian cultural transformation is a fascinating period of physical endurance, intellectual interaction, and social rejuvenation. Indian response to the West was ambivalent. It endeavoured, on the one side, to reassert India's great cultural past and, on the other, to purge its traditional character. Consequently, India sought to strike a delicate balance between the two.

As might be expected in any cultural encounter between two powerful civilizations, Western impact on India highlighted both the virtues and evils of Indian society and culture. Whilst the British industrial revolution inaugurated a new material era that transformed Indian economy, it also gave rise to poverty, overpopulation, and famine. Whilst it stirred the depths of the Indian mind, awakened its dormant spirit of scientific inquiry, and made new contributions to Indian life, it also compelled Indian society to defend its traditional inheritance, causing a cultural revivalism. In its totality it acted as a catalyst, setting in motion cultural processes which gradually led to an organized national consciousness and unity, and eventually to the modernization of traditional India.

Western influence on modern India, transmitted through English education Christian missions and, mainly, British domination, has indeed been both extensive and varied. Although Christian missionaries initiated cultural exchange in India, it was not until the British colonial administration began to train Indian personnel for utilitarian ends and the Indians themselves felt the pressure for change, that India began to break away from tradition to enter modernity. Despite many commentaries on the subject, the process and all its implications are yet to be evaluated dispassionately. Perhaps its full magnitude can only be seen after it has stood the test of time. India today is both old and new, and this makes her at once distinctive and complex. That Indian modernization began under Western impact is not denied, but how much of it is her own renewed vitality is often a subject of intense, if not acrimonious, debate. The two views are not really contradictory or even incompatible; the differences mainly arise when too much is claimed on one side and too much discounted on the other.

Historians have achieved no consensus, nor are they expected to, on the nature and consequences of the British impact on India. British rule of India was a long process with several clearly marked phases. Inevitably, cultural processes during this period proceeded in various directions and at various levels. In some respects, the British influence was positive; in others, negative. Again, some influences were the outcome of a conscious policy, whilst others were unintentional and incidental. But in all respects it was a stimulant on a stagnant society, with reactions ranging from imitation and assimilitation to rejection.

The restoration of law and order, the unification of the country under one central authority, the emergence of the middle classes, the development of transport and communications, the revival of international consciousness, in themselves are praiseworthy contributions. But what is more important is that because of these it was possible for Indians to pursue other cultural and intellectual activities. It is not for what the British actually contributed that they should be judged, but for making it possible for Indians to rejuvenate the best of their culture and determine their own destiny. By making them conscious of both their weaknesses and of their strengths, the British gave the Indians objectives and methods to approach these objectives. Knowledge of Western thought and method, and especially Western experience, gave Indians hope for the success of their new ideals. Without the awareness of the modernization processes which the West itself had gone through, it is extremely unlikely that Indian society could have been stirred into action. Precept without precedent seldom appears attractive.

The spirit of modern India is something like the spirit of nature itself.

It is ever new, constantly changing, yet old. Whilst they are actively engaged in the pursuit of scientific achievements, the Upanishads will continue to fascinate and inspire Indians, who will retain their search for the ultimate, without sacrificing material prosperity. Meanwhile, they will bear the weight of poverty with their characteristic quietness and happiness. Gandhi will always inspire them more than Marx, and their means will be as important as their ends. Yet what India represents today is the emergence of a new civilization, not merely the continuation of an old one.

India was in need of modernization, and the West introduced it to her. Modernism, however, must not be confused, as is so often done, with materialism or even Westernism. There is nothing inherently Western about modernism because it does not emanate from space but time. The modern Indian man, for example, may be agnostic, atheist, religious, or mystical. He is quite capable of experimenting with dangerous microbes or exploring outer space in search of truth. His motivation may be the spiritual conviction that man must know the truth about all things, or the faith that human suffering will be reduced if not eliminated. A modern saint, like a Karma Yogi, is often seen with hospital instruments or laboratory test-tubes praying inarticulately to an impersonal God called science or humanity. Modernism may have begun in the West but it is a universal and common human heritage. Even if there had been no British rule in India, modernism would still have come, as it came, for instance, to Japan. In an era of increasing scientific and technological advancement, the cultural isolation of one region could scarcely be possible. Without the impediment of colonial rule, Indian response to the West might have been even more unrestrained. Even so, although her choice of Western learning was somewhat limited by British imperial needs, the initiative to select from what was offered was mainly her own. India elected to absorb voluntarily. She resisted Western domination, but not Western learning.

NOTES

NOTES FOR PART I

Notes to Chapter I

1. Recent archaeological excavations in Turkey, conducted by the University of Istanbul, have revealed evidence that communities with a well-developed culture and economy had existed there as long ago as 7000 B.C., possibly even earlier. The full implications of this discovery have yet to be properly assessed. Jericho also belongs to about the same time and has yielded evidence of a society organized in fairly large units.
2. V. Gordon Childe, "Europe and the Near East: A Prehistorian's Interpretation of Diffusion" in Harvard Tercenary Conference of Arts and Sciences, *Independence, Convergence, and Borrowing,* p. 4.
3. Jean Filliozat, *Political History of India,* p. 85.
4. A team of archaeological experts from the Vikram University in Madhya Pradesh State has recently succeeded in unearthing the remains of a hitherto unknown Chalcolithic site, dating back to the third millennium B.C., in the village of Kayatha, fifteen miles east of Ujjain. These finds at Kayatha are of historic significance inasmuch as they indicate for the first time the existence of a fairly advanced culture and civilization in the Malwa region in such a remote period of history. The excavations reveal the remains of pottery, terracottas, copper tools, and some houses showing greater affinity with the Harappan and pre-Harappan elements of Rajasthan and Punjab.
5. V. Gordon Childe, *New Light on the Most Ancient East,* p. 169.

6. Herodotus, *The Histories,* III. 106.
7. J. B. Hutchinson, R. A. Silow, and S. G. Stephens, *The Evolution of Gossypium,* p. 88. Also see Vol. II, Ch. II, pp. 69–72.
8. Jacquetta Hawkes and Sir Leonard Woolley, *History of Mankind,* I, 396.
9. Two scholars, S. K. Ray, an Indian, and El Mansouri, an Egyptian, have pointed out striking similarities between the cultures of these two areas and have recently suggested, in independent studies, a historic and close relationship between ancient Egypt and prehistoric India, especially Bengal. S. K. Ray, *Pre-historic India and Ancient Egypt;* and S. M. El Mansouri, *Art-Culture of India and Egypt.*
10. A. L. Pusalkar, *Cultural Heritage of India,* I, 155.
11. Childe, *New Light on the Most Ancient East,* p. 170.
12. Childe, *Independence, Convergence, and Borrowing,* p. 19.
13. Childe, *New Light on the Most Ancient East,* pp. 183-84.
14. H. D. Sankalia, *Indian Archaeology Today,* p. 69.
15. Pusalkar, *Cultural Heritage of India,* I, 148.
16. John Garstang, *The Hittite Empire,* p. 205.
17. V. Gordon Childe, *The Aryans,* p. 19. The precise manner in which the kings of Mitanni and the vedic Aryans were connected will remain obscure until further inscriptions are brought to light through archaeological excavations.
18. Although the Phoenicians have left a rich legacy of ancient west Asian lore to the West, such as the alphabet, the knowledge available about them, as compared to the Romans or the Greeks, is scant. No Phoenician, or Punic, city has been resurrected which could give an overall picture of their ancient life. The sites of Sidon and Tyre, much destroyed and repeatedly rebuilt, may yet yield rich rewards. Potentially fruitful excavations, however, including underwater work, are now under way at the site called Motya, near Marsala in Sicily.
19. The Indian origin of ivory has been confirmed in recent years by the fact that some specimens of ivory from the collection of Nimzud have been recognized to be of Indian material. The Phoenicians were importing ivory from Dedan, in North Arabia, by the sixth century B.C. As there were no elephants in Arabia, ivory must have been imported from India or Somaliland by sea and thence across Arabia by camel. The case for its Indian origin is reinforced by the discovery of several pieces of ivory at Bahrein in the Persian Gulf, probably of the sixth or seventh century B.C.

See G. E. Bean, "Early Greek and Oriental Ivories," *Journal of Hellenic Studies,* LXVIII (1948), 1.

20. *Inaha-Ummagga Jataka,* No. 546.
21. Cecil Roth, *A Short History of the Jewish People,* p. 21.
22. See Michael Ridley, *The Seal of Aetea and the Minan Scripts.*
23. *Gaveru Jataka,* No. 339.
24. This subject is more fully discussed in Ch. V
25. For a summary of the arguments favouring the theory that India was the original home of the Aryans, see R. C. Majumdar (ed.), *The History and Culture of the Indian People,* I, 215–17.
26. Childe, *New Light on the Most Ancient East,* p. 188.
27. It has often been said that there is much secular poetry in the Vedas. However, these songs, themes, and humorous episodes have been applied to religious purpose.
28. Linguistic evidence indicates the Indo-European families fall into two distinct groups, according to the modification which certain consonants of the parent speech underwent in each, known as the *Centum* ("hundred" in Latin) and *Satem* ("hundred" in Avesta). The former group includes the Hellenic, Italic, Teutonic, and Celtic branches, and the latter the Indian, Iranian, Armenian, Balto-Slavic, and Albanian. Some scholars, however, like Sturtevant, have criticized the Centum-Satem hypothesis. Contemporary philologists attach less importance to this Centum-Satem division since the discovery of a Centum language in Central Asia in the tenth century A.D. and the discovery that in the nineteenth century B.C. the Hittites in Asia Minor spoke a language more nearly allied to Latin than to any Satem tongue.

    It was first thought that the Indo-European languages had arisen out of a parent speech and family trees were constructed. Realizing, however, that this was too much of an oversimplification, scholars later suggested that there was a continuum of diverging dialects, some of which were crystallized into languages. Even this view was exposed to exceptions. The present view is that the Indo-European languages have emerged, assuming divergent forms gradually, through the convergence of a loose and scattered continuum of distinct dialects. Whatever the course and nature of their convergence and divergence may have been, they are certainly interrelated by some common starting point or process.
29. For a fuller discussion, see V. Gordon Childe, *The Aryans,* pp. 3-16. The Florentine merchant, Filippo Sassetti, having lived in Goa for five years

between 1583 and 1588, declared that some relationship existed between Sanskrit and the principal languages of Europe. Later, Coeurdoux in 1767, and still later Sir William Jones in 1786, noticed affinities between Latin, Greek, and Sanskrit vocabularies and grammars, and put forward the theory of a common origin. The original Indo-European is extinct and has taken different forms in different environments over the intervening thousands of years. Of all the existing Indo-European languages, Lithuanian is closest to the basic idiom as reconstructed by comparative philology. Some scholars regard Sanskrit, with its three numbers, three genders, and eight cases of noun, as well as an extremely complicated verbal structure, as the nearest representative of the parent, highly inflected Indo-European language.

30. The word Aryas is also found in the western group.
31. For a discussion of the possible reasons for the discontinuance of the relationship, see R. C. Majumdar (ed.), *History and Culture of the Indian People,* I, 218ff.
32. "In this inversion," remarks Gordon Childe "we detect the hand of the prophet Zoroaster himself, who was perhaps the first great religious reformer:" *The Aryans,* p. 36.
33. Bopp was the first scholar to notice the connection between Avestan *Ahura* and Sanskrit *Astura,* and Avestan *deava* and Sanskrit *deva.*
34. Seleucia and Antioch did not exist as such during the Achaemenian period; both cities were founded by Seleucus Nicator in 300 and 312 B.C. respectively.
35. The Persians, if not the later Assyrians, were the first to create a permanent system of roads and to provide for their regular maintenance, cementing bridges, embankments, and stations at convenient stages.
36. "The Indians, the most populous nation in the known world, paid the largest sum: 360 talents of gold dust." Herodotus, *The Histories,* III, 95. Considering that only a small part of India was under the Persian Empire and that it formed only one satrapy the amount paid in revenue speaks highly of Indian prosperity at the time, even if allowance is made for the gross exaggeration to which Herodotus was very prone. Actually, a student of Indian history is amazed by the numerous references of foreign travellers to India's great riches. Arab and Chinese writers frequently mention them; Sir Thomas Roe, who visited the court of Jahangir in the seventeenth century complained, "Europe bleedeth to enrich Asia"; Hawkins, his contemporary, refers to the gold coins which flowed into India and "goeth out not." The French traveller Bernier, too, in the seventeenth century,

writes that gold and silver came from all over the globe "to be swallowed up, lost in some manner in Hindustan."

37. K. A. N. Sastri (ed.), *Age of the Nandas and Mauryas,* p. 390.
38. There is no real certainty that the pillars were made by Asoka. Some of them, it is likely, were in existence before him. He often ordered that his edicts be "inscribed on pillars whereever they may be found," or words to that effect.
39. Irrespective of his motives, which were wholly moral and partly practical, Asoka is the only monarch on record who renounced war after victory. H. G. Wells, who considers Asoka as one of the six greatest men of history—the only king included—says: "Amidst the tens of thousands of names of monarchs that crowd the columns of history, their majesties and graciousnesses and serenities and royal highnesses and the like, the name of Asoka shines, and shines almost alone, like a star." *Outline of History,* p. 247.
40. The origin of the name *Kharoshthi* is obscure but the term seems to mean script written on the skin of donkeys. See J. Przylushi, *Journal of the Royal Asoka Society,* p. 4.
41. E. B. Havell, *The History of Aryan Rule in India,* p. 105.
42. "Superficially these pillars," comments Hermann Goetz "remind one of Achaemenid columns, and yet they are different in every detail." *India,* p. 47.
43. The Greeks did not pronounce an initial aspiration, sharply or clearly, as they did not use a variety of sibilants.
44. Herodotus, *The Histories,* IV, 44.
45. Three centuries elapsed before this feat of a Red Sea journey was repeated.
46. *The Cambridge History of India,* p. 397. "Ktesias is responsible for most of the grotesque legends about India which fill the pages of classical and medieval writers to the days of Sir John Mandeville." H. G. Rawlinson, *Intercourse between India and the Western World,* p. 26.
47. A. R. Burn, *Persia and the Greeks,* p. 12. It was Ctesias who was responsible for introducing into Western lore the monster called the Martichora (a good Persian word meaning man-eater, which, corrupted into mantichora, passed by way of Aristotle, Pliny, and Aelian into the mediaeval bestiary). He described this monster, which he claimed to have seen at the court of the Persian king who had been sent one from India, as a creature the size of a lion with the face of a man. In contrast, Herodotus, who introduced

the phoenix into the West, at least confesses that "I myself have not seen this bird except in a picture." Aristotle, himself, whilst describing Ctesias' monster says "If one may believe Ktesias."

48. "In some ways—though few—the civilization of Persia," observes Will Durant, "was superior to that of contemporary Hellas; it produced a type of gentleman finer than the Greek in every respect except that of intellectual keenness and education, and a system of imperial administration that easily excelled the clumsy hegemonies of Athens and Sparta, and lacked only the Greek passion for liberty." *The Life of Greece,* p. 69.
49. In his Rede Lecture for 1875; Sir Henry Maine said, "Except the blind forces of nature, nothing moves in this world which is not Greek in origin." Cited in J. A. Symonds, *Studies of the Greek Poets,* p. 578.
50. For a quick reference to the genesis, development, influence, and recent partial decline of the classical Greek myth and the legend which has shaped much European thinking, see Philip Sherrard, *The Pursuit of Greece.*
51. *Rig Veda,* X, 71.
52. Although the *Iliad* and the *Odyssey* are attributed to Homer, little is known of Homer himself. He is considered, however, the first and possibly the greatest European poet, and the one who provided a link between the Mycenaean and classical Greek cultures. Both poems went through a long process of development during which they were enlarged and adapted by generations of bards before reaching their final form, as it is known today, in about the sixth century B.C.
53. Cyrus H. Gordon, *Before the Bible,* p. 238. In the *Iliad* the chief river of the Trojan plain was called by the gods "Xanthos" and by men "Scamander"; a certain bird was called "Chalkis" by the gods and "Kumindis" by men.
54. G. N. Banerjee, *Hellenism in Ancient India,* pp. 198–99. Also see Sir William Ramsay, *Asian Elements in Greek Civilization,* Ch. VI.
55. It should be noted that archaeologists have discovered enough evidence to endorse the existence of the cities of Troy, Mycenae, and others mentioned in the *Iliad* and of a Mycenaean civilization before 1200 B.C. somewhat akin to that described by Homer. Of the two Homeric poems, the *Odyssey* is mainly fictional whilst the *Iliad* purports to be fundamentally an historical poem.
56. J. W. McCrindle, *Ancient India,* p. 1. In a recent study, discussing the common background of Greek and Hebrew civilizations, it is suggested that Homer, like the authors of the Bible, had an east Mediterranean heritage. Both the *Gilgamesh* and the *Odyssey* relate the episodic wanderings of a

hero, in both the heroes reject a goddess' proposal of cohabitation, and in both the heroes interview the dead in Hades. The recapture of Helen in the *Iliad* is paralleled in the *Ugaritic Epic of Kret,* in which the pretty wife of Kret is withheld from him at Udum. Cyrus H. Gordon, *Before the Bible,* p. 19.

57. On the authority of Aristotle, we know that Thales was the forerunner of the absent-minded professor who, on a walk, was so intently looking up to heaven that he tumbled into a well.
58. Opinion on the question as to when Greek philosophy ended is divided. Many scholars hold the view that since the ideas and texts of Greek philosophy are still studied and debated, it never died, whereas others, taking a somewhat narrower view of its tradition and continuity observe that, as an organized study with its own students and professors, it came to an end in 529 when the Emperor Justinian closed the philosophical schools at Athens.
59. Gilbert Murray, *Greek Studies,* p. 71.
60. W. K. C. Guthrie, *A History of Greek Philosophy,* I, 4.
61. Greek philosophy has been divided into four main periods—the pre-Socratic from the early sixth to the middle fifth century B.C.; the Socratic up to the fourth century B.C.; the Hellenistic from the period of Alexander to the rise of the Roman Empire; and the period associated with the emergence of Neoplatonism, in which Greek philosophy became extinct. Zeller, *Outlines of the History of Greek Philosophy,* pp. 36–37.
62. A. K. Coomaraswamy, *Hinduism and Buddhism,* p. 8.
63. Guenon, "Introduction to the Study of the Hindu Doctrines," p. 31. Cited In Floyd H. Ross, *The Meaning of Life in Hinduism and Buddhism,* p. 12.
64. William Gould, George Arbaugh, and R. F. Moore, *Oriental Philosopies,* p. 1.
65. Original texts and details of the system of Indian materialism as of some other movements, are not available.
66. C. Kunhan Raja in S. Radhakrishnan (ed.), *History of Philosophy: Eastern and Western,* I, 31–38.
67. The influence of vedic thought on Indian science is discussed in Ch. V.
68. "As opposed to the other vedic texts which relate to the way of action: the karmamarga, they represent the way of knowledge, the jnanamarga," Lows Renou, *Vedic India,* p. 33.

69. Many more probably existed at an early time, but even now there are still over two hundred Upanishads, although the traditional number cited is one hundred and eight. Of these there are ten principal ones. The word Upanishad is coined from three Sanskrit words meaning literally sitting near, picturesquely describing groups of pupils sitting near the teacher to learn the truth. Some Upanishads are composed in verse, some in prose, and others in a combination of both.
70. S. N. Das Gupta in G. T. Garratt (ed.) *The Legacy of India,* pp 23–33.
71. Max Müller, *Tile Six Systems of Indian Philosophy,* pp. 215–19.
72. Will Durant, *Our Oriental Heritage,* p. 534.
73. The Orphic theology does not regard the body as the instrument of soul, but as its prison, or its tomb, and believes in transmigration, the grievous cycle of births. For the Pythagoreans the soul was a divine being, fallen and entombed in the body through a series of reincarnations, and it could revert to its original state by leading a life of ritual purity and virtue, by bringing itself into tune with the order and harmony of the universe, and by understanding how the principles of all things were derived from numbers. See A. H. Armstrong in H. Lloyd-Jones (ed) *The Greeks,* p. 127.
74. S. Radhakrishnan, *Eastern Religions and Western Thought,* p. 142.
75. Herodotus, *The Histories,* II, 123.
76. "Herodotus' derivation of the rebirth theory from Egypt is impossible, for the good reason that the Egyptians had no such theory." Herodotus had further concluded, also mistakenly, that the Greeks learned of Heracles from the Egyptians. See E. R. Dodds, *The Greeks and the Irrational,* p. 160.
77. Theodor Gomperz, *Greek Thinkers,* I, 127.
78. E. J. Urwick, *The Message of Plato,* pp. 13–14.
79. A. A. Macdonell, *Sanskrit Literature,* p. 422.
80. Whilst Macdonell accepts the high degree of probability of Indian thought influencing Pythagoras, his pupil, Keith, is of the opinion that "… the claim that Pythagoras learned his philosophic ideas from India though widely accepted rests on extremely weak foundations." A. B. Keith, *A History of Sanskrit Literature,* p. 500. For an elaboration of his ideas, see Keith, "Religion and Philosophy of the Vedas," *Journal of Royal Asiatic Society,* XXIX (1909), pp. 579ff.
81. The Ionian philosophers have been called empiricists—those who pay more attention to the facts of experience; and the Pythagorean and Eleatics

have been called rationalists—those who rely on axioms, then accepted as self-evident, and deduce incontestable truths. Thus between them, they represented the two major directions of Greek thought.

82. W. K. C. Guthrie, *A History of Greek Philosophy,* I, 402.
83. W. K. C. Guthrie, *The Greek Philosophers,* p. 50.
84. R. D. Ranade in S. Radhakrishnan (ed.), *History of Philosophy: Eastern and Western,* I, 37. Ranade goes on to call Samkara an Indian Parmenides.
85. T. Gomperz, *Greek Thinkers,* I, 206–07.
86. E. J. Urwick, *The Message of Plato,* pp. 1–14.
87. S. Radhakrishnan, *Eastern Religions and Western Thought,* p. 151.
88. Pythagoras appears to be an excellent example of such a combination. Zeller suggests that it was always in times of great crises, such as in the fifth century after the Peloponnesian War, that the dualistic-mystical tendency came to the fore.
89. Essentially, there were three stages in Greek religion: Chthonian, Olympian, and Mystic. The first worshipped subterranean, the second celestial, and the third resurrected gods. The first predominated before the Homeric Age, the second during it, the third after it. By the time of the Periclean Enlightenment the most vigorous element in Greek religion was the mystery. Will Durant, *The Life in Greece,* p. 188. Gilbert Murray has also made a similar demarcation in the progress of Greek religion. He calls the first stage the primitive, or the age of ignorance, which is typical of similar stages elsewhere and which may be regarded as the normal raw material out of which religion is made. The second stage is termed the Olympian or Classical, in which primitive vagueness was reduced to a kind of order; and the third stage is called the Hellenistic period, reaching roughly from Plato to St. Paul and the early Gnostics. *Five Stages of Greek Religion,* pp. 2–3.
90. F. M. Cornford writes: "Whether or not we accept the hypothesis of direct influence from Persia or Ionian Greeks in the sixth century B.C., any student of Orphic and Pythagorean thought cannot fail to see that the similarities between it and Persian religion are so close as to warrant our regarding them as expressions of the same view of life, and using the one system to interpret the other." *Religion to Philosophy,* p. 176. Guthrie finds resemblances too detailed to escape the hypothesis of direct influence. *Orpheus and Greek Religion,* p. 87.
91. Edward Zeller, *Outlines of the History of Greek Philosophy,* p. 34.
92. Will Durant, *The Life of Greece,* p. 191.

93. W. K. C. Guthrie, *Orpheus and Greek Religion,* p. 238.
94. Guthrie points out that Euripides, who was one of the most inquiring spirits in an age of inquiry and who might be called an eclectic, knew "the writings of the Orphics, and we may judge that he felt a certain sympathy for the ascetic ideal they upheld...." *Orpheus and Greek Religion,* p. 237.
95. A well-known thinker of this century, Whitehead, says that "the safest general characterization of the European philosophical tradition is that it consists of a series of footnotes to Plato." Cited in A. O. Lovejoy, *The Great Chain of Being,* p. 24.
96. *Brihadaranyaka Upanishad,* I, 3.28.
97. Plato, *Republic,* VII, 515–21.
98. Plato, *Phaedo,* 65–67.
99. Cited in E. R. Dodds, *The Greeks and the Irrational,* p. 139.
100. Radhakrishnan, *Eastern Religions and Western Thought,* p. 149.
101. E. R. Dodds, "Plato and the Irrational," *Journal of Hellenic Studies,* LXV, 24.
102. Some of them, such as Pococke, have asserted that Greek civilization, not excepting its language, is a local variation of an Indian culture taken to Greece by early colonists from India. *India in Greece.* Princep is recorded to have observed that "Greek was nothing more than Sanskrit turned topsy-turvy." D. S. Mahalanbois, "A New Light on Plato," *Modern Review,* August 1963, p. 142. Talking of Plato's mysticism, Strutfield says that "India, always the home of mystical devotion probably contributed the major share." *Mysticism and Catholicism* p. 74. Hopkins says "Plato is full of *samkhyan* thought worked out by him but taken from Pythagoras." Discussing the historical genesis of Greek antiquity, J. P. Mayer observes: "Egyptian, Persian and Indian cultural influences were absorbed into the Greek world from very early times." *Political Thought, The European Tradition,* p. 7. Sir William Jones has pointed out "it is impossible to read Vedanta or the many fine compositions in illustration of it without believing that Pythagoras and Plato derived their sublime theories from the same fountain with the Indian sages." Colebrooke, the great Orientalist, states significantly that "a greater degree of similarity exists between the Indian doctrine, and that of the earlier than the later Greeks." He goes on to conclude that Greek philosophy, especially between Pythagoras and Plato, was indebted to Indian thought. *Royal Asiatic Society Transactions,* I. A contemporary scholar of Western political thought, John Bowle, briefly

but categorically declares that Plato was influenced by Indian Ideas. *A New Outline of World History*, p. 91.

103. E. J. Urwick, *The Message of Plato*, p. 14.
104. *Ibid.*, pp. 27–28.
105. Plato, *Republic*, III and IV, 412–27.
106. Aristotle, *Politics*, Ch. XLI.
107. E. J. Urwick, *The Message of Plato*, pp. 15–39.
108. For Hindus, however, it has been the main principle of their metaphysics. The discovery of the means of putting a stop to further transmigration—the discontinuance of corporal being—and the liberation of the soul from body have been almost the foundations of Hindu philosophy.
109. E. R. Dodds, *Journal of Hellenic Studies*, LXV, 16.
110. Amongst contemporary philosophers in the Western world there has developed a body of thinkers who regard Plato's doctrine with some contempt, for it seeks to solve logical problems by postulating metaphysical entities. Not all scholars share this view, and even the critics of Plato disagree amongst themselves.
111. A. H. Armstrong, *The Greeks*, p. 131.
112. F. M. Cornford, *Before and After Socrates*, p. 89.
113. Some scholars regard Kautilya as belonging to a much later period.
114. B. A. Saletore, *Ancient Indian Political Thought and Institutions*, pp. 191–290.
115. *Bhagavad Gita*, II, 49.
116. A. K. Coomaraswamy, *Buddha and the Gospel of Buddhism*, p. 279.
117. Situated on the borders of Macedon and Thessaly, the 9600 foot high Mount Olympus was as sacred for the Greeks as were the Himalayas for the Indians. The Greeks believed that the summit of Olympus reached the upper air where Zeus had his throne surrounded by the other gods and goddesses of Greek mythology. The Canaanites also chose the mountain, Saphon, as the abode of their pantheon, and Mount Sinai as the meeting-place of Moses and Jehovah.
118. Gilbert Murray, *Five Stages of Greek Religion*, p. 49.
119. Opinion is divided as to when ancient Greek society perished. Some scholars hold that it died long before the Christian era, whereas others fix the date at 325, when Constantine founded Constantinople and Christian Byzantine civilization began to replace "pagan" Greek culture in the eastern

Mediterranean. Yet, there are others who date its end as late as the seventh century.

120. H. D. Kitto, *The Greeks,* pp. 169–94.
121. R. D. Ranade and R. N. Kaulin in S. Radhakrishnan (ed.), *History of Philosophy: Eastern and Western,* II, 26.
122. But, as A. H. Armstrong points out, "… though Greek philosophers did not as a rule expect or want to get any practical advantage for themselves from their philosophy, at least from the age of Socrates they were not impractical in the sense of being uninterested in ordinary human life and problems." H. Lloyd-Jones (ed.), *The Greeks,* p. 123–24.
123. Sir William Ramsay, *Asianic Elements in Greek Civilization,* p. 4.
124. M. P. Nilsson, *Greek Piety,* p. 137.
125. Enfield even says that "India was visited by Pythagoras, Anaxardes, Pyrrho, and others, who afterwards became eminent philosophers in Greece." There are authorities who suggest that Plato had found his way to the banks of the Ganges.
126. E. R. Dodds, *Humanism and Technique on Greek Studies,* p. 11.
127. The case of an influence in the other direction seems hardly tenable. Discussing the remarkable coincidences between the Greek and Hindu metaphysical systems, H. H. Wilson says: "That the Hindus derived any of their philosophical ideas from the Greeks seems very improbable; and if there is any borrowing in the case, the latter were most probably indebted to the former." Iswara Krishna, *Samkhra Karika,* H. T. Colebrooke (trans.). Also see H. H. Wilson, *The Commentary of Gaurapada* (Combined volume), p. ix.

Notes to Chapter II

1. The conventional view of the Persian Empire as a typical Oriental tyranny is as much a violation of the canons of historical criticism as it is illustrative of a massive prejudice which has persisted despite periodic refutations. It is derived from a superficial reading of Herodotus, who was full of Greek prejudices against the dominant Persians, and from the writers of late antiquity who sought to glorify Rome at the expense of her predecessor. In modern times, Western writers in search of antiquity for their young but dynamic civilization sought first to link it more firmly than it merited to ancient Greece, second to glorify it unreservedly, and finally to denounce its adversaries undeservedly.

The conflict between Persia and Greece has often been described as a struggle between East and West. In fact, such a concept did not exist then, and it is misleading. E. B. Havell writes: "The conflict of the free cities of Hellas with Darius of Persia was, however, the assertion of Aryan political principles against irresponsible autocracy rather than an opposition of intellectual and spiritual ideals, or a struggle between Western civilization and Eastern barbarism, as is usually represented." *The History of Aryan Rule in India,* p. 62. A contemporary writer, A. R. Burn, in his recent study, *Persia and the Greeks*, has also tried to assert that this conflict must not be analyzed in the modern concepts of national or cultural allegiance.

2. William Robertson, *An Historical Disquisition Concerning India,* p. 15.
3. It has been suggested that Alexander was poisoned but this can neither be proved nor disproved.
4. Some European scholars, such as V. A. Smith, however, have magnified his military successes and triumphant progress from the Himalayas to the sea against "the greatest Asiatic armies." In fact, Alexander had never come face to face with any of the powerful nations of India and his army evaded an encounter with the Magadha forces.
5. "The story of Alexander the Great appears to us as an almost embarrassingly perfect illustration of the man who conquered the world, only to lose his soul. After fighting, scheming and murdering in pursuit of the secure tenure of absolute power, he found himself at last on a lonely pinnacle over an abyss, with no use for his power and security unattainable...Alexander illustrates with startling clarity the ultimate loneliness of supreme power." E. Badian, *Studies in Greek and Roman History,* p. 204.
6. An Indian scholar, R. K. Mookerji, designating Alexander as the precursor of the recognized scourges of mankind, points out that this contact "was achieved at the cost of untold suffering inflicted upon India—massacre, rapine, and plunder on a scale till then without a precedent in her annals, but repeated in later days by more successful invaders like Sultan Mahmud, Tamerlane, and Nadir Shah." R. C. Majumdar (ed.), *History and Culture of the Indian People,* II, 53.
7. More cities and persons in a variety of countries and throughout all these past centuries have been named after Alexander than any other great conqueror in history. His personal name, Alexandros (defender of men, originally an epithet for a Greek goddess), has since been known in its numerous variations: Turkish and Arabic—Iskander; Indian and Persian —Sikander; Scottish—Alastair, Alec, and Sandy; French—Alexandre;

English—Alexander. Its feminine counterpart, Alexandra, is also a commonly used proper name. The only other name, although not of a conqueror but of a prophet, which has been borne by more male persons than that of Alexander is Muhammad, the founder of Islam.

8. Alexander, of course, encouraged such marriages mainly for political reasons. His own marriage to Roxane was not exactly a love match. Indeed, it is doubtful if Alexander cared for any woman other than his own mother, who is described as "terrible." These marriages were celebrated with unprecedented pomp, and Alexander gave rich gifts to married couples. He desired a new ruling class and a royal army of mixed blood with no fixed domicile. That the courtiers and commanders married mainly to please Alexander is suggested by the fact that after his death many nobles repudiated their Persian wives. Many bridegrooms died soon after their marriage. According to Badian, it was after his army had posthumously denounced Clitus for treason, thereby legitimizing Alexander's murder of him, that Alexander became more autocratic and "now regularly wore an adaptation of Persian royal dress, and before long he married an Iranian princess. This would have been unthinkable a few months earlier." *Studies in Greek and Roman History,* p. 198.
9. Callisthenes, who acted as Alexander's press agent and had done much for him, was tortured and executed by Alexander, ostensibly for treason but in reality for his opposition to Alexander's claims to divine honours and prostration. He had supported Alexander's claim to divinity.
10. Arrian, *Analasis Alexandri,* VII, 2. Calanus is mentioned by many other Greek writers. Diodorus in his *Bibliotheca Historica,* Ch. CVII, says that Calanus was held in high esteem by Alexander. Dandamis is reported to have rebuked Calanus for being lured into accompanying Alexander, denouncing him as unworthy of the friendship of God. Calanus accompanied Alexander and taught one of his generals, Lysimachus, who later became the King of Macedonia. However, Calanus fell ill at Susa and, having lost the desire to live, burned himself to death in the presence of the army amid trumpets and royal salutes. Before his end, however, he prophesized Alexander's death, saying to him, "we shall meet again at Babylon." Cited in W. W. Tam, *Alexander the Great* (Narrative), p. 110.
11. Jean Filliozat, *Political History of India,* p. 119.
12. E. B. Havell, *The History of Aryan Rule in India,* p. 63.
13. M. Cary and E. G. Warmington, *The Ancient Explorers,* p. 184.
14. Hemchandra Raychaudhuri, *Political History of Ancient India,* p. 262.

15. M. Rostovtzeff, *History of the Ancient World,* I, 349.
16. E. Badian in H. Lloyd-Jones (ed.), *The Greeks,* p. 236.
17. John Bowle, *An Outline of World History,* p. 97.
18. The Greek historian, Athenaisos, relates an interesting story, which is trivial in itself but points to familiarity between the Indian king and the Greek. Bindusara had asked Antiochus to send him a Sophist with sweet wine and dried figs. Whilst he was sent wine and figs, he was informed that "in Greece laws forbid a Sophist to be sold."
19. *Indo-Asian Culture,* October 1958, p. 121.
20. This conversion of a Greek prince to Buddhism by an Indian philosopher is symbolic of the East and West cultural collaboration. *Milinda Panho* (Questions of Milinde) is certainly a landmark in the history of Asian culture.
21. The enormous increase in the number of Greek coins and the exhibition of Indian goods by Antiochus together would suggest the pattern of trade between the Hellenic world and India. It further indicates that Greece imported goods from India and paid for them in cash.
22. W. W. Tarn, *The Greeks in Bactria and India,* pp. 316–23. Seleucus had entertained ideas of connecting the Caspian and Black Seas by a canal to improve trade between Asia and Europe. If he had not been assassinated soon after and had succeeded in doing so, the history of Asia could have been somewhat different.
23. It has been suggested that the temple at Taxila is Greek in style.
24. Because Graeco-Buddhist art flourished during the period of thriving trade between the Kushans and the Romans, it has been suggested that this art should be called "Romano-Buddhist" instead. See R. Ghirshaman, *Iran,* p. 2. During the Sassanian period there was indeed close contact between India and Iran. Magi priests came to India and gave further impetus to sun worship. Inscriptions in Pahlavi have been found on crosses in several places in South India. The well-known copper plate grant to the Syrian Church in South India carries in Pahlavi ten witness-signatures. *Journal of Royal Asiatic Society* (O. S. 1843), p. 353. The Pahlavi and Sanskrit languages borrowed a number of words from each other.
25. S. K. Saraswati, *A Survey of Indian Sculpture,* p. 71.
26. W. W. Tarn, *The Greeks in Bactria and India,* p. 393.
27. A. K. Coomaraswamy, *Buddha and the Gospel of Buddhism,* pp. 330–31.
28. H. Zimmer, *The Art of Indian Asia,* I, 347,
29. V. A. Smith, *A History of Fine Art in India and Ceylon,* p. 10.

30. Indeed, there is no iconographical representation of Asoka himself.
31. Saraswati, *A Survey of Indian Sculpture,* p. 66. For a discussion of these motifs and of Greek influences, direct or indirect, on Indian art, see Smith, *A History of Fine Art in India and Ceylon,* pp. 64–69.
32. Some scholars would put the date later. The word *Karsa* (pana) and the weight standard of the early punch-marked coins are probably Persian.
33. S. K. Chatterji, *Indian Drama,* p. 8.
34. *Rig Veda,* X, 95.
35. W. W. Tarn, *The Greeks in Bactria and India,* pp. 375–76.
36. *Ibid.,* p. 376. Indeed, later in the same chapter (p. 408) he says that "... there was nothing that was to be permanent there, not even the Buddha-statue."
37. Lily Ross Taylor, *The Divinity of the Roman Empire,* p. 1.
38. *Journal of Hellenic Studies,* XLVII (1927), 206–19.
39. *Cambridge Ancient History,* VII, 18.
40. W. W. Tarn, *Hellenistic Civilization,* pp. 45ff.
41. Taylor, *The Divinity of the Roman Empire,* p. 11.
42. For a fuller discussion of Greek hero-worship, See L. R. Farnell, *Greek Hero Cults and Ideas of Immortality.*
43. Ernest Barker in Cyril Bailey (ed.), *The Legacy of Rome,* p. 49.
44. *Cambridge Ancient History,* VII, 15.
45. E. Badian, *Studies in Greek History,* p. 202.
46. W. W. Tarn, *Alexander the Great* (Narrative).
47. E. R. Dodds, *The Greeks and the Irrational,* p. 237.
48. Will Durant, *The Story of Philosophy,* p. 97.
49. Dodds, *The Greeks and the Irrational,* p. 238.
50. Barker, *The Legacy of Rome,* p. 51.
51. It may be of some interest to note that the Stoics had resurrected the idea of Logos, especially the use of the term. It was the fundamental idea of a ruling cosmic principle, emanating from the ineffable and indefinable absolute, propounded by Heraclitus. In defining Logos, Heraclitus applied the technique of paradox. "It will be called Zeus; it will not be called Zeus." This technique is also found in the Upanishads, and indeed the bracketing of opposites is typically Indian. A. C. Bouquet, *Indo-Asian Culture,* October 1961, p. 213. Between Heraclitus and Zeno, however, it had become more common to use the term Nous, but Stoics preferred the earlier word, Logos.

Thus, the Logos-concept became central to their philosophy, dislodging the Nous of Aristotle.

52. Cited in H. Lloyd-Jones (ed.), *The Greeks*, pp. 132–33.
53. W. W. Tarn has described Posidonius as "the last great intellectual force which Hellenism, untouched by Rome, produced..." *Hellenistic Civilization*, p. 288.
54. E. Bevan, *Stoics and Sceptics*, p. 94.
55. Barber, *The Legacy of Rome*, p. 54.
56. *Ibid.*, p. 50.
57. John Bowle, *Western Political Thought*, p. 74.
58. John Bowle, *A New Outline of World History*, p. 99.
59. Dodds, *The Greeks and the Irrational*, p. 240.
60. "The dignity of character achieved and admired by the leaders of Graeco-Roman civilization owed more to it than to any other philosophy..." John Bowle, *Western Political Thought*, p. 76.
61. *Ibid.*, p. 70.
62. Bevan, *Stoics and Sceptics*, p. 69.

Notes to Chapter III

1. Michael Grant, *The World of Rome*, p. 4.
2. According to Kern, ancient Indians possibly called it Yavanapura, the city of the *Yavanas* (Greeks).
3. According to William Robertson, the chief object of Alexander in founding Alexandria was to secure the advantages arising from the trade with India, and Ptolemy, who was in Alexander's confidence, knew of Alexander's object. *An Historical Disquisition Concerning the Knowledge which the Ancients Had of India*, p. 35.
4. For a brief and up-to-date account of Alexandria, see E. Badian, *Studies in Greek and Roman History*, pp. 179–92.
5. M. Rostovtzeff in *Cambridge Ancient History*, VII, 194.
6. "An army could advance along the 'Royal Road' at the rate of nearly 20 miles a day, and the ease with which Alexander overthrew the Persian power is partly to be explained by the excellent system of communications which was available for his advancing army." Lee C. Bailey (ed.), *The Legacy of Rome*, p. 146.

7. See Bjorn Landstrom, *The Quest for India.*
8. M. P. Charlesworth, *Trade-Routes and Commerce of the Roman Empire,* p. 58.
9. The Roman forces at Carrhae were led by Marcus Crassus, Consultriumvir of Rome and Governor of Syria. The battle of Carrhae was one of the most disastrous in the history of Rome; about twenty thousand Roman soldiers, including Crassus and his son, were killed and ten thousand taken prisoner. It was at this battle that the Romans first saw articles of silk—the brilliantly coloured, gold-embroidered banners of the Parthians.
10. H. G. Rawlinson, *Intercourse Between India and the Western World,* pp. 90–91.
11. Strabo, *Geography,* II, 5, 12. Describing the location of India later, Strabo calls India "the greatest of all nations and the happiest in lot." II, 5, 32.
12. Charlesworth, *Trade-Routes and Commerce of the Roman Empire,* p. 59.
13. Rostovtzeff in *Cambridge Ancient History,* VII, 154.
14. I understand that a computer study of the work is under way at present (1967) in London.
15. A. B. Keith, *A History of Sanskrit Literature,* p. 461.
16. D. D. Kosambi, "An Introduction to the Study of Indian History," *Journal of Royal Asiatic Society,* p. 200. For a quick resume of the work regarding the dating of the Arthasastra, see K. A. N. Sastri, *The Age of the Nandas and Mauryas,* pp. 190–201.
17. In recent years it has come to be increasingly held that the tradition of Hippalus is false. Certainly, the evidence on which the tradition is based is too thin.
18. "The importance of this fact will be realised," comments Rawlinson, "when we recollect that, up to the opening of the overland route in 1838, it took travellers from five to eight months to reach India. India was nearer to Europe in the first century A.D. than at any time up to the middle of the nineteenth." G. T. Garratt (ed.), *The Legacy of India,* p. 16.
19. Paul-Louis, *Ancient Rome at Work,* p. 235.
20. Of the jewels, the Romans were especially fond of beryls and pearls. The two beryl mines that existed in South India at Padiyur and Vaniyambadi were a great source of wealth.
21. In the fifteenth century it sold at two shillings a pound which in terms of modern value would be well above a hundred shillings a pound. It is not easy to calculate a modern equivalent of denarii, but a Roman soldier

on duty in Egypt received two hundred and twenty-five denarii (or nine hundred sesterces) annually, or fifteen pounds of pepper per year; or for one Roman pound of cinnamon more than sixty-six Roman soldiers could be employed to fight in Egypt for a year.

22. Pliny, *Natural History,* VI, 26.
23. Tacitus, *The Annals of Imperial Rome,* II, 33; II, 53.
24. Charlesworth, *Trade-Routes and Commerce of the Roman Emipre,* p. 67.
25. Ancient Indians, it appears, originally used the term Yavana for the Ionian-Greeks, but later for all foreigners from the West. Somewhat in a similar manner, modern Indians use the term Angrez, the English, for all Westerners.
26. Sir Mortimer Wheeler, *Rome Beyond the Imperial Frontiers,* p. 209.
27. Dion Chrysostom, *Orations,* XXXII, 373. In another oration (XLIX, 538), he mentions that Indian Brahmins excel in self-control, righteousness, and love of God.
28. Pausanias, *Hellados Periegisis,* III, 12; IV, 34; VII, 29.
29. Arrian (96–180), who distinguished himself as a philosopher, statesman, soldier, and historian, also wrote the more important and famous *Anabasis of Alexander,* the life of Alexander. The Elder Pliny's (23–79) work deals with a variety of subjects. Ptolemy's treatise on geography forms the sequel to his famous work on astronomy. Both his works remained standard works until modern times. Yet, little is known of him except that he flourished in Alexandria about the middle of the second century A.D.
30. The Erythraean Sea was the name given by the Greek and Roman geographers to the Indian Ocean, including the Red Sea and the Persian Gulf. This work appears to have been composed about the middle or the second half of the first century. Some scholars have lately suggested that the work belongs to about 300.
31. B. P. Groslier, *Indo-China,* p. 49.
32. B. A. Saletore, *India's Diplomatic Relations with the West,* p. 230.
33. The commercial character of the Indian missions to Augustus is now quite evident. Strabo speaks of a communication to Augustus from an Indian king seeking assistance in any good enterprise. See *Geography,* XV, 1, 73.
34. For a discussion of the theme, see Saletore, *India's Diplomatic Relations with the West,* pp. 210–67.
35. E. Gibbon, *Decline and Fall of the Roman Empire,* I, 319.

36. Saletore, *India's Diplomatic Relations with the West,* p. 271.
37. Grant, *The World of Rome,* p. 189.
38. John Bowle, *A New Outline of World History,* p. 118.
39. H. G. Wells, *The Outline of History,* p. 273.
40. Gilbert Murray, *Hellenism and the Modern World,* p. 14.
41. Franz Cumont, *Oriental Religions in Roman Paganism,* pp. 2–3.
42. Tenney Frank, "Racial Mixture in the Roman Empire," *The American Historical Quarterly,* XXI (1961), 689–708. Tacitus has been accused of exposing Roman anti-Semitism, and of grossly distorting facts. S. Davis, *Race-Relations in Ancient Egypt,* pp. 161–63.
43. Hippolytus died as a martyr in 235. He was one of the most prolific writers of the early Church and was elected rival Bishop of Rome in 217 by those people who were opposed to Pope Callistus.
44. Jean Filliozat, "La doctrine brâhmanes d'apres saint Hippolyte," *Revue de l'Histoire des Religions* (1945), pp. 59–91; *Les relations exterieures de l'inde* (1956), pp. 31-60.
45. Wilhelm Holmqvist, *Acta Archaelogica,* XXV (Copenhagen,. 1954); *'Viking* (Oslo, 1957–58); William Holmqvist, Birgit Arrhemus, Per Lundstrom *Viltterhets Historie och Antikvitets Akademien* (Stockholm, 1961). Cited in Buddha Prakash, *India and the World,* p. 268.
46. Many Catholic monasteries in mediaeval Europe, however, served as schools, hospitals, orphanages, and old peoples homes.
47 Asoka was so influenced by the ethical tenets of the Buddhist "Law of Piety," even more than by the theory of nirvana which has often been mistakenly described as pessimistic, that he changed his name from Asoka, the Sorrowless One, to Piya-dasi (Sanskrit Priya-darsin), the Compassionate One.
48. The first two Buddhist Councils were held at Rajagaha and Vesali in 483 B.C. and 383 B.C. respectively.
49. V. A. Smith, *Oxford History of India,* p. 134.
50. *Mahavamsa,* XXIX, 37–39. This Convent of Alexandria is also mentioned in a later work, the *Thupavamsa.*
51. The doctrine of the Four Noble Truths is expounded in various Buddhist scriptures, such as the *Digha Nikaya,* the *Majjhima Nikaya,* the *Sutta Pitaka,* and the *Vinaya Pitaka.*
52. The name Milinda is an Indian adaptation of the Greek word Menandros. Ancient authors used various other Indian forms of the Greek King's name.

For example, Ksemendra's *Avadanakalpalata* calls him by the same name, Milindra, as that which is found in the Bstan-hygur collection, commonly known as Tanjur, of the Tibetan *Tripitaka*. The Shinkot casket inscription in the Kharoshthi script, which speaks of his missionary activities in spreading Buddhism in the northwest and beyond, gives his name as Menadra.

53. *Mahavamsa*, XII, 34–36.
54. Sir Charles Eliot, *Hinduism and Buddhism*, III, 450.
55. T. Watters, *On Yuan Chwang's Travels in India*, p. 257. According to Hsüan-tsang, Persia was rich but its people were by nature impulsive and violent. 'They did not care for learning and gave themselves entirely to works of art which were very popular in the neighbouring countries.
56. Cf. McCrindle, *Ancient India as described in Classical Literature*, p. 185. "Terebinthus proclaimed himself learned in all the wisdom of the Egyptians and gave out that his name was no longer Terebinthus but that he was a new Buddha (Buddas) and that he was born of a virgin. Terebinthus was the disciple of Scythianus, who was born in Palestine and who traded with India."
57. A. S. Altekar, *Indo-Asian Culture*, October 1958, pp. 120–21.
58. Cited in A. R. Vidler, *Objections to Christian Beljef*, p. 59. Bernard Shaw put it in his characteristic way: "What Christ said would have been just as true if he had lived in a country house with an income of £5,000 a year."
59. In recent years, Western theologians have renewed their effort to modernize the traditional Christian orthodoxy and present the faith in terms which are comprehensible to present-day man. To restate, reiterate, and defend the ancient dogma in exactly the same language is to strain the religious integrity and intellectual ability of the believer as much as of the preacher and of the layman. An expression of this view is found in the much discussed book by John A. T. Robinson, *Honest to God*.
60. In a recent publication, *The Death of Jesus*, Joel Carmichael has sought to prove that Jesus thought of himself as no more than the herald of an imminent material transformation of the world, and to achieve his purpose he led an armed insurrection, which led to his violent death.
61. H. G. Wells, *A Short History of the World*, p. 147.
62. It seems likely that the Roman rulers, having failed to evolve a universal religion for the Empire themselves, looked upon Christianity as a rival gaining success where they had failed, and thus were urged into taking a hostile attitude to its expansion.

63. Rudolf Bultmann, *Primitive Christianity in its Contemporary Setting*, p. 11.
64. Morton Enslin, *Christian Beginnings*, p. 147.
65. The word "Heaven" is sometimes used for "God" as a reverential Jewish way of avoiding the use of the divine name. The second of the ten Mosaic commandments, in any case, forbids the taking of God's name "in vain."
66. According to Carmichael, the concept of "Son of God" is an inadvertent development of the Greek expression of the term, "Servant of God," often used to describe Jesus by himself and his immediate disciples. The word used in Greek for servant, *pais,* also has the meaning child. Pais is used throughout the earliest Greek translations of the Old Testament for those people who are particularly in harmony with God's will: "The mere fact that the same word in Greek means both 'servant' and 'child' and that a similar expression was used in reference to Jesus, doubtless facilitated the transformation of the phrase 'servant' or 'child of God' and this gave a specific and, as it were, concrete aid to the magnifying effect of the early Christology." *The Death of Christ*, p. 205.
67. An important consequence of this discovery was that the earlier belief, that no really old perishable antiquities could ever be found in the area because of the prevailing dampness of the climate, was disproved. They had overlooked the extremely unusual geological fault of the Rift Valley that runs from Syria down into Africa and which reaches its lowest level around the Dead Sea. More than a thousand feet below sea level, the cliffs bordering the western side lie in a rain shadow. The sun shines into the basin for most of the year, and the caves in the limestone cliffs are kept dry as a desert. Inevitably, archaeologists poured into the area, and the western side of the Dead Sea, called in the Bible the Wilderness of Judah, has yielded rich harvests of antiquities, including wooden implements some six thousand years old, which have been preserved remarkably well.
68. One of the important consequences of the discovery of these texts, as some of them are written in Greek, may be the blurring of the sharp distinction usually made between the Judaism of the Holy Land and the Judaism of the Dispersion. There was much traffic between Jerusalem and Alexandria, and the quasi-monastic Therapeutai described by Philo look as though they were in some sense related to the Qumran sect. A. D. Nock, *Early Gentile Christianity and its Hellenistic Background*, p. x.
69. Murray, *Hellenism and the Modern World*, p. 17.

70. Nero is reported by Pliny the Elder to have been initiated into the cult of Mithras in 66 by a *magi* priest. He insisted on being worshipped as a sun god. About three centuries later, the Emperor Julian tried to make Mithraism the state religion but his death prevented this. Few other emperors kept direct contact with the Mithraic practices. Mithraism, however, was not a court religion, and was long regarded as too personal a creed to be included amongst public faiths.
71. W. K. C. Guthrie, *Orpheus and Greek Religion*, pp. 264–68.
72. *Ibid.*, p. 269.
73. Rudolf Bultmann, *Primitive Christianity*, pp. 177–78.
74. *Ibid.*, p. 178.
75. Of the three hundred bishops present at this council of Nicaea, only six were from the West.
76. The earliest known reference to the Christian ceremony is that in St. Paul's First Epistle to the Corinthians written some twenty-five years after the Crucifixion.
77. A. Powell Davies, *Dead Sea Scrolls*, p. 91.
78. Eliot, *Hinduism and Buddhism*, III, 430.
79. J. M. Creed in S. R. K. Glanville (ed.), *The Legacy of Egypt*, p. 300.
80. E. Bevan, *Stoics and Sceptics*, p. 69.
81. Franz Cumont, *Oriental Religions in Roman Paganism*, p. x.
82. See T. Frank, *Aspects of Social Behaviour in Ancient Rome*, p. 37.
83. Edward Gibbon, who had become a convert to Roman Catholicism whilst at Oxford, and not long after a profound sceptic, listed five principal causes of the success of Christianity: a) The inflexible, i.e. the intolerant, zeal of the Christians, derived from the Jewish religions; b) the doctrine of a future life; c) the miraculous powers ascribed to the primitive Church; d) the pure and austere morals of the Christians; and e) the union and discipline of the Christian republic. See *The Decline and Fall of the Roman Empire* (An Abridgement), p. 144. Gibbon found Christianity on the whole distasteful, and the pretensions of the bishops even more so, and the claims of Rome to maintain spiritual pre-eminence after the fall of the Empire a superstitious fraud. He found Christians' intolerance, whether practiced against other religions or against members of the Church, particularly unpleasant.
84. Eliot, *Hinduism and Buddhism*, III. 434.
85. Sidney Spencer, *Mysticism in World Religion*, p. 148.
86. *Encyclopaedia of Religion and Ethics*, V, 401.

87. Hendrik Kraemer, *World Cultures and World Religions,* p. 239.
88. R. Otto, *The Kingdom of God and the Son of Man,* p. 178.
89. *Ibid.*, p. 187.
90. S. Radhakrishnan, *Eastern Religion and Western Thought,* p. 162.
91. Otto, *The Kingdom of God and the Son of Man,* p. 206. *Kaushitahi Upanishad,* I, 2-7.
92. Otto, *The Kingdom of God and the Son of Man,* p. 398.
93. Theologians are divided two ways. One belief stresses the reality of the presence of the Kingdom of God transforming this life through judgement and mercy, thereby rendering the motif that "the Kingdom is yet to come" of minor significance. Whereas the other definitely holds the view that the Kingdom *is* yet to come.
94. Otto, *The Kingdom of God and the Son of Man,* p. 20.
95. *Ibid.*, p. 25.
96. T. W. Rhys Davids, *Journal of the Pali Text Society,* 1923, pp. 43–44. Cited in Radhakrishnan, *Eastern Religions and Western Thought,* p. 173.
97. Radhakrishnan, *Eastern Religions and Western Thought,* p. 176.
98. Most scholars now believe that Mark wrote first, but there are some others who argue for the priority of Matthew.
99. W. R. Inge, *Platonic Tradition in English Religious Thought,* p. 10.
100. *Sutta Nipata,* III, 11, 1–21; Gospel of St. Luke, Ch. 2.
101. There is, however, no reference to the virgin birth of Jesus in the Epistles which constitute the earliest Christian documents. The earliest Gospel of St. Mark does not mention it, nor does the Gospel of St. John, nor the Book of Revelation. On the contrary, Paul speaks of Jesus as "made of the seed of David according to the flesh" (Rom. 1 :3), that is to say, of the seed of Joseph, David's descendant. The story first appears in the Gospel of St. Luke, which tells us that Mary conceived her child by the Holy Ghost before consummation of her marriage with Joseph. The story is developed later in the Gospel of St. Matthew. A recent writer, Leslie D. Weatherhead, has in *The Christian Agnostic* suggested that what really happened was that Zacharias committed adultery with Mary in a "sacred marriage."
102. Main Hindu incarnations, Rama and Krishna, too, were born in the warrior caste.
103. Arthur Osborne, *Buddhism and Christianity in the Light of Hinduism,* p. 14. However, there are other gods and demi-gods who were the sons of

mothers whose names were variations of Mary: for example, Adonis, son of Myrrha; Hermes, son of Maia; Cyrus, son of Mariana or Mandane; Moses, son of Miriam; Buddha, son of Maya; and Joshua, son of Miriam. Because of this, Mary being somewhat of a stock substitute name for a divine mother, some scholars have suggested the possibility of a completely different name for Jesus' mother.

104. Christ wrote nothing, nor did the Buddha, nor Muhammad. It is indeed curious that the men whose ideas have influenced human thought most, did little to ensure the accuracy of their teaching by reducing it to writing under their supervision.

105. Osborne, *Buddhism and Christianity in the Light of Hinduism*, p. 10. In a recent publication, *Yoga and the Bible,* Joseph Leeming has endeavoured to show that the basic teachings of the New Testament and some parts of the Bible are essentially similar to the fundamental truths taught for ages by the teachers of *Shabad Yoga; Shabad,* meaning divine or inner sound, refers to the power which in the Bible is called the Word or Logos. The Yoga of the divine word, or *Shabad Yoga,* is a system of meditation and other spiritual practices, which takes its followers to the highest attainable states of spiritual consciousness.

106. The Hindus too expect the tenth *Avatar* (incarnation), the last of the series.

107. Max Müller, *Last Essays,* 1st Series, 1901, p. 285.

108. Radhakrishnan, *Eastern Religions and Western Thought,* p. 184.

109. Eliot, *Hinduism and Buddhism,* III, 443.

110. M. Huc wrote: "The cross, the mitre, the dalmatica; the cope, which the Grand Lamas wear on their journeys, the service with double choirs; the psalmody, the exorcisms; the censer, suspended from five chains; the benedictions, the chaplet, ecclesiastical celibacy, spiritual retirement, the worship of the saints; the fasts, the processions, the litanies, the holy-water—all these are analogies between the Buddhists and ourselves. Now, can it be said that these analogies are of Christian origin? We think so. We have indeed found, neither in the traditions nor in the monuments of the country, any positive proof of their adoption; still it is perfectly legitimate to put forward conjectures which possess all the characteristics of the most emphatic probability." Cited in N. Notovitch, *The Unknown Life of Christ,* pp. xiv–xv. More than a century before Hue in 1714 Father Diserdi was also struck by similarities between his own faith and Lamaistic practices. Still earlier, in 1661, Father Grueber, together with another priest, Dorville,

passed through Tibet on their return from Peking, and he noticed what Henry Princep describes as "the extraordinary similarity" between the doctrines and the rituals of the Buddhists of Lhasa and those of his own Roman faith. Cited in Arthur Little, *India in Primitive Christianity,* p. 220.

111. Osborne, *Buddhism and Christianity in the Light of Hinduism,* pp. 118–19.
112. It has been suggested that possibly a Christian mission under St. Thomas had come to the court of the Indo-Parthian King Gondophares at the beginning of the Christian era, although the mission seems to have left no impression. See S. N. Dasgupta (ed.), *A History of Sanskrit Literature,* I, ciii.
113. A recent report claiming the discovery of a small urn containing the remains of St. Thomas in Mosul, northern Iraq, has been disputed by Indian Christians who claim that the relics of the apostle were removed from Madras to Lisbon and that this fact is further corroborated by an important document recently found in Lisbon. This document is a four page letter, dated 27 December 1535, written to the King of Portugal from the Church of St. Thomas in Mylapore. It is signed by twelve Portuguese inhabitants. See *The Hindu Weekly,* 26 October 1964.
114. M. Vacherot, *Histoire Critique de l'École d'Alexandrie,* III, 250.
115. Dean Mansel, *The Gnostic Heresies of the First and Second Centuries,* p. 32.
116. Dean Milman, *History of Christianity,* II, 41.
117. It is curious that Apollonius, who was once considered a rival of Jesus, was born in the same year as Jesus, and was likewise said to have been born of the union of a god with his mother, to whom the coming birth was announced somewhat similarly as in the Christian tale. But the tale of miraculous conception is associated with a number of divine or semidivine personages.
118. J. Bidez in *Cambridge Ancient History,* XII, 614.
119. The word *gnosis* is Greek, meaning knowledge, and was a term used from the early days of philosophy to designate the science of the divine. Later, Porphyry called "the Antique or Oriental philosophy" gnosis to distinguish it from the Grecian systems. The term was also used in the technical sense of "superior or celestial knowledge" by the Jewish philosophers at Alexandria.
120. C. W. King, *The Gnostics and Their Remains,* p. x.
121. Rudolf Bultmann, *Primitive Christianity,* p. 162.

122. W. R. Inge, *Mysticism in Religion,* p. 106.
123. During the first four centuries, all that the Christian Church denounced as heretical may be traced to Indian speculative philosophy as its genuine fountain-head. Yet, a considerable part of what was accepted as orthodox also came from the same source. See King, *The Gnostics and Their Remains,* pp. vi–vii.
124. Kennedy says of Gnosticism, "It is Buddhist pure and simple—Buddhist in its governing ideas, its psychology, its metaphysics." Cited in Radhakrishnan, *Eastern Religions and Western Thought,* p. 205.
125. King, *The Gnostics and Their Remains,* p. 6.
126. *Ibid.,* p. 165.
127. *Ibid.,* pp. 16–21. Whittaker, who regards Gnosticism in contrast to Neoplatonism as a direct outgrowth of the East, says that the Gnostic claim that the spiritual men alone possess true knowledge could have given it, under favourable circumstances, "a starting point of Christian Brahmanism." Thomas Whittaker, *The Neo-Platonist,* p. 222.
128. Radhakrishnan, *Eastern Religions and Western Thought,* p. 200.
129. Sir Flinders Petrie, *Egypt and Israel,* p. 113.
130. Sidney Spencer, *Mysticism in World Religion,* p. 153.
131. *Stromata,* VI, 14, 114; VI, 7, 58.
132. Radhakrishnan, *Eastern Religions and Western Thought,* p. 233.
133. In antiquity the philosophers, who are now called Neoplatonists, called themselves simply Platonists. So did the philosophers of the seventh century and the Renaissance who drew their inspiration from Neoplatonism.
134. Amongst his predecessors are counted his teacher Ammonius Saccas; Posidonius, the Stoic teacher of Cicero; and Numenius, whose influence on Plotinus was considerable.
135. Indeed, other great men in history did likewise. Christ wrote nothing, nor did the Buddha; Muhammad was illiterate; Socrates was content to talk; Gandhi never systematically co-ordinated and formalized his great bulk of mixed writings.
136. These three had made a compact not to disclose any of the doctrines which Ammonius had revealed to them. Plotinus kept faith and divulged nothing of his teacher's system, but the compact was broken first by Erennius and later by Origen. It is interesting that the two persons who emerged in the third century as great religious teachers propounding divergent doctrines were students of Ammonius Saccas, who was born a Christian, but became a Platonist.

137. Stephen MacKenna (trans.), *Plotinus' The Enneads,* p. xiii.
138. Radhakrishnan, *Eastern Religions and Western Thought,* pp. 210–11.
139. George Goodwin, *The Great Mystics,* p. 27.
140. Even W. R. Inge thinks that in Plotinus, theory of vision there is "the direct influence of Oriental philosophy of the Indian type." *Christian Mysticism,* p. 901.
141. Bidez in *Cambridge Ancient History,* XII, 623.
142. Not only is there evidence that Indian scholars, both Buddhists and Brahmans, visited and resided in Western capitals, but there is evidence that Indian faiths were practiced in some parts of Asia Minor in pre-Christian times. The Syrian writer, Zenob, tells us of the worship of Krishna in Armenia at least in the second and third centuries B.C. Temples dedicated to Krishna were set up near the Lake Van. Zenob says that early in the fourth century A.D. there were about five thousand followers of Krishna in Armenia. It is also pointed out that the Hindus had resisted the demolition of temples by the early Christians.
143. W. R. Inge, *Mysticism in Religion,* p. 109.
144. He appears to have believed in two world-souls: one good, the other bad. He had adopted the theory of rebirth. Stutfield maintains that Indian mysticism had reached Alexandria which "blossomed forth in Plotinus" and passed into Christian thought through "the monk mystic and theosophical pantheist, the so-called Dionysus the Areopagite." *Mysticism and Catholicism,* p. 34.
145. "An influence of Indian thought on the Gnostics and Neoplatonists may be held to be more likely, and it would be unjust to rule it out of Court." A. B. Keith, *A History of Sanskrit Literature,* pp. 500-01.
146. Bidez in *Cambridge Ancient History,* XII, 633. The Christians in the fifth century destroyed the work of Porphyry, *Against the Christians,* written in fifteen books, but extracts from it which have survived in the Christian polemical writing, indicate that it was a powerful and intelligent attack on Christianity.
147. E. R. Dodds, *Proclus, the Elements of Theology,* p. xxv.
148. Radhakrishnan, *Eastern Religions and Western Thought,* p. 238.
149. He was venerated in the sixth century by St. Gregory, his words were used in the Third Council of Constantinople in 692 and at the Second Council of Nicaea, and St. John the Damascene became his follower. In the thirteenth century the Church denounced him, but his influence amongst the mystics of the fourteenth century rose again.

150. Radhakrishnan, *Eastern Religions and Western Thought*, p. 240.
151. It was St. Paul who began the process of stressing the divinity of Christ, and Athanasius (*ca.* 295–373) who formulated the doctrine of the Trinity accepted at Nicaea.

Notes to Chapter IV

1. Whilst references to Arab peoples and tribes are found in many biblical passages and in Genesis itself, the first mention of the name of these peoples, whose etymology is not clear, occurs in an inscription of the Assyrian King Shalmaneser III (853 B.C.).
2. The only certain source concerning the life of Muhammad (etymologically the name means "the much praised one") is the Quran itself, followed by the canonical biography, *Sira,* composed a century later in the eighth century. However, the year of the Prophet's birth is uncertain; 570 is accepted as an approximation. Muhammad was the posthumous son of the merchant Abdullah, and was brought up first by his grandfather Abd al-Mutta lib, and later by an uncle, Abu Talib, father of Ali, who was to become the fourth Caliph and the Prophet's son-in-law.
3. Richard Bell has advanced a new theory suggesting three periods in the composition of the Quran. See A. C. Bouquet, *Comparative Religion,* p. 275.
4. Reporting his victory to Caliph Umar, he remarked: "I have captured a city from the description of which I shall refrain. Suffice it to say that I have seized therein 4,000 villas with 4,000 baths, 40,000 poll-tax paying Jews and 4,000 palaces of entertainment for the royalty."
5. (1) The story makes its first appearance more than five hundred years after the event to which it relates;

   (2) on analysis the *story resolves into absurdities;*

   (3) the principal actor in the story, viz. John Philoponus, was dead long before the Saracens entered Egypt;

   (4) of the two great public libraries to which the story could refer (a) the Museum Library perished in the conflagration caused by Julius Caesar, or, if not, at a date not less than four hundred years anterior to the Arab Conquest, whilst (b) the Serapium Library either was removed prior to the year 391 A.D. or was then dispersed and destroyed; so that in any case it disappeared two and a half centuries before the conquest;

(5) the fifth, sixth, and early seventh century literature contains no mention of the existence of any such library;

(6) if, nevertheless, it had existed when Cyrus set his hand to the treaty surrendering Alexandria, yet the books would almost certainly have been removed—under the clause permitting the removal of valuables—*during the eleven months armistice which intervened* between the signature of the convention and the actual entry of the Arabs into the city; and

(7) if the Library had been removed, or if it had been destroyed, the almost contemporary historian and man of letters John of Nikiou, could not have passed over its disappearance in total silence.

The conclusion of the whole matter can be no longer doubtful. The suspicion of Renaudot and the scepticism of Gibbon are more than justified. One must pronounce that the Abu'l Faraj story is a *mere fable, totally destitute of historical foundation.* See Albert J. Butler, *The Arab Conquest of Egypt,* p. 424.

6. Palestine and Syria fell to the Arabs by 640, Iraq a year later, Egypt by 642, Tripolitania by 647, Persia by 650, Afghanistan by 661 in which year the seat of the Caliphate was moved from Medina to Damascus, Tunisia by 693, Algeria and Morocco by 705, and Spain in 711.
7. Many Arab historians, with some justification, decline to accord the title of Caliphate to the reigns of Muawiya and his successors, with the sole exception of Umar II (717–20) who is accepted as Caliph with kingship (*mulk*). The Caliphate is regarded to have lapsed until 750 when it was resumed with the ascendancy of the Abbasid dynasty of Iran.
8. George Sarton, *The Life of Science,* p. 145.
9. R. A. Nicholson, *A Literary History of the Arabs,* p. 259.
10. The name of the great capital, founded by Caliph Mansur, itself is said to be of Indian origin; *Bagh* is Sanskrit *Bhaga,* meaning God, and *da* in Sanskrit means to give. Baghdad thus meant given by God, or the gift of God.
11. Aziz S. Atiya, *Crusade, Commerce and Culture,* p. 224.
12. H. A. R. Gibb in A. J. Rustum and C. K. Zurak (eds.), *History of the Arabs and Arabic Culture,* p. 241.
13. F. H. Garrison, *An Introduction to the History of Medicine.*
14. Abu Sahl Ali bin Rabban al-Tabari has given at the end of his book, *Fardausul Hikmat,* written about 850, a short account of the Indian system of medicine.

15. Ibn Abi Usaybia, who wrote a general biography of physicians, entitled *Uyun al-Inba fi-Tabaqat al-Atibba,* found in *Al Hawi* and other works of Al Razi extracts from a number of Indian medical texts.
16. J. Needham, *Science and Civilization in China,* IV, 13.
17. Bettina Strauss in René Taton (ed.), *Ancient and Medieval Science,* p. 417.
18. Jose Maria Millas-Vallicrosa, in Guy S. Metraux and Francois Crouzet (eds.), *The Evolution of Science,* p. 129.
19. Of the other popular foods, the domestic fowl is also an Indian contribution to Western diet. Hieroglyphs from Indian village settlements would suggest that it has been domesticated for at least five thousand years. Some varieties are said to have originated from the Indian jungle fowl which still survives. The larger breeds have no similarity to any wild bird. Like horses, dogs, and camels, these have apparently completely passed over into the domesticated state or the wild ancestors have become extinct. For many centuries the domestic fowl was confined to India. In 1400 B.C. it spread to China—known in Egypt also about the same time—but it was another one thousand years or more before Europeans began to raise this bird.

    Tea, the national drink of the Anglo-Saxons, is an indirect Indian legacy to Western civilization. It is also a favoured drink of the Chinese, Japanese, Russians, and others. The original home of this shrub was Assam, India, and from there in the third century A.D. it travelled to China and by the middle of the seventeenth century it appeared in England. In the eighteenth century "tea gardens" began to appear in London and attracted especially women who preferred them to the stuffy tea houses in the congested city. Scholars too were attracted—Dr. Samuel Johnson and Boswell lent distinction to these gardens.
20. In 929 he adopted the title of Caliph and thus became the third of the three contemporary independent Caliphs in the Islamic world—the Abbasid in Baghdad, the Fatimid in North Africa, and the Umayyad in Spain. The Umayyads ruled from 736 to 1031.
21. J. B. Trend in Thomas Arnold and Alfred Guillaume (eds.), *The Legacy of Islam,* p. 5.
22. During the thirteenth century another Muslim centre of learning had come into prominence at Konya in Turkey during the reign of Alaeddin I (1219–1236). After Nicaea had fallen to the Crusaders in 1017, Konya became the capital of the Seljuk Sultans and attracted artists, poets, historians, jurists, theologians, and other scholars who were driven westward from Central

and Western Asia by the Mongol invasions. The effects of this school on Western learning are yet to be assessed systematically.

Notes to Chapter V

1. Recently a national commission consisting of historians, scientists, and linguists has been appointed to study and compile a history of Indian science under the supervision of the National Institute of Sciences in India.
2. F. S. Taylor, *Science: Past and Present,* p. 98.
3. B. B. Dey in S. Radhakrishnan (ed.), *History of Philosophy: Eastern and Western,* I, 470.
4. S. Radhakrishnan, *Indian Philosophy,* I, 29.
5. Heimann, *Facts of Indian Thought,* p. 37.
6. *Rig Veda,* X, 129.
7. Filliozat in René Taton (ed.), *Ancient and Medieval Science,* pp. 134–35.
8. *Taittiriyaka Upanishads,* II, 1, 3. Whilst the theory of many Upanishads and materialists is that the universe comprises these five elements, there are other texts, for instance the *Chandogya Upanishads* (VI, 4), which subscribe to the theory of three—fire, water, and earth—or four—without akasa—elements. In the *Bhagavad Gita* (VII, 4) three more elements—*buddhi* (intelligence), *ahamkara* (self-sense) and *manas* (mind)—are added to these five.
9. Sarton, *Introduction to the History of Science,* I, 69.
10. R. Garbe, *Philosophy of Ancient India,* p. 30.
11. S. K. Ramachandra Rao, *Development of Psychological Thought,* pp. 32–33.
12. Prabhavananda, *The Spiritual Heritage of India,* pp. 215–16.
13. B. N. Seal, *The Positive Sciences of the Ancient Hindus.* A. B. Keith has charged Seal with having read too many modern ideas into old texts. But then Keith himself has been accused, for example by Kosambi, of massive prejudice. However, Seal's work is unhistorical, devoted principally to logic and philosophical speculations despite its title, and is somewhat obscure.
14. There are a number of Indian scholars who place the date of the *Rig Veda* much farther back, *ca.* 3000 B.C., and thus claim greater antiquity for the origins of astronomy in India. The study of Hindu science is made exceptionally difficult because the lack of definite chronology often makes it extremely difficult to debate questions of priority.

15. Filliozat in Taton (ed.), *Ancient and Medieval Science,* p. 137.
16. *Ibid.,* p. 136.
17. Filliozat in Metraux and Crouzet (eds.), *The Evolution of Science,* p. 92. For a detailed discussion of the nakshatras and of Indian astronomy, see P. V. Kane, *History of Dharmesastra,* V, Part I, 495–512.
18. See *Nature,* CLXVIII (14 July 1951), 64; and *Science and Civilization in China,* III, 173–77.
19. Filliozat in Metraux and Crouzet (eds.) , *The Evolution of Science,* pp. 91–93.
20. For further discussion, see *ibid.,* pp. 94–96.
21. A passage from the *Aitareya Brahmana,* which dates from about two thousand years before Copernicus and centuries before Hipparchus, illustrates Indian interest in astronomy: "The sun never sets nor rises; when people think to themselves the sun is setting, he only changes about after reaching the end of the day, and makes night below and day to what is on the other side. Then when people think he rises in the morning, he only shifts himself about after reaching the end of the night, and makes day below and night to what is on the other side. In fact he never does set at all."
22. A. N. Singh in Radhakrishnan (ed.). *History of Philosophy: Eastern and Western,* I, 448–49.
23. Cited in B. K. Sarkar, *Hindu Achievements in Exact Science,* p. 30.
24. Over the door of the Academy was inscribed in Greek "A Credit in Mathematics is required" and one of Plato's sayings was "God is always doing Geometry."
25. Singh in Radhakrishnan (ed.), *History of Philosophy: Eastern and Western,* I, 431.
26. Heimann, *Facets of Indian Thought,* p. 24 and also pp. 95–104. It "is not a single cipher, positive or negative (growth and decay) but the unifying point of indifference and the matrix of the All and the None. Zero produces all figures, but is itself not limited to a certain Value. It is Sunya, the primary or final reservoir of all single shapes and numbers."
27. The Hindus called it sunya, and it passed on to the Arabs as *as-sifr* or *sifr.* It later became *zephirum, tziphar, zeuro, ceuro,* from which zero was but a short step. The English cipher and French *chiffre* are directly derived from the Arabic original *as-sifr,*
28. A. L. Basham, *The Wonder That Was India,* p. 496.

29. Filliozat is of the opinion that it could not have been written before the tenth century. Filliozat in Taton (ed.), *Ancient and Medieval Science,* p. 423. The Bakshali Manuscript consisting of seventy leaves of birch bark was found in 1881.
30. Singh in Radhakrishnan (ed.), *History of Philosophy: Eastern and Western,* I, 433. The *Aryabhatiya* is indeed a remarkable example of Indian accomplishment in mathematics. An eminent Indian scholar Singh goes even to the extent of saying that the *Aryabhatiya* "contains practically the whole of arithmetic that we teach today in our High Schools."
31. Filliozat in Metraux and Crouzet (eds.), *The Evolution of Science,* p. 104.
32. "This method is declared by a high mathematical authority (Hankel) to be the most delicate operation in the theory of numbers that had been achieved before the time of the great French astronomer Lagrange (eighteenth century)." A. A. MacDonell, *India's Past,* p. 192.
33. F. Cajori, *A History of Mathematics,* p. 97.
34. "If his works were not written in Greek no one would think for a moment that they were the product of a Greek mind." *Ibid.,* p. 60.
35. J. Struik, *A Concise History of Mathematics,* pp. 85–86.
36. How well developed algebra was in India can be easily realized when it is compared with the work of Diophantus, who is looked upon as a fountainhead of Western mathematical thought. According to Thomas Heath, the Europeans were anticipated by the Hindus in the symbolic form of algebra, and Williams points out that the Chinese were familiar with Indian mathematics, and, in fact, continued to study it long after the period of intellectual intercourse between India and China had ceased. Cited in Sarkar, *Hindu Achievements in Exact Science,* p. 14.
37. The Sulvasutra rules yield a rectangle equal to a given square, with $\sqrt{2}$ and $\frac{\sqrt{2}}{2}$ as the sides of the rectangle; they yield by geometrical construction a square equal to a given rectangle and satisfying the relation ab = $(b + [a-b]/2)^2$ ¼ $(a-b)^2$, corresponding to Euclid II, 5, Cajori, *A History of Mathematics,* p. 86.
38. Singh in Radhakrishnan (ed.), *A History of Philosophy: Eastern and Western,* I, 437–39.
39. Dey in Radhakrishnan (ed.), *A History of Philosophy: Eastern and Western,* I, 465.
40. Cited in L. White Jr., *American Historical Review,* April 1960, p. 516.

41. J. Needham, *Science and Civilization in China,* IV, 282.

42. P. Ray (ed.), *History of Chemistry in Ancient and Medieval India,* pp. 114–1.5.

43. This Nagarjuna is often confused with the great founder of the Madhyamika School of Buddhist philosophy, and a creator of Mahayana Buddhism.

44. White Jr., *American Historical Review,* April 1960, pp. 522–26. J. Needham's suggestion that this concept may have originated from naive observation of the water-driven chime clocks is not supported, as White points out, by any evidence at all. The idea of perpetual motion never appeared in China, nor is there any evidence that word of such clocks reached India where this concept really emerged.

45. Ayurvedic medicine is expounded, not only in popular recipe books, but also in textbooks intended for the many Ayurvedic Medical Colleges, which are at present more numerous than the modern medical colleges. In the Ayurvedic schools, whilst diagnoses and the corresponding methods of treatment are generally based on the traditional system, urinalyses are performed in accordance with modern ideas, and surgical methods are also up to date. The Ayurvedic medicine is also practiced because of its practical value for India. Short of medical doctors, India finds these Ayurvedic *vaidyas* (doctors) almost indispensable. Moreover, Ayurvedic drugs are relatively cheap, whilst modern drugs are too expensive for the majority of the people. It is, however, seriously expected that the study of traditional remedies, diets, and methods of treatment will help to enrich medicine as a whole, because many Indian drugs are being used with profit in modern therapy.

46. S. Dasgupta, *A History of Indian Philosophy,* II, 273. An excellent study on the history of ancient Indian medicine is Filliozat, *The Classical Doctrine of Indian Medicine,* originally published in French in 1949.

47. The following hymn is meant to cure leprosy by the use of a dark-coloured plant:

> Born in the night wast thou, O herb,
> Dark-coloured sable, black of hue:
> Rich-tinted, tinge this leprosy,
> And stain away its spots of grey!
>
> (*Artharva Veda,* I, 23)

48. Ayur Veda literally means the knowledge of longevity or science of life. These texts, modified and appropriately amended, are still regarded as authoritative.

49. Sarton, *Introduction to the History-of Science,* I, 77.
50. Filliozat, *The Classical Doctrine of Indian Medicine,* pp. 11–25.
51. A. L. Basham, *The Wonder That Was India,* p. 499.
52. For speculations in Indian medicine, see S. Dasgupta, *A History of Indian Philosophy,* II, Ch. XIII.
53. Filliozat in Metraux and Crouzet (eds.), *The Evolution of Science,* p. 96.
54. P. Kutumbiah, *Ancient Indian Medicine,* p. 34.
55. He points out the remarkable resemblances amongst the Indian theories and the Hippocratic treatise on The Winds and Plato's *Timaeus* which are indicative of Indian influence.
56. Jolly has given a list of analogies between Indian and Greek medical systems in his *Indian Medicine.*
57. Filliozat, *The Classical Doctrine of Indian Medicine,* p. 226.
58. Sarton, *A History of Science,* I, 373.
59. Filliozat, *The Classical Doctrine of Indian Medicine,* p. 232.
60. F. H. Garrison, *An Introduction to the History of Medicine,* p. 72.
61. Cited in G. N. Banerjee, *Hellenism in Ancient India,* p. 178.
62. Auscultation was introduced in Europe by R. T. H. Laennec (1781–1826).
63. The practice of inoculation was introduced in England in 1721, and it was Edward Jenner who discovered that small-pox could be prevented by vaccination.
64. Calder, *Medicine and Man,* p. 49.
65. Garrison, *An Introduction to the History of Medicine,* p. 72.
66. Sir James Young Simpson (1811–1870), is regarded as having introduced anaesthetics to Western medicine.
67. Filliozat in Taton (ed.), *Ancient and Medieval Science,* p. 157.
68. Garrison, *An Introduction to the History of Medicine,* p. 72.
69. T. Gomperz, *Greek Thinkers,* I, 285–86.
70. Heimann, *Facets of Indian Thought,* p. 39.
71. Ramsay Macdonald, a former Prime Minister of Britain (1924 and 1929–35) witnessed the death of plants as demonstrated by Bose in Calcutta and has described his experience thus:

    I spent part of my last day in Calcutta in the laboratory of Professor J. C. Bose at the Presidency College. I had heard him once in England deliver a weird lecture on the poisoning of metals, and I had not forgotten the impressive ending of his discourse when he recalled the ancient science of his people, and left us with expectation that the breath of awakening might even then be blowing across the subtle intelligence of India and be giving birth to a new epoch of scientific discovery.

In Calcutta that day, he took up the parable he left unfinished at the Royal Institution in Albemarle Street. By various strange devices he showed us how plants indicated that they felt blows inflicted upon them, how they shrank, how they shuddered, and, most mysterious of all, how they died. A flickering beam of light passed right and left along a scale as the sterns and leaves we were torturing protested against our cruelties, until the point was reached when no more response came. At that point a shudder passed through the fibers of the plant, just as the muscles of a human being contract in convulsive movement when his last breath passes his lips. All was then still. The organism was beginning to decay into its elements. Death had come.

J. R. Macdonald, *The Awakening of India,* pp. 303–04.

72. J. F. Royle, *Antiquity of Hindu Medicine,* p. 36.
73. In spite of such strict dietary rules, modern well-to-do Indians, on the whole, must be amongst the world's greatest over-eaters.
74. *Santi Parva,* XVI, 7–9. Cited in S. N. Mitra, *Anglo-Indian Studies,* p. 335.

Notes to Chapter VI

1. The pre-Buddhist Chinese sense of realism and of the concrete was so intense that they produced little mythology and few fairy tales of their own. The bulk of their finest fairy tales were originally brought by the Buddhist monks from India during the first millennium A.D. The Buddhists used them in their sermons to make their teaching more agreeable and lucid.
2. The story of "Pururavas and Urvasi" found in the *Rig Veda* (X, 95) is also the oldest literary rendering of the tale of Cupid and Psyche.
3. A. A. Macdonell, *India's Past,* p. 115.
4. J. P. Couchoud in J. Hackin, *et al., Asiatic Mythology,* p. 31.
5. By studying particularly Indian and Greek mythology, scholars hope to discover the means of learning about the succession of cultural epochs. Because, whilst the early civilizations of Egypt and Arabia, due to their geographical position, were overrun and destroyed, those of Greece and

especially of India, forming what may be called culs-de-sac, have survived. "Here, as if up the long shores of some hidden creek, would be forced the tidal wave of one epoch after another, each leaving on the coast a tide-mark that perhaps none of its successors would be able entirely to cover." See Nivedita and A. K. Coomaraswamy, *Myths of the Hindus and Buddhists,* p. 1.

6. A. B. Keith, *A History of Sanskrit Literature,* pp. 353–54.
7. Cited in G. N. Banerjee, *Hellenism in Ancient India,* p. 273.
8. Various illustrations of this view can be seen in Angelo de Gubernatis' *Zoological Mythology* (I, 30 f). For example: Aurora (the goddess of dawn), as the first to appear every day in the eastern sky and as the first to know the break of day, is naturally represented as one of the swiftest amongst those who are the guests of the sun prince during the night. And like her cows, which do not cover themselves with dust (this being an attribute which in the Indian faith distinguishes the gods from mortals, because the former walk in the heavens and the latter upon earth), she leaves no footsteps behind her in her onward flight. The word *aped* (*pad* and *pada* being synonymous) may mean not only she who has no feet, but also she who has no footsteps (that is, the measure of the foot), or, again, she who has no slippers, Aurora having, it appears, lost them; for the prince Mitras, whilst following the beautiful young girl, finds a slipper which shows her footstep, the measure of her foot, a foot so small that no other woman has a foot like it, an almost infirmable, almost imperceptible foot, which brings us back again to the idea of one who has no feet. The legend of the lost slipper, and of the prince who tried to find the foot predestined to wear it, the central interest in the popular story of Cinderella, seems to repose entirely upon the double meaning of the word *apad,* i.e., one who has no feet, or what is the measure of the foot, which may be either the footstep or the slipper. Moreover, in the story of Cinderella, the prince often cannot overtake the fugitive because a chariot bears her away.
9. Gomperz later said, "Practically the entire fairy-lore of the Occident is derived from India. No one disputes this assertion today, but no one as yet can give a completely clear account of the ways and means by which its journey was accomplished." See *Greek Thinkers,* p. 95.
10. Lang, *Custom and Myth,* pp. 12–13.
11. *Chandogya Upanishad,* I, 12, 1–5.
12. Manu, the intelligent, the father of the human race, was the son of gods.

From the remains of the offering he made for Visnu was born a woman, Ida. As Manu desired her, Ida turned herself into a cow seeking to avoid incest, as she regarded herself as Manu's daughter having been created by him. Manu then turned himself into a bull. Then Ida turned into a she-goat and Manu into a he-goat. Thus Manu, the father, each time took the male form corresponding to the female form assumed by Ida, his daughter. And in this way the animals were born.

13. *Rig Veda,* VII, 103.
14. Similarly, the distinction between the *katha* and the *akyayika,* as the invented story and the traditional legend respectively, is more or less academic. Some of the stories of the *Pancatantra* are indeed called kathas, but one of the versions of the entire work is styled *Tantrakhyayika,* whilst Gunadhya's work is designated *Brihatkatha.* Both these types, in turn, must be distinguished from the prose romance, the so-called katha and akhyayika, such as the *Harsa-carita* and the *Kadambari* in which all the graces and refinements of the Kavya are transferred from verse to prose, either to create an exuberantly fanciful story or to vivify and transform a legend or folktale.
15. Davids, *History and Literature of Buddhism,* pp. 54–55.
16. J. Hertel, *Das Pancatantra, seine Geschichte und seine Verbreitung,* index, pp. 451f.
17. F. Edgerton, *The Pancatantra,* p. 11.
18. Originally said to comprise twelve books, it is fairly certain that this work contained five books with a brief introduction and was called *Pancatantra,* but there is a considerable discussion of the meaning of the word *tantra.* It may denote nothing more than a book or its subject-matter, but since it occurs in the title *Tantrakhyayika* of one of the versions, it may indicate a text of polity as an art. There is no evidence at all of authorship. The name Visnusarman, applied in the introduction to the wise Brahman who instructs with these stories the ignorant sons of King Amarasakti of Mahilaropya in Deccan, is obviously as fictitious as the names of the king and the place. Hertel thinks that the work was composed in Kashmir, but his arguments are inconclusive.
19. Barzuyeh declined to accept any reward for his translation except a dress of honour and the freedom to append an account of his own life and opinions to the work.
20. V. Staden (ed.), *Vetalapantschavinsati,* p. xxvii.

21. Incidentally, the German translation of the *Pancatantra* was one of the earliest printed books in Europe.
22. For a chart illustrating the dissemination of Indian fables, see Max Müller, *Chips from a German Workshop*, IV, 171.
23. In 1844, M. Reinaud published the Persian text of the portions of the *Mujmil al-Tawarikh* with a French translation in the *Journal Asiatique* (1844, pp. 114 ff.), in his "Fragments Arabes et Persans inedits relatifs á l'Inde antérieurement au XIe siécle de l'ére chrétien." S. K. Chatterji in *Indo-Asian Culture*, July 1958, pp. 50–71.
24. One of the other sources from which *Hitopadesa* draws maxims is a purely metrical treatise, dealing directly with the principles of polity, *Nitisara.* In the Indian literature, *Hitopadesa,* like the *Pancatantra,* is classified as *Nitisastra.*
25. See D. M. Lang, *The Balavariani,* introduction and pp. 91–41.
26. *Ibid.*, p. 9.
27. M. Müller, *Chips from a German Workshop,* IV, 146.
28. W. R. S. Ralston, "Beauty and the Beast," *The Nineteenth Century,* IV (December 1878), 990–1012.
29. Cited in W. R. S. Ralston, *Russian Folk-tales,* p. 22. In this work Ralston refers to a variety of parallel stories in Russian and Indian traditions.
30. La Fontaine, *Fables,* Bk. VII. Fable 10.
31. *Pancatantra,* Bk. V, "The Brahman who Built Air-castles."
32. *Ibid.*, "The Brahman and the Mongoose."
33. Edgerton, *The Pancatantra,* pp. 17–19.
34. G. N. Banerjee has compiled a list of about thirty-five of those types of Indo-European fables which are common to the Hindus and the Persians on the one hand, and the Germans, the Norsemen, the Scots, the Irish, the Sicilians, the Greeks, and the Slavs on the other, and which may have migrated from India. See *Hellenism in Ancient India,* p. 281. Jacobs in his *History of the Aesopic Fable* has drawn parallels between the Indian and the Greek fable. He has selected thirteen Jatakas (Nos. 30, 32, 34 [with 45], 136, 143, 146, 189, 215, 294, 308, 374, 383, 426), and found parallels amongst such well-known Greek fables as "The Ass in the Lion's Skin," "The Wolf and the Lamb," "The Wolf and the Crane," and "The Fox and the Crow."
35. Banerjee, *Hellenism in Ancient India,* p. 286.
36. E. J. Thomas in H. T. Francis, *Jataka Tales,* p. iv.

37. Banerjee, *Hellenism in Allcient India,* p. 292.
38. Gokul Das De, *Significance and Importance of Jatakas,* p. 26.
39. Cited in Francis, *Jataka Tales,* p. iii.
40. A. A. Macdonell, *India's Past,* pp. 120–21. That Indian fables are pre-Buddhist has also been confirmed by M. Emmanuel Cosquin (*Contes Populaires de Lorraine*), who also postulates that Indian fables were continually transmitted to Europe orally from the early ages.
41. A. Weber, *The History of Sanskrit Literature,* pp. 211–22.
42. Banerjee, *Hellenism in Ancient India,* p. 291.
43. Edgerton, *The Pancatantra,* pp. 13–16.
44. The cosmological aspect in Indian music unlike that in its Western counterpart, is of great importance. Indian ragas are to be played at specified times, such as in the morning or evening, or during spring or autumn, etc.
45. Alain Danielou, *Northern Indian Music,* I, 115.
46. Ananda K. Coomaraswamy, *The Dance of Shiva,* p. 94.
47. It carries only one chapter on music proper, describing in detail the svaras (the seven notes of the gamut), srutis (microtonal intervals), *gramas* (scales), *murchhanas,* and *jatis.* Whilst the principles of his theory are still alive, the details of his system are things of the past. Other chromatic intervals, in addition to the seven pure notes, were obtained by the *murchhana* process, i.e. by changing the key note. It is uncertain if Bharata is the real name of the author. For the word *bharata* means a dance-actor, and was used as a common name in the title of all the treatises on stage technique, and Bharata is also regarded as the legendary guru of Sangita.
48. The *Sangita Ratnakara* deals with the whole range of musical form and composition and gives a detailed account of ancient musical theory. It mentions a number of musical writers, since the days of Bharata, but their works have not survived. Its fundamental scale, *suddha* raga, is *Mukhari,* the modern *Kanakangi.* Its author, in attempting to make his treatise as broad-based and exhaustive as possible, not only covered all the aspects of music and dancing, but also gave place in his work to styles and patterns prevalent in the various parts of the country. Scholars from all regions since have looked up to *Natyasastra* and *Sangita Ratnakara* for authority.
49. "While Western music speaks of the wonders of God's creation, Eastern music hints at the inner beauty of the Divine in man and in the world. Indian music requires of its hearers something of that mood of divine

discontent, of yearning for the infinite and impossible." Mrs. Mann, cited in H. A. Popley, *The Music of India,* p. 136.

50. "Indian classical music, compared with our Western music, is like a pure crystal. It forms a complete perfected world of its own, which any admixture could only debase. It has, quite logically and rightly, rejected those innovations which have led the development of Western music into the multiple channels which have enabled our art to absorb every influence under the sun. Freedom of development in Indian music is accorded the performer, the individual, who, within fixed limits, is free to improvise without any restraint imposed externally by other voices, whether concordance or discordant—but not to the basic style, which excludes polyphony and modulation." Yehudi Menuhin, "Indian and Western Music," *Hemisphere,* April 1962, p. 5.
51. *Geography,* X, 11, 17. Cited in Alain Danielou, *Northern Indian Music,* I, 21.
52. Menuhin, "Indian and Western Music," *Hemisphere,* April 1962, p. 6. The story of the discovery of Sanskrit is dealt with in Vol. II, Ch. V.
53. Alain Danielou's Hindu name is Shiva Sharan, and his books include *Northern Indian Music,* Volumes I and II, and *Introduction to the Study of Musical Scales and Hindu Polytheism.*
54. Abhedananda, *India and Her People,* 1940, pp. 216–21.
55. K. Sorabji, *Around Music,* pp. 147–48.
56. *Ibid.,* p. 149.
57. *Times,* London, 28 August 1963.
58. Menuhin, "Indian and Western Music," *Hemisphere,* April 1962.
59. A similar game on a 6 × 6 board is found in the bas-reliefs on the stupa of Bharhut.
60. H. J. R. Murray, *A History of Chess,* p. 115.
61. Murray, A *History oj Board Games,* p. 36.
62. H. Namkura, *Japan and India to Asia,* p. 9.
63. Patent No. 14636.

Notes to Chapter VII

1. It is not easy to make an exact count of the Gypsies who wander about ceaselessly, and it has been suggested that the official figures given are generally on the low side.

2. In recent years Gypsies have begun to organize themselves into a corporate body such as the International Gypsy Committee. The leaders of this Committee hope that one day they will have a seat at the United Nations. But at present they are mainly engaged in tackling the social and practical problems of their community. In December 1966, the Gypsies of Britain met at St. Paul's Cray, Kent, to form their first trade union under the auspices of the International Committee. Significantly, they met at the public-house outside of which hung the stern notice, "No Gypsies." *Time,* 12 December 1966.
3. This figure however is an official estimate, which is understated. Moreover, Gypsies were killed not only in the concentration camps, but everywhere, at home, on roads, in forests. Thus, some scholars, such as Jan Kochanowśki, estimate the number of Gypsies exterminated by the Nazis to be about two million.
4. Jean-Paul Clebert, *The Gypsies,* p. 59. This book is an excellent and exhaustive study of the history and daily life of the Gypsies up to the present day.
5. *Ibid,* p. 76.
6. G. Borrow, *The Zincali,* p. 15. Brian Vesey-Fitzgerald, probably the most reliable modern interpreter of Borrow, has suggested in his recent work, *Gypsy Borrow,* that Borrow, who looked so unlike his father and who had a "gypsy-mind" and a "gypsy temperament," was in fact a full-blooded Gypsy.
7. "Tradition says that it is there the origin of their phobia for wet places must be sought." Clebert, *The Gypsies,* p. 72.
8. George Borrow, *The Gypsies of Spain,* p. 14.
9. The following verse by the great Danish poet, Jeppe Aakjar, dated 1918 in his *Hjaertegrces og Ærenpris* (andet Oplag: Gyldendal, Københaun, 1921), is a fitting comment on the gentile treatment of Gypsies:

TATERNE

Vi voetlted deres Hytter, vi øden dem selv
bag Tugthucets gitrede Celler;
og da vi havde plaget dem grundigt ihjel,
vi lod dem opstaa i Noveller.

THE GYPSIES

We harried and ruined them and clapped them in jail
As soon as we had wrecked their hovels;

And when we had crushed them as dead as a nail,
We let them stand up in our novels.

Translated by J. Glyn Davies, October 1931, *Journal of the Gypsy Lore Society*, 3rd series, XII, 64.

10. It is not surprising to find that these Gypsies, who love freedom, nature, and wanderings so much, have not seriously endeavoured to found a national state of their own. Their only attempt to found a dynasty is associated with the family of Kwiek. Gregory Kwiek, a smith of Polish origin, declared himself "King of the Gypsies" about 1883. It was a feeble attempt and its brief history is full of accounts of intrigue, internecine strife, and "palace revolutions."

    The Gypsies first demanded a Romany state in 1875, then voiced the demand in subsequent congresses, but there never appears to have existed a systematic and well-organized movement. Apart from their own love of nomadism, the difficulties involved in working out a political organization consisting of Gypsies distributed across national frontiers, often in hostile countries, must have been too formidable.

11. From Irving Brown, *Deep Song*.
12. The name Romani for the language of the Gypsies first came to be used in writing in English in 1812, although the words *Romani* and *Romanes* had been in use by the Gypsies in Britain long before that.
13. "Gypsies and the Problem of their Acculturation," *Indo-Asian Culture*, XVI (1), 23.
14. Works on Indian history scarcely mention the Gypsies at all, with the exceptions of A. L. Basham's book, *The Wonder That Was India*, in which an Appendix on the Gypsies is given, and Dasratha Sharma's *The Earlier Chauhan Families*. A study by an Indian scholar, Chaman Lal, entitled *Gypsies: Forgotten Children of India*, is very useful, but this work is not a historical study in the real sense of the term. It is mainly a reiteration of the conclusions of well-known Western scholars, to which the author has made useful additions from his own personal experiences amongst Gypsies and the data he himself collected, with an emphasis on the Indian elements of the problem. Whilst it is true that Gypsies have not played any role in Indian history, as far as is known at present, their exodus from India must have been caused by certain events in India, an understanding and analysis of which must surely be considered important for Indian history itself. If the nature and history of the Gypsy migration were known, it would, no doubt, greatly help Gypsiologists.

15. John Sampson, "On the Origin and Early Migration of the Gypsies," *Journal of the Gypsy Lore Society,* 3rd series, II, 156–69.
16. Brian Vesey-Fitzgerald, *Gypsies of Britain,* pp. 8–9.
17. The wide acceptance of 1417 as the date of their arrival in Europe has given rise to considerable confusion because it inhibited or preconditioned research concerning Gypsy origin and migration.
18. In the *Miscellaneous Tracts Relating to Antiquity* is a letter of Simon Simeon, who, after visiting Cyprus in 1332, recorded that he found there a race of people called Cham, who were constantly wandering, living in small low black tents, and hiding in the mountains. There is mention of the *Zingari* in a letter of Theophilactus, who lived in the eleventh century. Records in the archives of Bucharest suggest that long before the eleventh century *Tziganes* were recognized as an entity by the inhabitants of the countries they lived in.
19. The Empress Catherine de Courtenay-Valois (1301–46) authorized the suzerains of Corfu to receive as vassals certain *homines vaginiti* coming from the Greek mainland and using the Greek rite.
20. E. O. Winstedt, "Some Records of the Gypsies in Germany," *Journal of the Gypsy Lore Society,* XI (1932), 98.
21. Clebert (*The Gypsies,* p. 29) gives the following dates for the appearance of Gypsies in Europe:

855?	Byzantium	1419	France Sisteron
or 1260 1399	Bohemia	1420?	Denmark
1322?	Crete	1422	Bologna Rome
1346	Corfu	1427	Paris
1348	Serbia	or 1430 1440?	Wales
1378	The Peloponnese Zagreb Basle	1447	Barcelona
		or 1492 1505	Scotland
1418	Transylvania Moldavia The Elbe	1509	Poland
		1515	Sweden

22. The majority of European Gypsies call themselves Rom, Romano Cxavo, Roma, Romane Cxave (Rama's Sons). Those who are an offshot of German and Italian Gypsies call themselves Manush (Sanskrit word for man), Stinti, and Sinthi, presumably after Sind in India.

    The equivalents of "Gypsy" are *Tsigeni* in Bulgaria, *Tigani* in Romania, *Ciganyok* in Hungary, *Zingari* in Italy, *Ziegeuner* in Germany, *Cigonas* in Lithuania, *Zincali* in Spain, and *Ciganos* in Portugal.

23. "Where we comes from the dear Lord only knows and He's too high and mighty to tell the likes of us." Charley Smith, A Gypsy. Cited in Brian Vesey-Fitzgerald, *Gypsies of Britain,* p. 1.
24. John Sampson, Jacob Bryant, in *Journal of the Gypsy Lore Society,* New Series, IV (1910–11), 162-94.
25. Romani dialects are numerous. The principal ones are Armenian Romani (spoken in Transcaucasia), Finnish, Hungarian, German, and Welsh Romani and the dialects of British, Catalan, and Andalusian Romanies.
26. Ralph Turner, "The Position of Romani in Indo-Aryan," *Journal of the Gypsy Lore Society,* V (1926), No. 4, 145–89. John Sampson opposed Turner's view. See "Notes on Professor Turner's The Position of Romani in Indo-Aryan," *Journal of the Gypsy Lore Society,* VI (1927), No. 2, 57–68.
27. Excommunication, however, is not only a Hindu practice. In any rigidly knit or closed community, excommunication is a normal feature of maintaining the purity of tradition and strict discipline.
28. In India the rules and laws governing caste and family have been drastically altered to remove social inequalities. The parallels drawn here relate to the old social organization, now in decline, in India.
29. Some German Gypsies, however, keep dogs and train them to steal meat from the butcher's shop.
30. "I have again experienced exactly the same mental impression," observes Clebert, "which I used to have in Indian temples, where the faithful remain, by turns indifferent and deeply moved, at the very feet of the idols." Clebert, *The Gypsies,* p. 143. Sara is regarded by all Christian, Protestant and Catholic Gypsies, as their own Black Virgin, the Kali, who was the first amongst them to receive the revelation of Christianity, and who preached the Gospel amongst Gypsies and non-Gypsies. Every year a Gypsy pilgrimage is held in May in France at Les Saintes-Maries-de-la-Mer where Sara is said to have had the vision of three Marys, and where a statue of Sara is now kept in a small church. Gypsies from all over Europe,

and even from America, attend, and the occasion has come to be a great Gypsy festival.

31. A number of their songs clearly illustrate this. For example:

> I have four great palaces
> Though you call me, 'Beggar, knave.'
> I've the hospital, the prison,
> The cathedral, and the grave.
>
> When rich and poor get drunk,
> You hear the people say,
> The poor man's very drunk,
> The rich man's very gay.
>
> The cobbler in the corner,
> Mending shoes beside his lamp,
> Says he cannot go to church,
> Because the church is damp.
>
> The cobbler in the corner,
> He's very, very ill,
> But if I'd said the tavern,
> He'd have gone and drunk his fill.

Despite frequent and almost unceasing persecutions, he is not always vindictive

> I hope God never gives
> Even to those I hate,
> Such sorrows as he sent to me,
> Such evil, evil fate.
> (From Irving Brown, *Deep Song*)

32. A Gitano song: "My father was a Dom, and so was my father's dad; you ask me who am I? Why, I'm a noble lad."
33. John Sampson, "Punjabi and Romani Parables," in Chaman Lal (ed.), *Gypsies,* pp. 182-87.
34. A version of this story is also common in the Philippines.

35. Amongst the famous Gypsy boxers are Tom Smith, the featherweight champion of 1844, Posh Price, Hooper the Tinman, and Tom Sayers.
36. Charles Leland and A. Barrere, *Dictionary of Slang, Jargon and Cant,* I, xiii.
37. Some scholars regard bloke as having been derived from the Dutch *blok* and not from *lok.*
38. Clebert, *The Gypsies,* p. 195.
39. *Ibid.,* pp. 98–99.
40. *Ibid.,* p. 14.
41. It is interesting that the archaeological finds of Untersiebenbrunn near. Vienna included golden broaches with coloured stones, belonging to the period around 400. Not only must these stones have come from India, but, what is more important, the technique of setting stones in metal is typically Indian. H. Kuhn, *Germanische Kunst der Völkerwanderung.*
42. The Hawaiians meet this difficulty by raising the strings and replacing the fixed frets by a metal bar that is shifted at will.
43. Brown, *Deep Song,* pp. 137–38.
44. Notwithstanding its name, this instrument corresponds to the dulcimer and to the cymbals.
45. Liszt was enchanted by Gypsy music, especially that of his famous Gypsy compatriot, Janos Bihari. Liszt published a book on Gypsy music *Des Bohemiens et de leur musique en Hongrie,* in 1859 in Paris.
46. A. L. Sinclair, "Gypsy and Oriental Music," *Journal of American Folk-Lore,* XX (76), 16.
47. Characterized by a very short step, with sharpened rhythm, this dance was composed in two parts: one of them slow, of indomitable haughtiness; the other, impetuous and of bouncing gaiety. Hussars and Gypsies enlivened the melody and the pace, supported by the clicking of heels and the rattle of spurs.
48. It has been disputed that Remenyi was a Gypsy. He is said to have been the descendant of an Hungarian merchant named Hoffman.
49. Clebert, *The Gypsies,* p. 116. Often traces are found amongst Gypsies of dances with a non-religious but magical function: for example the Gypsy women dancers called *dodole* who, in Yugoslavia, serve by their rhythms to prevent sterility in herds of cattle. These women have a widely beneficent role, since it is sufficient to touch them for maladies to disappear. The ground which they have trodden will cure patients of warts and gall-stones,

And, in Bulgaria, Gypsy women dancers are sprinkled with water to bring rain (the dance is called the *paparuda*).

50. The great American Romani, Rai Irving Brown, says: "It is my firm conviction that Beethoven learned something from the complex and swiftly changing rhythms of the Hungarian gypsies in Vienna; and Liszt has admitted his indebtedness in no uncertain terms." *Deep Song*, p. 117.
51. For this reason, in India, drums play a highly important role in accompanying a singer. A good Indian drummer is as much a virtuoso as a good European violinist, and is capable of producing extremely difficult and delicate effects on his instrument.
52. Brown, *Deep Song*, p. 122.
53. *Ibid.*, p. 130.
54. Duke of Beaufort (ed.), *The Badminton Library of Sports and Pastimes* (Volume on dancing), p. 215. On page 213, it is pointed out that "the kind of erotic dancing, which was practised from the earliest times in the East, and even in Europe by a class of women who, if not absolutely proved to be Gypsies, had, at any rate, many points of resemblance to to them. Thus the 'Syrian girl who haunts the taverns round,' described by Virgil suggests the Syrian and Egyptian dancer, who is of Indo-Persian, that is to say, of Luri, or Gypsy origin. Spanish girls of old times were conjectured to have come from the universal Hindoo-Romany stock."

Notes to Chapter VIII

1. The account of his initial expedition was first published in his *Sand-Buried Ruins of Khotan* (1903) and was subsequently published, incorporating a detailed report of the scientific results, as *Ancient Khotan* in two volumes in 1907. The account of the second expedition first appeared in his *Ruins of Desert Cathy* in two volumes in 1912, and later in *Ser-India* in five volumes in 1921, giving a detailed report of the explorations and scientific results. The account of his third journey appeared first in the *Geographical Journal* for August and September 1916, and later in his volumes on *Innermost Asia.*
2. For the nature of the Tun-huang manuscripts, see Arthur Waley, *Ballads and Stories from Tun-huang*, pp. 236–37.
3. Although during the period of Muslim domination Tokharestan signified the area between Badakshan and Balkh, in the ancient period it meant a much wider area, embracing all the territories on both banks of the Oxus River, which were economically allied to Balkh.

4. Scholars transliterate the name of the Chinese pilgrim differently. De Bary in the index to his *Sources of Chinese Tradition* suggests the *chuang* is the more correct reading of his name. (This is the way most Chinese actually pronounce the word today.) But both Mathews and Giles give *tsang* as the primary reading, at least in literary texts. Fairbank prefers *tsang* in *East Asia,* I, 146.
5. S. P. Tolstov, *Podrevnim del'tam oksa i Yaksarta* (The Ancient delta of the Oxus and Jaxartes), p. 6.
6. The Ancient name of Khotan appears in different forms in various sources, such as Yu-tien, which is the oldest, Yu-tun, and Kiu-tan. All are derivatives from the original form, Godana or Khotana. A Chinese name, perhaps a more learned form, was Kiu-sa-ta-na, Kustana. The versions found in old Kharoshthi documents are Kustana, Khotana, Khodana, and Khodamna.
7. Sambhota is the Sanskrit title meaning the good Bhotiya or Tibetan. The Tibetans call their country Bod from which is derived Bhota, by which name Indians called Tibet. The inhabitants of Bhota were thus known as Bhotias.
8. His two wives were also canonized as incarnations of Avalokitesvara's consort Tara, the goddess of mercy.
9. W. Y. Evans-Wentz, *The Tibetan Book of the Great Liberation,* p. 62.

Notes to Chapter IX

1. René Grousset, *A History of Chinese Empire,* p. 79.
2. Arthur Waley, *The Way and its Power,* p. 114.
3. P. C. Bagchi, *A Comprehensive History of India,* II, 766.
4. In Chinese the common term for India is *T'ien-chu,* which is a phonetic corruption of *Shen-tu,* as are the variants *Kan-tu, Hsien-tu,* or *Hsien-tou.* Later, during the T'ang period, a new term, *Yin-tu* or *In-tu,* was used.
5. The term Shen-tu can be philologically related to the word Sindhu (Indus). See B. Karlgren, *Analitical Dictionary of Chinese,* No. 869.
6. Waley, *The Way and its Power,* pp. 114–15.
7. The other main schools of ancient Chinese thought were those of Mo-tzu; the so-called School of Names (*ming-chia*); the Yin-Yang school; Legalism (*ja-chia*).
8. The *Lun Yu,* or *Analects,* is in fact a collection of his writings and sayings

made by his disciples. No actual writing of Confucius survives with the possible exception of his share as editor in the *Chun-Chiu* annals of the Lu state.

9. The story goes on to say that the first Chin Emperor was unwilling to embrace Buddhism and he had the Buddhist missionaries thrown into prison. But at night the prison was broken open by a golden man about sixteen feet high, who released the holy prisoners. The Emperor moved by this miraculous happening, sought forgiveness.
10. E. Zürcher, *The Buddhist Conquest of China* (Text), p. 20.
11. *Ibid.*, p. 23.
12. In some versions of the story it is stated that two Indian monks, Kasyapa Matanga and Dharmaratna (Chu-Fa-Lan), had returned with the envoys.
13. Despite the political disunion, China never lost cultural unity and the vision of a unified state, which would indicate the great value of the work of the Chin or Han dynasties in welding China together. Even today the Chinese call themselves the "Sons of Han."
14. Kenneth Ch'en, *Buddhism in China*, p. 58.
15. Arthur F. Wright, *Buddhism in China*, pp. 33–34.
16. Hu Shih, "East and West: The Indianization of China: A Case Study in Cultural Borrowing" in Harvard Tercenary Conference of Arts and Sciences, *Independence, Convergence, Borrowing*, p. 225.
17. In the Tripitaka catalogues, their names are recorded. Nanjio has listed the Tripitaka translators, both Chinese and foreign, whose names occur in the Ming dynasty catalogue rendered into English by him; these worked from the first century onwards. Amongst Nanjio's names are several who are said to have come from the "western region" and there is no doubt that they include monks from India.
18. The prefix *chu* is indicative of the Indian origin of the monks.
19. Many Buddhist texts no longer available in India in their original have survived in their Chinese renderings.
20. P. C. Bagchi, *India and China*, p. 34.
21. Some Sinologists doubt the historicity of Bodhidharma and claim that he was invented to give Ch'an Buddhism an air of authenticity.
22. Some scholars assert that although a strong patron of Buddhism, Harsha was not exactly a Buddhist ruler. He is called a Saiva in the *Harsha Charita* of Bana. Possibly he developed leanings towards Buddhism under Hsüan-

tsang's influence, but he does not seem to have actually embraced the faith. However, he practiced extreme religious tolerance, building temples for the Saivas, and monasteries for Buddhists; he was a brave soldier and a great commander, as well as a generous patron of art and learning, and a writer of repute. He erected a vihara and a bronze temple at the Nalanda University as well as several thousand stupas on the banks of the River Ganga. Like Asoka, he was responsible for a variety of humanitarian and public welfare activities and establishments.

23. There was another Bodhiruci who worked in northern China from 508 to 536. His original name was Dharmaruci, but was changed to Bodhiruci by order of the Empress Wu Tso-thien.
24. There are records of earlier pilgrims but little is known about them.
25. Tao-pu, Fe-sheng, Fa-wei, Tao-yo, and Tao-tai.
26. It is said that when he found that Harsha had died, and his throne had been usurped by his minister, he secured the military help of Nepal and Tibet, which were bound in matrimonial alliance with each other, as was Tibet with China, and defeated the usurper, Arunasva, taking him as a prisoner to China.
27. A set of the Liao edition of the Tripitaka was presented to Korea. Later, on the eve of printing their second edition of the canon, the Koreans made a comparison of the three editions—the Sung, Liao, and the first Korean—and found that the Khitan version was more accurate and comprehensive than the other two.
28. There are altogether fourteen printed editions of the Chinese Tripitaka, in which all the extant works are collected. The first edition dates from 972, and eight other editions appeared in China before 1869. An edition was published in Korea in 1010, and four editions were printed in Japan, of which the earliest appeared during the period from 1624 to 1643, and the last came out in 1924–30, known as the *Taisho Issaikyo,* consisting of eighty-three volumes containing 3,098 works.
29. In fact, some of the uprisings against the Mongols were fomented by monks or by common people ill the guise of monks. The White Lotus Society, a prominent Buddhist monastery, was a leading rebellious group. During the Mongol period secret societies claiming connections with Buddhism became active, but they were mainly inspired by political motives and considerations of power. However, information on this theme—the secret societies and Mongol Buddhism—is too insufficent to permit any definite evaluation at present.

30. The last imperial patron of Ch'an Buddhism in China was Emperor Yung-Cheng (1723–36).
31. Many Buddhist paintings, especially Lamaistic, were executed during the reign of Chien-Lung (1736–96).
32. H. G. Creel, *Chinese Thought,* p. 228.
33. René Grousset, *Chinese Art and Culture,* p. 137.
34. Wolfram Eberhard, *A History of China,* pp. 142–43.
35. Hu Shih, *Independence, Convergence, Borrowing,* p. 226.
36. Confucianist historians have insisted that the edict of 446 was due to the discovery of alcohol and women in one of the most famous Buddhist monasteries. The chief complaint of the Confucianist literati against Buddhism was that its monasticism "did away with the family, and thus struck at the very roots of ancestor-worship, and it gave men an opportunity to evade military service." The latter argument was an effective device to convince a soldier king like Toba. See René Grousset, *The Rise and Splendour of the Chinese Empire,* p. 113.
37. Hu Shih, *Independence, Convergence, Borrowing,* p. 230.
38. "Neo-Confucianism was stimulated in its development by a number of Buddhist ideas. Certain features of Taoism, such as its canon and pantheon, were taken over from Buddhism. Works and phrases in the Chinese language owe their origin to terms introduced by Buddhism, while in astronomical, calendrical, and medical studies the Chinese benefited from information introduced by Indian Buddhist monks. Finally, and most important of all, the religious life of the Chinese was affected profoundly by the doctrines and practices, pantheon and ceremonies brought in by the Indian religion." Kenneth Ch'en, *Buddhism in China,* p. 3.
39. There is an old Chinese proverb which says: "If the government gets hold of you, they will flog you to death; if the Buddhist get hold of you they will starve you to death."
40. Hu Shih, *Independence, Convergence, Borrowing,* p. 247.
41. *Ibid.,* p. 223.
42. *Ibid.,* p. 225.
43. Ch'en, *Buddhism in China,* p. 484.
44. Fung Yu-Lan, *Short History of Chinese Philosophy,* p. 242.
45. *Ibid.,* p. 254.
46. A. K. Coomaraswamy, *Buddha and the Gospel of Buddhism,* pp. 25–55.

47. Grousset, *Chinese Art and Culture*, p. 147. Grousset suggests that *dhyana* should perhaps be translated as "intuition" and not "meditation."

48. "I see no reason to doubt that the 'holy mountain-men' (sheng-hsien) described by Lieh Tzu are Indian *rishi;* and when we read in Chuang Tzu of certain Taoists who practised movements very similar to the *asanas* of Hindu *yoga,* it is at least a possibility that some knowledge of the *yoga* technique which these *rishi* used had also drifted into China." Waley, *The Way and its Power*, p. 114.

49. Hu Shih, *Independence, Convergence, Borrowing*, p. 234.

50. Printing fas invented in the middle of the eleventh century by Pi-cheng who is said to have made movable type moulded in terracotta. During the T'ang period wood-block printing appears to have been quite popular. The oldest Chinese printed book in existence today is a Buddhist text, the *Diamond Sutra* of 868, preserved in the British Museum. It is a scroll composed of leaves of paper glued end to end. The first people to spread printed books amongst the population were Buddhists, whose reasons for doing so were, naturally, missionary.

51. *Chinese Culture*, IV, No. 4 (March 1963), 53.

52. H. G. Creel, *Chinese Thought*, p. 216.

53. The writings of the Neoconfucianist School were collected in the fifteenth century by the Ming Emperor Yung-Lo in a compendium known as *Hsing-Li Ta Chuan,* Later, other collections and selections of Neoconfucianist writings were published. A modern and accessible one is that by Fung Yu-Lan, which has been translated into English.

54. Arthur Waley, *Analects of Confucius*, p. 73.

55. Creel, *Chinese Thought*, p. 220.

56. Ch'en, *Buddhism in China*, p. 472.

57. Wm. Theodore de Bary cited in David S. Nivison and Arthur F. Wright (eds.), *Confucianism in Action*, pp. 33–34.

58. *Ibid.*, p. 44.

59. Ch'en, *Buddhism in China*, p. 476.

60. H. G. Creel, *Chinese Thought*, p. 203.

61. D. Twichett cited in A. F. Wright, *Buddhism in Chinese History*, p. 104.

62. It has been estimated that before 1750 the number of books published in Chinese exceeded those of all other languages combined, and as late as 1850, Chinese books outnumbered those in any other language. Even in early times the number of Chinese books was prodigious.

63. "China has no epic and no dramatic literature of importance. The novel exists and has merits, but seldom became the instrument of great writers." Arthur Waley, *One hundred and seventy Chinese Poems,* p. 3.
64. Lai Ming, *A History of Chinese Literature,* p. 3.
65. The oldest examples of written Chinese are the inscriptions found on oracle bones and bronze vessels dating from the latter part of the Shang or Yin dynasty (traditional dates 1766–1123 B.C.), but these are very brief and of interest primarily to archaeologists.
66. Lai Ming, *A History of Chinese Literature,* p. 4.
67. An example of the efficacy of this form of preaching is given by Huei Chiao in his *Biographies of Great Buddhist Monks:* "When the Priests talked about the transience of life, the audience was seized by fear and trembled; when they described the scenes in Hell, the audience burst into tears of shock; when they examined the causes of tragedy, the audience felt that they were witness to the wrong-doings; when they preached the moral of their stories, the audience anticipated the punishment which was to follow; when they described happiness, the audience felt comforted and contented; when they portrayed sorrow the audience wheezed and sobbed. Thus, audiences were moved and won over. The people left their seats to kneel down and repent. And then everyone joined in in intoning Buddhist sutras and felt happy." Cited in Lai Ming, *A History of Chinese Literature,* p. 253.
68. René Grousset, *The Rise and Splendour of the Chinese Empire,* p. 170.
69. *Ibid.,* pp. 114–15.
70. *Ibid.,* p. 142.
71. Grousset, *Chinese Art and Culture,* pp. 187–88.
72. P. C. Bagchi, *India and China,* p. 163.
73. P. K. Acharya, *Hindu Architecture in India and Abroad,* VI, 367.
74. The earliest Chinese music manuscript yet known, found in the Tun-huang caves, belongs to the Tang period.
75. J. Needham, *Science and Civilization in China,* I, 213–14.
76. *Chinese Literature,* 4th issue, 1955, p. 164.
77. However, as the work progresses and if Needham finds further evidence, he does sometimes revise his opinion in subsequent volumes, e.g., concerning the trigonometric tables. See Needham, *Science and Civilization in China,* IV, Part 1, 51 footnote (a).
78. *Ibid.,* II, 419–26.

79. *Ibid.*, III, 202.

80. Needham, who finds it hard to adduce definite proof of Indian influence on Chinese science, says: "It is probable that drugs such as Chaulmoogra oil, used for leprosy, which have been for many centuries in Chinese pharmacopoeia, were of Indian origin." *Ibid.*, I, 212.

81. F. H. Garrison, *An Introduction to the History of Medicine*, p. 73.

82. Ch'en, *Buddhism in China*, p. 483. Hua T'o of the Han dynasty is often referred to in his biography as the father of Chinese surgery because of his surgical exploits, which included a laparotomy with anaesthesia, amputation of an infected portion of the intestines, then suturing the opening and applying some ointment to the wound. On another occasion he is said to have operated on the head of a patient. These exploits remind one of the surgical accomplishments of the Indian physician Jivaka, who was a contemporary of the Buddha, and whose deeds had come to be known to the Chinese through the translations of An Shih-kao in the second century. The earliest biography of Hua T'o appeared in the Wei-chih of Ch'en Shou (233–297), which suggests that the operations reputedly performed by Hua T'o were but echoes of those of Jivaka.

83. H. J. R. Murray, *A History of Board Games*, p. 36.

84. Cited in Needham, *Science and Civilization in China*, IV, Part 1, 328.

85. Suniti Kumar Chatterji, "India and China: Ancient Contact," *The Journal of the Asiatic Society*, (1), 1959, pp. 98–104.

86. The modern Indian names for pear and peach are different; they are *naspati* and *adu* respectively.

87. This was the only Chinese work translated into Sanskrit, although the Sanskrit version has not been found yet.

NOTES FOR PART II

Notes to Chapter I

1. It is from the name of this dynasty that the name of the country, Korea, is derived.
2. D. Bethune McCartee, a well-known American scholar, writes: "The art of spelling was invented neither by the Chinese nor by the Japanese. Its introduction into both these countries (and, as we are convinced, in Corea as well), was the result of the labours of . . . the early Buddhist missionaries. In all the three countries . . . the system of spelling is most undoubtedly of Sanskrit origin." Cited in W. E. Griffis, *Corea—The Hermit Nation,* p. 338.
3. In 607, a Japanese mission visited China, and a year later the Chinese sent a return mission. The Japanese Emperor addressed the Chinese Emperor Tang-ti of the Sui dynasty as "the Emperor of the East respectfully greets the Emperor of the west," but the Chinese Emperor returned "the Emperor greets the sovereign of Wa." Wa was the old name of Japan.
4. The ancient religion of Japan did not have a name, but after the introduction of Buddhism, it was called Shinto to distinguish it from other creeds.
5. Yamato is now a province in central Japan, but at the time it meant the whole of central Japan. Until Tokyo was made the capital of the country in 1869, the seat of government and the Imperial residence were always in that part of the country.
6. In Japan the reigning Queen in her own right is designated as "Emperor" to distinguish her from the Queen consort, who is addressed as "Empress."

7. The present temple is not really the original since it has been rebuilt many times on the original plan.
8. He died at Kongobuji, the leading monastery of the Shingon sect, but his followers believe he did not die but merely entered into *hyuji,* eternal *samadhi.* At a fixed time a properly qualified high priest comes and changes Kukai's gown in the inner sanctuary where he is believed to be staying in meditation.
9. D. C. Holtom, *Modern Japan and Shinto Nationalism,* p. 129.
10. H. Nakamura, *Japan and Indian Asia,* p. 8.
11. D. Suzuki in Chaman Lal (ed.), *India and Japan,* p. 11.
12. Nakamura, *Japan and Indian Asia,* p. 3.
13. The *Abhidharmakosa* of Vasubandhu and the *Vijnaptimatratasiddhi* of Dharmapala have become known to the West only through the French translations by L. de La Vallée Poussin, whereas in Japan numerous treatises have been composed upon them.
14. Even the bibliography appended to the *Immyo Zuigenki* (The Origin of Buddhist Logic) written by Hotan in the first half of the eighteenth century includes eighty-four Japanese works of logic.
15. The Sanskrit original of the poem runs as follows:

    Sarve Samskarah anityah
    Utpadavayadharminah
    Tesam vyupasamah sukham,
    Avadad mahasramanah.

    The Sanskrit verse is based on the last words of the Buddha in the *Sutra,* and its English rendering would be:

    The flowers, however fragrantly blooming
    Are doomed to wither, and who in this world
    Can hope to be permanently living?
    The remotest mountain path of existence is crossed today.
    Awakening from a dream so evanescent,
    I am no more subject to intoxication.

    One of the popular Japanese games played at New Year festivities is played with cards called *ihora karuta.* A pack consists of forty-eight cards—each with a short saying beginning with one of the forty-eight letters.
16. See Johannes Nobel, *Central Asia: The Connecting Link Between East and West,* Ch. V, for a brief account of this theme.

17. The print appears to have been made from a metal plate in the middle of the eighth century. The regular printing of Buddhist books from wooden blocks did not begin until later, during the early Kamakura period.
18. Sakira is an old name of Indra by which he is chiefly known in Japan.
19. Shinto mythology is founded on legendary stories that appear in two ancient collections: the *Nihongi* or *Nihonshoki* (Chronicles of Japan), and the *Kojiki* (Records of Ancient Things). The former, written in Chinese, was published in 720 by imperial order and is an official history. The latter, also written in Chinese characters but in a syntax which is purely Japanese, is a compilation of older stories put together in this collection between 704 and 714. Three other collections of stories and myths deserve mention: the *Kogoshui,* composed in about 807, the *Fudoki,* composed in the early eighth century, and the first ten books of the *Engishiki,* a ceremonial dating from 927. The last of these contains not only Shinto mythology, but more particularly Shinto religion. Before these collections were compiled, Shinto religion and mythology had already come under foreign influences, for example, Buddhism in Japan had been firmly established for a long time.
20. Gino K. Piovesana, *Recent Japanese Philosophical Thought,* p. 103.
21. Sir Charles Eliot, *Japanese Buddhism,* p. 191.
22. Coomaraswamy, however, does not subscribe to the the view that there exists a very close connection between Horyuji and Ajanta, and believes that the sources of the Japanese work are to be sought in Khotan rather than in India. But it seems as though the Japanese must have depended in some degree directly upon Indian sources; it would be impossible otherwise to explain such remarkable iconographic parallels as the Jikoku Ten (Dhrtarastra) of the Kondo standing on a crouching demon, with the Kubera Yaksa of Bharut; and difficult to account for the great admixture Brahmanical, especially many-armed, forms so characteristic of the mixed Shinto-Buddhist pantheon. A. K. Coomaraswamy, *History of Indian and Indonesian Art,* pp. 154–55.
23. H. J. R. Murray, *A History of Board Games,* p. 36.

Notes to Chapter II

1. Ancient Americans are popularly referred to as Red Indians, and by archaeologists as Amerindians. Whilst these two designations have the advantage of common usage and currency on their side, they often produce confusion, particularly for students of comparative history and

civilization. Ancient Americans are neither red nor Indians; they have lived in America, having originated from Asia, for a much longer period than Indo-Europeans have in Europe. Hence, it is perhaps more appropriate to call them Asiomericans rather than Amerindians. There seems little justification to perpetrate a mistake made by Columbus centuries ago.

2. Recently a Welsh writer, Mr. Richard Deacon, has claimed a Welshman, Madoc, son of Owain, King of Gwynedd, reached America three centuries before Columbus. An American scholar, Dr. Cyrus Gordon, believes that the Phoenicians discovered Brazil about two thousand years before Columbus reached the Bahamas. His conclusion is based on a new interpretation of an inscription found at Parahyba in 1872, and long regarded a forgery.
3. Bernal Diaz's is one of the two very personal accounts of what befell pre-Columbian civilization that have survived. He wrote the story of the conquest of Mexico late in life, less to vindicate or extol his own part in it than to correct the misrepresentations of others. The other account is about the Incas, written by Garcilaso de la Vega, son of a Spanish captain and the Princess Chimpu Occlo (first cousin of the last Inca monarch). He wrote down, also late in life, all he knew of the history and customs of his mother's peoples and of how their empire, the Tahuantinsuyu, collapsed. As he was of mixed descent and a devout Roman Catholic, he sought to reconcile Incas and Spaniards, and to contrast the horror and devastation caused by the Spaniards with the salvation they brought in the Christian religion.
4. Calder, *The Inheritors,* p. 151.
5. Honore, *In Quest of the White God,* p. 17.
6. For example, Hiram Bingham, Waldeck, Brasseru de Bourbourg, Le Plangeon, Alfred Maudslay, Ruz Lhullier, S. G. Morley, Edward Herbert Thompson, Tello, Zelia Nuttal, Manuel Gamio, Garcia Payon, and many others. These names are mentioned without any consideration of priority of work or importance.
7. *The Conquest of Mexico* (1843) and *The Conquest of Peru* (1847).
8. According to Emerson, Humboldt was one of those wonders of the world, like Aristotle, who appear from time to time as if to show the possibilities of the human mind.
9. Von Humboldt, *Research Concerning the Institutions and Monuments of the Ancient Inhabitants of America,* I, Part XXX, 22.
10. John Lang published a second edition of his work in 1877, in which

he claimed that two missionaries, John Williams and William Ellis, of the London Missionary Society had literally *stolen* his theory and had incorporated it into their respective publications, *A Narrative of Missionary Enterprises in the South Sea Islands* (London, 1837), and *Polynesian Researches* (London, 1831) without acknowledgment to him. See Lang, *Origin and Migration of the Polynesian Nation*, pp. 305–28.

11. Analyzing the development of societies, Gordon Childe remarks "...it is not in the least surprising that the development of societies observed in different parts of the Old World, to say nothing of the New, should exhibit divergence rather than parallelism... But a comparison of the sequence summarised discloses not only divergence and differentiation but also convergence and assimilation. To the latter phenomena it is hard to find an analogy in organic evolution." *Social Evolution*, p. 166.
12. R. Heine-Geldern and G. F. Ekholm in Sol Tax (ed.), *The Civilizations of Ancient America*, p. 301.
13. B. Rogers, "An Archaeological Pilgrimage to Santiago de Compostela," *Science*, Vol. 131, 1180.
14. Heine-Geldern and Ekholm in Sol Tax (ed.), *The Civilizations of Ancient America*, pp. 308–09.
15. Paul Kirchoff, "The Diffusion of a Great Religious System from India to Mexico." See *Sobretiro del XXXV Congress International de Americanistas*, p. 88.
16. *Ibid.*, p. 73.
17. D. A. Mackenzie, *Myths of Pre-Columbian America*, p. 58.
18. E. B. Tylor, "On Diffusion of Mythical Beliefs as Evidence in the History of Culture." See *Report of the British Association*, 1894, p. 774
19. Scholars such as Laurette Sejourne, however, definitely accept his historical reality because his qualities of leadership are often mentioned. Laurette Sejourne, *Burning Water—Thought and Religion in Ancient Mexico*, p. 25.
20. Some scholars see in Quetzalcoatl a Christian missionary who had reached America by accident.
21. Miguel Leon-Portilla in S. N. Kraemer (ed.). *Mythologies of the Ancient World*, p. 449.
22. M. Leon-Portilla, *ibid.*, p. 468.
23. M. Leon-Portilla, *ibid.*, p. 468.
24. M. W. De Visser, *The Dragon in China and Japan*. p. 5. Visser goes on to say that the Indian serpent-shaped Naga was identified in China with the

four-legged Chinese dragon, because both were divine inhabitants of seas and rivers, and givers of rain. Whilst it is certain that the cult of Naga was one of the most popular cults in ancient India, it is a subject of scholarly debate as to whether it is of Aryan or pre-Aryan origin. There was a form of Naga-worship prevalent in the Indus Valley period, but others argue that the form of Naga-worship, as it is known, dates from the vedic period. They refer to "Ahi-Budhnya," the serpent of the deep, mentioned in the *Rig Veda,* who was an atmospheric deity, and who, in some texts, is mentioned as a divinity of middle or aerial region.

25. Some writers have described the Maya elephant as a badly drawn bird. This confusion appears to have been caused because the Mayan sculptor apparently had never seen an elephant and must have used a manuscript picture as his model, which, in its turn, may have been drawn from memory.
26. "It would be ridiculous to assert that such a strange doctrine was of spontaneous origin in different parts of the Old and New worlds." D. A. Mackenzie, *Myths of Pre-Columbian America,* p. 70.
27. Heine-Geldern and Ekholm in Sol Tax (ed.), *The Civilizations of Ancient America,* p. 307.
28. W. H. Prescott, *Conquest of Peru,* p. 118.
29. Miles Poindexter, *The Ayar-Incas,* Vol. 11, 211–15.
30. *Ibid.,* pp. 271–87.
31. The chromosome complement in *Gossypium* is basically N = 13; all the wild species except one are diploid. The tetraploidal form has twice (2N=26) the number of the original number of chromosomes.
32. Hutchison, Silow, and Stephens, *Evolution of Gossypium,* p. 98.
33. "The genetic and cytological data justify the assumption of closer homology between the New World cottons and their nearest diploid relatives, and a more recent origin for allopolyploidy, than the proponents of the land bridge theory supposed. Firstly, all the allopolyploid species bear lint, and the only other lint-bearing species are the Old World cottons, carrying the A genom. Since the differentiation of the A genom has been shown to be bound up with the improvement of lint by civilized man, A-bearing, linted allopolyploids can only have arisen since the origin of human civilization. Secondly, on cytological, morphological, and phenogenetic behaviour, *G. raimondii* is more closely related to the New World cottons than any other species carrying the D genom. This also indicates a recent origin for the New World cottons, since it suggests that the American diploid

species were differentiated *inter se* before the occurrence of allopolyploidy. Such a recent origin rules out any theory of natural spread to account for the meeting of the diploid parents, solely on the inadequacy of the time available. Only one alternative remains, that they were carried across the Pacific by man among the seeds of his crop plants and with the tools of his civilization." Hutchinson *et al, Evolution of Gossypium*, p. 76.

34. Sir Joseph Hutchinson, see *Endeavour*, XXI, 14.
35. C. R. Stonor and Anderson, "Maize Among the Hill Peoples of Assam," *Annals of the Missouri Botanical Garden*, XXXVI (3), 356.
36. G. F. Carter, "Movement of People and Ideas across the Pacific" in J. Barrau (ed.), *Plants and the Migrations of Pacific Peoples*, p. 9.
37. Suggesting the most likely itinerary of early Buddhists sailing to America, Arnold and Frost say: "They followed the course of the current to America and would be thrown on the coast where it struck in it greatest force. The Pacific Counter Current turns off into two branches on nearing the coast at about 10 degrees north latitude, part going to the south and part north. If they took the southern branch they would come in contact with the Equatorial Current coming up from Peru, and inevitably be carried out to sea again. On the other hand, if they took the northern branch, they would be carried for some miles along the coast until about latitude 13 degrees, where the current runs in close, and there would be the most probable spot for them to land." Cited in R. Wauchope, *Lost Tribes and Sunken Continents*, p. 95.
38. *Journal of Royal Asiatic Society*, I, p. 2. Paper written by John Edye, and communicated by Sir John Malcolm.
39. Wauchope, *Lost Tribes and Sunken Continents*, p. 92.
40. Hawaiki and its dialectal equivalent is an ancient traditional term for a homeland throughout Polynesia, New Zealand, and Hawaii.
41. Recently, an Indian scholar, Chhabra, has noted certain resemblances between the symbols found in the petroglyphs from the Hawaiian Islands and those on the Harappan Seals. Some of the symbols in the petroglyphs are described as akin to early Brahmi script. B. Ch. Chhabra, "Vestiges of Indian Culture in Hawaii," *Vishveshvaranand Indological Journal*, I, part 11, 335–37.
42. D. A. Mackenzie, *Myths of Pre-Columbian America*, p. iv.
43. Heine-Geldern and Ekholm in Sol Tax (ed.), *The Civilizations of Ancient America*, p. 306.

Notes to Chapter III

1. The terms Further and Greater India are not of Indian, but of French or Dutch, coinage.
2. Cited in G. Coedès, *Journal of South East Asian History;* September, 1964, p. 1.
3. *Ibid.*, p. 4.
4. P. C. Bagchi, in K. A. Nilakanta Sastri (ed.), *A Comprehensive History of India,* II, 772.
5. B. P. Groslier, *Indo-China,* p. 47.
6. The author of the Periplus even mentions flourishing trade including malabathron (cinnamon) from which the well-known Roman unguent was extracted and which doubtless is a corruption of the Sanskrit *tamalapatra* (the dark leaf), between China and India through the unconscious mediation of the wild Sesatai people, who possibly lived in the north of Burma.
7. Paul Wheatley, *The Golden Khersonese,* pp. 185–86.
8. Arthur Waley, *The Way and Its Power,* p. 114, also see B. P. Groslier, *Indo-China,* p. 48.
9. The stupa as it is at present is an enlargement of the original Asokan one.
10. H. G. Quaritch Wales, *The Making of Greater India,* pp. 29–31.
11. Robert Heine-Geldern, cited in K. A. Nilakanta Sastri, *South Indian Influences in the Far East,* pp. 1–2.
12. *Ibid.*, p. 3.
13. This subject also raises the question of the existence of the many parallels between the ancient American civilizations on the one hand and those of East Asia and Southeast Asia on the other.
14. Groslier, *Indo-China,* p. 41.
15. G. Coedés, *Journal of South East Asian History,* pp. 1–26.
16. Groslier, *Indo-China,* p. 50.
17. There are historians who identify places all over the central uplands of Ceylon which are closely associated with the stories of Rama and Ravana. See M. D. Raghavan, *India in Ceylonese History, Society and Culture,* pp. 1–8.
18. On a full moon day in December the Buddhists of Ceylon commemorate the arrival of the tree. The sacred Bo-Tree, reputedly 2300 years old, is

in a state of decline. The original branches are dying and it is feared that in the course of time will wither away. At present the entire tree and its branches are supported by long poles and it is chemically treated to keep it alive.

19. The earliest known alphabet in Ceylon is substantially Asokan Brahmi.
20. The beautiful Buddha statue of Anuradhapura, draped in the Amaravati style of thin clinging material without folds, moved Jawaharlal Nehru so greatly that he carried a picture of the image with him for many years. Cited in Raghavan, *India in Ceylonese History, Society and Culture,* p. 93.
21. *Ibid.,* pp. 108–09.
22. G. H. Luce in Burma Research Society. *50th Anniversary Publication,* No. 2, p. 307.
23. R. C. Majumdar (ed.), *History and Culture of the Indian People,* III. 648.
24. It is only in this century that the history of the Pagan Period, as well as the earlier history of Burma, has come to be systematically studied. The main credit for pioneering the study is due to G. H. Luce and Pe Maung Tin who edited the *Inscriptions of Burma.*
25. The theory that Nanchao was the home of the Thais, who had been driven out of their original homeland by the Mongols, was first put forward by Terrien de Lacouperie. A modern writer, Hsu Yun Tsiao, has questioned it. See *The Journal of South Seas Society,* IV (2).
26. Walter Liebenthal, while subscribing to the theory of Indian influence on Nanchao, is of the opinion that it reached Tali, Nanchao, in the second half of the eighth century via Kamarupa and Tibet routes, for he holds the view that the Burma road was not opened to traffic "until between 791 and 858." *Journal of the Greater India Society*, XV (1), 8.
27. Majumdar, *History and Culture of the Indian People,* III, 648.
28. R. C. Majumdar, *Hindu Colonies in the Far East,* p. 257.
29. Cited in R. Le May, *Buddhist Art in Siam,* p. 10.
30. Le May, *The Culture of South-East Asia,* p. 63.
31. There has been some controversy about the exact location of this state. According to the Kedah annals it was on the west coast. But the evidence favours the east. For a discussion of the point, see D. Devahuti, *India and Ancient Malaya,* pp. 22–31.
32. A modern writer on Buddhist art describes somewhat graphically the various waves of Buddhist influence protruding out of India in divergent directions but converging upon Indo-China: "If we consider the development of

Buddhist art and culture in general, there is, on one hand, a movement from north-eastern and south-eastern India towards south and south-east Asia, which makes a slight turn to the north-east and so reaches the borderline we have mentioned; here in Indochina it encounters another branch coming from the north, by way of Burma. On the other hand, from the northern and north-western part of India there is a great migration right across Central Asia as far as China, where it divides: one line continues eastwards to Japan via Korea; another turns southwards until it reaches the Indian sphere of influence along the Annamese-Cambodian border. Thus the two jaws of a giant pincer movement meet in this area." See D. Seckel, *The Art of Buddhism*, p. 51.

33. Groslier, *Indo-China*, p. 41.
34. It has been suggested that the name Mekong has been derived from Ma-Ganga, Mother Ganges.
35. The Mison Stele inscription of King Prakasadharma dated 657, dealing with the foundation of Bhavapur, the capital of Kambuja.
36. Kaundinyas were a well-known class of Brahmans in South India during the first centuries A.D.
37. K. A. Nilakanta Sastri, *South Indian Influences in the Far East*, p. 48.
38. *Ibid.*, p. 36.
39. See *Journal of Indian History*, XLI (2), 415.
40. Groslier. *Indo-China*, p. 89.
41. Cited in Le May, *The Culture of South-East Asia*, p. 133.
42. Groslier, *Indo-China*, p. 170.
43. Devahuti, *India and Ancient Malaya*, p. 26.
44. Sir Richard Winstedt, *The Malays: A Cultural History*, p. 26.
45. Cited in Sastri, *South Indian Influences in the Far East*, p. 81.
46. This view, however, is disputed by Quaritch Wales, although Sastri seems to favour the interpretation of Evans.
47. Winstedt, *The Malays: A Cultural History*, p. 27.
48. Yavadvipa, to which Sugriva sent search parties looking for Sita, is a Sanskrit name mentioned in the *Ramayana*. Toward the end of the fifth century, Aryabhata, the Indian astronomer, wrote that when the sun rose in Ceylon it was midday in *Yavakoti* (Java) and midnight in the Roman land. In the *Surya Siddhanta* reference is also made to the *Nagari Yavakoti* with golden walls and gates.
49. Indonesians, mixed with Negroids, are found in Madagascar, where

Mongoloid features are strongest in the interior of the island. It is therefore suggested that there was migration from Indonesia to Madagascar, probably in the first century. A recent writer has even suggested that in the early centuries of the Christian era Africa was the scene of Indonesian colonization on a fairly large scale, influencing her culture. This is illustrated by reference to Madagascar both in regard to vocabulary and musical and cultural practices. Certain African instruments, and practices are compared with their Indonesian equivalents, including the drum-xylophone, clapperless bells, the *sese,* chorus-singing, *oriki* (Yoruba praise-songs), the *klama* songs of Ghana, and the vocabulary associated with the national *tshikona* flutes of the Venda in South Africa. It is the musical evidence which the author finds most convincing. See A. M. Jones, *Africa and Indonesia.*

50. R. C. Majumdar, *History and Culture of the Indian People,* II, 650.
51. It was during his reign, according to Lineham, who relied on the *Malay Annals,* that Singapura, modern Singapore, was founded. But Winstedt disputes it. See Sir Richard Winstedt, "A Note on the founding of Singapore," *Journal of South East Asian History,* September 1964.
52. Jules Leclercq, *L'ile de Java,* p. 147, cited in B. R. Chatterjee, *India and Java,* p. 37. At a very popular shrine of the Buddha in Surabaya, East Java, where Indonesians come in large numbers to worship the image of the Buddha and to offer gifts—the popularity of this Buddha as a generous dispenser of boons is very high in the area—the caretaker when asked how he, as a Muslim, could make his living out of image-worhip, simply replied that he was asked to do so by the Muslim, priest.
53. Sastri, *South Indian Influences in the Far East,* p. 100.
54. F. A. Wagner, *Indonesia,* p. 126.
55. Heinrich Zimmer, *The Art of Indian Asia,* I. 300.
56. This example has been taken from the writing of a contemporary Indonesian historian who uses it as an illustration for the same purpose. R. M. Sutjipto Wirjosuparto, *A Short Cultural History of Indonesia,* p. 22–23.
57. Gregorio F. Zaide, *Philippine Political and Cultural History,* I. 36.
58. Alfred L. Kroeber, *Peoples of the Philippines.* p. 11.
59. The three figures include Lao-tzu from China and two others representing Anglo-Saxon law and justice, and Spain.
60. Sastri. *South Indian Influences in the Far East,* p. 144.
61. An eminent historian of the Philippines suggests ethnic affinity between Indians and Filipinos, because of which certain racial qualities of the

Filipinos—their dignity of bearing, their stoical outlook on life, and their indifference to pain and misfortune—were inherited from the Hindus. Zaide, *Philippine Political and Cultural History,* I, 45.

Notes to Chapter IV

1. Edward C. Sachau, *Al Biruni's India*, pp. 22–23.
2. It is one of those strange coincidences of history that when the Indo-European world was in a state of decline, with flashes of intermittent brilliance, the rest of the world was well on the path of progress.
3. It is also suggested that the Rajputs, especially the Gurjaras, are the Huns or peoples who came in their wake.
4. Many Rajput rulers, however, cared a lot for social welfare. Some of them carried out great irrigation schemes, and most encouraged religion and learning.
5. There is evidence to suggest that there were larger and finer temples at centres such as Kanauj, Banaras, Prayag, and Ujjain. Khajuraho and the Orissan temples survived because they were not in the path of the Muslim conquerors, who destroyed almost all the ancient temples of northern India.
6. Syed Mahmud, *Hindu Muslim Cultural Accord,* p. 18.
7. *Ibid.,* p. 21.
8. *Ibid.*
9. The Christians in the area were also honourably named, but to distinguish them from the Muslims they were called *Nussarani Mappidas.*
10. Elliot and Dawson, I, 115–86.
11. Nominally though, the Mughals remained sovereigns of India until 1857 when the last ruler, Bahadur Shah II, was deported to Burma by the British. The East India Company ruled as an agent of the Mughal Emperor.
12. In South India, however, there arose the Vijaynagara Kingdom of which visiting foreigners, Persian, Italian and Portuguese, have left glowing accounts. It was constantly at war with the neighbouring Bahmani Kingdom and collapsed in the middle of the sixteenth century, under the attacks of a coalition of Deccan Sultans.
13. Today, at most, ten per cent of the Muslims of India and Pakistan are descended from foreigners. Even in these cases this means only that one of their many ancestors several centuries ago was a Turk or Arab or the like.

14. The date of Sankara is a matter of controversy: "According to Telang Samkara flourished about the middle or the end of the sixth century A.D. Sir R. G. Bhandarkar proposes A.D. 680 as the date of Samkara's birth, and is even inclined to go a few years earlier. Max Müller and Professor Macdonell hold that he was born in A.D. 788 and died in A.D. 820." S. Radhakrishnan, *Indian Philosophy*, II, 447.
15. Bhakti, however, began in South India (Tamilnad) long before Sankara. The earliest Tamil bhakti hymns are older than the Quran, and the cult reached Maharastra before Islam had made any impression there.
16. The accuracy of his dates is uncertain. In Arabic the word *Kabir* means great, and in the Quran it is one of the names of Allah.
17. Babur once visited Nanak and said: "In the face of this *jaqir* God is coming into sight."
18. Recently W. H. McLeod has put forward the view that the religion of Guru Nanak, and so of Sikhism as a whole, is basically Hindu in origin, and that Muslim influence, although evident, is not of fundamental significance. Sikhism is firmly embedded in the Sant tradition of northern India, in the beliefs of the so-called *Nirguna Sampradaya.* See W. H. McLeod, *The Influence of Islam upon the Thought of Guru Nanak* (a paper read at a seminar held at Simla in September 1966).
19. There are about ten million Sikhs in India at present, who are reputed for their enterprise and valour. Their main scripture is called the *Granth Sahib* or the *Granth. Granth* is a Sanskrit word meaning a treatise or book. It contains about twenty thousand hymns and verses, which were mainly compiled by the fifth Guru of the Sikh religion, Arjun, who was the head of the order from 1581 to 1606, until his execution by the Mughal Emperor Jahangir.
20. Despite much greater efforts and vastly improved technological facilities, even English has not become the language of the masses in modern times.

20a. A modern writer however refuses the view that the various styles of North Indian music were invented by the musicians of the Muslim period. A. Danielou. *Northern Indian Music*, p. 39.

21. Some of the better known artists were Mir Saiyid Ali and Khwaja Abdus, Samad of Shiraz, Biswanath, Basawan, Farrukh Beg, Jamshid, Khusrau Quli, Miskin, Zal, Tara, Mahesh, Jahan, Haribans, Makhu, Kesu, Khemakaran, Ram Lal, and Mukund.
22. The same is equally true of the influence of Western dress on India in

modern times. Whilst men have adapted the European suit to their style, Indian women have retained their traditional sari.

23. Such as the *sayyid, sheikh, pathan, malik, momin, mansoor, rayeen, qasale, raki, hajjam, dhobi, teli,* and *bhat* which divide Indian Muslims.
24. Murray T. Titus, *Islam in India and Pakistan,* p. 173.
25. R. C. Zachner, *Hindu and Muslim Mysticism,* pp. 93–94.
26. "Thus the evidence for Vedantin influence on Abu Yazid is not merely the fact that his master was a man from Sind, but the inexplicability of many of his utterances except against a Vedantin background." *Ibid.,* p.100.
27. Murray T. Titus, *Islam in India and Pakistan,* p. 156.
28. D. M. Lang, *The Wisdom of Balahvar,* pp. 24–29.
29. Sir Charles Eliot, *Hinduism and Buddhism,* III, 462.

Notes to Chapter V

1. W. Robertson, *An Historical Disquisition Concerning the Knowledge which the Ancients Had of Ancient India,* p. 173.
2. Sasetti, who was in India from 1578 to 1588. Cited in Robert Sewell, *A Forgotten Empire,* p. 211.
3. C. M. Cipolla, *Guns and Sails in Early Phase of European Expansion, 1400–1700.*
4. A. A. Macdonell, *India's Past,* pp. 237–38.
5. M. Winternitz, *A History of Indian Literature,* I, Part 1, 8.
6. "Gentoo" was derived from the Portuguese term "gentio" meaning heathen.
7. Forbes, *Oriental Memoirs,* II, 212.
8. Cited in A. J. Arberry, *Oriental Essays,* p. 83.
9. Jones made his translation from the "Bengali recension," which is regarded by scholars as less pure than the Devanagari recension. Boehtlingk was the first to edit the Devanagari recension of this play at Bonn in 1842. No other edition of the text of this recension was published until M. William's first edition in 1853. An edition of the same recension was published at Bombay in 1861, and one at Breslau in 1872 by Burkhard.
10. Prior to Jones' discovery of the linguistic affinity between the Indo-European languages, and independently of the English tradition in Indian studies, the French Orientalist, Joseph Deguignes, had published a paper in the *Memoires de l'Academie des Inscriptions et Belles Lettres* identifying the

Sandrokottos of the Greeks with the Chandragupta of the Indians and thus producing the basis of Indian chronology and suggesting common linguistic origins.

11. G. T. Garratt (ed.), *The Legacy of India,* p. 31.
12. M. Müller, *Chips from a German Workshop,* IV, 379.
13. F. Egerton regarded *Meghaduta* as "a glorious love-poem, surely one of the most beautiful known to man." Britain, however, continued to produce Indologists, many of whom, such as G. A. Grierson, Sir Monier Williams, A. A. Macdonell, R. T. Griffiths, F. W. Thomas, Rapson, A. B. Keith, Sir Ralph L. Turner, Sir Harold W. Bailey, and T. Burrow, have made notable contributions.
14. Jean Filliozat in *Indian Studies Abroad,* p. 8.
15. Other texts were discovered by the missions of Sir Aurel Stein, Germany's Von Le Coq and Grundwedel, and Japan's Tachibana. A fragmentary Sanskrit text was accompanied by its Kuchean version.
16. For example, Hermann Oldenberg's *Das Mahabharata—seine Entstehung, seine Inhalt, seine Form (The Mahabharata—its Origin, Contents and Form),* published in 1922. This work is the most comprehensive and striking of its kind.
17. Whilst Max Müller was engaged in bringing out his series of volumes of the *Rig Veda,* another German scholar, Theodor Aufrecht (1822–1907), Professor of Sanskrit at Edinburgh, published an edition of the complete text of the *Rig Veda* in Roman characters in 1861–1863.
18. *The Infinitive in Vedic, with the Verb System of Lithuanian and the Slav Languages,* published in 1871.
19. Arion Rosu, *Indo-Asian Culture,* January 1960, pp. 189–91.
20. For a fuller appraisal of Indological studies in the West, see V. Raghavan, *Sanskrit and Allied Indological Studies in Europe.* Also see *Indian Studies Abroad,* Bombay, 1964.
21. It was the occurrence of the word *Piyadassi* in the *Mahavamsa* that helped Prinsep and other scholars to identify King Piyadassi of the edicts with King Asoka.

Notes to Chapter VI

1. A. A. Macdonell, *A History of Sanskrit Literature,* p. 1.
2. M. Williams (ed.), *Sakuntala,* trans. E. B. Eastwick.

3. Marianne Von Herzfeld and C. Melvil Sym (trans.), *Letters from Goethe*, p. 514.
4. Alex Aronson, *Europe Looks at India*, p. 61.
5. *Ibid.*, p. 54.
6. Winternitz, *A History of Indian Literature*, I, *15*.
7. There have been other German statesmen, such as Von Thielmann, Rosen, and Solf, who devoted their leisure to reading Indian literature.
8. Johanne Novel, *Central Asia: The Connecting Link Between East and West*, p. 95.
9. Alex Aronson, *Europe Looks at India*, p. 56.
10. An English rendering of this verse would be:

    At the Ganges the air is filled
    with scent and light
    And giant trees are flowering
    And beautiful, quiet people
    Kneel before lotus flowers.

11. Arthur Schopenhauer, *The World as Will and Idea*, trans. R. B. Haldane and J. Kemp, pp. xii–xiii.
12. Will Durant, *The Story of Philosophy*, p. 339.
13. Aronson, *Europe Looks at India*, p. 86.
14. G. M. Trevelyan *English Social History*, p. 391. The other wealthy class of Britons from overseas at the time were the British owners of West Indian slave plantations, known as Creoles.
15. George D. Bearce, *op. cit.*, p. 23.
16. A. J. Arberry, *Oriental Essays*, p. 82.

16a. S. Foster Damon *William Blake—His Philosophy and Symbols*, p. 365. "Tharmas, the western Zoa, represents the Body and the senses. His name undoubtedly derived from Tamas (Tama, or Tamasee), the Hindu name for Desire. Blake had been reading the *Bhagvat-Geeta* (London, 1785), and had been so impressed by it that he made a water-colour drawing of *The Brahmins—Mr. Wilkin translating the Geeta* (No. 84 in Rossetti's list of Blake's paintings). In Lecture XIV of this book is a description of the three 'Goon': '*Satwa* truth, *Raja* passion, and *Tama* darkness; and each of them confineth the incorruptible spirit in the body' (p. 107). From other references to the Goon, it appears that they correspond almost precisely to the three lower Zoas: Satwa being Urizen, Raja being Luvah, and Tama being Tharmas. The fourth and highest Zoa, Urthona, is the 'incorruptible spirit' in the passage quoted above. Needless to say, Blake thought more highly of the Goon than the Brahmins: he desired a harmony of the four Zoas; they sought the subjection of three to Urthona." Considering however that Tharmas is close to Greek Thaumas, both verbally and in symbolic properties, Harper suggests that Blake possibly borrowed from both the Neoplatonic (through Taylor) and Indian (through Wilkins) sources. George Mills Harper, *The Neoplatonism of William Blake,* p. 181.

17. See the *Times Literary Supplement* (London), 9 April 1964, for a review of Désirée Hirst's *Hidden Riches.*
18. Carlyle who preached the gospel of stern manliness was, it is strongly suspected, in fact impotent.
19. L. G. Salinger in Boris Ford (ed.), *From Blake to Byron,* p. 193.
20. G. T. Garratt (ed.), *The Legacy of India,* pp. 33–34.
21. John Ruskin; *Lectures in Art,* p. 158.
22. N. Notovick, *The Unknown Life of Christ,* p. xxx.
23. G. Subga Rao, *Indian Words in English,* p. 100.
24. John Roach, "Liberalism and the Victorian Intelligentsia," *The Cambridge Historical Journal,* XIII, No.1 (1957), 64.
25. Sergiu Demetrian, *Indo-Asian Culture,* July 1965, p. 186.
26. Tudor Vianu, *Indo-Asian Culture,* October 1957, p. 189.
27. Aronson, *Europe Looks at India,* p. 127.
28. *Journals of Ralph Waldo Emerson,* VI, 494.
29. *Ibid,* IX, 197.
30. Robert Sencourt, *India in English Literature,* p. 224.
31. S. D. Kalelkar, "Thoreau and Mahatma Gandhi," *The Modern Review,* June 1963, p. 460.
32. Frank Macshane, "Walden and Yoga," *The New England Quarterly,* XXXVII, No. 3 (September 1964), 323.
33. Romain Rolland, *Life of Ramakrishna,* pp. 12–13.
34. S. D. Kalelkar, "Thoreau and Mahatma Gandhi," *Gandhi, Marg,* January 1964, p. 57.
35. Amiya Chakravarty in *Gandhi Marg,* January 1964, p. 67.
36. Romain Rolland in Radhakrishnan (ed.), *Mahatma Gandhi: Essays and Reflections,* p. 197.
37. R. S. Raju in S. Radhakrishnan (ed.), *History of Philosophy: Eastern and Western,* I, 534.

38. A. Aronson, *Rabindranath Through Western Eyes,* p. xii. Tagore's works were so popular in Europe that the librarians would receive requests for his works from all sections of people, many of whom did not even know his nationality. A well-known London library was once requested in a letter, "Please send me a copy of the Jewish writer's book *Gitanjali;* his name is Tagore, I think." Another reader asked, "Have you got the Russian Tagore's latest volume." A third one asked for "a copy please of that Arab poet's new volume of songs." Reported in *Hindu,* 23–29 March 1914; reproduced in 30 March 1964 issue. Yet there was the American Customs official who seriously asked Rabindranath Tagore if he could read and write.
39. W. B. Yeats, *Autobiography,* pp. 91–92.
40. Rabindranath Tagore, *Gitanjali,* pp. xiii–xiv.
41. *Ibid.,* p, xvii.
42. Kenneth Walker, *Diagnosis of Man,* p. 248.
43. Despite his having gained the highest office in the Indian State and despite his many great services to the nation, he had never been a professional politician. It is a tribute to Indian respect for learning that they should have chosen a philosopher, rather than a politician, to this supreme office. The late President of India, Dr. Zakir Hussain, was also principally an academician.
44. Edward Conze, "Dr. Koestler and the Wisdom of the East," *The Hibbert Journal,* LIX (1961), 178–81. It is a review of Koestler's widely read book, *The Lotus and the Robot.*
45. Geoffrey Gorer, *Exploring English Character,* p. 259.
46. G. T. Garratt, *op. cit.,* p 394.

Notes to Chapter VII

1. A. J. P. Taylor, *The Eastern Tradition,* pp. 62–63.
2. John Plamenatz, *On Alien Rule and Self-Government,* p. 16.
3. G. T. Garratt (ed.), *The Legacy of India,* p. 394.
4. W. C. Smith, *Modern Islam in India,* p. 15.
5. I. H. Qureshi in W. Th. de Barry (ed.), *Sources of Indian Tradition,* p. 740.
6. Mohammad Habib in Hamayun Kabir (ed.), *Maulana Abul Kalam Azad,* p. 91.
7. Comparing the progress of Islamic learning in India and Pakistan of today, a Pakistani professor of Arabic at Karachi University commented: "India is

far ahead in this respect... The stark fact is that Arabic-Islamic learning is simply neglected in our country... How unfortunate that in our schools and universities Islamic studies is not an academic study but an empty slogan just part of the Islam-morgering rampant everywhere." S. M. Yusuf, "The World of Islam," *Pakistan Times,* 19 June 1964.

8. Whilst there were democracies of an early variety in India and each in itself was small in size, they were spread over a much wider area and survived for many centuries. Hindu India, in any case, knew "government by discussion" at all levels, right down to the family council.
9. Some of the more famous of the many outstanding works are: Mount Stuart Elphinston's *History of India;* Vincent Smith's *Oxford History of India, Asoka,* and *Akbar;* Sir George Grieson's *Linguistic Survey of India;* Colonel Tod's *Annals and Antiquities of Rajasthan;* Romesh Chandra Dutt's *The Economic History of India.*
10. Cited in Romesh Dutt, *The Economic History of India,* II, 194.
11. Francis Buchanan, *Journey From Madras.*
12. Christopher Dawson, *Making of Europe,* p. 6.
13. The Spanish lay-brother, Joannes Goansalvez, cast a set of Malayan Tamil characters in 1577. He had joined the Jesuit Society in 1555 and published several books before his death in 1579. The first book ever printed in India from his press was entitled, *The Rudiments of Catholic Faith.*
14. H. N. Brailsford, *Subject India,* p. 97.

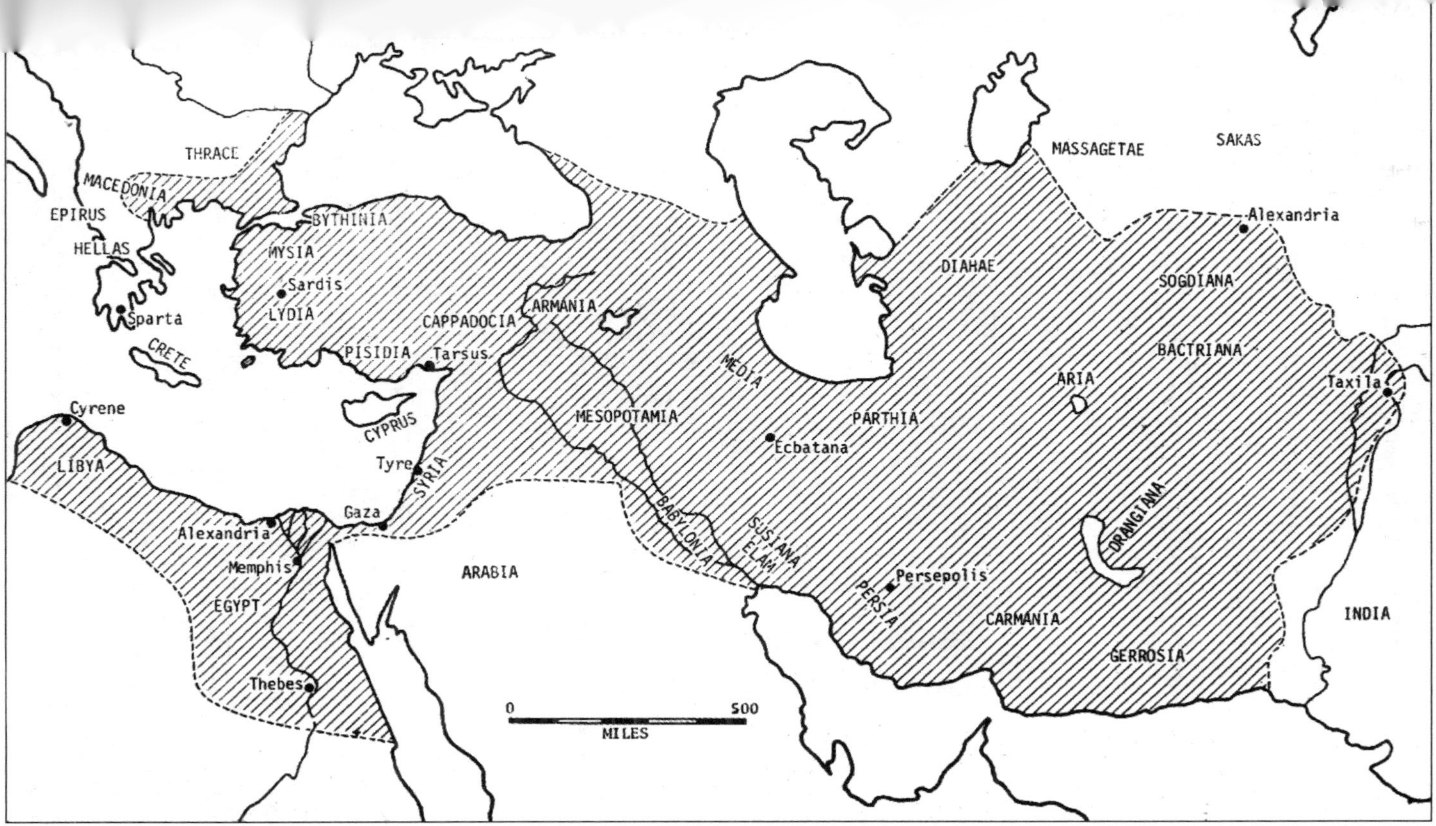

The Achaemenian Empire 500 B.C.

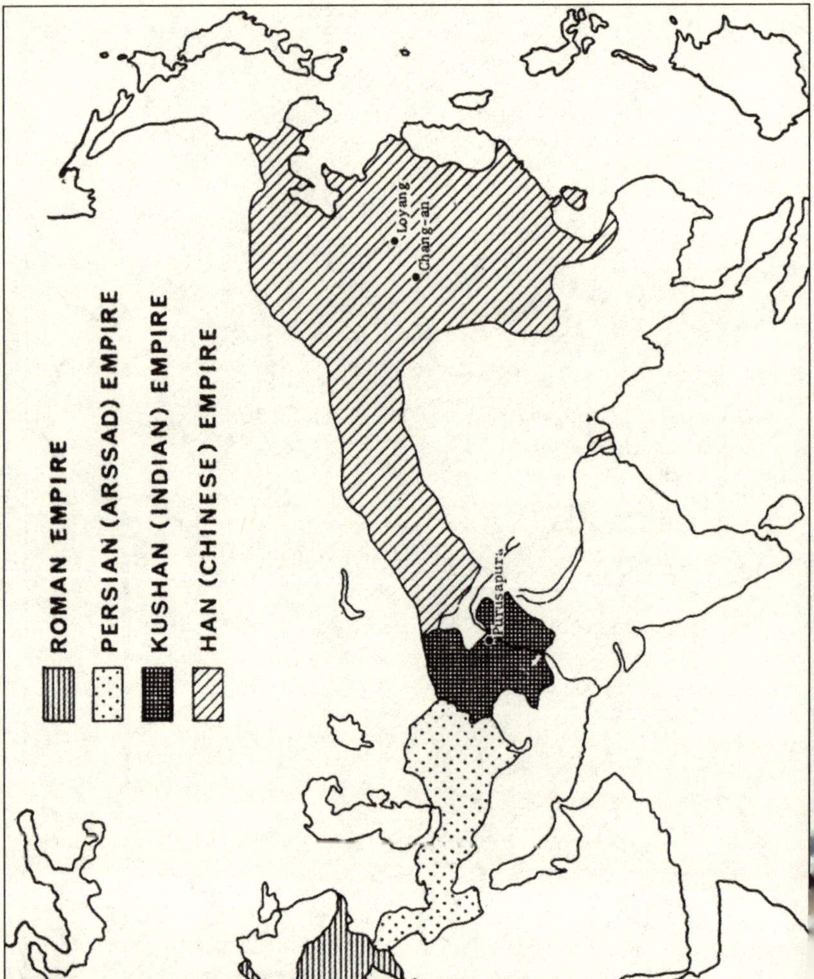
ROMAN EMPIRE
PERSIAN (ARSSAD) EMPIRE
KUSHAN (INDIAN) EMPIRE
HAN (CHINESE) EMPIRE
Loyang
Chang-an
Purusapura
Rome
Alexandria

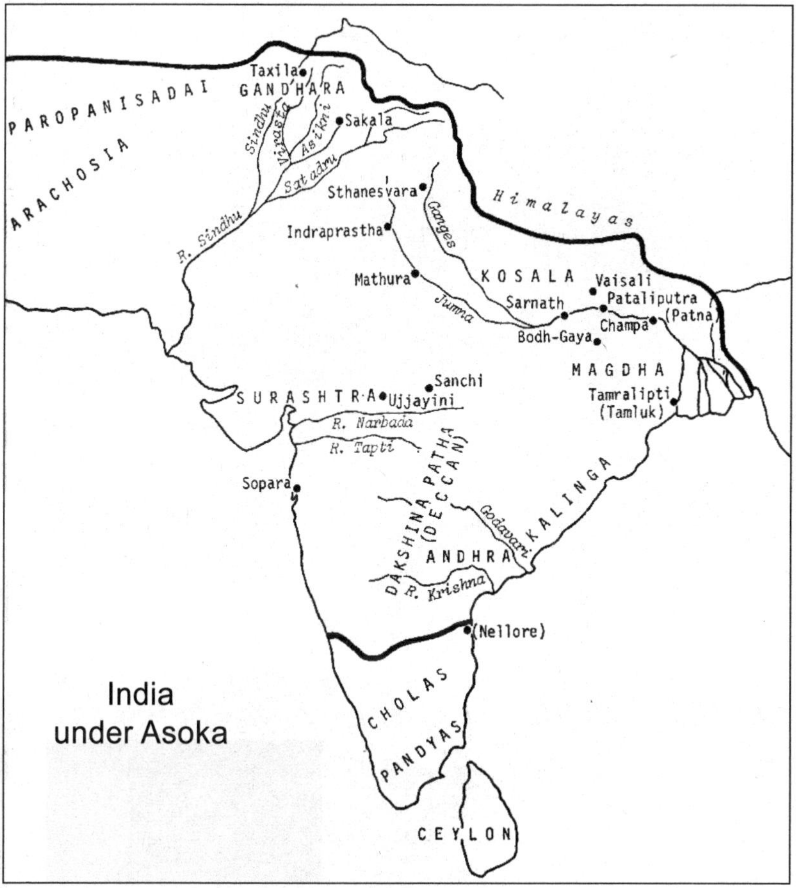
PAROPANISADAI
ARACHOSIA
Taxila
GANDHARA
Sindhu
Vitasta
Asikni
Sakala
Satadru
R. Sindhu
Sthanesvara
Indraprastha
Ganges
Himalayas
Mathura
Jumna
KOSALA
Vaisali
Pataliputra
(Patna)
Sarnath
Champa
Bodh-Gaya
MAGDHA
Sanchi
SURASHTRA
Ujjayini
Tamralipti
(Tamluk)
R. Narbada
R. Tapti
DAKSHINA PATHA
(DECCAN)
Sopara
Godavari
KALINGA
ANDHRA
R. Krishna
(Nellore)
CHOLAS
PANDYAS
CEYLON
India
under Asoka

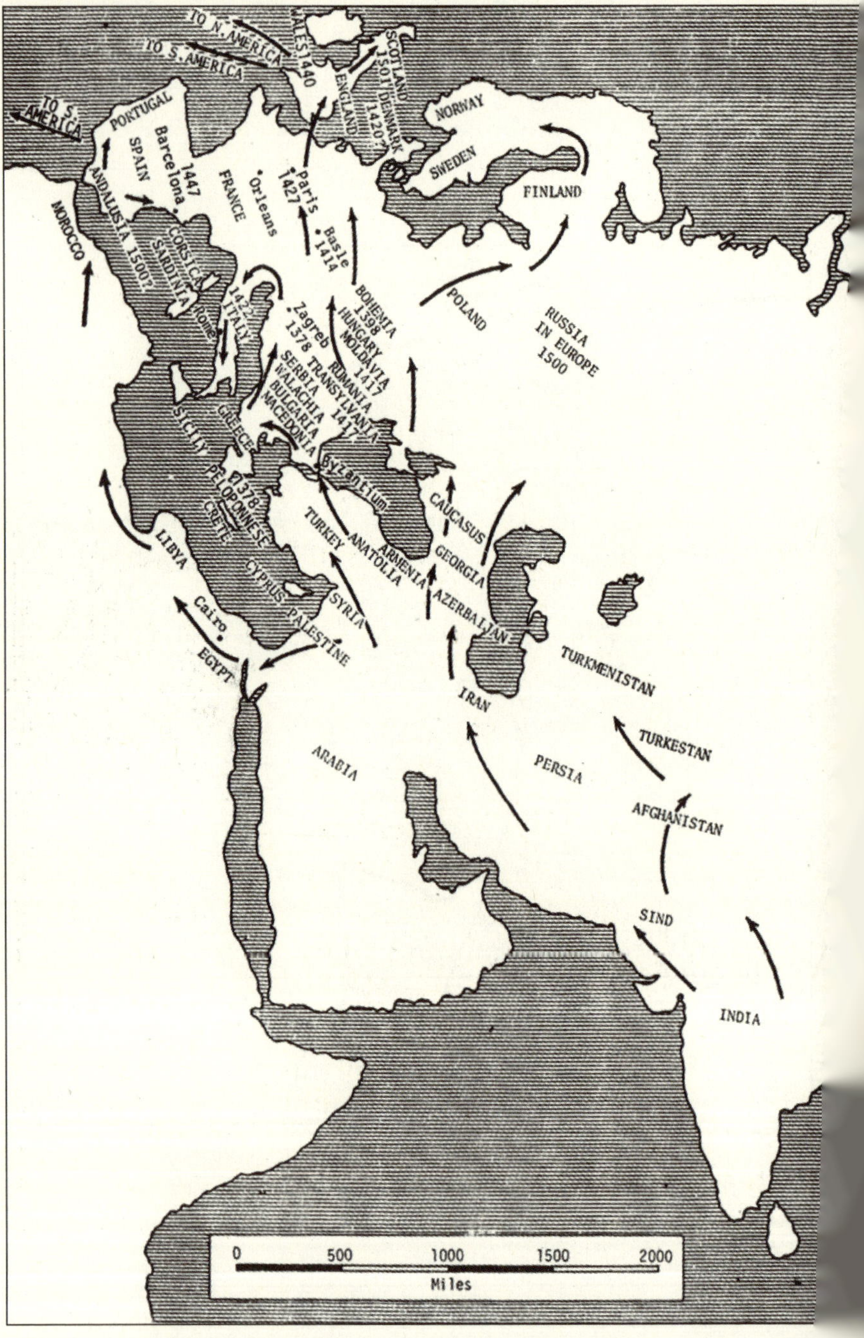

Romany migration from India

ISLAM 700-900 A.D.

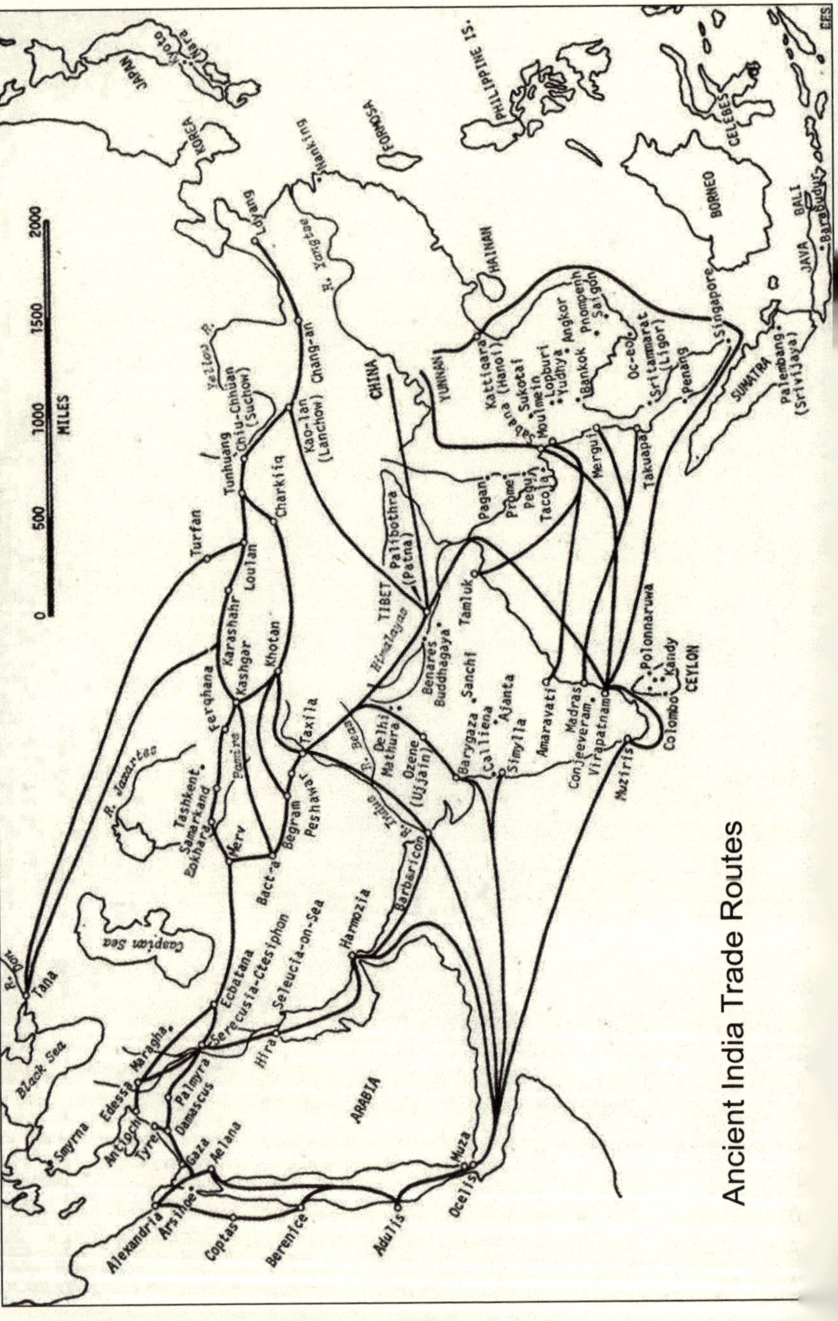

Ancient India Trade Routes

BIBLIOGRAPHY

Abnan, Soheil M. *Avicenna, His Life and Works.* London: 1958.

Abul-Fazl, Allami. *Ain-i-Akbari.* Edited by Henry Blochmann. Calcutta: 1873.

Acharya, Pasanna K. *Hindu Architecture in India and Abroad.* (Mānsāra Series, Vol. VI.) London: 1946.

Agrawala, Vasudeva S. *India As Known to Pānini.* Lucknow: 1953.

Ainalov, D. V. *The Hellenistic Origins of Byzantine Art.* New Brunswick: 1961.

Aiyangar, K. V. R. *Considerations on Some Aspects of Ancient Indian Polity.* Madras: 1935.

Akhilananda, Swami. *Hindu Psychology.* New York: 1947.

Akurgal, Ekrem. *The Art of the Hittites.* New York: 1962.

Al Attas, Syed Naguib. *Some Aspects of Sufism as Understood and Practiced Among the Malays.* Singapore: 1963.

Al Beruni's India. Translated by Edward C. Sachau. 2 vols. London: 1888.

Ali, Abdullah Yusub (tr.). *The Holy Quran.* 2 vols. New York: 1966.

Ali, Syed Ameer. *The Spirit of Islam.* London: 1965. First published London: 1891.

Alip, Eufronio M. *Political and Cultural History of the Philippines.* 2 vols. Manila: 1950–1952.

———. *Tagalog Literature.* Manila: 1930.

Allbutt, T. C. (ed.). *A System of Medicine.* London: 1896.

Allen, G. F. *The Buddha's Philosophy.* London: 1959.

Altekar, A. S. *State and Government in Ancient India.* Banaras: 1949.

Andrae, Tor. *Mohammed, The Man and His Faith.* London: 1936.

Anesaki, Masaharu. *Buddhist Art.* Boston: 1915.

———. *History of Japanese Religion.* Tokyo: 1963. First published London: 1930.

———. *Nichiren, The Buddhist Prophet.* Cambridge, Mass.: 1949.

Angus, S. *The Environment of Early Christianity.* London: 1931. First published 1914.

Anthropological Society of Washington. *Evolution and Anthropology.* Washington: 1959.

Anuruddha, R. P. *An Introduction into Lamaism.* Hosiarpur: 1959.

Arberry, A. J. *Aspects of Islamic Civilization.* London: 1964.

———. *Classical Persian Literature.* London: 1958.

——— (ed.). *The Legacy of Persia.* Oxford: 1953.

———. *Oriental Essays.* London: 1960.

———. *Revelation and Reason in Islam.* London: 1957.

———. *Sufism.* London: 1956.

Ardeshir, B., and P. Nanavutty (trs.). *Gathas.* London: 1952.

Armstrong, A. H. (ed.). *Plotinus,* London: 1953. (A volume of selections in a new English translation.)

——— (ed.). *The Cambridge History of Later Greek and Early Medieval Philosophy.* Cambridge: 1967.

Arnold. Channing, and Frederick J. Tabor Frost. *The American Egypt.* New York: 1909.

Arnold, Sir Thomas Walker. *The Caliphate.* Oxford: 1926.

——— and Alfred Guillaume (eds.). *The Legacy of Islam.* London: 1952. First published 1931.

Aronson, Alex. *Europe Looks at India.* Bombay: 1946.

———. *Rabindranath Through Western Eyes.* Allahabad: 1943.

Arrian, F. *History of Alexander; and Indica.* Translated by E. I. Robson. 2 vols. London: 1393.

Ashraf, K. M. *Life and Conditions of the People of Hindustan.* Delhi: 1959. First published 1935.

Aston, W. G. *Shinto: The Way of the Gods.* London: 1905.

Atiya, Aziz S. *Crusade, Commerce and Culture.* Bloomington, Ind.: 1962.

Atiyah, Edward. *The Arabs.* London: 1958. First published 1955.

Auboyer, Jeannine. *Daily Life in Ancient India.* London: 1961.

Badian, E. *Studies in Greek and Roman History.* Oxford: 1964.

Bagchi, Prabodha Chandra. *India and Central Asia.* Calcutta: 1955.

———. *India and China.* 2nd ed.; New York: 1951. First published Calcutta: 1927.

Bailey, Cyril (ed.). *The Legacy of Rome.* Oxford: 1951. First published 1923.

Bailey, H. W. *Indo-Scythian Studies.* Vol. IV. Cambridge: 1961–1963.

Ballantyne. J. R. *A Synopsis of Science from the Standpoint of the Nyaya Philosophy.* Vol. I. Mirzapore: 1852.

Bancroft, Hubert Howe. *The Native Races of the Pacific States of North America.* 5 vols. London: 1875–1876.

Banerjea,' Jitendra Nath. *The Development of Hindu Iconography.* 2nd ed.; Calcutta: 1956. First published 1941.

Banerjee, G. N. *Hellenism in Ancient India.* 3rd ed.; Delhi: 1961.

Bapat, P. V. (ed.). *2500 Years of Buddhism.* Dehli: 1956.

Barber, C. L. *The Story of Language,* London: 1964.

Barker, Sir Ernest. *The Politics of Aristotle.* Oxford: 1948.

———, Sir George Clark, and P. Vaucher (eds.). *The European Inheritance.* Vols. I, II, and III. Oxford: 1954.

Barnes, E. W. *The Rise of Christianity.* London: 1948.

Barnett, L. D. *Alphabetic Guide to Sinhalese Folklore from Ballad Sources.* Bombay: 1917.

——— (tr.). *Sañtideva.* London: 1947.

Barrau, J. *Plants and the Migrations of Pacific Peoples: A Symposium.* Honolulu: 1961.

Barrere, Albert, and Charles G. Leland (eds.). *A Dictionary of Slang, Jargon and Cant.* London: 1889.

Barthold, V. V. *Four Studies on the History of Central Asia.* Translated from the Russian by V. Minorsky and T. Minorsky. Leiden: 1956–1962.

———. *Le decouverte de L'Aise; histoire de l'orientalisme en Europe et en Russie.* Paris: 1947.

Barua, Benimadhab. *A History of Pre-Buddhist Philosophy.* Calcutta: 1921.

Basham, A. L. *The Wonder That Was India.* London: 1954.

Baynes, Cary F. (tr.). *The I Ching or Book of Changes.* 2 vols. New York: 1950. (The Richard Wilhelm translations rendered into English.)

Baynes, Norman H. *Byzantine Studies and other Essays.* London: 1955.

Beal, Samuel. *Buddhism in China.* London: 1884.

——— (tr.). *Si-Yu-ki: Buddhist Records of the Western World.* 2 vols. London: 1884. (From the Chinese of Hiven Tsiang, A.D. 629.)

———. *Travels of Hiven Tsiang.* Vols. I–IV. Calcutta: 1911.

Beaufort, Duke of, and Alfred E. T. Watson (eds.). *The Badminton Library of Sports and Pastime.* (Volume on Dancing by Lilly Grove). London: 1895.

Bell, Sir Charles. *The Religion of Tibet.* London: 1931.

Bell, Richard. *Introduction to the Quran.* Edinburgh: 1953.

Benfey, T. *Geschichte der Sprachwissenschaft,* Munich: 1869.

———. *Pantschatantra: Fünf Bücher Indischer Fablen, Märchen und Erzählungen.* 2 vols. Leipzig: 1859.

Benitez, Conrado. *The Old Philippine Industrial Development,* Manila: 1916.

Bernal, Ignacio. *Mexico Before Cortez: Art, History and Legend.* New York: 1963.

Bernal, J. D. *Science in History.* London: 1954.

Bernier, Francois. *Travels in the Mogol Empire: A.D.* 1656–1668. Translated by A. Constable. London: 1891.

Berque, Jacques. *The Arabs, Their History and Future.* Translated by Jean Stewart. London: 1964.

Bevan, E. R. *A History of Egypt Under the Ptolemaic Dynasty.* London: 1927.

———. *Later Greek Religion:* London: 192 7.

———. *Stoics and Sceptics.* Oxford: 1913.

——— and C. Singer (eds.). *The Legacy of Israel.* Oxford: 1927.

Beveridge, A. S. (tr.). *Tue Babar-nama.* London: 1921.

Beyer, H. O., and Jaime C. de Veyra. *Philippine Saga.* Manila: 1952.

Bhargava, K. D. *A Survey of Islamic Culture and Institutions.* Allahabad: 1961.

Bhatia, Balmokand. *Famines in India.* Bombay: 1963.

Bhatt, V. V. *Aspects of Economic Change and Policy in India 1800–1960.* New Delhi: 1963.

Bhattacharya, Benoytosh Vinayanosha. *The Indian Buddhist Iconography.* 2nd ed.; Calcutta: 1956. First published London: 1924.

Bhattachayya, H. (ed.). *Cultural Heritage of India.* Vols. I–IV. 2nd ed.; Calcutta: 1953–1958.

Bible. (Conpateruiz Version). New York: 1957.

Bible. (King James Version). Garden City: 1940.

Bible. (Old Testament). Philadelphia: 1955.

Bible. (Revised Standard Version containing Old and New Testaments). New York: 1952.

Bingham, H. *Lost City of the Incas.* London: 1951.

Birnbaum, Henrik, and Jaan Puhvel *Ancient Indo-European Dialects.* California: 1965.

Black, G. F. *A Gypsy Bibliography.* Edinburgh: 1909.

Bloch, Jules. *Les Tsiganes.* Paris: 1953.

Block, Martin (tr.). *Gypsies.* London: 1938. (The English translation of *Zigeuner: ihr Leben und ihre Seele.* Leipzig: 1936.)

Blofeld, J. E. C. *The Jewel in the Lotus: An Outline of Present-day Buddhism in China.* London: 1948.

Bloomfield, M. *The Religion of the Veda, the Ancient Religion of India.* London: 1908.

Boas, Franz. *Mind of Primitive Man.* New York: 1911. Rev. ed. 1938.

Bode, M. H. *The Pali Literature of Burma.* London: 1959.

Bohtlingt, Otto yon, and R. Roth. *Sanskrit-German Dictionary.* 7 vols. St. Petersburg: 1852–1875.

Bopp, Franz. *A Comparative Grammar of the Sanskrit, Zend, Greek, Latin, Lithuanian, Gothic, German and Slavonic Languages.* 3 vols. London: 1845–1850.

———. *Glossarium Sañscritum,* Berolini: 1830.

Borrow, G. *The Bible in Spain.* 3 vols. London: 1843.

———. *The Gypsies of Spain.* London: 1907. First published in two volumes in 1841.

———. *Lavengro,* 3 vols. London: 1851.

———. *Romano Lauo-Lil.* London: 1919. First published 1874.

———. *The Romany Rye.* 2 vols. London: 1857.

———. *The Zincali.* 2 vols. London: 1841.

Bosanquet, Bernard. *Science and Philosophy.* London: 1927.

Bosch, F. D. K. *Selected Studies in Indonesian Archaeology.* Translated by S. Lewis. The Hague: 1961.

Boss, Medard. *A Psychiatrist Discovers India.* Translated by Henry A. Frey. London: 1965.

Bouquet, A. C. *The Christian Faith and Non-Christian Religions.* Welwyn: 1958.

Bowers, Faubion. *Japanese Theatre.* New York: 1952.

Bowie, John. *A New Outline of World History.* London: 1962.

———. *Western Political Thought.* London: 1961. First published 1947.

Bowra, C. M. *The Greek Experience.* London: 1957.

Boxer, C. R. *The Christian Century in Japan 1549–1650.* Berkeley, Los Angeles, and London: 1951.

Boyer, A. M., E. J. Rapson, and E. Senart (trs. and eds.). *Kharoshthi Inscriptions*

Discovered by Sir Aurel Stein. Oxford: 1920–1927.

Braddell, Roland. *Study of Ancient Times in the Malay Peninsula. J. R. A. S.* (M. B.) Vols. XIV, XV, XVII.

Brennan, Louis A. *No Stone Unturned.* New York: 1959.

Briggs, L. P. *The Ancient Khmer Empire.* Philadelphia: 1951.

Brinkley, Captain F., and Baron Kikuchi. *A History of the Japanese People.* New York and London: 1912, 1914, 1915.

Brinkley, Frank. *Japan—Its History, Arts and Literature.* 8 vols. Boston and Tokyo: 1901–1902.

Brion, Marcel. *The World of Archaeology; Central Asia, Africa and the Near East.* Translated by Neil Mann. London: 1962.

———. *The World of Archaeology; India, China and America.* Translated by Miriam and Lionel Kochan. London and New York: 1961.

British Broadcasting Corporation (compiled by). *The Western Tradition.* London: 1949.

Brown, Irving. *Deep Song.* New York and London: 1929.

Brown, L. W. *The Indian Christians of St. Thomas.* Cambridge: 1956.

Brown, Percy. *Indian Architecture.* Bombay: 1962.

———. *Indian Painting Under the Mughals.* Oxford: 1924.

Brown, T. Burton. *Excavations in Azarbaijan 1948.* London: 1951.

Brown, W. Norman (ed.). *India, Pakistan, Ceylon.* New York: 1950.

——— (ed. and tr.). *The Saundarya lahari* (by Sankaracarya). Cambridge, Mass.: 1958.

Browne, Edward G. A. *A Literary History of Persia.* 4 vols. Cambridge: 1928.

Bruce, Joseph Percy. *Chu Hsi and His Masters.* London: 1923.

Brunton, Paul. *The Hidden Teaching Beyond Yoga.* London: 1962. First published 1941.

———. *Indian Philosophy and Modern Culture.* London: 1937.

Buck, Peter H. *Vikings of the Pacific.* Chicago: 1959.

Bühler, G. *Encylopaedia of Indo-Aryan Research.* Strasbourg: 1896.

———. *Indian Palaeography.* (An appendix to the Indian Antiquary, Vol. XXXIII.) Bombay: 1904.

Bultmann, Rudolf. *Primitive Christianity.* London and New York: 1956.

Burckhardt, Jacob. *History of Greek Culture.* Translated by Palmer Hilty. London: 1964.

Burke, Edmund. *Works.* 16 vols. London: 1803–1827.

Burke, Marie Louise. *Swami Vivekananda in America: New Discoveries.* Calcutta: 1958.

Burland, C. A. *Art and Life in Ancient Mexico.* Oxford: 1943.

Burlingame, E. W. (tr.). *Buddhist Parables.* New Haven: 1922.

Burma. Fiftieth Anniversary Publications. Vol. II. Rangoon: 1960.

Burrows, Millar. *More Light on the Dead Sea Scrolls.* London: 1958.

Burton, Sir Richard. *The Book of Thousand Nights and a Night.* 12 vols. London: 1897. First published Banares: 1885.

——— and F. F. Arbuthnot (trs.). *The Kama-sutra of Vatsyayana.* London: 1963.

Bushnell, G. H. D. *Peru.* London: 1956.

Butler, A. J. *The Arab Conquest of Egypt.* Oxford: 1902.

Cajori, Florian. *A History of Mathematics.* New York and London: 1894. 2nd ed.; New York: 1919.

Calder, Ritchie. *The Inheritors.* London: 1961.

———. *Medicine and Man.* London: 1958.

The Cambridge Ancient History. Vols. I–XII. London: 1923-1939.

Cannon, Garland, H. *Oriental Jones.* New Delhi and New York: 1964.

Carmichael, Joel. *The Death of Jesus.* London: 1963.

Carpenter, Frederic I. *Emerson and Asia.* Cambridge: 1930.

Carpentier, J. E. *Theism in Medieval India.* Lectures delivered in Essex Hall, Laden, October–December 1919. London: 1921.

Carter. G F. "Disharmony between Asiatic Flower-Birds and American Bird-Flowers." *Amer. Antiquity,* XX, No.2 (1954), 176–177.

———. "Plant Evidence for Early Contacts with America." *Southwest. J. Anthrop.,* VI (1950), 161–182.

———. "Plants across the Pacific." *Amer. Antiquity* (Mem.), XVIII, No. 3, Pt. 2 (1953), 62–71.

Carter, Thomas Francis. *The Invention of Printing in China and its Spread Westwards.* Revised by L. Carrington Goodrich. New York: 1955. First published 1925.

Cary, M *A History of the Greek World from 323 to 146 B.C.* 2nd ed.: London: 1951. First published 1932.

——— and T. J. Harrhoff. *Life and Thought in the Greek and Roman World.* London: 1957.

Cazamial Louis Francois. *A History of French Literature.* Oxford: 1955.

Chai, Ch'u and Chai Winberg. *The Changing Society of China.* New York: 1962.

Chakravarti, Chandra. *An Interpretation of Ancient Hindu Medicine.* Calcutta: 1923.

Chakravarti, Chintaharan. *Tantras: Studies on their Religion and Literature.* Calcutta: 1963.

Chan, Wing Tsit. *Religious Trends in Modern China.* Columbia: 1953.

Chand, Tara. *History of the Freedom Movement in India.* Vol. I. Delhi: 1961.

———. *Influence of Islam on Indian Culture.* Allahabad: 1936.

Chang, Chia-Sen (Dr. Carsun). *China and Gandhian India.* Calcutta: 1956.

———. *The Development of Neo-Confucaon Thought,* London: 1958.

Charlesworth, M. P. *Trade-Routes and Commerce of the Roman Empire.* Cambridge: 1924.

Chaterjee, Ashkok Kumar. *The Yogacara Idealism.* Varanasi: 1962.

Chatterjee, B. R. *India and Java.* 2nd ed. revised and enlarged (parts 1 and 2); Calcutta: 1933.

———. *Indian Cultural Influence in Cambodia.* Calcutta: 1928.

Chatterji, A. C. *India's Struggle for Freedom.* Calcutta: 1947.

Chattopadhyaya, Debiprasad. *Lokayata.* New Delhi: 1959.

Chaudhari, Haridas, and Frederick Spiegelberg (eds.). *The Integral Philosophy of Sri Aurobindo,* London: 1960.

Chen, Kenneth K. S. *Buddhism in China.* Princeton: 1964.

Chen, Shou-Yi, *Chinese Literature.* New York: 1961.

Chhabra, B. Chi. *Expansion of Indo-Aryan Culture.* Delhi: 1965.

Chiang-Kunag, Chou. *Mahayana Buddhism in China.* Allahabad: 1960.

Childe, V. Gordon. *The Aryalls—A Study of Indo-European Origins.* London: 1926.

———. *The Dawn of European Civilization.* London: 1961. First published 1925.

———. *New Light on the Most Ancient East.* 4th ed.; London: 1952. First published 1934.

———. *Social Evolution,* London: 1951.

———. *What Happened in History.* London: 1954.

Choksi, K. M. *Dentistry in Ancient India.* Bombay: 1953.

Chhabra, B. Chi. *Expansion of Indo-Aryan Culture.* Delhi: 1965.

Chou Hsiang-Kuang, *The History of Chinese Culture.* Allahabad: 1958.

Christy, Arthur C. *The Orient in American Transendentalism.* New York: 1932.

Cipolla, Carol M. *Guns and Sails in the Early Phase of European Expansion, 1400–1700.* London: 1964.

Clebert, Jean Paul. *The Gypsies.* Translated by Charles Duff. London: 1963.

Clements, E. *Introduction to the Study of Indian Music.* London: 1913.

Coe, Michael D. *Mexico.* London: 1962.

Coedés, G. *Les Peuples de la Peuinsule Indochinoise.* Dunod. Paris: 1962.

———. *The Making of South East Asia.* California: 1966.

——— and E. de Boccard. *Les États Hindoisés d'lndochine et d'lndonèsie.* Paris: 1948.

Cole, Sonia Mary. *Races of Man.* London: 1963.

Colebrooke, H. T. *Algebra, with Arithmetic and Mensuration from the Sanskrit of Brahmagupta and Bhascara.* 2nd ed.; Calcutta: 1927.

———. *Essays on the Religion and Philosophy of the Hindus.* London: 1927.

Colum, Padraic. *Orpheus. Myths of the World.* New York: 1930.

Congress Commemoration Volume. *To the Gates of Liberty.* Calcutta: 1948.

Conze, Edward. *Buddhism: Its Essence and Development.* Oxford: 1951.

——— (selected and tr.). *Buddhist Scriptures.* London: 1959.

———. *Buddhist Texts Through the Ages.* Oxford: 1955.

———. *Buddhist Thought in India.* London: 1962.

Cook, Arthur B. *Zeus—A Study in Ancient Religion.* 3 vols. Cambridge: 1914–1940.

Cook, O. F. "The Origin and Distribution of the Cocoa Palm." *Contr. U.S. National Herbarium* (Washington), VII, No. 2 (1901), 257–293.

Coomaraswamy, A. K. *The Arts and Crafts of India and Ceylon.* New York: 1964.

———. *Buddha and the Gospel of Buddhism.* Bombay: 1956. First published 1916.

———. *Ceylon Bronzes Chiefly in the Colombo Museum.* Colombo: 1914.

———. *The Dance of Shiva.* New York: 1959. First published in revised form, 1947.

———. *Hinduism and Buddhism.* New York: 1943.

———. *History of Indian and Indonesian Art.* London: 1927. New York: 1965.

———. *Medieval Sinhalese Art.* New York: 1956. First published 1908.

———. *The Origins of the Buddha Image.* New York: 1927.

———. *The Transformation of Nature in Art.* New York: 1934, 1956.

——— and Sister Nivedita (Margaret E. Noble). *The Myths of the Hindus and Buddhists.* London: 1916.

Coulborn, Rushton. *The Origin of Civilized Societies.* Oxford and Princeton: 1959.

Couling, S. *The Encyclopedia Sinica.* London: 1917.

Cowell, E. B. *The Buddha-Charita of Asvaghosha.* London: 1893.

——— (ed.), *The Jataka.* Vols. I–VI. London: 1957. First published 1895–1913.

Cowley, A. E. *The Hittites.* London: 1920.

Cox, G. W. *Introduction to the Science of Comparative Mythology and Folklore.* London: 1881.

———. *Mythology of the Aryan Nations.* 2 vols. London: 1870.

Cox, M. E. R. *Cinderella.* London: 1893.

Craveri, Marcello. *The Life of Jesus.* Translated from Italian by Charles L. Harkmann. New York: 1967.

Crawfurd, John. *History of Indian Archipelago.* 3 vols. Edinburgh: 1820.

Creel, H. G. *Chinese Thought.* Chicago: 1953.

———. *Confucius, The Man and the Myth.* New York: 1949.

Cresson, Andre. *The Essence of Ancient Philosophy.* Translated by Veronica Hull. New. York: 1963.

Croce, Benedetto. *History of Europe in the Nineteenth Century.* Translated by Henry Furst. London: 1965. First published 1934.

Crombie, A. C. (ed.). *Scientific Change.* London: 1963.

Crombie, I. M. *An Examination of Plato's Doctrines.* London: 1962–1963.

Crooke, W. *The Popular Religion and Folklore of Northern India.* 2 vols. London: 1896.

Culin, R. Stewart. *Chess and Playing Cards.* Washington: 1898.

———. *Games of the North American Indians.* Washington: 1907.

———. *Games of the Orient.* Rutland, Vt.: 1958. (First published under title *Korean Games.*)

Cumont, Franz Valery Marie. *The Oriental Religions in Roman Paganism.* New York: 1956. First published 1911.

Cunningham, A. *Ancient Geography of India.* Calcutta: 1924.

Cunningham, J. D. *A History of the Sikhs.* Oxford: 1918.

Dabbs, Jack A. *History of the Discovery and Exploration of Chinese Turkestan.* The Hague: 1963.

Dahlquist, Allan. *Megasthenes and Indian Religion.* Stockholm: 1962.

Dani, A. H. *Prehistory and Protohistory of Eastern India.* Calcutta: 1960.

Daniel, Norman. *Islam and the West.* Edinburgh: 1960.

Danielou, Alain. *Introduction to the Study of Musical Scales.* London: 1943.

———. *Northern Indian Music.* Vols. I and II. London and Calcutta: 1949.

———. *Yoga: The Method of Re-integration.* New York: 1956.

Danvers, F. C. *The Portuguese in India.* 2 vols. London: 1894.

Das, M. N. *The Political Philosophy of Jawaharlal Nehru.* New York and London: 1961.

Dasgupta, R. P. *A Study of Hindu and European Political Systems.* Calcutta: 1958.

Dasgupta, S. B. *An Introduction to Tantric Buddhism.* Calcutta: 1950.

Dasgupta, S. N. (ed.). *A History of Sanskrit Literature.* Vol. I. Calcutta: 1962.

Dasgupta, Surama. *Development of Moral Philosophy in India.* Calcutta: 1961.

———. *Indian Idealism.* Cambridge: 1933.

Dasgupta, Surendranath. *A History of Indian Philosophy.* Vols. I-V. Cambridge: 1952–1957. First published 1922.

Datta, B. Vibhuti. *The Science of the Sulba, A Study in Early Hindu Geometry.* Calcutta: 1932.

Datta, K. K. *Dawn of Renascent India.* Nagpur ; 1950.

Davar, Firoz C. *Iran and India Through the Ages.* Bombay and New York: 1963.

Davids, T. W. Rhys. *History and Literature of Buddhism,* 4th ed.; Calcutta: 1952. First published London: 1918.

——— (tr.). *The Questions of King Milinda.* 2 parts. New York: 1963.

Davidson, J. Leroy. *The Lotus Sutra in Chinese Art.* New Haven: 1954.

Davies, A. P. *The First Christian.* New York: 1957.

———. *The Meaning of the Dead Sea Scrolls.* New York: 1960.

Davis, Simon. *Race-Relations in Ancient Egypt.* London: 1951.

Dawson, Christopher Henry. *The Making of Europe.* London: 1946.

Dawson, Raymond (ed.). *The Legacy of China.* Oxford: 1964.

Dayal, Har. *The Bodhisattva Doctrine in Buddhist Sanskrit Literature.* London: 1932.

De Bary, Wm. Theodore. *Sources of Indian Tradition.* New York: 1958.

———. *Sources of the Japanese Tradition.* New York: 1958.

——— *et al.* (eds.). *Sources of Chinese Tradition.* New York: 1960.

De Burgh, W. G. *The Legacy of the Ancient World.* Vols. I and II. London: 1953. First published 1924.

Defréniery, C., B. R. Sanguinetti, and H. A. R. Gibb (eds. and trs.). *Travels of Ibn Battuta.* Cambridge: 1958.

De Gokuldas. *Democracy in Early Buddhist Samgha.* Calcutta: 1955.

———. *Significance and Importance of Jatakas.* Calcutta: 1951.

De Meester, Marie E. *Oriental Influences in the English Literature of the Nineteenth Century.* Heidelberg: 1915.

Deraniyagala, P. E. P. "Human and Animal Motif in Sinhalese Art." *J.R.A.S. (C.B.),* IV, Pt. 1.

Desai, A. R. *Recent Trends in Indian Nationalism.* Bombay: 1960.

———. *Social Background of Indian Nationalism.* Bombay: 1948.

Deussen, Paul. *Outline of Indian Philosophy.* Berlin: 1907.

———. *Outline of the Vedañta System of Philosophy.* Berlin: 1907.

———. *The Philosophy of the Upanishads.* Edinburgh: 1906.

Devandra, D. T. *Classical Sinhalese Sculpture.* London: 1958.

Devahuti, D. *India and Ancient Malaya.* Singapore: 1965.

———. *Harsha. A Political Study.* Oxford: in Press.

De Visser, M. W. *Ancient Buddhism in Japan.* 2 vols. Leiden: 1925–1935.

Dey, N. L. *Geographical Dictionary of Ancient and Medieval India.* London: 1927.

Dhalla, Maneckji Nusservanji. *Zoroastrian Civilization.* New York: 1922.

Diaz, Bernal. *The Conquest of New Spain.* Translated by J. M. Bohen. London: 1963. First published in Spanish 1632.

Dictionary of National Biography. Edited by Leslie Stephen. London: 1885.

Dixon, Roland B. *The Mythology of all Races: Oceania.* Edited by Louis Herbert Gray. Boston: 1916. (Vol. IX of the thirteen-volume series on world mythology.)

Dobie, M. R. *Ancient Persia and Iranian Civilization.* London: 1927.

Doblhofer, Ernst. *Voices in Stone.* Translated by Mervyn Savill. London: 1961.

Dodd, C. H. *The Parables of the Kingdom.* London: 1956. First published 1935.

Dodds, E. R. *The Greeks and the Irrational.* Berkeley: 1951,1956.

Dowson. John. *A Classical Dictionary of Hindu Mythology and Religion, Geography, History, and Literature.* London: 1879.

Dreyer, J. L. E. *A History of Astronomy from Thales to Kepler.* Cambridge: 1953.

Driver, Harold E. *Indians of North America.* Chicago: 1961.

Duchesne, Guillemin J. *The Western Response to Zoroaster.* Oxford: 1958.

Duff, Charles (St. Lawrence). *A Mysterious People.* London: 1965.

Dumoulin, Heinrich. *The Development of Chinese Zen.* New York: 1953.

Durant, Will. *The Story of Civilization.* 6 vols. New York: 1942.

———. *The Age of Faith.* New York: 1950.

———. *Caesar and Christ.* New York: 1944.

———. *The Life of Greece.* New York: 1939.

———. *Our Oriental Heritage.* New York: 1942.

———. *The Reformation.* New York: 1957.

———. *The Renaissance.* New York: 1953.

Dutt, Nalinaksha. *Early Monastic Buddhism,* 2 vols. Calcutta: 1941.

Dutt, Romesh Chunder. *The Early Hindu Civilization.* London: 1888. Calcutta: 1908.

———. *The Economic History of India.* 2 vols. London: 1902.

Dutt, R. Palme. *India Today.* London: 1940.

Dutt, Sukumar. *Buddhist Monks and Monasteries of India.* London: 1962.

Eberhard, Wolfram (tr.). *Chinese Fairy Tales and Folk Tales.* London: 1937.

———. *History of China.* 3rd ed.; London: 1955.

Eckardt, A. *A History of Korean Art.* London: 1929.

Edgerton, Franklin. *The Bhagavad Gita.* Cambridge. Mass.: 1966.

——— (ed. and tr.). *The Panchatantra.* London: 1965.

———. *Panchatantra Reconstructed.* 2 vols. New Haven: 1924.

Edmunds, A. J., and M. Anesaki. *The Buddhist and Christian Gospels.* 4th ed.; Philadelphia: 1935.

Edwards. C. R. "Sailing Rafts of Sechura-History and Problems of Origin." *Southwest. I. Anthrop.,* XVI (1960), 368–391.

Edwards. E. D. *Chinese Prose Literature of the Tang Period.* 2 vols. London: 1937–1938.

Ehrenberg, Victor. *The Greek State.* Oxford: 1960.

Ekholm, Gordon F. "A Possible Focus of Asiatic Influence in the Late Classic Cultures of Meso America." *Amer. Antiquity,* XVIII, No. 3, Pt. 2 (1953),72–89.

———. "A Possible Focus of Asiatic Influence in the Late Classic Culture of Mexico, *Mem. Soc. Amer. Arch.,* 9, 1953.

Eliade, Mircea. *Yoga: Immortality and Freedom.* Princeton: 1958.

Eliot, Sir Charles N. E. *Japanese Buddhism.* London: 1935, 1959.

———. *Hinduism and Buddhism.* 3 vols. London: 1954.

Ellis, William. *Polynesian Researches.* 4 vols. 2nd ed.; London: 1832–1834.

El Mansouri, S. M. *Art Culture of India and Egypt.* Calcutta: 1959.

Elsee, C. *Neoplatonism in Relation to Christianity.* Cambridge: 1908.

Encyclopaedia Britannica. Chicago: 1964.

Encyclopaedia of Islam. Leiden and London: 1960. First published 1911–1938.

Encyclopaedia of Religion and Ethics, 1908–1926. 13 vols. Edinburgh.

Enslin, M. *Christian Beginnings.* New York: 1956. First published 1938.

Epstein, I. (ed. and tr.). *The Babylonian Talmud.* 5 vols. London: 1935–1952.

Ernst, Earle. *The Kabuki Theatre.* Oxford: 1956.

Evans-Wentz, W. Y. *The Tibetan Book of the Dead.* London: 1927.

———. *The Tibetan Book of the Great Liberation.* London: 1954. (With psychological commentary by C. G. Jung.)

———. *Tibetan Yoga and Secret Doctrines.* London: 1935.

———. *Tibet's Great Yogi Milarepa.* London: 1951.

Fabri, Charles Louis. *An Introduction to Indian Architecture.* London and Bombay: 1963.

Fairbank, John K. (ed.). *Chinese Thought and Institutions.* 2nd ed.; Chicago: 1959.

Fairbank, J. K., E. O. Reischauer, and A. M. Craig. *A History of East Asian Civilization.* 2 vols. London: 1960.

Faris, Nabih Amin (ed.). *The Arab Heritage.* Princeton: 1944.

Farnell, Lewis Richard. *Greek Hero Cults Ideas of Immortality.* Oxford: 1921.

Farquhar, J. N. *Modern Religious Movements in India.* London: 1915.

———. *An Outline of the Religious Literature of India.* London: 1920.

Faruqi, Ziya-ul-Hasan. *The Deobund School and the Demand for Pakistan.* London and Bombay: 1963.

Figgis, John Neville. *The Divine Rights of Kings.* New York: 1965. (Introduction by G. R. Elton.) First published 1896.

Filliozat, Jean. *The Classical Doctrine of Indian Medicine.* Delhi: 1966. First published in French in 1949.

———. *India.* Translated from French by Margaret Ledesert. London: 1962.

———. *Political History of India.* Translated from French by Philip Spratt. Calcutta: 1957.

Finkelstein, Louis. *The Jews: Their History, Culture and Religion.* 2 vols. New York:. 1955.

Fisher, C. A. *South East Asia.* London: 1964.

Fiske, John. *Myths and Myth-makers.* Boston: 1873.

Fleet, J. F. (ed.). *Corpus Inscriptionum Indicarum, Gupta Inscriptions.* Vol. III. Calcutta: 1888.

Forbes, Charles. *Oriental Essays.* London: 1813.

Ford, Boris (ed.). *From Blake to Byron.* London: 1957.

Forke, A. *The World Conception of the Chinese.* London: 1925.

Fosberg, F. Raymond. "The American Element in the Flora of Hawaii." *Pacific Science,* V (1951), 204–206.

Fox-Strangways, A. H. *The Music of Hindostan.* Oxford: 1914.

Fradier, Georges. *East and West.* Paris: 1959.

Framjee, Firoze. *English Text Book on Theory and Practice of Indian Music.* Pona: 1938.

Francisco, Juan R. *Indian Influences in the Philippines.* Quezon City: 1964.

Frank, Tenney. *Aspects of Social Behavior in Ancient Rome.* Cambridge, Mass.: 1932.

Frazer, Sir James George. *The Golden Bough.* 12 vols. London: 1911–1927.

Friedrich, R. *The Civilization and Culture of Bali.* Edited by E. R. Rost. Calcutta: 1959. First published 1987.

Furtado, R. de L. *Three Painters: Amrita Sher-Gil, George Keyt and M. F. Hussain.* New Delhi: 1960.

Gallenkamp, Charles. *Maya.* New York: 1959.

Gamio, Manuel. *Cultural Evolution in Guatemala and its Geographic and Historic Handicaps.* Translated from the Spanish by Arthur Stanley Riggs. Washington: 1926.

Gandhi, M. K. *Autobiography.* Washington: 1948.

Gangoly, O. C. *Landscape in Indian Literature and Art.* Lucknow: 1964.

Garbe, Richard (ed.). *The Samkhya-pravacana-bhasya.* Cambridge, Mass.: 1895.

Gard, Richard A. *Buddhist Influences on the Political Thought and Institutions of India and Japan.* Claremont, Calif.: 1949.

Gardiner, Patrick. *Schopenhauer.* London: 1963.

Garratt, G. T. (ed.). *The Legacy of India.* Oxford: 1937.

Garrison, F. H. *An Introduction to the History of Medicine.* Philadelphia: 1961. First published 1913.

Garstang, John. *The Hittite Empire.* London: 1929.

Gaudefroy-Demombynes, Maurice. *Muslim Institutions.* London: 1950.

Geertz, Clifford (ed.). *Old Societies and New States.* New York: 1963.

Geiger, W. *The Mahavamsa.* Vols. I and II. London: 1912.

Getty, Alice. *The Gods of Northern Buddhism.* Tokyo: 1962. First published Oxford: 1914.

Gheerbrant, Alain. *The Incas.* New York: 1961.

——— (ed.). *The Incas: The Royal Commentaries of the Inca, Garcilaso de la Vega,* 1539–1616. Translated by Maria Jolas, London: 1963.

Ghirshman, Roman. *Iran: Parthians and Sassanians.* Translated by Stuart Gilbert and James Emmons. London: 1962.

Ghosh, Manomohan. *A History of Cambodia.* Saigon: 1960.

Ghosh, P. C. *The Development of the Indian National Congress 1892–1909.* Calcutta: 1960.

Ghoshal, U. N. *A History of Indian Political Ideas.* Bombay: 1959.

Gibb, H. A. R. *Arabic Literature, an Introduction.* London: 1926.

———. *Mohammedanism: An Historical Survey.* New York: 1955.

———. *Studies on the Civilization of Islam.* London: 1962.

——— and Harold Bowen. *Islamic Society and the West.* 2 vols. London: 1950, 1957.

Gibbon, E. *The Decline and Fall of the Roman Empire.* Edited by J. B. Bury. Vols. I-VII. London: 1909–1914. First published 1776–1788.

———. *The Decline and Fall of the Roman Empire.* London: 1960. (An abridgement by D. M. Low.)

Giles, H. A. *Confucianism and Its Rivals.* London: 1915.

——— (ed.). *Gems of Chinese Literature.* New York: 1965. First published 1923 in two volumes.

———. *A History of Chinese Literature.* New York: 1958. First published 1901.

———. *Religions of Ancient China,* London: 1918.

Giles, L. (tr.). *The Book of Mencius.* London: 1942.

——— (tr.). *Lao Tzu.* London: 1926.

——— (tr.). *Tao Tē Chīng.* London: 1954.

Gilkes, A. N. *The Impact of the Dead Sea Scrolls.* London: 1962.

Gladwin, H. S. *Men out of Asia.* New York: 1947.

Glanville, S. R. K. (ed.). *The Legacy of Egypt.* Oxford: 1953.

Glassenapp, Helmuth von. *Kant and the Religions of the East.* Germany: 1954.

Gokhale, B. G. *Asoka Maurya.* New York: 1966.

———. *Buddhism and Asoka.* Baroda: 1948.

Goldenveizer, Aleksandr. *History, Psychology and Culture.* New York: 1933.

Goldin, Judah (tr.). *The Living Talmud.* New York: 1957.

Goldstucker, Theodore. *Sanskrit and Culture.* Calcutta: 1955.

Goldziher, I. *The Influence of Buddhism Upon Islam.* English translation by T. Duka in the *Journal of Royal Asiatic Society,* January 1904, pp. 125–141.

Gomperz, Theodor. *Greek Thinkers.* Vols. I-II translated by Laurie Magnus; Vol. IV, by G. G. Berry. London: 1901–1912.

Gonda, J. *Sanskrit in Indonesia,* Nagpur: 1952.

Gordon, Antoinette, K. *The Iconography of Tibetan Lamaism.* New York; 1939. 2nd rev. ed.; Tokyo: 1959.

Gorer, Geoffrey. *Exploring English Character.* London: 1955.

Gosvami, O. *The Story of Indian Music.* Bombay: 1957.

Govinda (Lama) Angārika B. *The Psychological Attitude of Early Buddhist Philosophy.* London: 1961.

Granet, Marcel. *Chinese Civilization.* 3rd printing; New York: 1960. First published London: 1930.

Grant, Michael. *Myths of the Greeks and Romans.* London: 1962.

Grant, R. M. (ed.). *Gnosticism: An Anthology.* London: 1961.

———. *Gnosticism and Early Christianity.* New York: 1959.

Grattan, C. Hartley. *The South West Pacific to 1900.* Ann Arbor, Mich.: 1963.

Gray, Basil. *Buddhist Cave Paintings at Tun-Huang.* Chicago: 1959.

Gray, Denis. *Spencer Perceval.* Manchester: 1963.

Gregg, Richard B. *The Power of Non-Violence.* Philadelphia: 1934.

Grellmann, Heinrich. *Dissertation on the Gipsies.* London: 1787.

Griffis, William Elliot. *Corea: The Hermit Nation.* 6th ed.; New York: 1897. First published London: 1882.

Griffiths, Sir Percival Joseph. *The British Impact on India.* London: 1952.

Grimal, Pierre. *The Civilization of Rome.* Translated by W. S. Maguinness. London: 1963.

Grimm, Jacob L. C. and Wilhelm C. Grimm. *German Folk Tales.* Translated by V. P. Magoun Jr. and A. H. Krappe. Carbondale, Ill.: 1960.

Griswold, A. B. *Burma, Korea, Tibet.* London: 1964.

Groenveldt, W. P. *Historical Notes on Indonesia and Malaya.* Djakarta: 1960. (Compiled from Chinese Sources). The reprint of an article published in 1880.

Groome, F. H. *Gypsy Folk Tales.* London: 1889.

———. *In Gypsy Tents.* Edinburgh: 1880.

Groslier, Bernard Philippe. *Indochina.* Translated by George Lawrence. London: 1962.

Grote, George. *Plato and the Other Companions of Sokrates.* 3 vols. London: 1875.

Grousset, René. *Chinese Art and Culture.* Translated from the French by Haakon Chevalier. London: 1959.

———. *The Civilization of India.* Translated from the French by Catherine Alison Phillip. Delhi: 1964.

———. *In the Footsteps of the Buddha.* London: 1932.

———. *Introduction to the Study of Hindu Doctrines.* London: 1945.

———. *The Rise and Splendour of the Chinese Empire.* Translated from the French by A. Watson Gandy. California: 1953.

Grunebaum, G. E. Von. *Islam.* 2nd ed.; London: 1961. First published 1955.

———. *Medieval Islam: A Study in Cultural Orientation.* Chicago: 1953.

———. *Modern Islam: The Search for Cultural Identity,* Berkeley: 1962.

——— (ed.). *Unity and Variety in Muslim Civilization.* Chicago: 1955.

Gubematis, Angelo de. *Zoological Mythology.* London: 1872.

Gulabkunyerba Ayurvedic Soc., Shree. *The Caraka Sammita.* 6 vols. Jamnagar: 1949.

Gulik, Sidney Lewis. *The East and the West.* Rutland, Vt.: 1963.

Gurjar, L. V. *Ancient Indian Mathematics and Veda.* Poona: 1947.

Guthrie, W. K. C. *The Greek Philosophers from Tholes to Aristotle.* London: 1956.

———. *A History of Greek Philosophy.* Vol. 1. Cambridge: 1962.

———. *Orpheus and Greek Religion.* 2nd ed.; London: 1952.

Guy, Basil. *The French Image of China Before and After Voltaire.* Geneva: 1963.

Hackin, J. *et al. Asiatic Mythology.* London: 1963. First published 1932.

Haeckel, Ernst H. P. A. *Monism: As Connecting Religion and Science.* Translated by J. Gilchrist. London: 1894.

Hagen, Victor Wolfgang Von. *The Ancient Sun Kingdoms.* Cleveland: 1961.

———. *The Desert Kingdoms of Peru.* London: 1965.

Hall, D. G. E. (ed.). *Historians of South East Asia.* London: 1961.

———. *A History of South-East Asia.* London: 1955.

Hamilton, Angus, *Korea.* 2nd ed.; London: 1904.

Hamilton, Clarence M. *Buddhism, A Religion of Infinite Compassion.* New York: 1952.

Hanayama, Shinsho. *A History of Japanese Buddhism.* Tokyo: 1960.

Hans, H. *Bibliographie Zur Frage nach den Wechselbeziehung Zurschen Buddhismus und Christianismus.* Leipzig: 1922.

Happold, F. C. *Mysticism.* Hammondsworth: 1963.

Harden, Donald. *The Phoenicians.* London: 1962.

Hardie, J. Keir. *India.* London: 1909.

Harper, G. M. *The Neopkitonism of William Blake.* Chapel Hill: 1961.

Hartland, E. S. *Science of Fairy Tales.* London: 1889.

Harvey, G. E. *History of Burma.* London: 1925.

Haskins, Charles Homes. *Studies in the History of Mediaeval Science.* New York: 1960. First published 1924.

Hatt, Gudmund. "Asiatic Influences in America Folklore." *Det. Kgl. Danske Videnskabernes Selskab, Historisk-Filoogiske meddelelser,* XXXI, No. 6 (1949), 1–122.

———. "The Corn Mother in America and in Indonesia." *Anthropos.,* XLVI (1951),853–914.

———. "Early Intrusion of Agriculture in the North Atlantic Subarctic Region." *Univ. Alaska Anthrop. Pap.,* II, No.1 (1953), 51–107.

Havell, E. B. *The Art Heritage of India.* London: 1964.

———. *The History of Aryan Rule in India.* London: 1918.

Hazrat, Bikrama Jit. *Dara Shikuh: Life and Works.* Visvabharati: 1953.

Heath, Sir Thomas L. *Diophantos of Alexandria.* Cambridge: 1885.

Hedin, Sven. *Scientific Results of a Journey in Central Asia 1899–1902.* 6 vols. Stockholm: 1904–1907.

———. *Southern Tibet.* 13 vols. Stockholm: 1916–1922.

Heimann, Betty. *Facets of Indian Thought.* London: 1964.

———. *Indian and Western Philosophy.* London: 1937.

Heimsath, Charles H. *Indian Nationalism and Hindu Social Reform.* Princeton: 1964.

Heine-Geldem, Robert. "Asiatische Herkunft der Sudamerikanischen Matalitechik." *Paideuma,* V (1954), 347–423.

———. "Heyerdahl's Hypothesis of Polynesian Origins: A Criticism." *Royal Geographic Society Journal,* CXVI (1950), 183–192.

Hell, Joseph. *The Arab Civilization.* Cambridge: 1926.

Henke, Frederick Goodrich (tr. and ed). *The Philosophy of Wang-Yang-Ming.* 2nd ed. New York: 1964. First published 1916.

Henriques, Fernando *Prostitution and Society.* 2 vols. London: 1962–1963.

Hermann, A. *Historical Atlas of China.* Cambridge, Mass.: 1935.

Hertel, Johannes. *Das Pancatantra Seine Geschichte und seine Verbreitung.* 'Leipzig and Berlin: 1914.

Hervieux, Leopold. *Les Fabulistes Latins depms Le Siècle d'Auguste jusqu'à la fin du moyen age.* 5 vols. Pans: 1893–1899.

Heyden A., A. M. Van Der, and H. A. Schullard. *Atlas of the Classical World.* London: 1963.

Heyerdahl, Thor. *The Kon-Tiki Expedition.* London: 1950.

Hicks, R. D. *Stoic and Epicurean.* London: 1910.

Hiriyanna, M. *The Essentials of Indian Philosophy.* London: 1949.

———. *Outlines of Indian Philosophy.* London: 1932.

Hirst, Désirée. *Hidden Riches. Traditional Symbolism from the Renaissance to Blake.* London: 1964.

Hitti, Philip K. *History of the Arabs.* London: 1956.

———. *Islam and the West.* Princeton: 1962.

Hobson, J. A. *Imperialism: A Study.* London: 1902.

Hocart, A. M. *Kingship.* London: 1941.

Hodgen, Margaret T. *Early Anthropology in the 16th and 17th Centuries.* Pennsylvania: 1964.

Hodous, Lewis. *Buddhism and Buddhists in China:* New York: 1924.

Hernle, A. F. R. *Manuscript Remains of Buddhist Literature.* Oxford. 1916.

———. *Studies in the Medicine of Ancient India.* Oxford: 1907.

Holtom, D. C. *Modern Japan and Shinto Nationalism.* 2nd ed.; Chicago: 1947.

———. *The National Faith of Japan: A Study in Modern Shinto.* London: 1938.

Honore, Pierre. *In Quest of the White God.* London: 1963.

Hopkins, E. Washburn. *Epic Mythology.* Strasbourg: 1915.

———. *Ethics of India.* New Haven: 1924.

Hottinger, Arnold. *The Arabs.* London: 1963.

Hourani, G. F. *Arab Seafaring In the Indian Ocean in Ancient and Early Medieval Times.* Princeton: 1951.

Hoyland, John. *A Historical Survey of the Customs, Habits and Present State of the Gypsies.* New York: 1816.

Hoyle, Fred. *The Nature of the Universe.* Oxford: 1950.

Hui-li. *The Life of Hsuan-Tsang.* Peking: 1959.

Huizinga, Johan. *Men and Ideas.* Translated by James' S. Holmes and Hans van Marle. New York: 1959.

Hull, Denison B. (tr.). *Aesop's Fables.* Chicago: 1960.

Hultzsch, E. (ed.). *Corpus Inscriptionum Indicarum, Inscriptions of Asoka.* Vol. I. Oxford: 1925.

Humboldt, Alexander Von. *Researches Concerning the Institutions and Monuments of the Ancient Inhabitants of America.* London: 1814.

——— and Aimé Bonpland. *Personal Narrative of Travels to the Equinoctial Regions of the New Continent during the Years 1799–1804.* Translated by Helen Maria Williams. London: 1814–1829.

Hume, R. E. *The Thirteen Principal Upanishads.* London: 1934.

Humphreys, Christmas. *Buddhism.* London: 1951.

Hurvitz, Leon (tr.). *Wei Shou: Treatise on Buddhism and Taoism.* Kyoh: 1956.

Hu Shih. *The Chinese Renaissance.* New York: 1965.

Hutchinson, J. B., R. A. Silow, and S. G. Stephens. *The Evolution of Gossypium.* London: 1947.

Hutchinson, Sir Joseph. "The History and Relationship of the World's Cottons." *Endeavour,* XXI (1962).

Hutchinson, Lester. *European Freebooters in Mughal India.* Bombay: 1964.

Hutton; J. H. *Caste in India.* Cambridge: 1946.

Huxley, Aldous. *The Perennial Philosophy.* London: 1946.

Ikram, S. M. *Muslim Civilization in India.* New York and London: 1964.

Indian Council for Cultural Relations. *Indian Shidis Abroad.* Bombay: 1964.

Indica: The Indian Historical Research Institute Silver Jubilee Commemoration Volume. Bombay: 1954.

Inge, W. R. *Mysticism in Religion.* London: 1947.

———. *The Platonic Tradition in English Religious Thought.* London: 1926.

———, L. P. Jacks, M. Hiriyama, and D. T. Raju (eds.). *Radhakrishnan: Comparative Studies in Philosophy.* New York: 1951.

International Congress of Americanists. *The Civilization of Ancient America.* Chicago: 1951.

Irani, D. J. *Gathas.* London: 1924.

Isherwood, Christopher. *Ramakrishna and His Disciples.* London: 1965.

——— (ed.). *Vedanta for Modern Man.* London: 1952.

———. *Vedanta for the Westen World.* London: 1948.

I-tsing. *A Record of the Buddhist Religion as Practised* in *India and the Malay Archipelago.* Translated by J. Takakausu. Oxford: 1896.

Iyengar, K. R. Srinivasa. *Indian Writing in English.* New York: 1962.

Iyer, Raghavan (ed.). *South Asian Affairs.* No. l. London: 1960.

Jacobs, Hans. *Western Psychotherapy and Hindu Sadhana.* London: 1961.

Jaffar, S. M. *Some Cultural Aspects of Muslim Rule in India.* Peshawar: 1939.

Jairazbhoy, R. A. *Foreign Influences in Ancient India.* London: 1963.

Jameson, R. D. *Three Lectures on Chinese Folklore.* Peiping: 1932.

Janse, Olov R. T. *Archaeological Research in Indo-China.* Vols. I and II. Cambridge, Mass.: 1947.

Japanese National Commission for UNESCO. *Theatre in Japan.* Japan: 1963.

Jeans, Sir James. *The Mysterious Universe.* Cambridge: 1948.

The Jewish Encyclopedia. 12 vols. London: 1901–1906.

Johnson, A. H. *Whitehead's Philosophy of Civilization.* Boston: 1950.

Johnson, F. *Hitopadesa.* Revised by L. Barnett. London: 1928.

Johnston, E. H. *Early Samkhya; An Essay on Historical Development.* London: 1937.

Johnston, R. F. *Buddhist China.* London: 1913.

Jolly, Julius. *Indian Medicine.* Translated by C. G. Kashikar. Poona: 1951.

Jones, A. M. *Africa and Indonesia.* Leiden: 1964.

Jones, H. L. (tr.). *The Geography of Strabo.* 8 vols. London: 1917–1954.

Jones, Sir William, and Willard N. Augustus. *Music of India.* 2nd rev. ed.; Calcutta: 1962. First published 1793.

Joseph, John. *The Nestorians and Their Muslim Neighbours.* Princeton: 1961.

Journal of the American Oriental Society.

Journal of the Gypsy Lore Society. Old series. 3 vols., Edinburgh: 1888–1892. New series, 9 vols., Liverpool: 1907–1916. Third series, Edinburgh: 1922 to date.

Journal of Hellenic Studies. London.

Journal of the History of Ideas. Pennsylvania.

Journal of Indian History. Travancore.

Journal of the Royal Asiatic Society. London.

Journal of World History. UNESCO. Paris.

Kabir, Humayun. *The Indian Heritage.* Bombay: 1955.

——— (ed.). *Maulana Abul Kalam Azad.* Bombay: 1959. (A memorial volume.)

Kalhana, *Rjatarangini: A Chronicle of the Kings of Kasmir.* Translated by M. A. Stein. London: 1900.

Kālidāsa. *The Megha-Duta.* Edited by S. K. De. New Delhi: 1959. First published Bombay: 1916.

Kamath, M. A. *Hinduism and i Science,* Bangalore: 1947. (Foreword by Kunhan Raja.)

Kane, Pandurang Vaman. *History of Dharmasastra.* 5 vols. Poona: 1930–1962.

Kanga, D. D. *Where Theosophy and Science Meet.* 2 vols. Adyar: 1938–1939.

Kañgle, R. P. (ed.). *The Kantilya-Arthasastra.* Parts I and 2. Bombay: 1960–1963.

Karambelkar, V. W. *The Athar-veda and the Ayur-veda.* Nagpur: 1961.

Karlgren, Bernard. *The Chinese Language, an Essay on its Nature and History.* New York: 1949.

——— (tr.). *Shih Ching: The Book of Odes.* Stockholm: 1950.

Kato, Genchi. *A Study of Shinto.* Tokyo: 1926.

Kaul, Gwasha Lal. *Kashmir Through the Ages: 5000 B.C. to 1960 A.D.* Srinagar: 1960.

Kaye, G. R. *Indian Mathematics.* Calcutta and Simla: 1915.

Keay, Frank E. *A History of Hindi Literature.* 3rd ed.; Calcutta: 1920.

Keith, A. B. *A History of Sanskrit Literature.* Oxford: 1928.

———. *Indian Logic and Atomism.* Oxford: 1921.

———. *Sanskrit Drama.* Oxford: 1924.

Kern, H. (ed.). *The Jataka-Mala, by Arya Sura.* Cambridge, Mass.: 1914.

Kessel, Joseph. *Afghanistan.* Translated from the French by Bernadette Folliot. London: 1959.

Kielhorn, F. (ed.). *Mahabhashya* (by Pasañjab). 3 vols. Bombay: 1892–1909.

Kimura, Ryokan. *A Historical Study of the Terms Hinayalla and Mahayana and the Origin of Mahayana Buddhism.* Calcutta: 1927.

King, C. T. *The Gnostics and Their Remains.* London: 1864.

King, E. (Viscount Kingsborough.) *Antiquities of Mexico.* London: 1831–1848.

King, Martin Luther. *Why We Can't Wait.* London: 1964.

King, Winston L. *Buddhism and Christianity.* London: 1963.

Kitto, H. D. F. *The Greeks.* London: 1960.

Knight, Richard Payne. *The Symbological Language of Ancient Art and Mythology.* New York: 1892.

Kochanowski, Jan. *Gypsy Studies.* Parts 1 and 2. New Delhi: 1963.

Koebner, R., and H. D. Schmidt. *Imperialism.* Cambridge: 1964.

Kondapi, C. *Indians Overseas (1838–1949)* New Delhi: 1951.

Kosambi, D. D. *The Culture and Civilization of Ancient India in Historical Outline.* London: 1965.

———. *An Introduction to the Study of Indian History.* Bombay: 1956.

Kraemer, Hendrik, *World Cultures and World Religions.* London: 1960.

Kripalani, Krishna. *Rabindranath Tagore.* London: 1962.

Krishna, Isvara. *Sanklzya Karika: A Commentary of Gaurcpada.* Translated by H. T. Colebrooke and H. H. Wilson. Bombay: 1924.

Kroeber, A. L. *Anthropology.* London: 1924.

———. *The History of Philippine Civilization as Reflected in Religious Nomenclature.* New York: 1923.

———. *Peoples of the Philippines.* New York: 1928.

———. *Peruvian Archaeology.* New York: 1954.

——— *et al. Anthropology Today.* Chicago: 1953.

Krom, N. J. *Hindoe-Javaansche Geschiedenis. (Hindu-Javanese History.)* S'Gravenbadge: 1931.

Lach, Donald F. *Asia in the Making of Europe.* Vol. I, Books 1 and 2. Chicago: 1964.

La Fontaine, Jean de. *The Fables.* Translated by Walter Thornbury. London, Paris and New York: 1867–1870.

La Fontaine, Jean de. *Fables Choisies Mises En Vers.* Paris: 1962.

Lahovary, N. *Dravidian Origins and the West.* Bombay: 1963.

Lal, Chaman. *Gypsies.* Delhi: 1962.

———. *Hindu America.* Bombay, 1960.

———. *India and Japan: Friends of Fourteen Centuries.* Hoshiarpur: 1959.

La Motte, Etienne. *Histoire du Bouddhisme Indien.* Louvain: 1958.

Landau, Rom. *Islam and the Arabs.* London: 1958.

Landon, Kenneth Perry. *South East Asia, Crossroad of Religions.* Chicago: 1949.

Lane, Edward W. *The Thousand and One Nights.* London: 1839–1841.

Lang, Andrew. *Custom and Myth.* London: 1910. First published 1884.

Lang, D. M. *The Wisdom of Balahvar.* London: 1957.

Lang, John Dunmore. *Origins and Migrations of the Polynesian Nations.* 2nd ed.; Sydney: 1877. First published 1834.

Langdon-Davies, John. *A Short History of Woman.* London: 1928.

Latourette, K. S. *The Chinese: Their History and Culture.* London: 1946.

La Vallée Poussin, L. de. *Dynasties et Histoire de l'Inde depuis Kanishka jusqu'aux invasions Musulmanes.* Paris: 1935.

———. *The Way to Nirvana.* Cambridge: 1917.

Law, B. C. *The Historical Geography of Ancient India.* Paris: 1954.

Law, N. N. *Promotion of Learning in India During Muhammadan Rule.* London: 1916.

Lecky, W. E. H. *A History of European Morals.* 2 vols. London: 1869.

Lee, Samuel. *The Travels of Ibn Batuta.* London: 1829.

Leeming, Joseph. *Yoga and the Bible.* London: 1963.

Leeuwen Arend Th. van. *Christianity and World History.* Edinburgh: 1964.

Legge, J. *The Chinese Classics.* 5 vols. Oxford and London: *1871-1895.*

———(tr.). *A Record of Buddhistic Kingdoms.* Oxford: 1886. (An account of Fa-hien's travels in India.)

———. *Travels of Fa-hien.* Oxford: 1886.

Legouis, Emile. *A Short History of English Literature.* Oxford: 1934.

Leland, C. G. *The English Gypsies and Their Language.* London: 1873.

———. *The Gypsies.* Boston: 1924. First published 1882.

———. *Gypsy Sorcery and Fortune Telling.* London: 1891.

Le May, Reginald. *Buddhist Art in Siam.* Tokyo: 1963. First published Cambridge: 1938.

———. *The Culture of South-East Asia.* London: 1956.

Leon-Portilla, Miguel (ed.). *The Broken Spears: The Aztec Account of the Conquest of Mexico.* Boston: 1962.

Le Strange, Guy. *Baghdad during the Abbasid Caliphate from Contemporary Arabic and Persian Sources.* Oxford: 1924.

———. *The Lands of the Eastern Caliphate; Mesopotamia, Persia and Central Asia.* Cambridge: 1905.

Leur, J. C. van. *Indonesian Trade and Society.* 2nd ed.; Sumur Bandung: 1960.

Lévi, S. *Le Nepal.* 2 vols. Paris: 1905–1908.

Levy, Reuben (tr.). *The Epic of Kings.* Shahnama by Ferdowsi. Chicago: 1967.

Lewis, A. R. *Naval Power and Trade in the Mediterranean (500-1100).* Princeton: 1951.

Lewis, Bernard. *The Arabs in History.* London: 1962.

Lewis, H. Spencer. *The Mystical Life of Jesus.* 15th ed.; California: 1962. First published 1929.

Libby, Willard F. *Radio Carbon Dating.* Chicago: 1965.

Lillie, A. *India in Primitive Christianity,* London: 1909.

Lindsay, A. D. (tr.). *The Republic of Plato.* New York: 1950.

Lings, Martin. *A Moslem Saint of the Twentieth Century.* London: 1961.

Littmann. *Tauseudundeine Nacht in der Arabischen Literatur.* Tubingen: 1923.

Liu, Wu-chi. *Introduction to Chinese Literature.* London: 1966.

Livingstone, R. W. (ed.). *The Legacy of Greece.* Oxford: 1921.

Lloyd-Jones, H. (ed.). *The Greeks.* London: 1962.

Loeb, Edwin M. and Robert Heine-Geldern. *Sumatra.* Vienna: 1935.

Loenen, J. H. M. M. *Parmenides, Melissus, Gorgias.* Asen, Netherlands: 1959.

Lombard, F. A. *An Outline History of the Japanese Drama.* London: 1928.

Lovejoy, Arthur O. *The Great Chain of Being.* Cambridge, Mass.: 1953.

Lowie, Robert. *The History of Ethnological Theory.* London: 1937.

———. "Some Problems of Geographical Distribution." *Sudseestudien,* pp. 11–26. Basel: 1951.

Macaulay, Thomas Babington. *Critical and Historical Essays.* 2 vols. London: 1951.

Macauliffe, M. A. *The Sikh Religion.* 6 vols, Oxford: 1909.

McCrindle, J. W. *Ancient India as Described by Megasthenes and Arrian.* Calcutta: 1960. First published London: 1901.

——— (tr.), and S. N. Majundar (cd.). *Ancient India as Described by Ptolemy.* Calcutta: 1927.

MacCulloch, J. A. *The Childhood of Fiction.* London: 1905.

Macdonald, J. Ramsay. *The Awakening of India.* London: 1910.

Macdonell, A. A. and A. B. Keith. *Vedic Index of Names and Subjects.* London: 1912.

Macdonell, Arthur A. *A History of Sanskrit Literature.* London: 1905.

———. *India's Past.* Oxford: 1927.

———. *Vedic Mythology.* Strasbourg: 1897.

Macdowell, Edward. *Critical and Historical Essays.* Boston: 1912.

McEwan, C. W. *The Oriental Origin of Hellenistic Kingship.* Chicago: 1939.

MacGowan, Kenneth. *Early Man in the New World.* New York: 1950.

Mackay, E. J. H. *Further Excavations at Mohenjo-Daro,* Delhi: 1938.

MacKenzie, Donald A. *Myths of Pre-Columbian America.* London: 1923.

Mckenzie, J. *Hindu Ethics.* London: 1922.

McNickle, D'Arcy. *They Came Here First.* Philadelphia: 1949.

Macnicol, N. (ed.). *Hindu Scriptures.* London: 1938.

———. *The Making of Modern India.* London: 1934.

Mactic, J. N. *Myths and Legends of India.* Edinburgh: 1929.

Mahmud, Syed. *Hindu Muslim Cultural Accord.* Bombay: 1949.

Maitra, Susila Kumara. *The Ethics of the Hindus.* Calcutta: 1958.

Majumdar, R. C. *Ancient Indian Colonization in South-East Asia.* Baroda: 1963.

——— (ed.). *The Classical Accounts of India.* Calcutta: 1960.

———. *Hindu Colonies in the Far East.* Calcutta: 1963.

——— and A. D. Pusalker (eds.). *History and Culture of the Indian People.* Vols. I-VI. London: 1951.

Malalasekera, G. P. *The Pali Literature of Ceylon.* London: 1928.

Mangelsdorf, Paul C. "Ancester of Corn." *Science,* CXXVIII, No. 3335 (28 November 1958).

Mansel, H. L. *The Gnostic Heresies of the First and Second Centuries.* London: 1875.

Markham, C. R. *The Incas of Peru.* London: 1910.

Marlow, A. N. *Radhakrishnan.* London: 1962.

Marshall. John H. *Guide to Taxila.* 4th ed.; London: 1960. First published Calcutta: 1918.

Marshall, John, and Alfred Foucher. *The Monument of Sāñchi.* Calcutta: 1947.

Marlin, P. S. *Indians Before Columbus.* Chicago: 1947.

Mason, John Alden. *The Ancient Civilizations of Peru.* London: 1957.

Maspero, Henri. *Le Chine Antique.* Paris: 1955.

Mattingly, Harold. *Roman Imperial Civilization.* London: 1959.

Maude, Aylmer. *The Life of Tolstoy.* London: 1953. First published 1908–1910.

Maximoff, Matéo. *Savina.* Paris: 1956.

Mayer, J. P. *Political Thought. The European Tradition.* London: 1939.

Means, P. A. *Ancient Civilizations of the Andes.* New York: 1931.

Meester, Maria E. de. *Oriental Influences in the English Literature of the Nineteenth Century.* Heidelberg: 1915.

Mehta, Dharam Dev. *Some Positive Sciences in the Vedas.* New Delhi: 1959.

Mendis, G. C. *Early History of Ceylon.* Calcutta: 1940.

Menon, V. K. *The Development of W. B. Yeats.* Edinburgh: 1960.

Menon, V. Laxmi. *Ruskin and Gandhi.* Varanasi: 1965.

Merrill, Elmer Drew. "The Botany of Cook's Voyages, and Its Unexpected Significance in Relation to Anthropology, Biogeography and History." *Chronica Bontanica,* XIV (1954), 161–384.

Metraux, Guy S., and Francois Crouzet (eds.). *The Evolution of Science.* New York: 1963.

Miller, Robert James. *Monasteries and Culture Change in Inner Mongolia.* Wiesbaden: 1960.

Miller, William Robert. *Non-Violence. A Christian Interpretation.* London: 1964.

Ming, Lai. *A History of Chinese Literature.* London: 1964.

Mirza, M. W. *The Life and Works of Amir Khusrau.* Lahore: 1935.

Mitra, Sisirkumar. *Resurgent India.* Bombay: 1963.

Mizuno, Seiichi. *Chinese Stone Sculpture.* Tokyo: 1950.

Mode, Heinz. *The Harappa Culture and the West.* Calcutta: 1961.

Momigliano, Arnaldo (ed.). *The Conflict Between Paganism and Christianity.* Oxford: 1963.

Monier-Williams, M. *Hinduism.* Calcutta: 1951.

———. *Indian Wisdom.* 3rd ed.; London: 1876.

———. *Sakuntala by Kalidasa.* 2nd ed.; Oxford: 1876.

———. *A Sanskrit-English Dictionary.* Oxford: 1872, 1899.

Mookerji, R. K. *Indian Shipping and Maritime Activity.* London: 1910.

Moore, Charles A. (ed.). *Essays in East-West Philosophy.* Hawaii: 1951.

Moorhead, J. H., and S. Radhakrishnan (eds.). *Contemporary Indian Philosophy.* Rev. ed.; London: 1952.

Moraes, George. *A History of Christianity in India.* Vol. I. Bombay: 1964.

Morgan, Kenneth W. (ed.). *Islam: the Straight Path.* New York: 1958.

——— (ed.). *The Path of the Buddha.* New York: 1956.

Morley, S. G. *The Correlation of Maya and Christian Chronology.* Washington: 1910.

———. *Guide Book to the Ruins of Quirigua.* Washington: 1935.

———. *The Religion of the Hindus.* New York. 1953.

Morton, A. Q., and James McLeman. *Christianity and the Computer.* London: 1964.

Moscati, Sabatino. *Ancient Semitic Civilizations.* London: 1957.

———. *The Face of the Ancient Orient.* Chicago: 1960.

Mukerjee, Radhakamal. *The Culture and Art of India.* London: 1959.

Mukherji, Probhat K. *Indian Literature in China and the Far East.* Calcutta: 1932.

Müller, F. Max. *Chips from* a *German Workshop.* 4 vols. London: 1867–1875.

———. *Collected Works of F. Max Müller.* London: 1898.

———. *Comparative Mythology.* London: 1856.

———. *History of Ancient Sanskrit Literature.* Varanasi: 1964. First published London: 1859.

———. *India, what can it teach us.* London: 1883.

———. *Lectures on the Origin and Growth of Religion.* London: 1891. First published 1878.

——— *Ramakrishna: His Life and Sayings.* London: 1898.

———. *Ram Mohan to Ramakrishna.* Calcutta: 1952.

——— (ed.). *Sacred Books of the East.* 50 vols. Oxford: 1879–1910.

Vedic Hymns, by F. Max Müller and H. Oldenberg (2 vols.).

Hymns of the Atharva-Veda, by M. Bloomfield (1 vol.).

The Satapatha-Brahmana, by J. Eggeling (5 vols.).

The Grihya Sutras, by H. Oldenberg (2 vols.).

The Upanishads, by F. Max Müller (2 vols.).

The Bhagavad gita, by K. Trimbak Telang (1 vol.).

The Vedanta Sutras, by G. Thibut (3 vols.).

The Sacred Laws of the Aryas, by G. Bühler (2 vols.).

The Institutes of Vishnu, by J. Jolly (1 vol.).

The Minor Law Books, by J. Jolly (1 vol.).

Manu, by G. Bühler (1 vol.).

The Gaina-Sutras, by H. Jacobi (1 vol.).

The Saddharma-pundarika, by H. Kern (1 vol.).

Mahayana Texts, by E. B. Cowell, F. Max Müller, and J. Takakusu (1 vol.).

The Dhammapada and Sutta-Nipâta, by F. Max Müller and V. Fausböll (1 vol.).

Buddhist Suttas, by T. W. Rhys Davids (1 vol.).

Vinaya Texts, by T. W. Rhys Davids and H. Oldenberg (3 vols.).

The Questions of King Milinda, by T. W. Rhys Davids (2 vols.).

The Fo-sho-hing-tsan-king, from the Chinese translation of the Sanskrit, by S. Beal (1 vol.).

The Zend-Avesta, by J. Darmesteter and L. H. Mills (3 vols.).

Pahlavi Texts, by E. W. West (5 vols.).

The Quran, by E. H. Palmer (2 vols.).

Texts of Confucianism, by J. Legge (4 vols.).

Texts of Taoism, by J. Legge (2 vols.).

Analytical Index of Names and Subjects, by M. Winternitz (1 vol.).

———. *On Sanskrit Texts Discovered in Japan.* London: 1880.

———. *The Six Systems of Indian Philosophy.* London: 1899.

Murdoch, James. *History of Japan.* 3 vols. London: 1926.

Murray, Gilbert. *Five Stages of Greek Religion.* London: 1946.

———. *Hellenism and the Modern World.* London: 1953.

Murray, H. J. R. *A History of Chess.* Oxford: 1913.

———. *A History of Board-Games other than Chess.* Oxford: 1952.

Murray, M. A. *The Splendour That Was Egypt.* London: 1954.

Murti, T. R. V. *The Central Philosophy of Buddhism.* London: 1955.

Muzumdar, A. M. *Social Welfare in India.* Bombay: 1964.

Mylonas, George E. *Eleusis and the Eleusinian Mysteries.* Princeton: 1961.

Nag, Kilidas. *Discovery of Asia.* Calcutta: 1958.

———. *Greater India.* Calcutta: 1960.

———. *India and the Middle East.* Calcutta: 1954.

Nagarajan, S. "Arnold and the Bhagavad Gita: A Reinterpretation of 'Empedocles on Etna.'" *Comparative Literature,* XII (Fall 1960),335–347.

Nakamura, Hajime. *Japan and Indian Asia.* Calcutta: 1961.

———. *The Ways of Thinking of Eastern Peoples.* Rev. ed.; Honolulu: 1964.

Nanda, B. R. *Mahatma Gandhi.* Boston: 1958.

Narain, A. K. *The Indo-Greeks.* Oxford: 1957.

Naravane, V. S. *Modern Indian Thought.* Bombay: 1964.

Natarajan, S. *A Century of Social Reform in India.* London: 1959.

Natwar, Singh K. (ed.). *E. M. Forster. A Tribute.* New York: 1964.

Needham, J. (ed.). *Science, Religion and Reality.* London: 1926.

Needham, Joseph. *Science and Civilization in China.* Vois. I-IV. Cambridge: 1954–1962.

Nef, John U. *Cultural Foundations of Industrial Civilization.* Cambridge: 1958.

Nehru, Jawaharlal. *The Discovery of India.* New York: 1946.

———, Arnold Toynbee, and C. R. Attlee, *India and the World.* New Delhi: 1962.

Neill, Stephen C. *The Christian Society.* London: 1952.

Nethercot, Arthur H. *The First Five Lives of Annie Besant,* Chicago: 1960.

———. *The Last Four Lives of Annie Besant.* London: 1963.

Neuburger, M. *History of Medicine.* Translated by E. Playfair. London: 1910.

Neugebauer, O. *The Exact Sciences in Antiquity,* 2nd ed.; Providence, R. I.: 1957.

New Oxford. History of Music. Edited by D. A. Hughes and G. Abraham. Oxford: 1960.

Nicholson, R. A. *A Literary History of the Arabs.* London: 1898.

———. *The Mystics of Islam.* London: 1914.

——— (tr.). *Rumi, Poet and Mystic.* London: 1950.

———. *Studies of Islamic Mysticism.* London: 1921.

Niebuhr, Reinhold. *Faith and History.* London: 1949.

Nikhilananda, Swami. *The Bhagavad Gita.* New York: 1944.

——— (tr.). *The Gospel of Sri Ramakrishna.* Madras: 1964.

———. *Upanishads.* New York: 1949.

Nilsson, M. P. *Greek Piety.* Oxford: 1948.

Nivisin, D. S., and A. F. Wright (ed.). *Confucianism. in Action.* Stanford: 1959.

Nizami, K. A. *Some Aspects of Religion and Politics in India During the Thirteenth Century.* Aligarh: 1961.

———. *Studies in Medieval Indian History and Culture.* Allahabad: 1966.

Nobel, Johannes. *Central Asia: The Connecting Link Between East and West.* Nagpur: 1952.

Nock, A. D. *Early Gentile Christianity and its Hellenistic Background.* New York: 1964. First published 1928.

Nordenskjold, N. E. H. *Origin of the Indian Civilization in South America.* Gothenburg: 1931.

Norman, Dorothy (ed.). *Nehru: the First Sixty Years.* 2 vols, London: 1965.

Nutt, Alfred. *The Voyage of Bran.* 2 vols. London: 1895.

Nuttall, Zelia. *The Island of Sacrifice.* Lancaster: 1910.

Nyanatiloka. *Buddhist Dictionary,* Colombo: 1950.

Ojha, G. H. *Bharatiya Prachina Lipi-male.* Ajmer: 1918.

Oldenberg, Hermann. *Buddha; His Life, His Doctrine, His Order.* Translated by William Hoey. London and Edinburgh: 1882.

O'Leary, De Lacy. *How Greek Science Passed to the Arabs.* London: 1957.

Olmstead, A. T. *History of the Persian Empire.* Chicago: 1948.

O'Malley. L. S. S. (ed.). *Modern India and the West.* London: 1941.

Oman, J. C. *The Brahmans, Theists and Muslims of India.* London: 1907.

Orientalia Neerlandica. Leiden: 1948.

Osborne, Arthur. *Buddhism and Christianity in the Light of Hinduism*, London: 1959.

Otto, Rudolf. *The Kingdom of God and the Son of Man.* London: 1951.

Owen, Sidney J. *India on the Eve of the British Conquest.* Calcutta: 1954. First published London: 1872.

Pali Texts Society Translation Series. 13 vols. London: 1909–1925.

I. *Psalms of the Early Buddhists.* Translated by Mrs. Rhys Davids. 1909.

II. *A Compendium of Philosophy.* Translated, with introductory essay and notes, by Shwe Zan Aung and Mrs. Rhys Davids. 1910.

III. *The Mahāvamsa or Great Chronicle of Ceylon.* Translated by W. Geiger, assisted by M. Hayes-Bodes. 1912.

IV. *Psalms of the Early Buddhists.* Translated by Mrs. Rhys Davids. 1913.

V. *Points of Controversy or Subjects of Discourse.* Translation of the Kathā-Vatthu from the Adhidhamma-Pitaka by Shwe Zan Aung and Mrs. Rhys Davids. 1916.

VI. *Manual of a Mystic.* Translation from the Pali and Sinhalese work entitled the Yogāvachara's Manual by F. L. Woodword. Edited, with introductory essay, by Mrs. Rhys Davids. 1917.

VII. *The Book of the Kindred Sayings (Sanyutta-Nikāya) or Grouped Suttas. Part I. Kindred Sayings with Verses (Sagāthā-Vagga).* Translated by Mrs. Rhys Davids. 1917.

VIII-IX. *The Expositor (Atthasālini): Buddhaghosa's Commentary on the Dhammasangani, the First Book of the Abhidhamma Pitaka.* Translated by Maung Tin, edited and revised by Mrs. Rhys Davids. Vol. I, 1920. Vol. II, 1921.

X. *The Book of the Kindred Sayings (Sanyutta-Nikāya) or Grouped Suttas. Part II. The Nidāna Book (Nidāna-Vagga),* Translated by Mrs. Rhys Davids, assisted by F. L. Woodward. 1922.

XI. *The Path of Purity.* Translation of Buddhaghosa's Visuddhimagga by Pe Maung Tin. 1923.

XII. *Designation of Human Types (Puggala-Paññatti).* Translated by Bimala Charan Law. 1924.

XIII. *The Book of the Kindred Sayings (Sanyutta-Nikāya) or Grouped Suttas.* Translated by F. L. Woodward, edited by Mrs. Rhys Davids. 1925.

Panikkar, K. M. *Asia and Western Dominance.* London: 1953.

Panikkar, Raymond. *The Foundations of New India.* London: 1963.

———. *The Unknown Christ of Hinduism.* London: 1964.

Panini. *The Ashtadhyayi of Panini.* Edited and translated by S. C. Vasu. 2 vols. Delhi: 1962. First published Allahabad: 1891.

Pan Ku. *The History of the former Han Dynasty.* (The Imperial Annals.) Translated and edited by Homer H. Dubs. Vols. I and II. Baltimore: 1938, 1955.

Park, No-Yong. *Retreat of the West.* Boston and New York: 1937.

Parker, E. H. *Burma with Special Reference to her Relations with China.* Rangoon: 1893.

Parrinder, E. Geoffrey. *Comparative Religion.* London: 1962.

Parsons, E. A. *The Alexandrian Library.* London: 1952.

Partridge, Burgo. *A History of Orgies.* London: 1964.

Patterson, L. *Mithraism. and Christianity.* Cambridge: 1921.

Payne, G. H. (ed.). *Akbar and the Jesuits.* London: 1926.

Pennell, Elizabeth Robins. *Charles Godfrey Leland, A Biography.* London: 1906.

Perry, Ben E. *Studies in the Text History of the Life and Fables of Aesop.* Haverford: 1961.

Petech, L. *Medieval History of Nepal.* Rowe: 1958.

——— (ed.). *Northern India According to the Shui Ching Chu.* Rome. 1950.

Peterson, Peter (ed.). *Hitopadesa by Narayana.* Bombay: 1887.

Philips, C. H. (ed.). *Handbook of Oriental History.* London: 1951.

——— (ed.). *Historians of India, Pakistan and Ceylon.* London. 1961.

Philostratus. *The Life of Appollonius of Tyana.* Translated by F. C. Conybeare, London: 1912.

Piggott, Stuart. *Prehistoric India.* London: 1961.

Pirenne, Jacques. *The Tides of History.* Vols. I and II. London: 1962.

Pischel, Richard (ed.). *Kalidasa's Sakuntala.* 2nd ed.; Cambridge, Mass.: 1922.

Plamenatz, John. *On Alien Rule and Self-Government.* London: 1960.

Plowman, Max (ed.). *Poems and Prophecies.* London: 1959.

Pococke, E. (ed.). *India in Greece.* London: 1852.

Poindexter, M. *The Ayar-Iunas.* 2 vols. New York: 1930.

Polo, Marco. *The Travels of Marco Polo.* London: 1926. (Introduction by John Masefield.)

Pope, G. U. *The Sacred Kurral.* London: 1886.

Pople, H. A. *The Music of India.* Calcutta: 1950. First published 1921.

Post, L. A. and E. H. Warmington (ed.). *The Leob Classical Library Latin and Greek Volumes.* Cambridge, Mass and London: 1964.

Pothan, S. G. *The Syrian Christians of Kuala.* Bombay: 1963.

Pound, Ezra (tr.). *Confucian Analects.* London: 1956.

Prakash, Buddha. *India and the World.* Hoshiarpur: 1964.

Prakash, Satya. *Founders of Sciences in Ancient India.* New Delhi: 1965.

Prasad, Beni. *The Hindu-Muslim. Question.* Allahabad: 1961.

———. *History of Jahangir,* London: 1922.

Prasad, Isvari. *History of Medieval India.* Allahabad: 1925.

Prasad, Rajendra. *India Divided.* 3rd rev. ed.; Bombay: 1947.

Prescott. W. H. *The Conquest of Mexico.* 2 vols. London: 1913. First published in 3 volumes in 1843.

———. *The Conquest of Peru.* 2 vols. London: 1847.

Press, John (ed.). *Commonwealth Literature.* London: 1965.

Priaulx, Osmund de Beauvoir. *The Indian Travels of Appollonius of Tyana and the Indian Embassies to Rome.* London: 1873.

Price, A. F. (tr.). *The Diamond Sutra.* London: 1955.

Prinsep, James. *Essays on Indian Antiquities.* London: 1858.

Prip-moller, J. *Chinese Buddhist Monasteries.* Copenhagen: 1937.

Pritchard, James B. (ed.). *The Ancient Near East.* Princeton: 1950.

Przyluski, J. *Légende de l'Empereur Asoka.* Paris: 1923.

———. (Tr. into English by D. K. Biswas). *The Legend of Emperor Asoka.* Calcutta: 1967.

Rackham, H., and N. H. S. Jones (trs.). *Natural History* (Plinus Secundus), 11 vols. London: 1945.

Radhakrishnan, S. *The Bhagavad Gita.* New York: 1948.

———. *The Dhammapada.* London: 1950.

———. *Eastern Religions and Western Thought.* Oxford: 1939.

———. *Hindu View of Life.* London: 1927.

———(ed.). *History of Philosophy, Eastern and Western.* 2 vols. London: 1952.

———. *India and China.* 3rd ed.; Bombay: 1954.

———. *Indian Philosophy,* 2 vols. London: 1948.

———. *The Principal Upanishads.* London: 1953.

———. *Religion in East and West.* London: 1933.

——— and Charles A. Moore. *A Source Book in Indian Philosophy.* Princeton: 1957.

Radin, Paul. *The Method and Theory of Ethnology.* New York: 1933.

———. *The Story of the American Indian.* London: 1928.

Raghavan, M. D. *India in Ceylonese History, Society and Culture,* New Delhi: 1964.

Raghavan, V. *The Indian Heritage.* Bangalore: 1956.

———. *Prayers, Praises and Psalms.* Madras: 1938.

———. *Sanskrit and Allied Indological Studies in Europe.* Madras: 1956.

Raghu Vira (ed.). *Ramayana.* Lahore: 1938.

Raghu Vira and Lokeschandra. *Gilgit Buddhist Manuscripts.* New Delhi: 1959.

Rahula, Walpola. *History of Buddhism in Ceylon.* Colombo: 1956.

Ralston, W. R. S. *Russian Folk-Tales.* London: 1873.

Ramachandra Rao, S. K. *Development of Psychological Thought in India.* Mysore: 1962.

Randhawa, M. S. *Kangra Valley Painting.* Bombay: 1964.

Rao, M. V. Ramana. *A Short History of the Indian National Congress.* Delhi: 1959.

Rao, R. P. *Portuguese Rule in Goa 1510–1961.* Bombay: 1963.

Rapson, E. J. *Ancient India.* Cambridge: 1914.

Rau, G. Subba. *Indian Words in English.* Oxford: 1954.

Rawlinson, H. G. *India: A Short Cultural History.* Rev. ed.; London: 1952.

———. *Indian Historical Studies.* London: 1913.

———. *Intercourse between India and the Western World.* 2nd ed.; Cambridge: 1926.

Ray, H. C. *History of Ceylon.* Vol. I. Colombo: 1957.

Ray, Nihar Ranjan. *Introduction to the Study of Theravada: Theravada Buddhism in Burma.* Calcutta: 1946.

Ray, P. (ed.). *History of Chemistry in Ancient and Medieval India.* Calcutta: 1956.

Ray, Sunil Chandra. *Early History and Culture of Kashmir.* Calcutta: 1957.

Raychaudhuri, Hemachandra. *Political History of Ancient India.* Calcutta: 1953.

———. *Studies in India Antiquities.* Calcutta: 1958.

Raychaudhuri, Tapan. *Contributions to Indian Economic History.* Vol. I. Calcutta: 1960.

Reed, Howard S. *A Short History of the Plant Science.* Waltham, Mass.: 1942.

Regmi, D. R. *Ancient Nepal.* Calcutta: 1961.

Reichelt, Karl Ludwig. *Religion in Chinese Garment.* New York: 1951.

———. *Truth and Traditions in Chinese Buddhism.* Shanghai: 192 7.

Reischauer, A. R. *Studies in Japanese Buddhism.* New York: 1917.

Reischauer, Edwin O. *Ennin's Travels in T'ang China.* New York: 1955.

———. *Japan: Past and Present.* 2nd ed.; Tokyo: 1962.

Renou, Louis. *Religions of Ancient India.* London: 1953.

———. *Vedic India.* Translated by Philip Spratt. Calcutta: 1957.

Rhys, Ernest (Intro.). Aesop's *Fables* (and others). New York: 1913.

Ridley, Michael. *The Seal of Aetea and the Minoan Scripts.* Calcutta: 1963.

Riepe, Dale. *The Naturalistic Tradition in Indian Thought.* Seattle: 1961.

Ritchie, D. G. *Plato.* Edinburgh: 1902.

Rizvi, Saiyid Athar Abbas. *Muslim Revivalist Movements in Northern India in the Sixteenth and Seventeenth Centuries.* Agra: 1965.

——— and Lal Bhargava Moti. *Freedom Struggle in Uttar Pradesh.* Lucknow: 1962.

Roberts, Samuel. *The Gypsies.* London: 1836.

Robertson, William. *An Historical Disquisition Concerning the Knowledge which the Ancients Had of India.* London: 1791.

Robinson, John A. T. *Honest to God.* London: 1963.

Rogers, Millard B. "An Archeological Pilgrimage to Santiago de Compostela." *Science,* CXXXI, No. 3408 (22 April 1960).

Rolland, Romain. *The Life of Ramakrishna.* Translated by E. F. Malcolm-Smith. 6th ed.; Calcutta: 1960.

———. *Prophets of the New India.* Translated by E. F. Malcolm-Smith. New York: 1930.

Rosen, F. *The Algebra of Mohammed ben Musa.* London: 1831.

Rosenthal, Ethel. *The Story of Indian Music and its Instruments.* London: 1929.

Ross, Floyd H. *The Meaning of Life in Hinduism and Buddhism.* London: 1952.

Rostovtzeff, M. *Caravan Cities.* Oxford: 1932.

———. *History of the Ancient World.* Vols. I and II. Oxford: 1926.

———. *Social and Economic History of the Roman Empire.* Oxford: 1926.

Roth, Cecil. *The Historical Background of the Dead Sea Scrolls.* Oxford: 1958.

———. *The Jewish Contribution to Civilization.* Oxford: 1943.

———. *A Short History of the Jewish People.* London: 1936.

Rowe, J. Howland. *Inca Culture at the Time of Spanish Conquest.* Washington: 1946.

Rowland, Benjamin. *The Wall Paintings of India, Central Asia and Ceylon.* Boston: 1938.

Roy, Dhirendra N. *The Philippines and India.* Manila: 1930.

Royle, J. F. *Antiquity of Hindoo Medicine.* London: 1887.
———. *The Arts and Manufactures of India.* London: 1852.
———. *An Essay on the Antiquity of Hindoo Medicine.* London: 1837.
Rustum, A. J. and C. K. Zurayk (eds.). *History of the Arabs and Arabic Culture.* Beirut: 1940.
Ryder, A. W. *The Little Clay Cart.* Cambridge, Mass.: 1905.
———. (tr.). *The Panchatantra.* Chicago: 1925.

Sachs, Curt. *The Rise of Music in the Ancient World.* London: 1944.
Sakasena, Rama Babu. *A History of Urdu Literature.* Allahabad: 1927.
Sale, George (tr.). *The Koran.* London and New York: 1888.
Saleeby, Najeeb M. *The Origins of Malayan Filipinos.* Manila: 1911.
Saletore, B. A. *Ancient Indian Political Thought and Institutions.* London: 1963.
———. *India's Diplomatic Relations with the West.* Bombay: 1958.
Salmony, A. *Sculpture in Siam,* London: 1925.
Sambamoorthy, P. *History of Indian Music.* Madras: 1960.
———. *South Indian Music.* 3rd ed.; Madras: 1933.
Sampson, John. *The Dialect of the Gypsies of Wales.* Oxford: 1926.
Samuel, Viscount, and Herbert Dingle. *A Threefold Cord.* London: 1961.
Sanderson, Gorham D. *India and British Imperialism.* New York: 1951.
Sankalia, H. D. *Indian Archaeology Today.* Bombay: 1962.
———. *Prehistory and Protohistory in India and Pakistan.* Bombay: 1963.
———. *The University of Nalanda.* Madras: 1934.
Sankarananda, Swami. *Hindu States of Sumeria.* Calcutta: 1962.
Sansom, Sir George. *Japan: A Short Cultural History.* Rev. ed.; New York: 1943.
Saraswati, S. K. *A Survey of Indian Sculpture.* Calcutta: 1957.
Sarkar, Benoy K. *Hindu Achievements in Exact Science.* London: 1918.
Sarkar, H. B. *Indian Influences on the Literature of Java and Bali.* Calcutta: 1934.
Sarkar, Sasanka S. *Ancient Races of Baluchistan, Panjab and Sind.* Calcutta: 1964.
Sarma, D. S. *The Renaissance of Hinduism.* Banaras: 1944.
———. *What is Hinduism?* Madras: 1945.
Sarton, George. *A History of Science.* Vols I and II. Cambridge, Mass.: 1959.
———. *The History of Science and New Humanism.* New York: 1931.

———. *Introduction to the History of Science.* Vols. I-III. Baltimore: 1953. First published Washington: 1927.

———. *The Life of Science.* New York: 1948.

Sarup, L. *The Nighantu and the Nirukta.* London: 1920.

Sastri, K. A. Nilakanta (ed.). *Age of the Nandas and Mauryas.* Banaras: 1952.

———. (ed.). *A Comprehensive History of India.* Vol. II. Bombay: 1957.

———. *History of Sri Vijaya.* Madras: 1949.

———. *South Indian Influences in the Far East.* Bombay: 1949.

Sastri, Subrahmanya, and R. Bhat (trs. and eds.). *Brihak-Samhitā* (by Varahamihira). 2 vols. Banglore: 1947.

Satomi, Kishio. *Japanese Civilization.* London: 1923.

Sauer, J. D. "The Grain Amaranths: A Survey of their History and Classification." *Annals Missouri Botan. Garden.*, XXXVII (1950), 561–632.

Saunders, E. Dale. *Buddhism in Japan (with an outline of its origins in India).* Philadelphia: 1964.

Saunders, J. H. *The Wild Species of Gossypium and their Evolutionary History.* London: 1961.

Saunders, J. J. *A History of Medieval Islam.* London: 1965.

Schilling, Harold K. *Science and Religion.* New York: 1962.

Schilpp, Paul Arthur (ed.). *The Philosophy of Sarvepalli Radhakrishnan.* New York: 1952.

Schlegel, Frederick. *Lectures on the History of Literature Ancient and Modern.* London: 1818.

———. *Uber die Sprache und Weisheit der Inder.* Heidelberg: 1808.

Schopenhauer, Arthur. *The World as Will and Idea.* Translated and edited by R. B. Haldane and J. Kemp. 3 vols. London: 1883.

Schrödinger, Erwin. *Nature and the Greeks.* Cambridge: 1954.

Schwab, Raymond. *La Renaissance Orientale.* Paris: 1950.

Schweitzer, Albert. *The Quest for the Historical Jesus.* London: 1910.

Seckel, Dietrich. *The Art of Buddhism.* London: 1964.

Séjourné, Laurette. *Burning Water. Thought and Religion in Ancient Mexico.* New York: 1956.

Selincourt, Aubrey de (tr.). *Arrian's Life of Alexander the Great.* London: 1962.

———. *Herodotus, the Histories.* London: 1954.

Sen, Surendra Natha (ed.). *Indian Travels of Thevenot and Careri.* New Delhi: 1949.

Sencourt, Robert. *India in English Literature.* London: 1925.

Sewell, Robert. *A Forgotten Empire*. London: 1900.

Shah, C. L. J. *Jainism in Northern India*. London: 1932.

Sharif, M. M. (ed.). *A History of Muslim Philosophy*. 2 vols. Wiesbaden: 1963 and 1966.

Sharma, Bishan Sarup. *Gandhi As A Political Thinker*. Allahabad: 1956.

Sharma, Chandraddhar, *A Critical Survey of Indian Philosophy*. London: 1960.

Sharma, Dashratha, *Early Chauhan Dynasties*. Delhi: 1959.

Sharma, S. R. *The Crescent in India*. Bombay: 1937.

Sharp, Andrew. *Ancient Voyagers in the Pacific*. Wellington: 1956.

———. *Ancient Voyagers in Polynesia*. Auckland and Hamilton: 1963.

Shastri, D. *A Short History of Indian Materialism and Hedonism*. Calcutta: 1930.

Sherrard, Philip. *The Pursuit of Greece*. London: 1964.

Shinn, Roger L. *Christianity and the Problem of History*. New York: 1933.

Shorey, Paul. *Platonism Ancient and Modern*. California: 1938.

Shoso-In Gyobotsu Zuroku. Pictures of the Imperial properties in the Shoso-in, Nara. 18 vols. Tokyo: 1951.

Shukla, P. N. *Vastu-Sastra: Vol. I. Hindu Science of Architecture*. Lucknow: 1960.

———. *Vastu-Sastra: Vol. II. Hindu Canons of Iconography and Painting*. Lucknow: 1960.

Sila, Brajendranath. *The Positive Science; of the Ancient Hindus*. Delhi: 1958. First published London: 1915.

Singerist, H. E. *A History of Medicine*. London: 1951.

Singh, A. N., and B. Dutta. *The History of Hindu Mathematics*. Lahore: 1935.

Singh, Karan. *Prophet of Indian Nationalism*. London: 1963.

Singh, Rajendra (Brig.). *History of Indian Army*. New Delhi: 1963.

Singhal, D. P. *Nationalism in India and other Historical Essays*. Delhi: 1967.

Sircar, D. C. *Select Inscriptions bearing on Indian History and Civilization*. Calcutta: 1942.

Siren, O. *Chinese Painting. Leading Masters and Principles*. 7 vols. New York: 1956.

———. *Chinese Sculpture*. London: 1925.

———. *A History of Early Chinese Art*. 4 vols. London: 1929.

Smith, D. E., and L. C. Karpinski. *The Hindu Arabic Numerals*. Boston and London: 1911.

Smith, G. E. *Elephants and Ethnologists*. New York: 1924.

Smith, Stephenson Percy. *Hawaika: The Original Home of the Maori.* Christchurch, New Zealand: 1904.

Smith, Vincent, A. *A History of Fine Art in India and Ceylon.* Oxford: 1911.

———. *A History of Fine Art in India and Ceylon.* Revised and enlarged by Karl Khandalwala. 3rd ed.; Bombay.

Smith, Wilfred Cantwell. *Islam in Modern History.* Princeton: 1957.

———. *Modern Islam in India.* London: 1946.

Society of Antiquarians. *Archaeologia,* Vol. XCVII. Oxford: 1959.

———. *Miscellaneous Tracts Relating to Antiquity.* London: 1785.

Somadeva Bhatta. *Katha Sarit Sagara.* English translation entitled *The Ocean of Story* by C. H. Tawney in ten volumes, edited by N. M. Penzcr, London: 1927.

Soothill, W. E. (tr.). *Saddharmapundarika.* Oxford: 1930.

———. *The Three Religions of China.* London: 1913.

Sorabji, Kaikhusrau. *Around Music.* London: 1932.

———. *Mi Contra Fa.* London: 1947.

Soustelle, Jacques. *The Daily Life of the Aztecs.* Translated by Patrick O'Brian. London: 1955.

Spargo, J. W. *Linguistic Science in the Nineteenth Century.* Cambridge, Mass.: 1931.

Spence, Lewis. *The Myths of Mexico and Peru.* London: 1913.

———. *The Myths of the North American Indians.* London: 1914.

Spengler, Oswald. *The Decline of the West.* Translated by Charles F. Atkinson. 2 vols. New York: 1957.

Spinden, H. J. *Ancient Civilizations of Mexico and Central America.* New York: 1917.

———. *Maya Art and Civilization.* Colorado: 1957.

———. *Maya Dates and What They Reveal.* Brooklyn: 1930.

Sridharan, L. *A Maritime History of India.* Delhi: 1965.

Starkie, Walter. *Raggle-Taggle.* London: 1964. First published 1933.

———. *Scholars and Gypsies.* London: 1963.

Stcherbatsky, Th. *Central Concepts of Buddhism.* London: 1924.

———. *The Conception of Buddhist Nirvana.* Leningrad: 1927.

Steiger, G. N., H. O. Beyer, and C. Benitez. *A History of the Orient.* Boston: 1926.

Stein, Sir Mark Aurel. *Ancient Khotan.* 2 vols. Oxford: 1907.

———. *Innermost Asia.* Oxford: 1928.

———. *Memoirs on Maps of Chinese Turkestan and Kansu.* Dehradun: 1923.
——— (tr.). *Rejatarangini.* London: 1900.
———. *Ruins of Desert Cathay.* 2 vols. London: 1912.
———. *Sand-Buried Ruins of Khotan.* London: 1903.
———. *Serindia.* 5 vols. Oxford: 1921.
———. *Wall Paintings from Ancient Shrines in Central Asia.* Vols. I and II. Delhi: 1933.
Steinilber-Oberlin, E. *The Buddhist Sects of Japan.* London: 1938.
Sternbach, Ludwik. *The Hitopadesa and its Sources.* New Haven: 1960.
Stevens, Halsey. *The Life and Music of Bela Bartok.* New York: 1953.
Stevenson, S. *The Heart of Jainism.* London and New York: 1915.
Steward, Julian H. (ed.). *Handbook of Soutk American Indians.* Vols. I–VII. Washington: 1946–1959.
Stobart, J. C. *The Glory That Was Greece.* 3rd ed.; London: 1960. First published 1911.
Stockley, V. *German Literature as Known in England: 1750–1830.* London: 1929.
Stokes, Eric. *The English Utilitarians and India.* Oxford: 1959.
Stonor, C. R., and E. Anderson; "Maize among the Hill Peoples of Assam." *Annals Missouri Botan. Garden.*, XXXVI (1949), 355–396.
Stutfield, H. E. M. *Mysticism and Catholicism.* London: 1925.
Stutterheim, W. F. *Studies in Indonesian Archaeology.* The Hague: 1956.
Subrahmanya, Aiyyar. *The Grammar of South Indian Music.* Bombay: 1939.
Sukthankar, V. S., *et al.* (ed.). *Mahabharata.* Poona: 1933–1958.
Sutherland, Lucy S. *The East India Company in Eighteenth Century Politics.* Oxford: 1952.
Suzuki, Beatrice Lane. *Mahayana Buddhism.* London: 1948.
Suzuki, D. T. *A Brief History of Early Chinese Philosophy.* London: 1914.
———. *Essays in Zen Buddhism.* 3 vols. London: 1934–1949.
———. *An Introduction to Zen Buddhism.* New York: 1949.
———. *Living by Zen.* Tokyo: 1949.
———. *A Miscellany on/the Shin Teaching of Buddhism.* Kyoto: 1949.
———. *Studies in Zen.* New York: 1955.
———. *Zen Buddhism and its Influence on Japanese Culture.* Kyoto: 1938.
———. *The Zen Doctrine of No-Mind.* London: 1949.
———, Erich Fromm, and Richard de Martino. *Zen Buddhism and Psychoanalysis.* London: 1960.

Swain, Joseph Ward. *The Ancient World.* 2 vols. New York: 1950.
Swamikannu, Pillai. *An Indian Ephermeris,* 7 vols. Madras: 1952.
Sydow, C. W. V. *Selected Papers on Folklore.* Copenhagen: 1948.
Symonds, J. A. *Studies of the Greek Poets.* 3rd ed.; London: 1920. First published 1873.

Tachibana, S. *The Ethics of Buddhism.* London: 1926.
Tagore, Avanindranath, and Stella Kramrisch. *A. D. Coomaraswamy Commemoration Volume.* Calcutta: 1961.
Tagore, Rabindranath. *Drawings and Paintings.* Calcutta: 1961.
Takakusu, Junjiro. *The Essentials of Buddhist Philosophy.* Bombay: 1956.
———. *A Record of the Buddhist Religion as Practised in India and the Malay Archipelago.* Oxford: 1896.
Tam, W. W. *Alexander the Great* (Narrative). Cambridge: 1948.
———. *Alexander the Great* (Sources and Studies). Cambridge: 1958.
———. *The Greeks in Bactria and India.* 2nd ed.; Cambridge: ·1951.
———. *Hellenistic Civilization.* London: 1927.
Taton, Rene (ed.). *History of Science: Vol. I. Ancient and Medieval Science.* London: 1963.
———(ed.). *History of Science: Vol. II. The Beginnings of Modern Science.* London: 1964.
Tattwananda, Swami. *Ancient Indian Culture at a Glance.* Calcutta: 1962.
Taylor, F. Sherwood. *Science: Past and Present.* London: 1958.
Taylor, Lily Ross. *The Divinity of the Roman Emperor.* Middletown, Conn.: 1931.
Taylor, Thomas (tr.). *Porphyry on Abstinence from Anımal Food.* London: 1823.
Tax, Sol, and W. C. Bennet (ed.). *The Civilizations of Ancient America.* (Selected papers of the XXIX International Congress of Americanists.) Chicago: 1952.
Tello, J. *Andean Civilizations.* Edited by Julian H. Steward. New York: 1930.
Thapar, Romila. *Asoka.* Oxford: 1961.
Thomas, Edward J. *Early Buddhist Scriptures.* London: 1935.
———. *The History of Buddhist Thought.* 2nd ed.; New York: 1951.
———. *The Life of Buddha as Legend and History.* London: 1949.
Thomas, P. *The Story of the Cultural Empire of India.* Ernakulam: 1959.
Thompson, Edward. *Suttee.* London: 1928.

Thompson, John E. S. *The Rise and Fall of the Maya Civilization.* London: 1956.

Thompson, Stith. *The Folktale.* New York: 1946.

Thornbury, George Walter. *Life in Spain: Past and Present.* 2 vols. London: 1859.

Thornton, A. P. *The Imperial Idea and its Enemies.* London: 1959.

Tilak, B. G. *The Orion, or Researches into the Antiquity of the Vedas.* Bombay: 1893.

Titus, Murray T. *Islam in India and Pakistan.* Calcutta. 1959. First published 1930.

Tod, James. *Annals and Antiquities of Rajasthan.* 2 vols. London: 1829–1832.

Toynbee, Arnold. *An Historian's Approach to Religion.* New York: 1956.

———. *A Study of History.* 12 vols. London: 1934–1959.

Trevelyan, G. M. *English Social History.* 3rd ed.; London: 1955.

Tripathi, Rama Kanta. *Spinoza in the Light of the Vedanta.* Banaras: 1957.

Tripathi, R. P. *The Rise and Fall of the Mughal Empire.* Allahabad: 1960.

Tritton, A. S. *Islam: Beliefs and Practices.* London: 1951.

Trivedi, D. S. *Indian Chronology.* Bombay: 1959.

Tucci, Giuseppe. *Minor Buddhist Texts.* Rome: 1956.

———. *Preliminary Report on Two Scientific Expeditions in Nepal.* Rome: 1956.

———. *The Tombs of the Tibetan Kings.* Rome: 1950.

Turner, R. L. *The Position of Romani in Indo-Aryan.* Edinburgh: 1927. (Gypsy Lore Society Monograph No.4.)

Tweedie, M. W. F. *Prehistoric Malaya.* Rev. ed.; Singapore: 1955.

Tylor, Edward B. *Anthropology.* London: 1881.

———. *Primitive Culture.* 2 vols. London: 1871.

———. *Researches into the Early History of Mankind and the Development of Civilization.* London: 1865.

Tzu, Lao. *The Way of Life.* London: 1946.

UNESCO. *Humanism and Education in East and West.* Paris: 1953.

Urwick, E. J. *The Message of Plato.* London: 1920.

Vacherot, M. *Histoire Critique de l'école d'Alexandrie.* Paris: 1846.

Vahir, Syed Abdul. *Iqbal. His Art and Thought.* London: 1959.

Varma, V. P. *The Political Philosophy of Sri Aurobindo,* Bombay: 1960.

Vatsyayana. *Kamasutra.* Bombay: 1905.

Vermaseren, M. J. *Mithras, the Secret God.* London: 1963.

Verrill, A. Hyatt. *Old Civilizations of the New World.* Indianapolis: 1929.

Vesey-Fitzgerald, Brian. *Gypsies in Britain.* London: 1944.

———. *Gypsy Borrow.* London: 1953.

Vidler, A. R., *et al. Objections to Christian Belief.* London: 1963.

Vidyarthi, Mohan, Lal Venkateswana, and S. Vaidyanatha. *India's Culture through the Ages.* Bombay: 1928–1932.

Visser, M. W. De. *The Dragon in China and Japan.* Amsterdam: 1913. First published 1858.

Vlekke, Bernard H. M. *Nusantara.* Cambridge, Mass.: 1944.

Waddell, L. Austine. *The Buddhism of Tibet.* Cambridge: 1959.

———. *The Buddhism of Tibet or Lamaism.* Cambridge: 1959.

Wagner, Richard. *My Life.* London: 1963.

Wales, H. G. Quaritch. *The Making of Greater India.* 2nd ed.; London: 1961.

———. *Prehistory and Religion in South-east Asia.* London: 1957.

———. *Siamese State Ceremonies.* London: 1931.

Waley, Arthur (tr.). *The Analects of Confucius.* London: 1956,

———. *Ballads and Stories from Tun-Huang.* London: 1960.

———. (tr.). *The Book of Songs.* London: 1954.

———. *An Introduction to Chinese Painting.* London: 1923.

———. *Monkey.* London: 1942.

———. *The No Plays of Japan.* London: 1921.

———. *The Real Tripitaka.* New York and London: 1952.

———. *Three Ways of Thought in Ancient China.* London: 1939.

———. *The Way and Its Power.* London: 1942.

Walzer, Richard. *Greek into Arabic.* Oxford: 1962.

Wang, Kung-hsing. *The Chinese Mind.* New York: 1946.

Warmington, E. H. *The Commerce Between the Roman Empire and India.* Cambridge: 1928.

Warner, Langdon. *The Enduring Art of Japan.* Cambridge, Mass.: 1952.

Warren, Henry Clarke. *Buddhism in Translations.* Cambridge, Mass.: 1922.

Watson, Burton. *Early Chinese Literature,* New York and London: 1962.

———. *Records of the Grand Historian of China.* Translated from the *Shih-Chi* of Ssu-Ma Ch'ien. Vols. I and II. New York and London: 1961.

———. *Ssu-Ma Ch'ien Grand Historian of China.* New York and London: 1963.

Watt, W. Montgomery (tr.). *Al-Ghazali. The Faith and Practice of al-Ghazali.* London: 1953.

———. *Islam and the Integration of Society.* Evanston, Ill.: 1961.

Watters, Thomas. *On Yuan Chwang's Travels in India,* Delhi: 1961. First published London: 1904.

Watts, Alan W. *The Legacy of Asia and Western Man.* London: 1937.

———. *Psychotherapy, East and West.* New York: 1961.

Wauchope, Robert. *Lost Tribes and Sunken Continents,* Chicago and London: 1962.

Waxman, Meyer. *A History of Jewish Literature.* 4 vols. New York: 1938–1947.

Webb, G, C. E, *Gypsies: The Secret People.* London: 1960.

Weber, Albrecht. *The History of Indian Literature.* Translated by John Mann and Theodor Zachariae. 6th ed.; Varanasi: 1961. First published 1878.

Webster, T. B, L. *From Mycenae to Homer.* London: 1960.

Weigall, Arthur. *The Paganism in our Christianity.* London: 1928.

Welch, Holmes. *The Parting of the Way.* Boston: 1957.

Wells, H. G. *The Outline of History.* London: 1925.

Wells, Henry W. *The Classical Drama of India.* London: 1963,

Wells, Kenneth E. *Thai Buddhism: Its Rites and Activities.* Bangkok: 1934.

Wertheim, W. F. *Bali-Studies in Life, Thought, and Ritual.* The Hague and Bandung: 1960.

Westcott, G. H. *Kabir and the Kabir Panth,* Cawnpore: 1907.

Wheatley, Paul. *The Golden Khersonese.* Kuala Lumpur: 1961.

Wheeler, J. A, *Geometrodinamica.* New York and London: 1962.

Wheeler, J. T., and M. Macmillan. *European Travellers in India.* Calcutta: 1956.

Wheeler, Sir Mortimer. *The Indus Civilization.* Cambridge: 1953.

Wheeler, Post (ed. and tr.). *The Sacred Scriptures of the Japanese.* London: 1952.

Whitehead, Alfred N. *Adventures of Ideas.* New York: 1959, First published Cambridge: 1933.

———. *Science and the Modem World.* New York: 1959. First published 1926.

Whittaker, Thomas, *The Neo-Platonists: A Study in the History of Hellenism.* Cambridge: 1901.

Wichmann, Hans, and Siegfried Wichmann. *Chess: The Story of Chesspieces from Antiquity to Modern Times.* London: 1964.

Wickramasinghe, Martin. *Landmarks of Sinhalese Literature.* Colombo: 1963.

Wiener, Philip P., and A. Noland (eds.). "Ideas in Cultural Perspective." *Journal of the History of Ideas.* New Brunswick, N.J.: 1962.

Wilhelm, R. *A Short History of Chinese Civilization.* London: 1929.

Wilke, G. *Kulturbeziehungen Zwischen Indien, Orient and Europa.* 2nd ed.; Leipzig: 1923.

Wilkins, H. T. *Secret Cities of Old South America.* London: 1950.

Willetts, William. *Chinese Art.* 2 vols. London: 1958.

Willey, Gordon R. "New World Prehistory." *Science,* CXXXI, No. 3393 (8 January 1960).

Williams, Raymond. *Culture and Society, 1780–1950.* London: 1958.

Willson, A. Leslie. *A Mythical Image: The Ideal of India in German Romanticism.* Durham, N.C.: 1964.

Wilson, Anne C. *A Short Account of the Hindu System of Music.* London: 1904.

Wilson, Edmund. *The Scrolls from the Dead Sea.* London: 1955.

Wilson, Horace H. *Works.* 12 vols. London: 1862–1871.

Winstedt, Richard. *The Malays: A Cultural History.* 5th ed.; London: 1958.

Winter, H. J. J. *Eastern Science.* London: 1952.

Winternitz, M. *A History of Indian Literature:* Translated by S. Ketkar. Vol. I. 2nd ed.; Calcutta: 1927.

Wood, W. A. R. *A History of Siam,* London: 1926.

Woodcock, George. *The Greeks in India.* London: 1966.

Woods, J. H. (tr.). *The Yoga-System of Patañjali.* Cambridge, Mass.: 1914.

Woodward, F. L. *Some Sayings of the Buddha.* London: 1925.

Woolley, Sir Charles Leonard. *Mesopotamia and the Middle East.* London: 1961.

Wormington, H. M. *Ancient Man in North America.* 4th ed.; Denver: 1939.

Wright, Arthur F. *Buddhism in Chinese History.* Stanford: 1959.

——— (ed.). *Studies in Chinese Thought.* Chicago: 1953.

——— and Denis Twitchett (eds.). *Confucian Personalities.* Stanford: 1962.

Wright, Daniel. *History of Nepal.* Calcutta: 1877.

Wright, Elizar Jr. (tr.). *Fables of La Fontaine.* 2 vols. New York: 1841.

Yang, C. K. *Religion in Chinese Society.* Berkeley: 1961.

Yates, D. E. (ed.). *A Book of Gypsy Folk-Tales.* New York and London: 1948.

Yeats, W. B. *Autobiography.* London: 1926.

Yesudian, Selvarajan, and Elisabeth Haich. *Yoga: Uniting East and West.* London: 1956.

Yi-Pao Mei (tr.). *The Ethical and Political Works of Motse.* London: 1929.

Young, T. C. (ed.). *Near Eastern Culture and Society.* Princeton: 1951.

Yu-Lan Fung (tr.). *Chuang Tzu.* Shanghai: 1933.

———. *A History of Chinese Philosophy.* Translated by Derk Bodde. Vols. I–III. Princeton. 1956.

———. *A Short History of Chinese Philosophy.* London: 1948.

———. *The Spirit of Chinese Philosophy.* London: 1947.

Yutang, Lin (ed.). *The Wisdom of China and India.* New York: 1942.

———. *The Wisdom of Laotse.* New York: 1948.

Zaehner, R. C. *Hindu and Muslim Mysticism.* London: 1960.

———. *The Teachings of the Magi.* London: 1956.

Zaide, Gregario F. *Philippine Political and Cultural History.* Vols. I and II. Rev. ed.; Manila: 1957.

Zeller, Eduard. *Outlines of the History of Greek Philosophy.* New York: 1960.

Zimmer, Heinrich R., and J. Campbell. *The Art of Indian Asia.* 2 vols. New York: 1955.

Zimmer, Henry R. *Hindu Medicine.* Baltimore: 1948.

———. *Myths and Symbols in Indian Art and Civilization.* New York: 1953.

———. *Philosophies of India.* New York: 1951.

Zoete, Beryl D. E. *Dance and Magic Drama in Ceylon.* London: 1957.

———. *The Other Mind.* London: 1953.

Zürcher, E. *The Buddhist Conquest of China.* 2 vols. of text and notes respectively. Leiden: 1959.

INDEX